OOL

GEN 13

THE LAW OF CHARITIES

THE LAW OF CHARITIES

by

PETER LUXTON
De Montfort University, Leicester

Consultant Editor
JUDITH HILL
Farrer & Co, Solicitors

OXFORD
UNIVERSITY PRESS

OXFORD

UNIVERSITY PRESS

Great Clarendon Street, Oxford OX2 6DP

Oxford University Press is a department of the University of Oxford.
It furthers the University's objective of excellence in research, scholarship,
and education by publishing worldwide in

Oxford New York

Athens Auckland Bangkok Bogotá Buenos Aires Cape Town
Chennai Dar es Salaam Delhi Florence Hong Kong Istanbul Karachi
Kolkata Kuala Lumpur Madrid Melbourne Mexico City Mumbai Nairobi
Paris São Paulo Shanghai Singapore Taipei Tokyo Toronto Warsaw

and associated companies in Berlin Ibadan

Oxford is a registered trade mark of Oxford University Press
in the UK and in certain other countries

Published in the United States
by Oxford University Press Inc., New York

First published 2001

British Library Cataloguing in Publication Data

Data available

Library of Congress Cataloging in Publication Data

Luxton, Peter, 1952–
The law of charities / by Peter Luxton.
p. cm.
Includes bibliographical references.
1. Charitable uses, trusts, and foundations—Great Britain.
2. Charity laws and legislation—Great Britain.   I. Title.
KD1487.L874   2001   346.41'064—dc21   2001021838
ISBN 0–19–826783–5

1 3 5 7 9 10 8 6 4 2

Typeset by Hope Services (Abingdon) Ltd.
Printed in Great Britain
on acid-free paper by
Biddles Ltd,
Guildford and King's Lynn

For Margaret

PREFACE

The publication of this book, which is intended for both a professional and an academic readership, appears in the year which marks the four hundredth anniversary of the enactment of the Statute of Elizabeth 1601, whose Preamble (probably the most celebrated in English law) is still sometimes referred to by the courts in determining whether a purpose is charitable. In charity law, the Elizabethan Preamble remains the still point of the turning world; but the charity world is undoubtedly turning more quickly than ever before, and a different landscape is emerging.

For the professional lawyer, and for other professional persons involved with charities, the growth in importance of charity law over the last decade has been a remarkable phenomenon. The underlying reasons for such growth are probably the change in the Government's attitude to direct state involvement in the running of welfare and other public services since the 1980s, and the consequent emergence of the so-called 'contract culture'. Greater concern about the efficiency and effectiveness of charities led both to legislation and to changes in the role of the Charity Commission. Amongst other reforms, the Charities Act 1992 (now mostly consolidated with earlier legislation in the Charities Act 1993) considerably increased the legal responsibilities of charity trustees and reduced the Charity Commissioners' involvement in a number of areas (notably in relation to disposals of charity land); it also provided for the winding up of the major function of the Official Custodian for Charities. Reallocation of work within the Charity Commission has also meant that it is now concentrating more on what might be called its 'policing' functions; and its ability to give direct advice to charities (such as on the drafting of governing instruments) is somewhat reduced. Not surprisingly, these developments have resulted in charity trustees and managers increasingly seeking professional advice.

The last few years have also witnessed a change in the choice of legal structure for many new charities. Trustees of charitable trusts and the committee members of unincorporated charitable associations have always been potentially personally liable to third parties for breaches of contract, but the extent of their potential liability has grown as a result of the emergence of the contract culture and an increasingly litigious society. Many newer charities are therefore being created as companies with limited liability, and some older charities are effectively transforming themselves into such companies. An effect of this, and of the changing nature of charitable activities, especially with the growing importance of fund-raising and trading, has been the infiltration of company and commercial principles into charity law itself. Nevertheless, many aspects of charity law derive from the law of trusts; and trust-law thinking, with its concern, for example, to prevent conflicts of interests, still permeates much of this area. The tension in charity law between principles of property law on the one hand, and of company and commercial law on the other, is an issue of major significance to the practitioner and of considerable interest to the academic lawyer.

This book aims to break away from a primarily property-based standpoint and to present a picture of charity law that gives appropriate weight to the new influences affecting it, especially the influence of company law. Instead of basing the discussion of the law principally around the creation of charitable trusts, I have accorded matters of legal structure and governance a central place in the analysis. The significance of taxation for charities and donors is also given extensive treatment. Another feature of the book is its emphasis upon the importance of the work of the Charity Commissioners. Charities are naturally reluctant to spend their funds appealing to the courts against decisions of the Charity Commissioners, so there are nowadays relatively few judicial decisions on charity law. In practice, therefore, the approach of the Charity Commissioners is of vital importance, especially since they have decided to take on the role, so far as they are able, of developing charity law themselves, as witnessed by their current Review of the Register.

Several important statutes have altered the features of charity law even since the Charities Act 1992. The implications for charities of the Human Rights Act 1998, which came into force in October 2000, have yet to be addressed by the courts, but they are considered mostly in chapter 1. The Finance Act 2000, with its sweeping changes to the taxation of charitable giving, is considered mainly in chapters 3 and 19, and its important consequences for trading by charities, both directly and through subsidiary trading companies, are analyzed in chapter 20. Most recently, the Trustee Act 2000 has introduced a statutory duty of care for trustees, and has considerably altered the law relating to investment (with the effective repeal of the Trustee Investments Act 1961), to delegation, and to the use of nominees and custodians. These changes are fully dealt with in this book, particularly in chapters 9 and 16. In view of their growing importance for charities (especially since the Woolf reform of civil procedure), chapter 14 deals exclusively with mediation and dispute resolution. With the increased numbers of charities entering into contractual undertakings, the risk of insolvency is all the greater. The final chapter therefore examines the legal position on dissolution of charities.

In writing this book I was most fortunate to be able to draw upon the extensive professional knowledge and experience of charity law and practice of Judith Hill of Farrer & Co, who, in her capacity as Consultant Editor, read and commented upon every chapter. Judith's numerous suggestions enabled me to amend and improve the text in a number of important ways. I should also like to express my thanks to John Merrills and Jonathan Miller for helpful discussions of the Human Rights Act 1998; to Ram Singh, for his useful observations on mediation and dispute resolution; to Christopher Rycroft and Rebecca Allen at Oxford University Press for their invaluable help in seeing this book through its various stages; and to the copy editor, Charlotte Barrow, for her excellent work on the typescript. I should also like to thank Margaret Wilkie, to whom I have dedicated this book, for the unfailing support she has given me during the years of its preparation and writing. I would add only that the responsibility for any inaccuracies that the ensuing pages may contain rests with me alone. Thanks to the indulgences of my publishers at proof stage, I have been able to state the law as it was in the middle of February 2001. I have therefore been able to take account of the enactment of the Trustee Act 2000, which received the Royal Assent on 23 November 2000, and which came into force on 1 February 2001: Trustee Act 2000 (Commencement) Order 2001/49.

Peter Luxton
February 2001

Sheffield

CONTENTS—SUMMARY

VI CHARITABLE GIVING AND FUND-RAISING

VII DISSOLUTION OF CHARITIES

APPENDICES

CONTENTS

III LEGAL STRUCTURES AND GOVERNANCE

8. Legal Structures and the Distribution of Power

9. Trustees, Committee Members, and Directors

IV SUPERVISION AND CONTROL

10. The Charity Commissioners

Contents

VII DISSOLUTION OF CHARITIES

APPENDICES

TABLE OF CASES

TABLES OF LEGISLATION

Statutory Instruments

LIST OF ABBREVIATIONS

Articles and periodicals

ALJR	Australian Law Journal Reports
Ch Com News	Charity Commission News
Ch Com Rep	Annual Report of the Charity Commissioners for England and Wales
CL & PR	Charity Law & Practice Review
CLJ	Cambridge Law Journal
CLP	Current Legal Problems
Conv	Conveyancer and Property Lawyer
Decisions	Decisions of the Charity Commissioners
EHRR	European Human Rights Reports
Harv LR	Harvard Law Review
Hist J	*Historical Journal*
J Brit St	*Journal of British Studies*
JCLI	Journal of Current Legal Issues
JPL	Journal of Planning and Environment Law
LS	Legal Studies
Mich L Rev	Michigan Law Review
MLR	Modern Law Review
NILQ	Northern Ireland Legal Quarterly
NLJ	New Law Journal
P & CR	Property & Compensation Reports
PL	Public Law
Sol Jo	Solicitors Journal
TL & P	Trust Law & Practice
Trust Law Int	Trust Law International
Vict St	*Victorian Studies*

Statutes

AEA 1925	Administration of Estates Act 1925
CA	Charities Act
CA(NI) 1964	Charities Act (Northern Ireland) 1964
Companies Acts	Companies Acts 1985–1989
FA	Finance Act
FSA 1986	Financial Services Act 1986

ICTA 1988	Income and Corporation Taxes Act 1988
IHTA 1984	Inheritance Tax Act 1984
LP (Misc Provs) A 1989	Law of Property (Miscellaneous Provisions) Act 1989
LPA	Law of Property Act
TA	Trustee Act
Taxes Acts	Income and Corporation Taxes Act 1988, other Income and Corporation Tax Acts, Taxation of Chargeable Gains Act 1992, and all other enactments relating to capital gains tax
TCGA 1992	Taxation of Chargeable Gains Act 1992
TIA 1961	Trustee Investments Act 1961
TLATA 1996	Trusts of Land and Appointment of Trustees Act 1996
VATA 1983	Value Added Tax Act 1983

Miscellaneous

AGM	annual general meeting
CLA	Charity Law Association
Convention right	right under the Human Rights Convention
CPR	Civil Procedure Rules
EGM	extraordinary general meeting
ESC	Extra-statutory Concession

PART I

INTRODUCTION

1

THE SHAPING OF CHARITY LAW

A. Historical background

(1) Introduction

Good works that would today fall within the popular meaning of charity are **1.01** recorded in many societies in the past. Some acts of charity—particularly those which are spontaneous and direct—are manifestations of the better side of human nature and are no doubt as old as mankind itself. With such acts the law need not concern itself; indeed, such acts of benevolence may take place even before any form of society, let alone any recognizable legal system, has evolved. No legal machinery is needed to enable a donor, moved perhaps by compassion, to put alms into the hand of the beggar; no law has to be passed in order that a Good Samaritan may come to the aid of the injured traveller lying by the roadside. Such gifts or acts are by their nature transient and in themselves complete: they give rise to no continuing rights or obligations: they do not call for any method of legal supervision, protection or enforcement. The almsgiver and the Samaritan see the object of their pity, they do the good deed, and they go on their way.

1.02   In a wealthier society, philanthropic activity may become more extensive and more varied in scope. Once such activity extends beyond gifts to needy individuals, however, to the provision of benefits for groups (such as the poor of a particular village) or for a purpose which benefits society more generally (such as the repair of roads or sea-walls), the carrying out and effectiveness of the gift may to a large degree be dependent upon there being in place an appropriate system of law by which such charitable activity can be protected against the fraud and other wrongful acts of those charged with the responsibility of performing it. If the purposes of the gift are capable of endurance, and are to be carried out over decades or even centuries, its ultimate effectiveness may also depend upon the extent to which the society in question is prepared, through its legal system, to make provision for the modernization of purposes which have, over time, become outmoded.

1.03   In due course, the value of such good works to society may be recognized, so that there evolves some legal means to enable such works to be effected or facilitated. In some systems, however, the scope of legal intervention goes no further. There is no natural tendency for societies to evolve a system of direct public intervention, whereby the state will itself seek to protect gifts for such purposes, and compel those charged with carrying them out to discharge their duties properly. If such public intervention (which did occur in England) is regarded as progress, then the legal treatment of philanthropic activity in ancient Rome appears to reveal a stage of development which might be described as intermediate. Relatively complex types of charitable or philanthropic activity took place in ancient Rome. Plutarch records, for instance, that the will of Julius Caesar gave 'the gardens beyond the river' to the people[1]—a gift which Shakespeare has revealed to the citizens of Rome in the speech of Anthony:[2]

> Moreover, he hath left you all his walks,
> His private arbours, and new-planted orchards,
> On this side Tiber; he hath left them you,
> And to your heirs for ever; common pleasures,
> To walk abroad and recreate yourselves.

1.04   Yet, although the Romans possessed a developed legal system—one which even apparently recognized the doctrine which is known in modern English law as cy-près[3]—they had no particular method of protecting property given for 'chari-

---

[1] Plutarch, *The Lives of Caesar and Brutus*
[2] Shakespeare, *Julius Caesar*, Act III, Sc. 2, lines 248–52
[3] See H Picarda, (1992–3) 1 CL & PR 9, 14, citing Modestinus (d. 244 AD), who suggested that a legacy to a city for the holding of annual games in memory of the testator, should (the games being found to be illegal) be applied in some other lawful way to preserve the testator's memory

table' purposes.[4] The Romans did, however, permit a gift for 'charitable' purposes to one town to be made subject to a condition that the property should be applied to another town if the condition were not observed[5]—an indirect method of encouraging compliance with the terms of the gift which has a parallel in English law.[6]

The fact that in England the state did, over a period of centuries, take upon itself **1.05** the enforcement and protection of charitable gifts and institutions does not, however, necessarily mean that English law has, in this respect, for centuries been more advanced than its civil law counterparts, which never developed any comparable method of enforcement. To some extent, the relatively stable nature of English society since the Norman Conquest, and the evolution under it of that very flexible institution, the trust, have enabled English charity law to develop in the way it has; but this does not explain why, to this day, Continental systems have no general state machinery whose function is to protect and enforce charitable gifts in a way comparable to that of the Attorney-General in England. Even among common law systems, the degree of state intervention varies; a large number of the States of the USA, and some Australian States and Territories, whilst possessing an Attorney-General to protect charitable gifts, lack any public body comparable to the Charity Commission in England whereby charities can be subjected to more continuous supervision.

The fact that the public protection and enforcement of charitable activity in **1.06** England springs largely from the important role which trust law has played in the development of charity law has had one other important consequence on the nature of charity in English law. Protection for charity in England is directed towards charity, not as an act of goodness, but as an institution. This was the first and most crucial step by which 'charity' in its legal meaning began to divert from 'charity' in its popular sense. Charity became, not the act of giving—an act of charity—but the legal institution interposed between giver and recipient. Indeed, direct giving, without such filter, is not 'charitable' in English law. It is, perhaps, somewhat paradoxical that the act of the Good Samaritan—the epitome of an act of charity in the New Testament—is not 'charitable' in a technical, legal sense at all. In England then, charity law is necessarily a law of charitable institutions. In Continental systems, by contrast, and to some extent in federal systems, other indirect methods of regulation, notably by taxation, become more important.

---

   [4] See H Picarda, 'Charity in Roman Law: Roots and Parallels' (1992–3) 1 CL & PR 9; CEF Rickett, 'Charitable Giving in English and Roman Law' [1979] CLJ 118; AR Hands, *Charities and Social Aid in Greece and Rome* (Thames and Hudson, 1968)
   [5] H Picarda, (1992–3) 1 CL & PR 9, 12
   [6] cf *Christ's Hospital v Grainger* (1849) 1 Mac & G 460; see H Picarda, (1992–3) 1 CL & PR 9, 13

That is why, for example, the German lawyer treats the law of charitable purposes (*gemeinnüzige Zwecke*) as an aspect, not of property law, but of taxation.

(2) Charitable giving in the medieval period

1.07 In medieval times, most charitable gifts were administered by the church and protected by the ecclesiastical courts. Wealthy testators were encouraged to be generous to the church in the hope of entering the kingdom of heaven. There were therefore many gifts for the repair of churches and the maintenance of church institutions (including hospitals and almshouses). Many testators established chantries by their gifts.[7] Other charitable dispositions were to endow schools and other educational establishments, notably Oxford and Cambridge colleges. Some charities that survive to this day are older than the law of trusts,[8] which was developing significantly in the fourteenth century; but the charitable trust, which was also emerging during this period, is the most ancient of the present legal structures generally available to charities.

(3) From the Reformation to the Restoration

1.08 Following the Reformation and the break with Rome in the sixteenth century, charitable purposes tended to become more secular. This is reflected in the Preamble to the Statute of Elizabeth 1601, which mentions religion only in a limited way by reference to 'the repair of churches'; and even that appears to have been concerned more with the relief of rates than with matters of religion *per se*. The Tudor monarchs were concerned to prevent poverty, which they considered a cause of social disorder; and an aspect of this concern manifested itself in the foundation of new schools and the making of loans. The Tudors were also concerned to exert control over the whole country; this could be facilitated by the improvement of roads and bridges and the like: it is therefore not surprising to see these purposes expressly mentioned in the Preamble. It seems that one-third of charities that existed in this period are still in existence today.[9]

1.09 The Statute of Elizabeth 1601,[10] which re-enacted a statute of 1597,[11] was designed to provide a better system for the administration of charities; which shows that the importance of the proper administration of charities has been recognized for some four centuries. The Act established a commission to enable

---

[7] These were gifts to the church for the provision of a priest to say masses for the soul of the deceased

[8] eg St John's Hospital at Malmesbury, which is mentioned in a charter given to the borough in 939, may be the oldest surviving almshouse in the country: B Nightingale, *Charities* (Allen Lane, 1973) 5–6

[9] See KW Jordan, *Philanthropy in England 1480–1660* (George Allen & Unwin, 1959)

[10] 43 Eliz I c 4. It is also known as the Charitable Uses Act 1601

[11] 39 Eliz I c 6 (Statute of Charitable Uses 1597)

complaints to be heard.[12] The commissioners travelled around the country hearing complaints; they were empowered to issue decrees, and the Lord Chancellor could commit for contempt anyone who failed to observe them. The commissioners under the 1601 Act had jurisdiction only if the purpose fell within the ambit of its Preamble. Initially the system appears to have worked quite well; but the system largely broke down during the period of the Civil War and during the Interregnum. A few commissions were issued after this date; but, by the time of Charles I, a better and speedier method of protecting charities was perceived to be by an information to the Attorney-General. An information was brought formally in the name of the Attorney-General, but at the relation of a private individual.[13] From the end of the seventeenth century, this became the commonest way of proceeding; and the method under the 1601 Act fell into desuetude: the last commission under the Act of 1601 was issued in 1787,[14] and the Act of 1601 was abolished in 1853.

(4) The age of associated philanthropy

An important development is the change in the form of giving from the Restoration onwards.[15] Emerging in the late seventeenth century, and of increasing importance in the eighteenth, was the pursuit of charity through collective activity. Associations of persons would open up subscription lists to provide regular sources of funding for their charitable activities. This period has been called the age of 'associated philanthropy'.[16] **1.10**

The acquisition of land by means of associated philanthropy was indirectly encouraged by the Mortmain Act 1736,[17] which rendered void devises of land to charity unless the testator had complied with a complex procedure in his lifetime. Instead of making a legacy to be laid out in the purchase of land (which would be struck down by the statute), many testators would leave a sum by will to be applied for the building on land that was required to be purchased by means of the proceeds of subscriptions and donations. A legacy in this form was not caught by the Act.[18] The Mortmain Act therefore encouraged associated philanthropy whenever land was required; and it is perhaps not surprising, therefore, that, in the **1.11**

---

[12] For the history of the commissioners' activities, this account is heavily reliant on G Jones, *History of the Law of Charity, 1532–1827* (Cambridge Univ Press, 1969) 52–6

[13] ibid, 161

[14] ibid, 56

[15] D Owen, *English Philanthropy 1660–1960* (Harvard Univ Press, 1964) 3, 11–12

[16] See K Gray, *A History of English Philanthropy from the Dissolution of the Monasteries to the taking of the first census* (New York: Augustus M Kelly, repr 1967), 79–81

[17] 9 Geo II c 36

[18] *Vaughan v Farrers* (1751) 2 Ves Sen 182; *A-G v Bowles* (1754) 3 Atk 806 (both decisions of Lord Hardwicke); see G Jones, *History of the Law of Charity 1532–1827* (Cambridge Univ Press, 1969) 115

eighteenth century, associated philanthropy was responsible for the founding of many charity schools and hospitals.

1.12 The origins of voluntary societies lie mainly in three forms of organization,[19] the legal structures of which were adapted to the pursuit of associated philanthropy. The first was the joint-stock company, from which the charitable voluntary association derived the characteristics of the annual general meeting, and the relationships between the subscribers *inter se*, and between the subscribers and either the committee or the promoters.[20] The second was the chapel, where the property was generally vested in trustees, with the congregation (including the pew-rent payers)[21] having various rights, such as the right to elect or reject a minister or to inspect accounts. The third was the public house, which was the meeting place for informal community or trade groups; the public house was thus the venue for the formation of many debating societies, subscription libraries, friendly and building societies, and loan clubs; some of these developed in the nineteenth century into bodies of a charitable nature, such as public libraries and some friendly societies.

1.13 Industrialization in the early nineteenth century and the growth in city populations produced the great age of charitable societies,[22] and these offered Victorian ladies an opportunity to participate in philanthropic activity,[23] through participation in the charity bazaar[24] and in charity committees.[25] In the middle of the nineteenth century, municipalities co-ordinated the raising of money for social

---

[19] See RJ Morris, 'Voluntary Societies and British Urban Elites, 1780–1850: an Analysis' (1983) 26 *Hist J* 95, 104–105

[20] The joint-stock company's practice of financing their buildings was through proprietary members or shareholders; but this aspect contributed more to the development of self-help associations, such as building societies, which are not in law charitable

[21] The history of the funding of church building and maintenance is to some extent a microcosm of the history of fund-raising generally, in that there is a discernible trend from property, through gift, to contract. Before the middle of the 19th century, many churches raised funds from annual pew-rents (property). Increased costs from that time led to a general rise in the level of pew-rents; and by the 1860s these needed to be supplemented by quarterly collections (gifts). Even these collections proved insufficient, and by the 1890s the regular Sunday collections were introduced. More recently, some cathedrals have introduced a visitors' fee (contract): in 1986 Ely Cathedral became the first to charge a general admission fee to visitors: see W Schwarz, 'Fee to enter cathedral' Guardian 14 Jan 1986; 'Hard-up cathedral charges visitors' Guardian 3 Mar 1986

[22] D Owen. *English Philanthropy 1660–1960* (Harvard Univ Press, 1964) 91–2

[23] See KD Reynolds, *Aristocratic Women and Political Society in Victorian Britain* (Oxford Univ Press, 1998) esp chs 2 & 3

[24] See FK Prochaska, 'Charity bazaars in nineteenth-century England' (1977) 16 *J Brit St* 62

[25] An excellent parody of 19th-century philanthropic institutions of this nature is contained in Wilkie Collins' *The Moonstone* (1862), Second Period, First Narrative, ch 1, where Miss Clack refers to a meeting of the 'Select Committee of the Mothers'-Small-Clothes'-Conversion Society', whose object was 'to rescue unredeemed fathers' trousers from the pawnbroker, and to prevent their resumption, on the part of the irreclaimable parent, by abridging them immediately to suit the proportions of the innocent son'

amenities, as evidenced by the public park movement financed by public sub-scription and government funds.[26]

By the late eighteenth century, the method of enforcing charitable trusts by means   **1.14**
of an information was itself becoming unsatisfactory. As such proceedings were in
the Court of Chancery, the main drawback was the delay and expense of the litigation. In practice, the Attorney-General would not permit the action to proceed
unless someone (the relator) were responsible for his costs and for those of the
defendant should the action fail. The relator would also be personally liable if the
action was considered improper or unnecessary. Even if a successful action were
brought, and the relator awarded his costs, these would never cover the full costs of
the litigation, and some relators were brought to financial ruin as a consequence.[27]

(5) Victorian legal reforms

The reform of the administration of charities in the nineteenth century is an   **1.15**
aspect of the general reform of the administration of justice. Following pressure by
the Benthamite Lord Henry Brougham, the first of a series of parliamentary commissions was set up in 1818 to investigate breaches of charitable trusts. By 1835
these commissions had published twenty-four long reports. It was not until 1853,
however, that the first wide-ranging piece of legislation was passed: the Charitable
Trusts Act 1853. This Act enabled the newly established Charity Commissioners
to inquire into the management of endowed charitable trusts, and to obtain
accounts and statements from trustees. Where they considered legal proceedings
appropriate, they could certify cases to the Attorney-General; and no charity proceedings could be brought by anyone other than the Attorney-General without
the Charity Commissioners' consent. This Act led to the effectual demise of the
relator action in charity cases. The power to apply property cy-près was conferred
on the Commissioners a few years later.[28] The Act of 1853, however, applied only
to endowed charities, that is only to charitable trusts which held property of
which they were permitted to spend only the income. It did not apply to charities
(such as collecting charities) which were permitted to spend their capital as
income without forming an endowment.

(6) Street collecting

The later nineteenth century witnessed the growth of street collecting. There was   **1.16**
much opposition to this from some charitable sectors. A notable critic was the
Charity Organisation Society, which considered that collecting by such means
removed that element of personal involvement with a charity which, in its view,

---

[26] HL Malchow, 'Public gardens and social action in late Victorian London' (1985) 29 *Vict St* 97
[27] G Jones, *History of the Law of Charity 1532–1827* (Cambridge Univ Press, 1969) 161–2
[28] Charitable Trusts Act 1860, ss 2, 4

was the mainspring of associated philanthropy. Street collecting for charity was also perceived as akin to begging.[29]

1.17 No legislation to deal with street collecting was introduced until the First World War, when there was a perceived problem of abuse of funds from rogue collectors collecting for bogus service charities. This led to the swift enactment of the Police, Factories etc (Miscellaneous Provisions) Act 1916, section 5 of which enabled the police officer for the relevant authority to make regulations governing street collections. In 1972, this power was transferred (outside the Metropolitan Police District) to local authorities.[30] The House to House Collections Act 1939 was passed in order to deal with similar abuses. These two statutes will be repealed if and when Part III of the Charities Act 1993 is brought into force. The War Charities Act 1940, which originally dealt only with collections for the armed forces, and which was later extended to collections for the disabled, has, however, been repealed.[31]

(7) Charity in the age of the welfare state

1.18 The major developments in the provision of charity in the twentieth century, until the late 1970s, was the introduction and expansion of state provision taking over many of the functions previously performed by voluntary effort. This began with the Liberal Government's reforms of 1910–11, with Lloyd George's introduction of compulsory insurance against sickness and unemployment in 1911,[32] and continued under the Labour Government of 1945–51, with the introduction of the National Health Service in 1946.[33] The voluntary sector came to be seen as a mere junior partner in the major areas of welfare provision; and many considered that it had been entirely superseded by state provision and was no longer needed. A number of inquiries were instigated after the Second World War to consider the function of charity in the age of state welfare. The most important of these was the Nathan Committee, set up by the Conservative Government, which reported in 1952.[34] Nathan's remit was charitable trusts only; collecting charities were beyond its area of recommendations. Its recommendations were, however, enacted in the Charities Act 1960, which repealed the previous governing Act of 1853 and later Acts which had amended it.

---

[29] See a report of the meeting of the Charity Organisation Society in The Times 5 Feb 1895, 8, under the heading: 'Street begging by children for charities': see also Thomas J Barnardo's defence of child street collectors from this charge in a letter to The Times 7 Feb 1895

[30] Local Government Act 1972, s 251, Sch 29, Pt II, para 22

[31] CA 1992, s 78(2), Sch 7

[32] National Insurance Act 1911; see also Old Age Pension Act 1908, which introduced pensions for poor people of at least 70 years of age

[33] National Health Service Act 1946

[34] *Report of the Committee on the Law and Practice relating to Charitable Trusts*, Lord Nathan (chairman), Cmd 8710 (1952)

The Charities Act 1960 retained the Charity Commission,[35] and extended its **1.19**
scope to collecting charities as well. For the first time it established a public register of charities to be maintained by the Charity Commissioners.[36] It also extended
the legal scope of the cy-près jurisdiction,[37] and made numerous other minor
changes to charity law. The Act of 1960 was the governing Act until it was
repealed and replaced by the Charities Act 1993.

(8) Private welfare and public scrutiny

Moves to change the law based on the Charities Act 1960 sprang from a number **1.20**
of reports of private and governmental bodies, beginning with a report of the
National Council for Voluntary Organisations (NCVO) in 1986, *Malpractice in
Fundraising for Charity*,[38] which highlighted a number of concerns in that area,
and which made specific recommendations for reform. The report of the National
Audit Office, *Monitoring and Control of Charities in England and Wales*,[39] found
big gaps in the regulatory system, and 'disturbing evidence of a growth in the
extent of criminal charity-related fraud and abuse'.[40]

The philosophy of the Conservative Governments from 1979 onwards was to roll **1.21**
back the frontiers of the state, and to encourage private welfare. Not surprisingly,
therefore, the period since the 1980s has witnessed a vast expansion in the voluntary sector, and an increase in the varieties of methods of fund-raising, for example on the television (telethons and the BBC's Children in Need Appeal), and by
means of credit-card giving and payroll deduction. It was therefore evident that it
was important to tighten up the efficiency and effectiveness of the voluntary sector generally.

The Home Office appointed Sir Philip Woodfield to carry out an efficiency **1.22**
scrutiny of the supervision of charities, and his committee reported in 1987.[41]
There followed a report from the Committee of Public Accounts,[42] which
expressed grave concern at the risk of fraud, abuse, and maladministration of
charities, and heavily criticized the Charity Commission's passive attitude to its
role. Pending legislation, it also called for prompt and vigorous action to improve
supervision within the existing law. In 1989, the Government put forward a

---

[35] CA 1960, s 1(1)
[36] ibid, s 4(1)
[37] ibid, ss 13–15
[38] *Malpractice in Fundraising for Charity*, report of a working party of the NCVO, Harry Kidd
(chairman), (1986)
[39] National Audit Office, *Monitoring and Control of Charities in England and Wales* (1987)
[40] ibid, summary and conclusions, 4, para 4(w)
[41] *Efficiency Scrutiny of the Supervision of Charities*, report of the Woodfield Committee, Sir
Philip Woodfield (chairman), (HMSO, 1987)
[42] Committee of Public Accounts, *Monitoring and Control of Charities in England and Wales*
16th Report (HC Paper (1988) no 116)

White Paper, *Charities: a Framework for the Future*,[43] setting out its proposals for reform, which were largely along the lines of the Woodfield Report. Meanwhile, the Home Office, acting on recommendations in the Woodfield Report, had issued a consultation paper in 1988, suggesting changes in the law relating to public charitable collections.[44]

1.23   The Charities Bill 1992 was introduced to implement the White Paper. It was primarily debated in the House of Lords, which made a large number of amendments to it, many of which were accepted by the Government. It was passed and became the Charities Act 1992. This made important changes to the Charities Act 1960 and to the Commissioners' powers and introduced a new regime for charity collections and fund-raising. The Charities Act 1960 and most of the Charities Act 1992 (with the exception of the provisions relating to charity collections and fund-raising) were consolidated in the Charities Act 1993.

B. The sources of charity law

1.24   The modern law of charity is contained partly in case law and partly in legislation (both primary and subordinate). The definition of charity is, with the limited exception of the Recreational Charities Act 1958, to be found entirely in the case law. The law relating to the supervision and regulation of charities, however, whilst partly based in case law (for example, the cy-près doctrine), is, for the most part, a creature of statute.

1.25   The principal governing statute is currently the Charities Act 1993, as amended.[45] This is a consolidating Act, which brings together most of the changes to the legislation relating to charities effected by the Charities Act 1992. Outside the consolidation, and therefore still on the statute book, are the provisions relating to fund-raising (in Part II of the 1992 Act), and to public charitable collections (in Part III, though not yet brought into force at the time of writing[46]). Since these provisions are not restricted in their scope to charities in the strict sense, they may well be consolidated into their own separate Act in due course. The Recreational Charities Act 1958 also survived the consolidation, probably because it deals with an aspect of the definition of charity, and is therefore out of place in a measure

---

[43] Cm 694 (1989)

[44] Home Office Consultation Paper, *The Regulation of Charitable Appeals in England and Wales* (1988)

[45] The principal amendments have been made by the Deregulation and Contracting Out Act 1994, the Charities Amendment Act 1995, and the Trusts of Land and Appointment of Trustees Act 1996

[46] Until Pt III (or any other provision that might replace it) is brought into force, public charitable collections are still principally governed by the Police, Factories etc (Miscellaneous Provisions) Act 1916, s 5 (street collections) and the House to House Collections Act 1939

such as the Charities Act 1993 that is from first to last concerned with supervision and regulation.

The principal current legislation affecting charities therefore comprises (in chro- **1.26**
nological order) the following:

Police, Factories, etc (Miscellaneous Provisions) Act 1916, section 5
House to House Collections Act 1939
Charitable Trusts (Validation) Act 1954
Recreational Charities Act 1958
Charities Act 1992, Part II and (when brought into force) Part III
Charities Act 1993

Whilst the Charity Commissioners' decisions and practices are not themselves **1.27**
law, they provide important indications of the Commissioners' interpretation of
the law. To this extent, and also given the relatively small numbers of charity cases
which reach the courts, the Charity Commissioners' understanding of the law, as
indicated in its decisions, publications and guidance notes, is, for most practical
purposes, likely to prove decisive. For this reason, the views of the Charity
Commissioners are accorded a particularly important place in this book.

C. An overview of the charitable sector

It is impossible to state precisely how many charities there are in England and **1.28**
Wales. Part of the problem is identifying what entities to count. At the end of
1998, the number of charities registered with the Charity Commissioners
exceeded 186,000;[47] but only some 159,000 of these were main charities, the rest
being subsidiaries, branches, or constituent groups of charities.[48] Another
difficulty is that many charities exist which are not registered. In some cases this is
because they are not required to register,[49] and these may number 100,000.[50]
There are undoubtedly other charities which ought to be registered, but are not.
Even taking account of the fact that there are a few hundred registered charities
that cannot be traced and which may in fact be defunct,[51] it might be reasonable
to estimate that there are well over 250,000 main charities in England and Wales.
The number of registered charities has grown immensely in the last few decades.
By the end of 1971, for instance, there were only about 78,600 registered

---

[47] To be precise, 186, 248: [1998] Ch Com Rep, Ann i
[48] ibid
[49] See further ch 10, paras 10.03–10.34
[50] See Judith Hill and E Hackett, 'Exempt Charities' (1992–3) 1 CL & PR 209
[51] See [1994] Ch Com Rep 6, where it was reported that only 460 charities on the register proved
completely elusive

charities.[52] It is, however, important to bear in mind that the criteria for registration were changed in 1992,[53] and the increase in the numbers of registered charities since then may be partially due to the increased awareness of the need for registration which the Charities Act 1992 generated.[54]

1.29 Statistics compiled by the Charity Commissioners for 1992[55] showed that nearly one-quarter of registered charities (24 per cent) were for the relief of poverty. This was followed by charities for the advancement of education (16 per cent); social welfare and culture (15 per cent); health and sickness (10.8 per cent); children, young people and students (9.5 per cent); and religion (7.1 per cent). The remainder were listed under the headings of general and miscellaneous purposes for the benefit of the community, the elderly, overseas, and moral welfare. Many registrations in recent years have been of charities for social welfare and cultural purposes, for the benefit of young people, and for purposes such as the protection of the environment, helping the unemployed, the promotion of racial harmony, the relief of victims of AIDS, and the provision of drug relief. Charities for the relief of poverty still form the largest proportion of registered charities; but many of them are very old, and they now comprise a smaller proportion of the number of registered charities than in earlier years. In 1970, for example, charities for the relief of poverty had comprised nearly half of all registered charities.[56] The change in the criteria for registration in 1992, however, makes it necessary to treat these figures with caution. Furthermore, an increase in the mid-1990s in the number of charities concerned with health did not itself reflect an increase in activity in this area, but rather the registration of NHS Charities following a review: the Charity Commissioners estimated that some 25,000 of these (about half the total) needed to be registered.[57]

1.30 The capital[58] of individual charities varies enormously; but it is difficult to give precise figures because charities are not required to state the value of their capital in their public accounts. It is clear, however, that there is a small number of charities with assets worth millions or even billions of pounds. If account is taken of all assets,[59] the universities are in this super-league. So are the Church Commissioners for England (who have control of the assets of the Church of England): in

---

[52] [1971] Ch Com Rep 29 (para 97)

[53] CA 1992, s 2(5)

[54] [1992] Ch Com Rep 17 (para 64)

[55] [1992] Ch Com Rep 18 (table showing breakdown of registered charities by object type)

[56] The precise figure was 47%: [1970] Ch Com Rep 8–9 (para 20 and table)

[57] [1993] Ch Com Rep 10 (paras 30–1); [1994] Ch Com Rep 7–8 (which refers to the booklet, *NHS Charitable Funds: a Guide*, produced by the Charity Commission)

[58] ie that part of the charity's property which is not applicable as income of the charity, including land which the charity owns either for investment or occupation by it or the persons who benefit from the charity, and other investments (shares, bank deposit accounts, mortgages, and the like)

[59] ie including, for instance, the value of land and buildings occupied for the purposes of the charity rather than leased out for investment

1991 they had estates and assets worth £2.645 billion, producing an investment income of some £164 million.[60] Another example is the British Museum: in 1983 the value of its investment fund alone (which excludes, therefore, the value of its land, buildings, the museum objects, and other assets) was between £5 million and £6 million.[61] The largest charity in England and Wales is the Wellcome Foundation, which in 1988 had assets of £3,200 million.[62] There is a larger group of medium-sized charities, but the largest group of charities have very little in the way of capital assets.

At the end of 1998, the total annual income of registered charities was about £19.7 billion.[63] The annual income of all charities is bound to be significantly greater than this, but amounts are difficult to calculate with any precision, especially as it is difficult to avoid some element of double accounting (as where one charity makes a donation to another), and as it depends upon whether some receipts (such as fees charged to those using a charity's services) are included. The particular income of individual charities varies enormously: there are a few charities with very large incomes. An analysis of the income of registered charities during 1998 reveals that the largest 271 charities (a mere 0.17 per cent of those registered) account for some 40 per cent of the total annual income; and that 5 per cent of all registered charities receive approximately 85 per cent of the total recorded annual income. At the other end of the scale, some 70 per cent of registered charities have an annual income of £10,000 or less, and their combined income is less than 2 per cent of the annual income of all registered charities.[64]   **1.31**

Charities may obtain funding from a variety of sources: some are funded by an initial injection of capital from a settlor or body which produces an investment income sufficient to enable the charity to carry out its activities without needing to raise funds from additional sources. These types of charities are often endowed charitable trusts, many of which date back to medieval times. Other charities rely wholly or partly on revenue funding, through grants, membership subscriptions, the sale of goods or services, charges to users, fund-raising and spontaneous donations. In 1980, it was found that more than 70 per cent of the income of the charitable sector was derived from fees, charges, and grants from statutory bodies.[65]   **1.32**

Since the 1980s, however, the trend has been away from government funding of charities by means of grants; instead, the trend has been towards funding pursuant to contracts. A primary cause of this development, which has been termed 'the   **1.33**

---

[60]   *Harries v Church Commissioners for England* [1992] 1 WLR 1241, 1243
[61]   This was the figure stated by Megarry V-C in *Trustees of the British Museum v A-G* [1984] 1 WLR 418
[62]   See *Steel v Wellcome Custodian Trustees Ltd* [1988] 1 WLR 167
[63]   [1998] Ch Com Rep, Ann i
[64]   ibid
[65]   See J Posnett, *Charity Statistics 1983–4* (Charities Aid Foundation)

contract culture', was the election in 1979 of a Conservative Government amongst whose aims was the reduction of the state's direct involvement in welfare provision, which resulted in a greater role for voluntary bodies. One manifestation of this philosophy was the obligation placed upon local authorities, which had often provided such services themselves, to contract them out.[66] Another cause of the emergence of the contract culture has been identified as the increased professionalism in the voluntary sector, itself a result of the increasing competition for contract funding and of the recent legislation (in the Charities Acts 1992 and 1993) which have increased the demands on charity trustees and managers.[67] One significant legal consequence of this trend has been the need for charities to ensure that they have capacity to enter into such contracts, consistently with their objects and the restrictions of charity law, and to consider means of restricting the liability of their managers and members under such contracts.[68] Not surprisingly, many of the newer charities are choosing a corporate structure, which has the great advantage of providing its members with limited liability. For those proposing to set up a charity, selecting the appropriate legal structure and drafting the governing instrument are matters of the utmost importance.

D. Charitable status and legal structure

(1) Introduction

1.34 The term 'charity' is ambiguous; it can refer either to the status of being charitable, with the accompanying privileges and burdens, or it can refer to the particular institution which enjoys that status. Charity law refers essentially to the law relating to charitable status, regardless of an institution's legal structure. Charitable status can, however, be enjoyed only by a body which has a recognised legal structure, whether it be trust, unincorporated association, or corporation. The result is that all charitable institutions are subject to two sets of laws: those that relate to status, and those that relate to structure.

1.35 One of the fundamental problems with charity law is that the nature of charitable status was largely worked out in the context of one legal structure—namely the charitable trust. To this day, trusts law influences significantly the shaping of charity law, even in its use of the language of trusts. This is evident, for example, in the terminology of the principal governing statute, the Charities Act 1993, which refers to those persons having the general control and management of the administration of a charity as 'charity trustees',[69] even if they in fact happen to be direc-

---

[66] See J Warburton and D Morris, 'Charities and the contract culture' [1991] Conv 419
[67] ibid
[68] ibid

tors of a charitable company, or the committee members of an unincorporated charitable association. The encroachment of trusts law is also evident in relation to the manner in which charitable corporations hold their property. Although a company does not *per se* hold its property upon a trust in the strict sense, the courts have asserted jurisdiction over charitable companies incorporated under the Companies Acts on the footing that the effectual dedication of the property to charity by such a company's objects clause will be protected by equity.[70] We are witnessing the encroachment of trusts law by stealth.

The powerful influence of the trust has also led to confusion in some areas over whether the appropriate law should be that which relates to status or that which relates to structure. An example concerns the fiduciary duties of directors of charitable companies: should they be judged by the fiduciary standards laid down for trustees in the strict sense, or by those laid down for company directors generally? In the context of charities, even the applicability of some statutes becomes blurred. Could it be that some sections of the Trustee Act 1925 might apply to charitable companies that hold their assets on trust? The case law provides no clear answers. In such cases of conflict, the solution lies, it is suggested, in asking whether the issue concerns one of charitable status or legal structure.   **1.36**

The powerful influence of trusts law thinking in the charity sphere may be due in part to the fact that, whilst every charity must have a legal structure, there is no single structure in English law specifically designed for charities. This is surely a matter for surprise. For centuries, the Chancery judges have lavished attention on the minutiae of charitable status: there are vast numbers of cases exploring every facet of charitable status, there are thousands of cases on the meaning of charity and on the doctrine of cy-près; yet, for all this time, charities have had to make shift with a legal structure fashioned largely (in the case of the trust) for family property holding, or (in the case of the company) for commercial endeavour. Many charities, particularly those which exist as companies, are therefore subject to two sets of regulation, one status-related, and the other structure-related. Whilst, as has been mentioned, the law of trusts is invasive, the law relating to the legal structure of a particular charity is also playing its part in the development of charity law. The very fact that the legal structures used are not primarily designed for charities occasionally means that further conflict between rules of status and structure become apparent, and occasionally the latter have affected the former. The relationship between charitable status and legal structure is a theme which is discussed especially in chapter 8, but it also runs more generally throughout this book.   **1.37**

---

[69] CA 1993, s 97(1)
[70] *Liverpool and District Hospital for Diseases of the Heart v A-G* [1981] Ch 193

(2) A new corporate structure for charities?

1.38 During the 1990s proposals were put forward for the introduction of a new corporate structure designed specifically for charities,[71] and such a development was expressly welcomed in the Deakin Report.[72] The aim of the proposals is to enable those setting up a charity to obtain the benefits of separate corporate personality merely by registration of the corporate form with the Charity Commissioners, instead of with the Registrar of Companies. It is proposed that the new corporate structure should have two forms: the foundation, and the association with a membership structure. The proposal is that charities which adopt the new corporate structure, and those who control it, would be subject to a clear and coherent set of rules. The corporate entity would have a wide range of powers, including a wide power of investment; the standard of care of those controlling it would be specified; and there would be provisions relating to the disclosure of conflicts of interest, the rights of members, rules for the conduct of business, powers of amendment, and provisions for dissolution.

1.39 It is understood that a new corporate structure for charities on these lines is to be introduced in a Bill which will amend, and extend the scope of, the Deregulation and Contracting Out Act 1994. One of the aims of the Government's proposals is to confer on ministers a power allowing them to propose orders to amend, extend or supplement statutory provision so as further to enable or to facilitate things which the provision in question does not prohibit but which could not otherwise be done.[73] The Government specifically mentioned that this power could be used to introduce a new legal structure for charities:[74]

> The power would . . . cover cases such as the Charity Commission proposals to create a legislative vehicle for the incorporation of charities. For a number of reasons, incorporation is increasingly being seen as the most effective way for many charities to structure themselves. Many charities have been incorporated under the Companies Act 1985 and its statutory predecessors, others under industrial and provident society legislation. However these incorporated regimes were not structured with charities in mind, as their jurisprudence is more appropriate to commercial organisations or mutual traders. This can create operational and regulatory difficulties for charities.

---

[71] See *A New Legal Structure for Charities*, a paper prepared by a working party consisting of representatives of the CLA, the Univ of Liverpool, and the NCVOs (1996). See also J Warburton, 'Charity corporations: the framework for the future?' [1990] Conv 95, 101–5

[72] *Meeting the challenge of change: voluntary action into the 21st century*, report of the Commission on the future of the voluntary sector (Nicholas Deakin chairman) (NCVO, 1996) 84, (paras 3.4.1–3.4.3)

[73] *HL Select Committee on Delegated Powers and Deregulation 28th Report* (HL Paper (1998–9) no 111), Ann 2 Govt response to the 14th Report from the HL Select Committee on Delegated Powers and Deregulation (Session 1998–9) on Proposed Extension to the Deregulation and Contracting Out Act 1994, para 39

[74] ibid, paras 42–3

Use of the proposed power under the deregulation order-making procedure would provide a solution to this problem. Essentially it would allow the Charities Act(s) and/or the Companies Act(s) to be built on in order to allow a charity to become a body corporate, which could then be registered with and regulated by the Charity Commission. This would remove the operational and regulatory difficulties.

The Government had originally intended that orders should be permitted to remove burdens imposed by common law; but this proposal has since been withdrawn: an order under the extended deregulation legislation will still have to be anchored in a statutory provision.[75] As the common law does not recognize incorporation in the absence of a royal charter or statute, the inability of charities to incorporate except by one of these means might be considered to subject them to a burden imposed by common law. It nevertheless appears that a new incorporated structure for charities might still be introduced by order under the deregulation proposals, since any order could be treated as anchored in existing statutes, notably the Companies Acts. The Government has stated that, where appropriate, the Law Commission would advise on proposals in draft.[76] The Queen's Speech in November 1999 contained proposals for a deregulation Bill, but a draft Bill for comment by the Deregulation Committees was published only in April 2000.[77] **1.40**

In the meantime, the need for the introduction of a separate legal structure for charities has also been recognized in a Consultation Document produced by the Company Law Steering Group,[78] which, with a view to furthering the existing proposals,[79] has also produced Skeleton Draft Instructions for legislation to enable the creation of Charitable Incorporated Institutions (CIIs).[80] **1.41**

The introduction of a legal structure designed specifically for charities is undoubtedly to be welcomed. There is a distinct advantage in charities being able to choose a corporate form without having to become enmeshed in the complexities and commercial orientation of the Companies Act 1985. It might be mentioned in passing, however, that it is paradoxical that many of the overseas legal structures on which the proposals are partially based—notably the German *eingetragener Verein*,[81] and the Associations Incorporations Acts in force in a number of Australian States and Territories—are themselves not designed specifically for the **1.42**

---

[75] See Cabinet Office, *Proposed extension of the Deregulation and Contracting Out Act 1994: Survey of responses to the Government's consultation exercise and proposed next steps* (Sept 1999)

[76] ibid, para 45

[77] See *HL Select Committee on Delegated Powers and Deregulation* 15th Report (HL Paper (1999–2000) no 61); proposals reintroduced in Regulatory Reform Bill (Session 2000–1).

[78] Consultation Document, Company Law Steering Group, *Modern Company Law for a Competitive Economy: Developing the Framework*, (DTI, Mar 2000) ch 9

[79] ie those suggested in *A New Legal Structure for Charities* (n 71 above)

[80] The Skeleton Draft Instructions are available on the DTI's website

[81] For a brief discussion in English of the voluntary sector in Germany, see HK Anheier and W Seibel, 'Germany', ch 6 in LM Salamon and HK Anheier, *Defining the nonprofit sector: a cross-national analysis* (John Hopkins Nonprofit sector series 4, Manchester Univ Press, 1997). The *Verein* is considered ibid, 140–4

pursuit of charitable purposes, but as the vehicle for clubs and other associations whose aim is to further a lawful purpose other than for financial gain to the members or to the organization.[82]

1.43   The initial limited effect of the introduction of the new corporate form should be noted. It is envisaged that the new corporate structure would not replace, but would merely be additional to, existing charitable forms. New charities could choose it, and existing charities might be able to convert; but they could continue to exist as trusts, unincorporated associations or (unless prohibited from doing so) as companies limited by guarantee, as at present. It would be impractical to require all charities to adopt the new structure, since charitable status does not derive from registration either as a charity or as a legal entity, but merely from effectual dedication to charity; if charitable status were to be denied to bodies which did not register as such, the state would effectively be relinquishing its ability to protect charity funds. The benefits of the new structure would, however, be likely to appeal to many charities, so that in time the hope is that it might become the dominant form.

1.44   The Company Law Steering Group considers that, when the new legal structure is in place, it would be correct in principle to prohibit new charities from registering under the Companies Acts.[83] In practice, however, such prohibition would effectively require charitable status to be determined, on an application for registration under the Companies Acts, by the Registrar of Companies—which might be considered inappropriate. The Steering Group also raises the question whether, if new charities are to be prohibited from registering under the Companies Acts, charities which are currently so incorporated should be required to transfer their registration to the new legal structure.[84] The Group does not express a view on this, but it would seem that to compel such charities to re-register would be to impose on them an unnecessary burden.

1.45   Whilst the concept of registration as a separate legal entity with the Charity Commission is itself to be welcomed, there is, it is suggested, a need for further reflection on some of the other proposals which accompany it. One of the main themes of this book is the importance in charity law of distinguishing between matters of status and matters of structure; and, in some respects, the proposals do

---

[82] See, eg Associations Incorporation Act 1981 (Vic) (any lawful purpose); Associations Incorporation Act 1984 (NSW) (any lawful purpose); Associations Incorporation Act 1985 (SA) (any 'useful' object); Associations Incorporation Act 1991 (ACT) (specified purposes, including benevolent or charitable purposes); Associations Incorporation Act 1964 (Tas) (specified purposes, including benevolent or charitable purposes). See also Legal & Constitutional Cttee (Vic), *Report on the Public Liability of Voluntary Organisations*, 33rd Report to the Parliament, April 1989, ch 4; G Dal Pont, *Charity Law in Australia and New Zealand* (Oxford Univ Press, 2000) 374–5

[83] Consultation Document, Company Law Steering Group, *Modern Company Law for a Competitive Economy: Developing the Framework* (DTI, Mar 2000), DTI, paras 9.32–9.36 (294–6)

[84] ibid

not draw this distinction. There is no problem with a statute's laying down specific rules relating to the range of investments, conduct at meetings, the power to amend the constitution, and how the assets are to be distributed on dissolution, since these are all matters within which charity law permits some freedom of choice. But the standard of care of those controlling a charity, and the scope of the rule relating to conflicts of interests, should depend on the institution's status as a charity, not on its structure as a company. In other words, there must be a minimum standard of care, and a single rule relating to conflicts of interest, applicable to all those who control a charity's assets (whether they are trustees, committee members or directors) regardless of the charity's legal structure. There is no reason to prescribe these only in relation to one particular legal structure; any legislation relating to such matters ought to be contained in a separate statute of more general application to all those controlling a charity's assets. The Deakin Report evidently recognized the importance of this and recommended a codification of the law relating to the duties of charity trustees (which was clearly intended to include directors of charitable companies and committee members of unincorporated charitable associations) in the shape of a Charity Trustee Act, thus putting the relevant law into a single statute.[85] This approach implicitly recognizes that legislation relating to matters of charitable status needs to be contained in a separate statute from that which provides charities with available legal structures. This approach, it is submitted, is sound in principle, and is the one which should be adopted in any forthcoming legislative reforms.

(3) A European non-profit association?

Since the early 1990s, the Commission of the European Communities has been working on the development of a new legal structure, the European Association. **1.46** This would be an incorporated body established under Community legislation, which would ensure equal recognition for Associations in all Member States, and allow them to operate freely throughout the European Union.[86] The response to the draft regulations for such an Association did not, however, receive much support from those involved in the voluntary sector in the United Kingdom: the proposals were generally considered too rigid, too prescriptive in detail, and took little account of the practical problems involved in such an operation (for example, the absence of any provision for postal voting). Concern was also expressed about inadequate supervision of the proposed Association, and its possible use as a vehicle for fraud.[87] Work on developing the proposal further was put into the

---

[85] *Meeting the challenge of change: voluntary action into the 21st century,* The Report of the Commission on the Future of the Voluntary Sector, Nicholas Deakin (Charman) (NCVO, 1996) 85 (paras 3.5.1–3.5.3), 124 (rec 13)
[86] [1991] Ch Com Rep 4–5 (paras 18–20)
[87] [1992] Ch Com Rep 27 (para 106)

hands of an inter-governmental working group, but little progress seems to have been made.[88]

1.47 Continental systems make a broad division, which is not made in English law, between philanthropic grant-making 'foundations' and 'associations' (whether incorporated or unincorporated).[89] This is not in itself an insuperable problem, however, and the proposed introduction of a new corporate structure for English charities, with its twin forms of foundation and association, indicates that, in its provision of legal structures for charities, English law might be moving towards the Continental system. In other respects, however, a European Association such as that proposed raises particular problems for the United Kingdom.

1.48 First, the meaning of charity in England and Wales is broader than in Continental systems, which tend to limit it to the relief of poverty; and, whilst the Continental systems have institutions which perform what English law would consider to be charitable purposes within the other three heads of *Pemsel's* case, they do not (unlike English law) treat them as manifestations of a single concept.[90] Continental systems are more broadly concerned with regulating non-profit organizations generally, thereby including clubs, mutual associations and co-operatives, rather than with what the English lawyer would regard as charities.[91]

1.49 Secondly, Continental legal systems have no machinery for state enforcement of their 'charitable' institutions comparable to that in place in England and Wales through the Attorney-General and the Charity Commissioners. In the Civil Law systems, regulation of equivalent bodies tends to rely more on the intervention of members of voluntary associations, and on the indirect effect of withdrawal of tax reliefs when property is not applied to the stated objects.[92]

1.50 As it is the United Kingdom which is out of step with other Member States in these respects, it is difficult to see how substantial progress can be made on this issue without a fundamental rethink of the regulation of charities and other non-profit organizations within the United Kingdom, or even a fundamental rethink of the definition of charity itself.

---

[88] See [1993] Ch Com Rep 30 (para 118); [1995] Ch Com Rep 25 (paras 107–8); [1996] Ch Com Rep 31 (paras 220–2)

[89] [1989] Ch Com Rep 8 (para 17). See also KPE Lasok and D Beard, 'European Law and Charities' (1997) 71 NLJ Charities Appeals Suppl 13, 16; Jonathan Hill, 'Charitable foundations in French law', (1986) 1 TL & P 69; PC Hemphill, 'The Civil-Law Foundation as a Model for the Reform of Charitable Trusts Law', (1986) 1 TL & P 404

[90] See [1989] Ch Com Rep 8 (para 17)

[91] See [1990] Ch Com Rep 4 (para 17)

[92] See R Hüttermann, *Wirtschaftliche Betätigung und steuerliche Gemeinnützigkeit* (Verlag Dr Otto Schmidt KG, Cologne, 1991) Bundesministerium der Finanzen, *Gutachten der Unabhängigen Sachverstädigenkommission zur Prüfung des Gemeinnützigkeits- und Spendenrechts* Heft 40 (Stollfuss Verlag, Bonn, 1988)

E. Re-defining charity in English law

(1) A statutory definition?

There have for many years been calls for a re-defining of the meaning of charity in   **1.51**
English law.[93] Much of the criticism has not been directed towards moving
English law closer to the non-profit models of its Continental counterparts;
rather, commentators have tended to concentrate upon the anomalies and complexities of English charity law, its fairly tight restrictions on political objects and
political activity,[94] and its perceived inability to move sufficiently quickly to take
account of changes in society. The Deakin Report,[95] for instance, mentions the
fact that community development organizations, enterprise schemes, programmes to help the unemployed, mutual or self-help organizations such as credit
unions, and sporting organizations, are considered to lack the requisite element of
public benefit or to allow too much private benefit. It mentions that some human
rights and environmental groups have activities which are deemed too political to
be charitable; and that there have been problems and inconsistencies in relation to
what constitutes a sufficient section of the community.[96]

Since 1998, the Charity Commissioners have been embarked on the process of   **1.52**
reviewing the register of charities in an attempt to determine, within the law,
whether those organizations which currently benefit from charitable status should
continue to do so, and whether there is scope for the Commissioners to develop
further the boundaries of charitable status.[97] In undertaking this considerable
task, the Charity Commissioners adopt, as they have for several years, a flexible
approach to the application and interpretation of the law.[98] By use of this
approach, the Commissioners have, for instance, been able to register trusts to
promote good race relations, despite a decision of the Court of Appeal which suggested that such trusts were not charitable.[99] More recently, the Charity
Commissioners decided not to register two new rifle and pistol clubs,[100] thus

---

[93] A recent analysis containing an extensive review of the writings on this subject is C Mitchell, 'Redefining charity in English law' (1999) 13 Trust Law Int 21

[94] See A Dunn, 'Charity Law as a Political Option for the Poor' (1999) 50 NILQ 298

[95] *Meeting the challenge of change: voluntary action into the 21st century,* Report of the Commission on the Future of the Voluntary Sector (Chairman: Nicholas Deakin) (NCVO, 1996). For a commentary on the report, see Peter Luxton, 'The Deakin Report: its legal implications' (1996) 69 NLJ Christmas Appeals Suppl 15

[96] *Meeting the challenge of change: voluntary action into the 21st century,* Report of the Commission on the Future of the Voluntary Sector, Nicholas Deakin (chairman), (NCVO, 1996), 81, para 3.2.1

[97] See Charity Commissioners, RR1, *The Review of the Register of Charities* (1999). Two further re-view documents have since been published setting out the Commissioners' views on specified areas: see RR2, *Promotion of Urban and Rural Regeneration;* and RR3, *Charities for the Relief of Unemployment*

[98] See further ch 10, para 10.46

[99] *Re Strakosch* [1949] Ch 529; and see [1983] Ch Com Rep 10–11 (paras 15–20)

[100] *City of London Rifle and Pistol Club; Burnley Rifle Club* (1993) 1 Decisions 4, 10

effectively declining to follow a High Court decision of long- (albeit dubious) standing.[101] They have also come to the conclusion that the relief of unemployment—one of the Deakin Report's specific areas of criticism of the present definition of charity—is now to be treated as charitable.[102]

1.53 Nevertheless, so far as the existing law is clear, the Charity Commissioners are bound to apply it; so that, even with their progressive approach, the Commissioners' ability to develop charity law is far more circumscribed than that of the courts. The Charity Commissioners have themselves admitted, for instance, that only the courts could depart from the well-established principle, laid down in *Re Nottage*,[103] that the promotion of sport is not itself a charitable purpose.[104] The legal limits of the Commissioners' attempts to update charity law must therefore be recognized; and, to this extent, it must be admitted that there is merit in the Deakin Report's criticisms of English law's inability to develop charity law to meet the needs of modern society.

1.54 To deal with this problem of charity law's lagging some way behind social change, different suggestions have been put forward. The most extreme proposal was contained in the CENTRIS report[105] by Barry Knight in 1993, which recommended dismantling the whole legal concept of charity.[106] More restrained in its approach, the Deakin Report proposed that the legal concept of charity be retained, but recommended the abolition of the existing definition based upon the Preamble to the Statute of Elizabeth 1601 and upon *Pemsel*'s case,[107] and its replacement with an all-embracing statutory definition expressed as 'benefit to the community'. This definition, it says, would aim to be 'clear, workable and flexible'.[108] The community would need to be 'a sufficiently important sector of the public', and it seems to be implicit in this suggestion that some minority groups or black groups which are at present denied charitable status[109] would be brought within the new

---

[101] *Re Stephens* (1892) 8 TLR 792

[102] Charity Commission, *Charities for the Relief of Unemployment*, RR3 (1999); the Commissioners' new stance on unemployment, however, is not really the result of their own initiative, but is essentially derived from Lightman J's decision in *IRC v Oldham Training and Enterprise Council* [1996] STC 1218. See further Peter Somerfield, 'Review of the Register: Unemployment' (1999) 6 CL & PR 23

[103] [1895] 2 Ch 649

[104] See discussion of *The North Tawton Rugby Union Football Club*: [1995] Ch Com Rep 22

[105] CENTRIS Report by Barry Knight, *Voluntary Action in the 1990s* (Home Office, 1993)

[106] Discussed at [1993] NLJ Christmas Appeals Supp 16

[107] *Comrs for Special Purposes of the Income Tax v Pemsel* [1891] AC 531

[108] *Meeting the challenge of change: voluntary action into the 21st century*, Report of the Commission on the Future of the Voluntary Sector, Nicholas Deakin (chairman), (NCVO, 1996), para. 3.2.6

[109] This could be because they are in essence self-help organizations or because their purposes are too political. Furthermore, if a charity's purposes restrict its benefits to classes of persons defined by reference to colour, the colour restriction is struck out: Race Relations Act 1976, s. 34(1)

definition of charity. In 1975, a House of Commons Committee[110] similarly favoured replacing the existing definition of charity with a criterion that the purpose be 'beneficial to the community'.

A statutory definition of charity which is sufficiently succinct to allow for flexibility is, however, likely to lead to massive litigation in an attempt to establish what is in law charitable. This was one reason why the White Paper[111] on charities in 1989 rejected the idea of defining charitable purposes as 'purposes beneficial to the community'.[112] Lawyers seem to appreciate more than others the uncertainty that would result were the current meaning of charity in English law to be simply swept away.[113] As Sachs LJ once said:[114] **1.55**

> any statutory definition [of charity] might well merely produce a fresh spate of litigation and provide a set of undesirable artificial distinctions. There is indeed much to be said for flexibility in such matters.

The Nathan Report[115] of 1952 rejected any alteration in the content of the legal meaning of charity, but proposed that the *Pemsel* categories be put into statutory form in such a way as to preserve the existing case law.[116] In 1976, the Goodman Report[117] stated that it did not believe that it was possible to formulate a definition of charity which would enable the courts to look only at the words of the definition and not to the cases lying behind its evolution.[118] Like Nathan, it proposed that the existing case law be retained, but it suggested a more extensive statutory formulation of the *Pemsel* heads, including an updated list of the objects contained in the Preamble of 1601.[119] Even the more limited approach of these two reports was, however, rejected in the White Paper, which saw little point in a statutory definition that merely preserved the existing case law.[120] **1.56**

---

[110] Expenditure Committee *Charity Commissioners and their accountability 10th Report* (HC Paper (1975) no 495-I
[111] *Charities: a Framework for the Future*, White Paper, Cm 694 (1989)
[112] ibid, para. 2.15
[113] It is perhaps worth noting that the members of the Expenditure Committee admitted that they were not themselves lawyers: Expenditure Committee (n 110 above), para. 33. The more legally-constituted Nathan and Goodman Committees, by contrast, were more cautious. Indeed, the former noted that only its non-lawyer members advocated any change in the formulation of charity. See also AR Everton and A Dunn, 'Old Hats, New Models or Chapeaux Révisés?' (1999) 5 CL & PR 207
[114] *Incorporated Council of Law Reporting for England and Wales v A-G* [1972] Ch 73 at 94–5
[115] *Report of the Committee on the Law and Practice relating to Charitable Trusts*, Lord Nathan (chairman), Cmd 8710 (1952)
[116] ibid, ch 3
[117] Report of the Goodman Committee, *Charity Law and Voluntary Organisations* (Bedford Square Press, 1976)
[118] ibid, para. 31
[119] ibid, App I
[120] *Charities: a Framework for the Future*, White Paper, Cm 694 (1989), para. 2.14

1.57 To some extent, political considerations tend to preclude any change in the definition of charity. Discussion does, after all, provide a platform for those who wish to challenge the charitable status of public schools[121] or of some charities which provide overseas aid.[122] It is, therefore, not surprising that the White Paper declared the Government's intention not to change the law relating to the meaning of charity. What is charitable is necessarily a broad and complex issue, and it is bound to produce some uncertainties; so that, whilst a statutory definition might effectively sweep away some of the present areas of difficulty, it would undoubtedly replace them with different, and perhaps even greater, uncertainties. This is not to ignore the fact that some areas of charity law do need to be reformed; but, if uncertainty and litigation are to be avoided, it is probably better to retain the existing definition with discrete statutory modifications where required—there is already an example of this in the Recreational Charities Act 1958. A statute could, for instance, deem the promotion of sport to be a charitable purpose in its own right, and could also consign to history the anomaly which accords charitable status to trusts for a testator's poor relations.

1.58 A further important factor should also be borne in mind. Since very few cases on the definition of charity reach the courts, much of the detailed development of the meaning of charity in English law is carried out by the Charity Commissioners, who, as has been explained, are prepared to adapt the definition of charity in accordance with changes in society in the same way as the courts.[123] In so developing the definition of charity, the Charity Commissioners are effectively performing a quasi-judicial function; yet the Charity Commission remains, despite its virtual autonomy,[124] a part of the executive—a non-ministerial government department. At present the Commissioners' positive approach to developing charity law can to some extent be justified because, in reaching their decisions, the Commissioners have the guidance of substantial case law. If, however, the meaning of charity were to be changed and replaced by a statutory definition, its interpretation would also lie mainly with the Charity Commissioners, who would then lack the detailed guidance provided by the existing body of case law. The Charity Commissioners might view this as an opportunity to develop charity law free from the constraints of existing authorities; but any bold interpretations of the statute, without case law guidance, could be perceived as a mere naked usurpation

---

[121] As in Expenditure Committee, *Charity Commissioners and their accountability 10th Report,* HC Paper (1975) no 495-I, paras. 45–52

[122] eg those which have engaged in excessive political activity: see [1991] Rep Ch Com 19 (paras. 111–12)

[123] See Lord Simonds in *National Anti-Vivisection Society v IRC* [1948] AC 32, 74, and in *Gilmour v Coats* [1949] AC 426, 443

[124] Expenditure Committee, *Charity Commissioners and their accountability 10th Report,* HC Paper (1975) no 495-I, para. 23

by the executive of a function that is properly judicial. Paradoxically, therefore, the proper development of charity law might actually be hampered by a statutory definition.

There is also a related point. The Charity Commissioners have been criticized in recent years for determining charitable status on subjective grounds, rather than on a strict application of legal principles. The Charity Commissioners' approach may be due to the fact that only a minority of the current Commissioners are lawyers. It may also be that the criticisms made of the Commissioners in a series of reports which culminated in the Charities Acts 1992 and 1993, and the Commissioners' own internal re-organizations, have undermined the influence of lawyers within the Commission. Whatever the cause, it is indisputable that, in recent years, the Charity Commissioners have begun taking non-legal criteria into account in determining charitable status. It also appears that the Charity Commissioners have used these criteria to remove from the register some institutions which had previously been registered as charities.

The Charity Commissioners' present attitude is particularly evident in their review of the register, in which they have been engaging in consultation exercises and the commissioning of opinion polls in order to determine the public's views on charitable status. The most trenchant and telling criticism is that of Hubert Picarda QC, who has written:[125]

> The suggestion that consultation processes are necessary to establish the principles that underpin charity law is bizarre. The law has already been declared in a myriad of cases.
> Consultation with 'Joe Public', while possibly concordant with a 'touchy-feely' approach to government, is an inappropriate way of deciding what is in the public interest. . . . Decisions on charitable status must be determined on legally relevant evidence and well-established principles and not on unclear criteria or popular soundings.

Such criticisms provide an additional reason to eschew any wholesale statutory re-definition of charity. The broad language in which any statutory definition would need to be expressed would effectively give the Commissioners an even greater freedom to develop the meaning of charity than they enjoy at present, and there would no longer be any detailed objective legal criteria against which their subjective decisions could be assessed.

(2) A Charity Appeal Tribunal?

If a statutory definition of charity were to be introduced, it would need to be sufficiently flexible to keep pace with developments in society. At present, if the Charity Commissioners decline to register an institution as a charity, the only

1.59

1.60

1.61

1.62

---

[125] H Picarda, 'Charity review is a review too far' (1998) 12 *Lawyer* 9 June, 22

recourse is a costly appeal to the High Court, which, not surprisingly, few organizations are willing to risk. The Deakin report welcomed the Charity Commissioners' proposals that the law be amended to enable the Commission to apply to the High Court for a declaration on the charitable status of an organization seeking registration;[126] but it additionally recommended that this be complemented by the establishment of an independent Charity Appeal Tribunal comprised of experts in charity law and empowered to review the Charity Commissioners' decisions on charitable status.[127]

1.63 Whether, however, a tribunal would be able to develop the law of charity as Deakin proposes would depend very much on its status, on the composition of its members, and on its procedures. Deakin envisages a tribunal placed at a level between the Charity Commissioners and the High Court.[128] However, unless the tribunal's decisions were accorded a status equivalent to those of the High Court, it would still be bound by all existing case law, so that its ability to develop the law would be no more extensive than that of the Charity Commissioners. Furthermore, although an appeal to a tribunal might be at a lesser cost than to the High Court, there would still be additional legal expenses, since the charity concerned is likely to need the assistance of professional lawyers in handling the appeal. Indeed, in the absence of a full hearing with argument on each side, it is difficult to see how the decisions of the tribunal could be accorded the same authority as those of the High Court.

1.64 The idea of establishing a tribunal to hear appeals from the Charity Commissioners' decisions is not new. The Expenditure Committee also recommended setting up a tribunal, whose costs would be met from part of the proceeds of a special levy on registration.[129] Like Deakin, it saw the tribunal only as a step between the Charity Commissioners and the High Court. The Commissioners, in evidence to the Committee, expressed the view that such a tribunal would simply add another hoop through which organizations would have to pass in order to resolve a point of law, and would therefore be essentially duplicating their existing function.[130] The Goodman Report saw merit in a tribunal's hearing appeals from the Charity Commissioners on administrative matters (with a further appeal to the High Court on a point of law); but it believed that the High Court should be the final arbiter of whether the objects of an institution were charitable or not.[131]

---

[126] *Meeting the challenge of change: voluntary action into the 21st century*, Report of the Commission on the Future of the Voluntary Sector, Nicholas Deakin (chairman), (NCVO, 1996), para. 3.3.5

[127] ibid, para. 3.3.7

[128] ibid, para. 3.3.3

[129] Expenditure Committee, *Charity Commissioners and their accountability 10th Report*, HC Paper (1975) no 495-I paras. 79–85.

[130] ibid, para 81

[131] Report of the Goodman Committee, Charity Law and Voluntary Organisations (Bedford Square Press, 1976), paras 151, 154

The Goodman proposal seems to be the most firmly based: as an appeal mechan- **1.65**
ism, a tribunal is unlikely to be able to develop the legal concept of charity any
better than the Charity Commissioners. This does not, however, mean that the
idea of a tribunal should be rejected. At the very least, a tribunal may serve a useful function in correcting errors of individual decisions of the Charity
Commissioners. More importantly, with the current concerns that the Charity
Commissioners are adopting a cavalier attitude to the authorities in determining
charitable status, a legally qualified appeal tribunal would enable the more way-
ward decisions of the Commissioners to be put right without the expense of an
appeal to the High Court. Somewhat ironically, therefore, it would appear that
the strongest justification for such a tribunal is not that such a tribunal would be
better placed than the Commissioners to develop charity law, but rather that it
would be able to put a check on the Commissioners' tendency to make decisions
which are influenced by their own subjective attitudes and by opinion polls.

F. Charities and taxation

(1) The link between tax relief and charitable status

Since *Pemsel*'s case, the same meaning of charity which evolved in relation to the **1.66**
English law of trusts has been applied to taxing statutes. It did not have to be so:
the minority of the judges in that case would have limited 'charity' in taxing
statutes to the relief of poverty.[132] From a tax point of view, the decision became
more important in the years which followed, with the raising of the levels of taxation in the early twentieth century. The decision in *Pemsel*'s case means that all
bodies which qualify as charities in the law of trusts receive favourable treatment
from the public purse in the shape of specific tax reliefs and exemptions. This has
produced several consequences for charity law and for the way charities are run.

First, it has meant that many of the cases concerned with the meaning of charity **1.67**
are not involved with the validity of a disposition, but simply with whether a body
(say a company) can obtain tax relief by claiming its objects are wholly and exclusively charitable. It may be that the courts are less willing to accord charitable status to a body merely to confer tax relief. It is arguable that the restrictions on
public benefit developed from *Re Compton*[133] were an attempt to prevent charitable status from being used to provide tax relief for what were essentially private
purposes; but there is little indication of this in the cases themselves. Only Lord

---

[132] See *Comrs for Special Purposes of the Income Tax v Pemsel* [1891] AC 531 at 552 (Lord
Halsbury LC, giving the word what he considered to be its meaning in ordinary usage); see also Lord
Bramwell, ibid, at 563–9
[133] [1945] Ch 123

Cross in *Dingle v Turner*[134] openly stated that the courts should take tax considerations into account when determining charitable status; but the majority of their Lordships in that case expressly dissented from that view. The growing importance of tax relief for charities may also explain the exclusion, from the end of the nineteenth century, of political purposes from the ambit of what is charitable, and the restrictions on the political activities of charities.[135] Before that time, it was by no means clear that a political purpose precluded charitable status.[136]

1.68 Secondly, the link between charitable status and tax relief has encouraged two types of splintering. It has encouraged more politically concerned, campaigning-type charities to split into two, so as to hive off those of their purposes that are charitable to a charitable trust or company in order to obtain tax relief for at least some of their objects. It has also encouraged charities to trade via subsidiary trading companies rather than directly, in order to avoid tax on their trading income.

1.69 There is, however, no necessary link between charitable status and tax relief. The reliefs themselves are very specific, and changes in general taxation can cause charities to lose reliefs they had previously enjoyed.[137] Charities have never enjoyed any blanket relief from value added tax (VAT), although the VAT legislation contains a few categories of relief specifically applicable to them.[138] Relief under the VAT legislation (being designed to conform with the broader European concept of public benefit organizations) is also generally extended to certain other bodies which are not charities; and there are a few instances in which other UK taxes provide relief, not merely for charities, but also for various types of public bodies.[139] Some commentators have argued that charitable status should be separated from tax relief, the latter being accorded only to those charities which confer upon society a significant and undisputed benefit. It has, for instance, been suggested that tax legislation might effectively reverse *Pemsel's* case and restrict full tax relief to charities for the relief of poverty or distress and which 'genuinely benefit poor

---

[134] [1972] AC 601 (HL)

[135] See M Chesterman, 'Foundations of Charity in the New Welfare State' (1999) 62 MLR 333, esp 343–9

[136] eg *Russell v Jackson* (10) Hare 204 (secret trust to establish a school to educate children in the doctrines of socialism; the court directed an inquiry into the nature of the doctrines and whether they were illegal); *New v Bonaker* (1867) LR 4 Eq 655 (where a college was to engage a professsor to advocate the natural rights of black people; the court directed an inquiry whether the overseas trustees were willing to accept the trusts)

[137] See eg the rules introduced from 6 Apr 1999, which prevent the tax credit attributable to a dividend from being recoverable in the hands of a non-taxpayer: F (No 2) A 1997, s 34 and Sch 4. There is five-year transitional relief for charities in respect of qualifying distributions made before 6 Apr 2004: ibid, s 35

[138] eg VATA 1994, Sch 8, Gp 15, item 8 (charity advertising)

[139] eg qualifying donation by a company to even non-charitable scientific research organizations (ICTA 1988, s 339); and the exemption from income tax of such organizations as if they were charities applying their income to charitable purposes (ibid, s 508)

people',[140] while other charities (including, for instance, private schools and private hospitals) could have limited tax reliefs.[141] This argument is, of course, not based on legal principle but on an agenda which is overtly political. A two-tier system of tax reliefs has existed in Australia since 1928, when that country's legislature introduced the concept of the 'public benevolent institution'. Such an institution is one concerned with the relief of poverty, suffering, distress or misfortune,[142] or destitution or helplessness.[143] A body which falls within that definition is entitled to some tax reliefs denied to other charities, and gifts to such bodies also enjoy favourable tax treatment.

Just as the foregoing view advocates a league of 'super-charities', so a case has been put for validating trusts for purposes that might be worthwhile, but which do not qualify as charitable and are not deserving of the tax reliefs given to charities. Trusts for such purposes are usually void for uncertainty, unenforceability, or perpetuity;[144] and the argument is that legislation should provide a means by which these objections could be overcome. This could involve merely permitting such trusts to be carried out if the trustees so wish, as is allowed for trusts for individual animals and tombs; alternatively, legal machinery could be introduced by which such trusts could be enforced.[145] Such trusts could therefore exist, even if only for a perpetuity period of, say, twenty-one years, and would not enjoy any tax reliefs not otherwise enjoyed by private trusts. The United Kingdom legislature has shown no interest, however, in this sort of reform, which would of course have major implications for both charity law and trusts law. The sorts of purposes which might be susceptible to being saved by these methods would need to be defined clearly, and this might present formidable difficulties. They would presumably need at least a flavour of public benefit; and useless purposes would need to be excluded.[146] Enforcement presents additional problems; and it would need to be asked why the state should involve itself in enforcing trusts whose purposes cannot be shown to be beneficial to the public at large.[147]

1.70

---

[140] See M Chesterman, 'Foundations of Charity in the New Welfare State', (1999) 62 MLR 333, 340

[141] ibid

[142] *Perpetual Trustee Co Ltd v Commissioner of Taxation (Cth)* (1931) 45 CLR 224 at 233–4 (Dixon J)

[143] ibid, at 232 (Starke J)

[144] eg *Morice v Bishop of Durham* (1805) 10 Ves 552; *Re Astor's Settlement Trusts* [1952] Ch 534

[145] See NP Gravells, 'Public Purpose Trusts' (1977) 40 MLR 397; see also M Chesterman, *Charities, Trusts and Social Welfare* (Weidenfeld & Nicolson 1979) at 397–400

[146] cf *Brown v Burdett* (1882) 21 ChD 667

[147] Purpose trusts can, however, be enforced in some overseas jurisdictions: see P Matthews, ch 1 in *Trends in Contemporary Trust Law* (ed AJ Oakley) (Oxford Univ Press, 1997)

(2) The Treasury's Review of Charity Taxation

Introduction

1.71 A Treasury review of the taxation of charities was announced in 1997.[148] The announcement of the review was in the context of the planned abolition of advance corporation tax, with its detrimental effect on charities' dividend income. Implicit in the review was that the resulting loss of tax credit to charities would be to some extent made good by changes to the value added tax (VAT) regime which would be favourable to charities.[149] Views were sought, and the result, in March 1999, was the publication of a Treasury Consultation Document, entitled *Review of Charity Taxation*, which gave an indication of Government thinking in this area.[150]

1.72 The Consultation Document declared the government's responsibility 'to help create a culture of giving',[151] and it indicated a number of specific ways in which charitable giving might be simplified for donors (especially through improvements to the fiscal treatment of Gift Aid and payroll-giving), and in which charitable reliefs might be extended. It even invited suggestions on the merits of introducing, alongside existing reliefs, a US-style relief system for giving to charity whereby, instead of charities being able in some cases to claim the basic rate tax deducted, all individual donors would be able to claim, in their annual tax return, relief on all their charitable giving.[152]

1.73 Compared with what the charitable sector was hoping for, however, the suggestions for extending reliefs for charities themselves were modest. Substantial changes to VAT to relieve the burden on charities of irrecoverable VAT could not have been expected, since reliefs must comply with the European Community requirements for VAT. Charities had, however, been hoping that the Government would introduce a compensation scheme out of central funds, from which charities could to some extent be recompensed for their irrecoverable VAT. In the Consultation Document, however, this idea was given short shrift, the Government concluding that, 'for reasons of principle and of cost, this is not an

---

[148] *Hansard*, HC (series 6) vol 297, Budget Speech, col 307 (2 July 1997). For comment, see J Brown, 'Opportunity for Review' (1997) 71 NLJ Charities Appeals Suppl 24

[149] See CLA, *Government Review of Charity Taxation: Response to the Consultation Document by the Charity Law Association*, 1999, produced by a Working Party of the CLA, Judith Hill (chairman)

[150] See A Randall, 'Review of Charity Taxation—the Way Ahead' (1999) 74 NLJ Charities Appeals Suppl 20

[151] Foreword by Patricia Hewitt MP, Economic Secretary to the Treasury in HM Treasury, *Review of Charity Taxation: Consultation Document* (Mar 1999)

[152] ibid, 8–9 (paras 2.21–2.24)

idea we wish to pursue'.[153] The Document states that the cost to the Treasury could be some £460 million per year,[154] and, in the Government's view:[155]

> The figure would continue to rise in proportion to the size of the sector and its range of activities. We would therefore be faced with a permanent, high and rising demand on annual public expenditure, which would need to be found from elsewhere in the Government's budget, and would inevitably compete with other public spending priorities. A grant scheme would also increase administrative costs for charities and Government. It would add further complexities to the system, and run counter to our objectives of simplifying the tax system for charities and helping to minimise their compliance costs.

In its response, the Charity Law Association pointed out that it was not clear that **1.74** the impact on public spending would need to be anything near the total indicated, which figure took account of VAT incurred in respect of exempt activities; and it suggested that a compensation scheme might validly cover only non-business activities and could be introduced in a transitional period.[156]

Reform of charity taxation

The Consultation Document put forward a number of specific measures to **1.75** reform charity taxation. A few of these were effectively definite proposals, which were implemented shortly afterwards in the Finance Act 1999, notably the extension of the income tax, corporation tax, and capital gains tax relief on gifts by businesses of trading stock and equipment which they sell or use in the course of their business.[157]

Other ideas mooted in the Document have since been implemented in the **1.76** Finance Act 2000. One of these was a proposal that a company be permitted to make a donation by way of Gift Aid within a specified time after the end of its accounting period to which the donation relates.[158] A charity's subsidiary trading company is now able to return profits to the charity through Gift Aid without having to use the deed of covenant method.[159] Another was the suggestion that the rules relating to the taxation of a charity's trading income be relaxed to enable all

---

[153] ibid, 22 (para 5.8)
[154] ibid, 22 (para 5.10)
[155] ibid
[156] CLA, *Government Review of Charity Taxation: Response to the Consultation Document by the Charity Law Association* (1999) 10
[157] HM Treasury, *Review of Charity Taxation: Consultation Document* (Mar 1999) 14–15 (paras 3.13–3.15). See FA 1999, s 55, replacing the former exemption with the insertion of a new s 83A into ICTA 1988: see ch 19, paras 19.33–19.35
[158] See now FA 2000, s 40(7), substituting a new sub-s (7AA) in ICTA 1988, s 339
[159] HM Treasury, *Review of Charity Taxation Consultation Document* (Mar 1999) 20 (paras 4.16–4.17). See further, ch 20, paras 20.31–20.34

charities to claim tax exemption on a specified proportion of their profits.[160] This change[161] will clearly relieve many charities of the obligation to set up a subsidiary trading company, particularly small charities which wish to do no more than sell Christmas cards or raise funds from occasional small-scale business activities. It will not, however, relieve charities of the need to comply with the restrictions on non-primary purpose trading imposed by charity law. Additionally, charities which trade on a large scale will also still prefer to use separate trading companies in order to safeguard the charity's assets from the claims of creditors in the event of insolvency.

1.77 The Consultation Document saw Gift Aid as offering[162]

> an alternative, modern flexible relief which donors and charities find attractive and user-friendly, and which is within the reach of the vast bulk of donors and which, over time[,] might become the preferred choice of donors and charities.

It suggested that the minimum limit for Gift Aid donations be reduced from £250 to £100, and that payment be permitted to be made in instalments.[163] As is discussed in more detail in chapter 19, the Finance Act 2000 took these suggestions even further by abolishing the minimum limit for Gift Aid.

1.78 As regards payroll-giving, the Consultation Document mooted the idea of abolishing the maximum amount (which used to be £1,200 per annum)[164] and of the system being given a 'kick-start' by the Government's adding a specified percentage to sums contributed through payroll-giving, for a limited period.[165] It also said that it was attracted to the idea of allowing employers to distribute donations direct to charities nominated by the employees, if they wished, by removing the legal requirement to use an agency charity.[166] The Finance Act 2000 removed the ceiling on payroll-giving and introduced a scheme for the payment by the Government of a 10 per cent supplement for three years from 6 April 2000.[167]

1.79 The VAT treatment of membership subscriptions received by charities and other non-profit organizations was amended (as indicated in the Consultation Document), in the Finance Act 1999.[168] The Document indicated the

---

[160] HM Treasury, *Review of Charity Taxation: Consultation Document* (Mar 1999), 19 (paras 4.13–4.14)

[161] Embodied in FA 2000, s 46

[162] HM Treasury, *Review of Charity Taxation: Consultation Document* (Mar 1999), 7 (para 2.12)

[163] HM Treasury, *Review of Charity Taxation Consultation Document* (Mar 1999), 7 (paras 2.13–2.16)

[164] ibid, 11 (para 2.37)

[165] ibid, para 2.34

[166] ibid, paras 2.31–2.33 (p 10)

[167] FA 2000, s 38

[168] HM Treasury, *Review of Charity Taxation: Consultation Document* (Mar 1999), 24 (paras 5.19–5.21). See FA 1999, s 20, repealing VATA 1994, s 94(3); and see VAT (Subscriptions to Trade Unions, Professional and Other Public Bodies) Order 1999, SI 1999/2834

Government's wish to go further, however, and to look at ways for aligning the differing rules for direct taxation and VAT relating to membership subscriptions, and the possible introduction of a de minimis limit for VAT purposes (comparable to that applied in direct taxation), below which nominal benefits could be disregarded.[169]

1.80

The Consultation Document recognized that the existing scope of zero-rating in respect of the supply of charity advertising had failed to keep pace with changes in patterns of advertising, and that this has created a number of anomalies; and it indicated the Government's wish to extend the VAT relief for charity advertising.[170] This has since been effected by statutory instrument.[171]

1.81

Reform of non-domestic rates

The automatic 80 per cent rate relief enjoyed by charity shops (and a local authority's discretion to waive the remaining 20 per cent) has become in recent years, particularly since the recession of the early 1990s, a particularly thorny issue.[172] The Consultation Document examined the merits of such relief.[173] Whilst it recognized both the value of such relief to charities and the important part that charity shops play in raising funds, it went on to state that[174]

> we also acknowledge the real concerns of small independent shopkeepers that business rate relief gives charity shops that sell new, bought-in goods a competitive advantage. It was never the intention that charities should have relief on business premises that are predominantly used to sell new, bought-in goods and we do not want to extend the relief in this way.

The only suggestions the Document put forward in this context were whether the requirement that the trading be 'wholly or mainly' for charitable purposes should be clarified in order to give local authorities and charities greater guidance, and whether there should be more assurance-checking of compliance with the rules.[175] As yet, however, no legislative changes in this area have been introduced.

---

[169] HM Treasury, *Review of Charity Taxation Consultation Document* (Mar 1999) paras 5.22–5.23
[170] ibid, 25–26 (paras 5.24–5.27)
[171] Value Added Tax (Charities and Aids for the Handicapped) Order 2000, SI 2000/805, amending VATA 1994, Sch 8, Group 15
[172] See P Luxton, 'Reforming the Law on Charity Trading' in *Property Law: Current Issues and Debates* (ed P Jackson and DC Wilde) (Ashgate, 1999). On the current scope of rate relief for charities, see below, ch 3, paras 3.79–3.94
[173] HM Treasury, *Review of Charity Taxation: Consultation Document* (Mar 1999), 27–8 (paras 5.33–5.37)
[174] ibid, 27 (para 5.35)
[175] ibid, 28 (para 5.37)

G. Charities and the Human Rights Act 1998

(1) Background to the Act

1.82 The law of charities will undoubtedly be affected by the coming into force of the Human Rights Act 1998, which requires domestic courts to take account of rights contained in the treaty known as the European Convention for the Protection of Human Rights and Fundamental Freedoms (the Convention).[176] The Convention protects a range of human rights, which are very broadly expressed. It also set up three bodies, all based in Strasbourg: the European Commission of Human Rights (which ceased to exist in 1998), the European Court of Human Rights (ECHR), and the Committee of Ministers.

1.83 The Convention was ratified by the United Kingdom in 1951, but it was not incorporated into domestic law. The impact of the Convention on English courts has therefore been limited, although they have been able to make reference to the Convention in a limited number of ways, including the construction of ambiguous legislation.[177] Since 1961, individuals in the United Kingdom who allege that their human rights under the Convention have been abused have been able to petition to Strasbourg to have their complaint heard. If the Council or the ECHR found that a Convention right had been breached, the Member State involved would be obliged to pass amending legislation to bring its domestic law into line with the rights protected by the Convention. The right to petition did not arise, however, until the individuals had exhausted their remedies in domestic law, which effectively meant having pursued an appeal to the House of Lords. This requirement resulted in expense and delay before a matter could reach the ECHR. The idea expressed in a White Paper which led to the enactment of the Human Rights Act 1998 was that of 'bringing rights home', enabling people in the United Kingdom to enforce their rights under the Convention directly in the domestic courts;[178] however, as will be explained, the Act does not go so far as to make the rights enshrined in the Convention override United Kingdom domestic legislation. The Human Rights Act 1998 came into force on 2 October 2000.[179]

---

[176] See generally, J Wadham and H Mountfield, *Blackstone's Guide to the Human Rights Act 1998* (Blackstone Press Ltd, 1999)

[177] eg *R v Secretary of State for the Home Department, ex p Brind* [1991] 1 AC 696, 760

[178] *Rights Brought Home: the Human Rights Bill*, Cm 3782 (1997), paras 1.14–1.19; see also J Straw and P Boateng, *Bringing Rights Home: Labour's Plans to Incorporate the European Convention on Human Rights into United Kingdom Law*, Labour Party Consultation Paper (Dec 1996)

[179] Human Rights Act 1998 (Commencement No 2) Order 2000, SI 2000/1851

(2) Basic principles of the Act

Meaning of 'Convention rights'

The Human Rights Act 1998 refers to 'Convention rights', which expression   **1.84**
refers to those rights set out in Schedule 1 to the Act.[180] These comprise most (but
not all) of the rights contained in the Convention itself. These Convention rights
are, in summary: the right to life;[181] the prohibition of torture;[182] the prohibition
of slavery and forced labour;[183] the right to liberty and security;[184] the right to a fair
trial;[185] no punishment without law;[186] the right to respect for private and family
life;[187] freedom of thought, conscience and religion;[188] freedom of expression;[189]
freedom of assembly and association;[190] the right to marry;[191] the prohibition of
discrimination;[192] restrictions on political activity of aliens;[193] prohibition of
abuse of rights;[194] limitation on use of restriction on rights;[195] the protection
of property;[196] the right to education;[197] the right to free elections;[198] the abolition
of the death penalty;[199] and the death penalty in time of war.[200]

Some of the rights (such as the prohibition of torture) are absolute. Others (such   **1.85**
as the right to respect for private and family life and the right to freedom of expression) are qualified, so that states and public bodies may interfere with such
Convention rights to the extent required to protect a legitimate aim.

The approach of the ECHR to limitations has been to consider whether they are   **1.86**
'proportionate to the legitimate aim pursued'.[201]

---

[180] Human Rights Act 1998, s 1(1), (2), (3)
[181] ibid, Sch 1, Pt I, The Convention: Rights and Freedoms, Art 2
[182] ibid, Art 3
[183] ibid, Art 4
[184] ibid, Art 5
[185] ibid, Art 6
[186] ibid, Art 7
[187] ibid, Art 8
[188] ibid, Art 9
[189] ibid, Art 10
[190] ibid, Art 11
[191] ibid, Art 12
[192] ibid, Art 14
[193] ibid, Art 16
[194] ibid, Art 17
[195] ibid, Art 18
[196] ibid, Pt II, First Protocol, Art 1
[197] ibid, Art 2
[198] ibid, Art 3
[199] ibid, Pt III, Sixth Protocol, Art 1
[200] ibid, Art 2
[201] *Handyside v UK* (1976) 1 EHRR 737

Application of Convention rights and declarations of incompatibility

1.87 Since the Human Rights Act 1998 has come into force, domestic courts are required not to act in a way which is incompatible with a Convention right.[202] They are also obliged, so far as is possible, to decide cases before them (regardless of whether they turn on statute or case law) in a way which is compatible with Convention rights,[203] and they must also take decisions made at Strasbourg into account whenever they are relevant.[204] If legislation appears to conflict with a Convention right, the court must try to interpret it so as to make it compatible: in such circumstances, statutory interpretation is not a means of searching for the true or probable meaning, but rather for a possible meaning that would prevent incompatibility.[205] The exception is where the court cannot interpret a statute (or a provision made under a statute, such as a statutory instrument) in a way which is compatible with the Convention.[206] In such circumstances, the provision is not void, so the court must still give effect to it;[207] but the court[208] may make a 'declaration of incompatibility',[209] and the Act enables both primary and subordinate legislation to be amended, by expedited means, to remove the incompatibility. To this end, the Minister may, for instance, amend primary legislation by means of an order.[210]

Rights against 'public authorities'

1.88 The Act gives domestic litigants new, directly enforceable rights and remedies for breach of a Convention right against 'public authorities' and against other bodies which have some public functions in respect of the exercise of those functions.[211] The Act does not, however, define the expression 'public authority',[212] and there is bound to be litigation to determine its scope.

1.89 A person alleging that a public authority has acted (or proposes to act) in a way which is incompatible with a Convention right may bring proceedings against the authority under the Act in the appropriate court or tribunal, or may rely on the

---

[202] Human Rights Act 1998, s 6(1)
[203] ibid, s 3(1)
[204] ibid, s 2(1)
[205] See Lord Cooke of Thorndon, *Hansard*, HL (series 5) vol 582, col 1272 (3 Nov 1997)
[206] Human Rights Act 1998, s 6(1)
[207] ibid, s 4(6)(a)
[208] For this purpose, 'court' means the House of Lords, the Judicial Committee of the Privy Council, the Courts-Martial Appeal Court, and (in England and Wales) the High Court or the Court of Appeal: ibid, s 4(5)
[209] ibid, s 4(1)–(4)
[210] ibid, s 10
[211] ibid, s 7
[212] For a criticism of this omission, see I Leigh and L Lustgarten, 'Making Rights Real: the Court, Remedies, and the Human Rights Act' [1999] CLJ 509, 519–520

Convention right or rights concerned in any legal proceedings; but only if they are (or would be) a victim of the unlawful act.[213] If the proceedings are brought in an application for judicial review, the applicant is taken to have a sufficient interest in relation to the unlawful act only if they are, or would be, a victim of that act.[214] In relation to an act or a proposed act of a public authority, the court may grant such relief or remedy, or make such order, within its powers, as it considers just and appropriate.[215] Damages can be awarded, however, only if the court has the power to award damages, or the payment of civil compensation, in civil proceedings.[216]

(3) *Specific implications of the Act for charities*

It has been said that the incorporation of Convention rights into domestic law by the Human Rights Act 1998 'will subject the entire legal system to a fundamental process of review, and where necessary, reform by the judiciary'.[217] However, because the rights which it contains are expressed so generally, the extent of the impact of the Act in any particular area of law is difficult to predict; and so it is with the law of charities. Only litigation will in time reveal how much charity law will need to change; and such litigation is bound to be at a considerable cost, at least in part, to the charities and other bodies directly involved. Certainty in the law is evidently not a human right.[218]   **1.90**

Impact on charities which are 'public authorities'

It is important for a body to know whether it is a public authority, since if it is, and it acts illegally by breaching a Convention right, it may lay itself open to judicial review or to a claim for damages for breach of statutory duty.   **1.91**

The Charity Commissioners are without doubt a 'public authority', and the Act will have some impact on the way they operate. The Commissioners' internal prohibition on their own staff acting as charity trustees might, for instance, possibly breach Articles 10 (freedom of expression) and 11 (freedom of assembly and association).[219] Even before the Human Rights Act 1998 came into force on 2 October 2000, the Commissioners stated that they would, in considering an application for registration as a charity, construe the relevant legal authorities, where ambiguous or not binding, in a way which was compatible with the European Convention on Human Rights.[220] This approach was a matter of good practice   **1.92**

---

[213] Human Rights Act 1998, s 7(1)

[214] ibid, s 7(3)

[215] ibid, s 8(1)

[216] ibid, s 8(2)

[217] *R v DPP, ex p Kebeline* [1999] 4 All ER 801, 838 (Lord Hope of Craighead)

[218] See S Hocking and S Tucker, 'Will human rights become the convention in English law?' (1999) 13 *Lawyer* 15 Nov, 29

[219] See Anne-Marie Piper, '... keeping human rights in' (1999) 13 *Lawyer* 14 June, 31

[220] Decision of the Charity Commissioners, 17 November 1999: *Application by the Church of Scientology (England and Wales) for Registration as a Charity*, 7–9

(since any appeal against a Commissioners' decision would probably reach the courts after the implementation date), prudence (to avoid applications being dealt with differently according to whether they were brought before or after the date), and indirect legal obligation.[221]

1.93 The Act will also certainly affect those charities which can be considered to be 'public authorities' (including quasi-public bodies) for the purposes of the Act.[222] What is unclear is which charities fall within this definition and which do not. It may be confidently predicted, however, that the fact that all charities are for the public benefit is not itself sufficient to make all charities public authorities. The domestic courts may well treat a body as a public authority if it would satisfy the criteria for judicial review, but these criteria have themselves been left deliberately vague. The courts look at the purposes and functions of the institution, its importance to the public, whether it is established or governed by a statute, and whether any special provision is made for it in other legislation (such as taxing statutes).[223] The National Trust satisfies all these criteria; it is amenable to judicial review[224] and would surely be a public authority for the purposes of the Human Rights Act 1998. The same can probably be said of universities, since their purposes and functions are also of high public importance. At the other end of the scale, a charitable trust for a testator's poor relations is certainly not a public authority. In between these extremes there are many charities which possess one or two of the characteristics of a public authority, but not enough to put their position beyond doubt. It may also be difficult to decide in all cases when a charity which is a quasi-public body is exercising public or private functions. The Royal National Lifeboat Institution (RNLI), for instance, is an entirely voluntary body, which exists without direct state aid,[225] yet it performs a function which in many other countries is carried out by the state. In a parliamentary debate on the Human Rights Bill, the Home Secretary suggested that the RNLI would be a public authority in respect of those of its functions of a public nature.[226]

---

[221] See Human Rights Act 1998, ss 22(4), 7(1)(b). A person who claims that a public authority has acted (or proposes to act) in a way which is unlawful because it is incompatible with a Convention right may rely on Convention rights in any legal proceedings: s. 7(1)(b). These include proceedings brought by a public authority (eg the Charity Commissioners) *whenever* the act in question (eg the decision of the Charity Commissioners not to register the body as a charity) took place: s 22(4). The Charity Commissioners envisaged an association seeking to resist proceedings for recovery of tax on the basis that the Commissioners' refusal to register it as a charity had infringed its rights under European Convention of Human Rights: Decision of the Charity Commissioners, 17 November 1999: *Application by the Church of Scientology (England and Wales) for Registration as a Charity*, at p 9

[222] Human Rights Act 1998, ss 6–8

[223] *Scott v National Trust* [1998] 2 All ER 705, 716 (Robert Walker J)

[224] ibid

[225] It might be regarded as receiving indirect state aid through the tax relief accorded to it as a charity; but the according of tax relief to charities does not itself turn them into public authorities

[226] *Hansard*, HC (series 6) vol 314, cols 407–13, 17 June 1998

It is also important for a charity which is a public authority to know what actions it **1.94**
proposes to take might be unlawful for the purposes of the Act. A public authority
is not acting unlawfully for these purposes if it breaches a Convention right where[227]

(a) as a result of one or more provisions of primary legislation, the authority could
not have acted differently; or

(b) in the case of one or more provisions of, or made under, primary legislation
which cannot be read or given effect in a way which is compatible with the
Convention rights, the authority was acting so as to give effect to or enforce those
provisions.

The legislation referred to may be a statute which applies to a charity (such as one **1.95**
relating to employment law), but, in the case of a charity established by Act of
Parliament, it may also be the establishing statute itself. In such a case, the charity
may be able to point to its establishing statute to show that it had no choice but to
act in the way it did. A charity established by another method, such as by trust, a
scheme of the Commissioners, a royal charter (varied perhaps by an order in council) or under the Companies Acts, has no such escape route, since none of the constitutions thereby created comprises either primary or subordinate legislation. In
the light of this, a charity which is a public authority will effectively have no choice
but to depart from the terms of its constitution (unless it be contained in a statute
or statutory instrument) where this is necessary in order to avoid breaching a
Convention right.

The Act will broaden the scope for judicial intervention in relation to a charity **1.96**
that is a public authority beyond that which is obtainable in proceedings brought
by way of judicial review at present; and it confers on a victim of such a charity's
illegal act a right to bring an action for breach of statutory duty. These issues are
considered further in chapter 13.[228]

The visitatorial jurisdiction

The legality of the visitatorial jurisdiction in relation to eleemosynary corporations **1.97**
may be challenged under the Act. No case involving this jurisdiction has been heard
in Strasbourg; and, given its peculiar nature, it is difficult to predict, should its legality be challenged in an English court, whether such jurisdiction infringes the
Convention. The key issue is the scope of Article 6-1, which states that:

In the determination of his civil rights and obligations or of any criminal charge
against him, everyone is entitled to a fair and public hearing within a reasonable time
by an independent and impartial tribunal established by law. Judgment shall be
pronounced publicly but the press and public may be excluded from all or part of
the trial in the interests of morals, public order or national security in a democratic

---

[227] Human Rights Act 1998, s 6(2)
[228] See ch 13, paras 13.47–13.52 aand 13.54–13.55

society, where the interests of juveniles or the protection of the private life of the parties so require, or to the extent strictly necessary in the opinion of the court in special circumstances where publicity would prejudice the interests of justice.

1.98 A challenge to the legality of the visitatorial jurisdiction is most likely to arise in relation to its function of hearing disputes between the corporation and its members. It would seem difficult to contend that a process which involves determining whether the internal rules of an eleemosynary corporation have been breached, which could result in the expulsion or suspension of a member, does not involve a 'determination of his civil rights and obligations'.[229]

1.99 It is well established that a 'tribunal established by law' is not necessarily to be understood to signify a court of law of the classic kind, integrated into a country's standard judicial machinery.[230] Universities and other bodies which have Visitors are likely to be 'public authorities' for the purposes of the Act,[231] since their functions are of a public nature, and they are subject to judicial review. In many instances, the role of the Visitor is also recognized by statute, as in the case of universities.[232] In adjudicating on disputes, the Visitor can therefore probably be treated as a tribunal established by law. As a tribunal, it is a 'public authority' and so under an obligation not to act in a way which is incompatible with a Convention right.[233]

1.100 The requirement that judgment be pronounced publicly seems to pose no insuperable problem, since it is sufficient that the right to privacy can be waived by the individual.[234] The impartiality of a tribunal is presumed according to Strasbourg jurisprudence, unless there is proof to the contrary;[235] and the impression of lack of impartiality is itself sufficient.[236] In practice, however, impartiality is difficult to establish unless there is shown to be an absence of independence; and, in relation to the Visitor, it is independence which is the central issue.

Independence

1.101 As the source of the Visitor's jurisdiction is the charter of the institution which he visits, it might be argued that, in exercising his function of hearing disputes between the corporation and one of its members, the Visitor, having been effectively appointed by one side to the dispute, cannot be considered to be independent.

---

[229] See *Le Compte, Van Leuven and De Meyere v Belgium* (1981) 4 EHRR 433
[230] *X v UK* (1981) 4 EHRR 188; *Campbell and Fell v UK* (1984) 7 EHRR 165
[231] Human Rights Act 1998, s 6(3)
[232] Education Reform Act 1988
[233] Human Rights Act 1998, s 6(1), (3)(a)
[234] *Le Compte, Van Leuven and De Meyere v Belgium* (1981) 4 EHRR 433
[235] ibid; *Campbell v Fell v UK* (1984) 7 EHRR 165
[236] See *Langborger v Sweden* (1989) 12 EHRR 416 (Art 6(1) held breached by membership of a housing tribunal that had the possible appearance of lacking impartiality)

The issue of the independence of a tribunal was considered in Strasbourg in   **1.102**
Campbell and Fell v United Kingdom.[237] There the European Court of Human
Rights was called upon to decide whether a Prison Board of Visitors, in adjudicating on disciplinary offences committed by prisoners, and with power to make
disciplinary awards (including loss of remission), was independent, or whether
such disciplinary function breached (inter alia) Article 6-1. There were several
arguments against the Board's being considered independent. First, it was said
that there was a lack of independence because each member of such a Board was
appointed (and could be dismissed) by the Home Secretary, and that each
appointment was for not more than three years at a time (with the possibility of
re-appointment). Secondly, it was argued that the fact that the Board also performed other functions in prisons (including inquiring into the state of prisons,
directing the attention of the Governor to appropriate matters, and reporting to
the Home Secretary) itself pointed to a lack of independence, since such continuing contact might lead the members to associate themselves with the interests of
the prison. It was argued that all these circumstances showed that a Prison Board
of Visitors was not independent but merely an arm of the executive.

The court rejected these arguments, as it was satisfied that the Board was indeed   **1.103**
an independent tribunal. It said that,[238] in deciding whether a body can be considered to be 'independent' (notably of the executive and of the parties to the
case[239]), the court should have due regard to the manner of appointment of its
members and to the duration of their term of office,[240] to the existence of guarantees against outside pressures,[241] and to the question of whether the body presents
an appearance of independence.[242] The appointment of Board members by the
Home Secretary did not indicate lack of independence, and the shortness of the
appointment period could be explained by the fact that the members were
unpaid. The fact that the members could be removed by the Home Secretary did
not indicate lack of independence either, since the circumstances in which
removal might occur were narrow, and such removals were rare. The fact that the
Board performed other roles in the prison did not result in a lack of independence,
and it was not sufficient that the prisoners themselves might see it otherwise.

In the light of this decision, there are good reasons to believe that the Visitor of   **1.104**
an eleemosynary corporation may be regarded as an 'independent' tribunal. The
following factors would appear to be of particular importance:

---

[237] (1984) 7 EHRR 165
[238] ibid, 198–9, (para 78)
[239] See *Le Compte, Van Leuven and De Meyere v Belgium* (1981) 4 EHRR 433
[240] ibid
[241] See *Piersack v Belgium* (1982) 5 EHRR 169
[242] See *Delcourt v Belgium* (1970) 1 EHRR 355

(1) A Visitor cannot be removed or suspended by a decision of the corporation's members, since the Visitor's identity and jurisdiction are derived from the corporation's charter, any amendment to which requires the assent of Her Majesty.

(2) Despite the appellation 'Visitor', the notion that a Visitor of an eleemosynary corporation should physically visit the corporation is obsolete.

(3) Although a Visitor of an eleemosynary corporation usually has other functions besides hearing disputes between the corporation and its members, its degree of involvement with the corporation in such other matters is in practice minimal.

(4) In many instances, the exercise of the visitatorial jurisdiction to adjudicate on a dispute is in fact performed on behalf of the Visitor by one or more of the senior judiciary (for example the Judicial Committee of the Privy Council on behalf of Her Majesty).

1.105 In each of these instances, the 'independence' of such a Visitor would appear to be even stronger than that of the Prison Board of Visitors considered in the *Campbell and Fell* case.[243] Therefore, whilst modification to the visitatorial process may be needed in individual instances, to ensure compliance with every aspect of Article 6-1, it is suggested that the coming into force of the Human Rights Act 1998 does not mark the end of this very useful jurisdiction.

The meaning of charity

The advancement of religion

1.106 It has been argued that the Act has affected the meaning of the advancement of religion for the purpose of the law of charities.[244] The main basis for this contention is to be found in Articles 9 and 14 of the Convention, and Article 1 of the First Protocol.

1.107 Article 9 of the Convention provides:

> 1. Everyone has the right to freedom of thought, conscience and religion; this right includes freedom to change his religion or belief and freedom, either alone or in the community with others and in public or private, to manifest his religion or belief, in worship, teaching, practice and observance.
> 2. Freedom to manifest one's religion or beliefs shall be subject only to such limitations as are prescribed by law and are necessary in a democratic society in the interests of public safety, for the protection of public order, health or morals, or for the protection of the rights and freedoms of others.

---

[243] *Campbell and Fell v UK* (1984) 7 EHHR 165
[244] F Quint and T Spring, 'Religion, Charity Law & Human Rights' (1999) 5 CL & PR 153

Article 14 states: **1.108**

> The enjoyment of the rights and freedoms set forth in this Convention shall be
> secured without discrimination on any ground such as sex, race, colour, language,
> religion, political or other opinion, national or social origin, association with a
> national minority, property, birth or other status.

Article 1 of the First Protocol provides: **1.109**

> Every natural or legal person is entitled to the peaceful enjoyment of his possessions.
> No one shall be deprived of his possessions except in the public interest and subject
> to the conditions provided for by law and by the general principles of international
> law.
>   The preceding provisions shall not, however, in any way impair the right of a
> State to enforce such laws as it deems necessary to control the use of property in
> accordance with the general interest or to secure the payment of taxes or other con-
> tributions or penalties.

Over a period of two or three centuries, English law has abolished restrictions that   **1.110**
denied adherents of various religious groups the right to express and to practise
their religious faith, both publicly and in private, and that barred their admittance
to the universities and to other institutions and offices of state. In view of this, it is
arguable that Article 9 adds nothing to the religious toleration extended to persons of every faith in the United Kingdom, so that the more restricted meaning of
the advancement of religion for the purposes of the law of charity has nothing to
do with Article 9.[245]

However, even if English law conforms with Article 9 in respect of the personal   **1.111**
rights of individuals to freedom of religion, it might be argued that it breaches
Article 14 of the Convention and Article 1 of the First Protocol in that it discrim-
inates (by withholding the benefits of charitable status including tax exemptions)
against particular religious groups. Withholding tax relief from religious organizations which do not qualify as charities in English law might well impair their
ability to proselytize and to carry out their teaching; and a right to convince one's
neighbours, through teaching, is protected by Article 9 because it is intrinsic to
'the freedom to change' religion or belief.[246] The grounds of discrimination are
whether the doctrines of a group are monotheistic or polytheistic,[247] or not theis-
tic at all,[248] whether or not there is worship of a supreme being,[249] and whether or
not there is a benefit to a sufficient section of the community (for example,

---

[245] D Morris, 'Know your charitable rights' *NGO Finance Charity Law Annual Review 1998*
(Dec 1998) 18, 19
[246] *Kokkinakis v Greece* (1993) 17 EHRR 397
[247] cf *Bowman v Secular Society* [1917] AC 406, 449 (Lord Parker of Waddington)
[248] *Re South Place Ethical Society* [1980] 1 WLR 1565, 1571 (Dillon J)
[249] *R v Registrar General, ex p Segerdal* [1970] 2 QB 697, 709 (Buckley LJ); *Re South Place Ethical
Society* [1980] 1 WLR 1565, 1572 (Dillon J)

whether the worship is conducted in public,[250] and whether its adherents mix with the public[251] or are cloistered).[252] Two commentators have argued that:[253]

> benefits from recognition as a charity (including registration under the Charities Act 1993 where appropriate) flow both to the charity itself, to the individuals connected to it—whether they be members, supporters, beneficiaries, or trustees—and to the public-at-large. . . . A religious organization forced to operate without these benefits does so at a great disadvantage compared to religious organizations that enjoy them, and its supporters, beneficiaries, and trustees likewise must forego significant benefits and protections accorded the members, supporters, beneficiaries, and trustees of religious organisations [*sic*] that have been registered. Thus, while adherents of religious organizations that have not been recognized as charities may still be able to practise their religion, they must do so burdened by a number of 'hindrances' not suffered by adherents of religious organizations that have been recognized. It is these hindrances that would activate Article 9.

Three arguments might, however, be put forward against this line of reasoning.

1.112 First, whilst those who support or take part in a charity may derive personal benefit from doing so, the benefit of charitable status is a benefit to the community at large, and it is this public benefit which provides the rationale for the conferring of tax and other privileges of charitable status. The trustees, members and supporters of any charity, including a charity for the advancement of religion, are not 'beneficiaries' of it in the technical sense: they can have no personal interest in the charity's assets or in the tax exemptions which its status secures for it. If the charity exists in corporate form, so that it is a separate legal entity, it can have its own rights under the Convention, distinct from those of its members. These are, however, necessarily circumscribed: since a corporation is a legal fiction, it is difficult to see how it (as opposed to its members) can in any meaningful sense have a right to freedom of religion.[254] A corporation does, however, have other Convention rights, such as the right not to be deprived of its property without due process of law; so that, a charitable corporation which is the tenant under a lease might, for example, be able to complain of an infringement of Article 1 of the First Protocol should the landlord effect forfeiture through peaceable re-entry.[255] *Vis-à-vis* the state, however, its assets are effectually dedicated to charity, and so it cannot complain, for instance, of an expropriation of its assets under a lawful cy-près scheme. The foregoing argument is based on the nature of charities in English law,

---

[250] *Re Hetherington* [1990] Ch 1 (Browne-Wilkinson V-C)
[251] *Neville Estates Ltd v Madden* [1962] Ch 832, 853 (Cross J)
[252] *Gilmour v Coats* [1949] AC 426 (HL)
[253] F Quint and T Spring, 'Religion, Charity Law & Human Rights' (1999) 5 CL & PR 153, 166–7
[254] cf *Sutton's Hospital Case* (1612) 10 Co Rep 1a, 32b, where Coke CJ stated that a corporation cannot be excommunicated because it has no soul
[255] Whether a landlord's right of peaceable re-entry for breach of covenant will survive the Human Rights Act 1998 is itself uncertain

and it may be that the domestic courts, when determining whether there has been a breach of a Convention right, will not be prepared to give much weight to technical arguments of this kind.

The second argument, by contrast, has a broader foundation, being rooted in **1.113** Strasbourg jurisprudence. This is the principle of proportionality. The Strasbourg court acknowledges that the national courts are in principle better placed than an international court to evaluate local needs and conditions,[256] and it does so through its application of the doctrine of the 'margin of appreciation', whereby it recognizes 'that the convention, as a living system, does not need to be applied uniformly by all states but may vary in its application according to local needs and conditions'.[257] Although this technique is not as such available to national courts when considering Convention rights in their own countries,[258] the domestic courts will be able to apply an analogous principle. In his speech in *R v DPP, ex p Kebeline*, Lord Hope expressed the opinion that:[259]

> in the hands of the national courts also the convention should be seen as an expression of fundamental principles rather than as a set of mere rules. The questions which the courts will have to decide in the application of these principles will involve questions of balance between competing interests and issues of proportionality.

His Lordship said that in this area difficult choices may have to be made by the executive or the legislature between the rights of the individual and the needs of society; and in some circumstances the courts should recognize that there are some areas on which they should, on democratic grounds, defer to the considered opinion of the elected body or person whose act or decision is said to be incompatible with the Convention. The areas in which such choices will need to be made will be more easily recognized where the Convention itself requires a balance to be struck. In his view:[260]

> It will be easier for it to be recognised where the issues involve questions of social or economic policy, much less so where the rights are of high constitutional importance or are of a kind where the courts are especially well placed to assess the need for protection.

It is therefore suggested that, whilst the system of registration of charities under **1.114** the Charities Act 1993 and the tax reliefs given to charities by the taxing statutes undoubtedly favour some religious groups over others, there is no breach of Convention rights since such discrimination falls within the principle of proportionality. The legislature has had more than a century since the decision in *Pemsel*'s case to break the link in the taxing statutes between charitable status and

---

[256] *Buckley v UK* (1996) 23 EHRR 101, 129
[257] *R v DPP, ex p Kebeline* [1999] 4 All ER 801, 844 (Lord Hope)
[258] ibid
[259] ibid
[260] ibid

tax relief; furthermore, for some forty years since the Charities Act 1960, it has been content to base registration on the definition of charity developed by the courts. This appears to be one of those areas in which, in balancing the rights of the individual and the needs of society, the courts might well consider it appropriate to defer to the wishes of the legislature as expressed in the taxing statutes and in the Charities Acts. The Charity Commissioners have also expressed the view that a different treatment is justified by the margin of appreciation principle.[261]

1.115   Thirdly, the Charity Commissioners have stated that the different tests of public benefit (between the third and the fourth heads of *Pemsel*'s case) can be justified as falling within one of the legitimate aims identified in Article 9, namely, being necessary in a democratic society 'for the protection of the rights and freedoms of others'. In the Commissioners' view,[262]

> The different treatment is justified because English law is concerned with protecting and encouraging the concept of charity, the central characteristic of which is public benefit. Declining registration of those organisations which do not exhibit the characteristics of charity protects the position of those which do fulfil the criteria, and ensures that tax relief is available only to those organisations which are of public benefit of a charitable kind, and is a means of ensuring that those organisations exempted from tax are those which provide benefit to the public in some way (*ie* through their charitable purpose and activities).

1.116   The Charity Commissioners also consider that the difference in the tests of public benefit is both objective and reasonable and does not fall foul of Articles 9 and 14 taken together. The reason for this, the Commissioners state, is that[263]

> the test of public benefit acts as a filter by which the charitable and non-charitable organisations are distinguished. An essential element of charity is its public dimension. It is rational to state that where this element is lacking, an organisation will not be charitable. This applies to all organisations seeking acceptance as being charitable. The legal presumption of public benefit under the first three heads of charity is based on the accepted certainty established in case law based on experience that these purposes will lead to public benefit unless there is evidence to the contrary. Whereas this is not so for the broad category of fourth head purposes.

1.117   In the light of the foregoing, it is suggested that the present meaning of the advancement of religion in English law does not breach Convention rights. If, however, the courts were to take a different view, it would be necessary to determine the extent to which charity law would need to change. This too is by no means clear. First, it is not yet settled in Strasbourg jurisprudence whether the meaning of 'religion' in Articles 9 and 14 is wide enough to include the promotion of non-theistic ethical or philosophical beliefs. Secondly, it may be that English

---

[261] Decision of the Charity Commissioners, 17 November 1999: *Application by the Church of Scientology (England and Wales) for Registration as a Charity*, 12
[262] ibid, 42
[263] ibid

law already recognizes polytheism as being for the advancement of religion, since (whilst there is no case law in point) the Charity Commissioners have been prepared to register polytheistic religious groups. In view of these uncertainties, it may be that the only significant impact of the Act would be to admit as charitable for the advancement of religion those religious groups (such as the Church of Scientology) which are presently denied such status either because their faith does not involve reverence or worship, or because their activities cannot be shown to confer benefits on the community of a kind recognized in charity law (such as the intangible benefits of edification and intercessory prayer rejected by the House of Lords in *Gilmour v Coats*.)[264]

The Human Rights Act 1998 is not intended to affect the right of religious groups **1.118** to require employees to adhere to a group's particular religious faith or to conform to its doctrines. This is provided for by section 13(1) of the Act, which states:

> If a court's determination of any question arising under this Act might affect the exercise by a religious organisation (itself or its members collectively) of the Convention right to freedom of thought, conscience and religion, it must have particular regard to the importance of that right.

Political purposes and political activity

It might be argued that the Human Rights Act 1998 will compel the courts and **1.119** the Charity Commissioners to accord charitable status to some organizations which would previously have been denied such status on the ground that their objects are political.

At its narrowest, the argument is that the object of promoting the reform of **1.120** domestic English law to the extent necessary to give effect to Convention rights would cease to be a political purpose, and would be charitable under the fourth head of *Pemsel*'s case[265] as being to promote the better administration of the law. The argument is that what might once have been a political purpose may cease to be so if the law is changed,[266] since the court is then entitled to assume that what the legislature has laid down is for the public benefit.[267] Since compliance with its treaty obligations requires the Government to amend domestic legislation to comply with Convention rights, it might be considered no longer political to promote reform of domestic law so that it complies with such rights. Against this, however, it could be argued that there might be circumstances, even when a court has made a declaration of incompatibility, in which a government would choose

---

[264] [1949] AC 426 (HL)

[265] *Comrs for Special Purposes of the Income Tax v Pemsel* [1891] AC 531 (HL)

[266] cf *Re Bushnell* [1975] 1 WLR 1596 (from which it might be inferred that the object of promoting socialized medicine ceased to be political in respect of trusts created after the introduction of the National Health Service)

[267] *Bowman v Secular Society Ltd* [1917] AC 406, 422 (Lord Parker)

not to bring in corrective legislation. Indeed, the enactment of Convention rights in such a way that they do not override existing incompatible legislation seems to point to this very possibility. It therefore might not be safe to assume that the promotion of Convention rights is now to be treated as a charitable purpose.[268]

1.121 It might, however, be argued that the Act goes much further than this. It might be contended, first, that political objects must now be accorded charitable status; and, secondly, that charities may now engage in political activities beyond the legal restraints which have previously existed and which have been enforced by the Charity Commissioners.[269] Whether the Act has either of these effects turns on the applicability of Article 10 of the Convention, which provides as follows:

> 1. Everyone has the right to freedom of expression. This right shall include freedom to hold opinions and to receive and impart information and ideas without interference by public authority and regardless of frontiers. This Article shall not prevent States from requiring the licensing of broadcasting, television or cinema enterprises. 2. The exercise of these freedoms, since it carries with it duties and responsibilities, may be subject to such formalities, conditions, restrictions or penalties as are prescribed by law and are necessary in a democratic society, in the interests of national security, territorial integrity or public safety, for the prevention of disorder or crime, for the protection of health or morals, for the protection of the reputation or rights of others, for preventing the disclosure of information received in confidence, or for maintaining the authority and impartiality of the judiciary.

For this purpose, 'expression' includes, not merely words, but also images and actions that seek to convey an idea;[270] but there has been no consideration at Strasbourg of the impact of Article 10 on English charities. The nearest case is perhaps *Bowman v United Kingdom*.[271] This was an application brought by Mrs Bowman, who had been prosecuted for breaches of a United Kingdom statute that set a ceiling of £5 on the amount that unauthorized persons could spend on campaigning for particular candidates in the period before an election. Mrs Bowman, who was a director of the Society for the Protection of the Unborn Child (SPUC), had distributed leaflets describing the views on abortion of various constituency candidates, and she was prosecuted for exceeding the permitted expenditure limit. She applied to Strasbourg, complaining that the prosecution violated her right to freedom of expresion under Article 10. Her application was successful. In the present context, however, the decision is of limited value: first, because the court was concerned with her personal rights not those of SPUC; and, secondly, because SPUC was in any event not a charitable body.

---

[268] See GFK Santow, 'Charity in its political voice: a tinkling cymbal or a sounding brass?' (1999) 52 CLP 255, 279–281

[269] For a balanced discussion, see D Morris, 'Charities, Politics and Freedom of Speech' (1999) 5 CL & PR 219

[270] *Stevens v UK* (1986) 46 DR 245

[271] (1998) 26 EHRR 1

In the absence of authority, the application of Article 10 to charities is uncertain. **1.122**
It could be argued that this Convention right to freedom of expression means that
bodies cannot be denied charitable status merely because their objects are political. Against this, it might be contended that English law already recognizes this
right because it allows associations of persons to join together (whether as unincorporated associations or through the formation of companies) to promote any
political purposes that are not unlawful. Such restrictions on freedom of speech
are permitted because they involve matters (such as the prohibition of racial and
sexual discrimination) which fall within the proviso of Article 10-2. To deny
charitable status to bodies with political objects is not, therefore, to deny them
freedom of speech.

Apart from its impact on political objects, it could also be argued that Article 10 **1.123**
frees charities from any constraints on political activity. It is clear that the right to
freedom of expression in Article 10 extends to a body distinct from its members
or supporters, such as a company.[272] In the *Open Door Counselling* case,[273] the
ECHR held that Irish law had violated the right of two non-profit-making companies to freedom of expression under Article 10 when they had been prevented
from providing the public with information on the availability of abortion facilities outside Ireland. It does not follow from this, however, that Article 10 gives a
charity a right to engage in unrestricted political activity. The crucial point is that
an organization is permitted to apply its property only in accordance with the purposes agreed by those who created it. In the case of a non-charitable unincorporated association, this enforcement lies in the law of contract; in the case of a
non-charitable company, it lies in the doctrine of ultra vires. Similarly, a charity
(whether a trust, an unincorporated association or a company) must apply its
property only for its charitable purposes. To apply its property to other purposes
would be a breach of trust or ultra vires. The application of a charity's property to
a political purpose which cannot be considered to be ancillary to the promotion
of its exclusively charitable objects, can therefore be restrained by the state
(through the Attorney-General, the Charity Commissioners, or in some cases
through individual members themselves) on the basis of breach of trust or ultra
vires. Such restrictions are nothing to do with freedom of speech, and everything
to do with ensuring that funds given for charitable purposes are not misapplied by
those who undertook to apply them for such charitable purposes, in fraud of the
contributors. The individuals involved have, of course, the personal right to
freedom of expression, but similarly cannot use charitable funds for this purpose.
It is therefore suggested that the freedom of expression enjoyed by a charitable
institution (as opposed to that enjoyed by its members personally) is a freedom

---

[272] eg *Sunday Times v UK* (1979) 2 EHRR 245; *Open Door Counselling Ltd and Dublin Well
Woman Centre Ltd v Ireland* (1992) 15 EHRR 244
[273] *Open Door Counselling Ltd and Dublin Well Woman Centre Ltd v Ireland* (1992) 15 EHRR 244

exercisable only for the purpose of furthering its charitable objects. The *Open Door Counselling* case is entirely consistent with this analysis, since the provision of abortion advice was within the objects of each of the applicant companies.

1.124 If (contrary to what has been suggested above) the basic right to freedom of expression contained in Article 10-1 suggests that charities can now be registered with, or are free to pursue, political objects, it becomes important to determine if this basic right can be legitimately circumscribed. Although Article 10 is qualified, so that restrictions designed to protect morals, for instance, would be permitted, none of its expressed qualifications seems to offer any clear general ground for restricting the right of charities to express political views. An argument might be made that restrictions on political purposes and political activity can be justified as being 'for the protection of the reputation or rights of others' within Article 10-2, on the ground that such restrictions protect the reputation of charities in the mind of the public. The existing restrictions might also be justified by the margin of appreciation principle. Although it is essentially the courts which have decided that political purposes and activities are not permitted to charities, it might be argued that since Parliament effectively accepted the judicial definition of charity in the Charities Act 1993, this is an area in which the courts are entitled to defer to the decision of a democratic body.[274]

1.125 If political purposes and more extensive political activity are to be permitted to charities, the crucial issue is whether, and if so what, limits might still remain. It would be absurd to argue that a charity for the relief of poverty would have a right to express views on whether fox-hunting should be banned; or that an animal charity would be able to spend its funds campaigning to promote human rights in China. Criticisms of charity law's treatment of political purposes and activities often draw attention to the difficulty of determining where the line is to be drawn between what is permitted and what is not. This in itself, however, is hardly an adequate criticism of the underlying principle; and the line surely needs to be drawn somewhere. The latter point has sometimes been recognized, and it has been suggested that political activity should be permitted so far as it relates to 'matters of public interest in the community',[275] or so far as it is consistent with the established policy of the law as indicated by the passing of legislation in particular areas (such as race relations), or perhaps with government policy.[276] It has also

---

[274] cf *R v DPP, ex p Kebeline* [1999] 4 All ER 801, 844 (Lord Hope)

[275] See M Chesterman, 'Foundations of Charity in the New Welfare State' (1999) 62 MLR 333, 346–7, who draws an analogy with the Court of Appeal's recent decision in *Reynolds v Times Newspapers Ltd* [1998] 3 All ER 961, to extend the doctrine of qualified privilege in the law of libel to take account of the fact that 'the common convenience and welfare of a modern plural democracy such as ours are best served by an ample flow of information to the public concerning, and by vigorous public discussion of, matters of public interest to the community' (ibid, 1004 (Lord Bingham CJ delivering the judgment of the court))

[276] See GFK Santow, 'Charity in its political voice: a tinkling cymbal or a sounding brass?', (1999) 52 CLP 255, 279–81

been suggested that the law should be able to uphold as charitable even objects which are diametrically opposed to each other, provided that they are for the 'public benefit' in the view of a sizeable body of adherents;[277] with the result that, presumably, trusts to promote vivisection and trusts to promote anti-vivisection would both be capable of attaining charitable status. This last is a particularly controversial suggestion. Nevertheless, even if one or more of these relaxations in charity law were thought to be desirable, the problem would remain of whether the suggested criteria are capable of being formulated with sufficient clarity so as to be of practical assistance to those engaged in charities.

The danger in any relaxation which does not meet these requirements is that it would pave the way for serious abuse. It might be difficult or impossible to prevent bodies which are merely siphons for funding extreme political causes (of whatever persuasion) from obtaining registration as charities, thereby facilitating their raising of funds from the public ostensibly for charitable purposes. Any significant relaxation of the present restrictions on the political activities of charities could well undermine public confidence in charities, and so lead to a decline in charitable giving. It would also inevitably produce calls for the withdrawal of the tax advantages of charitable status. The present restrictions on the political activities of charities, being ultimately based on the notion that the political activity must be ancillary to the attainment of the charitable purposes, seem to provide a principled and workable compromise between freedom of expression and the fulfilment of charitable purposes. Any substantial modification to such restrictions could well upset this compromise, and would run the risk of eventually undermining the whole concept of charity in English law. **1.126**

H. Charitable trusts and investment

(1) Introduction

A charity may be either wholly or partly dependent for the carrying out of its purposes upon the income derived from its investments. It is also likely to be concerned, however, to have some capital growth, so that it may continue to produce an adequate investment income in the future. Some types of investment produce an income return but no capital growth, for example money in a bank or building society deposit account. Other investments may produce both an income and a capital return. A capital return may arise on marketable securities, for example shares on the Stock Exchange. An income return on shares takes the form of a dividend; but the shares themselves may increase in value, making a capital return. **1.127**

---

[277] J Stevens & DJ Feldman, 'Broadcast advertising by bodies with political objects: judicial review and the influence of charities law' [1997] PL 615, 622

Government stocks are similarly marketable securities, and may show capital appreciation. Fixed-interest forms of investment are generally safer, but the level of profit may not be great. Higher returns are possible with company shares, but these are riskier forms of investment, as they depend upon the performance of the company—the value of the shares may fall as well as rise, and there is never any guarantee of a dividend. Generally, however, unless the charity is very small, it will usually do better if the trustees are able to invest in the riskier forms of investment.

(2) Trustee Investments Act 1961

1.128 Before 1961, under the Trustee Act 1925, trustees were permitted to invest in government stocks and other safe sorts of fixed-interest securities;[278] but, until the Trustee Investments Act 1961, trustees (whether of private or charitable trusts) could not, under the general law, invest in company shares. They could invest in such shares if the trust instrument expressly permitted it (that is by conferring a special power of investment), but many of these older trusts did not contain such express investment powers. The pre-1961 restrictions on trustee investment had been laid down in an era of low inflation and financial stability. Post-war inflation, however, made it more difficult for the safer fixed-interest type securities to maintain the value of a trust fund. The Nathan Committee[279] recommended that charity trustees should be able to invest up to one half of the trust fund in shares and debentures of companies quoted on the Stock Exchange. This proposal was broadly implemented, and made applicable to all trusts, by the Trustee Investments Act 1961, under which trustees who had no power to invest in company shares and certain other 'riskier' forms of investment, were empowered (unless the trust instrument expressly forbade it) to invest a proportion of the fund in such investments within the confines of that Act.[280] They first had to divide the trust fund into two. Originally, the two parts had to be equal, and one half had to be invested in so-called narrower-range investments; the other half could be invested in so-called wider-range investments. Since investment in wider-range investments was merely permissive, the wider-range part could contain narrower-range investments. There were complex rules regarding withdrawals from, accruals to, and transfers between, the narrower- and wider-ranges. The Act itself conferred no general power to invest in land.

1.129 The powers conferred by the Act were additional to those conferred by the trust instrument itself.[281] If the trust instrument conferred a power of investment beyond that permitted under the Act, it was called a special power,[282] and invest-

---

[278] TA 1925, s 1 (repealed)

[279] *Report of the Committee on the Law and Practice Relating to Charitable Trust*, Lord Nathan (chairman), Cmd 8710 (1952), paras 289–96

[280] See Charity Commissioners', *Trustee Investments Act 1961*, CC32 (1995)

[281] TIA 1961, s 3(1)

[282] ibid

ments made pursuant to it were called special-range.[283] In practice, most modern trust instruments contained wide express powers of investment, which precluded the trustees from having to divide the fund into two to take advantage of its investment powers. Many other trusts, including many older charitable trusts, however, contain no express investment clause. The investments of many charitable trusts were therefore restricted to those authorized by the Act, unless the trustees obtained an extension of investment powers from the court or from the Charity Commissioners, which necessarily involved expense and delay.

(3) Criticisms of the Trustee Investments Act 1961

Several significant criticisms were levelled in recent years at the Trustee Investments Act 1961 and at the Charity Commissioners' approach to charity investment.

1.130

First, it became evident that the former obligation to divide the fund and place one half in narrower-range investments had resulted in a general loss of capital value of investments in that part. Although the performance of individual shares varies enormously, it is clear that a portfolio comprising a wide range of shares would have performed much better over the last few decades than a fund of which half had been invested in narrower-range.[284] The restrictions of the Trustee Investments Act 1961 were criticized in 1994 in the report produced by the Deregulation Task Force, on the basis that the Act 'interferes unwarrantedly in trustees' exercise of their discretion, and prevents them from maintaining the real value of their assets and investment income'.[285] This criticism was in part addressed by the relaxation in 1995, which permitted up to three-quarters of the fund to be invested in wider-range;[286] but this was essentially only an interim measure. Furthermore, whilst trustees of land or of the proceeds of sale of land had power to invest in land, trustees of other property had no general power to invest in land; yet for most of the period since the Trustee Investments Act 1961, land had been one of the best forms of investment.

1.131

1.132

---

[283] ibid, Sch 2, para 1

[284] See HM Treasury, *Investment Powers of Trustees: a Consultation Document* (May 1996), para 12

[285] Charities and Voluntary Organizations Task Force, *Charities and Voluntary Organisations Task Force Proposals for Reform* (Tessa Baring, chair), vol 1 (Summary Document), vol 2 (Full Report) (July 1994)

[286] Trustee Investments (Division of Trust Fund) Order 1996, SI 1996/845, made under TIA 1961, s 13, and which applied to private as well as to charitable trusts. This statutory instrument superseded one made the previous year which had relaxed the rule in regard to charitable trusts only, viz the Charities (Trustee Investment Act 1961) Order 1995, SI 1995/1092. The earlier statutory instrument came into force on 14 Apr 1995. It had been made by the Secretary of State pursuant to a power conferred upon him by CA 1993, s 70, to direct that a charitable trust fund could be divided between narrower- and wider-range under the TIA 1961 in different proportions from those applicable to private trusts

Secondly, doubt was cast on the philosophy underlying the Act's classification of investments according to their individual degree of risk. It was pointed out, for instance, that a number of the spectacular business collapses in recent years—such as those of Barings Bank, Maxwell Communications and Polly Peck—involved companies which would, until their fall, have been regarded as perfectly safe for investment by charities.[287] The Charity Commissioners were also criticized for applying the policy of the Act to special-range investments, thus effectively limiting what might be included in special-range. A challenge to the traditional view came from modern portfolio theory, which rejects the proposition that individual investments can be regarded as either prudent or speculative; instead, it applies the prudent-investor test to the investment portfolio overall. This approach has been gaining ground in the United States, where a growing number of States has introduced legislation to this effect;[288] and it has also received some recent judicial support in the United Kingdom.[289]

(4) The road to reform

Treasury Consultation Document, 1996

1.133 In the mid-1990s, the Conservative government then in power intended to reform the law of trustee investment by means of an Order to be made under the Deregulation and Contracting Out Act 1994; and, in compliance with the procedures which that Act prescribes,[290] a Treasury Consultation Document was issued before the Order was laid down. The Consultation Document, which was issued in 1996,[291] recommended the repeal of the Trustee Investments Act 1961 on the footing that it unnecessarily restricted trustees in their investments and therefore imposed upon them unnecessary administrative burdens.[292] It also made the point that the investment market is now far more regulated that it was in 1961, in that a person carrying on an investment business (including the giving of investment advice) must currently be authorized under the Financial Services Act 1986.[293] Investor protection is now being provided by different means. The Document therefore proposed that the statutory duty to divide the fund into two parts be abandoned, and with it any attempt to draw up lists of investments according to their degree of risk.[294] Lists rapidly become out of date as new investment prod-

---

[287] See D Morris, 'Charity Investment in the UK: some contemporary issues for the 1990s' [1995] 3 Web JCLI

[288] See HP Dale, and M Gwinnell, 'Time for a Change: Charity Investment and Modern Portfolio Theory' (1995–6) 3 CL & PR 65, 75–6

[289] See *Nestlé v National Westminster Bank plc* (ChD, 29 June 1988) (Hoffmann J, at first instance); *Steel v Wellcome Custodian Trustees Ltd* [1988] 1 WLR 167, 173 (Hoffmann J)

[290] Deregulation and Contracting Out Act 1994, s 3(1)

[291] HM Treasury, *Investment Powers of Trustees: a Consultation Document* (May 1996)

[292] ibid. 5–6 (paras 11–15)

[293] ibid, 9–10 (para 33)

[294] ibid, 10 (para 35(i))

ucts are constantly being produced, but more importantly, the Consultation Document saw the concept of lists as incompatible with modern portfolio theory.[295]

Under the new regime proposed by the Consultation Document, trustees would be given the same power to invest as if they were beneficial owners of the fund;[296] but they would continue to be under an obligation to have regard to the need for diversification (so far as is appropriate to the circumstances of the trust) and to the suitability of any proposed investment.[297] In exercising their powers of investment, they would remain subject to the existing duties and standards of care established by trust law, including the duty to take advice where necessary and to review portfolios.[298] The new wider power would be without prejudice to these duties and standards, and also to the more general rules and duties applicable to trustees under trusts law, such as the obligation to avoid any conflict of interest.[299]   **1.134**

The Document considered that the main effect on charities of these reforms would be a reduction in administrative inconvenience. Amongst other things, the changes would save many charities the time and expense of having to apply to the Charity Commissioners to have their investment powers widened.[300] The Document was of the opinion, however, that the proposed changes would be unlikely to lead to a substantial shift in the investment practice of charities, given charities' existing statutory power to invest the whole or any part of their fund in common investment or deposit funds.[301]   **1.135**

It then became apparent that it might not be possible to repeal the Trustee Investments Act 1961 by means of a Deregulation Order because, although that Act did impose burdens, this was in the broader context of widening trustees' investment powers: it was essentially an enabling Act. For this reason, although a draft Deregulation Order was brought forward in February 1997, it did not seek to repeal the 1961 Act; instead, it would merely have removed the requirement to divide the fund and extended the categories of authorized investments. Although the draft Order was approved by the Delegated Powers Scrutiny Committee of the House of Lords, it was lost when the General Election was called in the spring of 1997.[302]   **1.136**

---

[295] ibid, 6 (para 16(ii))
[296] ibid, 6 (para 16(iv))
[297] ibid, 10 (para 35(ii))
[298] ibid, 6 (para 16(iv))
[299] ibid, 6 (para 16(iv).
[300] ibid, 13 (para 47(ii))
[301] ibid, 12 (para 44)
[302] For a more detailed account of the abortive Deregulation Order, see Law Commission, *Trustees' Powers and Duties* (Law Com No 260, May 1999), pp 2–3 (paras 1.4–1.7), 18 (paras 2.20–2.21)

Law Commission Report on Trustees' Powers and Duties, 1999

1.137 The Law Commission had been examining trustees' powers and duties since 1995, and in 1997, having obtained the advice of the Trust Law Committee, it produced a consultation paper.[303] The Law Commission's examination was broader than that of the Treasury Consultation Document in that, whilst its main concern was trustee investment, it also considered a number of other powers and duties of trustees, including delegation, the power to employ nominees and custodians, the insurance of trust property, and charging by professional trustees. The Law Commission saw the extension of trustees' power to delegate and to employ nominees as directly linked to trustees' powers of investment, in that, unless such additional powers were conferred on trustees, they would not be able to take full advantage of any extended powers of investment.[304]

1.138 In its final report on this subject in 1999, and taking the same approach as the Treasury Consultation Document, the Law Commission proposed primary legislation to abolish the Trustee Investments Act 1961 as a key aspect of its proposals to reform the law governing trustees.[305] Instead of a fixed list of authorized investments, it was proposed that trustees should have all the powers of an absolute beneficial owner, but with appropriate statutory safeguards—notably the reproduction in the new statute of the duties relating to diversification and suitability contained in the Trustee Investments Act 1961, section 6(1),[306] a modfied duty to seek advice,[307] and the application of a new statutory duty of care, such duty being applied to the exercise of all the new powers which the Law Commission proposed to confer on trustees, including the powers of investment.[308] It also proposed that trustees who otherwise lack the power, should have a general power (inter alia) to invest in land.[309] The Law Commission considered that its proposals should apply to most trusts, including charitable trusts; but it recognized that some special types of trust, including common investment schemes and common deposit schemes for charities, are already subject to a specific statutory regime.[310] It did not think it would be appropriate to replace such a regime with a different scheme, and it therefore recommended that its proposals to reform the law of trustee investment should not apply to trusts whose trustees are given special statutory powers of investment by or under other enactments.[311]

---

[303] Law Commission, *Trustees' Powers and Duties* (Consultation Paper No 146 June 1997)
[304] See Law Commission, *Trustees' Powers and Duties* (Law Com No 260, (May 1999), 3 (paras 1.8–1.10)
[305] ibid, 17–19 (paras 2.19–2.23)
[306] ibid, 22–3 (paras 2.30–2.31)
[307] ibid, 23–5 (paras 2.32–2.34)
[308] ibid, 25–6 (paras 2.35–2.38)
[309] ibid, 26–9 (paras 2.39–2.44)
[310] CA 1993, ss 24–5
[311] Law Commission, *Trustees' Powers and Duties* (Law Com No 260, May 1999), 30–1 (paras 2.49–2.50)

The Law Commission appended a draft Bill to its report, which was introduced as   **1.139**
a Public Bill in the House of Lords in January 2000, and which passed into the
statute book as the Trustee Act 2000 in November of that year. It came into force
on 1 February 2001.[312] It puts the portfolio theory on a statutory basis in the law
of trustee investment. The impact of the Act on investment by trustees of charities is considered primarily in chapter 16; its impact on other aspects of the powers of charity trustees is dealt with mainly in chapter 9. It should be noted at the
outset, however, that the Trustee Act 2000 does not apply to charitable companies, as the Law Commission in its final report saw 'considerable technical
difficulties' in extending the Act to include them.[313]

---

[312] Trustee Act 2000 (Commencement) Order 2001/49.
[313] ibid, 7–8 (para 1.20, esp fn 37)

2

THE ADVANTAGES AND
DISADVANTAGES OF
CHARITABLE STATUS

2.01 The advantages of charitable status for those involved with charities are numerous and important, although it is also possible to identify what might be perceived as drawbacks which flow from such status. Some factors might be considered to fall into either category, depending upon one's point of view or the relevant circumstances. The cy-près doctrine, for instance, might be considered as either advantageous (in that it can save property for charity that might otherwise go on a resulting trust) or as restrictive (in that it limits the ability of those running the charity to deal with the charity's property as they think fit). Some of the factors to be borne in mind are considered in more detail, or from a particular aspect, in later chapters. It might be helpful to those concerned with setting up an institution, however, to consider together in this chapter the principal advantages and disadvantages of establishing it as a charity.

A. The main advantages of charitable status

(1) Tax exemptions and reliefs

2.02 Charities, and gifts to charity, enjoy significant tax exemptions and reliefs, and for many charities these privileges are undoubtedly the most important advantage of charitable status (the notable exception being VAT, in relation to which charities do not generally enjoy any privileged status). The fiscal exemptions and reliefs to charities themselves are considered in chapter 3; the fiscal privileges accorded to gifts to charity are dealt with mainly in chapter 19. As the fiscal advantages are very specific in scope, to derive maximum benefit from them, charities and donors may need to arrange their giving, or to organize their activities, in a particular way. Charities which wish to engage in trade, for example, may well find it necessary or desirable to form a subsidiary trading company to carry on the trade. The fiscal and other issues relating to charities and trading are considered in chapter 20.

2.03 To set against the foregoing advantages, it should be borne in mind that a number of tax privileges enjoyed by charities are also accorded to certain types of non-charitable bodies.[1] Furthermore, the fiscal advantages of charitable status are of less importance for a body which is largely funded by small donations, which spends the money it raises without investing it, and which does not own or occupy land.

(2) Enhanced public standing

2.04 Registration with the Charity Commissioners merely indicates that an institution's purposes are charitable, and is no guarantee that the institution operates effectively. Nevertheless, although there is no foundation for it in law, the possession by an institution of a charity registration number continues to inspire confidence in the public mind, and may elicit a better response in appeals for funds. A charity registration number may also be helpful or, indeed, a prerequisite, to a body's obtaining grants from some sources.

(3) Advisory and other supportive functions of the Charity Commissioners

2.05 One of the Charity Commissioners' general functions is to promote the effective use of charitable resources (inter alia) by giving information or advice to charity trustees on any matter affecting the charity.[2] Charity trustees who apply in writing for the opinion or advice of the Commissioners and who act in accordance with such opinion or advice are generally deemed to have acted in accordance with their trusts.[3] The Charity Commissioners may also establish schemes for the administration of charities and act for the protection of charities,[4] and they may by order authorize dealings with charity property even where such dealings would otherwise not be within the power of the charity trustees.[5] More specifically, the

---

[1] eg a scientific research organization whose research might facilitate an extension of any class of trade and which is approved by the Secretary of State, is, if its constitution prohibits any payment or transfer of profits to members, entitled to claim exemption from tax on its income as would be allowed under the ICTA 1988, s 505, in the case of a charity whose whole income is applied to charitable purposes: ibid, s 508. Such an organization can also be the recipient of a 'qualifying donation' (Gift Aid) made by a company: ibid, s 390(1)–(4), (9)

[2] CA 1993, s 1(3). See further ch 10, 10.119–10.128

[3] CA 1993, s 29. See further ch 10, para 10.120

[4] CA 1993, s 16

[5] ibid, s 26

Charity Commissioners may also approve dealings with land which might otherwise be objectionable as involving a conflict of interest.[6]

(4) Consent requirement for charity proceedings

Legal proceedings brought under the court's jurisdiction with respect to charities,[7] **2.06** or brought under the court's jurisdiction with respect to trusts in relation to the administration of a trust for charitable purposes, are 'charity proceedings' for the purposes of the Charities Act 1993.[8] As a general rule, charity proceedings can be brought only by specified classes of persons,[9] and only with the consent of the Charity Commissioners.[10] The restrictions on the bringing of such proceedings can be considered a form of protection for charities, and there is judicial support for this view.[11] The need for consent to bring charity proceedings has been described as 'a protective filter',[12] the purpose of which is 'to protect charities from being harassed and put to expense by a multiplicity of claims, which may or may not be well-founded, by persons who may or may not fairly be described as "busybodies".'[13] This protective filter does not exist for non-charitable bodies.

(5) Advantages for charitable (as opposed to private) trusts

Objects need not be certain   **2.07**

An express private trust must comply with the so-called three certainties:[14] namely, certainty of words (or intention), certainty of subject-matter, and certainty of objects. Charitable trusts are subject only to the first two certainties. The objects of a charitable trust (which refers to its purposes) do not need to be certain. Charitable trusts are, however, subject to an alternative requirement that their purposes must be wholly and exclusively charitable.[15] Provided the objects of a trust are wholly and exclusively charitable, any vagueness or uncertainty in those purposes is treated as a purely administrative matter, and can be remedied by the preparation of a scheme, either by the courts or by the Charity Commissioners.[16]

---

[6] ibid, s 36(1). See further ch 17, paras 17.47–17.49

[7] Charitable companies are included: see further ch 11, paras 11.16–11.29

[8] CA 1993, s 33(8)

[9] ibid, s 33(1)

[10] ibid, s 33(2). The Charity Commissioners' consent is not required if the charity is an exempt charity: ibid

[11] See *R v National Trust, ex p Scott* [1998] JPL 465, 467, where Tucker J held, in the circumstances of the case, that the National Trust (a charity) was 'protected' by CA 1993, s 33

[12] *Re Hampden Fuel Allotment Charity* [1989] Ch 484, 493–4 (Nicholls LJ)

[13] *Scott v National Trust* [1998] 2 All ER 705, 714 (Robert Walker J)

[14] *Knight v Knight* (1840) 3 Beav 148, 172 (Lord Langdale MR)

[15] See further ch 6 generally

[16] On the preparation of schemes in such instances, see ch 15, para 15.19

Possibility of cy-près application if objects fail

2.08   Where the objects of a private trust fail, the trustees will usually hold the property on a resulting trust for the settlor or his estate.[17] There may also be a resulting trust on the failure of the objects of a charitable trust, but (depending upon the circumstances), it is possible that the property will instead be applicable under a scheme through the doctrine of cy-près.[18]

Modernization of purposes through cy-près doctrine

2.09   Since the Charities Act 1960, it has been possible for charitable purposes to be modified through the cy-près doctrine to ensure that the property is more effectively applied to modern needs.[19] The cy-près doctrine has no application to private trusts.

Less stringent application of perpetuity rules

Rule against remoteness of vesting: general principles

2.10   Like private trusts, charitable trusts are subject to the rule against perpetuities known as the rule against remoteness of vesting. At common law, if a contingent gift is made to charity, it must be clear at the time the gift is made that it must vest (if it vests at all) within the perpetuity period; if there is the remotest possibility that it might vest outside that period, the gift is void for perpetuity *ab initio*.[20] If a gift made after 15 July 1964 is void for remoteness of vesting at common law, it may be saved by the Perpetuities and Accumulations Act 1964. Under that Act, a gift which might not vest until too remote a time is not treated as void for remoteness until such time (if any) as it becomes established that the vesting must occur, if at all, after the end of the perpetuity period: that is, it is necessary to 'wait and see'.[21]

2.11   Where the circumstances at the time of a testator's death make it impossible to comply with a condition precedent attached to a gift to charity, the condition is spent, and the gift to charity becomes absolute. This was so held in *Watson v National Children's Home*,[22] where the testator by his will gave one half of his es-

---

[17] Usually, but other outcomes are possible depending upon the construction of the instrument. It may be found that the settlor intended to give the beneficiary an absolute interest: see *Hancock v Watson* [1902] AC 14; *Re Andrews Trust* [1905] 2 Ch 48; *Re Osoba* [1979] 1 WLR 247 (CA)

[18] See further ch 15, paras 15.46–15.49 and para 15.51

[19] CA 1960, s 13(1), now re-enacted as CA 1993, s 14(1). See further ch 15, paras 15.65–15.81

[20] *Chamberlayne v Brockett* (1872) 8 Ch App 206, 211 (Lord Selbourne LC); *Re Lord Stratheden and Campbell* [1894] 3 Ch 265 (Romer J) (bequest of an annuity of £100 to the Central London Rangers on the appointment of the next Lieutenant Colonel); *Re Mills Declaration of Trust* [1950] 1 All ER 789; on appeal [1950] 2 All ER 292

[21] Perpetuities and Accumulations Act 1964, s 3(1)

[22] The Times, 31 Oct 1995

tate to the National Children's Home and the other half to the National Canine Defence League 'on the condition that the said League will look after my domestic pets in their kennels during the remainder of their natural lives'. In the event of the League's not agreeing to such condition, such half share was to go to the National Children's Home. By the time of the testator's death, his only pet, a dog, had died. Judge Colyer QC, sitting as a judge of the High Court, held that, on the construction of the words used, it was clear that the testator intended that the League should care for any domestic pets that the testator might have at his death. There being none, the half share went to the League absolutely. If his construction were wrong, his Lordship considered that the resulting ambiguity could be resolved by the admission of extrinsic evidence of the testator's intention;[23] and such evidence indicated the testator had intended that the League should still benefit if the testator had no pets at his death.

Gift to charity followed by gift over to non-charity

It is important to distinguish a gift subject to a condition subsequent from a de-   **2.12** terminable gift. The former is a gift of an absolute interest which can be cut short by the occurrence of the condition; it is created by words such as 'but if ', 'provided that', or 'on condition that'. The latter is a gift of an interest which is limited from the start in that it continues only until (if at all) the determining event occurs; it is created by words such as 'until', or 'so long as'.

If a gift is made to charity subject to a gift over to a non-charity on the occurrence   **2.13** of a condition subsequent, the possibility that the event giving rise to the gift over might occur outside the perpetuity period renders the gift over void at common law, so that the gift to charity becomes absolute.[24] For dispositions made after the coming into effect of the Perpetuities and Accumulations Act 1964, however, the gift over is not treated as void for perpetuity unless and until it becomes clear that its vesting must occur, if it occurs at all, outside the period of perpetuity which that Act prescribes (which, in the absence of human lives, will be twenty-one years).[25]

If a gift is made to charity determinable upon a future event, the gift to charity   **2.14** (being vested *ab initio*) will validly determine at common law even if the determining event might occur (and does in fact occur) outside the perpetuity period. If the testator provides for a gift over to a non-charity upon the determining event, such gift over is void if there is a possibility that the event might occur outside the perpetuity period.[26] The presence of an express gift over that was void for

---

[23] Administration of Justice Act 1982, s 21
[24] *Re Bowen* [1893] 2 Ch 491 (Stirling J) (bequest on trust to establish a day school in specified parishes in Wales subject to a gift over if the Government should establish 'a general system of education'); *Re Peel's Release* [1921] 2 Ch 218
[25] Perpetuities and Accumulations Act 1964, s 3(1), (4)
[26] *Re Chardon* [1928] Ch 464

perpetuity at common law did not preclude a reverter to, or resulting trust for, the testator's estate outside the perpetuity period[27] (since such interest was vested *ab initio*), even if the beneficiaries of the gift over were also the persons entitled upon the reverter or under a resulting trust.[28] Under the Perpetuities and Accumulations Act 1964, however, an express gift over is not treated as void for perpetuity unless and until it becomes clear that the determining event must occur (if at all) outside the period of perpetuity which that Act prescribes (which, in the absence of human lives, will be twenty-one years).[29] The possibility of a reverter or resulting trust for the testator's estate outside the perpetuity period is prevented by the Act's treating the charity's determinable interest, for the purposes of perpetuity, as if it were a condition subsequent, so that if the gift over in fact proves void for remoteness of vesting, the determinable gift to charity becomes absolute.[30]

Gift over from one charity to another

2.15 A limited exception to the latter rule applies where there is a gift over from one charity (or from one charitable purpose) to another, as the gift over is not subject to the rule against remoteness of vesting.[31] The most convincing explanation for this exception is that all charity is one; the rule against remoteness of vesting applies only to the vesting in the first charity (or charitable purpose); thereafter, the passing of the property from one charity to another is to be treated as a matter of administration only, which may therefore occur outside the period of perpetuity.[32]

2.16 The event upon which property is to pass from one charity to another does not have to be connected with the gift, so that it could (for instance) be expressed to be the falling into disrepair of the testator's tomb or family vault.[33] By such means, a testator can provide indirectly for a non-charitable purpose to be carried out in per-

---

[27] *A-G v Pyle* (1738) 1 Atk 435; *Re Blunt's Trusts* [1904] 2 Ch 767; *Re Cooper's Conveyance Trusts* [1956] 1 WLR 1096; but see *Hopper v Liverpool Corp* (1944) 88 Sol Jo 213

[28] *Re Randell* (1888) 38 Ch D 213

[29] Perpetuities and Accumulations Act 1964, s 3(1), (4)

[30] ibid, s 12

[31] *Christ's Hospital v Grainger* (1848) 16 Sim 83; affd (1849) 1 Mac & G 460. Appl *Royal College of Surgeons of England v National Provincial Bank Ltd* [1952] AC 631 (HL). There are also specific statutory exceptions to the rule against remoteness of vesting. These are for gifts over to charitable trusts which follow a non-charitable gift for the endowment of an historic building accepted by the Secretary of State, or of an historic garden accepted by the Historic Buildings and Monuments Commission for England: Historic Buildings and Ancient Monuments Act 1953, ss 8(5), 8(A)(5), 8(B)(5), as amended by National Heritage Act 1983, s 33 & Sch 4, para 10

[32] See the comments of Shadwell V-C in *Christ's Hospital v Grainger* (1848) 16 Sim 83, 100. In that case, the event which gave rise to the gift over occurred more than 200 years after the testator's death

[33] *Re Tyler* [1891] 3 Ch 252 (CA). In *Re Lopes* [1932] 2 Ch 130, the event that was to effect a gift over from one charity (the Zoological Society of London) to another (St Bartholomew's Hospital) was the Society's failure to comply with a condition (inter alia) that a picture of the testator's mother should hang in its boardroom. Farwell J made an order under which the Society undertook (inter alia) to permit access to its boardroom to persons authorized by the Hospital so that they could ascertain that the picture remained hanging there

petuity, since the charity initially given the property will have an interest in ensuring that the specified event does not occur. Any expenditure of the charity's funds on such a non-charitable purpose would prima facie comprise a breach of trust, although it might be open to the charity to contend that such expenditure should be treated as an incidental expense incurred in the preservation of a capital asset.

It is important that the wording of the gift does not impose an obligation on the first charity to carry out the non-charitable purpose (for example, the repair of the testator's tomb), since this will create a trust of imperfect obligation which may be void (inter alia) for perpetual trusts, which will in turn render void (for remoteness) the gift over to the second charity.[34] The testator should therefore take care to use words which merely create a condition subsequent (such as 'upon condition that if my tomb should fall into disrepair'), rather than words which create a gift subject to a condition in the sense of a trust obligation (such as 'upon condition that charity A keeps my tomb in repair'). **2.17**

Rule against perpetual trusts

Private trusts are also subject to a second rule against perpetuity called the rule against perpetual trusts, or the rule against inalienability. At common law, if there is the remotest possibility when a disposition is made that the capital will be tied up for longer than the perpetuity period, the disposition will be void for perpetual trusts. A non-charitable purpose trust will offend the rule unless in accordance with the disposition the capital can be spent either immediately or at least within the perpetuity period. The period of 'wait and see' introduced by the Perpetuities and Accumulations Act 1964 does not apply to the rule against perpetual trusts, so that dispositions remain subject to the common law rule.[35] **2.18**

Unlike private trusts, charitable trusts are exempt from the rule against perpetual trusts, so that capital can be tied up in a charitable trust for ever.[36] Charitable **2.19**

---

[34] *Re Dalziel* [1943] Ch 277 (Cohen J). The gift over in that case would have been void even if the disposition had been subject to the Perpetuities and Accumulations Act 1964. Although s 6 of that Act has a saving for expectant interests which might otherwise be void for remoteness, the section applies only where the interest is dependent upon a prior interest which is itself void for remoteness. The section does not therefore apply where the prior interest (as in *Re Dalziel*) is void for perpetual trusts

[35] Perpetuities and Accumulations Act 1964, s 15(4). It also seems that the possibility of specifying an alternative period of perpetuity (not exceeding eighty years) in s 1(1) of the Act is not available in respect of the rule against perpetual trusts: see *Underhill and Hayton's Law Relating to Trusts and Trustees* (ed D Hayton) (15th edn, Butterworths, 1995, 177–8. Trusts for the maintenance of individual graves (which are not charitable) may endure for 99 years under the Parish Council and Burial Authorities (Miscellaneous Provisions) Act 1970, s 1

[36] *Goodman v Mayor of Saltash Corp* (1882) 7 App Cas 633, 642 (Lord Selbourne), 650–1 (Earl Cairns); *Comrs for Special Purposes of the Income Tax v Pemsel* [1891] AC 531, 580–1 (Lord Macnaghten); *A-G v National Provincial & Union Bank Ltd* [1924] AC 262, 266 (Lord Haldane). Although their Lordships did not expressly limit their observations to the rule against perpetual trusts, it is evident that such was their intention. See also *A-G v Webster* (1875) LR 20 Eq 483 (where the court held valid a charitable trust created in 1585)

status is therefore vital to many dispositions if they are not to be invalidated by this rule.

Accumulations and retention of income

2.20 Unless the trust instrument gives the trustees a power to accumulate the income, the trustees are not permitted to accumulate it in the trust. If the trust instrument directs or empowers the trustees to accumulate income, such direction or power is subject to the statutory prohibitions upon accumulations of income for excessive periods.[37] If an excessive period of accumulation is specified, it is void only to the extent that it exceeds the appropriate statutory period of accumulation.[38] The income arising during the excess period goes to the persons who would have been entitled to it had no such accumulation been directed.[39] In the case of a private trust, this will often mean that such income goes on a resulting trust to the settlor or his estate. In the case of a charitable trust, however, the court may be able to apply such income cy-près, if there is a general charitable intention.[40] Even if the settlor directs accumulation for a permitted period, a charity which is absolutely entitled to the capital and income subject only to a direction to accumulate may disregard such direction and call for immediate payment.[41] Income which is lawfully accumulated by a charity loses its character as income; it is capitalized and becomes part of the charity's endowment. As such, it does not have to be applied in furtherance of the charity's objects. The restrictions on accumulations do not, of course, apply to charitable companies, which are permitted to accumulate income without limitation of time.

2.21 At first sight, it might appear that the restrictions upon excessive accumulations are a particularly serious impediment to charitable trusts, given that they may be of indefinite duration. In practice, however, the impact of the restrictions is less significant than might be supposed. This is because, in this context, the expression 'accumulations' does not mean any retention of income by the trustees. It has a narrow technical meaning, namely 'the addition of income to capital, thus increasing the estate of those entitled to the capital and against the interests of those entitled to the income. The mere retention of income . . . does not alter its nature: it remains income'.[42] Accumulation of income in this technical sense is therefore

---

[37] LPA 1925, s 164 and Perpetuities and Accumulations Act 1964, s 13. The restrictions on accumulations apply not merely to a trust to accumulate, but also to a power of accumulation: *Re Robb* [1953] Ch 459; *Baird v Lord Advocate* [1979] 2 WLR 369

[38] *Green v Gascoigne* (1864) 4 De GJ & Sm 565; see RH Maudsley, *The Modern Law of Perpetuities* (Butterworths, 1979) 207

[39] *Green v Gascoigne* (1864) 4 De GJ & Sm 565, 568 (Lord Westbury LC)

[40] *Martin v Maugham* (1844) 14 Sim 230; *Re Monk* [1927] 2 Ch 197; *Re Bradwell* [1952] Ch 575

[41] *Wharton v Masterman* [1895] AC 186 (HL), applying the rule in *Saunders v Vautier* (1841) 4 Beav 115 to charitable trusts

[42] *Re Earl of Berkeley* [1968] Ch 744, 772 (Harman LJ)

to be distinguished from the administrative retention of income, which is justified where the amount of income may fluctuate, so that the pattern will be one of retention in the fat years and distribution in the lean.[43] Retention of income to establish a maintenance fund to pay for repairs to buildings, for instance, is not an accumulation for the purposes of the rule[44] since this is expenditure of a revenue nature; but the application of income to a fund to be used for a capital outlay (such as the improvement of land or the construction of buildings[45]) is an accumulation and so subject to the rule against excessive accumulations.

The Law Commission has explained that,[46]   2.22

[b]y analogy, charities may retain income on an administrative basis provided that they can justify retention. It is the underlying duty of charities to apply such income for its charitable objects within a reasonable period of receipt. The regime is intrinsically flexible. It can, for instance, be relied upon as the basis for creating long term repair and maintenance funds for buildings, where appropriate, in just the same way as it can be relied upon to justify the retention of income for short term operational needs.

In a few instances, the trust instrument may give the trustees an express power to hold income in reserve; usually, however, the trustees wishing to retain income will have to rely on an implied power of retention.[47] In either case, where charity trustees retain income they must be able to satisfy the Charity Commissioners that such retention is justified, which means that it is in the charity's best interests.[48] Ultimately, retained income (unlike income which has been accumulated) must be applied to the charity's purposes.

Numbers and decisions of trustees

There is no maximum number of trustees of a charitable trust,[49] although it may,   2.23
of course, be impractical to have too large a number. Unless the trust instrument provides otherwise, decisions of trustees of charitable trusts may be made by a simple majority.[50]

---

[43] ibid, 780–1 (Widgery LJ)
[44] *Vine v Raleigh* [1891] 2 Ch 13
[45] ibid, 26
[46] Law Commission, *The Rule Against Perpetuities and Excessive Accumulations*, (Law Com No 251, 1998), 119 (para 9.32)
[47] See Charity Commission, *Charities' Reserves*, CC19 (May 1997), 8 (para 26)
[48] ibid, 10–13 (paras 34–43). On retention of income, see further ch 16, paras 16.102–16.105
[49] TA 1925, s 34(3)
[50] *Re Whiteley* [1910] 1 Ch 600, 608. The advantage of majority decisions is available to private trusts if the trust instrument so provides; otherwise decisions of trustees of private trusts must be unanimous: *Luke v South Kensington Hotel Ltd* (1879) 11 ChD 121; *Re Mayo* [1943] Ch 302

B. The main disadvantages of charitable status

(1) Generally

2.24 Charities are subject to a degree of public control by the Attorney-General and most charities must be registered with the Charity Commissioners and are subject to the supervision of the Commissioners. The Charities Act 1993 also imposes specific duties (including some criminal sanctions) on charity trustees, who are the persons having the general control and management of the administration of the charity,[51] including the duty to file accounts with the Charity Commissioners.[52] Only exempt charities are exempt from most of the obligations contained in the Charities Act 1993, and excepted charities are relieved of specific obligations thereunder.[53]

2.25 Charities and charity trustees are subject to the general restrictions of charity law on the application of their assets. A charitable trust for the relief of poverty, for instance, precludes the trustees from distributing the fund except to relieve the recipients' financial needs. Problems of this nature with disaster funds have meant that the primary public appeal fund raised following a disaster now usually takes the form of a private discretionary trust, under which the trustees can have greater flexibility in the allocation of the income and capital.[54] The restrictions on dealing with a charity's assets, and the restrictions on alterations of a charity's purposes, may also cause those concerned with an organization to take the view that charitable status is best avoided.[55] It has been said that '[t]he balance of advantage or disadvantage may be a fine one'.[56]

Although the rule prohibiting conflicts of interest applies to trustees, directors and committee members of non-charitable bodies, the rule is more severe in its application where the body is a charity. This is illustrated in a number of practical applications of the rule in the charitable sphere; one of the most important is the rule which (subject to certain limited relaxations in recent years) forbids charity

---

[51] CA 1993, s 97(1)
[52] ibid, s 49
[53] On the role of the Charity Commissioners, see generally ch 10
[54] Disaster funds are dealt with in ch 25
[55] In *IRC v Oldham Training and Enterprise Council* [1996] STC 1218, Oldham TEC, a company limited by guarantee, decided that it was not in its interests to oppose the appeal by the IRC against the Special Commissioners of the Inland Revenue, who had decided that its purposes were charitable. Shortly before the Special Commissioners' decision, Oldham TEC had changed its objects clause, which changes might not have been valid if its previous objects were held to be charitable: ibid, 1229 (Lightman J). In view of the importance of the appeal as a test case, however, it did nevertheless instruct counsel in order to assist the court to reach a decision after full argument on both sides
[56] ibid, 1230 (Lightman J)

trustees, directors and committee members from taking remuneration for acting as such.[57]

Charities are also subject to restrictions on their involvement in political activity, **2.26** with the result that the political aims of those running them are sometimes carried on through separate non-charitable organizations. The restrictions on political activity seem to have been a particular problem for charities whose object is the relief of poverty overseas, and it has also restricted the political involvement of some students' unions.[58]

Since members of a charitable association (incorporated or unincorporated) can **2.27** have no proprietary interest in the charity's assets, they are not entitled to a share in any surplus if the charity is dissolved. Unless the charity's constitution permits the members to dissolve the charity and to apply the assets to other charitable purposes, such assets will have to be applied under a scheme (which if necessary will be a cy-près scheme settled by the Charity Commissioners or the court).[59]

(2) Registered charities: statements in documents

If a registered charity had a gross income in its last financial year of more than **2.28** £10,000,[60] it must state the fact that it is a registered charity in legible characters[61] in all of the following documents:[62]

- (a) in all notices, advertisements and other documents issued by or on behalf of the charity and soliciting money or other property for the benefit of the charity;
- (b) in all bills of exchange, promissory notes, endorsements, cheques and orders for money or goods purporting to be signed on behalf of the charity; and
- (c) in all bills rendered by it and in all its invoices, receipts and letters of credit.

The Charity Commissioners have stated that this requirement is satisfied by any of the following descriptions: 'A Registered Charity'; 'Registered Charity No [followed by the charity number]'; 'Registered as a Charity'; or 'Registered with the Charity Commissioners'.[63]

It is an offence for any person to sign, issue or authorize the issue of, any such **2.29** document which does not contain the required statement.[64] The offence may

---

[57] On remuneration and conflicts of interest, see ch 9, paras 9.96–9.128

[58] On political activity generally, see ch 7, paras 7.40–7.88. The charitable status of students' unions is considered in ch 4, paras 4.26–4.29

[59] On schemes, see ch 15; on dissolution of charities, see ch 26

[60] CA 1993, s 5(1); sum substituted by Charities Act 1993 (Substitution of Sums) Order 1995, SI 1995/2696, reg 2(2), pursuant to CA 1993, s 5(6)

[61] The statement must be in English unless the document is otherwise wholly in Welsh, in which case the statement may be in Welsh if it consists of or includes the words '*elusen cofrestredig*' (the Welsh equivalent of 'registered charity'): CA 1993, s 5(2A), added by Welsh Language Act 1993, s 32(3)

[62] CA 1993, s 5(2)

[63] (2000) 12 Ch Com News 4

[64] CA 1993, s 5(4), (5); as amended by Welsh Language Act 1993, s 32(4), (5)

therefore be committed, not merely by a trustee, director, or Committee member of the charity, but also by any of a charity's agents, employees, or volunteers. Whilst most registered charities are no doubt keen to advertise the fact that they are registered as charities, the possibility of a criminal prosecution resulting from a contravention of this wide-ranging provision must be accounted a disadvantage of charitable status from the point of view of those involved with the running of a charity.

2.30   There are also specific publicity requirements for a charitable company formed under the Companies Act 1985.[65] These requirements flow, not from the institution's status as a charity, but from its structure as a company, and are therefore considered in chapter 8.[66] A registered charity which is incorporated under the Companies Act 1985 may therefore (depending on its gross income in its last financial year) find itself having to comply with two sets of statutory obligations relating to statements in documents: those imposed by company law and those imposed by charity law. It is important to note that these requirements are not precisely parallel. In practice, most registered charities choose to state their charity registration number on their business documents; but, as mentioned above,[67] statute does not require a statement of the registered number itself, merely a statement of the fact that the institution is a registered charity.[68] Under the publicity requirements in the Companies Act 1985, however, a company must specify in various business documents its company registration number:[69] a mere statement of the fact that it is a registered company is inadequate.

---

[65]   Companies Act 1985, ss 30(7), 349(1), 351; CA 1993, ss 67–8
[66]   See ch 8, para 8.73
[67]   See para 2.28 above
[68]   CA 1993, s 5(2)
[69]   Companies Act 1985, s 351(1). See further ch 8, para 8.73

3

CHARITIES AND TAXATION

Charities, and gifts to charity, enjoy significant tax exemptions and reliefs. **3.01** The following discussion concentrates on the fiscal advantages accorded to the charities themselves; the fiscal privileges enjoyed by gifts to charity are dealt with mainly in chapter 19. The tax implications of charity trading are analysed in chapter 20.

A. Taxation of charity income

(1) Scope of exemptions

Specific tax exemptions can be claimed by a charity by virtue of section 505(1) of **3.02** the Income and Corporation Taxes Act 1988 (ICTA). The exemptions are contained in the five surviving out of the original six lettered paragraphs.[1]

Exemption from tax under Schedules A and D in respect of rent and receipts from land

Under paragraph (a), there is[2]   **3.03**

    (a) exemption from tax under Schedules A and D in respect of any profits or gains arising in respect of rents or other receipts from an estate, interest or right in or over

---

[1] Para (a) was substituted by FA 1996, s 146; para (b) was repealed by FA 1988, s 148 & Sch 14, Pt V; paras (c)(ii)–(iib) were substituted for former para (c)(ii) by FA 1996, s 146; para (d) was substituted by FA 1996, s 79

[2] ICTA 1988, s 505(1)(a)

any land (whether situated in the United Kingdom or elsewhere) to the extent that the profits or gains—

    (i)   arise in respect of rents or receipts from an estate, interest or right vested in any person for charitable purposes; and

    (ii) are applied to charitable purposes only.

3.04   To be exempt, the receipts must be of an income, not a capital nature.[3] To determine this, it is necessary to examine the transaction's true nature, not just from the agreement which the parties have entered into, but also from surrounding circumstances.[4] A difficult decision in this regard is *Inland Revenue Commissioners v Church Commissioners for England*;[5] the Church Commissioners (a charity) owned various freehold and leasehold properties which were let or sub-let to a (non-charitable) company on long leases at £40,000 per annum. The Church Commissioners agreed to sell the properties to the company for yearly rentcharges issuing out of the property totalling £96,000 per annum. The company deducted tax at the standard rate, and the Church Commissioners sought to reclaim the tax deducted, under a forerunner of the present paragraph (a), on the ground that they were a charity. The Crown argued that the receipts were necessarily of a capital nature because it was initially possible to calculate the total amount to be paid; but this argument was rejected by the House of Lords. Their Lordships said that the character of the payments was to be determined by looking at the negotiations between the parties and the agreement which they had entered into. On the facts, they held that the receipts were of an income character: the charity was merely replacing receipts of rent for other payments of a revenue nature. The decision produces an anomaly since, although the sums were held to be income receipts of the charity, the House of Lords had previously held that they were capital payments of the company.[6]

Repealed exemption

3.05   With the repeal of Schedule B (tax on the occupation of woodlands), the exemption from tax under that Schedule formerly contained in paragraph (b) has itself been repealed.[7]

Specific exemptions from tax under Cases III, IV, and V of Schedule D on most types of investment income

3.06   Under paragraph (c)(ii)–(iii), there is exemption:[8]

    (ii)   from tax under Case III of Schedule D;

---

[3] eg *Vestey v IRC* [1962] Ch 861 (Cross J)
[4] ibid
[5] [1977] AC 329 (HL)
[6] *IRC v Land Securities Investment Trust Ltd* [1969] 1 WLR 604 (HL)
[7] Repealed by FA 1988, s 148 & Sch 14, Pt V, with effect from 6 Apr 1988
[8] Para (c)(i) was repealed by FA 1996, s 79 & Sch 7, para 19(1) and s 205 & Sch 41, Pt V(2)

(iia) from tax under Case IV or V of Schedule D in respect of income equivalent to income chargeable under Case III of that Schedule but arising from securities or other possessions outside the United Kingdom;

(iib) from tax under Case V of Schedule D in respect of income consisting of any such dividend or other distribution of a company not resident in the United Kingdom as would be chargeable to tax under Schedule F if the company were so resident; and

(iii) from tax under Schedule F in respect of any distribution,

where the income in question forms part of the income of a charity, or is according to rules or regulations established by Act of Parliament, charter, decree,[9] deed of trust or will, applicable to charitable purposes only, and so far as applied to charitable purposes only.[10]

A properly considered accumulation of income by a charitable trust (whether for **3.07** a specific charitable purpose or for the charity's general purposes), or a charity's retention of income pursuant to a responsible reserves policy, may comprise an application of the charity's income to exclusively charitable purposes to enable the charity to claim this exemption from income or corporation tax.[11] In *Inland Revenue Commissioners v Helen Slater Charitable Trust Ltd*, Oliver LJ, with whose judgment the other two members of the Court of Appeal agreed, stated:[12]

> Charitable trustees who simply leave surplus income uninvested cannot, I think, be said to have 'applied' it at all and, indeed, would be in breach of trust. But if the income is reinvested by them and held, as invested, as part of the funds of the charity, I would be disposed to say that it is no less being applied for charitable purposes than if it is paid out in wages to the secretary.

Income is also 'applied' by charitable corporation A if it is transferred outright to charitable corporation B, being itself both a corporation with exclusively charitable objects and an object of charity A.[13]

Except for the purposes of corporation tax, Case III of Schedule D comprises tax **3.08** in respect of[14]

(a) any interest of money, whether yearly or otherwise, or any annuity or other annual payment, whether such payment is payable within or out of the United

---

[9] In para (c), 'Act of Parliament' means an Act of the UK Parliament, 'charter' means a Royal Charter granted by the sovereign of the UK, and 'decree' means a decree of a court of the UK: *Camille & Henry Dreyfus Foundation Inc v IRC* [1954] 1 Ch 672, 706 (Jenkins LJ)

[10] ICTA 1988, s 505(1)(c). On whether income has been 'applied to charitable purposes only', see *IRC v Educational Grants Assoc Ltd* [1967] 1 Ch 993 (CA)

[11] *General Nursing Council for Scotland v IRC* (1929) SC 664, 671 (Lord Sands). Lord Blackburn there expressed a different view, but Lord Sands' opinion is supported by *IRC v Helen Slater Charitable Trust Ltd* [1982] Ch 49 (CA)

[12] [1982] Ch 49, 59, and approving the opinion of Lord Sands in *General Nursing Council for Scotland v IRC* 1929 SC 664, 671

[13] *IRC v Helen Slater Charitable Trust Ltd* [1982] Ch 49, 59–60, where Oliver LJ approved the observations of Slade J at first instance: [1981] Ch 79, 88

[14] ICTA 1988, s 18(1)

Kingdom, either as a charge on any property of the person paying the same by virtue of any deed or will or otherwise, or as a reservation out of it, or as a personal debt or obligation by virtue of any contract, or whether the same is received and payable half-yearly or at any shorter or more distant periods, but not including any payment chargeable under Schedule A; and
(b) all discounts; and
(c) income from securities which is payable out of the public revenue of the United Kingdom or Northern Ireland.

3.09 For the purposes of corporation tax, Case III of Schedule D comprises tax in respect of[15]

(a) any profits and gains which, as profits and gains arising from loan relationships, are to be treated as chargeable under this Case by virtue of Chapter II of Part IV of the Finance Act 1996;
(b) any annuity or other annual payment which—
(i) is payable (whether inside or outside the United Kingdom and whether annually or at shorter or longer notice) in respect of anything other than a loan relationship; and
(ii) is not a payment chargeable under Schedule A;
(c) any discount arising otherwise than in respect of a loan relationship.

The expression 'or other annual payment' includes only payments of an income, not of a capital, nature.[16] A receipt of sums paid under a deed of covenant is prima facie a receipt of an income nature; but such sums will be capital receipts in the charity's hands if they are designed to put the charity in funds to enable it to purchase the covenantor's business.[17]

3.10 A receipt by a charity under Gift Aid is treated as an annual payment made, in the case of a receipt from an individual, net of basic rate tax[18] (which the charity is able to reclaim), or, in the case of a receipt from a company, gross. For Gift Aid to apply, the sum paid must be a 'qualifying donation'. In April 2000,[19] the scope of Gift Aid was considerably widened. The changes made from that date are dealt with in more detail in chapter 19; but two of the most important may be mentioned here. First, the former requirement that the donation be of a specified minimum amount has been abolished.[20] Secondly, Gift Aid has effectively replaced the former method of giving tax relief on payments made under a deed of covenant. Before 1 or 6 April 2000,[21] a receipt by a charity of a payment made under a deed of covenant was

---

[15] ICTA 1988, s 18(3A) (inserted by FA 1996, s 104 & Sch 14, para 5)
[16] *Whitworth Park Coal Co Ltd v IRC* [1961] AC 31 (HL)
[17] *Campbell v IRC* [1970] AC 77 (HL)
[18] FA 1990, s 25 (as amended)
[19] ie from 1 Apr 2000 in respect of Gift Aid payments by companies and from 6 Apr 2000 in respect of Gift Aid payments by individuals
[20] FA 2000, ss 39(3)(a), 40(3), repealing FA 1990, s 25(2)(g) and ICTA 1988, s 339(3A) respectively
[21] ie before 1 Apr 2000 in respect of payments under deeds of covenant entered into by companies, and before 6 Apr 2000 in respect of payments under deeds of covenant entered into by individuals

exempt tax in the charity's hands as being an annual payment if the payment comprised 'a covenanted payment to charity'. The concept of 'a covenanted payment to charity' has now been abolished; a payment made on or after those dates under a deed of covenant (whenever entered into)[22] is entitled instead to tax relief under Gift Aid if it is a 'qualifying donation'.[23] The effect of these changes has been to simplify the tax treatment of donations for both donors and charities.

Exemption from tax under Schedule D in respect of public revenue dividends applied for repair of any cathedral, etc

Under paragraph (d), there is exemption from tax under Schedule D on public revenue dividends[24] on securities which are in the name of trustees, to the extent that the dividends are applicable and applied only for the repair of any cathedral, college, church or chapel, or any building[25] used only for the purposes of divine worship.[26] **3.11**

Exemption from tax under Schedule D in respect of the profits of primary purpose or 'beneficiary' trading

Under paragraph (e), there is exemption from tax under Schedule D in respect of the profits of any trade carried on by a charity (whether in the United Kingdom or elsewhere), if the profits are applied solely to the purposes of the charity, and either the trade is exercised in the course of the actual carrying out of a primary purpose of the charity, or the work in connection with the trade is mainly carried out by beneficiaries of the charity.[27] **3.12**

Exemption from tax in respect of the profits from certain types of lottery

Under paragraph (f), there is exemption from tax under Schedule D in respect of the profits accruing to a charity from a lottery which is promoted and conducted either as a small lottery incidental to exempt entertainments[28] or as a society's lottery,[29] provided the profits are applied solely to the charity's purposes.[30] **3.13**

---

[22] FA 2000, ss 39(10), 40(11)

[23] ibid, s 25; ICTA 1988, s 339

[24] For this purpose, 'public revenue dividends' means income from securities which is payable out of the public revenue of the UK or Northern Ireland, and income from securities issued by or on behalf of a government or a public or local authority in a country outside the UK: ICTA 1988, s 505(1A)

[25] In this paragraph, 'building' evidently means a building in the UK: *Camille & Henry Dreyfus Foundation Inc v IRC* [1954] 1 Ch 672, 705 (Jenkins LJ)

[26] ICTA 1988, s 505(1)(d)

[27] ibid, s 505(1)(e). In view of the limited scope of this exemption, for many charities involved in trading there can be fiscal advantages in forming a subsidiary company to carry on the trade. Charity trading and taxation is considered in ch 20, esp paras 20.04–20.17

[28] ie in accordance with the Lotteries and Amusements Act 1976, s 3

[29] ie in accordance with ibid, s 5

[30] ICTA 1988, s 505(1)(f)

Exemption from tax under Cases I or VI of Schedule D in respect of small trading income

3.14 The Finance Act 2000 introduced a new exemption which is intended to enable charities to engage in small amounts of non-purpose trading activities without the profits from such activities being liable to tax.[31] The exemption therefore saves such charities from having to set up subsidiary trading companies to carry on the trade.

3.15 A charity[32] may claim this exemption only if its income[33] (meanings its income under Cases I or VI of Schedule D) for a chargeable period is applied solely for the purposes of the charity.[34] Furthermore, either the charity's gross income[35] for that period must not exceed the requisite limit, or the charity must have had, at the beginning of that period, a reasonable expectation that its gross income for the period would not exceed that limit.[36]

3.16 The requisite limit is whichever is the greater of[37]

(a) £5,000; and
(b) whichever is the lesser of £50,000 and 25% of all of the charity's incoming resources for the chargeable period.

3.17 The phrase 'incoming resources' is not defined, but it is wider than 'income' and refers to a charity's total receipts for the period. It therefore includes investment income, donations and grants.[38]

3.18 In effect, the requisite limit is one quarter of a charity's incoming resources, but subject to the proviso that it is never less than £5,000 and never more than £50,000. The formula means that a charity's incoming resources need to exceed £20,000 if its requisite limit is to be more than £5,000. The maximum requisite limit of £50,000 is reached once a charity's incoming resources are £200,000. It

---

[31] FA 2000, s 46. The section applies for the year 2000–1 and subsequent years of assessment, or, in the case of charities which are companies, for accounting periods beginning on or after 1 Apr 2000: ibid, s 46(7). Certain income chargeable to tax under Case VI of Sch D does not, however, enjoy this exemption: ibid, s 46(2), where such income is listed

[32] In s 46, 'charity' means any body of persons or trust established for charitable purposes only: ibid, s 46(6)

[33] In s 46, 'income' in relation to a charity means any profits or gains or other income which is chargeable to tax under Cases I or VI of Sch D and which is not, apart from s 46, exempted from tax under that Case: ibid, s 46(6)

[34] ibid, s 46(3)

[35] In s 46, 'gross income' in relation to a charity means income (as defined (see n 33 above)) before deduction of any expenses: ibid, s 46(6)

[36] ibid, s 46(3)(a), (b)

[37] ibid, s 46(4). For a chargeable period of less than twelve months, the specified amounts are reduced proportionately: ibid, s 46(5)

[38] Inland Revenue, 'Getting Britain Giving: Inland Revenue Guidance Note for Charities' (Mar 2000) para 11.4

should be borne in mind that the exemption is lost completely if the charity's gross income exceeds (or if there is a reasonable expectation that it will exceed) the requisite limit.

The following are illustrations of how the statutory formula is used to determine whether a charity is entitled to exemption on its trading profits under the Finance Act 2000:

(1) Charity A has, for the chargeable period, an investment income of £2,000, it receives donations and legacies of £6,000, and it has a gross trading income under Case I of Schedule D (not otherwise exempt) of £4,000. The amount of its incoming resources for the chargeable period is the sum of these, namely £12,000. Since 25 per cent of that is £3,000, and this is less than £50,000, the figure falling within paragraph (b) is £3,000. The requisite limit for Charity A is therefore £5,000 (within paragraph (a)), since this is greater than £3,000 (within paragraph (b)). Charity A is entitled to the exemption on its trading income under the Finance Act 2000, since its trading income of £4,000 is within the requisite limit of £5,000.

(2) Charity B, for the chargeable period, has an investment income of £2,000, it receives donations and legacies of £4,000, and its gross trading income under Case I of Schedule D (not otherwise exempt) is £6,000. The amount of its incoming resources for the chargeable period is the sum of these, namely £12,000. Its requisite limit is therefore the same as that of Charity A, ie £5,000. However, unless Charity B can satisfy the Revenue that it had 'a reasonable expectation' at the beginning of its chargeable period that its gross income under Cases I and VI of Schedule D would not exceed £5,000, it will not be entitled to the exemption on its trading income, since the amount of such gross income (£6,000) exceeds the requisite limit of £5,000.

(3) Charity C has incoming resources for the chargeable period of £500,000. Since 25% of that is £125,000, and this is greater than £50,000, the figure falling within paragraph (b) is £50,000. The requisite limit for Charity C is therefore £50,000 (within paragraph (b)), since this is greater than £5,000 (within paragraph (a)). Therefore, so long as Charity C's gross income under Cases I and VI of Schedule D (not otherwise exempt) does not exceed £50,000, such income will be exempt under the Finance Act 2000.

(4) Charity D has incoming resources for the chargeable period of £120,000. Since 25% of that is £30,000, and this is less than £50,000, the figure falling within paragraph (b) is £30,000. The requisite limit for Charity D is therefore £30,000 (within paragraph (b)), since this is greater than £5,000 (within paragraph (a)). Whether Charity D can benefit from the new exemption depends upon whether its gross income under Cases I and VI of Schedule D (not otherwise exempt) falls within this limit.

(2) Qualifying and non-qualifying expenditure

In the mid-1980s there was concern that the tax exemptions for charities were **3.19** encouraging some individuals to use so-called charities as vehicles for tax avoidance, with no genuine intention of carrying on the charitable purposes. There was also concern about the scope for fraud, particularly that some moneys which a number of charities were paying to bodies which were overseas (and so outside the jurisdiction of the High Court) were not being applied to charitable purposes at all. The tax reliefs available to charity were therefore restricted by provisions in the Finance Act 1986, which are now contained in sections 505 and 506 of the Income and Corporation Taxes Act 1988.

3.20 Under the statutory regime, a charity loses its exemption under section 505(1) (and also its exemption under section 256 of the Taxation of Chargeable Gains Act 1992) if it incurs excessive amounts of non-qualifying expenditure. If in any chargeable period of a charity, a charity's relevant income and gains[39] are not less than £10,000, and its relevant income and gains exceed the amount of its qualifying expenditure, then the charity incurs, or is treated as incurring, non-qualifying expenditure. The exemptions are not available for so much of the excess as does not exceed the non-qualifying expenditure incurred, or treated as incurred, in that period.[40] If, for example, in a chargeable period a charity has £22,000 of relevant income and gains, but is treated as having incurred £4,000 of non-qualifying expenditure, the exemptions are not available on so much of the excess of its relevant income and gains (£22,000) as does not exceed the non-qualifying expenditure (£4,000). In this example, the effect is that tax is charged on an amount equal to the non-qualifying expenditure (£4,000), and the exemptions are available only on the remaining £18,000.

3.21 A payment made, or to be made, to a body situated outside the United Kingdom is not qualifying expenditure unless the charity concerned has taken such steps as may be reasonable in all the circumstances to ensure that the payment will be applied for charitable purposes.[41] In the Standing Committee debate which preceded the enactment of these provisions in their original form,[42] it was said that the Revenue would look at overseas payments as part of the normal process of dealing with the charity's annual claim for relief. Where appropriate, the Revenue may need to ask the charity for information about the objectives of the overseas body, and about arrangements for earmarking the payment for a purpose or checking on what it has been used for.[43]

---

[39] For this purpose, 'relevant income and gains' means income which, apart from ICTA 1988, s 505(1), would not be exempt from tax together with any income which is taxable notwithstanding that sub-section; and gains which apart from the TCGA 1992, s 256, would be chargeable gains together with any gains which are chargeable gains notwithstanding that section: ICTA 1988, s 505(5)

[40] ICTA 1988, s 505(3)

[41] ibid, s 506(3)

[42] ie FA 1986, s 31 and Sch 7

[43] Parl Debs, HC Official Report, Session 1985–6, vol 6, Standing Cttee G Debate Ninth Sitting, cols 495–6 (17 June 1986) (John MacGregor, Chief Secretary to the Treasury)

Non-qualifying expenditure is treated as including any amount invested or lent by **3.22**
a charity in a non-qualifying investment[44] or on a loan (not being an investment)
which is not a qualifying loan.[45]

Qualifying investments are any investment within the Trustee Investments Act **3.23**
1961[46] except mortgages of land,[47] or in a common investment fund or common
deposit fund,[48] any interest in land,[49] company shares or securities listed on a
recognized stock exchange or dealt in on the Unlisted Securities Market,[50] unit
trusts,[51] bank deposits at a commercial rate of interest,[52] certificates of deposit,[53]
and any loan or other investment which the Board are satisfied, on a claim being
made to them, is made for the benefit of the charity and not for the avoidance of
tax (whether by the charity or any other person).[54]

A loan is a qualifying loan if it is a loan not made by way of investment and if it **3.24**
consists of: a loan made to another charity for charitable purposes only;[55] or a loan
to a beneficiary of the charity which is made in the course of carrying out the purposes of the charity;[56] or money placed on current account with a bank;[57] or any
other loan which the Board are satisfied, on a claim being made to them, is made
for the benefit of the charity and not for the avoidance of tax (whether by the charity or by some other person).[58]

It will be noted that the only way in which a loan or investment by a charity in its **3.25**
own subsidiary trading company could in practice be a qualifying loan or a qualifying investment is if the charity can satisfy the Board that it is made for the

---

[44] A qualifying investment is defined in ICTA 1988, Sch 20, Pt I
[45] ibid, s 506(4). A qualifying loan is defined ibid, Sch 20, Pt II
[46] TIA 1961, Sch 1, which lists authorised investments, survives the repeal of much of that Act
by TA 2000, s 40(1) & Sch 2, para 1.
[47] ie excluding TIA 1961, Sch 1, Pt II, para 13: ICTA 1988, Sch 20, para 2
[48] ie in a common investment fund established under CA 1960, s 22, or CA 1993, s 24, or CA
(NI) 1964, or in a common deposit fund established under CA 1960, s 22A, or CA 1993, s 25; or
(in each case) in any similar fund established for the exclusive benefit of charities by or under any enactment relating to any particular charities or class of charities: ICTA 1988, Sch 20, para 3
[49] Other than a debt held as security for a debt of any description: ICTA 1988, Sch 20, para 4
[50] ibid, para 5
[51] ie unit trust schemes within the meaning of the FSA 1986: ICTA 1988, Sch 20, para 6
[52] ICTA 1988, Sch 20, para 7(1); but excluding a bank deposit which is made as part of an
arrangement under which a loan is made by the authorized institution to any other person: ibid,
para 7(2). In this paragraph, 'bank' has the meaning given by ibid, s 840A: ibid, Sch 20, para 7(3)
[53] As defined in ibid, s 56(5): ibid, Sch 20, para 8
[54] ibid, Sch 20, para 9(1). In this sub-paragraph, 'loan' includes a loan secured by a mortgage or
charge of any kind over land: ibid, para 9(2)
[55] ibid, para 10(1)(a)
[56] ibid, para 10(1)(b)
[57] Otherwise than as part of such an arrangement as is mentioned in para 7(2), ie under which a
loan is made by the authorized institution to any other person: ibid, Sch 20, para 10(1)(c). In this
paragraph, 'bank' has the meaning given by ibid, s 840A
[58] ibid, Sch 20, para 10(1)(d)

benefit of the charity and not for the avoidance of tax. This can cause problems for charities wishing to fund their subsidiary trading companies, and is considered further in chapter 20.[59]

B. Capital gains on disposals by a charity

3.26 A gain is not a chargeable gain if it accrues to a charity and is applicable and applied for charitable purposes.[60] In some circumstances, the non-qualifying expenditure rules mentioned above may operate to restrict this relief.[61]

C. Inheritance tax

3.27 When settled property is held upon trusts in which no qualifying interest in possession subsists, there is usually a charge to inheritance tax, both at each ten-year anniversary of the creation of the settlement,[62] and when property is transferred out of it.[63] No charges arise, however, where property is held for charitable purposes only, whether for a limited time or otherwise.[64]

D. Stamp duty

3.28 The instrument by which land is conveyed, transferred, leased, or agreed to be leased, to a body of persons established for charitable purposes only,[65] or to the trustees of a trust so established, or to the Trustees of the National Heritage Memorial Fund, is not chargeable to stamp duty.[66] If the instrument would be chargeable but for this exemption, it is not be treated as duly stamped unless it is stamped with a stamp denoting that it is not chargeable with any duty.[67]

---

[59] See esp ch 20, paras 20.20–20.27
[60] TCGA 1992, s 256(1)
[61] ICTA 1988, s 505(3), (5)(b), (6) & Sch 20, para 12(2)
[62] ITA 1984, s 64
[63] ibid, s 65(1)
[64] ibid, s 58(1)(a)
[65] For the purposes of exemption under FA 1982, s 129, the Historic Buildings and Monuments Commission for England is treated as established for charitable purposes only: FA 1983, s 46(3)(c)
[66] FA 1982, s 129(1)
[67] ibid, s 129(2)

E. Value added tax

(1) General principles

The VAT system

Under the Value Added Tax Act 1994, value added tax (VAT) is charged (inter **3.29** alia) on the supply of goods or services in the United Kingdom,[68] where it is a taxable supply made by a taxable person in the course or furtherance of any business carried on by him.[69] VAT levied by the supplier (inter alia) on goods or services supplied by him is known as 'output tax';[70] VAT which a taxable person pays (inter alia) on the supply to him of goods or services is known as 'input tax'.[71] The basic principle is that, at the end of each prescribed accounting period, a taxable person is entitled to credit allowable input tax[72] and then to deduct that amount from any output tax that is due from him.[73]

This basic principle is modified because the supply of certain goods and services is **3.30** not charged at the standard rate, but is zero-rated, exempt, or charged at a reduced rate. The supply of fuel for domestic use, or for use by a charity otherwise than in the furtherance of a business, is charged at a reduced rate.[74] Where a taxable supply is zero-rated, no VAT is charged on the supply, but it is in all other respects treated as a taxable supply, so that the rate at which VAT is treated as charged on the supply is nil.[75] The effect of zero-rating is that the supplier is entitled to recover any input tax he paid, but does not charge any output tax. The effect of a supply being exempt is that, whilst the supplier does not charge output tax, he cannot recover any input tax. Whether a charity benefits or loses from supplies being exempt depends upon its activities. A charity which does not incur very much input tax is likely to prefer to argue that its supplies are exempt; whereas a charity with high levels of input tax will generally prefer its supplies not to be exempt.

Basic elements for a charge to VAT

It is necessary to examine first the three basic elements for a charge to VAT: a tax- **3.31** able supply, a taxable person, and a business.[76]

---

[68] VATA 1994, s 1(1)(a)

[69] ibid, s 4(1)

[70] ibid, s 24(2)

[71] ibid, s 24(1)

[72] Allowable input tax is specified ibid, s 26

[73] ibid, s 25(2)

[74] ibid, Sch A1, as amended by FA 2000, Sch 35. The reduced rate also applies to certain supplies of energy-saving materials: VATA 1994, Sch A1

[75] VATA 1994, s 30(1)

[76] ibid, s 4(1)

Taxable supply

3.32 A taxable supply is a supply of goods or services made in the United Kingdom other than an exempt supply.[77] 'Supply' does not include anything done otherwise than for a consideration.[78] The giving away of goods or services by a charity, therefore, does not comprise a supply.

Taxable person

3.33 A person (which includes the trustees of a charitable trust and the directors of a charitable company) is a taxable person for the purposes of the Act while he is, or is required to be, registered under the Act.[79] A person who makes taxable supplies generally becomes liable to be registered if the value of his taxable supplies exceeds a specified annual amount, currently £52,000.[80] Exemption from such obligation to register may be obtained if the person seeking it can satisfy the Commissioners of Customs and Excise that any taxable supplies he makes would be zero-rated.[81] A person whose taxable supplies do not reach the minimum for compulsory registration may nevertheless obtain voluntary registration if he can satisfy the Commissioners that he makes (or intends to make) taxable supplies in the course of a business.[82] Voluntary registration may sometimes be desirable for a charity which incurs large amounts of input tax.

Business

3.34 For the purposes of the Act, 'business' includes any trade, profession or vocation;[83] but it is not confined to commercial organizations or enterprises which have a profit-motive,[84] and it extends to a continuing activity that is predominantly concerned with the making of supplies to others for a consideration.[85] For there to be a business, there must be 'a serious undertaking earnestly pursued';[86] and to determine this, it is necessary to look at the whole of the activities carried on.[87] There must be sufficiency of scale to the supplies, which must be continued over a period

---

[77] VATA 1994, s 4(2)
[78] ibid, s 5(2)(a)
[79] ibid, s 3(1)
[80] ibid, s 3(2), Sch 1, and the Value Added Tax (Increase of Registration Limits) Order 2000, SI 2000/804 (applicable from 1 Apr 2000)
[81] VATA 1994, Sch 1, para 14(1)
[82] ibid, Sch 1, paras 9–10
[83] ibid, s 94(1)
[84] *Comrs of Customs and Excise v Morrison's Academy Boarding Houses Assoc* [1978] STC 1, 5–6 (Lord Emslie)
[85] *NSPCC v Comrs of Customs and Excise* [1992] VATTR 417, 422. See J Warburton, 'Charities, Value Added Tax and Business' (1995–6) 3 CL & PR 37
[86] *Rael-Brook Ltd v Minister of Housing and Local Government* [1967] 2 QB 65, 76 (Widgery J); appl *Comrs of Customs and Excise v Royal Exchange Theatre Trust* [1979] 3 All ER 797, 802 (Neill J)
[87] *Comrs of Customs and Excise v Morrison's Academy Boarding Houses Assoc* [1978] STC 1, 5–6 (Lord Emslie)

of time; and the predominant concern of the person conducting the activity must be the making of supplies.[88] It is not enough that merely some of the activities have the attributes of a business, or that the activities are carried on in a business-like manner: the determining factor is the nature of the activities, not the efficiency with which they are undertaken.[89]

A charity's management of its investments, through the purchase and sale of **3.35** shares and other securities, does not therefore comprise a business for VAT purposes, since the making of investment supplies is not charity trustees' or directors' predominant concern.[90] The position remains the same regardless of the scale of the investments, and regardless of whether, in managing them, the charity uses what might be described as 'business methods'. The European Court recently confirmed this in *Wellcome Trust Ltd v Commissioners of Customs and Excise*,[91] where the charity (the largest in the United Kingdom) had raised over £2 billion from the sale of shares in order to diversify its investments. The sales, which were effected by inviting potential purchasers to submit tenders, had involved much planning, and the charity had consequently incurred considerable considerable legal and other fees. It sought to recover the input tax which it had paid in connection with such sales; but the European Court held that it was not entitled to recover, since the mere exercise of the rights of ownership could not by itself be regarded as constituting an 'economic activity' within Article 4(2) of the Sixth Council Directive on VAT.[92]

There can be a business even if the consideration for the supply is inadequate. **3.36** Thus the running by the Royal Society for the Prevention of Cruelty to Animals of an animal clinic where pet-owners were charged a fee was held to be a business, even though the fees were lower than those normally charged by commercial enterprises.[93] However, whilst the term 'business' cannot be defined exhaustively, the absence of any consideration for the supply is a matter of great importance in pointing away from a business.[94] Thus the provision of a gallery of works of art for viewing by the public free of charge has been held not to be a business.[95]

In *Commissioners of Customs and Excise v Royal Exchange Theatre Trust*,[96] the **3.37** trustees of a charitable trust for the promotion of the arts raised money from

---

[88] *NSPCC v Comrs of Customs and Excise* [1992] VATTR 417, 422
[89] *Comrs of Customs and Excise v Royal Exchange Theatre Trust* [1979] 3 All ER 797, 802–3 (Neill J)
[90] *NSPCC v Comrs of Customs and Excise* [1992] VATTR 417, 423
[91] [1996] STC 945 (ECJ)
[92] Council Directice (EEC) 77/388 on harmonization of laws of Member States relating to turnover taxes (Sixth Directive) [1977] OJ L145/1
[93] *RSPCA v Comrs of Customs and Excise* [1991] VATTR 407
[94] *Comrs of Customs and Excise v Royal Exchange Theatre Trust* [1979] 3 All ER 797, 802 (Neill J)
[95] *Whitechapel Art Gallery v Comrs of Customs and Excise* [1986] STC 156
[96] [1979] 3 All ER 797

individuals and from companies through public appeals, to finance the construction of a theatre in Manchester. Pursuant to a direction in the trust instrument, the trustees formed a charitable company limited by guarantee, acquired a lease of a building, built the theatre therein, and assigned the lease for no consideration to the charitable company. The issue in the case was whether the assignment of the lease to the company was a supply made by the trust in the course of a business carried on by the trust. The trustees contended that it was; and they had previously applied to be registered for the purposes of VAT in order that the trust could recover input tax charged to it on supplies made in connection with its proposed building operations. Neill J held that the assignment of the lease did not constitute a supply in the course of a business carried on by the trust. He considered that the trustees' activities looked at as a whole lacked any commercial element, and an important factor was the absence of monetary consideration for the assignment.

3.38 A charity is not carrying on a business by soliciting donations or by accepting grants (unless the grant is made on the basis that the charity will perform services).[97] If, however, a charity enters into sponsorship arrangements whereby it agrees to provide benefits to sponsors (other than mere acknowledgement of sponsorship), the charity will generally be making a supply of services.[98]

3.39 Without prejudice to the generality of the Act, the provision by a club, association or organization (for a subscription or other consideration) of the facilities or advantages available to its members, and the admission for a consideration of persons to any premises, are deemed to be the carrying on of a business.[99]

3.40 The export of any goods by a charity to a place outside the Member States of the European Union is, for the purposes of the Act, to be treated as a supply made by the charity in the United Kingdom, and in the course or furtherance of a business carried on by the charity.[100]

---

[97] *Hillingdon Legal Resources Centre Ltd v Comrs of Customs and Excise* [1991] VATTR 39

[98] A one-off supply in connection with a sponsorship deal, however, will probably not itself be a supply in the course of a business: see further ch 19, paras 19.90–19.94

[99] VATA 1994, s 94(2). Under s 94(3), it used to be provided that, where a body had objects which were in the public domain and were of a political, religious, philanthropic, philosophical or patriotic nature, it was not to be treated as carrying on a business only because its members subscribed to it, if a subscription obtained no facility or advantage for the subscriber other than the right to participate in its management or receive reports on its activities. The FA 1999, s 20, however, repealed VATA 1994, s 94(3), on 1 Dec 1999: Finance Act 1999, Section 20 (Appointed Day) Order 1999, SI 1999/2769. From that date, Group 9 of Sch 9 to VATA 1994 was amended: the Value Added Tax (Subscriptions to Trade Unions, Professional and Other Public Interest Bodies) Order 1999, SI 1999/2834 (discussed below, paras 3.65–3.66)

[100] VATA 1994, s 30(5)

(2) *Zero-rated supplies*

A supply of goods or services is zero-rated if it falls within one of the sixteen **3.41**
Groups set out in Schedule 8 to the Act.[101] Many of these could apply to charities
in appropriate circumstances, such as the zero-rating of food; but the following
survey concentrates upon those Groups which are of particular relevance to charities or to specific types of charities. These are Group 15, which deals specifically
with zero-rating for charities, and other Groups which provide for zero-rating of
the following: books;[102] talking books for the blind and handicapped and wireless
sets for the blind;[103] drugs, medicines, aids for the handicapped etc;[104] lifeboats
(within the transport Group);[105] construction of buildings, etc;[106] and protected
buildings.[107]

Charities

Group 15 provides for zero-rating of various supplies to charities. Item 1 applies **3.42**
to the sale, or letting on hire, by a charity of any goods donated to it for sale, letting or export.[108] Item 1A applies to the sale, or letting on hire, by a taxable person
of any goods donated to him for sale, letting or export, if he is a profits-to-charity
person in respect of the goods. Item 2 applies to the sale, export or letting by a
charity or a taxable person who is a profits-to-charity person in respect of the
goods. For these purposes, a taxable person is a 'profits-to-charity' person in
respect of any goods if[109]

(a) he has agreed in writing (whether or not contained in a deed) to transfer to a
charity his profits from supplies and lettings of the goods, or
(b) his profits from supplies and lettings of the goods are otherwise payable to a
charity.

These items, which apply to supplies made on or after 1 April 2000, are broader **3.43**
than those they replaced, in that the zero rate on the sale by a charity of donated

---

[101] ibid, s 30(2). The Groups comprise: 1. Food   2. Sewage services and water   3. Books
4. Talking books for the blind and handicapped and wireless sets for the blind   5. Construction
of buildings etc   6. Protected buildings   7. International services   8. Transport   9.
Caravans and houseboats   10. Gold   11. Bank notes   12. Drugs, medicines, aids for the
handicapped, etc   13. Imports, exports etc   14. Tax-free shops   15. Charities etc
16. Clothing and footwear
[102] VATA 1994, Sch 8, Gp 3
[103] ibid, Gp 4
[104] ibid, Gp 12
[105] ibid, Gp 8, Item 3
[106] ibid, Gp 5
[107] ibid, Gp 6
[108] Items 1, 1A, and 2 were substituted by Value Added Tax (Charities and Aids for the
Handicapped) Order 2000, SI 2000/805
[109] VATA 1994, Sch 8, Gp 15, Note (1E)

goods now applies to the supply of goods offered for sale, not merely to the public, but also to disabled persons or those receiving means-tested benefits.[110] The previous Item 1 had zero-rated the supply of donated goods by a taxable person which was obliged to transfer all the profits of that supply to a charity, but only if the obligation took the form of a deed of covenant. The effect of this was that, before 1 April 2000, the sale of donated goods by a charity's subsidiary trading company was zero-rated only if the subsidiary used the deed of covenant method to return its profits to the charity. Under the new measures, the need for a deed of covenant is removed. Instead, there must be a written agreement or another obligation (such as a declaration of trust) to transfer the profits.[111] The impact of these changes on trading by charities is dealt with more fully in chapter 20.

3. The export of any goods by a charity to a place outside the member States.

4. The supply of any relevant goods[112] for donation to a nominated eligible body[113] where the goods are purchased[114] with funds provided by a charity or from voluntary contributions.[115]

5. The supply of any relevant goods[116] to an eligible body which pays for them with funds provided by a charity or from voluntary contributions or to an eligible body which is a charitable institution providing care or medical or surgical treatment for handicapped[117] persons.[118]

---

[110] VATA 1994, Sch 8, Gp 15, Notes (1), (1C)

[111] See HM Customs and Excise, 'VAT: Changes to the zero rate for sales of donated goods by charities and others transferring the profits to charity', Budget 2000, BN 26/00

[112] 'Relevant goods' (in Items 4–6) includes medical, scientific, computer, video, sterilizing, laboratory or refrigeration equipment for use in medical or veterinary research, training, diagnosis or treatment; ambulances; medical and other equipment for the use of handicapped persons; certain motor vehicles designed or adapted to carry a handicapped person in a wheelchair; certain motor vehicles for use by an eligible body providing care for handicapped or terminally sick persons to transport such persons; and various specialized equipment for the sole use of rescue or first aid services undertaken by a charitable institution providing such services: VATA 1994, Sch 8, Gp 15, Note (3)

[113] 'Eligible body' in this Group includes a Health Authority or Special Health Authority in England and Wales; a hospital or research institution whose activities (in each case) are not carried on for profit; a charitable institution providing care or medical or surgical treatment for handicapped persons (but only if further criteria in Notes (4A), (4B), (5A) and (5B) are met, including the requirement that such care or treatment is provided in a relevant establishment—essentially a day-care centre); a charitable institution providing rescue or first-aid services; and a National Health Service Trust established under Pt I of the National Health Service and Community Care Act 1990: VATA 1994, Sch 8, Gp 15, Note (4)

[114] Items 4 and 5 include the letting on hire of relevant goods: ibid, Note (9)

[115] Item 4 does not apply where the donee of the goods is not a charity and has contributed in whole or in part to the funds for the purchase of the goods: ibid, Note (6)

[116] Item 5 includes computer services by way of the provision of computer software solely for use in medical research, diagnosis or treatment: ibid, Note (10)

[117] 'Handicapped' means chronically sick or disabled: ibid, Note (5)

[118] Item 5 does not apply where the body to whom the goods are supplied is not a charity and has contributed in whole or in part to the funds for the purchase of the goods: ibid, Note (7)

6. The repair and maintenance of relevant goods owned[119] by an eligible body.[120]

7. The supply of goods in connection with the supply described in item 6.

The next cluster of items in this Group is concerned with charity advertising, **3.44**
namely:

8. The supply to a charity of a right to promulgate an advertisement by means of a medium of communication with the public.[121]

8A. A supply to a charity that consists in the promulgation of an advertisement by means of such a medium.

8B. The supply to a charity of services of design or production of an advertisement that is, or was, intended to be, promulgated by means of such a medium.

8C. The supply to a charity of goods closely related to a supply within item 8B.

These items, which replace the former Item 8 in respect of supplies made on or **3.45**
after 1 April 2000,[122] have significantly widened the scope of zero-rating for charity advertising. First, the new relief covers all types of advertisements which are placed on someone else's advertising time or space; it therefore includes a charity's recruitment advertisements.[123] Secondly, all mediums of communication with the public are now included, provided the space is owned by a third party; broadly, this covers television, cinema, billboards, the sides of buses and other vehicles, newspapers and printed publications, and the Internet.[124] Thirdly, the supply of design or production of an advertisement also now qualifies for relief,[125] provided it is intended that the advertisement will be placed in purchased advertising time

---

[119] This includes goods hired or possessed: ibid, Note (9)

[120] Items 6 and 7 do not apply unless (a) the supply is paid for with funds which have been provided by a charity or from voluntary contributions, and (b) in a case where the owner of the goods repaired or maintained is not a charity, it has not contributed in whole or in part to those funds: ibid, Note (8)

[121] Neither Item 8 nor Item 8A includes a supply where any members of the public (whether individuals or other persons) who are reached through the medium are selected by or on behalf of the charity. For this purpose, 'selected' includes selected by address (whether postal address or telephone number, email address or other address for electronic communications purposes) or at random: ibid, Note (10A). In practice, therefore, items delivered by post (direct-mail packages) are not covered by this relief, although there may be relief for individual elements of the package under the provisions for printed matter and concessions eg appeal letters, discussed below. See HM Customs and Excise, 'Charity advertising and goods connected with collecting donations', Notice 701/58, para 2.4

[122] Value Added Tax (Charities and Aids for the Handicapped) Order 2000 SI 2000/805, reg 7, substituting new items to replace previous item 8 in VATA 1994, Sch 8, Gp 15

[123] See HM Customs and Excise, 'VAT: changes to the zero rate for the supplies of advertising to charities', Budget 2000, BN 27/00, para 2. Such recruitment advertisements for paid staff did not qualify for zero-rating under the old Item 8: *Comrs of Customs and Excise v Royal Society of Arts, Manufacture and Commerce* (The Times, 20 Dec 1997)

[124] HM Customs and Excise, 'Charity advertising and goods connected with collecting donations', Notice 701/58, para 2.3. None of Items 8–8C includes a supply used to create, or contribute to, a website that is the charity's own. For this purpose a website is a charity's own even though hosted by another person: VATA 1994, Sch 8, Gp 15, Note (10B)

[125] But neither Item 8B nor Item 8C includes a supply to a charity that is used directly by the charity to design or produce an advertisement: ibid, Note (10C)

or space;[126] examples of services now included are the design of a poster or the filming or recording of an advertisement to be broadcast.[127] By way of concession, the supply of specified goods used by charities in connection with collecting monetary donations is treated as zero-rated. The concession applies to certain printed stationery (essentially collecting envelopes[128] and pre-printed appeal letters), collection boxes, and lapel stickers and similar tokens of only nominal value.[129]

> 9. The supply to a charity, providing care or medical or surgical treatment for human beings or animals,[130] or engaging in medical or veterinary research, of a medicinal product[131] where the supply is solely for use by the charity in such care, treatment or research.
> 10. The supply to a charity of a substance directly used for synthesis or testing in the course of medical or veterinary research.

Books

3.46 There is zero-rating of the supply of the following: books, brochures, pamphlets and leaflets; newspapers, journals and periodicals; children's picture books and painting books; music (printed, duplicated or manuscript); maps, charts and topographical plans; and covers, cases and other articles supplied with the foregoing and not separately accounted for.[132]

Talking books for the blind and handicapped and wireless sets for the blind

3.47 The supply to the Royal National Institute for the Blind, the National Listening Library or other similar charities of tapes and tape-recording apparatus for the

---

[126] HM Customs and Excise, 'Charity advertising and goods connected with collecting donations', Notice 701/58, para 2.5. HM Customs and Excise have stated that a charity will not have to pay VAT retrospectively on the production costs of an advertisement that is not in fact used, provided that it was clearly the charity's intention to use those services for an advertisement which would have qualified for relief: ibid, para 2.8

[127] ibid, para 2.5. Under the previous Item 8, goods or services supplied to a charity to produce a poster promoting the aims of the charity were zero-rated within paragraph (c) only if supplied in connection with the publication of the advertisement, not just its preparation: *Comrs of Customs and Excise v Royal Society of Arts, Manufacture and Commerce* (The Times, 20 Dec 1997), where the charity was registered as one of a group for VAT, other companies in the group dealing with the production, printing and distribution of the posters, but not their publication. Scott Baker J said that the purpose of (the previous) Item 8 was to assist charities to acquire the service of publication of advertisements from a third-party supplier; it was not to help to promote in-house advertising

[128] It had previously been held that the supply by a printing company to a charity of collection envelopes for use by the charity in a fund-raising campaign, did not fall within the former Item 8, and so was not entitled to zero-rating: *TE Penny & Co Ltd v Comrs of Customs and Excise* VAT Tribunal Decision 15329

[129] HM Customs and Excise, 'Zero-rating of supplies of certain goods used in collection of monetary donations', Draft Extra Statutory Concession (Nov 2000)

[130] 'Animals' includes any species of the animal kingdom: VATA 1994, Sch 8, Gp 15, Note (2)

[131] 'Medicinal product' is defined ibid, Note (11)(a)

[132] ibid, Gp 3, Items 1–6. These items (a) do not include plans or drawings for industrial, architectural, engineering, commercial or similar purposes: ibid, Note

blind or severely handicapped, is zero-rated;[133] as is the supply to a charity of wireless receiving sets or cassette tape-recorders, being goods solely for gratuitous loan to the blind.[134] In each case, the supply includes the letting of those goods on hire.[135]

Drugs, medicines, aids for the handicapped, etc

This Group provides for zero-rating of the supply to an individual of any drug or medicine by a registered pharmacist or registered medical practitioner.[136] **3.48**

It also provides for zero-rating of various supplies to handicapped persons or to a charity for making available to handicapped persons.[137] These include the supply of medical or other equipment for the relief of handicapped persons[138] (including the installation of such equipment or appliances);[139] the supply of services to adapt a handicapped person's goods[140] or to provide or adapt a handicapped person's bathroom, washroom, or lavatory[141] (or to supply such services to a charity in respect of a building principally used by a charity for charitable purposes to facilitate the use of such rooms by handicapped persons);[142] to construct ramps or widen doorways or passageways to facilitate a handicapped person's entry to or movement within his residence[143] (or, in the case of a supply to a charity, to any building).[144] The supply of goods connected with the supply of the foregoing services is also zero-rated.[145] Also zero-rated are: the installation of a lift, either for a handicapped person,[146] or for a charity providing a residence or day-care centre for handicapped persons;[147] the supply of alarm systems which alert a specified person or control centre;[148] and the supply of services necessarily performed by such control centre.[149] **3.49**

There is also zero-rating of certain supplies of motor vehicles for handicapped persons. These comprise:[150] **3.50**

---

[133] ibid, Gp 4, Item 1
[134] ibid, Item 2
[135] ibid, Note
[136] ibid, Gp 12, Items 1 and 1(A)
[137] ibid, Items 2–20
[138] ibid, Item 2
[139] ibid, Item 7
[140] ibid, Items 3–4
[141] ibid, Items 10–11
[142] ibid, Item 12
[143] ibid, Item 8
[144] ibid, Item 9
[145] ibid, Items 6, 13
[146] ibid, Item 16
[147] ibid, Item 17
[148] ibid, Item 19
[149] ibid, Item 20
[150] ibid, Items 14–15

14. The letting on hire of a motor vehicle for a period of not less than 3 years to a handicapped person in receipt of a disability allowance by virtue of entitlement to the mobility component or of mobility supplement where the lessor's business consists predominantly of the provision of motor vehicles to such persons.

15. The sale of a motor vehicle which had been let on hire in the circumstances described in item 14, where such sale constitutes the first supply of the vehicle after the end of the period of such letting.

Lifeboats

3.51   One Item within the Group dealing with Transport[151] provides for zero-rating of:[152]

(a) The supply to and repair or maintenance for a charity providing rescue or assistance at sea of

(i) any lifeboat;[153]

(ii) carriage equipment designed solely for the launching and recovery of lifeboats;

(iii) tractors for the sole use of the launching and recovery of lifeboats;

(iv) winches and hauling equipment for the sole use of the recovery of lifeboats.

(b) The construction, modification, repair or maintenance for a charity providing rescue or assistance at sea of slipways used solely for the launching and recovery of lifeboats;

(c) The supply of spare parts or accessories to a charity providing rescue or assistance at sea for use in or with goods comprised in paragraph (a) above or slipways comprised in paragraph (b) above.

Construction of buildings, etc

3.52   Group 5 is important for many charities which engage in construction work. It provides for zero-rating of the first grant[154] by a person constructing a building designed as[155] (or converting a non-residential building or its non-residential part into[156]) a dwelling or a number of dwellings or a building intended for use solely for a relevant residential purpose or a relevant charitable purpose.[157] The supply of any services, other than the services of an architect, surveyor or any person acting as a consultant or in a supervisory capacity, is also zero-rated, but only in relation to construction.[158] The supply of such services is zero-rated in relation to conver-

---

[151] VATA 1994, Sch 8, Gp 8
[152] ibid, Item 3
[153] 'Lifeboat' means any vessel used or to be used solely for rescue or assistance at sea: ibid, Note (4)
[154] 'Grant' includes an assignment or surrender: ibid, Gp 5, Note (1)
[155] ibid, Item 1(a)
[156] ibid, Item 1(b)
[157] ibid, Item 1
[158] ibid, Item 2

sion only where the supply is to a relevant housing association[159] in the course of converting a building (or part) into a dwelling or dwellings or for use solely for a relevant residential purpose.[160] Such zero-rating is clearly important for charitable housing associations.

In this Group, 'use for a relevant residential purpose' means use as[161]   **3.53**

(a) a home or other institution providing residential accommodation for children;
(b) a home or other institution providing residential accommodation with personal care for persons in need of personal care by reason of old age, disablement, past or present dependence on alcohol or drugs or past or present mental disorder;
(c) a hospice;
(d) residential accommodation for students or school pupils;
(e) residential accommodation for members of any of the armed forces;
(f) a monastery, nunnery or similar establishment;
(g) an institution which is the sole or main residence of at least 90 per cent of its residents, except use as a hospital, prison or similar institution or an hotel, inn or similar establishment.

'Use for a relevant charitable purpose' means use by a charity in either or both of the following ways, namely[162]

(a) otherwise than in the course or furtherance of a business;
(b) as a village hall or similarly in providing social or recreational facilities for a local community.

In *Commissioners of Customs and Excise v St Dunstan's Educational Foundation*,[163]   **3.54** the Court of Appeal held that a sports centre constructed by a fee-paying school (whose pupils were drawn from the borough of Lewisham and neighbouring boroughs) was not entitled to zero-rating within sub-paragraph (b). Although the centre was used for some community purposes at the direction of the local council, it had been constructed primarily for the use of the pupils, and these did not benefit as members of the community but as pupils on whose behalf fees were paid to the school. The sports centre could not therefore be considered to have been intended to be used solely for the purpose of 'providing social or recreational facilities for a local community'.

---

[159] 'Relevant housing association' means (in England and Wales) a registered social landlord within the meaning of Pt I of the Housing Act 1996: VATA 1994, Sch 8, Gp 5, Note (21)
[160] VATA 1994, Sch 8, Gp 5, Item 3
[161] ibid, Note (4)
[162] ibid, Note (6)
[163] [1999] STC 381 (heard by the CA with the *Jubilee Hall* case, discussed below, para 3.56, in a conjoined appeal)

Protected buildings

3.55 Group 6 zero-rates:

> 1. The first grant[164] by a person substantially reconstructing[165] a protected building, of a major interest in, or in any part of, the building or its site.
> 2. The supply, in the course of an approved alteration[166] of a protected building,[167] of any services other than the services of an architect, surveyor or any person acting as consultant or in a supervisory capacity.
> 3. The supply of building materials to a person to whom the supplier is supplying services within item 2 of this Group which include the incorporation of the materials into the building (or its site) in question.

A 'protected building' means[168] a building which is designed to remain as or become a dwelling or number of dwellings[169] or is intended for use solely for a relevant residential purpose[170] or as a relevant charitable purpose[171] after the reconstruction or alteration and which, in either case, is a listed building[172] or a scheduled monument.[173]

3.56 Whether user was for a relevant charitable purpose was considered in *Jubilee Hall Recreation Centre Ltd v Commissioners of Customs and Excise.*[174] The charity was a company limited by guarantee whose objects were to promote facilities for recreation and other leisure-time occupation in the area of Greater London in the interests of social welfare for the benefit of the local community. It ran a sports and fitness centre (with a cafeteria attached) on the first floor of a listed building in Covent Garden. It ran the centre on a commercial basis, charging membership fees, with reductions for senior citizens, residents, children and the unemployed. Many of the members worked locally but lived elsewhere. The charity made extensive alterations to the premises for which listed building consents were obtained, and claimed that the building works were zero-rated within Item 2 of

---

[164] 'Grant' includes an assignment or surrender: VATA 1994, Sch 8, Gp 5, Note (3), applying the meaning of 'grant' contained in Note (1) to Gp 5

[165] For a building to be regarded as substantially reconstructed the reconstruction must satisfy one of the conditions set out VATA 1994, Sch 8, Gp 5, Note (4)

[166] 'Approved alteration' is defined ibid, Notes (6)–(8)

[167] For the purposes of Item 2, the construction of a building separate from, but in the curtilage of, a protected building does not constitute an alteration of the protected building: ibid, Note (10)

[168] ibid, Note (1)

[169] The conditions which must be satisfied if a building is to be treated as designed to remain or become a dwelling are set out ibid, Note (2)

[170] Defined ibid, Note (3), applying the meaning of 'use for a relevant residential purpose' contained in Note (4) to Gp 5

[171] Defined ibid, Note (3), applying the meaning of 'use for a relevant charitable purpose' contained in Note (6) to Gp 5

[172] Within the meaning of the Planning (Listed Buildings and Conservation Areas) Act 1990: VATA 1994, Sch 8, Gp 6, Note (1)(a)

[173] Within the meaning of the Ancient Monuments and Archaeological Areas Act 1979: VATA 1994, Sch 8, Gp 6, Note (1)(b)

[174] [1999] STC 381 (CA)

Group 6, because the premises were used for 'a relevant charitable purpose', namely[175]

(b) as a village hall or similarly in providing social or recreational facilities for a local community.

The Court of Appeal, reversing the first instance judgment of Lightman J,[176] and **3.57** restoring the decision of the tribunal, held that the supplies were not entitled to zero-rating. Sir John Vinelott said:[177]

the plain purpose of sub-paragraph (b) was . . . to extend the relief . . . to the case where a local community is the final consumer in respect of the supply of the services, including the reconstruction of a building, in the sense that the local community is the user of the services (through a body of trustees or a management committee acting on its behalf) and in which the only economic activity is one in which they participate directly; the obvious examples are the bring-and-buy or jumble sale, the performance of a play by local players and the like.
. . . Sub-paragraph (b) is intended to cover economic activities which are an ordinary incident of the use of a building by a local community for social, including recreational, purposes. The village hall is the model or paradigm of that case.

On this footing, the charity's use of the premises was not similar to that of a village **3.58** hall. His Lordship added that he also doubted whether persons who worked in the locality but lived elsewhere could necessarily be described as part of 'the local community'. He said:[178]

I myself feel considerable doubt whether a simple rule can be formulated. It is easy to see that the local butcher, baker or candlestick maker or, in contemporary society, the local bank manager, solicitor or accountant would ordinarily be regarded as part of the community in which they have their shop or place of work, although they may live outside. They would ordinarily be expected to take part in local activities. In the context of an urban area comprising primarily commercial premises with some residential premises the conception of a community comprising residents and all those who work in the area, seems to me extravagant.

(3) Exempt supplies

A supply of goods or services is an exempt supply if it falls within Schedule 9 to the **3.59** Act,[179] which lists thirteen Groups. The exemptions of most importance to charities are those for education;[180] subscriptions to professional and other public interest bodies;[181] sports, sports competitions and physical education;[182] health and

---

[175] Note (6) to Gp 5. This Note is applied to Gp 6 by Note (3) to Gp 6
[176] [1997] STC 414
[177] [1999] STC 381, 390
[178] ibid, 390
[179] VATA 1994, s 31(1)
[180] ibid, Sch 9, Gp 6
[181] ibid, Gp 9
[182] ibid, Gp 10

welfare;[183] burial and cremation;[184] works of art;[185] cultural services;[186] fund-raising events by charities;[187] and betting, gaming and lotteries.[188]

Education

3.60 Within Group 6, the provision by an eligible body of

(a) education;
(b) research, where supplied to an eligible body; or
(c) vocational training

is an exempt supply,[189] as is (in certain circumstances) the supply of any goods or services closely related to the foregoing by or to the eligible body.[190]

3.61 In *North of England Zoological Society v Commissioners of Customs and Excise*,[191] Carnwath J held that 'education' within paragraph (a), was to be interpreted narrowly. It did not include education in the sense of broadening the mind (which is included within the meaning of the word education in the second head of *Pemsel's* case[192]); rather it referred to education in the sense of a specified structured form of training, and so was restricted to a course, class or lesson of instruction. The result was that Chester Zoo was obliged to levy VAT on its admission charges.

3.62 For the purposes of this Group, an eligible body is defined to include most independent, voluntary, and grant-maintained schools; a university within the United Kingdom and any college, institution, school or hall of such a university; an institution falling within the Further and Higher Education Act 1992; a public body;[193] a body which is precluded from distributing and does not distribute any profits it makes, and applies any profits made from supplies of a description within this Group to the continuance or improvement of such supplies; and a

---

[183] VATA 1994, Sch 9, Gp 7
[184] ibid, Gp 8
[185] ibid, Gp 11
[186] ibid, Gp 13
[187] ibid, Gp 12
[188] ibid, Gp 4
[189] ibid, Gp 6, Item 1
[190] ibid, Item 3
[191] [1999] STC 1027
[192] *Re Lopes* [1931] 2 Ch 130, 136–7 (Farwell J) (Zoological Society held charitable). That case was applied by the Court of Appeal in *North of England Zoological Society v Chester RDC* [1959] 1 WLR 773, when it held that Chester Zoo was entitled to rate relief under the Rating and Valuation (Miscellaneous Provisions) Act 1955, because its object was the advancement of education
[193] The expression 'public body' is here given the same meaning as in VATA 1994, Sch 9, Gp 7, Note (5), ie (a) a government department within the meaning of s 41(6) of the same Act; (b) a local authority; (c) a body which acts under any enactment or instrument for public purposes and not for its own profit, and which performs functions similar to those of a government department or local authority

body not falling within the above, which provides the teaching of English as a foreign language.[194]

Also exempt within this Group is the provision of vocational training, and the supply of any goods or services essential thereto by the person providing the vocational training, to the extent that the consideration payable is ultimately a charge to funds provided pursuant to arrangements made under various statutory provisions.[195] 'Vocational training' means training, re-training or the provision of work experience for[196]   **3.63**

(a) any trade, profession or employment; or
(b) any voluntary work connected with
   (i) education, health, safety, or welfare; or
   (ii) the carrying out of activities of a charitable nature.

Also exempt within this Group is the provision of facilities by[197]   **3.64**

(a) a youth club[198] or an association of youth clubs to its members; or
(b) an association of youth clubs to members of a youth club which is a member of that association.

Subscriptions to professional and other public interest bodies

Group 9[199] exempts the supply to its members of such services, and, in connection with those services, of such goods as are both referable only to its aims and available without payment other than a membership subscription[200] by any non-profit-making organizations falling within one of five paragraphs, which describe trade union and similar organizations, professional associations, and certain other public interest bodies. The only paragraphs into which a charitable organization might fall are (c) and (e). Paragraph (c) specifies:[201]   **3.65**

an association, the primary purpose of which is the advancement of a particular branch of knowledge, or the fostering of professional expertise, connected with the past or present professions or employments of its members.

---

[194] ibid, Gp 6, Note (1). A supply by a body which is an eligible body only by virtue of falling within the last description (the teaching of English as a foreign language) does not fall within this Group in so far as it consists of the provision of anything other than the teaching of English as a foreign language: ibid, Note (2)

[195] ibid, Gp 6, Item 5. In England and Wales, the relevant statutory provision is the Employment and Training Act 1973, s 2

[196] VATA 1994, Sch 9, Gp 6, Note (3)

[197] ibid, Gp 6, Item 6

[198] For the purposes of Item 6, a club is a 'youth club' if (a) it is established to promote the social, physical, education or spiritual development of its members; (b) its members are mainly under 21 years of age; and (c) it satisfies the requirements of Note (1)((f)(i) and (ii)

[199] As amended by the Value Added Tax (Subscriptions to Trade Unions, Professional and Other Public Interest Bodies) Order 1999, SI 1999/2834

[200] 'Membership subscription' includes an affiliation fee or similar levy: VATA 1994, Sch 9, Gp 9, Note (3)

[201] ibid, Item 1, para (c)

This paragraph does not apply unless the association restricts its membership wholly or mainly to individuals whose present or previous professions or employments are directly connected with the purposes of the association.[202]

3.66 Paragraph (e)[203] comprises

> a body which has objects which are in the public domain and are of a political, religious, patriotic, philosophical, philanthropic or civic nature.

This Group does not include any right of admission to any premises, event or performance, to which non-members are admitted for a consideration.[204] The Group does include organizations and associations the membership of which consists wholly or mainly of constituent or affiliated associations which as individual associations would be comprised in the Group; and 'member' is to be construed as including such an association.[205]

Sports, sports competitions and physical education

3.67 Group 10[206] exempts

> 1. The grant of a right to enter a competition in sport of physical recreation where the consideration for the grant consists in money which is to be allocated wholly towards the provision of a prize or prizes awarded in that competition;[207]
> 2. The grant, by an eligible body established for the purposes of sport or physical recreation, of a right to enter a competition in such an activity;[208]
> 3. The supply, by an eligible body to an individual, except, where the body operates a membership scheme, an individual who is not a member, of services closely linked with and essential to sport or physical education in which the individual is taking part.[209]

For the purposes of this Group, an eligible body means a non-profit-making body which[210]

> (a) is precluded from distributing any profit it makes, or is allowed to distribute any such profit by means only of distributions to a non-profit making body;[211]

---

[202] VATA 1994, Sch 9, Gp 9, Note (4)

[203] Para (e) was added by the VAT (Subscriptions to Trade Unions, Professional and Other Public Interest Bodies) Order 1999 SI 1999/2834, which has effect in relation to supplies made after 30 Nov 1999

[204] VATA 1994, Sch 9, Gp 9, Note (1)

[205] ibid, Note (3)

[206] As amended by the VAT (Sports, Sports Competitions and Physical Education) Order 1999, SI 1999/1994, which has effect in relation to supplies made after 31 Dec 1999

[207] VATA 1994, Sch 9, Gp 10, Item 1

[208] ibid, Item 2

[209] ibid, Item 3. Item 3 does not include the supply of any services by an eligible body of residential accommodation, catering or transport: ibid, Note (1)

[210] ibid, Note (2A)

[211] In determining whether a body is an eligible body for this purpose, there is to be disregarded any distribution of amounts representing unapplied or undistributed profits that fall to be made to the body's members on its winding up or dissolution: ibid, Note (2C)

(b) applies in accordance with Note (2B)[212] any profits it makes from supplies of a description within Item 2 or 3; and

(c) is not subject to commercial influence.[213]

In Item 3, an eligible body does not include a local authority, a government **3.68** department,[214] or certain non-governmental public bodies.[215] An individual is to be considered a member of an eligible body for the purposes of Item 3 only where he is granted membership for a period of three months or more.[216] It has been held that 'member' and 'membership' for this purpose connote participation in the particular body.[217] For this purpose, therefore, a sports centre which ran a card scheme for 'members', which gave the holders benefits relating to the use of the centre (such as priority booking) but no right to participate in the constitution of the charity, was held not to be operating a 'membership scheme'. The result was that it did not have to pay VAT on its charges to non-members.[218]

Health and welfare

An exempt supply within Group 7 comprises: **3.69**

(i) the supply of services by a person registered or enrolled in any of the following: the register of medical practitioners or the register of medical practitioners with limited registration; the register of ophthalmic opticians or the register of dispensing opticians,[219] or either of the lists[220] of bodies corporate carrying on business as ophthalmic opticians or as dispensing opticians; any register kept under the Professions

---

[212] To come within Note (2B), the profits must be applied for one or more of the following purposes, namely: (a) the continuance or improvement of any facilities made available in or in connection with the making of the supplies of those descriptions made by that body; (b) the purposes of a non-profit-making body: ibid, Note (2B)

[213] For the purposes of this Group, a body is to be taken, in relation to a sports supply, to be subject to commercial influence only if there is a time in the relevant period when (a) a relevant supply was made to that body by a person associated with it at that time; (b) an emolument was paid by that body to such a person; (c) an agreement existed for either or both of the following to take place after the end of that period, namely— (i) the making of a relevant supply to that body by such a person, or (ii) the payment by that body to such a person of any emoluments: ibid, Note (4). 'Relevant period' broadly means a period of 3 years ending with the making of the sports supply, but in no case beginning before 14 Jan 1999: ibid Note (5). 'Relevant supply' is defined in Note (6), but there is expressly excluded (inter alia) a supply made by a charity or which (if it is made) will be made by a person who is a charity at the time when the sports supply is made: ibid, Note (7)(b). There are complex provisions specifying when a person is to be taken to be associated with a body for the purposes of this Group: ibid, Notes (8)–(15)

[214] ie within the meaning of VATA 1994, s 41(6)

[215] ie those listed in the 1993 edition of the publication prepared by the Office of Public Service and Science and known as 'Public Bodies'. See VATA 1994, Sch 9, Gp 10, Note (3)

[216] VATA, Sch 9, Gp 10, Note (2)

[217] *Basingstoke and District Sports Trust Ltd v Comrs of Customs and Excise* [1995] STI 1273. See J Warburton, 'Members, non-members and VAT', (1995–6) 3 CL & PR 133

[218] ibid

[219] ie kept under Opticians Act 1989

[220] ie kept under Opticians Act 1989, s 9

Supplementary to Medicine Act 1960; the register of osteopaths;[221] the register of chiropractors; the register of qualified nurses, midwives and health visitors;[222] and the register of dispensers of hearing aids or the register of persons employing such dispensers.[223]

(ii) the supply of any services or dental prostheses by a person registered in the dentists' register,[224] a person enrolled in any roll of dental auxiliaries,[225] or a dental technician;[226]

(iii) the supply of any services by a person registered in the register of pharmaceutical chemists.[227]

(iv) the provision of care or medical or surgical treatment and, in connection with it, the supply of any goods, in any hospital or other institution approved, licensed, registered or exempted from registration by any Minister of other authority pursuant to a public general Act of Parliament.[228]

(v) the provision of a deputy for a person registered in the register of medical practitioners or the register of medical practitioners with limited registration;[229]

(vi) human blood;[230]

(vii) products for therapeutic purposes, derived from human blood;[231]

(viii) human (including foetal) organs or tissue for diagnostic or therapeutic purposes or medial research;[232]

(ix) the supply, otherwise than for profit,[233] by a charity or public body[234] of welfare services[235] and of goods supplied in connection therewith;[236]

---

[221] ie maintained in accordance with Osteopaths Act 1993, s 2(3)
[222] ie kept under Nurses, Midwives and Health Visitors Act 1997, s 7
[223] ie maintained under Hearing Aid Council Act 1968, s 2. VATA 1994, Sch 9, Gp 7, Item 1
[224] ie registered under Dentists Act 1984, s 14(1)
[225] ie having effect under Dentists Act 1984, s 45
[226] VATA 1994, Sch 9, Gp 7, Item 2
[227] ie kept under Pharmacy Act 1954, s 2(1)(a). VATA 1994, Sch 9, Gp 7, Item 3
[228] VATA 1994, Sch 9, Gp 7, Item 4
[229] ibid, Item 5
[230] ibid, Item 6
[231] ibid, Item 7
[232] ibid, Item 8
[233] The expression 'otherwise than for profit' refers to the objects for which an organization is formed, not to the budgeting policy which it pursues or the motives of those running it. In *Comrs of Customs and Excise v Bell Concord Educational Trust* [1990] 1 QB 1040, the constitution of a charitable company limited by guarantee required it to apply all its income and capital to its charitable purposes, and forbade any payment to its members by way of dividend or otherwise. The Court of Appeal held that these circumstances were conclusive that the supplies were not for profit, even though a profit had in fact been made. See also *National Deposit Friendly Society v Skegness UDC* [1959] AC 293, 319, 320, where Lord Denning had applied such a construction to the same phrase used in a statute relating to rate relief
[234] 'Public body' means (a) a government department within the meaning of s 41(6) of VATA 1994; (b) a local authority, (c) a body which acts under any enactment or instrument for public purposes and not for its own profit, and which performs functions similar to those of a government department or local authority: VATA 1994, Sch 9, Gp 7, Note (5)
[235] In this Item, 'welfare services' means services which are directly connected with: (a) the provision of care, treatment or instruction designed to promote the physical or mental welfare of elderly, sick, distressed or disabled persons; (b) the protection of children and young persons; or (c) the provision of spiritual welfare by a religious institution as part of a course of instruction or a retreat, not being a course or a retreat designed primarily to provide recreation or a holiday: ibid, Gp 7, Note (6)
[236] ibid, Item 9. This Item does not include the supply of accommodation or catering except where it is ancillary to the provision of care, treatment or instruction: ibid, Note (7)

(x) the supply, otherwise than for profit, of goods and services incidental to the provision of spiritual welfare by a religious community to a resident member of that community in return for a subscription or other consideration paid as a condition or membership;[237]

(xi) the supply of transport services for sick or injured persons in vehicles specially designed for that purpose.[238]

Burial and cremation

3.70 Group 8 comprises the disposal of the remains of the dead,[239] and the making of arrangements for or in connection with such disposal.[240]

Works of art, etc

3.71 Group 11 essentially makes exempt a disposal of property which is not chargeable to inheritance tax following disposal to a national body specified in Schedule 3[241] to the Inheritance Tax Act 1984,[242] or by a disposal to the Board of the Inland Revenue in satisfaction of any inheritance tax payable.[243] It also exempts the disposal of an asset in a case where any gain accruing on that disposal is not a chargeable gain because an inheritance tax undertaking or a similar undertaking in respect of capital gains tax has been given and the disposal is to a national body specified in Schedule 3 to the Inheritance Tax Act 1984, or is a disposal to the Board of the Inland Revenue in satisfaction of any inheritance tax payable.[244]

Cultural services

3.72 Group 13[245] exempts the supply by either a public body[246] or an eligible body[247] of a right of admission to[248]

(a) a museum, gallery, art exhibition or zoo; or
(b) a theatrical, musical or choreographic performance of a cultural nature.

---

[237] ibid, Item 10
[238] ibid, Item 11
[239] ibid, Item 1
[240] ibid, Item 2
[241] ie Gifts for National Purposes, etc
[242] IHTA 1984, s 32(4)(a)
[243] ibid, s 230
[244] TCGA 1992, s 258(2)
[245] This Group was added by the VAT (Cultural Services) Order 1996, SI 1996/1256, with effect from 1 June 1996. See HM Customs and Excise 'Exemption from VAT of cultural services', Press Notice 33/96
[246] VATA 1994, Sch 9, Gp 13, Item 1. For the purposes of this Group, 'public body' means: (a) a local authority; (b) a government department within the meaning of s 41(6) of the same Act; or (c) a non-departmental public body which is listed in the 1995 edition of the publication prepared by the Office of Public Service and known as 'Public Bodies': ibid, Gp 13, Note (1)
[247] VATA 1994, Sch 9, Gp 13, Item 2
[248] ibid, Items 1 and 2

For the purposes of this Group, 'eligible body' means any body (other than a public body) which[249]

(a) is precluded from distributing and does not distribute any profit it makes;
(b) applies any profits made from supplies of a description falling within item 2 to the continuance or improvement of the facilities made available by means of the supplies; and
(c) is managed and administered on a voluntary basis by persons who have no direct or indirect financial interest in its activities.

3.73 It was recently held that London Zoo was not entitled to exemption on this ground because those who managed it on a daily basis had a financial interest in its activities. An appeal against this decision by London Zoo is presently pending in the European Court.[250]

Fund-raising events by charities

3.74 Group 12[251] exempts the supply of goods and services

(a) by a charity in connection with an event[252] that is organised for charitable purposes by a charity or jointly by more than one charity;[253] or
(b) by a qualifying body[254] in connection with an event that is organised exclusively for the body's own benefit;[255] or
(c) by a charity, or two or more charities, and a qualifying body in connection with an event that is organised exclusively for charitable purposes, or exclusively for the body's own benefit, or exclusively for a combination of such purposes and benefit.[256]

Additionally, in each case the primary purpose of the event must be the raising of money, and the event must be promoted as being primarily for that purpose.[257]

3.75 The exemptions within this Group do not apply if more than fifteen events of the same kind involving the charity or qualifying body are held at the same location in its financial year.[258] In determining whether this limit has been exceeded, there

---

[249] VATA 1994, Sch 9, Gp 13, Note (2)
[250] See R Pearson, (1999) *Lawyer* 1 Nov, 22
[251] VATA 1994, Sch 9, Gp 12, as substituted by the Value Added Tax (Fund-raising Events by Charities and Other Qualifying Bodies) Order 2000, SI 2000/802, which came into force on 1 Apr 2000, and which applies only to supplies made on or after that date: ibid, reg 1(1), (2)
[252] For the purposes of this Group, 'event' includes an event accessed (wholly or partly) by means of electronic communications: VATA 1994, Sch 9, Gp 12, Note (1)
[253] ibid, Item 1(a)
[254] The expression 'qualifying body' means: (a) any non-profit making organisation mentioned in item 1 of Group 9 (trade unions and certain professional and other public interest bodies); (b) any body that is an eligible body for the purposes of Group 10, and whose principal purpose is the provision of facilities for persons to take part in sport or physical education; or (c) any body that is an eligible body for the purposes of item 2 of Group 13 (certain non-profit museums, galleries, art exhibitions and zoos): VATA 1994, Sch 9, Gp 12, Note (3)
[255] ibid, Item 2(a)
[256] ibid, Item 3(a), (b)
[257] ibid, Items 1(b), (c), 2(b), (c), 3(c), (d)

is to be disregarded any event held in a week during which the aggregate gross takings do not exceed £1,000.[259] The VAT exemption for small-scale events such as jumble sales or coffee mornings is thereby preserved.[260]

This Group does not include any supply the exemption of which would be likely **3.76** to create distortions of competition such as to place a commercial enterprise carried on by a taxable person at a disadvantage.[261]

For the purposes of this Group, the term 'charity' is given an extended meaning, **3.77** as it includes a body corporate that is wholly owned by a charity if[262]

(a) the body has agreed in writing (whether or not contained in a deed) to transfer its profits (from whatever source) to a charity, or
(b) the body's profits (from whatever source) are otherwise payable to charity.

A charity's wholly owned subsidiary trading company is therefore itself treated as a charity for this purpose.

Betting, gaming and lotteries

Group 4 exempts the provision of any facilities for the placing of bets or the play- **3.78** ing of any games of chance,[263] and the granting of a right to take part in a lottery.[264] It does not include admission to any premises, or the granting of a right to take part in a game in respect of which a charge may be made by regulations,[265] or the provision by a club of such facilities to its members as are available to them on payment of their subscription but without further charge, or the provision of a gaming machine.[266]

---

[258] ibid, Note (4). In determining the number of events, an event is not to be disregarded solely because it was held before 1 Apr 2000: Value Added Tax (Fund-raising Events by Charities and Other Qualifying Bodies) Order 2000, SI 2000/802, reg 1(3)

[259] VATA 1994, Sch 9, Gp 12, Note (5)

[260] See Explanatory Note to ibid

[261] ibid, Note (11)

[262] ibid, Note (2)

[263] ibid, Gp 4, Item 1. 'Game of chance' has the same meaning as in the Gaming Act 1968 or in the Betting, Gaming, Lotteries and Amusements (Northern Ireland) Order 1985: VATA 1994, Sch 9, Gp 4, Note (2)

[264] VATA 1994, Sch 9, Gp 4, Item 2

[265] ie under the Gaming Act 1968, s 14 or under the Betting, Gaming, Lotteries and Amusements (Northern Ireland) Order 1985

[266] VATA 1994, Sch 9, Gp 4, Note (1). 'Gaming machine' is defined ibid, Note (3)

F. Rates

(1) Non-domestic rates

Premises wholly or mainly used for charitable purposes

3.79 An occupier of premises for business purposes is generally liable to pay non-domestic rates in respect of their occupation. If, however, the ratepayer is a charity or trustees for a charity, and the premises are wholly or mainly used for charitable purposes (whether of that charity or of that and other charities), it is liable to pay only 20 per cent of the non-domestic rate which would be paid if the premises were otherwise occupied for business purposes.[267]

3.80 Where business premises are unoccupied, the ratepayer is normally liable for half the amount of non-domestic rates which would have been payable had the premises been occupied.[268] This principle applies *mutatis mutandis* to charities. If the ratepayer of unoccupied premises is a charity or a trustee for a charity, and it appears that when next in use the premises will be wholly or mainly used for charitable purposes (whether of that charity or of that and other charities), it is liable to pay only 10 per cent of the non-domestic rate which would be paid if the premises were otherwise occupied for business purposes.[269] This is half of what the charity would have paid were it currently using the premises for charitable purposes.

3.81 A billing authority has a discretion to extend the proportion of a charity's exemption from non-domestic rates, and even to remit its liability to such rates altogether,[270] provided that[271]

(a) the ratepayer is a charity or trustees for a charity, and the hereditament is wholly or mainly used for charitable purposes[272] (whether of that charity or of that and other charities); or
(b) the hereditament is not an excepted hereditament,[273] and all or part of it is occupied for the purposes of one or more institutions or other organisations none of which is established or conducted for profit and each of whose main objects are charitable or are otherwise philanthropic or religious or concerned with education, social welfare, science, literature or the fine arts; or

---

[267] Local Government FA 1988, s 43(5), (6)
[268] ibid. s 45(1)–(4)
[269] ibid, s 45(5), (6)
[270] ibid, s 47(1)
[271] ibid, s 47(2)
[272] For the purposes of s 47, a hereditament not in use is treated as wholly or mainly used for charitable purposes if it appears that when next in use it will be wholly or mainly used for charitable purposes: ibid, s 48(1), (2)
[273] An hereditament is an excepted hereditament if all or part of it is occupied (otherwise than as a trustee) by a billing authority, or by a precepting authority (other than the Receiver for the Metropolitan Police District or charter trustees): ibid, s 47(9) (as amended)

(c) the hereditament is not an excepted hereditament, it is wholly or mainly used for purposes of recreation, and all or part of it is occupied for the purposes of a club, society or other organisation not established or conducted for profit.

Rate relief also extends to charity shops which sell mainly donated goods, the proceeds of which are applied for the charity's purposes. This is by way of a statutory extension to the meaning of use 'wholly or mainly for charitable purposes'. It is provided that;[274]   **3.82**

A hereditament shall be treated as wholly or mainly used for charitable purposes at any time if at the time it is wholly or mainly used for the sale of goods donated to a charity and the proceeds of sale of the goods (after deduction of expenses) are applied for the purposes of a charity.

In the context of this relief, 'mainly' probably means 'more than half';[275] but this is not entirely clear. In determining whether a charity shop is selling 'mainly' donated goods, a local authority will take into account the percentage of sales space occupied by the donated goods, the percentage of turnover and profits which the sale of donated goods represents, and the precentage of individual items sold which are donated goods.[276]

The relief for the sale by charity shops of donated goods was originally introduced[277] to reverse the effect of the decision of the House of Lords in *Oxfam v Birmingham City District Council*,[278] which had held that charity shops selling mostly donated goods were not entitled to rate relief as the law then stood.[279] That case remains of more general value, however, in explaining the circumstances in which premises are to be regarded as 'wholly or mainly used for charitable purposes'.   **3.83**

The issue in the *Oxfam* case[280] was whether Oxfam was entitled to rate relief in respect of several of its shops in the Birmingham area on the ground that they were wholly or mainly used for charitable purposes. Local groups of Oxfam ran hundreds of shops across the country, some of which occupied premises rent-free through the permission of their commercial owners, but many others were occupied at a full commercial rent, which was generally paid out of the shop takings. The shops sold some goods made in various parts of the developing world as part of Oxfam's overseas programme of encouraging village industries, and other items   **3.84**

---

[274] Local Government and FA 1988, s 64(10)

[275] See *Fawcett Properties Ltd v Buckingham County Council* [1961] AC 636 (Lord Morton)

[276] See HM Treasury, *Review of Charity Taxation: Consultation Document* (Mar 1999), 28 (para 5.37)

[277] In the Rating (Charity Shops) Act 1976

[278] [1976] AC 126 (HL)

[279] On rate relief and charity trading, see further ch 20, paras 20.40–20.41

[280] Their Lordships were considering rate relief under an earlier statute, General Rate Act 1967, s 40(1), but which also granted exemption for premises 'wholly or mainly used for charitable purposes'

which had been both purchased and sold by a non-charitable trading subsidiary company of Oxfam, which covenanted all its profits to Oxfam. Four-fifths of the goods sold in the shops, however, had been donated to Oxfam.

3.85 It was conceded by counsel for the rating authority that if the Oxfam shops had been mainly used for the sale of the 'village handicraft articles', they would have been entitled to relief; and counsel for Oxfam conceded that if the shops had been mainly used for the sale of articles purchased by its trading subsidiary, it would not have been entitled to relief. The House of Lords was, however, concerned with the question whether the premises could be said to be 'wholly or mainly used for charitable purposes' when their main use was for the sale of articles which had been donated.

3.86 Lord Cross (with whose speech three of the other Law Lords merely expressed agreement) said that user for charitable purposes referred to user for the purposes directly related to the achievement of the objects of the charity. A charity was entitled to rating relief in respect of premises which it occupied, even if they were not occupied for carrying on its main purpose, so long as the premises were occupied for an ancillary purpose.

3.87 A charitable hospital which provides homes for its nurses in order that they can live nearby would be using such homes for the purpose of the charity, since such provision would assist in the more efficient performance of its charitable activities, and would therefore be ancillary to its main charitable purpose of running a hospital.[281] Any organization which seeks to advance some cause must, if it is of any size, have an office from which its clerical and administrative work is done;[282] and it was conceded by council for the rating authority that Oxfam would have been entitled to rate relief as a charity in respect of premises used as its office wholly or mainly used to organize and carry out its charitable activities; and Lord Cross evidently considered that this concession had been rightly made, since such occupation would be ancillary to the carrying out of Oxfam's charitable purpose.

3.88 User for the purpose of getting in, raising or earning money for the charity, however, is not directly related to the achievement of the charity's objects. Therefore a charity which occupies premises for the purpose of carrying on a business to earn money for the charity is not occupying them for its charitable purposes. On this footing the House of Lords held that Oxfam was not entitled to rate relief in respect of its charity shops.

3.89 Lord Cross said that no distinction is to be drawn between using premises to get in money by managing existing trust property and using them to raise fresh

---

[281] *Glasgow City Corp v Johnstone* [1965] AC 609, 621 (Lord Reid)
[282] *United Grand Lodge of Ancient, Free and Accepted Masons of England v Holborn BC* [1957] 1 WLR 1080 (Lord Donovan)

money.[283] A charity which leases its land to tenants merely for the purpose of earning money for the charity is not using such land for its charitable purposes; it is simply running a business.[284] It makes no difference whether the land in question has been bought with a view to being leased out to raise money,[285] or forms part of estates which have been settled on trust for charitable purposes.

On this last point, Lord Cross evidently had doubts about the decision in *Aldous*   **3.90**
v Southwark Corporation,[286] which concerned the rating of certain hereditaments owned and occupied by the estate governors of Dulwich College. The estates (which originally comprised part of more extensive properties which had been settled on trust for charitable purposes several centuries earlier) had been subject to a statutory scheme for the advancement of education. The Court of Appeal held that the offices from which the estates were managed were occupied by the charity for its charitable purposes because the management and administration of such estates was itself a charitable purpose, being ancillary to the principal purpose of the advancement of education.

The Court of Appeal's decision must now be treated with caution. In the *Oxfam*   **3.91**
case, Lord Cross considered that the running of the Dulwich estates was analogous to the running of a business and had little to do with the furtherance of education.[287] He did not, however, think that the actual decision in the *Aldous* case was wrong: it might be justified on the basis that the various statutes and schemes (which were not set out in detail in the reports) could be regarded as having set up a trust for the management and exploitation of the charity property which was itself a separate charitable trust. In any event, the *Aldous* case offered no general guidance on the interpretation of the rating statute.[288]

Places of religious worship and premises used for ancillary purposes

Certain hereditaments are exempt from non-domestic rates. The exemption is in   **3.92**
the following form:[289]

> (1) A hereditament is exempt to the extent that it consists of any of the following—
>   (a) a place of public religious worship which belongs to the Church of England or the Church of Wales (within the meaning of the Welsh Church Act 1914)

---

[283] *Oxfam v Birmingham City DC* [1976] AC 126, 146 (Lord Cross)

[284] *Polish Historical Institution Ltd v Hove Corp* (1963) 10 RRC 73 (Wilberforce J), approved in *Oxfam v Birmingham City DC* [1976] AC 126, 143, 146 (Lord Cross), where their Lordships also disapproved of dicta of Lord Denning MR and Winn LJ in *Aldous v Southwark Corporation* [1968] 1 WLR 1671, 1676–7, 1682

[285] As in *Polish Historical Institution Ltd v Hove Corp* (1963) 10 RRC 73

[286] [1968] 1 WLR 1671

[287] *Oxfam v Birmingham City DC* [1976] AC 126, 146

[288] ibid, 147

[289] Local Government FA 1988, Sch 5, para 11, as amended by Local Government FA 1992, Sch 10, Pt I, para 3

or is for the time being certified as required by law as a place of religious worship;[290]

(b) a church hall, chapel hall or similar building used in connection with a place falling within paragraph (a) above for the purposes of the organisation responsible for the conduct of public religious worship in that place.

(2) A hereditament is exempt to the extent that it is occupied by an organisation responsible for the conduct of public religious worship in a place falling within sub-paragraph (1)(a) above and—

(a) is used for carrying out administrative or other activities relating to the organisation of the conduct of public religious worship in such a place; or

(b) is used as an office or for office purposes, or for purposes ancillary to its use as an office or for office purposes.

(3) In this paragraph 'office purposes' include administration, clerical work and handling money; and 'clerical work' includes writing, book-keeping, sorting papers or information, filing, typing, duplicating, calculating (by whatever means), drawing and the editorial preparation of matter for publication.

3.93 In *R v Registrar General, ex p Segerdal*,[291] the Church of Scientology sought mandamus against the Registrar General following his refusal to register under the Places of Worship Registration Act 1855 a building which the Scientologists described as a chapel. Lord Denning MR (with whom the other two judges agreed) said that a 'place of meeting for religious worship' within the 1855 Act connoted[292]

> a place of which the principal use is as a place where people come together as a congregation or assembly to do reverence to God. It need not be the God which the Christians worship. It may be another God, or an unknown God, but it must be reverence to a deity. There may be exceptions. For instance, Buddhist temples are properly described as places of meeting for religious worship. But, apart from exceptional cases of that kind, it seems to me the governing idea behind the words 'place of meeting for religious worship' is that it should be a place for the worship of God.

The Court of Appeal held that the refusal had been correctly made because they did not find in the beliefs of the Church of Scientology any reverence for God or a deity, but simply instruction in a philosophy.[293]

(2) Council tax

3.94 The Local Government Finance Act 1988 abolished domestic rates and replaced them with the community charge, which was in turn abolished and replaced by the council tax under the Local Government Finance Act 1992. The statute does not afford charity premises any special treatment, so resident occupiers of charity premises will be liable to pay council tax unless they fall within one of the exempt categories, for example, patients in residential care homes, mental nursing homes or hostels, or those who are severely mentally impaired.[294]

---

[290] ie under Places of Worship Registration Act 1855
[291] [1970] 2 QB 697 (CA)
[292] ibid, 707
[293] ibid, 707 (Lord Denning MR), 708–9 (Winn LJ)
[294] Local Government FA 1992, s 11, Sch 1

PART II

THE MEANING OF CHARITY

4

CHARITABLE PURPOSES

The term 'charity' is a term of art; but the definition of charity is not contained in **4.01** statute. The meaning of charity is to be found almost entirely in the case law, the sole exception being recreational charities, which may qualify as charitable if they satisfy the requirements of the Recreational Charities Act 1958.

Although there is no statutory definition of charity, some guidance is to be **4.02** obtained from the Preamble to the Statute of Charitable Uses 1601 (in this chapter referred to as the Preamble and the Statute of Elizabeth respectively).[1] The Preamble listed a number of objects which were regarded as charitable at the time. The list was not intended to be exhaustive;[2] but it has long been used as a touchstone as to what is in law charitable, and reference is still made to it today. Expressed in modern English, the purposes specified in the Preamble are as follows:

> The relief of aged, impotent and poor people; the maintenance of sick and maimed soldiers and mariners, schools of learning, free schools and scholars in universities; the repair of bridges, ports, havens, causeways, churches, sea-banks and highways; the education and preferment of orphans; the relief, stock or maintenance of houses of correction; the marriages of poor maids, the supportation, aid and help of young tradesmen, handicraftsmen and persons decayed; the relief or redemption of prisoners or captives; and the aid or ease of any poor inhabitants concerning payment of fifteens,[3] setting out of soldiers and other taxes.[4]

4.03   A simpler classification is that of Lord Macnaghten in *Pemsel*'s case.[5] His Lordship classified charitable purposes under four heads: the relief of poverty; the advancement of education; the advancement of religion; and other purposes beneficial to the community.[6] This classification has been broadly accepted in later cases;

---

[1] 43 Eliz I c 4. The Statute of Elizabeth was repealed by the Mortmain and Charitable Uses Act 1888 (s 13(1) and Sch); but it was expressly provided that references to charities in enactments and documents were to be construed as references to charities 'with the meaning, purview, and interpretation of the said preamble': ibid, s 13(2). The Mortmain and Charitable Uses Act 1888 was itself repealed by CA 1960 (s 38(1) and Sch 7, Pt II), which expressly provided that any reference in any enactment or document to a charity 'within the meaning, purview and interpretation of the Charitable Uses Act, 1601, or of the preamble to it, shall be construed as a reference to a charity within the meaning which the word bears as a legal term according to the law of England and Wales': ibid, s 38(4). As the meaning of charity as a legal term is contained in the case law, which is itself founded on the Preamble, the Preamble effectively survives within the case law: *Scottish Burial Reform and Cremation Society Ltd v Glasgow Corp* [1968] AC 138, 154 (Lord Wilberforce); *Incorporated Council of Law Reporting for England and Wales v A-G* [1971] Ch 626, 644 (Foster J) (first instance)

[2] *Turner v Ogden* (1787) 1 Cox 316, 317 (Kenyon MR); *Univ of London v Yarrow* (1857) 1 De G & J 72, 79 (Lord Cranworth LC: 'the objects enumerated [in the statute of Elizabeth] are not to be taken as the only objects of charity, but are given as instances'); *National Anti-Vivisection Society v IRC* [1948] AC 31, 64 (Lord Simonds: 'from the beginning it appears to have been assumed that the enumeration was not exhaustive')

[3] A 'fifteenth' was 'a tax of, theoretically, one fifteenth of the moveable property of every subject, granted from time to time to the King . . . Fifteenths originated in the twelfth century and are last heard of in the reign of James I': *Jowitt's Dictionary of English Law* (ed J Burke) (2nd edn, Sweet & Maxwell, 1977), vol I, 789–90

[4] The similarity between the Preamble and a passage from the 14th-century alliterative poem *The Vision of Piers Plowman* was noted by J Willard, 'Illustration of the Origin of Cy-Près' (1894–5) 8 Harv LR 69, 70–1

[5] *Comrs for Special Purposes of the Income Tax v Pemsel* [1891] AC 531

[6] Lord Macnaghten's classification appears to be based (without acknowledgement) upon a similar four-fold classification proposed by Sir Samuel Romilly *arguendo* in *Morice v Bishop of Durham* (1805) 10 Ves Jun 522, 532 viz, '1st, relief of the indigent; . . . 2dly, the advancement of learning: . . . 3dly, the advancement of religion; and 4thly, . . . the advancement of objects of general public utility': see *National Anti-Vivisection Society v IRC* [1948] AC 31, 41 (Lord Wright); *Re Macduff* [1896] 2 Ch 451, 467 (Lindley LJ)

although, particularly in cases under the fourth head, reference is still occasionally made to the Elizabethan Preamble. Commenting upon Lord Macnaghten's classification, Lord Wilberforce, in *Scottish Burial Reform and Cremation Society Ltd v Glasgow City Corporation*,[7] said, first, that since the classification is one of convenience, there may well be some purposes which do not fit neatly into one or other of the headings; secondly, that the words used must not be given the force of a statute to be construed; and, thirdly, that the law of charity is a moving subject which may well have evolved even since 1891.[8]

A. The relief of poverty

(1) The meaning of poverty

The Elizabethan Preamble lists the relief of aged, impotent and poor people, but **4.04** these words are to be construed disjunctively;[9] so that the relief of poor persons is charitable *per se*. Poverty in this context is not restricted to absolute destitution, but encompasses the notion of 'going short', due regard being had to a person's status in life.[10] What comprises poverty is therefore relative;[11] indeed a gift can be charitable for the relief of poverty even if the very poorest are in terms excluded,[12] or the recipients of benefits are charged a fee.[13]

---

[7] [1968] AC 138, 154

[8] See also *Re Strakosch* [1949] 1 Ch 529, 537 (Lord Greene MR: 'The preamble set out what were then regarded as purposes which should be regarded as charitable in law. It is obvious that as time passed and conditions changed common opinion as to what was properly covered by the word charitable also changed')

[9] *Re Glyn's Will Trusts* [1950] 2 All ER 1150n (Danckwerts J); *Re Robinson* [1951] Ch 198, 201 (Vaisey J); *Joseph Rowntree Memorial Trust Housing Assoc Ltd v A-G* [1983] Ch 159, 171–4 (Peter Gibson J)

[10] *Re Coulthurst* [1951] Ch 661, 666 (Lord Evershed MR)

[11] cf *Re De Carteret* [1933] Ch 103. In *Re Gardom* [1914] 1 Ch 662, 668, Eve J said, 'there are degrees of poverty less acute than abject poverty or destitution, but poverty nevertheless'

[12] *Re De Carteret* [1933] Ch 103 (provision of an annual allowance of £40 each to widows and spinsters whose annual income would otherwise be not less than £8 or more than £120 held charitable). An alternative view is that a minimum qualifying income does not in fact exclude the absolutely destitute, since such persons might be able to obtain the requisite income from another charity: see *Trustees of the Mary Clark Home v Anderson* [1904] 2 KB 645, 655 (Channell J). In that case a home for ladies of at least 50 years in reduced circumstances with an annual income of not less than £25 and not more than £55 was held entitled to tax relief as being an almshouse or a house provided for the relief of poor persons

[13] eg *Re Cottam's Will Trusts* [1955] 1 WLR 1299 (where a trust to provide flats for the elderly was held to be charitable for the relief of poverty even though the inhabitants were to pay economic rents)

Finding poverty requirement in words of instrument

4.05 The gift may be expressly 'for the relief of poverty' or 'for the poor', but other words may connote poverty. The use of the terms 'needy',[14] or 'of limited means',[15] is taken to refer to the poor; whereas 'deserving' by itself is not.[16] Poverty may also be inferred from the nature of the gift itself,[17] from the smallness of the amount given,[18] or from other indications in the will or other instrument. In *Re Gosling*,[19] provision of a superannuation fund for 'pensioning off old and worn out clerks' of a banking firm, was held charitable, being implicitly for the relief of poverty. Another example is *Re Cottam*,[20] where the testator had made a bequest to a local authority to provide flats for aged persons to be let at economic rents. This was interpreted to mean at less than a full commercial rent: namely, at cost price only. The court was able to infer that this was a trust for the relief of poverty, and held it charitable. Similarly, in *Re Young*,[21] a disposition for the relief of distressed gentlefolk was held charitable, as 'distressed' suggested a poverty requirement. In *Re Niyazi*,[22] Megarry V-C held that a trust to build working men's hostels in Cyprus was charitable for the relief of poverty. Although he thought the case to be near the borderline, he considered that the expression 'working men' in conjunction with the word 'hostels' was sufficient to indicate an element of poverty.

Extrinsic evidence of poverty inadmissible

4.06 That the gift is intended to be for the relief of poverty must, however, be at least implicit in the wording of the gift itself, since extrinsic evidence to show that the persons to benefit are in fact poor will not be admitted. This was illustrated in *Re Drummond*,[23] which concerned a bequest upon trust to assist the workers in a spinning factory with their holiday expenses. There was extrinsic evidence to show that the employees earned only £40 per week, which the judge admitted was a small wage even in 1913; but he declined to hold the disposition charitable, because no poverty requirement was imposed by the will itself. Similarly, in

---

[14] *Re Scarisbrick* [1951] Ch 622, 634 (Evershed MR: 'The phrase "in needy circumstances" is to my mind merely periphrastic for "poor" '). See also *Re Cohen* [1973] 1 WLR 415

[15] *Re Gardom* [1914] 1 Ch 662

[16] *Re Cohen* (1919) 36 TLR 16. The disposition may, of course, contain other indications that it is for the relief of poverty: see *Re Coulthurst* [1951] Ch 661

[17] *Biscoe v Jackson* (1887) 35 Ch D 460 (provision of a soup kitchen in Shoreditch). In *Re Glyn's Will Trusts* [1950] 2 All ER 1150n, Danckwerts J held that a bequest for building cottages for old women of the working classes aged 60 years or upwards was charitable for the relief of poverty because the context showed that the testatrix intended to benefit persons who were indigent

[18] *Re Lucas* [1922] 2 Ch 52 (Russell J) (gift of 5s per week each to the oldest respectable inhabitants of Gunville)

[19] (1900) 16 TLR 152 (Byrne J)

[20] [1955] 1 WLR 1299

[21] [1951] Ch 344

[22] [1978] 1 WLR 910

[23] [1914] 2 Ch 90

Re Sanders' Will Trusts,[24] a trust to provide dwellings for the working classes around Pembroke Dock in Wales was held not to be charitable. Although there was evidence outside the will that Pembroke Dock was a poor area of Wales, Harman J was unable to infer a poverty requirement from the will; the expression 'working classes', he considered, did not necessarily indicate poor persons.

A further example of a gift which failed to attain charitable status is *Re Gwyon*.[25]   **4.07**
The Reverend John Gwyon had given his residuary estate upon trust to establish a clothing foundation, the income from which was to be used to provide 'knickers' (a form of short trousers) for boys in Farnham; the waistband of each garment was to bear the legend 'Gwyon's Present', and, under the terms of the gift, these words had to remain legible before a boy was entitled to receive a second pair.[26] The disposition was held not to be charitable for the relief of poverty since the benefits were not restricted to boys who were poor.

(2) Methods of relieving poverty

Many older charities for the relief of poverty involved the direct distribution to the   **4.08**
poor of food,[27] fuel,[28] clothing, or sums of money,[29] or the provision of almshouses;[30] but the relief of poverty can be achieved in many different ways, including, for instance, the allotment of land for the cultivation of crops,[31] and the establishing of soup kitchens.[32] More recently, the Charity Commissioners have

---

[24] [1954] Ch 265

[25] [1930] 1 Ch 255

[26] This requirement was only one of the many extraordinary terms which the Rev Gwyon, by his will and five codicils, attached to his sartorial gift. In the more distant past, however, it was by no means uncommon for testators who made charitable dispositions to clothe the poor to require the recipients to wear garments bearing the testator's (ie the founder's) name or initials. See, eg, *The Hospital of the Lady Katherine Leveson and the Educational Foundation of Lady Katherine Leveson, at Temple Balsall, West Midlands* [1977] Ch Com Rep 39–40 (paras 133–136). The original charity in that case had been founded by the will of the testatrix, Lady Katherine Leveson, who died in the latter part of the 17th century. By her will, she left land to trustees to build and maintain an almshouse for 20 poor women, who were to receive gowns of grey cloth with the initials 'KL' in blue (the wearing of which was obligatory), with maintenance allowances

[27] cf *Biscoe v Jackson* (1887) 35 ChD 460 (soup)

[28] Many fuel allotment charities have been subject to schemes widening their original limited purpose of providing fuel for the poor: see, eg, *Re Hampton Fuel Allotment Charity* [1989] Ch 484. The Charity Commissioners were empowered by the Charities (Fuel Allotments) Act 1939 to prepare schemes for the sale of fuel allotments and for the application cy-près of the proceeds of sale

[29] ie 'dole' charities: see *Re Campden Charities* (1881) 18 ChD 310

[30] *Harbin v Masterman* [1894] 2 Ch 184 (CA); affd sub nom *Wharton v Masterman* [1895] AC 186 (HL)

[31] See, eg, *The Charity of Robert McDougal for the Allotments Committee Fund administered in connection with the Religious Society of Friends* [1972] Ch Com Rep 19–20 (paras 53–4), where, owing to a decline in the demand for the allotments, the Commissioners made a scheme enabling any surplus from the fund which could not be applied in assisting unemployed people who were in distress by the provision of allotments, to be applied to help such persons in such other ways as the trustees should think fit

[32] *Biscoe v Jackson* (1887) 35 ChD 460

registered as charities (as being for the relief of poverty) a number of neighbour-hood law centres whose aims are to give legal aid and advice to poor persons.[33] Also in modern times, the relief of poverty has sometimes taken the form of loans to the poor,[34] the relief of unemployment,[35] and even the use of a 'fair trade mark' to guarantee to consumers that the purchase of a particular brand of product will benefit people in need in poorer countries.[36] Whilst the provision of accommodation for the poor is a well-established purpose,[37] the last few decades have seen a growth in projects designed to relieve poverty by housing the poor in homes that they acquire for themselves.

4.09   In *Garfield Poverty Trust*, the Charity Commissioners were prepared to treat as charitable the purpose of relieving poverty by the making of loans to assist poor sections of the Exclusive Brethren to purchase freehold or leasehold housing accommodation.[38] The Commissioners found no objection in the possibility that the recipients of such loans might sell the property purchased at a profit, since such a profit was incidental, and not at the expense of the charity.[39] In order to ensure that a beneficiary should not continue to receive any benefit if he should cease to be poor, the position was to be reviewed regularly by the trustees.[40] Before registering the trust as charitable, the Charity Commissioners required the trustees to agree to certain conditions relating to the making of the loans.[41]

4.10   In *Habitat for Humanity Great Britain*,[42] the Charity Commissioners recognized an extension of this principle, and registered as a charity a company one of whose objects was the relief of poverty by assisting persons to build their own homes. The beneficiaries were to contribute 500 hours of unpaid labour in helping to build houses or to administer the local project. The charity would take a legal charge over each beneficiary's house in consideration for an interest-free loan repayable over twenty years, with five-yearly reviews, which gave an opportunity for the charity to consider the beneficiary's circumstances, and to call the loan in if these had improved. A beneficiary who disposed of the house within twenty years would have to repay the loan together with a proportion of the house's then mar-

---

[33]   *Camden Community Law Centre* [1974] Ch Com Rep 20–21 (paras 67–72)

[34]   *Re Monk* [1927] 2 Ch 197 (gift of residuary estate to provide a coal and loan fund for the poor and deserving of the testator's village)

[35]   See *IRC v Oldham Training and Enterprise Council* [1996] STC 1218, 1233 (Lightman J), referring to *Verge v Somervell* [1924] AC 496, 506, and *Re Tree* [1945] Ch 325

[36]   *The Fairtrade Foundation*, (1995) 4 Decisions 1

[37]   eg *Re Cottam's Will Trusts* [1955] 1 WLR 1299 (gift to provide flats to be let to aged persons at economic rents)

[38]   (1995) 3 Decisions 7–10 (relief of poverty amongst certain sections of the Exclusive Brethren)

[39]   ibid, 8

[40]   ibid, 9, ie a change in a beneficiary's circumstances might make it appropriate for the loan to be called in; cf *Joseph Rowntree Memorial Trust Housing Assoc v A-G* [1983] Ch 159

[41]   (1995) 3 Decisions 7, 9–10

[42]   (1995) 4 Decisions, 13–16

ket value, calculated according to the number of years since the loan had been made. The promoters proposed that the beneficiaries should come from that proportion of the population who, whilst being able to afford more than a fully subsidized rent, were nevertheless in housing need because the purchase of their own home was beyond their means. The income of such households would exclude them from social housing schemes, which gave priority to those on the lowest incomes.[43] The Charity Commissioners decided that this expressed object was plainly charitable for the relief of poverty. They considered that a person's inability to obtain adequate housing (either personally or for their dependants) because he or she (as a result of prevailing market prices) had insufficient income to obtain a commercial mortgage may constitute poverty in the charitable sense. The provision of facilities directed to relieving the need for adequate housing, a basic human need, could be properly regarded as the relief of poverty.[44] The Commissioners accepted that the quinquennial reviews safeguarded the charity's position where a beneficiary's position improved. Nevertheless, they were concerned that the form of inquiry should include ascertaining what capital assets the beneficiary owned, and that such assets should be taken into account. The promoters agreed to these terms, and the Commissioners registered the company as a charity.

(3) The Charity Commissioners' guidance notes

4.11 The Charity Commissioners have published guidance notes for trustees of charities for the relief of the poor.[45] The notes point out (inter alia) that the funds of such charities should not be used for purposes which would otherwise be met out of the rates, taxes or other public funds, and that trustees of such charities should therefore acquaint themselves with the system of statutory social benefits.[46] The Charity Commissioners also state that charity trustees proposing to give immediate aid in cases of emergency should take into account any arrangements made by the statutory authorities, and should ascertain, so far as circumstances permit, that emergency relief is not available from public funds.[47]

B. The advancement of education

(1) The scope of education

4.12 Aspects of the advancement of education are specifically mentioned in the Preamble, namely, 'schools of learning, free schools and scholars in universities'

---

[43] ibid, 13
[44] ibid, 14–15
[45] [1978] Ch Com Rep (para 63), App A
[46] ibid, App A, para 4
[47] ibid, App A, para 7

and also 'the education and preferment of orphans'. Despite the reference to 'free' schools, fee-paying schools (provided they do not distribute profits other than for charitable purposes) can be charitable;[48] and the advancement of education is independent of the relief of poverty.[49]

4.13   The advancement of education clearly includes formal teaching, the study or promotion of individual subjects, whether academic,[50] scientific,[51] medical,[52] professional,[53] managerial or vocational,[54] and the provision of scholarships;[55] and it also includes the giving of prizes in a school for academic achievement.[56] It is also charitable for the advancement of education (as well as under the fourth head of *Pemsel*) to provide public libraries,[57] museums,[58] art galleries and exhibitions of fine art,[59] botanical gardens,[60] and zoos.[61] The preparation of law reports has been held to be charitable.[62] A society to promote equal rights and responsibilities between men and women as citizens has been held charitable for the advancement of education.[63] Political propaganda, however, does not rank as education, and is not charitable.[64]

4.14   The advancement of education includes aesthetic education,[65] in other words[66] 'the promotion or encouragement of those arts and graces of life which are, after all, perhaps the finest and best part of the human character'. Thus a gift to build a theatre for the performance of the plays of Shakespeare and other classical drama-

---

[48]   *The Abbey, Malvern Wells Ltd v Ministry of Local Government and Planning* [1951] Ch 728
[49]   eg *A-G v Lonsdale* (1827) 1 Sim 105 (gift for a school for the education of the sons of gentlemen held charitable)
[50]   eg *Re Mariette* [1915] 2 Ch 284 (Classics); *Re British School of Egyptian Archaeology* [1954] 1 WLR 546 (Egyptology)
[51]   *Institution of Civil Engineers v IRC* [1932] 1 KB 149 (CA) (general advancement of mechanical science)
[52]   *Royal College of Surgeons v National Provincial Bank Ltd* [1952] AC 631 (surgery)
[53]   eg *Smith v Kerr* [1902] 1 Ch 774 (CA) (law)
[54]   *Re Koettgen's Will Trusts* [1954] Ch 252 (shorthand, typing, and book-keeping)
[55]   *Re Gott* [1943] Ch 193 (for postgraduate scholarships at Leeds University)
[56]   *Re Mariette* [1915] 2 Ch 284 (prize for Classics in a school)
[57]   *IRC v White* (1980) 55 TC 651 (maintenance for the public of a collection of books on craftsmanship)
[58]   eg *British Museum Trustees v White* (1826) 2 Sm & St 594; *Re Holburne* (1885) 53 LT 212 (art museum in Bath)
[59]   *Re Shaw's Will Trusts* [1952] Ch 163
[60]   *Townley v Bedwell* (1801) 6 Ves 194
[61]   *Re Lopes* [1931] 2 Ch 130 (trust for the upkeep and improvement of the Zoological Gardens and for the objects of the Zoological Society of London held charitable. The Society's objects were 'the advancement of zoology and animal physiology' and 'the introduction of new and curious subjects of the animal kingdom'. Farwell J held that latter object was to be read in connection with the first)
[62]   *Incorporated Council of Law Reporting v A-G* [1972] Ch 73
[63]   *Women's Service Trust* (Whitford J), noted [1977] Ch Com Rep, 14–15, paras 34–6)
[64]   See further ch 7, paras 7.09–7.33
[65]   *Royal Choral Society v IRC* [1943] 2 All ER 101, 105 (Lord Greene MR)
[66]   *Re Shaw's Will Trusts* [1952] Ch 163, 171–2 (Vaisey J)

tists has been held charitable,[67] as has a choral society whose object was the promotion, practice, and performance of choral works,[68] and a gift to promote the musical works of a composer of acknowledged merit.[69] Even a 'finishing school' has been held charitable.[70]

(2) Education and the young

In relation to the young, many things can be educational. A trust to provide treats **4.15** for schoolchildren can be charitable if such treats are either educational in themselves or advance education indirectly.[71] A trust to promote an annual chess tournament for boys and young men under the age of 21 in Portsmouth has been held charitable by Vaisey J, who admitted that the case was near the line:[72]

> One feels perhaps that one is on a rather slippery slope. If chess, why not draughts? If draughts, why not bezique? and so on, through to bridge, whist, and by another route stamp-collecting and the acquisition of birds' eggs.

There seems to be a clear implication in the case, however, that the trust was charitable only because it was restricted to the young. It may be inferred that a trust to promote chess-playing among adults would not be charitable for the advancement of education. It remains unsettled whether the promotion of bridge-playing in schools would be charitable.[73]

Again in the context of the young, Farwell J opined:[74]   **4.16**

> A ride on an elephant may be educational. At any rate it brings the reality of the elephant and its uses to the child's mind, in lieu of leaving him to mere book learning. It widens his mind, and in that broad sense is educational.

Although the promotion of sport is not itself charitable for the advancement of **4.17** education,[75] sport can be a means of advancing the education of the young.[76]

---

[67] *Re Shakespeare Memorial Trust* [1923] 2 Ch 398
[68] *Royal Choral Society v IRC* [1943] 2 All ER 101
[69] *Re Delius' Will Trusts* [1957] Ch 299 (Roxburgh J)
[70] *Re Shaw's Will Trusts* [1952] Ch 163 (Vaisey J)
[71] *Re Mellody* [1918] 1 Ch 228, where Eve J held a gift to provide an annual outing for school children charitable (i) because it promoted nature study, and (ii) because only those children who had good attendance records at school could participate. cf *Re Ward's Estate* (1937) 81 Sol Jo 397 (gift of sweets to children in a parish held not charitable since the award of the sweets was not linked to attendance at school)
[72] *Re Dupree's Deed Trusts* [1945] Ch 16, 20–21
[73] Picarda thinks it possible: see H Picarda, *The Law and Practice Relating to Charities* (3rd edn, Butterworths, 1999) 51. An anonymous note on *Re Dupree's Deed Trusts* at (1945) 61 LQR 12, suggests that the promotion of contract bridge should be charitable, because (like chess) it is a game of skill, and contains just that element of chance which is of special educational value, since it teaches the players to face with fortitude 'the slings and arrows of outrageous fortune'
[74] *Re Lopes* [1931] 2 Ch 130, 136–7
[75] *Re Nottage* [1895] 2 Ch 649, 656. See also *Birchfield Harriers* [1989] Ch Com Rep 13–16, paras 48–55, at 15, para 52: the Harriers' claim to charitable status as being for the advancement of physical education was rejected as the educational element in its purposes (such as coaching) was insufficient
[76] *IRC v McMullen* [1981] AC 1 (HL)

Therefore the provision of squash courts in a school (itself a charity) and prizes for sport in a school has been held to be charitable as being for the advancement of the pupils' education.[77]

(3) Public benefit

4.18 To rank as the advancement of education, the purpose must contain a sufficient public benefit, which is for the court, not the donor, to decide.[78] Were this otherwise, 'trusts might be established in perpetuity for the promotion of all kinds of fantastic (though not unlawful) objects, of which the training of poodles to dance might be a mild example'.[79]

4.19 What is predominantly amusement and entertainment is not the advancement of education.[80] A gift of a house and its contents upon trust to be maintained as a museum has been held not to be charitable, as the court found that the contents were a 'mass of junk'.[81] In another case, a theatre whose objects included the presentation (inter alia) of artistic dramatic work was held not to be charitable, since such object was vague and could include the presentation of works of no merit at all.[82] In *Re Hummeltenberg*,[83] it was argued that a college for the training of spiritualist mediums was charitable for the advancement of education; but the court, unable to discern any public benefit, held that it was not.

4.20 Where appropriate, such as where the subject is unfamiliar, the court will hear expert evidence of public benefit;[84] but there are many cases where the purpose is so obviously of benefit to the community that the matter speaks for itself, and no evidence of public benefit need be sought.[85] In those instances where the public benefit is not obvious, it can be difficult to predict which way the courts (or the Charity Commissioners) will go. Such was *Re Shaw's Will Trusts*,[86] where a bequest (by the wife of George Bernard Shaw) to promote in Ireland the arts of self-control, elocution, oratory, deportment, personal contact, and social intercourse, and to establish a university chair for those purposes, was held to be charitable for the advancement of education. Although the judge regarded it as near the borderline, he held it charitable as creating, in effect, a finishing school for the Irish.

---

[77] *Re Mariette* [1915] 2 Ch 284
[78] *Re Hummeltenberg* [1923] 1 Ch 237, 242 (Russell J)
[79] ibid
[80] See, eg, *Blackburn and East Lancashire Model Rly Society* [1977] Ch Com Rep 21–2 (paras 64–6) (model railway exhibitions merely public amusements and entertainments)
[81] *Re Pinion* [1965] Ch 85, 107 (Harman LJ)
[82] *Associated Artists Ltd v IRC* [1956] 1 WLR 752 (Upjohn J)
[83] [1923] 1 Ch 237. There was no argument in the case that the purpose might have been charitable as being for the advancement of religion
[84] As in *Re Pinion* [1965] Ch 85; *Re Dupree's Deed Trusts* [1945] Ch 16
[85] *Re Shaw's Will Trusts* [1952] 1 Ch 163, 167 (Vaisey J)
[86] [1952] Ch 163

A body is not precluded from being charitable for the advancement of education **4.21** merely because its members or other persons involved with it, including those educated by it, derive incidental personal enjoyment from its activities;[87] but if it is the educational aspect which is incidental, and the enjoyment of its members or others the primary purpose, the body cannot be charitable for the advancement of education.[88]

(4) The promotion of research

Research can be a charitable purpose for the advancement of education,[89] as can **4.22** the award of medals or prizes for outstanding contributions to research.[90] It seems, however, that a mere increase in knowledge is not in itself enough. In *Re Shaw*,[91] the playwright George Bernard Shaw had sought to create a trust by his will to research into the development of a phonetic alphabet. Harman J held this not to be charitable, since (inter alia) it involved a mere increase in knowledge, which his Lordship did not consider a charitable object unless combined with teaching or education.[92] So far as this dictum suggests that there has to be some ultimate public benefit from such increase in knowledge, it can be accepted as correct, and would therefore rightly deny charitable status to many frivolous or worthless purposes, such as the compilation of lists of Derby winners.[93] So far as the dictum suggests that the research must also involve teaching, however, it seems that Harman J went too far.

There was an evident retreat from *Re Shaw* in *Re Hopkins*,[94] which concerned a **4.23** bequest to the Francis Bacon Society for the purpose of finding the so-called Bacon-Shakespeare Manuscripts. The Society exists to show that it was Francis Bacon, and not the man from Stratford-upon-Avon, who wrote the plays attributed to William Shakespeare. Wilberforce J held the bequest charitable for the advancement of education. He said that research can be charitable for the advancement of education in three cases. First, if it is of educational value to the

---

[87] *Royal Choral Society v IRC* [1943] 2 All ER 101 (CA). See also *Re Lopes* [1931] 2 Ch 130, 136, where Farwell J, holding the advancement of zoology charitable, pointed out that, in order for a zoo to attract younger persons to be educated, it might be necessary to provide some form of amusement, such as riding on animals; but that such rides could themselves be educational

[88] See, eg, *Blackburn and East Lancashire Model Rly Society* [1977] Ch Com Rep 21–2 (paras 64–6)

[89] eg *Univ of London v Yarrow* (1857) 1 De G & J 72 (trust for research into diseases of animals held charitable)

[90] eg *The James Spence Medal* [1976] Ch Com Rep 25 (paras 89–90) (a charity founded in 1958 which directed that part of the income should be used to provide a gold medal to be awarded to persons making outstanding contributions to the advancement or clarification of paediatric knowledge)

[91] [1957] 1 WLR 729

[92] ibid, 738

[93] See J Brunyate, 'The Legal Definition of Charity' (1945) 61 LQR 268, 273

[94] [1965] Ch 669

researcher; secondly, if it is so directed as to lead to something which will pass into the store of educational material; and, thirdly, if it improves the sum of communicable knowledge in an area which education (including the formation of artistic taste) may cover.

4.24 In *Re Besterman's Will Trusts*,[95] Slade J held charitable a gift by will to the University of Oxford to complete research into the works of Voltaire, Rousseau and other authors of the Enlightenment. Having reviewed the authorities, his Lordship said that a trust for research will ordinarily qualify as a charitable trust only if three requirements are satisfied. First, the subject-matter of the proposed research must be a useful subject of study. Secondly, it must be contemplated that knowledge acquired as a result of the research will be disseminated to others. Thirdly, the trust must be for the benefit of the public, or a sufficiently important section of the public. In the absence of a contrary context, however, the court will be readily inclined to construe a trust for research as importing subsequent dissemination of the results thereof. His Lordship added that if a trust for research is to constitute a valid charitable trust, it is not necessary either that a teacher/pupil relationship should be in contemplation, or that the persons to benefit from the knowledge to be acquired should be persons who are already in the course of receiving 'education' in the conventional sense. Finally, he added that, in any case where the court has to determine whether a bequest for the purposes of research is or is not of a charitable nature, it must pay due regard to any admissible extrinsic evidence which is available to explain the wording of the will in question or the circumstances in which it was made.

4.25 Applying this approach in *McGovern v Attorney-General*,[96] Slade J, although holding some other objects of the Amnesty International Trust political and not charitable, said that he would have been prepared to treat as charitable for the advancement of education two of the purposes specified in the declaration of trust. One of these was the undertaking, promotion, and commission of research into the maintenance and observance of human rights. The other was the dissemination of the results of such research by the preparation and publication of the results, the creation of a library accessible to the public for the study of matters connected with the objects of the Trust and of the results of the research, and the production and distribution of documentary films showing the results of such research. His Lordship considered that the subject of the research was manifestly a subject of study which was capable of adding usefully to the store of human knowledge. An affidavit of the former Director of Amnesty International and the exhibits thereto indicated that the study of human rights had become an accepted academic discipline in many universities and in schools. The two purposes, when

---

[95] The Times, 21 Jan (1980). Slade J reproduced the relevant passage from his judgment in this case in his later decision in *McGovern v A-G*]1982] Ch 321, 352–3
[96] [1982] Ch 321

read together, made it clear that it was contemplated that the knowledge acquired as a result of the research would be disseminated to others. The mere theoretical possibility that the trustees might have implemented them in a political manner would not have rendered them non-charitable, as the clauses would have been entitled to a benignant construction and to the presumption that the trustees would act only in a lawful and proper manner appropriate to the trustees of a charity.[97]

(5) Students' unions

Many students' unions were initially established for students at a particular college or university on a fairly informal basis, so that there is a risk that all or some of the documentary records of their origins may be lost. Some students' unions are effectively under the close control of the educational establishment which the students attend, and large numbers of these are not separately registered as charities, but are treated as charitable both by the Charity Commissioners and the Inland Revenue, either because they are considered to be a component part of the educational institution where the students study (which will usually have charitable status), or because their purposes are treated as ancillary to the charitable purposes of such institution. **4.26**

A students' union is, however, not automatically a charity; indeed, a students' union, by providing social, athletic and kindred benefits for its members, might at first blush appear to be more in the nature of a club, and therefore lack the necessary element of public benefit.[98] It has, however, been held that a students' union may be charitable if its predominant object is the advancement of education, any personal and private benefits to its members being purely incidental.[99] **4.27**

To determine whether a particular students' union is charitable, it may be necessary to examine its origins as well as its constitution; and, to the extent that its objects are ambiguous, it may be necessary to look at its activities.[100] Affiliation to the National Union of Students and the payment of affiliation fees is not inconsistent with the union's having charitable status;[101] neither is a union's provision of facilities for a variety of students' political clubs.[102] Furthermore, whilst the union's activities after its formation may be relevant in determining whether it was formed for a charitable purpose, ultra vires activities must be disregarded.[103] Although it is a matter of evidence in each case, it seems that close regulation and **4.28**

---

[97] ibid, 353, referring to Gray J in *Jackson v Phillips* (1867) 96 Mass (14 Allen) 539
[98] cf *IRC v City of Glasgow Police Athletic Assoc* [1953] AC 380
[99] *London Hospital Medical College v IRC* [1976] 1 WLR 613 (Brightman J)
[100] ibid; *A-G v Ross* [1986] 1 WLR 252
[101] *A-G v Ross* [1986] 1 WLR 252, 262 (Scott J)
[102] ibid, 263
[103] ibid, 263–4

control of the union by the particular university or college (being itself a charity) is a factor (albeit only one factor) which points towards the charitable status of the union.[104] The fact that a students' union is established by a university in accordance with the provisions of its charter is, perhaps, also indicative that the union is a charity.[105]

4.29   The basis of a students' union's funding is also relevant. In *Attorney-General v Ross*,[106] Scott J noted that the North London Polytechnic's Students' Union was funded by an education authority in pursuance of its statutory function, that such funds were intended to further the authority's educational purposes, and that the funds were paid to the polytechnic, an educational charity, for transmission to the union, an integral part of the polytechnic. In these circumstances, he considered that the funds were 'stamped throughout with the flavour of educational purpose'.[107]

(6) Education in environmental matters

4.30   The Charity Commissioners are prepared to register as charities bodies whose purposes are for the advancement of public education in the protection and improvement of the natural environment and for the promotion of research in that field only if the objects are expressed in terms which are not too vague to be capable of being charitable objects. The Charity Commissioners have expressed difficulty with terms such as 'green', 'sustainable development', 'ecologically friendly', and 'ecological principles'.[108] The Commission has, however, registered The Wilderness Trust, which had been established to advance the education of the public by increasing knowledge and understanding of wilderness and the environment generally by the provision of instruction and of opportunities for direct experience of wilderness. The expression 'wilderness' was defined in the charity's governing instrument as meaning 'those areas of land or sea of scientific interest the primeval state of which has not been discernibly affected by the social or economic activities of man'.[109]

---

[104] In *London Hospital Medical College v IRC* [1976] 1 WLR 613, the students' union treated itself as part of and incidental to and under the control of the college; it had agreed not to alter its rules without the college's approval. Brightman J referred to these circumstances, although he reached his decision that the union was a charity without specifying what (if any) individual factors might have been of particular importance

[105] As in *Baldry v Feintuck* [1972] 1 WLR 552, where an article in the Univ of Sussex's charter stated: 'There shall be a Students' Union of the University'; but in that case the charitable status of the University of Sussex Union was simply assumed

[106] [1986] 1 WLR 252

[107] ibid, 265

[108] [1991] Ch Com Rep 13 (para 73)

[109] ibid

C. The advancement of religion

Although the nearest reference to the advancement of religion in the Preamble to **4.31** the Statute of Elizabeth 1601 is 'the repair of churches', the advancement of religion is a well-established charitable purpose. Within decades of the Preamble's enactment, a gift to maintain a preaching minister was held to be charitable, 'though this is no charitable Use mentioned in the Statute; yet . . . it is within the Equity of the Act';[110] and subsequent cases continued to expand the types of religious purposes which were charitable in English law. Before the age of religious toleration, the only permitted religion was that of the Established Church, with the result that gifts to promote other faiths, though charitable, were illegal and so applied cy-près under the sign manual for the benefit of the Established Church;[111] but the gradual removal of such prejudice in the eighteenth and early nineteenth centuries has enabled the courts to develop the notion of religion in the law of charity unhampered by the need to distinguish between that which is orthodox and that which, in the past, would have been accounted superstitious.

The question whether the meaning of this third head of *Pemsel*'s case needs to be **4.32** modified in the light of the Human Rights Act 1998 was considered in chapter one.[112] The following discussion proceeds on the conclusion there expressed, that the present meaning of the advancement of religion does not breach Convention rights protected by the Act.

(1) The meaning of religion

No distinction between religions

Equity's approach is one of toleration: equity makes no distinction between one **4.33** religion and another, or between one sect and another,[113] but operates on the principle that any religion is better than none.[114] This is illustrated in *Thornton v Howe*,[115] which concerned a devise of land for the publication of the works of one Joanna Southcote, who had claimed that she had been made pregnant by the Holy Ghost and would give birth to a second Messiah. Romilly MR said that, although

---

[110] *Pember v Inhabitants of Kington* (1639) 1 Eq Cas Abr 95
[111] *Da Costa v De Paz* (1754) 1 Dick 258 (Lord Hardwicke applied a bequest to promote the Jewish religion cy-près under the sign manual to an Anglican hospital for the support of preachers, and for the instruction in the Christian religion of the children in their care). On the history of charities for religious purposes, see generally G Jones, *History of the Law of Charity 1532–1827* (Cambridge Univ Press, 1969). On the use of the sign manual, see further ch 15, paras 15.01–15.02
[112] See ch 1, paras 1.106–1.118
[113] *Thornton v Howe* (1862) 31 Beav 14, 19–20 (Romilly MR); *Varsani v Jesani* [1999] Ch 219, 235 (para 30) (Morritt LJ)
[114] *Gilmour v Coats* [1949] AC 426, 457–8 (Lord Reid); *Neville Estates v Madden* [1962] Ch 832, 853 (Cross J)
[115] (1862) 31 Beav 14

very foolish, the devise was not immoral, and he held that it was charitable for the advancement of religion.[116] This decision suggests that just about any religion will be accepted; certainly, there are registered as charities a number of fringe religious sects and cults, and bodies associated with them.[117] One commentator has suggested that there is no reason why the principle of impartiality should not embrace heathenism, so that charitable status could be accorded to an altar for Baal or a grove for Diana.[118]

4.34 The case law has tended to concentrate on the established religions, which are very old; a new religion may find it more difficult to obtain registration as a charity. The Charity Commissioners have said that a new religion that is not simply an offshoot of an existing recognized religion cannot be presumed to be beneficial to the community.[119] This was one of the grounds they gave for refusing to register as a charity the Church of Scientology (England and Wales), since Scientology is based on a belief system which emerged only in the 1950s, and which is derived entirely from the writing of one man, L Ron Hubbard. This principle (which means that no religion at all is presumed to be better than a new one) is not to be found in the case law, and seems to run counter to *Thornton v Howe*.[120] If a distinction is to be drawn between new and old religions for the purpose of charity law, it may rather turn on the genuineness of the belief, since the courts and the Commissioners are entitled to be satisfied that the religion in question is genuinely held. When the charitable status of an entirely new religion is at issue, it may be reasonable for the courts or the Commissioners to demand evidence that the belief is geninely held, instead (as with established religions) of simply presuming that this is so.

---

[116] The judgment was not as indulgent as it might appear, since charitable status caused the devise to be void under the Mortmain Act 1736, which at that time was still in force

[117] eg *Holmes v A-G* The Times, 11 Feb 1981, where Walton J held charitable the Kingston Meeting Rooms Trust (Feltham), which was for the benefit of an ultra-Puritan sect known as the Exclusive Brethren (formerly the Plymouth Brethren). The Charity Commissioners had earlier conducted an inquiry into the religious charities of the Exclusive Brethren: [1976] Ch Com Rep, 33–36, Press Notice. In 1981, the Attorney-General applied to the Charity Commissioners for the removal from the register of two charities associated with the Unification Church, namely the Holy Spirit Association for the Unification of World Christianity and the Sun Myung Moon Foundation. The Charity Commissioners declined to remove the charities from the register because their objects were charitable in law, and moral or social disapproval of their activities was not a ground for denying them charitable status. The Attorney-General decided to appeal against the Commissioners' decision to the High Court, but later discontinued his action. See [1981] Ch Com Rep 25–27 (paras 71–73); [1982] Ch Com Rep 14 (paras 36–38) and 46–8, App C

[118] FW Newark, 'Public benefit and religious trusts' (1946) 62 LQR 244, 254

[119] Decision of the Charity Commissioners (17 Nov 1999), *Application for Registration as a Charity by the Church of Scientology (England and Wales)*, 45. For other aspects of this decision, see ch 10, para 10.59

[120] See above, para 4.33

If a gift is for the advancement of religion in general terms without specifying a **4.35** particular faith, it will be presumed to be for the established church,[121] but this presumption is easily rebutted by extrinsic evidence of the testator's or settlor's intention.[122]

Belief in a supreme being

With one recognized exception, namely Buddhism,[123] belief in a superior and **4.36** supernatural being is essential if the doctrine or creed is to comprise a religion. Certain Chinese obituary ceremonies involving the leaving of food and the saying of prayers to aid the spirit of the deceased, but not apparently involving belief in a superior being, do not meet this requirement.[124] It has been said that a trust for any kind of monotheistic theism would be a good charitable trust;[125] but it remains unsettled whether a polytheistic religion may be included.[126]

An atheistic or agnostic organization cannot comprise a charity for the advance- **4.37** ment of religion, although it may achieve charitable status under another head of charity. In *Re South Place Ethical Society*,[127] the Ethical Society existed to cultivate what it described as 'a rational religious sentiment'. It was clear, however, that 'religious' in this context did not connote a belief in a supreme being, but rather in the excellence of truth, love, and beauty. It was in fact an agnostic society, neither affirming nor denying the existence of God, or of a god. Dillon J held that the Society could not be a charity for the advancement of religion, saying that ethical principles concern man's relations with man, whereas religious principles concern man's relations with God.[128]

Although freemasonry holds out certain standards of truth and justice by which **4.38** members are urged to regulate their conduct, it has been held that these qualities themselves do not add up to the advancement of religion.[129]

---

[121] eg *Re Darling* [1896] 1 Ch 50

[122] *Re Barker's Will Trusts* (1948) 64 TLR 273 (gift merely 'for God's work' applied, in accordance with the testator's intention, to the purposes of the Baptist Church)

[123] In *R v Registrar General, ex p Segerdal* [1970] 2 QB 697, 707, Lord Denning MR treated Buddhism as an exception; but it might be argued that Buddhism does indeed recognize a supreme being, as was contended in an affidavit supplied to the court in *Re South Place Ethical Society* [1980] 1 WLR 1565, 1573, by Christmas Humphries QC, the eminent English Buddhist. In that case, Dillon J, whilst accepting that Buddhism was indeed a religion for the law of charities, chose to leave this particular point open

[124] *Yeap Cheah Neo v Ong Cheng Neo* (1875) LR 6 PC 381; FW Newark, 'Public benefit and religious trusts' (1946) 62 LQR 244, 251, 256

[125] *Bowman v Secular Society* [1917] AC 406, 449 (Lord Parker of Waddington)

[126] The Charity Commissioners treat Hinduism as a religion, even though it is polytheistic, with a trinity of gods comprising Brahma (the creator), Vishnu (the preserver), and Shiva (the destroyer). See, eg, [1976] Ch Com Rep 29 (paras 109–111)

[127] [1980] 1 WLR 1565

[128] ibid, 1571. His Lordship nevertheless held the Society to be charitable under the second and fourth heads of *Pemsel*'s case

[129] *United Grand Lodge of Ancient, Free and Accepted Masons of England v Holborn BC* [1957] 1 WLR 1080 (Donovan J). See also *R v Registrar General, ex p Segerdal* [1970] 2 QB 697, which

4.39 A trust to promote faith-healing as practised by a particular religious group has been held to be charitable for the advancement of religion.[130] The position of spiritualism, however, remains uncertain. In *Re Hummeltenberg*,[131] Russell J held that a college for the training of spiritualist mediums was not charitable; but the case was argued only under the second and fourth heads of *Pemsel's* case, not on the footing that it might be charitable for the advancement of religion.[132] In the light of the authorities, the Charity Commissioners do not recognize paganism as a charitable purpose.[133]

4.40 The Charity Commissioners have registered as a charity a trust for the advancement of religion in the Church of England by means which included exorcism.[134] This was only after the Commissioners had received a statement from the body indicating its firm intention to practise exorcism solely in accordance with the guidelines laid down by the Archbishop of Canterbury.

Worship of a supreme being

4.41 Religion involves, not merely belief in a supreme being, but also worship of that being.[135] The characteristics of worship are submission or supplication to the supreme being, veneration and reverence of that being, and praise, thanskgiving, prayer, or intercession;[136] and at least some of these elements must be present if a belief system is to obtain registration as a charity.[137] The Charity Commissioners

---

concerned the question of whether the Church of Scientology was entitled to registration under the Places of Worship Registration Act 1855 of a building which it used as a place of meeting for religious worship. Lord Denning MR expressed the view that the Church of Scientology's creed was more a philosophy of life than a religion involving the reverence or veneration of God or of a supreme being: ibid, 707

[130] *Re le Cren Clarke* (sub nom *Funnell v Stewart*) [1996] 1 WLR 288 (ChD). On the facts, it was also held charitable under the fourth head

[131] [1923] 1 Ch 237

[132] The Charity Commissioners have registered as charitable a non-denominational organization called The National Federation of Spiritualist Healers; but this seems to be explicable as being for the purpose of healing under *Pemsel's* fourth head

[133] In 1996, the Charity Commissioners registered as a charity The Pagan Hospice and Funeral Trust. It appears that this was on the ground that its purposes were caring for the sick and dying, rather than the promotion of paganism itself; but the Commissioners have since removed it from the register. They have also removed from the register a foundation set up in 1989 called Odinhof, the purpose of which is to promote the ancient teachings and philosophy of Odin and to advance education. See J Harlow, 'Pagans stripped of charity status' Sunday Times 31 Oct 1999. The Charity Commissioners have not published their views on the charitable status or otherwise of paganism, but it seems that they do not treat the promotion of paganism as being for the advancement of religion. If, however, it is accepted that paganism involves the worship of gods (both male and female), the promotion of paganism would appear to be prima facie charitable under the third head

[134] *Power, Praise and Healing Mission* [1976] Ch Com Rep 19–20 (paras 65–8)

[135] *Re South Place Ethical Society* [1980] 1 WLR 1565, 1572 (Dillon J)

[136] *R v Registrar General, ex p Segerdal* [1970] 2 QB 697, 709 (Buckley LJ)

[137] See Decision of the Charity Commisioners (17 Nov 1999), *Application for Registration as a Charity by the Church of Scientology (England and Wales)*, 26–7

recently decided not to register the Church of Scientology (England and Wales) as a charity because inter alia, although they accepted that Scientology involves belief in a supreme being, they did not consider that its activities of auditing (a one-to-one exploration of the individual's past life) and training (the intensive study of Scientology scripture) constituted worship for the purposes of charity law.[138] Auditing was essentially akin to counselling, and training was more like an educational activity.[139]

Must not be immoral

It might be 'that the tenets of a particular sect inculcate doctrines adverse to the very foundations of all religion, and that they are subversive of all morality'.[140] Such a sect, or a trust to promote the work of such a sect, will not be for the advancement of religion, and a bequest for such a purpose will be void.[141] This proposition would self-evidently deny charitable status to objects concerned with devil-worship, Satanism, or the arts of black magic. **4.42**

(2) Purpose must advance religion

A trust for religious purposes *per se* is not charitable under the third head: the trust must be for the advancement of religion, but this the courts seem ready to presume.[142] Advancement of religion means:[143] **4.43**

> the promotion of spiritual teaching in a wide sense and the maintenance of the doctrines on which it rests, and the observances that serve to promote and manifest it— not merely a foundation or cause to which it can be related.

It has also been said that[144] **4.44**

> [t]o advance religion means to promote it, to spread the message ever wider among mankind; to take some positive steps to sustain and increase religious belief; and these things are done in a variety of ways which may be comprehensively described as pastoral and missionary.

An example of the difference between 'religion' and 'the advancement of religion' has been furnished by Lord Denning:[145] **4.45**

---

[138] ibid, 27

[139] ibid

[140] *Thornton v Howe* (1862) 31 Beav 14, 20 (Romilly MR)

[141] ibid

[142] *Re White* [1893] 2 Ch 41 (CA); *Re Ward* [1941] Ch 308 (Clauson J); see also *Re Lloyd* (1893) 10 TLR 66 (gift for 'religious and benevolent' objects held charitable)

[143] *Keren Kayemeth Le Jisroel v IRC* [1931] 2 KB 465, 477 (Lord Hanworth MR); affd [1932] AC 650. See also *Re Thackrah* [1939] 2 All ER 4 (Bennett J)

[144] *United Grand Lodge of Ancient, Free and Accepted Masons of England v Holborn BC* [1957] 1 WLR 1080, 1090 (Donovan J)

[145] *National Deposit Friendly Society Trustees v Skegness UDC* [1959] AC 293, 322

> The word 'advancement' connotes, to my mind, the concept of public benefit. . . .
> When a man says his prayers in the privacy of his own bedroom, he may truly be
> concerned with religion but not with 'the advancement of religion'.

(3) Public benefit

4.46 The courts have stated on a number of occasions that it is prima facie assumed that
the advancement of religion is for the public benefit.[146] This evidently means only
that it is presumed that the doctrines inculcated by a particular religion are for the
public benefit; and, unless it is shown that such doctrines are immoral, the court
will treat them as charitable, no matter that it considers them foolish or even
devoid of foundation.[147] It is not, however, presumed that a religious purpose will
benefit a sufficient section of the community; so that, when 'public benefit' is used
in this latter sense, it is clear that, for a purpose to be charitable under this third
head of *Pemsel*, a public benefit must be shown.[148]

Enclosed orders

4.47 In *Gilmour v Coats*,[149] the testator had bequeathed property upon trust for the
purposes of a Carmelite convent. The Carmelites are a cloistered and purely contemplative order, and the nuns never venture beyond the convent walls. The
House of Lords held that this was not a charitable trust, as it was not a purpose
which benefited the public. The Roman Catholic Church had argued that there
was benefit: first, through intercessory prayer, in that the nuns prayed for God to
help members of the public; and, secondly, that their cloistered lives brought spiritual edification to the community. Lord Simonds, however, said that it was not
enough that the Roman Catholic Church believed that intercessory prayer and
spiritual edification benefited the public. Such benefits had to be proven as a matter of law; yet the value of the intercessory prayer was one of belief and was not susceptible to judicial proof, and any alleged public benefit in edification by example
was too vague and intangible to satisfy the prescribed test.[150]

Religious writings

4.48 The leading case is *Thornton v Howe*,[151] where Romilly MR said that Joanna
Southcote's writings, though foolish and in great measure incoherent and con-

---

[146] eg *National Anti-Vivisection Society v IRC* [1948] AC 31, 42 (Lord Wright), 65 (Lord
Simonds); *Re Watson* [1973] 1 WLR 1472, 1482 (Plowman J). For the Charity Commissioners'
view as to what evidence might rebut the presumption, see Decision of the Charity Commissioners
(17 Nov 1999); *Application for Registration as a Charity by the Church of Scientology (England and
Wales)*, discussed in ch 10, para 10.59
[147] *Thornton v Howe* (1862) 31 Beav 14, 20
[148] *Gilmour v Coats* [1949] AC 426 (HL)
[149] ibid
[150] ibid, 446. The public benefit aspect of this case is considered further in ch 5, para 5.16
[151] (1862) 31 Beav 14

fused, were not immoral or irreligious, and contained nothing which could shatter the faith of any sincere Christian;[152] and he held that a devise upon trust to print, publish and propagate such writings was charitable.

The decision of the House of Lords in *Gilmour v Coats*,[153] although not concerned **4.49** with publication of religious tracts or books, contrasts markedly with the liberal approach of the court in *Thornton v Howe*, and might be thought to have cast doubt on the validity of Romilly MR's judgment. After all, the Roman Catholic Church has many millions of adherents in every part of the globe, whereas Joanna Southcote's scribblings were of little concern to anyone other than the members of a particular fanatical religious sect.

The soundness of Romilly MR's views was, however, affirmed in *Re Watson*,[154] **4.50** which Plowman J treated as being on all fours with *Thornton v Howe*. In *Re Watson*, a testatrix left property upon trust 'for the continuance of the work of God as it has been maintained by Mr H G Hobbs and myself'. The said Hobbs was a friend of the testatrix and the leading light in their small group of non-denominational Christians. A Professor of Theology from King's College, London, gave evidence that Mr Hobbs' voluminous religious writings (a ton of which was stored in the testatrix's home) were of no intrinsic worth, but that they were not subversive of morality and might confirm Christians in their faith. Plowman J held the gift charitable in reliance on *Thornton v Howe*; unfortunately, whilst mentioned in Plowman J's judgment, *Gilmour v Coats* was not discussed.

It nevertheless seems that the cases can be reconciled. The crucial distinction **4.51** between them would appear to be that in *Gilmour v Coats* the benefits recognized as such by the law of charity were restricted to within the convent walls; whereas in each of *Thornton v Howe* and *Re Watson*, the benefits were (through publication) made available to the public at large. In all three cases, public benefit in the first sense was met; but *Gilmour v Coats* alone failed to satisfy the test of public benefit in the second sense. Another way of expressing this might be to say that, whilst the trusts in all three cases concerned religion, the trust purpose in *Gilmour v Coats* was not concerned with the advancement of religion.

Retreat houses

In one case, the provision of a retreat house for the Church of England has been **4.52** held not to be charitable on the ground that the benefit would accrue only to those who were to stay there, rather than to the public at large.[155] A later decision, however, took the view that a retreat house could be charitable if it reached out to the

---

[152] ibid, 19–20
[153] [1949] AC 426 (HL)
[154] [1973] 1 WLR 1472
[155] *Re Warre's Will Trusts* [1953] 1 WLR 725 (Harman J)

public.[156] There is a strong argument that the provision of an Anglican retreat house does benefit a sufficient section of the community since those who enter it do so for short periods only, and otherwise mix with their fellow citizens in the world.[157] Under this third head of *Pemsel*, such indirect public benefit ought to suffice.[158]

Religious ceremonies and masses

4.53   The issue of public benefit has also arisen in relation to carrying out of religious ceremonies and masses. The public benefit requirement is satisfied if a religious rite is in public.[159]

4.54   In the nineteenth century, the Privy Council held that a gift for the performance of Chinese religious ceremonies to the testatrix and her late husband was not charitable, as it lacked any public advantage, being of benefit or solace only to the family itself.[160] Additionally, although it is not clear from that case, it would appear that such a ceremony does not involve the worship of a superior being, and so is not 'religious' in the sense required for *Pemsel*'s third head.[161]

4.55   Most recently, in *Re Hetherington's Will Trusts*,[162] a testatrix made a bequest of £2,000 to the Roman Catholic Bishop of Westminster for the saying of masses for the souls of the testatrix, her husband, her parents, and her sisters, and gave the residue of her estate to a specific Roman Catholic church for masses for her soul. Browne-Wilkinson V-C held that both gifts were charitable for the advancement of religion. He considered that only a gift for the saying of masses in public would be charitable, as private masses would lack the element of public benefit. The will did not specify how the masses were to be conducted, but his Lordship decided that a benign construction should be put upon the gifts to enable them to be saved for charity by being construed as capable of being carried out by charitable means only. He therefore construed them as valid charitable gifts for the saying of masses in public.

(4) Religious societies

4.56   In the light of *Gilmour v Coats*,[163] the Charity Commissioners will require evidence that an abbey, monastery, or convent promotes religion in a way which

---

[156]   *Re Banfield* [1968] 1 WLR 846, 852

[157]   cf *Neville Estates Ltd v Madden* [1962] Ch 832, 853 (Cross J)

[158]   See also the trenchant criticisms of *Re Warre's Will Trusts* [1953] 1 WLR 725 in H Picarda, *The Law and Practice Relating to Charities* (3rd edn, Butterworths, 1999) 109–10

[159]   *Gilmour v Coats* [1949] AC 426, 459 (Lord Reid)

[160]   *Yeap Cheah Neo v Ong Cheng Neo* (1875) LR 6 PC 381

[161]   FW Newark, 'Public benefit and religious trusts' (1946) 62 LQR 245, 251, 256

[162]   [1990] Ch 1

[163]   [1949] AC 426 (HL), approving *Cocks v Manners* (1871) LR 12 Eq 574

confers a sufficient degree of public benefit before registering it as a charity.[164] Even if the apparent purposes of a religious society, as disclosed in its constitution, are not charitable in law (for example, the personal sanctification of the members of order by prayer and contemplation), it is necessary to determine whether those expressed purposes are its true purposes, and, if they are not, what those actual purposes are. To determine what its actual purposes are, it is permissible to look at the activities which the society carries on; if it is found that it engages in substantial activities of a charitable nature, the society will be a charity if such activities indicate that its purposes are wholly and exclusively charitable, any element of self-sanctification being merely incidental.[165]

The Charity Commissioners considered this issue recently in *The Society of the* **4.57** *Precious Blood*.[166] The Society was an enclosed community of Anglican Nuns which had applied to be registered as a charity. The primary purpose of the Society as indicated in its constitution was contemplation, and the first work of the Sisters was stated to be intercessory prayer. The Society was not entirely withdrawn from the outside world, however: it had associate members who were a part of the Society, but lived outside; it was involved with the community through a counselling and support service which it ran; it permitted members of the community (including school children) to visit the Abbey for educational purposes, including the study of archaeology and history; the Sisters gave talks to visitors on religious issues; and the Abbey offered retreat facilities to outsiders. Although retreat houses are not *per se* charitable,[167] the Charity Commissioners considered that the work of the Society revealed a substantial charitable element for the public benefit. In view of this, and the fact that the Society's constitution should not be taken to define its whole purposes, the Commissioners expressed the view that it might be argued that the charitable activities were an outward manifestation of the life of intercessory prayer, and were therefore its true purposes. However, in order to avoid any doubt, the Commissioners recommended to the Society that its constitution (which was capable of amendment) be changed to reflect more clearly that its actual purposes were charitable, the contemplative purposes being only a means, or a consequence, of the carrying out of such charitable purposes. The amendments were made, and the Society was subsequently registered as a charity.

A trust for a religious society may also advance religion indirectly. In **4.58** *Re Charlesworth*,[168] a bequest upon trust to provide a dinner at the annual meeting

---

[164] See *Caldey Abbey* [1969] Ch Com Rep 9 (para 19) (evidence that services in the abbey were open to the public at all times, and priests were sent out to serve in parishes on the mainland; the Commissioners were satisfied that these elements comprised sufficient public benefit)

[165] These principles can be derived from *Cocks v Manners* (1871) LR 12 Eq 574, and *Re Delaney* [1902] Ch 642

[166] (1995) 3 Decisions 11–17

[167] *Re Warre's Will Trusts* [1953] 1 WLR 725

[168] (1910) 26 TLR 214

of the members of a society of clergymen was held to be charitable; the society itself was charitable for the advancement of religion, and the gift would advance that purpose since, by relieving the members of the expense of the dinner, it would encourage them to attend the meetings, so furthering the society's work.

(5) Missionary purposes

4.59 The purpose of converting heathens is a charitable purpose for the advancement of religion, whether overseas[169] or in the United Kingdom.[170] A trust to publish and distribute religious writings, books, or tracts is also charitable,[171] provided there is nothing in them which is immoral or against all religion.[172]

(6) Church buildings, fabric, and music

4.60 The repair of churches is charitable within the letter of the Preamble,[173] and from this the courts have held to be charitable gifts for the enhancement of the fabric of a church,[174] the provision of church ornaments,[175] the maintenance of the church organ,[176] and the benefit of the choir.[177] A trust for the ringing of church bells is not charitable *per se*; therefore a bequest to have particular church bells rung half-muffled on the anniversary of the testator's death was a mere private benefit, and was held to be not charitable.[178] Difficult to reconcile with this general principle, however, is *Re Pardoe*,[179] where a gift to have the bells of a parish church rung on 29 May each year to commemorate the restoration of the monarchy was held to be charitable for the advancement of religion; perhaps the fact that the monarch is the head of the Established Church might give it some tenuous connection with the advancement of religion.

4.61 A gift to repair a churchyard is charitable by analogy with the repair of the church itself,[180] and (by a further analogy) the maintenance of a burial ground for mem-

---

[169] *A-G v City of London* (1790) 1 Ves 243; *Comrs for Special Purposes of the Income Tax v Pemsel* [1891] AC 531 (HL) (to advance the missionary establishments of the Moravian Church among the heathen nations of the world)

[170] *West v Shuttleworth* (1835) 2 My & K 684 (Pepys MR) ('to promote the knowledge of the Catholic Church religion amongst the poor and ignorant inhabitants of Swale Dale and Wenston Dale in the county of York')

[171] *Thornton v Howe* (1862) 31 Beav 14; *Re Watson* [1973] 1 WLR 1472

[172] *Thornton v Howe* (1862) 31 Beav 14, 20

[173] *A-G v Ruper* (1722) 2 P Wms 125, 126 (Jekyll MR)

[174] eg *Re King* [1923] 1 Ch 243 (trust to set stained-glass windows in a church)

[175] *Hoare v Osborne* (1866) LR 1 Eq 585

[176] *Adnam v Cole* (1843) 6 Beav 353

[177] *Re Royce* [1940] Ch 514

[178] *Re Arber* The Times, 13 Dec 1919

[179] [1906] 2 Ch 184 (Kekewich J)

[180] *A-G v Blizard* (1855) 21 Beav 233; *Re Vaughan* (1886) 33 Ch D 187

bers of a particular denomination is also charitable.[181] A gift to maintain an individual tomb (as opposed to all the tombs in a churchyard) is not charitable in English law, however, as it lacks any public benefit.[182]

(7) Gifts for the benefit of the clergy

A gift for the benefit or support of the clergy is charitable as being for the advancement of religion. Such gifts can include the training of the clergy,[183] the provision of clergymen and preachers,[184] the increase of clerical stipends,[185] and rest homes for the clergy of a particular diocese.[186] **4.62**

D. Other purposes beneficial to the community

Although Lord Macnaghten in *Pemsel's* case did not qualify his fourth head, it is clear that not all purposes beneficial to the community are charitable: they must still be purposes either expressed in, or analogous to purposes expressed in, the Preamble to the Statute of Elizabeth.[187] In other words, the purpose must still fall either within the letter or within 'the spirit and intendment' of the Preamble.[188] For this reason, a trust (inter alia) to promote the bonds of unity between the Union of South Africa and the United Kingdom was held not to be charitable: although the purpose was 'undoubtedly for the benefit of the community', it was not charitable 'in the same sense' as the purposes recited in the Preamble.[189] **4.63**

---

[181] *Re Manser* [1905] Ch 68. Such analogies have since extended beyond the third head and into the fourth: see *Scottish Burial Reform and Cremation Society Ltd v Glasgow City Corp* [1968] AC 138 (HL), discussed below, para 4.64

[182] *Doe d Thompson v Pitcher* (1815) 3 M & S 407; *Mellick v President of the Asylum* (1821) 1 Jacob 180; *Fowler v Fowler* (1864) 33 Beav 616 (Romilly MR); *Re Dalziel* [1943] Ch 277

[183] *Re Williams* [1927] 2 Ch 283

[184] *Pember v Inhabitants of Kington* (1639) 1 Eq Cas Abr 95 (to maintain a preaching minister); *Dundee Magistrates v Dundee Presbytery* (1861) 4 Macq 228 (HL)

[185] *A-G v Steward* (1872) LR 14 Eq 17

[186] *Re James* [1932] 2 Ch 25

[187] *A-G v National Provincial & Union Bank of England* [1924] AC 262, 265 (HL); *Re Macduff* [1896] 2 Ch 451, 470, 475 (Rigby LJ); *National Anti-Vivisection Society v IRC* [1948] AC 31, 41 (Lord Wright)

[188] *Re Macduff* [1896] 2 Ch 451, 467 (Lindley LJ: 'In deciding the case we must fall back upon the Statute of Elizabeth, not upon the strict or narrow words of it, but upon what has been called the spirit of it, or the intention of it'). See also *Univ of London v Yarrow* (1857) 1 De G & J 72, 79 (Lord Cranworth LC: 'The Court have always construed the [Statute of Elizabeth] as applying to objects of the same nature as those specified'); *Williams' Trustees v IRC* [1947] AC 447, 455 (Lord Simonds); *Re Strakosch* [1949] 1 Ch 529, 537 (CA); *Camille and Henry Dreyfus Foundation Inc v IRC* [1954] 1 Ch 672, 683 (Evershed MR: 'within the scope and meaning of the Elizabethan preamble')

[189] *Re Strakosch* [1949] 1 Ch 529, 537–8 (Lord Greene MR). See also *Anglo-Swedish Society v IRC* (1931) 47 TLR 295, where Rowlatt J held that, whilst a trust to promote a closer and more sympathetic understanding between the English and Swedish peoples was a trust of public utility, it was not charitable since he could not see how the purpose 'touched the area . . . marked out by the Statute of Elizabeth'

Similarly, '[h]ealthy and manly sports are certainly in fact beneficial to the public, but . . . are not generally entitled to qualify as charitable objects'.[190] Again, a bequest to vicars and churchwardens of two named churches 'for parish work' was evidently beneficial to the community, but failed because it did not fall within the spirit and intendment of the Preamble.[191] For the same reason, the House of Lords has held that a trust to establish an institute in London for the benefit of Welsh people in London with a view to the promoting the moral, social, spiritual, and educational welfare of Welsh people and fostering the study of the Welsh language and culture, was not charitable: the purpose, even if beneficial to the community, was not within the spirit and intendment of the Preamble.[192]

4.64 The courts initially appear to have developed the fourth head by drawing analogies with purposes specified in the Preamble; later, they became content to find an analogy with a purpose already held charitable as being itself analogous to a purpose within the fourth head.[193] The correctness of this approach was affirmed and applied by the House of Lords in *Scottish Burial Reform and Cremation Society Ltd v Glasgow City Corporation*.[194] The purpose of the Society was to provide cremation facilities in a secular context. The House of Lords held this to be a charitable purpose within the fourth head of *Pemsel* through a step-by-step approach. The Preamble itself states that the repair of churches is a charitable purpose. In *Re Vaughan*,[195] North J, saying that he could see no difference between a trust to repair God's House and a trust to repair God's Acre, held charitable a trust to repair a churchyard. By analogy with this case, a burial ground for dissenters (although not within the curtilage of a church) was held charitable in *Re Manser*.[196] By analogy with this, in *Re Eighmie*,[197] the court held charitable (although secular rather than religious) a trust for the maintenance of a cemetery owned and managed by a local authority. It was by drawing a further analogy with this last decision that the House of Lords, in the *Scottish Burial* case, was able to hold the provision of cremation facilities itself charitable within the fourth head. It is, however, dangerous to reason by analogy from one head of charity to another.[198]

---

[190] *National Anti-Vivisection Society v IRC* [1948] AC 31, 41–2 (Lord Wright)
[191] *Farley v Westminster Bank Ltd* [1939] AC 430, as explained by Lord Simonds in *Williams' Trustees v IRC* [1947] AC 447, 457
[192] *Williams' Trustees v IRC* [1947] AC 447 (HL)
[193] *Scottish Burial Reform and Cremation Society Ltd v Glasgow City Corp* [1968] AC 138, 147 (Lord Reid)
[194] [1968] AC 138
[195] (1886) 33 ChD 187, 192
[196] [1905] 1 Ch 279
[197] [1935] Ch 524
[198] *Gilmour v Coats* [1949] AC 426, 449 (Lord Simonds); *Neville Estates Ltd v Madden* [1962] Ch 832, 853 (Cross J)

Even in the *Scottish Burial* case itself, their Lordships were not all satisfied of the   **4.65**
merits of the step-by-step approach. Lord Upjohn considered that the result was
that the spirit and intendment of the Preamble had been 'stretched almost to
breaking point'.[199] A different approach was advocated by Russell LJ in
Incorporated Council of Law Reporting for England and Wales v Attorney-General.[200]
He said that,[201] when considering the fourth head in *Pemsel's* case, 'other purposes
beneficial to the community', or 'objects of general public utility',[202]

> the courts, in consistently saying that not all such are necessarily charitable in law,
> are in substance accepting that if a purpose is shown to be so beneficial or of such
> utility it is prima facie charitable in law, but have left open a line of retreat based on
> the equity of the Statute [of Elizabeth] in case they are faced with a purpose (e.g. a
> political purpose) which could not have been within the contemplation of the
> Statute even if the then legislators had been endowed with the gift of foresight into
> the circumstances of later centuries.
>
> In a case such as the present, in which in my view the object cannot be thought
> otherwise than beneficial to the community and of general public utility, I believe
> the proper question to ask is whether there are any grounds for holding it to be out-
> side the equity of the Statute.

This approach has been approved by some commentators as a welcome rational-
ization of this branch of the law,[203] and the Charity Commissioners have placed
reliance upon it;[204] it does not, however, so far appear to have affected the traditional judicial approach in the fourth head of looking for a purpose within the
spirit or intendment of the Preamble to the Statute of Elizabeth.[205]

The meaning of charity also changes over time. In the *National Anti-Vivisection*   **4.66**
Society case,[206] Lord Simonds said that a change in social habits and needs, or a
change in the law, or increased knowledge, may result in a purpose which once
appeared to be beneficial being seen to be truly detrimental to the community.[207]

---

[199] *Scottish Burial Reform and Cremation Society v Glasgow City Corporation* [1968] AC 138, 153
[200] [1972] Ch 73
[201] ibid, 88
[202] So called by Sir Samuel Romilly (then Mr Romilly) *arguendo* in *Morice v Bishop of Durham*
(1805) 10 Ves 522, 531. Romilly's phrase seems to be used increasingly in the modern cases, eg
Inland Revenue Commissioners v Oldham Training and Enterprise Council [1996] STC 1218, 1234
(Lightman J)
[203] See H Cohen, 'Four Heads are Better than . . .' [1978] NLJ Annual Charities Review, 6,
10–12
[204] eg *Council of Industrial Design* [1973] Ch Com Rep 23–24 (paras 68–70), at 24 (para 70),
where the Charity Commissioners applied Russell LJ's test as an alternative basis for holding that the
Council was established for charitable purposes
[205] Indeed, in Australia, Russell LJ's approach has been expressly rejected: *Royal National
Agricultural and Industrial Assoc v Chester* (1974) 3 ALR 486. See also *Brisbane City Council v A-G
for Queensland* [1979] AC 411, 422 (Lord Wilberforce) (PC). More recently, however, Lord
Browne-Wilkinson, expressing the view of the Judicial Committee, said that 'Russell LJ's aproach
has much to commend it': *A-G of the Caymen Islands v Wahr-Hansen* [2000] 3 All ER 642, 647 (PC)
[206] *National Anti-Vivisection Society v IRC* [1948] AC 31
[207] ibid, 74

In *Gilmour v Coats* he similarly stated that there may be circumstances in which the court will, in a later age, hold an object not to be charitable which in an earlier age has been held to possess that virtue; although he added that only a radical change of circumstances established by sufficient evidence should compel the court to accept a new view of the matter.[208]

4.67 In practice, since so few cases on charitable status reach the courts, the approach of the Charity Commissioners is of particular importance. In the light of the continuing adherence of the courts to the traditional approach, the Commissioners recognize that, when faced with a novel purpose which appears remote from any purpose which the existing law recognizes as charitable, they must look for some analogy. Nevertheless, the broad approach advocated by Russell LJ in the *Incorporated Council of Law Reporting* case has evidently encouraged the Commissioners to take 'a constructive approach in adapting the concept of charity to meet the constantly evolving needs of society'.[209] The Commissioners do not, therefore, restrict themselves to close analogies; they have stated that 'it was difficult to envisage a case otherwise suitable for registration where some analogy could not be found, given a generous as opposed to a restrictive view'.[210] Within the fourth head, the Commissioners are therefore looking for a clear charitable intent within the spirit of the Preamble; and, in taking account of their own decisions, as well as those of the courts, and of legislation passed by Parliament, they consider that they should act 'constructively and imaginatively'.[211]

4.68 In determining whether an object is for the public benefit within the fourth head, the Charity Commissioners may, where appropriate, invite argument from the promoters and may seek the view of other interested groups.[212]

4.69 The fourth head of *Pemsel* therefore covers a wide range of purposes; indeed, it is impossible to enumerate all the purposes for the benefit of the public which are capable of falling within the spirit and intendment of the Preamble. As Lord Evershed MR said in his dissenting judgment in *Re Cole*,[213]

> The truth may be that the possible variations of expressed intention by testators and settlors are as the sands of the sea, and that no catalogue of illustrations, however long, can exhaust or confine charity's scope.

---

[208] [1949] AC 426, 443
[209] [1985] Ch Com Rep 12 (para 27)
[210] [1985] Ch Com Rep 11 (paras. 24–7); see also (1994) 2 Decisions 5, 6–9, where the Commissioners repeated their continued adherence to this approach
[211] [1985] Ch Com Rep 12 (para 27)
[212] See, eg, the case of *Public Concern at Work*, where the Charity Commissioners sought the views of the Confederation of British Industry, the Securities and Investments Board and seven major companies as to whether certain objects in a draft objects clause were for the public benefit: these objects included the provision of advice and assistance to employees and officers who faced moral and ethical issues concerned with what might be essentially termed 'whistle-blowing': (1994) 2 Decisions 5, 10
[213] [1958] Ch 877, 891

(1) Relief of the aged

The 'relief of aged . . . people' is the first purpose specified in the Preamble. Many **4.70**
trusts or other charities for the relief of the aged are also for the relief of poverty
(many almshouses were for poor elderly residents); but the relief of elderly persons
is charitable independently of poverty, since the words 'aged, impotent and poor
people' in the Preamble, are to be construed disjunctively.[214] A recreational centre
for the elderly can therefore be charitable without its having to restrict its facilities
to those who are poor as well as old. The relief of aged persons is therefore more
appropriately treated under *Pemsel*'s fourth head. The relief of the aged can take
many forms, including the provision of medical care, day-centres for the elderly,
and the provision of housing or other accommodation.[215]

(2) Relief of disabled persons

The Preamble mentions 'the relief of . . . impotent . . . people'. In modern lan- **4.71**
guage, this refers to persons under a physical or mental disability. Like the relief of
the aged, the relief of the disabled is not limited to those who are also poor.[216] The
relief of the disabled can take many forms, including the provision of guide dogs
for the blind,[217] the provision to the disabled of means of personal transporta-
tion,[218] and the promotion of understanding of the causes of disablement and
understanding of the ways in which such causes may be eliminated or reduced.[219]

(3) Relief of distress

The mention in the Preamble of ' the relief of . . . impotent . . . people' provides a **4.72**
basis for the charitable status of relieving, not merely those who are disabled, but
also those who are in distress or merely weak.

Rest homes

Homes of rest for lady teachers,[220] and for persons engaged in a trade or profes- **4.73**
sion,[221] or a calling,[222] or for members of the public generally,[223] are charitable.

---

[214] *Re Glyn's Will Trusts* [1950] 2 All ER 1150n; *Re Robinson* [1951] Ch 198; *Joseph Rowntree Memorial Trust Housing Assoc Ltd v A-G* [1983] Ch 159

[215] *Joseph Rowntree Memorial Trust Housing Assoc Ltd v A-G* [1983] Ch 159

[216] eg *Re Lewis* [1955] Ch 104 (gift to 10 blind boys and 10 blind girls, Tottenham residents if possible, not to be restricted to such as were also poor)

[217] eg the Guide Dogs for the Blind Association (which makes no charge for the provision of guide dogs to blind persons, whatever their means); see also *Sarah Mary Collard Fund for the Provision of Guide Dogs* [1983] Ch Com Rep 20 (paras 57–8)

[218] *Motability* [1977] Ch Com Rep 18–19 (paras 51–6)

[219] *The Royal Assoc for Disability and Rehabilitation* [1977] Ch Com Rep 19–20 (para 57)

[220] *Re Estlin* (1903) 72 LJ Ch 687

[221] *IRC v Trustees of Roberts Marine Mansions* (1927) 43 TLR 270 (CA)

[222] *Re James* [1932] 2 Ch 25 (nuns); *Re White's Will Trusts* [1951] 1 All ER 528 (nurses); *Finch v Poplar Corp* (1967) 66 LGR 324 (seamen)

[223] *Re Chaplin* [1933] Ch 115

Temporary rest is included.[224] In some cases the provision of the home or rest home might be additionally explained as being for the promotion of other charitable purposes, such as the relief of poverty, the advancement of education or religion, or the promotion of public health; but the relief of distress provides an independent basis for their charitable nature. The potential residents must, however, comprise a sufficient section of the community.[225]

Welfare of children and young persons

4.74 The Preamble mentions 'the education and preferment of orphans', and the promotion of the welfare of children is a charitable purpose. As Lord Hailsham has stated:[226]

> the welfare of children, particularly of young children at risk of maltreatment by adults, has been, from the earliest days, a concern of the Crown, as parens patriae, an object of legal charities and in latter years the subject of a whole series of Acts of Parliament.

4.75 The provision and maintenance of an orphanage or a children's home is charitable.[227] A gift of the income of a fund for the 'general benefit and welfare' of the children in a home which included children who had been in trouble with the police and children beyond their parents' control was held not charitable, however, since the terms of the gift might enable it to be applied for things such as television sets which the court did not think came within the concept of charity to be found in the Preamble.[228]

4.76 The Preamble also mentions 'the marriages of poor maids'. Such gifts might be treated as being for the relief of poverty or for the welfare of young persons. Gifts for this purpose are charitable within the letter of the Preamble, but the purpose they formerly served is now obsolete, and they are likely to have been subject to an application cy-près.[229]

---

[224] *IRC v Trustees of Roberts Marine Mansions* (1927) 43 TLR 270 (CA)

[225] *Re Norgate* (1944) 88 Sol Jo 267n (rest home for vegetarians, teetotallers, pacifists, and conscientious objectors held not charitable)

[226] *D v NSPCC* [1978] AC 171, 228

[227] *Re Sahal's Will Trusts* [1958] 1 WLR 1243 (gift of house as a children's home held charitable)

[228] *Re Cole* [1958] Ch 877 (CA); appl (as regards the income of the fund 'for the benefit' of the children resident in a children's home) in *Re Sahal's Will Trusts* [1958] 1 WLR 1243

[229] But see the Maids' Money, Guildford, a charity created by a bequest by John How in 1674 for the marriage of poor maids, the winner to be decided at a ceremony on the throw of dice. Shortly after, there was a further bequest, Parson's Gift, for the loser; the income from the second having outstripped that of the first, it is better to lose. See B Nightingale, *Charities* (Allen Lane, 1973) 12–13

Prevention of alcoholism and drug addiction

To treat alcoholics, and to discourage alcoholism (provided the promotion of a **4.77** change in the law is not an expressed object[230]) is charitable.[231] The same principles apply to the treatment of drug addicts, and attempts to discourage the use of drugs other than for medical purposes.

Relief of refugees, emigrants, prisoners, and soldiers

The relief of refugees has been held charitable,[232] as has the assistance of poor emi- **4.78** grants.[233]

The Preamble lists 'the relief or redemption of prisoners or captives'. The relief of **4.79** prisoners is therefore within the letter of the Preamble;[234] as is the redemption of captives.[235] A trust for the relief of German soldiers disabled in the First World War has been held charitable.[236]

Another purpose contained in the Preamble is the 'setting out of soldiers'. In *Verge* **4.80** *v Somerville*,[237] the Privy Council decided that a trust for the relief of soldiers returning to New South Wales after the First World War was charitable because it would help to establish them in civilian life.

Distress arising from accident or disaster

The relief of distress provides a basis in the Preamble for the charitable status of **4.81** some disaster funds. To be charitable, the purpose of the fund must be to relieve the needs of those who have suffered, whether directly as victims or indirectly, such as members of victims' families.[238] 'Need' in this context does not itself connote poverty; a disaster fund may be charitable without also being for the relief of poverty, since the phrase 'aged, impotent and poor' in the Preamble is to be read disjunctively.[239] What is relieved is the person's distress, and although such relief

---

[230] *Re Hood* [1931] 1 Ch 240 250 (Lord Hanworth MR), 252 (Lawrence LJ) (CA); *IRC v Temperance Council* (1926) 136 LT 27
[231] *Inland Revenue Commissioners v Falkirk Temperance Café Trust* 1927 SC 261, 267 (Lord Sands), 269 (Lord Blackburn), 271 (Lord Ashmore); *Re Hood* [1931] 1 Ch 240, 249–50 (Lord Hanworth MR), 252 (Lawrence LJ)
[232] *Re Morrison* (1967) 111 Sol Jo 758
[233] *Re Tree* [1945] Ch 325
[234] *Re Prison Charities* (1873) LR 16 Eq 129 (Bacon V-C) (charities for the relief of poor prisoners, *ie* those imprisoned for debt)
[235] *A-G v Ironmongers' Company* (1840) 2 Beav 313; (1844) 10 Cl & Fin 908 (HL) (charity to redeem Christian slaves captured off the Barbary Coast)
[236] *Re Robinson* [1931] 2 Ch 122 (Maugham J)
[237] [1924] AC 496
[238] [1965] Ch Com Rep 17–19 (paras 54–8)
[239] *Re Glyn's Will Trusts* [1950] 2 All ER 1150n; *Re Robinson* [1951] Ch 198; *Joseph Rowntree Memorial Trust Housing Assoc Ltd v A-G* [1983] Ch 159

may include monetary help for those who are financially 'needy', it may include other forms of relief as well (for example, counselling services) which can benefit all those who have suffered, not merely the poor. Direct monetary payments, however, may be paid only to those who are in financial need.

4.82 To be charitable, the purposes of the disaster fund must be wholly and exclusively charitable; the inclusion of independent non-charitable purposes, such as 'worthy causes', amongst the objects of the fund will therefore prevent its being charitable.[240]

4.83 Unless a disaster fund is restricted to the relief of the distressed poor, the fund will be charitable only if the class of persons to benefit is a sufficient section of the community. Except for the purpose of the relief of poverty, those who are defined by reference to a nexus of employment are not a sufficient section of the public for the law of charity.[241] In the absence of a personal nexus, the matter is merely one of degree. Where the numbers of those who might benefit run into hundreds or more, there is no problem;[242] and even when the numbers are relatively small, the fund may be charitable: for example, a fund for the relief of the widows, orphans, and dependants of six fishermen who drowned when their boat capsized was held charitable.[243] A fund to relieve the distress of members of a single family, however, (unless restricted to the relief of poverty) would not be for a sufficient section of the community, and so could not be charitable.

4.84 Since many disaster funds are raised by means of public appeals, where it may be impossible to predict how much money will be raised, a well-drawn charitable disaster appeal will specify other charitable purposes to which any surplus in the fund will be applied after relieving the needs of those who have suffered distress.[244]

(4) The promotion of public health

4.85 The Preamble lists as charitable 'the maintenance of sick and maimed soldiers and mariners', and by analogy with this the promotion of public health is itself a charitable purpose. Thus a hospital is a charity, even if it charges fees, unless it is established for private profit.[245] The provision of an open area of land for use by the public for the purpose of sport or recreation is charitable for the promotion of public health.[246] By analogy with this, the Charity Commissioners have registered

---

[240] *Re Gillingham Bus Disaster Fund* [1958] Ch 300; affd [1959] Ch 62 (CA)
[241] *Re Hobourn Aero Components Ltd's Air Raid Distress Fund* [1946] Ch 194 (CA)
[242] eg *Pease v Pattinson* (1886) 32 ChD 154; *Re Hartley Colliery Accident Relief Fund* (1908) 102 LT 165n; *Re North Devon and West Somerset Relief Fund Trusts* [1953] 1 WLR 1260
[243] *Cross v Lloyd-Greame* (1909) 102 LT 163
[244] For a more detailed analysis of disaster appeal funds, see ch 25
[245] *Re Resch's Will Trusts* [1969] 1 AC 514 (PC)
[246] *IRC v Baddeley* [1955] AC 572 (HL)

as a charity a public ice-rink, inter alia, under the fourth head of *Pemsel*'s case.[247] The fact that an improvement in public health may be a consequence of the promotion of sport does not, in English law,[248] make the promotion of sport *per se* charitable as being for the promotion of public health.[249]

A trust to promote faith-healing as practised by a particular religious group has been held to be charitable (inter alia) under the fourth head.[250] **4.86**

In the past, the promotion of vegetarianism has been held to be a charitable purpose;[251] although this has since been doubted,[252] in the light of changing medical opinions on what constitutes a healthy diet and the causes of obesity and related health problems, it might now be plausibly argued that the promotion of vegetarianism is charitable as being for the promotion of public health under the fourth head. **4.87**

The Charity Commissioners have accepted that the giving of advice on contraception is charitable for the promotion of public health, and the means by which such primary purpose may be furthered can include the supply of contraceptive substances and appliances.[253] The Commissioners have also registered as a charity the British Pregnancy Advisory Service, whose purposes include the giving of advice, treatment, and assistance for women who are suffering from any physical **4.88**

---

[247] *Oxford Ice Skating Assoc* [1984] Ch Com Rep 11 (para 21). The Commissioners also considered it charitable under the Recreational CA 1958

[248] In Canada, however, the promotion of athletic sports has been held to be a charitable purpose for the promotion of health: *Re Laidlaw Foundation* [1984] 48 OR (2d) 549 (Ont High Ct)

[249] *Re Nottage* [1895] 2 Ch 649, 655 (Lindley LJ), accepted as correct in *IRC v McMullen* [1981] AC 1 (HL). See also *Birchfield Harriers* [1989] Ch Com Rep 13–16 (paras 48–55), where the Commissioners rejected the Harriers' claim to charitable status, and expressly rejected the argument that they should be regarded as charitable under the fourth head of *Pemsel* as being for the promotion of public health: ibid 15–16 (para 53). The Commissioners considered that the dominant purpose of the Harriers was not (as in *Oxford Ice Skating Assoc* [1984] Ch Com Rep 11 (para 21) the improvement of public health, but rather the encouragement of competitive sport

[250] *Re le Cren Clarke* (sub nom *Funnell v Stewart*) [1996] 1 WLR 288 (ChD); it was additionally held charitable for the advancement of religion. See also *Re Kerin* The Times, 24 May 1966. Contrast *Re Hummeltenberg* [1923] 1 Ch 237, which concerned a bequest to the London Spiritualistic Alliance Ltd towards a fund to establish a college for the training of spiritualist mediums, 'preference being given to healing mediums and those for diagnosis of disease'. Russell J said that, even if he were to assume that some mediums possessed powers of diagnosis or healing, the gift in question was not limited to the training of such persons, but could be applied to the training of non-therapeutic mediums: ibid, 241

[251] *Re Cranston* [1898] 1 IR 431; *Re Slatter* (1905) 21 TLR 295 (Joyce J)

[252] *National Anti-Vivisection Society v IRC* [1948] AC 31, 73 (where Lord Simonds said that he chose to express no opinion whether *Re Cranston* [1898] 1 IR 431, was rightly decided)

[253] *The Family Planning Assoc* [1969] Ch Com Rep 11 (para 25), where the Commissioners note that the passing of the National Health Service (Family Planning) Act 1967 indicated that Parliament regarded such a service for unmarried people as being for the benefit of the community, and that the Commissioners therefore accept that it is a service which could be provided by a charity. Objections to the Association's registration were made from various quarters, but were rejected by the Commissioners: [1976] Ch Com Rep 17–18 (paras 54–61)

or mental illness or distress as a result of or during pregnancy; the treatment could include the performance of an abortion.[254] The Charity Commissioners considered that to relieve women of such illness or distress was charitable as removing a risk to their health, and that it was no objection that pregnancy is a temporary, not a permanent, condition. A factor in favour of the Service's charitable status was evidently the qualification that the patients had to be suffering such illness or distress in addition to satisfying the legal requirements for an abortion.[255]

(5) Public works and amenities

4.89 The Preamble refers to 'the repair of bridges, ports, havens, causeways, . . . sea-banks and highways'. By analogy, purposes within the spirit of the Preamble include public works and amenities, and therefore comprise many services and provisions that are today undertaken by public (or privatized) authorities,[256] eg lighting, paving, cleaning, and policing the streets, and making sewers, drains, and waterworks in towns;[257] the establishment of a court house;[258] the provision of museums,[259] public libraries,[260] playing fields, parks,[261] and botanical gardens;[262] the maintenance and preservation of buildings of historical, aesthetic, or artistic value;[263] and even prizes for the best-kept gardens and cottages.[264] The National Trust has been held to be a charitable body.[265]

---

[254] *British Pregnancy Advisory Service* [1978] Ch Com Rep 26–7 (paras 82–5)

[255] ibid 27 (para 85)

[256] Many trusts for public purposes have therefore been made the subject of schemes under CA 1993, s 13(1)(e)(i). See 'Charities for the Maintenance of Highways, Bridges and Similar Works' [1968] Ch Com Rep 16–17 (paras 67–72), and ch 15, paras 15.71–15.72

[257] *A-G v Heelis* (1824) 2 Sim & St 67; *A-G v Eastlake* (1853) 11 Hare 205 (each of which encompassed all the provisions instanced in the text); *Jones v Williams* (1767) Amb 651 (waterworks for the use of the inhabitants of Chepstow: held charitable, but void as being within the Mortmain Act 1736)

[258] *A-G v Heelis* (1824) 2 Sim & St 67, 76–77 (Leach VC)

[259] *British Museum Trustees v White* (1826) 2 Sim & St 594

[260] *Re Scowcroft* [1898] 2 Ch 638

[261] *Re Hadden* [1932] 1 Ch 133 (playing fields and parks); *Brisbane City Council v A-G for Queensland* [1979] AC 411 (PC) (park and recreation purposes)

[262] *Townley v Bedwell* (1801) 6 Ves 194. See *The Priory, Ware, Herts* [1979] Ch Com Rep 24–6 (paras 74–81) (grant to local authority of an ancient manor house and grounds, the land to be used 'as a pleasure ground or recreation ground for public use'; the Commissioners held this to be a charitable purpose)

[263] *Re Cranstoun, National Provincial Bank v Royal Society for the Encouragement of Arts, Manufactures and Commerce* [1932] 1 Ch 537, where Farwell J held to be charitable both a gift to the Royal Society of Arts for the preservation of two Elizabethan cottages and an appeal fund which the Society had launched for the preservation of ancient cottages as specimens and models of English craftsmanship so as to teach the lessons of craftsmanship. See also *Settle and Carlisle Rly Trust* [1990] Ch Com Rep 23–6 (trust to assist in the preservation of the historical and architectural features of a railway line and to promote public knowledge of the heritage associated with the line accepted as charitable by the Commissioners)

[264] *Re Pleasants* (1923) 39 TLR 675. See [1973] Ch Com Rep 24–6 (paras 71–5)

[265] *Re Verrall* [1916] 1 Ch 100

The Charity Commissioners are prepared to treat as charitable trusts of gardens of **4.90** a private house, where the gardens are of horticultural or botanical interest, and where the owner will remain in occupation of the house itself; but the public benefit requirement must be satisfied, and the Commissioners have stated that they will need substantial reasons for concluding that the public benefit predominates over the private benefit accruing to the owner if the gardens are open to the public for less than three months a year.[266]

A charitable trust whose purpose is the promotion of public works or amenities **4.91** might also confer a private benefit upon another body (whether public or private) upon whom the expense of undertaking such works or of providing such activities might otherwise fall. Provided, however, the trustees do not apply any part of the charity's funds in relieving such body from its statutory duties, the circumstances might be such that any private benefit thereby conferred can be regarded as merely incidental and so not destructive of the trust's exclusively charitable nature.[267]

By analogy with the repair of highways mentioned in the Preamble, the Charity **4.92** Commissioners accept as charitable the provision (by non-profit making institutions) of transport services with minibuses in rural areas lacking public transport.[268]

An imaginative interpretation of the spirit of the Preamble enabled a Canadian **4.93** court recently to hold charitable under the fourth head of *Pemsel's* case a society whose object was the provision of free public access to the Internet.[269] It was held that the provision of such an 'information highway' was analogous, in an age of technology, to the repair of highways mentioned in the Preamble, since both were intended to improve means of communications between citizens.

(6) *The relief of rates and taxes*

The Preamble mentions 'the aid or ease of any poor inhabitants concerning pay- **4.94** ment of fifteens, setting out of soldiers and other taxes'. At the time the Preamble was enacted, parishes were obliged by the common law to make provision for various purposes, including the repair of churches (which the Preamble expressly mentions). A gift for the repair of a church was considered charitable as it would

---

[266] [1976] Ch Com Rep 13 (para 39)
[267] See *Settle and Carlisle Rly Trust* [1990] Ch Com Rep 23–26, where the Commissioners considered that, provided the trustees of the proposed Trust did not apply any of its funds in relieving British Railways Board from any responsibility which lay upon it to maintain the line in service, any private benefit conferred on the Board should be regarded as incidental within the test laid down by Lord Normand in *IRC v City of Glasgow Police Athletic Assoc* [1953] AC 380 (HL)
[268] [1976] Ch Com Rep 13 (para 40)
[269] *Vancouver Regional Freenet Assoc v Minister of National Revenue* (1996) 137 DLR 4th 406 (Can Fed CA); noted A Iwobi, 'Rolling down the information highway in search of charitable status' (1998) 5 Web JCLI

relieve parish funds for more pressing objects.[270] A gift which can be construed as being for the more general relief of parish funds is charitable on the same ground;[271] and this reasoning provides a further basis for upholding as charitable gifts for the promotion of public works,[272] and may explain the charitable status of some of the 'locality' cases.[273]

4.95 At a further level of abstraction, the authorities suggest that any gift for the relief of taxation is charitable. A gift for the exoneration of the National Debt has been held charitable,[274] as has a gift to the Chancellor of the Exchequer 'to be by him appropriated to the benefit and advantage of my beloved country Great Britain'.[275] Each of these might be considered to be charitable as relieving the burden of the taxpayer.[276]

(7) The protection of human life and property

4.96 The repair of sea-banks is a charitable purpose within the Preamble. Sea-banks protect the inhabitants of coastal areas from floods; by analogy, the provision of life-boats and the Royal National Lifeboat Institution are charitable. A more general analogy is any purpose aimed at protecting human life and property; hence provision for a local fire brigade has been held charitable.[277]

4.97 The Charity Commissioners recognize as charitable a body called Disaster Action, whose purposes are to promote the safety of the public against disasters involving multiple deaths or injury, whether on land, on water, or in the air. The charity both undertakes research into the prevention of and protection against such disasters, and provides support and succour to those affected by them.[278]

---

[270] See G Jones, *History of the Law of Charity 1532–1827* (Cambridge Univ Press, 1969) 31

[271] Although a gift for the relief of the poor of a parish is charitable, in the days of parish relief those in receipt of parochial relief would be excluded from its benefits because otherwise, the effect of the gift would be to relieve the ratepayers, not the poor: see *A-G v Marchant* (1866) LR 3 Eq 424, 431 (Kindersley V-C); *A-G v Clarke* (1762) Amb 422, 422–3 (Clarke MR). For an analysis of charity cases involving the relief of the rates, and their rationale, see A Dunn, 'Equity and Clemency: to what extent has equity ever developed or shown a 'human face' towards the needs of the vulnerable in society?' (PhD thesis, Univ of Leicester, 1996) ch 2, esp 28–38. See also A Dunn, 'As "cold as charity"?: poverty, equity and the charitable trust' (2000) 20 LS 222

[272] See above, para 4.89

[273] See below, paras 4.122–4.124

[274] *Newland v A-G* (1809) 3 Mer 684 (Lord Eldon LC)

[275] *Nightingale v Goulbourn* (1848) 2 Ph 594

[276] This ratio of *Nightingale v Goulbourn* was doubted in *Re Smith* [1932] 1 Ch 153 (CA), but has the support of H Picarda, *The Law and Practice Relating to Charities* (3rd edn, Butterworths, 1999) 149–150. In *Re Smith* itself, a gift 'unto my country England' was held charitable as being for the benefit of a locality; the court rejected the (more convincing) argument that it should be considered charitable as being for the relief of taxes

[277] *Re Wokingham Fire Brigade Trusts* [1951] Ch 373

[278] [1991] Ch Com Rep 13 (para 71)

(8) National or local defence and the preservation of public order
The promotion of the efficiency of the armed forces or the police

The Preamble refers to 'the setting out of soldiers', so gifts to promote the **4.98** efficiency of the armed forces, the air force, or the navy are charitable, ultimately because they tend to the defence of the nation and the security of the realm.

A gift to enable selected boys on a training ship to be trained with a view to their **4.99** taking commissions in the Royal Navy or becoming officers in the Mercantile Marine was held charitable for this reason.[279] A gift 'to promote the defence of the United Kingdom against the attack of hostile aircraft' was also held charitable on this ground.[280] An extreme case is perhaps one in which a trust to maintain a library for the use of the officers of a specified regiment, and to purchase plate for their mess, was held to be charitable as tending to promote the efficiency of the army.[281] Similarly, a gift to promote various field and outdoor sports amongst members of a regiment was held charitable, as the physical nature of the sports would increase the regiment's efficiency.[282] The promotion of the efficiency of the police is also charitable.[283] The promotion of peace, though treated as charitable in one case,[284] should probably be considered political and therefore not charitable.

In *Re Stephens*,[285] a testator had made a gift to the National Rifle Association for a **4.100** fund to be used for the teaching of shooting at moving objects 'so as to prevent as far as possible a catastrophe similar to that at Majuba Hill'. (Majuba Hill was a battle in the Boer War in which the English soldiers were defeated by reason of the excellent rifle shooting of the Boers.) Kekewich J said that, whilst he would not have thought the purpose of shooting at moving objects itself charitable, in this case the testator had a distinct object in view, namely to prevent a repetition of the catastrophe at Majuba Hill. His Lordship therefore held the gift charitable essentially on the basis that what the testator had in mind was a training in rifle shooting that would make the men instructed more effective soldiers in the event of their ever being called to serve in the army.

---

[279] *Re Corbyn* [1941] 1 Ch 400 (Morton J)
[280] *Re Driffill* [1950] 1 Ch 93 (Danckwerts J)
[281] *Re Good* [1905] 2 Ch 60
[282] *Re Gray* [1925] Ch 362, 365. The principle in this case and in *Re Good* were approved, although the decisions themselves received adverse comment, in *IRC v City of Glasgow Police Athletic Assoc* [1953] AC 380, 391 (Lord Normand), 401 (Lord Morton of Henryton)
[283] *IRC v City of Glasgow Police Athletic Association* [1953] AC 380, 401–2 (Lord Reid) (although the Association was found not to have the promotion of the efficiency of the police as its main object)
[284] *Re Harwood* [1936] Ch 285; but see *Re Koeppler's Will Trusts* [1986] Ch 423 (CA)
[285] (1892) 8 TLR 792 (Kekewich J)

4.101   On the authority of this case, a number of gun and rifle associations have been registered as charities. The Charity Commissioners have, however, recently declined to register two gun and rifle clubs as charities.[286] The Commissioners considered that the law as laid down in *Re Stephens* is obsolete,[287] both in view of the tactical and technological advances in modern warfare since the time of the Boer War, and because social and organizational changes affecting the recruitment and training of men and women for the army meant that it was unlikely that rifle and pistol clubs would be used as a manpower reserve in times of war and other national emergency.[288] The Commissioners added, however, that even if *Re Stephens* were to be treated as still good law, it was not authority for holding to be charitable the particular clubs in question. On the facts, the Commissioners considered the main purposes of the clubs to be the benefit of their members, and they were very little concerned with the defence of the realm.[289] Their purposes were therefore not wholly and exclusively charitable.

The administration of the law

4.102   The provision of a court house for a city or a county is charitable because it promotes the administration of the law.[290] The publication of law reports is also charitable under the fourth head, both because it assists the administration and development of the law by the courts, and also because it makes the law known, or at least accessible, to all members of the community.[291]

4.103   The Charity Commissioners have registered as charitable organizations whose object is to provide family counselling, mediation, or conciliation services, on the ground that such a purpose advances the administration of the law, and so is analogous to the provision of a court house or the provision of law reports.[292]

4.104   The Charity Commissioners treat as charitable the promotion of the sound administration of the law by providing legal advice and representation for prisoners who are believed to have suffered a miscarriage of justice and who cannot pay for such representation.[293] The Commissioners were not, however, prepared to

---

[286]   *The City of London Rifle and Pistol Club; The Burnley Rifle Club* (1993) 1 Decisions 4–13
[287]   ie following the principle explained by Lord Simonds in *National Anti-Vivisection Society v IRC* [1948] AC 31, 74; and in *Gilmour v Coats* [1949] AC 426, 443
[288]   (1993) 1 Decisions 4, 10. For a defence of the charitable status of rifle clubs, see P Clarke, 'The Charitable Status of Rifle Clubs: Out With a Bang?' (1992–3) 1 CL & PR 137, and 'Charitable Status of Rifle Clubs: the Explosion Occurs' (1993–4) 2 CL & PR 97
[289]   (1993) 1 Decisions 4, 12–13
[290]   *A-G v Heelis* (1824) 2 Sim & St 67, 76 (Leach MR)
[291]   *Incorporated Council of Law Reporting for England and Wales v A-G* [1972] Ch 73 (CA); see esp 85–86 (Russell LJ) 104 (Buckley LJ). The majority of the court (Sachs and Buckley LJJ) also held the Council's purposes charitable under the second head
[292]   *Mediation in Divorce (Richmond upon Thames); The National Family Conciliation Council* [1983] Ch Com Rep 13–14 (paras 28–34)
[293]   *JUSTICE* [1996] Ch Com Rep 12 (paras 60–65)

register as charitable an organization the original objects of which included the promotion of the preservation of law and order for the public benefit particularly in relation to the Jewish Community in the United Kingdom.[294] The Commissioners pointed out that the maintenance of law and order in relation to a specific section of the community, other than the inhabitants of a sufficient geographical area, is not a charitable purpose.[295] The Commissioners did, however, register the body after it had amended its objects so that they instead included the following purpose:

> to promote the efficiency of the police within the community at large and the promotion of good citizenship and greater public participation in the prevention of crime, with particular reference to the maintenance of public order and racially motivated, especially anti-Semitic, crime.

The Charity Commissioners have also registered as charities a number of neigh-   **4.105**
bourhood law centres, whose purposes essentially involve giving legal aid and advice to poor persons resident or working within the area.[296] The Commissioners consider that the fact that such centres might be doing work which could equally well be done by a solicitor in private practice will not affect its charitable status, since the need for centres arises mainly in deprived and distressed areas where the inhabitants would probably be deterred from consulting a solicitor in private practice by poverty, ignorance, or apprehension. The charitable status of such centres might be based on the promotion of the administration of the law; but, as they are designed for the less affluent, it is probably better to treat them primarily as charities for the relief of poverty.

The promotion of good race relations

In *Re Strakosch*[297] it was held that the appeasement of racial feelings between the   **4.106**
Dutch- and English-speaking sections of the South African community was not charitable, both because it was considered to be a political purpose and because the court considered it too vague to fall within the spirit and intendment of the Preamble. Since that case was decided, however, much has changed in relation to race relations, both in legislation and in social attitudes. The passing of the Race Relations Act 1968 meant that Parliament had effectively decided that the promotion of good race relations was for the public benefit, so the objection based on political purpose no longer applied. In the light of this, the Charity Commissioners reviewed their position in relation to the charitable status of the promotion of good race relations in 1983.[298] They decided that the promotion of good

---

[294] *Community Security Trust* (1995) 4 Decisions 8–12
[295] *IRC v Baddeley* [1955] AC 572
[296] *Camden Community Law Centre* [1974] Ch Com Rep 20–1 (paras 67–72)
[297] [1949] 1 Ch 529
[298] [1983] Ch Com Rep 9–11 (paras 15–20)

race relations, endeavouring to eliminate discrimination on grounds of race, and encouraging equality of opportunity between persons of different racial groups were charitable purposes. The Commissioners treated such purposes as charitable by analogy (inter alia) with the preservation of public order and the prevention of breaches of the peace.[299]

4.107 The Commissioners accept that the promotion of good race relations can be charitable even if it is primarily intended to eliminate racism in respect of one particular racial or ethnic group. A recent example of a body with such objects, which the Charity Commissioners registered as a charity, was Community Security Trust,[300] one of the objects of which was

> to promote good race relations between the Jewish community and other members of society by working towards the elimination of racism in the form of anti-Semitism.

(9) The promotion of agriculture, industry, and commerce

4.108 One of the purposes mentioned in the Preamble is 'the supportation, aid and help of young tradesmen [and] handicraftsmen'. By analogy with this, the courts have admitted the promotion of agriculture,[301] industry and commerce, as charitable under the fourth head of *Pemsel*. Basing himself more generally on the Statute of Elizabeth, however, Lord Cranworth LC said he did not entertain a doubt[302]

> that it would be a good charity to establish an institution for investigating and removing the causes of the potato disease, and of the vine disease, for it would tend to the improvement of those vegetables, and if any sound theory were to arise from its investigations it would be a most beneficial establishment for mankind in general.

4.109 Whereas the promotion of agriculture (including reafforestation[303]) generally is a charitable purpose *per se*,[304] the promotion of industry and commerce is charita-

---

[299] The Charity Commissioners also found such purposes analogous to the mental and moral improvement of man on the basis that discrimination on grounds of colour is immoral (*Re Hood* [1931] 1 Ch 240; *Re Price* [1943] Ch 422; *Re South Place Ethical Society* [1980] 1 WLR 1565); and to the promotion of equality of women with men (*Halpin v Seear* High Court 27 Feb 1976 (Whitford J); *Women's Service Trust* [1977] Ch Com Rep 14–15 (paras 34–6): [1983] Ch Com Rep 9, 11 (para 19)

[300] *Community Security Trust* (1995) 4 Decisions 8–12

[301] *IRC v Yorkshire Agricultural Society* [1928] 1 KB 611 (where a society formed to hold an annual meeting for the exhibition of farming stock, implements, and the like, for the general promotion of agriculture, was held charitable). Agriculture can be promoted by the holding of agricultural shows: ibid, 630 (Atkin LJ); *Brisbane City Council v A-G for Queensland* [1979] AC 411, 422–3 (Lord Wilberforce) (PC)

[302] *Univ of London v Yarrow* (1857) 1 De G & J 72, 80

[303] *Re Jacobs* (1970) 114 Sol Jo 515 (Foster J) (gift for the planting of trees in Israel)

[304] *IRC v Yorkshire Agricultural Society* [1928] 1 KB 611. See also [1976] Ch Com Rep 16 (para 53), and [1980] Ch Com Rep 31 (para 99), where the Charity Commissioners consider that, in this respect, the promotion of agriculture might be anomalous

ble only if the purpose can be shown to be for the benefit of the public at large.[305] The preservation and improvement of standards of craftsmanship both ancient and modern have been held charitable as being for the promotion of industry.[306] The Charity Commissioners have expressed their preparedness to register as a charity a body whose objects are directed to the advancement of industry and commerce by promoting, or assisting in promoting, opportunities for employment, particularly in areas where involuntary unemployment is causing suffering by reason of poverty or ill-health.[307] Industry and commerce may, however, be advanced by making workshops and other facilities available to craftsmen without any requirement of poverty.[308]

The Charity Commissioners do not regard the regulation of a trade as a charitable **4.110** purpose.[309]

Whether the promotion is of agriculture or industry and commerce, the Charity **4.111** Commissioners or the courts will need to be satisfied that the public benefit outweighs any element of private benefit which might be derived from those involved with it.[310] This aspect is considered further in chapter 5.[311]

(10) *The relief of unemployment*

Until recently, the Charity Commissioners did not regard the relief of unemploy- **4.112** ment as a charitable purpose *per se*, although such relief could be a means of achieving an avowed charitable purpose such as the relief of poverty or the promotion of agriculture, industry, or commerce. The Commissioners have now changed their approach in the light of dicta in *Inland Revenue Commissioners v Oldham Training and Enterprise Council*.[312] Lightman J there stated that[313]

> if the object of setting up the unemployed in trade or business was not charitable as being for the relief of poverty, it would fall within the fourth head of charity. It is a matter of general public utility that the unemployed should be found gainful activity and that the state should be relieved of the burden of providing them with unemployment and social security benefits, and this object is within the spirit, if not the

---

[305] *Crystal Palace Trustees v Minister of Town and Country Planning* [1951] Ch 132
[306] *IRC v White* (1980) 55 TC 651; noted [1980] Ch Com Rep 22–5 (paras 66–73)
[307] *Business in the Community* [1987] Ch Com Rep 4–5 (paras 16–19)
[308] *IRC v White* (1980) 55 TC 651; noted [1980] Ch Com Rep 22–5 (paras 66–73)
[309] *Wine Standards Board of the Vintners' Company* [1978] Ch Com Rep 30–1 (paras 95–8) (to ensure that persons engaged in the wine trade in the UK observed regulations relating to trading in wines whether made by HM Govt or by the EEC). See also *Fairtrade Foundation* (1995) 4 Decisions 1, 3–4, where the Commissioners declined to register the company's objects as first drafted because they suggested that the Foundation's purpose was the regulation of trade and work practices of businesses which employ workers in Third World countries
[310] *Hadaway v Hadaway* [1955] 1 WLR 16 (PC); *IRC v Yorkshire Agricultural Society* [1928] 1 KB 611; *IRC v Oldham Training and Enterprise Council* [1996] STC 1218
[311] See ch 5, paras 5.37–5.47
[312] [1996] STC 1218
[313] ibid, 1234

words, of the Elizabethan Statute, which includes amongst its list of charitable objects the 'supportation, aid and help of young tradesmen [and] handicraftsmen.'

4.113   The Charity Commissioners have since set out the criteria that an organization for the relief of unemployment must satisfy if it is to be regarded as charitable.[314] It must demonstrate that it is set up for the primary purpose of relieving unemployment for the public benefit, that its activities are directed to the relief of unemployment generally or to a significant section of the community in a way which can be demonstrated objectively, and that any benefit to private interests is strictly incidental to its primary purpose.[315] Within this, the Commissioners have provided a non-exhaustive list of activities in which an unemployment charity may engage, including:[316]

   (a) the provision of advice and training to unemployed individuals concerning employment, self-employment and the establishment of co-operative enterprises and the provision of CV writing, job search and job-club facilities for them;
   (b) the provision of practical support to unemployed people by way of accommodation, child care facilities or assistance with travel;
   (c) the provision by charities of land and buildings at below market or subsidised rents to businesses starting up;
   (d) the provision of capital grants or equipment to new businesses; and
   (e) the payment by a grant-making charity to an existing commercial business to take on additional staff from unemployed people.

4.114   The Charity Commissioners have also emphasized that trustees of such charities must ensure that the benefits provided are limited to the time that the recipient's unemployment is capable of being relieved. Support should therefore be tailored accordingly, for example, on a time-limited or income-achieved basis.[317] The Commissioners have also specified the following possible object to cover these activities:[318]

   the relief of unemployment for the public benefit in such ways as may be thought fit, including assistance to find employment.

(11)   The promotion of urban or rural regeneration

4.115   The Charity Commissioners have stated that they now recognize the promotion of urban and rural regeneration for the public benefit in areas of social and economic deprivation as a charitable purpose in its own right.[319] It is questionable, however, whether this represents any substantive development of the definition of

---

[314] Charity Commission, *Charities for the Relief of Unemployment*, RR3, (Mar 1999)
[315] ibid, 2–3
[316] ibid, 3
[317] ibid, 5–6
[318] ibid, 3
[319] Charity Commission, *Promotion of Urban and Rural Regeneration*, RR2, (Mar 1999), 2 (para 6)

charity. The problem is that the Commissioners do not consider that the phrase 'urban and rural regeneration' is by itself sufficiently certain to be capable of being controlled by the court; the promotion of such purposes without any further indication of the intended activities is therefore not charitable.[320] The Charity Commissioners will therefore normally be prepared to register an organization with such objects (even if they are restricted to areas of social and economic deprivation) only if the organization undertakes at least three or four[321] of the activities specified by the Commissioners in their publication *Promotion of Urban and Rural Regeneration*. Such activities must also cover a broad spectrum of regeneration work;[322] and the objects clause should normally stipulate the particular geographical area (local, national or international) in which the charity will operate.[323] The activities mentioned are:[324]

(a) the provision of financial or other assistance to people who are poor;
(b) the provision of housing for those in need and help to improve housing standards generally in those parts of an area of deprivation where poor housing is a problem;
(c) helping unemployed people to find employment;
(d) the provision of education, training and re-training opportunities and work experience, especially for unemployed people;
(e) the provision of financial or technical assistance or advice to new businesses or existing businesses where it would lead to training and employment opportunities for unemployed people;
(f) the provision of land and buildings on favourable terms to businesses in order to create training and employment opportunities for unemployed people;
(g) the provision, maintenance and improvement of roads and accessibility to main transport routes;
(h) the preservation of buildings in the area which are of historic or architectural importance;
(i) the provision, maintenance and improvement of recreational facilities;
(j) the provision of public amenities.

4.116 The Charity Commissioners elaborate on these activities in their model clauses, where such activities are listed as 'means' by which the object of the promotion for the public benefit of urban or rural regeneration in areas of social and economic deprivation are to be carried out.[325] Other means specified in the model clauses are the protection or conservation of the environment,[326] the provision of public health facilities and child-care,[327] and the promotion of public safety and

---

[320] ibid, 8–9 (para A21)
[321] ibid, 5 (para A1), 5–6 (para A4)
[322] ibid, 3 (para 8)
[323] ibid, 8 (para A19)
[324] ibid, 2–3 (para 7)
[325] ibid, 9–13 (paras A24–A25)
[326] ibid, 13, cl (j)
[327] ibid, cl (k)

prevention of crime.[328] The Commissioners recognize that this list might be added to in due course with the development of both practice and policy on urban and rural regeneration, and their model clauses contain a final clause specifying:[329]

> such other means as may from time to time be determined subject to the prior written consent of the Charity Commissioners for England and Wales.

4.117 The Charity Commissioners' insistence that, to obtain charitable status under this category, the organization must carry out (and, under the model clauses, list as means) at least a range of the activities specified, somewhat undermines their apparent recognition of urban or rural regeneration as a charitable purpose in its own right. If the objects of an organization are clearly charitable in themselves, they do not need the benefit of a restrictive interpretation by reference to activities or means to make them so.

(12) The promotion of the arts

4.118 The Charity Commissioners accept that the promotion of the arts, besides being charitable for the advancement of education,[330] can be charitable under the fourth head of *Pemsel*'s case.[331] They take the view that the public benefit element is self-evident in relation to charities for the promotion of the arts generally, and that there is no substantive difference between the second and fourth heads in relation to the public benefit requirement.

(13) Public memorials

4.119 There is little authority on whether it is charitable to provide a public statue or memorial. Apart from the difficulty of determining whether such an object is analogous to those stated in the Preamble, there may be a problem of public benefit. If the memorial or statue is of the testator himself, it will be difficult to overcome the objection that any benefit is likely to accrue only to the testator's immediate family or acquaintances. It might also be argued that such an object is the mere indulgence of the testator's own vanity, and is thereby lacking in altruism.[332] No such objection was made on this ground, however, in *Re Delius*,[333] which concerned a trust set up by Delius' widow to promote his music; and the fact that the settlor was the composer's widow rather than the composer himself hardly seems a satisfactory point of distinction.

4.120 It would appear that a trust to provide or to maintain a statue or memorial is not charitable *per se*, but might be charitable if it can be regarded as a means of fur-

---

[328] Charity Commission, *Promotion of Urban and Rural Regeneration*, RR2, (Mar 1999), 13, cl (l)
[329] ibid, cl (m)
[330] *Royal Choral Society v IRC* [1943] 2 All ER 101
[331] See [1991] Ch Com Rep 40–1
[332] cf *Re Endacott* [1960] Ch 232 ('some useful memorial to myself')
[333] [1957] Ch 299

thering a purpose which is charitable. The Charity Commissioners treated the Wellington Monument as charitable, but this was erected on land belonging to the National Trust (itself a charity) so that it had amenity aspects connected with the activities of that organization.[334] The Charity Commissioners have also registered as charitable a trust the purpose of which was to erect a statue to the late Earl Mountbatten on the ground that the provision and maintenance of a statue of a person of national or international respect and of historical importance could foster patriotism and good citizenship, and be an incentive to heroic and noble deeds.[335] A statue to a writer, composer, or artist could conceivably be treated as charitable as being educational, or an encouragement of artistic activity; but the figure would have to be outstanding, and what little precedent there is does not encourage.[336] The same might be said of statues of scientists or engineers. The provision of a statue to Brunel, for instance, ought to be capable of attaining charitable status.

The Charity Commissioners have registered as charitable a trust whose purpose is **4.121** the provision of plaques commemorating police officers killed during the execution of their duties in Great Britain and Northern Ireland.[337] The Commissioners thought that the provision of such memorials served the public benefit in promoting good citizenship by inculcating in the public an awareness of the hazards constantly undertaken by the police service on behalf of all of us.

(14) The benefit of a locality

A line of cases, the most important of which is the decision of the House of Lords **4.122** in *Goodman v Mayor of Saltash Corporation*,[338] has held that a trust for the inhabitants of a particular locality, such as a parish or a town, or to a particular class of such inhabitants, is charitable.[339] The proposition which is implicit in such cases is that such a disposition, lacking as it does an express charitable purpose, is

---

[334] See [1981] Ch Com Rep 25 (para 69)

[335] *The Earl Mountbatten of Burma Statute Appeal Trust* [1981] Ch Com Rep 24–5 (paras 68–70)

[336] *Re Jones* (1898) 79 LT 154 (trust to provide a monument to the philosopher John Locke held not charitable)

[337] *The Police Memorial Trust* [1984] Ch Com Rep 10 (para 17) (the appeal to establish the Trust was prompted by the death of WPC Yvonne Fletcher)

[338] (1882) 7 App Cas 633 (HL)

[339] ibid, 642 (Lord Selborne LC), 650–1 (Earl Cairns); 665 (Lord Watson). The decision of the House of Lords in that case was applied (reluctantly) in *Re Christchurch Inclosure Act* (1888) 38 Ch D 520 (CA) (rights of turbary for occupiers and future occupiers of certain cottages within a manor held charitable): see Lindley LJ (giving the judgment of the court), at 530 and 532; (appeal to House of Lords on a different ground, sub nom *A-G v Meyrick* [1893] AC 1). It was also followed in *Re Norwich Town Close Estate Charity* (1888) 40 Ch D 298 (CA): see Cotton LJ at 306–7. For cases ante-dating *Saltash* that appear to have been upheld on the limitation to a locality, see *Wrexham Corp v Tamlin* (1873) 28 LT 761 (Wickens V-C); *A-G v Webster* (1875) LR 20 Eq 483 (Jessel MR). A gift 'unto my country England' has been upheld as charitable on the ground that England is a locality: *Re Smith* [1932] 1 Ch 153 (CA)

charitable merely by dint of the express localization of its area of benefit. Other cases, however, have recognized that such a proposition is inconsistent with the principle that a trust is not charitable merely because it is beneficial to the community; it is also necessary to show that the purpose is itself charitable.[340] Furthermore, since the *Saltash* case, the House of Lords has held that if an express purpose of a trust is non-charitable, the restriction of its benefits to a particular parish or neighbourhood will not make it charitable.[341] The conflicting lines of authority could be reconciled if it were possible to infer that trusts for the benefit of a locality are presumed to be limited to charitable purposes; but it seems doubtful that all the cases can be explained on this basis.[342]

4.123 Many of the authorities were reviewed in *Peggs v Lamb*.[343] The freemen of Huntingdon and their widows had since time immemorial enjoyed pasturage and grazing rights over certain commons adjoining the borough, which rights had later been converted into monetary benefits. The Charity Commissioners had for many years treated the rights as charitable in nature; but, by 1991, the numbers of freemen had so dwindled, and the income from the property had so increased, that the Commissioners no longer considered an application of the income amongst the freemen alone to be consistent with an application for charitable purposes. At the Commissioners' suggestion, the trustees applied to the court to determine the terms upon which the property was held, and (if it were upon charitable trusts) for a scheme applying the income cy-près. Applying *Goodman v Mayor of Saltash Corporation*, as he was bound to do, Morritt J held that the rights of the freemen arose out of a charitable trust. He went on, however, to hold that this did not entitle the freemen to take the whole income amongst themselves. In the absence of a trust deed setting out the purposes of the trust, he held that it could be inferred that the whole interest in the land was given for charitable purposes for the benefit of the freemen. There being so few remaining freemen, his

---

[340] *A-G v National Provincial & Union Bank of England* [1924] AC 262, 265, (Lord Cave LC); *Williams' Trustees v IRC* [1947] AC 447, 455 (Lord Simonds); *IRC v Baddeley* [1955] AC 572, 591 (Viscount Simonds). Similarly, *Farley v Westminster Bank* [1939] AC 430 (HL) (gift to vicars and churchwardens 'for parish work' held not charitable). See also *Peggs v Lamb* [1994] Ch 172, 193 (Morritt J)

[341] *Houston v Burns* [1918] AC 337 (HL) ('for such public, benevolent or charitable purposes in connection with the parish of Lesmagahow or the neighbourhood' as the trustees should think proper). See also *Re Gwyon* [1930] 1 Ch 255, 261 (Eve J)

[342] eg the benefit of dredging for oysters taken by the freemen in *Goodman v Mayor of Saltash Corp* (1882) 7 App Cas 633: see *Williams' Trustees v IRC* [1947] AC 447, 459–50 (Lord Simonds). In *Re Allen* [1905] 2 Ch 400, 404, Swinfen Eady J said that 'a gift for public purposes in a specified locality is a valid charitable trust; although a gift for public purposes generally is void as being so general and undefined that it cannot be executed by the Court'. See also *Re Spence* [1938] Ch 96, where Luxmoore J held charitable a gift to a corporation of a 'public hall . . . for such public purposes as' the corporation might select. Some authorities might be explicable as being for public works or in aid of rates: see M Albery, 'Trusts for the benefit of the inhabitants of a locality' (1940) 56 LQR 49

[343] [1994] Ch 172

Lordship held that a cy-près circumstance was satisfied,[344] and he directed the settlement of a scheme to enlarge the class of persons by reference to which the charitable purposes were laid down from the freemen and their widows alone to the inhabitants of Huntingdon as a whole.

By inferring a charitable purpose on the facts before him, Morritt J was able to side-step, rather than to resolve, the difficulties of the *Saltash* decision. It is difficult to see how a first instance judge could have done more. The 'locality' cases therefore remain one of charity law's rather more awkward anomalies. They are, however, well established and the Privy Council has opined that they remain good law.[345]   **4.124**

(15) The care of animals

The care of animals is not a purpose mentioned in the Preamble, and the charitable status of such purpose is not apparently based on any analogy with the Preamble. It appears that the charitable status of a trust for the welfare of animals derives from a nineteenth-century case, *University of London v Yarrow*,[346] where a trust to establish an institution 'for studying and endeavouring to cure maladies of any quadrupeds or birds useful to man' was held charitable. This could be explained as being for the advancement of education, but the court did not refer to this, basing itself instead on the principle that it was beneficial to mankind and of the same nature as the purposes enumerated in the Statute of Elizabeth.[347] Although the trust was held to be limited to domestic animals, Lord Cranworth LC had no doubt that an institution to cure diseases among animals ordinarily kept for amusement (such as grouse) would be a good charity.[348]   **4.125**

Despite its doubtful parentage, a trust for the protection or welfare of animals is prima facie charitable,[349] and can be considered to fall within the fourth head of *Pemsel's* case. Thus a trust to look after animals generally, or a particular species of animal, is a good charitable trust.[350] A trust to look after a particular animal,   **4.126**

---

[344] ie what is now CA 1993, s 13(1)(d)

[345] *A-G of the Cayman Islands v Wahr-Hansen* [2000] 3 All ER 642, 646–7 (Lord Browne-Wilkinson)

[346] (1857) 1 De G & J 72

[347] ibid, 79–80 (Lord Cranworth LC). His Lordship appears to have treated the institution as an animal hospital, so that it promoted a purpose analogous to the maintenance of sick and maimed soldiers and mariners specified in the Statute of Elizabeth

[348] ibid, 80

[349] See *National Anti-Vivisection Society v IRC* [1948] AC 31, 67 (Lord Simonds); also *Marsh v Means* (1857) 3 Jur (NS) 790

[350] See, eg, *Re Wedgwood* [1915] 1 Ch 113 (CA) (trust for the protection and benefit of animals held charitable); *Re Moss* [1949] 1 All ER 495 (trust for the welfare of cats and kittens held charitable); *Re Green's Will Trusts* [1985] 3 All ER 455 (Nourse J) (principal object the rescue, maintenance, and benefit of cruelly treated animals, subsidiary object the prevention of cruelty to animals). The old cases which held the promotion of vegetarianism to be a charitable purpose might, perhaps, be treated as falling within the scope of this line of authorities, as being essentially concerned with animal welfare: *Re Cranston* [1898] 1 IR 431; *Re Slatter* (1905) 21 TLR 295

however, is not charitable.[351] The apparent inconsistencies in the meaning of charity perplexed Lord Sterndale MR, who admitted:[352]

> I confess I find considerable difficulty in understanding the exact reason why a gift for the benefit of animals, and for the prevention of cruelty to animals generally, should be a good charitable gift, while a gift for philanthropic purposes, which, I take it, is for the benefit of mankind generally, should be bad as a charitable gift.

What is clear is that the public benefit in a trust to look after animals is the benefit to mankind. This has been considered to be a benefit of an educative nature,[353] but it may now have a firmer basis by analogy with the moral improvement of mankind.[354] In *Re Wedgwood*,[355] for example, a trust for the protection and benefit of animals (by promoting humane methods of slaughtering them) was held to be charitable. In the Court of Appeal, Swinfen Eady LJ said that such a trust would tend to discourage cruelty, and thus to stimulate humane and generous sentiments in man, and by these means promote feelings of humanity and morality generally, and thus to elevate the human race.[356]

4.127   On the other side of the line is *Re Grove-Grady*,[357] which concerned a trust to establish a sanctuary for wild animals and birds where they would be free from molestation or destruction by man. The Court of Appeal held that this was not charitable. Lord Hanworth MR noted that the animals were to be left in their own wild state, and would be free to molest and harry one another; his Lordship did not see how this example of 'Nature, red in tooth and claw' was of benefit to mankind.[358] This decision, though well illustrating the requirement of benefit to mankind, is somewhat dated in its approach to environmental protection, as it is today recognized that it can be for the longer term benefit of the public that other species survive, and that this sometimes requires that the public be kept away. The

---

[351]   It may, however, be permitted to exist as a so-called trust of imperfect obligation if the trustees are willing to carry it out and the trust does not itself offend the perpetuity rules: see, eg, *Re Howard* The Times, 30 Oct 1908 (trust for a parrot during the lifetime of a specified servant held valid as a trust of imperfect obligation); *Re Haines* The Times, 7 Nov 1952 (trust to look after two cats held valid as a trust of imperfect obligation, despite the fact that the capital might be tied up for longer than 21 years, Danckwerts J taking judicial note of the fact that 16 years was a long life for a cat: *sed quere*)

[352]   *Re Tetley* [1923] 1 Ch 258, 266 (CA)

[353]   ibid, 266

[354]   cf *Re Price* [1943] Ch 422; *Re South Place Ethical Society* [1980] 1 WLR 1565, 1574 (Dillon J). The mental or moral improvement of mankind as a distinct charitable purpose is considered below, paras 4.129–4.136

[355]   [1915] 1 Ch 113

[356]   ibid, 122. See also *Tatham v Drummond* (1864) 4 De GJ & S 484, which concerned a testamentary gift to be applied 'towards the establishment . . . of slaughterhouses away from the densely-populated places in which they are now situated, and for the relief of and protection from cruelty of animals taken to be slaughtered'. Lord Westbury LC held the gift charitable, but void under the statute of mortmain then in force. See further *Re Cranston* [1898] 1 IR 431, 457 (Holmes LJ)

[357]   [1929] 1 Ch 557

[358]   ibid, 573–4 (though his Lordship does not himself use Tennyson's words)

Charity Commissioners accept that the preservation of flora and fauna is a charitable purpose.[359]

The most important decision on the charitable status of trusts for animals is   **4.128**
National Anti-Vivisection Society v Inland Revenue Commissioners,[360] where the
House of Lords, overruling a long-standing decision at first instance,[361] held that
anti-vivisection is not a charitable purpose. In the leading speech, Lord Simonds
observed that the necessary element of public benefit varies from age to age; but
that the disadvantages to mankind from abolishing vivisection outweighed the
moral benefits. Lord Wright said that[362]

> the whole tendency of the concept of charity in a legal sense under the fourth head
> is towards tangible and objective benefits, and that at least that approval by the com-
> mon understanding of enlightened opinion for the time being is necessary before an
> intangible benefit can be taken to constitute a sufficient benefit to the community
> to justify the admission of the object into the fourth class.

(16) The moral or spiritual welfare of mankind

In *Re South Place Ethical Society*,[363] the object of the eponymous Society was 'the   **4.129**
study and dissemination of ethical principles and the cultivation of a rational religious sentiment', but its members were agnostic about the existence of God, and
Dillon J held that the Society could not be charitable for the advancement of religion. He nevertheless held it charitable both for the advancement of education
and also under the fourth head of *Pemsel*'s case, as being for purposes tending to
promote the mental or moral improvement of the community. He also said that it
is on this latter basis that animal welfare trusts have been supported.[364] In holding
the Society charitable under the fourth head, his Lordship relied upon three cases.
None of them, however, is particularly convincing.

The first, *Re Scrowcroft*,[365] concerned a devise of a village club and reading room to   **4.130**
be maintained 'for the furtherance of Conservative principles and religious and
mental improvement and to be kept free from all intoxicants and dancing'.
Stirling J held it charitable, treating the furtherance of religious and mental
improvement as an essential portion of the gift.[366] He did not, however, provide
any authority to support the proposition that a trust for moral improvement is
charitable *per se*; and the decision is of doubtful validity.

---

[359] See, eg, *The Upper Teesdale Defence Fund* [1969] Ch Com Rep 10–11 (paras 23–4) (fund for
the preservation of the flora and fauna of Upper Teesdale treated as charitable)
[360] [1948] AC 31
[361] *Re Foveaux* [1895] 2 Ch 501
[362] *National Anti-Vivisection Society v IRC* [1948] AC 31, 49
[363] [1980] 1 WLR 1565
[364] ibid, 1574
[365] [1898] 2 Ch 638
[366] ibid, 641. It is likely that the trust would now have been held not charitable as being for a political purpose: *Bonar Law Memorial Trust v IRC* (1933) 49 TLR 220

4.131 In the second, *Re Hood*,[367] the Court of Appeal held charitable a gift to spread Christian principles and to extinguish the traffic in alcoholic drinks, the main reason being that it considered that the temperance element was to be construed merely as a means of furthering the advancement of religion. All the judges took the view, however, that the object of reducing intemperance would be beneficial to society at large. Lawrence LJ stated that temperance was a charitable object within the fourth class 'because many people regard temperance as contributing to the moral improvement of mankind',[368] and Romer LJ, agreeing, specifically referred to *Re Scowcroft*. No other authority for this principle was mentioned.

4.132 In the third, *Re Price*,[369] there was a gift by will to the 'Anthroposophical Society in Great Britain to be used at the discretion of the chairman and executive council of the society for carrying on the teachings of the founder, Dr Rudolph Steiner'. It was accepted that Steiner's teachings were directed to the extension of knowledge of the spiritual man and in the universe generally and of the interaction of the spiritual and the physical, and his writings had applied this knowledge to a wide range of studies, including religion and education. Cohen J held the gift valid as a private trust,[370] but went on to consider whether it might be valid as being charitable. He said that in his view, Rudolph Steiner's teachings were directed to the mental or moral improvement of man, and he held the gift charitable on this ground. Cohen J did not refer to either *Re Scowcroft* or *Re Hood*. He did, however, place reliance on *Re Macaulay's Estate*[371] at first instance, where Clauson J had said that there would be a strong case for holding charitable the object of philosophical and scientific research and for the general improvement of those engaged in such studies.

4.133 The decision in *Re Price* is as unsatisfactory as the two earlier cases. It does not seek any analogy with any purpose mentioned in the Preamble, and it does not set out any principle which might explain the charitable status of trusts for mental or moral improvement. The decision might be better explained as being for the advancement of education, the mental or moral improvement of those educated being merely a by-product. Cohen J also said that, provided Rudolph Steiner's teachings were not *contra bonos mores*, the court was not concerned to decide whether the gift would result in the mental or moral improvement of anyone, but only whether, on the evidence before the court, it might have that result.[372] He quoted the passage from *Thornton v Howe*[373] in which Romilly MR had said that,

---

[367] [1931] 1 Ch 240
[368] ibid, 252
[369] [1943] Ch 422
[370] On the principle of *Re Drummond* [1914] 2 Ch 90
[371] 10 July 1933 (Clauson J); affd [1943] Ch 435n (HL). On the facts, another object of the association in that case prevented its objects from being wholly and exclusively charitable
[372] *Re Price* [1943] Ch 422, 432
[373] (1862) 31 Beav 14

provided the tendency was not immoral, the court would not declare a gift for the advancement of religion void or take it outside the class of charitable bequests, and added that what was there said of religion would apply also to philosophy.[374] This misguided attempt to apply to the fourth head comments made in relation to the third further weakens the authority of *Re Price*.

The charitable provenance of trusts for the mental or moral improvement of **4.134** mankind is therefore as doubtful as that of trusts for the welfare of animals generally. Yet whereas the charitable status of the latter, albeit anomalous, seems secure, the charitable status of the former is by no means assured. Nevertheless, the Charity Commissioners have in recent years expressly relied upon these cases in treating as charitable on this ground the elimination of racial discrimination and the promotion of racial harmony,[375] and also an organization to provide assistance to employees faced with the moral and ethical issues of 'whistle-blowing'.[376]

In its most recent review of this line of authority, the Commissioners have clarified **4.135** their earlier position. This was in their decision to refuse to register as a charity the Church of Scientology (England and Wales).[377] The Church had argued that, so far as it was not a charity for the advancement of religion, it was charitable under the fourth head as being for the moral or spiritual welfare or improvement of the community. It had argued that there were clear parallels between the aims of the teachings of Scientology and the teachings of Rudolf Steiner considered in *Re Price*,[378] since Scientology's teachings were all directed to the moral or spiritual welfare or improvement of the community, which were translated into practical activity by its adherents (such as in the fields of rehabilitation of drug addicts and criminals). The Charity Commissioners rejected this argument. They accepted that the promotion of the moral or spiritual welfare or improvement of the community is a recognized category of charity within the fourth head;[379] but, having reviewed the authorities, notably *Re Price* and *Re South Place Ethical Society*, they found a distinct lack of judicial reasoning about the basis upon which this purpose is regarded as charitable.[380] In the event, they distinguished these cases on the grounds of public benefit. They explained that, in their earlier decisions based on the acceptance of this purpose as charitable,[381]

---

[374] *Re Price* [1943] Ch 422, 433
[375] [1983] Ch Com Rep 9–11 (paras 15–20) (see above, paras 4.106–107)
[376] *Public Concern at Work* (1994) 2 Decisions 5, 10
[377] Decision of the Charity Commisioners (17 Nov 1999), *Application for Registration as a Charity by the Church of Scientology (England and Wales)*
[378] [1943] Ch 422
[379] Decision of the Charity Commisioners (17 Nov 1999), *Application for Registration as a Charity by the Church of Scientology (England and Wales)*, 30
[380] ibid, 36
[381] ibid, 37

it is clear that the Commission has regarded the concept of moral or spiritual welfare or improvement as a flexible basis upon which a wide range of purposes beneficial to the public may by analogy be recognised as charitable, particularly where it was apparent that the benefit flowing from the organisations' purposes and activities are readily and easily accessible to the public and likely to achieve such a purpose.

4.136 The Charity Commissioners said that in both *Re Price* and *Re South Place Ethical Society*, the institutions were disseminating ideas which were broadly philosophical and which were generally accessible to, and capable of being applied within, the community, and which could be freely adopted from time to time, according to individual choice or judgement, by members of the public at large. This was very different from the Church of Scientology (England and Wales), which promoted a formal belief system, and whose doctrines, practices, and beliefs were not such as to be available to the public at large as they might choose from time to time, but were effectively limited to its own members.[382] The Charity Commissioners emphasized that the principal activities of that Church were the auditing and training of members, and there was insufficient evidence that its objects would be likely to promote the moral or spiritual improvement of the community.[383]

(17) Sports and games

4.137 A trust to promote sporting activities as such is not charitable. This was laid down in *Re Nottage*,[384] which concerned a bequest to the Yacht Racing Association of Great Britain upon trust to provide annually a cup, to be called 'The Nottage Cup', for the most successful racing yacht of the season. The bequest expressly stated that the testator's object was to encourage the sport of yacht racing, and such declaration proved in the event fatal. The Court of Appeal unanimously held that the bequest was not charitable. Lindley LJ said that it was a prize for a mere game or sport.[385] Lopes LJ was of the same opinion, and thought that the bequest was primarily calculated to amuse individuals apart from the community at large, and could not therefore be charitable, 'though such sport or game is to some extent beneficial to the public'.[386] He added:[387]

> If we were to hold the gift before us to be charitable we should open a very wide door, for it would then be difficult to say that gifts for promoting bicycling, cricket, football, lawn-tennis, or any outdoor game, were not charitable, for they promote the health and bodily well-being of the community.

---

[382] Decision of the Charity Commisioners (17 Nov 1999), *Application for Registration as a Charity by the Church of Scientology* (England and Wales), 31–2
[383] ibid, 39
[384] [1895] 2 Ch 649 (CA)
[385] ibid, 655–6
[386] ibid, 656
[387] ibid

The decision has since been applied in a number of cases concerning the promo-   **4.138**
tion of other sports;[388] and has effectively been approved by the House of Lords.[389]

A trust to promote a sporting activity can be charitable, however, if it can be con-   **4.139**
strued as a means of promoting a purpose which is charitable, such as the promotion of public health,[390] or of the efficiency of the armed forces[391] or the police,[392]
or the advancement of education.[393] An illustration of this principle is *Re
Mariette*,[394] where there was a bequest to build squash courts in a boys' school and
to provide prizes for sport in the school. The school itself was a charity, and Eve J
regarded sport as part of the boys' education; the bequest was therefore charitable
for the advancement of education.

Care is, however, needed in drafting the instrument, lest the court infer that the   **4.140**
promotion of sport is itself the intended purpose, and so deny it charitable status.
The danger of this is illustrated in *Inland Revenue Commissioners v City of Glasgow
Police Athletic Association*.[395] The Association's purposes were to provide sports
facilities to members of the Association. It was argued that the Association's purposes raised the morale and the efficiency of the Glasgow police force, and were
therefore charitable as promoting a charitable purpose, the promotion of the
efficiency of the police. The House of Lords, however, considered that the purposes of the Association revealed that it was merely a recreational club. The moral
of this case is for the draftsman to take care to separate in the governing instrument the purposes from the means by which they are to be fulfilled. The draftsman can then ensure that the purposes are indubitably charitable (for example,
the advancement of education or the promotion of the efficiency of the police, as
the case may be), and merely specify that the provision of sports facilities is a
means by which such purposes are to be achieved.

The leading case involving sport is *Inland Revenue Commissioners v McMullen*.[396]   **4.141**
This concerned the Football Association Youth Trust, whose object was to provide
sports facilities for students at schools and universities 'to assist both in their physical education and in the development of their minds'. The House of Lords held

---

[388] eg *Re Clifford* [1911] 81 LJ Ch 220 (gift to society whose object was the preservation and improvement of angling in a certain river); *Re Patten* [1929] 2 Ch 276 (gift for the encouragement of
cricket)
[389] *IRC v McMullen* [1981] AC 1, 15, where Lord Hailsham LC, having referred to the decision
in *Re Nottage* [1895] 2 Ch 649, expressly stated that nothing in his speech should be taken to cast
doubt on it
[390] *Re Hadden* [1932] 1 Ch 133; *Re Morgan* [1955] 2 All ER 632
[391] *Re Gray* [1925] Ch 362
[392] *IRC v City of Glasgow Police Athletic Assoc* [1953] AC 380 (although the Association itself was
held not to be charitable)
[393] *Re Mariette* [1915] 2 Ch 284; *IRC v McMullen* [1981] AC 1 (HL)
[394] [1915] 2 Ch 284
[395] [1953] AC 380 (HL)
[396] [1981] AC 1 (HL)

the trust charitable as being for the advancement of education; their Lordships did not seek to hear argument, nor therefore to reach any conclusion, as to whether it might also be charitable under the fourth head of *Pemsel's* case. The leading speech is that of Lord Hailsham LC, who, whilst affirming the basic principle in *Re Nottage* that the promotion of sport is not *per se* a charitable purpose, pointed out that in the case before him the facilities were for young persons, that is those of school age or just above.[397] He approved of the decision in *Re Mariette*, and said that the principle of that case was not to be read in a sense which confined its application to gifts to a particular institution.[398]

4.142 The Charity Commissioners have registered as charities a number of bodies whose purposes are the physical development and education of the young by the provision of sports facilities.[399]

4.143 The playing of games which do not involve physical exercise is not charitable unless the game is itself either educational[400] or can be construed as a means of furthering an avowedly charitable purpose under the principles just discussed.

(18) Recreation

4.144 A trust to provide a piece of land for use by the public, or at least the inhabitants of a particular area, as a recreation ground, is charitable for the promotion of public health, a purpose within the spirit of the Preamble to the Statute of Elizabeth.[401]

4.145 Problems, however, arose as a result of the decision of the House of Lords in *Inland Revenue Commissioners v Baddeley*.[402] A trust had been set up to promote the moral, social, and physical well-being of persons resident in West Ham and Leyton who were (or were likely to become) members of the Methodist Church, by the provision of facilities for moral, social, and physical training and recreation. The House of Lords held that this was not a charitable purpose. One reason was that the beneficiaries did not comprise a sufficient section of the community.[403] Another was that social well-being was not a charitable purpose: it was too vague to fall within the spirit and intendment of the Preamble. The decision caused con-

---

[397] cf *Re Dupree's Deed Trusts* [1945] Ch 16. Since the decision of their Lordships' House, increasingly large numbers of students at universities are mature students, and so of more than just above school age. It is therefore increasingly doubtful whether the presence of such students, who would presumably be able to take advantage of the sports facilities, could be ignored through the de minimis principle

[398] *IRC v McMullen* [1981] AC 1, 17

[399] eg The Cliff Richard Tennis Development Trust, which was established to promote and facilitate the playing of tennis amongst schoolchildren who would not otherwise have the opportunity to do so: [1991] Ch Com Rep 13 (para 74)

[400] As in *Re Dupree's Deed Trusts* [1945] Ch 16 (chess for boys and young men, discussed under the advancement of education, above, para 4.15)

[401] *Re Hadden* [1932] 1 Ch 133; *Re Morgan* [1955] 1 WLR 738

[402] [1955] AC 572

[403] This aspect of the decision is considered in ch 5 below, paras 5.20–5.21

cern that village halls and similar institutions, which had been considered as charitable in the past, might not after all be entitled to charitable status. It was for the removal of doubt in respect of these institutions, and to restrict the impact of *Baddeley*'s case, that the Recreational Charities Act 1958 was passed.

E. Recreational Charities Act 1958

Section 1(1) of the Recreational Charities Act 1958 states that   **4.146**

> it shall be, and be deemed always to have been, charitable to provide or assist in the provision of, facilities for recreation or other leisure-time occupation, if the facilities are provided in the interests of social welfare:
> Provided that nothing in this section shall be taken to derogate from the principle that a trust or institution to be charitable must be for the public benefit.

By section 1(2), the foregoing requirement of social welfare is not to be treated as **4.147**
satisfied unless

> (a) the facilities are provided with the object of improving the conditions of life for the persons for whom the facilities are primarily intended, and
> (b) either—
>   (i) those persons have need of such facilities . . . by reason of their youth, age, infirmity or disablement, poverty, or social and economic circumstances; or
>   (ii) the facilities are to be available to the members or female members of the public at large.

Subject to this requirement,[404]   **4.148**

> subsection (1) of this section applies in particular to the provision of facilities at village halls, community centres and women's institutes, and to the provision and maintenance of grounds and buildings to be used for purposes of recreation or leisure-time occupation, and extends to the provision of facilities for those purposes by the organising of any activity.

The Act expressly provides that it is not to be taken to restrict the purposes which **4.149**
are to be regarded as charitable independently of the Act.[405]

(1) 'facilities'

For a purpose to be charitable within the 1958 Act, it must involve the provision, **4.150**
or the assistance in the provision, of 'facilities'. It is clear from the statute that section 1(1) applies in particular to the provision and maintenance of grounds and buildings.[406] This suggests that the provision of other things can be the provision of facilities; but it is less clear what else is to be included: would, for instance, the

---

[404] Recreational Charities Act 1958, s 1(3)
[405] ibid, s 3
[406] ibid, s 1(3)

provision of sports equipment for recreation or other leisure-time occupation qualify? From a dictionary definition, it might be inferred that, in the context of the Recreational Charities Act 1958, the provision of 'facilities' means the provision of opportunities for the easy or easier performance of recreation or other leisure-time occupation.[407] It therefore appears that the provision of sports equipment can qualify, as can the provision of benches in a public park. It also appears that the giving of lessons to the public for the purpose of recreation or other leisure-time occupation falls within the Act's scope, since the lessons provide an opportunity for the easier performance of the activity being taught. The Charity Commissioners have accepted that, in connection with the promotion of rugby, facilities such as the provision of pitches, team games and coaching, are all 'facilities for recreation or other leisure-time occupation' within the meaning of the Act.[408] The Commissioners have indicated that the provision of facilities for horse-riding could be within the 1958 Act.[409] Provided the other requirements of the Act are satisfied, it is suggested that the object of providing lessons in flower-arranging or ballroom-dancing would be charitable under the 1958 Act.

4.151 The provision of the facilities must be the purpose of the trust itself; therefore the object of promoting or encouraging sport is not charitable under the Act, even if the provision of facilities for recreation is expressed to be the means by which such object is to be achieved. What is provided must itself be a facility; therefore the provision of a cup for the best racing-yacht of the season[410] would not fall within the Act, since it does not provide opportunities for the easier performance of such recreation or leisure-time occupation: it merely rewards what has been performed already.

(2) 'for recreation or other leisure-time occupation'

4.152 In *Fairfield (Croydon) Ltd,*[411] the Charity Commissioners considered that the phrase 'recreation or other leisure-time occupation' in section 1(1) gave rise to difficulties of interpretation which entitled it to refer to parliamentary material as an aid to construction.[412] On the basis of what a Home Office Minister had said

---

[407] *The Shorter Oxford English Dictionary* (3rd edn, Oxford Univ Press, 1978) ('Facility' . . . 2. Opportunity for the easy or easier performance of anything; usu. in *pl.* opportunities')
[408] *The North Tawton Rugby Union Football Club* (1997) 5 Decisions 7, 9 (although the Club itself failed to attain charitable status on other grounds)
[409] *Windmill Hill City Farm Limited* [1978] Ch Com Rep 28–30 (paras 90–4), 30 (para 93). In that case, the Charity Commissioners approved (subject to some modifications) the intended objects of a company which sought to improve the conditions of life of those living in rundown areas of cities by the establishment of 'City Farm' projects, the facilities for which were to include a community garden, a farmyard, a nature reserve, a riding school, an area for outdoor drama and sports, a community workshop, and a pre-school play centre
[410] cf *Re Nottage* [1895] 2 Ch 649
[411] (1997) 5 Decisions 14
[412] ie applying the principles in *Pepper v Hart* [1993] AC 593 (HL)

during the Bill's second reading,[413] the Commissioners came to the view that the phrase should not be construed restrictively; it was not confined to educational activities, but could include mere entertainment or amusement, such as the watching of films for enjoyment or relaxation, even though such provision would not be charitable at common law.[414] The charity in question principally ran a concert hall, a theatre, and an art gallery, and its objects fell within the Recreational Charities Act 1958. Adopting a wide interpretation of the Act, the Commissioners held that the charity was entitled, in pursuance of its objects, to include amongst its programme of events such non-educational activities as plays and films of no great artistic merit, pop concerts, pantomime, folk-song clubs, and exhibitions of arts and crafts by local groups. However, the Commissioners took the view that the necessary element of public benefit was to be determined by the fact that the facilities were being made available to the public in the interests of social welfare; and it seems to be implicit in their decision that the charity could, for example, provide pop concerts only as part of a balanced programme.

A bar, although perhaps a 'facility' within the meaning of the Act, is not, in the Commissioners' view, a facility 'for recreation or other leisure-time occupation'.[415] The inclusion of a bar facility will therefore prevent an institution's being charitable under the Act, unless the provision of the bar is merely ancillary to the provision of facilities that do qualify under the Act.[416]   **4.153**

(3) 'social welfare'

In a different statutory context, it has been said that the words 'social welfare' connote the concept of public benefit,[417] and that people engaged in improving their own conditions of life are not engaged in social welfare.[418] Charity, it has been said, involves an element of altruism.[419] In *Guild v Inland Revenue Commissioners*,[420] Lord Keith expressly acknowledged that it is not enough that the requirements of section 1(2) are met: the facilities must still be provided in the interests of social   **4.154**

---

[413] *Hansard*, HC (series 5) vol 582, col 322–3 (11 Feb 1958) (David Renton); see also *Hansard*, HL (series 5) vol 207, col 14 (21 Jan 1958) (Viscount Kilmuir LC)

[414] *Fairfield (Croydon) Ltd* (1997) 5 Decisions 14, 18

[415] *North Tawton Rugby Union Football Club* (1997) 5 Decisions 7, 10

[416] ibid; where, on the facts, the provision of the bar was more than ancillary

[417] *National Deposit Friendly Society Trustees v Skegness UDC* [1959] AC 293 (HL), 322 (Lord Denning), in relation to the Rating and Valuation (Miscellaneous Provisions) Act 1955

[418] ibid, 323 (Lord Denning). See also *Waterson v Hendon BC* [1959] 1 WLR 985, 993 (Salmon J)

[419] *Re Cranston* [1898] 1 IR 431, 446 (Fitzgibbon LJ); in *National Deposit Friendly Society Trustees v Skegness UDC* [1959] AC 293, 315, Lord MacDermott quoted and approved this passage from Fitzgibbon LJ's judgment, and added: 'there can be no doubt that unselfishness and benevolence are still of the essence of legal charity'. See also *Waterson v Hendon BC* [1959] 1 WLR 985, 991 (Salmon J): 'This object is not altruistic and is, in my judgment, not charitable.'

[420] [1992] AC 310, 321

welfare. Applying this principle, in *North Tawton Rugby Union Football Club*,[421] the Charity Commissioners decided that, even if the facilities could be said to improve the conditions of life for the persons for whom they were primarily intended, and even though the facilities were available to the public at large, they were not facilities provided in the interests of social welfare, since the facilities were essentially provided by the members for themselves. The necessary element of altruism was lacking, and this was sufficient to deny the Club charitable status under the Act.[422]

4.155 The objects of a trust or other instrument can be charitable within the 1958 Act even if they do not include any specific mention of the Act and even if they do not expressly state that the facilities are provided in the interests of social welfare.[423]

(4) 'improving the conditions of life': paragraph (a)

4.156 Under the 1958 Act, the facilities must be provided with the object of improving the conditions of life for the persons for whom the facilities are primarily intended.[424] It is enough that this requirement is met in fact: it is not necessary (although it is no doubt desirable) for the governing instrument to state this object expressly.[425]

4.157 This requirement is to be interpreted broadly, and it does not mean that the persons for whom the facilities are primarily intended must be in some way deprived. The law was, it is submitted, correctly stated by Bridge LJ in the Court of Appeal in *Inland Revenue Commissioners v McMullen*, where his Lordship observed that[426]

> Hyde Park improves the conditions of life for residents in Mayfair and Belgravia as much as for those in Pimlico or the Portobello Road, and the village hall may improve the conditions of life for the squire and his family as well as for the cottagers.

(5) 'need': paragraph (b)(i)

4.158 In the Court of Appeal in *Inland Revenue Commissioners v McMullen*,[427] the majority of the court had held that the Football Association Youth Trust was not charitable under the Recreational Charities Act 1958 because the word 'need' in sub-paragraph (i) of section 1(2)(b) connoted some element of deprivation,

---

[421] (1997) 5 Decisions 7, 11–12
[422] Similarly *Blackburn and East Lancashire Model Rly Society* [1977] Ch Com Rep 21–2 (paras 64–6) (promotion of model railways for mutual benefit of members was not in the interests of social welfare)
[423] *Kent Cricket Youth Trust* [1973] Ch Com Rep 27–8 (paras 80–2), 28 (para 82)
[424] Recreational CA 1958, s 1(2)(a)
[425] *Kent Cricket Youth Trust* [1973] Ch Com Rep 27–8 (paras 80–2), 28 (para 82)
[426] [1979] 1 WLR 130, 143. Although this was a dissenting view, it now appears to be sound in the light of *Guild v IRC* [1992] 2 AC 310 (HL)
[427] [1979] 1 WLR 130

whereas there was no evidence that students were, as a body, deprived compared with the rest of the population. Bridge LJ dissented; he did not see why only the deprived were capable of having their conditions of life improved.

The House of Lords reversed the Court of Appeal, but their Lordships only con- **4.159** sidered charitable status under the second head of *Pemsel*, namely, the advancement of eduction; they did not find it necessary to refer to the Recreational Charities Act 1958. The law was therefore in a somewhat unsatisfactory state, since the interpretation of 'need' in sub-paragraph (i) remained that of the majority of the Court of Appeal, whose judgments had otherwise been overturned on appeal. The position has now been clarified in *Guild v Inland Revenue Commissioners*,[428] where the House of Lords held that the word 'need' in sub-paragraph (i) of section 1(2)(b) does not connote deprivation. Their Lordships therefore effectively approved the dissenting judgment of Bridge LJ in the Court of Appeal in *Inland Revenue Commissioners v McMullen* in relation to the 1958 Act also.

As a result of *Guild v Inland Revenue Commissioners*, the requirement of 'need' can **4.160** be satisfied by the production of evidence to show that there is a shortage of the facilities in question. In the Court of Appeal in *Inland Revenue Commissioners v McMullen*, for instance, Bridge LJ would have accepted that this requirement was satisfied because there was evidence of a shortage of sports facilities in many schools and universities. In this respect, the approach of the Recreational Charities Act 1958 is unique in the law of charities. In all other contexts, whether the particular purpose designated by a settlor or testator is needed or not is irrelevant to its charitable status; it is relevant only to establish whether there is a failure of purpose or a circumstance which might give rise to the application of the cy-près doctrine.

The need for the facilities by the persons for whom such facilities are primarily **4.161** intended must be by reason of the factors mentioned in paragraph (b)(i). The Charity Commissioners rejected the claim of the athletics club known as Birchfield Harriers to charitable status under the Act because the facilities provided by the Harriers were neither provided for any of the special classes mentioned in that sub-paragraph, nor (because of restrictive membership requirements) for the benefit of the public at large within paragraph (b)(ii).[429]

(6) 'the facilities are to be available to the members or female members of the public at large': paragraph (b)(ii)

Since sub-paragraph (ii) refers to 'members or female members' of the public at **4.162** large, it is clear that, whilst facilities available to both men and women, or to

---

[428] [1992] 2 AC 310 (HL)
[429] *Birchfield Harriers* [1989] Ch Com Rep 13–16 (paras 48–55), at 16 (para 55)

women only, can satisfy it, facilities available to men only do not. This is sex discrimination written into the statute.

4.163   If the facilities are available to 'the public at large', it is no objection that the members of the public most likely to avail themselves of such facilities are those living nearby. It is, however, unclear whether facilities can be said to be available to 'the public at large' if their availability is expressly limited to persons resident in a particular geographical area.

4.164   Since sub-paragraphs (i) and (ii) are alternatives, a trust or other disposition can still be charitable under the Act, even if the persons for whom the facilities are primarily intended do not have need of them within sub-paragraph (i), provided that the facilities are available to the public at large within sub-paragraph (ii). In *Wynn v Skegness Urban District Council*,[430] the trustees sought relief from rates in respect of a holiday centre which they ran for the benefit of Derbyshire miners and their families. Under the terms of the trust, persons other than miners and their families could be admitted to surplus accommodation at cost price, the effect being to reduce the overheads and to keep down the charges to miners and their families; and such other persons had in fact been admitted on these terms. Ungoed-Thomas J held that the purposes of the trust were charitable under the 1958 Act. In his view, the miners and their families (the persons for whom the facilities were primarily intended) did have need of such facilities, so that the requirements of sub-paragraph (i) were met. He stated obiter, however, that, even if sub-paragraph (i) had not been satisfied, sub-paragraph (ii) would have been, since the facilities were available to the public at large. There was no requirement in these circumstances that the facilities should be primarily intended for the public at large.[431]

(7) Public benefit requirement

4.165   It is expressly provided that nothing in section 1 is to derogate from the principle that a trust or institution to be charitable must be for the public benefit.[432] In this context, 'public benefit' refers to the requirement of charity law that a sufficient section of the public at large should be capable of benefiting, and that the overall effects should not be harmful.[433] What comprises a sufficient section of the community for the purposes of the Recreational Charities Act 1958 is considered in the next chapter.[434]

---

[430]   [1967] 1 WLR 52
[431]   ibid, 64
[432]   Recreational CA 1958, s. 1(1)
[433]   *Wynn v Skegness UDC* [1967] 1 WLR 52, 63–4 (Ungoed-Thomas J)
[434]   See ch 5, paras 5.22–5.25

5

BENEFIT TO A SUFFICIENT SECTION OF THE COMMUNITY

A. Introduction

In the context of the law of charity, the expression 'public benefit' is somewhat **5.01** ambiguous. First, it can mean that the purpose itself must benefit the public. Such public benefit is necessary under all four heads of *Pemsel*'s case, and it indeed describes the fourth head. Public benefit in this sense has been considered in the definition of charitable purposes in chapter 4. Secondly, however, it can mean that the section of the community to benefit is sufficient. A trust for the advancement of education, for instance, satisfies the public benefit requirement in the first sense, but it will still not comprise a charitable trust if the persons to benefit are restricted to a class of persons which is not a sufficient section of the community in charity law. It is this second sense of the expression with which the present chapter is concerned.

Lord Campden once defined charity as 'a gift to a general public use, which **5.02** extends to the poor as well as to the rich'.[1] This is not very helpful, since a gift may be charitable, even if its benefits are not available to all members of the public. The public to benefit is assessed according to the section of the public who may benefit

---

[1] *Jones v Williams* (1769) 2 Amb 651

from a charity's activities, even if the purpose is by its very nature advantageous only to the few.[2] Some charitable purposes by their nature tend to be of greatest direct benefit to members of the particular locality: for example, the benefit of a bridge which is available for all the public may be a charity, and it is indifferent how many people use it.[3] Similarly, whilst the patients at a charitable hospital might be the greatest beneficiaries of its charitable activities, if its facilities are open to the public at large, the hospital benefits a sufficient section of the community, even if it charges admission fees.[4]

5.03 A related problem is the extent to which the terms of the gift, or of an institution's governing instrument, can expressly restrict the size of the community to benefit. It has been said that a gift cannot be charitable if it expressly restricts its benefit to millionaires,[5] so it may be be surmised that millionaires are not a sufficient section of the community for the law of charity. What does comprise a sufficient section of the community varies according to the head of charity concerned. The relief of poverty has long been charitable even if the persons to benefit are restricted to the testator's next of kin.[6] Outside the relief of poverty, what is a sufficient section of the community is in the first place a matter of evidence. A disaster fund for the relatives of lifeboatmen drowned in an accident was held charitable, even though there were only six victims.[7]

5.04 In the twentieth century, a rule of law, the so-called personal nexus test, was laid down, which denies charitable status, regardless of the number of persons who may benefit from it, to a gift or instrument which defines the objects to benefit by reference to a blood or contractual relationship. The personal nexus test, which does not apply to the relief of poverty,[8] has been developed in cases concerned with the advancement of education[9] and the fourth head of *Pemsel*,[10] and it seems to be less stringent in the context of the advancement of religion.[11] Furthermore, the fourth head of *Pemsel* is subject to an additional rule of law, which denies charitable status where the objects to benefit are defined as a 'class within a class'.[12] In this chapter, the necessary section of the community to benefit will be considered in relation to each head of *Pemsel* in turn, and also under the Recreational Charities Act 1958.

---

[2] *IRC v Baddeley* [1955] AC 572, 590 (Viscount Simonds)
[3] ibid, 592
[4] *Re Resch's Will Trusts* [1969] 1 AC 514 (PC)
[5] *Re White's Will Trusts* [1951] 1 All ER 528, 530 (Harman J)
[6] *Isaac v Defriez* (1754) Amb 595
[7] *Cross v Lloyd-Greame* (1909) 102 LT 163
[8] *Dingle v Turner* [1972] AC 601 (HL)
[9] *Re Compton* [1945] Ch 123; *Oppenheim v Tobacco Securities Trust Co Ltd* [1951] AC 297 (HL)
[10] *Re Hobourn Aero Components Ltd's Air Raid Distress Fund* [1946] Ch 194 (CA)
[11] *Neville Estates Ltd v Madden* [1962] Ch 832
[12] *IRC v Baddeley* [1955] AC 572 (HL)

B. The community to benefit

(1) The relief of poverty

Nexus test not applicable to relief of poverty

Ever since the emergence of the personal nexus test, there had been doubt whether **5.05** the relief of poverty could be charitable if the class of persons to benefit was defined by reference to a personal or contractual relationship. There was, nevertheless, a long line of cases back to the eighteenth century which had held that a trust for the testator's poor relations was charitable,[13] and that principle had later been extended, first to poor members of an association,[14] and then to poor employees.[15] It has been said that these cases 'stick out like a sore thumb' from the general rule.[16] It has also been said that the 'poor relations' cases might either be accepted as 'a hallowed, if illogical, exception', or they might be treated as justified 'on the basis that the relief of poverty is of so altruistic a character that the public element may be necessarily inferred thereby'.[17] The House of Lords, in *Dingle v Turner*,[18] recognized that the poor relations cases and their offshoots were anomalous; but it considered them to be too well established to be overruled. Their Lordships therefore held that the trust before them, which had been set up by the testator to provide pensions for poor employees of a company which he owned, was charitable for the relief of poverty despite the personal nexus.

Lord Cross, however, who delivered the only substantial speech in *Dingle v* **5.06** *Turner*, went rather further. He expressed agreement with Lord MacDermott's dissenting opinion in *Oppenheim v Tobacco Securities Ltd*[19] that the personal nexus rule was unsatisfactory. Lord Cross opined that the courts introduced the rule only in order to prevent the body concerned from obtaining tax relief. In his view, a trust to educate the children of employees of a company is really intended to provide an attractive fringe-benefit to the employer by way of tax-saving. Lord Cross expressed the belief that the courts ought to take fiscal consequences into account when deciding upon charitable status. He went on to explain that this

---

[13] See esp *Isaac v Defriez* (1754) Amb 595
[14] *Spiller v Maude* (1881) 32 ChD 158n (fund subscribed by members of a theatrical society to relieve any orphans of deceased members, to provide medical advice, and to pay annuities to incapacitated annuitants of small means held charitable by Jessel MR)
[15] See *Re Gosling* (1900) 16 TLR 152 (Byrne J) (superannuation fund for 'pensioning off old and worn out clerks' of a banking firm); *Re Sir Robert Laidlaw* (CA, 11 Jan 1935) (noted [1950] Ch 177, 195) (trust for relief of poverty among poor members of a company); *Gibson v South American Stores (Gath and Chaves) Ltd* [1950] Ch 177 (CA) (necessitous and deserving persons employed by a company, their widows and dependants); *Re Coulthurst* [1951] Ch 661 (CA) (poor employees of a bank)
[16] *IRC v Educational Grants Assoc Ltd* [1967] Ch 993, 1011 (Harman LJ)
[17] *Re Scarisbrick* [1951] Ch 622, 639 (Evershed MR)
[18] [1972] AC 601
[19] [1951] AC 297

was the reason why trusts for the relief of poverty are outside the *Oppenheim* test, as to provide relief for poor employees is hardly an attractive fringe-benefit. By the same token, he said, he considered that a trust to promote religion amongst the employees of a company could be charitable, provided the benefits were purely spiritual. The additional observations of Lord Cross represented, however, a minority view in *Dingle v Turner* itself. Only Lord Simon agreed with everything that Lord Cross said; and the other Law Lords, including Lord MacDermott himself, expressly dissociated themselves from Lord Cross's remarks that tax privileges should be taken into account.

Distinguishing between private and charitable gifts for poor relations

5.07 It can sometimes be difficult to determine whether a trust for poor relations is intended to be a charitable trust or a private trust.[20] It was at one time thought that the distinction lay in whether the capital of the trust was to be retained, only the income being applied for the benefit of the objects (in which case the gift was charitable), or whether the capital was immediately distributable among the objects (in which case the gift was not charitable).[21] This distinction was rejected, however, by the Court of Appeal in *Re Scarisbrick*,[22] and its rejection was approved by the House of Lords in *Dingle v Turner*.[23] In the latter case, Lord Cross (with whose speech on this point all the other Law Lords agreed) approved what had been said in *Re Scarisbrick*, where it had been laid down that the distinction between a charitable and a private trust[24]

> depended on whether, as a matter of construction, the gift was for the relief of poverty amongst a particular description of poor people or was merely a gift to particular poor persons, the relief of poverty among them being the motive of the gift.

The fact that it may be a trust for immediate distribution or perpetual is therefore merely a matter of evidence in determining into which category the gift falls.[25]

5.08 It was said in the Court of Appeal in *Re Scarisbrick* that even a trust for the relief of poverty will not be charitable if the persons to benefit are named,[26] or if the gift

---

[20] eg *Liley v Hey* (1842) 1 Hare 580, which concerned a devise upon trust to provide an annual distribution amongst such members of the families of 24 specified persons as the trustees should consider in needy circumstances. The heir-at-law contended (inter alia) that the gift was charitable and so void under the Mortmain Act 1736; but Wigram V-C held it valid as a beneficial gift to the objects

[21] *A-G v Price* (1810) 17 Ves 371 (Grant MR); but contrast the decision in *Liley v Hey* (1842) 1 Hare 580

[22] [1951] Ch 622 (CA)

[23] [1972] AC 601

[24] ibid, 616–17

[25] ibid, 617

[26] [1951] Ch 622, 651 (Jenkins LJ); see also *Re Compton* [1945] 1 Ch 123, 137, where Lord Greene MR made it clear that a gift to educate a number of named nephews and nieces of a testator could not be charitable

is to a narrow class of near relatives, such as a testator's statutory next of kin.[27] In conflict with this principle, however, is the more recent first-instance decision in *Re Segelman*.[28]

In *Re Segelman*, a testator had, by his will, established a trust fund to be used 'for **5.09** the assistance . . . for the poor and needy of the class of persons set out in' a schedule to the will. There was also a substitution of issue clause in the event that any of the persons set out in that schedule should predecease the testator or die within twenty-one years of his death. The schedule contained a list of six named persons, and after the name of each of five of them, it added 'and his issue'. At the time of the hearing, there were twenty-six persons who fell within the description in the schedule, which comprised only a selection of the testator's relatives. Chadwick J held that this was a charitable gift for the relief of poverty. He said he was influenced by the fact that the class of those eligible to benefit was not closed upon the testator's death, but remained open for a further period of twenty-one years; and he concluded from this that the testator could not have intended to make a gift to those afterborn issue as such, but rather his intention must have been to relieve poverty amongst the class of which they would be members.[29]

That such inference should be drawn from the presence of the substitution of **5.10** issue clause is somewhat surprising, since such a clause is typically found in a private trust, and it might be inferred from this that a private trust is what the testator intended. As a matter of law, however, the case is doubtful because, although the will referred to the persons falling within the schedule as a 'class', the persons to benefit within that schedule included not merely the issue of five of the named persons, but also the six named persons themselves. No previous case has held charitable for the relief of poverty a gift which included named persons amongst the objects to benefit; indeed, it is difficult to think of a description of objects which more unequivocally characterizes the nature of the benefit as private than a description which specifies the beneficiaries by name. It has been said that charitable trusts for 'poor relations' are anomalous;[30] yet the decision in *Re Segelman* not only extends the anomaly, but does so in an unwarranted way. With respect, therefore, the decision in *Re Segelman* on this point is inconsistent with *Re Scarisbrick* and the earlier cases, and must be considered to have been reached *per incuriam*.

---

[27] *Re Scarisbrick* [1951] Ch 622, 650–1 (Jenkins LJ)
[28] [1996] Ch 171
[29] ibid, 192
[30] *Caffoor v Commissioner of Income Tax, Colombo* [1961] AC 584, 602 (PC)

(2) The advancement of education

The personal nexus test

5.11 For the first time in charity law, the Court of Appeal laid down, in *Re Compton*,[31] a rule of law relating to the community to benefit. The case concerned a gift under the will of a testatrix, upon trust to educate the descendants of three named persons, 'to be used to fit the children to be servants of God serving the nation'. Clearly, 'education' satisfied the public benefit test in the first sense; but the Court of Appeal held that the trust could not be charitable because the beneficiaries were defined by reference to a purely personal relationship to a named *propositus*; and the inherent vice of the personal element was present however long the chain.[32] It had been argued in the case that the gift was charitable because it was beneficial to the community to have individuals so educated as to become God-fearing men and women and good citizens in accordance with the testatrix's direction; but the Court of Appeal rejected this argument, holding that such a direction could not change the character of the gift.[33] In essence, the court was rejecting the argument that the indirect benefit to society of having educated men and women within its ranks was a sufficient benefit to the community for the purpose of the second head of *Pemsel*'s case.[34]

5.12 The personal nexus principle was later extended to members of an association,[35] and it was affirmed by the House of Lords, again in relation to the advancement of education, in the leading case of *Oppenheim v Tobacco Securities Trust Co Ltd*.[36] A trust had been set up by a substantial shareholder in a tobacco company to provide for the education of the children of employees or former employees of the company or of any of its subsidiary or allied companies. The total number of employees involved was more than 110,000; yet the House of Lords held that, despite the large number of children who could receive a benefit, the trust was not charitable as it did not benefit a sufficient section of the community. Lord Simonds laid down two requirements for a charitable trust to satisfy the public benefit test.[37] First, he said that the number of possible beneficiaries must not be numerically negligible. This in itself is a restatement of the evidential requirement

---

[31] [1945] Ch 123

[32] ibid, 131 (Lord Greene MR). The other two members of the Court of Appeal, Finlay and Morton L JJ, merely expressed agreement with Lord Greene MR's judgment

[33] ibid, 136–7

[34] An indirect benefit to the community has been considered sufficient, however, in relation to the advancement of religion: see *Neville Estates Ltd v Madden* [1962] Ch 832 (below, paras 15.15–15.18); and it provides one explanation for the 'poor relations' and related anomalous cases under *Pemsel*'s first head (above, paras 5.05–5.06)

[35] See (in the context of the relief of distress) *Re Hobourn Aero Components Ltd's Air Raid Distress Fund* [1946] Ch 194 (CA)

[36] [1951] AC 297

[37] ibid, 306

already discussed. Secondly, he said that the quality which distinguishes such beneficiaries from other members of the community, so that they form by themselves a section of it, must be a quality which does not depend upon their relationship to a particular individual. No matter how numerous the group may be, if they are defined by reference to a particular *propositus* or several *propositi*, they cannot constitute a sufficient section of the community for the purpose of the law of charity. Lord MacDermott, however, dissented; he considered that public benefit should be purely a matter of evidence in each case. He pointed out the illogicality which results from an application of the rules laid down by the majority.[38] Thus (to use a modern illustration) a trust to educate the children of employees of British Nuclear Fuels would not be charitable, since the persons to benefit are defined by reference to a personal nexus (one of employment); whereas a trust to educate the children of workers in the nuclear industry would be charitable, since the persons to benefit are defined merely by reference to a calling. In essence, however, the two groups are substantially the same persons.

'Founder's Kin'

Before the decision in *Re Compton*,[39] the authorities had been interpreted to support the proposition that a bequest for the education of the donor's descendants at a school or college was charitable.[40] This proposition was derived principally from *Spencer v All Souls College*,[41] where the statutes of the founder of the College provided that in elections to fellowships preference was to be given to the founder's kin, 'this being a very common provision in the case of ancient foundations'.[42] In *Re Compton*, Lord Greene MR said that the validity of such a disposition 'had never been questioned from remote ages' and had not been questioned in that case.[43] Furthermore, his Lordship rejected the view that a more general proposition could be extracted from it,[44] and considered that cases which appeared to extend the principle beyond founder's kin fellowships on the endowment of a college for the advancement of learning had either been misinterpreted[45] or were unsound.[46]

5.13

---

[38] ibid, 317–19

[39] [1945] 1 Ch 123 (CA)

[40] *Tudor on Charities* (5th edn, Sweet & Maxwell, 1929) 30–1

[41] (1762) Wilm 163 (Wilmot J sitting as an assessor to the Archbishop of Canterbury, the Visitor of the College, upon appeal by certain 'founder's kin' against the decision of the warden and fellows who had elected other persons)

[42] *Re Compton* [1945] 1 Ch 123, 132 (Lord Greene MR)

[43] ibid, 132

[44] ibid, 131–6

[45] eg *A-G v Sidney Sussex College* (1869) 4 Ch 722, which Lord Greene MR considered a special case which in some respects resembled the 'Founder's Kin' cases, and *Re Lavelle* [1914] 1 IR 194, which he did not think carried the matter any further: *Re Compton* [1945] 1 Ch 123, 134

[46] eg *Re Rayner* (1920) 122 LT 577 (Eve J): see *Re Compton* [1945] 1 Ch 123, 134–5 (Lord Greene MR)

5.14 Lord Greene MR's judgment left the founder's kin cases as the only exception to the personal nexus rule in the context of the advancement of education; and the importance of these had already been narrowed in the nineteenth century when founder's kin fellowships in the Universities of Oxford and Cambridge were for the most part abolished pursuant to statutory powers conferred on the Colleges of those ancient universities.[47] Since the decision in *Re Compton*, the Privy Council has said that the principle upon which such cases were decided rested upon virtually no direct authority, and that they should probably be regarded as belonging more to history than to doctrine.[48] Nevertheless, the principle of these cases may have survived in so far as it has been held that the charitable status of a trust for the advancement of education directed primarily at the public at large is not destroyed merely by the testator's or settlor's direction that the trustees are to give preference to his descendants.[49]

(3) The advancement of religion

5.15 The requirement that a sufficient section of the community be capable of benefiting appears to be less stringent in the case of trusts for the advancement of religion. In *Dingle v Turner*,[50] Lord Cross said that a trust to promote some religion among the employees of a company might perhaps safely be held to be charitable, provided it was clear that the benefits were to be purely spiritual.[51] This suggests that the personal nexus test in *Oppenheim*'s case[52] might be of more limited application to the advancement of religion. Lord Cross's illustration was made in the context of his suggestion that the courts should take tax consequences into account in deciding upon charitable status, the notion being that such purely spiritual benefits would not comprise an attractive fringe-benefit. The status of this dictum is, however, uncertain, since Lord Cross's view that tax considerations should weigh with the courts in this field was one with which the majority of their Lordships in that case disagreed.

5.16 It does nevertheless seem to be established that, despite its rejection as a sufficient benefit in *Re Compton* in relation to the advancement of education, a tangible

---

[47] Oxford University Act 1854 (17 & 18 Vict c 81) s 28 (enabling the Colleges to convert founder's kin fellowships into scholarships and exhibitions); Cambridge University Act 1856 (19 & 20 Vict c 88) s 27 (to modify or abolish any right of preference). See *Re Compton* [1945] 1 Ch 123, 132 (Lord Greene MR)

[48] *Caffoor v Commissioner of Income Tax, Colombo* [1961] AC 584, 602 (Lord Radcliffe, giving the advice of the Judicial Cttee). See GD Squibb QC, *Founders' Kin: Privilege and Pedigree* (Oxford Univ Press, 1972)

[49] *Re Koettgen's Will Trusts* [1954] 1 Ch 252 (discussed below, paras 5.26–5.28). Upjohn J did not, however, base his reasoning on any analogy with the founder's kin cases, and did not mention them in his judgment

[50] [1972] AC 601

[51] ibid, 625

[52] *Oppenheim v Tobacco Securities Trust Co Ltd* [1951] AC 297 (HL)

indirect public benefit can suffice in the context of the advancement of religion. In *Neville Estates Ltd v Madden*,[53] Cross J held charitable a trust for the advancement of religion amongst members of the Catford Synagogue. The class was very small, and it was defined by reference to membership of the Synagogue; but the judge took notice of the fact that the members mixed with their fellow citizens in the world and that the benefit would accrue to the public at large.[54] A purely intangible indirect benefit does not, however, suffice, as was held in the leading case of *Gilmour v Coats*,[55] where the nuns were purely cloistered, and the public benefit which the Catholic Church claimed for the trust (namely the value of intercessory prayer and spiritual edification) was held to be incapable of judicial proof.

On the principle of *Neville Estates Ltd v Madden*, an Anglican retreat house ought to be considered charitable, since those spending time there do subsequently mix with their fellow citizens in the world. Unfortunately, when the charitable status of such retreat houses fell for judicial consideration in *Re Warre's Will Trust*,[56] Harman J held the retreat was not charitable. His Lordship relied on *Gilmour v Coats*, but that case seems to turn on the fact that the nuns never left their convent. Harman J's decision was nevertheless approved in *Re Banfield*,[57] where, however, Goff J was able to reach a different result. *Re Banfield* concerned the charitable status of the Pilsden community house. The purposes of the community involved members going out and doing good works in the community; and, on this basis, Goff J held it charitable because the community opened out to reach the public.[58] Despite his Lordship's distinguishing of *Re Warre's Will Trust*, the earlier case remains unsatisfactory.[59]   **5.17**

The direct benefit to be derived from a trust for the saying of masses for the soul of a deceased testator appears to be a private one. Nevertheless, provided the masses are to be said in public, the indirect public benefit suffices to meet the requirement that a sufficient section of the community be capable of benefiting.[60]   **5.18**

(4) Other purposes beneficial to the community

Personal nexus test

The personal nexus test was applied to the relief of distress (not being the relief of poverty) in *Re Hobourn Aero Components Ltd's Air Raid Distress Fund*,[61] where a   **5.19**

---

[53] [1962] Ch 832
[54] ibid, 853
[55] [1949] AC 426
[56] [1953] 1 WLR 725
[57] [1968] 1 WLR 846
[58] ibid, 852
[59] See ch 4, para 4.52
[60] *Re Hetherington, Gibbs v McDonnell* [1990] Ch 1
[61] [1946] Ch 194 (CA)

fund had been raised amongst workers in a factory in Coventry during the Second World War to provide for those amongst themselves who suffered loss in air raids. At the end of the war, a surplus remained in the fund, and the question arose as to what should be done with it. The Court of Appeal first had to consider whether the fund was in nature charitable; but they held that it was not, one reason being that the benefits were restricted to those in the employment of the company, that is, there was a personal nexus, albeit one of contract rather than of blood. Since this decision, it appears that the personal nexus test applies generally to all purposes falling under the fourth head.

Prohibition on a 'class within a class'

5.20   Purposes under the fourth head are subject to an additional public benefit requirement, which does not apply to the other three heads. In *Inland Revenue Commissioners v Baddeley*, Viscount Simonds commented:[62]

> It is, . . . in my opinion, particularly important in cases falling within the fourth category to keep firmly in mind the necessity of the element of general public utility, and I would not relax this rule. For here is a slippery slope. In the case under appeal the intended beneficiaries are a class within a class; they are those of the inhabitants of a particular area who are members of a particular church: the area is comparatively large and populous and the members may be numerous. But if this trust is charitable for them, does it cease to be charitable as the area narrows down and the numbers diminish?

Later in his speech he said that,[63]

> though I am well aware that in its application it may often be very difficult to draw the line between public and private purposes, I should in the present case conclude that a trust cannot qualify as a charity within the fourth class . . . if the beneficiaries are a class of persons not only confined to a particular area but selected from within it by reference to a particular creed.

5.21   Viscount Simonds' words could be interpreted narrowly so that the 'class within a class' prohibition applies only to purposes within the fourth head that restrict the persons to benefit by area and religion; but in principle it would seem that his Lordship must be taken to have intended that the presence of any two or more restrictions on the class of persons to benefit, whatever the nature of such restrictions might be, has the effect of preventing such class from comprising a sufficient section of the community within the fourth head. The 'class within a class' prohibition does not apply to the other three heads, so that a trust for the relief of the poor in a particular village is charitable for the relief of poverty even though, to qualify as an object of the charity, a person must satisfy the twin requirements of poverty and residence.

---

[62]   [1955] AC 572 591 (HL)
[63]   ibid, 592

(5)   Recreational Charities Act 1958

Meaning of 'public benefit' under the Act

The Recreational Charities Act 1958 expressly provides that nothing in section 1   **5.22**
is to derogate from the principle that a trust or institution to be charitable must be
for the public benefit.[64] In this context, 'public benefit' refers to the requirement
of charity law that a sufficient section of the public at large should be capable of
benefit, and that the overall effects should not be harmful.[65]

In *Oxford Ice Skating Association Ltd*,[66] the Charity Commissioners considered the   **5.23**
charitable status of a company's objects that included the provision of facilities for
an ice-skating rink in Oxford or its environs to be available to the members of the
public at large. The Inland Revenue had objected to the company's registration as
a charity on the ground that such a specialized facility would benefit only a relatively small number of the persons in the community, which would not satisfy the
public benefit requirement. The Charity Commissioners, however, accepted the
evidence of the promoters that the facilities would be available to a substantial
number of members of the public, the majority of whom would not require formal instruction or need to purchase special equipment; and they also accepted the
estimate that such an ice rink would be used by at least 6,000 people each week.
The Charity Commissioners concluded that the provision of a public ice-skating
rink is charitable both under the law as it was before 1958, and also, in the *Oxford*
case, by reason of the Recreational Charities Act 1958, having regard to the evidence of public benefit which had been provided.

The fact that an institution's facilities are open to the public at large does not, how-   **5.24**
ever, mean conclusively that the public benefit requirement is satisfied. In *North
Tawton Rugby Union Football Club*,[67] the Club had an open membership in that,
although the use of the rugby facilities was available only to members, it was open
to any member of the public to join because the subscription was of a modest
amount, and no minimum level of ability was required to join. The Charity
Commissioners did not consider that such type of membership structure would
itself preclude a finding that the facilities were available to the public at large.
Nevertheless, on the facts the Charity Commissioners decided that the main purpose of the Club was the benefit of its members; it was therefore a self-regarding
institution and did not satisfy the public benefit requirement.[68]

---

[64] Recreational CA 1958, s 1(1)
[65] *Wynn v Skegness UDC* [1967] 1 WLR 52, 63–4 (Ungoed-Thomas J)
[66] [1984] Ch Com Rep 10–11 (paras 19–25)
[67] (1997) 5 Decisions 7
[68] ibid, 12–13, applying *IRC v City of Glasgow Police Athletic Assoc* [1953] AC 380 (HL)

Restrictions by reference to race, nationality, ethnic or national origins, or religion

5.25 Although, under the fourth head of *Pemsel*, the section of the community to benefit cannot be a class within a class,[69] the Charity Commissioners have expressed the view that this prohibition does not apply to the section of the community to benefit under the Recreational Charities Act 1958.[70] The Commissioners are therefore prepared to register as charitable under that Act the objects of community associations and other recreational organizations that define the persons to benefit, not merely by reference to the criteria set out in section 1(2)(b)(i),[71] but additionally by reference to race, nationality, ethnic or national origins,[72] or religion, provided those further classes are capable of certain identification and it is possible to show that they are in consequence in social and economic need.[73] Where the organization is not open to the public at large, however, the Charity Commissioners will not treat the public benefit requirement as satisfied if there is anything to prevent any member of the beneficiary class from joining. There must therefore be no power to veto any proposed member of that class, the subscription must not be unreasonably high so as to constitute a bar to membership, and the number of members of that class must not be limited.[74] The Charity Commissioners have also approved a model form of objects for charitable community associations and other recreational organizations established primarily for identifiable racial minority groups where the Commissioners are satisfied that a special need exists.[75]

C. Preference for a private class

(1) Preference in governing instrument

5.26 Some governing instruments have attempted to circumvent the personal nexus rule in *Oppenheim*'s case by specifying a broad class of potential objects which does comprise a sufficient section of the community for the purpose of the law of

---

[69] *IRC v Baddeley* [1955] AC 572, 591–2 (Viscount Simonds) (HL)

[70] (1995) 4 Decisions 17–21. The Charity Commissioners reached this conclusion because they considered the ambit of the classes specified in s 1(2)(b)(i) to be sufficiently ambiguous on this point to cause them to invoke (in accordance with *Pepper v Hart* [1993] AC 593 (HL)) parliamentary material as an aid to construction. In this connection they quoted from a speech of the Home Office Minister introducing the Bill in the House of Commons: *Hansard*, HC (series 5) vol 582, col 322 (11 Feb 1958)

[71] ie that the persons for whom the facilities are primarily intended have need of such facilities 'by reason of their youth, age, infirmity or disablement, poverty or social and economic circumstances'

[72] But not by reference to colour: Race Relations Act 1976

[73] (1995) 4 Decisions 17, 19

[74] ibid, 20

[75] ibid, 21

charity, but adding a proviso that, in making their selection amongst that class, the trustees should give preference to a preferred group of beneficiaries. If the preferred group itself comprises a sufficient section of the community, there is no problem—the public benefit requirement remains satisfied.[76] The difficulty arises where the preferred group is defined by reference to a personal nexus (for example, children of a specified person or employees of a named company). If charity trustees were permitted to exercise a preference in a charitable trust in favour of a private class, the way would be open to drive a coach and horses through the personal nexus rule. If the purpose is the relief of poverty, there is no objection to the existence of a preference for the testator's next of kin or for members of a club or employees of a company and their relatives, since such purpose is not subject to the personal nexus rule. In principle, the problem with a preference for a private class could arise under any of the remaining three heads of *Pemsel*; in practice, however, it has arisen most frequently in relation to the advancement of education.

The issue first came before the court in *Re Koettgen*.[77] A testatrix had left her residuary estate upon trust for the furtherance of commercial education of British-born subjects whose means were insufficient for their obtaining such an education at their own expense. The testatrix further provided that, in selecting the beneficiaries, **5.27**

> It is my wish that the . . . trustees shall give a preference to any employees of JB & Co (London) Ltd, or any members of the families of such employees; failing a sufficient number of beneficiaries under such description then the persons eligible shall be any persons of British birth as the . . . trustees may select[,]

provided that no more than 75 per cent of the income each year could be made available to the preferred class.

Although there was a preference for a class which would not itself comprise a sufficient section of the community in the law of charity, Upjohn J held that the preference did not deprive the trust of its charitable nature. He said that the stage at which the public nature of the trust was to be decided was when the primary class of beneficiaries was ascertained. The primary class (British-born subjects of insufficient means) was a sufficient section of the community, and the trust was therefore of a sufficiently public nature. The direction to the trustees, when selecting from that primary class, to prefer the employees of the company and members of their families could not affect the validity of the primary trust, it being uncertain whether such persons would in any year exhaust 75 per cent of the trust fund. **5.28**

---

[76] eg *Re Beloved Wilks' Charity* (1851) 3 Mac & G 440, where the trust instrument directed the trustees to select a boy to be educated for holy orders in the Church of England, and provided that they should give preference to boys from specified parishes if a fit and proper candidate could be found in them
[77] [1954] Ch 252

In his Lordship's view, the will did not create a trust primarily for persons connected with the specified company, and the class of persons to benefit was not 'confined' to them. The trust was therefore a valid charitable trust.

(2) Priority in governing instrument

5.29   *Re Koettgen*[78] is a much criticized decision; and, whilst it has not been overruled, it has been distinguished in later cases. It has been held not to apply where the trustees, instead of being given a discretion to prefer, are placed under a positive duty to apply income or capital for the benefit of any members of the preferred class who are in existence or who come forward.

5.30   In *Caffoor v Commissioners of Income Tax, Colombo*,[79] the income from a trust deed was to be spent in educating in England deserving youths of the Islamic faith; and the recipients were to be selected in the following order: first, the male descendants of the grantor, failing whom, secondly, youths of the Islamic faith born in Ceylon. The Privy Council held that the trust was not charitable because it did not satisfy the public benefit requirement. Lord Radcliffe, giving the advice of the Board, considered that the decision in *Re Koettgen* 'edges very near to being inconsistent with' *Oppenheim v Tobacco Securities Trust Co Ltd*,[80] and he said it was unnecessary for their Lordships to say whether they would have put the same construction on the will there in question as Upjohn J did, or whether they regarded the distinction which he made as ultimately maintainable.[81] Lord Radcliffe nevertheless distinguished *Re Koettgen* on the ground that in the case before them the primary class was the family of the grantor.[82] The distinction therefore appears to be that Upjohn J had been dealing with a matter of preference, which went merely to the discretion of the trustees; whereas, in *Caffoor*'s case, the trustees had no discretion: any existing members of the private class had an absolute priority.

(3) De facto *application to private class*

5.31   The decision in *Re Koettgen*[83] was again distinguished in *Inland Revenue Commissioners v Educational Grants Association Ltd*.[84] This concerned a company set up by Metal Box Ltd, the principal object of which was the advancement of education. The objects clause of the company was couched in very general terms, and no particular class of persons to benefit was specified. In fact, however, the managers of the fund applied on average at least three-quarters of its income each year for the education of the children of the employees of Metal Box Ltd. The

---

[78] [1954] Ch 252
[79] [1961] AC 584
[80] [1951] AC 297 (HL)
[81] [1961] AC 584, 604
[82] ibid
[83] [1954] Ch 252
[84] [1967] Ch 993 [CA]

issue before the court was whether the company was entitled to tax relief on that part of its income expended for the benefit of children of employees of Metal Box Ltd, as tax relief was available only to the extent that the income was applied for charitable purposes only. The Court of Appeal, upholding Pennycuick J's judgment at first instance, held that the company was not entitled to tax relief on the income applied in this way.

The effect of the Court of Appeal's decision may be that, whilst a preference clause **5.32** on the lines of *Re Koettgen* does not preclude charitable status, if the trustees do in fact apply substantial amounts of income to members of the preferred class, such application is not an application for charitable purposes only. From this, it would follow that an application to a private class is a breach of trust. The effect may therefore be that a preference clause for a private class in a charitable trust is effectively void. If in fact the trustees apply the income to members of a preferred class, it may be necessary to decide if that application is a breach of trust. It will be if the persons were selected because they were members of a private class. If, however, the members of the preferred class are also members of the (wider) primary class, it might be argued that the trustees could validly select them as being members of that primary class. As was argued in the *Educational Grants* case, why should the children of employees of Metal Box Ltd, out of all the children in the United Kingdom, be the only persons in whose favour the managers of the fund could not exercise their discretion? The point was dealt with by Pennycuick J at first instance. He said that, in order to decide whether the income had been applied by way of public benefit,[85]

> I must, I think, look at the individuals and institutions for whose benefit the income has been applied, and seek to discern whether these individuals and institutions possess any, and if so, what, relevant characteristics by virtue of which the income has been applied for their benefit. One may for this purpose look at the minutes of the council, circular letters and so forth.

It would therefore seem that, if the trustees have in fact applied a large proportion of the income to members of a private class, a strong presumption is raised that those individuals were selected by reference to their membership of such class, so that the trustees would be committing a breach of trust. It would then be for the trustees to bring evidence before the court to rebut that presumption.

(4) The Charity Commissioners' approach

Although restricted in scope, the principle in *Re Koettgen*[86] remains binding on the **5.33** Charity Commissioners, and it is not surprising that, since that case was decided, they have received a number of applications to register as charities institutions

---

[85] [1967] Ch 123, 143–4
[86] [1954] Ch 252

whose objects (evidently drafted with regard to Upjohn J's judgment) contain a preference for a private class. Since the trust in *Re Koettgen* contained a 75 per cent ceiling upon an application of income to the preferred class, any trust which does not contain a restriction at least as strict will not be registered as charitable; but, even if an instrument contains an equivalent restriction, it will not necessarily achieve charitable status.

5.34 The Charity Commissioners' approach is well illustrated in their decision on the charitable status of the Cowan Charitable Trust.[87] The trust deed provided that the trustees should in their discretion apply the capital of the trust fund

> for charitable purposes and charitable institutions within the United Kingdom Provided that it is the wish of the Settlor (but without hereby creating or imposing any binding trust or obligation upon the Trustees) that the Trustees shall as between claims upon the Charity which shall appear to them to have equal merit prefer the claims of persons included amongst the Principal Beneficiaries[,]

subject to the qualification that no capital, and no more than 75 per cent of the income each year, could be applied exclusively for the benefit of the Principal Beneficiaries, 'save in so far as such benefit shall take the form of the relief of poverty amongst them'.

5.35 The Charity Commissioners decided that this trust was not entitled to be registered as a charity. They distinguished *Re Koettgen* on two grounds. First, the size of the primary beneficiary class in the Cowan Charitable Trust, unlike its equivalent in *Re Koettgen*, varied according to the particular charitable purpose to which the trustees were considering applying the trust moneys. The objection here would appear to be that the primary beneficiary class could include persons who were defined by reference to a personal nexus, and who could not therefore (except in relation to the relief of poverty) comprise a sufficient section of the community. Secondly, the mere fact that the trust deed used the expression 'charitable purposes' did not mean that the trust was necessarily wholly and exclusively charitable. Upon a construction of the trust deed, it was evident that the purposes of the trust included the conferring of private benefits on the Principal Beneficiaries. Its purposes, unlike those in *Re Koettgen*, were therefore not wholly and exclusively charitable.

5.36 The importance of the governing instrument giving the trustees merely a permissive power in favour of the preferred class, rather than placing them under an obligation to prefer such class, is clear from the Charity Commissioners' decision on the Haymarket Charitable Trust.[88] The draft deed declared trusts for the advancement of education by the giving of grants to or for the benefit of persons

---

[87] *The Cowan Charitable Trust* [1976] Ch Com Rep 14–16 (paras 45–9)
[88] *Haymarket Charitable Trust; The Harlow Meyer Educational Charitable Trust; Temple Educational Trust* [1978] Ch Com Rep 27–8 (paras 86–9)

chosen by the trustees to enable such persons to study at a school or college, and by the giving of grants to a school or college for the advancement of education. The draft deed directed that the trustees, in considering applications for grants from individuals, 'shall give preference' to persons whose parents or guardians were or previously had been employed by a number of specified companies. There was a further proviso restricting the amount of income applicable to such preferred persons in any year to 75 per cent. As it stood the Charity Commissioners would not have been prepared to register it as a charity, because the trustees were under a duty to give preference to the preferred class; but the Commissioners said that if the trust deed were amended to make the exercise of that power permissive, it would then be indistinguishable from *Re Koettgen*, and they would be prepared to register it as a charity.

D. Private benefit merely incidental

(1) General principles

Even if it is established that the purposes of an institution are for the benefit of the public, it will not attain charitable status if it is established primarily for the private benefit of its members. In many instances it is a question of weighing the public benefit (if any) against the potential for private benefit. If the private benefit is more than incidental, the public benefit requirement will not be satisfied.[89]   **5.37**

An illustration is *Hadaway v Hadaway*,[90] which concerned a bequest upon trust to found a bank whose object was 'to assist . . . planters and agriculturalists' by way of loans at low rates of interest. Even though the advancement of agriculture itself is a charitable purpose,[91] this particular trust was held not charitable because it was primarily directed at conferring private benefits. Viscount Simonds said that any indirect benefit to the community there might be was 'too speculative and remote'.[92]   **5.38**

A more recent case where private benefits outweighed public benefits is *Inland Revenue Commissioners v Oldham Training and Enterprise Council*.[93] One of the express objects of Oldham TEC was to promote industry, commerce, and enterprise in all forms for the benefit of the public in or around Oldham, and in furtherance of that object there was an ancillary object to provide support services and advice to and for new businesses. Lightman J considered that this object   **5.39**

---

[89] *IRC v City of Glasgow Police Athletic Assoc* [1953] AC 380 (HL)
[90] [1955] 1 WLR 16 (PC)
[91] *IRC v Yorkshire Agricultural Society* [1928] 1 KB 611
[92] [1955] 1 WLR 16, 20
[93] [1996] STC 1218

extended to enabling Oldham TEC to promote the interests of individuals engaged in trade, commerce, or enterprise, and the evidence of its activities showed that, by its provision of enterprise services, Oldham TEC did precisely this. Compared to such private benefits, the benefits to the community conferred by such activities were too remote. Oldham TEC's objects were therefore not wholly and exclusively charitable.

5.40 A case on the other side of the line is *Incorporated Council of Law Reporting v Attorney-General*,[94] where the Court of Appeal rejected the argument that the main purpose of the Council, which produces the Law Reports, was to advance the interests of the legal profession by supplying it with the tools of its trade. Buckley LJ said:[95]

> The benefit which the council confers on members of the legal profession in making accurate reports available is that it facilitates the study and ascertainment of the law. It also helps the lawyer to earn his livelihood, but that is incidental to or consequential on the primary scholastic function of advancing and disseminating knowledge of the law, and does not detract from the exclusively charitable character of the council's objects.

5.41 The issue of private benefit in relation to the advancement of education was considered by the Charity Commissioners in *The Centre for British Teachers in Europe Limited*.[96] This was a company whose object was to advance education by promoting the teaching of English in other European countries and by providing facilities for teachers in Britain and elsewhere to acquire experience of teaching in European schools and colleges. In furtherance of this object the company was empowered to recruit teachers and to assist education authorities to recruit teachers, and to provide information and welfare services for teachers. The issue to be resolved was whether one of the purposes of the company was really to benefit teachers by advancing them in their profession. The Charity Commissioners concluded that it was not, and that any benefit teachers might receive (both through being in salaried employment and through training) was merely incidental to the main purpose of teaching the English language. The company was not an employment agency but was itself the employer of teachers and provided teachers for foreign governments and authorities and received substantial fees out of which it paid its employees' salaries. Any profit was applied for the company's other charitable purposes, and no part could be distributed by way of profit or dividends. The fact that the teachers themselves were working for their own private benefit did not mean that they were not also carrying out the object of the company which employed them and thereby advancing education. The Charity Commissioners accordingly registered the company as a charity.

---

[94] [1972] Ch 73 (CA)
[95] ibid, 103
[96] [1976] Ch Com Rep 13–14 (paras 43–4)

D. Private benefit merely incidental

Another specific instance of private benefits in the context of students' unions was considered in chapter 4.[97] **5.42**

It has been held that the mere fact that persons who participated in a choral society's activities derived pleasure from doing so did not preclude the society from being charitable.[98] Such private benefit by way of personal amusement was merely a by-product of the carrying out of the society's charitable purposes. **5.43**

(2) Professional or trade associations

The need to weigh public and private benefits has often arisen with regard to associations concerned with the advancement of knowledge in a particular field in which most of the members have a professional interest.[99] A society formed to promote agriculture (a charitable purpose) was held charitable despite the fact that its members were for the most part involved in agriculture and might therefore derive a private benefit.[100] Atkins LJ said:[101] **5.44**

> if the benefit given to its members is only given to them with a view of giving encouragement and carrying out the main purpose which is a charitable purpose, then I think the mere fact that the members are benefited in the course of promoting the charitable purpose would not prevent the society being established for charitable purposes only.

On a number of occasions, the question of whether a body is primarily for the public benefit, or is really a trade organization to benefit the interests of its members, has fallen to be decided by the Charity Commissioners. The Commissioners decided to register the Council of Industrial Design, whose object was 'the advancement of British industry by the improvement of design in the products thereof', which object they considered beneficial to the public.[102] Although the carrying out of the purpose would result in a commercial benefit to the individual firms whose products would be exhibited, the Charity Commissioners noted that such firms were not members of the institution, and the members of its council were not self-regarding industrialists but the nominees of a Minister of the Crown who had an absolute power to remove them from office.[103] **5.45**

The Charity Commissioners also registered as charitable the Fairtrade Foundation, after it had agreed to revise its objects to the relief of poverty, suffering, and distress in any part of the world and the promotion of research into the causes and **5.46**

---

[97] See ch 4, para 4.27, discussing *London Hospital Medical College v IRC* [1976] 1 WLR 613
[98] *Royal Choral Society v IRC* [1943] 2 All ER 101, 104 (Lord Greene MR)
[99] *Royal College of Surgeons of England v National Provincial Bank Ltd* [1952] AC 631 (HL); *Royal College of Nursing v St Marylebone Corp* [1959] 1 WLR 1077. The respective Colleges were held charitable
[100] *IRC v Yorkshire Agricultural Society* [1928] 1 KB 611
[101] ibid, 631
[102] *Council of Industrial Design* [1973] Ch Com Rep 23–4 (paras 68–70)
[103] ibid, 24 (para 69). See also *Business in the Community* [1987] Ch Com Rep 4–5

189

effects of poverty particularly in relation to the conduct of business and the conditions of employment of poor people in any part of the world. In carrying out its objects, the Foundation intended to promote the use of a 'fair trade mark', which would guarantee to the consumer that the purchase of a particular product would benefit people in the Third World employed in its production. Although the mechanism might produce some commercial profits for businesses and retailers, the Charity Commissioners were satisfied that any such profits were necessarily incidental to the primary purpose of relieving need.[104]

5.47 On the other hand, the Charity Commissioners declined to register the Concrete Society Ltd because it seemed that its activities were primarily directed to the benefit of its members and other persons and organizations who profited from the use of concrete.[105] The Charity Commissioners also declined to register as a charity a company whose object was the promotion of research in connection with the wool textile industry.[106] An important factor there was that the company's articles showed that the research was intended to be private, carried out in secrecy, and available only to the membership; moreover, in practice its general research work was normally classified as confidential for at least twelve months. The Charity Commissioners did not consider this to be charitable research,[107] and the element of private benefit was not so slight as to be merely incidental to the benefit of the community.

E. Self-help

(1) Self-help incompatible with charitable status

5.48 A self-help organization is one which is primarily funded by its members, usually by way of subscription or other regular contributions, for the benefit of its members and (in some instances) of the members' families. Some of these associations, such as building societies and credit unions, exist to promote the economic interests of their members, and their purposes are not charitable. Other such associations exist for purposes which, in themselves, might be charitable—such as the provision of a library and reading room,[108] helping the sick, or relieving poverty. It is clear, however, that, except where its object is the relief of poverty,[109] a self-help

---

[104] *Fairtrade Foundation* (1994) 4 Decisions 1; and the Commissioners' further comment on this decision in *The Review of the Register*, RR1 (Mar 1999), 13–14 (Ann B, para 7)
[105] *The Concrete Society Ltd* [1976] Ch Com Rep 16 (paras 50–3). See also *National House-Builders Registration Council* [1969] Ch Com Rep 10 (para 22); *Wine Standards Board of the Vintners' Company* [1978] Ch Com Rep 30–1 (paras 95–8)
[106] *WIRA (formerly Wool Industries Research Assoc)* [1980] Ch Com Rep 30–1 (paras 97–101)
[107] ie as laid down in *Re Hopkins' Will Trusts* [1965] Ch 669
[108] *Re Dutton* (1878) 4 Ex D 54
[109] *Spiller v Maude* (1886) 32 ChD 158n

organization is not a charity.[110] Three reasons for this have been advanced. First, since the benefits of such an organization are entirely or largely restricted to the members and their immediate families, there is a personal nexus which precludes such persons from comprising a sufficient section of the community for the law of charity.[111] Secondly, self-help might be treated as a separate purpose in itself, and as such is not a purpose contemplated by the Preamble to the Statute of Elizabeth.[112] Thirdly, the courts have sometimes emphasized that charity must contain a degree of altruism, which is the very opposite of self-help.[113]

In order to ascertain whether self-help is present, the court will look at the fund's paramount and primary purpose.[114] A characteristic of a self-help organization is that it is primarily funded by those who receive its benefits; if it is so funded, its character will not be altered by its receipt of outside donations.[115] By the same token, if a society is not primarily funded by its members, but rather by outsiders, it is not prevented from being a charity merely because some of its funds derive from the subscriptions of its members, or because it levies fees for the charitable services which it provides.[116] Donations to an association, unless impressed with a trust, are taken to accrue to its general funds, which the court will not attempt to **5.49**

---

[110] The earliest decision is possibly *Anon* (1745) 3 Atk 277, though Atkins' reports are notoriously unreliable; furthermore it involved a voluntary society, and even a voluntary society with charitable purposes was not regarded at that time as giving rise to a fund which was effectually dedicated to charity. See also *Carne v Long* (1860) 2 De GF & J 75 (gift to a subscription library held not charitable and therefore void for perpetuity). The first clear expression of the incompatibility of mutual benefit and charitable status was in *Re Clark's Trust* (1875) 1 Ch 194 (Hall V-C). See also *Re Dutton* (1878) 4 Ex D 54, where a bequest to the trustees of the Tunstall Athenaeum Mechanics Institute was held not charitable: ibid, 57 (Kelly CB) ('[the Institute] is in reality a species of club in which a number of persons come together for literary purposes and mutual improvement'). See also *Cunnack v Edwards* [1896] 2 Ch 679, 681–2 (Lord Halsbury LC) (CA)

[111] *Re Hobourn Aero Components Ltd's Air Raid Distress Fund* [1946] 1 Ch 194 (CA); *Oppenheim v Tobacco Securities Trust Co Ltd* [1951] AC 297 (HL); *Re Mead's Trust Deed* [1961] 1 WLR 1244 (Cross J)

[112] *Re Hobourn Aero Components Ltd's Air Raid Distress Fund* [1946] 1 Ch 194, 203 (Lord Greene MR)

[113] eg Fitzgibbon LJ in *Re Cranston* [1898] 1 IR 431, 446, specifies as one of the essential attributes of a legal charity 'that it shall be unselfish—i.e. for the benefit of other persons than the donor'. These words were approved by Lord MacDermott in *National Deposit Friendly Society Trustees v Skegness UDC* [1959] AC 293, 315, where he added: 'there can be no doubt that unselfishness and benevolence are still of the essence of legal charity. . . The principle . . . is that a valid charity must be substantially altruistic and benevolent in its purpose.' See also Salmon J in *Waterson v Hendon BC* [1959] 1 WLR 985, 991 ('the object of the members of the society is not to do good to others but to themselves. This object is not altruistic and is, in my judgment, not charitable')

[114] *Re Hobourn Aero Components Ltd's Air Raid Distress Fund* [1946] 1 Ch 194, 202 (Lord Greene MR)

[115] ibid, 203 (Lord Greene MR). Only a very small proportion of the fund in that case derived from outside contributions

[116] *Re Resch's Will Trusts* [1969] 1 AC 514 (PC) (gift for general purposes of a hospital which charged substantial fees but which was not run for the private profit of individuals)

dissect into charitable and non-charitable parts.[117] A fund is no less one for the self-help of its members merely because their benefits are payable at the discretion of the trustees or committee rather than as of right.[118]

5.50 Although it has been said that charity must be provided by way of bounty rather than bargain,[119] this should be understood to mean only that there can be no charity if there is an entitlement to a benefit before it has been conferred.[120] Contractual entitlement of this nature points clearly to self-help, and prevents a co-operative housing association, for example, from being a charity. It is no objection to charitable status, however, that a person selected to benefit takes that benefit in the form of a contract.[121] A non-mutual housing association, whose members do not themselves receive benefits, and which exists to provide housing for the aged, is not prevented from being a charity merely because the beneficiaries selected must enter into a contract with the association to pay rent or other sums, even if they ultimately acquire a proprietary interest in their home.[122]

(2) Poverty qualification

5.51 The authorities suggest that the vitiating factor of self-help (like the personal nexus rule[123]) does not apply to a society whose purpose is the relief of poverty.[124] A society may therefore be a charity even though funded by its members, provided its rules restrict the payment of benefits to those members who are poor.[125] This concession applies only to the relief of poverty, not to the relief of the sick, infirm, or distressed.[126] It has been suggested that even a society for the relief of poverty

---

[117] In *Braithwaite v A-G* [1909] 1 Ch 511 a surplus on the dissolution of a non-charitable friendly society was composed of separate funds: one of these was the benefited members' fund; but most of the surplus was contained in the other, the honorary members' fund, which represented the subscriptions of honorary members. It was argued that, as the honorary members were not permitted under the society's rules to receive any benefits, the latter fund had been given for charitable purposes and should be applied cy-près; but the court declined to treat it separately from the society's other assets

[118] *Re Hobourn Aero Components Ltd's Air Raid Distress Fund* [1946] 1 Ch 194, 201 (Lord Greene MR)

[119] *IRC v Society for the Relief of Widows and Orphans of Medical Men* (1926) 11 TC 1, 22 (Rowlatt J)

[120] *Joseph Rowntree Memorial Trust Housing Assoc Ltd v A-G* [1983] Ch 159, 175 (Peter Gibson J, who points out that a co-operative housing association under which the persons requiring the dwellings had constitutional contractual rights to them, would not be charitable)

[121] ibid, 175 (Peter Gibson J)

[122] ibid, 175–6 (Peter Gibson J). On the charitable status of housing associations, see further ch 8, paras 8.219–8.221

[123] *Dingle v Turner* [1972] AC 601 (HL)

[124] *Spiller v Maude* (1886) 32 ChD 158n

[125] ibid. A friendly society for the relief of poverty can therefore be a charity: *Re Buck* [1896] 2 Ch 727 (Kekewich J)

[126] *Waterson v Hendon BC* [1959] 1 WLR 985 (society funded by members for the relief of members in sickness or infirmity: not charitable); *Re Hobourn Aero Components Ltd's Air Raid Distress Fund* [1946] 1 Ch 194 (fund for contributing employees in distress as the result of enemy action: not charitable)

amongst its members will not be charitable if the benefits are received by way of bargain rather than by way of bounty.[127] This view probably remains sound, since the entitlement of the recipients would arise, not from the exercise of the discretion of the trustees or committee at the time when the recipients fall into poverty, but from the contractual right which arose at an earlier date when they first joined.[128] A society for the relief of poverty may therefore be a charity even though persons selected to benefit are thereupon required to become members on payment of a modest fee. That would not turn what is in essence a charity into something not a charity.[129]

F. Private profit

A charity is not precluded from engaging in lawful trading activities[130] or from charging for its services[131] (unless perhaps the charges are so high that the poor are effectively excluded[132]). Any profits which it makes must, however, be applicable only for wholly and exclusively charitable purposes.[133] A body cannot, therefore, be a charity if its constitution permits the distribution of any profits for private benefit, for example, to its members or shareholders. For this reason, a charity cannot generally be created as a company limited by shares.   **5.52**

An exceptional case where a company limited by shares was held, for some purposes at least, to be a charity, was *The Abbey, Malvern Wells Ltd v Ministry of Local Government and Planning.*[134] A company limited by shares was formed to run a school for the private profit of its shareholders. Subsequently, it was decided that the school should be run as a charitable body. The usual method of achieving this would have been for the existing company to transfer the school to another company or a trust established (in either case) for wholly and exclusively charitable purposes. Instead, the shareholders merely vested their shares in trustees of a   **5.53**

---

[127] *IRC v Society for the Relief of Widows and Orphans of Medical Men* (1926) 11 TC 1, 22 (Rowlatt J)

[128] The view stated in the text is supported by the explanation of Rowlatt J's dictum provided by Peter Gibson J in *Joseph Rowntree Memorial Trust Housing Assoc Ltd v A-G* [1983] Ch 159, 174–5

[129] *Re Hobourn Aero Components Ltd's Air Raid Distress Fund* [1946] 1 Ch 194, 202 (Lord Greene MR)

[130] For trading by charities, see ch 20

[131] *IRC v Falkirk Temperance Café Trust* (1927) 11 TC 353; *Re Resch's Will Trusts* [1969] 1 AC 514 (PC)

[132] See *Re Resch's Will Trusts* [1969] 1 AC 514, 544, where the Privy Council held a fee-charging hospital charitable: 'The service is needed by all, not only by the well-to-do. So far as its nature permits it is open to all; the charges are not low, but the evidence shows that it cannot be said that the poor are excluded' (Lord Wilberforce, delivering the advice of the Board)

[133] See, eg, *Incorporated Council of Law Reporting for England and Wales v A-G* [1971] Ch 626 (CA)

[134] [1951] Ch 728

charitable trust. Danckwerts J nevertheless lifted the veil of incorporation and held that the company could be considered to be a charity for the purposes of entitlement to an exemption from a development charge under the planning legislation.[135]

5.54 A clause in the governing instrument which provides for, or provides scope for, the remuneration or other benefit of its trustees or directors, will deny an organization charitable status on the ground that this is an application for the private benefit of those persons, unless the applicants for registration can satisfy the Commissioners that such remuneration is necessary in the interests of the more efficient management of the charity.[136]

5.55 A charity's constitution may permit it to hire and employ staff in the course of carrying out its purposes; and the ability to apply its income or other funds in paying such persons' salaries does not deprive it of charitable status, since the payment of a salary is not a payment out of profits. If, however, the constitution provides for the payment of what might be regarded as an excessive salary, the Charity Commissioners might treat this as an application for the purposes of private profit and deny the body registration as a charity.

G. Charitable purposes overseas

5.56 To be charitable, a trust or institution must be based in the United Kingdom;[137] but the courts have on several occasions had to consider whether the promotion by such a body of a purpose which would be charitable if carried out in the United Kingdom, is charitable if it is to be performed overseas. The promotion of a purpose overseas raises issues of the community to be benefited (the population overseas or that in the United Kingdom), and also public policy. In the earliest cases, however, these issues were not directly addressed, as in *Whicker v Hume*,[138] where the House of Lords held charitable a bequest upon trust, to be applied at the trustees' discretion, 'for the benefit and advancement, and propagation, of education and learning in every part of the world so far as circumstances will permit'. Since then, the House of Lords has held charitable a conveyance of land upon trust to support the missionary establishments of the Moravian Church among heathen nations;[139] and other courts have held charitable a gift to the poor of

---

[135] See further the discussion of this case in ch 8, para 8.69

[136] This is considered in detail in ch 9, paras 9.97–9.115

[137] *Camille and Henry Dreyfus Foundation Inc v IRC* [1954] Ch 672 (CA). On jurisdictional issues, see further ch 11, paras 11.01–11.04

[138] (1858) 7 HL 124

[139] Comrs *for Special Purposes of the Income Tax v Pemsel* [1891] AC 531; it was put in argument (ibid, 536) that the trusts were for the benefit of foreign missions, whereas the intention of the legislature in granting tax exemptions was to relieve the inhabitants of the United Kingdom, but their Lordships' speeches did not deal with this directly

Obermoerlen in Germany,[140] and a testamentary gift to the German Government 'for the benefit of its soldiers disabled in the late war' (that is, the First World War).[141] A court has also held charitable a gift to trustees in the United Kingdom 'upon trust for charitable objects in the island of Cephalonia'.[142] In none of these cases, however, was there any significant discussion of the public benefit and public policy implications.

In *Keren Kayemeth Le Jisroel Ltd v Inland Revenue Commissioners*,[143] a company   **5.57** had been formed with the object of purchasing land in Palestine, Syria, and parts of Turkey for the purpose of settling Jews. The House of Lords rejected the argument that the object could be considered for the relief of poverty or the advancement of religion, and held that it could not be charitable under the fourth head of *Pemsel* because it was uncertain which Jews were to benefit, and the community to benefit could not therefore be identified.[144] The inference from this is that the court might have been prepared to hold the object charitable if the Jewish community had been sufficiently defined, and that it would not have been an objection that the community to benefit was not that of the United Kingdom.

In *Camille and Henry Dreyfus Foundation Inc v Inland Revenue Commissioners*,[145]   **5.58** the Court of Appeal held that a body incorporated in New York State was not entitled to tax relief on dividends arising in the United Kingdom because it was not a body of persons established in the United Kingdom for charitable purposes only. The problem of a charity in this country performing its objects overseas did not therefore arise; but Evershed MR did make some general observations. His Lordship said that it might be, on very general grounds, that the relief of poverty or distress in any part of the world, or the advancement of the Christian religion in any part of the world, would be regarded as being for the benefit of the community in the United Kingdom; but he saw 'formidable difficulties' (involving public policy) where the objects of the trust were the setting out of soldiers, or the repair of bridges or causeways, in a foreign country.[146] Jenkins LJ added to this list the reduction of the national debt of a foreign state;[147] but he expressly chose not to decide if the element of public benefit in those purposes carried out overseas which are recognized as charitable should be looked on as consisting in the direct benefit to the foreign population, or in 'some secondary and indirect benefit in the shape (for instance) of moral improvement, assumed to be conferred on the

---

[140] *Re Geck* (1893) 69 LT 819 (CA)
[141] *Re Robinson* [1931] 2 Ch 122 (Maugham J), where the judgment is chiefly concerned with the fact that the trustee, the German Government, was abroad
[142] *Re Vagliano* [1905] WN 179 (Lord Wrenbury)
[143] [1932] AC 650 (HL)
[144] ibid, 659 (Lord Tomlin)
[145] [1954] Ch 672, 684
[146] ibid, 684
[147] ibid, 704

public at home'.[148] Evershed MR's view that the public to benefit from the carrying out of a purpose overseas is the community in the United Kingdom was applied in *McGovern v Attorney-General*,[149] and this would seem to represent the present position; although, in view of the earlier observations of the House of Lords in *Keren Keyemeth*,[150] the point cannot be regarded as conclusively resolved.

5.59 In the light of the authorities, the relief of sickness and poverty, and of those who have suffered in a natural disaster, is undoubtedly charitable no matter in what part of the world the purposes are to be carried out;[151] and the same is true of the advancement of religion. The promotion of these purposes might be considered to involve a moral benefit for the community in the United Kingdom Some doubt remains, however, whether the advancement of education overseas is necessarily charitable. The Commissioners take the view that it is, because their approach is to ask first if the objects of the institution in question would be charitable if its purposes were to be carried out in England, and, if the answer is yes, then, in the first three heads of *Pemsel*, the public benefit element is to be presumed.[152]

5.60 Whether it is always charitable to advance education overseas is, however, by no means clear. Although *Whicker v Hume*[153] provides the highest authority that the advancement of education is charitable everywhere in the world, there was no discussion in that case of the community to benefit (and the objects of the trust could in fact have been performed at least in part in the United Kingdom). One of the arguments of counsel was that the trustees could, consistently with the large and vague words of the will, found scholarships in Turkey and Persia for the teaching there of the languages of those countries, and that this could not be called charitable. No response to this is to be found, however, in their Lordships' speeches. The only objection raised on the overseas aspect that their Lordships did address related to the feasibility of carrying the purposes into effect in every part of the world; and Lord Cranworth saw no difficulty in this since, although he considered this 'a silly provision', the bequest was for charitable purposes and the court was under a duty to ensure that the scheme it drew up was as extensive as the nature of the income permitted.[154] The decision therefore largely ignores those public benefit and public policy issues which are now recognized as important.

5.61 In more recent times, a bequest upon trust to promote the arts of self-control and eloquence in Ireland has been held charitable.[155] It is difficult to see, however, why

---

[148] [1954] Ch 672, 704–5
[149] *McGovern v A-G* [1982] Ch 321, 338
[150] *Keren Kayemeth Le Jisroel Ltd v IRC* [1932] AC 650 (HL)
[151] eg *The Independent Iran Fund* [1991] Ch Com Rep 13 (para 70) (relief of sickness and poverty amongst those injured and bereaved in the Iranian earthquakes of 1990)
[152] 'Charities operating overseas: charities for fourth head purposes' (1993) 1 Decisions 16
[153] (1858) 7 HL 124
[154] ibid, 162–3 (Lord Cranworth); see also Lord Chelmsford LC, 154–5
[155] *Re Shaw's Will Trusts* [1952] Ch 163

the advancement of education generally should be charitable in the United Kingdom if the country in which the purpose of the trust is to be carried out is a highly developed industrialized country such as, for instance, the United States of America, whose population enjoys an average standard of living higher than that of the population in this country. In the absence of specific authority, it is suggested that the advancement of education overseas should be charitable only if:

(a) it is also concerned with the relief of poverty or distress, or the advancement of religion; or

(b) it can otherwise be shown that there is a substantial indirect benefit to the community in the United Kingdom.

5.62 The Charity Commissioners have registered as charitable a trust whose purpose was to promote the relief of poverty, sickness, and distress and for the advancement of education (both academic and vocational) throughout the former Republics of the Soviet Union.[156] This might be considered to be charitable as falling within category (a) above.

5.63 The Charity Commissioners have registered as a charity a company whose object was advancing education by promoting the teaching of English in other European countries and by providing facilities for teachers to acquire experience of teaching in European schools and colleges.[157] They there noted that the advancement of education overseas, provided it is not of a purely private nature or carried out for private gain, has long been accepted as being for the benefit of the community and charitable.[158] Applying the foregoing analysis, however, it can be seen that, whilst the teaching of the English language overseas is a direct benefit to the residents of the overseas country who are taught English, the carrying out of that purpose also contains a substantial indirect benefit to the community in the United Kingdom, through the spread of its native language and, by that means, knowledge of its culture and institutions. The registration could therefore be considered to be justified as falling within category (b) above. Similarly, a trust to advance education by promoting the performance of the works of Shakespeare on the stage overseas might be considered to be charitable within this category.[159]

5.64 The foregoing criteria might also be applied to purposes falling under the fourth head of *Pemsel*. Some purposes within the fourth head would undoubtedly not be

---

[156] [1991] Ch Com Rep 13 (para 72)

[157] *The Centre for British Teachers in Europe Ltd* [1976] Ch Com Rep 13–14 (paras 43–4)

[158] ibid, 14 (para 44)

[159] In *Re Shaw* [1957] 1 WLR 729, George Bernard Shaw, whose will provided for the development of a phonetic alphabet, also specified that his trustees were to distribute copies of his work *Androcles and the Lion*, translated into the new alphabet, to overseas libraries. Although Harman J held that the purpose of the trust was not charitable for the advancement of education, the overseas aspect of the trust was not commented upon. Had the purpose been charitable, it might be argued that the public benefit requirement would have been satisfied within category (b) above

charitable, as being against public policy,[160] as indicated by Evershed MR in the *Dreyfus* case. The Charity Commissioners' approach is to ask if an institution whose objects fall within the fourth head would be charitable if its operation were confined to the United Kingdom; if it would be, the Commissioners presume it to be charitable even though it is operating overseas unless it would be contrary to public policy to recognize it.[161] The importance of satisfying the public benefit requirement should not, however, be overlooked. In *Re Jacobs*,[162] a gift for the planting of trees in Israel was held charitable as being for reafforestation and so for the promotion of agriculture. It does not appear that the court addressed either public policy or public benefit, but it might be argued that, as Israel might be treated as a developing country (at least at the time the disposition was made), the gift could be construed as one for the relief of poverty. The prevention of cruelty to animals overseas has been held charitable;[163] and this might be justified on the ground that, since the benefit to the community in such cases is an indirect moral benefit, such benefit can as well accrue to the community in the United Kingdom where the purpose is carried out overseas as where it is carried out in this country. Moral benefits, it might be said, know no frontiers.

5.65 The promotion of a purpose overseas which has a political element might fail to attain charitable status, even if it would otherwise meet the foregoing criteria, if is against public policy. A trust to promote socialized medicine might now be charitable in the United Kingdom, as the legislature of the United Kingdom effectively provided for this by the establishment of the National Health Service, and the public benefit of this is thereby presumed;[164] but by passing the National Health Service Act 1946, the legislature could not be taken to presume that the promotion of socialized medicine is of benefit to the public in this country if it is promoted overseas. To promote such a purpose in an overseas country which does not already have socialized medicine would remain a political purpose, and would not be charitable on that ground alone. It would also fail the public benefit test, since the carrying out of its purposes could damage this country's relations with the overseas country concerned.[165]

5.66 For the same reason, the Amnesty International Trust considered in *McGovern v Attorney-General*[166] would still fail to achieve charitable status. The objects of the

---

[160] eg *Habershon v Varnon* (1851) 4 De G & Sm 467 (trust to restore Jews to Jerusalem, then ruled by the Turks, held void as tending to promote revolution in a friendly state); but a similar trust was held valid at a time when Palestine was no longer ruled by the Turks: *Re Rosenblum* (1924) 131 LT 21

[161] 'Charities operating overseas: charities for fourth head purposes' (1993) 1 Decisions 16, 17

[162] (1970) 114 Sol Jo 515 (Foster J)

[163] *Armstrong v Reeves* (1890) 25 LR Ir 325; *Re Jackson* The Times, 11 June 1910

[164] cf *Re Bushnell* [1975] 1 WLR 1596

[165] *McGovern v A-G* [1982] Ch 321, 338

[166] [1982] Ch 321

trust (which expressly excluded the United Kingdom from its area of operation) included attempting to secure the release of prisoners of conscience and procuring the abolition of torture or inhuman or degrading treatment or punishment. These objects, which were held to be political, effectively sought to promote the attainment of some of the articles contained in the United Nations' Universal Declaration of Human Rights,[167] and similar rights are contained in the European Convention for the Protection of Human Rights and Fundamental Freedoms[168] to which the United Kingdom has long been a signatory. Neither of these treaties, at the time of the decision in the *McGovern* case, formed a part of English law. Although this has now changed with the enactment of the Human Rights Act 1998,[169] which effectively makes Convention rights a part of domestic law, the result in the *McGovern* case would be the same. The Act is necessarily, and for practical reasons, restricted in its effect to the territories of the United Kingdom;[170] the promotion of Convention rights in overseas countries which do not enshrine equivalent provisions in their systems therefore remains a political, and not a charitable, purpose. The objection based on absence of proven benefit to the community in the United Kingdom would therefore remain. Apart from this, it is arguable that the promotion of Convention rights remains a non-charitable purpose in English law even after the passing of the Human Rights Act 1998,[171] and so would not be charitable even if to be performed in other Member States which have enacted equivalent legislation.

---

[167] Cmnd 3320 (1967)

[168] Cmd 8969 (1953)

[169] In force 2 Oct 2000

[170] For judicial statements of the territorial principle of UK legislation, see *Cooke v Charles A Vogeler Co* [1901] AC 102, 107 (Earl of Halsbury LC); *Re Sawyers* (1879) 12 Ch D 522, 526 (James LJ), 528 (Brett LJ); *Clark v Oceanic Contractors Inc* [1983] 2 AC 30, 152 (Lord Wilberforce)

[171] See Ch 1, para 1.120

6

WHOLLY AND EXCLUSIVELY CHARITABLE

A. General principles

(1) Introduction

Meaning of 'wholly and exclusively charitable'

To attain charitable status, an institution's purposes or objects must be wholly and **6.01** exclusively charitable. This requirement originated in the law of trusts, in the principle that the execution of a trust must be under the control of the court, so that administration of it can be reviewed by the court, or so that the court itself can execute the trust.[1] Provided the purposes of a trust are wholly and exclusively charitable, its due administration can be directed and its property can, if necessary, be applied under a scheme.

Although a charity which is a corporate body or an unincorporated association **6.02** does not need charitable status for its validity, charitable status will subject it to the jurisdiction of the High Court over charities,[2] so far as that jurisdiction has not been ousted by any statute or charter under which it was formed; but the High

---

[1] *Morice v Bishop of Durham* (1805) 10 Ves 522, 539–40 (Lord Eldon LC)
[2] *Liverpool and District Hospital for Diseases of the Heart v A-G* [1981] Ch 193 (company limited by guarantee). On the jurisdiction of the court over charities, see ch 11

Court's charity jurisdiction over such charities (like its jurisdiction over charitable trusts) arises only if the institution's objects are wholly and exclusively charitable. Therefore, in order for a body to obtain charitable status, its objects must be wholly and exclusively charitable, whatever its legal structure might be.

6.03 To determine whether a trust's purposes or another institution's objects are wholly and exclusively charitable, it is necessary to consider all the purposes to which the property could be applied consistently with the terms of the instrument itself. Every such object must be wholly and exclusively charitable. A trust with some non-charitable purposes cannot be rendered charitable by the trustees giving an undertaking to apply the property only to those purposes which are wholly and exclusively charitable.[3] Conversely, if a trust's purposes are wholly and exclusively charitable, they do not cease to be so merely because the trustees might, in breach of trust, apply the property to private purposes.[4]

Application to purposes, not means

6.04 Whilst the purposes of an institution must be wholly and exclusively charitable, the ancillary means by which it attains those objects do not need to be. The promotion of agriculture through the holding of agricultural shows has been held charitable, for instance, even though it was common knowledge that all such shows include a number of miscellaneous activities, such as the provision of food and drink, the putting on of entertainments and side-shows of various kinds, and the sale of agricultural produce. The Privy Council accepted the conclusion of the judge at first instance that such activities could be treated as ancillary to the charitable purpose, being intended to assist in ensuring that such shows were successful.[5] If the evidence had been that such activities were more than ancillary to the carrying out of the charitable purposes, they would have been treated as independent (non-charitable) purposes, thereby denying the trust charitable status.

---

[3] *Morice v Bishop of Durham* (1805) 10 Ves 522. A trust whose purposes are not wholly and exclusively charitable will be void unless it can be construed as a valid private trust; but to exist as a private trust, the objects must be certain and there must be no breach of the rule against perpetual trusts

[4] An illustration is *IRC v Mullen* [1979] 1 WLR 130 (CA), where Bridge LJ (dissenting) would have held charitable a trust to provide sports facilities in schools and universities. It had been argued successfully at first instance that the trust should not be charitable because the trustees might provide such facilities at non-charitable schools run for private profit: [1978] 1 WLR 664 (Walton J). The Inland Revenue did not pursue this argument on appeal, however, and Bridge LJ was unimpressed by it, saying that such application would comprise a breach of trust, since the property would pass out of the control of the trustees and could be diverted by the new owners to purposes not within the trust: [1979] 1 WLR 130, 142

[5] *Brisbane City Council v A-G for Queensland* [1979] AC 411, 423–4 (Lord Wilberforce) (PC). See also *Re Lopes* [1931] 2 Ch 130, 136, 137, where Farwell J held that the objects of a zoo were educational and charitable, and none the less so because, in carrying out such objects, it was necessary for the zoo to provide food for persons who attended (inter alia) for educational purposes

(2) Construction of instruments

Benignant construction

Trust instruments

If a trust instrument is susceptible to more than one construction, one of which **6.05** will cause the instrument to be valid, the other void, the court leans in favour of the former. A benignant[6] construction in favour of charity may therefore save a trust which would otherwise be void for ambiguity or uncertainty,[7] and has in fact done so on a number of occasions.[8] The principle does not justify the insertion of words in order to restrict the plain meaning of an expression and thus give validity to an otherwise invalid bequest.[9]

A benignant construction was applied in *Guild v Inland Revenue Commissioners*,[10] **6.06** where the testator had left his residuary estate 'to the town council of North Berwick for the use in connection with the sports centre in North Berwick *or some similar purpose in connection with sport*'.[11] The House of Lords applied a benignant construction to the emphasized words, so that the testator, in specifying a 'similar' purpose, was to be taken to have intended to make provision for sports facilities of the nature provided by a sports centre and which were to be available to the public at large. On this construction, the whole gift was held to be charitable within the Recreational Charities Act 1958.[12]

In a few cases, however, the court has evidently not adopted a benignant approach **6.07** when, arguably, it might have done so.[13] An instance of this is *Re Cole*,[14] where the majority of the Court of Appeal held that a gift 'for the general benefit and general

---

[6] 'Benignant' is an ugly word, but it is used in the cases in this context, eg in *IRC v McMullen* [1981] AC 1, 14 (Lord Hailsham LC) and in *Guild v IRC* [1992] 2 AC 310, 322 (Lord Keith). 'Benign' or 'benevolent' might be more felicitous epithets

[7] *Whicker v Hume* (1858) 7 HL 124; *Weir v Crum-Brown* [1908] AC 162, 167 (Lord Loreburn LC); *Houston v Burns* [1918] AC 337, 341–2 (Lord Finlay LC); *Re Bain* [1930] 1 Ch 224, 230; *Hadaway v Hadaway* [1955] 1 WLR 16, 19; *IRC v McMullen* [1981] AC 1, 14 (Lord Hailsham LC); *Guild v IRC* [1992] 2 AC 310, 322–3 (Lord Keith)

[8] eg *Re Koeppler's Will Trusts* [1986] Ch 423 (CA); *Re Hetherington's Will Trusts* [1990] Ch 1. In *Whicker v Hume* (1858) 7 HL 124, the trust was for 'the advancement and propagation of education and learning all over the world.' Lord Chelmsford LC considered the word 'learning' to be susceptible of various meanings, both knowledge itself and the art of acquiring it. He adopted the latter sense, as carrying out the testator's intention: ibid, 153–4. See also *Re Bain* [1930] 1 Ch 224, 230–1 (Lord Hanworth MR)

[9] *Hadaway v Hadaway* [1955] 1 WLR 16, 19 (Viscount Simonds) (PC)

[10] [1992] 2 AC 310

[11] Emphasis supplied

[12] *Guild v IRC* [1992] 2 AC 310, 323 (Lord Keith)

[13] eg *Farley v Westminster Bank* [1939] AC 430 (HL) (gift to vicar for 'parish work' held not charitable on the ground that it could be applied for non-charitable purposes unconnected with the vicar's office); contrast *Re Simson* [1946] Ch 299. See further below, para 6.13. See also *Dunne v Byrne* [1912] AC 407 (PC)

[14] [1958] Ch 877 (Lord Evershed MR dissenting); appl *Re Sahal's Will Trusts* [1958] 1 WLR 1243

welfare' of the children for the time being in Southdown House, a children's home, was not charitable. In their Lordships' view, the terms of the disposition were too wide to be limited to exclusively charitable objects: they considered that the income could, consistently with the terms of the disposition, be applied in the purchase of television sets. The court was influenced by the fact that the residents of the home included what used to be called 'juvenile delinquents'.[15]

Other governing documents

6.08   An institution which has a legal structure other than that of the trust does not need to have wholly and exclusively charitable objects to be valid. Since a benignant construction is intended to save dispositions which would otherwise be void, it might be thought that it has no application to the objects of corporate bodies or of unincorporated associations. This was the view of Lightman J in *Inland Revenue Commissioners v Oldham Training and Enterprise Council*;[16] but this is inconsistent with *Guild v Inland Revenue Commissioners*,[17] where the House of Lords adopted a benignant construction even though the issue did not concern validity (the disposition having been made according to Scots law), but merely tax relief.

6.09   In the *Oldham* case, Oldham TEC itself was claiming charitable status in order to obtain tax relief, and it is generally acknowledged that it is in practice more difficult in such cases to convince the court that an institution's objects are charitable.[18] The restrictive approach evident in such cases is, however, rather one of determining the scope of charity; whereas the presumption in favour of a benignant construction does not extend the meaning of charity—it merely assists an uncertain or ambiguous instrument to fall within the existing definition of what is charitable in law. Moreover, having different rules of construction for different types of institution may have bizarre consequences. It could result in a legacy upon express trust for the objects of a corporation being held to be charitable (through the adoption of a benignant construction), even though the corporation itself (denied the benefit of such a construction) is not treated as having charitable objects. Where charitable status is at issue, it is suggested that it would be better to extend the principle of benignant construction to corporate bodies and unincorporated associations. The reason underlying the principle should now be recognized as being to save for charity, and therefore for the benefit of the public, property which might otherwise be lost to charity. The court could then truly be said to lean in favour of charity.

---

[15] *Re Cole* [1958] Ch 877, 888 (Romer LJ)
[16] [1996] STC 1218, 1235
[17] [1992] 2 AC 310
[18] See H Picarda, *The Law and Practice Relating to Charities* (3rd edn, Butterworths, 1999) 132, citing *Inland Revenue Commissioners v City of Glasgow Police Athletic Assoc* [1953] AC 380 (HL) as an example

Presumption that trustees will act in a lawful and proper manner

If the purposes of a trust are otherwise wholly and exclusively charitable, they will   **6.10**
not cease to be so merely because there is a theoretical possibility that the trustees
might carry them out in a political or other non-charitable manner. In such circumstances, it is to be presumed that the trustees will act only in a lawful and
proper manner appropriate to the trustees of a charitable trust.[19] It will, for example, be presumed that trustees of a trust for research into human rights will not
carry out the trust in a political manner.

(3) Gifts to office-holders

If a person is the holder of an office in a church or religious order which involves   **6.11**
the carrying out of a wholly and exclusively charitable purpose, a gift to such person by reference solely to the name of the office is prima facie construed to be a
gift, not to the individual who fills the office beneficially, but to the office-holder
upon trust for the wholly and exclusively charitable purposes of the office itself.[20]
The case law has been concerned almost entirely with holders of ecclesiastical
offices; but the principle could apply to the holder of another type of office in an
institution whose objects are wholly and exclusively charitable, for example to the
Vice-Chancellor of a university.[21]

Difficulties arise where the gift to the office-holder contains additional words   **6.12**
specifying the purposes to which the property is to be applied. If the superadded
words are merely precatory, they will not destroy the wholly and exclusively charitable nature of the gift.[22] If, however, they impose a trust obligation, they must be
construed to determine whether the specified purposes are too wide or vague to be
wholly and exclusively charitable. [23] If the purposes are not confined to those
which are in law charitable, they cannot be confined to charitable purposes merely
by reference to the character of the trustee.[24]

---

[19] *McGovern v A-G* [1982] Ch 321, 345–6, where Slade J approved the beneficent presumption
mentioned by Gray J in *Jackson v Phillips* (1867) 96 Mass (14 Allen) 539. See also *Re Koeppler's Will
Trusts* [1986] Ch 423, 437–8 (Slade LJ)

[20] *Thornber v Wilson* (1858) 4 Drew 350, 351 (Kindersley V-C); *Re Delany* [1902] 2 Ch 642,
646 (Farwell J); *Re Garrard* [1907] 1 Ch 382, 384 (Joyce J); *Re Barclay* [1929] 2 Ch 173, 191
(Lawrence LJ), 195 (Russell LJ); *Re Ray* [1936] 2 Ch 520 (Clauson J); *Re Flinn* [1948] Ch 241
(Jenkins J)

[21] In *Spensley's Will Trusts* [1954] Ch 233, 247, Jenkins LJ thought that a gift to the National
Trust in trust for such purposes as it should think fit might well be a valid charitable gift by analogy
with the principle stated in the text

[22] *Re Hetherington* [1990] Ch 1, 8 (Browne-Wilkinson V-C)

[23] *Dunne v Byrne* [1912] AC 407 (PC)

[24] *Re Davidson* [1909] 1 Ch 567, 569–70 (Cozens-Hardy MR), 571–2 (Farwell LJ); *Dunne v
Byrne* [1912] AC 407, 409–10 (Lord Macnaghten); *Re Spensley's Will Trusts* [1954] Ch 233, 243–4
(Jenkins LJ), 249 (Evershed MR)

6.13 In *Re Garrard*[25] a legacy to a vicar and churchwardens 'to be applied . . . as they shall . . . think fit' was held charitable; in *Re Bain*,[26] a gift to a vicar 'for such objects connected with the Church as he shall think fit' was held charitable; and in *Re Simson*,[27] a gift to a vicar 'for his work in the parish' was held charitable. However, in *Farley v Westminster Bank*,[28] a gift to a vicar 'for parish work' was held not to be charitable. The difference from the immediately preceding case is that 'his work in the parish' confined the gift to the vicar's own religious work, which was charitable; whereas 'parish work' could include non-charitable purposes outside the scope of the vicar's own duties—such as a coach trip to a pantomime or a civic reception for a footballer.

(4) Indefinite purposes
Indefinite but wholly and exclusively charitable purposes

6.14 A gift for 'charitable purposes' creates a valid charitable gift since, although no particular purposes are expressed, the only purposes to which the gift can be applied are charitable ones; the gift is wholly and exclusively charitable, and will be applied to more definite charitable purposes under a scheme.[29] Similarly, if a testator disposes of his residuary estate amongst charitable purposes and charitable institutions, the residue is dedicated to wholly and exclusively charitable purposes; even if, therefore, the testator did not specify the names of the charitable institutions or how much is to be applied to each institution or purpose, a scheme will be prepared to remedy this deficiency.[30]

6.15 Charitable purposes or charitable institutions (or both) may also be valid objects of a discretionary trust or a power. A settlor or testator may, for instance, validly give property to trustees 'to dispose of among such charitable purposes and institutions as they shall think fit'. It is a matter of construction of the instrument whether the charitable purposes and institutions are objects of a discretionary trust or of a mere power. A discretionary trust will arise if the instrument imposes a primary duty to distribute amongst the charitable objects. Even if the donees of the power are under no such duty, but have a mere power to distribute, it may be found that it is a fiduciary power, so that they must actively consider its exercise from time to time; they may exercise it only for its proper purpose; they must not act capriciously, arbitrarily, or in bad faith; and they must not take improper con-

---

[25] [1907] 1 Ch 382
[26] [1930] 1 Ch 224 (CA)
[27] [1946] Ch 299
[28] [1939] AC 430 (HL)
[29] *Moggridge v Thackwell* (1803) 7 Ves Jun 36 (Lord Eldon LC); affd HL, (1807) 13 Ves Jun 416
[30] *Mills v Farmer* (1815) 1 Mer 55 (Lord Eldon LC)

siderations into account.[31] If a mere power is given to persons as trustees, there is a strong presumption that it is conferred on them in their capacity as trustees and so is a fiduciary power.

It has sometimes been said that testamentary gifts for charitable objects are not **6.16** subject to a rule, otherwise of general application, against excessive delegation of testamentary power. Thus it was observed by Lord Simonds:[32]

> It is a cardinal rule, common to English and to Scots law, that a man may not delegate his testamentary power: to him the law gives the right to dispose of his estate in favour of ascertained or ascertainable persons. He does not exercise that right if in effect he empowers his executors to say what persons or objects are to be his beneficiaries. To this salutary rule there is a single exception: a testator may validly leave it to his executors to determine what charitable objects shall benefit, so long as charitable and no other objects may benefit.

However, in *Re Beatty's Will Trusts*,[33] Hoffmann J pointed out that it was important to bear in mind that Lord Simonds was speaking in the context of a gift for purposes ('charitable or benevolent') which was expressed in language which was so vague that it would be impossible for the court to say whether any specific application was within the terms of the will or not. In Hoffmann J's view,[34]

> a common law rule against testamentary delegation, in the sense of a restriction on the scope of testamentary powers, is a chimera, a shadow cast by the rule of certainty, having no independent existence.

In denying that the so-called rule against excessive delegation of testamentary **6.17** power has any existence outside the rule requiring certainty of objects, Hoffmann J effectively removed an unnecessary distinction between the rules applicable to dispositions made inter vivos and those made by will. On this footing, it is inappropriate to treat a testamentary gift for charitable purposes to be selected by the trustees as being exempt from a rule against excessive delegation of testamentary power. No question of excessive delegation can arise because such a gift, being wholly and exclusively charitable, can be controlled and (if necessary) executed by the court.

---

[31] *Re Gestetner Settlement* [1953] Ch 672 (Harman J); *Wishaw v Stephens* (Re *Gulbenkian's Settlement Trusts*) [1970] AC 508 (HL); *Re Manisty's Settlement* [1974] Ch 17 (Templeman J); *Re Hay's Settlement Trusts* [1982] 1 WLR 202 (Megarry V-C); *Mettoy Pension Trustees Ltd v Evans* [1990] 1 WLR 1587

[32] *Chichester Diocesan Fund and Board of Finance Inc v Simpson* [1944] AC 341, 371; see also remarks of Lord Macmillan, ibid, 349

[33] [1990] 1 WLR 1503

[34] ibid, 1509

Indefinite non-charitable purposes

6.18 If a settlor or testator gives property for 'benevolent purposes',[35] for 'deserving purposes',[36] for 'patriotic purposes',[37] for 'philanthropic purposes',[38] for 'public purposes',[39] or for 'worthy purposes',[40] the gift will not be charitable since none of these purposes is necessarily charitable in law: they could include non-charitable purposes.[41] This principle applies even if the trustees are given a discretion in the selection of such objects, since they cannot themselves make the trust charitable merely by undertaking to choose only charitable objects.[42]

(5) Charitable and/or other purposes

6.19 If a testator or settlor gives property for charitable purposes but links these with another purpose which is not charitable, it is necessary to decide if the gift is wholly and exclusively charitable. A particular gift, for example, one for 'charitable and deserving purposes', might not be charitable, since 'deserving purposes' are not necessarily charitable. The charitable status (and hence the validity) of such a disposition is a matter of construction. If the purposes are construed conjunctively, the gift is charitable, since the property may be applied only to purposes that are both charitable and deserving; the gift is wholly and exclusively charitable, and it is then of no consequence that 'deserving' has no objective meaning, since a charitable trust will not fail for uncertainty of objects. If, however, 'charitable and deserving' are construed disjunctively, so as to permit an application of the property to deserving purposes which are not charitable, the gift will not be wholly and exclusively charitable.

6.20 As in other instances where everything turns on construction, the authorities are of limited predictive value. Judges have held gifts for 'charitable or public' purposes,[43] for such 'charitable or benevolent' objects as the testator's executors might select,[44] for 'charitable or other purposes',[45] and (in effect) for 'charitable or

---

[35] *Morice v Bishop of Durham* (1805) 10 Ves 521; *James v Allen* (1817) 3 Mer 17; *Re Barnett* (1908) 24 TLR 788 (a gift 'towards the general benevolent objects or purposes of the Painter Stainers' Company'—not itself a charity—held not to be charitable)

[36] *Harris v Du Pasquier* (1872) 26 LT 689

[37] *A-G v National Provincial & Union Bank of England* [1924] AC 262 (HL)

[38] *Re Macduff* [1896] 2 Ch 451

[39] *Blair v Duncan* [1902] AC 37

[40] *Re Gillingham Bus Disaster Fund* [1959] Ch 62 (CA) ('worthy causes'); *Re Atkinson's Will Trusts* [1978] 1 WLR 586 ('worthy causes')

[41] See also *A-G of the Cayman Islands v Wahr-Hansen* [2000] 3 All ER 642 (PC) (purported trust to pay income (inter alia) to any 'institutions operating for the public good' held not charitable)

[42] *Re Jarman* (1878) 8 Ch D 584, 587 (Hall V-C); *Morice v Bishop of Durham* (1805) 10 Ves 521 (gift to the bishop 'for such objects of benevolence and liberality as he should most approve' held not charitable)

[43] *Blair v Duncan* [1902] AC 37 (HL); *Vezey v Jamson* (1822) 1 Sim & St 69, 71 (Leach V-C)

[44] *Chichester Diocesan Fund and Board of Finance Inc v Simpson* [1944] AC 341 (HL)

[45] *Ellis v Selby* (1836) 1 My & Cr 286

philanthropic' purposes,[46] not charitable and therefore void.[47] On the other hand, 'charitable and deserving objects'[48] have been held charitable, as have 'religious and charitable' institutions and purposes,[49] and 'charitable and benevolent' institutions.[50] This suggests that the courts tend to construe 'or' disjunctively, whereas 'and' is usually treated conjunctively. Yet there are cases where the courts have found precisely the opposite, where words linked by 'or' have been regarded as synonymous, whereas words linked by 'and' have been construed disjunctively.[51] It has been said that the more qualifications or characteristics enumerated, the more probable it is that the testator intended to multiply rather than to restrict the scope of his disposition.[52]

(6) Severance of charitable and non-charitable parts

6.21 If a disposition enables the trustees to apply the fund to charitable and to non-charitable objects so that, consistently with its terms, the trustees could apply the whole of the fund to the latter, the disposition will not be charitable.[53] Such a gift must be distinguished from one under which the trustees are obliged to distribute the fund both to charitable and to non-charitable objects, where it is clear that something must be allocated to charitable objects. A gift in this form will not fail merely because the proportions to be applied between the charitable and the

---

[46] *Re Macduff* [1896] 2 Ch 451
[47] See also *A-G of the Cayman Islands v Wahr-Hansen* [2000] 3 All ER 642 (PC) ('religious, charitable or educational . . . institutions or any . . . institutions operating for the public good': held not charitable)
[48] *Re Sutton* (1885) 28 Ch D 464
[49] *Baker v Sutton* (1836) 1 Keen 224. A gift for 'religious purposes' is treated as charitable: *Dunne v Byrne* [1912] AC 400, 411 (Lord Macnaghten) (PC); but a gift to 'religious societies' is not necessarily charitable, since it may not be for the advancement of religion or contain the necesary element of public benefit: ibid, 411, and see *Gilmour v Coats* [1949] AC 426 (HL). For this reason, the decision in *Re Lloyd* (1893) 10 TLR 66 ('religious and benevolent societies or objects' held charitable) is supportable only on the basis that there were further indications in the will that the testatrix intended exclusively charitable objects; but see also *A-G of the Cayman Islands v Wahr-Hansen* [2000] 3 All ER 642, 646
[50] *Re Best* [1904] 2 Ch 354
[51] *Re Bennett* [1920] 1 Ch 305 ('charity or other public objects' held charitable; the presence of the word 'other' was crucial); *Williams v Kershaw* (1835) LJ Ch 84 ('benevolent, charitable, and religious' purposes held not charitable; the absence of a conjunction between the first two expressed purposes led to a disjunctive construction); *A-G v National Provincial & Union Bank of England* [1924] AC 262 ('for such patrotic purposes or objects and charitable object or objects in the British Empire as my trustees may select' construed disjunctively and held not charitable); *A-G of the Bahamas v Royal Trust Co* [1986] 1 WLR 1001 (PC) ('education and welfare' of Bahamian children and young people held not charitable, as welfare could not be considered to be restricted to 'educational welfare')
[52] *Re Eades* [1920] 2 Ch 353, 357 (Sargant J); see also *Williams v Kershaw* (1835) LJ Ch 84
[53] *Hunter v A-G* [1899] AC 309, 323, where Lord Davey said that the testator 'has not fixed upon any part of the property a trust for charitable uses, and I cannot, therefore, devote any part of it to charity'. See also *Re Tetley* [1923] 1 Ch 258, 269 (Lord Sterndale MR), 273 (Warrington LJ), and 275–6 (Younger LJ); the decision of the Court of Appeal was affirmed on appeal to the House of Lords, *sub nom A-G v National Provincial & Union Bank of England* [1924] AC 262

non-charitable objects are not specified. If either the charitable or the non-charitable objects are sufficiently specific to enable the court to ascertain how much would be needed to carry them out, an appropriate apportionment of the fund will be directed.[54] Failing this, the fund will be divided equally between the charitable and non-charitable purposes on the basis that equality is equity.[55] By this means, the part allotted to charitable purposes is valid as being wholly and exclusively charitable, and is unaffected by any invalidity affecting the non-charitable part.

6.22 The same principle applies where the gift is both for charitable objects and individual beneficiaries. A bequest upon trust 'to be divided between charitable purposes and such of my relatives in such shares as my trustees shall think fit' creates a valid discretionary trust, although no part of it is effectually dedicated to charity until the trustees exercise their discretion. If the trustees exercise their discretion, the part allocated to the charitable purposes is fixed.[56] If the trustees fail to exercise their discretion, the court will execute the trust in the manner best calculated to give effect to the testator's intention.[57] In the absence of evidence of the testator's intention, the court will order an equal division between the charitable objects on the one side, and the testator's relatives on the other, again applying the equitable maxim 'Equality is Equity'.[58] Similarly, in *Re Coxen*,[59] the will provided that an unspecified part of a large fund applicable to charitable purposes was to be spent on an annual dinner for the trustees. Jenkins J held that, even if the provision for the dinner were not charitable,[60] he would be prepared to quantify the capital needed to produce an income sufficient for that invalid purpose, the balance (now a certain amount) being applicable to the charitable purposes.

6.23 The authorities on severance all concern gifts on trust. There appears to be no example of the court's using severance in relation to an institution, so as to divide its funds into charitable and non-charitable parts. It might be argued that, as a rule of trusts law, severance would in any event have no application to corporate bodies

---

[54] *Re Vaughan* (1886) 33 ChD 187 (for charitable purposes and for repair of a tomb: apportionment directed). Contrast *Re Porter* [1925] Ch 746 (Eve J), where income from a fund was to be applied for the maintenance of a masonic temple (not charitable), any balance being applied to masonic charities. No apportionment was here possible since the non-charitable purpose could have used up the entire income; the whole gift was therefore held void

[55] *Hoare v Osborne* (1866) LR 1 Eq 585 (for charitable purposes and for repair of a tomb). See also *Re Clarke* [1923] 2 Ch 407, where Romer J held that a gift by a testator of his residuary estate for such of four separate purposes as his executors should select, created a trust for equal distribution between the four parts, subject to variation by the executors exercising their discretion. As the first three purposes were charitable, each took one-quarter; the last purpose was not charitable, and was held in trust for those entitled under an intestacy

[56] *Re Clarke* [1923] 2 Ch 407 (Romer J)

[57] *McPhail v Doulton* [1971] AC 424, 457 (HL)

[58] *Salusbury v Denton* (1857) 3 K & J 529

[59] [1948] Ch 747

[60] In the event, Jenkins J held that all the provisions were charitable: see below, para 6.27

or unincorporated associations. However, although the rule originates in the law of trusts, its purpose is to favour the status of charity, and there is no reason why severance should not be applicable to institutions other than trusts. In practice, the rule has little significance to such institutions because, although a body may have several objects, its governing document will rarely allocate any part of its funds to particular objects; in which case, even if some of its objects are charitable, there is the possibility that all its funds might be expended on the non-charitable objects, so that severance cannot be applied. Whether an institution is a charity is in practice to be determined by an examination of all its objects; and, unless each and every one of these is charitable, the institution will not be a charity.

If, exceptionally, the objects clause of a charitable company specified four objects, **6.24** only three of which were charitable, and it was further provided that the corporation's assets were to be held as to one-quarter for each of those specified objects, the one-quarter share to be devoted to charitable objects would, it would appear, be effectually dedicated to charity according to the objects clause. If such company were to change its objects clause so that the object relating to that one-quarter share ceased to be charitable, its assets at that date devoted to that one-quarter share would have to continue to be applied for charitable purposes. An alteration of the objects clause for this purpose would not, however, need the prior written consent of the Charity Commissioners, since the company itself would not be a charity.[61]

(7) Primary gift for charity subject to uncertain part elsewhere

There is a rule of trusts law of general application that if a gift of the whole of a **6.25** fund has a trust engrafted upon it in relation to a part only, the failure of the trust for any reason causes the gift to become absolute.[62] If the gift were for charitable purposes, and the trust were for non-charitable purposes which were void (whether for uncertainty of objects or because no specified portion of the fund had been allotted to it), the gift to charity would become absolute. The whole fund would thus be applicable to wholly and exclusively charitable purposes.

(8) Non-charitable purpose merely ancillary

If the terms of an instrument specify that a fund is to be applied to several pur- **6.26** poses, the fund will be charitable only if every one of those purposes is charitable. If even one purpose is non-charitable, the fund as a whole will not be charitable, no matter how many of the other purposes are.[63] Sometimes, however, an

---

[61] CA 1993, s 64(2). See further ch 8, paras 8.119–8.125

[62] *Curtis v Rippon* (1820) 5 Madd 434; *Lassence v Tierney* (1849) 1 Mac & G 551; *Hancock v Watson* [1902] AC 14 (HL)

[63] If, as discussed above (para 6.21), the court is able to sever the charitable and non-charitable parts, the former will comprise separate dispositions which are wholly and exclusively charitable

instrument purports to specify several purposes, one of which is non-charitable, but the court upholds the wholly and exclusively charitable nature of the disposition on the footing that the non-charitable purpose is merely ancillary to the other, charitable, purposes. Expressed in this way, a decision to uphold such dispositions as charitable appears to be a qualification to the wholly and exclusively charitable requirement. In substance, however, when the courts refer to such a purpose as 'ancillary', they mean that it is not truly a purpose in itself, but merely a means of achieving the other, wholly and exclusively charitable, purposes.[64] A number of cases whose purposes included apparently non-charitable political purposes might be explained (not all convincingly) in this way.[65] This is the reverse of the process whereby the courts and the Charity Commissioners sometimes find that purported 'means' of achieving specified charitable objects are in fact non-charitable purposes in their own right.

6.27 An illustration of the principle that a disposition can be held charitable despite its containing a non-charitable ancillary purpose is *Re Coxen*.[66] In that case the testator by his will gave £200,000 to the Court of Aldermen of the City of London upon trust to pay (1) £100 per annum to provide a dinner for the trustees when they met on trust business; (2) one guinea to each trustee who attended the whole of the meeting; and (3) the balance of the income for the benefit of various hospitals. Although the last of these directions was charitable, the first two were not. A trust simply to provide an annual dinner for the Aldermen or to pay them a guinea each periodically would not be charitable as it would be merely for their private benefit.[67] However, in this case the annual dinner was to be provided to the Aldermen as trustees of a charitable trust when they met on trust business, and the guineas were payable only to a member who was present during the whole of a committee meeting. The dinner and the fees could therefore be fairly regarded as in the nature of remuneration to the trustees for their services in administering the trust, and would be conducive to the attainment of the charitable purpose. The object of providing the dinner and the fees was therefore the attainment of the charitable purpose, not the conferring of private benefits upon the Aldermen personally.

6.28 In *Re Coxen*, the charitable purpose to which the non-charitable directions were ancillary was itself specified in the same disposition. It does not, however, have to be. In *Re Charlesworth*[68] there was a bequest on trust to pay the expenses of the

---

[64] See *National Anti-Vivisection Society v IRC* [1948] AC 31, 76 (Lord Normand)

[65] eg *Re Scowcroft* [1898] 2 Ch 638 (promotion of Conservative principles might be considered ancillary to the testator's charitable purposes of advancing education and religion); *Re Hood* [1931] 1 Ch 240 (CA) (promotion of temperance could be considered ancillary to the testator's purpose of the advancement of religion). See further ch 7, paras 7.36–7.39

[66] [1948] Ch 747 (Jenkins J)

[67] cf *Re Barnett* (1908) 24 TLR 788

[68] (1910) 26 TLR 214

dinner at the annual meeting of the members of a religious society. All the members of the society were in holy orders, and they met quarterly to discuss questions affecting the clergy. Eve J held the bequest charitable as he thought that it would encourage members to attend the meetings, and it would therefore further the work of the society and so be for the advancement of religion. This principle seems to fall in line with those cases which have upheld as charitable a gift for a purported non-charitable purpose (such as the promotion of sport) because it could be construed as being merely the means of furthering (and therefore ancillary to) a purpose which is charitable (such as the advancement of education).[69]

B. Statutory validation of imperfect trust provisions

By virtue of the Charitable Trusts (Validation) Act 1954, certain dispositions **6.29** made before 16 December 1952 ('the relevant date') which would otherwise be void because not exclusively charitable are rendered charitable by being modified so as to restrict the application of the property for charitable purposes. The courts have in the past experienced great difficulty in applying the Act; indeed, Cross J once declared that 'the Act is a very odd one, and it is no answer to an argument founded on it that it produces a result which is surprising or even absurd'.[70] Because the statute is of retrospective effect only, the years since its enactment have rendered it increasingly moribund.[71] Furthermore, it can validate only a disposition which comprises a description of 'purposes', so that the objects clauses of companies lie beyond its grasp.[72]

So far as trust instruments executed before the relevant date are concerned, how- **6.30** ever, the Act continues to apply; and it is possible that, were the trustees of an instrument not exclusively charitable only now to seek registration as a charity, the Act could be crucial in determining whether such registration could be granted.[73] The provisions of the Act might, for example, be relevant today where the disposition in question was made before 16 December 1952, but was subject to a prior life interest. In these circumstances the rights of the person entitled on the basis that the remainder is void will not accrue until the death of the person with the prior interest, as specified in the provisions in the Act relating to adverse claims.

---

[69] eg *Re Mariette* [1915] 2 Ch 284

[70] *Re Saxone Shoe Co Ltd's Trust Deed* [1962] 1 WLR 943, 956 (Cross J)

[71] See L Sheridan, 'Charitable Trusts (Validation) Act 1954: a Case for Reform' (1993–4) 2 CL & PR 1

[72] *Re Harpur's Will Trusts* [1961] Ch 38; affd [1962] Ch 78 (CA)

[73] eg in the case of *Grays Sports Ground, Grays, Essex*, the Charity Commissioners treated the Act as validating for charity a trust of a sports ground, even though the deed of trust had been executed more than 50 years earlier in 1921. The trust was therefore entitled to registration as a charity: [1973] Ch Com Rep 26–7 (paras 76–9)

Because the statute is not entirely obsolete, a survey of its application is still considered necessary.

(1) Dispositions and covenants to which the Charitable Trusts (Validation) Act 1954 applies

6.31   The Act applies[74]

> to any disposition of property to be held or applied for objects declared by an imperfect trust provision, and to any covenant to make such a disposition, where apart from this Act the disposition or covenant is invalid under the law of England and Wales, but would be valid if the objects were exclusively charitable.

'Covenant' includes 'any agreement whether under seal or not'.[75]

6.32   The Charity Commissioners do not consider a disposition to be void if the governing instrument (which might be the rules of an association) provides a means by which the purposes can be amended to exclusively charitable purposes.[76] The presence of such machinery means that the Act does not apply.

6.33   A disposition in settlement or other disposition creating more than one interest in the same property is treated for the purposes of the Act as a separate disposition in relation to each of the interests created.[77]

6.34   As the Act applies only to instruments taking effect before 16 December 1952, it is important to ascertain when an instrument takes effect. This is the date of declaration of an inter vivos trust; and, as a will is of no effect during the testator's lifetime, a testamentary instrument takes effect on the testator's death. In the case of an appeal for property or funds, the Act itself provides:[78]

> A document inviting gifts of property to be held or applied for objects declared by the document shall be treated for the purposes of this section as an instrument taking effect when it is first issued.

A covenant entered into before the commencement of the Act (30 July 1954) is not enforceable by virtue of the Act unless subsequently confirmed by the covenantor; but a disposition made in accordance with such a covenant is treated for the purposes of the Act as confirming the covenant and any previous disposition made in accordance with it.[79]

---

[74]   Charitable Trusts (Validation) Act 1954, s 2(1)
[75]   ibid, s 1(4)
[76]   *The Bath Club Servants' Benevolent Fund* [1969] Ch Com Rep 8–9 (para 18)
[77]   Charitable Trusts (Validation) Act 1954, s 2(3), discussed in *Re Chitty's Will Trust* [1970] Ch 254 *sub nom Re Thomas's Will Trust* [1969] 3 All ER 1492 (Buckley J)
[78]   Charitable Trusts (Validation) Act 1954, s 1(3)
[79]   ibid, s 3(6)

(2) The meaning of 'imperfect trust provision'

'Imperfect trust provision' means:[80]　　　　　　　　　　　　　　　　　　　　**6.35**

> any provision declaring the objects for which property is to be held or applied, and
> so describing those objects that, consistently with the terms of the provision, the
> property could be used exclusively for charitable purposes, but could nevertheless be
> used for purposes which are not charitable.

The meaning of 'charitable purposes' in this context is to be determined according to the law as it stood at the date the instrument took effect, that is, if the provision is contained in a will, at the testator's death,[81] or if it is contained in an inter vivos instrument, at the date of execution.

It is clear that a disposition upon trust for 'charitable or benevolent purposes', if **6.36** those words are construed disjunctively,[82] would fall within this definition,[83] since the whole of the property could, at the trustees' discretion, be applied to exclusively charitable purposes.[84] A trust where property is 'to be divided equally between charitable and benevolent purposes' would not, however, qualify, since in these circumstances the whole of the property could not be applied to exclusively charitable purposes.[85]

What is by no means clear, however, is whether a disposition can rank as an 'im- **6.37** perfect trust provision' if the settlor or testator has not specified charitable purposes separately, but has simply used an expression which is sufficiently broad to admit an application to charitable purposes only. Would a disposition 'for worthy causes',[86] or 'for public purposes',[87] for example, fall within the scope of the Act? The issue was raised, but not resolved, in *Re Gillingham Bus Disaster Fund*,[88] where different views were expressed.[89] Later cases suggest that a trust for an indefinite purpose which could permit the application of the whole to either charitable or non-charitable purposes will comprise an 'imperfect trust provision' if the expres-

---

[80]　ibid, s 1(1)

[81]　*Re Bushnell* [1975] 1 WLR 1596, 1603, 1606–7 (Goulding J)

[82]　*Chichester Diocesan Fund and Board of Finance Inc v Simpson* [1944] AC 341 (HL)

[83]　See *Re Saxone Shoe Co Ltd's Trust Deed* [1962] 1 WLR 943, 956–7

[84]　How the property has in fact been applied is not relevant to determining whether there is an imperfect trust provision. In *Grays Sports Ground, Grays, Essex*, the Commissioners treated the trust as charitable under the Act even though for fifty years the property had never in fact been applied for charitable purposes: [1973] Ch Com Rep 26–7 (paras 76–9)

[85]　*Vernon v IRC* [1956] 1 WLR 1169

[86]　cf *Re Gillingham Bus Disaster Fund* [1959] Ch 62 (CA); *Re Atkinson's Will Trusts* [1978] 1 WLR 586; [1978] 1 All ER 1275

[87]　Cross J posed the same question in relation to this phrase in *Re Saxone Shoe Co Ltd's Trust Deed* [1962] 1 WLR 943, 957

[88]　[1958] Ch 300; aff'd [1959] Ch 62 (CA)

[89]　Harman J at first instance held that the Act was applicable only if the disposition showed that part of the fund was to be devoted to charitable purposes; in the Court of Appeal, however, the only judge who expressed a view, Ormerod LJ (dissenting), would have held a trust 'for worthy causes' to fall within the scope of the Act

sion used contains 'at least some flavour of charity',[90] such as has been considered to be present, for instance, in the phrase 'welfare purposes'.[91] A trust for what are found to be 'quasi-charitable purposes'[92] therefore comes within the Act. For this reason, a trust where the board of directors of a company was given a discretion to use the fund 'as a benevolent or welfare fund or for welfare purposes for the past, present and future employees of the fund' was held to fall within the Act: the expressions used connoted some element of charity,[93] and the purposes were statutorily confined to the relief of poverty. In contrast to this, the Act cannot save a trust where a charitable flavour is absent, such as one where the trustees are permitted to apply the property 'to whatever purposes they may think fit'.[94]

6.38   To comprise an 'imperfect trust provision', the description must be of purposes, not of institutions[95] or individuals.[96] The statute cannot therefore apply to the objects clause of a corporation or to a private discretionary trust.[97] Similarly, the statute cannot save a discretionary trust whose objects comprise both charitable purposes and the employees of a company if it is evident that the employees are intended to benefit as individuals. A trust for the relief of poverty amongst the employees of a company, however, is a trust for a purpose (a charitable purpose) rather than a (private) trust for persons.[98] A trust 'for the relief of poverty of the employees of [specified company] and for the general benefit of such persons' could therefore fall within the Act.[99]

(3) Method of validation

6.39   The Act validates an imperfect trust provision contained in an instrument taking effect before 16 December 1952 by treating it as if, before that date, the whole of its declared objects were charitable, and, in respect of the period thereafter,[100] 'as if the provision had required the property to be held or applied for the declared objects in so far only as they authorise use for charitable purposes'.

6.40   Depending upon the nature of the disposition, there are two legitimate ways in which such validation can be effected: by deletion and by limitation. Deletion

---

[90] *Re Saxone Shoe Co Ltd's Trust Deed* [1962] 1 WLR 943, 958 (Cross J); cf *Leahy v A-G for New South Wales* [1959] AC 457, 474–6, where the Privy Council had expressed a similar view on the equivalent legislative provision in New South Wales

[91] *Re Saxone Shoe Co Ltd's Trust Deed* [1962] 1 WLR 943, 958 (Cross J)

[92] ibid

[93] *Re Wykes* [1961] Ch 229 (Buckley J)

[94] *Re Saxone Shoe Co Ltd's Trust Deed* [1962] 1 WLR 943, 958 (Cross J)

[95] *Re Harpur's Will Trusts* [1961] Ch 38; affd [1962] Ch 78 (CA)

[96] *Re Saxone Shoe Co Ltd's Trust Deed* [1962] 1 WLR 943, 957 (Cross J)

[97] *Re Flavel's Will Trusts* [1969] 1 WLR 444 (Stamp J), where an employee benefit fund void for offending the rule against remoteness of vesting could not be saved by the Act

[98] *Dingle v Turner* [1972] AC 601 (HL)

[99] cf Cross J's approach in *Re Mead's Trust Deed* [1961] 1 WLR 1244 (criticized below, para 6.41)

[100] Charitable Trusts (Validation) Act 1954, s 1(2)

results in a gift on trust for 'charitable or benevolent' purposes being deemed merely 'for charitable purposes': limitation results in its being deemed 'for charitable or (so far as they are charitable) benevolent purposes'. Limitation, which involves a smaller adjustment to the specified purposes, is closer to the testator's or settlor's intentions, and is the approach that has been favoured judicially. For example, in *Re South Place Ethical Society*,[101] 'religious or civil purposes' were construed, in accordance with the Act, as 'purposes religious or civil, being charitable'.

This latter approach cannot always be adopted, however. In *Re Mead's Trust Deed*,[102] the purposes of the trust were for a sanatorium for members of a particular trades union, a convalescent home for members of the union recovering from illness, and a home for aged members of the union who were no longer able to support themselves. The first two purposes were not restricted to the relief of poverty; and, on this footing, they were not charitable purposes, both because the class to benefit did not comprise a sufficient section of the community, and because there was an element of self-help. Cross J, however, held that the trust was saved for charity by the Act, the effect of which was to impose a poverty requirement in respect of all three purposes. This approach, which might be termed 'limitation by addition', seems difficult to reconcile with the statute, since it involves altering the purpose of the trust; and the judgment has been criticized on this ground.[103] It seems that the only legitimate means to save the gift under the Act in that case would have been to delete the first two (non-charitable) purposes. **6.41**

The Charity Commissioners' approach

In many instances, of course, the effect of the Act upon a particular instrument is decided not by the courts but by another body, usually the Charity Commissioners in an application for registration. The Charity Commissioners' reports contain examples where they have treated the Charitable Trusts (Validation) Act as excising the non-charitable purposes.[104] **6.42**

A noteworthy example of the Charity Commissioners' approach, which utilized a mixture of deletion and limitation, is the case of *Sir Howell Jones Williams Trust*.[105] Clause 4 of the trust deed, executed in 1937, provided for the establishment of an **6.43**

---

[101] [1980] 1 WLR 1565. This aspect of the case is not dealt with in the version of the judgment reported in All ER, *sub nom Barralet v A-G* [1980] 3 All ER 918
[102] [1961] 1 WLR 1244
[103] H Picarda, *The Law and Practice Relating to Charities* (3rd edn, Butterworths, 1999) 239–40
[104] See, eg, the case of *Muswell Hill, St James, Village Hall and Workmen's Club, Greater London*, which concerned a village hall and workmen's club founded in 1891. The Charity Commissioners had registered the trust as a charity in 1962 on the ground that, although the purpose of a working men's club was not charitable, a village hall was, so that the declared trusts could be treated as exclusively charitable, thereby confining the purposes to a village hall. The property was eventually applied by way of a scheme to recreational purposes: [1976] Ch Com Rep 22–3 (paras 78–84). See also *Saffron Walden Pig Market, Essex* [1980] Ch Com Rep 37–8 (paras 126–134)
[105] [1977] Ch Com Rep 23–6 (paras 71–80)

institute and meeting place in London for the benefit of Welsh people with a view to creating a centre in London 'for promoting the social spiritual and educational welfare of Welsh people'. In clause 5, several other purposes were also specified, all of which were connected with the provision of various kinds of benefits for the beneficiary class within the institute. The House of Lords had held in 1945 that the trust was not established for charitable purposes only;[106] but the Charity Commissioners decided in 1977 that the trust deed contained an 'imperfect trust provision' within the 1954 Act. The Commissioners decided that clause 4 should be read as if the word 'social' had been deleted from clause 4. They also effectively struck out of clause 5 the phrases 'social intercourse', and 'discussion or entertainment', which imported non-charitable purposes. They did, however, insert the word 'charitable' before the word 'purposes' in clause 5(F), so as to limit its scope to 'any of the *charitable* purposes of the Association' (emphasis supplied).

6.44 Because the Act does not itself amend the wording of a trust instrument to which it applies, there is some risk that future trustees might be confused about the trust's true purposes and perhaps apply the property in breach of trust. Another confusion which might arise would be if the trustees of a trust that is made charitable only by the operation of the Act wish to incorporate the charity: they will not be able to transfer its assets to a corporation whose objects are identical to those declared in the original trust instrument, since these will not be exclusively charitable, and the statute will not make them so. The objects of the incorporated charity must be only those objects of the original trust instrument as are charitable by virtue of the Act.

6.45 To avoid confusion, it is the Charity Commissioners' practice, on the application of the trustees, to make a scheme under which the trust's purposes are amended to those exclusively charitable purposes to which the property is applicable under the Act.[107]

(4) Savings for adverse claims

6.46 Although the Charitable Trusts (Validation) Act 1954 is retrospective,[108] it was not intended to upset transfers already made on the basis that the provision in the trust instrument was void as not being exclusively charitable. There is accordingly a saving for disposals of the trust property or income made by the trustees before 16 December 1952 to the persons who would have been entitled by reason of the invalidity of the disposition containing an imperfect trust provision.[109]

---

[106] *Trustees of Sir Howell Jones Williams' Trust v IRC* [1947] AC 447 (HL)
[107] [1965] Ch Com Rep 8
[108] To the date of the publication of *Report of the Committee on the Law and Practice relating to Charitable Trusts*, Lord Nathan (chairman), Cmd 8710 (1952)
[109] Charitable Trusts (Validation) Act 1954, s 2(2)

A disposition containing an imperfect trust made before 16 December 1952 **6.47** would, at the time it was made, have been void, with the result that those entitled by reason of the invalidity would have an immediate claim. The Act did not intend to deprive such persons of their claims, provided they brought them in time. Even without the intervention of the Act, however, by 16 December 1952, claims not made within the previous six years would already have become statute-barred under the general law. The Act therefore preserved the claims only of those claiming under an instrument which took effect after 16 December 1946 (unless, in the case of an earlier instrument, the disposition was itself subject to a prior interest until after that date).[110]

The time limit for bringing claims, however, was laid down as either within one **6.48** year of the passing of the Act (that is before 30 July 1955) or within one year (if later) of the first accrual of the claimant's right or the right of some person through whom he claims.[111] If proceedings to recover the property are not begun in time, the claimant's title to the property is extinguished.[112] Time will not run where there has been fraud[113] or a written acknowledgement of the person's rights.[114] Furthermore, the claimant's right 'shall not be deemed to accrue'[115] so long as he is under a disability[116] or has a future interest only, or so long as the disposition is subject to another disposition made by the same person, and the whole of the property or the income arising from it is held or applied for the purposes of that other disposition.[117]

The operation of these saving provisions can be illustrated by the hypothetical ex- **6.49** ample of a testator who died in 1950 and who by his will gave his entire estate to A for life, remainder upon trust for purposes which declare an imperfect trust provision. The person entitled to the disposition in remainder on the footing that it is void was originally B; but B died in 1975, giving all her property by will to C. The Charitable Trusts (Validation) Act validates the disposition in remainder by restricting its application to charitable purposes exclusively; but it saves C's claim by giving C one year from the death of A to bring proceedings. If C does not claim

---

[110] ibid, s 3(1)

[111] ibid, s 3(2). For the circumstances in which a person is deemed to claim through another person, see Limitation Act 1980: Charitable Trusts (Validation) Act 1954, s 3(4) (as amended)

[112] Charitable Trusts (Validation) Act 1954, s 3(2)

[113] ibid, s 3(2)(a)

[114] ibid, s 3(2)(b)

[115] In *Re Chitty's Will Trust* [1970] Ch 254, 259, *sub nom Re Thomas's Will Trust* [1969] 3 All ER 1492, 1495, Buckley J considered that these words in s 3(3) should be read as 'shall be deemed not to accrue'

[116] Within the meaning of the Limitation Act 1980, s 38: Charitable Trusts (Validation) Act 1954, s 3(4) (as amended)

[117] Charitable Trusts (Validation) Act 1954, s 3(3). The sub-section was discussed and applied in *Re Chitty's Will Trust* [1970] Ch 254, *sub nom Re Thomas's Will Trust* [1969] 3 All ER 1492

within that period, C's right is barred and C's title extinguished, and the property subject to the disposition in remainder vests indefeasibly in trust for exclusively charitable purposes in accordance with the Act.

7

POLITICAL PURPOSES AND POLITICAL ACTIVITY

This chapter considers the extent to which the possession of political objects, or **7.01** the pursuing of political activity, is incompatible with charitable status. The potential impact of the Human Rights Act 1998 on these issues was considered in chapter 1, where it was concluded that such impact is likely to be minimal.[1] This chapter is therefore posited on that footing.

A. Political purposes

A political object is incompatible with charitable status, and the court cannot **7.02** inquire into whether the object is of public benefit. The case law reveals that a 'political object' is one which expressly aims to change the law, or one which seeks to promote either a particular theory or attitude which involves seeking a change in the law or a change in government policy. Outside these confines, an object may be considered political in a broad sense, in that it has a propaganda element, but the court is entitled to determine whether the purpose is charitable in law and involves a benefit to the public.

(1) Express object to change the law

A trust or other body which has as one of its main objects a change in the law of **7.03** the United Kingdom cannot be charitable. One reason for this was put forward

---

[1] See ch 1, paras 1.119–126

by Lord Parker in *Bowman v Secular Society Ltd*,[2] where his Lordship stated that:[3]

> a trust for the attainment of political objects has always been held invalid, not because it is illegal . . . but because the court has no means of judging whether a proposed change in the law will or will not be for the public benefit.

Lord Parker gave a number of illustrations of the political objects which he had in mind:[4]

> The abolition of religious tests, the disestablishment of the Church, the secularization of education, the alteration of the law touching religion or marriage, or the observation of the Sabbath.

7.04 In his dissenting speech in the leading case of *National Anti-Vivisection Society v Inland Revenue Commissioners*,[5] Lord Porter pointed out that these are all objects which involve the doing away with a positive injunction of the law, and which could not therefore have been effected without an Act of Parliament.[6]

7.05 A second reason for denying charitable status to a trust which seeks to change the law is that, since charitable trusts are enforced by the Attorney-General on behalf of the Crown, charitable status would mean that the Attorney-General might be required to enforce trusts whose objects were highly prejudicial to the welfare of the State.[7] The latter explanation has been considered to be an illustration of the difficulties that would be caused if the courts began to encroach on the function of the legislature, that is that one arm of the State (the judicial) would be set against another (the legislative).[8] In the *National Anti-Vivisection Society* case,[9] the Society had as one of its expressed objects the repeal of a statute,[10] and this was itself sufficient to deny it charitable status.

7.06 The Human Rights Act 1998 is unique in English law in that the Convention rights which it enshrines do not override other domestic legislation with which they may be found to be incompatible.[11] If a court cannot interpret other legislation in a manner which is consistent with the rights contained in the Act, it may make a declaration of incompatibility.[12] Following the Act, it might be argued that the object of promoting the reform of domestic English law to the extent necessary to give effect to Convention rights should cease to be a political purpose, and

---

[2] [1917] AC 406 (HL)
[3] ibid, 442
[4] ibid
[5] [1948] AC 31 (HL)
[6] ibid, 54–5 (Lord Porter (dissenting))
[7] ibid, 62–3 (Lord Simonds)
[8] *McGovern v A-G* [1982] Ch 321, 337 (Slade J)
[9] [1948] AC 31
[10] ie Cruelty to Animals Act 1876
[11] Human Rights Act 1998, s 3
[12] ibid, s 4

should be charitable under the fourth head of *Pemsel*'s case[13] as being to promote the better administration of the law. If this argument is sound, both potential objections to the charitable status of such a purpose are effectively removed by the Act.[14]

Whether a gift for an object is political in involving a change in the law is to be   **7.07**
assessed at the time the gift is made which, in the case of a gift by will, is the testator's death. A gift which is so tainted as being political does not lose that taint merely because it follows a life interest and the law changes before the death of the tenant for life.[15]

(2) Express object to prevent a change in the law

Although a trust to uphold the law is charitable as being within the spirit and   **7.08**
intendment of the Preamble to the Statute of Elizabeth,[16] a trust with the express object of preventing the law from being changed is open to the same objection *mutatis mutandis* as a trust with the express object of changing the law. It has been held that, just as the court has no means of assessing whether a change in the law would be for the public benefit, so it has no means of assessing whether it is for the public benefit to keep the law as it is.[17] For this reason, a trust with the object of, for example, seeking to prevent any change in the constitutional links between Northern Ireland and the rest of the United Kingdom would not be charitable.

(3) Propaganda

In his dissenting speech in *National Anti-Vivisection Society v Inland Revenue*   **7.09**
Commissioners,[18] Lord Porter took the view that an object should be denied charitable status as being political only if its attainment (like those purposes enumerated by Lord Parker in *Bowman v Secular Society Ltd*[19]) would necessarily involve changing the law. In Lord Porter's view, an object which, although capable of attainment by a change in the law, can be achieved by other means (such as by

---

[13] *Comrs for Special Purposes of the Income Tax v Pemsel* [1891] AC 531 (HL)

[14] But for a counter-argument, see ch 1, para 1.120

[15] cf *Re Bushnell* [1975] 1 WLR 1596. The objects of the trust in that case involved political propaganda rather than a necessary change in the law, but it can be inferred from it that the object of promoting socialized medicine ceased to be political in respect of trusts created after the introduction of the National Health Service

[16] See the case of *Public Concern at Work* (1993) 2 Decisions 5, 10, where the Charity Commissioners accepted that to promote compliance with the law is a charitable purpose under the fourth head of *Pemsel* by analogy with trusts to enforce the law. The Commissioners referred to a passage in H Picarda, *The Law and Practice Relating to Charities* (now in 3rd edn, Butterworths, 1999, 181) that 'adherence to the law is the duty of every citizen'. See *Re Vallance* (1876) 2 Seton's Jdgts, 7th edn, 1304; *Re Herrick* (1918) 52 ILT 213 (to promote prosecutions for cruelty to animals is a charitable purpose)

[17] *Re Hopkinson* [1949] 1 All ER 346, 350

[18] [1948] AC 31, 55

[19] [1917] AC 406, 442

persuading mankind to engage in or to refrain from a particular activity), might still be considered to be charitable.[20] His Lordship said:[21]

> I cannot accept the view that the anti-slavery campaign or the enactment of the Factory Acts or the abolition of the use of boy labour by chimney-sweeps, would be charitable so long as the supporters of these objects had not in mind or at any rate did not advocate a change in the laws, but became political and therefore non-charitable if they do so. To take such a view would to me be to neglect substance for form.

Lord Simonds, however, in his speech, did not agree that the expression 'political object' should be confined in the manner that Lord Porter suggested;[22] and Lord Simonds' opinion appears to be that of the majority.[23]

7.10 It could, nevertheless, be argued that the majority of their Lordships were not necessarily disagreeing with Lord Porter's general view. The decision of the majority turns on the fact that one of the objects of the National Anti-Vivisection Society was to repeal a statute, and the majority were unable to construe this object as merely ancillary to the Society's other objects, even if those other objects had themselves been charitable. Had the Society not had an express object of changing the law, it is evident that the majority of their Lordships would still have held the Society's objects non-charitable, but only because, on weighing the evidence, they could not be shown to be for the public benefit—indeed, the majority thought that the objects would have been to the disadvantage of mankind. It therefore appears that, in the absence of the express object of repealing a statute, the majority would not have treated the objects of the Society as 'political objects' within the meaning given to that phrase by Lord Parker in *Bowman v Secular Society Ltd*.[24] If this be correct, the decision in *National Anti-Vivisection Society v Inland Revenue Commissioners* does indeed support Lord Porter's view that, where a particular object can be attained by means other than legislation, the court will assess whether the attainment of such object is or is not for the public benefit.

7.11 Later decisions, however, have not interpreted the *National Anti-Vivisection Society* case in this way, and have taken it to be authority for the proposition that, even if an object does not expressly seek a change in the law, it will still be a 'polit-

---

[20] *National Anti-Vivisection Society v IRC* [1948] AC 31, 55 (Lord Porter (dissenting))
[21] ibid, 55
[22] ibid, 62 (Lord Simonds)
[23] Viscount Simon agreed with Lord Simonds' opinion: *National Anti-Vivisection Society v IRC* [1948] AC 31, 40; Lord Wright considered that Lord Parker's statement in the *Bowman* case 'was not limited to party political measures, but would cover activities directed to influence the legislature to change the law in order to promote or effect the views advocated by the society': ibid, 51–2; Lord Normand said that Lord Parker's words were not limited to 'matters of acute political controversy', and he commented that if the promoters of a project for new legislation 'have patiently prepared the way by a gradual education of the public, they may succeed in eliminating much of the opposition': ibid, 78
[24] [1917] AC 406

ical object' if it promotes a particular theory or attitude that involves seeking a change in the law or (by an extension of this principle) a change in government policy.[25] Such an object, which can be termed 'political propaganda', might be directed either at Parliament or the government directly, or indirectly through trying to influence public opinion so that the public itself is encouraged to agitate for such a change.

This, however, leaves a number of cases, including *National Anti-Vivisection* **7.12**
Society v Inland Revenue Commissioners[26] itself, where the body's objects involve the promotion of a cause and where the courts have inquired whether the object in question is for the public benefit or not.[27] For purposes of exposition, it therefore seems necessary to distinguish between:

(a) an object which promotes a particular theory, attitude, or cause that involves seeking a change in the law or a change in government policy (political propaganda); and

(b) an object which promotes a particular theory, attitude, or cause *simpliciter*, without seeking to change the law or government policy.

The modern case law treats an object within category (a) as a 'political object' **7.13**
within Lord Parker's dictum in *Bowman v Secular Society Ltd*,[28] so that the court will deny it charitable status without assessing public benefit. An object within category (b), however, is not treated as a 'political object', so that it is capable of attaining charitable status: the court will ascertain whether the purpose is charitable and has a sufficient element of public benefit; if the latter requirement is absent, the court may designate the purpose merely propaganda. These categories will be dealt with in turn.

Political propaganda

In relation to very old charities

Although, in modern times, an object which promotes a particular theory, atti- **7.14**
tude, or cause that involves seeking a change in the law or a change in government policy ranks as a 'political object' and is not charitable, this has not always been so. In the nineteenth century, a much more relaxed attitude to political objects is apparent. The courts of that era did not consider a trust to be non-charitable merely because it promoted a particular political ideology. Thus in *Russell v Jackson*,[29] Turner V-C treated as charitable a secret trust to educate children in the

---

[25] *McGovern v A-G* [1982] Ch 321
[26] [1948] AC 31
[27] See *Re Hopkins' Will Trusts* [1965] Ch 669
[28] [1917] AC 406, 442
[29] (1852) 10 Hare 204

doctrines of socialism—a purpose whose political character would undoubtedly prevent its being held charitable today.

7.15 The difference in attitude is of more than historical interest, for some long-lived charities that were founded before the 'political objects' objection was introduced in the twentieth century retain their charitable status to this day, despite their objects being political in nature. The Charity Commissioners never sought to remove them from the register of charities and to have their property applied cy-près on the ground that their objects had ceased to be in law charitable.[30] Longevity evidently has its privileges. Such highly favoured charities include, for instance, the Lord's Day Observance Society and Anti-Slavery International (formerly known as the Anti-Slavery Society).

7.16 Such privilege is even more wide reaching, because the Charity Commissioners effectively treat it as extending also to any successor charity with substantially similar objects, such as a charitable company to which the original charity transfers its assets to obtain the benefits of incorporation, even though the successor is a new charity with a different charity registration number. A modern illustration is Anti-Slavery International itself, which is the incorporated and latest successor to the original society established in 1839. Its current (revised) objects include: 'the elimination of slavery, the slave trade and all forms of unlawful forced labour and unlawful deprivation of freedom'.

7.17 A completely new body set up today with such objects would surely be refused charitable status; yet Anti-Slavery International, undoubtedly because it was the successor to an old charity whose objects pre-dated the prohibition on political purposes, was registered as a charity with these objects in 1995. The approach of the Charity Commissioners is evidently to apply the tightening of the law in respect of political objects only to completely new bodies, when they seek registration as charities.

In relation to modern institutions

7.18 The modern judicial approach to political propaganda vitiating charitable status was expounded in *McGovern v Attorney-General*.[31] This concerned a trust set up by Amnesty International (not itself a charity) with several purposes. One of these purposes, the relief of prisoners of conscience, was clearly charitable, and some of the others (namely, research into the observance of human rights, and the publication of such research) were evidently charitable.[32] The problem, however, was

---

[30] ie under CA 1993, s 13(1)(e)(ii)
[31] [1982] Ch 321
[32] Slade J stated that he would have held the promotion of research into the observance of human rights and the dissemination of the results of such research charitable had they been the trust's only purposes: *McGovern v A-G* [1982] Ch 321, 353. In *Webb v O'Doherty* (1991) 3 Admin LR 731, Hoffmann J was perhaps more cautious: he considered that research into the observance of human

that the trust contained two purposes which were less clearly charitable, namely, attempting to secure the release of prisoners of conscience, and procuring the abolition of torture or inhuman or degrading treatment or punishment. The definition of a 'prisoner of conscience' expressly excluded any person lawfully imprisoned or detained within the United Kingdom, so that the object of relieving prisoners of conscience could not be objected to on the ground that it might set one arm of the state against another.[33] Slade J accepted that the dangers of the court encroaching on the functions of the legislature would not be nearly so great in relation to a trust whose purposes were to be carried out abroad.[34] Nevertheless, he denied the trust charitable status on the ground that the court had no means of judging whether advocating a change in the laws of another country would be for the benefit of the public, this being (even in the case of a trust to be executed abroad) the public in the United Kingdom.[35] Furthermore, he said that, before ascribing charitable status to an English trust whose main object was to secure the alteration of a foreign law, the court would be bound to consider the consequences for this country as a matter of public policy. The activities of such a trust might well prejudice this country's relations with the country concerned, and the court would have no means of assessing the extent of such a risk, which would be more a matter for political than for legal judgement.[36] Finally, Slade J said that the object of procuring the abolition of torture or inhuman or degrading treatment or punishment was not charitable because it sought to procure changes in the laws of this country.[37] In his Lordship's view, a trust to procure a reversal of government policy or of particular decisions of governmental authorities (whether in this country or overseas) is a political purpose and not charitable.[38]

Political propaganda masquerading as education

If the objects of the body are directed to seeking to influence the attitude of the **7.19** public by promoting a particular point of view, the purpose is one of propaganda not education. If the underlying aim of such propaganda is to seek a change in the law or a change of government policy, the object comprises political propaganda.

---

rights 'may well be' charitable. The Charity Commissioners have registered trusts whose purposes comprised the promotion of research into the observance of human rights (*Parliamentary Human Rights Trust*) and to advance research and education of the public concerning human rights and the development of international law and its role in the effective protection of human rights (*John Galway Foster Human Rights Trust*): [1987] Ch Com Rep 3 (para 12)

[33] ie the substance of the objection mentioned by Lord Simonds in *National Anti-Vivisection Society v IRC* [1948] AC 31, 62–3: see *McGovern v A-G* 1982] Ch 321, 336–7 (Slade J)

[34] *McGovern v A-G* 1982] Ch 321, 338

[35] *Camille and Henry Dreyfus Foundation Inc v IRC* [1954] Ch 672, 684 (Evershed MR). For a discussion of charitable objects to be performed overseas, see further ch 5, paras 5.56–5.66

[36] *McGovern v A-G* 1982] Ch 321, 338–9. See also C Forder, 'Too political to be charitable?' [1984] Conv 263

[37] *McGovern v A-G* [1982] Ch 321, 352

[38] ibid, 339–40

The courts and the Charity Commissioners are astute to deny charitable status to '[p]olitical propaganda masquerading . . . as education'.[39] For this reason, a trust or body to educate the public in the aims of a particular political party,[40] or in a particular political ideology,[41] is denied charitable status.

7.20 **Propaganda element discernible on the face of the instrument** Even if the object refers expressly to education or to research, the purpose of political propaganda may be apparent on the face of the instrument itself. This is illustrated by the case of the *Animal Abuse, Injustice and Defence Society* (commonly known as Animal AID), a company limited by guarantee.[42] The Charity Commissioners refused to register Animal AID as a charity because its objects were not wholly and exclusively charitable. Several of its objects were not charitable, including object (G), which was

> to promote . . . medical, surgical and scientific research, education and learning for the purpose of replacing animals . . . in medical, surgical and scientific experiments and . . . to promote . . . any research . . . for the purpose of showing that any experiments . . . on animals . . . are harmful to mankind or are unnecessary . . . and to publish the results of such research and experimentation.

The wording of this object itself made it clear that the research would be conducted only to confirm a pre-existing theory and not to challenge or validate the theory. This was not research which comprised the advancement of education, but was merely propaganda.

7.21 **Ambiguity on the face of the instrument** Even if no political propaganda is apparent from the governing instrument itself, the court will not accept that a purpose is educational merely because it describes itself as such. The courts and the Charity Commissioners will need to be satisfied that the ostensible purpose is for the advancement of education within the meaning of the law of charity. A purpose which describes itself as educational may therefore be treated as ambiguous, so enabling the courts and the Commissioners to examine the body's present and past activities (if it is already in existence[43]) or its proposed activities (if it is newly created[44]). This approach is nevertheless somewhat suspect, since an object which is expressed to be merely 'the advancement of education' would appear to be a charitable purpose both wholly and exclusively, and unambiguously.[45] If, however, an existing body, with a view to seeking registration as a charity, has changed either its objects or its management (or both), it cannot be assumed that its activ-

---

[39] *Re Hopkinson* [1949] 1 All ER 346, 350 (Vaisey J)
[40] eg *Bonar Law Memorial Trust v IRC* (1933) 49 TLR 220 (Conservative Party); *Re Hopkinson* [1949] 1 All ER 346 (Labour Party)
[41] eg *Re Bushnell* [1975] 1 WLR 1596 (socialism)
[42] (1994) 2 Decisions 1
[43] As in *Animal Abuse, Injustice and Defence Society* (1994) 2 Decisions 1
[44] As in *Margaret Thatcher Foundation* [1991] Ch Com Rep 13 (para 75), 39 (App D)
[45] See further ch 10, paras 10.54–10.55

ities will be carried on in the same manner as before. In such circumstances, evidence of prior political or other non-charitable activities will not necessarily lead to the conclusion that the new objects are not charitable in law.[46]

The mere fact that the trustee is politically active is not itself an indication that the **7.22** trust's purposes are not wholly and exclusively charitable, since he would be obliged to administer the trust without regard to his personal views.[47] If the Charity Commissioners register a trust where the trustees are politically active, they might, in appropriate circumstances, inform the trustees of their duty to administer the trust without regard to their personal views, and they might warn the trustees of their potential personal liability if such duty is breached.[48]

A recent example of political propaganda dressed up as education is *Southwood v* **7.23** *Attorney-General*,[49] where the expressed purpose of the trust was '[t]he advancement of the education of the public in the subject of militarism and disarmament'. At first instance, Carnwath J said that, whilst peace as a general objective was not a matter of political controversy, the question whether such an objective would be secured by disarmament was more controversial. The expressed purpose being ambiguous, the court was entitled to look at the activities of the promoters before the execution of the trust. It was clear from background papers prepared by the promoters that the aim was to challenge the current policies of western governments. The trust was therefore denied charitable status. Carnwath J's decision was affirmed by the Court of Appeal,[50] which also construed the nature and scope of the objects in the light of the promoters' intentions at the time the trust was declared. Chadwick LJ, with whose judgment the other members of the court agreed, did not, however, refer expressly to ambiguity as the ground for admitting evidence of the promoters' intentions. Instead, he explained that the declaration of trust, like any other written instrument, had to be construed with a proper regard to the circumstances in which it came to be executed. This might suggest that extrinsic evidence of promoters' intentions might be admissible even when the expressed objects are unambiguous; but it is more likely that Chadwick LJ intended his comments to be understood in the context of an instrument which was ambiguous on the face of it.

The same approach is evident in a number of decisions of the Charity **7.24** Commissioners. In the case of the *Margaret Thatcher Foundation*,[51] the

---

[46] See, eg, the Charity Commissioners' decision on the case of the *Institute for the Study of Terrorism* [1988] Ch Com Rep 7 (paras 27–34)
[47] See *Re MacDougall* [1957] 1 WLR 81, 90–1 (Upjohn J); see also *Institute for the Study of Terrorism* [1988] Ch Com Rep 7 (paras 27–33, esp para 34)
[48] See, eg, *Institute for the Study of Terrorism* [1988] Ch Com Rep 7, 8 (para 34)
[49] CA, 28 June 2000, aff The Times, 26 Oct 1998 (Carnwath J)
[50] 28 June 2000
[51] [1991] Ch Com Rep 13 (para 75), 39 (App D)

Commissioners were asked to consider whether they would register as a charity a proposed institution of that name if its object were

> the education of the general public and in particular, without prejudice to the generality of the foregoing, the increase of knowledge, understanding and appreciation of the principles of freedom under a rule of law, of democracy and of responsibility towards both the ethical and physical environment.

In order to determine whether this object was charitable in the legal sense, the Charity Commissioners looked at a statement provided by the promoters which indicated the activities that the proposed institution intended to undertake. The Commissioners concluded that a substantial part of the proposed activities was concerned, not with objective analysis, but with arguing and advancing a particular political viewpoint, and so such object would not be charitable.

7.25 Propaganda disguised as education was also apparent in the case of the *Animal Abuse, Injustice and Defence Society*,[52] which has already been mentioned. Another of the objects of Animal AID, object (B), was 'To educate the public on all aspects involving animals and wildlife'. The Charity Commissioners considered that the wording of this object raised the question whether Animal AID's activities were to be confined to education in the sense understood in charity law. This ambiguity in the object enabled the Commissioners to look at Animal AID's actual activities. It was clear from such activities and from its publications that Animal AID was disseminating propaganda in the sense that it was publishing selected and slanted information in support of a pre-conceived point of view—that experiments on and the exploitation of animals should be stopped. This purpose was therefore not charitable.

Promotion of a theory, attitude or cause simpliciter

7.26 Political propaganda, as has been seen,[53] is a 'political object', and will therefore deny a trust or other body charitable status, as the court cannot inquire whether the purpose is of benefit to the public. It is, however, important to distinguish a 'political object' of this kind from an object which promotes a particular theory or attitude but without seeking to change the law or government policy. The court is entitled to ascertain whether an object of the latter category comprises a charitable purpose (such as the advancement of education) or is merely propaganda; and, to do so, it will determine whether the object is of benefit to the public.

7.27 **Need for a wholly and exclusively charitable purpose** The purpose must itself be charitable in law. If the purpose is too vague to be restricted to charitable purposes only, it will fail to satisfy the requirement of being wholly and exclusively charitable. Thus in *National Anti-Vivisection Society v Inland Revenue*

---

[52] (1994) 2 Decisions 1: see above, para 7.20
[53] See above, paras 7.12–7.25, esp paras 7.12–7.13

Commissioners,[54] Lord Wright considered that, apart from the fact that one of the Society's expressed objects was political, in that it sought a change in the law, the promotion of anti-vivisection could not in any event be regarded as a charitable object within any of the four heads of *Pemsel*'s case.

Uncertainty as to the scope of its purpose was one reason for the failure of the trust **7.28** in *Re Strakosch*.[55] The testator there had directed that part of his residuary estate should be held by his trustees upon trust to be applied

> to a 'fund' for any purpose which in their opinion is designed to strengthen the bonds of unity between the Union of South Africa and the Mother Country and which incidentally will conduce to the appeasement of racial feeling between the Dutch and English speaking sections of the South African community.

The court held[56] that 'the very wide and vague scope of the gift' precluded its falling within the spirit and intendment of the Preamble to the Statute of Elizabeth. It could not be considered to be confined to educational purposes (on the footing that the appeasement of racial feeling is education in its widest sense), since the '[t]he appeasing of racial feeling within the community is a political problem, perhaps primarily political'.[57]

Similarly, in *Anglo-Swedish Society v Inland Revenue Commissioners*,[58] Rowlatt J **7.29** held that 'the promotion of a closer and more sympathetic understanding between the English and Swedish peoples', although an object of public utility, was not a purpose within the Preamble: it was rather a trust 'to promote an attitude of mind, a view of one nation by another'.[59]

Assessment of public benefit As in the assessment of public benefit in other **7.30** areas of the law of charity, the mere fact that the settlor believes the purpose to be of benefit to the public is of no account.[60] The court will make its own assessment of whether the purpose is for the public benefit.

This approach is evident from the speeches in the House of Lords in *National* **7.31** *Anti-Vivisection Society v Inland Revenue Commissioners*,[61] where Lord Wright considered that the promotion of anti-vivisection could not in any event be

---

[54] [1948] AC 31
[55] [1949] Ch 529 (CA)
[56] ibid, 536–38 (Lord Greene MR). The Charity Commissioners have since accepted that the promotion of good race relations is a charitable purpose: [1983] Ch Com Rep 11 (para 20); and this position is also accepted by the Inland Revenue: [1987] Ch Com Rep 4 (para 14). See further ch 4, paras 4.106–4.107
[57] *Re Strakosch* [1949] 1 Ch 529, 538 (Lord Greene MR)
[58] (1931) 47 TLR 295 (KB)
[59] *ibid*
[60] *National Anti-Vivisection Society v IRC* [1948] AC 31, 65–6 (Lord Simonds); *Re Shaw* [1957] 1 WLR 729, 740 (Harman J)
[61] [1948] AC 31

regarded as charitable. Its only claim to charitable status could be that it was a purpose beneficial to the community within the fourth head of *Pemsel*'s case,[62] but to ascertain whether it was of such benefit involved 'balancing conflicting values', and the tangible benefits to mankind from vivisection in his view clearly outweighed any intangible and vague moral benefits that might flow from anti-vivisection.[63] Similarly, Lord Simonds in the same case said that the court should not shut its eyes to the finding of fact that the carrying out of the Society's objects would be injurious to mankind in that it would be detrimental to medical science and research and consequently to public health.[64]

7.32 In contrast to this, in *Re Shaw*,[65] Harman J considered that the trust's purpose of developing a phonetic alphabet was not educational, but comprised propaganda to persuade the public that the adoption of the new script would be 'a good thing'.[66] He concluded that the objects of the alphabet trust were 'analogous to trusts for political purposes', and were therefore not charitable.[67] The phonetic alphabet trust might therefore be treated merely as having fallen on the wrong side of the line.

7.33 A different attitude from that displayed in *Re Shaw*,[68] is, however, apparent in the decision of Wilberforce J in *Re Hopkins' Will Trusts*.[69] In that case there was undoubtedly a propaganda element in the trust, since the purpose of searching for the Bacon-Shakespeare manuscripts was premised on the controversial (but by no means implausible[70]) theory that the works attributed to William Shakespeare were in fact written by somebody other than the man from Stratford-upon-Avon. The trust was held charitable, however, because '[t]he discovery of such manuscripts, or of one such manuscript, would be of the highest value to history and to literature'.[71] Similarly, if a trust were established to promote vegetarianism merely by encouraging the public to abstain from the consumption of flesh and fowl, the courts and the Charity Commissioners would not be precluded from determining whether the purpose (if itself charitable) was for the public benefit (perhaps involving the promotion of public health).[72]

---

[62] *Comrs for Special Purposes of the Income Tax v Pemsel* [1891] AC 531
[63] *National Anti-Vivisection Society v IRC* [1948] AC 31, 49
[64] ibid, 60, 65
[65] [1957] 1 WLR 729
[66] *Re Shaw* [1957] 1 WLR 729, 738
[67] ibid, 742
[68] [1957] 1 WLR 729
[69] [1965] Ch 669
[70] See C Ogburn, *The Mysterious William Shakespeare: the myth and the reality* (2nd edn, EPM Publications Inc, Virginia, 1992)
[71] *Re Hopkins' Will Trusts* [1965] Ch 669, 679
[72] A bequest to two vegetarian societies was held charitable in *Re Cranston* [1898] 1 IR 431; but Lord Simonds, in *National Anti-Vivisection Society v IRC* [1948] AC 31, 73, chose to express no

(4) Political education

Although the promotion of a particular political theory is not charitable, it can be   **7.34**
charitable for the advancement of education to promote the discussion of political issues, provided that a variety of opposing political opinions are to be expressed
and debated.[73] Thus a trust to educate the public in forms of government and
political matters generally—what might be termed political science—can be
charitable.[74] A trust to promote educational research does not cease to be charitable merely because an incidental effect of the publication of the research might be
to provide material which might be used by others in a political campaign.[75]

The difficulty of distinguishing between political education and political propa-   **7.35**
ganda arose in *Re Koeppler's Will Trusts,*[76] which concerned a bequest for the purposes of an institution known as Wilton Park. This was construed to mean for the
furtherance of the work of the Wilton Park Project, which comprised the holding
of conferences on European and international political, economic, and social
issues, before an audience drawn from member states of various international
organizations. Slade LJ, giving the judgment of the Court of Appeal, said that,
even when the conferences touched on political matters, they constituted no more
than 'genuine attempts in an objective manner to ascertain and disseminate the
truth'.[77] He said that the trust was entitled to a 'benignant construction', in the
sense that the court was entitled to presume that the trustees would only act in a
lawful and proper manner appropriate to the trustees of a charity, and would not,
for instance, seek to use the trust to propagate tendentious political opinions.[78]

(5) Political purpose merely ancillary

If several purposes are set out in the governing instrument, all of them must be   **7.36**
charitable if the body is to attain charitable status; the presence of even a single
political purpose will prevent the body's objects being wholly and exclusively
charitable. If, however, the court is able to treat the apparent political purpose
not as a purpose at all, but merely as a means of achieving the other (wholly and

---

opinion whether *Re Cranston* was rightly decided. See also *Re Slatter* (1905) 21 TLR 295 (gift to further principles of food reform advocated by specified vegetarian societies held charitable). In the
light of changing scientific attitudes to nutrition and following the BSE crisis, a court might today
consider a trust to educate the public in vegetarianism to be charitable as being either for the advancement of education or (within the fourth head of *Pemsel*) for the promotion of public health

[73] See eg *A-G v Ross* [1986] 1 WLR 252, 263 (Scott J)
[74] *Re Trusts of the Arthur MacDougall Fund* [1957] 1 WLR 81
[75] *Webb v O'Doherty* (1991) 3 Admin LR 731, (Hoffmann J, referring to the use that might be
made of research into the observance of human rights)
[76] [1986] Ch 423 (CA)
[77] ibid, 437
[78] ibid, 437–8

exclusively) charitable purposes, the trust or other body will be charitable.[79] Where the court is able to do this, it usually states that it is treating the political purpose as merely ancillary or subsidiary to the charitable objects. An illustration of this was provided by Lord Normand in *National Anti-Vivisection Society v Inland Revenue Commissioners*,[80] where he said that:[81]

> A society for the prevention of cruelty to animals, for example, may include among its professed purposes amendments of the law dealing with field sports or with the taking of eggs or the like. Yet it would not, in my view, necessarily lose its right to be considered a charity, and if that right were questioned, it would become the duty of the court to decide whether the general purpose of the society was the improvement of morals by various lawful means including new legislation, all such means being subsidiary to the general charitable purpose. If the court answered this question in favour of the society, it would retain its privileges as a charity.

7.37   A case where this principle had been applied was *Re Hood*,[82] where the testator had given property upon trust 'to advance the Christian religion and ultimately to extinguish this enemy of my country's welfare'. The 'enemy' referred to was alcohol, so the trust appeared to have a temperance aim, and it had previously been held that the promotion of temperance was not a charitable purpose.[83] The Court of Appeal nevertheless held the trust before it charitable by construing the temperance aim as merely ancillary to the wholly and exclusively charitable object of advancing the Christian religion. On the other hand, in the *National Anti-Vivisection Society* case,[84] the House of Lords was unable to treat the Society's object of altering the law as ancillary to the attainment of a good charitable object. The Commissioners for the Special Purposes of the Income Tax Acts had found that the repeal of a statute was a main object of the Society, and the House of Lords treated this finding as conclusive.[85]

7.38   A difficulty with the notion of a political purpose as ancillary to charitable purposes is that it can be difficult to ascertain what might be regarded as merely ancillary rather than an independent object. A political purpose cannot be treated as ancillary to the charitable purposes if it would permit political activity which goes beyond that which the charity in question might lawfully engage in. It might be contended that a trust for the advancement of religion (such as that in *Re Hood*[86]) provides greater scope for an ancillary political purpose; as one commentator has

---

[79]   See *Re Scowcroft* [1898] 2 Ch 638, where Stirling J applied this principle to hold as charitable a gift to maintain a reading room (in a Conservative Club) for the furtherance of Conservative principles and religious improvement

[80]   [1948] AC 31

[81]   ibid, 76

[82]   [1931] 1 Ch 240 (CA)

[83]   *IRC v Temperance Council* (1926) 136 LT 27

[84]   *National Anti-Vivisection Society v IRC* [1948] AC 31

[85]   ibid, 61 (Lord Simonds)

[86]   [1931] 1 Ch 240 (CA)

remarked, 'since the main concerns of all religions cover eternity and infinity, it could easily be said that all human life, and therefore politics, is ancillary to God's purpose'.[87] It is, however, difficult to appreciate how the furtherance of one political doctrine can be considered to be ancillary to the advancement of religion.[88]

7.39

If the body in question is established as a company, it may contain an independent objects clause,[89] in which case a political object has to be treated as such, as the court is then precluded from treating any object as ancillary to any other.[90]

B. Political activity

(1) General principles

7.40

The basic principle is that a charity is not permitted to apply any of its funds for a political purpose. This is illustrated in several cases involving attempted donations by students' unions to political campaigns, which in each instance were restrained by injunction.[91]

7.41

This principle is, however, subject to the qualification that a charity is permitted to engage in political activity to the extent that such activity is made in furtherance of, and ancillary to, the charity's stated objects, and also within its powers.[92] There must be a reasonable expectation that the activity will further the charity's purposes to an extent justified by the resources devoted to those activities.[93]

7.42

An educational charity, for example, may, in the furtherance of its educational purposes, 'encourage students to develop their political awareness or . . . acquire knowledge of, and . . . debate, and . . . form views on, political issues'.[94] Charitable status is therefore no bar in itself to a students' union encouraging students in this way by providing facilities for a variety of students' political clubs (such as a Labour club or a Conservative club).

---

[87] I Williams, *The Alms Trade: Charities, Past, Present and Future* (Unwin Hyman, 1989) 116

[88] The decision in *Re Scowcroft* [1898] 2 Ch 638 (discussed above, para 7.36) is therefore difficult to justify

[89] ie a '*Cotman v Brougham* clause': *Cotman v Brougham* [1918] AC 514

[90] See observations of Cohen LJ in *Tennant Plays Ltd v IRC* [1948] 1 All ER 506, 511; see also *Oxford Group v IRC* (1949) 31 TC 221, 245–6 (Croom-Johnson J at first instance) 253–4 (Cohen LJ in CA)

[91] See *Baldry v Feintuck* [1972] 1 WLR 552 (proposed donation by the Students' Union of the University of Sussex to a campaign against Government proposals to withdraw free school milk); *Webb v O'Doherty* (1991) (1991) 3 Admin LR 731 (proposed donation by the Anglia Student Union (Cambridge) to an anti-Gulf War campaign)

[92] See Charity Commission, *Political Activities and Campaigning by Charities*, CC9 (Feb 1997), 8 (para 10)

[93] ibid, 8–9 (para 11)

[94] *A-G v Ross* [1986] 1 WLR 252, 263 (Scott J)

(2) The Charity Commissioners' guidelines

7.43 The Charity Commissioners have produced detailed guidance on the extent to which charities may engage in political activity.[95] Essentially, the guidelines represent the Charity Commissioners' views on which particular activities are, or are not, permitted, in the light of the more general statements laid down in case law: namely, that the charity has the power to engage in the activity, and that the activity is made in furtherance of, and is merely ancillary to, the charity's purposes.

7.44 In view of the importance of the need to keep within the legal restrictions on political activities by charities, the Charity Commissioners recommend that any charity undertaking political activities should have adequate arrangements in place for the commissioning, control, and evaluation of such activities conducted by their trustees.[96]

Campaigning

7.45 Campaigning may comprise the mobilization of public opinion to influence government policy.[97] The Charity Commissioners emphasise that a charity should not seek to organize public opinion to support or oppose a political party which advocates a particular policy favoured or opposed by the charity. A charity is not prevented from promoting its own policy merely because it happens to coincide with that of a particular political party; but the charity should take care to ensure that the independence of its view is explained and understood.[98]

7.46 Any information which the charity provides to the public in support of the campaign as a whole must be accurate and sufficiently full to support its position.[99] The only qualification to this is where a charity uses a communications medium the nature of which makes it impractical to set out the full basis of its position; here, it need not set out the full factual basis and argument for its stance, but must be able to set out its full position if called upon to do so.[100] Subject to these requirements, the campaign may have an emotional content; but (except where the nature of the medium makes it impracticable to set out the basis of the charity's position) it is unacceptable for a charity to seek to persuade government or the public on the basis of material which is *purely* emotive.[101]

---

[95] Charity Commission, *Political Activities and Campaigning by Charities*, CC9 (Feb 1997); Charity Commission,CC9(a) *Political Activities and Campaigning by Local Community Charities*, CC9(a) (Feb 1997)

[96] Charity Commission, *Political Activities and Campaigning by Charities*, CC9 (Feb 1997), 10 (para 15)

[97] ibid (para 16)

[98] ibid, 11 (para 19)

[99] ibid (para 20)

[100] ibid

[101] ibid, 12 (para 21)

Permissible political activity

Influencing government or public opinion

A charity may seek to influence government or public opinion through well- **7.47**
founded, reasoned argument based on research or direct experience on issues either
relating directly to the achievement of the charity's own stated purposes or relevant
to the well-being of the charitable sector.[102] A charity may provide information to
its supporters or the public on how individual Members of Parliament or parties
have voted on an issue, provided they do so in a way which will enable its supporters or the public to seek to persuade those Members or parties to change their position through well-founded, reasoned argument rather than *merely* through public
pressure.[103] A charity may provide its supporters, or members of the public, with
material to send to Members of Parliament or the Government, provided that the
material amounts to well-founded, reasoned argument.[104] A charity may also organize and present a petition to either House of Parliament or to national or local government; the purpose of the petition should be stated on each page.[105]

A charity must not participate in party political demonstrations,[106] and it must **7.48**
not seek to influence government or public opinion on the basis of material which
is merely emotive (except where the nature of the medium makes it impracticable
to set out the basis of the charity's position).[107]

A charity must not invite its supporters or the public to take action in support of its **7.49**
position without providing them with sufficient information to enable them to
decide whether to give their support and to take the action requested. In particular,
a charity must not invite its supporters or the public to write to their Members of
Parliament or the Government without providing them with sufficient information
to enable them to advance a reasoned argument in favour of the charity's position.[108]

A charity for the advancement of education must not step over the boundary **7.50**
between education and propaganda. The former involves providing balanced
information designed to enable people to make up their own minds; the latter
involves providing one-sided information designed to promote a particular point
of view.[109]

---

[102] ibid (para 24)
[103] ibid, 12–13 (para 25)
[104] ibid, 13 (para 26)
[105] ibid (para 27)
[106] ibid (para 29)
[107] ibid (para 31)
[108] ibid, 13–14 (para 32)
[109] ibid, 14 (para 33). See also *Oxfam: Report of an Inquiry submitted to the Charity Commissioners*
(HMSO, 1991), which reported that Oxfam had, in various publications, engaged in impermissible political activities by campaigning to change the policies of governments in the UK and overseas
in relation to Cambodia and South Africa

Responding to proposed legislation

7.51 A charity may provide and publish comments on possible proposed changes in the law or government policy, whether contained in a Green or White Paper or otherwise.[110] It may, in response to a Parliamentary Bill, supply to members of either House for use in debate such relevant information and reasoned arguments as can reasonably be expected to assist the achievement of its charitable purposes.[111]

Advocating and opposing changes in the law and public policy

7.52 A charity may advocate (or oppose) a change in the law or public policy which can reasonably be expected to help it to achieve (or to hinder it from achieving) its charitable purposes. The charity may present government with a reasoned written argument in support of its position, and it may publish its views and seek to influence public opinion in favour of its position by well-founded reasoned argument.[112]

Supporting, opposing, and promoting legislation

7.53 A charity may support (or oppose) the passage of a Bill which can reasonably be expected to help it to achieve (or to hinder it from achieving) its charitable purposes.[113] It may spend its funds on the promotion of public general legislation provided it has the power to do so and the legislation can reasonably be expected to further its charitable purposes.[114]

Commenting on public issues

7.54 A charity may comment publicly on social, economic, and political issues if these relate to its purposes or the way in which the charity is able to carry out its work.[115]

Supporting political parties

7.55 A charity may advocate a particular solution if it can reasonably be expected to further the purposes of the charity, even though that solution is advocated by a political party; but it must make it plain that its views are independent of the political party.[116] A charity must not support a political party.[117]

---

[110] Charity Commission, *Political Activities and Campaigning by Charities*, CC9 (Feb 1997), 14 (para 34)
[111] ibid, (para 35)
[112] ibid (para 36)
[113] ibid, 15 (para 37)
[114] ibid (para 38)
[115] ibid (para 39)
[116] ibid (para 40)
[117] ibid (para 41)

Acting with other bodies

A charity may affiliate to a campaigning alliance, even if the alliance includes non-   **7.56**
charitable organizations, if certain conditions are met. First, the charity must carefully consider the alliance's activities, and the implications for itself of being
associated with them, and should affiliate only if affiliation can reasonably be
expected to further the charity's own purposes.[118] Secondly, the charity must dis-
sociate itself from any activities undertaken by the alliance that it would be
improper for the charity to undertake directly; the charity must also take reasonable steps to ensure that its name, and any funds that it has contributed, are not
used to support them.[119]

Providing information

A charity may provide factual information to its members and those interested in   **7.57**
its work in seeking to inform their Members of Parliament and others on matters
related to the purposes of the charity.[120] It may employ Parliamentary staff to provide information to Members of Parliament on matters relevant to its purposes.[121]

Forthcoming elections

A charity may respond to forthcoming elections, whether local, national, or to the   **7.58**
European Parliament, by analysis and comment on the proposals of political parties which relate to its purposes or the way in which it is able to carry out its work,
provided that it comments in a way which is consistent with the Charity
Commissioners' guidelines and complies with all the relevant provisions of electoral law.[122] A charity may also bring to the attention of prospective candidates
issues relating to its purposes or the way in which it is able to carry out its work,
and raise public awareness about them generally, provided that the promotional
material is educational, informative, reasoned, and well-founded.[123] It must not

---

[118] ibid (para 42). A students' union charity may therefore subscribe to membership of the
National Union of Students (not itself a charity): *A-G v Ross* [1986] 1 WLR 252, 262 (Scott J). On
the other side of the line, see *Webb v O'Doherty* (1991) 3 Admin LR 731 (proposed donation to an
anti-Gulf War campaign); *Baldry v Feintuck* [1972] 1 WLR 552 (proposed donation to campaign
opposing the Government's plans to withdraw free school milk). See also *Oxfam: Report of an
Inquiry submitted to the Charity Commissioners*, (HMSO, 1991), which notes that Oxfam had in
1989 joined the South Africa Coalition, a group working to initiate change in the apartheid system
in South Africa. The Charity Commissioners took the view that this particular initiative went
beyond the furtherance of Oxfam's charitable objects and took the charity into an area of political
activity inappropriate for a charity
[119] Charity Commission, *Political Activities and Campaigning by Charities*, CC9 (Feb 1997),
15–16 (para 42)
[120] ibid, 16 (para 43)
[121] ibid (para 44)
[122] ibid (para 48)
[123] ibid, 16–17 (para 49)

seek to persuade members of the public to vote for or against a candidate or for or against a political party.[124]

Conducting and publishing research

7.59 A charity which conducts research must ensure that it is properly conducted using a methodology appropriate to the subject. Research undertaken to test a hypothesis must be undertaken objectively to test that hypothesis. The aim in publishing the results of the research must be to inform and educate the public.[125] A charity must not undertake research for another body where it is clear that that body intends to use the research for party political or propagandist purposes.[126]

Seeking support for government grants

7.60 A charity may seek the support of Members of Parliament where a question arises whether a government grant to the charity is to be made or continued.[127]

Charities' involvement in demonstrations and direct action

7.61 If a charity's involvement in a campaign is restricted to the provision of reasoned argument or information (such as the handing out of leaflets in public places), the general principles contained in the guidelines apply.[128] If, however, an event goes beyond this, and includes things such as marches, rallies, or peaceful picketing, additional considerations apply.[129] Such events may involve the charity in significant risks:[130] they may damage public support for the charity,[131] and may result in the charity, its officers, or others taking part, in the commission of a public order offence.[132] A charity should assess whether or not it needs to seek its own legal advice on the lawfulness of what it has in mind, with a view to satisfying itself that there is no significant risk of any civil or criminal proceedings being brought against it.[133]

7.62 If a charity decides to proceed, the charity trustees should take reasonable steps to ensure that the event in question receives thorough and appropriate advance preparation (including, where necessary, liaison with the police and other authorities); is at all times fully under the control of the charity or the event's organizers; is peaceful; does not give rise to a significant risk of civil or criminal proceedings

---

[124] Charity Commission, *Political Activities and Campaigning by Charities*, CC9 (Feb 1997), 17 (para 50)
[125] ibid (para 51)
[126] ibid (para 54)
[127] ibid (para 56)
[128] ibid, 18 (para 57)
[129] ibid (para 58)
[130] ibid (para 61)
[131] ibid 19 (para 62)
[132] ibid (para 63)
[133] ibid, 19–20 (para 66)

being brought against the charity, its trustees or members, or those participating; and does not generally bring the charity into disrepute (for example as a result of being intimidatory, provocative or excessively disruptive of the life of the community).[134]

A charity should consider carefully before requiring its staff to take part in a **7.63** demonstration or other form of direct action. It should bear in mind that an implied term of employment contracts is that the employer must not require the employee to do an unlawful act. It should take care that any instructions that it gives its staff are capable of being fully carried out in a way which will not involve, or be likely to involve, the staff in any unlawful act.[135]

There is generally no objection to members or officers of a charity participating in **7.64** demonstrations or direct action organized by others where they participate in their personal capacity. Charities should, however, take reasonable steps to ensure that there is no misunderstanding as to the basis of such participation, and should do nothing (such as the supplying of placards or badges) which might suggest that participants are taking part as official representatives of the charity.[136]

Ethical investment

Another form of political activity is ethical investment, which is more fully dealt **7.65** with in chapter 16.[137]

Additional guidelines for local community charities

The Charity Commissioners have produced separate guidelines for local commu- **7.66** nity charities.[138] Such charities are subject to the same legal restrictions on political activity as other charities, and the guidelines relating to them do not differ in principle from the general guidelines considered above. Such guidelines must therefore be complied with in any event, and the general provisions already discussed will not therefore be repeated here.

The general restrictions on the political activities of charities can, however, raise **7.67** special difficulties for local community charities. In particular, such charities may understandably wish to take positive action on issues affecting the local community, and the mobilization of public opinion to influence government may take the form of mobilizing local opinion with a view to influencing the actions of local councillors. The following matters (taken from the Charity Commissioners' guidance to local community charities) may be of particular importance to local charities.

---

[134] ibid, 20 (para 67)
[135] ibid, 21 (para 69)
[136] ibid (para 70)
[137] See ch 16, paras 16.61–16.66
[138] Charity Commission, *Political Activities and Campaigning by Local Community Charities*, CC9(a) (Feb 1997)

The issues that a local charity may engage in

7.68 The issues on which a local charity may campaign will depend upon the nature of its objects.[139] It may campaign on issues which directly affect its objects. Depending on a local charity's objects, such issues might include the provision of recreational, arts, and education facilities; youth clubs; rights for the disabled or elderly; equal opportunity matters; and the preservation of local buildings and open spaces. A local charity may also campaign in relation to issues which affect the way in which it carries out its work, such as building and fire regulations, licensing laws, and charity legislation.[140]

Advocacy work

7.69 A local charity may provide information and reasoned argument to central government and local authorities to influence or challenge their decisions in the exercise of their functions, where to do so can reasonably be expected to further the charity's purposes. The Charity Commissioners list a number of examples of what might be done.[141] They consider that a local charity for the homeless could provide assistance in connection with an appeal against a decision of a local authority not to award accommodation, or that a civic trust could seek to influence decisions by local authorities concerning the listing of buildings of architectural merit. A local charity may comment on particular decisions of central government or the local authority in exercise of statutory powers and support the legal challenge of such decisions, where to do so can reasonably be expected to further the charity's purposes.[142]

Arranging public meetings

7.70 A local charity may organize public meetings to test public feeling on issues which affect the achievement of its purposes or the way it goes about its work, provided it complies with the relevant provisions of electoral law.[143]

Supporting political parties

7.71 In order to raise funds, local charities may in their publications (for example, newsletters) carry paid advertisements by political parties, election candidates or campaigning groups, provided that these are on proper commercial terms. Charities should not discriminate in this regard between organizations or individuals on the basis of the views they hold, unless they consider that these would

---

[139] Charity Commission, *Political Activities and Campaigning by Local Community Charities*, CC9(a) (Feb 1997), 8 (para 15)
[140] ibid 9 (para 16)
[141] ibid, 14 (para 35)
[142] ibid (para 36)
[143] ibid (para 37)

conflict with the charity's purposes or would alienate the charity's beneficiaries or supporters.[144]

A local charity, like any other charity, is not precluded from advocating a particu-   **7.72**
lar solution merely because it is also favoured by a political party. The Charity
Commissioners' general guidelines should be complied with; but local charities in
receipt of funding from a local authority should consider whether such advocacy
is consistent with the terms of such funding. Charities which are regulated companies for the purposes of the Local Authorities (Companies) Order 1995[145] may
not publish material which appears to be designed to affect public support for a
political party.[146]

A local charity may invite members of either House of Parliament, local council-   **7.73**
lors, leaders of local authorities and mayors, to act as patrons or honorary presi-
dents.[147]

Use of charity premises

A local charity may permit its premises to be used as a polling station.[148]   **7.74**

A local charity whose purposes include the provision of premises to community   **7.75**
groups (such as a community association or village hall) may allow its premises to
be used by local political or campaigning groups, provided that it does so on the
same terms as other non-commercial user organizations. Charities should not
generally discriminate between organizations on the basis of the views they hold,
but may be justified in refusing use of the premises to particular organizations or
individuals where there is a risk of public disorder or of alienating the charity's
beneficiaries or supporters.[149]

In order to raise funds, local charities of all types may permit non-charitable orga-   **7.76**
nizations, including local political and campaigning groups, candidates for election, and local Members of Parliament or councillors to use their premises (when
not being used for their own charitable purposes) for the holding of surgeries with
their constituents, provided such use is on proper commercial terms. Charities
should not generally discriminate between such organizations or persons on the
basis of the views they hold, but may be justified in refusing use of the premises to
particular organizations or individuals whose aims and activities conflict with the

---

[144] ibid, 15 (para 39); cf similar criteria applied in relation to ethical investment: see further ch 16, paras 16.62, 16.64
[145] SI 1995/849
[146] Charity Commission, *Political Activities and Campaigning by Local Community Charities*, CC9(a) (Feb 1997), 15 (para 40)
[147] ibid (para 41)
[148] ibid, 18 (para 57)
[149] ibid, 19 (para 58)

charity's purposes, or where there is a risk of public disorder or of alienating the charity's beneficiaries or supporters.[150]

7.77 Certain local charities (notably schools) may be statutorily required to allow election candidates to use their premises for the holding of election meetings free of charge.[151]

Trustees nominated by local authorities

7.78 Trustees nominated by a local authority (whether or not they are councillors or officers of the authority) must not act as representatives or nominees of the authority or of any political party of which they are a member. They must, as trustees, act only in the best interests of the charity. If, in relation to a particular issue, they have a conflict of interests between their duty to the charity as trustee, and the duty they owe as councillors or officers to the authority and the people within its area, they should not take part in the trustees' discussion or vote on that issue.[152] This is considered more fully in chapter 9.[153]

(3) Use of separate charitable and non-charitable organizations

7.79 A body with political objects may attempt to secure the tax exemptions and reliefs available to charities by setting up a separate organization with wholly and exclusively charitable purposes. Conversely, if those running a charity wish to engage in political activity which is forbidden to the charity itself, they may do this by setting up a separate non-charitable body to pursue such activities. In the latter instance, the appropriate form for the political body will be either the unincorporated association or the company limited by guarantee.

7.80 Any transactions between a charity and such political bodies must, however, be conducted on a purely commercial basis as if the bodies were dealing with each other at arm's length. The charity may not, therefore, make donations of its own funds to the non-charitable body, and must, for instance, charge the latter a proper fee should it wish to make use of the charity's premises. If a director or trustee of the charity is also a director or committee member of the political organization, he should take appropriate steps to avoid a conflict of interests between the two bodies; for the same reason, it is desirable that the majority of the directors of the political body should not also be directors or trustees of the charity.[154] The political body must not have the same name as the charity. Apart from statu-

---

[150] Charity Commission, *Political Activities and Campaigning by Local Community Charities*, CC9(a) (Feb 1997), (para 59)

[151] ie under Representation of the People Act 1983, ss 95–6; Charity Commission, *Political Activities and Campaigning by Local Community Charities*, CC9(a) (Feb 1997), 19 (para 60)

[152] Charity Commission, *Political Activities and Campaigning by Local Community Charities*, CC9(a) (Feb 1997), 20 (para 61)

[153] See ch 9, para 9.128

[154] For avoidance of conflicts of interests generally, see further ch 9, para 9.96

tory restrictions on the same name where both bodies are companies incorporated under the Companies Acts,[155] the creation of a political body with a similar name to a charity might be fraud on the contributors, who might be misled into giving to the former when they intended to give to the latter. The charity might also have a passing off action against the other body.[156]

(4) Consequences of improper political activity

Improper political activity comprises a breach of trust. Where the charity is a company, an application of the charity's funds or property in improper political activity is outside the scope of the charity's objects and so ultra vires. An actual or threatened improper political activity may give rise to a variety of consequences and remedies. **7.81**

Advice and warning from the Charity Commissioners

If it appears to the Charity Commissioners that a charity may have engaged in unlawful political activity, they may invite the charity to discuss the matter with them.[157] Even where it is clear that a charity has engaged in impermissible political activity, the Charity Commissioners' approach is usually only to advise and warn trustees that the activities in question are not permissible, and to seek an assurance from them that the charity will forthwith cease to engage in such activities.[158] The Charity Commissioners are evidently very patient; for they have continued only to warn even when the charity concerned has engaged in other non-permissible political activity at a later date.[159] The Commissioners may also advise the trustees that such non-charitable activities might continue to be conducted by a separate non-charitable organization financed from moneys not contributed for charitable purposes.[160] **7.82**

---

[155] See ch 8, paras 8.87–8.88

[156] cf *British Diabetic Assoc v Diabetic Society Ltd* [1995] 4 All ER 812

[157] eg, as in the case of *War on Want* [1978] Ch Com Rep 11 (paras 22–5), where the charity had started publishing a magazine called *Poverty and Power*, which contained political propaganda

[158] eg the case of *Christian Aid Division* [1978] Ch Com Rep 12 (para 27). See also the case of *RSPCA* [1979] Ch Com Rep 10 (para 20)

[159] An example is *War on Want*, where the Charity Commissioners warned the charity in 1978 that some of their activities were of a political nature not open to a charity, as a result of which the charity ceased such activities, accepted the Commissioners' guidance with regard to certain projects which it aided, and agreed to seek the Commissioners' further advice about the type of research and education which it could validly carry out: [1978] Ch Com Rep 11–12 (paras. 22–5). Three years later, the same charity was found to be engaging in a national campaign 'to fight poverty and unemployment', which was essentially political in nature. The Charity Commissioners again merely warned the trustees, who gave an assurance that the charity would in future refrain from impermissible political activities: [1981] Ch Com Rep 22–3 (paras 57–60). See also the case of Oxfam, which was warned by the Charity Commissioners about certain political activity in 1978: [1978] Ch Com Rep 12 (para 26); and again in 1991: *Oxfam: Report of an Inquiry submitted to the Charity Commissioners* (HMSO, 1991)

[160] See, eg, *War on Want* [1978] Ch Com Rep 11, 12 (para 25). The relation between the charity and the non-charitable company with which it was involved proved less than satisfactory, however: the charity initially found it difficult to work out a proper relation with the non-charitable

7.83 In *Oxfam: Report of an Inquiry,*[161] it was found that the charity had used some of its funds in producing publications and supporting campaigns of a political nature beyond that which was permissible to it. The Charity Commissioners decided not to refer the matter to the Attorney-General with a view to seeking reimbursement of such misapplied funds from the trustees personally, since the Commissioners accepted that the trustees had acted in good faith. The Commissioners merely required that Oxfam's unacceptable political activities should cease; but the Commissioners warned that they would not hesitate to pursue the question of reimbursement if Oxfam were to continue such activities.[162]

Injunction

7.84 Any improper political activity, or application of the charity's money or other property on such activity, may be restrained by injunction, whether permanent or interlocutory.[163] An injunction may restrain improper political activity which is either merely threatened,[164] or which has already occurred. The injunction may be sought by the Attorney-General *ex officio* or (with the agreement of the Attorney-General) by the Charity Commissioners.[165] An application for an injunction ranks as charity proceedings,[166] and may therefore be brought by the charity, or any of the charity trustees, or any person interested in the charity, or by any two or more inhabitants of the area of the charity if it is a local charity, but not by any other person.[167] Charity proceedings may be brought only by order of the Charity Commissioners, unless the charity concerned is an exempt charity.[168] Since virtually all universities are exempt charities, students' unions which are a constituent part of such universities are also exempt charities. Members of such students' unions, for instance, can therefore bring proceedings themselves to restrain proposed misapplications of a union's funds without obtaining an order from the Charity Commissioners.[169]

Loss of tax exemptions

7.85 An application by a charity of its income on impermissible political activity is not an application to charitable purposes only, so the charity is not entitled to relief

---

company: [1981] Ch Com Rep 22, 23 (para 60); and a host of further problems later led to a Charity Commission investigation: *War on Want: Report of an Inquiry submitted to the Commissioners* (HMSO, 1991)

[161] *Oxfam: Report of an Inquiry submitted to the Charity Commissioners* (HMSO, 1991)
[162] ibid; see the Charity Commissioners' letter to Oxfam of 9 May 1991, 2–3 of Report
[163] See *Baldry v Feintuck* [1972] 1 WLR 552 (temporary injunction)
[164] As in ibid ; *Webb v O'Doherty* (1991) 3 Admin LR 731
[165] CA 1993, s 32
[166] ibid, s 33(8)
[167] ibid, s 33(1)
[168] ibid, s 33(2)
[169] As happened in *Baldry v Feintuck* [1972] 1 WLR 552

from income tax on that part of its income so applied.[170] Any disposal of an asset for the purposes of such impermissible political activity may give rise to a chargeable gain for the purposes of capital gains tax,[171] and a liability to inheritance tax may also arise.[172]

Personal liability of trustees

If the charity takes part in a campaign of direct action and the charity incurs **7.86** financial loss as a result (as, for example, where it is liable for the acts of its trustees or other officers where a demonstration gets out of control), the trustees may be personally liable in respect of the financial losses unless they have taken reasonable steps as recommended by the Charity Commissioners[173] in relation to the preparation, form and conduct of such direct action.[174] The trustees' liability includes the making good of any loss of tax relief to the charity resulting from the misapplication.

Action against recipient

In some cases it may be possible to recover any funds or other property misapplied **7.87** to political purposes by means of a tracing action; but the Charity Commissioners are unlikely to seek to trace unless the amount recovered is likely to justify the expense involved. If a charitable company misapplies its funds to political purposes, the application is ultra vires;[175] but, as the company's funds are dedicated to charity, this does not preclude the bringing either of a proprietary or a personal remedy against the recipient, subject to the usual defences. The personal remedy may be either an action for damages in the law of restitution,[176] or an action *in personam* in equity.[177]

Impact on charitable status

The fact that a charity engages in political activity incompatible with charitable **7.88** status is not a ground for depriving it of charitable status.[178] If, however, the actual purposes of an organization are themselves in doubt, it is legitimate to take into

---

[170] ICTA 1988, s 505(1)
[171] TCGA 1992, s 256(1)
[172] IHTA 1984, ss 58(1)(a), 65(1)
[173] ie as set out in Charity Commission, *Political Activities and Campaigning by Charities*, CC9 (Feb 1997), 18–21 (paras. 57–70), discussed above, para 7.61–7.64
[174] Charity Commission, *Political Activities and Campaigning by Charities*, CC9 (Feb 1997), 20 (para 68)
[175] cf *IRC v Educational Grants Assoc Ltd* [1967] Ch 123, 139–40 (Pennycuick J); affd [1967] Ch 993 (CA)
[176] *Westdeutsche Landesbank Girozentrale v Islington LBC* [1996] AC 669 (HL)
[177] *Ministry of Health v Simpson* [1951] AC 251 (HL)
[178] See [1978] Ch Com Rep 13 (para 29), where the Charity Commissioners mention that there is a good deal of misunderstanding on this

account, in determining whether the organization is or is not a charity, the nature of the activities which it has in fact carried on since its formation.[179] If an organization has several charitable objects, and one which appears to be political, evidence of the organization's political activity since it was established may therefore be used to determine whether the political aim is an independent object (so that the organization is not a charity) or merely ancillary to the wholly and exclusively charitable objects.[180]

---

[179] *A-G v Ross* [1986] 1 WLR 252, 263–4 (Scott J)
[180] ibid (Scott J)

Part III

LEGAL STRUCTURES AND GOVERNANCE

8

LEGAL STRUCTURES AND
THE DISTRIBUTION OF POWER

A. Introduction

(1) Need for property to be effectually dedicated to charity

8.01 In English law, 'charity' refers neither to the act of giving, nor to a state of mind, but to the effectual dedication of property to charitable purposes. Effectual dedication occurs when property is subject to an obligation that it be applied for the public benefit in such a way that the right to compel such application passes to the Attorney-General on behalf of the Crown as *parens patriae*. A mere power to appoint property for charitable purposes does not therefore result in effectual dedication to charity.[1] Although individuals may have a right to institute proceedings to ensure that property dedicated to charity is applied for its charitable purposes,[2] such proceedings do not comprise the enforcement of individual proprietary rights, but rather the enforcement, in a manner which the Charities Act 1993 permits, of rights vested in the Crown as *parens patriae*.

8.02 For effectual dedication to occur, there must initially be identifiable property or funds. The separation of property for charity in this way occurs through the creation of a separate legal structure. An express undertaking by a person to hold specific property for charitable purposes subjects such person to an obligation enforceable in equity, and creates an express charitable trust. Other legal structures for effectual dedication of property to charity include the unincorporated association and the corporation. The term 'charity' is often used to refer to the legal structure by which charitable property is held; and, using the expression in this sense, 'a charity' is an institution which separates (and, in a sense, insulates) the individuals who provide or distribute the funds from those who benefit from them. By itself, however, the term 'charity' has been described as an abstract conception distinct from the institutional mechanism provided for holding and administering its funds.[3] In this sense, 'charity' refers to the status of being charitable; and the body of rules which relates to charitable status, regardless of the particular institution's legal structure, is exclusively the province of charity law. In contrast to this, the body of rules which relates to the particular legal structure varies according to the legal structure adopted. The analysis of legal structure in this chapter is therefore an exploration of the boundary, and the relationship, between these distinct bodies of rules, that is, between charitable status and legal structure.

Gift upon a condition

8.03 A gift of property 'on condition' that it be applied to charitable purposes will, if the fulfilment of the condition would result in the whole of the property being

---

[1] *Down v Worrall* (1833) 1 My & K 561, 563–4 (Leach MR)
[2] ie 'charity proceedings' within the meaning of CA 1993, s 33
[3] *Re Vernon's Will Trusts* [1972] Ch 300, 304

applied for charitable purposes, generally be construed as imposing an obligation on the donee, thereby effectually dedicating the property to charity by means of a charitable trust.[4]

However, a gift of property 'on condition' that a specific amount be applied to **8.04** charitable purposes, thus leaving a surplus to which the donee is entitled beneficially, will normally be construed as a condition precedent, and as creating no enforceable right in favour of charity. The donee may therefore choose whether to accept the condition (and so take the gift), or to decline the condition (and so lose the gift). In such an instance, no property is effectually dedicated to charity unless and until the donee accepts the gift subject to the condition.[5]

Covenant and contract

A conveyance of land to a corporation (a local authority) subject to a covenant **8.05** that it be used 'as a recreation ground and for no other purpose' (which was itself conceded to be a charitable purpose) did not effectually dedicate the land to charity. The covenant, which was contained in a deed *inter partes*, conferred private rights only upon the covenantee; the Attorney-General, not being a party to the deed, had no locus standi to intervene to prevent a proposed application of the land for non-charitable purposes.[6] The issue was purely one of contract, not of property. Similarly, in *Attorney-General v Barratt Manchester Ltd*[7] it was held that an agreement between a landowner and a local planning authority under the planning legislation, that the land should be preserved as an open space as a public amenity, did not give rise to a charitable trust.

Contract does not, however, necessarily preclude effectual dedication to charity. **8.06** Effectual dedication may occur if that is the intention of the contracting parties, as in the case of an unincorporated charitable association, whose property is effectually dedicated to charity through the machinery of the trust, the contract merely governing the rights and obligations of the parties in relation to matters of administration. Even such contractual rights cannot be enforced without the approval of the state, whether the Charity Commissioners or the Attorney-General.[8] Similarly, a covenant to pay money to a charity may generate a separate proprietary right, a chose in action,[9] which is enforceable by the charity; the chose

---

[4] *Goodman v Mayor of Saltash Corp* (1882) 7 App Cas 633, 642 (Lord Selborne LC); *Re Richardson* (1887) 56 LJ Ch 784

[5] *A-G v Wax Chandlers' Co* (1873) LR 6 HL 1, 19 (Lord Cairns)

[6] *Liverpool City Council v A-G* The Times, 1 May 1992, applying *A-G v Poole Corp* [1938] Ch 23 (CA)

[7] The Times 11 July 1991; see LA Sheridan, *Keeton & Sheridan's The Modern Law of Charities* (4th edn, Barry Rose, 1992) 130, n 22

[8] ie 'charity proceedings': CA 1993, s 33

[9] cf *Fletcher v Fletcher* (1844) 4 Hare 67

in action is therefore itself property effectually dedicated to charity as soon as the covenant is entered into. A contract may also be ancillary to the creation of an inter vivos charitable trust: as where a settlor sells land to a local authority that undertakes in the contract to use the land for charitable purposes only. The contractual obligation on the trustee does not preclude the creation of a charitable trust; it is merely one of the terms, that is part of the consideration, on which the trustee acquires the land.[10]

8.07 In *The Priory, Ware, Herts*,[11] the Charity Commissioners accepted that the grant by an individual of a long lease of a manor house and land to a local authority had effectually dedicated the property to charity, even though no trusts had been declared in the lease. Recitals in the lease indicated that the land was granted in consideration of the lessor's regard for the welfare of the local inhabitants. The authority had entered into covenants in the lease to apply the property for specified purposes that were charitable, and had erected a tablet on a wall of the manor house which stated that it had been given by the donor for the benefit and enjoyment of the townspeople in perpetuity. The Commissioners considered that in this case the covenants in the lease could be accepted as evidence of a trust, particularly when supported by the external evidence of the commemorative tablet.[12]

Mandate theory

8.08 The normal inference where a number of persons contribute to a fund to be applied to the same charitable purposes is that the terms upon which the fund is held form a contract between the contributors, who thereby become members of an unincorporated association, and that the fund is thereby effectually dedicated to charity. If, however, the situation can be analysed exclusively as one of agency, no effectual dedication will occur. A principal who transfers a fund to an agent and gives the latter a mandate to apply the fund for charitable purposes only does not effectually dedicate the property to charity, since the obligation is enforceable only by the principal himself, who is entitled to demand that the property, until applied, be returned to him.[13] Nor is there any effectual dedication to charity merely because several persons transfer funds to an agent and the terms of each mandate are the same.

8.09 If, however, the agent mixes the funds (with the authority of the principals), the mandate becomes irrevocable, in that no contributor is entitled to demand his money back, although the recipient can be restrained from applying the mixed funds outside the terms of the mandate.[14] This analysis was applied by the Court

---

[10] *Brisbane City Council v A-G for Queensland* [1979] AC 411, 421–2 (Lord Wilberforce) (PC)
[11] [1979] Ch Com Rep 24–6 (paras 74–81)
[12] ibid, 25–6 (paras 78–9)
[13] cf *Conservative and Unionist Central Office v Burrell* [1982] 1 WLR 522, 529 (Brightman LJ)
[14] ibid, 529–30 (Brightman LJ)

of Appeal in *Conservative and Unionist Central Office v Burrell*.[15] The court considered that Central Office lacked the characteristics of an unincorporated association, since there were no mutual understandings between all the members, no mutual rights and obligations, and no rules governing control where it clearly lay (with the leader).[16] The absence of evidence relating to when Central Office was formed or of any document evidencing such agreement also suggested that no unincorporated association had come into existence.[17] The mandate theory provided an alternative basis to explain how Central Office held its funds. Brightman LJ himself, however, pointed out technical difficulties with the mandate theory: first, the rights of the contributors might be good only against the original recipient and not against his successors; secondly, legacies are not susceptible to the mandate analysis: an agency cannot be created by will because an agency between a testator and his chosen agent cannot be set up at the moment of death.[18]

It remains to be seen whether the courts will be willing to apply the mandate **8.10** theory to multiple contributors where the mandate permits the application of the funds to charitable purposes only. Even if a mandate arises initially, it seems reasonable to infer that the moment at which the separate contributions are mixed, when each individual contributor loses his right to a return of any unspent part of his contribution, is the moment at which the contributions are effectually dedicated to charity. Furthermore, in contrast to the approach in *Burrell*'s case, without evidence of a charity's origins, the application of funds for charitable purposes raises a presumption that the funds were effectually dedicated to charity at some time in the past.[19]

(2) Basic legal structures for effectual dedication

In English law, a charity may exist in one of several legal structures, the three basic **8.11** forms being the trust, the unincorporated association, and the corporation. More specialist structures—the friendly society and the industrial and provident society—also exist for certain types of charities. Subject to this, the choice of basic structure—trust, unincorporated association or company incorporated under the Companies Acts—lies with those who create the charity, or who control it. Each legal structure will now be considered in turn.

---

[15] [1982] 1 WLR 522

[16] ibid, 527 (Lawton LJ)

[17] ibid, 527 (Lawton LJ). But see P Creighton, 'A Note on *Conservative and Unionist Central Office* v. *Burrell (Inspector of Taxes)*' [1983] Conv 150, 152: 'It may be as misleading to deny the organisation its status as an unincorporated association because its origins are obscure as it would be to deny the existence of a living human being on the ground that his birth certificate could not be found'

[18] *Conservative and Unionist Central Office v Burrell* [1982] 1 WLR 522, 530 (Brightman LJ). See also criticisms by P Creighton, 'A Note on *Conservative and Unionist Central Office* v. *Burrell (Inspector of Taxes)*' [1983] Conv 150

[19] *A-G v St Cross Hospital* (1853) 17 Beav 435, 464

B. The charitable trust

(1) Introduction

8.12 Usually a charitable trust is created expressly; but it can arise by way of presumption. Thus, if the instrument by which a charity was created cannot be found, or its origins are obscure, but there is evidence that property has been devoted to charitable purposes for a long period, the long user raises a presumption that the property is held upon charitable trusts.[20] The court will then presume whatever is required (such as a lost grant[21]) in order to give the charity legal validity.

8.13 The traditional charitable trust is created by a settlor (or testator) who transfers (or bequeaths or devises) funds or other property to trustees upon trust for wholly and exclusively charitable purposes. The structure of a charitable trust is very simple. The governing document is the trust instrument, which sets out the express purposes of the trust and the administrative powers of the trustees. A charitable trust is therefore relatively easy to set up; no stamp duty is payable on the instrument by which the conveyance, transfer, or lease, or the agreement for it, is effected, although it must be stamped by the Inland Revenue with a stamp denoting that it is not chargeable with any duty.[22] The charitable trust should also be registered (if appropriate) with the Charity Commissioners.[23]

8.14 The trustees are obliged to carry out the purposes of the trust as specified in the trust instrument, subject only to any modification either of the purposes (for example, by means of a cy-près scheme), or of the administrative provisions. Such modification will need to be effected either with the approval of the court or of the Charity Commissioners, or pursuant to the exercise of a power of amendment in the trust instrument.[24] Subject to this, the purposes of the trust are static, the whole character of the charity being essentially stamped by the settlor or testator who created it. The law of trusts imposes duties and confers powers on the trustees, who therefore generally have responsibility for the entire management of the charity. It is possible for the settlor to create a trust which gives the power to make decisions (for example, as regards the selection of persons to receive any benefit under the charitable trust) to third parties, but this begins to blur the distinction between those who are trustees and those who are not. The simple nature of a trust therefore makes it difficult to allocate power between different groups, as is possible in a corporation (where the distinction can be drawn between directors or managers on the one hand, and members on the other). For this reason, the

---

[20] *A-G v St Cross Hospital* (1853) 17 Beav 435, 464
[21] *Goodman v Mayor of Saltash Corp* (1882) 7 App Cas 633 (HL); *Peggs v Lamb* [1994] Ch 172
[22] FA 1982, s 129
[23] CA 1993, s 3
[24] If the court or the Charity Commissioners make a scheme for a charitable trust, the scheme itself will thereafter be the governing instrument

trust form is more appropriate to a foundation-type charity, one which already has sufficient capital from which it makes grants or other applications for charitable purposes. Indeed, the trust is the only structure available to a charity created by will. Charitable trusts, unlike charitable companies, are subject to the rule against accumulations, and are not therefore permitted to accumulate income outside the permitted period of accumulation,[25] although they may be able to retain income in the form of a reserve.[26]

(2) Amending clause in governing instrument

The trust instrument may confer a power on its trustees or governors to revoke or **8.15** alter any of the clauses which it contains. The scope of such power to amend will depend upon the width of the amending clause itself. The power to amend may be limited to administrative matters or matters of internal management; but it may also include a power to amend the charitable trust's purposes.

It is always desirable that a clause which permits alterations to the charitable trust's **8.16** purposes permits only alterations of a non-fundamental nature. The reason for this is that any fundamental alteration to the charity's purposes may be outside the contemplation of outsiders who have already made donations, whether spontaneously or as a result of a fund-raising campaign. Fundamental alterations would not therefore carry such earlier contributions to the amended purposes, the result being that such contributions must continue to be held upon trust (that is, upon what is now a special trust) for the pre-amendment purposes. The corollary of this is that lesser alterations to the charitable trust's purposes are indeed taken to be within the contemplation of donors, and so are effective to carry earlier donations to the amended purposes. Whether an alteration is fundamental or not may sometimes be uncertain;[27] and the merit of expressly limiting the amendment power to non-fundamental changes of purpose and to administrative changes is that it avoids the risk of inadvertently subjecting existing funds to a special trust.

Because the concept of a fundamental alteration is based upon what might be con- **8.17** sidered to be within the reasonable contemplation of donors, it is desirable for the trust instrument to define 'a fundamental alteration' by reference to the reasonable contemplation of donors. This is done in the amendment clause contained in the model constitution for a charitable trust prepared on behalf of the Charity

---

[25] LPA 1925, s 164; Perpetuities and Accumulations Act 1964, s 13
[26] On the difference between accumulations and reserves, see ch 2, paras 2.20–2.22
[27] As *In Re Holloway's Trusts* (1909) 26 TLR 62, where the deed declaring the trusts of a college provided that the rules and regulations could be revoked or altered after the death of the founder and 20 years after the deed was made by a three-quarters majority of the governors; but not so as to alter the 'fundamental principles' there laid down. It was held that a clause in the original deed prohibiting the appointment of a woman governor was not fundamental, and so could be removed by the majority procedure

Law Association.[28] The amendment clause enables the trust deed to be amended by a supplemental deed on a resolution passed by a specified percentage of the trustees (which would normally be more than a simple majority[29]); but it provides that no amendment is valid if it would make a 'fundamental change' to objects or to the amending clause itself, or which would destroy the charitable status of the trust. A 'fundamental change' is defined in the trust deed as 'such a change as would not have been within the reasonable contemplation of a person making a donation to the Trust'.[30] The clause further provides that no amendment may be made to certain other clauses (those concerning benefits to trustees,[31] the personal interest of a trustee in any matter[32], and the investment of funds not required for immediate use[33]) without the prior written consent of the Charity Commissioners.

(3) Proceedings of trustees

8.18 Under the general law, there is no maximum number of trustees of a charitable trust.[34] The general law similarly requires no minimum number; but two trustees of a charitable trust are needed to dispose of land, since a sole trustee (unless a trust corporation) cannot give a valid receipt for the proceeds of sale or other capital money arising under a trust of land.[35]

8.19 The trust instrument should, as a matter of good practice, specify a minimum number of trustees' meetings each year,[36] and the number of trustees which comprises a quorum.[37] Unless the trust instrument provides otherwise, the decisions of the trustees of a charitable trust may be made by a simple majority.[38] Where it is envisaged that there will be a large number of charity trustees, the advantages of majority rule are manifest. Also as a matter of good practice, the trust instrument should provide for the chairman of the trustees, or another trustee chosen by the trustees, to preside at each meeting; and, in the event of a tie, it should confer on the chairman of the meeting a second or casting vote.[39]

---

[28] Trust Deed for a Charitable Trust, cl 8
[29] ibid, see note to cl 8
[30] ibid, cl 11.1 (interpretation)
[31] ibid, cl 6.2
[32] ibid, cl 6.3
[33] ibid, cl 6.4
[34] TA 1925, s 34(3) (exempting charitable trusts from the maximum number of four applicable to private trusts of land)
[35] TA 1925, s 14(2)(a), as amended by Trusts of Land and Appointment of Trustees Act 1996, s 25(1) and Sch 3, para 3(3)
[36] See, eg, the CLA's Trust Deed for a Charitable Trust cl 5.1
[37] See, ibid, cl 5.2
[38] *Re Whiteley* [1910] 1 Ch 600, 608
[39] See, eg, the CLA's Trust Deed for a Charitable Trust cl 5.6

It may sometimes be difficult to assemble the requisite number of trustees for a **8.20**
meeting in person. Such difficulty can be overcome if the trust deed provides for
a meeting by means of a telephone- or video-conference at which the trustees are
in simultaneous contact with each other; such provision is contained in the model
Trust Deed for a Charitable Trust drafted on behalf of the Charity Law
Association.[40] Another method is for the trust instrument to provide that a written resolution signed by all the trustees is to be as valid as a resolution passed at a
meeting.[41]

(4) Contracts with third parties

A charitable trust does not itself give rise to a distinct legal entity which can be **8.21**
identified as 'the charity'. A charitable trust, like any trust, is, after all, merely an
obligation imposed on one or more persons in equity to hold property, in this case
for charitable purposes. Any contract entered into by the charity trustees with
respect to the charitable funds is therefore entered into by them personally. The
trustees are therefore personally liable on such contracts, subject only to their entitlement to have any such liability met first out of the assets of the charitable trust.[42]
If, therefore, it is envisaged that a charity about to be formed will be entering into
substantial contracts with third parties, trading on a large scale, or employing a
large number of staff, the trust structure may not be the most suitable.

C. The charitable unincorporated association

(1) Introduction

An unincorporated association refers to a group of persons who contract together **8.22**
to pursue a common purpose. If the purpose is to carry on a business for profit for
themselves, it is a partnership. If it is a non-business purpose, it may be a non-
charitable association (for example, a members' club) or a charitable association.
It will be a charitable association if, under the contract between the members, the
association's property is to be devoted to wholly and exclusively charitable purposes.

The contract between the members of a charitable unincorporated association is **8.23**
contained in what are commonly called the Rules of Association, which therefore
comprise the association's governing instrument. In accordance with the rules, the
members will usually appoint a few of their number as the day-to-day managers
of the association, who together form what is generally known as a Committee.
Because the structure of a unincorporated charitable association is partly based on

---

[40] ibid, cl 5.3
[41] ibid, cl 5, which provides for this
[42] See further ch 9, paras 9.192–9.200

the law of contract, it is better able than the trust to provide for a division of rights and responsibilities between the various groups, namely the Committee and the general meeting.

8.24   The association is likely to have money or other property accrued from members' subscriptions, donations, and perhaps profits from fund-raising activities such as bazaars. It will probably have a bank account in the association's name. Since, however, an unincorporated association (like a trust) has no distinct legal persona, the legal title to any such property must be vested in the members or in one or more other persons. If the association has more than three or four members, it becomes impracticable to have the assets vested in the names of all of them. Often, therefore, the association's assets will be vested in the names of two or three of the members, who are generally called the Trustees.

8.25   The traditional terminology used by unincorporated associations can be confusing even to those who run them. The problem arises because section 97(1) of the Charities Act 1993 imposes certain obligations on 'the persons having the general control and management of the administration of a charity', and it designates these persons the 'charity trustees'. The obligations imposed by the Act are therefore applicable not only to trustees of charitable trusts in the strict sense, but also to the general managers of a charitable unincorporated association. These will be the members of the Committee. The so-called Trustees are merely the persons in whom the association's assets are vested. Their role as such is a purely passive one: they hold the property subject to the directions of the Committee and (so far as power is reserved to them) the general body of members. This can cause great confusion in practice, as members sometimes wrongly believe that the Trustees of the association are the 'trustees' for the purposes of the Charities Act 1993, which is patently not so.

8.26   The Constitution for a Charitable Unincorporated Association drafted on behalf of the Charity Law Association seeks to avoid such confusion by stating expressly that[43] 'The Committee as charity trustees have control of the Association and its property and funds' and by specifying in an interpretation clause that 'charity trustees' has the meaning prescribed by the Charities Act 1993, section 97(1).[44]

(2) Role of trust in dedicating association's property to charity

8.27   Although contract plays an important role in charitable associations, it is clear that the members of such an association (unlike the members of a non-charitable unincorporated association) are not contractually free to apply the property held by the association in any way other than according to the charitable purposes there specified. Neither the members of the association nor the Committee can be

---

[43] Constitution for a Charitable Unincorporated Association, r 6.1
[44] ibid, r 15.1

treated as having a beneficial interest in the association's property (whether raised by way of subscription, donations, or otherwise). The constitution may usefully remind members of this by expressly stating that the association's property and funds do not belong to the members or to the Committee.[45]

Sometimes the association's constitution will provide expressly that its assets are to be held upon trust for its (wholly and exclusively) charitable objects, so that the association combines the concepts of trust and contract.[46] Even in the absence of an express declaration of trust, however, it is possible to infer a trust for the association's purposes specified in its Rules; indeed, in modern times, it appears that the assets of every charitable unincorporated association are to be treated as being held upon trust, whether express or implied.[47] **8.28**

Since members have no proprietary interest in the association's assets, any rights they enjoy *qua* members can only be rights arising under the association's constitution. The enforcement of such rights therefore comprises 'charity proceedings',[48] and needs the authorization of the Charity Commissioners.[49] **8.29**

(3) Holding of assets

Because the membership of the Committee is likely to change fairly regularly, it may be inconvenient to vest the assets of the association in the names of the Committee members. It may therefore be appropriate to vest the assets in a nominee (which should be a corporate body) or holding trustees (or a trust corporation as a sole holding trustee), in which case provision for this should be made in the constitution.[50] Provision for all these methods is made in the Constitution for a Charitable Unincorporated Association drafted on behalf of the Charity Law Association,[51] which also provides that land may be held by the Official Custodian for Charities under an order of the court or of the Charity Commissioners.[52] **8.30**

(4) Objects and powers

The association's constitution must specify the association's objects, which must be wholly and exclusively charitable. In order to avoid confusion between objects and powers, the constitution should separately specify the association's powers, stating that they may be exercised only in promoting the association's objects. The Constitution for a Charitable Unincorporated Association drafted on behalf of **8.31**

---

[45] See, eg, ibid, r 9.1
[46] See M Chesterman, *Charities, Trusts and Social Welfare* (Weidenfeld & Nicolson, 1979) 198
[47] See further ch 11, paras 11.10–11.15
[48] CA 1993, s 33(8)
[49] ibid, s 33(2)
[50] On custodian and holding trustees, see ch 9, paras 9.66–9.74
[51] r 9.6
[52] ibid, r 9.6.5

the Charity Law Association lists nineteen separate powers.[53] These are powers to promote or carry out research;[54] to provide advice;[55] to publish or distribute information;[56] to co-operate with other bodies;[57] to support, administer, or set up other charities;[58] to raise funds (but not by way of taxable trading);[59] to borrow money and give security for loans (but only in accordance with the restrictions imposed by the Charities Act 1993);[60] to acquire or hire property of any kind;[61] to let or dispose of property of any kind (but only in accordance with the restrictions imposed by the Charities Act 1993);[62] to make grants or loans of money and to give guarantees;[63] to set aside funds for special purposes or as reserves against future expenditure;[64] to deposit or invest funds;[65] to delegate the management of investments to a financial expert subject to certain requirements;[66] to insure the association's property against any foreseeable risk and to take out other insurance policies to protect the association where required;[67] to insure members of the Committee against the costs of a successful defence to a criminal prosecution or against personal liability in specified circumstances;[68] to employ paid or unpaid agents, staff, or advisers;[69] to enter into contracts to provide services to or on behalf of other bodies;[70] to pay the costs of forming the association;[71] and to do anything else within the law which promotes or helps to promote the objects.[72]

8.32 The powers so specified are the powers of the association. Depending on the allocation of power in the constitution, many of these powers are likely to be exercisable by the Committee; but some may be expressly reserved to the general meeting.[73]

---

[53] ibid, r 3
[54] ibid, r 3.1
[55] ibid, r 3.2
[56] ibid, r 3.3
[57] ibid, r 3.4
[58] ibid, r 3.5
[59] ibid, r 3.6
[60] ibid, r 3.7
[61] ibid, r 3.8
[62] ibid, r 3.9
[63] ibid, r 3.10
[64] ibid, r 3.11
[65] ibid, r 3.12
[66] ibid, r 3.13
[67] ibid, r 3.14
[68] ibid, r 3.15
[69] ibid, r 3.16
[70] ibid, r 3.17
[71] ibid, r 3.18
[72] ibid, r 3.19. This is an 'incidental activities' provision
[73] This is discussed below, paras 8.42–8.45

(5) Committee

Appointment and discharge

As it is generally impractical for an association to be managed by the whole body **8.33** of members, an association's constitution should make provision for a small number of persons to comprise the Committee. The Constitution for a Charitable Unincorporated Association drafted on behalf of the Charity Law Association provides for a Committee to consist of at least three individuals (with provision for a maximum number to be specified), all of whom must be members (but must not be paid employees) of the association.[74] An association's constitution should additionally provide for one Committee member to be the Chair.

The constitution will also need to determine the method for becoming a **8.34** Committee member. It may, for instance, provide for all the Committee members to be elected by the members at general meeting. Provision may also need to be made, however, for nominated Committee members, as where another body (such as a local authority) has power to nominate one or more persons.[75] In order to maintain a working number of Committee members in the event of deaths or retirements between general meetings, or to enable the Committee to appoint persons with particular knowledge or skills, it is also advisable for the Committee to be given an express power to co-opt members to be additional Committee members. It is usual for the constitution to provide that co-opted members are to hold office until the next annual general meeting.[76]

In order to ensure that there is some continuity in the membership of the **8.35** Committee, the constitution should provide a system for retirement of elected Committee members by rotation. The constitution drafted on behalf of the Charity Law Association, for instance, provides for one-third (or the number nearest one-third) of the elected Committee members to retire at each annual general meeting, those longest in office retiring first, and the choice between any of equal service being made by drawing lots.[77] It also requires every Committee member to sign a declaration of willingness to act as a charity trustee of the association before becoming eligible to vote at any meeting of the Committee;[78] this is to ensure that so far as possible those taking on the responsibility of membership of the Committee are aware of the legal responsibilities involved.[79]

---

[74] r 6.2
[75] On nominative trustees generally, see ch 9, para 9.21 (appointment), and para 9.128 (conflicts of interests)
[76] The Constitution for a Charitable Unincorporated Association drafted on behalf of the CLA makes provision for a Chair and for specified numbers of all three types of Committee members, normally elected Committee members, nominated Committee members, and co-opted Committee members: r 6.2
[77] ibid r 6.3
[78] ibid, r 6.4
[79] ibid, p 14 (Notes to r 6.4)

8.36   The constitution should also provide for the circumstances in which a Committee member automatically ceases to be a member of the Committee. The constitution drafted on behalf of the Charity Law Association provides for this in the event that the Committee member is disqualified under the Charities Act 1993;[80] is incapable, whether mentally or physically, of managing his or her own affairs;[81] is absent from a specified number of consecutive meetings of the Committee;[82] ceases to be a member of the association (but with provision for reinstatement by resolution of all the other members of the Committee on resuming membership of the association);[83] and resignation by written notice to the Committee (but only if at least two members of the Committee will remain in office).[84] It also provides for removal by a resolution passed by all the other members of the Committee after inviting the views of the Committee member concerned and considering the matter in the light of any such views.[85] Such safeguards should ensure that any such removal cannot be challenged on the ground that it infringes the rules of natural justice.

8.37   An appointment or discharge of a Committee member by resolution of the Committee members, the members of the association, or other persons, should be recorded in a memorandum in accordance with section 83 of the Charities Act 1993.[86]

Committee meetings

8.38   As a matter of good practice, the constitution should make provision for a minimum number of Committee meetings each year,[87] and specify a quorum at such meetings.[88] It may also provide for meetings either in person or by electronic means.[89] It should provide for the Chair (or if the Chair is unable or unwilling to do so) some other member of the Committee chosen by the members present, to preside at each Committee meeting.[90] It should also provide for determination of issues by a simple majority of the votes cast at a Committee meeting; as an alternative, it may also provide that a resolution in writing and signed by all

---

[80]   ibid, r 6.5.1

[81]   ibid, r 6.5.2

[82]   ibid, r 6.5.3

[83]   ibid, r 6.5.4

[84]   ibid, r 6.5.5

[85]   ibid, r 6.5.6

[86]   For further discussion of the requirements and effect of the statutory memorandum, see ch 9, paras 9.48–9.49

[87]   See Constitution for a Charitable Unincorporated Association, r 7.1, which makes such provision

[88]   ibid, r 7.2, which makes such provision

[89]   ibid, r 7.3, which does so provide. See further the comments on the parallel provision made in the CLA's Trust Deed for a Charitable Trust, cl 5.3, discussed above, para 8.20

[90]   See Constitution for a Charitable Unincorporated Association, r 7.4, which provides for this

Committee members is as valid as a resolution passed at a meeting.[91] It is also usual to provide that, in the event of a tie, the chair of the meeting has a second or casting vote.[92]

(6) Members

Membership

The constitution may restrict its membership to individuals, or it may open it to organizations as well. The Charity Law Association's Constitution for a Charitable Unincorporated Association provides that membership is open to any individual or organization interested in promoting the charity's objects.[93] The constitution may also provide for different classes of membership, with different subscription rates.[94] It is also useful to require the Committee to maintain a register of members.[95]   **8.39**

It is a good policy to specify that a member whose subscription is a specified period of time in arrears automatically ceases to be a member.[96] The constitution may also specify that a member may resign by written notice to the association.[97] It may also be desirable to remove a member whose views are considered to be harmful to the association. The Charity Law Association's model constitution provides that the Committee may terminate the membership of any individual or organization whose continued membership would, in the reasonable view of the Committee, be harmful to the association (but only after notifying the member concerned in writing and considering the matter in the light of any written representations which the member puts forward within fourteen clear days after receiving notice).[98] Such procedure should ensure that no allegations can be made that the removal breached the rules of natural justice.[99] It may also be useful to specify that membership of the association is not transferable.[100]   **8.40**

---

[91] ibid, r 7.5
[92] ibid, r 7.6
[93] ibid, r 4.1
[94] The CLA's Constitution for a Charitable Unincorporated Association gives such power to the Committee: ibid, r 4.2
[95] ibid, r 4.3
[96] ibid, r 4.4
[97] ibid, r 4.5
[98] ibid, r 4.6
[99] On the expulsion of members of unincorporated non-profit associations generally, see *Dawkins v Antrobus* (1881) 17 ChD 615 (CA) (expulsion from a club), where the requirements for expulsion were stated to be (1) that the rules and proceedings are not contrary to natural justice; (2) that the expulsion is in accordance with the rules; (3) that the proceedings are not in bad faith. See also Z Chafee Jr, 'The internal affairs of associations not for profit' (1930) 153 Harv LR 993
[100] Constitution for a Charitable Unincorporated Association, r 4.7

General meetings

8.41 The constitution should make provision for general meetings of members, both for an annual general meeting, and for extraordinary general meetings; it should also provide for the giving of a minimum period of notice of such meetings, specifying the business to be transacted. It should also state the quorum for such meetings, and provide for the Chair or some other member elected by those present to preside at the meeting. It should also indicate the size of the majority of votes cast necessary to determine an issue; in practice, a simple majority of the votes cast by the members present is generally suitable for most issues; but it may be thought appropriate to require a larger majority (for example, two-thirds or three-quarters of those present and voting) on matters which affect the basic nature of the charity (for example, amendments to the constitution, or a resolution that the association be dissolved).[101]

(7) Division of power and responsibility between Committee and general meeting

8.42 It is important that the association's constitution allocate the association's powers between the Committee and the general meeting. The constitution will usually vest specific powers and responsibilities in each of the Committee and the general meeting, but subject thereto will necessarily leave the day-to-day running of the association in the hands of the Committee. How specific powers and responsibilities should be allocated between the Committee and the general meeting, however, is largely a matter of preference for the draftsman. It will also need to be considered to what extent the general meeting should be able to pass resolutions on the general policy of the association which, while not binding on the Committee, do nevertheless take the form of suggestions, exhortations, or warnings to the Committee.

8.43 The Constitution for a Charitable Unincorporated Association drafted on behalf of the Charity Law Association imposes specific responsibilities on, and reserves specific powers to, the general meeting. It provides for the members at the annual general meeting to receive the association's accounts for the previous financial year,[102] and to receive the report of the Committee on the association's activities since the previous annual general meeting.[103] It provides for the election at the annual general meeting of elected Committee members to replace those retiring from office,[104] and for the election from among the members of the association of

---

[101] See eg ibid, r 5 ; r 12.1 requires a two-thirds majority at a general meeting for amendments to the constitution; but only a simple majority is required for a dissolution: r 14.1

[102] ibid, r 5.8.1

[103] ibid, r 5.8.2

[104] ibid, r 5.8.3

the Chair of the association for the following year.[105] It does not, however, empower the general meeting to remove Committee members, such power being reserved to the Committee itself.[106] The model constitution also provides for the appointment at the annual general meeting of an auditor or independent examiner for the association where required.[107] It also empowers the annual general meeting to confer on any individual (with his consent) the honorary title of Patron, President, or Vice-President of the association.[108]

Under the model constitution, the general meeting also has a residual power 'to discuss and determine any issues of policy or deal with any other business put before them'.[109] The constitution does not, however, specify whether such issues or other business may be put before the general meeting only by the Committee, or by any member of the association. This will need to be laid down in standing orders, rules, and regulations, which the Committee is empowered to make.[110] It may well be thought inappropriate that the general meeting should be able to pass resolutions relating to issues of policy which are binding on the Committee. On the other hand, it may be considered advisable to give the members of the association the ability to put down issues of policy for discussion at general meetings, and to empower the general meeting to make merely non-binding policy suggestions to the Committee. A possible compromise would be to enable a member, by notice, to put down policy-orientated resolutions for discussion at the general meeting, but to provide that such resolutions must be signed by a specified minimum number of the association's members. Under the Charity Law Association's model constitution, the only action which can be taken by a general meeting dissatisfied with the manner in which the Committee conducts the association's affairs is through its voting on the appointment of Committee members at the general meeting. The ultimate sanction of the general meeting, however, is to decide that the association itself should be dissolved, in which case the Committee is obliged to follow such decision and to wind up the association's affairs. [111]

8.44

The Charity Law Association's model constitution gives to the Committee various powers in the administration of the charity.[112] These comprise the power to appoint a Treasurer and other honorary officers,[113] to delegate their functions to sub-committees,[114] to make standing orders to govern proceedings at general

8.45

---

[105] ibid, r 5.8.4
[106] ibid, r 6.5.6
[107] ibid, r 5.8.5. For discussion of the statutory obligations relating to the auditing or examination of charity accounts, see ch 10, paras 10.92–10.98
[108] Constitution for a Charitable Unincorporated Association, r 5.8.6
[109] ibid, r 5.8.7
[110] ibid, rr 8.3, 8.4, and 8.5
[111] ibid, r 14.1
[112] ibid, r 8
[113] ibid, r 8.1
[114] ibid, r 8.2. See further discussion of delegation in ch 9, paras 9.145–9.175

meetings,[115] to make rules about the Committee and sub-committees,[116] to make regulations about the running of the association,[117] and to resolve or establish procedures to assist the resolution of disputes within the association.[118] Finally, it gives the Committee the power to exercise any powers of the association which are not reserved to a general meeting.[119] Under this constitution, therefore, the residual power of the association resides in the Committee, not in the general meeting.

(8) Alteration of objects

8.46 The association will be charitable only if its constitution provides that its assets can be applied solely to wholly and exclusively charitable purposes. As a matter of contract alone, there would be nothing to prevent the members from altering the objects in any way they wished, so as to substitute other charitable (or even non-charitable) objects, or even to permit the distribution of the assets among themselves. This could clearly never be permitted; and, indeed, in *Re Tobacco Trade Benevolent Association Charitable Trusts*,[120] it was held that, in the absence of an express power to do so, a charitable association has no power to alter its constitution in any way. This can be explained on the basis that the association's assets are bound, not merely by the contract between the members, but by a trust, implied if not expressed, for the association's charitable objects, thus precluding any alteration which might result in the application of the association's assets for non-charitable purposes.

8.47 A power to amend may be expressed negatively, as in *Motor and Cycle Trades Benevolent Fund v Attorney-General*.[121] Rule 19 of the unincorporated charity's constitution provided that no rule should be made, altered, or rescinded except by a four-fifths majority of votes at a general meeting. The trustees sought to alter the rules to confer wider powers of investment than those conferred by the Trustee Investments Act 1961. Whitford J held that, although rule 19 was expressed in the negative, it plainly contemplated that new rules could be made, and that the purported addition to the rules conferring wider powers of investment had been properly made.

8.48 Nevertheless, for the avoidance of doubt, an association's constitution should include an express positive power to amend. The model constitution of a charitable unincorporated association prepared on behalf of the Charity Law Association provides for amendments to the constitution to be made at a general meeting by

---

[115] Constitution for a Charitable Unincorporated Association, r 8.3
[116] ibid, r 8.4
[117] ibid, r 8.5
[118] ibid, r 8.6
[119] ibid, r 8.7
[120] [1958] 1 WLR 1113
[121] Noted at [1982] Ch Com Rep 42

Non-payment of subscription

The articles may provide for automatic termination of membership if a member **8.140** is a specified period in arrears with the payment of the appropriate subscription, with provision for reinstatement on payment of the amount due.[351]

Removal

It may be desirable to remove a member whose views are considered to be harm- **8.141** ful to the association. The Charity Law Association's model constitution provides that membership is terminated if the member concerned is removed from membership by resolution of the directors on the ground that in their reasonable opinion the member's continued membership is harmful to the charity (but only after notifying the member in writing and considering the matter in the light of any written representations which the member concerned puts forward within fourteen clear days after receiving notice).[352] Such procedure is important to ensure that the removal does not breach the rules of natural justice. It may also be useful to specify that membership of the association is not transferable.[353]

Register of members

Entries on register

Every company must keep a register of its members.[354] There must be entered on **8.142** the register the names and addresses of the members; the date on which each person was registered as a member; and the date at which any person ceased to be a member.[355] In the case of a company which does not have a share capital (such as a charitable company limited by guarantee) but has more than one class of members, there must be entered on the register, with the names and addresses of the members, the class to which each member belongs.[356] If a company defaults in complying with these requirements, the company and every officer of it who is in default is liable to a fine and, for continued contravention, to a daily default fine.[357] Any entry relating to a former member may be removed from the register twenty years after he ceased to be a member.[358]

If the number of members of a private company limited by guarantee falls to one, **8.143** there must thereupon be entered in the register of members with the name and address of the sole member a statement that the company has only one member,

---

[351] See, eg, ibid, Art 1.5.3
[352] ibid, Art 1.5.4; for meaning of 'clear days' see above, para 8.138
[353] See, eg, the CLA's Memorandum and Articles of Association for a Charitable Company Limited by Guarantee, Art 1.6
[354] Companies Act 1985, s 352(1)
[355] ibid, s 352(2)
[356] ibid, s 352(4)
[357] ibid, s 352(5)
[358] ibid, s 352(6)

and the date on which the company became a company having only one member.[359] If the membership increases from one to two or more, there must be entered in the register with the name and address of the former sole member, a statement that the company has ceased to have only one member together with the date on which that event occurred.[360] If a company defaults in complying with these requirements, the company and every officer of it who is in default is liable to a fine and, for continued contravention, to a daily default fine.[361]

Other obligations relating to register

8.144 A company's register of members must (with some specified exceptions) be kept at its registered office.[362] The company must send notice in the prescribed form to the Registrar of Companies of the place where its register of members is kept, and of any change in that place.[363] If a company makes default for fourteen days in complying with this requirement, the company and every officer of it who is in default is liable to a fine and, for continued contravention, to a daily default fine.[364]

8.145 If a company has more than fifty members, it must keep an index of the names of the members of the company and must, within fourteen days after any alteration is made in the register of members, make any necessary alteration in the index.[365] The index must be kept at the same place as the register of members.[366]

8.146 Except when the register of members is closed as permitted by the Companies Act 1985,[367] the register and index of members' names must be open to the inspection of any member of the company without charge, and of any other person on payment of such fee as may be prescribed.[368] Any member or other person may request a copy of the register or any part of it on payment of such fee as may be prescribed, and the company must send the requested copy to such person within ten days.[369] There are penalties for non-compliance,[370] and the court may order an immediate inspection of the register and index, or direct that the copies required be sent to the person requiring them.[371]

---

[359] Companies Act 1985, s 352A(1)
[360] ibid, s 352A(2)
[361] ibid, s 352A(3)
[362] ibid, s 353(1)
[363] ibid, s 353(2)
[364] ibid, s 353(4)
[365] ibid, s 354(1)
[366] ibid, s 354(3)
[367] A company may close the register for up to 30 days each year, on giving notice by advertisement in a newspaper circulating in the district in which the registered office is situated: ibid. s 358
[368] ibid, s 356(1)
[369] ibid, s 356(3)
[370] ibid, s 356(5)
[371] ibid, s 356(6)

Contract in memorandum and articles

Section 14(1) of the Companies Act 1985 states that, subject to the provisions of **8.147** that Act, the memorandum and articles, when registered, bind the company and its members to the same extent as if they respectively had been signed and sealed by each member, and contained covenants on the part of each member to observe all the provisions of the memorandum and articles. The effect of the sub-section is to create a statutory contract between the company and the members, and between the members *inter se*.[372] The right of an individual member of a company to enforce the articles is, however, limited by the rule in *Foss v Harbottle*,[373] and it may also be limited by the need to obtain consent to 'charity proceedings',[374] both of which are discussed below.[375]

General meetings

Annual general meeting

A company incorporated under the Companies Acts must hold an annual general **8.148** meeting each year, and must specify the meeting as such in the notices calling it.[376] However, so long as a company holds its first annual general meeting within eighteen months of its incorporation, it need not hold it in the year of its incorporation or in the following year.[377] Not more than fifteen months may elapse between the date of one annual general meeting and the next.[378] If there is default in holding a meeting in accordance with these requirements, the company and every officer of it who is in default is liable to a fine.[379] A private company (which includes a company limited by guarantee and not having a share capital), may, however, by elective resolution,[380] dispense with the holding of annual general meetings.[381]

Unless the articles require a longer period, an annual general meeting may be **8.149** called by twenty-one days' notice in writing.[382] A provision in the company's articles for a shorter period of notice (other than for an adjourned meeting) is void.[383] An annual general meeting for which less than the required period of notice is

---

[372] *Hickman v Kent or Romney Marsh Sheep-Breeders' Assoc* [1915] 1 Ch 881
[373] (1843) 2 Hare 461
[374] CA 1993, s 33
[375] See paras 8.161–8.169
[376] Companies Act 1985, s 366(1)
[377] ibid, s 366(2)
[378] ibid, s 366(3)
[379] ibid, s 366(4). The Secretary of State has power to call a meeting in default: ibid, s 367
[380] For the meaning of, and requirements for, an 'elective resolution', see ibid, s 379A
[381] ibid, s 366A(1). Where, pursuant to an election, no AGM has been held, any member of a company may require the holding of an AGM by giving three months' notice before the end of the year: ibid, s 366A(3)
[382] ibid, s 369(2)(a)
[383] ibid, s 369(1)(a)

given is nevertheless deemed to have been duly called if it is so agreed by all the members entitled to attend and vote at it.[384] In some circumstances, a general meeting may be called by the court.[385]

Extraordinary general meetings

8.150   The articles will usually give the directors a power to call an extraordinary general meeting at any time; and they may also give a minimum number of members the right to call such a meeting on giving a minimum period of notice.[386]

8.151   Notwithstanding anything in the company's articles, the directors must, on a members' requisition, forthwith proceed duly to convene an extraordinary general meeting of the company.[387] In the case of a charitable company, a members' requisition is a requisition of members having not less than one-tenth of the voting rights at annual general meetings.[388] The requisition must state the objects of the meeting, and must be signed by the requisitionists and deposited at the company's registered office.[389] If the directors fail duly to proceed to call a meeting within twenty-one days of such deposit, the requisitionists may themselves convene one within three months.[390]

8.152   Unless the articles require a longer period, an extraordinary general meeting may be called by fourteen days' notice in writing.[391] A provision in the company's articles for a shorter period of notice (other than for an adjourned meeting) is void.[392] An extraordinary general meeting for which less than the required period of notice is given is nevertheless deemed to have been duly called (in the case of a company not having a share capital) if it is so agreed by a majority of members at that meeting together representing 95 per cent of the total voting rights.[393] In some circumstances, an extraordinary general meeting may be called by the court.[394]

Proceedings at general meetings

8.153   So far as the articles do not provide otherwise,[395] the Companies Act 1985 provides that notice of a meeting must be served on every member of the company in

---

[384]   Companies Act 1985, s 369(3)(a)
[385]   ibid, s 371(1)
[386]   See the CLA's Memorandum and Articles of Association for a Charitable Company Limited by Guarantee, Art 2.10, which provides that an EGM may be called at any time by the directors, and must be called within 28 days on a written request for a specified number (left blank) of members
[387]   Companies Act 1985, s 368(1)
[388]   ibid, s 368(2)
[389]   ibid, s 368(3)
[390]   ibid, s 368(4)
[391]   ibid, s 369(2)(b)(ii); unless the company is unlimited, when the period of notice in writing is only seven days: ibid, s 369(2)(b)(i)
[392]   ibid, s 369(1)(b)
[393]   ibid, s 369(3)(b); s 369(4)(b)
[394]   ibid, s 371(1)
[395]   ibid, s 370(1)

the manner in which notices are required to be served by Table A,[396] that not less than 5 per cent in number of the members of the company may call a meeting,[397] that two members personally present are a quorum,[398] that any member elected by the members present at a meeting may be chairman of it,[399] and that every member has one vote.[400] These statutory provisions should be modified as necessary to suit the particular charitable company limited by guarantee. In most cases, for example, it will be desirable to specify a quorum of more than two members.[401]

Notwithstanding any provision to the contrary in the articles of a private company limited by guarantee having only one member, one member present in person or by proxy is a quorum.[402]   **8.154**

The statutory right of a member to appoint a proxy to attend and vote (and, in the case of a private company, to speak) at a meeting in his place,[403] does not apply to a company not having a share capital unless the articles otherwise provide.[404] Furthermore, unless the articles provide otherwise, a member of a private company is not entitled to appoint more than one proxy to attend on the same occasion,[405] and a proxy is not entitled to vote except on a poll.[406]   **8.155**

A provision in a company's articles is void in so far as it would have the effect of excluding the right to demand a poll at a general meeting on any question other than the election of the chairman or the adjournment of the meeting.[407]   **8.156**

If members representing no less than one-twentieth of the total voting rights of all the members so requisition in writing, the company must (at the expense of such requisitionists) give to the members of the company entitled to receive notice of the next annual general meeting notice of any resolution which may properly be moved and is intended to be moved at that meeting, and to circulate to such members any statement of not more than 1,000 words with respect to the matter   **8.157**

---

[396] ibid, s 370(2)
[397] ibid, s 370(3)
[398] ibid, s 370(4)
[399] ibid, s 370(5)
[400] ibid, s 370(6)
[401] See, eg, the CLA's Memorandum and Articles of Association for a Charitable Company Limited by Guarantee, Art 2.2
[402] Companies Act 1985, s 370A
[403] ibid, s 372(1)
[404] ibid, s 372(2)(a). No provision for proxy voting is contained in the CLA's Memorandum and Articles of Association for a Charitable Company Limited by Guarantee, but the Notes thereto point out that provision for this may be necessary where, for instance, the charity's membership is numerous and widespread: see Note to Art 2.1 (p 18). Table C of the Companies (Tables A to F) Regulations 1985, SI 1985/805, effectively substitutes reg 59 of Table A with its own express Art 8, which provides that on a show of hands every member present in person has one vote; and that on a poll every member present in person or by proxy has one vote
[405] Companies Act 1985, s 372(2)(b)
[406] ibid, s 372(2)(c)
[407] ibid, s 373(1)(a)

referred to in any proposed resolution or the business to be dealt with at that meeting.[408]

8.158   A company must record minutes of all proceedings of general meetings in books kept for that purpose.[409] Any such minute, if purporting to be signed by the chairman of the meeting at which the proceedings took place, or by the chairman of the next succeeding meeting, is evidence of the proceedings.[410]

8.159   Anything which in the case of a private company may be done by resolution of the company in general meeting may be done, without a meeting and without any previous notice being required, by resolution in writing signed by or on behalf of all the members of the company who at the date of the resolution would be entitled to attend and vote at such a meeting.[411] A copy of any written resolution so proposed to be agreed must be sent to the company's auditors.[412] The company must record resolutions so agreed (and the signatures) in the same way as minutes of proceedings of the general meeting.[413]

8.160   The books containing the minutes of proceedings of any general meeting must be kept at the company's registered office, and must be open to the inspection of any member without charge;[414] and any member (on payment of such fee as may be prescribed) is entitled to be furnished with a copy of any such minutes within seven days of the request being made.[415]

(9) The rights of individual members

8.161   Although section 14(1) of the Companies Act 1985 provides that the memorandum and articles form the basis of a statutory contract between the company and the members and the members *inter se*, it is clear that an individual member of a charitable company does not have a right, as a member, to bring proceedings to enforce every provision in the memorandum and articles, or to complain of every wrong done to the company. There are two restrictions upon an individual member's right to bring such an action: first, there is a rule of general applicability in company law known as the rule in *Foss v Harbottle*;[416] secondly, there is the need to obtain the consent of the Charity Commissioners to the taking of 'charity proceedings' under the Charities Act 1993.[417]

---

[408]   Companies Act 1985, s 376(1)
[409]   ibid, s 382(1)
[410]   ibid, s 382(2)
[411]   ibid, s 381A(1)
[412]   ibid, s 381B(1)
[413]   ibid, s 382A(1)
[414]   ibid, s 383(1)
[415]   ibid, s 383(3)
[416]   (1843) 2 Hare 461. See J Warburton, 'Charities, Members, Accountability and Control' [1997] Conv 106, esp 112–118
[417]   CA 1993, s 33

In one respect, however, the rights of an individual member of a charitable com-   **8.162**
pany are greater than those enjoyed by a member of a non-charitable company.
This is because 'charity proceedings' can be brought (inter alia) by 'any person
interested' in the charity,[418] and a member of a charitable company probably ranks
as a 'person interested'. Provided, therefore, that the member can obtain the
Charity Commissioners' consent to take proceedings, the member may be able to
complain of wrongs done to the company of which, because of the rule in *Foss v
Harbottle*, he would otherwise be unable to complain.

The rule in *Foss v Harbottle*

The right of an individual member to enforce the articles is limited by the rule in   **8.163**
Foss v Harbottle,[419] which provides that, subject to certain exceptions, the minority of members by votes cannot complain of wrongs done to the company
(whether by the directors, the majority of the members, outsiders, or other wrong-
doers) or of irregularities in the conduct of the company's internal affairs. The rule
has been said to be based on the desirability of avoiding pointless[420] or oppres-
sive[421] litigation, or numerous actions,[422] which would both flood the courts and
damage the companies concerned.[423] These reasons apply with at least equal force
to companies which are charities, and there is no reason to doubt the applicability
of the rule to such companies.

One example of the application of the rule is in regard to the ratification of an act   **8.164**
of the directors which, although beyond the power of the directors, is intra vires
the company and promotes the company's charitable objects; such an act is
ratifiable by ordinary resolution at general meeting.[424] This is essentially a matter
of internal management, and the rule in *Foss v Harbottle* applies to prevent an individual member from applying to the court.

The rule is, however, subject to a number of exceptions, the scope of which   **8.165**
remains, unfortunately, far from clear. The exceptions include acts which are illegal or ultra vires. The rule would not therefore prevent a member of a charitable
company from bringing proceedings to restrain the charity from pursuing objects
other than the charitable objects stated in the objects clause of its memorandum.

Another exception comprises what is generally called 'a fraud on the minority',   **8.166**
but which, especially in the context of a charitable company (where the members
have no proprietary interest in the company) might be better termed 'a fraud on

---

[418] ibid, s 33(1)
[419] (1843) 2 Hare 461
[420] ibid, 494
[421] *Gray v Lewis* (1873) 8 Ch App 1035, 1050–1
[422] *Mozley v Alston* (1847) 1 Ph 790, 799
[423] *La Cie de Mayville v Whitley* [1896] 1 Ch 788, 807
[424] On ratification of directors' acts of this nature, see discussion above, para 8.118

the company'.[425] In practice, cases exploring this exception have involved fraud committed by the company's directors. In a commercial company, directors' fiduciary duties are owed to the company itself, not to the individual members. To the extent that the breach comprises a fraud on the company, it is clear that an individual member can bring an action to complain of it. The difficulties which have arisen in company law in determining the scope of this exception have mostly concerned what acts are, for this purpose, to be to be regarded as 'fraudulent'. An exercise by the directors of their powers in bad faith, or for a collateral purpose, comprises a 'fraud' which can be challenged by the minority.[426] Similarly, it seems that incidental benefits taken by the directors for themselves in circumstances where such benefits ought to have been obtained for the company can be recovered for the company by a minority action within the scope of this exception.[427] On the other hand, a failure by the directors to exercise the standard of care required of directors does not comprise a 'fraud' for this purpose, so the minority cannot complain if the majority do not object.[428] To the extent that the fiduciary duties of directors of a charitable company are owed to the company, the ability of an individual member to complain of a fraud on the company also comprises an exception to the rule in *Foss v Harbottle*.

8.167   Since the rule is based upon control by a bare majority, other exceptions to it include acts which require the approval of a special resolution or the unanimous consent of the members. A further exception to the rule is in respect of a member's *personal* rights under the memorandum and articles. Thus a shareholder has a right, *qua* member, to compel the company to permit him to vote at a general meeting as provided for in the articles.[429] Even though a member of a charitable company has no proprietary interest in the company, a member of a charitable company does have a contractual right, conferred by section 14(1) of the Companies Act 1985, to vote in accordance with the articles. It may therefore be concluded that an individual member of a charitable company cannot be prevented by the rule in *Foss v Harbottle* from applying to the court to enforce his right to vote at a general meeting.

'charity proceedings'

8.168   Even if his action falls outside the scope of the rule in *Foss v Harbottle*, however, an individual member, or a minority of the members, will not be permitted to bring an action against the company without the Charity Commissioners' consent if

---

[425]   See KW Wedderburn, 'Shareholders' rights and the rule in *Foss v. Harbottle*' [1957] CLJ 194, 199, and [1958] CLJ 93ff
[426]   *Re Smith and Fawcett Ltd* [1942] Ch 304, 306 (CA); *Cannon v Trask* (1875) 20 Eq 669
[427]   *Cook v Deeks* [1916] 1 AC 554
[428]   *Pavlides v Jensen* [1956] Ch 565
[429]   *Pender v Lushington* (1877) 6 ChD 70

such action comprises 'charity proceedings' within the Charities Act 1993.[430] In principle, all rights enjoyed by a member of a charity ought to be treated as constitutional rights, and so as rights in favour of, rather than against, the charity. As such, the enforcement of all members' rights ought to be considered to rank as 'charity proceedings'. The statutory contract in the memorandum and articles created by section 14(1) of the Companies Act 1985, however, undoubtedly gives the members contractual rights against the company, and it is therefore difficult to contend that the enforcement of such rights falls within the definition of 'charity proceedings'.[431] It is therefore suggested that an individual member of a charitable company formed under the Companies Acts is, for instance, entitled to bring an individual action against the company to compel it to permit him to vote, without such action being thwarted either by the rule in *Foss v Harbottle*[432] or by the absence of Charity Commissioners' consent.

Provided he can obtain the Charity Commissioners' consent, however, a member **8.169** may be able to bring 'charity proceedings' as a 'person interested in the charity'.[433] Through 'charity proceedings', therefore, a member may be able to complain, *qua* 'person interested', of wrongs done to the company of which, by virtue of the rule in *Foss v Harbottle*, he would not be able to complain *qua* member.

(10) Directors

Appointment and discharge

By statute, every private company must have at least one director,[434] but it is desir- **8.170** able that a charitable company have several directors, preferably at least three. The articles should specify the minimum number of directors.[435] There is no statutory maximum number of directors, but it is impractical to have too large a number; the articles might therefore also usefully specify a maximum number.[436] Every company must also have a secretary;[437] a sole director may not also be the secretary.[438]

The names and requisite particulars of the first directors of the company must be **8.171** contained in a statement in a prescribed form delivered with the memorandum

---

[430] CA 1993, s 33(8)
[431] See further ch 13, para 13.30
[432] See *Pender v Lushington* (1877) 6 Ch D 70
[433] CA 1993, s 33(1)
[434] Companies Act 1985, s 282(3)
[435] See, eg, the CLA's Memorandum and Articles of Association for a Charitable Company Limited by Guarantee, Art 3.2. Table C of the Companies (Tables A to F) Regulations 1985, SI 1985/805, specifies a minimum of two (unless otherwise determined by ordinary resolution): reg 64
[436] See, eg, the CLA's Memorandum and Articles of Association for a Charitable Company Limited by Guarantee, Art 3.2
[437] Companies Act 1985, s 283(1)
[438] ibid, s 283(2)

and articles to the Registrar of Companies.[439] The statement must be signed by or on behalf of the subscribers of the memorandum and must contain a consent signed by each of the persons named in it as director to act in such capacity.[440]

8.172 The articles should specify the length of service of directors, or provide for their regular retirement by rotation. The Charity Law Association's Memorandum and Articles of Association for a Charitable Company Limited by Guarantee makes provision for one-third (or the number nearest to one-third) of the directors to retire at each annual general meeting, those longest in office retiring first, the choice between any of equal service being made by drawing lots.[441]

8.173 Provision for the appointment of later directors will usually be made in the articles. The power to appoint new directors to fill vacancies arising may, for instance, be given to the members at the annual general meeting.[442] The articles generally give the board of directors a power to co-opt any duly qualified person to fill any casual vacancy; and the power to appoint additional directors may be given either to the board[443] or to the general meeting.[444] The articles should also make provision for resignation of directors, and for the termination of their appointment by other means, whether through disqualification, incapacity, absence from meetings, or removal.[445]

8.174 Under section 303 of the Companies Act 1985, a company may by ordinary resolution remove a director before the expiration of his period of office, notwithstanding anything in its articles or in any agreement between it and him.[446] Special notice is required of such a resolution, or of a resolution to appoint somebody instead of a director so removed at the meeting at which he is removed.[447] Where notice has been given of a resolution so to remove a director, that director has a right to make written representations to the company which must be sent to every

---

[439] Companies Act 1985, s 10(2)(a). The requisite particulars are set out in Companies Act 1985, Sch 1. The statement must also contain the name or names of the person or persons who are to be the secretary or joint secretaries of the company: ibid, s 10(2)(b)

[440] ibid, s 10(3). The statement must also contain a consent signed by the person or each of the persons named in it as secretary, or as one of joint secretaries, to act in such capacity: ibid

[441] Art 3.5. See also Table C of the Companies (Tables A to F) Regulations 1985, SI 1985/805, regs 73–4, which provides for all the directors to retire at the first AGM, and for the retirement of one-third of the directors at each subsequent general meeting (those longest in office retiring first, with similar provision for drawing lots in respect of those of equal service)

[442] See, eg, the CLA's Memorandum and Articles of Association for a Charitable Company Limited by Guarantee, Art 2.8.4

[443] ibid, Art 3.7

[444] As in reg 78 of Table C of the Companies (Tables A to F) Regulations 1985, SI 1985/805

[445] See the CLA's Memorandum and Articles of Association for a Charitable Company Limited by Guarantee, Art 3.6; also reg 81 of Table C of the Companies (Tables A to F) Regulations 1985, SI 1985/805

[446] Companies Act 1985, s 303(1)

[447] ibid, s 303(2)

member of the company.[448] The removal of a director under section 303 does not deprive him of compensation or damages payable to him in respect of the termination of his appointment as director.[449] This potential liability will need to be borne in mind by those charitable companies which, exceptionally, pay directors' remuneration.

In order to avoid the pitfalls of section 303 (that is, the possible liability to pay compensation and the need to circulate a director's representations), the articles can themselves make express provision for removal of a director by the general meeting. The Charity Law Association's Memorandum and Articles of Association for a Charitable Company Limited by Guarantee provide for the removal of a director by resolution passed by a minimum number or percentage of the members present and voting at a general meeting after the meeting has invited the views of the director concerned and considered the matter in the light of any such views.[450] The requirement of inviting and considering the views of the director is to ensure that the removal cannot be challenged on the ground that it contravenes the rules of natural justice. **8.175**

Under the Companies Act 1985, the acts of a director or manager are valid notwithstanding any defect that may afterwards be discovered in his appointment or qualification.[451] This statutory provision may be usefully repeated in the articles.[452] **8.176**

Directors' meetings

The articles may state that the directors must hold a minimum number of board meetings each year.[453] The articles will usually specify, or make provision for the directors to specify, the quorum for directors' meetings.[454] They will also often empower the directors to regulate their own proceedings as they think fit,[455] and provide for majority voting at board meetings[456] (with the chairman, in the case of equality of votes, having a second or casting vote[457]). **8.177**

---

[448] ibid, s 304(1), (2)
[449] ibid, s 303(5)
[450] Art 3.6.6
[451] Companies Act 1985, s 285
[452] See, eg, the CLA's Memorandum and Articles of Association for a Charitable Company Limited by Guarantee, Art 3.8
[453] See, eg, ibid, Art 4.1
[454] See, eg, Table A of the Companies (Tables A to F) Regulations 1985, reg 89; the CLA's Memorandum and Articles of Association for a Charitable Company Limited by Guarantee, Art 4.2
[455] See, eg, Table A of the Companies (Tables A to F) Regulations 1985, reg 88; the CLA's Memorandum and Articles of Association for a Charitable Company Limited by Guarantee, Art 5.5
[456] See, eg, Table A of the Companies (Tables A to F) Regulations 1985, reg 88; the CLA's Memorandum and Articles of Association for a Charitable Company Limited by Guarantee, Art 4.5
[457] See, eg, Table A of the Companies (Tables A to F) Regulations 1985, reg 88; the CLA's Memorandum and Articles of Association for a Charitable Company Limited by Guarantee, Art 4.6

To whom are directors' fiduciary duties owed?

8.178 Although it is clear that directors of a non-charitable company owe their duties to the company itself, there has been very little judicial (or even extra-judicial) discussion of the question of to whom the fiduciary duties of directors of a charitable company are owed. What judicial authority exists suggests that the fiduciary duties of such directors (like those of trustees of charitable trusts) are owed to the public,[458] and are therefore enforceable by the Attorney-General, by the Charity Commissioners, or by other persons (including 'persons interested') in 'charity proceedings'. A closer analysis, however, suggests that whilst many fiduciary duties of a director of a charitable company are owed to the public, some are owed exclusively to the company itself.

8.179 The intervention of the state in the affairs of a charitable company is intended to ensure that the company's property is applied to its exclusively charitable objects. Therefore, so far as the fiduciary duties of a director of such a company relate to the application of the company's property to such exclusively charitable objects, they are owed to the public. The company's property will not be applied to such objects if it is applied, for example, for the private benefit of the directors. A breach of fiduciary duty which involves such misapplication cannot be ratified by the charitable company's general meeting, or even by the unanimous agreement of its members, since it is not open to any such organ or body to authorize, or to ratify, the application of the company's property other than in ways which promote the company's charitable objects.

8.180 There are, however, some breaches of fiduciary duty by the directors which might not impinge on a charitable company's application of its property to its exclusively charitable objects. These essentially concern matters of internal management. Directors who exceed their powers to borrow under the articles, for example, will be in breach of their fiduciary duty; but, provided the borrowing is intra vires the company and promotes the company's charitable objects, such borrowing does not impinge on the company's application of its property to its exclusively charitable objects.[459] Such a breach of fiduciary duty ought therefore to be capable of ratification by the general meeting. Another example of a fiduciary duty which does not impinge on the company's application of its property to its exclusively charitable objects, but relates only to internal management, is the duty of the directors to give proper consideration to an application for membership of the charity. To treat such fiduciary duties as owed exclusively to the company does not, however, preclude state intervention in every case, however, since in some cases such breaches of fiduciary duty might be evidence of 'misconduct or mis-

---

[458] *Re French Protestant Hospital* [1951] Ch 567
[459] For ratification of directors' acts in these circumstances, see above, para 8.118

management in the administration of a charity',[460] so as to enable the Charity Commissioners, following an inquiry,[461] to exercise their remedial powers.[462]

In some instances, admittedly, it can be difficult to determine on which side of the line the duty should fall; and this is particularly true of incidental profits made by a director who has taken personal advantage of an opportunity which has arisen during his time as director. A variety of 'corporate opportunities' may present themselves to a charitable company, many of which the board may quite properly choose not to pursue. If such opportunities were treated as assets of the company, their rejection by the board would constitute a destruction of the charity's property instead of its application to its exclusively charitable objects—a view which is patently absurd. Nevertheless, in order to avoid a potential conflict of interest, it is important that directors should not be permitted to exploit such rejected opportunities for themselves personally. The traditional view of English law (laid down in non-charity cases) is that directors who take personal advantage of such opportunities are accountable to the company for any profit they make, even if the board has rejected such opportunity for the company because the latter lacks the resources to exploit it.[463] The profit made from the opportunity might therefore be treated as property to which the company is entitled, even if the opportunity to make it could not be. The Privy Council, however, has suggested that the rejection of the opportunity by the board in good faith, after full disclosure by the director concerned, can have the effect of removing the opportunity from the scope of the director's fiduciary duty so as to entitle him to retain any profit which may result.[464] Even if this view were to be accepted into English law, however, it would be difficult to see how it could be applied to the directors of charitable companies, since it is not open to the board of directors or the general meeting to give away the charity's property (in this case the profit made from the 'corporate opportunity') other than in pursuit of its exclusively charitable objects. It is therefore suggested that the fiduciary duty of directors of a charitable company in relation to 'corporate opportunities' is owed to the public, not to the company itself.

8.181

---

[460] CA 1993, s 18(1)(a), (2)(a)

[461] ibid, s 8

[462] ibid, s 18

[463] *Regal (Hastings) Ltd v Gulliver* [1967] 2 AC 134 (HL) (dec 1942)

[464] *Queensland Mines Ltd v Hudson* (1978) 52 ALJR 399 (PC). The decision may, however, turn on the fact that the board meeting comprised all the members of the company, who all voted in favour of rejecting the opportunity for the company and permitting the director to go ahead personally; the decision could therefore be treated as one made by the unanimous agreement of the members: see GR Sullivan, (1979) 42 MLR 711. This reasoning cannot, of course, be applied to a charity, whose members are not entitled to give away an asset of the charity (the profit) other than in pursuit of the company's exclusively charitable objects

(11) Division of powers and responsibilities between board and general meeting

Powers and responsibilities of the board

8.182   The articles of association usually confer specific powers on the board of directors. Under the Charity Law Association's model form of articles of association, the directors have powers, in the administration of the charity, to appoint any member (who may be a director) to act as secretary to the charity in accordance with the Companies Act 1985 and to remove them;[465] to appoint a chairman, treasurer, and other honorary officers from among their number;[466] to delegate their functions (within prescribed limits);[467] to make standing orders, rules, and regulations to govern proceedings at general meetings, and meetings of committees, and to govern the administration of the charity and the use of its seal (if any);[468] and to establish procedures to assist the resolution of disputes within the charity.[469]

8.183   Apart from this, the articles of association will usually give the board a general express power to manage the charity. The Charity Law Association's model articles, for instance, having conferred specific powers on the board, give the directors the power 'to exercise any powers of the Charity which are not reserved to a general meeting'.[470]

8.184   If the charitable company adopts Table C, the general power of the directors will be contained in regulation 70 of Table A of the Companies (Tables A to F) Regulations 1985.[471] This more expansively-worded regulation provides (emphasis added):

> Subject to the provisions of the Act, the memorandum and the articles and to any directions given by special resolution, *the business of the company shall be managed by the directors* who may exercise all the powers of the company. No alteration of the memorandum or articles and no such direction shall invalidate any prior act of the directors which would have been valid if that alteration had not been made or that direction had not been given. The powers given by this regulation shall not be limited by any special power given to the directors by the articles and a meeting of directors at which a quorum is present may exercise all powers exercisable by the directors.

For a charitable company, which is not carrying on a business, but is pursuing charitable objects, the italicized words are hardly appropriate. If, therefore, this regulation is to be adopted, it should be modified by substituting for the italicized

---

[465] CLA's Memorandum and Articles of Association for a Charitable Company Limited by Guarantee, Art 5.1
[466] ibid, Art 5.2
[467] ibid, Art 5.3
[468] ibid, Arts 5.4, 5.5, and 5.6
[469] ibid, Art 5.7
[470] ibid, Art 5.8
[471] SI 1985/805

words a more apt form of words, such as 'the general control and management of the administration of the charity shall lie with the directors . . .'. This follows the form of words used to define 'charity trustees' in the Charities Act 1993.[472]

Regulation 70 of Table A enables the general meeting to give directions to the board by special resolution. Such directions can therefore restrict the freedom of the directors in their management of the charity and can compel the directors to pursue a particular course of action. It might well be thought that the conferring of such a power on the general meeting of a charitable company gives the members excessive power, and no equivalent power is contained in the Charity Law Association's model form of articles of association;[473] these merely provide that the general meeting is to 'discuss and determine any issues of policy or deal with any other business put before them'.[474] **8.185**

The members of the board of directors are 'charity trustees' for the purposes of the Charities Act 1993,[475] and are subject to all the duties which that Act imposes on charity trustees.[476] The Companies Act 1985 imposes specific duties and prohibitions on directors,[477] and other specific duties are usually imposed on the directors by the company's articles.[478] The directors of a company are also subject to various fiduciary duties; specific fiduciary duties are considered in chapter 9, and the problem of the extent to which the fiduciary duties of the directors of a charitable company are owed to the company has been analysed above.[479] **8.186**

Powers and responsibilities of the general meeting

Some powers of the company are reserved to the general meeting by the Companies Act 1985. Amongst the most important of these is the power to alter the memorandum[480] and the articles of association[481] (which power, in the case of a charitable company, is partially restricted by the Charities Act 1993[482]). Other important powers reserved to the general meeting by statute are the powers to **8.187**

---

[472] CA 1993, s 97(1)
[473] Memorandum and Articles of Association for a Charitable Company Limited by Guarantee
[474] ibid, art 2.8.7
[475] CA 1993, s 97(1)
[476] See further ch 9, paras 9.141–9.143
[477] eg disclosure of interests in contracts with the company: Companies Act 1985, s 317; prohibitions on loans to directors: ibid, s 330(2); and various duties relating to the preparation (ibid, s 226(1)) and approval (ibid, s 233(1)) of the company's accounts, and the preparation (ibid, s 234(1)) and approval (ibid, s 234A) of a directors' report
[478] eg to hold a minimum number of board meetings each year: see CLA's Memorandum and Articles of Association for a Charitable Company Limited by Guarantee, Art 4.1
[479] See above, paras 8.178–8.181
[480] Companies Act 1985, s 2(7); the objects clause can be altered by special resolution: ibid, s 4(1)
[481] ibid, s 9(1)
[482] CA 1993, s 64(2), discussed above, paras 8.122–8.125, and 8.131

appoint auditors,[483] to remove a director by ordinary resolution,[484] and (by special resolution) to effect a voluntary winding up.[485]

8.188   The articles will also usually reserve specific powers to the general meeting. Under the Charity Law Association's Memorandum and Articles of Association for a Charitable Company Limited by Guarantee, the members at an annual general meeting receive the accounts of the charity for the previous financial year[486] and the directors' report on the charity's activities since the previous annual general meeting;[487] they accept the retirement of those directors who wish to retire or who are retiring by rotation;[488] they elect persons to be directors to fill the vacancies arising;[489] they appoint auditors[490] (which repeats the obligation imposed by statute); they may confer on any individual (with his consent) the honorary title of Patron, President, or Vice-President of the charity;[491] and they discuss and determine issues of policy or deal with any other business put before them.[492]

8.189   The general meeting has power to ratify directors' acts which, although intra vires the company, are beyond the directors' powers under the articles. The general meeting has power to ratify directors' acts which are both beyond their powers as directors and ultra vires the company, but (in this instance) only with the prior written consent of the Charity Commissioners.[493]

8.190   If there is deadlock on the board of directors, or the directors are unable or unwilling to exercise their powers, such powers are by default exercisable by the general meeting.[494] If the general meeting were to continue to exercise these powers for any length of time, the members would themselves become 'charity trustees' for the purposes of the Charities Act 1993, since they would then be 'the persons having the general control and management of the administration of the charity'.[495]

(12) Public involvement and the limits of corporate control

8.191   In a charitable company, it is not sufficient merely to determine the distribution of power within the company itself; it is also important to determine the extent to which the state involves itself in the running of a charitable company. In other

---

[483] Companies Act 1985, s 384(1), 385(2)
[484] ibid, s 303(1)
[485] Insolvency Act 1986, s 84(1)(b)
[486] CLA's Memorandum and Articles of Association for a Charitable Company Limited by Guarantee, Art 2.8.1
[487] ibid, Art 2.8.2
[488] ibid, Art 2.8.3
[489] ibid, Art 2.8.4
[490] ibid, Art 2.8.5
[491] ibid, Art 2.8.6
[492] ibid, Art 2.8.7
[493] CA 1993, s 65(4). For further discussion of ratification, see above, paras 8.116–8.118
[494] *Barron v Potter* [1914] 1 Ch 895
[495] CA 1993, s 97(1)

words, it is necessary to determine what (if any) decisions a charitable company can make without the risk of what might be called 'state intervention', that is, an action brought by the Attorney-General, the Charity Commissioners, or by a 'person interested' in 'charity proceedings', and what decisions are invariably subject to the possibility of such intervention.

It has already been seen, in the specific context of directors' fiduciary duties, that **8.192** a line needs to be drawn between those fiduciary duties which relate to the application of the charity's property to its exclusively charitable objects, and those which do not.[496] Duties in the former category are owed to the public, and breaches of such duties are therefore beyond the power of the company to authorize in advance or to ratify subsequently. Duties in the latter category, on the other hand, can be so authorized or ratified by the general meeting. It is suggested that this principle is of wider application, so that those breaches of a charitable company's articles which relate to the application of the company's property to its exclusively charitable objects are susceptible to state intervention, whereas those which do not (and which relate merely to matters of internal management) are not susceptible to such intervention.

On this footing, for example, no member of the public could (as a 'person inter- **8.193** ested') bring 'charity proceedings' to complain of a breach of the articles which comprises a mere procedural irregularity, such as the holding of a general meeting without proper notice. The enforcement of such an article is therefore a private matter for the company itself, and so to be determined in accordance with the general rules of company law. In this particular instance, it would appear that an individual member does, as an exception to the rule in *Foss v Harbottle*,[497] have a personal right, *qua* member, to complain that no notice of a meeting has been given in accordance with the articles.[498]

Breach by a charitable company of even those articles which relate merely to inter- **8.194** nal management might nevertheless be evidence of 'misconduct or mismanagement in the administration of the charity', so as to entitle the Charity Commissioners, after an inquiry, to exercise their remedial powers.[499]

H. Friendly societies

A friendly society has been described as 'a voluntary association of individuals, **8.195** unincorporated or incorporated, subscribing for provident benefits'.[500] These

---

[496] See above, paras 8.178–8.181
[497] (1843) 2 Hare 461
[498] *Baillie v Oriental Telephone Co* [1915] 1 Ch 503
[499] CA 1993, s 18
[500] *Halsbury's Laws* (4th edn) (re-issue), (Butterworths, 1995), vol 19(1), Friendly Societies, para 103

benefits may take a variety of forms, and may be either financial (such as life assurance, accident, sickness and funeral benefits, or other benefits for members in financial difficulties) or social benefits.

(1) Friendly societies and charitable status

8.196 A friendly society will enjoy charitable status only if its purpose is the relief of poverty. A qualification of poverty in order to benefit may be express or inferred;[501] but in its absence, the society will fail to attain charitable status because its purposes will not be charitable,[502] and, because its benefits are restricted to its members and their widows or families, it will lack the requirement of public benefit, in that such persons do not comprise a sufficient section of the community for the purposes of the law of charity. Additionally, there will be present the vitiating element of self-help,[503] which is sometimes referred to as mutual benefit,[504] the objection apparently being an absence of altruism.[505] Self-help often involves an element of contractual entitlement,[506] but it has been held that mutuality can still be present (and so charitable status denied) even if the trustees or committee have a discretion in the application of the fund.[507] It had been judicially suggested that contractual entitlement to benefits will preclude a self-help society from being a charity, even if a requirement of poverty in order to benefit is expressly imposed, that is that the beneficiaries must receive their benefits by way of bounty rather than bargain;[508] but this dictum has been rejected in so far as it suggests that the beneficiaries cannot be required to contribute to the cost of the benefits they receive.[509] If the objects of the society do not constitute it a charity, the fact that it receives donations and subscriptions cannot make it one.[510]

---

[501] See *Re Buck* [1896] 2 Ch 727, where the rules of a friendly society stated that its object was to provide a fund for the relief of sick and distressed members, their widows and children; and other rules provided that such persons could benefit only if they were 'in distressed circumstances'. Kekewich J held the society charitable as being for the relief of poverty. See also *Spiller v Maude* (1886) 32 ChD 158n (Jessel MR), which concerned the York Theatrical Fund Society (a friendly society)

[502] *Cunnack v Edwards* [1896] 2 Ch 679, 681–2 (Lord Halsbury LC) (CA) (concerning a friendly society called the Helston Equitable Annuitant Society); *Re Hobourn Aero Components Ltd's Air Raid Distress Fund* [1946] 1 Ch 194, 203 (Lord Greene MR)

[503] *Re Hobourn Aero Components Ltd's Air Raid Distress Fund* [1946] 1 Ch 194, 200 (Lord Greene MR); see also *Re Mead's Trust Deed* [1961] 1 WLR 1244 (Cross J)

[504] See *Re Clark's Trust* (1875) 1 ChD 497, 500 (Hall V-C) (concerning a bequest to the trustees of the Ringwood Friendly Society)

[505] *Waterson v Hendon BC* [1959] 1 WLR 985, 991 (Salmon J)

[506] *Re Buck* [1896] 2 Ch 727

[507] *Re Hobourn Aero Components Ltd's Air Raid Distress Fund* [1946] 1 Ch 194, 201 (Lord Greene MR)

[508] *IRC v Society for the Relief of Widows and Orphans of Medical Men* (1926) 11 TC 1, 22 (Rowlatt J)

[509] *Joseph Rowntree Memorial Trust Housing Assoc Ltd v A-G* [1983] Ch 159, 174–5 (Peter Gibson J)

[510] *Re Hobourn Aero Components Ltd's Air Raid Distress Fund* [1946] 1 Ch 194, 203 (Lord Greene MR). See also *Braithwaite v A-G* [1909] 1 Ch 511, 518 (Swinfen Eady J), which concerned the Benefit Society for Girls Educated at the School of Industry, Kendal (a registered friendly society)

(2) Forms of friendly society

A friendly society may exist in one of three forms. **8.197**

Registered society under Friendly Societies Act 1974

A friendly society may be registered under the Friendly Societies Act 1974 as an **8.198** unincorporated association of individuals. Since 1 February 1993, however, no new society may be registered under this Act. Any society wishing to be registered must now do so under the Friendly Societies Act 1992, which provides for both registration and incorporation. Societies which were already registered under the 1974 Act, however, may remain registered societies under that Act.

Although most societies registered under the 1974 Act are friendly societies, some **8.199** other classes of society were also permitted to register under it.[511] These include a couple of classes which might attain charitable status under the Charities Act 1993 if their purposes are wholly and exclusively charitable, namely, benevolent societies for any benevolent or charitable purpose;[512] and what the 1974 Act calls 'old people's home societies', which are societies to provide homes for members and others over the age of fifty.[513]

Registration and incorporation under Friendly Societies Act 1992

A friendly society may be registered and incorporated under the Friendly Societies **8.200** Act 1992. This Act permits friendly societies, by registering, to obtain incorporation, which had not previously been available to them.[514] Incorporation automatically follows upon registration; a new society which prefers not to incorporate can therefore exist only as an unregistered society. A society incorporated under the 1992 Act is a corporate body, but not a company registered under the Companies Acts, although it will be subject to some provisions of those Acts.[515] The Friendly Societies Act 1992 also established a regulatory authority, the Friendly Societies Commission,[516] but it is expected that the functions of this body will be transferred to the Financial Services Authority in 2001.[517]

---

[511] Friendly Societies Act 1974, s 7(1), as amended by Friendly Societies Act 1992, s 95 and Sch 16

[512] Friendly Societies Act 1974, s 7(1)(c)

[513] ibid, s 7(1)(e)

[514] Friendly Societies Act 1992, ss 5, 6

[515] eg Companies Act 1985, ss 312 (approval by members of proposed payment to director for loss of office) and 316(3) (supplementary) are adapted and applied to friendly societies by Friendly Societies Act 1992, s 27 and Sch 11, para 8

[516] Friendly Societies Act 1992, ss 1–4 and Sch 1

[517] Pursuant to Financial Services and Markets Act 2000, s 334(1), which makes provision for such transfer by order of the Treasury

8.201 At least seven persons are required to establish a society under the 1992 Act.[518] They must agree upon the society's purposes and the extent of its powers in a memorandum,[519] they must agree a set of rules for the society's regulation,[520] and they must send three copies of the memorandum and rules to the central office.[521]

8.202 The memorandum must specify: the name of the society;[522] whether the registered office is to be situated in England and Wales, or in Scotland, or in Northern Ireland;[523] the address of its registered office;[524] the purposes of the society and the extent of its powers;[525] and, if any of those purposes include the carrying on of any business outside the United Kingdom, it must state that fact.[526] The purposes of the society must be wholly and exclusively charitable if the society is to enjoy charitable status.

8.203 The rules must provide for various matters, including the terms of admission and cessation of membership; the election, appointment, and removal of officers; the powers and duties of the committee of management; the investment of the society's funds; the manner of settling disputes; the form, custody, and use of any corporate seal; the calling and holding of meetings; the entitlement of members to participate in any surplus assets on winding up; and the procedure for altering the memorandum and rules.[527] If the society is to comprise a charity, its rules must forbid any application of surplus assets to its members on a winding up; rather, they should provide for their application to such other charitable body with similar purposes as the members might decide. In the absence of an express provision, the assets on dissolution of a charitable friendly society are applicable cy-près.[528]

8.204 The rules of an incorporated friendly society bind each of the members and officers of the society and all persons who claim on account of a member or under the rules.[529] Any other person who is a party to a transaction with such a society is not bound to inquire as to any limitation on the powers of the committee of man-

---

[518] Friendly Societies Act 1992, Sch3, para 1(1)
[519] ibid, s 5(6) and Sch 3, para 1(1)(a)
[520] ibid, para 1(1)(b)
[521] ibid, para 1(1)(c); 'central office' means the central office of the registry of friendly societies except in relation to Scotland, where it means the assistant registrar of friendly societies: ibid, s 119(1). The address of the central office for England and Wales is Victory House, 30–34 Kingsway, London WC2B 6ES. The Financial Services and Markets Act 2000, s 335(2), makes provision for the transfer of the functions of the central office to the Financial Services Authority by order of the Treasury. Such transfer is expected to take place in 2001
[522] Friendly Societies Act 1992, Sch 3, para 4(1)(a)
[523] ibid, para 4(1)(b)
[524] ibid, para 4(1)(c)
[525] ibid, para 4(1)(d)
[526] ibid, para 4(1)(e)
[527] ibid, para 5(3)
[528] *Re Buck* [1896] 2 Ch 727
[529] Friendly Societies Act 1992, s 9(1)

agement to bind the society.[530] In favour of any other person who gives valuable consideration for an act of the society (being within the capacity of the society) and who does not know that the act is beyond the powers of the committee of management, the committee's powers to bind the society are deemed to be free of any limitation in the society's constitution.[531] This does not, however, affect the right of a member of such society to bring proceedings to restrain an act which is beyond the powers of the committee of management.[532]

The memorandum or rules may be altered, or provisions may be deleted or addi- **8.205** tions made, in the manner prescribed in the society's rules.[533] Three copies of a record of the alteration, signed by the secretary, must be sent to the central office, together with a statutory declaration by the secretary that the alteration was made in accordance with the procedure laid down in the society's rules.[534]

An incorporated friendly society may be dissolved either by the consent of the **8.206** members, or by being wound up either voluntarily or by the court under the Friendly Societies Act 1992.[535] Following a dissolution or winding up of the society, the central office must cancel its registration under the Friendly Societies Act 1992.[536]

Unregistered friendly society

A friendly society may be unregistered, in which case the provisions of the **8.207** Friendly Societies Acts do not apply to it. Such a society will be an unincorporated association of individuals, and its property will usually be vested in trustees. An unregistered society is entitled to claim exemption from income and corporation tax (on both income and chargeable gains) if its income does not exceed £160 a year.[537] If the rules of an unregistered friendly society do not make provision for their amendment, no amendment made can affect the existing rights of any member who does not consent to the alteration.[538] The decision of the majority of members to register an unregistered friendly society binds the minority.[539]

---

[530] ibid, s 9(2)
[531] ibid, s 9(4)
[532] ibid, s 9(6)(a)
[533] ibid, s 5(6) and Sch 3, para 6(1)
[534] ibid, para 6(4)
[535] ibid, ss 5–26 and Schs 2–10
[536] ibid, s 26(1)
[537] ICTA 1988, s 459, as amended by F (No 2) A 1992, s 56 and Sch 9, para 4
[538] *Souter v Davies* (1895) 39 Sol Jo 264 (DC)
[539] *M'Kenny v Barnsley Corp* (1894) 10 TLR 533 (CA)

(3) Exempt charities

8.208 So far as it is a charity, any registered society or branch within the meaning of the Friendly Societies Act 1974 is an exempt charity for the purposes of the Charities Act 1993.[540]

I. Industrial and provident societies

8.209 A society registered under the Industrial and Provident Societies Act 1965 is a body corporate with limited liability.[541] A society registered under an earlier Act relating to industrial and provident societies is deemed to be registered under the Industrial and Provident Societies Act 1965.[542] The Act of 1965 together with later statutes governing industrial and provident societies[543] are collectively known as the Industrial and Provident Societies Acts 1965–78. Registration vests in the society all property currently held by any person in trust for it, and legal proceedings may be brought or continued by or against the society in its registered name.[544]

8.210 A society may be registered with rules which authorize it to carry on any industry, business, or trade (including dealings with land), but only if either:

(a) it is a bona fide co-operative society, or

(b) in view of the fact that the business of the society is being, or is intended to be, conducted for the benefit of the community, there are special reasons why the society should be registered under the 1965 Act rather than as a company under the Companies Act 1985.[545]

8.211 The element of mutuality in category (a) prevents a co-operative society from being a charity. A credit union, for example, may apply to be registered as such under the 1965 Act,[546] but it cannot have the status of a charity.[547] The objects of a registered society within category (b), however, may be charitable. Guidance notes issued by the Registry of Friendly Societies state that, in order to satisfy the

---

[540] CA 1993, s 3(5)(a) and Sch 2, para (y)

[541] Industrial and Provident Societies Act 1965, s 3

[542] ibid, s 4

[543] ie Industrial and Provident Societies Act 1967, Friendly and Industrial and Provident Societies Act 1968, Industrial and Provident Societies Act 1975, and Industrial and Provident Societies Act 1978

[544] Industrial and Provident Societies Act 1965, s 3

[545] ibid, s 1(1)(a), (2)(a)

[546] The Industrial and Provident Societies Acts 1965–78 apply to credit unions except as modified by the Credit Unions Act 1979: ibid, s 31(3)

[547] The principal objects of a credit union are the promotion of thrift among its members by the accumulation of their savings, the creation of sources of credit for the members' benefit at a fair and reasonable rate of interest, and the use and control of members' savings for their mutual benefit: Credit Unions Act 1979, s 1(3)

requirement that the society be 'conducted for the benefit of the community', the society must show (inter alia) that it will benefit persons other than its members and that its business is in the interests of the community. Special reasons why the society should be registered under the 1965 Act include whether it is non-profit making and whether its rules prohibit the distribution of its assets amongst the members, whether its rules vest control of the society in its members equally (and not according to their financial interest), whether the rules provide that interest payable on share and loan capital will not exceed a rate necessary to obtain and retain the capital needed to carry out the society's objects, and whether there is any artificial restriction of membership with a view to increasing the value of proprietary rights and interests. Some societies which are 'conducted for the benefit of the community' may have purposes which are wholly and exclusively charitable, and many societies obtaining registration on this ground are housing associations.

If the society's registered office is in England, Wales or the Channel Islands, registra-   **8.212**
tion is currently with the central office of the Chief Registrar of Friendly Societies,[548] but it is expected that the functions of the Chief Registrar will be transferred to the Financial Services Authority in 2001.[549] To obtain registration, a society must send to the Registrar an application signed by seven members and the secretary, together with two printed copies of the society's rules.[550] The last name of a registered society must be 'Limited',[551] unless the Registrar is satisfied that the society's objects are wholly charitable or benevolent, in which case he may allow registration with that word omitted.[552] In practice, no society is permitted to use the word 'company' in its name.[553] There are also restrictions on names which the Registrar considers undesirable.[554] Any amendment of the rules must be registered with the Registrar, and a registered society must also (inter alia) file annual returns with the Registrar.

The rules of a registered society (other than a credit union) must provide (inter   **8.213**
alia) for the following:[555] the society's name[556] and objects;[557] the place of its registered office;[558] the terms of admission of members;[559] the holding of meetings, voting rights, and making, altering, and rescinding the society's rules;[560] the

---

[548] Industrial and Provident Societies Act 1965, s 73(1)(b), (c)(i)
[549] Financial Services and Markets Act 2000, s 335(1)
[550] Industrial and Provident Societies Act 1965, s 2(1)(b)
[551] ibid, s 5(2)
[552] ibid, s 5(5)
[553] The statutory prohibition applies, however, only to societies which convert from being companies registered under the Companies Acts: Industrial and Provident Societies Act 1965, s 53(5)
[554] Industrial and Provident Societies Act 1965, s 5(1)
[555] ibid, s 1(1)(b) and Sch 1
[556] ibid, Sch 1, para 1
[557] ibid, para 2
[558] ibid, para 3
[559] ibid, para 4
[560] ibid, para 5

appointment and removal of a committee, and of managers and other officers, and their remuneration;[561] whether (and, if so, the terms upon which) the society may enter into loans or receive money on deposit from members or others;[562] the audit of accounts by auditors appointed by the society;[563] whether, and if so how, members may leave the society;[564] the mode of application of the society's profits;[565] the use and custody of the society's seal;[566] and the authority and manner of investing the society's funds.[567]

8.214 The rules of a registered society bind the society and all its members and persons claiming through them respectively to the same extent as if each member had subscribed his name and affixed his seal to them, and there were contained in those rules a covenant on the part of each member and any person claiming though him to conform to the rules subject to the statutory provisions.[568] The contract thereby created is similar to that which arises between the company and the members and between the members *inter se* under a company registered under the Companies Acts 1985.[569] The discussion of the impact of the statutory contract in relation to companies registered under the Companies Act 1985[570] therefore applies *mutatis mutandis* to a registered society under the Industrial and Provident Societies Act 1965.

8.215 Since registration under the 1965 Act confers corporate status, a registered society's legal capacity is limited to its stated objects. The modifications to the ultra vires rule contained in the Companies Act 1985 do not apply to registered societies; but the case law relevant to the construction and effect of the objects and powers of companies registered under the Companies Act 1985 applies to registered societies.[571] A registered society which is also a charity will be acting ultra vires if it purports to give gratuitous guarantees to secure loans made to its noncharitable subsidiary; such guarantees will therefore be void.[572]

---

[561] Industrial and Provident Societies Act 1965, para 6
[562] ibid, para 8
[563] ibid, para 10
[564] ibid, para 11
[565] ibid, para 12
[566] ibid, para 13
[567] ibid, para 14
[568] ibid, s 14(1)
[569] ie under Companies Act 1985, s 14
[570] See above, paras 8.147 and 8.161
[571] See, eg, *Halifax Building Society v Meridian Housing Assoc Ltd* [1994] 2 BCLC 540, which concerned an industrial and provident society registered under the 1965 Act, and where Arden J applied *Rolled Steel Products (Holdings) Ltd v British Steel Corp* [1986] Ch 246 (CA)
[572] *Rosemary Simmons Memorial Housing Assoc Ltd v United Dominions Trust* [1986] 1 WLR 1440 (Mervyn Davies J) (concerning a charitable housing association registered under the 1965 Act)

So far as it is a charity, any registered society within the meaning of the Industrial **8.216**
and Provident Societies Act 1965 is an exempt charity for the purposes of the
Charities Act 1993.[573]

J. Charitable housing associations

(1) Introduction

A housing association is essentially a non-profit organization whose purpose is the **8.217**
provision of housing. The term 'housing association' is not a term of art, and the
legislation which applies to such associations depends upon the particular type of
association concerned. The term 'housing association' is therefore a broad
description of the association's purposes, not a description of its legal structure.
Nevertheless, because such associations are governed by their own particular legislation according to the legal structure which they adopt, it is convenient to deal
with such associations in this chapter.

A housing association may adopt one of several legal structures: a trust, an unin- **8.218**
corporated association, a company under the Companies Act 1985, or a corporate
body under the Industrial and Provident Societies Act 1965 ('the 1965 Act');
exceptionally, a charitable housing association may be incorporated by special Act
of Parliament.[574] Most housing associations are in fact registered as industrial and
provident societies under the 1965 Act. A housing association which adopts a corporate structure has capacity to enter only into transactions which are within the
scope of its objects and within its express or implied powers.[575] A charitable housing association registered and incorporated under the 1965 Act has been held to
be acting ultra vires in purporting to give gratuitous guarantees to secure loans
made to its non-charitable subsidiary; such guarantees were gratuitous *vis-à-vis*
the charity itself, and were therefore ultra vires and void.[576]

(2) Housing associations and charitable status

Whatever legal structure it adopts, a housing association cannot be a charitable **8.219**
organization unless its purposes, objects clause, or rules, as the case may be,
restrict the application of its assets to wholly and exclusively charitable purposes.

---

[573] CA 1993, Sch 2, para (y)
[574] eg Peabody Trust, incorporated by Peabody Donation Fund Act 1948
[575] See, eg, *Halifax Building Society v Meridian Housing Assoc Ltd* [1994] 2 BCLC 540, where the
housing association was registered as an industrial and provident society under the 1965 Act
[576] *Rosemary Simmons Memorial Housing Assoc Ltd v United Dominions Trust* [1986] 1 WLR
1440 (Mervyn Davies J)

Some associations are fully mutual,[577] and are in the nature of self-governing co-operatives; these cannot be charities since their purposes are not charitable, the benefits are not available to a sufficient section of the community, and (even if there is a poverty requirement in order to benefit) they contain the vitiating factor of self-help.[578] A housing association which is essentially a self-help organization does not cease to be one merely because its funds derive partially from outside sources, such as grants from the Housing Corporation or from local authorities.[579] Many non-mutual housing associations, however, are altruistic organizations, in that the members are not themselves the 'beneficiaries', and have no economic interest in the association; because of the privileges accorded to charities, many such associations are formed as charities. Indeed, it has been said that housing associations 'historically have been charities motivated by an interest to provide housing for the poorer classes'.[580]

8.220 The provision of housing is not itself a charitable purpose, but the object of providing housing for the poor or for the elderly can be a charitable purpose as being for the relief of 'aged, impotent and poor people'[581] within the Preamble to the Statute of Elizabeth, or within one of the four heads of charity in *Pemsel*'s case.[582] Charitable status is not denied merely because the poor or aged persons benefited are contractually obliged to contribute to the cost of the housing so provided, for example by way of rent or the payment of a capital sum by way of premium;[583] nor is it denied merely because such persons acquire a proprietary interest in their homes (for example, through the grant to them of leases for a term of years).[584] In order to meet the identified housing needs of the elderly, it might be necessary to grant a long-term lease with concomitant security of tenure, and the risk that the tenant cannot be removed even if his financial circumstances improve; and the ability to grant such a lease will not deprive a housing association of its charitable status.[585]

---

[577] To comprise a 'fully mutual association', the association must restrict membership to tenants or prospective tenants, and preclude the grant or assignment of leases to non-members: Housing Act 1996, s 63(1), applying the definition in Housing Associations Act 1985, s 1(2). For special provisions relating to fully mutual associations, see Housing Act 1996, Sch 1, para 2(2)(c)

[578] *Over Seventies Housing Assoc v Westminster LBC* (1974) 230 EG 1593 (mutual housing association set up 'for persons of limited means upon terms appropriate to their means' held not charitable)

[579] *Joseph Rowntree Memorial Trust Housing Assoc Ltd v A-G* [1983] Ch 159

[580] *Governors of the Peabody Donation Fund v Higgins* [1983] 1 WLR 1091, 1093 (Cumming-Bruce LJ) (CA)

[581] The expression 'aged, impotent and poor' is to be read disjunctively: *Re Glyn* (1950) 66 TLR (Pt 2) 510, 511 (Danckwerts J); *Re Robinson* [1951] Ch 198 (Vaisey J); *Joseph Rowntree Memorial Trust Housing Assoc Ltd v A-G* [1983] Ch 159, 174 (Peter Gibson J)

[582] [1891] AC 531 (HL)

[583] *Joseph Rowntree Memorial Trust Housing Assoc Ltd v A-G* [1983] Ch 159 (Peter Gibson J), distinguishing dictum of Rowlatt J in *IRC v Society for the Relief of Widows and Orphans of Medical Men* (1926) 11 TC 1, 22

[584] *Joseph Rowntree Memorial Trust Housing Assoc Ltd v A-G* [1983] Ch 159

[585] ibid, applying *Re Monk* [1927] 2 Ch 197

In order to preserve the essential charitable nature of a charitable housing associa-   **8.221**
tion for the poor or elderly, there should be an appropriate restriction on the tenants' right to assign (for example, to elderly persons, or to persons who would
themselves qualify as objects of the charity). It has nevertheless been held that an
association's rules which permitted assignment to a tenant's spouse on the tenant's
death (who might not herself be a qualifying person) did not deprive the association of charitable status, as the incidental disadvantage of this was outweighed by
the advantage to the association of ensuring that the tenancies were not such as to
give the tenants security of tenure or a statutory right to acquire the freehold.[586]

Shared ownership schemes

The Charity Commissioners have expressed their views on the ability of charita-   **8.222**
ble housing associations to enter into shared ownership schemes, in particular the
form of scheme known as Do-it-Yourself Shared Ownership (DIYSO).[587] Such
schemes are designed both to create vacant units in the housing association and
local authority sectors in order to house a homeless household, and to encourage
home-ownership by enabling first-time buyers who cannot buy outright to purchase a property on the open market on a shared ownership basis.

The Charity Commissioners have pointed out two concerns about charitable   **8.223**
housing associations entering into DIYSO schemes.[588] First, there is the problem
of the ability of such associations to enter into such schemes with persons who are
not qualified as beneficiaries, where the object is to make that person's existing
accommodation available to somebody else who is a beneficiary. Secondly, there is
the problem of the ability of such associations to enter into shared ownership
schemes with persons who originally qualify as beneficiaries, where the scheme
makes no provision for the possibility that that person may cease to be a
beneficiary during the lifetime of the scheme.

The Charity Commissioners consider that there is no objection in principle to a   **8.224**
charitable housing association's entering into a shared ownership scheme with a
person who is not qualified as a beneficiary, provided that the purpose of doing so
is to procure vacant accommodation for persons who are beneficiaries, and provided that this is an efficient use of the association's property and resources in
achieving that purpose. The association must constantly bear in mind its charitable housing objectives; if the scheme is intended to free housing stock belonging
not to the association itself but to another housing association, it should approach
such a scheme with considerable caution. It should ensure that its participation in

---

[586] *Joseph Rowntree Memorial Trust Housing Assoc Ltd v A-G* [1983] Ch 159
[587] [1993] Ch Com Rep 25 (paras 98–102). See also S Hayes & J Gubbins, 'Shared Ownership:
a Charitable Option?' (1992–3) 1 CL & PR 225
[588] [1993] Ch Com Rep 25 (para 100)

such schemes does not become so regular as to become an end in itself; apart from exceptional circumstances, such schemes should form only a small part of a charitable housing association's total activities. It must also ensure that it has the necessary powers under its constitution to enter into such a scheme.[589]

8.225 The Charity Commissioners consider that the ability of a charitable housing association to enter into a shared ownership scheme with a person who is qualified as a beneficiary is not affected by the fact that the scheme permits the beneficiary to purchase further shares in the property should that beneficiary's means improve sufficiently to enable him to 'staircase'. The Commissioners nevertheless recommend that charitable housing associations should at least consider whether it might be workable and acceptable to potential shared owners to stipulate either (1) that the association may require the shared owner to purchase all the remaining equity in the property or that the property be sold, in the event that his financial position changes so substantially that he ceases to be qualified as a beneficiary; or (2) that, should there be a substantial change in a shared owner's financial position, the association may require the rent to be increased to a full market rent. If such stipulations are found not to be acceptable to potential shared owners and cause problems in respect of repayment of any Housing Association Grant, the charitable housing association may proceed with the scheme without such stipulations, but only if it is satisfied that such a scheme is the best way of meeting the needs of beneficiaries, and that it is an effective use of the association's own resources.[590]

(3) Registration of charitable housing associations

8.226 A housing association which is registered as a social landlord under the Housing Act 1996 ('the 1996 Act') enjoys certain privileges, notably eligibility for statutory funding in the form of grants and loans from the registering authority and from local authorities. A charitable housing association may therefore choose to register as a social landlord under the 1996 Act.[591]

Registration is made with what the statute calls the 'relevant authority', which must maintain a register of social landlords which is open to public inspection.[592]

---

[589] [1993] Ch Com Rep 26 (para 101(1))

[590] ibid, 26 (para 101(2))

[591] The Housing Act 1996, Pt I, largely re-enacted (with some changes in terminology) the provisions relating to the registration of housing associations previously contained in the Housing Associations Act 1985, but it also gave new powers to the relevant authorities, gave new rights to acquire to housing association tenants, and established an ombudsman in this area. For a brief summary of the changes made by the 1996 Act in relation to housing associations, see J Driscoll, 'What is the future for social housing; reflections on the public sector provisions of the Housing Act 1996' (1997) 60 MLR 823, 826. See generally, J Alder & C Handy, *Housing Associations: the Law of Social Landlords* (3rd edn, Sweet & Maxwell, 1997)

[592] Housing Act 1996, s 1(1). Every housing association previously registered under the Housing Associations Act 1985 was automatically registered as a social landlord: ibid, s 1(2)

Where the social landlord is a charity registered with the Charity Commissioners **8.227** with a registered office in Wales, or is a company or an industrial and provident society with a registered office in Wales, the relevant authority is the Secretary of State; otherwise, the relevant authority is the Housing Corporation.[593]

A registered charity which is a housing association is automatically eligible for reg- **8.228** istration as a social landlord.[594] Some such associations are therefore registered both with the Charity Commissioners and with the relevant authority. In practice, however, most non-mutual housing associations are registered as industrial and provident societies, and such registration renders a charitable housing association an exempt charity for the purposes of the Charities Act 1993.[595] An exempt charity is not entitled to be registered as a charity.[596]

A society registered under the Industrial and Provident Societies Act 1965 or a **8.229** company registered under the Companies Act 1985 (and not being a registered charity) is eligible for registration as a social landlord only if (in each case) it satisfies specified conditions.[597] There are three conditions.[598] First, the body must be non-profit making.[599] Secondly, it must be established for the purpose of, or have among its objects or powers, the provision, construction, improvement, or management of:

(a) houses to be kept available for letting; or
(b) houses for occupation by members of the body, where the rules of the body restrict membership to persons entitled or prospectively entitled (as tenants or otherwise) to occupy a house provided or managed by the body; or
(c) hostels.

Thirdly, any additional purposes or objects must be limited to the ancillary purposes set out in the 1996 Act, which include the provision of land, amenities, and services; the acquisition, repair and improvement, or construction of houses to be disposed of on shared ownership terms; the management of houses or flats held on leases; and the giving of advice on the forming and running of housing associations and the like.[600] The Secretary of State may by order specify additional permissible purposes or objects,[601] and additions have thereby been made.[602]

---

[593] Housing Act 1996, ss 1(1A), 56
[594] ibid, s 2(1)(a)
[595] CA 1993, Sch 2, para (y)
[596] ibid, s 3(2), (5)(a). Although s 3(5) states that such charities 'are not required to be registered', s 3(2) makes it clear that they are not entitled to be registered
[597] Housing Act 1996, s 2(1)(b), (c)
[598] ibid, s 2(2)
[599] The expression 'non-profit making' is defined ibid, s 2(3)
[600] ibid, s 2(4)
[601] ibid, s 2(7)
[602] Social Landlord (Permissible Additional Purposes or Objects) Order 1996, SI 1996/2256, reg 3

8.230 Upon registering a body as a social landlord, the relevant authority must give notice of registration to the Charity Commissioners (if the body is a registered charity),[603] or to the appropriate Registrar if it is an industrial and provident society.[604] If the body is a company Registered under the Companies Act 1985, the relevant authority must give notice to the Registrar of Companies.[605] If body is both a registered charity and a company registered under the Companies Act 1985, the relevant authority must give notice to both the Charity Commissioners and the Registrar of Companies.[606] In each case, the recipient of the notice must record the registration.[607] A body which is at any time registered as a social landlord is, for all purposes other than rectification of the register, conclusively presumed to be, or to have been while so registered, a body eligible for registration as a social landlord.[608]

8.231 There is provision for the removal of a body from the register of social landlords if the body ceases to be eligible for registration,[609] if it has ceased to exist or does not operate,[610] or if it requests removal.[611] On removing a body from the register, the relevant authority must give notice of the removal to the same persons as must be notified of registration, these being the Charity Commissioners (if it is a registered charity), the appropriate Registrar (if it is an industrial and provident society), or the Registrar of Companies (if it is a company registered under the Companies Act 1985), and the recipients must similarly record the removal.[612] The relevant authority is required to establish and publish criteria for registration[613] and removal.[614] A body may appeal to the High Court against a decision to refuse registration or to remove it from the register of social landlords.[615] The relevant authority must give notice of any such appeal to the Charity Commissioners (if it is a registered charity), to the appropriate Registrar (if it is an industrial and provident society), or to the Registrar of Companies (if it is a company registered under the Companies Act 1985), as the case may be.[616]

---

[603] Housing Act 1996, s 3(3)(a)

[604] ibid, s 3(3)(b)

[605] ibid, s 3(3)(c). It is anticipated that in 2001 the functions of the Chief Registrar of Friendly Societies will be transferred to the Financial Services Authority pursuant to provisions made in the Financial Services and Markets Act 2000, s 335(1)

[606] Housing Act 1996, s 3(3)(c)

[607] ibid, s 3(3)

[608] ibid, s 3(4)

[609] ibid, s 4(2)(a)

[610] ibid, s 4(2)(b)

[611] ibid, s 4(4)

[612] ibid, s 4(6)

[613] ibid, s 5(1)

[614] ibid, s 5(5)

[615] ibid, s 6(1)

[616] ibid, s 6(3)

(4) Regulation of registered social landlords

The Housing Act 1996 regulates registered social landlords in respect of various   **8.232**
matters.

Removal or appointment of director, trustee, or committee member

There is provision for the relevant authority to remove, or to appoint, on specified   **8.233**
grounds, a director, trustee, or committee member of a registered social landlord
which is a registered charity, an industrial and provident society, or a company
registered under the Companies Act 1985.[617] There are, however, restrictions on
the removal of a director or trustee of a registered charity;[618] and before the relevant authority may appoint a director or trustee of a registered charity, it must first
consult the Charity Commissioners.[619]

Alteration of memorandum or articles

If a registered social landlord is a registered charity, not being a company incorpo-   **8.234**
rated under the Companies Act 1985, its objects may not be altered without the
consent of the Charity Commissioners.[620] If a registered social landlord is such a
company (whether a registered charity or not), no alteration of its memorandum
or articles (other than a change of name or the alteration of its registered office) is
valid without the consent of the relevant authority.[621]

Winding-up and transfer of assets

The relevant authority may petition, on specified grounds, for the winding up of   **8.235**
a registered social landlord which is a company incorporated under the
Companies Act 1985 (including a company which is a registered charity) or
which is an industrial and provident society.[622] If the registered social landlord is
not a registered charity, any surplus property on dissolution is transferred to the
relevant authority;[623] if the registered social landlord is a charity, the relevant
authority may dispose of such property only to another registered social landlord
which is also a charity and whose objects appear to the relevant authority to be, as
nearly as practicable, akin to those of the body which is dissolved or wound up.[624]

---

[617] ibid, Sch 1, paras 4 (removal), 6–8 (appointment)
[618] ibid, para 5
[619] ibid, para 6(2)(b)
[620] ibid, para 10
[621] ibid, para 11
[622] ibid, para 14
[623] ibid, para 15(2)
[624] ibid, para 15(4)

Accounting and audit requirements for a registered social landlord which is a registered charity

8.236 A registered social landlord which is a registered charity is, in respect of its housing activities, and separately from any other activities it may have, subject to additional accounting and auditing requirements (which correspond to those imposed by the Friendly and Industrial and Provident Societies Act 1968); but these do not affect any obligations of the charity under sections 41–5 of the Charities Act 1993.[625] The charity must, in respect of its housing activities, keep proper books of account showing its transactions and its assets and liabilities, and it must establish and maintain a satisfactory system of control of its books of accounts, its cash holdings and all its receipts and remittances. The books of account must be such as to enable a true and fair view to be given of the state of affairs of the charity in respect of its housing activities, and to explain its transactions in the course of those activities.[626]

8.237 The charity must for each period of account[627] prepare a revenue account giving a true and fair view of the charity's income and expenditure in the period, so far as arising in connection with its housing activities, and a balance sheet giving a true and fair view as at the end of the period of the state of the charity's affairs. The revenue account and balance sheet must be signed by at least two directors or trustees of the charity.[628]

8.238 The charity must in each period of account appoint a qualified auditor to audit the accounts so prepared by the charity.[629] The auditor must report to the charity on the accounts; for this purpose, he must carry out necessary investigations, and has a right of access to the books, deed, and accounts of the charity, and is entitled to require information and explanations from officers of the charity as the auditor thinks necessary to perform the duties of auditor.[630]

8.239 Every person directly concerned with the conduct and management of the affairs of a registered social landlord who in that capacity is responsible for the preparation and audit of accounts must ensure that such accounting and audit requirements are complied with.[631] Criminal sanctions can be imposed on such a person and on the registered social landlord for breach of some of these requirements[632]

---

[625] Housing Act 1996, para 18(1)
[626] ibid, para 18(2)
[627] A period of account is 12 months or such other period not less than 6 months or more than 18 months as the charity may, with the consent of the relevant authority, determine: ibid, para 18(8)
[628] ibid, para 18(3)
[629] ibid, para 18(4)
[630] ibid, para 18(5), (6), (7)
[631] ibid, para 19(1)
[632] ibid, para 19(2)

(subject to certain defences[633]); but a prosecution may be brought only by or with the consent of the relevant authority or the Director of Public Prosecutions.[634]

Miscellaneous matters

Other regulation of registered social landlords includes the control of payments to **8.240** members,[635] officers, and employees;[636] changes of rules and amalgamations of industrial and provident societies;[637] and the instituting of inquiries.[638]

---

[633] ibid, para 19(3)
[634] ibid, para 19(4)
[635] ibid, paras 1, 3
[636] ibid, para 2
[637] ibid, paras 9, 12
[638] ibid, s 7 and Sch 1, Pt IV (paras 20–29)

9

TRUSTEES, COMMITTEE MEMBERS, AND DIRECTORS

A. Introduction

(1) The meaning of 'charity trustee'

9.01 An initial problem in considering the position of charity trustees is to determine who ranks as a charity trustee. Much confusion can arise from the fact that the expression 'charity trustee' is susceptible to more than one meaning, and it is often necessary to determine the meaning from the context in which the expression is used. There are three possible meanings.

Trustee of a charitable trust

9.02 The expression 'charity trustee' can be used narrowly to refer to a trustee of a charitable trust. This meaning would exclude the director of a charitable corporation, since there is no trust in the strict sense: the corporate charity's assets are vested in the corporation, not in its directors. The expression 'trustee' in the Trustee Act 1925 evidently refers to a trustee in this strict sense, and it is clear that the Trustee Act 2000 has no application to directors of charitable companies.[1]

Fiduciary in whom the charity's management or assets (or both) are vested under the terms of the governing instrument

9.03 The expression 'charity trustee' can be used to refer to all persons in whom either the management and administration of a charity, or its assets (or both) are vested under the terms of the governing instrument. In this context, the word 'trustee' is used loosely to include fiduciaries who manage and administer a charity (such as directors of charitable companies or Committee members of unincorporated charitable associations), and also those in whom the assets are vested (such as the trustees of an unincorporated charitable association). Other fiduciaries (such as third party agents hired by the charity) are excluded from this definition, since they do not have either the assets or the management and administration of the charity vested in them under the terms of the governing instrument.

Special meaning in the Charities Act 1993

9.04 The expression 'charity trustee' bears a special meaning in the Charities Act 1993. In that Act, 'except in so far as the context otherwise requires, "charity trustees"

---

[1] See Law Commission, *Trustees' Powers and Duties* (Law Com No 260, 1999) 7 (para 1.20 & n 37)

means the persons having the general control and management of the administration of a charity';[2] and 'charity' includes any institution, corporate or not.[3] This
definition therefore includes the trustees of a charitable trust, the directors of a
charitable corporation, and the members of the Committee of an unincorporated
charity. This is the sense in which the expression 'charity trustee' is used in this
chapter, unless the context indicates otherwise. The definition does not, however,
include the soi-disant 'trustees' of an unincorporated charity who merely hold the
charity's assets subject to the directions of the Committee. Such persons are, nevertheless, trustees for the purposes of the law of trusts, and are subject to the
fiduciary obligations to which equity subjects trustees, such as the duty not to
make an unauthorized profit from the use of the trust assets.

If an institution, such as a school, is a part of a larger organization, it can some-   **9.05**
times be difficult to identify who are its 'charity trustees'. A voluntary-controlled
or voluntary-aided school is required to have governors, and these are subject to
statutory duties similar to those imposed on charity trustees; but, if the school is,
for example, part of a religious order, it may be difficult to determine if the 'charity trustees' of the school are the governors of the school or the trustees of the
order.[4]

If the governing instrument divides the general control and management of a   **9.06**
charity's administration between different persons or groups of persons, allotting
different functions to each, it is arguable that each is a 'charity trustee' for the purposes of the Charities Act 1993, but only in respect of those duties and powers
which are vested in him. It seems doubtful whether this possibility is contemplated by the statutory definition of 'charity trustee'; and it seems difficult to interpret the statute to permit this meaning. The Charity Commissioners nevertheless
consider that different persons can be 'charity trustees' in respect of different functions, as is clear from the Commissioners' model scheme for new common investment funds. This allocates responsibilities for the administration and
management of such a fund (which is itself a charity) between a corporate trustee
and a corporate manager (or amongst them and a board of individuals), and
expressly recites that each is a 'charity trustee' within the meaning of the Charities
Act 1993 in respect of the duties and powers so vested in it or him.[5] If the expression 'charity trustee' is indeed so divisible, then division can surely occur only

---

[2] CA 1993, s 97(1)
[3] ibid, s 96(1)
[4] See Judith Hill, 'Roman Catholic Religious Orders as Charities' (1997–8) 5 CL & PR 1, 10,
referring to *Andrews v The Trustees of the Roman Catholic Diocese of Westminster* (The Times, 18 Aug
1989) (CA), which suggests that in such circumstances it is the the school governors who are the
'charity trustees'. See also D Morris, *Schools: an Education in Charity Law* (Dartmouth, 1996)
73–80
[5] Charity Commission, *Common Investment Funds: Policy Statement* (1996), Ann B, cls 8
(Trustee), 18 (Manager); Ann C, cl 14 (Board). See further ch 16, paras 16.89 and 16.91

where the responsibilities of day-to-day management are (as in the case of such model scheme) divided fairly evenly between two or three persons or groups, so that each has a share of the charity's 'general' control and management. The mere fact that a governing instrument vests a single duty in someone other than the charity trustees cannot render him a 'charity trustee' in respect of that duty, since his control and management of the charity's administration could hardly be described as 'general'.

(2) Determining the scope of the duties and powers of charity trustees by reference to their source

9.07 In view of these differences in treatment, it is necessary to consider in each case the source of the obligation or power, and to inquire if it is based on status (that is, with reference to the fact that the institution concerned is a charity) or structure (that is, on whether the institution is a trust, a company, or an unincorporated association).

9.08 The duties imposed, and the powers conferred, on charity trustees by the Charities Act 1993 are clearly status-based, and apply not only to trustees in the strict sense, but also to directors of charitable companies and to committee members of unincorporated charitable associations. Some other statutes are evidently structurally based. The duties and powers applicable to trustees in the Trustee Acts 1925 and 2000, for example, are applicable only to persons who are trustees in the strict sense, and therefore do not apply to directors of charitable companies. Similarly, the provisions of the Companies Act 1985 which apply to directors (and which therefore apply to directors of charitable corporations) do not, of course, apply to trustees of charitable trusts. The scope of some other statutes remains ambivalent. It was conceded in one case, for example, that the provisions of the Trustee Investments Act 1961 applied to a charter company;[6] this was on the basis that the corporation in question was in the position of a trustee with regard to its funds, but the point has never been judicially resolved. Yet again, the courts have been prepared to treat company directors as trustees for some purposes (for example, as regards their misapplication of the company's funds for the purposes of the Limitation Acts).[7]

(3) The meaning of 'trustee for a charity'

9.09 In contradistinction to a 'charity trustee', the Charities Act 1993 also refers to a person who is a 'trustee for a charity'.[8] That expression is not defined in the Act. It would seem an appropriate term to describe the 'trustee' of an unincorporated

---

[6] *Soldiers', Sailors' and Airmen's Families Association v A-G* [1968] 1 WLR 313, 317 (Cross J)
[7] *Re Lands Allotment Co* [1894] 1 Ch 616; see further ch 13, para 13.10
[8] See, eg, CA 1993, s 16(1)(b), which refers to 'a charity trustee or trustee for a charity'

charity who holds the assets but has no management powers which would make him a 'charity trustee' for the purposes of that Act.

B. Capacity and suitability to be a charity trustee

(1) Generally

A person who has been disqualified under the Charities Act 1993 cannot be a **9.10** 'charity trustee' or a 'trustee for a charity'.[9] Such disqualification is not therefore related to the legal structure of the charity concerned, but applies equally to forbid persons from being trustees of charitable trusts, trustees or Committee members of unincorporated charitable associations, and directors of charitable companies. Disqualification is considered more fully later in this chapter.[10] A person may, however, be subject to more general limitations on capacity, and for this purpose it is necessary to distinguish both between individuals and corporate trustees, and between charitable trusts and charitable corporations.

Trustee of a charitable trust

Generally, any person who has capacity to hold property is capable of being **9.11** appointed a trustee of a charitable trust *strictu sensu*. An individual who has attained the age of majority has the requisite capacity; but a minor cannot be appointed to be a trustee of any property (either realty or personalty). A purported appointment of a minor as trustee is therefore void, but without prejudice to the power to appoint a new trustee to fill the vacancy.[11]

A corporation formed by royal charter or under a specific statute has capacity to **9.12** be appointed a trustee of a charitable trust unless the terms of its charter or of the statute in question (as the case may be) deny it such capacity. The memorandum of association of a corporation formed under the Companies Acts may confer a capacity to be a trustee of a charitable trust; such power must, however, be expressly contained in the company's memorandum. If, therefore, property is given upon special charitable trusts to a charitable company incorporated under the Companies Acts, the company will have capacity to act as trustee of such property only if such power is contained in its constitutional documents. Where such power is absent, it may be conferred by appropriate amendment to the company's memorandum or articles of association (or both), which requires the prior written consent of the Charity Commissioners.[12] Provided a corporation has capacity to

---

[9] ibid, s 72
[10] See below, paras 9.50–9.60
[11] LPA 1925, s 20
[12] CA 1993, s 64(2)

be a trustee, it may be a trustee jointly with another person (whether an individual or another corporation).[13]

Director of a charitable corporation

9.13 Although a minor lacks capacity to be a trustee of a charitable trust, a minor (subject to any restriction in the company's articles[14]) may be appointed a director of a company incorporated under the Companies Acts, including therefore a charitable company. A minor who is a director of a charitable company is therefore a 'charity trustee' for the purposes of the Charities Act 1993, even though he could not have been appointed a 'trustee' in the narrow sense. A company may itself be a director of another company.[15]

9.14 A person may be disqualified from being a director by order of the court under the Company Directors Disqualification Act 1986 on various grounds, and these are discussed further below.[16]

(2) Trust corporations

9.15 A trust corporation means the Public Trustee or a corporation either appointed by the court (or by the Charity Commissioners under the Charities Act 1993[17]) in any particular case to be a trustee, or entitled by rules made under the Public Trustee Act 1906,[18] to act as custodian trustee.[19] A trust corporation is therefore often a bank. A trust corporation may be a charity trustee; but since it will not in practice agree to act unless it is able to charge a fee, it is unlikely to be considered a suitable charity trustee except in exceptional circumstances.[20] Where a trust corporation is appointed a trustee of a charity, it is likely to be in the limited capacity of custodian trustee, considered further below.[21]

(3) Local authorities

9.16 A local authority is entitled by statute[22] to act as the trustee of charities for the benefit of the inhabitants of the area of the local authority, other than ecclesiastical charities and charities for the relief of poverty.[23] The trusteeship of a local

---

13 Bodies Corporate (Joint Tenancies) Act 1899
14 There are no such restrictions in Tables A or C
15 *Re Bulawayo Market and Offices Co Ltd* [1907] 2 Ch 458
16 See below, paras 9.58–9.60
17 CA 1993, s 35(1)
18 Public Trustee Act 1906, s 4(3)
19 TA 1925, s 68(18); LPA 1925, s 205(1)(xxviii); AEA 1925, s 55(xxvi); Supreme Court Act 1981, s 128
20 [1989] Ch Com Rep 25 (para 91); [1981] Ch Com Rep 24 (para 64)
21 See below, paras 9.66–9.74
22 Local Government Act 1972, s 139(1). See also Local Government and Housing Act 1989, ss 67–73 (companies under the control or subject to the influence of local authorities)
23 Local Government Act 1972, s 139(3)

authority has the advantage that, as a body corporate, it enjoys perpetual succession, thereby avoiding the need to appoint replacement trustees and the consequent need to vest the charity's property in the new and continuing trustees. The Charity Commissioners have also noted that a local authority will sometimes subsidize the charity's operation out of its own statutory funds, either directly by way of grant or indirectly, as by the supply of professional services without charge.[24] The Commissioners have noted, however, that such an appointment can lead to problems of conflicts of interests, with the result that the local authority might wrongly make decisions as trustee on the basis of what is in the best interests of its chargepayers, or even on party political grounds, rather than on the basis of what is in the best interests of the charity, which should be its sole consideration; there could also be a conflict of interests in respect of land transactions.[25] At a time of increasing demand on local authority resources, the Charity Commissioners have pointed out the pressure for such authorities to exploit the value of their assets,[26] so the potential for a conflict of interests is all the greater. Apart from this, there is also the risk that the local authority might simply confuse its objectives as a statutory body with its role of trustee of the charity.[27]

The Charity Commissioners have stated that they will therefore examine carefully **9.17** any proposal to appoint a local authority a sole trustee of a charitable trust. They will accept such an appointment only if they are satisfied, after having considered all other possibilities, that such appointment would be the most beneficial arrangement for the charity having regard to the need to avoid conflicts of interests to safeguard the charity's property, and the interests of the beneficiaries. Furthermore, when the Commissioners make a scheme for some other purpose in relation to a charity which is administered by a local authority as sole trustee, they have stated that they will consider whether other trusteeship arrangements might not be more appropriate. In suitable cases, the Charity Commissioners will suggest to the local authority that it might retire in favour of a body of individual trustees, through perhaps retaining the right to appoint some of those trustees.[28]

C. Appointment, retirement, and removal of charity trustees

(1) Power to appoint, re-appoint, or remove trustees

Express power in the governing instrument

The governing instrument will usually specify the names of the initial trustees; it **9.18** may also specify who has the power to appoint, re-appoint, or remove a trustee. In

---

[24] (1993) 1 Decisions 29 (para 9)
[25] ibid
[26] [1991] Ch Com Rep 8 (para 44)
[27] ibid, 9 (para 44)
[28] (1993) 1 Decisions 29 (para 9)

the case of a charity set up by a settlor inter vivos, the trust deed will sometimes reserve a power of appointment to the settlor during his lifetime.

9.19 The names and particulars of the initial directors of a charitable company must be contained in a statement delivered to the Registrar of Companies with the memorandum.[29] The statement must be signed by the subscribers to the memorandum and must contain the signed consent to act of each person named as director.[30] The initial directors are also usually named in the articles of association; alternatively the articles may provide that the first directors are to be the subscribers to the memorandum.[31] The model articles in Table A provide for all the directors to retire from office at the first annual general meeting.[32]

9.20 The articles of a charitable company will also usually provide for the appointment of future directors and for the retirement of directors by rotation.[33] The articles will usually confer on the existing directors a power to fill a vacancy or to appoint an additional director, in each case by co-opting any person who is qualified to be a charity trustee.[34]

9.21 The governing instruments of some charities provide for one or more of the trustees to be appointed by a particular body or organization. A person appointed pursuant to such a power is sometimes known as a 'nominative' or 'representative' trustee.[35] The Charity Commissioners have commented that a nominative power can be useful in enabling vacancies to be filled more swiftly, and in ensuring that the trustees represent a cross-section of the community or of users of the facilities which are to be provided; but nominative trusteeships can give rise to potential conflicts of interests, which are discussed more fully below.[36] The use of the expression 'representative trustee' in governing instruments is best avoided, since it can mislead (and apparently has in fact misled) some trustees so designated into believing that they are the representatives of the interests of the body which appointed them;[37] whereas, to avoid a breach of trust, they must, as trustees, act in the interests of the charity itself.[38]

---

[29] Companies Act 1985, s 10(2)(a)
[30] ibid, s 10(3)
[31] See, eg, Art 3.3 of the Memorandum and Articles of Association for a Charitable Company Limited by Guarantee produced on behalf of the CLA
[32] Companies (Tables A to F) Regulations 1985, SI 1985/805, Table A, reg 73
[33] See, eg, ibid, regs 73–80
[34] See, eg, Art 3.7 of the CLA's Memorandum and Articles of Association for a Charitable Company Limited by Guarantee
[35] See [1991] Ch Com Rep 8 (para 41)
[36] See below, para 9.128
[37] [1991] Ch Com Rep 8 (para 41), where the Charity Commissioners note that a number of cases arose during the year which suggested that there might be confusion in the minds of certain Representative or Nominative Trustees as to their role and function
[38] ibid (para 42)

If the trustees have a power to appoint a trustee, the continuing trustees may re- **9.22** appoint an outgoing trustee at the end of his term of office; but only if the number of continuing trustees is at least the minimum number required under the governing instrument to be trustees and to form a quorum.[39]

Even if a purported appointment of a trustee is defective, a purported appointee **9.23** who intermeddles in the trust by doing acts characteristic of a trustee can incur liability for breach of trust as a constructive trustee.[40] A defective appointment will not prevent a purported appointee from being a 'charity trustee' for the purposes of the Charities Act 1993 if he is one of 'the persons having the general control and management of the administration of the charity'.[41] The definition is clearly satisfied by one who has *de facto* general control and management, even though his acts are not clothed with any shred of legal authority. The votes of a person whose appointment as trustee is defective are void.[42] In order to prevent the decisions of trustees' meetings being invalidated by the vote of such a person, the charity's governing instrument may provide that a technical defect in the appointment of a trustee does not invalidate decisions taken by the trustees, provided the trustees are unaware of the defect at the time.[43]

Statutory powers

Trustees of charitable trusts

Subject to any express power in the trust instrument, a trustee may be appointed **9.24** under the statutory power in section 36(1) of the Trustee Act 1925. The statutory power to appoint a new trustee arises where an existing trustee is dead, or remains out of the United Kingdom for more than twelve months, or desires to be discharged, or refuses or is unfit to act, or is incapable of acting, or is an infant. In these circumstances, more than one new trustee can be appointed, with the result that the total number of trustees may be increased. The power to appoint under the section is conferred on the person nominated for that purpose by the trust instrument, and subject thereto on the surviving or continuing trustee or trustees or the personal representatives of the last such trustee.

Under section 36(6) of the Trustee Act 1925, one or more additional trustees may **9.25** be appointed even where no vacancy in the trusteeship arises. Such additional appointments can be made under this power where there are not more than three trustees (none of them being a trust corporation). The power to appoint is

---

[39] [1986] Ch Com Rep 27 (para 6)
[40] *Pearce v Pearce* (1856) 22 Beav 248
[41] CA 1993, s 97(1)
[42] *Pearce v Pearce* (1856) 22 Beav 248
[43] See the model constitutions for charities produced on behalf of the CLA: Trust Deed for a Charitable Trust, cl 4.9; Constitution for a Charitable Unincorporated Association, r 6.7; Memorandum and Articles of Association for a Charitable Company Limited by Guarantee, Art 3.8

similarly conferred on the person nominated in the trust instrument, subject to which it is exercisable by the trustee or trustees for the time being.

9.26 These provisions apply, however, only to trustees in the strict sense; they cannot therefore be used to appoint directors of a charitable corporation.

Directors of charitable companies

9.27 A director of a charitable company may be removed at any time by ordinary resolution, notwithstanding anything in the articles or in any agreement between the director and the company.[44]

Appointment or removal by the Charity Commissioners

9.28 The jurisdiction of the Charity Commissioners derives from the Charities Act 1993. The Charity Commissioners have the same jurisdiction and powers as the High Court for the purpose of appointing or removing a charity trustee or trustee for a charity.[45] They cannot, however, exercise this jurisdiction except on an application of the charity, or on an order of the court directing a scheme for the administration of a charity,[46] or (except in the case of an exempt charity) on the application of the Attorney-General.[47] If, however, the charity is not an exempt charity and its income does not exceed £500 a year, the Charity Commissioners may exercise their jurisdiction to appoint or remove a trustee on the application of any one or more of the charity trustees, or of any person interested in the charity, or of any two or more inhabitants of the area of the charity if it is a local charity.[48]

9.29 The Charity Commissioners may appoint, suspend, or remove a charity trustee or charity trustees of their own motion in various special circumstances. They may do so where they have instituted an inquiry[49] and are satisfied that there has been misconduct or mismanagement in the administration of the charity or that it is necessary or desirable to act to protect the property of the charity or for securing a proper application for the purposes of the charity of that property or of property coming to the charity.[50]

9.30 The Charity Commissioners may also remove a charity trustee by order of their own motion where, within the last five years, the trustee, having previously been

[44] Companies Act 1985, s 303
[45] CA 1993, s 16(1)(b). *Sed quaere*, whether this enables the Charity Commissioners to appoint or remove directors of a charitable corporation: see discussion of inherent jurisdiction of High Court below, paras 9.32–9.35
[46] ie under CA 1993, s 16(2)
[47] ibid, s 16(4)
[48] ibid, s 16(5)
[49] Under ibid, s 8
[50] ibid, s 18(1)(i) (suspension); s 18(1)(ii) (appointment of additional charity trustees); s 18(2)(ii) (removal of trustee or charitable trustee responsible for or privy to the misconduct or mismanagement or who has by his conduct contributed to it or facilitated it)

adjudged bankrupt, or had his estate sequestered, has been discharged; or, having previously made a composition or arrangement with, or granted a trust deed for, his creditors, has been discharged in respect of it; where the trustee is a corporation in liquidation; where the trustee is incapable of acting by reason of mental disorder within the meaning of the Mental Health Act 1983; where the trustee has not acted, and will not declare his willingness or unwillingness to act; or where the trustee is outside England and Wales, or cannot be found, or does not act, and his absence or failure to act impedes the proper administration of the charity.[51]

The Charity Commissioners may by order made of their own motion appoint a person to be a charity trustee:[52]   **9.31**

    (a) in place of a charity trustee removed by them under [section 18] or otherwise;

    (b) where there are no charity trustees, or where by reason of vacancies in their number or the absence or incapacity of any of their number the charity cannot apply for the appointment;

    (c) where there is a single charity trustee, not being a corporation aggregate, and the Commissioners are of opinion that it is necessary to increase the number for the proper administration of the charity;

    (d) where the Commissioners are of opinion that it is necessary for the proper administration of the charity to have an additional charity trustee because one of the existing charity trustees who ought nevertheless to remain a charity trustee either cannot be found or does not act or is outside England and Wales.

High Court

The High Court has an inherent jurisdiction to appoint a trustee or to remove a trustee who has committed a breach of trust or whose continuance as trustee would be detrimental to the trust. The power derives from the court's jurisdiction over trusts, and is therefore clearly exercisable where the charity exists as a charitable trust. In practice, the court may well be unlikely to exercise its inherent jurisdiction other than in the circumstances contemplated by the Charities Act 1993 for the removal of a charity trustee by the Charity Commissioners of their own motion.[53] That the courts should not be eager to remove charity trustees who are doing their best is evident from the following observations of Neuberger J:[54]   **9.32**

---

[51] ibid, s 18(4)

[52] ibid, s 18(5)

[53] ie ibid, s 18(2). See *Scargill v Charity Commissioners* (High Ct, 4 Sept 1998) 132 of official jdgt (Neuberger J); *Letterstedt v Broers* (1884) 9 App Cas 371, 385–7, 389–90 (Lord Blackburn)

[54] *Scargill v Charity Commissioners* (High Ct, 4 Sept 1998) 133 of official jdgt. On the facts of the case before him, however, Neuberger J upheld the Charity Commissioners' order to remove Scargill and a co-trustee because they had (inter alia) required the charity to make a sustantial grant to another charity despite the fact that such a grant required (as they knew, and as had been drawn to their attention more than once) the consent of another body, and that such consent (as they also knew) had not been obtained

I think it is legitimate for the court [to] bear in mind that making or upholding an order removing a person as charitable trustee could, at least in some circumstances, discourage people who might otherwise be prepared to do that which is self-evident [*sic*] in the public interest, namely to act as charitable trustees. It would be wrong to require unrealistically high standards of legal skill, financial analysis, or detailed factual knowledge, from charitable trustees. The court should, in principle, not be anxious to find fault with charitable trustees who, while doing their best, make honest, even stupid, mistakes.

9.33   If the charity is an unincorporated association, the persons in whom the charity's assets are vested (who are usually called 'the trustees') will be trustees for this purpose. It does not matter whether such 'trustees' are also the persons who are empowered to make decisions with regard to the application of the assets, or are merely holding them subject to the directions of another body of persons. Similarly, it is not necessary to determine the precise juridical nature of the trusts involved (that is, whether the charitable trusts are express or implied) since the property is undoubtedly held upon trust, and that is itself sufficient to give the court jurisdiction.

9.34   It is less clear whether the High Court has inherent jurisdiction to appoint a 'trustee' of an incorporated charity. There appears to be no reported case where this has been done. The uncertainty is the result of the broader problem concerning the jurisdiction of the High Court over charitable corporations, which is considered in chapter 11. The starting point is section 16(1) of the Charities Act 1993, which gives the Charity Commissioners 'the same jurisdiction and powers as are exercisable by the High Court in charity proceedings' (inter alia) for the purpose of 'appointing, discharging or removing a charity trustee or trustee for a charity'.[55] A charity trustee for this purpose indisputably includes a director of a charitable company.[56] Section 16(1) might be supposed to be based on the premise that the High Court does have jurisdiction and power to appoint and remove a director of a charitable company. If, however, it is considered that the High Court has no such jurisdiction, the section could be interpreted to deny such jurisdiction to the Charity Commissioners also. Set against this, section 18 expressly confers on the Charity Commissioners in certain circumstances a jurisdiction and power of their own motion to appoint and remove 'charity trustees'. The section 18 jurisdiction, unlike that in section 16, is not expressed to be coextensive with that of the High Court; and from this it might be inferred that the Commissioners' jurisdiction under section 18 is intended to be wider than that under section 16. This points to the conclusion that the High Court has no inherent jurisdiction to appoint or remove directors of charitable corporations.

---

[55]   CA 1993, s 16(1)(b)
[56]   See ibid, s 97(1) (definition of 'charity trustee'), s 96(1) (definition of 'charity')

The High Court also has a statutory jurisdiction under section 41(1) of the **9.35** Trustee Act 1925 to appoint a new trustee or trustees of any trust where it is found inexpedient, difficult, or impracticable to do so without the court's assistance. Unless proceedings are already before the court, the application to the court to appoint a new trustee requires the prior consent of the Charity Commissioners.[57] The Trustee Act 1925 applies, however, only to trusts, and does not therefore confer a statutory jurisdiction to appoint new directors of a charitable company.

Parochial charities

Where the charity trustees of a parochial charity in a parish, not being an ecclesias- **9.36** tical charity nor a charity founded within the preceding forty years, do not include persons elected by the local government electors, ratepayers, or inhabitants of the parish or appointed by the parish council or parish meeting, the parish council or parish meeting may appoint additional charity trustees, to such number as the Charity Commissioners may allow.[58] If there is a sole charity trustee not so elected or appointed of any such charity, the number of charity trustees may, with the approval of the Charity Commissioners, be increased to three, of whom one may be nominated by the sole trustee and one by the parish council or parish meeting.[59]

(2) Disclaimer

A person cannot be compelled to accept the office of trustee without his consent.[60] **9.37** A person appointed a trustee against his will is entitled to disclaim.[61] To provide clear evidence, a disclaimer should be effected by deed,[62] but it may also be inferred from conduct.[63] A person appointed a trustee will be deemed to have accepted if he performs acts characteristic of a trustee.[64] Once he has accepted office, a trustee cannot disclaim.[65] For the avoidance of doubt as to whether a person appointed a trustee has accepted or not, the trust instrument might oblige a future trustee on appointment to sign a declaration of willingness to act as a trustee of the trust. The model charity constitution prepared on behalf of the Charity Law Association obliges a future trustee to sign such a declaration before being eligible to vote at meetings of trustees.[66]

---

[57] ibid, s 33
[58] ibid, s 79(2)
[59] ibid
[60] *Robinson v Pett* (1734) 3 P Wms 249
[61] *Re Birchall* (1889) 40 ChD 436
[62] *Re Schär* [1951] Ch 280
[63] *Re Clout and Frewer's Contract* [1924] 2 Ch 230
[64] *Conyngham v Conyngham* (1750) 1 Ves Sen 522
[65] *Re Lister* [1926] Ch 149
[66] Trust Deed for a Charitable Trust, cl 4.6. Equivalent provisions applicable to Committee members and directors are contained in the CLA's other model constitutions: Constitution for a Charitable Unincorporated Association, r 6.4; Memorandum and Articles of Association for a Charitable Company Limited by Guarantee, Art 3.4

(3) Maintaining charity trustees' numbers

9.38 If the governing instrument specifies a minimum number of charity trustees or a minimum number to comprise a quorum at charity trustees' meetings,[67] the charity trustees must ensure that their number does not fall below that specified. In the absence of any such requirement in the governing instrument, the trustees should ensure that their number is kept up, in the words of the Charity Commissioners, 'to an effective working strength', having regard to the administrative requirements of the charity and the legal rule[68] (unless modified by the governing instrument) requiring a decision to be made by a majority of a charity's trustees.[69] It may be necessary or desirable to appoint a new trustee when an existing trustee retires or dies; but the existing trustees should be mindful that it can sometimes be advantageous to appoint an additional trustee increase the number of trustees. The Charity Commissioners have stated that the addition of a new trustee to the trustee body can often provide fresh insight into the way the charity is being administered. They also express the view that the appointment of an additional trustee can help to avoid the situation where a dominant personality, who may not even be a trustee, effectively takes control of a charity and acts without regard and referral to the legally appointed trustees.[70]

(4) Term of appointment

9.39 In many instances, the governing instrument will itself state the term for which trustees should hold office. This may be either for life, or for a lesser period. In the case of a charitable trust, the settlor may consider it appropriate to appoint the first trustees for life; alternatively, the trust instrument might specify that the first and future trustees should hold office for a specified number of years, subject to earlier removal or retirement.[71] In order to ensure continuity, it may be desirable to appoint the first trustees for terms of different lengths.[72]

9.40 Life appointments as directors are less appropriate in the case of a charitable company. The articles may appoint a director to office for a specified number of years. Alternatively, the appointments may be for an unspecified term, but subject to a

---

[67] See eg, Art 4.2 of the Memorandum and Articles of Association for a Charitable Company Limited by Guarantee, cl 5.2 of the Trust Deed for a Charitable Trust, and cl 7.2 (Committee Meetings) of the Constitution for a Charitable Unincorporated Association, produced on behalf of the CLA

[68] *Re Whiteley* [1910] 1 Ch 600, 608

[69] [1986] Ch Com Rep 26–7 (para 5)

[70] [1993] Ch Com Rep 21 (para 84)

[71] See alternative options for cl 4.3, and cl 4.4, of the Trust Deed for a Charitable Trust produced on behalf of the CLA

[72] ibid, cl 4.3, and see Notes thereto (ibid, p 10)

requirement that a proportion of the board retires at each annual general meeting, with those who have served longest retiring first.[73]

If the governing instrument does not specify a time limit for appointments, the **9.41** appointment of a trustee will be for that person's life, or until his resignation or bankruptcy, or until the occurrence of some other legally disabling circumstance.[74] In practice, trustees appointed by local authorities under the provisions of section 79 of the Charities Act 1993 are normally appointed for a term of four years.[75]

(5) Retirement and resignation

A method of resignation may be specified in the charity's governing documents. **9.42** Such a clause may provide for resignation to be effected by notice in writing given to the charity trustees; but, in order to prevent the number of trustees falling below an acceptable number, the power to resign should be conditional upon there being at least two charity trustees (which, in the case of a charitable corporation, means at least two directors) who will remain in office.[76] A potential drawback of retirement by notice in accordance with a procedure laid down in the trust instrument is that such retirement will not activate the vesting provisions of the Trustee Act 1925.[77] If, therefore, the charity's assets include land which is vested in the names of the trustees, it will still be necessary to convey the land out of the names of the old trustees into the names of the continuing (and any new) trustees. In the absence of such conveyance, the retiring trustee will not have been effectively discharged.

No conveyance is needed if the retirement occurs on the appointment of a new **9.43** trustee by deed,[78] or if the trustee retires by deed under section 39 of the Trustee Act 1925.[79] A trustee of a charitable trust may retire in accordance with section 36(1) of that Act where a new trustee is appointed in his place.[80] Such a trustee may also retire under section 39(1) of the same Act without any new trustee being appointed to replace him. The latter sub-section enables a trustee to be discharged from the trust where, after his discharge, either at least two individual trustees or a trust corporation will remain as trustees. The retiring trustee will be discharged

---

[73] See, eg, Art 3.5 of the Memorandum and Articles of Association for a Charitable Company Limited by Guarantee produced on behalf of the CLA. This provides for one-third of the board to retire at each AGM

[74] [1986] Ch Com Rep 27 (para 6)

[75] ibid, referring to the predecessor of the CA 1993, s 79, viz CA 1960, s 37

[76] See, eg, cl 4.7.4 of the Trust Deed for a Charitable Trust, and Art 3.6.5 of the Memorandum and Articles of Association for a Charitable Company Limited by Guarantee, produced on behalf of the CLA

[77] TA 1925, s 40

[78] ibid, s 40(1)

[79] ibid, s 40(2)

[80] Discussed above, para 9.24

if he executes a deed declaring his desire to be discharged from the trust, provided that his co-trustees (and any other person who is empowered to appoint trustees) by deed consent to the discharge of the trustee and to the vesting of the trust property in the co-trustees alone.

9.44 A trustee who retires is entitled to an indemnity from the trust fund in respect of any liabilities properly incurred whilst a trustee. By way of reminder, however, it is worthwhile specifying such a right in the governing instrument.[81]

9.45 A trustee remains liable for breaches of trust committed during his period of office as trustee, even after he ceases to be a trustee. A trustee is not liable for breaches of trust committed after he ceased to be a trustee unless he retired in order to facilitate a breach of trust.[82] The same principle probably applies to directors who retire in order to facilitate a breach of fiduciary duty by their co-directors.

9.46 Under general principles of company law, even if the articles of a company contain no express power, a director may resign irrevocably merely by giving notice to the secretary,[83] and acceptance of even an oral notice of resignation is valid, despite anything in the articles, if it is accepted by the general meeting.[84] These principles would appear to be equally applicable to charitable companies.

(6) Recording appointments, removals, and resignations

9.47 To help to ensure that the body of trustees is legally constituted at all times, the Charity Commissioners recommend that a record be kept of the date on which and the method by which each trustee is appointed or re-appointed and the date on which a trustee ceases to hold office, whether through resignation, death, formal removal, or disqualification.[85]

Effect of memorandum of appointment or discharge of trustee of a charitable trust

9.48 In the nineteenth century, many non-conformist chapels existed as trusts, often with more than twenty trustees. The terms of such trusts traditionally gave the right to appoint new trustees to the congregation (that is, to the general members of the chapel). In practice, such a system could cause conveyancing problems when it came to disposing of the congregation's land, since the purchaser would have to satisfy himself that he was taking a conveyance from trustees who had been properly appointed. This problem was overcome in a series of statutes from

---

[81] See, eg, clause cl 4.8 of the Trust Deed for a Charitable Trust produced by the CLA
[82] *Head v Gould* [1898] 2 Ch 250
[83] *Maitland's* case (1853) 4 De GM & G 769
[84] *Latchford Premier Cinema Ltd v Ennion* [1931] 2 Ch 409
[85] [1993] Ch Com Rep 23 (para 88)

1850,[86] under which a memorandum by deed of the appointment by the meeting was conclusive evidence that the appointment had been duly made. The original Act applied to land held by trustees of a congregation or body of person for religious or educational purposes, and these purposes were extended in later Acts. These statutes were repealed on 1 January 1961, although they continued to have effect as regards land held upon trusts subject to their provisions at that date.[87]

The statutes were, however, replaced by provisions of general application (that is, provisions not limited to trusts for certain religious and educational charities) which are now contained in section 83 of the Charities Act 1993. This section provides that where, under the trusts of a charity, trustees of property held for the purposes of the charity may be appointed or discharged by resolution of a meeting of the charity trustees, members, or other persons, a memorandum declaring a trustee to have been so appointed or discharged shall be sufficient evidence of that fact if the memorandum is signed either at the meeting by the person presiding or in some other manner directed by the meeting and is attested by two persons present at the meeting.[88] Where a document purports to have been so signed and attested, then on proof (whether by evidence or as a matter of presumption) of the signature, the document is presumed to have been so signed and attested unless the contrary is shown.[89] Provided the memorandum is executed as a deed, it has the like operation under section 40 of the Trustee Act 1925 to vest the trust property in the new and continuing trustees as if the appointment or discharge had been effected by deed.[90]

9.49

D. Disqualification from acting as a charity trustee or trustee for a charity

(1) Disqualifying circumstances

Certain persons are prohibited from acting as a charity trustee or as a trustee for a charity. A person who has been convicted of any offence involving dishonesty or deception (excluding a spent conviction under the Rehabilitation of Offenders Act 1974) is disqualified;[91] so is an undischarged bankrupt and a person sequestration of whose estate has been ordered and who has not been discharged,[92]

9.50

---

[86] These were: the Trustees Appointment Act 1850 (13 & 14 Vict c 28) (Sir Mortin Peto's Act); the Trustees Appointment Act 1869 (32 & 33 Vict c 26); and the Trustees Appointment Act 1890 (53 & 54 Vict c 19) (Fowler's Act)

[87] See CA 1960, s 35(6). But the continuing effect of the repealed statutes is in doubt: see H Picarda, *The Law and Practice Relating to Charities* (3rd edn, Butterworths, 1999) 460–1

[88] CA 1993, s 83(1)

[89] ibid, s 83(3)

[90] ibid, s 83(2)

[91] ibid, s 72(1)(a)

[92] ibid, s 72(1)(b)

unless leave has been granted under section 11 of the Company Directors Disqualification Act 1986 for him to act as a director of the charity. Similarly disqualified is a person who has made a composition or arrangement with, or granted a trust deed for, his creditors and has not been discharged in respect of it.[93]

9.51 Disqualification also applies to a person who has been removed from the office of charity trustee or trustee for a charity by an order made by the Charity Commissioners[94] or by the High Court, on grounds of any misconduct or mismanagement in the administration of the charity for which he was responsible or to which he was privy, or which he by his conduct contributed to or facilitated.[95] The Charity Commissioners must keep a register of all persons removed from office on this ground;[96] and such register must be available for public inspection.[97]

9.52 Also disqualified is a person who has been removed[98] by the Court of Session in Scotland from being concerned in the management or control of any body.[99]

9.53 A person who is subject to a disqualification order under the Company Directors Disqualification Act 1986[100] or to any order made under section 429(2)(b) of the Insolvency Act 1986 (failure to pay under county court administration order) is also disqualified,[101] unless leave under the order has been granted for him to act as a director of the charity.[102]

(2) Waiver of disqualification

9.54 Except in one instance, the Charity Commissioners have power to waive a disqualification upon the application of the disqualified person. A waiver may be either general, or in relation to a particular charity or a particular class of charities.[103] The exception is that no such waiver can be granted in relation to any charity which is a company if the person concerned is prohibited from acting as a director of the charity by virtue of a disqualification order under the Company Directors Disqualification Act 1986, or under sections 11(1) or 12(2) of that Act (undischarged bankrupts; failure to pay under county court administration order).[104]

---

93 CA 1993, s 72(1)(c)
94 Under ibid, s 18(2)(i), or its statutory predecessor, CA 1960, s 20(1)
95 CA 1993, s 72(1(d)
96 ibid, s 72(6)
97 ibid, s 72(7)
98 Under the Law Reform (Miscellaneous Provisions) (Scotland) Act 1990, s 7
99 CA 1993, s 72(1)(e)
100 Discussed further below, paras 9.58–9.60
101 CA 1993, s 72(1)(f)
102 ibid, s 72(3)
103 ibid, s 72(4)
104 ibid

It is thought that the power of waiver might be appropriately used, for instance, to **9.55**
enable a former prisoner to act as a trustee of a charitable trust to provide assistance in the rehabilitation of offenders.

(3) Effect of acting while disqualified

A person who acts as a charity trustee or a trustee for a charity while disqualified **9.56**
commits an offence, for which the maximum penalty is two years' imprisonment
or a fine (or both) on conviction on indictment.[105] No such offence is committed,
however, where the charity concerned is a company and the disqualification is
under section 72(1) paragraphs (b) (bankrupty) or (f) (company director's
disqualification order or failure to pay under county court administration order)
only.[106]

Any acts done as a charity trustee or as trustee for a charity by a disqualified per- **9.57**
son are not invalid by reason only of the disqualification.[107] The Charity
Commissioners are, however, empowered by order to direct a disqualified person
to repay to the charity the whole or any part of any sums (or to pay the monetary
value of any benefits) received by way of remuneration, expenses or benefit in kind
received while he was acting as a charity trustee or trustee for a charity,[108] but only
in respect of the time when he was disqualified.[109]

(4) Disqualification of company directors

As has been mentioned above, a director subject to a disqualification order under **9.58**
the Company Directors Disqualification Act 1986 is automatically disqualified
from being a charity trustee or a trustee for a charity under the Charities Act
1993.[110]

A person may be disqualified from being a director of a company by order of the **9.59**
court on a number of specified grounds. These comprise: conviction of an
indictable offence in connection with the promotion, formation, management, or
liquidation of a company or with the management of its property;[111] persistent
default in making returns or delivering accounts or other documents to the
Registrar of Companies;[112] that he has been guilty (whether or not he has been
convicted) of fraudulent trading[113] or (whilst an officer or liquidator of a company) of any other fraud in relation to the company or breach of his duty as such

---

[105] ibid, s 73(1)
[106] ibid, s 73(2). For disqualification under s 72(1) paras (b) or (f), see above, paras 9.50 and 9.53
[107] CA 1993, s 73(3)
[108] ibid, s 73(4)
[109] ibid, s 73(5)
[110] ibid, s 72(1)(f)
[111] Company Directors Disqualification Act 1986, s 2
[112] ibid, s 3
[113] ie under Companies Act 1985, s 458

officer or liquidator;[114] unfitness (where the court is satisfied that he has been a director of a company that has become insolvent and that his conduct while director, either of that company alone or taken together with his conduct as director of any other company, makes him unfit to be concerned in the management of a company);[115] and where he has been found liable to contribute to the assets of the company on grounds of wrongful or fraudulent trading.[116]

9.60 It will be noted that, whilst bankruptcy is not itself a ground for disqualification from being a director of a company under the Company Directors Disqualification Act 1986, it is a ground for disqualification from being a charity trustee or a trustee for a charity under the Charities Act 1993.[117]

E. Incorporation of charity trustees

9.61 Incorporation of the charity trustees refers to incorporating the body of trustees themselves. This does not result in the incorporation of the charity, which may continue to exist in the form of a trust. Incorporation of the trustees results in the trustees becoming a separate and continuing entity, distinct from the persons who from time to time occupy the position of trustees. This has the advantage that it becomes unnecessary, upon a change of trustees, to vest the charity's assets into the names of the new and continuing trustees. Incorporation by charity trustees was first made possible in 1872,[118] but it was from the start very little used. Between 1872 and 1960, it appears that only 55 charitable trustees were incorporated under that Act.[119] The reason for the Act's neglect appears to be that it expressly provided that incorporation of the trustees as a body corporate did not remove their personal liability as trustees; whereas incorporation of the charity itself (which had been possible since the Companies Act 1862) could achieve this end. Furthermore, the problem of having to vest assets in new trustees could be overcome by vesting them in the Official Custodian for Charities. Additionally, as one commentator has pointed out, the concept of an unincorporated charity having incorporated trustees is difficult to grasp and may confuse the trustees.[120]

9.62 The 1872 Act was repealed in 1992, but its provisions were re-enacted with modifications now contained in Part VII of the Charities Act 1993. The Charity

---

[114] Company Directors Disqualification Act 1986, s 4
[115] ibid, ss 6–9
[116] ibid, s 10
[117] CA 1993, s 72(1)(b)
[118] Under the Charitable Trustees Incorporation Act 1872
[119] The figure is quoted by H Picarda, *The Law and Practice Relating to Charities* (3rd edn, Butterworths, 1999) 431
[120] See Judith Hill, 'The Trust Versus the Company under the CA 1992 & 1993', (1993–4) 2 CL & PR 133, 139

Commissioners are empowered to grant the trustees of a charity a certificate of
incorporation upon an application to them by the trustees of the charity if the
Charity Commissioners consider that incorporation would be in the interests of
the charity.[121] The certificate may be granted subject to such conditions or directions as the Commissioners think fit to insert.[122]

On the grant of such certificate, the trustees of the charity become a body corpo- **9.63**
rate known by such name as is specified in the certificate.[123] After incorporation,
the trustees may sue and be sued in their corporate name.[124] Documents can be
executed by the corporate body by affixing its common seal (if it has one), by being
signed by the majority of the trustees and expressed (in whatever form of words)
to be executed by the body, or by any two or more of the trustees who may be
authorized by the trustees to execute documents in the name and on behalf of the
body of the trustees.[125]

The Charity Commissioners also have powers to amend the certificate of incor- **9.64**
poration (either on the application of the corporate body or of their own
motion).[126] They may also dissolve the incorporated body in certain circumstances, such as where it has no assets or does not operate or where the purposes of
the charity have been achieved or are incapable of being achieved.[127]

The concept of incorporating the trustees gained a new (if somewhat short-lived) **9.65**
lease of life as a result of the winding up, following the Charities Act 1992,[128] of
most of the functions of the Official Custodian for Charities. As a result of that
Act, the Official Custodian was required to divest herself of assets (other than
land) held on behalf of charities, and to re-transfer them to the charities concerned. The Charity Commissioners indicated to charity trustees that incorporation as a body corporate could be a solution to the problem of vesting; and some
use appears to have been made of this device.[129] Following the completion of the
divesting by the Official Custodian, however, the provisions appear again to have
fallen into desuetude. There are, moreover, alternative ways in which trustees can
cope with the vesting of trust assets without having to incorporate themselves as a
separate body, or to incorporate the charity itself.[130] First, use could be made of

---

[121] CA 1993, s 50(1)
[122] ibid, s 50(1)
[123] ibid, s 50(3)(a)
[124] ibid, s 50(4)(a)
[125] ibid, s 60
[126] ibid, s 56(1)
[127] ibid, s 61(1)
[128] CA 1992, ss 29–30
[129] See H Picarda, *The Law and Practice Relating to Charities* (3rd edn, Butterworths, 1999) 432,
n 10, stating that from 1 Jan 1993 to 8 June 1995, 130 certificates were issued
[130] See further, Judith Hill, 'The Trust Versus the Company under the CA 1992 & 1993',
(1993–4) 2 CL & PR 133, 138–9

another custodian trustee[131] (a trust corporation can be a custodian trustee, holding the property but leaving the decisions to the management trustees); unlike the Official Custodian for Charities, however, who has no power to charge fees,[132] a professional custodian trustee is likely to charge a fee commensurate with the skill and work involved. Before the Trustee Act 2000, a power in the trust instrument was needed to use a custodian trustee or a holding trustee, but the Charity Commissioners would readily permit the instrument to be amended to include it. Since the Trustee Act 2000, trustees have a default power to appoint a custodian;[133] but, except in the case of an exempt charity, the trustees of a charitable trust must, in selecting the custodian, act in accordance with any guidance given by the Charity Commissioners.[134] Secondly, the Official Custodian for Charities could vest the charity's assets in the names of nominees.[135] Before the Trustee Act 2000, a power in the trust instrument was needed to vest replacement assets in the names of the nominees when the original assets transferred to the nominees were sold; but, again, the Charity Commissioners were prepared to permit an amendment to the instrument to include such a power. Since the Trustee Act 2000, trustees have a default power to appoint a nominee;[136] but, except in the case of an exempt charity, the trustees of a charitable trust must, in selecting the nominee, act in accordance with any guidance given by the Charity Commissioners.[137]

F. Managing, custodian, and holding trustees

9.66 The functions of trustees can be divided between managing trustees, who are responsible for the management of the charitable trust, and a custodian or holding trustee, in whom the charity's assets are vested, but who takes no part in its management. The advantages of such a division are to avoid the need to vest the charity's assets in the new and continuing trustees every time there is a change of trustees,[138] and also to achieve a greater degree of security for the charity's assets.

9.67 A custodian trustee must be distinguished from a mere nominee. Charity trustees may vest trusts assets (such as shares) in a nominee if the governing instrument itself permits. In the absence of such express power, an appointment of a nominee

---

[131] Public Trustee Act 1906
[132] CA 1993, s 22(1)
[133] TA 2000, s 17
[134] ibid, s 19(4)
[135] CA 1992, s 29(5)
[136] TA 2000, s 16
[137] ibid, s 19(4)
[138] An advantage that can be also achieved by incorporating the trustees as a corporation under CA 1993, Pt VII

before the Trustee Act 2000 required an order of the Charity Commissioners;[139] but such an order is now sought less frequently, since the Trustee Act 2000 has given trustees a statutory power to appoint a nominee.[140] Since a charity trustee who appoints a nominee is not himself a beneficial owner, it seems (although the matter is the subject of dispute) that any transfer of the charity's assets to the nominee does not give rise to a bare trust; rather, the nominee is the trustee's agent.[141] Like a custodian trustee, the nominee may be subject to assessorial liability as a constructive trustee if he dishonestly assists the trustee in a breach of trust.[142] If a nominee is considered to be merely an agent of the charity trustee, the fiduciary duties imposed on him are in some respects less stringent than those imposed on a custodian trustee, who is after all a trustee.[143]

It is important to distinguish between a custodian trustee in the strict sense, the **9.68** appointment of which is authorized by statute, under the Public Trustee Act 1906,[144] and a holding trustee[145] (often confusingly also called a custodian trustee), whose appointment derives from the trust instrument itself. The duty of care under the Trustee Act 2000[146] applies to a trustee when appointing a person to act as a custodian and when reviewing the acts of a custodian;[147] but the expression 'custodian' is there used in contradistinction to a 'custodian trustee'[148] and appears to refer to certain bodies which are not custodian trustees for the purposes of the Public Trustee Act 1906.[149]

(1) Custodian trustee appointed under the Public Trustee Act 1906

A custodian trustee appointed under the Public Trustee Act 1906 means any **9.69** banking or insurance company, or other body corporate entitled to act by virtue

---

[139] ie an order under CA 1993, s 26. The Charity Commissioners took the view that TA 1925, s 23 (now repealed by TA 2000), did not authorize charity trustees to appoint nominees: see (1994) 2 Decisions 30

[140] TA 2000, s 16(1)(a). If the charitable trust is not an exempt charity, the trustees must act in accordance with any guidance issued by the Charity Commissioners: ibid, s 19(4). See further ch 16, paras 16.69–16.71

[141] Contrast *Underhill & Hayton's Law of Trusts and Trustees* (ed DJ Hayton) (15th edn, Butterworths, 1995) 778–9; and *Hanbury & Martin's Modern Equity* (ed JE Martin) (15th edn, Sweet & Maxwell, 1997) 69–70

[142] *Royal Brunei Airlines Ltd v Tan* [1995] 2 AC 378 (PC)

[143] eg it seems that the 'self-dealing rule', under which a purchase by a trustee of the trust property is voidable automatically, does not apply to a purchase from the trust by an agent acting for the trustees, since such a person is not both vendor and purchaser, and the court will permit the sale to stand if satisfied that the fiduciary did not abuse his position, made full disclosure, and paid a fair price: see *Holder v Holder* [1968] Ch 353; *Edwards v Meyrick* (1842) 2 Hare 60

[144] Public Trustee Act 1906, s 4(3)

[145] See below, para 9.74

[146] TA 2000, s 1(1)

[147] ibid, Sch 1, para 3(1)(c), (e)

[148] Defined ibid, s 39(1)

[149] See ibid, ss 16–27

of rules made under the Act.[150] Rules have been made authorizing corporations which satisfy specified criteria. The most important categories for the purposes of charitable trusts are:

(a) the Treasury Solicitor;

(b) any corporation which is constituted under the law of the United Kingdom or of any part thereof, or under the law of any other Member State of the European Economic Community or any part thereof, which is empowered by its constitution to undertake trust business, which has at least one place of business in the United Kingdom, and which is either—

   (i) a company incorporated by special Act of Parliament or by Royal charter, or

   (ii) a company registered (with or without limited liability) in the United Kingdom under the Companies Act 1948 or 1985 or under the Companies Act (Northern Ireland) 1960 or in another Member State of the European Economic Community and having a capital (in stock or shares) for the time being issued of not less than £250,000 (or its equivalent in the currency of the State where the company is registered), of which not less than £100,000 (or its equivalent) has been paid up in cash, or

   (iii) a company which is registered without limited liability in the United Kingdom under the Companies Act 1948 or 1985 or the Companies Act (Northern Ireland) 1960 or in another Member State of the European Economic Community and of which one of the members is a company within any of the classes defined in this sub-paragraph;

(c) any corporation which is incorporated by special Act of Parliament or Royal Charter or under the Charitable Trustees Incorporation Act 1872 or the Charities Act 1993 which is empowered by its constitution to act as a trustee for any charitable purposes, but only in relation to trusts in which its constitution empowers it to act;

(d) any corporation which is constituted under the law of the United Kingdom or of any part thereof and having its place of business there, and which is authorized by the Lord Chancellor to act in relation to any charitable, ecclesiastical, or public trusts as a trust corporation, but only in connection with any such trust so authorized;

(e) a local authority,[151] but only in relation to charitable or public trusts (and not trusts for an ecclesiastical charity or for a charity for the relief of

---

[150] Public Trustee Act 1906, ss 4(3) and s 14(1)(f); Public Trustee Rules 1912, r 30; amended and consolidated by SI 1975/1189, and later amended by SI 1976/836, SI 1981/358, SI 1984/109, SI 1985/132, and SI 1987/1891

[151] ie the corporation of any London borough (acting by the council); a county council, district council, parish council, or community council; the Council of the Isles of Scilly; and the Common Council of the City of London

poverty) for the benefit of the inhabitants of the area of the local authority concerned and its neighbourhood, or any part of that area.

The Public Trustee himself, however, is forbidden to accept any trust exclusively for religious or charitable purposes.[152]

The Public Trustee Act 1906 provides that, as between a custodian trustee and the managing trustee, the custodian trustee is to have the custody of all securities and documents of title relating to the trust property, but the managing trustee is to have free access to them and is entitled to copy them.[153] The custodian trustee must concur in the performance of all acts necessary to enable the managing trustees to exercise their powers, including their powers of management, unless the matter in which he is required to concur is a breach of trust or involves personal liability upon him; but, unless he so concurs, the custodian trustee is not liable for any act or default on the part of the managing trustees or any of them.[154] All sums payable to or out of the income or capital of the trust property must be paid to or by the custodian trustee; except that the custodian trustee may allow the income derived from the trust property to be paid to the managing trustees or to such person as they direct, in which case the custodian trustee is not answerable for its loss or misapplication.[155] The power of appointing new trustees, when exercisable by the trustees, is exercisable by the managing trustees alone, but the custodian trustee has the same power of applying to the court for the appointment of a new trustee as any other trustee.[156] In determining the number of trustees for the purposes of the Trustee Act 1925, the custodian trustee is not counted;[157] this is important in relation to those provisions in the Trustee Act 1925 relating to minimum numbers of trustees.[158] **9.70**

A custodian trustee, like other trustees, is not entitled to make an unauthorized profit, and cannot contract with the managing trustees for his own benefit.[159] A custodian trustee appointed under the Public Trustee Act 1906, however, is authorized to charge fees not exceeding those chargeable by the Public Trustee.[160] **9.71**

---

[152] Public Trustee Act 1906, s 2(5); and see *Re Hampton* (1918) 88 LJ Ch 103
[153] Public Trustee Act 1906, s 4(2)(c); and see *IRC v Silverts Ltd* [1951] Ch 521
[154] Public Trustee Act 1906, s 4(2)(d)
[155] ibid, s 4(2)(e)
[156] ibid, s 4(2)(f)
[157] ibid, s 4(2)(g)
[158] eg TA 1925, s 37(1)(c), which states that a trustee will not be discharged unless there will be as trustees either a trust corporation or at least two individuals. The restrictions on maximum numbers of trustees do not apply to a charitable trust: ibid, s 34(3)
[159] *Re Brooke Bond & Co Ltd's Trust Deed* [1963] Ch 357 (where, however, the court permitted the custodian trustee to retain the profit)
[160] Public Trustee Act 1906, s 4(3)

(2) The Official Custodian for Charities

9.72   The Official Custodian for Charities (the Official Custodian) is a corporation sole with perpetual succession, and uses an official seal which is judicially noted.[161] The function of the Official Custodian was reduced under the Charities Act 1992, which required the Official Custodian to divest herself of all property other than land and any other property vested in her under an order of the Charity Commissioners under what is now section 18 of the Charities Act 1993 (power to act for the protection of charities following an inquiry).[162] As trustee of any property vested in him in trust for a charity, the Official Custodian must not exercise any powers of management, but has the same powers, duties, and liabilities, is entitled to the same rights and immunities, and is subject to the control and order of the court, as a custodian trustee appointed under section 4 of the Public Trustee Act 1906.[163] Unlike custodian trustees appointed under the 1906 Act, however, the Official Custodian has no power to charge fees.[164]

9.73   The Official Custodian is not liable as trustee for any charity in respect of any loss or of the misapplication of any property unless it is occasioned by or through the wilful neglect or default of the Official Custodian or of any person acting for him; but the Consolidated Fund is liable to make good to a charity any sums for which the Official Custodian may be liable by reason of any such neglect or default.[165]

(3) Holding trustees

9.74   As has been indicated, many so-called custodian trustees are not custodian trustees within the meaning of the Public Trustee Act 1906, but are merely holding trustees under a division of responsibilities laid down in the trust instrument. A division between managing and custodian trustees is in effect what occurs in most unincorporated charitable associations, where the powers of management are vested in a Committee (who effectively comprise the managing trustees) and the responsibility of holding the charity's assets is given to one or more persons or a body corporate, often called 'the Trustees'. The division of powers between the managing and the holding trustees in such circumstances depends entirely on the trust instrument or rules of association. A holding trustee who is not a custodian trustee within the Public Trustee Act 1906 does not enjoy any of the protection which that statute confers, and does not have any statutory right to levy a fee for

---

[161]   CA 1993, s 2(1)
[162]   See CA 1992, s 20. On the divestment of the Official Custodian's investment function, see further ch 16, para 16.73
[163]   ibid, s 22(1)
[164]   ibid
[165]   ibid, s 2(5)

its services.[166] A charity's governing instrument may, however, permit the payment of reasonable fees to any nominee or holding trustee.[167]

G. Standard of care and skill

(1) General position in equity

The general standard of care and skill required of any trustee is that of the ordinary prudent man of business acting in the management of his own affairs.[168] This general standard is modified in the context of investment.[169] A prudent man of business may take risks;[170] but the distinction is between a prudent degree of risk on the one hand, and hazard on the other.[171] A trustee who is honest and reasonably competent is not to be held responsible for a mere error of judgement, from which no businessman, however, prudent, can expect to be immune.[172] A trustee is not therefore liable merely because his decision is wrong and results in a loss to the trust or to the trust's performing less well than it might otherwise perform: a trustee is to be judged 'not so much by success as by absence of proven default'.[173] If trustees make a decision and it subsequently appears that there are good and sufficient reasons for supporting their decision, they will not be liable for any loss merely because they made the decision on the wrong grounds.[174] The court will look objectively at the circumstances to see if there are good and sufficient reasons for supporting the trustees' decision.[175]

9.75

If the trust has a controlling interest in a company, and facts come to the trustee's knowledge that the company's affairs are not being conducted as they should be, or which put him on inquiry, the trustee, acting as a prudent man of business, must take appropriate action. He must not content himself with the receipt of information on the affairs of the company such as an ordinary shareholder would receive at an annual general meeting. One means of ensuring that he has sufficient

9.76

---

[166] Under TA 2000, s 30, however, the Secretary of State is empowered to make regulations providing for the remuneration of a trustee of a charitable trust which is a trust corporation or who acts in a professional capacity. See further below, para 9.98

[167] See the model constitutions for unincorporated charities prepared on behalf of the CLA: Trust Deed for a Charitable Trust, cl 3.16; Constitution for a Charitable Unincorporated Association, r 9.4 (which permits the payment of reasonable fees to any trust corporation appointed a holding trustee or to any nominee)

[168] *Speight v Gaunt* (1883) 9 App Cas 1, 19

[169] The trustee must not, for instance, speculate: *Learoyd v Whiteley* (1887) 12 App Cas 727, 733 (Lord Watson)

[170] *Re Godfrey* (1883) 23 ChD 483, 493 (Bacon V-C)

[171] *Bartlett v Barclays Bank Trust Co Ltd (No 1)* [1980] Ch 515, 531 (Brightman J)

[172] ibid, 531, where Brightman J applied dicta in *Re Chapman* [1896] 2 Ch 736, 778 (Lopes LJ)

[173] *Nestlé v National Westminster Bank plc* [1993] 1 WLR 1260, 1284 (Leggatt LJ)

[174] *Cowan v Scargill* [1985] Ch 270, 294 (Megarry V-C)

[175] *Nestlé v National Westminster Bank plc* [1993] 1 WLR 1260, 1270 (Dillon LJ)

information to enable him to make an informed decision is to put himself (or where there are several trustees, one of their number) on the board of directors; alternatively, a nominee could be put on the board to report back to the trustees from time to time on the company's affairs.[176] In appropriate circumstances, it might be sufficient instead to rely on the receipt of copies of the agenda and minutes of board meetings, if held regularly, the receipt of monthly management accounts in the case of a trading concern, or quarterly reports. What is appropriate action in each case will, however, depend on the particular facts, and it is impossible to lay down a general rule.[177] In each case, the trustees need to take, so far as is reasonably practicable, such steps as should ensure to them an adequate flow of information to enable them to make use of the controlling interest should it be necessary to protect the trust asset, namely the shareholding.[178] These points need especially to be borne in mind by charity trustees where the charity is trading by means of a subsidiary trading company.

9.77 A higher standard of care than that of the prudent man of business is required of a paid trustee;[179] and the Charity Commissioners have stated that if the trustee were a trust corporation or a professional person being remunerated for his skills, they would normally expect such higher duty of care.[180] Judicial pronouncements suggest that a higher standard is to be based on the holding out of a particular expertise rather than the fact of remuneration itself.[181] A solicitor who acts as a charity trustee may therefore be subject to such a higher standard of care even if he acts gratuitously. Since the standard of care of a professional trustee is based on the special care and skill which he professes to have, there may be a sliding standard of care, with the highest standard being expected of the trust corporation.[182]

(2) The statutory duty of care applicable to trustees

9.78 The Trustee Act 2000 imposes a 'duty of care'[183] on trustees in particular circumstances. Whenever such duty of care applies to a trustee, he must exercise such care and skill as is reasonable in the circumstances, having regard in particular:[184]

---

[176] *Re Lucking's Will Trusts* [1968] 1 WLR 86 (Cross J)

[177] *Bartlett v Barclays Bank Trust Co Ltd (No 1)* [1980] Ch 515, 533 (Brightman J)

[178] ibid, 533–4 (Brightman J)

[179] *Re Waterman's Will Trusts* [1952] 2 All ER 1054; *Bartlett v Barclays Bank Trust Co Ltd (No 1)* [1980] Ch 515; see also 23rd Report of the Law Reform Committee, *The Powers and Duties of Trustees*, Cmnd 8733 (1982), paras 2.12–2.16

[180] [1989] Ch Com Rep 25 (para 90)

[181] *Bartlett v Barclays Bank Trust Co Ltd (No 1)* [1980] Ch 515, 534 (Brightman J). It should be noted that this case, like most of the reported decisions, concerned a private trust, where a professional trustee is usually paid, and where the position of an unpaid professional trustee has not been considered

[182] This seems to be implicit in ibid, 534 (Brightman J)

[183] TA 2000, s 1(2)

[184] ibid, s 1(1)

(a) to any special knowledge or experience that he has or holds himself out as having, and

(b) if he acts as trustee in the course of a business or profession, to any special knowledge or experience that it is reasonable to expect of a person acting in the course of that kind of business or profession.

The duty of care applies to a trustee in relation (inter alia) to investment;[185] to the **9.79** acquisition of land;[186] to the appointment of agents, nominees, and custodians;[187] and to the exercise of any power to insure.[188] The duty of care does not apply if or in so far as it appears from the trust instrument that the duty is not meant to apply.[189]

It would appear that in most of the specified instances in which the duty of care **9.80** applies, the position under the statute is merely to codify the existing position in equity. The Law Commission, which recommended the introduction of the statutory duty of care, expressly noted this was probably the position, for example, in relation to investment.[190] It pointed out that the present law already recognizes a gradation of the standard of care from an unpaid layman to the paid professional trustee.[191] In most areas, therefore, the existing case law will continue to provide more detailed guidance on trustees' standard of care.

In relation to delegation, however, the duties and standards of care of trustees were **9.81** out of line, because the Trustee Act 1925[192] had changed the law in ways which had long been criticized as unnecessarily complex and illogical.[193] The Law Commission intended that the introduction of a uniform statutory duty of care applicable to each of the functions to which it was applied would both amend the pre-existing law relating to delegation and also provide a clear and accessible statement of the standard of care to be expected from trustees.[194] In the exercise of those powers not covered by the statutory duty of care (for example, in relation to the exercise of their discretion in allocating the charity's funds to its charitable purposes), the duties and standard of care of trustees of charitable trusts remain those laid down in equity.

---

[185] ibid, s 2 & Sch 1, para 1. See further ch 16, paras 16.14–16.16
[186] TA 2000, s 2 & Sch 1, para 2. See further ch 17, paras 17.04 and 17.16
[187] TA 2000, s 2 & Sch 1, para 3. See further below, paras 9.153 and 9.159 (agents); 16.71 (nominees); and above, 9.68 (custodians)
[188] TA 2000, s 2 & Sch 1, para 5. See further below, para 9.179
[189] TA 2000, s 2 & Sch 1, para 7
[190] Law Commission, *Trustees' Power and Duties* (Law Com No 260 1999) 38 (para 3.16)
[191] ibid, 42 (para 3.24)
[192] See esp TA 1925, ss 23(1), 23(2), 23(3) & 30(1) (now repealed by TA 2000, s 40 & Sch 4)
[193] Law Commission, *Trustees' Power and Duties* (Law Com No 260 1999) 34–6 (paras 3.5–3.7)
[194] ibid, 36–7 (paras 3.8–3.10)

(3) Directors of charitable companies

9.82 Whilst the Trustee Act 2000 applies to trustees of charitable trusts, and (because a trust is necessarily involved) to Committee members of charitable unincorporated associations, the Act has no application to charitable corporations.[195] In relation to the exercise by directors of their powers, the general duties and standard of care of directors of such companies therefore remains as it was before the Act was passed. In the absence of specific authority, it would appear that, as fiduciaries, such directors should be subject to the same duties and standard of care as have been laid down in equity for trustees of charitable trusts.

H. Excluding or relieving liability

(1) Relief granted by the court

High Court's inherent jurisdiction

9.83 The standard of care and skill of the prudent man of business applies to charity trustees; but the High Court has an equitable jurisdiction, inherited from the Court of Chancery, to relieve a trustee from personal liability, and it is sympathetic to the plight of charity trustees in particular. It has been recognized since the time of Lord Eldon LC that the court needs to be lenient to charity trustees who have acted honestly, where the loss to the charity arises merely from a mistake.[196] Originally, such leniency was justified partly by the difficulty which might arise in determining from the charity's governing instrument how its funds ought to be applied;[197] but, with the availability of the Charity Commissioneers to advise charity trustees on such matters prospectively,[198] this explanation carries less weight in modern times. Lord Eldon LC stated, however, that 'To act on any other principle would be to deter all prudent persons from becoming trustees of charities';[199] and this rationale still holds good for unpaid trustees. This approach underlies the attitude of the Charity Commissioneeers; for example, in the context of schemes, they have said that a failure by charity trustees to keep within the terms of the trust 'may often be evidence of the need to alter the purposes of the charity rather than of dereliction of duty on the part of the trustees'.[200]

---

[195] For an explanation, see Law Commission, *Trustees' Power and Duties* (Law Com No 260 1999), 7 (para 1.20 & n 37)

[196] *A-G v Exeter Corp* (1826) 2 Russ 45, 54 (Lord Eldon LC); *A-G v East Retford Corp* (1833) 2 My & K 35, 37–8 (Leach MR)

[197] *A-G v Exeter Corp* (1826) 2 Russ 45, 54 (Lord Eldon LC)

[198] CA 1993, s 29

[199] *A-G v Exeter Corp* (1826) 2 Russ 45, 54 (Lord Eldon LC)

[200] [1970] Ch Com Rep 16 (para 44)

A modern example of the court's use of its inherent jurisdiction to relieve a char-   **9.84**
ity trustee is *Re Freeston's Charity*,[201] where the charity trustee (itself a charitable
corporation) mistakenly but honestly appropriated for itself, for a period of over
twenty-six years, part of the trust income which should have been paid to another
charity, a foundation. Fox J said that in dealing with a charitable corporation
which had acted mistakenly but honestly the court has a considerable measure of
discretion.[202] He thought that the court should decline to order an account in
respect of the period before the issue of proceedings[203] (in 1970), and, there being
some evidence of delay on the part of the foundation thereafter, he ordered an
account only in respect of the previous six years (to 1971).

Statutory relief

Statutory relief may also be sought. Under section 61 of the Trustee Act 1925 the   **9.85**
court is empowered to grant relief (either wholly or in part) to a trustee who is or
may be personally liable for breach of trust from liability for such breach, if he has
acted honestly and reasonably and ought fairly to be excused for the breach, and
for omitting to obtain the directions of the court in the matter in which he committed such breach. The onus of proving that he acted honestly and reasonably is
on the trustee.[204] The section enables relief to be given even if no breach has been
proved to have occurred, but it does not enable the court to relieve from liability
for future breaches.[205] Relief is discretionary, and whether it will be granted
depends on the facts of each particular case;[206] but the court is most reluctant to
grant relief to a paid trustee.[207] The wording of the section poses some problems,
since if a trustee has acted honestly and reasonably he is likely to have satisfied the
prudent man of business test and so avoid any liability in the first place. Acting on
the advice of a person qualified to give it is not necessarily sufficient to satisfy the
reasonableness criterion;[208] the trustee must have actively considered the advice
and have satisfied the prudent man of business test. The Charity Commissioners
have stated that, on legal questions concerning the rights of trustees against persons outside the charity, they advise the trustees that they should consult a solicitor and that, if they do so, and act reasonably on the basis of his advice, they will
not be liable for breach of trust.[209]

---

[201] [1978] 1 All ER 481 (Fox J), affd [1979] 1 WLR 741 (CA)
[202] *Re Freeston's Charity* [1978] 1 All ER 481, 491 (Fox J). The courts seem particularly willing
to grant relief to a corporate trustee of a charity: *A-G v Caius College* (1837) 2 Keen 150, 169
[203] As in *A-G v Wax Chandlers' Co* (1873) LR 6 HL 1, 14 (Lord Chelmsford)
[204] *Re Stuart* [1897] 2 Ch 583
[205] *Re Rosenthal* [1972] 1 WLR 1273
[206] *Re Pauling's Settlement Trust* [1964] 1 Ch 303, 359 (Upjohn LJ)
[207] ibid, 339 (Willmer LJ)
[208] *Marsden v Regan* [1954] 1 All ER 475, 481 (Evershed MR) (CA)
[209] [1982] Ch Com Rep 12 (para 25)

9.86 If the charity is a company incorporated under the Companies Acts, the court has a jurisdiction to relieve a director, wholly or in part, from liability for negligence, default, breach of duty, or breach of trust, provided that the director can establish that he acted honestly and reasonably and, having regard to all the circumstances, ought fairly to be excused.[210] This relieving power is adopted from section 61 of the Trustee Act 1925, and it is therefore likely that the court would exercise its discretion under this section in the same way.

(2) Exclusion provision in the charity's governing instrument

9.87 It remains to be considered to what extent a charity trustee's liability for breach of trust can be excluded or limited by a clause in the governing instrument itself.

9.88 If the charity is a company incorporated under the Companies Acts, section 310 of the Companies Act 1985 lays down that any provision, whether contained in the company's articles or in any contract with the company or otherwise, for exempting (inter alia) any officer of the company from, or indemnifying him against, any liability which by virtue of any rule of law would otherwise attach to him in respect of any negligence, default, breach of duty, or breach of trust of which he may be guilty in relation to the company is (with some specified exceptions) void.[211]

9.89 In *Movitex v Bulfield*,[212] however, which concerned a commercial company, it was held that the predecessor to section 310[213] did not invalidate an article in the company's constitution which purported to modify the scope of a director's duties so as to permit him to retain a profit from transactions involving the company in which he had an interest.[214] In that case, Vinelott J considered that an article modifying or reducing the content of directors' duties was valid, provided that it was not contrary to statute and concerned a matter which was ratifiable by the company in general meeting.[215] His Lordship's rationale was that the so-called 'no conflicts' rule did not connote a positive duty that a director should not permit himself to be placed in a position of conflict of duty and interest: rather it was to be construed as a disability;[216] and, as such, it fell outside what is now section 310.

9.90 This decision suggests that a charitable company's articles might also validly modify the scope of a director's duties in such a way as to prevent him from being

---

[210] Companies Act 1985, s 727(1)

[211] ibid, s 319(1), (2). The most notable exception for present purposes is that permitting the purchase of indemnity insurance: ibid, s 310(3)(a). Indemnity insurance is discussed below, paras 9.183–9.191

[212] (1986) 2 BCC 99, 403

[213] ie Companies Act 1948, s 205

[214] *Movitex Ltd v Bulfield* (1986) 2 BCC 99, 403 (Vinelott J)

[215] ie not within one of the exceptions to *Foss v Harbottle* (1843) 2 Hare 461

[216] See *Tito v Waddell (No 2)* [1977] Ch 106, 248 (Megarry V-C), disc *Movitex Ltd v Bulfield* (1986) 2 BCC 99, 403, 430–2

subject to a liability for his acts which he might otherwise incur. The difficulty is to determine what modifications are permissible. Following *Movitex v Bulfield*,[217] it has been suggested that the non-excludable duties of directors, apart from those imposed by statute, probably include the duties of good faith and proper purpose, proper care and skill, and the duty not to misappropriate the company's property.[218] From this analysis, it would therefore appear that a director's liability for gross negligence cannot be excluded by the articles, and that this principle should be applicable, not merely to directors of companies, but also to other fiduciaries, including trustees. This was a view which had commanded a fair body of academic support.[219] It might also be considered to be supported by the recent relaxation of the rules relating to charity trustee indemnity insurance, which was evidently based on the assumption that liability for gross negligence could not be excluded.

In *Armitage v Nurse*,[220] however, Millett LJ, giving the judgment of the Court of Appeal, whilst accepting that there is an irreducible core of obligations owed by trustees to the beneficiaries, rejected the notion that such core obligations included the duties of skill and care, prudence, and diligence. His Lordship stated: 'The duty of the trustees to perform the trusts honestly and in good faith for the benefit of the beneficiaries is the minimum necessary to give substance to the trusts, but in my opinion it is sufficient.'[221] In that case, the Court of Appeal upheld the validity of a clause in a private trust which excluded the trustee from liability for loss or damage to the trust fund or its income from any cause whatsoever 'unless such loss or damage shall be caused by his own actual fraud'. Actual fraud was held to connote dishonesty (including bad faith and wilful misconduct), and was not to be equated with so-called 'equitable fraud', which in this context 'involves some dealing by the fiduciary with his principal and the risk that the fiduciary may have exploited his position to his own advantage'.[222] Such a clause can protect even a trustee who consciously takes a risk that loss will result, provided that the trustee acts in good faith and in the honest belief that he is acting in the interests of the beneficiaries.[223] Millett LJ pointed out, however, that such a clause would not protect a trustee who had purchased the trust property from the trust against an action for its recovery (or even for equitable compensation) because such action would not be brought in respect of any 'loss

9.91

---

[217] (1986) 2 BCC 99
[218] See *Boyle and Birds' Company Law* (3rd edn, Jordans, 1995) 488–9
[219] P Matthews, 'The Efficacy of Trustee Exemption Clauses in English Law' [1989] Conv 42; *Hanbury & Martin's Modern Equity* (ed JE Martin) (15th edn, Sweet & Maxwell, 1997) 483–4; contrast *Underhill & Hayton's Law of Trusts and Trustees* (ed DJ Hayton) (15th edn, Butterworths, 1995) 560–1
[220] [1998] Ch 241 (CA)
[221] ibid, 253–4 (Millett LJ)
[222] ibid, 253
[223] ibid, 252; expl *Walker v Stones* [2000] 4 All ER 412, 443–5 (CA)

or damage' to the trust, since such an action does not depend on proof of loss or damage.[224]

9.92 There is no reason in principle why an exclusion clause in similar terms could not be included in the governing instrument of a charity; but the Charity Commissioners are likely to resist its inclusion in the constitution of a new instrument, particularly in respect of a paid trustee.[225] In their report for 1989, they stated that, where the trustee is remunerated, they would 'scrutinise very closely' any purported limitation of liability clause;[226] and developments since then suggest that there should be no relaxation of this attitude. The charity trustees might after all be as well protected by indemnity insurance (which can include insurance against negligence, whether ordinary or gross), and this is certainly to the advantage of the charity itself, which otherwise cannot recover its loss. The objection which the Charity Commissioners might take to such a clause is that it would be authorizing the application of charitable property to non-charitable purposes. It is unlikely, however, that the Charity Commissioners would raise this objection in the case of a charitable trust created by will, where the objection would be that the trust would not be wholly and exclusively charitable. Against this, it might be contended that certain relaxations of the 'no conflicts' rule contained in the charity's constitution might be permissible on the ground that they involve not an exclusion of liability for breach of duty but a relief from a disability, as has already been argued. They do not, therefore, involve any application of the charity's assets to non-charitable purposes.

9.93 If the governing instrument of a charitable trust contains a clause excluding the liability of the trustees for 'wilful default', that phrase will be given the same interpretation as it had in section 30(1) of the Trustee Act 1925, now repealed by the Trustee Act 2000.[227] Section 30(1) stated that a trustee was answerable and

---

[224] *Armitage v Nurse* [1998] Ch 241, 253

[225] TA 2000 does not invalidate trustee exclusion clauses, yet it seems unjustifiable that trust corporations and trustees who are paid, professional persons should be able to exclude their liability as trustees. The issue of trustee exclusion clauses was examined in a Consultation Paper by the Trust Law Committee: *Trustee Exemption Clauses* (Nov 1998), in association with the Society of Trust and Estate Practitioners and Trust Law International. The Committee's provisional view was that such clauses should not be effective to exempt paid trustees from liability even for ordinary negligence. In the Second Reading of what became the TA 2000, Lord Goodhart expressed concern that the Bill did not seek to restrict the validity of such clauses: *Hansard*, HL (series 5) vol 612 col 383 (14 April 2000); and this criticism was supported by Lord Wilberforce: ibid, col 392. In response, Lord Irvine LC, who presented the Bill, cautioned that the economic consequences of such a change needed to be assessed, and said that he would be referring the matter to the Law Commission: ibid, col 394. The Lord Chancellor later confirmed at Committee Stage that reference would be made before the summer recess: *Hansard*, HL, committee, cols 13–14 (7 June 2000). It might be questioned whether such reference was necessary, given the Trust Law Committee's existing analysis of this issue. For criticism, see A Kenny, 'Trust law reform' (2000) 76 NLJ Charities Appeal Suppl 15, 18

[226] [1989] Ch Com Rep 25 (para 90)

[227] TA 2000, s 40(3) & Sch 4, Pt II

accountable only for his own acts, receipts, neglects, or defaults, and not for those of any other trustee, nor for any banker, broker, or other person with whom any trust moneys or securities might be deposited, nor for the insufficiency or deficiency of any securities, nor for any other loss, unless the same happened through his own wilful default.[228] The expression 'wilful default' in this context had been held to mean 'a consciousness of negligence or breach of duty, or a reck-lessness in the performance of a duty'.[229] Although this interpretation had been criticized,[230] the Court of Appeal recently considered it to be correct.[231] On grounds of simplicity, there is much to be said for this, as it means that the expres-sion 'wilful default' bears the same meaning if contained in the articles of associa-tion of a charitable company[232] as it does in relation to the trustees of a charitable trust in the strict sense. It also appeared that the expression 'for any other loss' was to be construed *ejusdem generis* with the preceding words; the trustee would there-fore remain subject to the prudent man of business test in failing to supervise an agent who was appointed to manage a business in which the trust had a share-holding, since in such circumstances, the trust assets (the shares) would not them-selves be deposited with the agent.[233]

(3) Relief to a director of a charitable company by ratification of general meeting?

Under general principles of company law, some breaches of duty on the part of a director can be ratified by the passing of an ordinary resolution at a general meet-ing. Some acts have been held to be ratifiable, provided in every case that the direc-tor has acted bona fide in the interests of the company. For example, the sale by the directors of one of the company's assets at a substantial undervalue was held, in the absence of fraud on the directors' part, to be so ratifiable.[234] Certain other acts are never capable of ratification by the general meeting, such as one which involves the company's performing an act which is ultra vires or illegal,[235] or one which

9.94

---

[228] TA 1925, s 30(1) (repealed)

[229] *Re Vickery* [1931] 1 Ch 572, 584 (Maugham J), following *Re City Equitable Fire Insurance Co* [1925] Ch 407 (Romer J); and *Re Trusts of Leeds City Brewery Ltd's Debenture Stock Trust Deed* [1925] Ch 532n. See also *Lewis v Great Western Rly Co* (1877) 3 QBD 195

[230] This was on the ground that 'wilful default' in the Trustee Acts 1859 (Lord St Leonard's Act) and 1893 had been interpreted so as not to derogate from the prudent man of business test (*Re Brier* (1884) 26 ChD 238, also *Re Chapman* [1896] 2 Ch 763) but merely to reverse the burden of proof. It has also been pointed out that in *Re City Equitable Fire Insurance Co* [1925] Ch 407 Romer J was considering 'wilful default', not in the statutory context, but rather in regard to directors' liability under a company's articles of association. See G Jones, 'Delegation by Trustees: a Reappraisal' (1959) 22 MLR 381; JE Stannard, 'Wilful Default' [1979] Conv 345; *Hanbury & Martin's Modern Equity* (ed JE Martin) (15th edn, Sweet & Maxwell, 1997) 563–4

[231] *Armitage v Nurse* [1998] Ch 241, 252, where Millett LJ expressed the view that it was consis-tent with the earlier authorities

[232] cf *Re City Equitable Fire Insurance Co* [1925] Ch 407

[233] *Re Lucking's Will Trusts* [1968] 1 WLR 866 (Cross J)

[234] *Pavlides v Jensen* [1956] Ch 565

[235] *Re Exchange Banking Co, Flitcroft's case* (1882) 21 ChD 519 (CA)

would infringe a member's individual rights conferred by the articles. This problem is part of the broader issue of the extent to which a minority of members can sue in respect of wrongs done to the company or of irregularities in the manner in which the company conducts its internal affairs.[236]

9.95 The application of these principles to charitable companies, however, is by no means clear. A purported ratification by the general meeting of a director's act of negligence could be characterized as a purported gift by the charity to the director of an amount equivalent to the sum which, if the ratification were valid, he would be relieved of having to make good to the company. In other words, it could be construed as a purported application of the charity's assets to a private, rather than to a charitable, purpose, which would therefore be ultra vires and void. It might, however, be argued that ratification of some acts which would have breached the 'no conflicts' rule (such as a director's taking personal advantage of a corporate opportunity[237]) could be treated as merely removing the director from a disability, and might therefore be upheld. Furthermore, the ratification by the general meeting of acts which are intra vires the company, though beyond the directors' powers, is a matter of internal management and therefore valid.[238]

I. Duty to avoid a conflict of interests

9.96 Like a trustee of a private trust, a charity trustee owes a duty of undivided loyalty to the trust, the only difference being that the charity trustee's duty is owed to the public rather than to individual beneficiaries.[239] The duty is owed not merely by trustees of a charitable trust, but also by other fiduciaries, such as the directors of a charitable corporation.[240] The rule is based on the principle that a fiduciary is not permitted to put himself into a position where his interest and duty conflict. It will be considered in relation first to charity trustee remuneration, and then in relation to other profits.

(1) Remuneration

Introduction

9.97 The office of trustee is essentially gratuitous.[241] Equity is concerned to prevent the trustee putting his own interest (in receiving a reward from acting as a trustee) in conflict with the interest of the trust. The basic principle therefore, is that, unless

---

[236] See *Foss v Harbottle* (1843) 2 Hare 461, and the exceptions thereto
[237] cf *Queensland Mines Ltd v Hudson* (1978) 18 ALR 1
[238] See further ch 8, paras 8.118 and 8.178–8.181
[239] *Bray v Ford* [1896] AC 44 (HL)
[240] *Re French Protestant Hospital* [1951] Ch 567
[241] *Re Duke of Norfolk's Settlement Trusts* [1982] Ch 61 (CA); *Guinness plc v Saunders* [1990] 2 AC 663 (HL)

the governing instrument expressly provides otherwise, the charity trustee is not entitled to any remuneration from his position, nor for his loss of time or personal trouble.[242]

In the case of private trusts, this equitable principle has recently been modified by **9.98** statute. The Trustee Act 2000 has given a trust corporation and a trustee (other than a sole trustee) who acts in a professional capacity (with the written consent of the other trustees) a right (subject to any provision in the trust instrument) to receive reasonable remuneration out of the trust funds for services provided to or on behalf of the trust.[243] This provision expressly excludes, however, a trustee of a charitable trust.[244] In its report which recommended the reforms now embodied in the Trustee Act 2000, the Law Commission, whilst recognizing that it could sometimes be in the best interests of a charity to be able to remunerate trustees, appreciated that there was force in certain reservations which had been expressed about the wisdom of giving a default charging power to professional trustees of charitable trusts.[245] Such a power might be perceived to run counter to the principle that charities exist for the public benefit, and might damage public confidence in charities; it would also suggest that the inclusion of such a charging clause is 'best practice', whereas in charitable trusts such clauses are not standard.[246] In the event, the Law Commission considered that, whilst there should be further consultation within the charity sector, it would be more convenient (in avoiding the need for further primary legislation) to give the Secretary of State power to make regulations by way of statutory instrument providing for the remuneration of charity trustees.[247] Such a power is therefore contained in section 30 of the Trustee Act 2000. As originally drafted, it would have enabled regulations to be made to remunerate lay, as well as professional, trustees. Uneasiness was expressed, during the passage of the Trustee Bill through Parliament, that such an important measure as the remuneration of trustees of charitable trusts should be capable of being effected merely by means of delegated legislation, particularly given the potential for it to be used to remunerate lay trustees.[248] The Government accepted that there was no intention that the power should be used to provide for the remuneration of lay trustees, and that it was envisaged that any regulations would essentially parallel the provisions for the remuneration of professional trustees of private trusts. Accordingly, section 30 as enacted restricts the Secretary of State's power to the making of regulations for the remuneration only of trustees who are

---

[242] *Brocksopp v Barnes* (1820) 5 Madd 90 (Leach MR)

[243] TA 2000, s 29

[244] ibid, s 29(1)(b), (2)(b)

[245] Law Commission, *Trustees' Power and Duties* (Law Com No 260, 1999) 79–80 (paras 7.21–7.22)

[246] ibid, 80 (para 7.22)

[247] ibid, 80 (para 7.23)

[248] 2nd Reading, Trustee Bill 2000, *Hansard*, HL (series 5) vol 612, col 388 (14 Apr 2000) (Lord Phillips of Sudbury)

trust corporations or act in a professional capacity. No regulations have as yet been made. For the present, therefore, the power of trustees of charitable trusts to charge remuneration for their services continues to depend on general principles of equity.

9.99 The court has an inherent jurisdiction to sanction the payment of remuneration to trustees, which it has exercised in relation to private trusts.[249] It has exercised this jurisdiction on the basis that it is in the interests of a trust that it be well administered, and that better administration might in some circumstances be secured by remunerating the trustees. The court has applied the same rationale to charitable trusts. In *Re Coxen*,[250] for instance, the court held that a provision in the trust instrument for an annual dinner for the charity trustees to be paid for out of the charity's funds did not deprive the trust of its exclusively charitable nature, since such provision tended to promote the charity's efficient administration.

9.100 Charging clauses in private trusts often permit trustees to be remunerated in respect of time spent in attending to the business of the trust, and no objection is made to such a clause if contained in the original instrument. Bearing in mind the fact that many charities hold assets and investments many times larger than most private trusts, the fact that many charities operate as business enterprises, and the fact that recent legislation has placed increased duties (and even criminal penalties in some instances) upon charity trustees, it has become more important for charity trustees and those setting up charities to know whether the trust instrument can validly provide for their remuneration in respect of time and effort spent in acting in their capacity as charity trustees.

9.101 In the wake of the Charities Act 1993, the Charity Commissioners reviewed both the legal position and their own policy in relation to the remuneration of charity trustees.[251] The Charity Commissioners' interpretation of the law and their own avowed stance have not changed since their previously stated position of a few years before;[252] but, in setting out the circumstances in which they will authorize the remuneration of charity trustees, the Charity Commissioners are now more expansive, and there is evidence of a slight softening of their approach. Their starting-point is that the office of trustee carries no automatic right to remuneration; they will nevertheless authorize the remuneration of charity trustees in those cases where it can be shown to be both 'necessary and reasonable in the interests of the charity'.[253] The Commissioners interpret this to mean that the payment of remuneration must be 'both necessary to ensure the good administration of the charity

---

[249] *Re Duke of Norfolk's Settlement Trusts* [1982] Ch 61 (CA); *Marshall v Holloway* (1820) 2 Swan 432 (Lord Eldon MR)
[250] [1948] Ch 747
[251] (1994) 2 Decisions 14–23
[252] [1989] Ch Com Rep 24–6 (paras 87–95); [1981] Ch Com Rep 23–4 (paras 61–4)
[253] *Re Smallpiece Trust, Smallpiece v A-G* [1990] Ch Com Rep 36 (Judge Paul Baker QC, sitting as a judge of the High Court)

and reasonable in relation to the services rendered to the charity by trustees and the income of the charity'.[254] The burden of producing evidence that these requirements have been met lies on the trustees, and the Charity Commissioners require 'cogent evidence' if such burden is to be discharged.[255] The Commissioners have also stated that it is, in their view, inappropriate for a trust corporation which charges fees to be a charity trustee unless there are exceptional circumstances;[256] although a trust corporation may charge fees if it is a custodian trustee.[257]

McCall has contended that the permissible scope of a trustee remuneration clause **9.102** should depend upon whether such a clause is contained in the original instrument or is sought to be introduced at a later date.[258] In the former case, he argues that a wider power to remunerate should be valid since it is provided for by the settlor himself;[259] whereas, in the latter case, a narrower power can be justified because the trustees have already accepted office on the basis that they are not to be paid. He therefore considers that decisions laying down the scope of the power to remunerate after the trust has been created[260] should not be taken as laying down the permissible scope of a remuneration clause contained in the original instrument. Whilst the Charity Commissioners do not accept McCall's view that a charity's governing instrument might validly provide for remuneration for all charity trustees when a new charity is established, they do agree that the two sets of circumstances are to be treated differently.[261]

Charging clause in the original instrument

The Charity Commissioners have no objection to the presence of a charging clause **9.103** which is contained in the governing instrument (whether it be a trust instrument or memorandum and articles of association) when the charity is set up, '[p]rovided that this provision is couched in terms which tie the nature and level of remuneration to the services undertaken by the trustee or director (even as trustee/director)'.[262] If the nature or level of such remuneration is not so limited, the Charity Commissioners take the view that the body (whether a trust, association, or company) is not established for exclusively charitable purposes, since the trustee will be obtaining a benefit from the charity not matched by an equivalent benefit from him to the charity; the trustee will effectively be a beneficiary of the charity,[263] and the

---

[254] (1994) 2 Decisions 18
[255] ibid, 15
[256] [1989] Ch Com Rep 25 (para 91); [1981] Ch Com Rep 24 (para 64)
[257] See above, paras 9.69 and 9.71
[258] C McCall, 'Remuneration of Charity Trustees' (1992–3) 1 CL & PR 191
[259] cf *Re Coxen* [1948] Ch 747
[260] eg *Re Smallpiece Trust, Smallpiece v A-G* [1990] Ch Com Rep 36
[261] (1994) 2 Decisions 14
[262] ibid 15
[263] *Re Barker* (1886) 31 ChD 665; *Re Pooley* (1888) 40 ChD 1; *Re White* [1898] 1 Ch 297

Commissioners will therefore decline to register the body as a charity.[264] It is therefore important that any trustee remuneration clause expressly limits the award of remuneration to such sums as are both necessary and reasonable in the interests of the charity. A clause which merely provides that the trustees may award themselves such remuneration as they shall determine, or that the directors of a charitable company shall be entitled to receive such remuneration as shall be voted to them in a general meeting of the members, will not meet the Charity Commissioners' criteria. If, however, an overbroad charging clause is contained in a testamentary trust, rather than contending that the trust is void as not being wholly and exclusively charitable, the Commissioners merely ask the trustees for an undertaking that they will not avail themselves of the clause,[265] or advise them that it can be used only for remuneration which is both 'necessary and reasonable'.

9.104 The model charity constitution documents produced on behalf of the Charity Law Association include trustee remuneration clauses for trustees of a charitable trust and for Committee members of an unincorporated charitable association.[266] The model clause permits any trustee with specialist skills or knowledge, and any firm or company of which he is a member or employee, to charge and be paid reasonable fees for work carried out for the trust on the instructions of the other trustees, provided that the prescribed procedure is followed in selecting the trustee, firm, or company and in setting the amount of the fees, and subject to the further proviso that not more than one half of the trustees may take advantage of this procedure in any one financial year. The prescribed procedure (which is the general procedure to be adopted whenever a trustee has a personal interest) essentially requires the trustee to declare an interest before discussion on the matter begins, and to withdraw from the meeting and from the vote.[267] No equivalent charging clause is contained in the Charity Law Association's model constitutional documents for a charitable company limited by guarantee; but there is no objection in principle to the inclusion of a similar charging clause in the memorandum or articles of such a company.

9.105 Where the funds are raised for charitable purposes from the public by means of a charitable appeal before a trust instrument has been prepared, the trustees or the Committee entrusted with the funds are taken to have the implied authority of the donors to declare the trusts to which such contributions are to be subject.[268]

---

[264] (1994) 2 Decisions 14, 15, referring to *Re Coxen* [1948] 1 Ch 747. See also [1989] Ch Com Rep 25 (para 89)
[265] See C McCall, 'Remuneration of Charity Trustees' (1992–3) 1 CL & PR 191, 196, highlighting what he sees as an apparent inconsistency in the Charity Commissioners' approach
[266] See cl 6.1 of the Trust Deed for a Charitable Trust, and r 9.2.6 of the Constitution for a Charitable Unincorporated Association
[267] See cl 6.3 of the Trust Deed for a Charitable Trust, and r 9.3 of the Constitution for a Charitable Unincorporated Association. See further below, para 9.121
[268] *A-G v Mathieson* [1907] 2 Ch 383, 394 (Cozens-Hardy MR)

The Charity Commissioners consider that there may be some doubt whether such implied authority extends to enabling the trustees to insert a power of remuneration into the terms of the trust as regards money previously collected; but 'for practical reasons' they will normally accept such a power as valid if the charity submits a complete trust document with its application for registration.[269] If, however, the trustees approach the Charity Commissioners before the declaration has been executed, the Commissioners will advise the trustees that they have no authority to include a power of remuneration and that the authority of the Commissioners is needed; and the Commissioners treat the case as if it were an application by an existing charity seeking a power of remuneration.[270] It might seem somewhat unsatisfactory that the Charity Commissioners are prepared to accept a charging clause merely because it is a *fait accompli*, and their policy could suggest that it is in the interests of the charity trustees to execute the trust instrument before approaching the Charity Commissioners! It would seem, however, that the Commissioners' principal concern is with moneys sent in by donors spontaneously, before any appeal has been launched. If the charity is continuing to raise funds after applying to the Charity Commissioners, the Commissioners do not seek to distinguish between the application of the remuneration clause in relation to funds already raised and funds to be raised in the future, and they will accept the declaration of trust as including the power of remuneration and as applying to all the charity's funds.[271]

No charging clause in the original instrument

If the charity is already in existence and the governing instrument contains no **9.106** power of remuneration, the trustees[272] or directors[273] are not entitled to be paid, since they are not permitted to make an unauthorized profit from their fiduciary position. The same principle also precludes the trustees or directors from seeking to use any power of amendment contained in the trust instrument or memorandum and articles of association to include a remuneration clause.[274] Neither can the principle be circumvented by appointing the trustee as a salaried employee of the trust or company, since such a position would flow from the trusteeship.[275]

If authorization to charge is not contained in the original instrument, the trustees **9.107** will need the approval of the court or of the Charity Commissioners to amend the

[269] (1994) 2 Decisions 14, 16
[270] ibid
[271] ibid
[272] *Robinson v Pett* (1734) 3 P Wms 249; *Re Thorpe* [1891] 2 Ch 360; *Re White* [1898] 2 Ch 217
[273] *Hutton v West Cork Rly Co* (1883) 23 ChD 654; *Re George Newman & Co* [1895] 1 Ch 674; *Guinness v Saunders* [1990] 2 AC 663 (HL)
[274] *Re French Protestant Hospital* [1951] Ch 567. If the charity is a company, any such amendment would be ineffective without the prior written consent of the Charity Commissioners: CA 1993, s 64(2). See ch 8, paras 8.123–8.125
[275] cf *Re Macadam* [1946] Ch 73

instrument. The court has an inherent jurisdiction to authorize the payment of remuneration (or an increased level of remuneration[276]) to trustees of a private trust in respect of services rendered,[277] where the court feels that it is in the interests of the beneficiaries.[278] The jurisdiction is exercisable, not merely on the appointment of a trustee,[279] but also after his appointment.[280] In *Smallpiece v Attorney-General*[281] Judge Paul Baker QC, sitting as a judge of the High Court, refused permission to a charitable company to amend its constitution so as to permit a small amount of remuneration for the charity trustees (its Council members). The judge emphasized that remuneration would be awarded only exceptionally. The overriding consideration is the good administration of the charity.[282]

9.108 In practice, the Charity Commissioners deal with such applications themselves, and will not authorize applications to the court directly.[283] Authorization can be given by the Charity Commissioners either by way of a scheme[284] or by an order.[285] A scheme is more appropriate (because it amends the instrument itself) where a continuing power to charge is sought; an order may be made to sanction an exceptional payment. If the charity is a company, the consent of the Charity Commissioners is needed to amend the memorandum and articles of association.[286]

9.109 Whilst adhering to the view that every case will depend upon the circumstances of the particular charity involved, the Charity Commissioners have indicated a number of factors which may be relevant, but they emphasize that this is not intended to be a comprehensive list.[287] If the charity's instrument already has a provision concerning the remuneration of trustees, a particular case to justify varying it will need to be made. The size of the charity's funds and activities is relevant, as there must generally be a degree of complexity in the administration of the charity to justify the remuneration of the trustees; and a charity must have

---

[276] *Re Duke of Norfolk's Settlement Trusts* [1982] Ch 61 (CA); *Re Codd* [1975] 1 WLR 1139 (Graham J)

[277] *Re Duke of Norfolk's Settlement Trusts* [1982] Ch 61 (CA) (Fox LJ)

[278] *Bainbridge v Blair* (1845) 8 Beav 558 (Lord Langdale MR); *Forster v Ridley* (1864) 4 De GJ & Sm 452 (CA)

[279] *Brocksopp v Barnes* (1820) 5 Madd 90 (Leach MR); *Re Masters* [1953] 1 WLR 81, 83 (Danckwerts J); *Re Worthington* [1954] 1 WLR 526, 528 (Upjohn J)

[280] *Re Duke of Norfolk's Settlement Trusts* [1982] Ch 61 (CA); *Re Codd* [1975] 1 WLR 1139 (Graham J)

[281] [1990] Ch Com Rep 36

[282] *Re Duke of Norfolk's Settlement Trusts* [1982] Ch 61 (CA); *Re Smallpiece Trust* [1990] Ch Com Rep 36; *Re Charlesworth* (1910) 101 LT 908; *Marshall v Holloway* (1820) 2 Swan 432; *Bainbridge v Blair* (1845) 8 Beav 588

[283] Such an application would be 'charity proceedings' within the CA 1993, s 33, and would therefore require the consent either of the Charity Commissioners or of a judge of the High Court

[284] CA 1993, s 16

[285] ibid, s 26

[286] ibid, s 64(2)

[287] (1994) 2 Decisions 19–20

sufficient income each year to remunerate the trustees without affecting its capacity to undertake its charitable objects. The nature of the charity's activities is another factor: whether the charity provides a service requiring continual oversight rather than simply distributing income at periodic trustee meetings; whether the charity carries out one activity or is involved in a number of operations; and whether the charity has any subsidiary business that requires oversight. The Charity Commissioners will also have regard to the degree of involvement required of the trustees in the day-to-day running of the charity, including whether the charity has employees to carry out the bulk of such day-to-day running and whether the nature of the charity's activities requires the active participation of a trustee at all times; if the number of trustees is small and the burden onerous, the Charity Commissioners will inquire whether the individual load can be lightened by the appointment of additional trustees. The specialist nature of the skills required of the trustees in the administration of the charity is a further consideration: the nature of the charity's property and of its activities may make it essential that it has trustees with particular expertise, but it may be that the necessary expertise could be supplied by staff or external advisers. Finally, the Charity Commissioners will have regard to the cost of obtaining necessary specialist skills by employing people to provide them compared with the cost of remunerating the trustees themselves.

9.110 The principle against remunerating a trustee cannot be circumvented by paying the trustee a fee as an agent or employee. Similarly, the Charity Commissioners will not generally permit a charity trustee to receive remuneration from acting as director of the charity's subsidiary trading company[288] or of any other non-charitable company which runs lotteries ostensibly for the benefit of the charity.[289] If it intended to obtain the services of a professional person who will require to be paid for his services, the trustees should consider hiring him as their agent or employee, rather than attempting to appoint him a trustee.

Professional charging clauses

9.111 Formerly, charging clauses were construed strictly,[290] so that an express charging clause which entitled a trustee acting in a professional capacity to levy his 'professional charges' would be treated as authorizing remuneration only in respect of those services rendered by such trustee in his professional capacity.[291] Such a trustee would be able to charge for *all* his services as trustee only if the charging clause provided for this in clear terms. This presumption has, in effect, now been

---

[288] ibid, 20–21; see further ch 20, para 20.39
[289] [1981] Ch Com Rep 34 (para 105)
[290] *Re Gee* [1948] Ch 284
[291] *Harbin v Darby* (1860) 28 Beav 325; *Re Chapple* (1884) 27 ChD 584; *Re Chalinder and Herrington* [1907] 1 Ch 58

reversed by the Trustee Act 2000. Where a charitable trust contains a professional charging clause, a trustee which is a trust corporation or 'is acting in a professional capacity' is now treated as entitled under the trust instrument (unless it provides otherwise) to receive payment in respect of services, even if they are services which are capable of being provided by a lay trustee; but (unless the trustee is a trust corporation) only if the majority of the trustees have so agreed.[292] Subject to this, if a trust instrument authorizes a trustee to charge for 'his services as trustee', he would now be able to charge for all his services; but, if it merely authorizes him to charge for his '*professional* services as trustee', he would still be restricted to charging for those services in respect of which he acted in a professional capacity.

9.112 It was not the intention of the Law Commission that trustees engaged in *any* profession or business should come within the scope of these provisions; but rather, in the Law Commission's words, that there should be 'a close nexus between the particular profession or business of the trustee and the services which he or she provides to the trust as trustee'.[293] The Law Commission thought that the matter should be put beyond doubt by an express provision. Accordingly, the Trustee Act 2000 specifies what is meant by 'acting in a professional capacity'. It provides that, for this purpose:[294]

> a trustee acts in a professional capacity if he acts in the course of a profession or business which consists of or includes the provision of services in connection with—
>> (a) the management or administration of trusts generally or a particular kind of trust, or
>> (b) any particular aspect of the management or administration of trusts generally or a particular kind of trust,
> and the services it provides to or on behalf of the trust fall within that description.

It was probably intended that persons such as teachers, social workers, or personnel officers should not be regarded as 'acting in a professional capacity'; but whether the statutory wording is sufficient to exclude them has been doubted.[295]

9.113 Before the Trustee Act 2000, payments received under professional charging clauses were treated, for some purposes, not as remuneration for services rendered, but as gifts. Such treatment may have owed something to the nineteenth-century notion of trustees as enthusiastic amateurs;[296] but, whatever the explanation, it had some unfortunate consequences where the trust arose under a will: first, if the trustee witnessed the will, his right to charge was void;[297] and,

---

[292] TA 2000, s 28(1), (2), (3). A person acts as a lay trustee if he is not a trust corporation and does not act in a professional capacity: ibid, s 28(6)

[293] Law Commission, *Trustees' Power and Duties* (Law Com No 260, 1999) 76 (para 7.14)

[294] TA 2000, s 28(5)

[295] 2nd Reading, Trustee Bill 2000, *Hansard*, HL (series 5) (vol 612) col 390 (14 Apr 2000) (Lord Phillips of Sudbury)

[296] Law Commission, *Trustees' Power and Duties* (Law Com 260, 1999) 78 (para 7.19)

[297] Wills Act 1837, s 15

secondly, a trustee's charges did not obtain priority over legacies and other debts of the deceased.[298] These anomalies have now been removed by the Trustee Act 2000, which provides that in those cases, any payments to which a trustee is entitled in respect of services are to be treated, not as gifts, but as remuneration for services.[299]

Expenses

A trustee is entitled to be reimbursed for out-of-pocket expenses (such as travel expenses) incurred in the administration of the trust.[300] Reimbursement of such expenses does not comprise remuneration. The Charity Commissioners recognize that trustees' expenses may, in appropriate circumstances, include indirect expenses, such as the costs of engaging a baby-minder to enable poor persons to participate as trustees of a charitable trust.[301] Directors of charitable companies who act gratuitously are similarly entitled to reimbursement for out-of-pocket expenses; but, under general principles of company law, a company director is not entitled to be reimbursed for expenses incurred in the performance of his office,[302] unless the articles provide otherwise.[303]   **9.114**

So-called 'expenses' might be treated as remuneration if they are not related to expenditure actually incurred. If a charity trustee receives a fixed sum for attending trustees' meetings, regardless of what his actual expenses are, such sum (or at least that part not referable to expenses actually incurred) effectively comprises remuneration, even though it might have been designated as 'expenses'. In these circumstances, it would be necessary to inquire whether such remuneration was properly paid, and whether therefore the trustee might lawfully retain it.   **9.115**

(2) Other benefits and profits

Purchases by trustee from the charity

The 'no conflicts' rule forbids a trustee from being both vendor and purchaser. Under the so-called 'self-dealing rule',[304] a trustee who purchases trust property from the trust, or who acquires a lease of land belonging to the trust, is liable to have the transaction set aside regardless of the adequacy of the price or other   **9.116**

---

[298] AEA 1925, s 34(3)

[299] TA 2000, s 28(4)

[300] A trustee's entitlement to be reimbursed out of the trust funds for expenses properly incurred when acting on behalf of the trust has now been put on a statutory basis: TA 2000, s 31

[301] See 2nd Reading of Trustee Bill 2000, *Hansard*, HL (series 5) (vol 612) col 388 (14 Apr 2000) (Lord Phillips of Sudbury)

[302] *Young v Naval Military and Civil Service Co-operative Society of South Africa* [1905] 1 KB 687

[303] Reg 83 of Table A expressly permits reimbursement of travel and other expenses of attending company directors' meetings: Companies (Tables A to F) Regulations 1985, SI 1985/805, applied to Table C with modifications made by Table C, reg 9

[304] *Tito v Waddell (No 2)* [1977] Ch 106, 224–5 (Megarry V-C)

circumstances of the sale.[305] This has sometimes been characterized by the courts as a disability of a trustee rather than a duty, since the transaction is voidable without the need to prove a breach of trust.[306] Since a trustee is a 'connected person', a charity which wishes to sell its land to one of its trustees must obtain either an order of the court or of the Charity Commissioners.[307] Such requirement does not apply to the purchase of land by a charity from one of its trustees; but since such a purchase might give rise to a conflict of interests, it is desirable for the charity to obtain the Charity Commissioners' consent to the transaction in advance.

Sales by trustee to the charity

9.117 Sales by a trustee of a charitable trust to the charity itself involve self-dealing,[308] and are therefore voidable regardless of the fairness of the price or of other circumstances, unless the trustee has made full disclosure.[309] Instead of seeking to set the purchase aside, however, the charity may merely claim the trustee's profit. In the absence of full disclosure, the trustee will be accountable for the profit if he acquired the property in question after becoming a trustee.[310] If he acquired it earlier, and can satisfy the court that the sale price was fair, the older view is that he will be allowed to retain the profit even in the absence of full disclosure;[311] it has, however, been argued that, as the trustee is both vendor and purchaser, he should be accountable for the profit unless he made full disclosure, regardless of the time he acquired the property in question.[312]

9.118 It has long been the practice of the Charity Commissioners to include in schemes a clause providing that no trustee is to take or hold any interest in property belonging to the charity otherwise than as a trustee, and that no trustee shall receive remuneration or be interested in the supply of goods or services to the cost of the charity.[313] The Commissioners are, however, prepared to relax this rule where, in small villages, the only persons suitable to be charity trustees are also the only persons living locally who can supply the charity with such goods or services.[314] In such circumstances, the Commissioners will permit an alternative form of clause

---

[305] *Campbell v Walker* (1800) 5 Ves Jr 678; *ex p Lacey* (1802) 6 Ves Jr 625
[306] *Tito v Waddell (No 2)* [1977] Ch 106, 248 (Megarry V-C); *Movitex Ltd v Bulfield* (1986) 2 BCC 99, 403, 430–2
[307] CA 1993, s 36(1), Sch 5
[308] *Tito v Waddell (No 2)* [1977] Ch 106, 224–5 (Megarry V-C)
[309] *Gillett v Peppercorne* (1840) 3 Beav 78 (Lord Langdale MR). In the context of a charitable trust, it would seem that disclosure involves obtaining the consent of the Charity Commissioners under CA 1993, s 26(1); but in some circumstances, it may be sufficient to follow a procedure laid down in the governing instrument (see below, para 9.118)
[310] *Bentley v Craven* (1853) 18 Beav 75
[311] *Re Cape Breton Co* (1885) 29 ChD 795
[312] See *Underhill and Hayton's The Law Relating to Trusts and Trustees* (ed DJ Hayton) (15th edn, Butterworths, 1995) 18–19
[313] [1970] Ch Com Rep 33 (para 92)
[314] ibid (paras 92–3)

which permits the appointment of suitable persons as trustees without preventing them from supplying work or goods to a charity.[315] Such clause provides that the trustee must absent himself from any meeting of the trustees at which they are discussing any transaction in which he is interested in the supply of services, work, or goods to the cost of the charity, and also that the other trustees must be satisfied that any transaction arising out of their deliberations is advantageous to the charity.[316] A suitable clause relating to the supply of goods and services by a director of a charitable company to that company is set out in the model constitution prepared on behalf of the Charity Law Association.[317]

Other benefits

Several provisions of the Companies Act 1985 prohibit or regulate the company's **9.119** making payments or transferring other benefits to a director.[318] Where the company is a charity, however, section 66(1) of the Charities Act 1993 makes the approval of certain dealings with directors ineffective without the prior written consent of the Charity Commissioners.[319] These dealings are:[320] payments to directors in respect of loss of office or retirement[321] (including where this is made in connection with a transfer of the company's undertaking or property[322]); the incorporation in a director's service contract of a term whereby his employment will or may continue for a period of more than five years;[323] an arrangement whereby assets are acquired by or from a director or a person connected with him;[324] and the provision of funds to meet certain expenses incurred by directors.[325] Any affirmation by a charitable company for the purposes of section 322(2)(c) of the Companies Act 1985 (affirmation of voidable arrangements under which assets are acquired by or from a director or person connected with him) is also ineffective without the Charity Commissioners' prior written consent.[326]

The various model charity constitutions prepared on behalf of the Charity Law **9.120** Association, whilst containing a general prohibition upon a trustee, Committee member, or director receiving any payment of money or other material benefit

---

[315] ibid (para 93)
[316] ibid
[317] See cl 5.3 of the Memorandum and Articles of Association for a Charitable Company Limited by Guarantee
[318] Companies Act 1985, Pt X
[319] CA 1993, s 66(1)(a)
[320] ibid, s 66(2)
[321] Companies Act 1985, s 312
[322] ibid, s 313(1)
[323] ibid, s 319(3)
[324] ibid, s 320(1)
[325] ibid, s 337(3)(a)
[326] CA 1993, s 66(1)(b)

(whether direct or indirect) from the charity, nevertheless specifically authorize certain types of benefits.[327] These permitted benefits include indemnity insurance, the payment of interest at a reasonable rate on money lent to the charity, the payment of a reasonable rent or hiring fee for property lent or hired to the charity, the reimbursement of reasonable out-of-pocket expenses actually incurred in running the charity, an indemnity in respect of any liabilities properly incurred in running the charity (including the costs of a successful defence to criminal proceedings), and (in exceptional cases) other payments or benefits with the prior written approval of the Charity Commissioners.

General procedure for avoiding conflict of interests

9.121   A general procedure for avoiding potential conflicts of interests is contained in the model constitutional documents for charities prepared on behalf of the Charity Law Association. The relevant clause provides that a trustee with a personal interest in a matter to be discussed at a meeting of the trustees or any committee must declare an interest before discussion on the matter begins, and withdraw from the meeting for that item unless expressly invited to remain in order to provide information. It also provides that the trustee must not be counted in the quorum during that part of the meeting, and must withdraw during the vote and have no vote on the matter.[328] The model articles for a charitable company limited by guarantee additionally provide that such provision may not be amended without the prior written consent of the Charity Commission.[329] This serves as a reminder of the statutory prohibition upon the alteration of any provision in a charitable company's memorandum or articles which directs or restricts the manner in which the company's property may be used or applied without the Charity Commissioners' prior written consent.[330]

(3) User-participation in charity management

9.122   Recent years have witnessed a growing demand for user-participation in the management of charities.[331] Pressure for this has come particularly from disabled persons who wish to become trustees of charities for the disabled. As the report points out, however, 'Charity Law remains something of an obstacle to user involvement

---

[327] See Trust Deed for a Charitable Trust, cl 6.2; Constitution for a Charitable Unincorporated Association, r 9.2; and Memorandum and Articles of Association for a Charitable Company Limited by Guarantee, cl 5.2 of Memorandum

[328] See Trust Deed for a Charitable Trust, cl 6.3, and Memorandum and Articles of Association for a Charitable Company Limited by Guarantee, cl 5.4 of Memorandum

[329] Memorandum and Articles of Association for a Charitable Company Limited by Guarantee, cl 5.5 of Memorandum

[330] CA 1993, s 64(2)(b)

[331] See the Deakin Report: *Meeting the challenge of change: voluntary action into the 21st century*, The Report of the Commission on the Future of the Voluntary Sector (Chair: Nicholas Deakin), NCVO (1996) 108–10 (para 4.6)

in governance'.[332] Deakin does not describe what these obstacles are, but they could (in some instances) involve the vitiating elements of self-help or political purpose. More generally, however, there is the principle of trusts law that a fiduciary is not permitted to place himself in a position of conflict.[333] It follows from this that, like any trustee, a charity trustee must not exercise his discretions so as to benefit himself. Therefore it is clear that a charity trustee of a grant-awarding charity would be precluded from awarding a grant to himself. Even if he were only one of several trustees and absented himself from the meeting at which the grant was discussed, he would also be prohibited from receiving such a grant. In such circumstances, the rule is absolute. If there are sound reasons for such a rule in private trusts, there are even stronger reasons for it in relation to charitable trusts. After all, public confidence in charities would be severely undermined if the trustees were seen to be exercising their discretions so as to provide direct financial benefits for themselves.

There are, however, many circumstances where it is less clear to what extent the **9.123** 'no conflicts' rule applies. As described below,[334] there seem to be circumstances where the rule is not absolute, and where evidence may be admitted that the trustee did not abuse his position. There is, unfortunately, a dearth of reported case law involving charity trustees. One particular instance, the position of parent-governors of schools, has been examined by the Charity Commissioners.[335] Such governors might be in a position of conflict so far as decisions affect their own children. The Charity Commissioners take the view that, provided certain safeguards are met, the benefits of having such persons as governors outweigh the potential danger of conflicts of interests. The safeguards are: first, that not more than one-third of the governors should be parent-governors; secondly, that at no meeting of the governors should the parent-governors form a majority; and, thirdly, that parent-governors should not take part in decisions concerning the award of scholarships to, or the admission of, their own children.

In many instances, of course, charity trustees are not exercising their discretions in **9.124** favour of individuals, but in favour of types or classes of objects. A charity for the disabled might, for instance, make certain types of equipment available to persons with a certain type and degree of disability. Would a trustee of such a charity who would otherwise be eligible to receive such equipment, be precluded from doing so? In the absence of reported case law involving charities, it is instructive to compare recent developments in relation to trustee-employees of pension funds, where the strict application of this rule would require the trustee-employee to forgo, for instance, any increased pension decided upon by the trustees. The

---

[332] ibid, 110 (para 4.6.7)
[333] *Bray v Ford* [1896] AC 44
[334] See para 9.124
[335] [1988] Ch Com Rep 10 (para 40)

approach of the courts has not been consistent. Vinelott J has, in two reported decisions,[336] held that the strict Chancery approach applies, since he considered it 'outrageous'[337] that a person with a power to distribute a fund amongst a class that includes himself should be able to distribute any part of it for his own benefit. On the other hand, Lindsay J[338] has held that the strict approach should not be applied to trustees who had not deliberately pushed themselves forward as trustees, 'but rather were selected as persons able and willing to serve their colleagues in some way'.[339]

9.125   The Charity Commissioners have stated that where the governing instrument provides for trustees to be nominated by the users of the charity's facilities, such trustees should not participate in meetings which would involve them participating in a decision which would give rise to an irreconcilable conflict of interests.[340] The application of the no-conflicts rule would, however, result in the exclusion of user-trustees from most of the important decisions taken by the trust, and thereby exclude from the decision-making a voice which has at least some moral claim to be heard. The Charity Commissioners have noted the problem of user-participation in relation to the social housing market, and have indicated that they are currently undertaking a review of their policy in this area; they hope to consult widely on the matter.[341]

9.126   In the light of the present uncertainty, and in the absence of any reported court ruling in relation to charities, the safest course of action is to seek the approval of the Charity Commissioners to amend the governing instrument to authorize the appointment of beneficiary-trustees only on the footing that they are excluded from taking part in any meeting at which they could be placed in a position of conflict of interests. A new charity might adopt the model clause in the Charity Law Association's model constitutional documents for charities which lays down a general procedure for avoiding a conflict where a charity trustee has a personal interest in a matter to be discussed at a meeting of the charity trustees.[342]

(4) Local authority members as sole charity trustees

9.127   A local authority as sole trustee can give rise to conflicts of interests, so that the Charity Commissioners are not generally prepared to accept a governing instru-

---

[336] *Re William Makin & Sons Ltd* [1993] OPLR 171; *British Coal Corp v British Coal Superannuation Scheme* [1995] 1 All ER 912
[337] *British Coal Corp v British Coal Superannuation Scheme* [1995] 1 All ER 912, 925
[338] *Re Drexel Burnham Lambert Pension Plan* [1995] 1 WLR 32
[339] ibid, 42. Ironically, in the light of the Robert Maxwell saga, the Pensions Act 1995 generally requires one-third 'beneficiary' representation on the board of trustees of a pension fund, and expressly abrogates the no-conflicts principle in the context of pension funds: Pensions Act 1995, s 39
[340] [1991] Ch Com Rep 8 (paras 41, 43); and see *Users on Board* CC24 (2000)
[341] See [1996] Ch Com Rep 7 (paras 22–5)
[342] The relevant clauses are discussed above, para 9.121

ment which appoints a local authority as sole charity trustee unless they are satisfied that, having considered all other possibilities, such arrangement would be the most beneficial for the charity.[343] The issue has been dealt with above.[344]

(5) *Representative or nominative trustees*

There is potential for a conflict of interests where, in accordance with the terms of the governing instrument, one or more of the charity trustees are appointed by a particular body or organization. It is important that a trustee so appointed makes his decisions as trustee in accordance with the interests of the charity, not the interests of the body which appointed him.[345] The expression 'nominative trustee', which is sometimes used in governing instruments, is probably best avoided, since it gives the misleading impression that the trustee is there to represent the interests of the body which appointed him, which is most certainly not the case. The Charity Commissioners have stated that where there is an irreconcilable conflict of interests, such as in relation to a property transaction, the representative trustee should be excluded from the particular trustee meetings while the matter in question is considered. The remaining trustees, including any other representative trustees, must also act exclusively in the interests of the charity.[346]

9.128

J. Other fiduciary duties

(1) *Duty to participate in the management of the charity*

Each charity trustee has a duty to participate actively in the management of the charity.[347] A charity trustee who passively leaves the administration of the charity to his co-trustees or to others will be personally liable for any loss,[348] and inactivity of some trustees is evidence of misconduct or mismanagement in the administration of the charity, which will enable the Charity Commissioners (after an inquiry) to use their powers to act for the protection of charities.[349]

9.129

---

[343] (1993) 1 Decisions 29 (para 9)

[344] See above, paras 9.16–9.17

[345] [1991] Ch Com Rep 8 (para 42)

[346] ibid, para 43. See also Charity Commission, *Political Activities and Campaigning by Local Community Charities* CC9(a) (Feb 1997), para 61

[347] *Bahin v Hughes* (1886) 31 ChD 390 (CA)

[348] ibid. See also Civil Liability (Contribution) Act 1978

[349] CA 1993, s 18. The potential adverse consequences for a charity where some of its trustees fail to participate in the running of the charity are illustrated in the case of Valley Books Trust, where the founding trustee effectively ran the charity without reference to the other trustees, two of whom were resident in the USA: see [1995] Ch Com Rep 16 (paras 62–6)

Duties on appointment of new trustee

9.130   To satisfy his obligations from the outset, a new trustee should therefore take the
first opportunity to meet his co-trustees and anyone else concerned with the
administration of the charity in order to be briefed about its activities, its funding,
and the nature and condition of its property. The trustees should also ensure
(unless the property is vested in custodian or holding trustees) that all necessary
steps are taken to vest the property in the new and continuing trustees. They
should also examine the latest accounts of the charity; and, where necessary, an
explanation of their content and layout should be obtained. Where necessary, new
trustees (particularly *ex officio* trustees) should formally signify their acceptance by
signing the minute book.[350]

(2)   Duty not to deviate from the terms of the trust or to exceed their powers

9.131   The Charity Commissioners suggest a number of simple steps which all trustees
should take, but which in their experience are often overlooked, which should
help to ensure that the trustees keep within the terms of the trust and do not act
beyond their powers:[351]

> Every trustee should have a personal copy of the governing document(s) of the char-
> ity and be well acquainted with its main provisions. At least one copy of the govern-
> ing document(s) should be available for reference at meetings of the trustees so that
> in taking decisions they do not lose sight of the purposes of the charity nor of the
> limitations on their powers. It is essential that formal minutes of meetings of the
> trustees are taken and that, in particular, the minutes record all the decisions made,
> by whom and by what date any further action has to be taken.

(3)   Fiduciary duties relating to the exercise of their powers

Generally

9.132   Under general principles of trusts law, trustees must periodically consider the
exercise of their powers; any powers they have must be exercised in good faith and
for their proper purpose; no improper considerations must be taken into account;
and there must be no element of capriciousness.[352] In relation to charities, these
duties relate to the status of the trustees as the persons responsible for the general
management and administration of the charity, and should therefore apply to all
charity trustees, including directors of charitable companies and Committee
members of charitable unincorporated associations.

9.133   In reaching decisions relating to the exercise of their fiduciary powers, trustees
have to try to weigh up competing factors, which are often incommensurable in

---

[350]   [1986] Ch Com Rep 26 (para 3)
[351]   [1993] Ch Com Rep 22 (para 88)
[352]   *Re Hay's Settlement Trusts* [1982] 1 WLR 202; *Re Manisty's Settlement* [1974] Ch 17

character; but they are not a court or an administrative tribunal, and are not under any general duty to give a hearing to both sides (and in many situations 'both sides' is a meaningless expression).[353]

Under the general law, trustees do not have to give reasons for their decisions, and this principle has been applied to charitable trusts.[354] This does not mean that the courts have a greater liberty to examine and correct decisions of trustees who choose to give reasons; merely that it is easier to examine a decision if the reasons for it have been disclosed.[355] If a decision taken by trustees is directly attacked in legal proceedings, the trustees may be compelled either legally (through disclosure or subpoena) or practically (in order to avoid adverse inferences being drawn) to reveal the substance of the reasons for their decision.[356] But not everything said in the hurly-burly of debate will be taken as a ground of decision.[357]   **9.134**

Duty to act impartially between persons qualified to benefit from the charity

In the same way that trustees of a private trust are under a duty to act impartially between the beneficiaries or objects (or classes of objects) of the trust,[358] so charity trustees must act impartially between those who, whilst not 'beneficiaries' or 'objects' in the strict sense, nevertheless qualify as persons in whose favour the trustees could exercise their discretion.[359] If, therefore, the purpose of a charity is the relief of poverty by the provision of pensions for a company's poor retired employees and their families,[360] then in exercising their powers of investment (and in particular in considering the competing merits of income and capital growth), the trustees should balance the needs of present pensioners against the potential needs of those who may become pensioners at some future date.   **9.135**

Duty to take account of beneficiaries' legitimate expectations?

In *Scott v National Trust*,[361] Robert Walker J appeared to suggest that the public law doctrine of legitimate expectation has its counterpart in the law of trusts. The case itself concerned the rights of huntsmen to object to a decision of the council of the National Trust to ban deer-hunting on some of the Trust's land. His Lordship's remarks, though obiter (since the huntsmen were not themselves   **9.136**

353 *Scott v National Trust* [1998] 2 All ER 705, 718 (Robert Walker J)
354 *Re Beloved Wilkes's Charity* (1851) 3 Mac & G 444
355 *Dundee General Hospitals Board of Management v Walker* [1952] 1 All ER 896, 900 (Lord Normand) (HL)
356 *Scott v National Trust* [1998] 2 All ER 705, 719
357 ibid, 719, and referring to *R v London County Council, ex p London and Provincial Electric Theatres Ltd* [1915] 2 KB 466, 490–1 (Pickford LJ)
358 *Nestlé v National Westminster Bank plc* [1993] 1 WLR 1261 (CA); the duty of impartiality underpins the rule in *Howe v Lord Dartmouth* (1802) 7 Ves Jr 137
359 [1986] Ch Com Rep 27 (para 8)
360 *Dingle v Turner* [1972] AC 601 (HL); *Re Coulthurst* [1951] Ch 661
361 [1998] 2 All ER 705. For other aspects of this case, see ch 13, paras 13.32 and 13.34–13.46

objects of the National Trust), were clearly intended to be of wide application. He said:[362]

> if (for instance) trustees (whether of a charity, or a pension fund, or a private family trust) have for the last ten years paid £1,000 per quarter to an elderly, impoverished beneficiary of the trust it seems at least arguable that no reasonable body of trustees would discontinue the payment, without any warning, and without giving the beneficiary the opportunity of trying to persuade the trustees to continue the payment, at least temporarily. The beneficiary has no legal or equitable right to continued payment, but he or she has an expectation. So I am inclined to think that legitimate expectation may have some part to play in trust law as well as in judicial review cases.

9.137 This suggestion that charity trustees may have a special duty towards persons who have enjoyed the benefits of the charity over a period of time is novel and its scope uncertain. The existence of such a duty raises the spectre of charity trustees having to give advance notification to such 'beneficiaries' before the charity trustees can take decisions which might adversely affect them. Such a duty might be difficult to comply with where large numbers of such beneficiaries are involved, and could in some cases result in price-sensitive or other information filtering into the public domain, with its potential to prejudice the value of the charity's assets or otherwise to damage the charity itself.

9.138 It is also not clear whether Robert Walker J was seeking to import the public law doctrine of legitimate expectation into trusts law, or whether he meant to draw a parallel between that doctrine and the notion of reasonable expectation which has developed in the context of pension funds.[363] It is more likely that he intended the latter; but care is needed in extracting principles of general application from the pension fund cases, since pension funds have special elements which distinguish them from other private trusts and from charitable trusts. The crucial point is that beneficiaries of a pension fund can be treated as having provided consideration for their interests, either through having made contributions directly into the fund, or through having worked for the company concerned, and their pension rights might therefore be considered a form of deferred pay. Most objects of a charity, by contrast, will be volunteers, so the rationale for applying the principle of reasonable expectation is absent.

9.139 This leaves the possibility that the doctrine of reasonable expectation might be applicable to objects of a charity who have provided consideration, such as the parents of a child at a fee-paying charity school, or an aged person who has entered into a contract for accommodation with a non-mutual charitable housing association. To treat persons who pay for a charity's services and those who do not as having different rights in relation to the charity, however, would surely be invidi-

---

[362] [1998] 2 All ER 705, 718
[363] *Re Courage Group's Pension Scheme* [1987] 1 WLR 495, 515

ous. It is also wrong in principle, since, unlike the objects of a pension fund, the objects of a charity must be selected as objects before entering into any contract with the charity: any contract they may enter into merely indicates the basis on which such benefits are to be received.[364]

It is therefore suggested that neither the public law doctrine of legitimate expecta- **9.140** tion nor the pension trust principle of reasonable expectation should be imported into the law of charities. The fact that charity trustees act without sounding out the views of those currently receiving benefits from the charity might be a factor to be taken into account in all the circumstances when the court is having to decide, according to existing principles, if the charity trustees made their decision properly; but everything must depend on the nature of the charity and what those circumstances are, and there is no merit in trying to impose a distinct and additional duty on charity trustees.

K. Specific duties and powers under the Charities Acts 1992 and 1993

(1) Duties under the Charities Acts 1992 and 1993

The Charities Acts 1992 and 1993 impose a variety of obligations on charity **9.141** trustees and upon other persons, and these are given detailed treatment in the appropriate chapters of this book. The Charities Act 1992 introduced thirteen new criminal offences.[365] Most of these were re-enacted in the Charities Act 1993, but those relating to the control of fund-raising and public charitable collections are still to be found in Parts II and III respectively of the Charities Act 1992.[366] Certain offences under the Charities Act 1993 cannot be instituted except by, or with the consent of, the Director of Public Prosecutions.[367]

---

[364] *Joseph Rowntree Memorial Trust Housing Assoc Ltd v A-G* [1983] Ch 159 (Peter Gibson J)
[365] See F Quint, 'Criminal and Other Sanctions under the CA 1992' (1992–3) 1 CL & PR 101
[366] See chs 21 passim & 22, paras 22.01–22.03 and 22.55–22.82
[367] CA 1993, s 94(1). This safeguard was introduced because of fears expressed in debate during the passage of the Charities Bill 1992 that, as many of the new criminal offences were offences of strict liability, they had the potential to operate in a draconian manner. Offences in CA 1993 requiring the consent of the DPP are those contained in the following sections of that Act: s 5 (signing certain documents which fail to state that the charity is a registered charity); s 11 (supply of false or misleading information to the Charity Commissioners, or suppressing or destroying documents); s 18(14) (failing to comply with an order of the Charity Commissioners not to part with property, or to pay any debt to the charity, or restricting the transactions into which the charity may enter or the payments which may be made in the administration of the charity, without the Charity Commissioners' approval); s 49 (certain offences relating to charity accounts, reports, and returns); and s 73(1) (acting as a charity trustee while disqualified)

9.142 Some obligations[368] contained in the Charities Acts are imposed specifically upon 'charity trustees'[369] (and therefore apply, for example, to directors of charitable companies, as well as to charity trustees of charitable trusts). Other obligations[370] are imposed merely upon 'trustees' (and therefore apply only to trustees of charitable trusts in the strict sense). Yet others are imposed upon anybody who performs a particular act, which could in some instances be the charity trustee himself.[371] Breach of some of the obligations imposed by the Charities Acts can give rise to criminal as well as civil sanctions.[372] In some instances, the only sanction under the Charities Acts is invalidity.[373] Some other duties imposed by the Charities Acts, such as a failure to apply for a cy-près scheme,[374] are enforceable only by civil sanctions. Depending on the nature of the breach, civil remedies may in any event be available; these include an action to account, or for damages for breach of trust or breach of fiduciary duty, or for an injunction to restrain a breach of trust or breach of fiduciary duty. Such proceedings can be brought by the Attorney-General, the Charity Commissioners,[375] or (in 'charity proceedings'[376]) by other persons with locus standi.

9.143 Breach of the duties imposed by the Charities Acts may comprise 'misconduct or mismanagement in the administration of the charity',[377] so enabling the Charity Commissioners, following an inquiry, to exercise their remedial powers to protect charities, including the suspension[378] or removal[379] of any trustee or charity

---

[368] eg the duty to apply for registration of any charity which is not registered nor excepted from registration: CA 1993, s 3(7)(a); and obligations relating to charity accounts, reports, and returns: ibid, ss 41–9. See further ch 10, paras 10.28, 10.85–10.118

[369] As defined in CA 1993, s 97(1)

[370] eg the duty, where appropriate, to apply for a cy-près scheme; this duty is imposed only on a 'trustee' of 'a trust for charitable purposes': ibid s 13(5). This suggests that the duty is imposed on trustees of charitable trusts in the strict sense only

[371] Thus, in relation to a registered charity, an offence is committed by *any person* who signs a document which is required to state the fact that the charity is a registered charity and which fails to do: ibid, s 5(5) (see further ch 2, para 2.28–2.29). An offence is committed by *any person* who knowingly or recklessly provides the Charity Commissioners with false or misleading information, or who wilfully alters, suppresses, conceals, or destroys any document which he might be required to produce to the Charity Commissioners: ibid, s 11(1), (2)

[372] eg persistent failure without reasonable excuse to submit to the Charity Commissioners an annual report or an annual return, or to supply to any person on request a copy of the charity's most recent accounts: ibid, s 49

[373] eg disposals of charity land which fail to comply with the requirements of ibid, ss 36 or 37; see further ch 17, paras 17.83–17.85, 17.95 and 17.109–17.110

[374] CA 1993, s 13(5)

[375] ibid, s 32

[376] ibid, s 33

[377] ibid, s 18(1), (2)

[378] ibid, s 18(1)(i)

[379] ibid, s 18(2)(i)

trustee, the appointment of additional charity trustees,[380] and the establishing of a scheme for the administration of the charity.[381]

(2) Powers under the Charities Act 1993

The Charities Act 1993 confers some powers on charity trustees. Thus it provides **9.144** a procedure to enable trustees of a charity to incorporate themselves as a body corporate.[382] It also lays down procedures by which charity trustees of a small charity may transfer their property to other charities or may modify the trusts of the charity,[383] or (if the charity has a permanent endowment other than land) may spend the capital.[384]

L. Delegation of powers

If there is a large body of trustees, it may be convenient for that body to delegate **9.145** particular management decisions of the charity to a small committee of their own number. Charity trustees may also wish to delegate decisions requiring particular expertise to an appropriate agent; this is especially important in relation to the delegation of investment powers.[385] Trustees may find that delegation of some of their functions, notably investment, is a practical necessity. If the trustees of a very large charitable trust fund are not able to apply their minds to every investment decision which must be made, it is inevitable that day-to-day investment decisions have to be delegated to advisers.[386]

Trustees' legal powers to delegate are, in equity, very restricted: the general princi-**9.146** ple is enshrined in the Latin proposition, *delegatus non potest delegare*: a trustee, being a delegate, cannot himself delegate his duties or powers, either to his co-trustees or to a third party. Important inroads into this principle have, however, been made by statute. Apart from this, delegation may, to some extent, be authorized by a provision contained in the charity's governing instrument or in a scheme, or it may be otherwise sanctioned by the Charity Commissioners.

(1) Statutory power to delegate

Position pre-Trustee Act 2000

Until the Trustee Act 2000, the trustees of a charitable trust (including, therefore, **9.147** the Committee members of an unincorporated charity) had the statutory power

---

[380] ibid, s 18(1)(ii)
[381] ibid, s 18(2)(ii)
[382] ibid, s 50; see above, paras 9.61–9.65
[383] CA 1993, s 74. See further ch 15, paras 15.136–15.147
[384] CA 1993, s 75. See further ch 15, paras 15.148–15.151
[385] On delegation of trustees' investment function, see also ch 16, paras 16.67–16.68
[386] *Steel v Wellcome Custodian Trustees Ltd* [1988] 1 WLR 167, 174 (Harman J)

to delegate contained in the Trustee Act 1925. By virtue of section 23(1), trustees might, instead of acting personally, employ and pay an agent, whether a solicitor, banker, stockbroker, or other person, to transact any business or do any act required to be transacted or done in the execution of the trust, including the receipt and payment of money, and would not be responsible for the default of such agent if employed in good faith.[387] This sub-section enabled trustees to appoint an agent even where the use of an agent was not strictly necessary;[388] but the agent still had to be appointed in his proper field,[389] that is, a stockbroker to deal with financial business, or a solicitor to conduct legal work. Since the business or act had to be such as was 'required' to be done, it was clear that the sub-section did not enable trustees to delegate to the agent the exercise of their discretions as trustees.[390] It also seems that the appointment of the agent in good faith did not itself relieve trustees from any subsequent duty to supervise the agent in the performance of his duties;[391] so that, if a trustee had put the trust property in the agent's hands, the trustee would have been liable on the basis of wilful default.[392]

9.148 Delegation of trustees' discretion to an agent was, however, permissible where the trust property was outside the United Kingdom. Section 23(2) of the Trustee Act 1925 empowered trustees to appoint an agent to deal with trust property situated abroad or to exercise any discretion, trust, or power vested in them in relation to any such property, and the trustees were not responsible for any loss arising thereby by reason only of their having made such an appointment.[393]

Trustee Act 2000

9.149 The Trustee Act 2000 repeals section 23 of the Trustee Act 1925, and Part IV of the new Act contains a much more detailed regime relating to trustees' powers of delegation. The new provisions do not distinguish between property within and outside the United Kingdom. As a respondent to the Law Commission's

---

[387] TA 1925, s 23(1) (repealed)

[388] *Re Vickery* [1931] 1 Ch 572, 581 (Maugham J); contrast the earlier position as laid down in *Speight v Gaunt* (1884) 9 App Cas 1, and *Learoyd v Whiteley* (1887) 12 App Cas 727, which had held that an agent could be appointed only if it was reasonably necessary or in accordance with ordinary business practice

[389] *Ex p Belchier* (1754) Amb 218 (Lord Hardwicke); *Fry v Tapson* (1884) 28 ChD 268

[390] ie thereby leaving intact the position in equity established in *Speight v Gaunt* (1884) 9 App Cas 1; see (1994) 2 Decisions 28

[391] It can be argued that the proviso that the trustee was not to be liable for the default of the agent 'if employed in good faith' was merely intended to clarify that the trustee was not *vicariously* liable for the acts of his agent. On this basis, the proviso did not affect the trustee's *personal* liability: see *Hanbury & Martin's Modern Equity* (ed JE Martin) (15th edn, Sweet & Maxwell, 1997) 562. Contrast *Steel v Wellcome Custodian Trustees Ltd* [1988] 1 WLR 167, 174

[392] TA 1925, s 30(1); see *Re Vickery* [1931] 1 Ch 572. For the meaning of 'wilful default', see above, para 9.93. TA 1925, s 30, is also repealed by TA 2000

[393] TA 1925, s 23(2) (repealed)

Consultation Paper pointed out, the overseas exception to the non-delegation rule was 'a relic of an age of slow communication', and is inappropriate now that global communication is instantaneous. [394]

Part IV confers (inter alia) broader powers of delegation upon trustees than its pre- **9.150** decessor. These statutory powers are, however, additional to other powers conferred on trustees (for example, by other statutes or by the trust instrument), and are also subject to any restriction or exclusion contained in the trust instrument or in any enactment or any provision of subordinate legislation.[395] It should also be noted at the outset that an agent's appointment is not invalidated by the fact that trustees exceed their statutory powers of delegation.[396]

Delegable functions

Section 11(1) of the Trustee Act 2000 sets out the basic principle that the trustees **9.151** of a trust may authorize any person to exercise any or all of their 'delegable functions' as their agents.[397] What, therefore, are these 'delegable functions'?

In the case of private trusts, the delegable functions relate to most of the trustees' **9.152** administrative powers, but not to what might be termed their 'distributive powers', that is their decisions as to the distribution of the trust's income or capital for the benefit of its objects.[398] The Law Commission report that led to the new Act considered that it was inappropriate to draw the same distinction for charitable trusts, because the legal concept of 'charitable purposes' is much wider than the particular charitable objects for which the trust exists. To prohibit trustees of charitable trusts from delegating those functions which relate to charitable purposes would therefore narrow, not widen, their delegable powers.[399] Instead, the Law Commission suggested that the distinction should be drawn between those aspects of the management of charitable trusts that relate to the generation of income to finance the charitable purposes, and the execution of those purposes.[400] Hence they recommended that trustees of charitable trusts should have power to delegate matters which relate to income generation, even though this entails the delegation of their discretions; but that in relation to the delegation of other matters, they should have no greater powers than they had under the law as it then stood, so that they should be able to delegate only those functions which are purely ministerial.[401] The Trustee Act 2000 gives effect to these proposals.

[394] Law Commission Report, *Trustees' Powers and Duties* (Law Com No 260, 1999) para 4.13
[395] TA 2000, s 26
[396] ibid, s 24
[397] ibid, s 11(1)
[398] ibid, s 11(2)
[399] Law Commission Report, *Trustees' Powers and Duties* (Law Com No 260, 1999) para 4.38
[400] ibid, para 4.39
[401] ibid, para 4.42

9.153 In the case of a charitable trust, therefore, the delegable functions, set out in section 11(3), are:[402]

   (a) any function consisting of carrying out a decision that the trustees have taken;
   (b) any function relating to the investment of assets subject to the trust (including, in the case of land held as an investment, managing the land and creating or disposing of an interest in the land);
   (c) any function relating to the raising of funds for the trust otherwise than by means of profits of a trade which is an integral part of the carrying out of the trust's charitable purpose;
   (d) any other function prescribed by an order made by the Secretary of State.[403]

For the purposes of paragraph (c), section 11(4) provides that a trade is an integral part of the carrying out of a trust's charitable purposes if, whether carried on in the United Kingdom or elsewhere,[404] the profits are applied solely to the purposes of the trust and either[405]

   (a) the trade is exercised in the course of the actual carrying out of a primary purpose of the trust, or
   (b) the work in connection with the trade is mainly carried out by beneficiaries of the trust.

The statutory duty of care[406] applies to trustees when entering into an arrangement authorizing any person to exercise all or any of their delegable functions as their agent.[407]

General restrictions on delegation

9.154 The persons whom the trustees may under this statutory power authorize to exercise their functions as their agent include one or more of their number.[408] They may not authorize two or more persons to exercise the same function unless they are to exercise the function jointly.[409] A person may be authorized to exercise functions as the trustees' agent even though he is also appointed to act as their nominee or custodian.[410]

9.155 It is also provided, in section 12(3) of the Trustee Act 2000, that trustees may not use the statutory power to authorize 'a beneficiary' to exercise any function as their

---

[402] TA 2000, s 11(3)

[403] The power to make an order under para (d) is exercisable by statutory instrument, which is to be subject to annulment in pursuance of a resolution of either House of Parliament: ibid, s 11(5)

[404] The sub-section is grammatically unsound: the phrase 'whether carried on in the United Kingdom or elsewhere' is clearly intended to refer to 'the trade', not to 'the profits'

[405] TA 2000, s 11(4)

[406] ibid, s 1(1)

[407] ibid, s 2 & Sch 1, para 3(1)(a)

[408] ibid, s 12(1)

[409] ibid, s 12(2)

[410] ibid, s 12(4)

agent (even if the beneficiary is also a trustee).[411] Although a charitable trust does not have human 'beneficiaries' in the strict sense, the use of the word 'beneficiaries' in section 11(4) specifically in the context of charitable trusts shows that this expression is there being used loosely to refer to those classes of persons whom a charitable trust is intended to benefit.[412] If it has the same meaning in section 12(3), the trustees of charitable trusts which directly benefit identifiable classes of persons (such as the disabled) will not be able to rely on the statutory power to appoint as an agent a person who may fall into the class of recipients or potential recipients. A charity for the sightless, for instance, would not be able to use the statutory power to appoint as their agent a blind solicitor.

A person who is authorized under section 11 to exercise a function is (whatever **9.156** the terms of the agency) subject to any specific duties or restrictions attached to the function.[413] An agent to whom the trustees delegate their investment function, for example, must therefore have regard to the standard investment criteria laid down in section 4.[414] Similarly, if trustees of a charitable trust rely on section 11 to delegate functions in relation to land, the agent, in carrying out those functions, must comply with the requirements of the Charities Act 1993.[415] If an agent is authorized under section 11 of the Trustee Act 2000 to exercise a power which is subject to a requirement to obtain advice, the agent is not subject to such requirement if he is the kind of person from whom it would have been proper for the trustees to obtain advice.[416]

Trustees may authorize a person to exercise their functions as their agent on such **9.157** terms as they may determine.[417] Trustees may not, however, appoint an agent on a term which permits the agent to appoint a substitute, or which restricts the liability of the agent or such substitute, or which permits the agent to act in circumstances capable of giving rise to a conflict of interests, unless it is reasonably necessary for them to do so.[418]

---

[411] ibid, s 12(3)
[412] The wording of s 11(4) follows that of ICTA 1988, s 505(1)(e), where the expression 'beneficiaries' is similarly used
[413] TA 2000, s 13(1)
[414] ibid
[415] ie as set out in CA 1993, ss 36–9. See Law Commission Report, *Trustees' Powers and Duties* (Law Com No 260, 1999) para 4.41, and Explanatory Note to cl 13 of the Draft Bill appended thereto
[416] TA 2000, s 13(2). *Sed quaere* whether, for the purposes of CA 1993, s 36(3), an agent would be free from the obligation to obtain and consider a written report on a proposed disposition of charity land from a qualified surveyor if the agent is himself so qualified. It depends whether the requirement to obtain and consider a surveyor's report is 'a requirement to obtain advice' within the TA 2000, s 13(2). In substance it is
[417] TA 2000, s 14(1). This is subject to ss 14(2), 15(2), and 29–32
[418] ibid, s 14(2), (3)

Delegation of asset management functions

9.158 There are special restrictions on the delegation by trustees of what are called their 'asset management functions', which means their functions relating to the investment of assets, the acquisition of property for the trust, and the creation, management, and disposal of trust property.[419] Trustees may not delegate their asset management functions except by an agreement which is in, or evidenced in, writing;[420] the trustees must also prepare a policy statement giving guidance on the exercise of such functions, with which statement the agent must, in his agreement, undertake to comply.[421]

Review of, and liability for, agents

9.159 Section 22 of the Trustee Act 2000 imposes duties on trustees to supervise an agent. The trustees must keep under review the arrangements under which the agent acts, and how they are being put into effect.[422] In appropriate circumstances, they must consider whether they should give directions to the agent, or revoke his authorization.[423] Where the trustees have delegated asset management functions, they must also assess whether the policy statement is being complied with, and whether there is any need to revise it.[424] Under section 23, a trustee is not liable for the act or default of the agent unless he has failed to comply with the statutory duty of care[425] when appointing the agent or with the duties of subsequent supervision imposed by section 22.[426] Sections 22 and 23 apply to trustees, however, only so far as there is no contrary provision in the trust instrument.[427]

Execution of instruments: s 82 of Charities Act 1993

9.160 The Charities Act 1993[428] expressly enables charity trustees (in addition to and not in derogation of any other powers[429]) to delegate to any two or more of their number the power to execute assurances, or other deeds or instruments, in the names and on behalf of the trustees, for giving effect to transactions to which the trustees are a party. The authority may be general or limited in such manner as the

---

[419] TA 2000, s 15(5)
[420] ibid, s 15(1)
[421] ibid, s 15(2)
[422] ibid, s 22(1)(a)
[423] ibid, s 22(1)(b), (4)
[424] ibid, s 22(2)
[425] ie under ibid, s 1(1) & Sch 1, para 3(1)(a)
[426] ibid, s 23(1). There are parallel provisions concerning a trustee's liability for the act or default of a substitute: ibid, s 23(2)
[427] ibid, s 21(3)
[428] CA 1993, s 82
[429] ibid, s 82(5)

trustees think fit. Any deed or instrument executed in pursuance of an authority so given is deemed to be of the same effect as if executed by the whole body.[430]

It is provided that any such authority suffices for any deed or instrument if it is given in writing or by resolution of a meeting of the trustees, notwithstanding the want of any formality that would otherwise be required.[431] Any such authority may be given so as to make the powers conferred exercisable by any of the trustees, or it may be restricted to named persons or in any other way.[432] Subject to any such restriction, and until it is revoked, such authority has effect, notwithstanding any change in the charity trustees, as a continuing authority given by the charity trustees from time to time of the charity and exercisable by such trustees.[433] **9.161**

In any authority under this section to execute a deed or instrument in the names and on behalf of charity trustees, there is, unless the contrary intention appears, to be implied authority also to execute it for them in the name and on behalf of the Official Custodian for Charities or of any other person, in any case in which the charity trustees could do so.[434] **9.162**

Where a deed or instrument purports to be executed in pursuance of this section, then in favour of a purchaser who (then or afterwards) in good faith acquires for money or money's worth an interest in or charge on property or the benefit of any covenant or agreement expressed to be entered into by the charity trustees, it is conclusively presumed to have been duly executed by virtue of the section.[435] **9.163**

The section does not itself confer any authority on those trustees so authorized to execute a deed to deliver it as a deed on behalf of the body of trustees as a whole. It used to be thought that an agent could not at common law deliver a deed on behalf of his principal unless his authority was itself conferred by deed;[436] but it now appears that this view was misconceived, and that the common law required no such authorization by deed.[437] In any event, any such rule of law which might have existed has since been abolished by statute.[438] Where charity trustees have conferred authority on two or more of their number to execute deeds in accordance with section 82 of the Charities Act 1993, it is reasonable to presume, where no express authority to deliver the document as a deed has been conferred, that **9.164**

---

[430] ibid, s 82(1)
[431] ibid, s 82(2)(a)
[432] ibid, s 82(2)(b)
[433] ibid, s 82(2)(c)
[434] ibid, s 82(3)
[435] ibid, s 82(4)
[436] eg *Berkeley v Hardy* (1826) 5 B & C 355 (authority under hand only, and a deed of authorization was not to be presumed); *Harrison v Jackson* (1797) 7 TR 207 (execution by partner purportedly on behalf of his co-partners)
[437] *Longman v Viscount Chelsea* (1989) 58 P & CR 189 (CA); but contrast *Venetian Glass Gallery Ltd v Next Properties Ltd* [1989] 2 EGLR 42
[438] LP (Misc Provs) A 1989, s 1(1)

such authority is to be implied. For the avoidance of doubt, however, it is desirable that the conferring of the authority to execute deeds also contains an express authority to deliver such deeds on behalf of all the trustees.

9.165 Since section 82 confers the power to delegate the execution of instruments on 'charity trustees', it might at first sight appear that directors of charitable companies (who for the purposes of the Charities Act 1993 are 'charity trustees',[439] may avow themselves of this power. The section is not, however, appropriate to a corporate charity, since deeds and other instruments will be executed by the company itself, not in the names and on behalf of its directors. A document may be executed by a company by the affixing of its common seal;[440] but a document signed by a director and the secretary of the company, or by two directors, and expressed (in whatever form of words) to be executed by the company, has the same effect as if executed under the common seal.[441] A document executed by a company which makes it clear on its face that it is intended by the person or persons making it to be a deed has effect, upon delivery, as a deed; and it is presumed, unless a contrary intention is proved, to be delivered upon its being so executed.[442]

Individual delegation

9.166 The examples of statutory delegation so far considered have all involved delegation by the trustees collectively: three trustees, A, B, and C, for instance, might, pursuant to their statutory powers, delegate certain of their functions to (for example) D. There is, however, also statutory provision for delegation by a trustee individually; this would enable A to delegate all or any of his functions to D, without affecting the functions of the other trustees, B and C. Provision for individual delegation is contained in section 25 of the Trustee Act 1925 as substituted by the Trustee Delegation Act 1999.[443] Under the new section, notwithstanding any rule of law or equity to the contrary, a trustee may, by power of attorney, delegate the execution or exercise of all or any of the trusts, powers, and discretions vested in him as trustee either alone or jointly with any other person or persons.[444] Such delegation may be for a period not exceeding twelve months.[445] The persons who may be donees of a power under this section include a trust corporation.[446] The donor of a power of attorney given under this section is liable for the acts or

---

[439] CA 1993, s 97(1)

[440] Companies Act 1985, s 36A(2). S 36A was inserted by Companies Act 1989, 130(2) as from 31 July 1990

[441] Companies Act 1985, s 36A(4)

[442] ibid, s 36A(5). For protection of purchasers, see ibid, s 36A(6)

[443] See Trustee Delegation Act 1999, s 5(1)

[444] TA 1925, s 25(1), which affects powers of attorney created after the commencement of the Trustee Delegation Act 1999

[445] TA 1925, s 25(2)(b)

[446] ibid, s 25(3)

defaults of the donee in the same manner as if they were the acts or defaults of the donor.[447]

(2) Delegation under a power in the governing instrument

Power to delegate may be contained in the governing instrument.[448] Such a power **9.167** may be limited so as to permit delegation in respect of particular matters only, or it may be very broad so as to permit the trustees to delegate any of their functions.[449] A power which merely permits the trustees to employ a clerk or other officers does not in itself authorize the trustees to delegate the administration of the charity to those officers.[450] The Charity Commissioners emphasize that, where trustees properly delegate decisions on day-to-day management matters to committees or employees, the limits of delegation should be precisely defined in writing and clear arrangements made and followed for reporting back decisions taken;[451] and they remind trustees of the need for trustees to monitor and control this process closely.[452] Since the trustees who delegate are liable for the acts performed by any committee which they appoint, it is also desirable that any such committee contains at least one trustee.[453]

If the power is very wide, enabling the trustee to delegate all his duties and powers **9.168** to the delegate, or if the delegation goes beyond matters of management and administration and extends into matters such as the selection of objects to benefit, the delegate will himself become a trustee for the purposes of the law of trusts. If the delegation vests in the delegate the general control and management of the charity, such a person will be a 'charity trustee' for the purposes of the Charities Act 1993.[454] However, even if the appointment effectively makes the delegate a trustee, the trustees who appointed him will remain liable for the acts and omissions of the delegate unless the governing instrument validly restricts their liability.

---

[447] ibid, s 25(7)

[448] See [1993] Ch Com Rep 21 (para 83)

[449] The model charity constitutions prepared on behalf of the CLA confer a very wide power to delegate: see cl 5.7.2 of the Trust Deed for a Charitable Trust; art 5.3 of the Memorandum and Articles of Association of a Charitable Company Limited by Guarantee; and r 8.2 of the Constitution for a Charitable Unincorporated Association

[450] [1986] Ch Com Rep 27–8 (para 10)

[451] The model charity constitutions prepared on behalf of the CLA require all proceedings of committees to be reported promptly to the trustees: see cl 5.7.2 of the Trust Deed for a Charitable Trust; art 5.3 of the Memorandum and Articles of Association of a Charitable Company Limited by Guarantee; and r 8.2 of the Constitution for a Charitable Unincorporated Association

[452] [1993] Ch Com Rep 21 (para 83)

[453] A requirement that every committee contain a minimum number of trustees is contained in the model charity constitutions prepared on behalf of the CLA: see cl 5.7.2 of the Trust Deed for a Charitable Trust; art 5.3 of the Memorandum and Articles of Association of a Charitable Company Limited by Guarantee; and r 8.2 of the Constitution for a Charitable Unincorporated Association

[454] CA 1993, s 97(1)

9.169 From the point of view of the charity trustees, it is therefore important that any express power of delegation does contain some restriction on their personal liability in the event of loss resulting from the acts or omissions of the delegates. The Charity Commissioners are unlikely to approve the registration of (or a proposed amendment to) a governing instrument excluding the personal liability of the trustees except in the most unusual circumstances, where a limited exclusion would be in the best interests of the charity.[455]

(3) Delegation under a scheme or otherwise sanctioned by the Charity Commissioners

9.170 A power to delegate may be contained in a scheme. Since the Charity Commissioners have concurrent jurisdiction with High Court in the making of schemes for the administration of a charity,[456] the Charity Commissioners may, and indeed have, approved schemes involving the delegation of trustees' powers. The criterion for the approval of such a power, as in other instances where amendment of administrative provisions in the governing instrument (as opposed to the charity's purposes) is sought, is what is expedient in the best interests of the charity.[457] The Charity Commissioners have, for instance, made schemes empowering the trustees (*inter alia*) to appoint professional investment advisers to whom the power to buy and sell investments could be delegated, in order to assist the trustees in administering a substantial capital endowment.[458]

9.171 In another instance, a hospital charity needed to borrow substantial amounts in order to carry out works of modernization, but the trustees and the committee of management which ran it were forbidden by the deed of gift which established it from raising money by mortgaging the hospital premises. At that time, the Charity Commissioners' consent to mortgage had to be obtained.[459] A mortgagee was willing to make a loan subject to the condition that professional managers were brought in to run the hospital. The Charity Commissioners authorized the delegation of the trustees' powers to a firm of management consultants for a period of five years, with an option to renew. Under the arrangement the consultants undertook to act within the objects and powers of the charity and to be

---

[455] cf the court's approval of a scheme excluding trustees' liability in *Steel v Wellcome Custodian Trustees Ltd* [1988] 1 WLR 167, discussed below, paras 9.173–9.175

[456] CA 1993, s 16; see further ch 15, paras 15.28–15.34

[457] cf *Re JW Laing Trust* [1984] Ch 143; and see ch 15, para 15.23

[458] See eg [1989] Ch Com Rep 22–3 (paras 77–9), referring to the scheme made by the Charity Commissioners in respect of the Tottenham Grammar School Foundation

[459] ie under CA 1960, s 29, which empowered the Charity Commissioners to consent to mortgaging the permanent endowment despite anything in the trusts of the charity: ibid, s 29(3). The comparable modern provision is the CA 1993, s 38, which enables the Charity Commissioners' consent to be dispensed with where the charity trustees have obtained and considered proper advice. The modern procedure also applies notwithstanding anything in the trusts of the charity: ibid, s 38(5)

subject to the overall control and direction exercised by the committee of management. In the circumstances, the Commissioners considered that such an arrangement was in the best interests of the charity.[460]

The Commissioners may alternatively by order sanction a delegation of the **9.172** trustees' powers which would otherwise not be within the powers of the charity trustees, provided that such a delegation is expedient in the interests of the charity.[461]

It is rare for a scheme to contain an exclusion of the trustees' personal liability for **9.173** the acts and omissions of those to whom the powers are delegated, since this will not usually be in a charity's best interests. A restriction on the charity trustees' liability was approved, however, in *Steel v Wellcome Custodian Trustees Ltd*,[462] where the court approved a scheme relating to the investment of the charity's fund. The scheme contained, inter alia, a power to delegate the investment of the entire fund to external advisers subject to certain conditions, namely, that the trustees were to be entitled to revoke the delegation after twelve months; that the advisers were to report at least quarterly on the performance of the investments entrusted to them, and were to notify the trustees within fourteen days of any acquisition or disposal; and that the trustees were to use reasonable endeavours to ensure that the advisers observed the guidelines. The power of delegation in the scheme could be exercised 'without liability for any loss', but again this was subject to certain qualifications:[463] the trustees were to be liable if they failed to take reasonable care in choosing their agents or in fixing or enforcing the terms of their engagement; they were also to be liable if they failed to require an agent to take remedial action in respect of breaches of the agency agreement in circumstances in which they had or ought to have had notice of the breach and in which, as reasonably prudent men of business, they could have been expected to require remedial action to be taken.

As his Lordship pointed out,[464] the fund was unusual both in its enormous size (its **9.174** total value being at that time some £3.2 billion) and in the fact that 90 per cent of it was invested in the shares of one company. Nevertheless, the decision illustrates that there is no rule of law which prevents the governing instrument of a charity from excluding to a limited extent the liability of the trustees for the acts of those to whom they have lawfully delegated powers of management, provided that the delegation is subject to the appropriate safeguards, that is, the delegation is for a limited period, the delegates are required to report back at regular (and not

---

[460] [1984] Ch Com Rep 17 (paras 43–5) (discussing the Ospedale Italiano, ie the Italian Hospital)
[461] CA 1993, s 26(1)
[462] [1988] 1 WLR 167 (Harman J)
[463] ibid, 170–1
[464] ibid, 170

excessively long) intervals, and the trustees use reasonable endeavours to ensure that the delegates observe the guidelines.

9.175 The fact that in the *Steel* case the trustees retained personal liability for seeing that the delegates observed the guidelines laid down reinforces what the Charity Commissioners had themselves stated some years earlier, namely, that:[465]

> while a trust instrument may permit a trustee to delegate some of his duties, he is never entitled to abrogate his responsibilities entirely: ultimately the trustees must ensure that the assets of the charity are properly managed and adequately safeguarded.

M. Insurance

(1) Insuring the charity's property

Power to insure

9.176 Trustees of a trust of land have a power to insure trust property for its full value, because they have in relation to the land all the powers of an absolute owner.[466]

9.177 Trustees have for many years had a power to insure under section 19 of the Trustee Act 1925. In its original form, however, this power was limited in three ways: first, it was limited to personalty; secondly, it gave trustees power to insure personal property only for an amount not exceeding three-quarters of its value; and, thirdly, it gave them power to insure out of income only.[467] The Charity Commissioners' view was that section 19, and therefore its restrictions, did not apply to charitable trusts.[468] Whether that section did apply to charitable trusts or not was never resolved judicially; but this is now a matter of historical interest only, because the Trustee Act 2000[469] has substituted a new section 19 into the Trustee Act 1925, which, whilst applying to charitable trusts, has removed the former restrictions. Under the new section 19(1), a trustee may

> (a) insure any property which is subject to the trust against risks of loss or damage due to any event, and
> (b) pay the premiums out of the trust funds.

---

[465] [1981] Ch Com Rep 34 (para 108)

[466] Trusts of Land and Appointment of Trustees Act 1996, s 6(1)

[467] TA 1925, s 19(1) (original form)

[468] [1972] Ch Com Rep 28 (para 82). The Charity Commissioners considered that s 19(2) (which disapplied sub-s (1) in the case of a bare trust) indicated that the original s 19 was intended to be restricted to private trusts only. If, however, the trustees of a charity were concerned that, in insuring for full value, they might be contravening s 19(1), the Commissioners were prepared to give their consent to such payment under what is now CA 1993, s 26 (power to authorize dealing with charity property) or their advice that, in making such payment, the trustees would be acting in accordance with the trusts, under what is now CA 1993, s 29

[469] TA 2000, s 34(1)

The expression 'trust funds' means any income or capital funds of the trust.[470] The new power therefore enables trustees to pay the premiums out of either income or capital. It will also be seen that the substituted provision is not limited to personalty, and it permits insurance to be for the property's full value.

Duty to insure?

Although trustees have long had a power to insure, it has never been clear whether **9.178** equity imposes on them a duty to do so;[471] it is, however, likely that the court would today recognize that there is a duty to insure where it is in all the circumstances reasonable to do so. The Charity Commissioners have stated that, in their opinion, charity trustees are under a duty, as ordinary prudent men, to insure the property of the charitable trust for its full value.[472] The Commissioners do recognize, however, that in the case of a museum or art gallery, the full costs of insurance of the exhibits or works of art may be prohibitively high, in that it might leave the charity with insufficient funds to fulfil other activities essential to its purposes. In such circumstances, they suggest that the trustees seek their guidance as to whether a failure adequately to insure would be a breach of trust, or an act of negligence.[473]

Although the Trustee Act 2000 amended the law relating to trustees' powers to **9.179** insure, it did not introduce any statutory duty to insure. In their Report which led to the new Act, the Law Commission recognized that there might be uncertainty about when such a duty would arise, with the result that trustees might waste trust assets by insuring in circumstances where insurance was not necessary.[474] It also noted the concern that some trusts might lack the resources to insure, particularly small museums and art galleries.[475] It did, however, recommend that, once trustees have resolved to exercise their power to insure, their manner of doing so should be subject to the new statutory duty of care.[476] This proposal was implemented in the Trustee Act 2000, which provides that such duty of care[477] applies to a trustee[478]

---

[470] TA 1925, s 19(5), as substituted by TA 2000, s 34(1)
[471] *Re McEacharn* (1911) 103 LT 900 (Eve J, holding that trustees are under no obligation to insure, even where a prudent person would do so); contrast *Re Betty* [1899] 1 Ch 821, 829 (North J, suggesting that trustees ought to insure the trust property at the expense of the estate)
[472] [1972] Ch Com Rep 28 (para 83). See generally, Charity Commission's leaflet, *Charities and Insurance*, CC49 (1996). Charity trustees are under a duty imposed by the general law to take out certain other types of insurance, eg if the charity has employees, the charity trustees must take out employer's liability insurance; if it owns or operates vehicles, they must have the necessary minimum care insurance: ibid, paras 53–4. Charities which own or occupy buildings should take out public liability cover: ibid, paras 49–51
[473] Charity Commission, *Charities and Insurance*, CC49 (1996), para 47
[474] Law Commission Report, *Trustees' Powers and Duties* (Law Com No 260, 1999) para 6.8
[475] ibid
[476] ibid, para 6.9
[477] The statutory duty of care is set out in TA 2000, s 1(1): see above, paras 9.78–9.79
[478] TA 2000, s 2 & Sch 1, para 5

(a) when exercising the power under section 19 of the Trustee Act 1925 to insure property;

(b) when exercising any corresponding power, however conferred.

9.180 The statutory duty of care does not apply if, or in so far as, it appears from the trust instrument that the duty is not meant to apply.[479]

Insurance and schemes

9.181 Problems can arise where a charity is given property which it is too expensive for it to insure. In one instance, the governors of a school had been given valuable Greek manuscripts which were not suitable for use in teaching, and the cost of insuring them was too great. The Charity Commissioners considered that the manuscripts had been given to the school, not for its general purposes, but for use in teaching. They did, however, agree to proceed with a scheme authorizing the governors to sell the manuscripts at auction, and making provision for the proceeds of sale.[480]

9.182 In another case, a bequest to the Royal Academy of Music included, amongst other musical instruments, three made by Stradivarius, these being so valuable it was not practicable to permit their use by students. The cost of insurance would also have been many thousands of pounds a year, at a time when the Academy had insufficient ordinary instruments for daily practice. After discussion with the trustees, the Charity Commissioners made a scheme empowering the trustees to sell the most valuable instruments and to apply the proceeds for the acquisition of other instruments for student use, and ultimately for the promotion of the musical education of the Academy's students.[481]

The Commissioners' common-form clause used in schemes directs[482]:

> that the trustees shall insure the property of the charity to the full value thereof against fire and other usual risks and shall suitably insure in respect of public liability and employer's liability, in so far as the property of the charity is not required to be kept insured by lessees or tenants.

(2) Indemnity insurance

9.183 The Charity Commissioners have no objection to a charity's paying the premiums on an insurance policy to cover the loss, damage or destruction of the charity property resulting from the acts and defaults of its trustees.[483] Before their review of their policy on indemnity insurance in 1991, however, they had taken the view that the charity's funds could not be applied to provide indemnity insurance to the

---

[479] TA 2000, Sch 1, para 7

[480] *Baroness Burdett-Coutts' Bequest to Highgate School* [1987] Ch Com Rep 11 (para 48)

[481] *The Royal Academy of Music—the John Rutson Bequest* [1986] Ch Com Rep 30–1 (App B, para (a))

[482] [1972] Ch Com Rep 28 (para 84)

[483] [1991] Ch Com Rep 7 (para 36)

charity trustees against their own liability. It is clear, as a matter of law, that insurance cannot cover the charity trustees against their own criminal acts, since this would be against public policy.[484] What was less clear was the extent to which a charity could lawfully provide such insurance to cover charity trustees for non-criminal acts. The Charity Commissioners' earlier attitude was that such insurance was not permissible, since the payment of the premiums would comprise an application of charity funds which would be for the personal benefit of the trustees, and not an application of the funds for charitable purposes. The enactment of the Charities Acts 1992 and 1993, however, produced heightened awareness of the responsibilities of trustees;[485] and, in the light of growing public concern that persons might be deterred from becoming charity trustees because of fear that, through misjudgement rather than malicious intent, their personal assets might be at risk, the Charity Commissioners undertook a review of this area.[486] The result of the review was that they reformulated their policy on charity trustee indemnity insurance.[487]

It may be surmised (although the Charity Commissioners do not acknowledge this to be the reason) that the changes made to the companies' legislation in 1989 provided an additional spur to modifying the Charity Commissioners' approach. **9.184** By an amendment made in 1989 to the Companies Act 1985,[488] a company was authorized to purchase and maintain insurance for any officer (including a director) of the company against any liability for negligence, default, breach of duty, or breach of trust in relation to the company.[489] This amendment did not exclude insurance for directors of charitable companies, so that it became difficult for the Commissioners to maintain either that directors of charitable companies could not take advantage of the statute, or that the ability of a charity to provide such indemnity insurance should depend upon its having been set up in corporate form. In their report for 1991 the Charity Commissioners stated that the withdrawal of the statutory restriction did not of itself authorize a charitable company to provide indemnity insurance for its directors, as such insurance would be a personal benefit to the directors, and the memorandum and articles of a charitable company would usually preclude the directors from taking any personal benefit.[490] For the directors of an existing company to take advantage of the relaxation would therefore require an amendment to the memorandum and articles, and the Charity Commissioners stated that they would have no objection to

---

[484] ibid, para 37
[485] [1993] Ch Com Rep 7 (para 18)
[486] See [1990] Ch Com Rep 3 (para 11); [1991] Ch Com Rep 7 (para 34)
[487] See generally C Baxter, 'Trustees' Personal Liability and the Role of Liability Insurance' [1996] Conv 12
[488] Companies Act 1985, s 310(3)(a), as inserted by Companies Act 1989, s 137(1)
[489] Companies Act 1985, s 310(1)
[490] [1991] Ch Com Rep 7–8 (para 38)

such an amendment, provided that the insurance was limited to that which will now be described.[491]

9.185 In their report for 1991, the Charity Commissioners stated that, a contract of insurance being one of utmost good faith, insurance would probably not be obtainable to cover charity trustees against acts which they knew to be wrong, though not criminal.[492] However, in the same report, the Commissioners expressed a view from which they have since partially retreated: namely that they would have no objection if, in appropriate cases, a charity paid for insurance, either directly or by reimbursing the trustees for the premiums, to cover a trustee from personal liability for acts either properly undertaken in the administration of a charity or undertaken in breach of trust but under an honest mistake.[493] They added that trustees would need to satisfy themselves that the degree of exposure to liability, and the cost of effecting insurance, justified the expenditure.[494]

9.186 The Charity Commissioners evidently later considered that the statement contained in their 1991 report was too wide-ranging, because they have since adopted a much more cautious stance.[495] The Charity Commissioners originally required a clause empowering the charity to provide indemnity insurance for its trustees to contain a limitation excluding any claim 'for wilful default or wrongdoing or wilful neglect or default' on the part of the trustee insured. Doubts were, however, raised whether such form of words would permit a charity to pay for insurance to indemnify a trustee who had committed a breach of trust but had acted honestly.[496] The Charity Commissioners concluded that the following was an appropriate form of wording:[497]

> The Insurers shall not be liable for loss arising from any act or omission which the trustee knew to be a breach of trust or breach of duty or which was committed by the trustee in reckless disregard of whether it was a breach of trust or breach of duty or not.

9.187 In devising this new form of wording, the Charity Commissioners said that they were mindful of the fact that, were indemnity insurance to be excluded in all cases where the trustees could be shown to have acted without due care, the result would be to deny insurance cover to trustees who, though proven to have acted

---

[491] [1991] Ch Com Rep 7–8 (para 38)

[492] ibid, 7 (para 37)

[493] ibid

[494] ibid

[495] [1993] Ch Com Rep 8 (paras 19–20); (1994) 2 Decisions 24–7

[496] cf 'wilful default' in *Re City Equitable Fire Insurance Co* [1925] Ch 407 (Romer J); in the context of TA 1925, s 23(1), as interpreted by Maugham J in *Re Vickery* [1931] 1 Ch 572; and in the context of an accident insurance policy in *Morley v United Friendly Insurance plc* [1993] 3 All ER 47, 55 (Beldam LJ). See further above, para 9.93

[497] (1994) 2 Decisions 26; see also Charity Commission, *Charities and Insurance*, CC49 (1996), para 21

without sufficient care, had nevertheless acted honestly.[498] It does, however, seem that the new form of words effectively denies trustees of much of the value of indemnity insurance cover. The practical difficulty with the Charity Commissioners' current approach is that it leaves room for an insurance company to argue about whether the trustees acted in reckless disregard or not. In the light of this, charities should consider carefully whether trustee indemnity insurance can be justified as being in the charity's interests, when other measures might be taken to reduce the risk of trustees' personal liability.[499] It is clearly more important that a charity insure its own funds against losses which might arise from breaches of trust, since the scope of such insurance cover can be wider than that of indemnity insurance for trustees.[500]

The Model Trust Deed for a Charitable Trust prepared on behalf of the Charity Law Association permits the trustees to insure themselves[501]   **9.188**

> against the costs of a successful defence to a criminal prosecution brought against them as charity trustees or against personal liability incurred in respect of any act or omission which is or is alleged to be a breach of trust or breach of duty (unless the Trustee concerned knew that, or was reckless whether, the act or omission was a breach of trust or breach of duty).

The Charity Commissioners have also expressed their view on the scope for indemnity insurance to cover the directors of a charitable company from personal liability for wrongful trading.[502] They point out that the expression 'wrongful trading' necessarily includes a sufficient lack of care which makes it coincide substantially with the terms of their approved exclusion clause. They recognize, however, that the coincidence is not complete, so that they would not object to a charitable company purchasing insurance for the directors to indemnify them against any liability arising from 'wrongful trading', provided that an equivalent exclusion clause is applied to the cover, that is, so that the insurers are not liable for loss arising if the directors of the charitable company continued to trade knowing that it was insolvent or in reckless disregard of whether it was solvent or not.[503]   **9.189**

If a national charity has numerous autonomous branches, it is not necessary for each branch of the charity to make out a case for the purchase of indemnity insurance if the national charity itself can satisfy the Charity Commissioners that such purchase is expedient in the interests of both the national charity and its branches. The Charity Commissioners can then give a single authority for both the national   **9.190**

---

[498] (1994) 2 Decisions 26
[499] [1996] Ch Com Rep 7–8 (paras 26–7); Charity Commission, *Charities and Insurance*, CC49 (1996)
[500] See Farrer & Co, *Charity Group Newsletters*, Autumn 1993, Autumn 1994
[501] cl 3.15
[502] Insolvency Act 1986, s 214
[503] (1994) 2 Decisions 27; see also Charity Commission, *Charities and Insurance*, CC49 (1996), para 30

charity and its branches.[504] A separate application is needed, however, if the autonomous branches prefer to have a different policy from that of the national charity.[505]

9.191 Whether a trust or an unincorporated charity has power to provide indemnity insurance for the trustees depends upon the terms of the governing instrument be. The Charity Commissioners have stated that they will raise no objection to the inclusion of a provision for such insurance in a new instrument submitted for registration, provided that the insurance is limited as set out above.[506] Where the governing instrument of an existing charity contains no power to pay for indemnity insurance, the Charity Commissioners have stated that they are willing to approve an amendment to the constitution to provide for it only if they are satisfied that such insurance is expedient in the interests of the charity. In the Commissioners' view:[507]

> If the activities of the charity were so simple and uncomplicated that the possibility of loss either by deliberate wrong doing or by negligence could be dealt with by proper administrative controls the necessary power would not generally be given. The trustees would need to demonstrate that there were special circumstances to justify the provision of such insurance. These could include the nature of the charity's activities, the degree of risk of personal liability to which its trustees were exposed, the number of trustees, the amount of indemnity required, and the cost to the charity of effecting liability insurance for all of them.

N. Liability to third parties

(1) Trustees of a charitable trust strictu sensu

9.192 It must be emphasized at the outset that much of the law concerning the liability of trustees to third parties has been developed in relation to private, rather than charitable, trusts. The principles which have emerged can, however, be applied to charitable trusts with little modification. Some differences necessarily flow from the nature of a charitable trust: there is, for instance, no question of a charity trustee's recovering by way of indemnity from the personal assets of a beneficiary,[508] since there is no human *cestui que trust* who can be subjected to such personal obligation.

9.192 As a charitable trust is not an incorporated body it lacks a separate legal *persona*; therefore contracts which the charity enters into with third parties must be

---

[504] Charity Commission, *Charities and Insurance*, C49 (1996), para 22
[505] ibid, para 23
[506] [1991] Ch Com Rep 8 (para 40)
[507] ibid, para 39
[508] cf (in the context of a private trust) *Hardoon v Belilos* [1901] AC 118 (PC) (Lord Lindley)

entered into by its trustees, who thereby incur personal liability which, unless limited by the appropriate means, extends to the entire value of the trustees' personal assets.[509] The trustees' liability to the third party may be limited by the terms of the contract with the third party.[510] A trustee who contracts merely 'as trustee' will remain personally liable without limit; but it seems that if the trustee contracts 'as trustee and not otherwise' his liability is restricted to his right of indemnity out of the trust assets.[511] The trustees are personally liable on a contract even if it is not within the purposes of the charity,[512] or is beyond their powers as trustees, or is otherwise made in breach of trust (for example, because the trustees did not meet the prudent man of business test). Such liability arises because trustees contract as individuals, so that their contractual capacity is unlimited.[513] If two or more trustees enter into the contract with a third party, their liability is joint and several; and if one trustee is made to pay the entire amount, he may be able to recover a contribution from his co-trustees.[514]

Trustees of a charitable trust who incur personal liability under contracts entered into as trustees are entitled, provided they have acted properly within the terms of the trust,[515] to be indemnified out of the assets of the charity, unless the trust instrument provides otherwise.[516] The model constitution for a charitable trust prepared on behalf of the Charity Law Association contains an express form of indemnity for a trustee in respect (inter alia) of any liabilities incurred in or about the administration of the trust.[517] **9.194**

It would be difficult to justify excluding the right of indemnity to a charity trustee who acts unpaid; but such an exclusion might be considered appropriate if, exceptionally, the trustee is remunerated for his work as trustee.[518] The right to indemnity is equitable in origin, but in modern times such right is in the process of being subsumed within the developing law of restitution. In the present **9.195**

---

[509] For suggestions for reform generally, see Trust Law Committee Consultation Paper, *Rights of creditors against trustees and trust funds* (April 1997)

[510] *Re Robinson's Settlement* [1912] 1 Ch 717, 729

[511] See E Ford, 'Rights of creditors against trustees and trust funds' (1997) 70 NLJ Easter Appeals Suppl 28, 35

[512] In relation to a charitable trust or charitable unincorporated association, it is wrong to use the term 'ultra vires' to describe transactions entered into by the trustees or Committee members outside the charity's purpose. '[T]he doctrine of ultra vires is one which has been developed entirely as a result of the juridical concept of the limited capacity of corporations and has no application whatever to the activities of individuals': *De Vigier v IRC* [1964] 1 WLR 1073, 1083 (Lord Upjohn)

[513] ibid (Lord Upjohn)

[514] Civil Liability (Contribution) Act 1978

[515] *Re Grimthorpe* [1958] Ch 615, 623 (Danckwerts J)

[516] *Re German Mining Co, ex p Chippendale* (1854) 4 De GM & G 19, 52

[517] Trust Deed for a Charitable Trust, cl 6.2.5

[518] cf the position in company law, where a paid director is not entitled to be indemnified against expenses incurred in the performance of his office: *Young v Naval Military and Civil Service Co-operative Society of South Africa* [1905] 1 KB 687. See above, para 9.114

context, the right is designed to prevent the charitable trust from being unjustly enriched at the expense of the trustee, and it therefore exists only in so far as the charitable trust is itself benefited. The right to an indemnity is reduced if, and to the extent that, the trustee is indebted to the trust fund itself.[519] A trustee also has a statutory right of reimbursement out of the trust funds for expenses properly incurred by him when acting on behalf of the trust.[520]

9.196 A third party who contracts with a trustee of a charitable trust generally has no direct right of action against the charity assets.[521] A third party may, however, acquire a direct right if the trust instrument itself confers such a right.[522] It has been suggested that this could be effected by a clause in the trust instrument which specifies that the trust fund is to be liable where the obligations to the third party were incurred in the proper administration of the trust, and which expressly confers a right of indemnity on the third party against the trust assets in the event of default by the trustee.[523] In the absence of a direct right of action against the charity's own assets, the third party may have recourse to them indirectly through subrogation to the trustee's own right of indemnity.[524] The right of subrogation cannot, however, be invoked unless it is reasonably clear that any direct claim against the trustee would prove fruitless—as, for instance, where the trustee is bankrupt.[525] A weakness of the subrogated claim is that it cannot place the third party in a better position than the trustee himself, and so it is restricted to the extent of the trustee's own right of indemnity. No subrogated claim can therefore be made if the charity's governing instrument excludes the trustee's right of indemnity, and the right of subrogation is reduced to the extent that the trustee may himself be indebted to the trust.[526] If, however, there are two or more charity trustees, not all of whom are indebted to the charity, the creditor is entitled to be subrogated to the rights of those who are not indebted.[527]

9.197 To meet any indemnity, a charity which lacks sufficient income or investments which can be realized may be obliged to dispose of the endowment itself, even if this is a building used for the purposes of the charity (such as a village hall) or which the charity exists to preserve (such as almshouses), thereby effectively bringing the charity to an end.[528] Charity trustees who wish to sell charity land to

---

[519] *Re Finch* [1902] 1 Ch 342, 345
[520] TA 2000, s 31(1)
[521] *Strickland v Symons* (1884) 26 ChD 245
[522] *Underhill & Hayton's Law of Trusts and Trustees* (ed DJ Hayton) (15th edn, Butterworths, 1995) 803
[523] See precedent set out ibid
[524] *Staniar v Evans* (1886) 34 ChD 470
[525] *Owen v Delamere* (1872) LR 15 Eq 134
[526] *Ex p Edmonds* (1862) 4 De GF & J 488, 498; *Re Blundell* (1890) 44 ChD 11
[527] *Re Frith* [1902] 1 Ch 342, 346
[528] See observations of Earl Ferrers during the passage of the Charities Bill in 1991: *Parl Debs, (HL Official Report)*, Public Bill Committee, 5th Sitting, cols 188–9 (11 Dec 1991)

meet the indemnity must dispose of it in accordance with the statutory requirements laid down in the Charities Act 1993.[529] To the extent that the charity's assets
are insufficient to satisfy the indemnity, the loss falls on the trustees personally.[530]

Trustees of a charitable trust who enter into expensive contracts with third parties **9.198**
may therefore incur great personal risk. Even though they have taken all proper
advice and have acted honestly and reasonably (so that they are not in breach of
their duties as trustees) circumstances may arise which may put them in breach of
contract with the third party. A charity which maintains an historic building, for
instance, may discover that urgent repairs are needed to it which the charity can
afford only through a public appeal fund; in view of the urgency, however, the
charity trustees may decide to enter into a contract with a building company
before the appeal has raised the total amount required.[531] The works of a building
contract, furthermore, can easily escalate, as works of repair may uncover other
defects which also need to be put right, thereby adding to the cost.[532] Again, a
charity may depend upon an annual grant, and the trustees, having received indications in good faith from the awarding body that their application is likely to be
successful, may decide to renew the contracts of their staff. If the grant were not
after all forthcoming, the trustees would be personally liable in full for salaries,
overdrafts, and redundancy payments to the extent that the charity's assets prove
insufficient.[533]

The problem of personal liability under contract could in theory be dealt with by **9.199**
the trustees taking out a policy of insurance at the cost of the charity; but it is
difficult to imagine that any insurance company would be willing to insure a risk
of this sort. If the contracts with third parties are substantial, the charity trustees
should consider incorporating the charity with limited liability.

---

[529] ie either the sale must be made after the charity trustees have obtained and considered the report of a qualified surveyor, or the sale must be made after an order of the court or of the Charity
Commissioners: CA 1993, s 36

[530] An amendment was put down in the House of Lords during the Committee Stage of the
Charities Bill (which became the CA 1992) that would have limited the personal liability of charity
trustees or trustees for a charity who had acted reasonably and complied with the statutory requirements relating to registered charities to the value of the charity's assets: *Parliamentary Debates
(House of Lords Official Report)* Public Bill Committee, Charities Bill, 5th Sitting, cols 184–193
(11 Dec 1991). The Government opposed the amendment on the grounds that it would severely
limit the ability of charities to enter into contracts, that it would adversely affect the position of third
parties, that it was likely that the matter could be dealt with by appropriate insurance (ibid, col 189
(Earl Ferrers)), that the trustees could already specifically limit their liability in the contract itself,
and that the Government intended to examine the nature of the problem fully after the Bill had
completed its course: ibid, Report, Charities Bill, cols 438–443 (16 Feb 1992) (Earl Ferrers). The
amendment, which had been passed in Committee, was rejected at Report

[531] cf ibid, Public Bill Committee, Charities Bill, 5th Sitting, cols 188 (11 Dec 1991) (Lord
Mottistone)

[532] cf ibid, col 190 (Earl Ferrers)

[533] cf ibid, Report, Charities Bill, cols. 440 (16 Feb 1992) (Lord Bishop of Newcastle)

9.200 Trustees who incur liability in tort while acting in the proper execution of the trust are entitled to recover any damages out of the trust assets by way of indemnity, provided that they are themselves not personally at fault.[534]

(2) *Committee members and ordinary members of a charitable unincorporated association*

9.201 The law governing the liability of the Committee members and the ordinary members of a charitable unincorporated association, like that affecting the liability of trustees of a charitable trust, has been largely developed in a series of cases which do not concern charities. In this instance, the law has been developed essentially by authorities which were considering non-charitable associations. In contrast to charitable trusts, however, when considering charitable associations, it is more difficult, and potentially misleading, to press the analogy from the non-charitable sphere too far. It may well be that, were the courts to consider some of the following issues specifically where members of a charitable association were defendants, some legal differences in treatment would emerge.

9.202 As an unincorporated association has no separate legal personality, and English law does not recognize its funds as a separate juridical entity,[535] contracts must be entered into on its behalf by human intermediaries. These will usually be the members of a Committee appointed by the general body of members (the ordinary members) in accordance with the rules of the association to manage its day-to-day affairs. The Committee members who contract with a third party incur personal liability if they contract as principals; but they are generally not liable under[536] (nor are they entitled to enforce[537]) a contract which they enter into as agents for the ordinary members. In the former case, the Committee members have a right of indemnity out of the charity's assets according to the principles of the law of trusts or restitution which were considered in the examination of trustees of charitable trusts.[538] In the latter case, it is the ordinary members who incur liability and who should have a corresponding right of indemnity out of the charity's assets. In either case, the third party can reach the charity's assets by subrogation to the defendants' right of indemnity, a method whose disadvantages have already been discussed.[539] Several distinct legal doctrines—contract, trust, restitution, and agency—are therefore potentially here involved.

9.203 Under general principles of agency, if the Committee are in fact agents for the ordinary members, and the Committee enter into a contract with a third party

---

[534] *Benett v Wyndham* (1862) 4 De DF & J 259
[535] See discussion in HAJ Ford, *Unincorporated Non-Profit Associations*, (Oxford Univ Press, 1959) 86 & ch 9
[536] *Ferguson v Wilson* (1866) LR 2 Ch App 77
[537] *Fairlie v Fenton* (1870) LR 5 Ex 169
[538] See above, paras 9.194–9.195
[539] See above, para 9.196

which indicates that they are contracting as agents (for example, if they sign 'on behalf of . . .' or '*pro procurationem*') they will incur no personal liability. The difficulty is generally in deciding whether the circumstances give rise to an agency. The point was first considered, and was later developed, in a number of nineteenth-century decisions dealing with gentlemen's clubs.[540] In *Flemyng v Hector*,[541] a wine merchant supplied wine on credit to the Westminster Reform Club; he later attempted to recover its cost from one of the members, arguing that the Committee, which had been appointed by the members to manage the Club's affairs, was the agent of the members. The action failed because the Club was organized on a ready-money basis, with the members paying their debts quotidianly, so that it was impossible to imply into the Club's rules any provision that the Committee were authorized to deal on credit. Following this decision, however, it soon became evident that in some circumstances an agency might be inferred: the transaction entered into by the Committee might be of a type (such as the employment of staff or the taking of a lease at a rent) which would necessarily involve the giving of credit;[542] or credit might be given at a time when there was no subsisting fund out of which payment could be made, and the ordinary members must have realized that this was so.[543] The law seemed set to establish that, regardless of whether the ordinary members were aware of a particular contract, they would be taken to have authorized the Committee to act as their agents whenever the Committee entered into a contract which would further the objects of the association.[544] Unfortunately, some other authorities lost sight of the basic distinction between associations which were organized on a ready-money basis and those which were not, and treated *Flemyng v Hector* as having laid down a principle of general application for all clubs.[545] It was these other authorities which were favoured by the Privy Council in *Wise v Perpetual Trustee Co Ltd*,[546] whose advice can be considered to have thrown the law back somewhat. It was there decided that a Committee has no power to enter into contracts binding on the ordinary members merely because the management of the association is vested in the Committee under the club's rules; and later cases applied this reasoning to other types of associations.[547] It therefore appears that the ordinary members of an association are liable only if they can be said to have authorized or later ratified the particular contract in question: actual, not usual, authority, is the basis for ordinary members' liability.

---

[540] See generally, HAJ Ford, *Unincorporated Non-Profit Associations* (Oxford Univ Press, 1959) ch 4, on which much of the following account relies

[541] (1836) 2 M & W 172

[542] *Todd v Emly* (1836) 2 M & W 172

[543] *Barnett v Lambert* (1846) 15 M & W 489; *Bailey v Macaulay* (1819) 13 QB 815

[544] *Cockerell v Aucompte* (1857) 2 CBNS 440

[545] See esp the influential decision in *Re St James' Club* (1852) 2 De GM & G 383

[546] [1903] AC 139

[547] *Bradley Egg Farm Ltd v Clifford* [1943] 2 All ER 378

9.204 Since the ordinary members' liability generally depends on actual authority, they will not normally be liable on any contracts which the Committee enter into where such authority is absent. Where such authority is lacking, there is either a valid contract between the third party and the Committee members personally, or there is no contract at all. If the Committee expressly or impliedly represented that they were acting in the capacity of agents when they had no actual authority so to act, the third party, even in the absence of a contract with the Committee members personally, may be able to sue them for damages for breach of warranty of authority, unless the absence of authority was known to the third party.[548] There will be no contract and no action for breach of warranty of authority if there is clear evidence that the parties did not intend that the Committee members should be personally liable.[549] Otherwise, there is much to be said for the view that, if the Committee members contract without actual authority, they should be personally liable under the contract, but should be estopped from being able to enforce it against the third party.[550] This is not, however, the established position, which holds that, in these circumstances, unless the words or conduct of the parties suggest otherwise, there is no contract and no liability on the part of the Committee to the third party.[551]

9.205 It is therefore evident that, at least when dealing with non-charitable associations, English law has (as a general rule) settled on placing contractual liability on the Committee, rather than on the ordinary members. It is, however, unfortunate that none of these cases concerned an association of a charitable nature, as there are several reasons why it could be persuasively argued that, when dealing with charitable associations, different principles from the members' club cases should apply, the common thread running through them being that members of a charitable association (unlike their counterparts in a non-charitable association) cannot be the beneficial owners of the association's assets.[552] The members may pay a subscription, but they cease to have any beneficial interest in it when it is paid, and they have no right to any surplus funds when the association is dissolved. Any rights which they acquire as members are in nature either personal or constitutional, not proprietary.

9.206 The peculiar nature of the rights of members of a charitable association has several consequences. First, one explanation for the decisions in some of the members' club cases—that to hold the members liable in contract would result in their pay-

---

[548] *Halbot v Lens* [1901] 1 Ch 344
[549] cf *Jones v Hope* (1880) 3 TLR 247n
[550] cf *Holman v Pullin* (1884) C & E 254 (QBD)
[551] See dicta ibid
[552] At least in the case of a members' club or other 'inward-looking' association, the modern analysis is that the members hold the association's assets beneficially subject to contract (*Re Recher's Will Trusts* [1972] Ch 526), although there are other possibilities: cf *Re Denley's Trust Deed* [1969] 1 Ch 373

ing twice[553]—assumes that the ordinary members, through the agency of the Committee, are buying the goods for themselves, and cannot therefore be used to justify a similar result where the association is a charity.[554] Secondly, as the members of a charitable association lack any proprietary interest in any contracts entered into, they are less directly concerned than the Committee with the contract-making function;[555] to treat the ordinary members as principals under such contracts smacks of artificiality. Thirdly, cases such as *Flemyng v Hector* appear to be examples of an application of the general principle that no man shall enjoy the advantages of property without incurring its liabilities[556]—a principle which cannot, of course, be applied to charitable associations.[557] A general imposition of contractual liability on members of a charitable association might also deter potential new members from joining, with a resulting detriment to the charitable sector.

It is therefore suggested that, in this area, trust law should predominate over principles of agency. In entering into contracts with third parties, Committee members should normally be treated, not as agents for the ordinary members, but as trustees of a charitable trust. Indeed, it is arguable that the contract will normally be made with the Committee members personally even if they contract 'on behalf of the XYZ Charitable Association', since the superadded words could be construed in this context, not as signifying that the third party is dealing with agents, but merely that he is dealing with trustees, thereby indicating that he may have recourse to the charity's funds—via subrogation if necessary—in the event of the contract's being breached. **9.207**

There is very little authority exploring the liability of members of a charitable association in tort. If the tort is caused by the actions of the Committee members, or of some of them, those responsible will be liable.[558] The ordinary members will be vicariously liable for the tortious acts of the Committee members if the latter are their agents, but the scope of ordinary members' liability in tort in such circumstances has not been directly addressed, perhaps because it is procedurally easier for the claimant to bring the action against those who directly committed the tort, or against the Committee members as being the persons primarily **9.208**

---

[553] See *Re St James' Club* (1852) 2 De GM & G 383 (Lord St Leonards LC: 'The member pays on the spot, and were he also liable to those supplying the articles, he would pay twice over')

[554] Quite apart from this, if the charity's funds have been swelled by outside donations, it may not be easy to determine whether or not purchases have been made out of members' subscriptions

[555] cf judgment of Scott LJ in *Bradley Egg Farm Ltd v Clifford* [1943] 2 All ER 378

[556] See TC Williams, 'Club Trustees' Right to Indemnity: a Criticism of *Wise v Perpetual Trustee Co., Ltd*' (1903) 19 LQR 386, referring to *Hardoon v Belilos* [1901] AC 118 (PC)

[557] HAJ Ford, *Unincorporated Non-Profit Associations* (Oxford Univ Press, 1959) 78

[558] *Brown v Lewis* (1896) 12 TLR 455; *Mercantile Marine Service Association v Toms* [1916] 2 KB 243

responsible for it.[559] It is submitted that liability in tort, as in contract, is better dealt with on the footing that the Committee members are trustees of a charitable trust rather than agents for the ordinary members.

9.209 The model constitution for a charitable unincorporated association produced on behalf of the Charity Law Association contains an express form of indemnity for any Committee member in respect of (inter alia) any liabilities properly incurred in running the association.[560]

(3) Directors of charitable companies

9.210 Because of the doctrine of separate corporate personality, directors of charitable companies do not generally incur personal liability on contracts entered into by the company. In some circumstances, however, the veil of incorporation is lifted so as to impose personal liability on directors. The veil can be lifted either under statute (as where there is fraudulent or wrongful trading) or judicially; but only the former need be considered here, as there is no reported instance of liability being imposed on a director through the judicial doctrine.

Fraudulent trading

9.211 Where, in the course of the winding up of a company, it appears that any business of the company has been carried on with intent to defraud creditors of the company or creditors of any other person, or for any fraudulent purpose, the court, on the application of the liquidator, may declare any persons who were knowingly parties to the carrying on of the business in that manner liable to make such contributions (if any) to the company's assets as the court thinks proper.[561] In this context, fraud means actual dishonesty.[562] Fraudulent trading is also a criminal offence.[563] It should be noted that the statutory liability is not limited to the company's directors or members: any other person who is a party to the fraudulent trading may be held personally liable to contribute to the company's assets.[564] In practice, however, the element of dishonesty is often hard to establish, and creditors might well prefer an action against the company's directors for wrongful trading.

---

[559] See HAJ Ford, *Unincorporated Non-Profit Associations* (Oxford Univ Press, 1959) 61–3; Legal & Constitutional Committee (Victoria), *Report on the Public Liability of Voluntary Organisations*, 33rd Report to the Parliament, Apr 1989, ch 3 (unincorporated associations). See also *Smith v Yarnold* [1969] 2 NSWR 410, 415 ('The liability of the committeemen . . . does not depend wholly upon a logical approach to the law of . . . tort, none the less it is the only method by which justice can be done towards the plaintiff')

[560] Constitution for a Charitable Unincorporated Association, r 9.2.5

[561] Insolvency Act 1986, s 213

[562] *Re Patrick & Lyon Ltd* [1933] Ch 786, 790; *Re Augustus Barnett & Son Ltd* [1986] BCLC 170

[563] Companies Act 1985, s 458

[564] *Re Cooper (Gerald) Chemicals Ltd* [1978] Ch 262

Wrongful trading

This action also applies where a company is in an insolvent winding up. If at some   **9.212**
time prior to the commencement of the winding-up it appears that a director
knew or ought to have concluded that there was no reasonable prospect that the
company would avoid going into insolvent liquidation, the court may, on the
application of the liquidator, declare such director liable to make such contribution to the company's assets as it thinks proper.[565] 'Director' for this purpose
includes a shadow director,[566] who is a person in accordance with whose directions
or instructions the directors of the company are accustomed to act.[567]

---

[565] Insolvency Act 1986, s 214; and see *Re Produce Marketing Consortium Ltd* [1989] 3 All ER 1
[566] Insolvency Act 1986, s 214(7)
[567] ibid, s 251

PART IV

SUPERVISION AND CONTROL

10

THE CHARITY COMMISSIONERS

A. Introduction

The Charity Commissioners are the main body concerned with the supervision **10.01**
of charities. The Commissioners were initially established in 1853,[1] and their

---

[1] Charitable Trusts Act 1853, ss 1–8

functions and powers are now contained in the Charities Act 1993.[2] The Commissioners are civil servants appointed by the Home Office.[3] There must always be at least three Commissioners, one of whom is the Chief Charity Commissioner.[4] At least two of these must be legally qualified.[5] There is also provision for the appointment of not more than two additional Commissioners;[6] and two part-time Commissioners have been appointed. The Commissioners are assisted by a staff of several hundred persons. There are three branches of the Charity Commissioners: London, Liverpool,[7] and Taunton.[8]

10.02 Under the Charities Act 1993, the general function of the Charity Commissioners is that of 'promoting the effective use of charitable resources by encouraging the development of better methods of administration, by giving charity trustees information or advice on any matter affecting the charity and by investigating and checking abuses'.[9] The general object of the Commissioners is 'so to act in the case of any charity (unless it is a matter of altering its purposes) as best to promote and make effective the work of the charity in meeting the needs designated by its trusts'.[10] It is, however, expressly stated that the Commissioners do not themselves have power to act in the administration of a charity'.[11] The Charities Act 1993 also imposes specific duties, and confers specific powers, on the Charity Commissioners. The work of the Commissioners can be considered to fall under four broad headings: supervisory (including the maintenance of the register of charities and the receipt of charity accounts); policing (including the investigation of breaches of trust and maladministration); quasi-judicial[12] (including making decisions upon charitable status and the preparation of cy-près and other schemes); and advisory (including the giving of advice to charity trustees on matters affecting their duties, or to persons in the process of setting up charities).

---

[2] CA 1993, s 1(1). The constitution of the Charity Commissioners is contained in CA 1993, Sch 1: ibid, s 1(2)

[3] ibid, Sch 1, para 1(3)

[4] ibid, para 1(1)

[5] ibid, para 1(2)

[6] ibid, para 1(5)

[7] The Liverpool office was opened in 1970: [1971] Ch Com Rep 6 (paras 13–14). In 1994, it moved from the city centre to a new building in the Queen's Dock area of Liverpool: [1994] Ch Com Rep 22

[8] The Taunton branch (the South West Regional Office) was opened as recently as 1989: [1989] Ch Com Rep 4 (para 11). It moved to a purpose-built office in 1991: [1991] Ch Com Rep 4 (para 14)

[9] CA 1993, s 1(3)

[10] ibid, s 1(4)

[11] ibid

[12] cf *Jones v Charity Commissioners of England and Wales* [1972] 1 WLR 784, 785, where Ungoed-Thomas J described the Charity Commissioners as 'a statutory body exercising what may be considered a semi-judicial jurisdiction'

B. Exempt charities

An exempt charity is exempt from most (but not all) of the obligations imposed **10.03**
by the Charities Act 1993, and therefore from most of the powers of the Charity
Commissioners. The rationale for the exemption is that such charities are already
subject to some means of supervision by a body other than the Charity
Commissioners. The scope of the exemptions is considered further below;[13] but it
is first important to identify which charities are exempt.

(1) List of exempt charities

Schedule 2 to the Charities Act 1993 contains a list of exempt charities, but only **10.04**
some are specifically named; others are exempt either because they have been declared to be exempt by Order in Council, or because they fall within one of the
general categories of exempt charities; yet others are made exempt by other provisions of the Charities Act 1993 or by other legislation.

**An institution which would have been exempt before the Charities Act 1960
under enactments other than the Charitable Trusts Acts 1853–1939**

The first category of exempt charities comprises[14] **10.05**

> any institution which, if the Charities Act 1960 had not been passed, would be ex-
> empted from the powers and jurisdiction, under the Charitable Trusts Acts 1853 to
> 1939, of the Commissioners or Minister of Education (apart from any power of the
> Commissioners or Minister to apply those Acts in whole or in part to charities other-
> wise exempt) by the terms of any enactment not contained in those Acts other than
> section 9 of the Places of Worship Registration Act 1855.

Certain institutions were exempt before the passing of the Charities Act 1960. **10.06**
Some exemptions were contained in the charities legislation which that statute repealed, namely the Charitable Trusts Acts 1853 to 1939;[15] provision was made for
additional exemptions in other statutes. The exempt status of charities falling into
the latter category was preserved by the Charities Act 1960, and that saving is now
contained in paragraph (a) of Schedule 2 to the Charities Act 1993. Within this
paragraph fall a number of institutions, including several of the so-called 'red-
brick' universities.[16]

---

[13] See below, paras 10.17–10.21
[14] CA 1993, Sch 2, para (a)
[15] The Charitable Trusts Acts 1853–1939 comprised the following Acts: Charitable Trusts
Act 1853, Charitable Trusts (Amendment) Act 1855, Charitable Trusts Acts 1860, 1862, 1869,
and 1887, Charitable Trusts (Recovery) Act 1891, Charitable Trusts (Places of Religious Worship)
Act 1894, Charitable Trusts Acts 1914 and 1925, and Charities (Fuel Allotments) Act 1939. All
these Acts were repealed entirely by CA 1960, s 48(2) & Sch 7, Pt I
[16] See Birmingham University Act 1900, s 14; Liverpool University Act 1903, s 14; Victoria
University of Manchester Act 1904, s 11; University of Leeds Act 1904, s 12; University of Sheffield

10.07 A registered place of worship is not exempt, but is not required to be registered under the Charities Act 1993.[17]

Specified universities and colleges

10.08 The Charitable Trusts Acts 1853–1939 provided for the exempt status of a number of institutions.[18] The Charities Act 1960 broadly preserved the exempt status of these institutions, and this saving is continued (with some later additions[19]) by paragraph (b) of Schedule 2 to the Charities Act 1993, which exempts

> the universities of Oxford, Cambridge, London, Durham and Newcastle, the colleges and halls in the universities of Oxford, Cambridge, Durham and Newcastle, Queen Mary and Westfield College in the University of London and the colleges of Winchester and Eton.

Any university, university college or connected institution declared exempt by Order in Council

10.09 Within the category of exempt charities is any university, university college, or institution connected with a university or university college, which Her Majesty declares by Order in Council to be an exempt charity for the purposes of the Charities Act 1993.[20] Various Orders in Council have been made pursuant to this provision.[21] By virtue of these Orders, this category effectively includes all the re-

---

Act 1905, s 11; University of Bristol Act 1909, s 12; University of Reading Act 1926, s 10; University of Nottingham Act 1949, s 9; University of Southampton Act 1953, s 10

[17] CA 1993, s 3(5). A 'registered place of worship' means land or buildings falling within Places of Worship Registration Act 1855, s 9: CA 1993, s 3(14). Places of meeting for religious worship had been exempt from the provisions of Charitable Trusts Act 1853: ibid, s 62

[18] The exempt status of the Universities of Oxford, Cambridge, London, and Durham, and of any hall or college of the Universities of Oxford, Cambridge, and Durham, goes back to Charitable Trusts Act 1853: ibid, s 62

[19] Universities of Durham and Newcastle Act 1963, s 18; Queen Mary and Westfield College Act 1989, s 10

[20] CA 1993, Sch 2, para (c)

[21] The following universities, university colleges and allied institutions have been declared exempt charities under paragraph (c) of Schedule 2: University of Keele, University of Sussex, University of Wales, University College of Wales, Aberystwyth, University College of North Wales, University College of South Wales and Monmouthshire, University College of Swansea, and the following institutions connected with the University of London: (1) General: Chairman, Council, and Governors of Bedford College for Women; Birkbeck College; Imperial College of Science and Technology; London School of Economics and Political Science; Principal and Governors of Queen Elizabeth College; Queen Mary College; Royal Holloway College; Royal Veterinary College; School of Oriental and African Studies; School of Pharmacy, University of London; Principal and Governors of Westfield College London; College of St Gregory and St Martin at Wye; (2) Medical: Charing Cross Hospital Medical School; Council of Governors of Guy's Hospital Medical School; King's College Hospital Medical School; London Hospital Medical College; Middlesex Hospital Medical School; Royal Dental Hospital of London School of Dental Surgery; Royal Free Hospital School of Medicine; Medical College of St Bartholomew's Hospital in the City of London; St George's Hospital Medical School; St Mary's Hospital Medical School; St Thomas's Hospital Medical School; University College Hospital Medical School; Westminster Medical

maining 'old' universities and also those 'new' universities[22] that existed as corporate bodies before the Education Reform Act 1988, and which did not therefore become higher education corporations pursuant to that Act (these effectively comprising a number of former polytechnics in London).[23]

School; (3) Postgraduate Medical: British Postgraduate Medical Federation; Postgraduate Medical School of London; Institute of Cancer Research: Royal Cancer Hospital; Institute of Cardiology; Institute of Child Health; Institute of Dental Surgery; Institute of Dermatology; Institute of Diseases of the Chest; Institute of Laryngology and Otology; Institute of Neurology; Institute of Obstetrics and Gynaecology; Institute of Ophthalmology; Institute of Orthopaedics; Institute of Psychiatry; Institute of Urology; London School of Hygiene and Tropical Medicine; also exempt is the Welsh National School of Medicine, an institution connected with the University of Wales. All the foregoing universities, university colleges and allied institutions are exempt under the Exempt Charities Order 1962, SI 1962/1343. Exempt under later orders are: University of East Anglia, University of Essex, University of Kent, University of Lancaster, University of Warwick, University of York, University College, and St David's College, Lampeter: Exempt Charities Order 1965, SI 1965/1715; University of Surrey, University of Aston in Birmingham, University of Bradford, Loughborough University of Technology, and the University of Manchester Institute of Science and Technology (University of Manchester): Exempt Charities Order 1966, SI 1966/1460; Bath University of Technology, City University, Brunel University, University of Salford, and Chelsea College of Science and Technology (University of London): Exempt Charities Order 1967, SI 1967/821; Open University: Exempt Charities Order 1969, SI 1969/1496; University College London: Exempt Charities Order 1978, SI 1978/453; United Medical Schools of Guy's and St Thomas's Hospitals (University of London): Exempt Charities Order 1982, SI 1982/1661; United Medical and Dental Schools of Guy's and St Thomas's Hospitals (University of London): Exempt Charities Order 1983, SI 1983/1516; University of Wales College of Medicine (Coleg Meddygaeth Prifysgol Cymru): Exempt Charities Order 1984, SI 1984/1976; Institute of Education (University of London): Exempt Charities Order 1987, SI 1987/1823; Goldsmith's College (University of London): Exempt Charities Order 1989, SI 1989/2394; Cranfield University: Exempt Charities Order 1993, SI 1993/2359; London Guildhall University: Exempt Charities Order 1994, SI 1994/1905; University of Greenwich: Exempt Charities (No 2) Order 1994, SI 1994/2956; University of Derby: Exempt Charities Order 1995, SI 1995/2998; London Business School: Exempt Charities Order 1996, SI 1996/1637; University of Westminster: Exempt Charities (No 2) Order 1996, SI 1996/1932; University of North London: Exempt Charities (No 3) Order 1996, SI 1996/1933; South Bank University: Exempt Charities Order 1999, SI 1999/3139; Royal College of Art: Exempt Charities Order 2000, SI 2000/1826

[22] The expression 'new university' is not a term of art, but is generally used to refer to those former polytechnics and former colleges of higher education which have, pursuant to the Further and Higher Education Act 1992, s 77, chosen, with the consent of the Privy Council, to include the word 'university' in their name

[23] Until the changes made pursuant to the Education Reform Act 1988, the polytechnics within the area of the former Inner London Education Authority (ILEA) enjoyed a unique position amongst polytechnics since they were already corporate bodies (namely, companies limited by guarantee). See speech of Baroness Cox in the Second Reading of the Education Reform Bill 1988: Hansard series 5, vol 497, col 97 (16 May 1988). It was not therefore necessary to transform these 'ILEA' polytechnics into higher education corporations; hence, following their attaining the status of universities, such former 'ILEA' polytechnics have been made exempt charities by virtue of Orders in Council made under para (c) of Sch 2 to CA 1993

Any higher education corporation or further education corporation

10.10 The list of exempt charities is deemed to include any higher education corporation within the meaning of the Education Reform Act 1988.[24] That Act made
provision for the transfer of polytechnics and other institutions of higher education out of local authority control. At that time, most of those institutions had no
separate corporate identity,[25] and so, in order to achieve its aim, the Act made provision for the transfer of such institutions to newly created higher education corporations.[26] Any further education corporation within the meaning of the Further
and Higher Education Act 1992 is also an exempt charity.[27] This broadly means
sixth form colleges and the old colleges of further education.[28]

10.11 So far as it is a charity, any institution which is administered by or on behalf of any
higher education corporation or further education corporation, and is established
for the general purposes of, or for any special purposes of or in connection with,
that corporation, is also an exempt charity for the purposes of the Charities Act
1993.[29]

Maintained schools and any Education Action Forum

10.12 The governing body of any foundation, voluntary, or foundation special school,
and any foundation body established under section 21 of the School Standards
and Framework Act 1998[30] is an exempt charity for the purposes of the Charities

---

[24] CA 1993, s 3(5A)(a), inserted by Teaching and Higher Education Act 1998, s 44 (1) & Sch 3,
para 9. See also Education Reform Act 1988, s 125A(1) (inserted by Teaching and Higher
Education Act 1998, s 41(1), which came into force on 1 Oct 1998: Teaching and Higher
Education Act 1998 (Commencement No 3) Order 1998, SI 1998/2215, Art 2). A successor company to a higher education corporation (within the meaning of the Education Reform Act 1988,
s 129(5)) is also exempt: CA 1993, Sch 2, para (i)

[25] The exceptions were the 'ILEA' polytechnics, discussed above, para 10.09

[26] The institutions which became higher education corporations on 1 Apr 1989, were designated
as such by orders made pursuant to the Education Reform Act 1988: Education (Higher Education
Corporations) Order 1988, SI 1988/1799 (which specifies, amongst other institutions, Leicester
Polytechnic, North East London Polytechnic, and Portsmouth Polytechnic); Education (Higher
Education Corporations) (No 2) Order 1988, SI 1988/1800; Education (Higher Education
Corporations) (No 3) Order 1988, SI 1988/1801; Education (Higher Education Corporations)
(No 4) Order 1988, SI 1988/2283; Education (Higher Education Corporations) (No 5) Order
1989, SI 1989/17. Most higher education corporations which previously existed as polytechnics
have since chosen, with Privy Council permission, to call themselves universities, pursuant to
Further and Higher Education Act 1992, s 77

[27] CA 1993, s 3(5A)(b), inserted by Teaching and Higher Education Act 1990, s 44(1) & Sch 3,
para 9. See also Further and Higher Education Act 1992, s 22A (inserted by Teaching and Higher
Education Act 1998, s 41(2), and brought into force on 1 Oct 1998, by Teaching and Higher
Education Act 1998 (Commencement No 3) Order 1998, SI 1998/2215, Art 2)

[28] See Judith Hill & E Hackett, 'Exempt Charities' (1992–3) 1 CL & PR 209, 221

[29] Education Reform Act 1988, s 125A(2), inserted by Teaching and Higher Education Act
1998, s 41(1)

[30] School Standards and Framework Act 1998, s 23. The expression 'foundation body' is defined
ibid, s 21(4)

Act 1993.[31] An Education Action Forum is also an exempt charity:[32] an Education Action Forum refers to a corporate body established to improve standards in those maintained schools which are designated to participate in an education action zone established by order of the Secretary of State.[33]

Various bodies concerned with qualifications and curriculum

Other exempt educational institutions are the Qualifications and Curriculum Authority[34] and the Qualifications, Curriculum and Assessment Authority for Wales.[35]

10.13

Various museums and art galleries

The Trustees of the British Museum and the Trustees of the Natural History Museum are exempt charities within Schedule 2 to the Charities Act 1993,[36] as are the Boards of Trustees of the following institutions: the Victoria and Albert Museum;[37] the Science Museum;[38] the Armouries;[39] the Royal Botanic Gardens, Kew;[40] the National Museums and Galleries on Merseyside;[41] the National Gallery;[42] the Tate Gallery;[43] the National Portrait Gallery;[44] and the Wallace Collection.[45] Also exempt are the Trustees of the Imperial War Museum,[46] and the Trustees of the National Maritime Museum.[47]

10.14

---

[31] CA 1993, s 3(5B)(i), added by School Standards and Framework Act 1998, s 140(1) & Sch 30, para 48

[32] CA 1993, s 3(5B)(ii), added by School Standards and Framework Act 1998, s 140(1) & Sch 30, para 48

[33] School Standards and Framework Act 1998, ss 10 (education action zones), 11–12 (Education Action Forums)

[34] CA 1993, Sch 2, para (da), added by Education Act 1993; see now Education Act 1997, s 57(1) & Sch 7, para 7(a)

[35] CA 1993, Sch 2, para (f), as substituted by Education Act 1993; see now Education Act 1997, s 57(1) & Sch 7, para 7(b)

[36] CA 1993, Sch 2, para (p); derived from Museums and Art Galleries Act 1992, s 11(2) & Sch 8, Pt I, para 4

[37] CA 1993, Sch 2, para (k), derived from National Heritage Act 1983, s 40(1) & Sch 5, para 4

[38] CA 1993, Sch 2, para (l), derived from National Heritage Act 1983, s 40(1) & Sch 5, para 4

[39] CA 1993, Sch 2, para (m), derived from National Heritage Act 1983, s 40(1) & Sch 5, para 4

[40] CA 1993, Sch 2, para (n), derived from National Heritage Act 1983, s 40(1) & Sch 5, para 4

[41] CA 1993, Sch 2, para (o), derived from Local Government Reorganization (Miscellaneous Provisions) Order 1990, SI 1990/1765, art 3

[42] CA 1993, Sch 2, para (q), derived from Museums and Galleries Act 1992, s 11(2) & Sch 8, Pt II, para 10(1)

[43] CA 1993, Sch 2, para (r), derived from Museums and Galleries Act 1992, s 11(2) & Sch 8, Pt II, para 10(1)

[44] CA 1993, Sch 2, para (s), derived from Museums and Galleries Act 1992, s 11(2) & Sch 8, Pt II, para 10(1)

[45] CA 1993, Sch 2, para (t), derived from Museums and Galleries Act 1992, s 11(2) & Sch 8, Pt II, para 10(1)

[46] CA 1993, Sch 2, para (u), derived from Imperial War Museum Act 1920, s 5

[47] CA 1993, Sch 2, para (v), derived from National Maritime Museum Act 1934, s 7

Connected institutions

10.15 Any institution which is administered by or on behalf of an institution included under paragraphs (a)–(v) of Schedule 2 to the Charities Act 1993,[48] and is established for the general purposes of, or for any special purposes of or in connection with, that institution is itself an exempt charity.[49]

Other exempt charities

10.16 The following bodies are also listed as exempt charities in Schedule 2 to the Charities Act 1993: the Church Commissioners and any institution administered by them;[50] any registered society within the meaning of the Industrial and Provident Societies Act 1965 and any registered society or branch within the meaning of the Friendly Societies Act 1974;[51] the Board of Governors of the Museum of London,[52] the British Library Board,[53] and the National Lotteries Charities Board.[54] Also exempt is a common investment fund whose scheme admits only exempt charities, whether established under section 24 of the Charities Act 1993[55] or under any other enactment.[56]

(2) Scope of exemptions

10.17 As has been already mentioned, an exempt charity is exempt from most (but not all) of the obligations imposed by the Charities Act 1993. This includes exemption from the requirements of registration with,[57] and the submission of an annual report and accounts to, the Charity Commissioners, and from the obligation to have the charity's accounts audited.[58] In addition, the Charity Commissioners have no power to require an exempt charity to change its name.[59]

10.18 The Charity Commissioners have no power to institute an inquiry into an exempt charity;[60] and the Commissioners cannot require a person having custody of documents relating only to an exempt charity to furnish them with copies or

---

[48] The institutions included under CA 1993, Sch 2, paras (a)–(v), are those discussed above, paras 10.05–10.09 and 10.13–10.14
[49] CA 1993, Sch 2, para (w)
[50] ibid, para (x)
[51] ibid, para (y)
[52] ibid, para (z), added by Museum of London Act 1965, s 11
[53] CA 1993, Sch 2, para (za), added by British Library Act 1972, s 4(2)
[54] ibid, para (zb), added by National Lottery etc Act 1993, s 37(2) & Sch 4, para 12
[55] CA 1993, s 24(8)
[56] ibid, s 24(9). On common investment funds, see further ch 16, paras 16.72–16.94, esp 16.79
[57] ibid, s 3(5)(a)
[58] ibid, s 46(1), which disapplies ss 41–5 to an exempt charity. See further below, paras 10.115–10.116
[59] CA 1993, s 6(9)
[60] ibid, s 8(1)

extracts.[61] The Commissioners' power to act for the protection of a charity (such as suspending or removing trustees, making vesting or freezing orders, or appointing a receiver and manager) do not extend to an exempt charity.[62]

The Commissioners' jurisdiction to make schemes, to appoint and remove charity trustees, and to transfer property, is also more limited in the case of an exempt charity.[63] For instance, the Charity Commissioners are empowered to initiate a scheme for a charity, other than an exempt charity, where they are satisfied that the charity trustees ought, in the interests of the charity, to apply for a scheme; the Commissioners have no such power to initiate a scheme in respect of an exempt charity.[64] The Commissioners' power to give directions about dormant bank accounts does not apply to any account held in the name of or on behalf of an exempt charity.[65] **10.19**

The Commissioners' power to order a charity trustee or a trustee for a charity to repay to the charity any sums received by him from the charity when he was disqualified, by way of remuneration, expenses, or any benefit in kind, does not apply where the charity concerned is an exempt charity.[66] **10.20**

Other freedoms enjoyed by an exempt charity comprise the following: an exempt charity is not subject to the restrictions in the Charities Act 1993 on dispositions of charity land[67] and on mortgaging of charity land[68] (although it is subject to certain requirements concerning statements in instruments on dispositions of land by or to a charity[69]); an exempt charity may bring charity proceedings without an order of the Charity Commissioners;[70] and finally, exempt charities are not subject to a restriction applicable to other charities, namely that, notwithstanding anything in the trusts of a charity, no expenditure incurred in preparing or promoting a Bill in Parliament may be defrayed out of charity moneys without obtaining the consent of the court or of the Charity Commissioners.[71] **10.21**

(3) Provisions applicable to exempt charities

Exempt charities are still charities for the purposes of the general law of charities. They are therefore still subject to the general jurisdiction of the courts in relation **10.22**

---

[61] ibid, s 9(4)
[62] ibid, s 18(16)
[63] ibid, s 16(5)
[64] ibid, s 16(6)
[65] ibid, s 28(10)
[66] ibid, s 73(4)(a)
[67] ibid, s 36(10)(a)
[68] ibid, s 38(7)
[69] ibid, s 37(1). See further below, para 10.25, and ch 17, paras 17.87–17.95. The duty imposed on charity trustees to provide a certificate on the disposal of charity land does not, however, apply if the charity is an exempt charity: CA 1993, ss 36(10)(a), 37(2). See further ch 17, para 17.96
[70] ibid, s 33(2)
[71] ibid, s 17(7)

to charities, and the general equitable duties and the standard of care imposed on charity trustees generally apply equally to trustees of exempt charities.

10.23 Exempt charities are also charities for the purposes of the Charities Acts 1992 and 1993; and, although free from the monitoring and policing function of the Charity Commissioners, exempt charities and their trustees remain subject to many of the general provisions of the Charities Acts 1992 and 1993.[72] In the earlier of those Acts, the provisions relating to control of fund-raising for charitable institutions[73] and (when brought into force) to public charitable collections,[74] apply equally to exempt and non-exempt charities. In the later Act, such general provisions to which exempt charities are subject include, for instance, the duty in appropriate circumstances to take steps to secure the application of the charity's property cy-près.[75] The general provisions relating to disqualification from being a charity trustee or a trustee for a charity apply even where the charity in question is an exempt charity.[76]

10.24 In particular, trustees of an exempt charity are expressly required to keep proper books of account with respect to the affairs of the charity, and, if not required by or under the authority of any other Act to prepare periodical statements of account, they must prepare consecutive statements of account consisting on each occasion of an income and expenditure account relating to a period of not more than fifteen months and a balance sheet relating to the end of that period.[77] Such books and statements of account must be preserved for at least six years, unless the charity ceases to exist and the Charity Commissioners consent in writing to their being destroyed or otherwise disposed of.[78] If any person makes a written request to the charity trustees of a charity (including an exempt charity) for a copy of the charity's most recent accounts, and pays such reasonable fee as may be requested, the trustees must comply with such request within two months.[79]

10.25 Some instruments disposing of land by or to a charity must also contain specified statements if the disposition is to be valid; and even exempt charities are subject to these obligations. Certain instruments, including contracts for the sale, lease, or other disposition of land by or to a charity, and any conveyance, transfer, lease, or other instrument effecting such a disposition, must make specified statements,

---

[72] See Judith Hill, & E Hackett, 'Exempt Charities' (1992–3) 1 CL & PR 209, where these provisions are usefully summarized
[73] CA 1992, Pt II
[74] ibid, Pt III
[75] CA 1993, s 13(5)
[76] ibid, ss 72, 73 (except s 73(4))
[77] ibid, s 46(1)
[78] ibid, s 46(2)
[79] ibid, s 47(2)

including, where the charity is exempt, a statement that the charity is an exempt charity.[80] The precise requirements are considered further in chapter 17.[81]

(4) Provisions of which an exempt charity may avail itself

Since it is a charity for the purposes of the Charities Act 1993, an exempt charity **10.26** may avail itself of many of the Charity Commissioners' powers. These include authorizing dealings with charity property where this is expedient in the interests of the charity.[82] Even if the charity is exempt, a charity trustee or trustee for a charity may seek the Charity Commissioners' advice in writing, and secure the protection thereby afforded.[83] The exempt charity may itself apply to the Commissioners to exercise their jurisdiction to make schemes and to act for the protection of the charity.[84] One or more exempt charities may (whether with other charities or not) apply to the court or to the Charity Commissioners to make a common investment scheme.[85] Charity trustees of an exempt charity, like other charity trustees, may apply to the Commissioners for their authorization to make an *ex gratia* payment.[86]

C. Registration of charities

The Charity Commissioners are required to maintain a register of charities; but **10.27** the manner in which it is maintained is left to their discretion.[87] The register, which was first established in 1961,[88] was for many years operated manually through a card index system before computerization in the early 1990s.[89] The register is open to public inspection;[90] and it may be accessed by members of the public without charge at the Commission's website or from computer terminals at each of the Commission's branches. The register of charities must contain the name of the charity and such other information as the Charity Commissioners think fit.[91] The Commissioners will enter on the register basic information describing the charity's purposes; its contact address; whether it awards grants, provides services, or raises funds; and its annual income.[92]

---

[80] ibid, s 37(1)
[81] See ch 17, paras 17.87–17.95
[82] CA 1993, s 26(1)
[83] ibid, s 29
[84] ibid, s 16(4)(a)
[85] ibid, s 24(2)
[86] ibid, s 27. On *ex gratia* payments, see ch 18, paras 18.07–18.18
[87] CA 1993, s 3(1)
[88] Under CA 1960, s 4(1)
[89] [1990] Ch Com Rep 5–6 (paras 25–8)
[90] CA 1993, s 3(8)
[91] ibid, s 3(3)
[92] See Charity Commission, *Central Register of Charities*, CC45 (1995)

10.28 Charity trustees[93] are under a duty to register the charity with the Charity Commissioners, unless the charity is excepted from registration.[94] A copy of the charity's trusts (together with any other documents or information as may be prescribed by regulation) must accompany the application for registration.[95] The charity trustees must also notify the Charity Commissioners if the institution ceases to exist or if there is any change in its trusts or in the particulars of it entered in the register, and must supply to the Commissioners particulars of any such change and copies of any new trusts or alterations of the trusts.[96] If charity trustees fail to apply for registration of a charity (not being a charity excepted from registration), they may be required to do so by an order of the Commissioners.[97] If the charity trustees still refuse to comply, the Commissioners may apply to the High Court, which may treat the matter as contempt of court.[98]

(1) Charities not required to register

10.29 A charity is not required to register if it falls within one of four excepted categories,[99] namely an exempt charity;[100] a charity excepted by order or regulations;[101] a charity which has neither any permanent endowment,[102] nor the use or occupation of any land, and whose income from all sources does not in aggregate amount to more than £1,000 a year;[103] and a charity in respect of any registered place of worship.[104] These four categories will now be considered in turn.

Exempt charities

10.30 Although an exempt charity is the first specified category of charities 'not required to be registered',[105] an exempt charity is in fact not permitted to register.[106]

---

[93] See the definition in CA 1993, s 97(1), considered further in ch 9, paras 9.04–9.06
[94] CA 1993, s 3(7)(a). On charities excepted from registration see below, paras 10.31–10.34
[95] ibid, s 3(6). The Commissioners produce a printed form of application: RE 1
[96] CA 1993, s 3(7)(b)
[97] ibid, s 9(1)
[98] See, eg, *Re Gilchrist Educational Trust* [1895] 1 Ch 367
[99] CA 1993, s 3(5)
[100] ibid, s 3(5)(a)
[101] ibid, s 3(5)(b)
[102] Chesterman (referring to the predecessor of this exception in CA 1960) has pointed out that the criterion of lacking a permanent endowment seems to be a survival from the time when the charities legislation did not cover collecting charities: M Chesterman, *Charities, Trusts and Social Welfare* (Weidenfeld & Nicolson, 1979) 388
[103] CA 1993, s 3(5)(c)
[104] ibid, s 3(5)
[105] ibid, s 3(5)
[106] ibid, s 3(2)

Charities excepted by order or regulation[107]

A charity within the second excepted category may be excepted in one of two **10.31**
ways. First, it may obtain an exception individually (and either permanently or
temporarily) by an order of the Charity Commissioners.[108] Secondly, it may be a
charity of a description permanently or temporarily excepted by regulations made
by the Secretary of State.[109] Regulations have been made excepting certain voluntary schools,[110] certain charities for Boy Scouts and Girl Guides,[111] certain
charities for the advancement of religion,[112] certain charities for the promotion of
the efficiency of the armed forces,[113] and all universities that are not exempt
charities.[114]

Any charity which has neither any permanent endowment, nor the use or
occupation of any land, and whose income from all sources does not in
aggregate exceed £1,000 a year.[115]

Although the Charities Act 1993 nowhere defines 'income', it is generally as- **10.32**
sumed, with reasonable foundation, that it includes voluntary receipts (such as
donations, legacies, and grants) and is not restricted to 'income' in the sense in
which that term is used in the Income and Corporation Taxes Act 1988.[116] It is
clear that the figure of £1,000 is to be calculated by reference to the charity's gross
revenues, or what the Charity Commissioners estimate these are likely to be;
and it is also clear that nothing is to be brought into account for the yearly value
of land occupied by a charity apart from any pecuniary income received from that
land. The wide meaning attached to 'income' may well result in a charity's income
fluctuating wildly from one year to the next, according to the size of individual

---

[107] ibid, s 3(5)(b). On relief from certain accounting obligations for charities excepted from registration under para (b), see below, para 10.118
[108] ibid, s 3(13)(a). The Charity Commissioners have, eg, excepted charities vested in diocesan
trustees of the Roman Catholic Church and the Church in Wales: [1963] Ch Com Rep 10 (para 24)
[109] CA 1993, s 3(13)(b)
[110] Charities (Exception of Voluntary Schools from Registration) Regulations 1960
(SI 1960/2366)
[111] Charities (Exception of Certain Charities for Boy Scouts and Girl Guides from Registration)
Regulations 1961 (SI 1961/1044)
[112] Charities (Exception from Registration) Regulations 1996 (SI 1996/180). A charity for the
advancement of religion is permanently excepted from the duty to be registered if the application of
its income in a particular manner is conditional upon a grave, tomb, or personal monument being
kept in good order and if the income of the charity does not amount to more than £1,000 a year:
ibid, reg 5. Certain charities connected with specified religious bodies are also excepted from the
duty to be registered until 1 Oct 2002: ibid, reg 4, as amended by the Charities (Exception from
Registration) (Amendment) Regulations 2001, SI 2001/260, reg 2
[113] Charities (Exception from Registration and Accounts) Regulations 1965 (SI 1965/1056)
[114] Charities (Exception of Universities from Registration) Regulations 1966 (SI 1966/965).
The University of Buckingham falls within this exception
[115] CA 1993, s 3(5)(c). For the relief from certain accounting requirements for charities excepted
from registration under para (c), see below, para 10.117
[116] On the meaning of 'income' in CA 1993, see further below, para 10.89

donations or legacies which it happens to receive, or the amount of fund-raising in which it engages. For example, a charity which engages in substantial fund-raising in its first year only, will not be excepted from registration under this paragraph in that first year if it raises more than £1,000, whereas in subsequent years it may qualify as an excepted charity (if the other requirements of the paragraph are met), provided that any income produced by investments purchased from its prior fund-raising activities or from other sources does not exceed £1,000. A charity's obligation to register may therefore itself fluctuate from year to year. In practice, charity trustees of a charity whose income is likely to fluctuate in this way are best advised to register the charity initially, and not to request the Commissioners to remove it from the register in any year merely because the income falls below £1000 in that year, lest it surpass this figure the next year.

10.33 Although an excepted charity is not required to register, an excepted charity (not being an exempt charity) may apply for registration, in which event the Charity Commissioners have a discretion whether to register it or not.[117] One reason for charity trustees of an excepted charity seeking registration might be to enable them to seek grants which the awarding body concerned is prepared to make only to registered charities. Another reason might be to enable the charity to describe itself as a registered charity in its literature or fund-raising campaigns, in the hope that this will give donors greater confidence that the charity is properly run (which, of course, the registration machinery does not guarantee).

Registered places of worship[118]

10.34 A 'registered place of worship' means any land or buildings falling within the Places of Worship Registration Act 1855.[119]

(2) Special trusts

Meaning of 'special trusts'

10.35 Whether a charity is or is not itself excepted from the requirement to register, it may need to register as a separate charity any funds that it holds subject to a 'special trust', which is defined as:[120]

property which is held and administered by or on behalf of a charity for any special purposes of the charity, and is so held and administered on separate trusts relating only to that property

---

[117] CA 1993, s 3(2)
[118] ibid, s 3(5)
[119] ibid, s 3(14). See further ch 3, para 3.93. On the relief from certain accounting obligations for charities excepted from registration on this ground, see below, para 10.118
[120] CA 1993, s 97(1)

but this is subject to the proviso that a special trust does not by itself constitute a charity for the purposes of Part VI of the Charities Act 1993, which imposes obligations relating to charity accounts, reports, and returns.[121] The expression 'trusts', in relation to a charity, means:[122]

> the provisions establishing it as a charity and regulating its purposes and administration, whether those provisions take effect by way of trust or not, and in relation to other institutions has a corresponding meaning.

A special trust therefore comprises property that is not held upon trust for the charity's general purposes, or (where the charity is a company) that is not held by it beneficially to be applied for its exclusively charitable objects; and a special trust can arise by virtue of the objects clause of a company, as well as under a trust in the strict sense.

Creation

An outright inter vivos gift or legacy to an existing charity that does not subject **10.36** the property given to special trusts, does not create a new charity, but merely swells the general assets of the existing recipient charity. A gift or a legacy upon special charitable trusts, however, will, under general principles of the law of trusts,[123] create a separate charitable trust. The Charity Commissioners have stated that whether a separate fund of property is a separate 'charity'[124]

> all depends on the intention of the person who makes the gift. Did he intend by his gift to set up a new charity or contribute to an existing one? . . . Grants by the lottery distribution bodies to existing charities may more naturally be perceived as contributions to the funds of those charities, even if the trusts which attach to the contributions are restricted.

If an existing charity receives property upon special charitable trusts, it (or its **10.37** trustees if it is a trust or an unincorporated body) will be a trustee of that property upon the terms imposed by the settlor. If, for instance, an existing charity raises money from a public appeal and the terms of the appeal make it clear that the money is to be applied, not for the charity's general purposes, but for special, perhaps more limited, purposes, the money so raised will be subject to special trusts to apply it for those purposes, in which case the fund thereby formed will be a separate charity and cannot be treated as part of the charity's general assets. If an existing charity is proposing making an appeal to the public, the terms of the appeal need to be drafted with care. If the appeal clearly indicates that the money is

---

[121] ibid

[122] ibid, s 97(1)

[123] But subject to the power of the Charity Commissioners to give directions for the purposes of CA 1993, considered below, para 10.38–10.44: CA 1993, s 96(5), (6)

[124] Written answer to a question submitted to representatives of the Charity Commission at a 'Brains Trust' held by the CLA on 10 Dec 1998, and contained in the Minutes of that meeting

for the general purposes of the charity, no special trusts will be created merely because the appeal indicates a few ways in which the funds so raised might be applied. If, however, the terms of the appeal would suggest to a reasonable donor that the money is be applied to the projects indicated only, then the funds are likely to be treated as held upon special trusts.[125]

Charity Commissioners' power to direct whether special purposes form a distinct charity

10.38 A special charitable trust (even if it is not excepted from the need to register) does not necessarily need to be registered with the Charity Commissioners with a separate registration number from that of the main charity. By virtue of section 96(5), of the Charities Act 1993,[126] the Charity Commissioners may direct that for all or any of the purposes of that Act an institution established for any special purposes of or in connection with a charity (being charitable purposes) is to be treated as forming part of that charity or as forming a distinct charity. Any such direction can relate only to the Charities Act 1993, and cannot, for example, affect the nature of the institution as a separate body or otherwise for the purposes of the law of trusts. If the law of trusts treats it as the same institution, the question of the Charity Commissioners' exercising their power does not arise.

10.39 Since the Charity Commissioners can make a direction 'for all or any' of the purposes of the Charities Act 1993, the direction may be of varying scope. On the one hand, the Commissioners may direct that the subsidiary institution is to form part of the main charity for all the purposes of the Charities Act 1993, with the result that the subsidiary would have no separate entry in the register of charities. On the other hand, the direction may provide that the subsidiary is to form part of the main charity for the purposes of registration only. The effect of a direction in the latter form is that the subsidiary is registered as a separate charitable institution in the register of charities, but under the same registration number as the main charity.

(3) Groups of charities

General principles

10.40 Several charities may have different or overlapping purposes, but may choose to co-ordinate their activities as a group. Unless one of the charities can be treated as a main charity, with the others as its subsidiaries (which would enable the Charity Commissioners to direct that they form part of the main charity for the purposes

---

[125] See (in the context of fund-raising for schools) D Morris, 'Fund-raising for maintained schools' [1995] Conv 453, 463; D Morris, *Schools: an Education in Charity Law* (Dartmouth, 1996) 134–7

[126] Re-enacting CA 1960, s 45(5)

of the Charities Act 1993[127]), each institution, until recently, had (unless excepted from registration) to be registered as a separate charity with a separate registration number. There is now scope in some circumstances for this obligation to be relieved, as a result of the addition of section 96(6) to the Charities Act 1993.

Charity Commissioners' power to direct that two or more charities having the same trustees are to be treated as a single charity

Section 96(6) was inserted into the Charities Act 1993 by amending legislation[128] **10.41** in order to reduce a flood of registration applications following the reorganization of the National Health Service (NHS). The Charity Commissioners used to register under one number all NHS charitable trusts controlled by each health authority. This practice was questionable, as health authorities are not themselves charities. The problem was, however, exacerbated with the creation of the so-called NHS Trusts,[129] which are not trusts, but corporate bodies. As the NHS Trusts are not charities, it was impossible for NHS charitable trusts to be treated as their subsidiaries for the purposes of registration. It was envisaged that the 25,000 or so NHS charitable trusts[130] would need to be registered separately. This would have been an enormous task and provoked much opposition. The insertion of the new sub-section (the scope of which is described below)[131] has now made separate registrations unnecessary, and it has also put the Charity Commissioners' earlier practice on a more secure legal footing. The Commissioners' power is not, however, restricted to NHS charitable trusts, and it can therefore be used to enable any groups of charities having the same trustees to be registered under the same number.

Under section 96(6) of the Charities Act 1993 the Charity Commissioners may **10.42** direct that for all or any of the purposes of the Charities Act 1993 two or more charities having the same trustees are to be treated as a single charity.[132] This sub-section differs from sub-section (5)[133] in that the purposes of the charities may be entirely different; but there is instead a requirement that the charities have the same trustees. Again, the direction may relate 'to all or any' of the purposes of the Charities Act 1993. This enables the Charity Commissioners to ensure that each charity in the group is separately registered, but that all are registered under the same number.

---

[127] ie under CA 1993, s 96(5); discussed above, paras 10.38–10.39
[128] ie Charities Amendment Act 1995
[129] Under the National Health Service and Community Care Act 1990. See further H Picarda, *The Law and Practice Relating to Charities* (3rd edn, Butterworths, 1999) 825–6
[130] [1994] Ch Com Rep 7
[131] See below, paras 10.42–10.44
[132] CA 1993, s 96(6), inserted by Charities Amendment Act 1995
[133] Discussed above, paras 10.38–10.39

10.43 In exercising their discretion under section 96(6), the Commissioners have stated:[134]

> The discretion about group registration will normally be exercised in accordance with the wishes of the trustees, but our policy is that if charities are group registered, they should also be grouped (not, of course, consolidated) for accounting purposes (and if they are registered separately they should account separately).
>
> If two or more charities are grouped for registration and accounting purposes, their income/expenditure is aggregated for the purpose of determining the application of the size thresholds in the legislation.
>
> But group registration cannot be used to force an excepted charity to register, if its trustees do not wish it to be registered.

10.44 Although section 96(6) enables the Charity Commissioners to direct that the charities be treated as a single charity 'for all' the purposes of the Charities Act 1993, if a direction were to be made with this effect, it would give rise to objections both theoretical and practical. None of the charities individually would require to be registered, but only the 'single charity' of which each is a part. Unless the individual charities have been made the subject of a 'single charity' uniting scheme,[135] such 'single charity' would be merely a construct of the statute itself, and would have no separate institutional existence: to call it a 'single charity' is merely a convenient way of describing the whole group. Such 'single charity' would, nevertheless, require to be registered as a charity—which would be absurd, since it would have no constitutional documents, no name, and no separate purposes. If such a 'single charity' were to be registered, then its objects would presumably be composed of the aggregate of those of all members of the group, which other members would thereby become its subsidiaries.

(4) The Charity Commissioners' decision as to registration

10.45 Apart from the limited instance of an excepted charity (other than an exempt charity) that applies for registration,[136] the Charities Act 1993 does not give the Charity Commissioners any express discretion as to registration; on the face of the statute, therefore, registration appears to be a purely administrative function. In practice, however, the Charity Commissioners' role goes beyond the merely ministerial.

Charity Commissioners' development of the meaning of 'charity'

10.46 The register is a register of charities in the legal sense: registration will not be accorded to institutions whose purposes are, for example, merely philanthropic or

---

[134] Written answer to a question submitted to representatives of the Charity Commission at a 'Brains Trust' held by the CLA on 10 Dec 1998, and contained in the Minutes of that meeting

[135] On uniting schemes, see ch 15, paras 15.39–15.42

[136] CA 1993, s 3(2); see above, para 10.33

benevolent, unless those purposes are wholly and exclusively charitable. The Charity Commissioners must make a decision in each case whether the institution in question is established for wholly and exclusively charitable purposes based on case law and statute. The registration process therefore involves the exercising of a quasi-judicial function; and, to the extent that the purposes of the institution in question do not fall clearly within any precedents, the decision of the Charity Commissioners might be characterized as the exercise of a discretion.[137] The Commissioners adopt the same flexible approach as the courts, and are prepared to develop the law of charity in accordance with changes in society.[138]

Determining charitable status in an individual case

The Charity Commissioners have stated their approach boldly and without qualification:[139]   **10.47**

> We consider whether the purposes of the organisation are charitable in law and this involves us looking at both its objects and its activities.

This statement is somewhat eliptical, as a decision to register or to deny registration to a particular institution is in fact a two-stage process. First, it is necessary to ascertain what the institution's purposes are; and, secondly, it is necessary to determine whether those purposes are charitable.   **10.48**

Ascertaining an institution's purposes

The basic principle is that, where the objects of an institution are comprehensively set out in a document, then (in the absence of ambiguity or uncertainty) its objects are to be ascertained by reference to that document (usually its governing instrument) and from that document alone. It is irrelevant to inquire into the   **10.49**

---

[137] See M Chesterman, *Charities, Trusts and Social Welfare* (Weidenfeld & Nicolson, 1979) 116–17

[138] See the speeches of Lord Simonds in *National Anti-Vivisection Society v IRC* [1948] AC 32, 74, and in *Gilmour v Coats* [1949] AC 126, 443. The Charity Commissioners relied upon those words in declining to register two new rifle and pistol clubs, even though this effectively meant departing from *Re Stephens* [1892] 8 TLR 792 (Kekewich J): *City of London Rifle and Pistol Club*; *Burnley Rifle Club* (1993) 1 Decisions 4, 10. See ch 4, paras 4.100–4.101. See also [1966] Ch Com Rep 10 (para 29). The Charity Commissioners are taking the same approach in their review of the register as they take to individual applications for registration: see Charity Commission, *The Review of the Register*, RR1 (Mar 1999), 3 (paras 9, 11), and Ann B, which sets out some examples of where the Commissioners have applied this approach in the past. Besides their new approach to rifle and pistol clubs described earlier in this note, these include: the promotion of good community relations: [1983] Ch Com Rep 9–11 (paras 15–20); the provision of recreational facilities for ethnic and other minorities: (1995) 4 Decisions 17–21; public benefit in relation to charities operating overseas: (1993) 1 Decisions 16; the promotion of ethical standards in business and corporate responsibility: *Public Concern at Work* (1994) 2 Decisions 5, 10; and the relief of poverty of deprived producers and workers overseas by the awarding of a 'fair trade mark': *The Fairtrade Foundation* (1995) 4 Decisions 1

[139] [1996] Ch Com Rep 15 (para 79)

motives of the founders or how they contemplated or intended that the institution should operate or how it has in fact operated.[140]

10.50 It can sometimes be difficult to determine whether what appears to be an object is in fact a power, and vice versa. Even though the principal expressed purposes or objects of the institution may appear, or purport to be, wholly and exclusively charitable, if the governing instrument contains other provisions or powers which could enable the property to be applied for non-charitable purposes,[141] then the institution's purposes or objects will not be wholly and exclusively charitable.[142] The Charity Commissioners examine the whole instrument, and they will refuse registration if what are apparent powers are in substance non-charitable purposes. The risk that ostensible powers will be construed as independent objects is greater if the powers are described in the same clause as the expression of the institution's purposes, for instance, if the powers are contained within the objects clause where the institution is a company.[143]

10.51 The principle that the objects of an institution are to be ascertained solely by reference to its governing instrument admits of only two exceptions.

10.52 First, if the institution's purposes are ambiguous when read in the context of the instrument, extrinsic evidence may be brought, which may include evidence of the intention of those who control the institution[144] and of the manner in which the purposes have been,[145] or are capable of being,[146] carried out. Extrinsic evidence may therefore be brought to indicate whether one of the expressed purposes, which is not in itself a charitable purpose, is properly an independent purpose (which therefore prevents the trust from being wholly and exclusively

---

[140] *IRC v Oldham Training and Enterprise Council* [1996] STC 1218, 1234 (Lightman J)

[141] eg the Charity Commissioners will treat a trustee remuneration clause in this way, unless payment to the trustees is necessary in the interests of the charity, and the clause restricts the payments to reasonable amounts: see (1994) 2 Decisions 14–23; and see further ch 9, paras 9.101–9.110

[142] eg *The Cowan Charitable Trust* [1976] Ch Com Rep 14–16 (paras 45–9), where the Commissioners were asked to register a trust which provided for its capital to be distributed at the trustees' discretion 'for charitable purposes and charitable institutions'. The Commissioners declined to register the trust, because the trust instrument went on to specify that the trustees were to prefer the claims of persons who in fact constituted a private class, which showed that the purposes lacked the necessary element of a sufficient community to benefit

[143] See, eg, *Oxford Group Ltd v IRC* [1949] 2 All ER 537 (CA) (where the expression of powers in the objects clause in the memorandum of a company was construed as an independent non-charitable object). On objects and powers of charitable companies under the Companies Acts, see further ch 8, paras 8.89–8.97

[144] *Re Whiteley* [1910] 1 Ch 600

[145] See *Southwood v A-G* The Times, 26 Oct 1998 (Carnwath J), where the need for ambiguity is clearly stated. The Court of Appeal in the same case made no express reference to the need for ambiguity, but it was considering a trust instrument which was in fact ambiguous on its face: *Southwood v A-G* (CA, 28 June 2000). See further ch 7, para 7.23

[146] *Incorporated Council of Law Reporting for England and Wales v A-G* [1972] Ch 73, 91. Extrinsic evidence is admissible to show that the objects can be carried out only in a way which is wholly and exclusively charitable

charitable) or merely ancillary to purposes which are wholly and exclusively charitable (which does not preclude charitable status). Activities of an organization after its formation can never be relevant, however, unless they are intra vires.[147] Furthermore, since the main purposes of an organization are to be assessed at the time of its formation, evidence of activities at or shortly after that time has a greater probative value than evidence of activities carried out subsequently.[148] In so far as the activities of the institution reveal the intention of those who control it, such activities are relevant, to this limited extent, in determining charitable status.[149]

Secondly, if there is no governing instrument, or if it has been lost, or if what instrument does exist is clearly not intended to be comprehensive, the applicants must produce evidence to the Charity Commissioners that the property in question is subject to charitable trusts.[150] This may be satisfied by evidence that the property in question has been applied for wholly and exclusively charitable purposes for a sufficiently long period.[151]

10.53

More controversially, however, it appears that the Charity Commissioners, when determining what an institution's objects are, consider themselves free to refer to its activities in every case, even when the governing instrument is itself unambiguous. The Commissioners will therefore decline to register even an institution with clearly exclusively charitable objects if they consider that the institution is likely to apply its property to non-charitable purposes or to carry out its activities in an improper manner.[152] An institution whose charitable purposes are very wide (for example, 'for charitable purposes' or 'for the advancement of education') is particularly likely to have to satisfy the Charity Commissioners both that its existing or proposed activities are charitable (for example, that propaganda activities are not to wear the mask of education)[153] and that they are not markedly narrower than the purposes expressed (as it is not uncommon, particularly for charities which intend to raise funds from the public, to try to give the impression that their activities are wider than they really are).[154]

10.54

The Charity Commissioners' exercise of their discretion to refuse registration on this last ground undoubtedly serves a useful function in enabling the registration

10.55

---

[147] *A-G v Ross* [1986] 1 WLR 252, 264 (Scott J)
[148] ibid, 264
[149] See further J Fryer, 'The Charity Commission: determination of charitable status on the sole basis of the stated objects' (1985) NLJ Christmas Appeals Suppl 10
[150] *The Barmouth Sailors' Institute* [1966] Ch Com Rep 31, App A6
[151] *A-G v St Cross Hospital* (1853) 17 Beav 435, 464; *A-G v Gould* (1860) 28 Beav 485, 501. See also *Caldey Abbey* [1969] Ch Com Rep 9 (para 19)
[152] J Fryer, 'The Charity Commission: determination of charitable status on the sole basis of the stated objects' (1985) NLJ Christmas Appeals Suppl 10, 16–18
[153] [1966] Ch Com Rep 13 (para 38). See further ch 7, paras 7.19–7.25 esp 7.23
[154] See [1966] Ch Com Rep 13 (para 39)

system to operate as a prophylactic against potential abuse.[155] The Commissioners' authority to refuse registration for this reason is, however, of dubious legitimacy. The existence of such authority is denied by the authorities which, as has been seen,[156] have laid down that, in determining what an institution's purposes are, extrinsic evidence cannot be used unless there is ambiguity. Furthermore, the Charities Act 1993 does not confer upon the Charity Commissioners any express power to decline to register an institution whose purposes are charitable merely because the Commissioners consider that those setting it up or running it lack good faith.[157] There is also no legal requirement that, for an institution to be charitable, its objects must be expressed with any degree of specificity, since certainty of objects has never been a requirement of charitable trusts. Provided an institution's objects are wholly and exclusively charitable, they are charitable in law, no matter how broadly they may be expressed.[157a]

Determining whether those purposes are charitable

10.56 Once an institution's objects have been ascertained, it is necessary to decide if they are charitable. For an institution to be charitable, its purposes must be wholly and exclusively charitable.[158] Another way of expressing this is to say that there must be a clear intention, either expressed or implied, that its property is to be devoted to purposes that are wholly and exclusively charitable. In ascertaining this intention, a fair interpretation must be put upon the whole of the objects clause taken together.[159] Where an institution's expressed purposes are not wholly and exclusively charitable, a recital of charitable intention in the instrument cannot make them charitable.[160] Where, however, the purposes are ambiguous, a recital of charitable intention may have this effect.[161]

---

[155] It might, eg, be used to prevent the registration of a so-called 'captive charity', viz a charity formed with the aim of providing a private gain for its managers, such as a charity set up by a professional fund-raiser or commercial participator in order to hire out its own services at a fee or to increase its own profits. See *Malpractice in Fundraising for Charity*, report of a working party of the NCVO, Harry Kidd (chairman) (1986), paras 2.6, 5.39–5.49

[156] See above, paras 10.49–10.52

[157] The introduction of a statutory requirement of good faith as a condition of registration was considered, but rejected, in two reports preceding the changes in charity law which were made in the early 1990s. One reason was the difficulty of defining such a concept; another was fear of subjectivity on the part of the Charity Commissioners, which might be a step towards subjecting charity registration to the arbitrary approval of officials or politicians: see Kidd Report, para. 5.40. A further objection was that a charity denied registration on this ground alone would remain a charity. An argument against the introduction of a probationary period of registration was that final registration might then be seen as a seal of approval of the activities of registered charities: Report of the Woodfield Committee, *Efficiency Scrutiny of the Supervision of Charities* (1987), 27 (para 74). These objections were evidently persuasive, as the matter was not discussed in the White Paper, *Charities: a Framework for the Future*, CM 694 (1989) and no such criterion was introduced into what became the CA 1992

[157a] See ch 6, paras 6.14

[158] See ch 6, paras 6.01–6.03

[159] *Hunter v A-G* [1899] AC 309, 320

[160] *Re Sanders' Will Trusts* [1954] Ch 265

[161] *A-G v Jesus College, Oxford* (1861) 29 Beav 163, 168

Although evidence outside the four corners of the governing instrument cannot **10.57** generally be used to determine what an institution's objects are, such evidence is admissible to determine whether such purposes are charitable. Such evidence can therefore be used to determine whether the requirements for charitable status are satisfied: namely, that the purpose is itself charitable, that there is a sufficient public benefit, and that such benefit is made available to a sufficient section of the community. To this end, it is proper to have regard to evidence about the purposes which the pursuit of those objects will serve.[162] What the body has done in pursuance of its objects 'may afford graphic evidence of the potential consequences of the pursuit of its objects'.[163]

Where a purpose falls within the first, second, or fourth head of *Pemsel*'s case,[164] **10.58** public benefit is not presumed; it may, however, be self-evident, as where the purpose is expressed in very general terms (such as 'the relief of poverty' or 'the advancement of education'), or where its worth is generally acknowledged.[165] In borderline cases, whether a purpose is charitable and for the public benefit may need to be proved by the use of expert evidence. Expert witnesses have been used, for instance, when the court had to decide whether the promotion of a chess tournament for young men and boys in Portsmouth was educational,[166] and whether a collection to be maintained as a museum was of public utility or of educative value.[167]

Where a purpose falls under the third head of *Pemsel*'s case, namely, the advance- **10.59** ment of religion, public benefit is assumed.[168] Rather alarmingly, however, the Charity Commissioners now consider that it is appropriate, when deciding whether such presumption has been rebutted, to take into account concern amongst some sectors of the public about an institution's practices, as evidenced by unsolicited letters sent to them and views expressed in the press, even though, as they admit, the truth or accuracy of such claims may be questionable.[169] This practice is to be deprecated; it is unacceptable that the assessment of public

---

[162] *Incorporated Council of Law Reporting for England and Wales v A-G* [1972] Ch 73, 99 (Buckley LJ, who examined evidence relating to the need for reliable law reports and the reasons for publishing them)

[163] *IRC v Oldham Training and Enterprise Council* [1996] STC 1218, 1235 (Lightman J)

[164] ie the relief of poverty, the advancement of education, and other purposes beneficial to the community

[165] eg *Re Delius* [1957] Ch 299

[166] *Re Dupree's Deed Trusts* [1945] Ch 16 (where a schoolmaster gave evidence that chess was educational)

[167] *Re Pinion* [1965] Ch 85 (CA)

[168] *National Anti-Vivisection Society v IRC* [1948] AC 31, 42 (Lord Wright), 65 (Lord Simonds); *Re Watson* [1973] 1 WLR 1472, 1482 (Plowman J)

[169] See Decision of the Charity Commissioners (17 Nov 1999), *Application for Registration as a charity by the Church of Scientology (England and Wales)*, 46, where such evidence contributed to the Charity Commissioners' conclusion that the presumption of public benefit under the third head of *Pemsel*'s case was rebutted, so that the applicant should have to demonstrate public benefit in fact

benefit, and thereby charitable status, should turn on unsubstantiated rumour. The *lettre de cachet* has no place in charity law. The Commissioners' present attitude is also strikingly at variance with their own avowed stance of a few years earlier.[170]

Disclosure of information by tax authorities

10.60 The Commissioners of Customs and Excise and the Commissioners of the Inland Revenue may disclose to the Charity Commissioners information as to (inter alia) the purposes of an institution and the trusts under which it is established or regulated, in order to assist the Charity Commissioners in determining whether the institution ought to be treated as established for charitable purposes.[171]

Submission of executed instruments only

10.61 In view of the foregoing, there is a risk that the trustees may incur time and money in having the trust instrument prepared and executed, only to have registration refused. The Charity Commissioners used to operate a clearing system, whereby draft trust instruments could be submitted to them for approval before execution. This facility was, however, withdrawn in April 1996; so that now the Commission will be prepared to consider instruments in draft only in special circumstances.[172] As part of the change in the registration procedure, the Charity Commissioners send an information pack[173] (which is written in lay terms) to anyone who asks about setting up a charity.[174] The Commissioners consider that the guidance contained in the pack on what is required in a governing document, including an adequate amendment provision, is sufficient to avoid most problems.[175] Nevertheless, the new registration procedure has undoubtedly increased the involvement of private lawyers in the preparation of charities' governing documents.

(5) Effects of registration

10.62 An institution is for all purposes other than rectification of the register conclusively presumed to be or to have been a charity at any time when it is or was on the register of charities.[176] During the period of its registration as a charity, an institution is therefore entitled to claim the tax exemptions and rating reliefs available to

---

[170] See [1990] Ch Com Rep 15 (para 77), and below, para 10.138

[171] CA 1993, s 10(2)(b). See further below, para 10.156

[172] eg where novel charitable objects are proposed or where an organization proposes to deviate from an agreed model: [1995] Ch Com Rep 19 (para 82); and [1996] Ch Com Rep 15–16, esp paras 83, 88

[173] 'Starting a Charity and Applying for Registration'

[174] [1996] Ch Com Rep 15 (para 85)

[175] ibid, 16 (para 88)

[176] CA 1993, s 4(1)

charities. Although registration is not itself retrospective, the effect of this deeming provision is that, unless the court is hearing an appeal against the institution's registration or continued registration on the alleged ground that it is not a charity, it must assume that a registered charity was also in law a charity during the period prior to its registration when its purposes were the same as those in respect of which it was registered.[177] Furthermore, even if the purposes of the institution are subsequently held by the court not to be charitable (which will lead to its removal from the register) its status as a charity is preserved until such removal takes place.[178] There is, however, no contrary presumption that an institution which is not on the register is not a charity.[179] An institution which can satisfy the taxing or rating authorities that it is a charity is therefore entitled to claim the exemptions and reliefs available to charities even if it is not registered with the Charity Commissioners.

(6) Objections to registration

Any person who is or may be affected by the registration of an institution as a charity may, on the ground that it is not a charity, object to its being entered by the Charity Commissioners on the register, or apply to them for it to be removed from the register.[180] The persons most likely to object in practice are the Commissioners of the Inland Revenue[181] or rating authorities, or those who would be entitled to the property under a resulting trust, by way of a residuary gift, or under an intestacy (as the case may be) should the registered institution be held not to be a charity. It has been suggested that, although an ordinary taxpayer or ratepayer in the area in which the charity operates might contend that he is a person affected (since

10.63

---

[177] *Re Murawski's Will Trusts* [1971] 1 WLR 707; noted T Lloyd, (1971) 87 LQR 468

[178] Between 1895 and 1948, the promotion of anti-vivisection was regarded as a charitable purpose on the authority of Chitty J's judgment in *Re Foveaux* [1895] 2 Ch 501. The effect of the House of Lords' decision in *National Anti-Vivisection Society v IRC* [1948] AC 31, however, was to overrule the earlier case, and to hold that anti-vivisection had never been a charitable purpose. Had the present registration machinery been in place during this period, the Charity Commissioners would have removed anti-vivisection societies from the register following the House of Lords' decision; but the better view (albeit one at variance with that of the Charity Commissioners) is that such institutions would continue to have been deemed charities during their period of registration: see further ch 15, paras 15.78–15.79. Similar consequences would ensue today if the courts were to overrule *Re Stephens* (1892) 8 TLR 792 and hold the promotion of rifle shooting not to be a charitable purpose. For a more detailed analysis of the problems which arise when an institution is removed from the register, see: Maintenance of the Register Discussion Document, *Maintenance of an Accurate Register of Charities*, Charity Commission (1999), paras 13–16, Ann B. See also ch 15, paras 15.73–15.79, where the difficulties are considered in relation to the applicability of the cy-près doctrine

[179] *Re Murawski's Will Trusts* [1971] 1 WLR 707

[180] CA 1993, s 4(2), which also provides for regulations to be made by the Secretary of State as to the manner in which such objection or application is to be made; but no regulations have been promulgated

[181] As in *IRC v McMullen* [1981] AC 1 (HL)

registration increases the tax or rate burden), such a purely fiscal interest would probably not suffice.[182]

10.64 The question of who qualifies as a person 'affected by the registration' of an institution as a charity has been considered on several occasions by the Charity Commissioners. In one case, a non-charitable body, the Oxford Union Society, had set up a charitable trust with a view to conveying to it all or part of the Society's land.[183] Three members of the Society (who had a potential interest in its property) applied for the removal of the trust from the register of charities on various grounds. The Charity Commissioners concluded that the application was misconceived and rejected it, but they also doubted whether the objectors could properly claim to be persons 'affected by the registration', because it was not registration as such which affected them, but rather the Society's proposals to benefit the trust.

10.65 In another case, the Charity Commissioners received an application for the removal from the register of the British Pregnancy Advisory Service (BPAS) from a man who had previously applied unsuccessfully to the High Court for an injunction to prevent his estranged wife from having an abortion which the BPAS had facilitated.[184] The applicant claimed to be a person affected by the registration because he had lost the chance to be a father; but the Charity Commissioners considered this argument to be weak, and concluded that he was not a person affected by the registration.[185]

10.66 When the Cult Information Centre[186] applied (in the event successfully) to be registered as a charity, with the aim of educating the public (mainly students) about the techniques used to recruit people into cults, the Charity Commissioners received objections to its registration as a charity from two existing registered charities (the Holy Spirit Association for the Unification of World Christianity, and the National Council of Hindu Temples) and from a body that was not a registered charity (the Church of Scientology). The Charity Commissioners decided that the objections should be rejected, both on their merits and because it was doubtful that the objectors could be regarded as persons who were or might be affected by the registration of the Cult Information Centre as a charity so as to confer upon them a right to object. The Commissioners said it was difficult to see how legitimate educational activities could affect the objectors in any way which would entitle them to object to the Cult Information Centre's registration.

---

[182] H Picarda, *The Law and Practice Relating to Charities* (3rd edn, Butterworths, 1999) 610
[183] *Oxford Literary and Debating Union Charitable Trust* [1976] Ch Com Rep 18–19 (paras 62–4)
[184] *British Pregnancy Advisory Service* [1978] Ch Com Rep 26–7 (paras 82–5)
[185] ibid, 27 (para 84)
[186] (1993) 1 Ch Com Rep 1–3

(7) Appeals against the Charity Commissioners' decisions

An appeal against any decision of the Charity Commissioners as to whether or not **10.67** to register an institution, or as to whether or not to remove an institution from the register, may be brought in the High Court by the Attorney-General, or by the persons who are or who claim to be the charity trustees of the institution,[187] or by any person whose objection to registration or whose application for removal[188] is disallowed by the decision.[189]

If the Commissioners decide to register, or not to remove, an institution, then, if **10.68** there is an appeal against such decision in the High Court, 'until the Commissioners are satisfied' whether their own decision is or is not to stand, the entry in the register must be maintained, but is in suspense and must be marked to indicate that this is so.[190] An institution is deemed not to be on the register during any period when the entry relating to it is thereby in suspense.[191] The phrase 'until the Commissioners are satisfied' could be interpreted to mean that the Charity Commissioners are entitled to ignore a decision of the High Court! It would seem, however, that the Commissioners are bound to recognize such a decision, and that these words are intended merely to give them a power to maintain a registration after a judgment of the High Court against the registration or in favour of the removal of the institution from the register, pending the possibility of an appeal to the Court of Appeal or to the House of Lords.[192]

The effect of an institution's registration being marked 'in suspense' is to deny it, **10.69** during the period that its entry is so marked, of the benefit of being deemed a charity for all purposes (which benefit would otherwise flow from being entered on the register).[193] Removal of a suspension does not have retrospective effect. If, therefore, the last court to which an appeal is made holds that the institution is a charity, and the Charity Commissioners remove the suspension, the institution obtains the benefit of being deemed a charity for all purposes only from the date of removal of the suspension. Since, however, a decision of the court that the institution is a charity will have retrospective effect, the institution may thereby be found to have been a charity during the entire period of its suspension (together

---

[187] See, eg, *Holmes v A-G* The Times, 11 Feb 1981, where the trustees of a trust for the benefit of the Exclusive Brethren successfully appealed against the Charity Commissioners' decision to remove the trust from the register on the ground that the original registration had been a mistake

[188] ie under CA 1993, s 4(2)

[189] ibid, s 4(3). An example of an (eventually unsuccessful) appeal by the Commissioners of the Inland Revenue against a decision of the Charity Commissioners to register an institution is *IRC v McMullen* [1981] AC 1. The Commissioners of the Inland Revenue had objected to the registration, and no question arose as to their standing on the appeal

[190] CA 1993, s 4(4)

[191] ibid

[192] See Lord Nathan, *The CA 1960* (Butterworths, 1962), 53–4. For an analysis of the legislative background, see J Fryer, 'A charity up for suspension' (1985) 129 Sol Jo 880

[193] ie CA 1993, s 4(1), does not apply to a charity whose registration is in suspense

with any period prior to its entry on the register). Since an institution can be a charity even when it is not entered in the register of charities, such institution will then be entitled to claim the tax and rating reliefs available to charities (and which are not restricted to charities which are registered) from the date that it became a charity, which may include the whole period of suspension.

10.70   The principle that registration as a charity is not retrospective applies similarly if the Charity Commissioners refuse to enter an institution on the register, or remove an institution from the register, in either case on the ground that it is not a charity. If, on appeal, the institution is held to be a charity, so that the Commissioners thereupon enter it (or re-enter it) in the register, the institution is deemed to be a charity from the date of that entry (or re-entry). Again, however, the decision of the court will be retrospective, so that tax and rating relief may be obtained from the date that the institution became a charity.

10.71   The Charity Commissioners are not precluded by a decision on appeal which affects the registration of an institution or its removal from the register from considering the matter afresh, if it appears to them that there has been a change of circumstances or that the decision is inconsistent with a later judicial decision, whether given on such appeal or not.[194]

(8) Power to direct change of name

10.72   There are five grounds upon any one of which the Charity Commissioners are empowered to direct that a charity (other than an exempt charity[195]) change its name, within a specified period, to such other name as the charity trustees may determine with the Commissioners' approval.[196] The grounds for directing a change of name are:

(1)   In the case of a registered charity, if its name is the same, or in the Commissioners' opinion, too like, that of another charity (whether registered or not) at the time when the registered name was entered in the register.[197] In this case, any direction of the Commissioners must be made within twelve months of the registered name's being entered in the register.[198]

(2)   If the name is, in the Commissioners' opinion, likely to mislead the public as to the true nature of the charity's purposes as set out in its trusts, or of its activities in pursuit of those purposes.[199]

---

[194]   CA 1993, s 4(5)
[195]   ibid, s 6(9)
[196]   ibid, s 6(1)
[197]   ibid, s 6(2)(a)
[198]   ibid, s 6(3)
[199]   ibid, s 6(2)(b)

(3) If the name includes any word or expression for the time being specified in regulations made by the Secretary of State and which is, in the Commissioners' opinion, likely to mislead the public in any respect as to the status of the charity.[200]

(4) If the name is, in the Commissioners' opinion, likely to give the impression that the charity is connected in some way with Her Majesty's Government or any local authority, or with any other body of persons or any individual, when it is not so connected.[201]

(5) if the name is, in the Commissioners' opinion, offensive.[202]

10.73 A direction requiring a change of name must be given to the charity trustees,[203] who must give effect to it notwithstanding anything in the trusts of the charity.[204] When the name of a charity is changed pursuant to such a direction, the charity trustees must forthwith notify the Charity Commissioners of the charity's new name and of the date on which the change occurred.[205] A change of name pursuant to such a direction does not affect any rights or obligations of the charity; and any legal proceedings commenced by or against the charity in its former name may be continued in its new name.[206]

10.74 Where the charity is a company, the change of name must be effected by resolution of the directors of the company.[207] Any resolution passed by the directors in compliance with a direction must be registered with the Registrar of Companies.[208] Unless the new name breaches the statutory prohibitions on the registration of certain company names,[209] the Registrar of Companies must enter the new name on the register in place of the former name, and must issue an amended certificate of incorporation; and the change of name has effect from the date on which the altered certificate is issued.[210]

(9) Removal from the register

Duty of charity trustees

10.75 It is the duty of the charity trustees (or the last charity trustees) of any institution which is for the time being registered to notify the Charity Commissioners if it

---

[200] ibid, s 6(2)(c). The current regulations are the Charities (Misleading Names) Regulations 1992, SI 1992/1901, which list 45 such words or expressions

[201] CA 1993, s 6(2)(d)

[202] ibid, s 6(2)(e)

[203] For the purposes of this section, the expression 'charity trustees' is, in relation to a charity which is a company, a reference to the directors of the company: CA 1993, s 6(8)

[204] ibid, s 6(4)

[205] ibid, s 6(5)

[206] ibid, s 6(6)

[207] ibid, s 7(1)

[208] ie in accordance with the Companies Act 1985, s 380: CA 1993, s 7(2)

[209] Under the Companies Act 1985, s 26

[210] CA 1993, s 7(3)

ceases to exist, or if there is any change in its trusts or in the particulars of it entered in the register, and to supply to the Commissioners particulars of any such change and copies of any new trusts or alterations of the trusts.[211]

Grounds for removal

Institution ceases to be a charity

10.76 The Charity Commissioners must remove from the register any institution which no longer appears to them to be a charity; where the removal is due to any change in the institution's purposes or trusts, such removal takes effect from the date of that change.[212]

10.77 Removal on this ground is somewhat unusual. It could take place because the Charity Commissioners decide that the institution's purposes are not in law charitable, and that the original registration had therefore been a mistake.[213] It could also take place because the Commissioners consider that the purposes, although charitable when the institution was registered initially, have since ceased to be charitable, as where a later case overrules an earlier authority on which the decision to register had been founded.[214] Although the Charity Commissioners consider themselves able to treat the definition of charities as a moving subject, and have declined to register institutions as charities on the ground that the courts would no longer consider their purposes to be charitable, there does not appear to be any recorded instance of the Charity Commissioners removing a charity from the register on this ground in the absence of a decision of the courts.[215]

10.78 Removal could also take place on the basis that an institution has ceased to be a charity if a charitable company were to alter its objects so that they ceased to be wholly and exclusively charitable[216]; any property of the company held immediately before the alteration would appear to remain effectually dedicated to the un-

---

[211] CA 1993, s 3(7)(b)

[212] ibid, s 3(4)

[213] eg, as in the case of *Scott Baden Commonwealth Ltd* [1967] Ch Com Rep 48, App D, Pt II. See also M Chesterman, *Charities, Trusts and Social Welfare* (Weidenfeld & Nicolson, 1979) 364. For a successful appeal by trustees against a decision of the Charity Commissioners to remove a charity from the register on this ground, see *Holmes v A-G* The Times, 11 Feb 1981

[214] It is difficult to find a modern example; but had the register of charities been in existence at the time of the decision in *Re Foveaux* [1895] 2 Ch 501, the Charity Commissioners would no doubt have registered charities whose objects were for the promotion of anti-vivisection. The decision of the House of Lords in *National Anti-Vivisection Society v IRC* 1948] AC 31, which held such a purpose not to be charitable, would have meant that the Commissioners would have been obliged to remove charities for the promotion of anti-vivisection from the register of charities

[215] See *City of London Rifle and Pistol Club, Burnley Rifle Club* (1993) 1 Decisions 4, 10, where the Charity Commissioners declined to register two new rifle clubs because they considered that courts would no longer treat *Re Stephens* (1892) 8 TLR 792 as authoritative; but they did not remove from the register existing rifle clubs which had obtained registration on the basis of that case

[216] See ch 8, paras 8.119–8.120

amended (charitable) objects through the imposition of a constructive trust, which would form a separate charitable institution subject (unless excepted) to the obligation to register.

Although the Charity Commissioners are not obliged to notify a charity of their intention to remove it from the register, it appears that it is their practice to do so, at least where removal is on the ground that the institution no longer appears to the Charity Commissioners to be a charity.[217]   **10.79**

Institution ceases to exist or does not operate

The Charity Commissioners must remove from the register any charity which ceases to exist or does not operate.[218] This is the basis for most removals,[219] and the number of such removals has increased in recent years owing to the Commissioners' continued work on ensuring the accuracy of the register, following the tightening of the accounting and reporting obligations on charities contained in the Charities Act 1993.[220] The Commissioners have no power to remove a charity merely because its administration is poor, and the Commissioners have other powers under the Charities Act 1993 to remedy poor practice, for example by replacing the trustees.[221]   **10.80**

An unincorporated charity ceases to exist if it has no property, as where it has disposed of all its property in the course of carrying out its charitable purposes, or pursuant to a power in its constitution (for example, upon a transfer of its assets on incorporation[222]), or (where it is a small endowed charity) following a resolution under section 75 of the Charities Act 1993[223] or where its property has been applied to another charity pursuant to a cy-près scheme,[224] or where (being a small charity) it has disposed of its property following a resolution under section 74 of the Charities Act 1993.[225]   **10.81**

A charitable company registered under the Companies Act 1985 remains in existence, even if it has no assets, until it is removed from the register of companies. The Registrar of Companies may strike a defunct company off the register of   **10.82**

---

[217] As in *Scott Baden Commonwealth Ltd*, [1967] Ch Com Rep 48, App D, Pt II

[218] CA 1993, s 3(4)

[219] [1997] Ch Com Rep 12 (para 60)

[220] See [1996] Ch Com Rep 13 (para 74). The peak was in 1996, when some 10,000 charitites were removed from the register: ibid

[221] See [1997] Ch Com Rep 12 (para 60)

[222] See [1996] Ch Com Rep 13 (para 74)

[223] The section enables small endowed charities (as there defined) to spend capital by following a specified procedure: see ch 15, paras 15.148–15.151

[224] For an illustration, see *Tape Recording Topics International* [1980] Ch Com Rep 45–6 (paras 166–171)

[225] The section enables small charities (as there defined) to transfer property or modify their objects by following a specified procedure: see ch 15, paras 15.138–15.147

companies.[226] Such a defunct company can, however, be removed from the register of charities (without having to be struck off the register of companies) on the ground that it does not operate.[227]

Excepted charity

10.83 If an excepted charity (not being an exempt charity) has been entered on the register of charities at the request of the charity, it may at any time, and must at the request of the charity, be removed from the register.[228] It clearly makes sense for the Charity Commissioners to have only a power to remove an excepted charity from the register, since, were a duty of removal imposed, a charity with no permanent endowment or without the use or occupation of land, whose annual income fluctuates around £1,000 from year to year would lose its registration in any year in which its income from all sources does not exceed £1,000.[229] In effect, it might suffer a fluctuation in its registration from one year to the next.

Public inspection of cancelled entries

10.84 Entries cancelled when institutions are removed from the register must (like the register itself) be kept open to public inspection at all reasonable times.[230]

D. Submission of accounts

(1) Introduction

10.85 The accounting obligations imposed on charities vary according to the charity's legal structure.[231] Most unincorporated charities (that is, charitable trusts and unincorporated charitable associations) are subject to the accounting regime contained in Part VI of the Charities Act 1993, which came into force on 1 March 1996.[232] These statutory provisions are supported by the Charities (Accounts and Reports) Regulations 1995,[233] the Charities (Accounts and Reports) Regulations 2000,[233a] and the Charities (Annual Return) Regulations 1997.[234] These legal re-

---

[226] Companies Act 1985, s 652

[227] ie under CA 1993, s 3(4). For an example of a charity's removal on the ground that it had ceased to operate, see *The Institute of Electoral Research Limited* [1973] Ch Com Rep 31–2 (paras 98–102), where the sole surviving director of the charitable company was unwilling to take action to revive its activities or to remedy its apparent insolvency. See also *RECALL Ltd* [1987] Ch Com Rep 8–9 (paras 33–4), where the charitable company had undertaken no significant activities and had no assets to do so. See also ch 26, para 26.12

[228] CA 1993, s 3(2)

[229] ibid, s 3(5)(c). See above, paras 10.32–10.33

[230] CA 1993, s 3(8)

[231] See R Vincent, 'Charity Accounting under the CA 1993' (1996–7) 4 CL & PR 43

[232] CA 1993 (Commencement and Transitional Provisions) Order 1995, SI 1995/2695

[233] SI 1995/2724

[233a] SI 2000/2868

[234] Made by the Charity Commissioners under CA 1993, Pt VI

quirements are complemented by a revised Statement of Recommended Practice, 'Accounting and Reporting by Charities' (generally referred to as the Charities SORP 2000), issued by the Charity Commission in 2000 under the auspices of the Accounting Standards Board, and applicable to accounting periods beginning after 31 December 2000. The Charity Commission has also produced a range of explanatory leaflets.[235]

The accounting obligations imposed by Part VI vary according to the charity's income and expenditure, with the most stringent regime applying to charities with a gross annual income or expenditure of more than £250,000. Charities which are incorporated under the Companies Act 1985 must prepare an annual report and (in some cases) an annual return under Part VI, but are otherwise outside its provisions; they are instead subject to the accounting regime imposed by Part VII of the Companies Act 1985, which applies to all companies incorporated under it, whether charitable or not, although with some minor modifications for charitable companies.[236] **10.86**

Most of the provisions in Part VI of the Charities Act 1993 do not apply to an exempt charity[237] or to a charity which is excepted from the duty to register as a charity and which is not registered.[238] An exempt charity may, however, be subject to a different accounting regime imposed by another statute, for example if it is an industrial and provident society.[239] **10.87**

A registered social landlord which is a registered charity is, in respect of its housing activities, subject to specific accounting and auditing requirements under the Housing Act 1996, in addition to any obligations imposed on it by the Charities Act 1993, Part VI.[240] **10.88**

Meaning of 'income' and 'gross income'

Several of the provisions in Part VI of the Charities Act 1993 and in the Charities (Accounts and Reports) Regulations 2000,[241] refer to a charity's 'gross income',[242] **10.89**

---

[235] *Charity Accounts 2001: the framework* CC61; *Charities SORP 2000: what has changed* CC62; *The carrying out of an Independent Examination: Directions and Guidance Notes* (revised) CC63; *SORP 2000: Receipts and Payments Accoaunts Pack* CC64; *SORP 2000: Accruals Accounts Pack* CC65; *SORP 2000: Example reports and accounts* CC66

[236] See further below, paras 10.106–10.114

[237] CA 1993, s 46(1). But an exempt charity is subject to the accounting obligations contained in CA 1993, s 46(1), (2). See further below, paras 10.115–10.116

[238] CA 1993, s 46 (3), (4), (8). But the Charity Commissioners can require the charity trustees of an excepted charity to prepare an annual report: CA 1993, s 46(5), (6), (7). See further below, paras 10.117–10.118

[239] See further ch 8, paras 8.209–8.216, esp para 8.212

[240] See further ch 8, paras 8.236–8.239

[241] SI 2000/2868

[242] See CA 1993, ss 42(3) (annual statement of accounts); 43(1), (3) (annual audit or examination); 45(3), (3A) (annual reports); and 48(1A) (annual returns by registered charities). See also Charities (Accounts and Reports) Regulations 2000, SI 2000/2868, reg 7(3)

which is stated in the Act, in relation to a charity, to mean 'its gross recorded income from all sources including special trusts'.[243] The Act does not, however, define what is meant by 'income' itself. Rents received in respect of land, dividends received from shares, interest received on a bank deposit account, and other types of profit produced on the charity's investments, or from sales of goods, or from the levying of fees, are indisputably income. What is uncertain, however, is whether 'income' includes voluntary donations of money or gifts in kind.[244] If 'income' is used in the sense which it bears in tax law, purely voluntary gifts would be excluded,[245] whereas money paid under an obligation, such as under a deed of covenant, would rank as income. It may be inferred that 'income' is intended to include gifts, legacies, grants, voluntary subscriptions, and the like, since section 42(3) of the Charities Act 1993 enables the charity trustees (if in any financial year the charity's gross income does not exceed £100,000) to elect to prepare (inter alia) 'a receipts and payments account', which clearly envisages that voluntary receipts are to be included. Not surprisingly, the Charity Commissioners treat 'income' for the purposes of the Charities Act 1993 as bearing this wider meaning.[246]

(2) Accounting obligations under Part VI of the Charities Act 1993

Duty to keep accounting records

10.90 Charity trustees of a charity must ensure that accounting records are kept in respect of the charity which are sufficient to show and explain all the charity's transactions.[247] Such records must disclose at any time, with reasonable accuracy, the financial position of the charity at that time, and enable the trustees to ensure that any statements of accounts prepared by them[248] comply with the statutory requirements.[249] The accounting records must in particular contain entries showing from day to day all sums of money received and expended, and the matters in respect of which the receipt and expenditure take place, and a record of the charity's assets and liabilities.[250]

---

[243] CA 1993, s 97(1)

[244] See C McCall, 'How Big is Big? A Surprising Omission from the CA 1992' (1993–4) 2 CL & PR 111

[245] For the purposes of income tax, there must be a taxable source. For this reason, a sum of money received, for example, from one's grandmother as a birthday present does not rank as the recipient's income, even if it is made annually. CA 1993, s 3(5)(c) refers to 'income from all *sources*' (emphasis supplied); but this does not necessarily mean only taxable sources

[246] See, eg, Charity Commission, *Charity Accounts: Charities under the £10,000 Threshold*, CC52 (1996), para 11; Charity Commission, *Accounting for the Smaller Charity*, CC54 (1995), para 8.1; Charities SORP 2000, para 17 (App 1). See also above, para 10.32

[247] CA 1993, s 41(1)

[248] ie under ibid, s 42(1)

[249] ibid, s 41(1)

[250] ibid, s 41(2)

Annual statement of accounts

If a charity's gross income in any financial year exceeds £100,000,[251] the charity **10.91** trustees must prepare in respect of each financial year a statement of accounts in the prescribed form.[252] The form is currently set out in the Charities (Accounts and Reports) Regulations 2000.[253] Where a charity's gross income does not exceed this amount, the charity trustees may prepare such a statement of accounts, but they may instead, in respect of that year, elect to prepare a receipts and payments account and a statement of assets and liabilities.[254]

Annual audit or examination of charity accounts

If the gross income or total expenditure of a charity in a financial year, or in either **10.92** of the two immediately preceding financial years, exceeds £250,000,[255] the charity's accounts for that year must be audited by what might conveniently be termed 'a registered auditor', that is, a person who is either eligible for appointment as a company auditor,[256] or who is a member of a prescribed body, and is under the rules of such body eligible for appointment as auditor of the charity.[257]

If the foregoing does not apply to the financial year of a charity, but its gross in- **10.93** come or total expenditure in that year exceeds £10,000, the charity trustees may elect, instead of being audited by a qualified auditor, to be examined by an independent examiner, which means an independent person who is reasonably believed by the trustees to have the requisite ability and practical experience to carry out a competent examination of the accounts.[258] The Charity Commissioners may give guidance to charity trustees in connection with the selection of a person for appointment as an independent examiner, and they may give such directions as they think appropriate with respect to the carrying out of an examination; and such guidance or directions may either be of general application or apply to a particular charity only.[259]

If a charity subject to these requirements defaults in complying with them for ten **10.94** months from the end of a financial year, or if it appears to the Charity

---

[251] This amount was substituted by SI 1995/2696
[252] CA 1993, s 42(1)
[253] SI 2000/2868, reg 3. This reg applies to statements of accounts in respect of a financial year beginning after 31 Dec 2000 (or on or before that date if the charity trustees so determine); ibid, reg 3(1). Different requirements apply to a 'special case charity' ie a charity which is a registered social landlord or which conducts a further or higher education institution: Charities (Accounts and Reports) Regulations 2000, SI 2000/2868, reg 5
[254] CA 1993, s 42(3)
[255] ibid, s 43(1). This amount was substituted by SI 1996/2696
[256] In accordance with Companies Act 1989, s 25
[257] CA 1993, s 43(2)
[258] ibid, s 43(3), as amended by Deregulation and Contracting Out Act 1994, s 28
[259] CA 1993, s 43(7)

Commissioners that it is desirable for a charity's accounts to be audited by a registered auditor, the Charity Commissioners may by order require the charity's accounts for that year to be audited by such a person.[260] If the Commissioners make such an order because of the default of the charity trustees, the Charity Commissioners will themselves appoint the auditor,[261] and the expenses of such an audit (including the auditor's remuneration) are recoverable by the Commissioners from the charity trustees (who are personally liable, jointly and severally, for those expenses), or (to the extent that it is not practical to seek recovery from the charity trustees), from the charity's funds.[262]

10.95 Regulations prescribe the duties of an auditor carrying out an audit of charity accounts,[263] and make provision for the making of an independent examiner's report.[264] An auditor's report (unless qualified) gives 'positive assurance', in that it must state (inter alia) whether in the auditor's opinion the statement of accounts gives 'a true and fair view' of the charity's state of affairs.[265] In contrast, an independent examiner's report gives merely 'negative assurance',[266] in that the examiner is required to state (inter alia) 'whether or not any matter has come to his attention in connection with the examination which gives him reasonable cause to believe that in any material respect'[267] there has been non-compliance with the accounting requirements, or other irregularities, such as material expenditure apparently not in accordance with the trusts of the charity.[268] For most charities which do not exceed the £250,000 threshold, however, this advantage in an audit is likely to be outweighed by the heavier audit fees incurred.

10.96 The regulations also give an auditor or independent examiner a right of access to any books, documents, and other records which relate to the charity concerned, and which the auditor or independent examiner considers it necessary to inspect.[269] The regulations further provide that an auditor or independent examiner is entitled to require such information and explanations from past or present charity trustees or trustees for the charity, or from past or present officers and

---

[260] CA 1993, s 43(4)

[261] ibid, s 43(5)

[262] ibid, s 43(6)

[263] Charities (Accounts and Reports) Regulations 1995, SI 1995/2724, reg 6, made pursuant to CA 1993, s 44(1)(b), and amended by Charities (Accounts and Reports) Regulations 2000, SI 2000/2868, reg 4

[264] Charities (Accounts and Reports) Regulations 1995, SI 1995/2724, reg 7, made pursuant to CA 1993, s 44(1)(c), and amended by Charities (Accounts and Reports) Regulations 2000, SI 2000/2868, reg 4

[265] Charities (Accounts and Reports) Regulations 1995, SI 1995/2724, reg 6(1)(e)

[266] See G Morgan, 'Independent examination: assessing the new regime' (1999) Sol Jo Charities and Appeals Suppl, 34, 36

[267] Charities (Accounts and Reports) Regulations 1995, SI 1995/2724, reg 7(e)

[268] ibid, reg 7(g)

[269] ibid, reg 8(1), made pursuant to CA 1993, s 44(1)(d)

employees of the charity, as he considers it necessary to obtain.[270] If any person fails to afford an auditor or independent examiner any access to books, documents, or other records, or fails to provide information or explanations when required, the Charity Commissioners may by order give to that person or to the charity trustees for the time being such directions as the Commissioners think appropriate for securing that the default is made good.[271]

The regulations impose an unequivocal duty on an auditor, in cases where there **10.97** is evidence of serious breaches by the charity trustees of their duties under the Charities Act 1993, or under the general law, to engage in 'whistleblowing' on the charity whose accounts he is auditing. This duty is imposed by regulation 6(5):[272]

> The auditor shall communicate to the Commissioners, in writing, any matter of which the auditor becomes aware in his capacity as such which relates to the activities or affairs of the charity or of any institution or body corporate connected with the charity and which the auditor has reasonable cause to believe is, or is likely to be, of material significance for the exercise, in relation to the charity[,] of the Commissioners' functions under section 8 (general power to institute inquiries) or 18 (power to act for protection of charities) of the 1993 Act.

No equivalent duty is placed on an independent examiner. An examiner who dis- **10.98** covers specified breaches or defaults during the course of the examination is merely required to put a statement to this effect in the report to the charity trustees themselves.[273] The breaches and defaults specified are: any material expenditure or action which appears not to be in accordance with the trusts of the charity; failure to afford to the examiner any information or explanation to which he is entitled; and inconsistency between information contained in a statement of accounts prepared under section 42(1) and any report of the charity trustees prepared under section 45 of the Charities Act 1993.[274]

Annual reports

The charity trustees of a charity must prepare, in respect of each financial year, an **10.99** annual report containing a report by the trustees on the charity's activities during that year and other information prescribed by regulation.[275]

The regulations provide that, if a charity's gross income in a financial year does not **10.100** exceed £250,000, the report is to be a brief summary of the main activities and

---

[270] Charities (Accounts and Reports) Regulations 1995, SI 1995/2724, reg 8(2), made pursuant to CA 1993, s 44(1)(e)
[271] CA 1993, s 44(2)
[272] Charities (Accounts and Reports) Regulations 1995, SI 1995/2724
[273] ibid, reg 7
[274] ibid, reg 7(g)
[275] CA 1993, s 45(1)

achievements of the charity during the year in relation to its objects.[276] If such gross income in a financial year does exceed this figure, the report must be a review of all activities, including material transactions, significant developments, and achievements of the charity during that year in relation to its objects, any significant changes in those activities during that year, any important events affecting those activities which have occurred since the end of that year and any likely future developments in those activities and where only fund of the Charity was in deficit at the beginning of the financial year, the steps taken by the Charity trustees to eliminate that deficit.[277] In each case, the annual report must be dated and signed by one or more of the charity trustees, each of whom must have been authorized to do so.[278]

10.101 The annual report must also contain (inter alia) the following information: the name of the charity; its number in the register (and in the case of a charitable company, the number with which it is registered as a company); its principal address (and in the case of a charitable company, the address of its registered office); a description of the objects of the charity; and the names of the charity trustees (including the name of any other person who has been a charity trustee at any time during the financial year) and of any other person or body entitled to appoint a charity trustee of the charity.[279] If in any financial year a charity's gross income exceeds £250,000, the annual report must additionally contain (inter alia) a description of the charity's organizational structure, and a description of the charity's assets and of assets held by it for another charity (including particulars of any special arrangements for the safe custody and segregation of such assets and of the objects of the charity on whose behalf the assets are held).[280] The prescribed contents of the annual report are modified in the case of a common investment fund or a common deposit fund which is deemed to be a charity under section 24(8) of the Charities Act 1993.[281] In these instances, the annual report must be a review of the investment activities and policies of the trustees during that year. In particular, it must specify the name and address of any person to whom the trustees have delegated their management functions, and provide a description of any powers delegated by the trustees.

---

[276] Charities (Accounts and Reports) Regulations 2000, SI 2000/2868, reg 7(3)(a), made pursuant to CA 1993, s 45(2)(a)

[277] Charities (Accounts and Reports) Regulations 2000, SI 2000/2868, reg 7(3)(b), made pursuant to CA 1993, s 45(2)(a)

[278] Charities (Accounts and Reports) Regulations 2000, SI 2000/2868, reg 7(3)(c), made pursuant to CA 1993, s 45(2)(a)

[279] Charities (Accounts and Reports) Regulations 2000, SI 2000/2868, reg 7(4)(a)–(j), made pursuant to CA 1993, s 45(2)

[280] Charities (Accounts and Reports) Regulations 2000, SI 2000/2868, reg 7(4)(m)–(n), (8), made pursuant to CA 1993, s 45(2)

[281] Charities (Accounts and Reports) Regulations 1995, SI 1995/2724, reg 10(4), made pursuant to CA 1993, s 45(2). See also Charities (Accounts and Reports) Regulations 2000, SI 2000/2868, reg 7(1). On common investment funds and common deposit funds generally, see ch 16, paras 16.72–16.99

It must also state whether any such delegate has complied with the terms of the scheme, and it must describe the procedures adopted by the trustees to ensure that delegated powers are exercised in accordance with the scheme and with the investment policy of the trustees.

If in a financial year a charity's gross income or total expenditure exceeds £10,000, **10.102** the charity trustees must transmit the annual report to the Charity Commissioners, and they must transmit it within ten months of the end of that year, unless the Commissioners allow a longer period.[282] If in a financial year a charity's gross income or total expenditure does not exceed this figure, the annual report does not need to be transmitted to the Charity Commissioners unless the latter so request, in which case it must be transmitted within three months of the date of the request or within ten months of the end of that year, whichever is the later, unless the Commissioners allow a longer period.[283] Any annual report transmitted to the Commissioners pursuant to this obligation, together with the documents attached to it, must be kept by the Commissioners for such period as they think fit.[284] Any person who, without reasonable excuse, is persistently in default in complying with the obligation to transmit the annual report to the Commissioners[285] is guilty of an offence.[286]

Annual returns by registered charities

If in any financial year of a registered charity its gross income or total expenditure **10.103** exceeds £10,000, it must prepare in respect of that year an annual return in such form, and containing such information, as may be prescribed by regulations made by the Charity Commissioners.[287] Any such return must be transmitted to the Commissioners by the same date as the annual report.[288] The Commissioners may dispense with the obligation to prepare an annual report in respect of a particular charity or a particular class of charities, either generally or in respect of a particular financial year.[289]

Any person who, without reasonable excuse, is persistently in default in relation **10.104** to the obligation to transmit the annual return to the Commissioners by the requisite date is guilty of an offence.[290] For the time being, however, the

---

[282] CA 1993, s 45(3), as amended by Deregulation and Contracting Out Act 1994
[283] CA 1993, s 45(3A), inserted by Deregulation and Contracting Out Act 1994
[284] CA 1993, s 45(6)
[285] ie in accordance with ibid, s 45(3), (3A), taken with s 45(4) or (5), as the case may be
[286] ibid, s 49
[287] ibid, s 48(1), (1A). See Charities (Annual Return) Regulations 1997, made by the Commissioners pursuant to CA 1993, s 48(1), and which came into force on 16 Jan 1997. These regulations are set out in (1997) 5 Decisions 30–1
[288] CA 1993, s 48(2)
[289] ibid, s 48(3)
[290] ibid, s 49

Commissioners consider that the most appropriate way to deal with defaults is by the use of their inquiry and protection powers under sections 8 and 18 of the Charities Act 1993.[291]

Preservation of documents

10.105 The charity trustees must preserve accounting records,[292] any statement of accounts (or receipt and payments account and statement of assets and liabilities),[293] and any annual report not required to be transmitted to the Charity Commissioners,[294] for at least six years from the end of the financial year in which (in the case of accounting records) they are made or to which (in other cases) they relate.[295] Where a charity ceases to exist, the last charity trustees of the charity must continue to preserve such documents as remain subject to the foregoing obligation, unless the Commissioners consent in writing to their being destroyed or otherwise disposed of.[296]

(3) Charities incorporated under the Companies Act 1985

10.106 Sections 41–4 of the Charities Act 1993 do not apply to a charity which is a company incorporated under the Companies Act 1985.[297] Such a charitable company is not, therefore, subject to the duties which the Charities Act 1993 imposes in respect of keeping accounting records,[298] the preparation of annual statements of accounts,[299] and the annual auditing or examination of charity accounts.[300] Instead, such a charitable company must comply with the accounting and audit regime imposed on companies registered under the Companies Act 1985 and which is contained in Part VII of that Act.

Keeping of accounting records

10.107 Part VII of the Companies Act 1985 imposes obligations on a company relating to the keeping of accounting records: such records must be sufficient to show and explain the company's transactions, and must disclose with reasonable accuracy at any time the company's financial position, and enable the directors to ensure that any balance sheet and profit and loss account prepared under Part VII comply with the requirements of that Act.[301]

---

[291] See [1998] Ch Com Rep 24–5. The Commissioners' inquiry and protection powers are considered further below, paras 10.138–10.172
[292] ie under CA 1993, s 41
[293] ie under ibid, s 42
[294] ie under ibid, s 45
[295] ibid, ss 41(3), 42(4), 45(7)
[296] ibid, ss 41(4), 42(5), 45(8)
[297] ibid, ss 41(5), 42(7), 43(9)
[298] ibid, s 41
[299] ibid, s 42
[300] ibid, ss 43–4
[301] Companies Act 1985, s 221(1)

Preparation of balance sheet and profit and loss account

The directors of a company must prepare for each financial year of the company a **10.108**
balance sheet as at the last day of that year, and a profit and loss account (which are
together referred to as the company's 'individual accounts').[302] The balance sheet
must give a 'true and fair view' of the state of affairs of the company as at the end
of the financial year; and the profit and loss account must give a 'true and fair view'
of the profit or loss of the company for the financial year.[303]

Preparation of directors' report

The directors must also prepare a report for each financial year, which report must **10.109**
contain a fair review of the development of the company's business and its subsidiary undertakings during the financial year and of their position at the end of
it, and also other prescribed information, including contributions for charitable
purposes and other matters relating to the health, safety, and welfare at work of the
company's employees.[304]

Audit obligations

With some slight modifications, the audit obligations for charitable companies **10.110**
are the same as for other companies. The basic obligation is that the company's auditors must make a report to the company's members on all annual accounts of the
company.[305] Certain categories of small company[306] are exempt from the obligation to have their accounts audited.[307] If a charitable company is a small company,
it is exempt if its balance sheet total is not more than £1.4 million, and its gross income is not more than £90,000.[308] If such a charitable company's gross income exceeds £90,000 but not £250,000,[309] it is exempt if the directors cause to be
prepared a report (usually called a 'compilation report') in respect of the company's individual accounts for that year in accordance with section 249C of the
Companies Act 1985, and made to the company's members.[310]

Unlike auditors of an unincorporated charity, auditors of a charitable company **10.111**
who discover that the charity trustees have committed serious breaches of duty,
whether under the general law or under statute, are not under an express duty to
report the matter to the Charity Commissioners. The Statement of Auditing

---

[302] ibid, s 226(1)
[303] ibid, s 226(2)
[304] ibid, s 234(1), (3), (4), and Sch 7
[305] ibid, s 235(1)
[306] A 'small company' is defined ibid, s 247(3)
[307] ibid, s 249A
[308] ibid, s 249A(1), (3), (5)(a)
[309] ibid, s 249A(4), (5)(b)
[310] ibid, s 249A(2)

Standards produced by the Auditing Practices Board recommends that in these sorts of circumstances the auditor should consider whether the matters in question are of sufficient importance that the auditor ought to disclose the matter to 'a proper authority in the public interest'. The 'proper authority' in such circumstances would clearly be the Charity Commissioners; but when disclosure might be considered to be 'in the public interest' is not clear, and auditors of charitable companies who discover evidence of serious wrongdoing or other breaches of duty might therefore have a difficult decision to make.[311]

Laying accounts and reports before general meeting

10.112   The directors of a company must, in respect of each financial year, lay before the company in general meeting copies of the company's annual accounts, the directors' reports, and also the auditors' reports on those accounts,[312] and they must also deliver copies of such accounts and reports to the Registrar of Companies[313] within the period allowed.[314]

Accounting obligations imposed by Charities Act 1993

10.113   The charity trustees of a charitable company incorporated under the Companies Act 1985 must comply with the duties imposed by section 45 of the Charities Act 1993 in respect of the preparation and transmission to the Charity Commissioners of an annual report. If, therefore, in a financial year, neither the charitable company's gross income nor its total expenditure exceeds £10,000, the annual report does not have to be transmitted to the Commissioners unless they so request.[315] Any annual report transmitted to the Commissioners must have attached to it a copy of the charity's annual accounts prepared for the financial year in question under Part VII of the Companies Act 1985, together with a copy of any auditors' report or reports on those accounts made for the purposes of section 249A(2) of the Companies Act 1985.[316] This replaces the usual obligation to attach to the annual report a statement of accounts (or account and statement) prepared in accordance with section 42(1) or (3) of the Charities Act 1993, (as the case may be).

10.114   Charitable companies are also subject to the duty imposed by section 48 of the Charities Act 1993 to prepare and transmit to the Charity Commissioners an annual return if, in any financial year of a charity, its gross income or total expenditure exceeds £10,000.

---

[311] See S Wethered, 'Whistle blowing—a new regime' (1996–7) 4 CL & PR 95; N Wells, 'Charity auditors as whistleblowers' (1999) Sol Jo Charities and Appeals Suppl, 38

[312] Companies Act 1985, s 241(1)

[313] ibid, s 242(1)

[314] ibid, s 244

[315] CA 1993, s 45(3A)

[316] ibid, s 45(5). Details of the preparation of the report required for the purposes of the Companies Act 1985, s 249A(2), are set out in s 249C thereof

(4) Exempt and excepted charities

Exempt charities

Sections 41–5 of the Charities Act 1993 do not apply to exempt charities.[317] **10.115**
Exempt charities are therefore not subject to the specific duties of the Act relating
to the keeping of accounting records,[318] to the preparation of annual statements of
accounts,[319] the annual auditing or examination of accounts,[320] or the preparation
and transmission to the Commissioners of an annual report.[321] However, the
Charities Act 1993 does require charity trustees of an exempt charity to keep
proper books of account with respect to the affairs of the charity; and, if not required by or under the authority of any other Act to prepare periodical statements
of account, they must prepare consecutive statements of account consisting on
each occasion of an income and expenditure account relating to a period of not
more than fifteen months and a balance sheet relating to the end of that period.[322]

The books of account and statements of accounts relating to an exempt charity **10.116**
must be preserved for at least six years, unless the charity ceases to exist and the
Charity Commissioners consent in writing to the documents being destroyed or
otherwise disposed of.[323]

Excepted charities

Nothing in sections 43–5 of the Charities Act 1993 applies to a charity which is **10.117**
excepted from registration under paragraph (c) of section 3(5) (that is, to a charity which has neither any permanent endowment, nor the use or occupation of
land, and whose income from all sources does not in aggregate amount to more
than £1,000 a year), and which is not registered.[324]

A charity which is excepted under section 3(5)(b) (that is, which is excepted by **10.118**
order or regulations) or which is excepted under the same sub-section in respect of
a registered place of worship, and which (in either case) is not registered, is not
subject to the obligation in section 45 to prepare and transmit an annual report,[325]
but the charity trustees of such a charity must prepare an annual report if so requested by the Charity Commissioners.[326]

---

[317] CA 1993, s 46(1)
[318] ibid, s 41
[319] ibid, s 42
[320] ibid, ss 43–4
[321] ibid, s 45
[322] ibid, s 46(1)
[323] ibid, s 46(2)
[324] ibid, s 46(3), (8)
[325] ibid, s 46(4)
[326] ibid, s 46(5), (6), (7)

E. Advice

10.119 The Charity Commissioners have the general function of promoting the effective use of charitable resources by (inter alia) giving charity trustees information or advice on any matter affecting the charity.[327] The Commissioners fulfil this function partly in the giving of general advice to all charity trustees in the form of free leaflets and guidance notes, which are available both in print and on the Internet, and partly by the giving of general or particular advice to charity trustees of particular charities.

10.120 Section 29 of the Charities Act 1993 specifically provides that the Charity Commissioners may, on the written application of any charity trustee, give him their opinion or advice on any matter affecting the performance of his duties as such.[328] A charity trustee or trustee for a charity acting in accordance with the opinion or advice of the Commissioners so given with respect to a charity is deemed, as regards his responsibility for so acting, to have so acted in accordance with his trust, unless, when he does so, either he knows or has reasonable cause to suspect that the opinion or advice was given in ignorance of material facts, or the decision of the court has been obtained in the matter or proceedings are pending to obtain one.[329] The section does not, therefore, confer protection on charity trustees who apply to the Charity Commissioners other than under section 29, or who do not specifically apply to the Commissioners at all, but act merely in reliance on the Commissioners' general guidance notes. In practice, however, a charity trustee who has acted on the basis of the Charity Commissioners' general advice or on information contained in the Commissioners' leaflets is likely to be considered to have acted reasonably, and so not to be liable for any consequent breach of trust.

10.121 The Charity Commissioners' advice under section 29 does not need to be contained in a formal order; indeed, there is nothing to prevent such advice from being oral; in practice, however, the Commissioners give such advice in a letter signed by an officer of at least the rank of Assistant Commissioner.[330]

10.122 It is also not the Commissioners' practice to approve of any action by opinion or advice under section 29 unless they believe that it lies within the trusts as they exist. The Charity Commissioners have stated that if the trustees seek the Commissioners' authority to carry out some action not within their trusts and the Commissioners wish to sanction it, they will not use section 29, but will

---

[327] CA 1993, s 1(3)
[328] ibid, s 29(1)
[329] ibid, s 29(2)
[330] [1970] Ch Com Rep 23 (para 64)

instead either rely on section 26³³¹ (sanctioning a proposed action) or, more usually, make a scheme.³³²

The Charity Commissioners' advice under section 29 is limited to telling trustees **10.123**
whether or not a particular course of action, perhaps with modifications suggested
by the Commissioners, would or would not be in law a breach of trust.³³³ The
Commissioners will not advise on policy matters which are properly within
the discretion and responsibility of the charity trustees as trustees, or on legal
advice on litigation against a third party. The Charity Commissioners therefore
see their advisory function as supplementing rather than duplicating professional
advice; but only the Commissioners can give advice which confers statutory protection on the trustees.³³⁴ The Commissioners' advice is therefore both authoritative and objective,³³⁵ and the Commissioners see themselves as uniquely qualified
to give advice on highly technical matters (such as cy-près).³³⁶

If charity trustees seek advice on policy matters, the Charity Commissioners will **10.124**
advise that the issue is for the trustees, and that if they come to a reasonable decision, made in good faith, and after taking into account all proper considerations,
they will not commit a breach of trust.³³⁷ If legal advice against a third party is
sought, the Commissioners restrict their advice to telling the trustees that they
must consult a solicitor, and that if they do so and act reasonably on the basis of
his advice they will not be liable for breach of trust.³³⁸ Similarly, the
Commissioners have stated that they cannot advise trustees on all the activities of
their charities which require special expertise, such as how to conduct surgical operations or how to rescue seafarers from sinking ships!³³⁹

The Charity Commissioners have provided a few instances where they have given **10.125**
advice under section 29 of the Charities Act 1993.³⁴⁰ These include advising on
the payment of gratuities to staff when a charity was being wound up under a provision in its constitution, and advising whether certain proposed activities would
fall within the objects of the charity. On the other hand, where the trustees of a
charity established for the provision of a public water supply sought the Charity
Commissioners' advice on the extent to which third parties might exercise their
private rights to take water from the reservoir, the Commissioners advised them

---

331 Considered below, paras 10.129–10.133
332 [1970] Ch Com Rep 23 (para 64)
333 [1982] Ch Com Rep 12 (para 26)
334 [1986] Ch Com Rep 5 (para 20)
335 See [1987] Ch Com Rep 9–10 (para 40)
336 [1989] Ch Com Rep 9 (para 39)
337 [1982] Ch Com Rep 11–12 (para 25)
338 ibid 12 (para 25)
339 ibid (para 26)
340 ibid (para 27)

that this was not a matter on which they could give advice except to tell them to seek legal advice.

10.126 Advice under section 29 is often given as a preliminary to, or as part of, other work of the Commissioners, such as the making of a scheme or order, the registration of a charity, or the conducting of an inquiry.[341]

10.127 Legal proceedings to challenge the Commissioners' advice rank as 'charity proceedings'.[342] Any of the charity trustees has locus standi to bring such proceedings;[343] but the consent of the Commissioners[344] or (if they refuse) leave of a judge of the Chancery Division[345] must be obtained.

10.128 The Charity Commissioners owe no common law duty of care to potential objects of the charity, and cannot therefore be liable in negligence to such persons even if their advice is wrong.[346] The reasons for this are the existence of a remedy in the form of the appeals machinery; the undesirability of the increased legal costs which would result from negligence actions in addition to rights of appeal in charity proceedings; the consideration that it would be contrary to the good of charities for the Charity Commissioners' decisions to be attacked by so wide and indeterminate a class; and (least significantly) the apparent absence of any authority for such an action since the Charity Commissioners were originally established.[347]

F. Consents

(1) Sanctioning of proposed action in the administration of a charity: Charities Act 1993, section 26

10.129 Where it appears to the Charity Commissioners that any action proposed or contemplated in the administration of a charity is expedient in the interests of the charity, they may by order sanction that action, whether or not it would otherwise be within the powers exercisable by the charity trustees in the administration of the charity; and anything done under the authority of such an order is deemed to be properly done in the exercise of those powers.[348]

---

[341] [1986] Ch Com Rep 5 (para 17)
[342] CA 1993, s 33. See further ch 13, paras 13.22–13.23
[343] CA 1993, s 33(1)
[344] ibid, s 33(2)
[345] ibid, s 33(5)
[346] *Mills v Winchester Diocesan Board of Finance* [1989] Ch 428 (Knox J)
[347] ibid
[348] CA 1993, s 26(1). An order under this section does not confer any authority in respect of certain consecrated buildings: ibid, s 26(7)

Any such order may be made so as to authorize a particular transaction, compro- **10.130**
mise, or the like, or a particular application of property, or so as to give a more
general authority, and (without prejudice to the generality of the Charity
Commissioners' power to sanction a proposed action) may authorize a charity to
use common premises, or employ a common staff, or otherwise combine for any
purpose of administration, with any other charity.[349]

Any order so made may give directions as to the manner in which any expenditure **10.131**
is to be borne and as to other matters connected with or arising out of the action
thereby authorized.[350] Where anything is done in pursuance of any authority
given by any such order, any directions given in connection therewith are binding
on the charity trustees for the time being as if contained in the trusts of the charity.[351] Any such directions may, on the application of the charity, be modified or
superseded by a further order.[352] The directions may include directions for meeting any expenditure out of a specified fund, for charging any expenditure to
capital or to income, for requiring expenditure charged to capital to be recouped
out of income within a specified period, for restricting the costs to be incurred at
the expense of the charity, or for the investment of moneys arising from any transaction.[353]

An order made under this section may authorize any act notwithstanding that it **10.132**
is prohibited by any specified disabling Acts,[354] or that the trusts of the charity provide for the act to be done by or under the authority of the court; but no such order
may authorize the doing of any act expressly prohibited by Act of Parliament other
than the specified disabling Acts or by the trusts of the charity, and nor may such
an order extend or alter the purposes of the charity.[355]

The Charity Commissioners have stated that in practice they prefer to limit the **10.133**
use of their power under this section to sanctioning a single transaction or a limited series of transactions, and to use the procedure of establishing a scheme, with
its attendant publicity, in order to confer authority of a more general nature.[356]
The power can be used to authorize a particular dealing in which there is a potential for a conflict of interests.

---

[349] ibid, s. 26(2)
[350] ibid, s 26(3)
[351] ibid, s 26(3)
[352] ibid, s 26(3)
[353] ibid, s 26(4)
[354] ie Ecclesiastical Leases Acts 1571, 1572, 1575 & 1836: CA 1993, s 26(6)
[355] CA 1993, s 26(5)
[356] [1970] Ch Com Rep 23 (para 63)

(2) Consent to dealings with charity land

10.134 Although the Charities Act 1993 states that the consent of the court or of the Charity Commissioners is required whenever there is a disposal of charity land,[357] it goes on to provide that such consent is not needed where the charity trustees obtain and consider the advice of a properly qualified surveyor.[358] In practice the Charity Commissioners expect the charity trustees to use this alternative method whenever possible. The court's or the Commissioners' consent to a disposal must be obtained, however, if the disposal is to a connected person,[359] so that the Commissioners' involvement with charity land disposals is now largely limited to disposals of this nature. The Commissioners' limited involvement in charity land disposals is considered more fully in chapter 17.[360]

G. Schemes and cy-près

10.135 This aspect of the Charity Commissioners' work is dealt with in chapter 15.

H. Powers to preserve charity documents

10.136 By virtue of section 30 of the Charities Act 1993, the Charity Commissioners may provide books in which any deed, will, or other document relating to a charity may be enrolled.[361] The Commissioners may accept for safe keeping any document relating to a charity, and the charity trustees or other persons having the custody of such documents (including those relating to a charity which has ceased to exist) may, with the consent of the Charity Commissioners, deposit them with the Commissioners for safe keeping, unless some other enactment requires them to be kept elsewhere.[362]

10.137 Where a document is enrolled by the Charity Commissioners or deposited with them under section 30, evidence of its contents may be given by means of a copy certified by one of their officers; and a document purporting to be such a copy must be received in evidence without proof of the official position, authority, or handwriting of the person certifying it or of the original document.[363] Regulations made by the Secretary of State may provide for such deposited documents as may be prescribed to be destroyed or otherwise disposed of after such

---

[357] CA 1993, s 36(1)
[358] ibid, s 36(2)
[359] ibid, s 36(2)(a)
[360] See ch 17, paras 17.22–17.27 and 17.47–17.49
[361] CA 1993, s 30(1)
[362] ibid, s 30(2)
[363] ibid, s 30(3)

period or in such circumstances as may be so prescribed.[364] To date, however, no such regulations have been made. These provisions also apply to any document which the Charity Commissioners have by order obtained from any person as being a document relevant to the discharge of the Commissioners' functions.[365]

I. Investigations

(1) Informal inquiries

10.138

The Charity Commissioners have said that about three-quarters of the causes for concern brought to their attention prove to be unfounded, and they caution that care is essential in ensuring that undue credence is not given to allegations (particularly those made in the media) before they have been assessed and investigated.[366] If the Charity Commissioners receive a complaint about the administration of a charity, and the complaint appears on its face to have some justification, the Commissioners' practice, if the complainant agrees, is to send a copy of the complaint to the trustees and to invite their comments.[367] The Commissioners are thereby able to hear both sides before expressing their own view. This procedure also gives the trustees an opportunity to consider the matter and to make improvements or to correct errors where this seems desirable.[368] The Commissioners find that most trustees co-operate readily, and that it is only rarely that the Commissioners have to exercise their powers to intervene or to institute a formal inquiry under section 8 of the Charities Act 1993.[369] The Commissioners also find that most difficulties arise from inadequate financial controls or from poor management or administration.[370]

10.139

Before opening a formal inquiry, the Charity Commissioners carry out a short preliminary evaluation to see whether there is a prima facie cause for concern which calls for investigation, or whether the matter could be more helpfully dealt with in another way.[371]

---

[364] ibid, s 30(4)

[365] ie to documents transmitted to the Charity Commissioners under ibid, s 9: ibid, s 30(5)

[366] [1990] Ch Com Rep 15 (para 77). But contrast the Charity Commissioners' recent willingness to take account of media comment in determining public benefit: see above, para 10.59

[367] [1979] Ch Com Rep 36 (para 125)

[368] ibid

[369] ibid 37 (para 126)

[370] [1994] Ch Com Rep 11

[371] ibid. In 1994, the Charity Commissioners opened 1,600 evaluation cases, of which slightly over one-half resulted from monitoring and other internal Commission operations. Slightly under half of these cases revealed no significant cause for concern; nearly one-fifth were dealt with by advice and information; a quarter led to inquiries being opened; and the rest (about one-seventh) were outstanding at the end of the year: [1994] Ch Com Rep 11

(2) Formal inquiries

10.140 The Charity Commissioners may from time to time institute inquiries with re-gard to charities or a particular charity or class of charities, either generally or for particular purposes; but no such inquiry may extend to an exempt charity.[372] The Commissioners cannot institute an inquiry to determine whether the purposes of a particular body are charitable or not; but the wording of the sub-section is very wide, and authorizes an inquiry to enable the Charity Commissioners to ascertain (inter alia) whether the property of a charity is being applied for the purposes of the trusts of the charity.[373] An inquiry is not limited to findings of fact; and an in-quiry into whether property is being applied for an authorized charitable purpose may often involve a question of law on which the inquirer must necessarily form and express a conclusion.[374]

10.141 The Charity Commissioners may either conduct such an inquiry themselves or appoint a person to conduct it and to make a report to them.[375] Although the statute refers to 'a person', this is evidently taken to authorize the appointment of joint inquirers. The bulk of such inquiries are conducted by the Commissioners' own staff acting in the Commissioners' names; but the Commissioners occasion-ally appoint a specific person (or persons) to conduct an inquiry where the case is particularly complex, important, or of great public interest.[376] Such inquirer could be one of the Commissioners' own senior staff,[377] or someone outside the Commission. If two persons are appointed, one may be from the Commission, another an outsider.[378]

---

[372] CA 1993, s 8(1). In 1994, the Charity Commissioners completed 523 inquiry cases. In just under a half of these, the Commissioners were satisfied that there was no substantial cause for con-cern. In the remainder, there was substantial cause for concern, and in two-thirds of the cases it arose from maladministration, eg inadequate management or financial controls, and misunderstandings and difficulties with associated trading organizations: [1994] Ch Com Rep 11. In 1995, 609 new inquiries were started, in nearly half of which a cause for concern was substantiated: [1995] Ch Com Rep 13

[373] *Rule v Charity Commissioners* (High Ct, 10 Dec 1979) (Fox J) noted [1979] Ch Com Rep 12–16 (paras 24–36): see 13 (para 28). An appeal by members of the Exclusive Brethren to the Court of Appeal was subsequently withdrawn: [1981] Ch Com Rep 12 (para 31)

[374] *Rule v Charity Commissioners* (Fox J) see [1979] Ch Com Rep 13–14 (para 29)

[375] CA 1993, s 8(2)

[376] [1990] Ch Com Rep 12 (para 60). In 1990, eg, the Charity Commissioners commissioned four inquiries to be conducted by specific persons. These included inquiries into Oxfam, War on Want and the Royal British Legion

[377] As in the case of the inquiry into the Royal British Legion, which a senior lawyer with the Commission was appointed to conduct: see [1990] Ch Com Rep 12 (para 63)

[378] As in the case of the inquiry into War on Want, which was conducted by a partner in a firm of chartered accountants and by a senior lawyer with the Commissioners' investigation staff: see [1990] Ch Com Rep 12 (para 62). The Charity Commissioners have described this as probably the most complex inquiry ever conducted on their behalf: [1991] Ch Com Rep 20 (para 120). An in-quiry into the religious charities of the Exclusive Brethren in 1976 had been conducted by a prac-tising silk: [1979] Ch Com Rep 12 (para 24)

For the purposes of any such inquiry, the Charity Commissioners, or a person appointed by them to conduct it, may direct any person (subject as provided):[379]   **10.142**

> (a) to furnish accounts and statements in writing with respect to any matter in question at the inquiry, being a matter on which he has or can reasonably obtain information, or to return answers in writing to any questions or inquiries addressed to him on any such matter, and to verify any such accounts, statements or answers by statutory declaration;
> (b) to furnish copies of documents in his custody or under his control which relate to any matter in question at the inquiry, and to verify any such copies by statutory declaration;
> (c) to attend at a specified time and place and give evidence or produce any such documents.

For the purposes of any such inquiry, evidence may be taken on oath, and the persons conducting the inquiry may for that purpose administer oaths, or may instead require the person examined to make and subscribe a declaration of the truth of the matters about which he is examined.[380]

The Charity Commissioners may pay to any person the necessary expenses of his   **10.143**
attendance to give evidence or to produce documents for the purposes of the inquiry; and a person cannot be required to go more than ten miles from his place of residence unless those expenses are paid to him. [381]

The Charity Commissioners may have printed and published the report or other   **10.144**
statement of the results of the inquiry as they think fit,[382] or may publish such report or statement in some other way which is calculated in their opinion to bring it to the attention of persons who may wish to make representations to them about the action to be taken.[383] The Commissioners are not, therefore, obliged to publish the results of the inquiry; and they might refrain from publishing a report the main conclusions of which relate to a view of the law which they feel unable to accept.[384] On the other hand, unlike the position under the previous law, the

---

[379] CA 1993, s 8(3)

[380] ibid, s 8(4)

[381] ibid, s 8(5)

[382] ibid, s 8(6). eg, the report of the inquirer into the Royal British Legion was published by the Charity Commissioners themselves: *Royal British Legion: Final Report of the Inquirer* (Charity Commission, 1992). The report of the inquirers into War on Want was published separately by HMSO: *War on Want: Report of an Inquiry* (HMSO, 1991). The report of the inquirer into Oxfam was also published by HMSO in 1991: see *Oxfam: Report of an Inquiry Submitted to the Charity Commissioners* (HMSO, 1991), mentioned [1991] Ch Com Rep 19 (para 111)

[383] CA 1993, s 8(6). An interview on television or radio, eg, might be a suitable means of bringing the report to the attention of relevant persons in an appropriate case. (Some Inquiry Reports are now being put on the Charity Commissioners' website: eg Charity Commission Inquiry Report, *Voice of Methodism Association* (2000))

[384] As, eg, the report of the inquirer into the Exclusive Brethren: see *Rule v Charity Commissioners* (High Ct, 10 Dec 1979) (Fox J), disc [1979] Ch Com Rep 12–16 (paras 24–36); see 14–15 (paras 31–2)

Commissioners may publish a report even if they do not propose to take any action on it.[385] A report may be referred to in any legal proceedings; and, to the extent that the report is not challenged, it is to be treated as evidence in an appeal.[386] Any view of the law which the report may express carries no weight in such proceedings, however, and any statement of facts may be challenged by any party to the proceedings.[387]

10.145 Where inquiries are made into local charities, the relevant council may contribute to the Commissioners' expenses.[388] This is, however, the council's choice: it cannot be required to do so.

Judicial review of section 8 inquiries

10.146 In *Rule v Charity Commissioners*,[389] Fox J considered a claim brought by certain members of the Exclusive Brethren seeking certain declarations and injunctions against the Charity Commissioners on the alleged ground that the conduct of an inquiry by the Commissioners into the Exclusive Brethren had (inter alia) been unfair and contrary to natural justice. Fox J indicated the existence of four basic principles. First, in order to determine what fairness required, a clear distinction must be made between inquiries which involve a charge or accusation or subjection to pains and penalties on the one hand, and purely fact-finding inquiries on the other. A purely administrative inquiry falls into the latter category. Secondly, the investigator is the master of his own procedure and is entitled to obtain information in any way he thinks fit. Thirdly, the investigator must give those affected a fair opportunity for commenting on or contradicting relevant statements which are prejudicial to them. Fourthly, no higher duty than that is placed upon the investigator. In particular, he is not required to put his conclusions to the persons affected.[390]

10.147 Even if the court does find evidence of unfairness in the conduct of an inquiry, the court will not necessarily make a declaration that the inquiry was conducted in a manner contrary to natural justice or unfairly. In *Rule v Charity Commissioners*,[391] Fox J said: 'It seems to me that the court will not normally make a declaration in the air. There must be practical consequences to justify making the declaration.'[392] In that case, he thought that, even if there had been evidence of unfairness, there

---

[385] See E Cairns, 'Preventing Abuse: Commissioners' Increased Powers' (1992–3) 1 CL & PR 127, 129

[386] *Jones v A-G* [1974] Ch 148, 162 (Orr LJ, delivering judgment of CA)

[387] *Jones v A-G* [1974] Ch 148; *Rule v Charity Commissioners* (High Ct, 10 Dec 1979) (Fox J), noted [1979] Ch Com Rep 12–16 (paras 24–36): see 14–15 (para 31)

[388] CA 1993, s 8(7)

[389] (High Ct, 10 Dec 1979) (Fox J), noted [1979] Ch Com Rep 12–16

[390] *Rule v Charity Commissioners* (High Ct, 10 Dec 1979): see [1979] Ch Com Rep 14 (para 30)

[391] (High Ct, 10 Dec 1979) (Fox J), noted [1979] Ch Com Rep 12–16

[392] *Rule v Charity Commissioners* (High Ct, 10 Dec 1979): see [1979] Ch Com Rep 14 (para 31)

would be no practical value in making the declaration sought, since the Exclusive Brethren could themselves bring proceedings in the High Court to determine whether their doctrines affected their charitable status; and, in such proceedings, the legal views expressed in the report would carry no weight, and its findings of fact could be challenged.[393]

(3) Power to call for documents and to search records

Under section 9 of the Charities Act 1993 the Charity Commissioners may by order require any person to furnish them with any information in his possession which relates to any charity and is relevant to the discharge of their functions or of the functions of the Official Custodian for Charities.[394] They may also by order require any person who has in his custody or under his control any document which relates to any charity (other than a document which relates only to an exempt charity[395]) and is relevant to the discharge of their functions or of the functions of the Official Custodian for Charities, either to furnish them with a copy of or extract from the document, or (unless the document forms part of the records or other documents of a court or of a public or local authority) to transmit the document itself to them for their inspection.[396] The Charity Commissioners are entitled to keep such copy or extract without payment; and where a document transmitted to them for their inspection relates only to one or more charities and is not held by any person entitled as trustee or otherwise to the custody of it, the Commissioners may keep it or may deliver it to the charity trustees or to any other person who may be so entitled.[397]

10.148

Any officer of the Charity Commissioners, if so authorized by the Commissioners, is entitled without payment to inspect and to take copies of or extracts from the records or other documents of any court, or of any public registry or office of records, for any purpose connected with the discharge of the functions of the Commissioners or of the Official Custodian for Charities.[398]

10.149

Supply of false or misleading information to the Charity Commissioners

Any person who knowingly or recklessly provides the Charity Commissioners (or to any person conducting a section 8 inquiry[399]) with information which is false

10.150

---

[393] *Rule v Charity Commissioners* (High Ct, 10 Dec 1979): see [1979] Ch Com Rep 14–15 (para 31)

[394] CA 1993, s 9(1)(a)

[395] ibid, s 9(4)

[396] ibid, s 9(1)(b)

[397] ibid, s 9(3)

[398] ibid, s 9(2). Where the information is recorded otherwise than in legible form, these rights include the right to require the information to be made available in legible form for inspection or for a copy or extract to be made of or from it: CA 1993, s 9(5)

[399] ibid, s 11(4)

or misleading in a material particular commits an offence if the information is either provided in purported compliance with a requirement imposed by or under the Charities Act 1993, or is otherwise provided in circumstances in which the person providing it intends, or could reasonably be expected to know, that it would be used by the Commissioners for the purpose of discharging their functions under the Charities Act 1993.[400]

10.151 Any person who wilfully alters, suppresses, conceals, or destroys any document which he is or is liable to be required, by or under the Charities Act 1993, to produce to the Charity Commissioners (or to a person conducting a section 8 inquiry[401]), commits an offence.[402]

10.152 Any person committing either of the foregoing offences is liable, on summary conviction, to a fine not exceeding the statutory maximum, or, on conviction on indictment, to imprisonment for a term not exceeding two years, or to a fine, or both.[403]

(4) Disclosure of information

10.153 Section 10 of the Charities Act 1993 contains new provisions for information disclosure between the Charity Commissioners and certain other public bodies.[404] Nothing in the section, however, affects any power of disclosure otherwise exercisable.[405]

Disclosure by and to specified bodies and persons

10.154 Certain specified bodies and persons may, subject to any express restriction imposed by or under any other enactment,[406] disclose to the Charity Commissioners any information received by that body or person under or for the purposes of any enactment, where the disclosure is made to enable or assist the Commissioners to discharge any of their functions.[407] The specified bodies and persons are any government department (including a Northern Ireland department); any local authority; any constable; and any other body or person discharging functions of a public nature (including a body or person discharging regulatory functions in relation to any description of activities).[408]

---

[400] CA 1993, s 11(1)
[401] ibid, s 11(4)
[402] ibid, s 11(2)
[403] ibid, s 11(3)
[404] ibid, s 10
[405] ibid, s 10(8)
[406] For the purposes of this section, 'enactment' includes an enactment comprised in subordinate legislation within the meaning of the Interpretation Act 1978: CA 1993, s 10(9)
[407] CA 1993, s 10(1)
[408] ibid, s 10(6)

The Charity Commissioners may also disclose to such specified body or person   **10.155**
any information received by them under or for the purposes of any enactment,
where the disclosure is made by the Commissioners for any purpose connected
with the discharge of their functions, and for the purpose of enabling or assisting
that body or person to discharge any of its or his functions.[409] This is subject to the
qualification that the Commissioners may not make disclosure of information
which was obtained by them from such a body or person or from the Commissioners of Customs and Excise or the Commissioners of Inland Revenue under
this section, if such disclosure would breach any express restriction on disclosure
imposed by the body or person making the disclosure.[410]

Disclosure by Customs and Excise and Inland Revenue

The Commissioners of Customs and Excise and the Commissioners of Inland   **10.156**
Revenue (in either case 'the relevant body') may disclose to the Charity
Commissioners only the following information[411] relating to an institution:[412]

(a) the name and address of any institution which has for any purpose been treated
by the relevant body as established for charitable purposes;
(b) information as to the purposes of an institution and the trusts under which it is
established or regulated, where the disclosure is made by the relevant body in order
to give or to obtain assistance in determining whether the institution ought for any
purpose to be treated as established for charitable purposes;[413] and
(c) information with respect to an institution which has for any purpose been
treated as so established but which appears to the relevant body—
(i) to be, or to have been, carrying on activities which are not charitable, or
(ii) to be, or to have been, applying any of its funds for purposes which are not
charitable.

It is therefore evident that, whilst Customs and Excise and the Inland Revenue
may make limited disclosure to the Charity Commissioners, the section makes no
provision for the Charity Commissioners to make any disclosure to either of
them.

---

[409] ibid, s 10(4). In relation to a disclosure by the Charity Commissioners, the final category of
bodies and persons (viz any other body or person discharging functions of a public nature) is to be
construed as including a reference to any such body or person in a country or territory outside the
UK: ibid, s 10(7)

[410] ibid, s 10(5)

[411] ibid, s 10(2)

[412] ibid. In relation to the IRC, this is a reference to an institution in England and Wales: ibid,
s 10(3)

[413] The IRC may, for instance, disclose such information to the Charity Commissioners in order
to seek the latter's view on the charitable status of a body, in order to assist the IRC in deciding if the
body is entitled to be treated as a charity for tax purposes. Any view expressed by the Charity
Commissioners on the body's charitable status pursuant to such disclosure, unlike registration by
the Charity Commissioners under ibid, s 4, is not conclusive. For an example of the IRC's using the
s 10(2)(b) procedure to seek the Charity Commissioners' views on a body's charitable status, see *IRC
v Oldham Training and Enterprise Council* [1996] STC 1218

J. Remedial powers following inquiry

10.157 Section 18 of the Charities Act 1993 confers on the Charity Commissioners various powers which they may exercise following an inquiry. The Commissioners cannot exercise these powers in respect of an exempt charity.[414]

(1) Where the circumstances in either paragraphs (a) or (b) of section 18(1) are satisfied

10.158 Where, at any time after they have instituted an inquiry under section 8 with respect to any charity, the Commissioners are satisfied:[415]

(a) that there is or has been any misconduct or mismanagement[416] in the administration of the charity; or
(b) that it is necessary or desirable to act for the purpose of protecting the property of the charity or securing a proper application for the purposes of the charity of that property or of property coming to the charity,

the Commissioners may of their own motion do one or more of the following things:[417]

(i) by order suspend any trustee, charity trustee, officer, agent or employee of the charity from the exercise of his office or employment pending consideration being given to his removal (whether under this section or otherwise);

This power cannot be used to suspend a person for more than twelve months; but the suspension order may provide for matters arising out of the suspension, and in particular for enabling any person to execute any instrument in the suspended person's name or otherwise act for him and, in the case of a charity trustee, for adjusting any rules governing the proceedings of the charity trustees to take account of the reduction in the number capable of acting.[418]

(ii) by order appoint such number of additional charity trustees as they consider necessary for the proper administration of the charity;

---

[414] CA 1993, s 18(16)

[415] ibid, s 18(1)

[416] The reference to misconduct or mismanagement extends (notwithstanding anything in the trusts of the charity) to the employment for the remuneration or reward of persons acting in the affairs of the charity, or for other administrative purposes, of sums which are excessive in relation to the property which is or is likely to be applied or applicable for the purposes of the charity: ibid, s 18(3). It has been accepted that 'misconduct' will normally involve some dishonesty, whereas 'mismanagement' will not necessarily do so: *Scargill v Charity Commissioners* (High Ct, 4 Sept 1998) (Neuberger J), 124–5 of official judgment. They are ordinary English words, however, and whether there is misconduct or mismanagement is a question of fact: *Scargill v Charity Commissioners*, 123–4, approving comments of Dillon LJ in *Re Sevenoaks Stationers Ltd* [1991] Ch 164, 176, in relation to the Company Directors Disqualification Act 1986, s 6

[417] CA 1993, s 18(1)

[418] CA 1993, s 18(11)

(iii) by order vest any property held by or in trust for the charity in the official custodian, or require the persons in whom any such property is vested to transfer it to him, or appoint any person to transfer any such property to him;

(iv) order any person who holds any property on behalf of the charity, or of any trustee for it, not to part with the property without the approval of the Commissioners;

(v) order any debtor of the charity not to make any payment in or towards the discharge of his liability to the charity without the approval of the Commissioners;

(vi) by order restrict (notwithstanding anything in the trusts of the charity) the transactions which may be entered into, or the nature or amount of the payments which may be made, in the administration of the charity without the approval of the Commissioners;

It is an offence for a person to contravene an order made under paragraphs (iv) to (vi) above;[419] but this does not preclude the bringing of proceedings for breach of trust against any charity trustee or trustee for a charity in respect of a contravention of an order under paragraphs (iv) or (vi).[420]

(vii) by order appoint . . . a receiver and manager in respect of the property and affairs of the charity.[421]

The Charity Commissioners must, at such intervals as they think fit, review any **10.159** order made by them under any of the paragraphs (except paragraph (ii)); and, if on such review it appears to them that it would be appropriate to discharge the order in whole or in part, they must so discharge it (whether subject to any savings or other transitional provisions or not).[422]

(2) Where the circumstances in both paragraphs (a) and (b) of section 18(2) are satisfied

Where, at any time after they have instituted an inquiry under section 8 with re- **10.160** spect to any charity, the Commissioners are satisfied:[423]

(a) that there is or has been any misconduct or mismanagement[424] in the administration of the charity; and

---

[419] ibid, s 18(14). A person who commits such offence is liable on summary conviction to a fine not exceeding level 5 on the standard scale: ibid, s 18(14)

[420] ibid, s 18(15)

[421] ibid, s 18(1). The appointment must be in accordance with ibid, s 19, discussed below, paras 10.163–10.168. On the equitable power of the High Court to appoint a receiver, see ch 11, para 11.08

[422] CA 1993, s 18(13)

[423] ibid, s 18(2)

[424] The reference to misconduct or mismanagement extends (notwithstanding anything in the trusts of the charity) to the employment for the remuneration or reward of persons acting in the affairs of the charity, or for other administrative purposes, of sums which are excessive in relation to the property which is or is likely to be applied or applicable for the purposes of the charity: ibid, s 18(3)

(b) that it is necessary or desirable to act for the purpose of protecting the property of the charity or securing a proper application for the purposes of the charity of that property or of property coming to the charity,

the Commissioners may of their own motion do either or both of the following (additional) things:[425]

(i) by order remove any trustee, charity trustee, officer, agent or employee of the charity who has been responsible for or privy to the misconduct or mismanagement or has by his conduct contributed to it or facilitated it;
(ii) by order establish a scheme for the administration of the charity.

10.161 An order for the removal of a charity trustee or trustee for a charity under section 18 has the like effect as an order made under section 16 of the Charities Act 1993.[426]

10.162 Before the Charity Commissioners can exercise their jurisdiction under section 18(2), they must give notice of their intention to each of the charity trustees, except any that cannot be found or has no known address in the United Kingdom.[427] Any such notice may be given by post addressed to the recipient's last known address in the United Kingdom.[428]

(3) Supplementary provisions relating to receiver and manager appointed for a charity

10.163 The Charity Commissioners may, under the power in section 18(1),[429] appoint to be a receiver and manager of the property and affairs of a charity such person (other than an officer or employee of theirs) as they think fit.[430]

10.164 Without prejudice to the generality of the Charity Commissioners' power in section 89(1) to include incidental or supplementary provisions in their orders, they may make provision with respect to the functions to be discharged by the receiver and manager appointed by the order; and those functions must be discharged by him under the supervision of the Commissioners.[431]

---

[425] CA 1993, s 18(2). For examples of the exercise of the Commissioners' power to establish a scheme pursuant to this paragraph, see Charity Commission Inquiry Report, *Voice of Methodism Association* (Charity Commission, 2000) where, following inquiries into two charities, the Commissioners made a scheme amalgamating them under a single body of trustees. See also the scheme made by the Commissioners following their inquiry into *Iran Aid* (2000); under the scheme the charity was dissolved and its assets transferred to a new charitable company, the Iran Aid Foundation. See further T Baldwin, 'Millions lost in Iranian charity black hole', The Times 15 Sept 2000, 3
[426] CA 1993, s 18(7)
[427] ibid, s 18(12)
[428] ibid, s 18(12)
[429] ie ibid, s 18(1)(vii)
[430] ibid, s 19(1)
[431] ibid, s 19(2)

In connection with the discharge of those functions, any such order may provide **10.165** for the receiver and manager to have such powers and duties of the charity trustees of the charity concerned (whether under the Charities Act 1993 or otherwise) as are specified in the order, and for such powers or duties to be exercisable or performed by him to the exclusion of those trustees.[432]

A receiver and manager has the same right as a charity trustee to apply to the **10.166** Charity Commissioners in writing for their advice, and he enjoys the same protection as a charity trustee if he acts in accordance with such advice.[433] The Commissioners may also apply to the High Court for directions in relation to any particular matter arising in connection with the discharge by the receiver and manager of his functions.[434] On such an application by the Charity Commissioners, the High Court may either give such directions or make such orders declaring the rights of any persons (whether before the court or not), as it thinks just; and the costs of any such application must be paid by the charity concerned.[435]

The Secretary of State may make regulations providing for the appointment and **10.167** removal of persons appointed receiver and manager of a charity, for the remuneration of such persons out of the charity's income, and for receivers and managers to make reports to the Charity Commissioners.[436] Such regulations may, in particular, authorize the Charity Commissioners to require security to be given by the person so appointed for the due discharge of his functions, to determine the amount of such a person's remuneration, and to disallow any amount of remuneration in such circumstances as the regulations may prescribe.[437] Regulations have been made to deal with these matters.[438] The regulations require (inter alia) the receiver and manager to make a report to the Commissioners within three months of his appointment, setting out the estimated total value of the charity's property, such information about its property and affairs as he believes should be included, and his strategy for discharging his functions.[439] He must also make a report within one month of each anniversary of his appointment,[440] and within three months of his ceasing to hold office.[441]

---

[432] ibid, s 19(3)
[433] ibid, s 19(4)(a), applying ibid, s 29
[434] ibid, s 19(4)(b)
[435] ibid, s 19(5)
[436] ibid, s 19(6)
[437] ibid, s 19(7)
[438] Charities (Receiver and Manager) Regulations 1992, SI 1992/2355, which came into force (pursuant to CA 1960, as amended by CA 1992) on 1 Nov 1992
[439] Charities (Receiver and Manager) Regulations 1992, SI 1992/2355, reg 5(2)
[440] ibid, reg 5(3)
[441] ibid, reg 5(4)

10.168 The Charity Commissioners have indicated that they have found the power to appoint a receiver and manager very useful in preventing a charity's collapse or in saving valuable assets that would otherwise have been lost, and the power has been increasingly used.[442] The Commissioners have, however, said that, because the costs of the appointment are normally borne by the charity, such an appointment is appropriate only in a minority of cases;[443] and it may be inferred from the examples which they give in their Reports that it is used only in the case of very large charities. The Commissioners have also made innovative use of the power to resolve a problem of conflict of interests, where the trustees of a charity in financial difficulties received an offer for the charity's business from a commercial company with which it had a close connection. With the trustees' agreement, the Charity Commissioners appointed a receiver and manager for the limited purpose of carrying out a financial evaluation of the charity's affairs, considering the options for its future administration and considering the bid received. The receiver and manager was able to negotiate a seven-fold increase in the original offer, and recommended to the Commissioners that this was the best price obtainable and otherwise in the best interests of the charity. The Commissioners approved this recommendation, and gave their consent to the sale at the new price.[444]

(4) Appeals

10.169 An appeal against an order of the Charity Commissioners under section 18 may be brought in the High Court either by the Attorney-General, or, within three months of the order's being published, by the charity or any of the charity trustees, or by any person removed from any office or employment by the order.[445] With two qualifications, no appeal may be brought other than by the Attorney-General except with a certificate of the Commissioners that it is a proper case for an appeal or with the leave of a judge of the Chancery Division.[446] The qualifications are that no such certificate or leave is required for an appeal by a charity or any of the charity trustees against an order appointing a receiver and manager,[447] or for an appeal by a person against an order removing him from his office or employment.[448]

---

[442] In 1996, the Charity Commissioners made nine such appointments, a considerable increase on previous years: [1996] Ch Com Rep 26 (para 169). For particular instances in which the power has been used, see [1993] Ch Com Rep 17 (paras 62–4); [1994] Ch Com Rep 16; and [1995] Ch Com Rep 16 (paras 62–6) (*Valley Books Trust*). The 1994 report details two particular cases, *The Fellowship Charitable Foundation*, and *The Royal Masonic Hospital*, in each of which a receiver and manager was appointed to act to the exclusion of the trustees: [1994] Ch Com Rep 16. A receiver and manager was appointed in 1998 in respect of the charity Iran Aid: see Charity Commissioners, *Scheme relating to Iran Aid* (2000). See most recently, Charity Commission Inquiry Report, *Voice of Methodism Association* (Charity Commission, 2000)
[443] [1996] Ch Com Rep 26 (para 169)
[444] [1995] Ch Com Rep 9–10 (paras 28–9)
[445] CA 1993, s 16(11), (12), appl to s 18 orders by ibid, s 18(8)
[446] ibid, s 16(13), appl (with qualifications) to s 18 orders by ibid, s 18(8)
[447] ie under ibid, s 18(1)(vii): ibid, s 18(9)(a)
[448] ie under ibid, s 18(2)(i) or (4)(a): ibid, s 18(9)(b)

Unless the appeal is brought by the Attorney-General himself, an appeal against **10.170** the order of the Charity Commissioners under section 18 should be brought in the first instance against the Attorney-General alone. If the Attorney-General is not minded to take the same course as the Charity Commissioners, he can so inform them, in which case the Commissioners can also be joined as parties.[449]

On an appeal to the High Court against an order made by the Charity Commis- **10.171** sioners under section 18, the judge is entitled to look at the Commissioners' report as part of the essential background of the case.[450] The right of appeal is in terms against the order and not against the report, because it is the making of the order which affects the rights of the trustees and others concerned; but the report is not to be treated as something separate from the order which is founded on it.[451] It is for the appellant who appeals against the section 18 order to show that it was wrongly made.[452] It is open to the appellant to challenge the order's factual or legal basis (or both), which will normally be contained in the report.[453] To the extent that the appellant does not challenge the contents of the report, they are to be treated as evidence in the appeal.[454] It is open to the appellant to rely on fresh evidence which was not before the Charity Commissioners.[455] Where the appellant challenges findings of fact or puts in new evidence in the appeal (or both), the appeal is effectively a *de novo* hearing, so that the onus of proving whether the order ought to be made lies with the Charity Commissioners.[456]

K. Other power to remove or appoint a charity trustee

In some instances, such as where the charity trustee is bankrupt or is a company in **10.172** liquidation, or is incapable of acting, the Charity Commissioners have power by order made of their own motion to remove or appoint a charity trustee without first having to institute an inquiry.[457] The Commissioners may also by order (but not of their own motion) exercise the same jurisdiction and powers as the High Court to appoint, discharge, or remove a charity trustee or trustee for a charity, or to remove an officer or employee.[458] These powers are dealt with in chapter 9.[459]

---

[449] *Jones v Charity Commissioners of England and Wales* [1972] 1 WLR 784, 785 (Ungoed-Thomas J); revsd (but not on this point) *sub nom Jones v A-G* [1974] Ch 148 (CA)
[450] *Jones v A-G* [1974] Ch 148, 159–60 (Orr LJ, delivering jdgt of CA)
[451] ibid, 162
[452] ibid, 162
[453] ibid, 161
[454] ibid, 162
[455] ibid, 162
[456] *Scargill v Charity Commissioners* (High Ct, 4 Sept 1998) (Neuberger J) 37–9 of official jdgt
[457] CA 1993, s 18(4)–(7)
[458] ibid, s 16(1)(a)
[459] See ch 9, paras 9.28–9.31

L. Power to order taxation of a solicitor's bill

10.173 The Charity Commissioners may order that a solicitor's bill of costs for business done for a charity, or for charity trustees or trustees for a charity, is to be taxed, together with the costs of the taxation, by a taxing officer in such division of the High Court as may be specified in the order, or by the taxing officer of any other court having jurisdiction to order the taxation of the bill.[460] On any such order, the taxation is to proceed, and the taxing officer is to have the same powers and duties, and the costs of the taxation are to be borne, as if the order had been made, on the application of the person chargeable with the bill, by the court in which the costs are taxed.[461] No such order for taxation may be made after payment of the bill unless the Charity Commissioners are of opinion that it contains exorbitant charges; and no such order is in any case to be made where the solicitor's costs are not subject to taxation on an order of the High Court by reason either of an agreement as to his remuneration or the lapse of time since payment of the bill.[462]

---

[460] CA 1993, s 31(1)
[461] ibid, s 31(2)
[462] ibid, s 31(3)

11

THE COURT'S JURISDICTION OVER CHARITIES

A. Territorial jurisdiction

(1) Overseas charitable institutions

The High Court has a charitable jurisdiction over an institution only if its purposes are wholly and exclusively charitable and if it is based in England and Wales; and the word 'charity' in the Charities Act 1993 is territorially limited in the same way. For the purposes of the Charities Act 1993,[1] **11.01**

> 'charity' means any institution, corporate or not, which is established for charitable purposes and is subject to the control of the High Court in the exercise of the court's jurisdiction with respect to charities.

At first instance, in *Construction Industry Training Board v Attorney-General*,[2] Pennycuick V-C accepted that the second half of this definition was to some extent, perhaps primarily, directed to the issue of territorial jurisdiction, and considered that its purpose was to emphasize that the High Court does not have jurisdiction over a charitable corporation established in a foreign jurisdiction.

The High Court does not have a charity jurisdiction over a body which is incorporated outside England and Wales,[3] even if it carries on activities in England and **11.02**

---

[1] CA 1993, s 96(1)
[2] [1971] 1 WLR 1303, 1308; affd [1973] Ch 173 (CA)
[3] *Camille and Henry Dreyfus Foundation Inc v IRC* [1954] 1 Ch 672 (CA) (body incorporated under law of New York State was resident outside the UK and had never conducted any operations there)

Wales and has assets within the jurisdiction.[4] The objection to administering a foreign charity is the same regardless of the charity's legal structure, namely that those who are responsible for the administration of the charity are beyond the court's control.[5] If the institution is a trust whose purposes would be charitable in England and Wales, the High Court might theoretically have a charitable jurisdiction over its trustees if these are in England and Wales, even if the trust's assets are situated abroad; but, in any event, the scope of such jurisdiction would be limited, since the High Court could not order the preparation of a scheme in respect of a foreign trust. It is most unlikely that in modern times the High Court would assert any charity jurisdiction over a trust unless its assets were within the United Kingdom.

(2) Domestic charities operating overseas

11.03   It is important to distinguish between a body which is established overseas, and over which the High Court has no charitable jurisdiction (a foreign charity) from one which is established in England and Wales and which merely carries on its charitable purposes overseas (an English charity). The High Court does have charity jurisdiction over the latter, and can direct a cy-près scheme in respect of its assets even though the objects of the charity are resident abroad.[6]

(3) Gifts for charitable purposes to overseas trustees

11.04   If a testator gives assets to overseas trustees upon trust for charitable purposes overseas, the court will direct an inquiry as to whether the intended trustees are willing to accept the trusts.[7] If the intended overseas trustee is an individual, the practice is to ask for an undertaking.[8] Where the intended trustee is overseas, the court has no power to direct a scheme to supply details of the trust;[9] the practice

---

[4] *Gaudiya Mission v Brahmachary* [1997] 4 All ER 957 (CA) (a religious body incorporated in India with objects recognized as charitable and which also had a temple in London). See further ch 13, para 13.22

[5] *Mayor of Lyons v East India Co* (1836) 1 Moo PCC 175, 297 (Lord Brougham)

[6] *Re Colonial Bishoprics Fund 1841* [1935] Ch 148 (Luxmoore J); *A-G v City of London Corp* (1790) 3 Bro CC 171 (Lord Thurlow LC). Similarly, in *Re Vagliano* [1905] WN 179, a testator had made a gift to trustees in the UK upon trust for charitable purposes in Cephalonia. As the fund and two of the trustees were in England, Lord Wrenbury directed a scheme of application. See also *Re Robinson* [1931] 2 Ch 122, 129; *Gaudiya Mission v Brahmachary* [1997] 4 All ER 957, 965 (Mummery LJ)

[7] *New v Bonaker* (1867) LR 4 Eq 655, where the testator gave funds to the President and the Vice-President of the USA and to the Government of Pennsylvania upon trust to build and endow a college where a professor was to be engaged to advocate the natural rights of black people. Kindersley V-C directed an inquiry whether the intended trustees were willing to accept the trusts

[8] *Re Robinson* [1931] 2 Ch 122, 129–30 (Maugham J) (testamentary gift to the German Government for the benefit of its soldiers disabled in the First World War; it was held that the gift could be paid over to the German Government upon its giving a diplomatic assurance)

[9] *Provost of Edinburgh v Aubery* (1754) Amb 236 (bequest to Provost of Edinburgh for maintenance of poor labourers of Edinburgh and neighbouring towns); *A-G v Lepine* (1818) 2 Swan 181 (bequest for the benefit of a school for the poor in the parish of Dollar); *A-G v Sturge* (1854) 19 Beav

in such a case is to hand over the fund to the trustee to be applied according to the trusts of the will without directing a scheme.[10] If the overseas trustee appointed cannot act, or refuses to act,[11] then, unless the testator has made provision for a substitute trustee, the court may order the fund to be paid to such other person as the intended trustee should appoint.[12] If the testator does not himself specify a trustee, the court may (where the foreign country has a law of trusts) direct the fund to be paid to trustees to be administered by the courts of that foreign jurisdiction.[13]

B. Institutional jurisdiction

A description of the court's jurisdiction over institutions involves an analysis both **11.05** of the juridical basis for the court's intervention and of the scope of that jurisdiction. The scope of the jurisdiction determines the powers which the court can exercise and the remedies which it can grant in respect of a particular institution.

(1) Charitable trusts

The Court of Chancery asserted jurisdiction over charities through its jurisdic- **11.06** tion over trusts; it was therefore purely a jurisdiction over charitable trusts. As the trust was the creation of the Court of Chancery, which was concerned with the protection of property rights, in exercising its jurisdiction over the charitable trust the court was concerned with the protection of the settlor's expressed purposes; hence the very limited ability of the courts to apply property cy-près until the relaxations introduced in the Charities Act 1960.

Since the charitable trust is a creature of equity, in exercising its jurisdiction over **11.07** such a charity the High Court has available to it the full range of equitable powers and remedies which derive from the inherent jurisdiction of the Court of Chancery. These include establishing a scheme for the administration of a charity,[14] the appointment and removal of trustees,[15] and an order for an account.[16]

The High Court has vested in it the inherent equitable jurisdiction of the Court **11.08** of Chancery to appoint a receiver. In a modern charity case, in confirming that the

---

597 (gift to a school established by the testatrix in Genoa); *Forbes v Forbes* (1854) 18 Beav 552 (gift to build a bridge over the River Don in Scotland); *Re Marr's Will Trusts* [1936] Ch 671, 675

[10] *Emery v Hill* (1826) 1 Russ 112 (bequest to the treasurer of a society established in Scotland for the propagation of Christian knowledge); *Minet v Vulliamy* (1819) 1 Russ 113n; *Re Robinson* [1931] 2 Ch 122, 129

[11] *New v Bonaker* (1867) LR 4 Eq 655

[12] *Provost of Edinburgh v Aubery* (1754) Amb 236

[13] *A-G v Lepine* (1818) 2 Swan 181, 182 (Lord Eldon LC)

[14] See ch 15, paras 15.03–15.06

[15] See ch 9, paras 9.32–9.33

[16] *A-G v Cocke* [1988] Ch 414

High Court had jurisdiction to appoint a receiver for a school, and (rather exceptionally) authorizing the receiver to appoint and remove the school's foundation governors, Megarry V-C said that '[t]he remedy is one to be moulded to the needs of the situation; within proper limits, a receiver may be given such powers as the court considers to be appropriate to the particular case'.[17] His Lordship pointed out, however, that the powers given to a receiver will depend on the terms of the appointment, the terms of the trusts and other provisions governing the charity and its assets, and the circumstances of the case; and that, in ordinary circumstances, a receiver would be well advised to seek the directions of the court.[18] Since section 18 of the Charities Act 1993 gave the Charity Commissioners jurisdiction in specified circumstances to appoint a receiver and manager,[19] a power which they had not possessed under the Charities Act 1960, it is unlikely that in future many applications to appoint a receiver will be made to the court.

11.09 Property which was given for charitable purposes, but without the interposition of a trust, was not capable of being controlled by the Court of Chancery—probably on the basis that, since equity acts *in personam*, it could not impose such obligations where there was no person against whom its obligations could be enforced.[20] Such property vests in the Crown, which permits it to be applied to charitable purposes.[21]

(2) Unincorporated charitable associations

11.10 There can be little doubt today that the courts will always assert a general jurisdiction over the assets of unincorporated charitable associations; but there is a surprising dearth of case law dealing specifically with this issue.

11.11 The assets of a charitable unincorporated association, like those of its non-charitable counterpart, will usually be vested in trustees. In the case of a non-charitable association, this is merely a means of property-holding, each member having a beneficial interest under a trust. By contrast, it is clear that the members of a charitable association can have no proprietary rights over those assets of the association which have been given to it for the furtherance of its charitable purposes.[22]

---

[17] *A-G v Schonfeld* [1980] 3 All ER 1, 5
[18] ibid, 5
[19] See ch 10, paras 10.158–10.159, 10.163–10.168
[20] See Buckley, appearing as counsel, *arguendo*, in *Re Bennett* [1960] 1 Ch 18, 23
[21] *Re Smith* [1932] 1 Ch 153. See ch 15, paras 15.01–15.02
[22] See *Strickland v Weldon* (1885) 5 ChD 901, where five members of a church building committee brought an action on behalf of themselves and the other members of the committee against a former member, claiming an account of moneys which he had received in respect of the building fund. Pearson J held (inter alia) that even if all the subscribers had been named in the writ as plaintiffs, the action would still have been defective as only the A-G could represent a charity and sue on its behalf. In contrast to this, a member will, of course, retain rights over property lent to the association, or if he has taken a mortgage over the association's assets, although such dealings might be set aside as involving conflict of interests

Sometimes the charitable association's constitution will provide expressly that its assets are to be held upon trust for its (wholly and exclusively) charitable objects. Even in the absence of an express declaration of trust, it may be possible to infer a trust for the association's purposes specified in its rules. Indeed, since the association has no distinct legal personality, the only means by which equity can prevent the members from applying the association's assets to themselves is by the imposition of a trust.

It is only in modern times that the courts have asserted a general jurisdiction over **11.12** the assets of unincorporated charitable associations. In the early part of the nineteenth century, it had been held that the court had no charitable or trust jurisdiction over a purely voluntary charity, that is, a charity funded entirely by subscriptions which could be spent immediately.[23] If an endowed charity raised money through subscriptions and donations, the court would have jurisdiction over the endowed funds only.[24] The rationale for this approach appears to have been that a voluntary charity had no permanence; it could be brought to an end at any time by the subscribers' withholding their voluntary subscriptions.[25] Any decree issued by the Court of Chancery in respect of such a fund might therefore be defeated by the contributors' deciding to bring such fund to an end.[26] Since equity will not act in vain, no decree would therefore be issued. An additional reason for the court's reluctance to assert jurisdiction over voluntary charities also appears to turn on the fact that much of the litigation concerned disputes among the congregations and members of voluntary churches and chapels;[27] the court was evidently keen not to become entangled in making pronouncements on orthodox doctrine.[28]

---

[23] *Anon* (1745) 3 Atk 277 (essentially a self-help society); *A-G v Fowler* (1808) 15 Ves Jun 85; *Re Macclesfield School, ex p Pearson* (1818) 6 Price 214, 224–5 (Lord Richards CB) ('This is not . . . one of those constitutional permanent charities which the law of the land places under the care of the sovereign'). Also *Leslie v Birnie* (1826) 2 Russ 114

[24] See *Re Macclesfield School, ex p Pearson* (1818) 6 Price 214, where subscribers to a school established by voluntary subscription objected to the appointment to the school, by the majority of the trustees, of a minister not of the established church. The minister's salary was to be paid out of the subscribed funds, and the court held that, this being a voluntary charity, it had no power to intervene

[25] *Leslie v Birnie* (1826) 2 Russ 114, 119 (Lord Eldon LC) ('The Court has nothing to do with the voluntary subscriptions which may be paid to-day, and withheld tomorrow; its jurisdiction is founded only on its right to declare the trust of the chapel and how the chapel is to be used')

[26] See words of Lord Richards CB in *Re Macclesfield School, ex p. Pearson* (1818) 6 Price 214, 221: 'This Court being called on to interfere with respect to this particular charity, must not fail to recollect that it has no existence except from the daily and voluntary contributions of the subscribers, who may with-hold their subscriptions to-morrow, when there would be an end of the institution altogether. If we had any jurisdiction in a case of this description, it would be a most injurious thing to make an order now, in its nature decretal, in a case wherein, before that order should reach Macclesfield, the institution might in consequence be put an end to'

[27] As in *Leslie v Birnie* (1826) 2 Russ 114

[28] See *Re Macclesfield School, ex p Pearson* (1818) 6 Price 214, 225 (Graham B)

11.13 In the early nineteenth century the court also denied that the governors of a voluntary charity had the power, by a declaration of trust, to convert property purchased out of general donations and subscriptions into an endowment, unless the consent of all those who had contributed to the purchase had been obtained.[29] This principle was, however, modified in the early twentieth century by the application of the notion that the contributors were to be taken to give the committee members an implied authority to declare trusts in respect of the funds (and therefore, depending upon the terms upon which such trusts were declared, to create an endowment).[30]

11.14 Since this time, the courts appear to have departed from their former view, their decisions suggesting that they are now prepared to assert jurisdiction over purely voluntary charities. There is indirect support for this analysis in *Re Finger's Will Trusts*,[31] where Goff J construed a legacy to the National Radium Commission, an unincorporated charity which had ceased to exist before the death of the testatrix, as a gift to the unincorporated association upon trust for the work it carried on, and so directed a scheme of administration to apply the legacy to its charitable purposes.[32] There is further support from the cases involving purported alteration of a charitable association's rules. In the absence of an entrenchment clause, it might be thought that, since a charitable association is primarily based on contract, there is nothing to preclude the members from altering the rules at any time so as to amend the charitable objects of the association to other wholly and exclusively charitable objects. In *Re Tobacco Trade Benevolent Association Charitable Trusts*,[33] however, it was held that, in the absence of an express power to do so, a charitable association has no power to alter its constitution in any way.[34] This can be explained on the basis that the trust freezes the rules of the association.

11.15 These cases indicate that the assets of all unincorporated charitable associations are to be regarded as bound by a trust which, if not express, will be in origin either implied or constructive. In modern times, therefore, it is probably safe to conclude that every charitable association's structure embodies the twin concepts of

---

[29] *Re Macclesfield School, ex p Pearson* (1818) 6 Price 214

[30] *A-G v Mathieson* [1907] 2 Ch 383; in the words of counsel *arguendo* (ibid, 389), the committee members could be treated as standing *in loco fundatoris*

[31] [1972] Ch 286

[32] ibid, 297–8. See also *Re Vernon's Will Trusts* [1972] Ch 300n, 303, where Buckley J said that 'Every bequest to an unincorporated charity by name without more must take effect as a gift for a charitable purpose'. Buckley J did not, however, regard such a gift as necessarily upon trust, since he said that a bequest for such a charitable purpose 'will not fail for lack of a trustee but will be carried into effect either under the sign manual or by means of a scheme.' A charitable gift which fails cannot be applied under the sign manual if it is given on trust

[33] [1958] 1 WLR 1113

[34] See also *Re Jewish Orphanage Charity Endowments Trust* [1960] 1 WLR 344, and *Motor and Cycle Trades Benevolent Fund v A-G*, unrep, noted at [1982] Ch Com Rep 42 (App B, para (c)). Both cases are discussed in ch 8, paras 8.46–8.51

contract and trust.[35] This being so, the High Court has the same range of powers and remedies in relation to its jurisdiction over a charitable unincorporated association as it has in respect of a charitable trust.

(3) Charitable corporations

A source of continual theoretical difficulty is the basis of the court's jurisdiction **11.16** over charitable companies. The inherent jurisdiction over charities enjoyed by the Court of Chancery (until its abolition in 1875) was a jurisdiction over charitable trusts. This jurisdiction is now vested in the High Court. Originally, it was assumed that the Court of Chancery had jurisdiction over a charitable corporation because it held its property on trust;[36] but this assumption can no longer be made. The Charities Act 1993 (like its predecessor, the Charities Act 1960) does not clarify this point. Section 96(1) provides that, except in so far as the context otherwise requires, 'charity' means

> any institution, corporate or not, which is established for charitable purposes and is subject to the control of the High Court in the exercise of the court's jurisdiction with respect to charities.

Had the definition stopped at the words 'charitable purposes', the matter would have been beyond doubt. The problem is therefore the effect of the words that follow, which suggest that there may be institutions established for charitable purposes that are not subject to the control of the High Court in its exercise of its charity jurisdiction.

Even if the High Court is able to assert jurisdiction over a charitable corporation, **11.17** the scope of its jurisdiction will be more limited than that which it has in respect of a charitable trust, since the High Court has no inherent power to modify an Act of Parliament or to alter the terms of a Royal charter.

Charities incorporated under the Companies Acts

Most charitable corporations are incorporated under the Companies Acts **11.18** 1985–9, and it is a well-established principle of company law that a company incorporated under those Acts does not hold its property upon trust for its purposes.[37] That principle was laid down in the context of a non-charitable company; but it appears to apply equally to a charitable corporation, even where the

---

[35] See M Chesterman, *Charities, Trusts and Social Welfare* (Weidenfeld & Nicolson, 1979) 198

[36] *Lydiatt v Foach* (1700) 2 Vern 410, 412, where the Lord Keeper stated: 'The corporation are but trustees for the charity, and might improve for the benefit of the charity, but could not do any thing to the prejudice of the charity, in breach of the founder's rules.'

[37] *Salomon v Salomon & Co* [1897] AC 22. There is, however, nothing in the Companies Acts to prevent a company from becoming an express trustee of property held upon charitable trusts. The discussion in the text does not concern such special trusts (which give rise to no jurisdictional problems), but concerns only the charitable corporation's own assets

property includes outright gifts (such as legacies) from third parties.[38] If that principle applies equally to a charitable corporation incorporated under those Acts, there would appear to be a risk that the court has no charitable jurisdiction over it.

11.19 Nevertheless, whilst the courts have seldom addressed this issue directly, they have consistently proceeded on the footing that such a jurisdiction exists.[39] Thus in *Re Dominion Student Hall Trust*,[40] the court was asked to sanction a scheme to apply cy-près the property of a charitable company incorporated under the Companies Acts. Evershed J was concerned to ascertain that the circumstances for a cy-près application were satisfied, and appears to have tacitly assumed that a trust existed. In *Inland Revenue Commissioners v Educational Grants Association Ltd*,[41] Salmon LJ referred to a charitable company limited by guarantee under the Companies Acts as a 'trust'.[42] If the incorporated charity previously existed in the form of a charitable trust, there is the possibility that the charitable trusts might be treated as continuing in respect of assets held at the date of incorporation, the company merely becoming a trustee of such assets. Such trusts would not, however, apply to assets acquired after incorporation, so that the problem of jurisdiction remains.[43]

11.20 In the absence of evidence that the assets of a charitable company incorporated under the Companies Acts are held on trust, the courts have in recent years developed a more subtle approach to this problem of jurisdiction. In the absence of a trust, it would appear that such a company must hold its property beneficially, subject however to the limitation (which the Attorney-General will enforce[44]) that it must apply the property only to furthering its charitable objects. The court's jurisdiction might therefore be viewed as based upon the notion that the charitable corporation, though not a trustee of its assets in the strict sense, is nevertheless subject to fiduciary duties in respect of them, which duties are enforceable by the Attorney-General in the High Court in respect of its jurisdiction over charities. The assets of a charitable corporation might therefore be described as subject to a quasi-trust,[45] or as being subject to a trust in the broad sense. Thus in *Von Ernst et Cie SA v Inland Revenue Commissioners* Buckley LJ considered[46] that the earlier

---

[38] See the speech of Lord Parker in *Bowman v Secular Society Ltd* [1917] AC 406, 440–1. Although the corporation concerned was not one established for charitable purposes, his Lordship's words do not appear to be restricted to non-charitable companies

[39] See, eg, *Re Church Army* (1906) 75 LJ Ch 467, 474 (Cozens-Hardy MR); *Re Society for Training Teachers of the Deaf & Whittle's Contract* [1907] 2 Ch 486 (Neville J)

[40] [1947] Ch 183

[41] [1967] Ch 993, 1015 (CA)

[42] See further, M Chesterman, *Charities, Trusts and Social Welfare* (Weidenfeld & Nicolson, 1979) 394

[43] See 'Charity Companies', [1971] Ch Com Rep 9–11 (paras 22–30)

[44] *Construction Industry Training Board v A-G* [1973] Ch 173 (CA)

[45] *Brigham v Peter Bent Brigham Hospital* 134 F 513 (1904)

[46] [1980] 1 WLR 468, 475

authorities supported the view that 'a company incorporated for exclusively charitable purposes is in the position of a trustee of its funds or at least in an analogous
position'.

Buckley J's view was developed further by Slade J in *Liverpool and District Hospital* **11.21**
for Diseases of the Heart v Attorney-General.[47] In that case, the charity had been incorporated under the Companies Acts to provide a hospital to treat heart disease
and to do research into heart disease. It was wound up in 1978, and a surplus of
assets remained. By statute, surplus assets on a voluntary winding up must (unless
the articles provide otherwise) be distributed to the members;[48] clause 9 of the
company's memorandum prohibited any surplus assets on a winding up from
being distributed among the members, and required them to be transferred to
some other institution or institutions with similar objects as should be determined by the members or, in default, by the High Court. It was not clear whether
any members of the corporation were still alive. The liquidator applied to the
court for directions as to whether the assets should be distributed to the members
in accordance with the statute,[49] or applied cy-près by the court. Counsel for the
Attorney-General argued that the company held its assets in trust for its charitable purposes, and that therefore the statutory provisions (then contained in the
Companies Acts) regarding application of the surplus could not apply. Slade J rejected that argument; but he nevertheless held,[50] supporting the view put forward
by Buckley LJ in *Von Ernst et Cie SA v Inland Revenue Commissioners*,[51] that the authorities established that a company formed under the Companies Acts 'is in a position *analogous to that of a trustee* in relation to its corporate assets, such as
ordinarily to give rise to the jurisdiction of the court to intervene in its affairs'.[52]
Clause 9 of the memorandum, by comprising a members' agreement that the
property should not be distributed among themselves, was sufficient to deprive the
members of the right they would otherwise have enjoyed under the statutory provisions (then contained in the Companies Acts) to share the surplus assets among
themselves. The final question was therefore whether the court had jurisdiction to
order a cy-près scheme. Slade J held that it did. The court's cy-près jurisdiction
was similarly not restricted to property held in trust in the strict sense. He stated:[53]

> In my judgment the so-called rule that the court's jurisdiction to intervene in
> the affairs of a charity depends on the existence of a trust, means no more than this: the
> court has no jurisdiction to intervene unless there has been placed on the holder of

---

[47] [1981] Ch 193. Se also *Rabin v Gerson Berger Assoc Ltd* (CA, 27 Jan 1987)
[48] Then Companies Act 1948, s 302, later Companies Act 1985, s 597; now Insolvency Act
1986, s 107
[49] ibid
[50] [1981] Ch 193, 209
[51] [1980] 1 WLR 468, 479 (CA)
[52] [1981] Ch 193, 209. The emphasized words are in the original
[53] [1981] Ch 193, 214

the assets in question a legally binding restriction, arising either by way of trust in the strict traditional sense or, in the case of a corporate body, under the terms of its constitution, which obliges him or it to apply the assets in question for exclusively charitable purposes; for the jurisdiction of the court necessarily depends on the existence of a person or body who is subject to such obligation and against whom the court can act in personam so far as necessary for the purposes of enforcement.

Charities incorporated by special Act of Parliament

11.22   If a charity is incorporated by a special Act of Parliament, the Act may impose an express trust on the corporation's assets.[54] In the absence of an express trust, the circumstances might be such that a trust can be inferred.[55] If the charity existed as a charitable trust or in another unincorporated form before being incorporated by the Act of Parliament, it might be argued (as in the case of an existing charity incorporated by Royal charter) that the charitable trusts survive the incorporation in respect of assets held at the date incorporation took place. Even if an express or implied trust can be found in respect of assets held at the date of incorporation, it would not extend to assets acquired from that date, so that the problem of jurisdiction resembles that of charities incorporated under the Companies Acts.

11.23   The meaning of the statutory predecessor to section 96(1) of the Charities Act 1993[56] was considered in *Construction Industry Training Board v Attorney-General.*[57] The Construction Industry Training Board (CITB), which was a corporation established by special Act of Parliament, applied to the Charity Commissioners to be registered as a charity. The Charity Commissioners refused to register it on the ground that, although its purposes (to provide courses and training for persons employed or to be employed in the construction industry) were charitable, so that it met the first part of the statutory definition of 'charity', it was not (in their view) 'an institution . . . subject to the control of the High Court in the exercise of the court's jurisdiction with respect to charities', so that it failed to meet the second part of the definition.

11.24   At first instance,[58] Pennycuick V-C accepted that the second half of the definition was primarily directed to the issue of territorial jurisdiction; to emphasize that the

---

[54] As in *Re Manchester Royal Infirmary* (1889) 43 ChD 420, where North J held that the trust funds held by a corporation incorporated under the special Act (which imposed an express trust) were funds vested in it as a 'trustee' within the meaning of the Trust Investment Act 1889; see *Liverpool and District Hospital for Diseases of the Heart v A-G* [1981] Ch 193, 206 (Slade J)

[55] cf *Re Shipwrecked Fishermen & Mariners' Royal Benevolent Society* [1959] Ch 220. The Society had been incorporated by special Act of Parliament in 1850, which had specified the authorized investments of the Society's money. Vaisey J held that this statute had been impliedly modified by TA 1925, s 57(1), which was therefore to be read into the earlier Act; and he therefore held that he had jurisdiction under s 57 to widen the Society's powers of investment

[56] CA 1960, s 45(1)

[57] [1973] Ch 173; [1972] 2 All ER 1339

[58] [1971] 1 WLR 1303, 1308; noted T Lloyd, 'What is a charity?' (1971) 87 LQR 468

High Court does not have jurisdiction over a charitable corporation established in a foreign jurisdiction. He therefore accepted the argument of the CITB that it was a 'charity' within the meaning of the section. In the Court of Appeal, Russell LJ expressed the view that the second half of the definition was intended to exclude a charity created by an Act of Parliament which itself provided for a system of accountability to a separate body, and thereby ousted the jurisdiction of the court.[59] The statute setting up the CITB made it accountable to the Department of Education and Science, which had a measure of control over the CITB's functions and could remove members of the board in certain cases. Russell LJ would have held this degree of control sufficient to remove the jurisdiction of the court, so that, in his view, the CITB did not satisfy the statutory definition of a 'charity'.

Russell LJ's view, however, was a dissenting one. The other two judges agreed with him that the charitable corporation could be subject to the jurisdiction of the court; but expressed themselves more vaguely. Buckley LJ thought that the court had jurisdiction over a charitable company because it could restrain a charitable company from applying its property other than to its charitable objects.[60] Similarly, Plowman J thought that there was nothing in the Act which established the CITB that would prevent the Attorney-General from taking proceedings to prevent the misapplication of its admittedly charitable funds.[61] They both held that the Act which had established the CITB had not removed sufficient of the court's jurisdiction over the CITB to preclude it from ranking as a 'charity' within what is now section 96 of the Charities Act 1993. **11.25**

If there is a weakness in the reasoning of the majority, it is that the jurisdiction of the court to prevent a corporation applying its property to objects outside its objects clause is a jurisdiction which it has over companies generally to prevent an application of their property ultra vires. It is not a jurisdiction which is based on the court's jurisdiction with respect to charities.[62] The better view, it is submitted, is that the explanation of the basis for the court's jurisdiction over charities incorporated under the Companies Acts provided in the *Liverpool Hospital* case[63] should also be applied to charities incorporated by special Act of Parliament. Where a special Act of Parliament is involved, however, the scope of the court's charitable jurisdiction will vary according to the terms of the particular statute by which the charity was incorporated. **11.26**

---

[59] [1973] Ch 173, 181–2
[60] ibid, 186–7
[61] ibid, 188
[62] See M Chesterman, *Charities, Trusts and Social Welfare* (Weidenfeld & Nicolson, 1979) 392–3
[63] *Liverpool and District Hospital for Diseases of the Heart v A-G* [1981] Ch 193

Charities established by Royal charter

11.27 The court does not have a general jurisdiction to re-found or to re-establish charities founded by Royal charter; but such charities can be regulated and controlled by the court, especially on financial grounds.[64] Such jurisdiction appears to be based upon the principle that the governors of such a charity are to be considered as trustees of such of the charity's revenues as are under their control, and to protect such revenues the court assumes a jurisdiction of necessity to regulate or control the charity itself.[65]

11.28 Apart from this, it is possible that the majority of charter companies can be considered to continue to hold upon trust those assets which were vested in them at the date the charter was granted.[66] Most charities which exist as charter companies will have begun life without a charter—either as express charitable trusts or as unincorporated charitable associations, so that their assets will have been held upon trust, whether express or implied. Unless, as would have been rare in the past, the trusts or other governing instrument of such charity permitted the trustees or committee to bring the charity to an end by transferring its assets to another charity, the incorporation of the charity by the grant of a Royal charter would not cause its trusts to determine; and the effect would be to transfer the assets from the existing trustees to a newly created corporate trustee. The court's inherent jurisdiction over such a charity would therefore continue in respect of the assets held at the date the charter was granted, except so far as its exercise would require the charter to be varied, as the power to modify a charter lies exclusively with the sovereign. This analysis does not, however, explain the basis for any jurisdiction which the court might have over the assets acquired by the corporation after the charter was granted.

11.29 The High Court's jurisdiction with respect to charities to make a scheme relating to a body corporate established by Royal charter or to the administration of property held by such body (including a scheme for the cy-près application of any such property) is recognized by the Charities Act 1993.[67] The same Act has also overcome the practical problem that the High Court has no inherent jurisdiction to make a scheme which involves a modification of the charter itself: the High Court may now make a scheme which depends upon the alteration of the charter, but so framing the scheme that it cannot come into effect unless and until the charter is amended.[68]

---

[64] *Re Whitworth Art Gallery Trusts* [1958] 1 Ch 461, 467 (Vaisey J)
[65] See *A-G v Governors of the Foundling Hospital* (1793) 2 Ves 41, 48 (Lord Commissioner Eyre), quoted in *Re Whitworth Art Gallery Trusts* [1958] 1 Ch 461, 468
[66] See *Re French Protestant Hospital* [1951] Ch 567 (charitable corporation established by Royal charter; Danckwerts J seems to have assumed that a trust existed). In *Soldiers', Sailors' and Airmen's Family Assoc v A-G* [1968] 1 WLR 313, a chartered company conceded that it was in the position of trustee in regard to its funds, which were therefore held subject to TIA 1961. See also *Re Whitworth Art Gallery Trusts* [1958] Ch 461
[67] CA 1993, s 15(1)
[68] ibid, s 15(1). See further, ch 15, paras 15.07–15.11

12

THE VISITATORIAL JURISDICTION

A. Introduction

12.01 The function of the Visitor is to interpret the internal laws of an ecclesiastical or eleemosynary corporation, and to hear and determine disputes which relate to such laws. The Visitor was historically an ecclesiastical body which monitored, and corrected abuses in, church government. Ecclesiastical corporations (for example, Dean and Chapters) are therefore subject to the visitatorial jurisdiction of the bishop. Lay corporations may be either civil (such as municipal or commercial corporations) or eleemosynary. Civil corporations are purely secular in origin, and are not subject to any visitatorial jurisdiction; rather they are subject to the common law and to the jurisdiction of the courts. Eleemosynary corporations are corporations established to distribute the bounty of the founder.[1] The commonest types of eleemosynary corporations were originally hospitals (in the older sense of institutions to relieve the poor, aged, and infirm) and colleges (being institutions for the promotion of learning among indigent persons).[2] The early eleemosynary corporations were subject to significant ecclesiastical influence, one lasting effect of which is that such corporations, like ecclesiastical corporations, are subject to the visitatorial jurisdiction. In the case of an eleemosynary corporation, the Visitor would be either the founder or his heirs, or persons nominated by the founder. The rights of a founder's heirs have apparently been abolished by statute,[3] and it seems

---

[1] *Thomas v Univ of Bradford* [1987] 1 AC 795, 827 (Lord Ackner). In *Re Armitage* [1972] Ch 438, 444, Goulding J said that an eleemosynary charity 'covers all charities directed to the relief of individual distress, whether due to poverty, age, sickness or other similar afflictions'

[2] *Philips v Bury* (1694) Skin 447, 484 (Holt CJ)

[3] AEA 1925, s 45(1)(a); but the effect of the section is not clear: see P Pettit, *Equity and the Law of Trusts* (8th edn, Butterworths, 1997) 284, n 16

that the visitatorial jurisdiction which would have been exercisable by such heirs is now vested in the Crown.[4]

12.02 The Universities of Oxford and Cambridge are themselves civil corporations, and so do not have Visitors;[5] but the colleges of those universities are eleemosynary corporations, and subject to the visitatorial jurisdiction.[6] Many of the institutions which became universities in the 1990s[7] were created as companies limited by guarantee under the Companies Acts (such as a number of London polytechnics), or as higher education corporations under the Education Reform Act 1988;[8] they are therefore civil, and not eleemosynary, corporations, and do not have, and cannot make provision for, Visitors.[9]

12.03 The remaining universities in England and Wales, which, starting with the University of London, were established from the earlier part of the nineteenth century onwards, are nearly all founded by Royal charter; they are therefore eleemosynary corporations in their own right, and so are entitled to have a Visitor.[10] The founder of a charter university is the sovereign; therefore, unless the charter nominates some other person as the Visitor, the Visitor will be the sovereign in person (whose power is, in practice, exercised by the Lord Chancellor or

---

[4] See H Picarda, *The Law and Practice Relating to Charities* (3rd edn, Butterworths, 1999) 560

[5] The court therefore has jurisdiction to hear an application from a decision of one of the ancient universities by way of judicial review. See, eg, *R v University of Cambridge, ex p Evans* (QB, 22 Aug 1997), where a lecturer at the university sought judicial review of a decision to refuse her a personal readership. Sedley J pointed out that the Vice-Chancellor of Cambridge University is able to take the advice of a Commissary—in that case, Lord Oliver

[6] Some Oxford colleges are subject to the visitation of the Bishop of Lincoln (in whose diocese Oxford once was), from which their ecclesiastical origin is evident: see H Picarda, *The Law and Practice Relating to Charities* (3rd edn, Butterworths, 1999) 560. Some Oxford and Cambridge colleges have other *ex officio* visitors: the visitor of Clare Hall, Cambridge, for instance, is the Vice-Chancellor of the Supreme Court: see *R v Visitors to the Inns of Court, ex p Calder, ex p Persaud* [1994] QB 1, 33 (Nicholls V-C) (CA)

[7] See ch 10, paras 10.09–10.10

[8] See Education Reform Act 1988, s 123

[9] As public bodies, such new universities are, however, subject to the general principles of judicial review: *R v Manchester Metropolitan Univ, ex p Nolan* [1994] ELR 380 (DC). If, therefore, one of the newer universities made a decision which departed from its own rules, the court might entertain an application by way of judicial review: see *Thirunayagam v London Guildhall Univ* (CA, 14 Mar 1997) (Hirst LJ). The court will not, however, entertain a claim which relates to examination results, regardless of whether the university has a Visitor or not: ibid, appl *Thorne v Univ of London* [1966] 2 QB 237. See, to similar effect, *Madekwe v London Guildhall Univ* (CA, 5 June 1997). Where a student at such a new university has a claim in contract of a sort which is suitable for adjudication in the courts (such as a claim which relates to alleged breaches of the university's student regulations), the claim will not be struck out merely because proceedings by way of judicial review might have been more appropriate: *Clark v University of Lincolnshire and Humberside* [2000] 3 All ER 752 0(CA)

[10] The exception is the University of Newcastle upon Tyne, which is a creature of statute: namely, the Universities of Durham and Newcastle upon Tyne Act 1963. This provides for the Lord Chancellor to be Visitor

by such other person as he may advise Her Majesty to nominate[11]). Many university charters expressly nominate the sovereign as Visitor, if not personally, then either through Her Majesty in Council[12] or through the Lord President of the Council. Some other university charters nominate other persons; and a few reserve the appointment of a Visitor (either by Her Majesty[13] or by another) until the need arises.

The Inns of Court are peculiar in that they are not corporations, they have no statutes, and they were not established by founders who nominated Visitors. They are nevertheless voluntary societies which have for centuries 'submitted to government analogous to that of other seminaries of learning', and they have throughout that period been subject to the control of all the judges of the High Court acting as Visitors.[14] In their capacity as Visitors to the Inns of Court, the judges sit as a domestic tribunal, not as a court of law,[15] and they have jurisdiction over both disciplinary[16] and educational[17] matters. **12.04**

An advantage of the visitatorial jurisdiction is that instead of 'the formality, publicity and expense of proceedings in court', it provides a forum 'which can determine the matter informally, privately, cheaply and speedily'.[18] It has the further advantage of finality, because the scope for judicial review is severely curtailed.[19] Against this, however, it might be argued that the quality of the justice may be variable, depending upon the quality of the particular person who fills the office of Visitor, or at least upon the quality of any legal advice that he may obtain. There is also no guarantee of informality; the Visitor may choose the procedure, which (depending on the legal complexity of the appeal and whether there is any substantial dispute as to the facts) may be almost as complex as the procedure in the **12.05**

---

[11] *Thomas v Univ of Bradford* [1987] 1 AC 795, 811 (Lord Griffiths); *Patel v Univ of Bradford Senate* [1978] 1 WLR 1488 (Megarry V-C); *A-G v Dedham School* (1857) 23 Beav 350. In *Thomas v Univ of Bradford (No 2)* [1992] 1 All ER 964, the Lord Chancellor appointed the Vice-Chancellor of the Chancery Division, Browne-Wilkinson V-C

[12] As in the case of the University of London. Strictly, the committee of the Privy Council, when acting as Visitor on behalf of the sovereign, does not itself make a decision, but instead expresses an opinion for the guidance of Her Majesty in Council: see *R v HM the Queen in Council, ex p Vijayatunga* [1990] 2 QB 444, 451 (CA) (Bingham LJ)

[13] eg, under the charter of the University of Aston in Birmingham, Her Majesty reserves to herself, her heirs, and successors the right to appoint a Visitor in specified circumstances. Until such appointment, the visitatorial power is vested in Her Majesty: see *Casson v Univ of Aston in Birmingham* [1983] 1 All ER 88

[14] *R v Gray's Inn* (1780) 1 Doug 353, 354 (Lord Mansfield CJ)

[15] *R v Visitors to the Inns of Court, ex p Calder, ex p Persaud* [1994] QB 1, 33 (Nicholls V-C) (CA)

[16] ibid, 34

[17] *R v Board of Examiners of the Council of Legal Education, ex p Joseph* [1994] ELR 407 (CA)

[18] *Patel v Univ of Bradford Senate* [1978] 1 WLR 1488, 1499–1500 (Megarry V-C)

[19] See *R v Lord President of the Privy Council, ex p Page* [1993] 1 AC 682, 704 (Lord Browne-Wilkinson); *Thomas v Univ of Bradford* [1987] 1 AC 795, 825 (Lord Griffiths)

High Court.[20] It should also be borne in mind that legal aid, which might be available to an impecunious litigant (such as a student) in a court of law, is unobtainable by a party to visitatorial proceedings.

12.06   It has been argued in chapter 1[21] that the visitatorial jurisdiction will probably survive the coming into force of the Human Rights Act 1998, and this chapter is based on that premise.

B.   The jurisdiction of the Visitor

(1)   The nature of the jurisdiction

12.07   The nature of the visitatorial jurisdiction is *forum domesticum*, the private jurisdiction of the founder.[22] 'The jurisdiction stems from the power recognised by the common law in the founder of an eleemosynary corporation to provide the laws under which the object of his charity is to be governed and to be sole judge of the interpretation and application of those laws, either by himself or by such person as he should appoint as a visitor.'[23] Matters governed by the internal laws of the foundation also include 'those internal powers and discretions that derive from the internal laws such as the discretion necessarily bestowed upon those in authority in the exercise of their disciplinary functions over members of the foundation'.[24] In the leading case of *Philips* v *Bury*,[25] Holt CJ stated that the office of Visitor was to judge according to the statutes of the college, to expel and deprive upon just occasions, and to hear appeals.

12.08   The jurisdiction of the Visitor is exclusive; and the determination of the Visitor (in the absence of impropriety or excess of jurisdiction[26]) is final and not examinable in any court.[27] In those few areas, however, where statute has superseded the jurisdiction of the Visitor, as in the protection of employees,[28] the court or tribunal hearing the action should not, where a question of interpretation of the

---

[20]   See, eg, *Thomas v Univ of Bradford (No 2)* [1992] 1 All ER 964 (Lord Browne-Wilkinson on behalf of the Visitor)

[21]   See ch 1, paras 1.97–1.105

[22]   *Green v Rutherford* (1750) 1 Ves Sen 462

[23]   *Thomas v Univ of Bradford* [1987] 1 AC 795, 814–5 (Lord Griffiths); *Ex p Kirkby Ravensworth Hospital* (1808) 15 Ves 305, 311 (Sir Samuel Romilly)

[24]   *Thomas v Univ of Bradford* [1987] 1 AC 795, 820 (Lord Griffiths)

[25]   (1694) Skin 447

[26]   *Patel v Univ of Bradford Senate* [1978] 1 WLR 1488, 1499–1500

[27]   *Philips v Bury* (1694) Skin 447; *A-G v Talbot* (1747) 3 Atk 662; *St John's College, Cambridge v Todington* (1757) 1 Burr 158; *R v Dean and Chapter of Chester* (1850) 15 QB 513; *R v Hertford College, Oxford* (1878) 3 QBD 693; *Thomson v Univ of London* (1864) 33 LJCh 625, 634 (Kindersley V-C); *Thorne v Univ of London* [1966] 2 QB 237; *Patel v Univ of Bradford Senate* [1978] 1 WLR 1488, 1493–4 (Megarry V-C); *Herring v Templeman* [1973] 2 All ER 581 (affd by CA on other grounds: [1973] 3 All ER 569); *Hines v Birkbeck College* [1986] Ch 524

[28]   As under the Employment Rights Act 1996

university's charter and statutes arises, adjourn pending a decision by the Visitor, but should interpret such documents itself.[29] To this limited extent, the court's jurisdiction appears to be concurrent with that of the Visitor. For any period during which the person occupying the office of Visitor is also the person visited, the visitatorial power is in suspension and the court has jurisdiction.[30]

(2) General and special Visitors

A Visitor may be either a general Visitor (who may visit the corporation in rela- **12.09**
tion to any matter concerning its internal workings) or a special Visitor (who may visit only for a specified purpose). A corporation may have two or more Visitors with separate jurisdictions; perhaps both a special Visitor and a general Visitor,[31] or even several Visitors appointed for different purposes.[32]

A general Visitor has an original jurisdiction enabling him to exercise his visitato- **12.10**
rial powers of his own volition (a general visitation); but this jurisdiction is virtually obsolete.[33] He also has a standing jurisdiction upon his receiving a petition or upon an appeal being made to him.[34] A general Visitor has the right physically to visit the corporation; but in modern times this rarely occurs. A 'visit' therefore usually refers merely to an act within the Visitor's jurisdiction. The power to hear and adjudicate upon complaints is incidental to the office of a general Visitor.[35]

Unless a Visitor's powers are expressly restricted by the charter, the Visitor will **12.11**
usually be considered to be a general Visitor, with full visitatorial powers.[36]
Furthermore,

> [t]he mere fact that, in certain respects, his powers are limited in the way they can be
> exercised—for example by committing to some other body in the first instance the
> right to determine questions with an appeal to the visitor—does not cut him down
> from being a general visitor to a special visitor.[37]

Therefore, a restriction in the charter which limits a general Visitor's jurisdiction to visit on his own initiative will not restrict his power to hear complaints.

---

[29] *Thomas v Univ of Bradford* [1987] 1 AC 795, 824 (Lord Griffiths)
[30] *R v Bishop of Chester* (1728) 2 Stra 797
[31] *St John's College, Cambridge v Todington* (1757) 1 Burr 158
[32] *A-G v Middleton* (1751) 2 Ves Sen 327, 329
[33] Picarda has pointed out that a general visitation appears to have been exercised only once in modern times, and that was in Australia: see H Picarda, 'Practice and Procedure in Visitatorial Appeals' (1992–3) 1 CL & PR 63, 64, noting RJ Sadler, 'University Visitor: Visitatorial Precedent and Procedure in Australia' (1981) 7 Univ Tas LR 2
[34] *Philips v Bury* (1694) Skin 447, 478 (Holt CJ)
[35] *St John's College, Cambridge v Todington* (1757) 1 Burr 158, 202 (Lord Mansfield)
[36] *Oakes v Sidney Sussex College, Cambridge* [1988] 1 WLR 431, 442; *R v Bishop of Worcester* (1815) 4 M & S 415, 420, 421; *St John's College, Cambridge v Todington* (1757) 1 Burr 158, 201 (Lord Mansfield); *Thomson v Univ of London* (1864) 33 LJCh 625, 633–4; *R v Dunsheath, ex p Meredith* [1951] 1 KB 127, 131; *Thorne v Univ of London* [1966] 2 QB 237, 242 (CA)
[37] *Oakes v Sidney Sussex College, Cambridge* [1988] 1 WLR 431, 442 (Browne-Wilkinson V-C)

(3) The scope of a Visitor's jurisdiction

12.12 The Visitor is interpreter[38] and judge of the foundation's internal laws.[39] A general Visitor therefore has jurisdiction to hear and determine claims and disputes which relate to the corporation's internal affairs.[40] The Visitor's interpretation of the corporation's statutes may determine whether the Visitor has jurisdiction in respect of the matter the subject of the dispute; to this extent only, the Visitor is judge of the scope of his own jurisdiction, subject only to the supervisory jurisdiction of the High Court under judicial review.[41]

Jurisdiction in respect of rights claimed under the domestic law

12.13 Since the jurisdiction of the Visitor relates to the domestic law of the foundation, it used to be thought that it applied only to the corporators themselves, because only they are subject to such domestic laws.[42] On this understanding of the law, it was vital to determine who precisely the corporators were; and, to this end, it was necessary to examine the corporation's charter and statutes.[43] This view of the law has now been shown to be unsound. In the light of the decision of the House of Lords in *Thomas v University of Bradford*,[44] it is now clear that 'the jurisdiction of a visitor does not depend on membership of the body as such, but on whether the rights being claimed arise under the domestic law'.[45] A Visitor therefore has jurisdiction in relation to the status of persons who are not corporators where such laws set out the conditions governing the appointment and removal of such persons.[46] Thus in *Oakes v Sidney Sussex College, Cambridge*,[47] the plaintiff, an undergraduate of the college, brought an action against it for not permitting him to return to complete his degree. His action was struck out because the right he was seeking to enforce was within the law of the college, and so within the exclusive jurisdiction of the Visitor. It did not avail him that, as an ordinary undergraduate and not a scholar, he was not a corporator for the purpose of the college statutes.

---

[38] *A-G v Stephens* (1737) 1 Atk 358

[39] *Thomas v Univ of Bradford* [1987] 1 AC 795, 816 (Lord Griffiths)

[40] *A-G v Talbot* (1747) 3 Atk 662, 674 (Lord Hardwicke)

[41] See *Ershad v Council of Legal Education (Inns of Court School of Law)* (DC, 5 Feb 1993) (Lexis Transcript), where students who had failed the Bar Vocational Course sought judicial review of the decision of the Council of Legal Education. Potts J considered that the matter was properly one for the Visitors; but, instead of striking out the proceedings, he adjourned them to enable the applicants to apply to the Visitors. In the event that the Visitors should refuse jurisdiction, his Lordship said that the applicants could revive their application for judicial review of the Council's decision

[42] See dictum of Megarry V-C in *Patel v Bradford Univ Senate* [1978] 1 WLR 1488, 1495

[43] The charters of modern universities usually define the corporators very broadly to include the university's officers and senior administrators, the members of its governing bodies, its academic staff, and its graduates and existing undergraduates

[44] [1987] 1 AC 795

[45] *Oakes v Sidney Sussex College, Cambridge* [1988] 1 WLR 431 (Browne-Wilkinson V-C)

[46] *A-G v Magdalen College, Oxford* (1847) 10 Beav 402; *Thomas v Univ of Bradford* [1987] 1 AC 795, 815 (Lord Griffiths)

[47] [1988] 1 WLR 431

It is not the nature of the action which is brought which determines whether it is **12.14** within the exclusive jurisdiction of the Visitor, but whether in substance it turns on rights contained in, or an interpretation of, the foundation's internal laws. The court has therefore declined to hear an action brought by a student against a university for alleged negligence in marking examination papers, on the ground that this matter was in substance one within the exclusive jurisdiction of the Visitor.[48] Similarly, an action against a university and one of its officers for alleged defamation in the course of an inquiry into whether the plaintiff had cheated in an examination was struck out on the ground (inter alia) that it fell within the exclusive jurisdiction of the Visitor.[49]

A dispute involving persons who are not corporators and which does not concern **12.15** any rights or liabilities (if any) which such persons may have under the corporation's charter or statutes, is not susceptible to the visitatorial jurisdiction, but is instead justiciable by the courts. The courts will therefore interfere in disputes concerning rights of property, or rights as between the corporation and a third person *dehors* the corporation, or with regard to any breach of trust committed by the corporation.[50] The reason why the court, rather than the Visitor, has jurisdiction over trusts, whether or not such trusts benefit members of the foundation, is that the terms of the trust are to be derived from the construction of the trust instrument, and not by an application of the laws of the foundation.[51]

Matters outside the Visitor's jurisdiction might therefore be expected to include, **12.16** for instance, a dispute between a foundation and a supplier;[52] and a university's seeking an injunction to exclude a former student from its premises.[53]

Rights under contracts of employment

The visitatorial jurisdiction extends to matters which affect, not merely an indi- **12.17** vidual's status within the corporation (for example, as master of a college), but also (except where statute provides otherwise[54]) his contract of employment.[55] There is much old authority holding that the jurisdiction includes the appointment and removal of Fellows at Oxford and Cambridge colleges,[56] although these cases were concerned with the status of being a Fellow rather than rights of employment.

---

[48] *Thorne v Univ of London* [1966] 2 QB 237
[49] *Foecke v Univ of Bristol (a Body Corporate) and others* (CA, 30 July 1996) (Lexis Transcript)
[50] *Thomson v Univ of London* (1864) 33 LJCh 625, 634 (Kindersley V-C). On breach of trust, see also the remarks of Lord Langdale MR in *A-G v Magdalen College, Oxford* (1847) 10 Beav 402, 409
[51] *Thomas v Univ of Bradford* [1987] 1 AC 795, 823 (Lord Griffiths)
[52] *ex p Death* (1852) 18 QB 647
[53] *Univ of Essex v Ratcliffe* The Times, 28 Nov 1969
[54] See the Education Reform Act 1988, discussed below, paras 12.20–12.22
[55] *Thomas v Univ of Bradford* [1987] 1 AC 795, 815 (Lord Griffiths)
[56] ibid

More modern cases have applied the same principle even where the individual concerned has a contract of employment, as in the case of academic staff at modern universities; but the jurisdiction of the Visitor to determine disputes involving the appointment and removal of academic staff at universities has since been considerably reduced by statute.[57]

12.18 Statute apart, the general principle was expressed by Hoffmann J in *Hines v Birkbeck College* where his Lordship said:[58]

> In my judgment the dispute is no less domestic because the rules, customs or procedures in issue are alleged to constitute terms of a contract or because their construction or the questions of fact involved in their application are equally conveniently justiciable in a court.

The leading modern case is *Thomas v University of Bradford*,[59] although the impact of the decision itself on a university's ability to dismiss its academic staff without being subject to the common law has since been reduced by statute.[60] The plaintiff, who had been dismissed by the university from her post as lecturer, brought an action against the university claiming a declaration that her dismissal had been invalid for failing to comply with the university's charter, statutes, ordinances, and regulations, and also claiming damages for breach of contract, or alternatively arrears of salary. The House of Lords held that, as the entire dispute centred upon the statutes and ordinances of the university, it fell within the exclusive jurisdiction of the Visitor, and the court had no jurisdiction to entertain it. The court did not acquire jurisdiction merely because the dispute also affected the plaintiff's contract of employment.[61] Had the matter in dispute under the contract of employment related to purely common law or statutory rights, instead of rights under the university's internal rules and regulations, it would have been within the jurisdiction of the courts and not the Visitor.[62] It therefore appears that the contract of employment of a member of a foundation could confer, in addition to special rights given to him as a member, purely contractual rights; such contractual rights would be enforceable by the courts and not by the Visitor.[63]

12.19 A foundation's charter and statutes will not generally enshrine the terms of appointment, employment, and dismissal of non-academic-related employees, such as secretaries, porters, cleaners, and other ancillary staff, including those concerned with maintenance or security. If the contracts of employment of such staff

---

[57] ie by the Education Reform Act 1988, discussed below, paras 12.20–12.22
[58] [1986] Ch 524, 543
[59] [1987] 1 AC 795 (HL)
[60] ie, by the Education Reform Act 1988, discussed below, paras 12.20–12.22
[61] *Thomas v Univ of Bradford* [1987] 1 AC 795, 821
[62] See *Re Wislang's Application* [1984] NI 63, 80–1 (Kelly LJ), whose judgment was approved by Lord Griffiths in *Thomas v Univ of Bradford* [1987] 1 AC 795, 817
[63] *Re Wislang's Application* [1984] NI 63, 80–1 (Kelly LJ)

are free-standing contracts, in that they are not governed by the foundation's internal laws, they fall outside the visitatorial jurisdiction and are justiciable exclusively by the courts.[64]

Impact of Education Reform Act 1988

The general principles laid down in the *Thomas* case no longer apply to universities and other institutions affected by the Education Reform Act 1988. This Act excludes from the jurisdiction of the Visitor any dispute relating to the appointment or employment, or the termination of the appointment or employment, of a member of the academic staff[65] of a qualifying institution.[66] A qualifying institution is essentially any university (including any constituent college, hall, or other institution) or any other body authorised by charter to grant degrees, which at the relevant date[67] was in receipt of grants from the University Funding Council or the Secretary of State (in the case of a university, on the advice of the University Grants Committee).[68] The same Act also required universities to amend their statutes to provide (inter alia) for members of the academic staff[69] to be dismissed for redundancy or for good cause, and to set up disciplinary procedures dealing with appointment or dismissal,[70] procedures to deal with appeals by such members of staff who are dismissed or disciplined,[71] and grievance procedures which can be invoked by such members of staff in matters concerning their appointment.[72]   **12.20**

The Education Reform Act 1988 does, however, qualify the exclusion of the Visitor's jurisdiction in two ways. First, the visitatorial power was not ousted in respect of any dispute referred to the Visitor before the date that the statutes of the university were amended to provide for the matters set out above.[73] Secondly, the Visitor may hear or determine appeals and redress grievances under the procedures introduced into universities' statutes pursuant to the 1988 Act.[74]   **12.21**

Not affected by the Education Reform Act 1988, since it is not a qualifying institution (not having been in receipt of public grants) is the University of Buckingham. Other non-qualifying institutions, to which the general principles   **12.22**

---

[64] *R v Industrial Disputes Tribunal, ex p Queen Mary College, Univ of London* [1957] 2 QB 483
[65] This includes academic-related staff: Education Reform Act 1988, ss 203(4), 206(4)
[66] ibid, s 206(1)
[67] ie the period of three years from 1 Aug 1987
[68] Education Reform Act 1988, s 202(3)
[69] This includes academic-related staff: ibid, s 203(4)
[70] ibid, s 203(1)(c)
[71] ibid, s 203(1)(d)
[72] ibid, s 203(1)(e)
[73] ibid, s 206(2). See *Pearce v Univ of Aston in Birmingham* [1991] 2 All ER 461 (CA)
[74] Education Reform Act 1988, s 206(3); the procedures are those specified in s 203(1)(d) and (e)

laid down in *Thomas* are still applicable, include many public schools created as charter corporations. Furthermore, even though the Visitor's jurisdiction has been removed in respect of disputes involving the appointment and removal of academic and academic-related staff at universities subject to the Act, the Visitor retains jurisdiction over other matters affecting such staff, for example, as to who is entitled to hold an office (such as dean) within a faculty.[75] The *Thomas* decision also remains good in respect of university students, who are still precluded from bringing a claim in contract before the courts to the extent that the matter centres upon the university's charter and statutes.[76] The introduction of the requirement for all university students to contribute to their tuition fees may increase the numbers of disputes between universities and individual students; and the decision in the *Thomas* case ensures a continuing important role for the Visitor in disputes of this kind.

C. The duties of the Visitor

12.23 The manner in which the Visitor should exercise his powers is essentially to be left to the discretion of the Visitor. The courts have rejected any attempt to prescribe the way in which such powers should be exercised, since they 'fall to be exercised in an almost infinite variety of situations'.[77] In exercising his jurisdiction to investigate and correct wrongs done in the administration of the foundation's internal laws, the Visitor may on occasion need to act rather more like an appeal court than a review court, although the Visitor's role cannot be properly characterized either as supervisory or appellate.[78] The Visitor 'should investigate the basic facts to the extent that in the exercise of a proper judgment he concludes to be appropriate'.[79] The Visitor is less constrained than the courts, in that he may 'interfere with any decision which he concludes to be wrong, even though he feels unable to categorise it as *Wednesbury*[80] unreasonable'.[81] On the other hand, 'many decisions giving rise to dispute will be subject to considerations which quite properly inhibit the visitor from embarking on an independent fact-finding role'.[82]

---

[75] H Picarda, 'Practice and Procedure in Visitatorial Appeals' (1992–3) 1 CL & PR 63, 65
[76] See, eg, *R v Univ of Nottingham, ex p Ktorides* (CA, 28 July 1997); *Cotran v Buckingham Univ* (CA, 24 Feb 1998)
[77] *R v Judicial Cttee of the Privy Council, ex p Vijayatunga* [1988] QB 322 (DC) (Kerr LJ), 333
[78] ibid (Simon Brown J) 344, whose judgment was approved on appeal: *R v HM the Queen in Council, ex p Vijayatunga* [1990] 2 QB 444 (CA) (Bingham LJ). See also *Thomas v Univ of Bradford* [1987] 1 AC 795, 824, where Lord Griffiths referred to an 'appeal' to the Visitor
[79] *R v HM the Queen in Council, ex p Vijayatunga* [1990] 2 QB 444, 457 (Bingham LJ)
[80] See *Associated Provincial Picture Houses Ltd v Wednesbury Corp* [1948] 1 KB 223
[81] *R v Judicial Cttee of the Privy Council, ex p Vijayatunga* [1988] QB 322, 344–5 (Simon Brown J)
[82] ibid

In *R v Visitors to the Inns of Court, ex p Calder, ex p Persaud*,[83] however, the Court **12.24** of Appeal, in proceedings for judicial review, quashed decisions of the judges of the Inns of Court made in their capacity as Visitors. The matter before the Visitors had concerned two barristers who had been found guilty of professional misconduct by a Disciplinary Tribunal of the Council of the Inns of Court. The Court of Appeal (which did not consider the role of Visitors to the Inns of Court to be different from that of any other Visitor) quashed the Visitors' decision on the ground that the judges, in exercising their visitatorial jurisdiction, had mistaken the nature of their role and had acted as a review body rather than as an appellate tribunal. This misdirection seems to be crucial to the Court of Appeal's decision, which otherwise would undermine the accepted rule that the Visitor is entitled to determine his own manner of proceeding. If, therefore, the Visitors had been aware that they could decide to proceed either as a review body or as an appeal tribunal, and had considered the former to be the more appropriate, it is submitted that their decision could not have been subject to judicial review. Indeed, more recently, a divisional court[84] has expressed the view that there is nothing in the Court of Appeal's decision to cast doubt on the established principles or on the practical examples as to their application set out in the Court of Appeal's earlier decision in *R v HM the Queen in Council, ex p Vijayatunga*.[85]

In *ex p Vijayatunga*,[86] Bingham LJ illustrated the correct approach by reference to **12.25** a hypothetical case. He supposed a college whose statutes empower it to terminate a student's membership if he or she, inter alia (1) fails, after receiving twenty-eight days' written notice to do so, to pay any sum owed to the college; or (2) is guilty of persistent insobriety such as, in the opinion of the college, to render him or her unfit to remain a member; or (3) fails in the opinion of the college to attain the required academic standard.

His Lordship said that in case (1), the Visitor's role would be essentially that of a **12.26** first-instance judge: he would be the judge of both fact and law. The Visitor would therefore determine if the debt were owed, whether the requisite notice was given, whether the student failed to pay, and whether there was any defence (such as estoppel or a promise of extra time).

In case (2) the Visitor would satisfy himself (if it were in issue) that there was reli- **12.27** able evidence of persistent, and more than trivial, insobriety, and that the college's decision had been reached in good faith and not for any extraneous reason. If he were satisfied on those points, he would not substitute his own opinion on fitness for that of the college:[87]

---

[83] [1994] QB 1 (CA)
[84] *R v Honourable Society of the Middle Temple, ex p Bullock* (CA, 17 Jan 1996) (Brooke J)
[85] [1990] 2 QB 444
[86] ibid, 457–8
[87] *R v HM the Queen in Council, ex p Vijayatunga* [1990] 2 QB 444, 457–8 (Bingham LJ)

That is because it is his responsibility to see that the college acts lawfully in accordance with the statutes, not to act as an independent arbiter of matters entrusted by the statutes to the judgment of the college and on which its judgment is likely to be better, because better informed and more experienced, than his.

This restates the important and well-established principle that the Visitor should not interfere in those matters in which the corporators have a discretion, provided that the discretion has been exercised honestly.[88]

12.28   In case (3), the Visitor would again satisfy himself (if it were in doubt) that there was reliable evidence of poor academic performance and that the college's decision had not been tainted by bad faith or extraneous motives. If so satisfied, he could go no further, for the same reasons as in case (2). 'He could not legitimately override the college's bona fide assessment, based on reliable evidence, of the student's academic performance.'[89]

12.29   In the *Vijayatunga* case[90] itself, a candidate of the University of London, whose doctoral thesis had been rejected by the examiners, claimed that the examiners had not been properly qualified to assess her thesis. A committee of the Privy Council, acting for Her Majesty in Council as Visitor, dismissed the petition on the ground that it would not interfere in matters of technical or scientific judgement. The candidate applied for judicial review of the committee's decision, arguing that, in failing to inquire into the suitability of the examiners, the committee had abdicated its role of Visitor by deferring to the very body whose conduct it was its duty to investigate. The Court of Appeal, dismissing the candidate's appeal from the judgment of the Divisional Court, held that the committee had been entitled, if not bound, to conclude that the university's procedures for appointing examiners had been followed, so that there was no manifest procedural impropriety. In those circumstances, the committee was entitled to conclude that the choice of examiners was a matter for expert judgement with which it (the committee) should not interfere.

12.30   Bingham LJ's general principles were applied in *R v Honourable Society of the Middle Temple, ex p Bullock*,[91] where a candidate who failed the Bar Vocational Course alleged that the Council of Legal Education had not taken account of mitigating circumstances. Tucker J, sitting as a Visitor, had decided that he could not interfere unless the Council had acted unlawfully or irrationally. The candidate's application for judicial review of the Visitor's decision was dismissed, Brooke J evidently treating the circumstances as falling within case (3) in Bingham LJ's illustration.

---

[88]   *R v Hertford College, Oxford* (1878) 3 QBD 693, 701 (CA)
[89]   *R v HM the Queen in Council, ex p Vijayatunga* [1990] 2 QB 444, 458 (Bingham LJ)
[90]   [1990] 2 QB 444 (CA)
[91]   (DC, 17 Jan 1996)

A Visitor is a 'public authority' for the purposes of the Human Rights Act 1998, **12.31** and so it is unlawful for him to act in a way which is incompatible with a Convention right.[92]

D. The remedies available to a Visitor

As judge of the laws of the foundation, a Visitor has a power to right a wrong done **12.32** to a member or office-holder in the foundation where those laws have been mis-applied. Thus a Visitor who concludes that a member of the foundation has been dismissed without good cause can order the member's reinstatement, and can also order payment of arrears of salary between the date of the dismissal and reinstate-ment. Alternatively, where the Visitor concludes that the dismissal was without good cause, but that reinstatement would not be conducive to the health of the foundation, he can order the foundation to pay monetary compensation in lieu of reinstatement.[93]

The Visitor also has power to award costs.[94]   **12.33**

E. Judicial control over Visitors

The court's jurisdiction over Visitors is supervisory, not appellate;[95] its control **12.34** over Visitors is therefore limited. A Visitor is not subject to judicial review if he acts within his jurisdiction in good faith and in accordance with the rules of nat-ural justice.[96] The court will not interfere in matters which are wholly of academic judgement, such as the choice of examiners to examine a thesis.[97] Under the Human Rights Act 1998, however, a Visitor will be subject to judicial review if he acts in a way which is incompatible with a Convention right.[98]

It used to be thought that *certiorari* was not available against a Visitor because the **12.35** law administered by him is not common law or statute law, but that contained in

---

[92] Human Rights Act 1998, s 6(1), (3)(a). For the meaning of 'Convention right', see ch 1, paras 1.84–1.86
[93] *Thomas v Univ of Bradford* [1987] 1 AC 795, 823–4 (Lord Griffiths), 828 (Lord Ackner)
[94] *Thomas v Univ of Bradford (No 2)* [1992] 1 All ER 964
[95] *Thomas v Univ of Bradford* [1987] 1 AC 795, 825 (Lord Griffiths); *R v HM the Queen in Council, ex p Vijayatunga* [1990] 2 QB 444, 459 (Mann LJ) (CA)
[96] *R v Lord President of the Privy Council, ex p Page* [1993] 1 AC 682, 701 (Lord Browne-Wilkinson); *R v Bishop of Ely* (1788) 2 TR 290, 338
[97] *R v HM the Queen in Council, ex p Vijayatunga* [1990] 2 QB 444 (CA)
[98] Human Rights Act 1998, ss 6(1), 7(1). For the meaning of 'Convention right', see ch 1, paras 1.84–1.86. It should not be difficult for the member of the eleemosynary corporation who was in-volved in the proceedings before the Visitor to satisfy the 'victim' requirement of s 7(3)

the corporation's charter and statutes.[99] However, in *Thomas v University of Bradford*,[100] the House of Lords recognized that *certiorari* could be used to quash a decision of the Visitor on an application for judicial review if, in the words of Lord Griffiths, the decision of the Visitor 'amounted to an abuse of his powers'.[101] Subsequently, in the *Page* case,[102] his Lordship explained that he used the phrase 'an abuse of his powers' to connote 'some form of misbehaviour that was wholly incompatible' with the visitatorial role.[103] *Certiorari* could therefore be used to quash a decision of the Visitor made in excess of jurisdiction or in breach of the rules of natural justice.[104] Lord Griffiths was at pains to point out that the phrase did not include a mere error of law.[105] Also in the *Page* case, Lord Browne-Wilkinson explained why the court cannot review a decision of the Visitor on a point of law: the reason is that[106]

> the visitor is applying not the general law of the land but a peculiar domestic law of which he is the sole arbiter and of which the courts have no cognisance. If the visitor has power under the regulating documents to enter into the adjudication of the dispute (i.e., is acting within his jurisdiction in the narrow sense) he cannot err in law in reaching this decision since the general law is not the applicable law. Therefore he cannot be acting ultra vires and unlawfully by applying his view of the domestic law in reaching his decision. The court has no jurisdiction either to say that he erred in his application of the general law (since the general law is not applicable to the decision) or to reach a contrary view as to the effect of the domestic law (since the visitor is the sole judge of such domestic law).

12.36 For the same reason, the Visitor's decision cannot be reviewed under the *Wednesbury* principle;[107] it cannot therefore be challenged on the ground that the Visitor has allegedly failed to take into account relevant matters, or has taken into account irrelevant matters, or has reached an irrational conclusion.[108] In its freedom from challenge on a point of law or under the *Wednesbury* test, 'the position of the visitor is anomalous, indeed unique'.[109]

---

[99] See JW Bridge, 'Keeping Peace in the Universities: the Role of the Visitor' (1970) 86 LQR 531, 545. An analogy used to be drawn with the court's inability to issue *certiorari* against an ecclesiastical court: *R v Chancellor of St Edmundsbury and Ipswich Diocese, ex p White* [1948] 1 KB 195 (CA); but the analogy has since been rejected: see *R v Judicial Cttee of the Privy Council, ex p Vijayatunga* [1988] QB 322, 332–3 (DC) (Kerr LJ)

[100] [1987] 1 AC 795

[101] ibid, 825

[102] *R v Lord President of the Privy Council, ex p Page* [1993] 1 AC 682

[103] ibid, 693 (Lord Griffiths)

[104] ibid, 705 (Lord Slynn)

[105] ibid, 693 (Lord Griffiths)

[106] ibid, 702–3 (Lord Browne-Wilkinson)

[107] *Associated Provincial Picture Houses Ltd v Wednesbury Corp* [1948] 1 KB 223

[108] *R v Lord President of the Privy Council, ex p Page* [1993] 1 AC 682, 704 (Lord Browne-Wilkinson)

[109] ibid

Prohibition is available to restrain a Visitor who intends to act beyond his juris-   **12.37**
diction[110] (even if the parties have submitted to such extended jurisdiction[111]), or
to breach the rules of natural justice (as in the exceptional case where, being also
the person visited, he purports to be a judge in his own cause).[112]

Mandamus will also lie against a Visitor who breaches the rules of natural justice.   **12.38**
Thus, even if the Visitor has power to exercise his jurisdiction as he sees fit, mandamus can lie against him if he fails to adhere to the principle *audi alteram partem*,
and does not give the parties interested an opportunity to be heard.[113] Mandamus
can also be granted against a Visitor who simply refuses to act,[114] since, if he does
not do so, no one else can.[115] As *certiorari* used to be thought not to be available,
mandamus could be utilized effectively to quash a decision of the Visitor, in that
it could require the parties to act on the footing that the Visitor's decision was invalid.[116]

Certiorari, prohibition and mandamus are not available if the Visitor is the sover-   **12.39**
eign in person, since the prerogative orders do not lie against the Crown. It has
been suggested that, in such instances, the appropriate remedy is a declaratory
judgment of the court, since this does bind the Crown.[117]

An action for damages lies against a Visitor who exceeds his jurisdiction.[118]   **12.40**

---

[110] *R v Bishop of Chester* (1791) 1 W Bl 22, 23; *Bently v Bishop of Ely* (1729) 1 Barn KB 192;
Bishop of Chester v Hayward (1787) 1 Durn & E 650
    [111] *Green v Rutherford* (1750) 1 Ves Sen 462, 471
    [112] *Bently v Bishop of Ely* (1729) 1 Barn KB 192; *R v Bishop of Chester* (1748) 1 W Bl 22. *R v Bishop
of Ely* (1788) 2 TR 290, 338. This breaches the rule *nemo iudex in re sua*
    [113] *R v Bishop of Ely* (1788) 2 TR 290, 336, 338
    [114] *Thomson v Univ of London* (1864) 33 LJ (Ch) 625; *R v Bishop of Ely* (1794) 5 Durn & E 475
    [115] *R v Lord President of the Privy Council, ex p Page* [1993] 1 AC 682, 708 (Lord Slynn)
    [116] *Appleford's Case* (1672) 1 Mod Rep 82; see *R v Lord President of the Privy Council, ex p Page*
[1993] 1 AC 682, 698 (Lord Browne-Wilkinson)
    [117] See JW Bridge, 'Keeping Peace in the Universities: the Role of the Visitor' (1970) 86 LQR
531, 546, n 14, and the texts there cited
    [118] *Green v Rutherford* (1750) 1 Ves Sen 462, 470

13

LEGAL PROCEEDINGS

A. The role of the Attorney-General

(1) Ex officio *proceedings*

Giving the advice of the Privy Council in *Wallis v Solicitor-General for New Zealand*,[1] Lord Macnaghten said:[2]   **13.01**

> It is the province of the Crown as parens patriæ to enforce the execution of charitable trusts, and it has always been recognised as the duty of the law officers of the Crown to intervene for the purpose of protecting charities and affording advice and assistance to the Court in the administration of charitable trusts.

The Attorney-General, representing the Crown and acting *ex officio*, may intervene to protect a charity's property if it has been, or there is a threat of its being, applied, in breach of trust for non-charitable purposes. In such matters, the Attorney-General may be considered to protect the public interest in ensuring that property is not lost to charity.   **13.02**

---

[1] [1903] AC 173
[2] ibid, at 181–2

(2) Relator action

13.03 The Attorney-General may also be a party to proceedings brought in his name, and with his consent, by a relator. Such proceedings by way of information to the Attorney-General were in fact the principal means of enforcing charitable trusts for the century or so before the establishment of the Charity Commissioners in 1853.[3] The action would be nominally brought in the name of the Attorney-General,[4] but would in reality be that of the informer, who, as relator in the action, could be liable in costs.[5] Following the introduction in the Charitable Trusts Act 1853 of what are now called 'charity proceedings', the relator action in proceedings involving charities has become obsolete. Such proceedings can still be brought, however, and the Charities Act 1993 expressly provides that the restrictions on 'charity proceedings' do not apply to the taking of proceedings by the Attorney-General, with or without a relator.[6]

(3) Reference from the Charity Commissioners

13.04 The Attorney-General may take legal proceedings with reference to a charity upon being informed by the Charity Commissioners that it is desirable for legal proceedings to be taken with reference to any charity (other than an exempt charity) or its property or affairs, and for the proceedings to be taken by the Attorney-General.[7]

(4) Limitation of actions brought by the Attorney-General

13.05 Under the Limitation Act 1980, no period of limitation there prescribed applies to an action by a beneficiary under a trust in respect of any fraud or fraudulent breach of trust to which the trustee was a party or privy, or an action to recover from the trustee[8] trust property or its proceeds in the possession of the trustee, or previously received by the trustee and converted to his use.[9] Subject to this, section 21(3) provides that:

> an action by a beneficiary to recover trust property or in respect of any breach of trust . . . shall not be brought after the expiration of six years from the date on which the right of action accrued.

---

[3] See G Jones, *History of the Law of Charity 1532–1827* (Cambridge Univ Press, 1969) 160–4
[4] *A-G v Logan* [1891] 2 QB 100, 106
[5] *A-G v Newcombe* (1807) 14 Ves 1; 2 Ves Jun Supp 227, 356; *A-G v Earl of Mansfield* (1827) 2 Russ 501
[6] CA 1993, s 33(6)
[7] ibid, s 33(7)
[8] The Limitation Act 1980, s 38, gives the same meaning to the terms 'trust' and 'trustee' as is contained in TA 1925, s 68(17)
[9] Limitation Act 1980, s 21(1)

This limitation period does not apply to actions brought by the Attorney-General **13.06**
and involving charitable trusts. This was held in *Attorney-General v Cocke*,[10] where
the Attorney-General brought an action by writ against the defendants, who were
the executors and trustees of a charitable trust created under the will of a testator
which had been proved nearly thirty-five years earlier. The Attorney-General
sought accounts and inquiries in relation to the testator's estate, injunctions restraining the disposition of the assets held on the charitable trusts, and the appointment of new trustees in place of the defendants. Harman J held that the limitation
period under section 21(3) does not apply to an action brought by the Attorney-
General in respect of a charitable trust, because the Attorney-General is not personally a beneficiary of a charitable trust. Even if he could be considered to be acting
on behalf of the public at large, who benefit from such a trust, members of the public have no property rights under it, and they too cannot in any meaningful sense be
treated as 'beneficiaries' for the purposes of the statute.[11] Harman J considered that
some earlier cases which had held that the Attorney-General was bound by periods
of limitation were of no modern significance, since they turned on the rather
different wording of statutes of limitation which preceded the modern form of
words originally introduced in the Limitation Act 1939.[12]

Harman J left open the possibility that a few charitable trusts can be treated as hav- **13.07**
ing individual beneficiaries; and, although he did not give instances, he might
have had in mind the so-called 'poor relations' cases. However, even if one of the
poor relations brought a relator action alleging a breach of trust, the action would
still nominally be that of the Attorney-General, so the impact of the Limitation
Act 1980 would be unchanged.

It was further argued in *Attorney-General v Cocke* that the action to account could **13.08**
not lie because the Limitation Act 1980 provides:[13]

> An action for an account shall not be brought after the expiration of any time limit
> under this Act which is applicable to the claim which is the basis of the duty to ac-
> count.

As the Attorney-General had alleged no breach of trust or other wrongdoing, it
was argued that there was no claim which founded the basis of the duty to account. Harman J rejected this argument also, holding that no wrongdoing needed
to be alleged: the basis of the duty to account was the fiduciary relationship between the trustees and the person entitled to enforce the trust, namely the

---

[10] [1988] Ch 414. See J Warburton, 'Attorney-General Unlimited' [1988] Conv 292
[11] *A-G v Cocke* [1988] Ch 414, 419–20 (Harman J). See also *Thomson v Trustees of the Honourable Society of the Inner Temple* (Mayor and City of London's Court, 30 May 1967)
[12] eg *College of St Mary Magdalen, Oxford (President and Scholars) v A-G* (1857) 6 HL Cas 189 (Lord Cranworth LC); *A-G v Payne* (1859) 27 Beav 168 (Romilly MR); *How v Earl Winterton* [1898] 2 Ch 626; *Re Blow, St Bartholomew's Hospital (Governors) v Cambden* [1914] 1 Ch 233
[13] Limitation Act 1980, s 23

Attorney-General on behalf of Her Majesty as *parens patriae.*[14] In so holding, Harman J was able to draw support from *Tito v Waddell (No 2)*,[15] where Megarry V-C had held that a claim to set aside a transaction entered into in breach of the self-dealing and fair-dealing rules was not an action for breach of trust, and so was outside the period of limitation specified in (what is now) section 21(3).

13.09 Where no period of statutory limitation applies, an equitable claim is generally subject to the doctrine of laches, but there is old authority holding that laches does not apply to claims brought by the Attorney-General in respect of charitable trusts.[16] The question whether the Attorney-General can be bound by the doctrine of acquiescence has been expressly left open.[17]

13.10 It has been held that if company directors breached their duties by misapplying the company's funds, they would be treated as trustees for the purposes of an earlier Limitation Act, so that any action against them would have to be brought within the six-year period.[18] Even if this general position remains the same under section 21(3) of the Limitation Act 1980, the principle in *Attorney-General v Cocke* would exclude the operation of that sub-section to directors of charitable companies, so that the Attorney-General would not be subject to any statutory period of limitation in respect of actions for breach of fiduciary duty which he brings against such directors.

B. The role of the Charity Commissioners

(1) Power to institute legal proceedings

13.11 Section 32 of the Charities Act 1993 has given the Charity Commissioners a new power to institute legal proceedings themselves.[19] Under the section, the Commissioners may exercise the same power with respect to the taking of legal proceedings with reference to charities or the property or affairs of charities, or the compromise of claims with a view to avoiding or ending such proceedings, as are exercisable by the Attorney-General acting *ex officio.*[20] This is subject to one exception, namely to the power of the Attorney-General[21] to present a petition for

---

[14] *A-G v Cocke* [1988] Ch 414, 420–1 (Harman J). See also *Re Richardson* [1919] 2 Ch 50

[15] [1977] Ch 106, 248

[16] *A-G v Christ's Hospital* (1834) 3 My & K 344; *College of St Mary Magdalen, Oxford (President and Scholars) v A-G* (1857) 6 HL Cas 189, 207 (Lord Cranworth LC: 'laches cannot be imputed in cases of charity . . . the parties most interested are . . . least able to assert their rights')

[17] *Re Freestone's Charity* [1979] 1 All ER 51, 63 (Goff LJ)

[18] *Re Lands Allotment Co* [1894] Ch 616

[19] CA 1993, s 32. The power was first introduced by CA 1992, s 28, which inserted s 26A into CA 1960

[20] CA 1993, s 32(1)

[21] Under ibid, s 63(1)

the winding up of a charity.[22] The practice and procedure to be followed in relation to any proceedings taken by the Charity Commissioners under their new power are to be the same in all respects (and in particular as regards costs) as if they were proceedings taken by the Attorney-General acting *ex officio*.[23] No rule of law or practice is to be taken to require the Attorney-General to be a party to any such proceedings.[24] The powers exercisable by the Charity Commissioners under section 32 are exercisable by them of their own motion, but only with the agreement of the Attorney-General on each occasion.[25] It is expressly provided that the restrictions on 'charity proceedings' do not apply to the taking of proceedings by the Charity Commissioners in accordance with section 32.[26] There is not, as yet, any reported instance of the Charity Commissioners' having used their section 32 power to take legal proceedings or to compromise claims.

Since the Attorney-General cannot be treated as a beneficiary of a charity,[27] it must follow that the Charity Commissioners cannot be treated as beneficiaries either. It is therefore clear that, like the Attorney-General, the Commissioners are not subject to the period of limitation specified in section 21(3) of the Limitation Act 1980. **13.12**

(2) *Consent to charity proceedings*

Except where legal proceedings are taken by the Attorney-General (with or without a relator), no charity proceedings[28] may be entertained or proceeded with in any court without the authorization by order of the Charity Commissioners.[29] This is dealt with more fully below.[30] **13.13**

(3) *Reference to the Attorney-General*

Where it appears to the Charity Commissioners, on an application for an order for their consent to the bringing of charity proceedings[31] or otherwise, that it is desirable for legal proceedings to be taken with reference to any charity (other than an exempt charity) or its property or affairs, and for the proceedings to be taken by the Attorney-General, the Charity Commissioners must so inform the Attorney-General, and send him such statements and particulars as they think necessary to explain the matter.[32] **13.14**

---

[22] ibid, s 32(2)
[23] ibid, s 32(3)
[24] ibid, s 32(4)
[25] ibid, s 32(5)
[26] ibid, s 33(6)
[27] *A-G v Cocke* [1988] Ch 414
[28] As defined in CA 1993, s 33(8)
[29] ibid, s 33(2)
[30] See below, para 13.33
[31] ie under CA 1993, s 33
[32] ibid, s 33(7)

C. Charity proceedings

(1) The development of 'charity proceedings'

13.15   The concept of 'charity proceedings' is now contained in section 33 of the Charities Act 1993, which (in essence) requires the Charity Commissioners' consent to proceedings concerning a charity's administration. The effect of the section is to prevent such proceedings from being brought except by a number of specified classes of claimant, and then only with the consent of the Charity Commissioners. It is 'a protective filter' designed 'to avoid charities being concerned with frivolous and ill founded claims'.[33]

13.16   The ancestor of the modern provision was contained in the Charitable Trusts Act 1853.[34] It was said that the 1853 Act[35]

> was never intended to interfere with the rights or powers of the trustees of a charity in their character of owners of property, or to interfere with their rights in the character of masters who are employing servants. Its object was to prevent strangers from coming in as relators in suits in Chancery, or as Petitioners under *Sir Samuel Romilly's Act*,[36] to complain of the management of a charity, unless the Charity Commissioners are first satisfied that such proceedings ought to be taken.

13.17   Under the Act of 1853, the Charity Commissioners' consent was required only in respect of legal proceedings relating to 'any Charity', and the Act itself restricted the expression 'Charity' to 'every Endowed Foundation and Institution'.[37] Voluntary charities (that is, those which had no endowment, but relied entirely on membership subscriptions) were therefore excluded from its scope. Individual members of such voluntary charities could therefore enforce any rights arising under the rules of association without needing recourse to a relator action (with the consent of the Attorney-General) or charity proceedings (with the consent of the Charity Commissioners). This seems to explain several old decisions in which individual actions by members of voluntary charities were entertained without either the Attorney-General's being made a party or (after 1853) without the consent of the Charity Commissioners. In relation to such charities, subscribers' rights were treated as personal rights, which the courts would enforce between the members simply as a matter of contract.[38] A decision upholding the validity of a

---

[33] *Re Hampden Fuel Allotment Charity* [1989] Ch 484, 494 (Nicholls LJ); see also *Scott v National Trust* [1998] 2 All ER 705, 714 (Robert Walker J)

[34] Charitable Trusts Act 1853, s 17, of which it was stated: 'In my opinion, the section relates exclusively to administration': *Rendall v Blair* (1890) 45 ChD 139, 160 (Fry LJ). This was re-enacted in CA 1960, s 28, the immediate forerunner of CA 1993, s 33

[35] *Holme v Guy* (1877) 5 ChD 901, 910 (James LJ)

[36] ie Charities Procedure Act 1812

[37] Charitable Trusts Act 1853, s 66

[38] See *Howard v Hill* (1888) 59 LT(NS) 818, 819, where Kekewich J said that 'the court has a right to interfere with a voluntary institution of this character to this extent: that persons who, by

voting agreement between subscribers to a charity can also be explained on this basis.[39] Since 1961,[40] however, with the widening of the definition of 'charity' for the purposes of the Charities Act 1960,[41] 'charity proceedings' now include proceedings brought in relation to purely voluntary charitable associations. In view of this, some of the older cases relating to the rights of members of such associations must be treated with care.

The Attorney-General is unlikely to intervene where there has been a breach of a **13.18** mere matter of the internal administration of a charity that does not involve an application of its property to other than its charitable purposes. Even before the Charitable Trusts Act 1853 statutorily restricted the scope for individual litigation, the courts were keen not to become involved in matters relating purely to a charity's internal regulation. They could therefore refuse to entertain an action brought by a third party complaining of an act or omission which related to the internal administration of a charity unless that act itself infringed an individual (or personal) right of the plaintiff (whether it be a right at common law or in equity).

An individual right could be a right conferred by the trust instrument itself, for ex- **13.19** ample a constitutional right of a member to vote at meetings, or to give consent to a transaction; or such a right could be conferred outside the trust instrument, for example a contractual right which a third party has as an employee of the charity or as a supplier of goods to the charity, or a claim by a legatee to be entitled to the charity's property under a resulting trust. A person who could not establish a personal right to bring an action, but who simply sought to prevent or to undo an act which merely contravened the terms of the trust instrument, would be prevented from doing so without the Charity Commissioners' consent. This remains the position today, as such proceedings would constitute 'charity proceedings' within the Charities Act 1993.[42] The Charity Commissioners will be unwilling to give their consent to charity proceedings in these circumstances, since the court is reluctant to intervene in matters of purely internal administration.

The court's desire not to become involved in a charity's internal administration **13.20** mirrors a similar desire of the courts not to become involved in the internal management of a company, where it has given rise to an analogous principle, known as

---

subscribing money or otherwise, have established themselves in the position of governors, or whatever they like to call themselves, are entitled to come to the court and say, "our rights which are secured to us by the rules of the institution must be protected" '

[39] See *Bolton v Madden* (1873) LR 9 QB 55, 57, where Blackburn J, whilst expressing disapproval of this sort of arrangement, held that a subscriber to a charity may give his votes as he pleases, 'answering only to his own conscience and reputation for the way he exercises his power'

[40] CA 1960, s 45(1) ('charity'); s 28 ('charity proceedings')

[41] ibid, s 45(1)

[42] CA 1993, s 33(8)

the rule in *Foss v Harbottle*.[43] One of the principles enshrined in this rule, and derived from a partnership doctrine,[44] is that matters of internal regulation are under the control of the majority, thereby precluding applications to the court to regulate many matters of internal management.[45] A member of a charitable company who wishes to enforce an administrative provision of the company's constitution may therefore have to surmount two obstacles, both the (structurally based) rule in *Foss v Harbottle* and the (status-based) requirement to obtain the Charity Commissioners' consent to bring charity proceedings.

13.21 An additional reason for discouraging litigation in the charitable sphere has no doubt been the wish to spare, or to deny, charities an involvement in litigation where the benefit secured would be trifling in comparison with the prejudice to the charity's funds of having to bear the costs of an expensive suit.[46]

(2) The meaning of 'charity proceedings'

13.22 It is first necessary to determine whether any proceedings which are to be instituted by or against the charity or its trustees comprise 'charity proceedings'. 'Charity proceedings' means:[47]

> proceedings in any court in England or Wales brought under the court's jurisdiction with respect to charities, or brought under the court's jurisdiction with respect to trusts in relation to the administration of a trust for charitable purposes.

An institution established under the laws of another legal system is not a 'charity' for this purpose, even if it carries out all or some of its objects in England; therefore an action brought in the English courts by or against such an institution does

---

[43] (1843) 2 Hare 461. See further ch 8, paras 8.163–8.167
[44] See KW Wedderburn, 'Shareholders' rights and the rule in *Foss v. Harbottle*' [1957] CLJ 194, 196
[45] See *Carlen v Drury* (1812) 1 V & B 154, 158 (Lord Eldon LC: 'The Court is not to be required on every Occasion to take the Management of every Playhouse and Brewhouse in the Kingdom')
[46] See *A-G v Shearman* (1839) 2 Beav 104, where the majority of trustees of a charitable trust had executed a lease. The minority considered (inter alia) the rent to be inadequate, and in a relator action asked the court to declare the lease void and to refer the matter to the Master for the appointment of new trustees. Lord Langdale MR stated (at 111–12): 'I am of opinion that a prosecution of the accounts and inquiries . . . would be prejudicial and not beneficial to the charity, unless more effectual means than the court possesses could be found of altogether relieving the charity from costs and other prejudice to arise from the prolonged litigation in a matter of such small value; . . . I think it quite proper to discourage long and expensive litigation in charity cases for matters of such small value'; and he ordered the relators to pay the costs of the rehearing. In *Muman v Nagasena* [1999] 4 All ER 178, the Court of Appeal stayed proceedings for possession of land on the ground that they comprised 'charity proceedings' which had been commenced without the necessary authority, and directed that the stay should not be lifted until the parties had attempted mediation. The court expressed the hope that no more of the charity's money would be wasted in the costs of legal proceedings. On mediation, see further ch 14, paras 14.11–14.13 and 14.19
[47] CA 1993, s 33(8)

not comprise 'charity proceedings'.[48] In *Gaudiya Mission v Brahmachary*,[49] it was accepted that Gaudiya Mission ('the Mission', which was not a registered charity in this country) was a corporate body registered in India with objects that would have been entitled to charitable status in England. The Mission had various centres throughout India and also a centre in London. The Mission brought an action against the trustees of the Gaudiya Mission Society Trust (the Trust), which was registered as a charity in England, claiming that it was entitled to the Trust's assets, and that the Trust was passing itself off as the plaintiff mission. The Court of Appeal held that, as an overseas institution, the Mission was not a charity within the meaning of the Charities Act 1993, that its action did not comprise 'charity proceedings', that therefore the leave of the Charity Commissioners was not required, and that the Attorney-General was not a necessary party to the proceedings.

None of the following ranks as charity proceedings: an action to determine **13.23** whether a gift or legacy creates a charitable trust;[50] an action brought against the interests of a charity;[51] a charity's action against a third party (or vice versa) in tort[52] or for breach of contract,[53] or based upon any other right at common law[54] or in equity.[55] By statute, charity proceedings do not include the taking of proceedings in a pending cause or action.[56] If, therefore, money belonging to a charitable trust

---

[48] *Gaudiya Mission v Brahmachary* [1997] 4 All ER 957 (CA), applying *Camille and Henry Dreyfus Foundation Inc v IRC* [1954] Ch 672 (CA), affd [1956] AC 39 (HL), and disapproving of dicta of Turner LJ and Lord Cairns LJ in *Re Duncan* (1867) LR 2 Ch App 356. See further ch 11, paras 11.01–11.02

[49] [1997] 4 All ER 957 (CA)

[50] *Re Shum's Trusts* (1904) 91 LT 192 (summons to determine if land held on charitable trusts or on a resulting trust for the settlor's estate); *Re Belling* [1967] Ch 425; *Hauxwell v Barton-upon-Humber UDC* [1974] Ch 432

[51] *Holme v Guy* (1877) 5 ChD 901; *Benthall v Earl of Kilmorey* (1883) 25 ChD 39. An action by a third party for a declaration as to the validity of a contract entered into with a charity does not comprise charity proceedings: *Haslemere Estates Ltd v Baker* [1982] 1 WLR 1109

[52] eg the tort of passing off: *British Diabetic Association v Diabetic Society of Great Britain* [1995] 4 All ER 812 (Ch D)

[53] *Haslemere Estates Ltd v Baker* [1982] 1 WLR 1109, 1122 (Megarry V-C)

[54] Examples given by James LJ in *Holme v Guy* (1877) 5 ChD 901, 910, include an action for possession against a tenant holding over, distress against a defaulting tenant, and (as in that case itself) an action for an injunction to prevent a former employee from trespassing on the charity's land. In *Bassano v Bradley* [1896] 1 QB 645, an action by trustees of a charity to recover arrears of a rent-charge issuing out of the defendant's land was held not to comprise charity proceedings under Charitable Trusts Act 1853, s 17

[55] In *Rendall v Blair* (1890) 45 ChD 139, 160, Fry LJ expressed the view that an action to enforce 'an individual equitable right, not relating to the administration of the trusts of the charity', would be outside Charitable Trusts Act 1853, s 17. In *Rooke v Dawson* [1895] 1 Ch 480, 488, Chitty J experienced some difficulty in determining precisely what Fry LJ had in mind, but thought it might possibly include 'the case of an equitable right to specific performance of a contract'

[56] CA 1993, s 33(4)

has been paid into court under any statutory provision,[57] an application to the court to deal with it does not fall within the meaning of charity proceedings.[58] On the other hand, an action brought against a trustee for breach of fiduciary duty (whether actual or apprehended) probably does fall within the definition of charity proceedings,[59] as do an application to the Charity Commissioners for an order authorizing the disposal of charity land,[60] and (it appears) an application for leave for judicial review.[61]

13.24   The object of the forerunner of the present section (section 17 of the Charitable Trusts Act 1853)[62]

> was to stop the enormous abuses which had grown up in the administration of charities in reference to proceedings which used to be instituted to the good of no one. It would, however, be a very strong thing to say that if there is a matter in which the Court of Chancery ought to act, it cannot act until it is set in motion by the sanction of the Charity Commissioners.

This dictum is one explanation for a couple of cases in the decades after the Charitable Trusts Act 1853 was passed, which were prepared to entertain petitions from charity trustees[63] (or, if no trustees remained, even local inhabitants[64]) in matters which would appear to concern the administration of charities, even

---

[57]   eg TA 1925, s 63(1) or its predecessors, Trustee Relief Act 1847, s 1, and TA 1893, s 42; in *Re Lister's Hospital* (1855) 6 De GM & G 184, the money had been paid into court pursuant to the Lands Clauses Consolidation Act 1845

[58]   As in both *Re Lister's Hospital* (1855) 6 De GM & G 184 and *Re St Giles & St George Bloomsbury Volunteer Corps* (1858) 25 Beav 313

[59]   See *Construction Industry Training Board v A-G* [1973] Ch 173, 187 (CA). In *Rooke v Dawson* [1895] 1 Ch 480, the trust deed provided for the award of a scholarship to the pupil achieving the best performance in an examination. The trustees declined to award the scholarship to the plaintiff, who had obtained the highest mark and who sought a declaration that he was entitled and an order directing the trustees to make him the award. Chitty J decided that, there being no contract between the plaintiff and the trustees, the former's action was not to enforce any personal right, but rather to enforce the administration of the trusts of the charitable deed. As the Charity Commissioners' certificate had not been obtained under Charitable Trusts Act 1853, s 17, his Lordship held that the action could not proceed

[60]   *Haslemere Estates Ltd v Baker* [1982] 1 WLR 1109; but the order of the Charity Commissioners to authorize such disposals is now required in practice only when the disposal is to a connected person: CA 1993, s 36(2); see ch 17, paras 17.47–17.49

[61]   *R v National Trust, ex p Scott* [1998] JPL 465; and see *Scott v National Trust* [1998] 2 All ER 705, 716 (Robert Walker J). See further below, paras 13.34–13.53

[62]   *Re Lister's Hospital* (1855) 6 De GM & G 184, 186 (Lord Cranworth LC)

[63]   So in *Re Lister's Hospital* itself, trustees of a hospital charity, some of whose lands had been purchased by a railway company, were held entitled, without the Charity Commissioners' sanction under Charitable Trusts Act 1853, s 17, and without the Attorney-General's being a party to the proceedings, to petition the court to have the sale proceeds applied in the purchase of other lands

[64]   As in *Re St Giles & St George Bloomsbury Volunteer Corps* (1858) 25 Beav 313, which concerned a petition to the court to direct a scheme of application of the assets of a volunteer corps. The corps had been established in a number of parishes, but had been disbanded many years earlier and the last trustee had died. The petition was presented by the rectors of two of the parishes. Sir John Romilly MR, applying the principle in *Re Lister's Hospital* (1855) 6 De GM & G 184, held that the certificate of the Charity Commissioners was not necessary in order to make the order

without the Attorney-General's being made a party to the proceedings or the consent of the Charity Commissioners being obtained.[65]

(3) Who may bring charity proceedings?

Charity proceedings may be taken with reference to a charity either by the charity, **13.25** or by any of the charity trustees, or by any person interested in the charity, or by any two or more inhabitants of the area of the charity if it is a local charity, but not by any other person.[66]

If the charity is a corporation, it can bring proceedings in its own name. If it is an **13.26** unincorporated body, it will lack the legal capacity to bring an action itself, and proceedings will have to be brought on its behalf by its trustees.[67]

The phrase 'any person interested in the charity' is uncertain. It cannot be meant **13.27** to include merely a public-spirited person, since there would then be no reason for the express inclusion of inhabitants of the area of a local charity. It has been stated that[68]

> If a person has an interest in securing the due administration of a trust materially greater than, or different from, that possessed by ordinary members of the public . . . that interest may, depending on the circumstances, qualify him as a 'person interested'.

But this is vague; and, on the occasions when the courts have considered the expression, they have declined to provide a definition.[69] Indeed, it has been suggested that the court should not attempt 'to delimit with precision a boundary which Parliament has left undefined'.[70]

It has, however, been held that the executors of a charity's settlor are not 'persons **13.28** interested'.[71] Whether the settlor or a donor is a person interested has yet to be decided; different views have been expressed.[72] A local authority which itself provided facilities for the relief of hardship or distress of persons within its own area was held to be 'a person interested' in a charity whose purpose was the relief of

---

[65] The alternative explanation is that in each case the moneys involved had already been paid into court by the trustee or his executor

[66] CA 1993, s 33(1)

[67] *Re Pritt* (1915) 85 LJ Ch 166

[68] *Re Hampton Fuel Allotment Charity* [1989] Ch 484, 493 (Nicholls LJ)

[69] *Haslemere Estates Ltd v Baker* [1982] 1 WLR 1109, 1122

[70] *Re Hampton Fuel Allotment Charity* [1989] Ch 484, 493 (Nicholls LJ)

[71] 'Executors succeed to the property of the deceased; not to her spirit and disembodied wishes': *Bradshaw v Univ College of Wales, Aberystwyth* [1988] 1 WLR 190 (Hoffmann J)

[72] In *Bradshaw v Univ College of Wales, Aberystwyth* [1988] 1 WLR 190, Hoffmann J evidently thought that the settlor would not qualify. LA Sheridan, *Keeton & Sheridan's Modern Law of Charities* (4th edn, Barry Rose Law Publishers Ltd, 1992), 379, considers that a settlor should not rank as a person interested since a settlor, merely by virtue of being the settlor, has no greater managerial interest in the charity he has founded than has anybody else. In *Re Hampton Fuel Allotment Charity* [1989] Ch 484, however, Nicholls LJ expressly left the point open

hardship or distress of persons resident in part of that area.[73] In contrast to this, a person is not interested in a charity by virtue of an interest which is adverse to the charity, such as a contract with the charity trustees.[74] Thus the phrase does not include 'every tenant of charity land, or those who have easements or profits or mortgages or restrictive covenants over charity land, or those who contract to repair or decorate charity houses, or those who agree to buy goods from the charity or sell goods to the charity'.[75]

13.29   *Brooks v Richardson*[76] concerned the affairs of the Royal Masonic Hospital, which was run by an unincorporated charity established by trust deed. The charity's property was vested in trustees, but the charity was run by a board of management (the board). The charity's constitution made provision for persons to become governors of the charity (which depended upon the payment of a subscription), and it also provided for an annual general meeting of governors to elect various officers, to fill vacancies on the board, to receive an audited balance sheet and annual report from the board, and generally to direct and control the charity's affairs. The plaintiff, who was a governor, objected to a decision of the board to sell the hospital, and he brought an action against the other governors, who were members of the board, and against the charity's chief executive officer, to restrain the sale. He also sought declarations that the defendants were not entitled to refuse to put a motion of no confidence in the board to the charity's general meeting, and that the first defendant was not qualified to act as a member of the board or as a trustee because he had not paid the requisite subscription. A preliminary issue was raised, however, that such action ranked as 'charity proceedings' and that the plaintiff therefore required the Charity Commissioners' consent to bring them (which he had not applied for), and that the Attorney-General also needed to be a party to the proceedings. The plaintiff's argument was that the charity's constitution had a dual effect: that it created a charitable trust, but also constituted the basis of a contract between all the subscribers to the charity (that is, the governors) which regulated their rights and obligations *inter se*, and which each of them was entitled to enforce. The plaintiff argued that in seeking the relief in these proceedings he did not need to invoke the court's jurisdiction with respect to charities or trusts; he was merely invoking the court's jurisdiction to enforce contracts. Warner J, however, rejected this argument. He held that there was no contract

---

[73]   *Re Hampton Fuel Allotment Charity* [1989] Ch 484
[74]   *Haslemere Estates Ltd v Baker* [1982] 1 WLR 1109, where a company which claimed to have entered into a contract to purchase land from charity trustees was held entitled to bring an action for a declaration as to the validity of the contract, since such a declaration did not rank as charity proceedings; but was held not entitled to apply for an order of the Charity Commissioners to sanction a disposal of the land to it, since such application did rank as charity proceedings and the company was not a person interested
[75]   *Haslemere Estates Ltd v Baker* [1982] 1 WLR 1109, 1122 (Megarry V-C)
[76]   [1986] 1 WLR 385

between the governors. The rights acquired as governor, whether through making a donation or not, were not contractual rights but rights to take part in the government of the charity for the benefit of the charity. He said it was noteworthy that the constitution described a governor's rights to take part in the government of the charity as 'privileges', not as 'rights'. His Lordship rejected the analogy of a members' club, because the rights of a member of such a club are rights that he acquires for his own benefit.[77] He also held that there was no reason why the Attorney-General should not be a party to the proceedings.

Two points arise from this decision. First, although Warner J reached the conclusion on the nature of a governor's rights by analysis of the trust deed, it would seem that any rights which relate to participation in the government of an unincorporated charity are necessarily constitutional in nature and cannot be made to confer personal contractual rights on the holder. Secondly, the decision relates only to the rights conferred under the constitution of an unincorporated charity. In the case of a charity incorporated under the Companies Acts, it is statutorily provided that the memorandum and articles, when registered, 'bind the company and its members to the same extent as if they respectively had been signed and sealed by each member and contained covenants on the part of each member to observe all the provisions of the memorandum and of the articles'.[78] A member is, however, unable to enforce every provision of the memorandum or articles; indeed, to permit a member to do so would run counter to the rule in *Foss v Harbottle*,[79] which prevents actions from being brought by minorities to prevent or remedy internal irregularities.[80]   **13.30**

Gunning v Buckfast Abbey Trustees Ltd[81] concerned a fee-paying school run by Benedictine monks as part of the activities of a charitable trust. The trustee decided to close the school because of declining numbers of pupils. Some parents of pupils at the school brought charity proceedings against the trustee (joining the Attorney-General as second defendant), claiming that the trustee's decision was void because it had been made without the consent of the Chapter of the Abbey or the Abbott's Council, which (it was claimed) was required by the trust deed. As a preliminary issue, the trustee argued that the parents' interest in the charity arose only by virtue of their contractual relationship with the trustee, which was, on the authority of *Haslemere Estates Ltd v Baker*,[82] insufficient. Arden J, however, held that the mere fact that such a contract existed did not itself bar the parents from   **13.31**

---

[77] ibid, 390
[78] Companies Act 1985, s 14(1). See further *Boyle & Birds' Company Law* (ed J Birds, E Ferran, and C Villiers) (3rd edn, Jordans, 1995) 70–3
[79] (1843) 2 Hare 461
[80] See *Boyle & Birds' Company Law* (ed J Birds, E Ferran, and C Villiers) (3rd edn, Jordans, 1995) 492–506; and see further ch 8, paras 8.161–8.169
[81] The Times, 9 June 1994
[82] [1982] 1 WLR 1109

bringing charity proceedings. They would be barred if they sought to use the charity proceedings to assist them to pursue an adverse claim against the trustee; this was not, however, the object of these proceedings. Her Ladyship accepted the submissions of counsel for the parents and for the Attorney-General that the parents were persons interested in the charity both through the benefit to themselves of having their children educated as they wished, and because of their natural and moral concern for their children's education as well as the legal obligation to educate them. These elements gave them an interest which was materially different from that enjoyed by a member of the public.

13.32 In *Scott v National Trust*,[83] the plaintiffs, who comprised persons who had formerly hunted under licence on National Trust land and tenant farmers, had obtained the consent of the Charity Commissioners to bring proceedings by originating summons against the National Trust. The National Trust applied to have the summons struck out on the ground that the plaintiffs were not 'persons interested' within section 33(1) of the Charities Act 1993. Robert Walker J dismissed the National Trust's application. He considered that the plaintiffs were 'persons interested' because they could be treated as partners with the National Trust in the management of the land and the preservation of its deer, whose preservation could be fairly regarded as falling within one of the National Trust's statutory purposes.[84] The plaintiffs' interest was therefore materially greater than or different from that possessed by ordinary members of the public in securing the charity's due administration.[85]

(4) Consent of the Charity Commissioners

13.33 Generally, no charity proceedings relating to a charity (other than an exempt charity)[86] are to be entertained or proceeded with in any court unless the taking of the proceedings is authorized by order of the Charity Commissioners.[87] The Commissioners may not, without special reasons, authorize the taking of charity proceedings where, in their opinion, the case can be dealt with by them under the

---

[83] [1998] 2 All ER 705

[84] ibid, 715; see National Trust Act 1907, s 4(1)

[85] [1998] 2 All ER 705, 713–15

[86] In *Baldry v Feintuck* [1972] 1 WLR 552, some members of the students' union of Sussex University applied to the court for an injunction to stop the union from altering its constitution so as to enable it to apply its funds to non-charitable objects, or to charitable objects that were not an object of the students' union. It was conceded that the union was a charity, and it had been treated as such by the Inland Revenue, but the union was evidently not registered as a charity with the Charity Commissioners. The Charity Commissioners' consent to the proceedings does not appear to have been sought or obtained; and, whilst the report offers no explanation for this, it would appear to be justified on the basis that the students' union, being constituted by the ordinances of the university, was treated as a subsidiary charity of the university, and therefore as a part of an exempt charity. This does not, however, explain the omission to join the Attorney-General as a party to the proceedings

[87] CA 1993, s 33(2)

powers conferred on them by the Charities Act 1993.[88] If the Charity Commissioners' order for the taking of charity proceedings has been applied for and refused, such proceedings may nevertheless be entertained or proceeded with if leave to take the proceedings has been obtained from a judge of the Chancery Division.[89]

D. Judicial review

(1) Charities that are subject to judicial review

A person aggrieved by a decision of a body exercising public functions in a matter **13.34** of sufficient concern to the public may apply to the court for the public law remedy of judicial review. As Robert Walker J recently stated in *Scott v National Trust*,[90] a successful application for judicial review is generally founded on the public officer or body in question exceeding his or its statutory powers or on procedural irregularity or unfairness, or unreasonableness in the extreme sense indicated by Lord Greene MR in the *Wednesbury* case.[91]

Judicial review is available only to challenge the decision-making process of bodies **13.35** which either derive their power from statute or the Royal prerogative, or exercise public functions;[92] and to be subject to judicial review, the decision must affect the rights and legitimate expectations of citizens, and be of a kind which the law requires to be exercised in accordance with the rules of natural justice.[93] Whilst the element of public benefit runs through all charities, it is clear that not all charities are to be treated as exercising public functions.[94] In *R v National Trust, ex parte Scott*,[95] Tucker J was evidently prepared to treat the National Trust, which was conceded to be a charity,[96] as prima facie amenable to judicial review, as he considered its decision to ban deer-hunting on some of its estates 'as being

---

[88] ibid, s 33(3), excluding, however, for this purpose, the Commissioners' powers under s 32 (ie to take legal proceedings or to compromise claims)

[89] CA 1993, s 33(5). The first application to a judge of the Chancery Division for leave to bring charity proceedings following a refusal of the Commissioners to authorize such proceedings came to the Commissioners' notice in 1979: see [1979] Ch Com Rep 21 (paras 56–8). The application (under the predecessor of s 33(5), viz CA 1960, s 28(5)) had been brought by a dissenting Governor of Dulwich College Picture Gallery; in the event, the judge refused leave

[90] [1998] 2 All ER 705, 710–11

[91] *Associated Provincial Picture Houses Ltd v Wednesbury Corp* [1948] 1 KB 223; and see *Council of Civil Service Unions v Minister for the Civil Service* [1985] AC 374, 410–11 (Lord Diplock) (the *GCHQ* case)

[92] *R v Panel on Take-overs and Mergers, ex p Datafin plc* [1987] QB 815 CA

[93] *Leech v Deputy Governor of Parkhurst Prison* [1988] AC 533, 561 (Lord Bridge) (HL)

[94] cf *R v East Berkshire Health Authoirty, ex p Walsh* [1985] QB 152, 164, where Donaldson MR said there was no warrant 'for equating public loss with the interest of the public'

[95] [1998] JPL 465

[96] See *Re Verrall* [1916] 1 Ch 100

arguably taken by a statutory body exercising public functions, so as to justify the engagement of public law remedies'.[97] This statement should not be taken to suggest that only a statutory body is susceptible to judicial review, as this is manifestly not so.[98] In later proceedings involving the National Trust's hunting ban, *Scott v National Trust*,[99] Robert Walker J said that he did not think it was helpful, or even possible, to consider the broad question of whether any charity, or even any charity established by statute, is subject to judicial review. He did however take cognizance of the fact that[100]

> the National Trust is a charity of exceptional importance to the nation, regulated by its own special Acts of Parliament. Its purposes and functions are of high public importance, as is reflected by . . . special statutory provisions (in the fields of taxation and compulsory acquisition). . . . It seems to me to have all the characteristics of a public body which is, prima facie, amenable to judicial review, and to have been exercising its statutory public functions in making the decision which is challenged.

(2) Locus standi and leave to apply for judicial review

13.36   Even if it is decided that a particular charity does exercise public functions, so that its decisions are capable of being judicially reviewed, an applicant seeking judicial review must be able to establish locus standi. The applicant must be aggrieved by the decision, which requires him to have a sufficient interest in it; and, for leave to bring such proceedings, he must be able to establish an arguable case.

13.37   In *R v National Trust, ex p Scott*,[101] members of two hunts and the chairman of the Tenant Farmers' Group applied for leave for judicial review of the decision of the Council of the National Trust to end deer-hunting on National Trust land and not to renew licences for hunting red deer after that season. Tucker J considered that the applicants had a sufficient interest in the Council's decision to give them locus standi to make their application. He also considered that the applicants had an arguable case for judicial review, both because the Council of the National Trust did not give the applicants an opportunity to make representations before making its final decision, and because the applicants had a legitimate expectation, created by past practice, that their hunting leases would be renewed until and unless deer-hunting was outlawed. [102]

---

[97]   *R v National Trust, ex p Scott* [1998] JPL 465, 466. The National Trust was incorporated originally under the Companies Acts, and then by the National Trust Act 1907

[98]   eg *R v Panel on Take-overs and Mergers, ex p Datafin plc* [1987] QB 815

[99]   [1998] 2 All ER 705

[100]   ibid, 716

[101]   [1998] JPL 465

[102]   These points did not arise for decision in the subsequent proceedings before Robert Walker J in *Scott v National Trust* [1998] 2 All ER 705. As to the possible application in the law of charities of the analogous pension-fund doctrine of reasonable expectation, see ch 9, paras 9.136–9.140

(3) Restrictions on availability of judicial review

Where there is an alternative remedy of charity proceedings

Even if the charity in question is exercising public functions which would under general principles make it susceptible to judicial review, if the application comprises 'charity proceedings', the application may effectively be barred. In the two sets of proceedings involving the National Trust, however, the respective judges expressed differing views in regard to the precise relationship between judicial review and charity proceedings.[103] **13.38**

In *R v National Trust, ex p Scott,* Tucker J pointed out that the National Trust's status as a charity meant that the members of its Council were charity trustees for the purposes of the Charities Act 1993.[104] He took the view that the substance of the complaint was against a decision made by the charity trustees in the exercise of their discretionary powers in the management of the National Trust's property, and so related to the conduct of its affairs as a charity. In Tucker J's opinion, the submission that the National Trust was a public body performing public functions could relate only to the National Trust's administration of its affairs, with the result that the proceedings were charity proceedings.[105] As the requisite consent of the Charity Commissioners to such proceedings had not been obtained, he held that he had no jurisdiction to entertain the application, which was therefore dismissed. **13.39**

The effect of Tucker J's decision is that applications for judicial review of decisions of charitable bodies will (unless the charity is an exempt charity) comprise charity proceedings, and so will be subject to the additional hurdle of Charity Commissioners' consent as well as the need to obtain the leave of a judge for judicial review. As a matter of principle, the existence of two sets of leave in cases of this nature is difficult to justify.[106] **13.40**

Following Tucker J's decision, the applicants sought the Charity Commissioners' leave to commence charity proceedings. The Commissioners granted leave to commence proceedings by way of originating summons, but refused to authorize an application for judicial review because, in their opinion (which was clearly different from that of Tucker J), judicial review proceedings would not be charity proceedings.[107] The plaintiffs applied for leave to take judicial review proceedings against the National Trust and for injunctive relief. The application was heard by Robert Walker J in *Scott v National Trust.*[108] **13.41**

---

[103] *R v National Trust, ex p Scott* [1998] JPL 465 (Tucker J); *Scott v National Trust* [1998] 2 All ER 705 (Robert Walker J)

[104] CA 1993, s 97(1)

[105] *R v National Trust, ex p Scott* [1998] JPL 465, 467

[106] See commentary to *R v National Trust, ex p Scott* [1998] JPL 465, ibid, 468

[107] See *Scott v National Trust* [1998] 2 All ER 705, 716 (Robert Walker J)

[108] [1998] 2 All ER 705

13.42   Commenting on the divergence of opinion between Tucker J and the Charity Commissioners on the question of whether judicial review proceedings would be charity proceedings, Robert Walker J said that Tucker J's view was to be preferred, but he did not find it necessary to express a concluded opinion.[109] Robert Walker J nevertheless refused leave to apply for judicial review because it was well established that judicial review will not normally be granted where an alternative remedy is available, whether by appeal or otherwise.[110] He said that the special procedure which Parliament has laid down for the judicial monitoring of charities—charity proceedings in the Chancery Division—is the procedure that should be followed 'in all but the most exceptional cases'.[111] He speculated that a possible exception might be where a local authority held land on charitable trusts and questions about its dealings with that land were caught up with other questions about its dealings with land which it owned beneficially (though subject, of course, to statutory constraints). But he could see no good reason for making an exception in the case before him:[112] the plaintiffs had gone some considerable way down the road of their originating summons proceedings, and he had already held that they had a sufficient interest so to do. In these circumstances, his Lordship thought that it would be less convenient (not more) if they had to go through the double filter of consent to charity proceedings (under section 33 of the Charities Act 1993) and leave for judicial review (under section 31 of the Supreme Court Act 1981) in order to bring the substance of their complaint before the High Court. He thought that the right course was for the plaintiffs to proceed with their charity proceedings (the originating summons), and that to have judicial review proceedings would be 'simply wasteful duplication', and he accordingly refused to grant the plaintiffs leave for judicial review proceedings.

13.43   The upshot of these decisions is that whereas Tucker J treated judicial review proceedings as charity proceedings, so as to require the plaintiffs to go through a double filter, Robert Walker J treated the availability of charity proceedings as an alternative route to bringing the substance of the matter before the court, which thereby precluded judicial review proceedings from being brought. On the other hand, Robert Walker J's reference to the plaintiffs' having already gone a considerable way down the road of their originating summons seems to suggest that he was not laying down as a matter of law that the availability of charity proceedings necessarily precludes proceedings by way of judicial review. Furthermore, whilst the presence of a double filter is difficult to justify, it can hardly be a reason to deny the plaintiff access to judicial review.

---

[109]   1998 2 All ER 705, 716
[110]   ibid, 716, referring to *R v Chief Constable of the Merseyside Police, ex p Calveley* [1986] QB 424 (CA)
[111]   *Scott v National Trust* [1998] 2 All ER 705, 716
[112]   ibid, 716–17

The present position is therefore anything but satisfactory, particularly given that **13.44** whether a person can be considered to have a sufficient interest to bring charity proceedings is often uncertain. This was no doubt the reason why, following Tucker J's rejection of their application for judicial review, the huntsmen began parallel proceedings by way of originating summons. In view of the uncertainty, they were clearly taking every precaution to avoid being thwarted by what they might well regard as a technicality.[113]

Neither of the judgments in the National Trust litigation does much to clarify the **13.45** differences in nature between judicial review proceedings and charity proceedings; although Robert Walker J did say that he was inclined to think that legitimate expectation, which is of enormous importance in judicial review,[114] has 'some part to play' in trusts law also.[115] It appears that, for Tucker J, it was the nature of the remedy which the huntsmen sought, namely judicial review (as opposed, for example, to damages) which brought their action within the definition of charity proceedings. Some of the older cases did indeed decide that whether proceedings comprised charity proceedings or otherwise depended on the remedy sought.[116] This does not itself indicate into which category the remedy of judicial review falls; but, in any event, the more modern approach to charity proceedings is to look at the nature of the claim, and to determine whether it is adverse to the charity.[117] Charity proceedings can be brought by a person who (in a technical sense) is merely 'interested' in the charity, and has no adverse claim; whereas proceedings for judicial review can be brought only by a person aggrieved. There is surely a persuasive case for treating an action for judicial review of the decision of a charity as in nature adverse to the charity in question. In the National Trust litigation, for instance, although the huntsmen evidently had no contractual rights against the charity, they were essentially in dispute with it in regard to their right to hunt; their claim to a public law remedy was in substance adverse to the charity. Since a claim adverse to a charity does not comprise charity proceedings,[118] there is no logic or merit in treating such action as charity proceedings merely because the remedy sought is judicial review.

If a charity is an exempt charity, it is not subject to the restrictions on charity pro- **13.46** ceedings contained in the Charities Act 1993.[119] An applicant for judicial review

---

[113] ibid, 717

[114] See the *GCHQ* case: *Council of Civil Service Unions v Minister for the Civil Service* [1985] AC 374, 401, 408

[115] *Scott v National Trust* [1998] 2 All ER 705, 718. On the relevance of legitimate or reasonable expectation in trusts law, see ch 9, paras 9.136–9.140

[116] *Benthall v Earl of Kilmourey* (1883) 25 ChD 39; *Rendall v Blair* (1890) 45 ChD 139; see also *Scott v National Trust* [1998] 2 All ER 705, 713

[117] *Haslemere Estates Ltd v Baker* [1982] 1 WLR 1109, 1122 (Megarry V-C)

[118] ibid

[119] CA 1993, s 33(2)

against an exempt charity does not therefore risk his application being rejected on the ground that charity proceedings are an alternative available remedy, although the possibility of other remedies against the exempt charity (for example, a claim for damages in contract) will preclude judicial review.

Where judicial review concerns a breach of a Convention right

13.47 The Human Rights Act 1998 makes it unlawful for a public authority to act in a way which is incompatible with a Convention right.[120] Although there is no definition of 'public authority' in the Act, it is likely that any body which is a public body for the purposes of judicial review will be treated as a public authority for the purposes of the Act, which would include a number of charities (including the National Trust).[121]

13.48 A person who claims that a charity which is a public authority has acted (or proposes to act) in a way which is incompatible with a Convention right may bring proceedings against such charity in the appropriate court or tribunal.[122] If, however, the proceedings are brought on an application for judicial review, the applicant is to be taken to have a sufficient interest in relation to the unlawful act only if he is, or would be, a victim of that act.[123] Case law in Strasbourg has established that a person ranks as a 'victim' for this purpose only if he is (or there is a risk that he might be) actually and directly affected by the act or omission in question.[124] A representative body with special expertise will normally have locus standi to bring proceedings by way of judicial review, which has enabled such proceedings to be brought by some charities;[125] but it is possible that a representative group (such as a charity) would not comprise a 'victim' for present purposes, unless perhaps its members included persons who could be considered to be victims.[126]

13.49 It appears that the courts have more scope to review decisions of public authorities where Convention rights are in issue than they currently have in judicial review proceedings, since the Strasbourg courts start from the presumption that Convention rights should be protected.[127] The *Wednesbury* test[128] will probably

---

[120] Human Rights Act 1998, s 6(1). An act is not 'unlawful' if the public authority was constrained by legislation to act as it did: ibid, s 6(2): see further ch 1 paras 1.94–1.95

[121] For further discussion of which charities might be 'public authorities' for the purposes of the Human Rights Act 1998, see ch 1, paras 1.88–1.96

[122] Human Rights Act 1998, s 7(1)(a)

[123] ibid, s 7(3)

[124] *Klass v Germany* (1978) 2 EHRR 214

[125] eg *R v Sefton Metropolitan BC, ex p Help the Aged* [1997] 4 All ER 532; *R v Lord Chancellor, ex p Child Poverty Action Group* [1998] 2 All ER 755

[126] See P Cane, 'Standing up for the public' [1995] PL 276; J Wadham & H Mountfield, *Blackstone's Guide to the Human Rights Act 1998* (Blackstone Press, 1999) 38–41

[127] J Wadham, & H Mountfield, *Blackstone's Guide to the Human Rights Act 1998* (Blackstone Press, 1999) 14

[128] *Associated Provincial Picture Houses Ltd v Wednesbury Corp* [1948] 1 KB 223; and see the

have no application where the review concerns an alleged breach of Convention rights.

If the Human Rights Act 1998 had been in force when the huntsmen in the **13.50** National Trust litigation brought their initial action, it might have been open to them to argue that the National Trust (evidently a public authority) had breached Convention rights in banning them from hunting deer on its land, and that they were victims of that breach. They might have been able to allege that the National Trust had breached Article 6 of the Convention (that is, the right to a fair hearing in determining their civil rights) and (rather less plausibly, perhaps) that it had breached Article 1 of the First Protocol (that is, the right not to be unlawfully deprived of their possessions, namely their licences). Provided such unlawful acts could be established, the huntsmen themselves would have had no difficulty in showing that they were the 'victims' of such acts; but the tenant farmers who had joined in the application might not have satisfied this criterion.

Proceedings against a public authority alleging breach of Convention rights must **13.51** be brought within one year from the date on which the act complained of took place, unless the court considers a longer period should be allowed, but subject to any rule imposing a stricter time limit in relation to the procedure in question.[129] There is a stricter time limit in respect of proceedings by way of judicial review, namely three months from the date when the grounds for the application first arose, unless the court considers that there is good reason for extending the period.[130]

The better view is that proceedings brought against a charity by way of judicial re- **13.52** view in respect of an alleged breach of a Convention right are not 'charity proceedings'[131] and do not need the Charity Commissioners' consent.[132] In this respect, therefore, it makes no difference whether the review proceedings involve a breach of Convention rights or not.

Where charity has a Visitor

If a charity is an eleemosynary corporation with a Visitor, the Visitor has jurisdic- **13.53** tion exclusive of the courts in matters governed by the corporation's internal laws. No proceedings for judicial review can therefore be brought against such a charity, the appropriate proceedings being an application to the Visitor. Judicial review is restricted in such cases to review of the decisions of the Visitor. The

---

GCHQ case, *Council of Civil Service Unions v Minister for the Civil Service* [1985] AC 374, 410–411 (Lord Diplock)

[129] Human Rights Act 1998, s 7(5)
[130] See RSC Ord 53, r 4(1), scheduled to CPR 1998, Pt 50
[131] CA 1993, s 33
[132] See the general discussion of charity proceedings and judicial review, above, paras 13.38–13.46

universities of Oxford and Cambridge and the newer universities[133] are civil corporations, and do not have Visitors; they are, however, considered to be public bodies and are thereby subject to the general principles of judicial review.[134] The scope of judicial review in relation to the visitatorial jurisdiction is considered more fully in chapter 12.

E. Breach of Convention rights and private law proceedings

13.54 A person who claims that a public authority has acted (or proposes to act) in a way which is unlawful because it inconsistent with a Convention right may bring proceedings against the authority under the Human Rights Act 1998 in any court or tribunal,[135] provided that he is (or would be) a victim of that act.[136] Such proceedings (as has been discussed) can be public law proceedings by way of judicial review; but they can also be private law proceedings against the public authority for breach of statutory duty. The Act specifically provides that, in relation to any act (or proposed act) of a public authority which the court finds is (or would be) unlawful,[137] it may grant such relief or remedy, or make such order, within its powers as it considers just and appropriate.[138] No award of damages (meaning damages for an unlawful act of a public authority[139]) is to be made unless, taking account of all the circumstances of the case, the court is satisfied that the award is necessary to afford just satisfaction to the person in whose favour it is made.[140] The circumstances to be taken into account include any other relief or remedy granted, or order made, in relation to the act in question (by that or any other court),[141] and the consequences of any decision (of that or any other court) in respect of that act.[142]

13.55 It is suggested that proceedings against a charity for a breach of statutory duty under the Human Rights Act 1998 are not 'charity proceedings',[143] since the claim is essentially the enforcement of a right against the charity. The prior consent of the Charity Commissioners is not therefore required.

---

[133] ie those which took advantage of the power conferred by the Further and Higher Education Act 1992 to call themselves universities

[134] *R v Manchester Metropolitan Univ, ex p Nolan* [1994] ELR 380 (DC)

[135] Human Rights Act 1998, ss 6(1), 7(1)

[136] ibid, s 7(1). The meaning of 'victim' was considered above, paras 13.48–13.50. An act is not 'unlawful' if the public authority was constrained by legislation to act as it did: ibid, s 6(2): see further ch 1, paras 1.94–1.95

[137] This means unlawful under Human Rights Act, s 6(1): ibid, s 8(6)

[138] ibid, s 8(1)

[139] ibid, s 8(6)

[140] ibid, s 8(3)

[141] ibid, s 8(3)(a)

[142] ibid, s 8(3)(b)

[143] CA 1993, s 33

14

MEDIATION AND DISPUTE RESOLUTION

A. Introduction

Charities may be involved in a variety of disputes, but these are essentially of three **14.01** kinds. First, there are internal disputes between those involved in the charity, either as groups or as individuals. There may, for instance, be disputes between rival groups of members, or between the trustees and the members, or between the charity and one or more of its employees. Secondly, there may be disputes between a charity and a third party, such as a contractor or supplier, or a local authority, a landlord or a tenant. Thirdly, there may be disputes between different charities.

It may be necessary, or sometimes appropriate, to resolve a dispute through litiga-**14.02** tion. Litigation may ultimately be the only option to a charity if the other party is not amenable to settling the dispute in some other way, notably through the use of mediation. Litigation may also be necessary as a last resort if the charity has a substantial and indisputable claim (for example, in contract) against another party who proves entirely intractable. Litigation may also be appropriate where it may help to resolve a point of law of importance to the charity in relation to other potential disputes in which it might be involved (for example, if the point relates to one of many leases which a charity has granted in standard form).

In many circumstances, however, litigation is likely to prove unhelpful. The very **14.03** nature of charities tends to inspire a deep personal commitment on the part of those involved with them, but this can sometimes go too far and spill over into fruitless disputation. Where an action comprises 'charity proceedings', it cannot proceed without the consent of the Charity Commissioners or leave of a judge of

the Chancery Division.[1] If no leave is given, the claimant will either have no redress at all, or will have to attempt some other means of reaching a settlement.

B. A charity's internal procedures

14.04   Some kinds of internal dispute may often be satisfactorily resolved through the
use of an institution's own internal procedures. Some types of charities have well-
established procedures for dealing with disputes internally, for example the
statutes of many universities make provision for grievance procedures, which can
be invoked by individual students or staff who wish to complain that the university has not dealt with them properly or fairly. The constitutions of many other
sorts of charities, however, have no history of making express provision for internal dispute resolution.[2] If a charity has members in addition to the charity trustees
themselves, it might be advisable for it to consider the merits of introducing an
internal dispute resolution procedure by way of amendment to the governing
instrument. The Charity Law Association's model constitution for a charitable
unincorporated association empowers the Committee to resolve or establish procedures to assist the resolution of disputes within the association;[3] and its model
constitution for a charitable company limited by guarantee empowers the directors to establish procedures to assist the resolution of disputes within the charity.[4]
These provisions effectively place the responsibility of finding a solution to internal disputes on the Committee and the directors respectively.[5]

14.05   In the absence of internal dispute procedures, it is still possible for the parties to
avoid litigation if they agree to the involvement of an independent third party
in the resolution of the dispute through one of the procedures which are together
referred to as alternative dispute resolution.

---

[1] CA 1993, s 33

[2] In 1976, the Charity Commissioners noted that many administrative provisions in governing
instruments of religious charities established primarily for the benefit of immigrant members of the
community and their descendants are often so badly drafted or so elaborate that their full implications were probably not appreciated when they were adopted. This can itself lead to disputes later
on: [1976] Ch Com Rep 29–30 (paras 109–12)

[3] CLA, Constitution for a Charitable Unincorporated Association, r 8.6

[4] CLA, Memorandum and Articles of Association for a Charitable Company Limited by
Guarantee, art 5.7

[5] CLA, Constitution for a Charitable Unincorporated Association, p 16 (Note to r 8.6);
Memorandum and Articles of Association for a Charitable Company Limited by Guarantee, p 22
(Note to art 5.7)

C. Alternative dispute resolution

Alternative dispute resolution (ADR) describes the procedures which are available   **14.06**
to resolve, or to attempt to resolve, disputes without resort to litigation. ADR
comprises three separate processes: arbitration, conciliation, and mediation. In
the United Kingdom, the first two of these have been used for many years; whereas
the last, mediation, is relatively new.[6]

All three methods of ADR involve the bringing in of an independent third party,   **14.07**
and none of them can be used without the agreement of all the parties. From this
point, however, the different methods of ADR differ significantly. Arbitration
differs from the other two in that an arbitrator's decision binds the parties;
whereas any resolution of a dispute where conciliation or mediation is used depends upon the parties' agreement. Conciliation differs from mediation essentially in that the role of the conciliator is a more passive one; whereas a mediator
will be more active in suggesting solutions to the disputants, the conciliator is
merely there to aid them in resolving their disagreement themselves.

(1) Arbitration

Arbitration is useful where the parties need to obtain a decision. If a dispute is to   **14.08**
be referred to an arbitrator, it must be with the agreement of the parties, although
they may agree to this in advance: many leases, for example, make provision for
the referral of disputes involving rent review to an arbitrator. Arbitration may also
be used in other contexts, notably in industrial disputes.

Although arbitration avoids litigation, it is itself a judicial process, governed by   **14.09**
the Arbitration Act 1996; and an arbitrator is answerable to the court and must
abide by the rules of natural justice. An arbitrator is essentially determining an
issue between the parties, and his decision should therefore fall between the limits of the parties' differences. A most important difference between arbitration on
the one hand, and conciliation and mediation on the other, is that the award of the
arbitrator is binding on the parties; and, provided the arbitrator has acted within
his terms of reference[7] and there is no 'serious irregularity' of a specified kind[8]
which the court considers 'has caused or will cause substantial injustice' to the applicant,[9] his award cannot be challenged in court.[10]

---

[6] See R Singh, 'Mediation and charities' (1995) NLJ Christmas Appeals Suppl 28; R Singh,
'Alternative dispute resolution: a gift for charities' (1996–7) 4 CL & PR 73; F Quint, 'Alternative
Dispute Resolution in the Charitable Sector' in *The Henderson Top 2000 Charities* (Hemmington
Scott Publishing Ltd, 1995), 1–4
[7] Arbitration Act 1996, s 67
[8] ie as set out in Arbitration Act 1996, s 68(2)(a)–(h)
[9] ibid, s 68(2)
[10] This is subject to the qualification that a party may appeal from the arbitrator on a question of
law, but (unless the parties agree) only with the court's leave: Arbitration Act 1996, s 69(1), (2)

(2) Conciliation

14.10 The role of a conciliator is to aid the parties to reach their own solution to the dispute. A conciliator may indicate to the parties what their options are, and may try to nudge the parties towards a settlement; but unlike a mediator, a conciliator is not permitted to make recommendations to the parties involved. Conciliation is not significantly used outside industrial disputes, where it provides a statutory procedure for the attempted settling of a dispute before it goes to a tribunal.

(3) Mediation

14.11 A mediator takes a more active role than a conciliator, and may suggest solutions to the parties. The resolution of the dispute still depends, however, upon the agreement of the parties themselves.

14.12 The advantages of mediation over legal proceedings are several. First, mediation is cheaper and quicker: it is usually possible to arrange an early date for mediation, and the mediation itself often takes merely one day. Secondly, it is less formal and less confrontational: the mediation process generally does less damage than legal proceedings to future relations between the parties, since, unlike the legal process, the outcome does not involve a winner and a loser, because it is the result of the parties' agreement. A further advantage is that mediation is confidential to the parties; and this is particularly important for charities, which might find it preferable to litigation, with its risk of adverse publicity. The Charity Commissioners have stated that they have no objection to a charity's paying the reasonable costs of a mediation service, if, without mediation, the dispute is likely to continue and to result in even greater cost to the charity in the long run.[11]

14.13 Mediation in the United Kingdom began only with the establishment of the Advisory Conciliation and Arbitration Service (ACAS) in 1974. In 1993, the Centre for Dispute Resolution (CEDR) introduced a Charities Group to settle differences in the charity sector, and the National Council for Voluntary Organisations (NCVO) introduced a pilot dispute resolution service in 1995 (which, however, excluded disputes between charities). Since 1998, CEDR and NCVO have formed a joint mediation service for voluntary organizations, which is supported by the Active Community Unit of the Home Office. The cost of mediation using this service varies according to the size of the organization and whether the dispute is an internal one. All mediators used in this service are CEDR-accredited and work to CEDR's service guarantee. The CEDR–NCVO mediation service was specifically referred to recently in *Muman v Nagasena* by Mummery LJ, who said:[12]

---

[11] [1996] Ch Com Rep 23 (para 152)
[12] [1999] 4 All ER 178, 184 (CA)

It has received a grant from the Home Office, which is the government department responsible for the Charity Commission. The purpose of that grant is to subsidise the costs of mediating charity disputes. The purpose of the scheme is to achieve, by voluntary action confidentially conducted, a healing process under which disputes within a charity can be resolved at a modest fee and without diminishing the funds which have been raised for charitable purposes.

D. The role of the Charity Commissioners

Often one of the parties to a dispute involving a charity will inform the Charity **14.14** Commissioners. In many instances, however, the claims made lack any substance. The Charity Commissioners have explained the problem thus:[13]

> The internal disputes we see, arise typically from personality clashes, differences of view over the charity's policy and direction, or disagreement about its constitutional requirements. We receive complaints, accusations and counter-accusations of misconduct from the parties involved. When we examine these claims few can be sustained with objective evidence. Many are made with a view to discrediting opponents. Often a resolution depends on the attitudes of the parties involved and not, whatever they believe, on the exercise of some statutory power we are assumed to possess.

In appropriate cases, the Charity Commissioners have in the past made strenuous **14.15** efforts to encourage the parties to resolve internal charity disputes by mediation; but if the parties prove intractable (as they often are in disputes amongst members of religious charities), resort to the courts may ultimately be the only solution. Internal disputes in religious charities may involve interpretation or application of doctrine; where such discord leads to schisms, the outcome can too often be litigation.[14] The fact that the Commissioners may have authorized 'charity proceedings' in a particular case, however, is no safeguard to the parties that they will be awarded their costs[15]—and this should serve as a warning to charity trustees and their members to take mediation seriously.

---

[13] [1996] Ch Com Rep 22 (para 147). Also on internal charity disputes, see [1984] Ch Com Rep 18 (paras 48–50)

[14] See, eg, the disputes between members of the fundamentalist Christian sect known as the Exclusive Brethren: [1974] Ch Com Rep 22–3 (paras 78–81); [1976] Ch Com Rep 33–6 (paras 128–31, and Press Notice)

[15] See *Guru Arjan Dev Gurudawara Sikh Temple, Derby* [1985] Ch Com Rep 28–9 (paras 86–9). The Charity Commissioners had made great efforts to resolve a dispute between groups of members of the Sikh Temple, including the making of three visits to Derby by one of the Commissioners' staff to try to seek agreement between them. The Commissioners' attempts at mediation were in vain, and they eventually authorized the bringing of charity proceedings by one of the groups, which sought various reliefs including the establishment of a scheme. The judge approved a scheme for the interim administration of the charity, and ordered the costs of the Attorney-General to be met on a common fund basis out of the Temple's funds; but he ordered the other parties to bear personally their respective costs

14.16   In 1996, the Charity Commissioners began research to identify the 'early warning signs' of internal disputes, in order to see whether (and if so why) some particular types of charities are particularly prone to such disputes. The Commissioners have also produced standard guidance for those bringing a complaint to them. The guidance explains what powers the Commissioners have to intervene in such cases, and emphasizes that the responsibility for the policies and activities of a charity lies with the trustees. The guidance also points out that the Commissioners will not take up any complaint which is the product of discontent with a decision properly made in the management of a charity.[16]

14.17   The Commissioners take the view that they do not themselves have the power to arbitrate or to adjudicate in charity disputes. The Commissioners reached this conclusion for two reasons: first, because the Charities Act 1993 expressly denies them the power 'to act in the administration of a charity';[17] and, secondly, because they formerly[18] possessed a limited power to arbitrate, but this was repealed and not replaced, the inference being that Parliament did not intend the Commissioners to function as an arbitrator.[19] The Commissioners, however, do consider that they have a power to mediate;[20] and, in 1998, they established a small team to provide a specialized service to deal with charity disputes, including the secondment to them of a trained mediator.[21]

E.   Alternative dispute resolution in the course of litigation

14.18   The 'overriding objective' of the Civil Procedure Rules 1999 ('the Rules')[22] is 'enabling the court to deal with cases justly'.[23] Furthermore, '[t]he court must further the overriding objective by actively managing cases'.[24] One of the means by which the court will actively manage cases is specified in a (non-exhaustive) list, and includes:[25]

---

[16] [1996] Ch Com Rep 22 (para 148); see also Charity Commission, *Resolving Charity Disputes: Our Role*, CC 25 (Mar 2000)

[17] CA 1993, s 1(4)

[18] ie until CA 1960. Under Charitable Trusts Act 1853, s 64, disputes among members of exempt charities could be referred to the Charity Commissioners for arbitration. More generally, under ibid, s 23, the Charity Commissioners had a power to compromise claims which trustees of charitable trusts might have against third parties. The trustees or the third party (with the trustees' consent) could submit a proposal for compromise to the Charity Commissioners, who could, following an inquiry, make an order compromising the claim as the Commissioners should think fit. The order would bar the parties' right to the courts in respect of such dispute. The Charitable Trusts Act 1853 was repealed by CA 1960, s 48(2) and Sch 7, Pt I

[19] [1996] Ch Com Rep 22 (para 151)

[20] ibid, 23 (para 152)

[21] [1998] Ch Com Rep 15–16

[22] Introduced 26 Apr 1999

[23] Civil Procedure Rules 1999, r 1.1(1)

[24] ibid, r 1.4(1)

[25] ibid, r 1.4(2)(e)

encouraging the parties to use an alternative dispute resolution procedure if the court considers that appropriate and facilitating the use of such procedure.

In order, so far as possible, to remove from the courts those disputes that can be effectively resolved either through negotiation or through ADR, the Rules have also introduced pre-action protocols. These seek to obtain information about the case to enable the court to allocate the case to a track.[26] Once a case has been defended in its entirety, the court sends the parties an allocation questionnaire, and the first question asks the parties if they wish there to be a one-month stay to attempt to settle the case. Solicitors acting for a charity must therefore be aware of the availability of alternative forms of dispute resolution and inform the charity of such alternatives.

In *Muman v Nagasena*,[27] some members of a charity brought an action for posses-   **14.19** sion of premises owned by the charity against the occupier and licensee, the Patron of the charity, on the ground that he had been replaced as Patron at a meeting of the charity. The Court of Appeal held that the proceedings were charity proceedings, and that, as they had not been authorized by either the Charity Commissioners or a judge, they should be stayed. Mummery LJ, with whom the other two members of the court agreed, also directed that, separately from the need to obtain authorization to proceed, the stay should not be lifted until the parties had attended mediation to try to resolve the issues between them. He also expressed the hope that no more of the charity's money would be wasted in the costs of legal proceedings.

---

[26] ie small claims track, fast track, or multi-track
[27] [1999] 4 All ER 178 (CA)

Part V

CHARITY PROPERTY

15

CY-PRÈS AND SCHEMES

A. Jurisdiction to make a scheme

(1) Prerogative jurisdiction

15.01 If property is given for charitable purposes without the interposition of a trust, the Crown may have jurisdiction over it. If property is given for charitable purposes that are uncertain, and without being subjected to a trust, it will vest in the Crown, which, by convention, and through the exercise of the royal prerogative, will direct the property under the sign manual[1] to be applied to specific charitable purposes.[2] A modern example of the exercise of the prerogative jurisdiction is *Re Smith*,[3] where a gift 'to my country England' was held charitable and applied under a scheme by the sign manual. Another example is *Re Slevin*,[4] where a legacy was made to a charity which ceased to exist after the testator's death, but before the legacy had been paid over. It was held that the legacy became the property of the charity, so that, on the charity's ceasing to exist, the legacy fell to be applied to some analogous purpose of charity under the prerogative jurisdiction of the Crown.[5] The prerogative jurisdiction was also used where property was given for charitable purposes which were unlawful, as where property was given for religious purposes other than for those of the established church;[6] but the spread of religious toleration has long rendered such cases largely redundant.

15.02 In 1986, Her Majesty delegated the power to dispose of charitable gifts under the sign manual to the Attorney-General.[7] A request for a sign manual direction should be made through the Treasury Solicitor.[8]

(2) Judicial jurisdiction

15.03 The jurisdiction of the High Court to make schemes in relation to charities is derived from the inherent jurisdiction of the Court of Chancery over charitable

---

[1] ie the signature of the sovereign. 'It is called the Sign Manual because it is the actual signature of the sovereign, as distinguished from the operation of signing documents by the Signet': *Jowitt's Dictionary of English Law* (ed J Burke) (2nd edn, Sweet & Maxwell, 1977), vol II, 1659

[2] *A-G v Peacock* (1676) Cas temp Finch 245; *sub nom A-G v Matthews* 2 Lev 167; *Moggridge v Thackwell* (1803) 7 Ves 36, 86; affd (1807) 13 Ves 416; *Re Weir Hospital* [1910] 2 Ch 124, 136 (Farwell LJ)

[3] [1932] 1 Ch 553 (CA)

[4] [1891] 2 Ch 230 (CA)

[5] The report does not state the legal form in which the dissolved charity had existed; presumably this was as a corporation

[6] *Da Costa v De Paz* (1754) 1 Dick 258, where an unlawful bequest to provide instruction in the Jewish religion was applied by the Crown under the sign manual for the instruction of children in the religion of the Church of England

[7] [1989] Ch Com Rep 12 (para 38)

[8] [1989] Ch Com Rep 12 (para 39). In 1989, 89 applications were made to the Attorney-General for sign manual directions involving property with a combined value of almost £1.25m. Of this sum, nearly £0.5m consisted of bequests to 'cancer research' where no particular cancer charity was named in the will: ibid

trusts; and this jurisdiction is, by statute, exercisable in certain circumstances by the Charity Commissioners.[9]

Modern cases indicate an expansion of the judicial jurisdiction at the expense of the prerogative. For instance, even when no trust is expressed, the courts have sometimes asserted jurisdiction by inferring the existence of a trust. A gift for the purposes of an unincorporated charitable association is therefore presumed to be made upon trust for the institution's purposes.[10]   **15.04**

A trust has even been presumed in relation to unlawful gifts, where the court has been able to treat the unlawful object stated in the instrument as merely a mode of carrying out what is in truth a lawful charitable purpose. Thus in *Attorney-General v Vint*,[11] there was a bequest to provide the elderly inmates of a workhouse with a pint of porter. There was evidence that alcohol was not permitted in a workhouse, but the court directed that the fund should be applied for the provision of tea, sugar, and the like.   **15.05**

The judicial jurisdiction to make a scheme has also been held not to be limited to the existence of a trust in the strict sense, but to exist also where property is effectually dedicated to charity under the constitution of a charitable company.[12]   **15.06**

(3) Charities established by Royal charter

Unless the charter itself provides otherwise, the court has no inherent jurisdiction to re-found or to re-establish a charitable corporation founded by Royal charter; any alteration of the charter itself must be effected by the Crown through the revocation of the existing charter and the grant of a new one. The court can, however, regulate and control such a charity, especially on financial grounds, and the court is entitled to have regard to altered circumstances.[13] It seems that this jurisdiction is based upon the existence of a trust.[14] The court does, therefore, have an inherent jurisdiction, to this limited extent, to make a scheme for the trusts of such a charity. A scheme of the Charity Commissioners affecting a charity   **15.07**

---

[9] CA 1993, s 16(1)(a)

[10] *Re Vernon's Will Trusts* [1972] Ch 300n

[11] (1850) 3 De G & Sm 704

[12] *Liverpool and District Hospital for Diseases of the Heart v A-G* [1981] Ch 193

[13] *Re Whitworth Art Gallery Trusts* [1958] Ch 461, 467–8 (Vaisey J), referring to *A-G v Earl of Clarendon* (1810) 17 Ves 491; *Berkhampsted School Case*, (1865) LR 1 Eq 102; *Re Berkhampsted Grammar School* [1908] 2 Ch 25; *A-G v Governors of the Foundling Hospital* (1793) 2 Ves 41

[14] See *A-G v Governors of the Foundling Hospital* (1793) 2 Ves 41, 48, where Lord Commissioner Eyre, speaking of charities established by charter, said, 'but if those, established as governors, have also the majority of the revenues, this court does assume a jurisdiction of necessity, so far as they are to be considered as trustees of the revenues'. See also *A-G v Smart* (1748) 1 Ves Sen 72; *A-G v Middleton* (1751) 2 Ves Sen 326

founded by Royal charter may establish trusts which provide for the body corporate to continue in existence as the trustee of the charity.[15]

15.08 If a charity incorporated by the grant of a Royal charter has previously existed as a trust or as an unincorporated association, the court will generally have jurisdiction to make a scheme in respect of assets held at the date the charter was granted, since the incorporation does not destroy the charitable trusts—it merely provides for the incorporation of the trustee.[16] The position is different if the constitution of the unincorporated charity enables its entire capital and income to be applied to another charitable body with similar charitable objects; the transfer of the assets to the incorporated charity pursuant to such power would destroy the charitable trusts subject to which they were formerly held.[17] In each case, the court's inherent jurisdiction over assets acquired after the grant of the charter remains unclear.

15.09 Section 15 of the Charities Act 1993 has widened the court's jurisdiction in respect of charitable charter companies. Where the Royal charter can be amended by the grant and acceptance of a further charter (a supplemental charter), a scheme relating to the body corporate or to the administration of its property (including a cy-près scheme) may be made by the court under its jurisdiction with respect to charities notwithstanding that the scheme cannot take effect without the alteration of the charter. The scheme must be so framed that it (or such part of it as cannot take effect without the alteration of the charter) does not purport to come into operation unless or until the sovereign thinks fit to amend the charter in such manner as will permit the scheme or that part of it to have effect.[18] In practice, such schemes are generally made by the Charity Commissioners, who have concurrent jurisdiction with the High Court in charity proceedings for the purpose of establishing a scheme for the administration of a charity.[19]

15.10 Where, under the court's jurisdiction with respect to charities or under powers conferred by the Charities Act 1993, a scheme is made with respect to a body corporate, and it appears to the sovereign expedient, having regard to the scheme, to amend any Royal charter relating to that body, the sovereign may, on the applica-

---

[15] See, eg, the scheme made by the Charity Commissioners under the procedure contained in (what is now) CA 1993, s 17, in *The Hospital of Sir John Hawkins, Knight, in Chatham* [1983] Ch Com Rep 22–4 (paras 65–72), esp 24 (para 71)

[16] *A-G v Dedham School* (1857) 23 Beav 350. See also H Picarda, *The Law and Practice Relating to Charities* (3rd edn, Butterworths, 1999) 370

[17] cf *Re Roberts* [1963] 1 WLR 406

[18] CA 1993, s 15(1)

[19] ibid, s 16(1)(a). The Charity Commissioners' practice is to establish a scheme only after discussion with the Privy Council Office. For examples of the exercise of the power contained in s 15(1), see [1965] Ch Com Rep 8–9; [1967] Ch Com Rep 15–18; *The Benevolent Institution for the Relief of Aged and Infirm Journeymen Tailors* [1978] Ch Com Rep 37 (paras 129–31); *Cuddesdon Theological College, Oxford* [1978] Ch Com Rep 38 (paras 132–6); *The Newspaper Press Fund* [1980] Ch Com Rep 40–1 (paras 144–5); *The Almshouses (Municipal Charities), Stratford-upon-Avon* [1981] Ch Com Rep 30–1 (paras 90–3)

tion of that body, amend the charter accordingly by Order in Council in any way in which the charter could be amended by the grant and acceptance of a further charter; and any such Order in Council may be revoked or varied in like manner as the charter it amends.[20]

In appropriate circumstances, the Charity Commissioners may decide to proceed **15.11** with a scheme involving a charity founded by Royal charter, not under section 15, but under section 17, of the Charities Act 1993. The section 17 procedure (which is discussed further below[21]) may be preferable if the Charity Commissioners are establishing a single scheme for several charities including both a charity established by Act of Parliament and a charity founded by Royal charter. Exceptionally, the section 17 procedure may be used even if the only charity involved in the scheme is one founded by Royal charter; in which case the charity would be relieved of the need to seek a supplemental charter.[22]

(4) Charities established or regulated by a special Act of Parliament

The court has no inherent jurisdiction to make a scheme in respect of a charity in- **15.12** corporated by an Act of Parliament to the extent that the scheme would involve an alteration of the statute itself.[23] The court does have jurisdiction to make a scheme in respect of matters not laid down by the Act of Parliament, or to the extent that the Act itself confers on the court an express power to amend.[24]

The Charities Act 1993 provides that the jurisdiction of the court with respect to **15.13** specified types of charities is not to be excluded or restricted by the operation of certain statutes, and that a scheme established for any such charity may modify or supersede the provision made by any such enactment or instrument as if made by a scheme of the court.[25] The court may exercise its jurisdiction with respect to charities:[26]

(a) in relation to charities established or regulated by any provision of the Seamen's Fund Winding-up Act 1851 which is repealed by the Charities Act 1960;

(b) in relation to charities established or regulated by schemes under the Endowed Schools Acts 1869 to 1948, or section 75 of the Elementary

---

[20] CA 1993, s 15(2). For recent examples of the exercise of this power, see Royal College of Ophthalmologists (Charter Amendment) Order 1998, SI 1998/2252; Royal College of Physicians of London (Charter Amendment) Order 1999, SI 1999/667; Licensed Victuallers' National Homes (Charter Amendment) Order 2000, SI 2000/1348
[21] See below, paras 15.15–15.17
[22] See *The Hospital of Sir John Hawkins, Knight, in Chatham* [1983] Ch Com Rep 22–4 (paras 65–72)
[23] *Re Shrewsbury Grammar School* (1849) 1 Mac & G 324
[24] ibid
[25] CA 1993, s 15(3)
[26] ibid, Sch 4, para 1

Education Act 1870 or by schemes given effect to under section 2 of the Education Act 1973 or section 554 of the Education Act 1996;

(c) (repealed);

(d) in relation to fuel allotments;[27]

(e) in relation to charities established or regulated by any provision of the Municipal Corporations Act 1883 which is repealed by the Charities Act 1960, or by any scheme having effect under such provision;

(f) in relation to charities regulated by schemes under the Local Government Act 1899;

(g) in relation to charities regulated by orders or regulations under section 2 of the Regimental Charitable Funds Act 1935; and

(h) in relation to charities regulated by section 79 of the Charities Act 1993, that is, certain parochial charities, or by any such order as is mentioned in that section.

15.14 The Charity Commissioners are empowered to make a scheme for the administration of a charity established or regulated by Act of Parliament under section 17 of the Charities Act 1993. This power is considered below.

(5) The Charity Commissioners' jurisdiction under section 17 of the Charities Act 1993

15.15 Section 17 of the Charities Act 1993 gives the Charity Commissioners statutory power to make a scheme for the administration of a charity established or regulated by statute and in certain other special circumstances.[28] The power is exercisable where it appears to the Commissioners that a scheme should be established for the administration of a charity, but that it is necessary or desirable for the scheme to alter the provision made by an Act of Parliament, or to make any other provision which goes or might go beyond the powers otherwise exercisable by them, or that it is for any reason proper for the scheme to be subject to parliamentary review.[29] A scheme so settled by the Charity Commissioners may be given effect by order of the Secretary of State, and a draft of the order must be laid before Parliament.[30] Many schemes have been made taking effect in this way.[31] Exceptionally, the Charity Commissioners have proceeded under section 17 even

---

[27] Notwithstanding anything in Commons Act 1876, s 19, a scheme for the administration of a fuel allotment may make certain provisions relating to the disposal, exchange or use of the allotment: CA 1993, s 15(3) & Sch 4, para 2

[28] CA 1993, s 17. In most cases, the Charity Commissioners cannot make a scheme pursuant to s 17 of their own motion, but only on an application of the charity, the Attorney-General, or certain other persons: ibid, s 17(6). See further below, para 15.17

[29] CA 1993, s 17(1)

[30] ibid, s 17(2). The effect is that the Secretary of State's order giving effect to the scheme is subject only to the negative resolution of either House of Parliament

[31] See, eg, *Leicester Freemen's Estate* [1977] Ch Com Rep 39 (para 132); *The Queen's College at Birmingham* [1977] Ch Com Rep 42 (para 145); *Arundell Street Fund, Westminster* [1978] Ch Com

when the scheme did not involve the alteration of a provision contained in an Act of Parliament,[32] and the section may be appropriately used where a scheme involves two or more charities, even if only one of them was established by an Act of Parliament.[33]

If the scheme alters a statutory provision of a public general Act of Parliament and such alteration could not have been made but for the power in section 17, the order is not to be made unless the draft has been approved by resolution of each House of Parliament.[34]   **15.16**

Any provision of a scheme brought into effect under section 17 may be modified or superseded by the court or the Charity Commissioners as if it were a scheme brought into effect by order of the Commissioners under section 16.[35] The Charity Commissioners cannot make a scheme under section 17 except in the same circumstances as if they were proceeding (without an order of the court) under section 16.[36] In most cases, therefore, an application must first have been made to the Commissioners by the charity, the Attorney-General, or one or more   **15.17**

Rep 38–9 (paras 137–8); *The New College of Cobham, at Cobham, Kent* [1978] Ch Com Rep 39–40 (paras 139–42); *Charity of Richard Cloudesley, Islington, Greater London* [1982] Ch Com Rep 22–3 (paras 69–74); *The Booth Charities, Salford, Greater Manchester* [1985] Ch Com Rep 17–18 (paras 44–8); *The William Lamb (London) Trust* [1986] Ch Com Rep 32 (App C); *The University of Liverpool* [1988] Ch Com Rep 15 (paras 66–8); *Bridge House Estates* [1992] Ch Com Rep 13–14 (paras 46–9)

[32] See *The Priest and Poor of Ginge Petre, Essex (Sir William Petre's Almshouses)* [1977] Ch Com Rep 40–2 (paras 137–44). The charity had been founded in 1557, most unusually under letters patent. Although the scheme settled by the Charity Commissioners in respect of it did not alter the provisions of an Act of Parliament, it was thought right to proceed by order made by the Secretary of State under (what is now) s 17, because the scheme dissolved the ancient corporation and varied the provisions for trusteeship provided by the letters patent. See also *The Hospital of Sir John Hawkins, Knight, in Chatham* [1983] Ch Com Rep 22–4 (paras 65–72), where, although the charity had been founded by Royal charter, it was agreed that a scheme for its future regulation should be brought into effect under (what is now) s 17

[33] See, eg, *Sutton's Hospital in Charterhouse, Greater London* [1983] Ch Com Rep 21–2 (paras 61–4), where the Charity Commissioners proceeded by way of a single scheme under (what is now) s 17, which replaced several existing charities whose various origins lay in letters patent, in Acts of Parliament, and in schemes made under parliamentary procedures by the High Court and under the Charity Commissioners' ordinary jurisdiction. See also the single scheme uniting charities with different origins in *The Jarvis Eleemosynary Charity, Staunton-on-Wye, Bredwardine and Letton, Hereford and Worcester* [1982] Ch Com Rep 21 (paras 65–8)

[34] CA 1993, s 17(3). The provisions of this sub-s were invoked for the first time in *The Hospital of the Lady Katherine Leveson and the Educational Foundation of Lady Katherine Leveson, at Temple Balsall, West Midlands* [1977] Ch Com Rep 39–40 (paras 133–6). For a further example of the use of this sub-s, see *Lord Hastings Hospital Trust, Stoke Poges, Bucks* [1980] Ch Com Rep 41 (paras 146–9)

[35] CA 1993, s 17(4). This is subject to the qualification that, where s 17(3) applies to a scheme, the order giving effect to it may direct that the scheme is not to be modified or superseded by a scheme brought into effect otherwise than under s 17, and may also direct that sub-s (3) is to apply to any scheme modifying or superseding the scheme to which the order gives effect: CA 1993, s 17(5).

[36] CA 1993, s 17(6). On the scope of the Commissioners' jurisdiction under s 16, see below, paras 15.28–15.33

other specified categories of persons; and the Commissioners must give notice to the charity trustees.

(6) Companies registered under the Companies Acts

15.18 Although a charitable company incorporated under the Companies Acts does not hold its assets on trust in the strict sense, such a company is in a position analogous to that of a trustee in relation to its corporate assets, so that the court has jurisdiction to intervene in its affairs.[37] In appropriate circumstances, this suffices to give the court jurisdiction to order a cy-près scheme.[38]

B. Types of schemes

(1) Schemes relating to purposes

Not involving cy-près

15.19 Not all schemes involving a charity's purposes are schemes of cy-près. A cy-près scheme involves an alteration of the charitable purposes, whereas sometimes the scheme merely fills in the detail which might have been omitted from the purposes specified in the will or other governing instrument.[39] A scheme will therefore be needed where the property is given for general purposes which, although wholly and exclusively charitable, do not indicate the precise purposes to which the property is to be applied, for example, a trust set up merely for 'charitable purposes', or 'for the advancement of education'. In practice, such schemes are drawn up by the Charity Commissioners rather than the courts. A gift for general charitable purposes not upon trust will be applied under a scheme directed by the sign manual.[40]

Cy-près schemes

15.20 A scheme is a cy-près scheme if it involves an alteration of the charitable purposes. Where property is applicable cy-près, the substituted purposes should be as near as possible to those originally specified, but the court or the Charity Commissioners will not be defeated merely because there is no other very similar purpose to which the property can be applied; neither are they constrained to

---

[37] *Liverpool and District Hospital for Diseases of the Heart v A-G* [1981] Ch 193, 209, in which Slade J placed reliance on (inter alia) *Re Dominion Students' Hall Trust* [1947] Ch 183 (Evershed J), and on *Construction Industry Training Board v A-G* [1973] Ch 173 (CA)

[38] *Liverpool and District Hospital for Diseases of the Heart v A-G* [1981] Ch 193, 214 (Slade J). For further discussion of this case, see ch 11, para 11.21

[39] *Re Robinson* [1931] 2 Ch 122, 128 (Maugham J)

[40] *Re Smith* [1932] 1 Ch 153 (CA) (not upon trust, so applicable under the prerogative jurisdiction). On the use of the sign manual, see above, paras 15.01–15.02

apply the property to the nearest possible purpose. This is illustrated in *Attorney-General v Ironmongers' Company*,[41] where the charity's purpose, the redemption of Christian slaves captured by Barbary pirates, being no longer capable of being carried out, its property was applied cy-près for the benefit of charity schools.

Even an application to the nearest practicable purpose might be unsuitable or **15.21** ineffective, for example, if that purpose is already being adequately provided for by other means.[42] It might be said that the courts or the Charity Commissioners will go in ever increasing circles until they find the nearest practicable purpose which is both suitable and effective.[43] The Charity Commissioners' approach to the exercise of their cy-près jurisdiction is considered later in this chapter.[44]

(2) Administrative schemes

A scheme may not involve the charitable purposes themselves, but merely the **15.22** charity's administrative provisions. An administrative scheme may be used, for example, merely to simplify the administration of several charities serving a common area and providing overlapping benefits by the appointment of a single body of trustees to administer all the charities, but otherwise leaving them as separate charities, each with their own objects.[45]

The distinction between a scheme which involves the charitable purposes and one **15.23** which involves merely the charity's administrative machinery is not always easy to draw; it is, however, important, since the circumstances in which an administrative scheme may be ordered are wider than those in which the court may make a scheme altering the purposes cy-près. The court has a broad inherent jurisdiction to alter or delete administrative provisions in a charitable trust on the ground that such alteration or deletion is expedient in the best interests of the charity;[46] whereas its jurisdiction to order a cy-près scheme is restricted to the circumstances specified in section 13 of the Charities Act 1993.[47]

(3) Determining whether an alteration is merely administrative or involves purposes

Some provisions in a charitable trust appear to be administrative in nature, and **15.24** cannot be considered to be purposive merely because the settlor intends that they should be. In *Re JW Laing Trust*,[48] the trust, which had been set up inter vivos for

---

[41] (1834) 2 My & K 576
[42] [1989] Ch Com Rep 21 (para 74)
[43] See ibid
[44] See below, paras 15.35–15.38
[45] See [1969] Ch Com Rep 14–15 (paras 32–5). This is an example of a purely administrative 'uniting scheme': see further below, paras 15.39–15.42
[46] *Re JW Laing Trust* [1984] Ch 143, discussed below, para 15.24
[47] See below, paras 15.59–15.81
[48] [1984] Ch 143

'charitable purposes', contained a requirement that the trustees had to distribute the entire fund within ten years of the settlor's death. At the time it was set up, the trust fund was worth some £15,000; and nobody could have foreseen at the time that the settlor would live a further sixty years, and that, by his death, the fund's value would have increased to some £24 million. Peter Gibson J held that the deletion of the requirement could not affect the purposes of the charity, and so could not fall within what is now section 13(1) of the Charities Act 1993. He nevertheless thought that its deletion could be effected by means of a scheme of administration. He said that the court could, and should, take into account all the circumstances of the charity, including how it had been distributing its money, in considering whether it was expedient to regulate the administration of the charity by removing the restriction. Having taken these factors into account, he held that the requirement should be deleted as being inexpedient in the very altered circumstances since the charity had been established.

15.25 Other cases make it clear, however, that the alteration of some provisions may be either administrative or purposive in nature, depending upon the intention of the settlor. The identity of a particular trustee selected by the settlor is not usually treated as essential to the settlor's purpose; so that the death[49] or dissolution of the specified trustee before the testator's death,[50] or the intended trustee's refusal to accept the trusteeship,[51] will not usually affect the purposes of the trust. Such events are normally treated as mere failures in the administration of the charitable trust, which will not cause a failure of the charity's purposes: equity will not permit a trust to fail for want of a trustee. If necessary, a scheme will be ordered applying the property to the same purposes through the machinery of a different trustee.[52]

15.26 If, however, there is clear evidence that the identity of the trustee was essential to the settlor's gift, the death or dissolution of the trustee, or its refusal to act, or at least to accept the terms of the charitable trust as they stand,[53] will cause a failure of the charitable purposes themselves. If, for example, a testator appoints as trustee a charitable institution, it may be found that the carrying out of the trusts by that particular institution is part of the testator's purpose. If, for example, the court finds that the testator's intention was to make the gift dependent upon that specified institution serving as the instrument for bringing the gift into effect, the closure of the institution before the testator's death is a failure of the charitable purposes of the gift.[54]

---

[49] *A-G v Hickman* (1732) 2 Eq Cas Abr 193; *Moggridge v Thackwell* (1803) 7 Ves 36 (Lord Eldon LC)

[50] *Re Vernon's Will Trusts* [1972] Ch 300n; *Re Finger's Will Trusts* [1972] 1 Ch 286

[51] *Reeve v A-G* (1843) 3 Hare 191. The intended trustee institution will be obliged to refuse to act if (like the societies in *Reeve v A-G*) it has no power under its constitution to accept property given to it upon special trusts

[52] *Marsh v A-G* (1860) 2 J & H 61

[53] *Re Lysaght* [1966] Ch 191; *Re Woodhams* [1981] 1 WLR 493

[54] *Re Vernon's Will Trusts* [1972] Ch 300n, 303 (Buckley J); *Re Ovey* (1885) 29 ChD 560

If, exceptionally, the court finds that the identity of the particular trustee is essen- **15.27**
tial to the testator's purpose, his declining the trusteeship will cause the purpose to
fail ab initio, so that the charitable trust can be saved only if the court can find a
general charitable intention to justify a scheme cy-près.[55] In *Re Woodhams*,[56] the
testator left the residue of his estate (on the expiration of a life interest) to be
divided equally between two music colleges. Each share of residue was effectively
made conditional upon the respective college being willing to accept it as trustee
upon trust to provide annual scholarships for the musical education of a promis-
ing orphan boy from one of a number of specified children's homes. The number
of orphans had fallen since the will had been made, and neither college was willing to accept its respective trusteeship unless the terms of the trust were widened
to provide scholarships for the musical education of any boys of British nationality. Vinelott J found that the testator had intended that the charitable gifts should
be administered by the named colleges and by no one else; the gifts therefore failed
ab initio. By contrast, his Lordship found that the restriction to orphans was not
an essential part of the gifts. As other changes in the circumstances of the colleges
indicated that a more radical scheme might be required than the mere deletion of
the restriction to orphans, his Lordship referred the settlement of a scheme to the
Charity Commissioners.

C. Role of the Charity Commissioners

(1) Scope of the Charity Commissioners' jurisdiction

The Charity Commissioners may of their own motion by order establish a scheme **15.28**
for the administration of a charity in some circumstances following an inquiry
into that charity:[57] this is dealt with in chapter 10.[58] More generally, section 16 of
the Charities Act 1993 provides that the Charity Commissioners may by order exercise the same jurisdiction and powers as are exercisable by the High Court in
charity proceedings for the purpose (inter alia) of 'establishing a scheme for the
administration of a charity'.[59] A scheme 'for the administration of a charity' includes schemes relating to purposes, including cy-près schemes.[60]

The Charity Commissioners have no jurisdiction under section 16 of the **15.29**
Charities Act 1993 to try or determine the title at law or in equity to any property

[55] *Re Lysaght* [1966] Ch. 191; *Re Woodhams* [1981] 1 WLR 493. On general charitable intention, see below, paras 15.43–15.51
[56] [1981] 1 WLR 493
[57] CA 1993, s 18(2)(ii)
[58] See ch 10, paras 10.160–10.162
[59] CA 1993, s 16(1)(a). The Charity Commissioners' power to make schemes dates from 1860,
when the Charitable Trusts Act of that year conferred upon them concurrent power with the Court
of Chancery
[60] See Charity Commission, *Making a Scheme* CC 36, (1999)

as between a charity or trustee for a charity and a person holding or claiming the property or an interest in it adversely to the charity, or to try or determine any question as to the existence or extent of any charge or trust.[61] If, for example, the purpose of a charitable trust fails ab initio, only the court can determine whether the property should be applied to charity (under a scheme) or should be held on a resulting trust. If the court decides in favour of the former, it may refer the settlement of a scheme to the Charity Commissioners.[62]

(2) When the Charity Commissioners may exercise their jurisdiction under section 16 of the Charities Act 1993

15.30 The Charity Commissioners may not exercise their jurisdiction under section 16 to make a scheme except in five specified instances. The first two which are listed below apply to exempt charities as well as to non-exempt charities. The last three instances apply only to non-exempt charities. The circumstances are:

(a) on the application of the charity;[63]

(b) on an order of the court under subsection (2);[64]

(c) in the case of a charity other than an exempt charity, on the application of the Attorney-General;[65]

(d) in the case of a charity which is not an exempt charity and whose income from all sources does not in aggregate exceed £500[66] a year, on the application of any one or more of the charity trustees, or of any person interested in the charity, or of any two or more inhabitants of the area of the charity if it is a local charity;[67] and

(e) where (except in the case of an exempt charity) the Charity Commissioners are satisfied that the charity trustees ought in the interests of the charity to apply for a scheme, but have unreasonably refused or neglected to do so and the Commissioners have given the charity trustees an opportunity to make representations to them, the Commissioners may proceed as if an application for a scheme had been made by the charity. The Charity Commissioners do not have such power to act to alter the purposes of a charity, however, unless forty years have elapsed from the date of its foundation.[68]

---

[61] CA 1993, s 16(3)

[62] As in *Re Woodhams* [1980] 1 WLR 493; see CA 1993, s 16(2)

[63] ibid, s 16(4)(a). Even an exempt charity is therefore entitled to apply to the Charity Commissioners for a scheme

[64] ibid, s 16(4)(b)

[65] ibid, s 16(4)(c)

[66] The Secretary of State is empowered by order to substitute a different amount: ibid, s 16(15)

[67] ibid, s 16(5)

[68] ibid, s 16(6)

Where a charity cannot apply to the Charity Commissioners for a scheme by reason of any vacancy among the charity trustees or the absence or incapacity of any of them, but such an application is made by such number of the charity trustees as the Charity Commissioners in the circumstances consider appropriate, the Commissioners may nevertheless proceed as if the application were an application made by the charity.[69]

Where the court directs a scheme for the administration of a charity to be established, the court may by order refer the matter to the Charity Commissioners for them to prepare or settle a scheme in accordance with such directions (if any) as the court sees fit to give. Any such order may provide for the scheme to be put into effect by order of the Commissioners as if prepared under section 16(1) and without any further order of the court.[70]   **15.31**

(3) Restrictions on the Charity Commissioners' exercise of their jurisdiction under section 16 of the Charities Act 1993

Before exercising any jurisdiction under section 16 of the Charities Act 1993, otherwise than on an order of the court, the Charity Commissioners must give notice of their intention to do so to each of the charity trustees, except any that cannot be found or has no known address in the United Kingdom or who is party or privy to an application for the exercise of the jurisdiction. Any such notice may be given by post, in which event it may be addressed to the recipient's last known address in the United Kingdom.[71] There is, however, no prescribed form of notice.   **15.32**

The Charity Commissioners must not exercise their jurisdiction under section 16 in any case (not referred to them by order of the court) which, by reason of its contentious character, or of any special question of law or of fact which it may involve, or for other reasons, they may consider more fit to be adjudicated on by the court.[72]   **15.33**

(4) Appeals from the Charity Commissioners' order under section 16 of the Charities Act 1993

An appeal against an order of the Charity Commissioners under section 16 may be brought in the High Court: **15.34**

  (1) By the Attorney-General.[73]
  (2) Within three months beginning with the day following that on which the order is published, by the charity or any of the charity trustees, or by any person removed from any office or employment by the order (unless he is

---

[69] ibid, s 16(7)
[70] ibid, s 16(2)
[71] ibid, s 16(9)
[72] ibid, s 16(10)
[73] ibid, s 16(11)

removed with the concurrence of the charity trustees or with the approval of the special Visitor, if any, of the charity).[74] But no such appeal may be brought except with a certificate of the Charity Commissioners that it is a proper case for an appeal or with the leave of a judge of the Chancery Division.[75]

(3) Where an order of the Charity Commissioners under section 16 establishes a scheme for the administration of a charity, by any person interested in the charity (who has the like right of appeal as a charity trustee),[76] and, in the case of a local charity in any area, by any two or more inhabitants of the area and by the council of any parish or (in Wales) by any community comprising the area or any part of it.[77]

(5) The Charity Commissioners' guidance on the exercise of the cy-près doctrine

15.35 The Charity Commissioners have published the guidance given to their staff on the application of the cy-près doctrine.[78] The Charity Commissioners (like the courts) will not select an application to the nearest practicable purpose if that might be unsuitable or ineffective (as where that purpose is already being adequately provided for by other means); instead, they will select the nearest practicable purpose which is both suitable and effective.[79] The Charity Commissioners have stated that they might not, for instance, appropriate the proceeds of sale of an almshouse or a school solely for the relief of poverty or for educational purposes respectively if the area of benefit were already adequately provided with poor or educational charities.[80] Similarly, the Charity Commissioners comment that there would be no point in extending the area of benefit of a charity if the adjoining areas to which it might be extended already had adequate provision in the terms of the charity's purposes. Instead, the purposes might be extended within the existing area of benefit.[81] They have also said that the physical location of a charity within its existing area of benefit might also be a factor in determining a practical cy-près application: adjoining areas might not be readily combined with the existing area of benefit.[82]

15.36 The Charity Commissioners observe that Lord Macnaghten's classification of charities under four heads in *Pemsel*'s case[83] is not a definition, and there is no rule of law which prohibits a charity whose purposes fall within one head from being

---

[74] CA 1993, s 16(12)
[75] ibid, s 16(13)
[76] ie under CA 1993, s 16(12)
[77] ibid, s 16(14)
[78] [1989] Ch Com Rep 20–2 (paras 73–5)
[79] See [1989] Ch Com Rep 21 (para 74)
[80] ibid
[81] ibid
[82] ibid
[83] [1891] AC 531

given a scheme so that its new purposes include other heads.[84] They point out that the extent to which a charity's purposes can be altered depends upon the circumstances, and that there is greater scope for alteration when the existing purposes already include elements of more than one head of charity—for instance, trusts for the education of poor persons or a trust both for the poor and for the public benefit.[85] They note that, whilst closed schools would normally, on cy-près principles, be made subject to a scheme for educational purposes, if the trust is clearly local in nature, consideration might be given to widening the objects rather than altering the area of benefit.[86]

The Charity Commissioners have also cautioned against the automatic placing of greater weight on one part of a charity's objects than on another. They state that, where the beneficiary class of a charity is defined by reference to a number of components, for instance poor women resident in the parish of X, care should be taken not to attach undue importance to one component as against the remainder, unless the charity's foundation or trust deed indicates otherwise.[87]   **15.37**

Finally, the Charity Commissioners reject the idea that certain elements of a trust are sacrosanct, such as the age limit included in educational schemes, religious qualifications in essentially secular charities, and sex qualifications, particularly in relation to schools. They take the view that no part of a charity's trusts is unalterable.[88]   **15.38**

(6) Uniting schemes

The Charity Commissioners may sanction what they call 'uniting schemes', which are designed to simplify the administration of similar charities serving a common area and to prevent overlapping of their benefits by uniting them under a new scheme.[89]   **15.39**

There are, however, different degrees of uniting charities. At one end of the scale, a uniting scheme may merely appoint a single body of trustees to administer all the charities, leaving them in other respects as separate charities, each with its own objects.[90] At the other end of the scale there is a uniting scheme which, through the application of the cy-près doctrine, merges the purposes of the formerly separate charities into a single and newly formed charity. A scheme of the latter sort is permissible only where the cy-près circumstances set out in section 13(1) of the Charities Act 1993 apply—most appropriately where property applicable for   **15.40**

---

84   [1989] Ch Com Rep 21 (para 75)
85   ibid
86   ibid, (para 75(i))
87   ibid, 22 (para 75(iii))
88   ibid (para 75(v))
89   See [1969] Ch Com Rep 14–15 (paras 32–5)
90   ibid, 14 (para 32)

similar purposes can more effectively be used in conjunction and made applicable to common purposes.[91]

15.41 When dealing with a uniting scheme of an administrative nature, the Charity Commissioners prefer to achieve a closer union than can be obtained by merely appointing a single body of trustees, and are prepared to frame their scheme so that a common purpose or set of purposes is provided for all the charities, and under which, for all administrative purposes, the charities become a single charity with undivided endowments.[92] Where the Charity Commissioners have taken this course, they have provided in the uniting scheme that 'the charities shall be administered and managed together as one charity under the title of . . .'.[93]

15.42 Where the Charity Commissioners approve what might be termed a 'single charity' uniting scheme, a new institution is thereby created for the purposes of the Charities Act 1993.[94] The Charity Commissioners, however, take the view that this does not extinguish the separate charities which have been thereby united, since the Commissioners have no power to extinguish an endowed charity merely by a scheme of an administrative nature.[95] The individual charities therefore continue to exist,[96] and so remain entitled to legacies made to them individually. A legacy to one of them vests in, and should be paid to, the trustees of the united charity.[97]

D. General charitable intention

(1) The meaning of 'general charitable intention'

15.43 One of the most frequently quoted descriptions of the meaning of the phrase 'general charitable intention' is that of Parker J in *Re Wilson*.[98] His Lordship (speaking in the context of testamentary trusts) said that there are two classes of cases.[99] First, there are those cases where, in form, the gift is given for a particular

---

[91] CA 1993, s 13(1)(c). See further below, paras 15.65–15.67
[92] [1969] Ch Com Rep 14 (para 32)
[93] ibid, 14 (para 32). The Charity Commissioners consider that the balance of advantage lies in giving to the united charities a title which is in the singular (eg the Ryder Street Charity) rather than in the plural (eg the Ryder Street United Charities), since the latter might leave the trustees and others in doubt as to how the united charities should be administered: ibid, 14–15 (para 35)
[94] ibid, 14 (para 33)
[95] *Re Faraker* [1912] 2 Ch 488, where it appears that the Charity Commissioners had settled a uniting scheme of this sort. See also [1969] Ch Com Rep 14 (paras 33–4). It is questionable, however, whether *Re Faraker* justifies the Commissioners' practice: see below, paras 15.98–15.101. See also the discussion below, para 15.66, as to whether a cy-près scheme effected under CA 1993, s 13(1)(c) might now destroy an endowed charity
[96] [1969] Ch Com Rep 14 (para 34)
[97] ibid, para 33
[98] [1913] 1 Ch 314
[99] ibid, 320

charitable purpose, but it is possible, taking the will as a whole, to say that the paramount intention is to give the property in the first instance for a general charitable purpose and to graft on to the general gift a direction as to the intentions of the testator as to the manner in which the general gift is to be carried into effect. If this is the construction and the particular purpose is impossible, the gift will be applied cy-près.[100] Secondly, there are cases where, on a construction of the will, no such paramount general intention can be inferred; if it is impossible to carry out that particular purpose the whole gift fails.[101]

Some cases have sought to express the same distinction as was made by Parker J by inquiring whether the mode of attaining the charitable purpose is of the substance of the gift.[102] An excellent description of the meaning of 'general charitable intention' is that suggested by Sheridan and Delany, namely:[103] **15.44**

> an intent to benefit any or a type of charity, however narrow or unlimited, which is wide enough to include the stated (impossible) purpose (if any) and at least one other (possible) purpose.

A much wider conception of the phrase is to found in the judgment of Vinelott J in *Re Woodhams*, where he said:[104]

> one way of approaching the question whether a prescribed scheme or project which has proved impracticable is the only way of furthering a desirable purpose that the testator or settlor contemplated or intended is to ask whether a modification of that scheme or project, which would enable it to be carried into effect at the relevant time, is one which would frustrate the intention of the testator or settlor as disclosed by the will or trust instrument interpreted in the light of any admissible evidence of surrounding circumstances.

It is important to ascertain whether the settlor's specified purpose was intended to be merely a means of furthering a wider charitable purpose; and, if so, whether a scheme can be drawn up which can apply the property within the ambit of that wider purpose. The true ambit of the settlor's purpose in each case is a matter of the construction of the particular instrument, so that rules of law cannot be laid down. The case law does, however, offer some guidance. The authorities suggest that the greater the detail in which the settlor sets out his purpose, the narrower the ambit of his intention to benefit charity is likely to be;[105] but, even if the ambit is narrow, provided it includes a practicable charitable purpose that comprises a suitable and effective method of application, the property is still applicable cy-près. The fact that a charitable gift comprises residue (and is therefore of an **15.45**

---

[100] ibid, 320–1
[101] ibid, 321
[102] See *Mills v Farmer* (1815) 19 Ves. 483 (Lord Eldon LC); *Re Rymer* [1895] 1 Ch 19 (Lindley LJ)
[103] LA Sheridan & VTH Delany, *The Cy-près Doctrine* (Sweet & Maxwell, 1959) 36
[104] [1981] 1 WLR 493, 503. See also Buckley J's definition in *Re Lysaght* [1966] Ch 191, 202
[105] *Re Good's Will Trusts* [1950] 2 All ER 653

indeterminate amount) might indicate that the ambit of the settlor's purpose is wider than it would have been had he made a gift of a specified sum;[106] but the court will usually consider this factor alone insufficient.[107] The ambit of the testator's charitable purpose may also be wider if the charitable disposition in question is one of several in the same will.[108] However, it seems that the court will not endeavour to find a general charitable intention in respect of a specific legacy which fails if the residue of the estate is also given for charitable purposes.[109]

(2) Circumstances in which a general charitable intention must be found

15.46 Before the Charities Act 1960, a distinction was drawn between failure of the charitable purpose ab initio, and failure thereafter. Failure ab initio means failure before or at the moment the charitable disposition vests in interest; supervening failure is failure at any later time.[110] Where a gift upon charitable trusts follows a life interest, failure of the charitable purposes during the running of the preceding life interest is therefore a supervening failure. It may therefore be necessary for the court to ascertain precisely when failure occurred: whether at the testator's death[111] or only subsequently.

Initial failure

15.47 It is well established that, in the event of a failure of the charitable purpose ab initio, the property is applicable cy-près only if the court can discern a general charitable intention on the part of the settlor or testator.[112]

Supervening failure

15.48 Where the failure is merely supervening, it is now firmly established that the property is applicable cy-près without any need to inquire whether the settlor or testator had a general charitable intention.[113] Once property has been effectually dedicated to charity, the court presumes that the settlor or testator intended that the gift to charity was intended to be perpetual, so that no reversion is left in his

---

[106] *Re Goldschmidt* [1957] 1 WLR 513; *Re Royce* [1940] Ch 514; cf *Re Raine* [1956] Ch 417, 423 (Vaisey J)

[107] *A-G v Painter-Stainers' Co* (1788) 2 Cox Eq Cas 51, 59 (Lord Thurlow LC); but see *Re Douglas* [1905] 1 Ch 279 (Kekewich J), which has been roundly condemned as wrong: H Picarda, *The Law and Practice Relating to Charities* (3rd edn, Butterworths, 1999) 344 (n 11), 345 (n 4)

[108] *Re Satterthwaite's Will Trusts* [1966] 1 WLR 277; but this factor did not lead to a finding of a general charitable intention in respect of gifts to charities which had ceased to operate in *Re Harwood* [1936] Ch 285 (Farwell J)

[109] *Re Goldschmidt* [1957] 1 WLR 513

[110] See *Re Wright* [1954] Ch 347 (CA); *Re Tacon* [1958] Ch 447 (CA)

[111] eg as in *Re Woodhams* [1981] 1 WLR 493

[112] *Biscoe v Jackson* (1887) 35 ChD 460 (CA)

[113] *A-G v Craven* (1856) 21 Beav 392; *Re Wright* [1954] Ch 347 (CA); *Re Tacon* [1958] Ch 447 (CA)

estate and therefore no possibility of a resulting trust. The presumption in favour
of effectual dedication to charity is strong, and cogent evidence is needed to rebut
the presumption. It may be that nothing short of a valid[114] express gift over on failure of the specified charitable purpose will suffice.[115]

In *Re Peel's Release*,[116] an inter vivos deed vested land in trustees for use as a school. **15.49**
The deed contained an express statement that, should the precise charitable pur-
pose be defeated, the land was to be held for the settlor's heirs and assigns. The
heirs and assigns admitted that this express reverter clause was void for perpetuity,
but argued that the presence of the clause nevertheless indicated that the testator
had thereby excluded the operation of the cy-près doctrine, so that the property
should be held for them on a resulting trust. Sargant J rejected this argument because he found that the deed contained a contradictory statement that the land
was to be used for teaching 'for ever thereafter', which indicated that the settlor
intended the gift to charity to be absolute and perpetual, and this statement over-
rode the purported gift over. By contrast, in *Re Cooper's Conveyance Trusts*,[117]
where again the charitable trust failed after it had come into effect, Upjohn J held
that the property went on a resulting trust for the next of kin on the ground that
the will contained an express gift over which, though itself void for perpetuity, was
sufficient evidence to negative any general charitable intention or intention to
give the property out and out to charity. It is doubtful, however, whether this
latter decision can stand against more recent cases in the Court of Appeal.[118]

Surplus

Several cases have held that, if the specified charitable purpose has been fully car- **15.50**
ried out, any surplus is applicable cy-près only if a general charitable intention can
be found;[119] although only in a couple of cases has the court held that the surplus
should be held on a resulting trust rather than be applied cy-près.[120] There is, however, also contrary authority which holds that no general charitable intention need
be sought to apply a surplus cy-près.[121] To the extent that a surplus is analogous to

---

[114] See Perpetuities and Accumulations Act 1964, s 12, which renders void a gift over (other than
from one charity or charitable purpose to another) taking effect outside the permitted period of perpetuity
[115] But see P Luxton, 'Cy-près and the ghost of things that might have been' [1983] Conv 107
[116] [1921] 2 Ch 218; appl *Bath and Wells Diocesan Board of Finance v Jenkinson* The Times,
6 Sept 2000 (Evans-Lombe J) (High Ct)
[117] [1956] 1 WLR 1096
[118] ie *Re Wright* [1954] Ch 347 (CA); *Re Tacon* [1958] Ch 447 (CA)
[119] *Re Stanford* [1924] 1 Ch 73 (Eve J); *Re Monk* [1927] 2 Ch 197 (CA); *Re Robertson* [1930]
2 Ch 71; *Re Royce* [1940] Ch 514 (Simonds J)
[120] *Re Stanford* [1924] 1 Ch 73 (surplus remaining out of £5,000 bequeathed to publish an ety-
mological dictionary); *Re British Red Cross Balkan Fund* [1914] 2 Ch 419 (surplus in a fund raised
by a public appeal)
[121] *Re King* [1923] 1 Ch 243 (Romer J)

a supervening failure, it is difficult to see why a general charitable intention should be needed only in the former circumstance. However, to the extent that it is reasonably practicable to determine the amount needed to carry out the specified purpose at the date of vesting, any surplus might be more properly treated as an initial failure *pro tanto*, where a general charitable intention is indeed required.[122]

Preservation of general charitable intention by s 13(2) of the Charities Act 1993

15.51 Although the Charities Act 1960 widened the circumstances in which property is applicable cy-près, it did not abolish the need for a general charitable intention in those circumstances in which it was required before that Act took effect.[123] This provision is now contained in section 13(2) of the Charities Act 1993, which states that the occasions on which property can be applied cy-près in sub-section (1):[124]

> shall not affect the conditions which must be satisfied in order that property given for charitable purposes may be applied cy-près except in so far as those conditions require a failure of the original purposes.

The effect of this saving is that failure ab initio must now be distinguished from all other cy-près occasions, for it is only if there is failure ab initio that there is a possibility that the property will be lost to charity in the event of there being no general charitable intention on the part of the settlor.[125]

E. Cy-près circumstances

(1) Introduction

15.52 Before the Charities Act 1960, cy-près was permissible only if the charitable purposes were, or had become, impossible or impracticable to perform, or in the event of a surplus. Section 13(1) of the Charities Act 1960 widened the circumstances in which property might be applied cy-près, and this sub-section was re-enacted as section 13(1) of the Charities Act 1993.

15.53 Section 13(1) of the Charities Act 1993 states:

> Subject to subsection (2) below, the circumstances in which the original purposes of a charitable gift can be altered to allow the property given or part of it to be applied cy-près shall be as follows—

---

[122] See the discussion in H Picarda, *The Law and Practice Relating to Charities* (3rd edn, Butterworths, 1999) 343–6

[123] *Re JW Laing Trust* [1984] Ch 143, dealing with CA 1960, s 13(2)

[124] CA 1993, s 13(2)

[125] *Re Good's Will Trusts* [1950] 2 All ER 653

and it goes on to list five cy-près circumstances (or 'pigeon-holes' as they have been called[126]) in paragraphs (a) to (e).

'the original purposes'

The expression 'the original purposes' in section 13(1) refers to the charitable **15.54** trusts as a whole. Where a charitable trust provides for the payment of a fixed annual sum of the income of the fund to charity A and the payment of the residue of that income to charity B, this comprises a single charitable gift; therefore the phrase 'the original purposes' refers to the charitable trusts as a whole, not severally to each part.[127] If, however, a trust provides for the division of income between charities in aliquot shares, or for charities in succession, it comprises separate charitable gifts, since the possibility or otherwise of carrying out the trusts of one share would hardly react on the possibility or otherwise of carrying out the trusts relating to another.[128] In these latter instances, the expression 'the original purposes' will therefore need to be considered only in relation to each separate part.

The 'purposes' of a charitable gift within section 13(1) means 'those charitable ob- **15.55** jects on which the property given is to be applied'.[129] It does not, therefore, include a requirement to distribute the property by a particular date.[130]

Before 1961, it was often necessary for the court to ascertain precisely what the **15.56** original charitable purposes were, in order to determine if they were, or had become, impossible or impracticable, and so whether the court had jurisdiction to order a cy-près scheme.[131] With the widening of the cy-près circumstances in 1961, this is no longer necessary where the court is satisfied that the property is applicable cy-près under one of the other circumstances set out in section 13(1).[132]

'the spirit of the gift'

Several of the cy-près circumstances set out in section 13(1) of the Charities Act **15.57** 1993 refer to 'the spirit of the gift'.[133] In *Re Lepton's Charity*,[134] Pennycuick V-C said that the expression 'the spirit of the gift' in (the predecessor[135] to)

---

[126] *Varsani v Jesani* [1999] Ch 219, 232 (para 21), per Morritt LJ, adopting a graphic phrase of counsel's

[127] *Re Lepton's Charity* [1972] Ch 276, 285 (Pennycuick V-C)

[128] ibid, 285

[129] *Re JW Laing Trust* [1984] Ch 143, 149 (Peter Gibson J)

[130] ibid

[131] *Craigdallie v Aikman* (1813) 1 Dow 2; 2 Bligh 530, 539 (Lord Eldon LC); *A-G v Pearson* (1817) 3 Mer 353, 413–19; *General Assembly of Free Church of Scotland v Overtoun, Macalister and Young* [1904] AC 515, 643–5 (Lord Davey)

[132] *Varsani v Jesani* [1999] Ch 219, 232–3 (paras 21–2) (Morritt LJ)

[133] ie CA 1993, s 13(1), paras (a)(ii), (c), (d), & (e)(iii)

[134] [1972] Ch 276

[135] ie CA 1960, s 13(1)

section 13(1) may be an echo of the words used in *Re Campden Charities*,[136] and that it is 'equivalent in meaning to the basic intention underlying the gift, that intention being ascertainable from the terms of the relevant instrument read in the light of admissible evidence'.[137]

15.58 The absence of any founding document does not preclude the existence of any 'spirit of the gift'.[138] In *Varsani v Jesani*,[139] Morritt LJ said that the expression means 'the basic intention underlying the gift or the substance of the gift rather than the form of words used to express it or conditions imposed to effect it'.[140] He noted that the phrase is used in section 13(1) 'only in contexts which require the court to make a value judgment'; and he added that '[t]he court is not bound to follow the spirit of the gift but it must pay regard to it when making the value judgment required by some of the provisions of section 13(1)'.[141]

(2) Cy-près circumstances under section 13(1) of the Charities Act 1993
Fulfilment or failure

15.59 Under paragraph (a) of section 13(1) of the Charities Act 1993, cy-près is permissible where the original purposes, in whole or in part,[142]

(i) have been as far as may be fulfilled; or
(ii) cannot be carried out, or not according to the directions given and to the spirit of the gift.

15.60 Paragraph (a)(ii) was applied in *Re Lepton's Charity*.[143] In that case, a testator, who had died in 1715, had provided in his will for the income of a trust he had thereby set up to be applied each year in the payment of £3 to the dissenting minister of Pudsey, the balance of the income being applied to the poor and aged residents of Pudsey. At the time of the testator's death, the charity had produced an income of £5 per year, but by the date of the present judgment the annual income had increased to nearly £800. It was sought to increase the annual amount paid to the minister. Pennycuick V-C found that the intention underlying the gift was to divide a sum which, according to the values of 1715 provided a modest, but not a

---

[136] (1881) 18 ChD 310, 333. It was suggested in the *Report of the Committee on the Law and Practice relating to Charitable Trusts*, Lord Nathan (chairman), Cmd 8710 (1952) (the Nathan Report), that the origin of the concept 'the spirit of the gift' may have been the Educational Endowments (Scotland) Act 1882, s 15, which referred to 'the spirit of the intention of the founders': see Nathan Report, 73–4 (paras 311–12) and 92 (para 365(c)). These alternative origins were pointed out in *Varsani v Jesani* [1999] Ch 219, 233–4 (para 24); but Morritt LJ thought that the origin was of no significance: ibid, 234 (para 24)
[137] *Re Lepton's Charity* [1972] Ch 276, 285; appl *Peggs v Lamb* [1994] Ch 172, 197 (Morritt J)
[138] *Peggs v Lamb* [1994] Ch 172, 197
[139] [1999] Ch 219 (CA)
[140] ibid, 234 (para 24). See also Chadwick LJ in the same case, 238
[141] ibid, 234 (para 24) (Morritt LJ)
[142] CA 1993, s 13(1)(a)
[143] [1972] Ch 276

negligible, amount for the minister in such a manner that the minister took three-fifths. That intention was plainly defeated when, in modern conditions, the annual income having greatly increased, the minister continued to take a derisory £3. Pennycuick V-C held that, in these circumstances, the original purposes could not be carried out according to the spirit of the gift within paragraph (a)(ii),[144] and he made an order for a scheme under which the minister's income was increased to £100 per annum.

Paragraph (a)(ii) is also appropriate where the trustee specified by the testator refuses to act as trustee of the charitable trusts as laid down in the governing instrument, and where, exceptionally, the identity of the trustee is found to be essential to the testator's purpose. The refusal of the trustee to act causes the charitable trust to fail ab initio, since the bequest will be, in effect, conditional on the willingness of the trustee to accept the trusts as indicated in the will.[145] The identity of the particular trustee would be a direction given, in accordance with which the original purpose could not be carried out according to the spirit of the gift.[146] The property will therefore be applicable cy-près if a general charitable intention can be found.[147]   **15.61**

Before the Charities Act 1960, the courts had allowed the removal of impractical conditions attached to charitable gifts by means of cy-près schemes. In *Re Robinson*,[148] the testatrix had given money to endow an evangelical church, subject to 'an abiding condition' that a black gown be worn in the pulpit. The condition was held to be impracticable, as defeating the main evangelical purpose of the gift, and was deleted by the court. If similar facts arose today, the court could probably delete such condition (not itself a purpose of the trust) under section 13(1)(a)(ii), as being a direction according to which the original purpose (the endowment of an evangelical church) could not be carried out.[149] In *Re Dominion Students' Hall Trust*,[150] the charitable trust restricted the class of persons who could benefit to male students of the overseas dominions of the British Empire who were of European origin. The court deleted such restriction as tending to defeat the charity's main object. Such restriction could today be treated either as part of the original purposes, or as a direction; and, in either event, it could be deleted under paragraph (a)(ii).[151]   **15.62**

---

[144] Alternatively, he considered that the circumstances would fall within paragraph (e)(iii). See below, para 15.80

[145] *Re Woodhams* [1981] 1 WLR 493 (Vinelott J); *Re Lysaght* [1966] Ch 191 (Buckley J) (although CA 1960, s 13, was not there considered)

[146] See *Re JW Laing Trust* [1984] Ch 143 (Peter Gibson J).; cf *Re Woodhams* [1981] 1 WLR 493; *Re Lysaght* [1966] Ch 191 (although no reference is made in the judgment to what was then CA 1960, s 13)

[147] *Re Lysaght* [1966] Ch 191; *Re Woodhams* [1981] 1 WLR 493

[148] [1923] 2 Ch 332

[149] *Re JW Laing Trust* [1984] Ch 143

[150] [1947] Ch 183

[151] *Re JW Laing Trust* [1984] Ch 143

15.63 In *Re JW Laing Trust*,[152] the court had to consider an application to have deleted from the terms of a charitable trust a requirement that the entire fund be distributed within ten years of the settlor's death.[153] Peter Gibson J there pointed out that not every provision, even if only administrative, which a donor makes applicable to his gift can be treated as a condition and hence as a purpose. He distinguished *Re Robinson*[154] and *Re Dominion Students' Hall Trust*[155] on the ground that, even if the stipulations in those cases could not be treated as conditions, they were 'directions' within paragraph (a)(ii). The argument in favour of cy-près in *Re JW Laing Trust*, however, was based entirely on paragraph (e)(iii): no argument was put to fit the application within paragraph (a)(ii). It may nevertheless be inferred from Peter Gibson J's reasoning that he would not have been prepared to treat the obligation to distribute the fund within ten years of the settlor's death as a 'direction', because otherwise the alteration of every administrative provision of a charitable trust would, in his view, necessarily involve a cy-près scheme. Against this, it might be argued that there is a cy-près circumstance within paragraph (a)(ii) only where the existence of the direction prevents the purposes from being carried out according to the spirit of the gift. In many instances, an administrative provision (whether it be called a direction or not) merely causes inconvenience in the performance of the purposes, but does not prevent their being carried out. The principle that can be extracted from the earlier cases is that, whether or not a provision is a direction within paragraph (a)(ii) depends, not upon whether it is intrinsically 'purposive' or 'administrative', but upon whether it prevents the purposes from being carried out according to the spirit of the gift. To determine this, it is necessary to look to the basic intention underlying the gift and to the importance of the provision in the testator's or settlor's overall plan. If the trust contains a provision requiring that the property be distributed by a certain date, the court should inquire whether such provision is essential to the testator's purpose in the same way that it makes this inquiry of other provisions attached to a charitable gift, such as the wearing of the gown in *Re Robinson*, or the identity of the particular trustee in *Re Lysaght*.[156] The evidence in *Re JW Laing Trust* was that the settlor attached little importance to the distribution requirement. It is this factor which indicates that its deletion would not have fallen within paragraph (a)(ii). The distribution requirement was a purely administrative provision whose deletion would not involve a cy-près scheme.

---

[152] Re JW Laing Trust [1984] Ch 143
[153] The case is discussed above, para 15.24
[154] [1923] 2 Ch 332
[155] [1947] Ch 183
[156] [1966] Ch 191

Use for part of property only

Cy-près is permissible where the original purposes provide a use for part only of **15.64** the property available by virtue of the gift.[157]

More effective user with other property for common purposes

Under paragraph (c) of section 13(1) of the Charities Act 1993, cy-près is permis- **15.65** sible where the property available by virtue of the gift and other property applicable for similar purposes can be more effectively used in conjunction, and to that end can suitably, regard being had to the spirit of the gift, be made applicable to common purposes.

In *Re Faraker*,[158] the Charity Commissioners had by a scheme purported to con- **15.66** solidate a charity known as Hannah Bayly's Charity (an endowed charity for the benefit of poor widows of Rotherhithe) with thirteen other charities, for the consolidated purpose of benefiting the poor of Rotherhithe generally.[159] At that time, as there continued to be poor widows in Rotherhithe, neither the courts nor the Charity Commissioners had jurisdiction to alter the purposes of Hannah Bayly's Charity; which, it was held, therefore continued to exist despite the consolidation. Nowadays, in similar circumstances, the Charity Commissioners might be able to effect a lawful cy-près scheme under paragraph (c) of section 13(1), on the ground that this might comprise a more effective use of the property held by Hannah Bayly's Charity, regard being had to the spirit of the gift.

The Charity Commissioners have pointed out that the word 'similar' in paragraph **15.67** (c) does not mean 'the same', so that the purposes of the amalgamated charities do not have to be wholly coincidental. They have stated that adjustments can be made to beneficiary classes and areas of benefit where the practical considerations are clearly in favour of it.[160] Furthermore, although the Charity Commissioners accept that it is generally sound practice not to change a charity's objects so as to exclude any part of its existing purposes, they consider that this principle should not be taken to excessive lengths so as effectively to frustrate radical reorganization of trusts where this would be appropriate. They suggest that it is, for instance, sensible, when making regulating schemes for schools, to amalgamate the varied and various prize funds into a single fund so that the identity of the separate funds is lost. Such an amalgamation, they consider, may be administratively and practically sound, as the individual prize funds established many years ago may now be

---

[157] Charities Act 1993, s 13(1)(b)
[158] [1912] 2 Ch 488
[159] ie *semble* under a 'single charity' uniting scheme: see above, paras 15.39–15.42. For further discussion of *Re Faraker*, see below, paras 15.98–15.101
[160] [1989] Ch Com Rep 22 (para 75)

insufficient to provide the prizes intended. The Charity Commissioners also observe that this process can be applied to other groupings of charities.[161]

Area or class ceased to be suitable

15.68 Paragraph (d) of section 13(1) of the Charities Act 1993 applies where the original purposes

> were laid down by reference to an area which then was but has since ceased to be a unit for some other purpose, or by reference to a class of persons or to an area which has for any reason since ceased to be suitable, regard being had to the spirit of the gift, or to be practical in administering the gift.

15.69 A recent case in which a scheme was ordered under paragraph (d) is *Peggs v Lamb*,[162] which concerned an ancient charitable trust for the benefit of the freemen of Huntingdon. Over the centuries, the number of freemen had declined considerably, and application was made to the court for a cy-près scheme. Morritt J found that the original purposes of the gift were general charitable purposes for the benefit of qualifying freemen of Huntingdon and their widows. Although the charity had no founding instrument, he held that this did not preclude the existence of a spirit of the gift, which he found to be the benefit of the borough of Huntingdon. In the circumstances, his Lordship held that paragraph (d) was satisfied, that is, the original purposes had been laid down by reference to a class of persons who had since ceased to be suitable, regard being had to the spirit of the gift. He directed the settlement of a scheme to enlarge the class of persons to benefit from the freemen alone to the inhabitants of Huntingdon as a whole.

15.70 Apart from the power to make schemes in accordance with section 13(1), the court may in certain instances also exercise its jurisdiction with respect to charities to enlarge the area of operation of a charity. This power is exercisable where the purposes were laid down by reference to an area which is specified in Schedule 3 to the Charities Act 1993, when they may be enlarged to any such area as is therein mentioned.[163] This means that:[164]

> (1) Greater London may be enlarged to any area comprising Greater London.
> (2) Any area in Greater London and not in, or partly in, the City of London, may be enlarged to:
>> (i) Any area in Greater London and not in, or partly in, the City of London;
>> (ii) the area of Greater London exclusive of the City of London;
>> (iii) any area comprising the area of Greater London, exclusive of the City of London;

---

[161] [1989] Ch Com Rep 22 (para 75), (iv)
[162] [1994] Ch 172
[163] CA 1993, s 13(4)
[164] ibid, Sch 3

(iv) any area partly in Greater London and partly in any adjacent parish or parishes (civil or ecclesiastical), and not partly in the City of London.

(3) A district may be enlarged to any area comprising the district.

(4) Any area in a district may be enlarged to:

(i) Any area in the district;

(ii) the district;

(iii) any area comprising the district;

(iv) any area partly in the district and partly in any adjacent district or in any adjacent Welsh county or county borough.[164a]

(5) A parish (civil or ecclesiastical), or two or more parishes, or an area in a parish, or partly in each of two or more parishes, may be enlarged into any area not extending beyond the parish or parishes comprising or adjacent to the existing area.

(6) In Wales, a community, or two or more communities, or an area in a community, or partly in each of two or more communities, may be enlarged into an area not extending beyond the community or communities comprising or adjacent to the existing area.

Since laid down, purposes have been adequately provided for by other means, or ceased to be charitable in law, or ceased to be suitable or effective

15.71 The final cy-près circumstance is set out in paragraph (e) of section 13(1) of the Charities Act 1993. This paragraph permits cy-près where the original purposes, in whole or in part, have, since they were laid down,

(i) been adequately provided for by other means; or

(ii) ceased, as being useless or harmful to the community or for other reasons, to be in law charitable; or

(iii) ceased in any other way to provide a suitable and effective method of using the property available by virtue of the gift, regard being had to the spirit of the gift.

'been adequately provided for by other means'

15.72 Sub-paragraph (i) is an extension of the pre-1961 law, since alternative adequate provision was formerly not itself sufficient to justify a cy-près scheme. Thus, in *Attorney-General v Day*,[165] the mere fact that a local authority had been subjected to a duty to maintain a road did not enable property subject to an existing charitable trust for the maintenance of the road to be applied cy-près. The sub-paragraph has therefore been of particular importance in relation to charitable trusts for purposes which have been taken over by the central or local government authorities since the trusts were created.[166] The Charity Commissioners have,

---

[164a] For the enlargement of any area in a Welsh county or county borough see ibid, Sch 3, para 4A, inserted by Local Government (Wales) Act 1994.

[165] [1900] 1 Ch 31

[166] [1968] Ch Com Rep 17 (para 68)

with the agreement of the trustees, used the power contained in sub-paragraph (e)(i) to make schemes for a number of charities established for the repair of roads and bridges, substituting other general purposes for the benefit of the local inhabitants, such as the promotion of the arts, the provision of seats or shelters, the preservation of old buildings, or the improvement of local amenities.[167]

'ceased, as being useless or harmful to the community or for other reasons, to be in law charitable'

15.73   There is no reported case in which a cy-près scheme has been made under sub-paragraph (e)(ii) on the ground that the original purpose has ceased in law to be charitable. In *Peggs v Lamb*,[168] which concerned a charitable trust for the freemen of Huntingdon, Morritt J said that there would come a time, if it had not already arrived, when the class of freemen (which had rapidly dwindled) would cease to be a section of the public at all, in which event a case for a scheme might be made under sub-paragraph (e)(ii). In the circumstances, however, he did not need to decide if such a time had indeed arrived, since he was able to order a scheme under paragraph (d). With respect, however, it is submitted that, once a purpose has been held to be charitable, it does not cease to be so merely because the number of persons to benefit ceases to comprise a sufficient section of the community. The circumstances in *Peggs v Lamb* more properly fall under paragraph (d) or sub-paragraph (a)(ii).

15.74   Sub-paragraph (e)(ii) might be invoked if a statute declared a purpose to be no longer charitable; but there is no instance of this to date.[169] It is not enough that a statute merely declares a purpose to be unlawful, since a purpose can be charitable even though it is unlawful under the general law.[170] In the past, property given for charitable but unlawful purposes has been applicable cy-près either by the courts or under the Royal prerogative; and the effect of a statute outlawing the charitable purpose might today cause the property to be applicable cy-près under sub-

---

[167] [1970] Ch Com Rep 16 (para 43). A specific example is *Hermitage Lands or Highway Charity, in the Ancient Townships of Calveley and Wardle, Cheshire* [1972] Ch Com Rep 19 (paras 50–2), where land had been conveyed in 1776 to trustees upon trust to use the income for the repair and support of a causeway or pavement in the parish of Bunbury. Under a scheme prepared by the Charity Commissioners, the trustees of the Bunbury Parochial Charities were appointed trustees of the Hermitage Land Charity, and the income was to be applied for any charitable purposes for the general benefit of the inhabitants of Calveley and Wardle for which provision was not made out of rates, taxes, or other public funds. The new objects would include such purposes as the repair or provision of a public clock, beautifying or improving the neighbourhood, helping in the provision of a recreation ground or village hall, or providing a bus shelter

[168] [1994] Ch 172; discussed above, para 15.69

[169] This might occur were statute to remove the charitable status of independent schools. The Labour Party in opposition has in the past threatened to introduce a Bill to do this, but has currently ruled this out. See J Jaconelli, 'Independent Schools, Purpose Trusts, and Human Rights' [1996] Conv 24, 30–2

[170] eg *Da Costa v De Paz* (1754) 1 Dick 258. See above, paras 15.01 and 15.05

paragraph (a)(ii). Nevertheless, the passing of a statute making a purpose illegal under the general law might suggest that the purpose would no longer be regarded as charitable—perhaps because it would be 'harmful to the community'—in which event, it might be contended that the effect of the statute would be to make the property applicable cy-près under sub-paragraph (e)(ii).

According to the declaratory theory of judicial decisions, the effect of overruling **15.75** is retrospective, so that the law is treated as having always been as laid down in the later decision, unless and until it is itself overruled by a higher court. It might therefore be argued that if a decision of a lower court that a specified purpose is charitable were later overruled by an appellate court, the effect would be that the purpose would be treated as never having been charitable. According to this declaratory theory, the effect of the House of Lords holding in *National Anti-Vivisection Society v Inland Revenue Commissioners*[171] that anti-vivisection is not a charitable purpose, was to treat as a mistake of law the first-instance decision in *Re Foveaux*,[172] which had stood for over fifty years, and which had held that such a purpose was charitable. On this reasoning, anti-vivisection institutions which had previously enjoyed charitable status would have ceased to be charitable as a result of the decision of their Lordships' House, but their purposes would not have ceased in law to be charitable: they would be considered never to have been charitable at all. It would follow that, even if their Lordships' decision had been made after the enactment of section 13 of the Charities Act 1960, the assets of such institutions would not have become applicable cy-près under paragraph (e)(ii). This argument is in some ways appealing. It might be considered unfair that the law should compel such institutions to apply their property cy-près merely because of Chitty J's mistaken decision in *Re Foveaux*. In the case of charitable corporations, the argument works well, in that it enables those institutions to retain their property for the purposes of anti-vivisection. This analysis has its own difficulties, however, in that the purposes of anti-vivisection societies which had previously existed as trusts would, as a result of their Lordships' ruling, have become void, since the law does not generally recognize the validity of non-charitable purpose trusts.

More recently, the House of Lords has recognized that the declaratory theory is a **15.76** fiction, which, although necessary, should no longer preclude recovery of money paid at a time when there was a settled understanding of the law but which became a mistake of law only because the law on which such settled understanding was based was subsequently overturned by another court.[173] It might similarly be argued, without doing violence to the theory, that if an institution's purposes are

---

[171] [1948] AC 31 (HL)
[172] [1895] 2 Ch 501 (Chitty J)
[173] *Kleinwort Benson Ltd v Lincoln City Council* [1999] 2 AC 349, esp 377–84 (Lord Goff)

treated as charitable on the basis of a settled understanding of the law, which understanding is found to be mistaken because of an overruling by a later court, that institution's purposes should be considered to have 'ceased . . . to be in law charitable' within the meaning of paragraph (e)(ii). On this reasoning, had the *Anti-Vivisection Society* case been decided after 1960, the assets of anti-vivisection societies which had previously been regarded as charities would have been applicable cy-près. The drawback with this analysis, however, is that it denies such institutions the opportunity to continue carrying out their existing (now non-charitable) objects, and it seems very unfair to donors who gave to further the particular purpose no longer considered charitable.

15.77 An added complexity is section 4(1) of the Charities Act 1993. By virtue of this subsection, an institution is conclusively presumed to be a charity for all purposes other than rectification while it is on the register of charities.[174] This being so, it might be argued that, if the courts were later to hold the purposes of such a body not to be charitable, the Charity Commissioners would be obliged to remove it from the register,[175] but that (by virtue of the deeming effect of the statute) its property would then be applicable cy-près under sub-paragraph (e)(ii). If this is correct, then, pending the application of the property by way of a scheme, it is submitted that such property would be held by the trustees, not subject to the purposes (which are no longer charitable) expressed in the governing instrument, but rather on a constructive trust for indefinite, but wholly and exclusively charitable purposes. The trustees would then be under a duty to take steps to have such property applied cy-près under this sub-paragraph. If this view is sound, the property of gun- or rifle-clubs which are registered as charities would be applicable cy-près in this manner, were the courts to depart from previous authority[176] and to hold that the purposes of such clubs are not in law charitable. The Charity Commissioners take the view that such purposes will no longer be held charitable by the courts, and the Commissioners have declined to register applications from two such clubs.[177] The Charity Commissioners have not, however, removed existing gun- and rifle-clubs from the register of charities on this ground. In practice, therefore, it seems that nothing short of a statute or a decision of the courts will suffice to cause the property of a registered charity to be applicable cy-près under sub-paragraph (e)(ii). An objection to the foregoing argument based on section 4(1), however, is that it would seem to require an institution's property to be applied cy-près even if the initial registration was the result of a mistake, whether it be a mistake of law (such as that in *Re Foveaux*) or because, in the application for registration, the Charity Commissioners were supplied with false, mistaken, or misleading information.

---

[174] On the effects of registration, see further ch 10, para 10.62
[175] CA 1993, s 3(4)
[176] *Re Stephens* (1892) 8 TLR 792
[177] (1993) 1 Decisions 4–13

The Charity Commissioners' view is that if an institution is removed from the reg-   **15.78**
ister on the ground that it was never charitable in the first place, the registration
was from the first a mistake.[178] They consider that such registration must therefore
be considered to have been ultra vires, so that, when such mistake is corrected by
the removal of such institution from the register of charities, any issue relevant to
that institution during the period it was on the register must be decided without
reference to the fact that it was once registered as a charity. This neatly explains
why the property of an institution which was registered by mistake should not be
applied cy-près; but this interpretation has its own drawbacks. The Charity
Commissioners' view is that a mistaken registration for this purpose includes even
one made on a settled understanding of the law as it appears at the time, but which
is later shown to be wrong in a later decision of a higher court. Yet it would seem
harsh if an institution which is registered as a charity on this footing were later required to pay tax as if it had not been a charity during the time it had been on the
register. It is arguable, however, that any claim by the revenue authorities for such
retrospective tax might breach the Human Rights Act 1998.[179]

An intermediate view might be possible: namely, that whilst section 4(1) deems   **15.79**
the institution itself to have been a charity while on the register, it does not actually deem its *purposes* to have been charitable during that period. This would mean
that (subject to any objections under the Human Rights Act 1998) an institution
removed from the register because its initial registration was found to have been a
mistake would retrospectively lose those tax exemptions (such as those enjoyed by
charities in respect of income tax) which depend upon an application of income
or assets for charitable purposes only. But in respect of matters which turn on the
institution's having been a *charity*, such as the reliance of the charity trustees on
the advice of the Charity Commissioners,[180] or the authorization by the
Commissioners of *ex gratia* payments,[181] the institution would be able to continue
to rely on its having been registered under section 4(1) during the time in question. This intermediate view means that a mistaken registration of an institution
as a charity under section 4(1) does not result in an application of the institution's
property cy-près, since removal from the register on this ground enables its *purposes* to be treated as non-charitable during the period of registration. It is submitted that, under the existing charity legislation, this is, on balance, the preferred
outcome, albeit one reached by a somewhat tortuous route. There is clearly a need
for amending legislation to clarify the effect of registration as a charity under
section 4(1).

---

[178] See Charity Commission, *Maintenance of an Accurate Register of Charities*, Review of the
Register Discussion Document, (1999), Ann B (paras 13–16); Charity Commission, *Maintenance
of an Accurate Register of Charities*, RR 6, (Nov 2000) 13–14 (Ann C)
[179] Notably Art 1 of the First Protocol (Protection of Property)
[180] CA 1993, s 29
[181] ibid, s 27

'ceased in any other way to provide a suitable and effective method of using the property available by virtue of the gift, regard being had to the spirit of the gift'

15.80   In *Re Lepton's Charity*,[182] Pennycuick V-C considered that, apart from paragraph (a)(ii), the circumstances were such that the original purposes, had, since they were laid down, ceased to provide a suitable and effective method of using the property available, regard being had to the spirit of the gift, within paragraph (e)(iii). A direction in a charitable trust to distribute the capital by a particular date is not, however, a method of using the property, and so cannot be deleted under paragraph (e)(iii).[183]

15.81   In *Varsani v Jesani*,[184] the court had to consider a charitable trust set up to promote the faith of a particular Hindu sect as practised according to the teachings of its founder, whom the adherents believed to be a Supreme Being. The sect later split into two, following allegations of misconduct against the founder's successor; a minority of the members of the sect refused to acknowledge the successor's divine status, and ceased to worship at the charity's temple in London. The majority group sought, and the judge at first instance granted, an order for a cy-près scheme under section 13(1)(e)(iii) of the Charities Act 1993. The order was affirmed by the Court of Appeal. Morritt LJ[185] said that there was no doubt what the original purposes of the charity were; but the teachings and tenets of the founder did not deal with whether belief in a particular successor or in such successor's divine attributes was an essential tenet of the faith. Litigation to resolve this (which was sought by the minority group) could not resolve the impasse in this matter of faith. In the circumstances, he held that it was not necessary to determine whether either of the groups continued to adhere to the original purposes of the charity, since it was self-evident that those original purposes had ceased to provide a suitable and effective method of using the property (regard being had to the spirit of the gift) within sub-paragraph (e)(iii).[186] Chadwick LJ said that the spirit underlying the original gift was a desire to provide facilities for a small but united community of followers of the sect in and around Hendon to worship together in the particular faith; and that the original purposes were no longer a suitable and effective method of using the property because the community had become divided and could no longer worship together.[187] The Court of Appeal therefore directed a scheme for the division of the charity's property between the majority and the minority groups.[188]

---

[182] [1972] Ch 276. The facts of this case are set out above, para 15.60
[183] *Re JW Laing Trust* [1984] Ch 143
[184] [1999] Ch 219 (CA)
[185] ibid, 233 (para 23), 234 (para 25). The other two judges in the Court of Appeal expressed their agreement with Morritt LJ, Chadwick LJ adding a short judgment of his own
[186] ibid, 233 (para 23) (Morritt LJ)
[187] ibid, 238
[188] ibid, 234 (para 25) (Morritt LJ)

F. Clauses in governing instruments to avoid need for schemes or cy-près

There is no need to have recourse to the Charity Commissioners or to the courts **15.82** for a scheme of cy-près or a scheme of administration if the governing instrument of the charity itself reserves an appropriate power to the charity trustees to alter the governing instrument. If the charity is a corporation, the consent of the Charity Commissioners will be required to exercise any power to alter the objects clause or any other provision in its memorandum or articles of association which directs or restricts the manner in which its property may be used or applied.[189] Clauses in governing instruments to provide for alteration of the purposes, objects, or administrative provisions of the charity are considered in chapter 8.[190]

G. Gifts to charitable institutions

(1) Introduction

There are two possible ways in which a gift to a specified charitable institution can **15.83** take effect, namely:

(a) as a beneficial gift to the particular institution; or
(b) as a gift on trust.

If it is construed as a beneficial gift to the particular institution, the gift will prima facie lapse if the institution has ceased to exist by the time of the testator's death, although it may be applied cy-près if a general charitable intention can be found. If it is construed as a gift on trust, it is necessary to ascertain the terms of the trust; these could be either the general charitable objects of the legatee institution, or the work that the institution is (or was) carrying on (which may be narrower than the institution's general purposes).

Incorporated and unincorporated charities

In ascertaining whether a gift to a charity should be construed as a beneficial gift **15.84** to the particular institution, or as a gift on trust,[191] it appears that the intention of the testator is not necessarily decisive. A distinction was drawn in *Re Vernon's Will Trusts*,[192] between gifts to incorporated and unincorporated charities. Buckley J

---

[189] CA 1993, s 64(2)

[190] See ch 8, paras 8.15–8.17 (charitable trusts), and 8.46–8.51 (charitable unincorporated associations). Charities formed as companies under the Companies Acts need no power of amendment in their constitutions, since they have statutory powers to alter the objects clause of their memorandum or the articles; but these powers are hedged about with restrictions: see ch 8, paras 8.119–8.125

[191] As explained above, para 15.83

[192] [1972] Ch 300n

said that the former are prima facie to be construed as gifts to such institutions beneficially (that is, as simple legacies); whereas he considered that every bequest to an unincorporated charity by name without any purpose being indicated must take effect as a gift for a charitable purpose (that is, as a trust legacy), on the ground that no individual or aggregate of individuals could claim to take such a bequest beneficially.

15.85 This distinction has not met with universal approval. In *Re Roberts*, Wilberforce J stated:[193]

> The mere fact that there is a gift to an unincorporated charity does not seem to me to be enough to enable me to come to the conclusion that it is a gift for charitable purposes.

The distinction was reluctantly applied, but its consequences side-stepped, in *Re Finger's Will Trusts*.[194] In that case, the testatrix had given legacies to the Radium Commission, an unincorporated charity, and to the National Council for Child Welfare, an incorporated charity. Both institutions had ceased to exist before the testatrix's death: the former had been disbanded, the latter dissolved. The gift to the Radium Commission was treated, in accordance with *Re Vernon's Will Trusts*,[195] as a trust legacy, and Goff J ordered that it be subject to a scheme of administration to apply it to the same purpose.[196] The gift to the other charity was held to be a simple legacy, which would have lapsed; but Goff J found a general charitable intention and applied the legacy cy-près.[197] More recently, the distinction made in *Re Vernon's Will Trusts*[198] was applied in *Re ARMS (Multiple Sclerosis Research) Ltd*,[199] where legacies made to an incorporated charity by testators who died after the charity had gone into insolvent liquidation were held to be beneficial gifts to that institution, and were therefore payable to the liquidator for the benefit of the charity's creditors.

(2) Legacy to specific charitable institution

Institution has ceased to exist

Before testator's death

15.86 A simple legacy to a charity which has ceased to exist by the testator's death is treated as subject to lapse, in the same way as if it were a gift to an individual who had predeceased the testator. The gift will therefore normally either fall into the testator's residuary estate (if it is a specific gift), or (if it is itself a gift of residue) will

---

[193] [1963] 1 WLR 406, 414
[194] [1972] Ch 286
[195] ibid, 300n
[196] ibid, 286, 294–8
[197] ibid, 298–300
[198] ibid, 300n
[199] [1997] 1 WLR 877, discussed further below, para 15.88 and in ch 26, para 26.23

pass to the testator's next of kin. Exceptionally, the legacy will be applied cy-près, if the court finds that the testator had a general charitable intention.[200] It has been stated that it is difficult to find a general charitable intention when the testator has taken the trouble to name a particular institution.[201]

After testator's death but before payment has been made

If the charity is still in existence at the testator's death, a simple legacy to it will not **15.87** lapse. The legacy becomes the property of the charity, and it will go with the assets of the charity.[202] In *Re Slevin*,[203] the court held that the charity's assets (and the legacy with it) passed to the Crown, to be applied to charity under the sign manual.[204] The decision does not state the nature of the institution, however; and it seems that this will occur today only if the charity is a company whose assets can be made the subject of a judicial scheme cy-près, and where such company is dissolved without its assets having been applied to other charitable purposes, either in accordance with a clause in its constitution or by the court under a scheme cy-près.

If the charity is an insolvent company, this construction results in the legacy **15.88** benefiting the charity's creditors. In *Re ARMS (Multiple Sclerosis Research) Ltd*,[205] the charity, which had been incorporated under the Companies Acts, had got into difficulties through overspending, and was being wound up with debts of some £1.5 million. The liquidator claimed various legacies made by testators who had died after the winding-up order had been made as being beneficial gifts which were therefore available to the creditors. Neuberger J, applying *Re Vernon's Will Trusts*,[206] held that a bequest without limitation or trust, to a limited company, takes effect if the company exists at the testator's death, and there was nothing in any of the wills to rebut the presumption of a beneficial gift. The result, therefore, was that the legacies swelled the assets of the charity available to its creditors.

Institution has never existed

The court is more willing to find a general charitable intention and apply a legacy **15.89** cy-près if it is made to an ostensibly charitable institution which has never

---

[200] As was found in respect of the legacy to the incorporated charity in *Re Finger's Will Trusts* [1972] Ch. 276
[201] *Re Spence* [1979] Ch 483. See also *Clark v Taylor* (1853) 1 Drew 642 (which wrongly states that the institution closed after the testator's death, whereas it in fact closed before); *Fisk v A-G* (1867) 4 Eq 521; *Re Ovey* (1885) 29 ChD 560; *Re Rymer* [1895] 1 Ch 19 (CA). See also *Re Harwood* [1936] 1 Ch 285, 287 (Farwell J)
[202] *Re Slevin* [1891] 2 Ch 230, 243 (CA)
[203] [1891] 2 Ch 230 (CA)
[204] ibid, 243. For an explanation of the sign manual, see above, para 15.01
[205] [1997] 1 WLR 877, discussed above, para 15.85 and ch 26, paras 26.33–26.24
[206] [1972] Ch 300n

existed[207] or merely to a specific type of society.[208] It seems that in these instances the principle is that the testator, by naming a fictitious institution, is presumed to have intended to further a purpose; and, unless there is evidence to rebut the presumption, the court will direct a scheme to carry that purpose into effect.[209] In *Re Harwood,*[210] the testatrix had made bequests to many charitable institutions, and also to the Peace Society of Belfast and the Peace Society of Dublin. It was found that no institutions bearing those names had ever existed. Farwell J found a general charitable intention in respect of those two legacies, and applied them for peace purposes cy-près. The testatrix had also made a bequest to the Wisbech Peace Society, which institution had existed but had ceased to exist before the testatrix's death. Because the testatrix had specified a particular institution, Farwell J was unable to find a general charitable intention in respect of this legacy, which therefore lapsed and fell into residue.[211] The court cannot find a general charitable intention if the name of the non-existent institution specified in the will suggests that a wholly and exclusively charitable institution was not intended.[212]

Mere misdescription

15.90   If it is found that no institution answering the exact description contained in the will exists, it is possible that the testator has merely misdescribed an existing institution that he meant to benefit. In these circumstances, extrinsic evidence is admissible to ascertain what institution was intended.[213] This process is independent of, and distinct from, the cy-près doctrine.

15.91   If, however, the object of the testator's bounty is accurately described in the will and that description fits one object only, extrinsic evidence is, with one qualification, not admissible to show that another was intended to benefit. The qualification to this rule derives from a dictum of Lord Loreburn in *NSPCC v SNSPCC.*[214] The testator had made a bequest to the National Society for the Prevention of Cruelty to Children (NSPCC), a society which operated in England and which was correctly described in the will. The bequest was, however,

---

[207] Older cases include *Bennett v Hayter* (1839) 2 Beav 81; *Re the Clergy Society* (1856) 2 K & J 615; *Re Maguire* (1870) LR 9 Eq 632; *Re Davis* [1902] 1 Ch 876
[208]   *Loscombe v Wintringham* (1850) 13 Beav 87
[209]   *Re Davis* [1902] 1 Ch 876, 882 (Buckley J)
[210]   [1936] 1 Ch 285
[211]   See above, para 15.86
[212]   *Re Satterthwaite's Will Trusts* [1966] 1 WLR 277; *Re Jenkins's Will Trusts* [1966] Ch 249
[213]   The best illustration is probably *Bunting v Marriott* (1854) 19 Beav 163, where no fund of the precise name described in the will existed, but two funds with slightly different names did exist; Romilly MR was able to identify the one intended. See also *Wilson v Squire* (1842) 1 Y & CCC 654. In *Coldwell v Holme* (1854) 2 Sm & Giff 31, an institution answering the precise description had existed, but it had ceased to exist before the testatrix had even made her will. Stuart V-C considered that she should be presumed to have been aware of this at the time; the problem was therefore one of misdescription, and he was able to identify the institution intended to benefit
[214]   [1915] AC 207

claimed by another society, namely the Scottish National Society for the Prevention of Cruelty to Children (SNSPCC), which argued that all the evidence indicated that it, and not the English society, was the society which the testator intended to benefit. The evidence was that the testator was a Scotsman who had lived all his life in Scotland. All his interests were Scottish, and the bequest in dispute was placed amongst a series of bequests to Scottish charities. Moreover, the SNSPCC had a branch near the testator's home, and the testator knew of the society's existence. The English-based NSPCC, on the other hand, had no branch in Scotland, and did not even operate there. All members of the House of Lords, however, agreed that such evidence was not sufficient. Earl Loreburn, with whom three other of their Lordships agreed, said that it would be dangerous to lay down an absolute rule forbidding the admission of extrinsic evidence in every case where the object is correctly described, because unforeseen circumstances might arise where such a rule would lead to injustice. Nevertheless,[215]

> the accurate use of a name in a will creates a strong presumption against any rival who is not the possessor of the name mentioned in the will. It is a very strong presumption and one which cannot be overcome except in exceptional circumstances.

Counsel for the SNSPCC had argued that the name of a society is really descriptive of its objects, and so the presumption should be less strong than in the case of a legacy to an individual person. Earl Loreburn thought that this was perhaps a circumstance to be considered, although he said that he could see little difference.[216]

In *Re Meyers*,[217] Harman J seized upon Earl Loreburn's dictum to help to justify   **15.92** why a corporate charity which was correctly described and in existence was not entitled to receive the legacy made to it in the testator's will. The circumstances were no doubt the exceptional ones that Earl Loreburn had in mind, for the legatee hospital carried on no work and existed merely as a name on the register of companies.[218]

(3) Gift upon trust

For the institution's purposes

As has been mentioned earlier in this chapter,[219] Buckley J stated in *Re Vernon's*   **15.93** *Will Trusts*[220] that a bequest to an unincorporated charity by name without more necessarily take effect as a gift for charitable purposes. If those purposes are still capable of being carried out, a scheme will direct a means of applying the legacy to

---

[215] ibid, 212
[216] ibid, 213
[217] [1951] Ch 534
[218] See further discussion of *Re Meyers* [1951] Ch 534 below, para 15.96
[219] Above, para 15.84
[220] [1972] Ch 300n

those purposes.[221] If, however, the carrying out of the purposes depended on the continued existence of the charity, its failure will cause the charitable purposes to fail; and the legacy can be saved for charity by an application cy-près only if the testator disclosed a general charitable intention.

For the work that the institution had been carrying on

15.94   If the gift is construed as one to carry on the work of the legatee institution, and that institution's work has been taken over before the testator's death by another body which is carrying on that work at the testator's death, the legacy will go to that body as trustee for the purpose of carrying out that work.

15.95   In *Re Morgan*,[222] there was a gift by will 'for the benefit of the Liskeard Cottage Hospital'; this was at the time the will was made an unincorporated charity, but by the time of the testator's death its property had been taken over by the National Health Service. Roxburgh J held that the legacy was for the work of the institution, and should therefore be paid to the Hospital Management Committee that carried on the work of the hospital. He did not reach this decision on the ground that the institution had been unincorporated, but because, on construction, the words 'for the benefit of' indicated a purpose trust, the purpose being the work that the hospital was carrying on.

15.96   Similarly, in *Re Meyers*,[223] a will contained a number of legacies to different hospitals, some of which were incorporated. The effect of the nationalization of these hospitals before the testator's death was to put an end to those which existed as unincorporated associations. Those which were incorporated, however, were still in existence at the testator's death because they had not yet been struck off the register of companies: they continued, albeit merely as shadows of their former selves. Harman J was faced with what he admitted was a 'formidable argument'[224] that while the incorporated charities existed the court had no power to give their legacies to other bodies.[225] In the event, Harman J surmounted this problem by construing all the legacies as trust legacies. He did not distinguish between those institutions which were incorporated and those which were not:[226]

> I am doing no violence to the language which the testator has used, in the context in which he has used it, in saying that in every case when he gave money to a hospital he did not regard the fact whether it was corporate or not, but he gave to the work that that hospital was carrying on.

---

[221] *Re Finger's Will Trusts* [1972] Ch 286
[222] [1950] Ch 637
[223] [1951] 1 Ch 534, appr *Re Glass* [1950] Ch 643n (Vaisey J)
[224] [1951] 1 Ch 534, 540
[225] See above, paras 15.91–15.92
[226] [1951] 1 Ch 534, 542

(4) Gift to a charitable institution which survives in a different form

It may be found that the charitable institution has not in fact ceased to exist, but survives in a modified form; in which event it is necessary to determine whether the legacy belongs to such institution as modified.   **15.97**

Endowed charity's assets applied cy-près under scheme

It is sometimes stated that an application of an endowed charity's assets under a cy-près scheme cannot destroy the charity, so that an endowed charity will continue to exist wherever its assets are currently being applied. The soundness of this proposition, however, is by no means clear.   **15.98**

The leading case on the apparent indestructibility of an endowed charity is *Re Faraker*.[227] A testatrix who died in 1911 by her will gave a legacy to Mrs Bailey's Charity, Rotherhithe. A charity known as 'Hannah Bayly's Charity' had been founded in the eighteenth century as an endowed charity for the benefit of poor widows of Rotherhithe, and this was identified as the institution which the testatrix meant to benefit. The action arose because in 1905 Hannah Bayly's Charity had been consolidated with thirteen other charities under a scheme settled by the Charity Commissioners; and under the terms of the consolidated charity provision was to be made for the poor of Rotherhithe generally. It was argued that as a result of this scheme Hannah Bayly's Charity had ceased to exist and that in consequence the legacy lapsed. All three members of the Court of Appeal were agreed in holding that Hannah Bayly's Charity had not ceased to exist because it was an endowed charity.   **15.99**

What, however, tends to be overlooked in relation to *Re Faraker* is the fact that, as there were at all times poor widows of Rotherhithe, the endowed charity could not be brought to an end either by the courts or the Charity Commissioners as the law then stood. The Charity Commissioners had therefore acted ultra vires in 1905 in purporting to approve a scheme which would permit the income of the funds from Hannah Bayly's Charity to be applied other than specifically to poor widows of Rotherhithe. At that time, all that the Charity Commissioners could have lawfully done *vis-à-vis* Hannah Bayly's Charity would have been to prepare a purely administrative scheme whereby its funds would be held by the same trustees as those of the other charities; but such trustees would have had to keep the funds of Hannah Bayly's Charity entirely separate from those of the other charities, and apply them only to the designated purposes of Hannah Bayly's Charity.   **15.100**

Later cases which have considered *Re Faraker*, however, have not sought to distinguish the case on this ground.[228] In *Re Lucas*[229] the principle was applied where the   **15.101**

---

[227] [1912] 2 Ch 488. For further discussion of this case, see above, paras 15.42 and 15.66

[228] See *Re Lucas* [1948] Ch 424, 427, *Re Roberts* [1963] 1 WLR 406, and *Re Vernon's Will Trusts* [1972] Ch 300n

[229] [1948] Ch 427

property of the original charity had been applied for altered and slightly wider purposes under a lawful cy-près scheme. It is suggested that if an endowed charity's assets are applied cy-près after 1960, the charity will not necessarily continue in existence thereafter; and, whether it does, depends upon how extensive the scheme is. If the purposes are substantially altered, the charity should be treated as having come to an end. An example of this would be where a scheme substitutes new purposes which, although cy-près the original purposes, are nevertheless far removed from them. This will occur where, exceptionally, the substituted purposes fall under a different head of charity within the four-fold classification in *Pemsel*'s case.[230] In practice this is likely to occur only 'where there has been a failure of a purpose under the fourth head and no purpose eujsdem generis can be identified'.[231] An extreme example is *Attorney-General v Ironmongers' Co*,[232] where the property of a charity whose purpose was the redemption of Christian slaves captured by Barbary pirates was applied cy-près for the benefit of charity schools. If, however, the alteration is not substantial, such as the deletion of a particular restriction from its stated purposes,[233] the more effective use of property in conjunction where it is made applicable to common purposes,[234] or an extension of the area of benefit or of the class of persons to benefit,[235] the endowed charity should be treated as continuing. The schemes which had been prepared in both *Re Faraker*[236] and *Re Lucas* might be considered to have involved less than substantial alterations.

Institution's objects altered in accordance with a provision in governing instrument

15.102 If a gift to a charitable corporation is construed as being to the particular institution beneficially (as where there are no words to rebut the presumption of a simple legacy[237]), it would appear that the institution will be entitled to the legacy if it remains on the register of companies, regardless of whether its objects clause has been altered to include different charitable purposes, or even to cause the company to cease to be charitable. In these circumstances, the purposes of the institution are treated merely as attributes, the essence of the gift being the particular institution itself.

---

230 [1891] AC 531
231 H Picarda, *The Law and Practice Relating to Charities* (3rd edn, Butterworths, 1999) 393
232 (1841) Cr & Ph 208 (HL)
233 eg the deletion of a colour bar in *Re Dominion Students' Hall Trust* [1947] Ch 183, discussed above, para 15.62
234 CA 1993, s 13(1)(c)
235 ibid, s 13(1)(d); *Peggs v Lamb* [1994] Ch 172
236 Which today might be lawfully effected under CA 1993, s 13(1)(c)
237 See above, paras 15.83–15.84

If the gift is construed as a trust legacy,[238] it is submitted that whether the named institution remains entitled to the gift depends upon the extent to which its purposes have been altered. If the alteration is small, so that the institution's purposes remain substantially what they were, the institution will remain entitled to a legacy made by a testator who died before the alteration was effected. The legacy will then be paid to the charity, to be held on trust for its general purposes (as amended). If, however, the charity's purposes are substantially altered, as where one head of charity is substituted for another, it is no longer possible for the institution to receive the property on trust for its general purposes, as this would substantially defeat the intention of the settlor. If the institution's previous charitable purposes are still capable of fulfilment, the legacy will be applied under a scheme (not a cy-près scheme) to those purposes. If they are no longer capable of fulfilment, the legacy will fail unless a general charitable intention on the testator's part can be found. **15.103**

Institution's assets transferred to another charity in accordance with a provision in its governing instrument

Pursuant to a power in the trust instrument, the trustees may be able to transfer the entire fund to another institution with similar (or indeed other) charitable purposes. In *Re Roberts*,[239] the trust instrument conferred on the trustees of the Sheffield Boys' Working Home a power to sell its property and distribute the proceeds to other charities. Pursuant to this power, the trustees sold the property and paid over most of the proceeds of sale to the Sheffield Town Trust. Wilberforce J held that the exercise of this power involved a termination of the institution. The Sheffield Town Trust was not, therefore, entitled to take a legacy to the Sheffield Boys' Working Home made by a testatrix who died after the sale of its property. **15.104**

H. Public charitable appeals

(1) Introduction

Surplus

If a surplus remains in a charitable public appeal fund after the specified purpose for which the money was raised has been carried out, such surplus is treated as applicable cy-près without inquiry as to general charitable intention,[240] either on the **15.105**

---

[238] See above, paras 15.83–15.84

[239] [1963] 1 WLR 406. See also *Re Stemson's Will Trusts* [1970] Ch 16, where the same principle was applied when a charitable company's assets were transferred, on dissolution, to another charity, pursuant to a power contained in the transferor company's memorandum

[240] eg *Spiller v Maude* (1881), rep (1886) 32 ChD 158n (Jessel MR); *Pease v Pattinson* (1886) 32 ChD 154; *Re Hartley Colliery Accident Relief Fund* (1908) 102 LT 165n; *Re Welsh Hospital (Netley) Fund* [1921] 1 Ch 655; *Re North Devon and West Somerset Relief Fund Trusts* [1953] 1 WLR 1260

basis that the donors are presumed to have intended this,[241] or simply because it is considered that no general charitable intention need be sought.[242] The one case to the contrary is *Re British Red Cross Balkan Fund*,[243] where the surplus was returned rateably to subscribers; but this decision is out of line with the array of contrary authorities, and is probably wrong.[244] For the avoidance of doubt, it is good practice to specify in the terms of the appeal a description of other charitable purposes to which any surplus funds are to be applied.

Failure

15.106 Where funds are raised for a charitable purpose by means of a public appeal, there is a risk that insufficient sums may be raised to enable the specified purposes to be carried out. The potential difficulties to which this can give rise can be overcome by providing expressly in the terms of the appeal that, in the event of insufficient funds being raised for the primary purpose, the funds which have been collected will be applied to other charitable purposes—either specified purposes, or such other charitable purposes as the trustees of the appeal fund may select. If such alternative provision is made and the sums raised do indeed prove inadequate, the charity trustees will be able to apply the funds to the secondary purposes without having to go through the procedures specified in section 14 of the Charities Act 1993.

15.107 In the absence of an expressed secondary purpose, the difficulty is to determine how the funds raised should be dealt with in the event of a failure of the purposes specified. If the failure occurs after the funds have been raised, the failure is supervening, so that on general principles, the funds would be treated as effectually dedicated to charity and applicable cy-près.[245]

15.108 A failure which results merely from insufficiency of funds is, however, treated as an initial failure, so that, on general principles, the sums would need to be returned to the donors unless they disclosed a general charitable intention. In *Re University of London Medical Sciences Institute Fund*, before the enactment of

---

[241] *Re Welsh Hospital (Netley) Fund* [1921] 1 Ch 655; *Re North Devon and West Somerset Relief Fund Trusts* [1953] 1 WLR 1260

[242] See *Re Ulverston and District New Hospital Building Trusts* [1956] Ch 622, 636; *Re British School of Egyptian Archaeology* [1954] 1 WLR 546, 553 (Harman J); also (in context of testamentary trust) *Re Monk* [1927] 2 Ch 197, 211–12 (Sargant LJ). On surpluses generally, see above, para 15.30

[243] [1914] 2 Ch 419

[244] It has been described as an aberration: see H Picarda, *The Law and Practice Relating to Charities* (3rd edn, Butterworths, 1999) 354. See also the criticisms in *Barlow Clowes International Ltd v Vaughan* [1992] 4 All ER 22, 29 (Dillon LJ, who describes this aspect of the decision as 'suspect'). The principle of the *Balkan Fund* case has, however, been applied to non-charitable appeals: *Re Hobourn Aero Components Ltd's Air Raid Distress Fund* [1946] Ch 86, 97 (Cohen J, at first instance; this issue did not arise on appeal to the CA: [1946] Ch 194)

[245] On failure generally, see above, paras 15.46–15.48

the Charities Act 1960, the Court of Appeal treated a legacy of £25,000 to an appeal fund made in response to a public appeal as given conditionally on the charitable purpose being carried out; as the purpose had been found to be impracticable and had been abandoned, it was held that the legacy should be returned to the executors.[246] In other cases, there was judicial disagreement about the treatment of donations made by identifiable donors inter vivos: in *Re Hillier*[247] Evershed MR said that identifiable donors were presumed to have given their contributions with a paramount intention of charity,[248] and Denning LJ thought that such donors should be treated as having given their contributions out and out to charity.[249] On the other hand, in *Re Ulverston and District New Hospital Building Trusts*,[250] Jenkins LJ thought that funds raised solely for a specific purpose precluded the finding of any general charitable intention on the part of identifiable donors.

None of the cases involving failed charity collections ever held that there should **15.109** be a resulting trust in favour of anonymous donors.[251] One view was that donations from such sources were to be considered to have been abandoned; such contributions would therefore pass as bona vacantia to the Crown,[252] and so would be applicable cy-près under the prerogative jurisdiction. Another view was that contributions from anonymous donors should be treated as having been made either with a paramount intention of charity,[253] or as having been given out and out to charity.[254]

A resulting trust of anonymous contributions was held to arise in *Re Gillingham* **15.110** *Bus Disaster Fund*.[255] This did not involve a collection for a charitable purpose,

---

[246] *Re University of London Medical Sciences Institute Fund* [1909] 2 Ch 1 (CA)

[247] [1954] 1 WLR 700 (CA)

[248] See Evershed MR in *Re Hillier* [1954] 1 WLR 700, 712 (CA), who also thought that, where the circumstances of the appeal are such that contributors will appreciate that their contributions will be mingled with thousands of others, including some from anonymous sources, that is a relevant and admissible factor in determining such contributors' true intentions: ibid, 712. cf *Re Dover's Battle of Britain Memorial Hospital Fund* The Times, 29 June 1955, cited *arguendo* in *Re Ulverston and District New Hospital Building Trusts* [1956] Ch 622, 627

[249] See Denning LJ in *Re Hillier* [1954] 1 WLR 700, 714–16 (CA). Russell LJ dissented, as he considered that the voluntary nature of the proposed hospital, for the building of which the appeal had been launched, was an essential quality of the appeal; he would therefore have returned the contributions to the identifiable donors: ibid, 718

[250] [1956] Ch 622 (CA)

[251] In *Re Ulverston* [1956] Ch 622, Jenkins LJ said that he could envisage circumstances in which an anonymous contributor might be able to prove that he had made a contribution of a specified amount so as to entitle him to claim its return, but his suggestions were dismissed as 'somewhat fanciful and unreal' in *Re West Sussex Constabulary's Widows, Children and Benevolent Fund Trust* [1971] Ch 1, 13 (Goff J)

[252] This seems to have been the view favoured in *Re Ulverston* [1956] Ch 622 by Jenkins LJ (with whose jdgt Hodson LJ agreed)

[253] *Semble* this was the view of Evershed MR in *Re Hiller* [1954] 1 WLR 700 (CA)

[254] See dicta of Denning LJ in *Re Hillier* [1954] 1 WLR 700, 714–16

[255] [1958] Ch 300; affd [1959] Ch 62

and the decision was criticized in a later case on the ground that equity will not impute to the donors an intention which it considers would be absurd on the face of it.[256] The decision in the *Gillingham* case, which meant that the money had to be paid into court to await reclamation by anonymous donors, nevertheless gave rise to some concern that the same outcome might be reached in respect of anonymous donations to charitable purposes. This led to the passing of section 14 of the Charities Act 1960, which has now been re-enacted, with some modifications, as section 14 of the Charities Act 1993.[257] The section applies to property given for charitable purposes notwithstanding that it was so given before the commencement of that Act.[258]

(2) Section 14 of the Charities Act 1993

15.111   Section 14(1) states:

> Property given for specific charitable purposes which fail shall be applicable cy-près as if given for charitable purposes generally, where it belongs—
> (a) to a donor who after—
>   (i) the prescribed advertisements and inquiries have been published and made, and
>   (ii) the prescribed period beginning with the publication of those advertisements has expired,
> cannot be identified or cannot be found; or
> (b) to a donor who has executed a disclaimer in the prescribed form of his right to have the property returned.

The meaning of certain phrases in this sub-section will now be considered in turn.

Meaning of 'property given'

15.112   In section 14, except in so far as the context otherwise requires, references to property given include the property for the time being representing the property originally given or property derived from it.[259]

15.113   It might be argued that payments made under a deed of covenant are not 'given', since such payments are not voluntary, but are made under a legal obligation. The better view, however, is that 'given' in the section is not used in its technical sense, but merely means 'transferred',[260] so that such payments can be included.

---

[256] *Re West Sussex Constabulary's Widows, Children and Benevolent Fund Trust* [1971] Ch 1, 14 (Goff J)

[257] CA 1993, s 14, came into force 1 Aug 1993. It re-enacts CA 1960, s 14, with the amendments which would have been made by CA 1992, s 15, had that section of the 1992 Act (now repealed) been brought into force

[258] CA 1993, s 14(11)

[259] ibid, s 14(10)

[260] cf House to House Collections Act 1939, s 11, where 'to give' has been held to include the payment of money in the purchase of goods: *Cooper v Coles* [1986] QB 230

Meaning of 'for specific charitable purposes'

As has been discussed,[261] the case law before 1961 held that anonymous donors **15.114** must be treated as having given with a paramount intention of charity, or to charity out and out, or to have abandoned any interest in their contributions, and even identifiable donors were sometimes considered to have given with a paramount intention of charity.[262] It nevertheless seems that such contributions are given primarily for the specific purposes of the appeal, and would therefore satisfy the requirement that they be given 'for specific charitable purposes'.

Meaning of 'which fail'

Section 14(1) of the Charities Act 1993 is applicable only where property has been **15.115** given for specific charitable purposes 'which fail'. For the purposes of the section, charitable purposes are deemed to 'fail' where any difficulty in applying property to those purposes makes that property or the part not applicable cy-près available to be returned to the donors.[263]

If this definition is treated as exhaustive,[264] section 14 has little significance for **15.116** anonymous donations, since, as has been seen, none of the cases which preceded the Charities Act 1960 held that the failure made the contributions of anonymous donors available to be returned to them.[265] Since the main importance of the section lies in its treatment of anonymous donations, this interpretation would rob the section of most of its significance; it would indeed be largely a dead letter.[266] It may, however, be contended that the definition is intended to be merely expansive or illustrative;[267] in which case, the section applies even in those cases where the property would otherwise have gone to the Crown or have been applicable cy-près under general principles. It is submitted that, as the former interpretation would deny the section much of its meaning, the courts would prefer the latter. In any event, the statutory predecessor of the section[268] has in practice been applied by the court[269]

---

[261] See above, paras 15.109–15.110

[262] See above, para 15.107

[263] CA 1993, s 14(7)

[264] The expression 'deemed' may indicate that the definition which follows is exhaustive: see *St Aubyn (LM) v A-G (No. 2)* [1952] AC 15, 53 (Lord Radcliffe, speaking in the context of a taxing statute)

[265] *Re Ulverston and District New Hospital Building Trusts* [1956] Ch 622; *Re Hillier* [1954] 1 WLR 700

[266] See D Wilson, 'Section 14 of the Charities Act 1960: a Dead Letter?' [1983] Conv 40

[267] cf *Barclay's Bank Ltd v IRC* [1961] AC 509, 523 (Viscount Simonds, who said, in the context of a taxing statute, that he regarded the primary function of the word 'deem' as being 'to bring about something which would otherwise be excluded')

[268] ie CA 1960, s 14

[269] *Re Henry Wood National Memorial Trusts* [1966] 1 WLR 1601

and (on numerous occasions) by the Charity Commissioners[270] on the assumption that it is applicable to donations from unidentifiable donors.

15.117 A surplus can fall within section 14 only if it can be treated as a 'failure' of the purpose. A surplus might be considered to be an initial failure *pro tanto* in respect of sums raised after it is clear that an amount sufficient for the purpose has been raised, but this would in practice be difficult to establish.[271] Only in one case, moreover, has the surplus of funds raised by a charitable public appeal been held to go on a resulting trust,[272] and this decision is probably wrong.[273] On the footing that a surplus is not a failure, section 14 does not apply. Any surplus funds from a public appeal would in any event be applicable cy-près without the need for a general charitable intention, and could be applied under a scheme prepared by the Charity Commissioners under their jurisdiction conferred by section 16 of the Charities Act 1993.

Meaning of 'as if given for charitable purposes generally'

15.118 This means that the cy-près scheme is not restricted by the ambit of all or any of the donors' intentions.

Meaning of 'where it belongs . . . to a donor'

15.119 Except in so far as the context otherwise requires, references in section 14 to a donor include persons claiming through or under the original donor.[274]

Meaning of 'the prescribed advertisements and inquiries'

15.120 'Prescribed' means prescribed by regulations made by the Charity Commissioners, and such regulations may make provision for the form and content of the advertisements required by section 14(1)(a).[275] This information is set out fully below.[276]

---

[270] See, eg, *Mile End Memorial Hall Fund* [1965] Ch Com Rep 8 (paras 19–21); *Stewartby United Church Building Fund* [1969] Ch Com Rep 20 (paras 54–7); *Bedford Church Hall Fund, Hartshorne, St Peter, Derbyshire* [1971] Ch Com Rep 22–3 (paras 72–5); *South Scarborough Swimming Pool Association* [1980] Ch Com Rep 38–9 (paras 135–36); *South Petherton Swimming Pool Fund, Somerset* [1982] Ch Com Rep 20 (paras 62–3)
[271] cf above, para 15.50
[272] *Re British Red Cross Balkan Fund* [1914] 2 Ch 419
[273] See above, para 15.105
[274] CA 1993, s 14(10)
[275] ibid, s 14(8). The Charity Commissioners must publish regulations made by them under s 14 in such manner as they shall think fit: ibid, s 14(9)
[276] See below, paras 15.122–15.124

Meaning of 'the prescribed period'

The regulations prescribe a period of three months.[277]

15.121

(3) Prescribed forms and information pursuant to section 14 of Charities Act 1993

Advertisements

The current regulations[278] require the advertisements to be published in English in every case. Additionally, where the appeal was published[279] in another language, the advertisements must be published in that language; and they may also be published in Welsh, even if the appeal was not made in Welsh.[280] An advertisement must be published in the specified manner,[281] which means that it must be published in a newspaper or other periodical which is both written in the same language as the advertisement, and sold or distributed throughout the area in which the appeal was made.[282] Where the purposes of the appeal were directed towards the benefit of an area contained wholly or mainly within a local authority district or a London borough or the City of London, a copy of every advertisement so published must also be published by fixing copies of it to two public notice boards in the relevant area.[283]

15.122

The advertisement must be set out in the form specified in Schedule 1 to the Regulations or in an equivalent form in any other required or permitted language.[284] The form is as follows:[285]

15.123

FORM OF ADVERTISEMENT PRESCRIBED FOR THE PURPOSES OF SECTION 14(1)(a)(i) OF THE CHARITIES ACT 1993

'ADVERTISEMENT

Name of charity (if applicable):

Registered charity number (if applicable):

Purpose for which money or other property was given:

NOTICE is given that money and other property given for this purpose cannot be used for that purpose because [state reasons].

---

[277] Charities (Cy-près Advertisements, Inquiries and Disclaimer) Regulations 1993, reg 5. These regulations came into force on 24 June 1993
[278] ibid. The regulations are set out in (1993) 1 Decisions 30–7
[279] The expression 'published' is here used widely to refer to the means by which the appeal was made, which could, for instance, be on television or radio, or by appeal leaflets
[280] Charities (Cy-près Advertisements, Inquiries and Disclaimer) Regulations 1993, reg 2(2)
[281] ibid, reg 3
[282] ibid, Sch 2, para 1
[283] ibid, para 2
[284] ibid, reg 2(1)
[285] ibid, Sch 1

2 If you gave money or other property for that purpose you are entitled to claim it back. If you wish to do so you must tell [insert name] of [insert address] within 3 months of [specify date: see note below]. If you wish the money or other property to go to a similar charitable purpose and to disclaim your right to the return of the money or other property, you must ask the person named above for a form of disclaimer.

3 If you do not either make a claim within the 3 months or sign a disclaimer, the Charity Commissioners may make a Scheme applying the property to other charitable purposes. You will still be able to claim the return of your money or other property (less expenses), but **only if you do so within 6 months from the date of any Scheme made by the Commissioners**.

4 Date of this notice [**specify date: see note below**]'

[**Note:** [**This Note does not form part of the prescribed advertisement**] If this advertisement is to be published in a newspaper or other periodical, the words 'the date of publication' should be inserted in paragraphs 2 and 4 above.

If this advertisement is to be published on a public notice board, the date inserted here should be the date on which the advertisement was fixed to the public notice board.]

Inquiries

15.124   A prescribed inquiry must be made in writing, and sent by post to the address of each donor recorded in the records of the trustees of the property, and it must contain at least the information specified in Schedule 3 to the Regulations.[286] This information is as follows:[287]

INFORMATION TO BE CONTAINED IN INQUIRIES TO BE MADE IN PURSUANCE OF SECTION 14(1)(a)(i) OF THE CHARITIES ACT 1993

1 The name and address of the charity to which the property was given by the donor;

2 A description of the specific charitable purpose for which the property was given by the donor;

3 The reasons why that purpose has failed;

4 A description of the property (including the amount of any money) given for that purpose by the donor;

5 A statement of the donor's right to have the property returned;

6 A statement that the donor may disclaim the right to have the property described in paragraph 4 above returned by executing a disclaimer in the prescribed form;

7 A statement that, where the donor disclaims his right in respect of such property, the property may be applied for other charitable purposes similar to those for which it was given by a Scheme established by the Commissioners or by the court; and

---

[286] Charities (Cy-près Advertisements, Inquiries and Disclaimer) Regulations 1993, reg 4
[287] ibid, Sch 3

> 8 A statement that, where the donor has not replied in writing to the inquiry within three months from the date of service of the inquiry, he will be treated for the purposes of section 14(1)(a) as a donor who cannot be identified or found, but that he will be able to claim the property, less expenses, within six months from the date of any Scheme made by the Commissioners or the court.

Disclaimer

A disclaimer executed in pursuance of section 14(1)(b) must either be executed in English in the specified form,[288] or be executed in the equivalent form in Welsh.[289] The prescribed form in English is as follows:[290]   **15.125**

> FORM OF DISCLAIMER PRESCRIBED FOR THE PURPOSES OF SECTION 14(1)(a)(ii) OF THE CHARITIES ACT 1993
>
> 'DISCLAIMER   I HEREBY DISCLAIM my right to the return of the sum of £ . . . . ./the property consisting of (insert description of property)* given by me for (insert name of charity to which, or description of purposes for which, the money or property was given).
>
> Signed
>
> Name in capitals
>
> Address
>
> Date
>
> Signed†
>
> Name in capitals
>
> Address
>
> Date
>
> * Delete as appropriate
>
> † This paragraph may be repeated if further signatures are required.

(4) Protection of trustees

Where the prescribed advertisements and inquiries have been published and made, the trustees are not liable in respect of the property to any person from whom they receive no claim before the expiry of the prescribed period, beginning with the publication of those advertisements.[291]   **15.126**

---

[288] ie in the form specified ibid, Sch 4
[289] ibid, reg 6
[290] ibid, Sch 4
[291] CA 1993, s 14(2)

(5) Property which may be treated as belonging to unidentifiable donors

15.127 By virtue of section 14(3) of the Charities Act 1993, for the purposes of that section property is conclusively presumed (without any advertisement or inquiry) to belong to donors who cannot be identified, in so far as it consists[292]

   (a) of the proceeds of cash collections made by means of collecting boxes or by other means not adapted for distinguishing one gift from another; or

   (b) of the proceeds of any lottery, competition, entertainment, sale or similar money-raising activity, after allowing for property given to provide prizes or articles for sale or otherwise to enable the activity to be undertaken.

15.128 By virtue of sub-section (4), the court may by order direct that property not falling within sub-section (3) is, for the purposes of section 14, to be treated (without any advertisement or inquiry) as belonging to donors who cannot be identified where it appears to the court either[293]

   (a) that it would be unreasonable, having regard to the amounts likely to be returned to the donors, to incur expense with a view to returning the property; or

   (b) that it would be unreasonable, having regard to the nature, circumstances and amounts of the gifts, and to the lapse of time since the gifts were made, for the donors to expect the property to be returned.

(6) Rights of donors who are identifiable and found within the prescribed period

15.129 Section 14 of the Charities Act 1993 does not specify the extent of the claim of donors who (not falling within sub-section (3) or (4)) are identifiable and found within the prescribed period. This is therefore dealt with under the general law, so that, unless the donor can be shown to have given out and out to charity or with a general charitable intention, he will (during the prescribed period) have a beneficial interest under a resulting trust.

15.130 In the presumably rare cases where the donor can show that his contribution was used to purchase an asset, the donor will be entitled to trace into that asset, thus taking the benefit of any increase in its value.[294] If it can be shown that the asset was acquired through the contributions of two or more identifiable donors who claim within the prescribed period, such donors will be entitled to a charge *pari passu* on the asset, or to take the asset between them as tenants in common in equity if they agree.[295] Some of the funds raised in *Re Hillier*[296] had been applied in the purchase of land which was subsequently sold at a profit; but no point was

---

[292] CA 1993, s 14(3)

[293] ibid, s 14(4)

[294] *Re Diplock* [1948] Ch 465 (CA)

[295] *Sinclair v Brougham* [1914] AC 398, 442 (Lord Parker). This case was doubted (and arguably overruled) by the more recent House of Lords' decision in *Westdeutsche Landesbank Girocentrale v Islington LBC* [1996] AC 669, but the principle itself probably survives. See also *Re Tilley's Will Trusts* [1967] Ch 1179

[296] [1954] 1 WLR 700

made in argument as to the exact rights of the subscribers with regard to such profit.[297]

Where innocent volunteers' moneys are wrongfully[298] mixed in an active bank ac-   **15.131**
count, the normal rule as between innocent volunteers is that of 'first in, first out',
that is, withdrawals are treated as being made in the same order as payments in.[299]
The rule would not, therefore, seem to be applicable where the mixing is not
wrongful but might be reasonably contemplated by the donors, as is the case in
most charitable appeals.[300] Quite apart from this, the 'first in, first out' rule is one
of convenience only, and will not apply where it would be impracticable for it to
do so, or where it would lead to an injustice.[301] If there are numerous identifiable
donors, the application of the rule might well prove impracticable. Where the
'first in, first out' rule does not apply, the claimants share *pari passu* in proportion
to the amount of their contributions.[302]

(7) Claims after property has been applied cy-près under section 14 of the Charities Act 1993

At first sight, it appears that, after the prescribed period has expired, the rights of   **15.132**
a donor who cannot be identified or cannot be found are lost permanently, since
sub-section (1) of section 14 says that the property of such person is then applicable cy-près 'as if given for charitable purposes generally'. It appears, however, that
whilst such rights are lost at the end of the prescribed period, some of them may
be revived by sub-section (5) later, when the property is actually applied cy-près.
Sub-section (5) revives (to a limited extent) the claims of donors who were
unidentifiable or who could not be found other than by virtue of their falling
within sub-section (3) or under a direction made under sub-section (4). Since a
direction under sub-section (4) can be made by the court only, and not by the
Charity Commissioners, there are many appeals in which the total amount raised
overall cannot justify the expense of applying to the court for such a direction. In

---

[297] ibid, 707 (Evershed MR)

[298] ie as in *Re Diplock* [1948] Ch 465 (which involved a wrongful distribution of an estate to various charities), or *Re Hallett's Estate* (1880) 13 ChD 696 (where a solicitor wrongfully mixed moneys held by him in a fiduciary capacity for one client and moneys belonging to a trust in a single
general bank account which he held for his own purposes). See *Barlow Clowes International Ltd v
Vaughan* [1992] 4 All ER 22, 45 (Leggatt LJ)

[299] ie the rule in *Clayton's Case: Devaynes v Noble, Clayton's Case* (1816) 1 Mer 529

[300] This was the view of Leggatt LJ in *Barlow Clowes International Ltd v Vaughan* [1992]
4 All ER 22, and it could explain the basis of distribution in the non-charitable appeal in *Re Hobourn
Aero Components Ltd's Air Raid Distress Fund* [1946] Ch 86, 97 (Cohen J), and the charitable appeal
in *Re British Red Cross Balkan Fund* [1914] 2 Ch 419, although the latter case may be doubted on
other grounds: see above, paras 15.50 and 15.105

[301] *Barlow Clowes International Ltd v Vaughan* [1992] 4 All ER 22 (CA)

[302] *Sinclair v Brougham* [1914] AC 398 (HL); *Barlow Clowes International Ltd v Vaughan* [1992]
4 All ER 22, 27 (Dillon LJ)

the absence of such a direction, there remains the possibility of claims being made to the property when it is applied cy-près.

15.133 Sub-section (5) initially provides that, where property is applied cy-près by virtue of section 14, the donor is deemed to have parted with all his interest at the time when the gift was made.[303] It goes on, however, to qualify this by stating that, where property is so applied as belonging to donors who cannot be identified or cannot be found, and is not so applied by virtue of sub-section (3) or (4), the scheme must specify the total amount of that property,[304] and the donor of any part is entitled, if he claims within six months of the scheme's being made, to recover from the charity for which the property is applied a sum equal to that part, less any expenses properly incurred by the charity trustees after that date in connection with claims relating to his gift.[305] The scheme may include directions as to the provision to be made for meeting any such claim.[306] The combined effect of these provisions is that, if the donor does not claim within the six months, he loses for ever his right to have his gift or any part of it returned.

15.134 The amount set aside under sub-section (5) for meeting claims may, of course, be only a fraction of what was originally contributed by the donors, since (quite apart from the expenses incurred in connection with claims relating to the donors' gifts) a part of the total fund may previously have been applied in meeting expenses in connection with the appeal, or have been used to purchase property which has since declined in value. The likely possibility of a shortfall is dealt with in sub-section (6), which provides that if the aggregate amount of such claims exceeds the amount set aside for meeting them after deduction of expenses, then the Charity Commissioners may direct that each of the donors in question is entitled to a proportionately reduced amount.[307]

15.135 Section 14 does not, however, deal expressly with the opposite case, where the value of the fund has, perhaps through being invested, increased. It seems to be implicit in sub-section (5)(b), however, that the value of a donor's claim cannot exceed the amount of his contribution. Any surplus would therefore be applicable cy-près.

---

[303] CA 1993, s 14(5)
[304] ibid, s 14(5)(a)
[305] ibid, s 14(5)(b)
[306] ibid, s 14(5)(c)
[307] ibid, s 14(6). This sub-s originates in CA 1992, before which it was unclear whether in such circumstances the applicable principle as between the innocent volunteer contributors should be first in, first out (as in *Re Hallett* (1880) 13 ChD 696, Fry J at first instance), or proportionately (as in *Re Diplock* [1948] Ch 465 (CA), where the mixing took place outside an active bank account))

I. Small charities

Sections 74 and 75 of the Charities Act 1993 lay down procedures which charity **15.136**
trustees of a small charity may follow in order either to transfer property to another charity or to modify its objects, or (in the case of a small endowed charity)
to enable it to spend capital.[308]

(1) Power to transfer property and modify objects

Charities within s 74 of Charities Act 1993

Section 74 applies to a charity if three conditions are met: first, if its gross income **15.137**
in its last financial year did not exceed £5,000;[309] secondly, if it does not hold land
on trusts which stipulate that the land is to be used for the purposes, or any particular purposes, of the charity; and thirdly, if it is neither an exempt charity nor a
charitable company.[310]

Resolutions which charity trustees may make

Under section 74, charity trustees of a charity may, by a resolution passed by a **15.138**
two-thirds majority of such charity trustees as vote on it,[311] resolve to take three
different types of action. The possible actions are as follows.

Transfer of charity's property to another charity or charities

The charity trustees may resolve to transfer all the charity's property to another **15.139**
charity,[312] or to divide it between two or more other charities;[313] the transferee
charities must be specified in the resolution, and must be either registered or not
required to be registered.[314]

---

[308]   These sections re-enact CA 1992, ss 43–4, which came into force on 1 Sept 1992, and which
themselves re-enacted, with important modifications which broadened the application of, and
simplified the procedures contained in, the original provisions introduced in CA 1985. See A-
M Piper and M Palmer, 'Charities: a new miniature code' (1992–3) 1 CL & PR 239. On the back-
ground to CA 1985, see *Hansard*, HL (series 5) vol 442 cols 278–309 (6 May 1983), Second
Reading of the Parochial Charities (Neighbourhood Trusts) Bill. See also M Sladen, 'The Charities
Act 1985' [1986] Conv 78. On the modern provisions, see also Charity Commission, *Small
Charities: Alteration of Trusts, Transfer of Property, Expenditure of Capital*, CC44 (Sept 1995)

[309]   The Secretary of State may by order substitute a different sum: CA 1993, s 74(11)

[310]   ibid, s 74(1). In s 74, 'charitable company' means a charity which is a company or other body
corporate: ibid, s 74(12)(a)

[311]   ibid, s 74(3)

[312]   ibid, s 74(2)(a)

[313]   ibid, s 74(2)(b)

[314]   ibid, s 74(2)(a), (b). Charities not required to be registered are set out in s 3(5), and therefore
include an exempt charity. In s 74, references to the transfer of property to a charity are references
to its transfer to the charity trustees, or to any trustee for the charity, or to a person nominated by
the charity trustees to hold it in trust for the charity, as the charity trustees may determine: ibid,
s 74(12)(b)

15.140 The charity trustees do not have power to pass such a resolution unless they are satisfied:[315]

    (a) that the existing purposes of the transferor charity have ceased to be conducive to a suitable and effective application of the charity's resources; and

    (b) that the purposes of the charity or charities specified in the resolution are as similar in character to the purposes of the transferor charity as is reasonably practicable.

Before passing the resolution, the charity trustees must have received written confirmation from the charity trustees of the transferee charity, or (as the case may be) of each of the transferee charities, specified in the resolution, that those trustees are willing to accept a transfer of property under the section.[316]

Modification of charitable purposes

15.141 The charity trustees may resolve to modify the trusts of the charity by replacing all or any of the charity's purposes with such other purposes, being in law charitable, as are specified in the resolution.[317]

15.142 The charity trustees do not have power to pass such a resolution unless they are satisfied:[318]

    (a) that the existing purposes of the charity (or, as the case may be, such of them as it is proposed to replace) have ceased to be conducive to a suitable and effective application of the charity's resources; and

    (b) that the purposes specified in the resolution are as similar in character to those existing purposes as is practical in the circumstances.

Modification of administrative powers or procedures

15.143 The charity trustees may resolve that any provision of the trusts of the charity relating to any of the powers exercisable by the charity trustees in the administration of the charity, or regulating the procedure to be followed in connection with its administration, should be modified in such manner as is specified in the resolution.[319]

Procedure after resolution has been passed

15.144 Where the charity trustees have passed a resolution under section 74 of the Charities Act 1993, they must give public notice of it in such manner as they think reasonable in the circumstances, and send a copy to the Charity Commissioners, together with a statement of their reasons for passing it.[320] The Charity Commissioners, when considering the resolution, may require the charity trustees to

---

[315] CA 1993, s 74(4)(a), (b)
[316] ibid, s 74(4)
[317] ibid, s 74(2)(c)
[318] ibid, s 74(5)
[319] ibid, s 74(2)(d)
[320] ibid, s 74(6)

provide additional information or explanation as to the circumstances in which they have determined to act, or relating to their compliance with the provisions of section 74 in connection with the resolution.[321] The Commissioners must take into account any representations made to them by persons appearing to them to be interested in the charity where those representations are made within six weeks from the date when the Commissioners receive a copy of the resolution.[322] The Charity Commissioners must, within three months of receiving a copy of the resolution, notify the trustees in writing whether they concur or do not concur with the resolution.[323]

Duties of charity trustees if Charity Commissioners concur

Where the Charity Commissioners notify their concurrence with a resolution that involves a transfer of the charity's property to another charity or charities,[324] the charity trustees must arrange for all the property of the transferor charity to be transferred in accordance with the resolution.[325] The charity trustees must ensure that such property will be held and applied by the transferee charity for its purposes, but subject to any restrictions on expenditure to which it is subject as property of the transferor charity.[326] The trustees must arrange for such property to be so transferred by such date as may be specified in the notification.[327] **15.145**

Where the Charity Commissioners notify their concurrence with a resolution that involves a modification of the charitable purposes,[328] or administrative powers or procedures,[329] then the trusts of the charity are deemed to have been modified in accordance with the terms of the resolution as from such date as may be specified in the notification.[330] **15.146**

Vesting orders

For the purpose of enabling any property to be transferred to a charity under section 74, the Charity Commissioners have power, at the request of the charity trustees of that charity, to make orders vesting any property of the transferor charity either in the charity trustees of the transferee charity or in any trustees for that charity, or in any other person nominated by those charity trustees to hold the property in trust for that charity.[331] **15.147**

---

[321] ibid, s 74(7)(a), (b)
[322] ibid, s 74(7)
[323] ibid, s 74(8)
[324] ie under CA 1993, s 74(2)(a) or (b)
[325] ibid, s 74(9)(a)
[326] ibid, s 74(9)(a)(i), (ii)
[327] ibid, s 74(9)
[328] ie under ibid, s 74(2)(c)
[329] ie under ibid, s 74(2)(d)
[330] ibid, s 74(9)(b)
[331] ibid, s 74(10)

(2) Power to spend capital

Charities within section 75

15.148 Section 75 of the Charities Act 1993 applies to a charity (not being an exempt charity or a charitable company[332]) if it has a permanent endowment which does not consist of or comprise any land, and if its gross income in its last financial year did not exceed £1,000.[333]

Resolution to permit expenditure of capital of permanent endowment

15.149 If the charity trustees of a charity within section 75 consider that the property of the charity is too small, in relation to its purposes, for any useful purpose to be achieved by the expenditure of income alone, they may resolve that the charity ought to be freed from the restrictions with respect to expenditure of capital to which its permanent endowment is subject.[334] Any such resolution requires a two-thirds majority of such charity trustees as vote on it.[335] Before passing such a resolution, the charity trustees must consider whether any reasonable possibility exists of effecting a transfer or division of all the charity's property under section 74 (disregarding any such transfer or division as would, in their opinion, impose on the charity an unacceptable burden of costs).[336]

Procedure after resolution has been passed

15.150 Where the charity trustees have passed such a resolution, they must give public notice of it in such manner as they think reasonable in the circumstances, and send a copy to the Charity Commissioners together with a statement of their reasons for passing it.[337] The Charity Commissioners, when considering the resolution, may require the charity trustees to provide additional information or explanation as to the circumstances in which they have determined to act, or relating to their compliance with the provisions of section 75 in connection with the resolution.[338] The Charity Commissioners must take into account any representations made to them by persons appearing to them to be interested in the charity where those representations are made within six weeks from the date when the Commissioners receive a copy of the resolution.[339] The Charity Commissioners

---

[332] In s 75, 'charitable company' means a charity which is a company or other body corporate: CA 1993, s 75(10)
[333] ibid, s 75(1). The Secretary of State may by order substitute a different sum: ibid, s 75(9)
[334] ibid, s 75(2)
[335] ibid, s 75(3)
[336] ibid, s 75(4)
[337] ibid, s 75(5)
[338] ibid, s 75(6)(a), (b)
[339] ibid, s 75(6)

must, within three months of receiving a copy of the resolution, notify the trustees in writing whether they concur or do not concur with the resolution.[340]

Effect of Charity Commissioners' concurrence

Where the Charity Commissioners notify their concurrence with the resolution, the charity trustees have, as from such date as may be specified in the notification, power by virtue of section 75 of the Charities Act 1993 to expend any property of the charity without regard to any restrictions with respect to expenditure of capital to which its permanent endowment is subject.[341]   **15.151**

J. Dormant bank accounts

By virtue of section 28 of the Charities Act 1993, the Charity Commissioners are empowered to direct a bank, building society, or certain other financial institutions holding charity funds in an account which is dormant, to transfer such funds to such other charity[342] or charities (and, in the latter case, in such amounts) as the Charity Commissioners may direct.[343] This power does not apply to any account held for an exempt charity.[344]   **15.152**

The Charity Commissioners can make such a direction only when they are informed by a 'relevant institution' that it holds one or more accounts in the name or on behalf of a particular charity ('the relevant charity'), that such account or each of such accounts is dormant, and where the Charity Commissioners are unable, after making reasonable inquiries, to locate the charity or any of its trustees.[345] No obligation as to secrecy or other restriction on disclosure (however imposed) is to preclude a relevant institution from disclosing any information to the Charity Commissioners for the purpose of enabling them to discharge their functions in relation to dormant accounts.[346]   **15.153**

A 'relevant institution' means:[347]   **15.154**

    (i) the Bank of England;

---

[340] ibid, s 75(7)

[341] ibid, s 75(8)

[342] For the purposes of ibid, s 28, references to the transfer of any amount to a charity are references to its transfer to the charity trustees, or to any trustee for the charity, as the charity trustees may determine: ibid, s 28(8)(c)

[343] ibid, s 28(2)

[344] ibid, s 28(10)

[345] ibid, s 28(1)

[346] ibid, s 28(7)

[347] ibid, s 28(8)(b)

    (ii) an institution which is authorised by the Financial Services Authority[348] to operate a deposit-taking business under Part I of the Banking Act 1987;

    (iii) a European deposit-taker as defined in regulation 82(3) of the Banking Coordination (Second Council Directive) Regulations 1992;

    (iv) a building society which is authorised by the Building Societies Commission under section 9 of the Building Societies Act 1986 to raise money from its members; or

    (v) such other institution mentioned in Schedule 2 to the Banking Act 1987 as the Secretary of State may prescribe by regulations.

An account is dormant for this purpose if no transaction has been effected in relation to the account within the previous five years, excluding any payment into the account or a transaction performed by the institution holding the account (for example, a bank).[349] The exclusion means that an account is not prevented from being treated as dormant merely because the charity holds an investment which generates income that is paid (upon standing instructions) directly into the charity's bank account.

15.155   The Charity Commissioners may specify in a direction such other charity or charities as they consider appropriate, having regard, in a case where the purposes of the relevant charity are known to them, to those purposes and to the purposes of the other charity or charities; but the Charity Commissioners must not specify any charity unless they have received from the charity trustees written confirmation that those trustees are willing to accept the amount proposed to be transferred to the charity.[350]

15.156   Any amount so received by a charity[351] is received on terms that it is to be held and applied by the charity for the purposes of the charity, but that it is nevertheless to be subject to any restrictions on expenditure to which it was subject as property of the relevant charity.[352] The receipt of any charity trustees or trustee for a charity in respect of any amount so received is a complete discharge of the institution in respect of that amount.[353]

15.157   Where the Charity Commissioners have been informed by a relevant institution that an account is dormant, but, before any transfer has been made pursuant to any direction, the institution has cause to believe that the account is no longer dormant, it must forthwith notify the Charity Commissioners in writing; and if

---

[348] Substituted by Bank of England Act 1998, s 23 & Sch 5, Pt I, para 42; Bank of England Act 1998 (Commencement) Order 1998, SI 1998/1120

[349] CA 1993, s 28(8)(a)

[350] ibid, s 28(3)

[351] This is to be construed as a reference to a receipt by the charity trustees, or by any trustee for the charity: ibid, s 28(8)(c)

[352] ibid, s 28(4)

[353] ibid, s 28(6)

it appears to the Commissioners that the account is indeed no longer dormant, they must revoke any direction as to transfer already made.[354]

The Charity Commissioners' powers to launch an inquiry[355] or to call for docu- **15.158** ments and to search records[356] extend to a dormant account only if there has been no payment into the account in the previous five years.[357] A bank, for instance, cannot therefore be required to furnish statements or answer questions or inquiries in respect of any charity account unless there has been no payment into the account within that period.

---

[354] ibid, s 28(5)
[355] Under ibid, s 8
[356] Under ibid, s 9
[357] ibid, s 28(9)

16

CHARITY INVESTMENT

A. The meaning of 'investment'

(1) General

Neither the Trustee Act 2000 nor any other statute provides a definition of the **16.01** term 'investment' for the purpose of investment by trustees generally or by charity trustees in particular.[1] Assistance must therefore be sought from case law. In *Re Wragg*,[2] Lawrence J said[3]

---

[1] In the context of security regulation, the FSA 1986, Sch 1, Part 1, restricts the meaning of 'investment' to the assets, rights, and interests listed in Sch 1, Part 1; but even an exhaustive list is hardly a definition. The TIA 1961 Sch 1, Parts I–III, merely listed items which ranked as authorized investments

[2] [1919] 2 Ch 58

[3] ibid, 64–5

the verb 'to invest' when used in an investment clause may safely be said to include as one of its meanings 'to apply money in the purchase of some property from which interest or property is expected and which property is purchased in order to be held for the sake of the income it will yield.'

This explanation would exclude the purchase of an asset which can provide, or which is acquired in order to provide, capital appreciation only. In *Re Lilly's Will Trusts*,[4] however, Harman J accepted counsel's submission that anything was an 'investment' which was 'a mode of laying out money with a view to obtaining a return',[5] which suggests that even an asset producing solely a capital return is included. Today, it is generally recognized that an investment may involve a capital or an income return, or both.[6] Some sort of return must, however, be intended; thus a clause in a trust instrument giving the trustees power to invest in freehold property was held not to authorize them to purchase freehold premises in order to permit the beneficiaries to live in the premises rent-free.[7]

16.02 The Charity Commissioners consider an investment to be[8]

an asset which is purchased with the hope of maintaining or enhancing its value, but with the main purpose of obtaining an incoming resource derived from ownership of the asset. An incoming resource need not necessarily take the form of interest or dividends. It might take the form of an assured capital appreciation—such as where interest or earnings are not distributed and are, therefore, reflected in the intrinsic capital value of the asset itself, or where loan stock is issued to or purchased by trustees at a discount to its repayment value.

(2) Investment distinguished from trading

16.03 The Charity Commissioners distinguish between investment and trading. They treat the acquisition of any asset (including derivatives, currencies, and commodities) primarily with a view to sale at a profit as the acquisition of stock in trade rather than investment.[9] If, for instance, a charity acquired Old Masters, vintage cars, antique furniture, or cases of old port, solely in the hope of selling them at a future date at a profit, the charity would not be 'investing', but would be trading. The scope for charities to trade is restricted both by charity law and by the limits on tax relief.[10]

---

[4] [1948] 2 All ER 906

[5] ibid, 907

[6] *Cowan v Scargill* [1985] Ch 270 (Megarry V-C). See also *Harries v Church Commissioners for England* [1992] 1 WLR 1241, 1246, where Nicholls V-C said that charity trustees should endeavour to secure 'the maximum return, whether by way of income or capital growth'

[7] *Re Power's Will Trusts* [1947] Ch 572 (Jenkins J). The decision led to the inclusion in trust instruments of express powers authorizing the purchase of property for this purpose; but this is now no longer necessary for trustees of land and trustees of the proceeds of sale of land: see TLATA 1996, s 6(3), and TA 2000, s 8(1)(b)

[8] (1995) 3 Decisions 18–19

[9] ibid, 18

[10] Charity trading is considered more generally in ch 20, below

(3) Investment distinguished from functional property

A distinction must also be made between assets held as investments and those held **16.04** merely for functional purposes. The latter are assets which the charity uses in carrying out its charitable purposes; they include the hostels for the destitute owned by the Salvation Army,[11] the historic houses and open spaces owned by the National Trust,[12] and the wheelchairs and minibuses owned by a charity for the disabled. Other assets which might be held by a charity for functional purposes are those which facilitate the charity's better administration; they include office accommodation,[13] and office equipment such as computers and furniture. Such assets are not 'investments' since they are acquired for use *in specie*, not for the purpose of generating money.

B. Powers of investment of trustees of charitable trusts

(1) The general power of investment

The default investment powers of trustees are now contained in Part II of the **16.05** Trustee Act 2000.[14] The basic provision (subject to certain exceptions) is that a trustee may make any kind of investment that he could make if he were absolutely entitled to the assets of the trust.[15] This power is called 'the general power of investment'.[16] The Law Commission considered that it was implicit in this power that trustees would be able to hold investment property jointly with other persons.[17]

(2) Restriction or exclusion of general power of investment

Instruments made after 2 August 1961

The general power of investment is additional to powers conferred on trustees **16.06** otherwise than by the Trustee Act 2000, but is subject to any restriction or exclusion imposed by the trust instrument (if made after 2 August 1961) or by any enactment or any provision of subordinate legislation.[18] A provision contained in a

---

[11] *Harries v Church Commissioners for England* [1992] 1 WLR 1241, 1246

[12] ibid

[13] ibid

[14] For the background to the Trustee Act 2000 and the investment powers of trustees before its coming into force, see ch 1, paras 1.127–1.139

[15] TA 2000, s 3(1)

[16] ibid, s 3(2)

[17] See Law Commission, *Trustees' Powers and Duties* (Law Com No 260, 1999) 21 (para 2.28, esp fn 55), 97 (Explanatory Notes to cl 3 of Draft Bill). Trustees could not previously make such joint investments, since they are under a duty to take reasonable steps to secure that the trust property is vested in them or under their control. *Sed quere* whether s 3 is sufficient to oust such general duty

[18] TA 2000, s 6(1). For the purposes of the Act, an enactment or a provision of subordinate legislation is not to be regarded as being, or as being part of, a trust instrument: ibid, s 6(2); and 'subordinate legislation' has the same meaning as in the Interpretation Act 1978: TA 2000, s 6(3)

trust instrument made before the coming into effect of Part II of the Trustee Act 2000, and which confers power to invest under the Trustee Investments Act 1961, is to be treated as conferring the general power of investment on a trustee.[19]

16.07   In an explanatory note on the clause in its Draft Bill, which became section 6 of the Trustee Act 2000, the Law Commission stated that the intention was that,[20]

> for example, an express power of investment authorising trustees to invest '*only* in government bonds' would be taken to exclude the general power of investment. On the other hand, an express power to invest 'in shares quoted on the London Stock Exchange, but not in shares of X plc' would take effect as the general power of investment, subject to the restriction on investing in X plc.

Instruments made before 3 August 1961

16.08   The date is that on which the Trustee Investments Act 1961 took effect. That Act freed trustees from any restrictions on powers of investment which might be contained in any instrument made before 3 August 1961;[21] and the Law Commission did not wish the repeal of the 1961 Act to 're-activate' restrictions in trust instruments made before that date.[22] The Trustee Act 2000 therefore provides that no provision relating to the powers of a trustee contained in a trust instrument made before 3 August 1961 is to be treated as restricting or excluding the general power of investment.[23]

16.09   If a trust instrument made before that date conferred a special power (however expressed) to invest property in any investment for the time being authorized by law for the investment of trust property, the Trustee Investments Act 1961 provided that it took effect as a power to invest property in accordance with its provisions.[24] Under the Trustee Act 2000, such a provision is to be treated as conferring the general power of investment on a trustee.[25]

Special statutory powers of investment

16.10   The Law Commission's Draft Bill would not have conferred the general power of investment on trustees who, immediately before its commencement, had what the Draft Bill called special statutory powers of investment.[26] This meant powers of investment conferred by an enactment or subordinate legislation on trustees of

---

[19] TA 2000, s 7(3)(b)

[20] Law Commission, *Trustees' Powers and Duties* (Law Com No 260, 1999) 99 (n on cl 6 of Draft Bill)

[21] TIA 1961, s 1(3)

[22] Law Commission, *Trustees' Powers and Duties* (Law Com No 260, 1999) 31 (para 2.51)

[23] TA 2000, s 7(2)

[24] TIA 1961, s 3(2)

[25] TA 2000, s 7(3)

[26] Law Commission *Trustees' Powers and Duties* (Law Com No 260, 1999) cl 7(1)–(3) of Draft Bill

a particular trust or a particular kind of trust.[27] It seems that the Law Commission's aim was to exclude from Part II the investment functions of pension trustees and of trustees of unit trusts, which are already governed by special statutory regimes.[28]

This restriction would also have excluded from the general power of investment **16.11** those charitable trusts whose powers of investment are conferred by an Act of Parliament or subordinate legislation.[29] The restriction would thereby have excluded from the general power of investment certain classes of charitable trusts for religious and educational purposes.[30] It was recognized during the progress of the Trustee Bill through Parliament that the restriction was undesirable, and it was agreed that trusts with special statutory powers of investment should not be excluded from the general power of investment. As a result, the restriction was dropped,[31] so that the general power of investment under the Trustee Act 2000 applies to trusts (both charitable and non-charitable) with special staturoty powers of investment.

(3) Exclusions from Part II of the Trustee Act 2000

A special statutory regime already exists to govern the investment functions of **16.12** trustees managing a fund under a common investment scheme[32] or a common deposit scheme.[33] The Law Commission did not consider it appropriate to replace these with a different scheme.[34] Accordingly, the Trustee Act 2000 provides that (with limited exceptions) Part II does not apply to trustees managing a fund under such schemes.[35]

(4) Investment in land

The general power of investment does not permit a trustee to make investments **16.13** in land other than in loans secured on land.[36] Trustees (except of a trust to which the Universities and College Estates Act 1925 applies[37]) are, however, given a separate power to acquire freehold or leasehold land in the United Kingdom as an investment.[38] It appears that the reason for separating out the power to invest was to

---

[27] ibid, cl 7(3) of Draft Bill

[28] ie Pensions Act 1995, s 34, and FSA 1986, s 81. See Law Commission, *Trustees' Powers and Duties* (Law Com No 260, 1999) 19–20 (para 2.25) and 30–1 (para 2.49)

[29] See comments of Lord Irvine LC in Committee Stage of Trustee Bill, HL, 7 June 2000, col CWH1

[30] ibid

[31] ibid, col CWH2

[32] CA 1993, s 24

[33] ibid, s 25

[34] Law Commission, *Trustees' Powers and Duties* (Law Com No 260, 1999) 30–1 (para 2.49)

[35] TA 2000, s 38

[36] ibid, s 3(3). On the acquisition of land generally, see further ch 17, paras 17.02–17.13

[37] TA 2000 s 10(1)(b)

[38] TA 2000, s 8(1)(a)

facilitate the making of consequential amendments to existing enactments in Schedule 2 to the Trustee Act 2000.[39]

C. Duties relating to the exercise of investment powers

(1) The general statutory duty of care

16.14 The Trustee Act 2000 introduces a 'duty of care' which applies to a trustee when (inter alia) exercising the general power of investment or any other power of investment, however conferred, or when carrying out a duty to which he is subject under section 4 or 5 of the Act (duties relating to the exercise of a power of investment or to the review of investments).[40]

16.15 The duty of care requires the trustee to exercise such care and skill as is reasonable in the circumstances, having regard in particular[41]

(a) to any special knowledge or experience that he has or holds himself out as having, and
(b) if he acts as a trustee in the course of a business or profession, to any special knowledge or experience that it is reasonable to expect of a person acting in the course of that kind of business or profession.

This statutory duty of care appears to represent, as the Law Commission itself considered, no more than a codification of the existing duty of care at common law.[42] The Law Commission nevertheless thought it appropriate to apply the statutory duty of care to the exercise of trustees' powers of investment so as to provide a uniform duty in relation to the exercise of the other new powers which it was recommending.[43]

16.16 Further guidance on the duty of care is therefore to be obtained from existing case law. In equity, a trustee has a duty 'to take such care as an ordinary prudent man of business would take if he were minded to make an investment for the benefit of the people for whom he feels morally bound to provide'.[44] Since equity does not countenance a sleeping trustee, a trustee would in any event be under a general equitable duty periodically to review the exercise of all his powers, including the power of investment.

---

[39] Law Commission, *Trustees' Powers and Duties* (Law Com No 260, 1999) 99 (Explanatory Note to Draft Bill)
[40] TA 2000, ss 1(2), 2 & Sch 1, para 1
[41] ibid, s 1(1)
[42] Law Commission, *Trustees' Powers and Duties* (Law Com No 260, 1999) 25 (para 2.35). The higher standard of care of professional trustees had already been recognized in *Bartlett v Barclays Trust Co Ltd (Nos 1 and 2)* [1980] Ch 515, 534 (Brightman J)
[43] Law Commission, *Trustees' Powers and Duties* (Law Com No 260, 1999) 25 (para 2.35)
[44] *Re Whiteley* (1886) 33 ChD 347, 355 (Lindley LJ)

(2) Specific statutory investment duties

Standard investment criteria

In exercising any power of investment, whether arising under Part II of the Trustee **16.17** Act 2000 'or otherwise',[45] a trustee must have regard to the standard investment criteria,[46] and must from time to time review the investments of the trust and consider whether, having regard to such criteria, they should be varied.[47]

The standard investment criteria in relation to a trust are:[48] **16.18**

(a) the suitability to the trust of investments of the same kind as any particular investment proposed to be made or retained and of that particular investment as an investment of that kind, and
(b) the need for diversification of investments of the trust, in so far as is appropriate to the circumstances of the trust.

Although slightly differently worded, these are essentially the familiar duties formerly contained in the Trustee Investments Act 1961, now made applicable to trustees' investment powers generally.

The need to diversify is most important where the fund is very large, in order to **16.19** spread the risk; it might therefore be a breach of this duty for the trustees to put all their investments in company shares into the shares of one company.[49] The Charity Commissioners' view, expressed before the Trustee Act 2000 was enacted, was that investments in any one equity or fixed-interest stock should not normally represent more than 5 per cent of a charity's portfolio;[50] and the applicability of this rule of thumb would seem to have survived the new legislation. The duty to diversify is less appropriate if the fund is very small, perhaps only a few thousand pounds; in such circumstances, it might be appropriate for the charity trustees to place the entire sum available for investment in a common investment fund.

Advice

Before exercising any power of investment, whether arising under Part II of the **16.20** Trustee Act 2000 or otherwise, and when reviewing the investments of the trust, a trustee must (unless the exception applies) obtain and consider proper advice

---

[45] TA 2000 s 4(1). Pt II contains the general power of investment. The expression 'or otherwise' is very wide: it includes the specific power to invest in land in s 8, and also any express power of investment contained in the trust instrument or authorized by the Charity Commissioners under CA 1993, s 26
[46] TA 2000, s 4(1)
[47] ibid, s 4(2)
[48] ibid, s 4(3)
[49] This risk of substantial investment in a single company, however reputable it might appear to be, has been highlighted by the collapses in recent years of business enterprises such as the Barings Group and Polly Peck International plc
[50] Charity Commission, *Investment of Charitable Funds*, CC14 (Aug 1995), 6

about the way in which, having regard to the standard investment criteria, the power should be exercised or the investment should be varied (as the case may be).[51] The exception is that a trustee does not need to obtain such advice if he reasonably concludes that in all the circumstances it is unnecessary or inappropriate to do so.[52]

16.21 Proper advice is the advice of a person who is reasonably believed by the trustee to be qualified to give it by his ability in and practical experience of financial and other matters relating to the proposed investment.[53]

16.22 The position is now different from that which pertained under the Trustee Investments Act 1961, since trustees are no longer under an absolute duty to seek advice in respect of any particular kinds of investment. It is unlikely, however, that a trustee could reasonably conclude that it is unnecessary or inappropriate to obtain advice where the trust fund is very large. If a trustee invests a large fund without advice, he may be in breach of such duty to obtain advice; he may also be in breach of the duty of care laid down in the Act,[54] which applies to a trustee when (inter alia) exercising the general power of investment or any other power of investment, however conferred.[55]

16.23 The level of advice required will depend on the nature and size of the trust. The Charity Commissioners recommend that trustees who have substantial sums to invest (for example, £100,000 or more) should consider appointing an independent investment manager who is regulated under the Financial Services Act 1986 to advise them on investment policy and on the selection of appropriate investments.[56]

(3) Equitable duties

16.24 The foregoing statutory duties supplement the pre-existing fiduciary duties to which trustees are subject, including the duty to act in the best interests of the trust and the duty to avoid a conflict of interests. The statutory duties also express in a very general way the equitable duties of trustees in relation to the selection of investments, and reference must therefore continue to be made to case law for more detailed guidance.

16.25 A convenient summary of the basic duty of charity trustees relating to investment is contained in the judgment of Nicholls V-C in *Harries v Church Commissioners*

---

[51] TA 2000, s 5(1), (2)

[52] ibid, s 5(3)

[53] ibid, s 5(4). There is no specific restriction on who is qualified to give such advice. Under the new regime, and in contrast to TIA 1961, there is no statutory requirement for the advice to be given or confirmed in writing

[54] TA 2000, s 1(1). On the duty of care, see further above, paras 16.14–16

[55] TA 2000, Sch 1, para 1

[56] Charity Commission, *Investment of Charitable Funds*, CC14 (Aug 1995), 5. On delegation of investment decisions, see below, paras 16.67–16.68

for England.[57] In that case, his Lordship stated that charity trustees should endeavour to secure[58]

> the maximum return, whether by way of income or capital growth, which is consistent with commercial prudence . . . having regard to the need to diversify, the need to balance income against capital growth, and the need to balance risk against return.

In making investments, trustees are more restricted than ordinary investors who **16.26** are investing their own money. The basic law governing investment by trustees of charitable trusts is the same as that governing investment by trustees generally. In equity, a trustee is under a duty to invest the trust property, but (unless restricted by the terms of the trust instrument) has a discretion as to which investments to make.

It has been a long-standing principle that the investments made by a trustee must **16.27** not be speculative, since a trustee is not permitted to speculate with trust funds:[59] he must avoid, it has been said, all investments that are attended with hazard.[60] There are, however, statements in more recent cases that trustees are to be judged according to modern economic and financial conditions; and that they should therefore be judged by modern portfolio theory, which applies the prudent-investor test to the overall investment portfolio instead of to individual investments.[61] By abolishing the distinction between authorized and unauthorized investments, the Trustee Act 2000 effectively puts portfolio theory on a statutory basis. It is now clear that, whilst trustees are still not permitted to speculate with trust funds, whether their investments are speculative is to be judged, not merely by looking at each investment in isolation, but also by considering each investment in relation to the trust's overall range of investments. There are, nevertheless, some types of investment that are so speculative that to invest in them at all would be a breach of trust. The risk for trustees of charitable trusts since the Trustee Act 2000 came into force is that the Charity Commissioners might consider that really speculative ventures are not 'investments' at all. It could hardly be an investment, for instance, to apply charity funds in the purchase of lottery tickets.

The trustees should also avoid being over-cautious in their investment policy; for **16.28** they will be committing a breach of trust if they invest in a way that produces a

---

[57] [1992] 1 WLR 1241
[58] ibid, 1246
[59] See Dillon LJ in *Nestlé v National Westminster Bank plc* [1993] 1 WLR 1260, 1268: 'Trustees should not be reckless with trust money'
[60] *Learoyd v Whiteley* (1887) 12 App Cas 727, 733 (Lord Watson)
[61] See the first-instance judgment of Hoffmann J in *Nestlé v National Westminster Bank plc* (29 June 1988); *Steel v Wellcome Custodian Trustees Ltd* [1988] 1 WLR 167, 173; and Lord Nicholls, 'Trustees and their broader community: where duty, morality, and ethics converge' (1995) 9 Trust Law Int 71

smaller return than would have been obtained by an ordinary prudent investor.[62] Trustees must therefore steer a middle path, pursuing an investment policy that is neither too speculative on the one hand, nor yet too cautious on the other. Like the baby bear's porridge, their policy must be 'just right'.

(4) Retention of investments not authorized by the charity's governing instrument

Investment that has ceased to be authorized

16.29 The abolition by the Trustee Act 2000 of the distinction which had been made under the Trustee Investments Act 1961 between authorized and unauthorized investments[63] has the effect that the term 'unauthorized investment' is now relevant only in relation to charitable trusts with governing instruments under which the trustees' powers of investment are restricted.

16.30 Section 4 of the Trustee Act 1925 provided that a trustee was not liable for breach of trust by reason only of his continuing to hold any investment which had ceased to be an investment authorized by the trust instrument or by the general law. The effect of section 4 was to prevent the trustee from being liable from the date when the investment ceased to be authorized merely because he had not by then disposed of it. It was unlikely that the section relieved a trustee of his general fiduciary duty to review the exercise of his investment powers periodically.[64] A trustee who retained an investment for an excessively long period after it had ceased to be authorized was probably in breach of trust, despite section 4.

16.31 Section 4, with the rest of Part I of the Trustee Act 1925, was repealed by the Trustee Act 2000. The question is whether such repeal has removed trustees from the protection which they formerly enjoyed. It is possible to envisage that a trust instrument created after the Trustee Act 2000 came into force might expressly restrict the trustees' power to invest in shares to investments in companies which have paid a dividend on all their shares in the last five years. Does the repeal of section 4 make the trustees automatically liable for breach of trust if they retain shares in a company even one day after it ceases to satisfy such a criterion? To impose liability in those circumstances would appear harsh, since it would arise without any fault on the trustees' part. It would seem appropriate for the trustees to be under a duty to sell the unauthorized investments only with reasonable promptitude. In some circumstances, it might be commercially better to retain an unauthorized investment for a while until there is an upturn in the market. With the

---

[62] See *Nestlé v National Westminster Bank plc* [1993] 1 WLR 1283 (Leggett LJ)

[63] For a summary of the main provisions of the TIA 1961 (now partially repealed), see ch 1, paras 1.128–1.129

[64] *Re Chapman* [1896] 2 Ch 763; *Wright v Ginn* [1994] OPLR 83; cf *Rawsthorne v Rowley* [1909] 1 Ch 409n

repeal of section 4 of the Trustee Act 1925, a trustee would now be taking a risk in doing so; although in some circumstances a trustee might be able to obtain relief from personal liability under section 61 of that Act. It is suggested that, where new charitable trusts contain express restrictions on the trustees' investment powers, thought should now be given to putting an express exoneration clause into the instrument, adapting the relevant terms of the now-repealed section 4.

Gifts of unauthorized investments

If a charitable trust restricts the trustees' powers of investment to particular types **16.32** of investment, the trustees cannot retain any unauthorized investment which comes to the charity by way of a gift, whether inter vivos or testamentary. They will be obliged to realize it and reinvest in authorized investments. Similarly, even if there is no such restriction in the trust instrument, so that the trustees of the charity have all the investment powers of absolute owners, they will not be able to invest pursuant to such powers any property which is given to them upon special charitable trusts which impose restrictions on their powers of investment.

D. Investment by charitable companies

The constitutions of most charitable companies contain an express investment **16.33** clause, so there has been relatively little judicial consideration of the scope of a charitable company's powers of investment where no such clause is present. Whether a charitable company could rely on the investment powers given by the Trustee Investments Act 1961 was never clarified; but the better view seems to be that that statute applied to charitable companies only to the extent that they held property on charitable trusts.[65] This is clearly the position under the Trustee Act 2000. The Law Commission had provisionally recommended in its Consultation Paper that the new powers of trustees (including the extended powers of investment) should be conferred on the directors of charitable companies.[66] In its final report, however, the Law Commission noted that there would be technical difficulties in extending such powers in this way, and the recommendation was

---

[65] See *Re Manchester Royal Infirmary* (1889) 43 ChD 420 (company incorporated and regulated under special Acts of Parliament held to be trustees and so to have the investment powers conferred by Trust Investment Act 1889); *Soldiers', Sailors' and Airmen's Family Association v A-G* [1968] 1 WLR 313 (charter company held to have the powers of investment under TIA 1961). These decisions may not establish any general principle, but may simply turn on the fact that the charities in question could be regarded as holding their assets on trust. The position remains unclear in respect of companies incorporated under Companies Act 1985, which do not generally hold their assets on trust: see *Liverpool and District Hospital for Diseases of the Heart v A-G* [1981] Ch 193. See further ch 11, paras 11.18–11.21

[66] See Law Commission, *Trustees' Powers and Duties* (Consultation Paper No 146, June 1997), 6–7 (paras 1.17–1.19). See also the final report: Law Commission, *Trustees' Powers and Duties* (Law Com No 260, 1999) 7 (para 1.20)

dropped. The final report notes that the assets of a charitable company are not vested in its directors, but in the company itself, so that powers to deal with the assets are the powers of the company.[67] The investment powers and duties specified in the Trustee Act 2000 apply to a charitable company only in respect of any assets which it holds as trustee upon charitable trusts. The Act therefore applies to assets held by such a corporation subject to special charitable trusts.

16.34 The Law Commission noted that a charitable company would come within the scope of its proposals only if such company's investment powers were set out with reference to the powers of trustees or to the Trustee Investments Act 1961.[68] This suggests that it was intended that, in such circumstances, the company would now have the general power of investment conferred on trustees by the Trustee Act 2000. An express statement to this effect found its way, however, neither into the draft Bill which the Law Commission appended to its report, nor into the Trustee Act 2000. It might, nevertheless, be inferred that, where a charitable company's powers of investment are expressed to be those conferred by the Trustee Investments Act 1961, its powers of investment are to be those conferred on trustees, with the result that such company would now have the general power of investment under the Trustee Act 2000. Such analysis would seem to be consistent with the intention of the Law Commission. Failing that, an argument might be made that such companies would at least continue to have the powers of investment contained in the Trustee Investments Act 1961 on the ground that, although much of that Act has been repealed,[69] many of its provisions continue to have effect so far as they are applied by or under certain other enactments.[70] An express reference to the powers of investment contained in the Trustee Investments Act 1961 might therefore be treated as a reference to surviving provisions. If neither of these arguments is sound, charitable companies whose investment clauses confer the powers of investment contained in the Trustee Investments Act 1961 are now in the unfortunate position of having merely those investment powers which are implied by law.

16.35 Directors of charitable companies are not trustees in the trusts law sense, and are therefore not subject to the statutory duties in the Trustee Act 2000 relating to investment, namely the duty of care, and the duties relating to diversification, choice of suitable investments, and the obtaining and considering of appropriate advice. Nevertheless, such directors are fiduciaries, and the court would probably treat them as subject to equivalent duties in equity. Directors of a charitable company would therefore be well advised to act according to the statutory standard laid down for trustees. Such duties are effectively imposed in the Charity Law

---

[67] Law Commission, *Trustees' Powers and Duties* (Law Com No 260, 1999) 7 (para 1.20, n 37)
[68] ibid, 7 (para 1.20, n 37)
[69] TA 2000, s 40 & Sch 4, Part I
[70] ibid, s 40 & Sch 2

Association's Memorandum of Association for a Charitable Company Limited by Guarantee, which confers on the company a general power:[71]

> To deposit or invest funds in any manner (but to invest only after obtaining advice from a financial expert and having regard to the suitability of investments and the need for diversification)

For this purpose, the model clause states that[72]

> a 'financial expert' means an individual, company or firm who is an authorised person or an exempted person within the meaning of the Financial Services Act 1986.

It will be noted that this is slightly stricter than the position under the Trustee Act 2000, which does not define who is competent to give appropriate advice.

E. Specialized types of investment

(1) Introduction

The general power of investment which trustees of charitable trusts enjoy in default of any express provision in the trust instrument, whilst making all investments available to trustees of charitable trusts, does not of course mean that all investments are necessarily suitable. Similarly, an express investment clause in the constitution of a charitable company may confer upon the company a power of investment equivalent to the general power of investment conferred on trustees, but the directors will still be effectively restricted to choosing suitable investments. Trustees will be in breach of trust if they make an unsuitable investment, even though the investment in question is authorized by the governing instrument, and an unduly speculative investment is likely to be considered unsuitable. **16.36**

The Charity Commissioners cannot refuse to register a body as a charity merely because its governing instrument authorizes very wide powers of investment whose exercise would be inappropriate given the size of the charity concerned, unless those powers suggest that the assets of the charity will be applied to non-charitable purposes.[73] If, however, a charity specifically takes powers which appear to amount to speculation, the Charity Commissioners will warn the charity that such powers are inappropriate. If the trustees insist on their inclusion, the Commissioners will monitor the charity to ensure that its charitable funds are not placed at risk.[74] Since trading does not comprise investment, the power to carry out trading in any substantial manner is appropriate in a charity's constitution **16.37**

---

[71] Cl 4.12 of the Memorandum and Articles of Association for a Charitable Company Limited by Guarantee, produced on behalf of the CLA

[72] ibid, Art 9.1

[73] (1995) 3 Decisions 20

[74] ibid

only where such trade is in furtherance of the charitable objects.[75] The Commissioners will therefore warn any charity that specifically takes powers which could facilitate non-charitable trading that such powers are inappropriate, and will similarly monitor the charity.[76]

16.38 Such monitoring or warning by the Charity Commissioners is less likely to occur in practice after the coming into force of the Trustee Act 2000. The reason is that most charitable trusts now enjoy the wide investment powers which that Act confers, and the Charity Commissioners can hardly object to the inclusion in the governing instrument of a charitable trust or charitable company of an express power of investment couched in the same wide language as section 3(1) of the Trustee Act 2000. The Charity Commissioners are probably going to be alerted to the likelihood of unsuitable investments in the future only in those instances where the governing instrument specifically authorizes investment in a specified investment or type of investment (such as the making of unsecured loans) which the Commissioners believe to be inherently unduly speculative.

(2) Lending

16.39 A general power to invest trust moneys at the trustees' discretion enables them to invest funds by way of a secured loan, but it does not entitle them to lend money merely on the strength of the borrower's personal promise to repay.[77] Trustees commit a breach of trust if they lend money without taking security, notwithstanding that they have power to do so under the trust instrument and that interest is charged.[78] The explanation is that, even if an unsecured loan can be regarded as an investment (as where interest is charged), it is extremely hazardous in that there is a risk that the borrower, however financially sound he may appear, might be unable to repay.

16.40 In practice, most lending by charities is for the purpose of funding their subsidiary trading companies. If a charity proposes to invest in a subsidiary trading company, either initially or by way of additional capital, its trustees will need to comply with the duties imposed on them in relation to investment, including considering the advisability and appropriateness of the investment, and ways in which the risk of loss to the charity can be minimized. The trustees should therefore ensure that any loan the charity makes to its subsidiary is both secured and at a proper rate of interest,[79] and also that the charity does not invest in such subsidiary too high a proportion of its funds.[80]

---

[75] *Tennant Plays Ltd v IRC* [1948] 1 All ER 506
[76] (1995) 3 Decisions 20
[77] *Khoo Tek Keong v Ch'ng Joo Tuan Neoh* [1934] AC 529 (PC)
[78] *Holmes v Dring* (1788) 2 Cox Eq Cas 1 (Lord Kenyon)
[79] Charity Commission, *Charities and Trading*, CC35 (Feb 1997) 19 (para 55)
[80] ibid, 18–19 (paras 52–3). For a more detailed discussion of the funding of trading subsidiaries by way of loan, see ch 20, paras 20.24–20.26

(3) Underwriting

The underwriting of shares involves the risk that the underwriter may have to pur- **16.41**
chase the shares in the event that the issue is not fully subscribed; and the Charity
Commissioners had originally expressed the general opinion that all underwrit-
ings of shares were 'too speculative' and so inappropriate for charity trustees.[81]
They later qualified this view, and effectively recognized that, where the primary
purpose of an underwriting is not to obtain a quick profit from a commission, but
to enable the charity to obtain the underlying shares, such an arrangement might
be unobjectionable.[82] The Charity Commissioners then laid down the following
additional criteria:[83]

(a) the underlying shares would be a suitable long term holding for the charity's investment portfolio, at the given cost, should they be required to be taken up;
(b) the acquisition of the shares would be permissible under the investment powers
of the charity;
(c) funds would be available for taking up in full all the shares underwritten.

(4) Derivatives and swap transactions

'Derivatives' are instruments which confer a right to buy or sell a security at a **16.42**
specified price, and they include options and futures. Derivatives are marketable
securities, since they can be traded in their own right: they are therefore negotiable
instruments. To the extent that derivatives are bought in order to obtain a profit
from a possible change in the value of the underlying stock, they involve speculation. For this reason, and also because they regard the purchase and sale of derivatives as trading, the Charity Commissioners' view is that such transactions are
not generally a suitable use of charity funds.[84] Within the category of derivatives,
and subject to the same general strictures, the Charity Commissioners place both
foreign currency deposits and 'swap transactions'.[85] The latter comprise the making of a monetary loan under an arrangement whereby the borrower, whilst paying an initial rate of interest, is entitled to elect (or swap) to another rate of interest
(eg a variable rate) at some future time; such transactions necessarily involve a degree of speculation on the future movement of interest rates.

Although derivatives are normally unsuitable for charities, there are exceptional **16.43**
circumstances in which they might be permissible forms of charity investment. In
Trustees of the British Museum v Attorney-General,[86] a case decided under the old

---

[81] [1985] Ch Com Rep 23 (para 69)
[82] [1986] Ch Com Rep 17 (paras 80–81)
[83] ibid, para 80
[84] (1995) 3 Decisions 25
[85] See Charity Commission, *Investment of Charitable Funds*, CC14 (1995) 7. For criticisms of
the Charity Commissioners' approach, see HP Dale, & M Gwinnell, 'Time for Change: Charity
Investment and Modern Portfolio Theory', (1995–6) 3 CL & PR 65, 91
[86] [1984] 1 WLR 418

regime of the Trustee Investments Act 1961, Megarry V-C authorized a scheme extending the investment powers of the charity to include traded options, although this was subject to the restriction that investment in such options was not to exceed 5 per cent of the value of the free part of the trust fund (in effect about two-thirds of its value). The trust fund in that case was, however, of an extraordinarily high value; and the Charity Commissioners were, at the time, keen to point out that the decision should not be taken to authorize all charity trustees to speculate with trust funds in that way.[87] Nevertheless, the decision showed that there was nothing intrinsically objectionable to the purchase of derivatives, even though such purchase might at that time have been considered appropriate only to a handful of charities.

16.44 More influential in developing the law on investment in derivatives has been the decision of the House of Lords in *Hazell v Hammersmith and Fulham London Borough Council*,[88] which concerned the legality of swap transactions. The arrangements in question had been entered into by a local authority, not a charity; but the Charity Commissioners drew attention to Lord Templeman's observations in that case relating to the circumstances in which such a transaction is speculative, and pointed out that such remarks 'may be relevant to any analysis of the duty of charity and other trustees'.[89] In the *Hazell* case, Lord Templeman (with whose speech the other Law Lords agreed) recognized that there are many such swap transactions 'which eliminate or reduce speculation'[90] in that the ability to move from one method of interest calculation to another could be considered to reduce uncertainty. On the other hand, his Lordship said that there are other such transactions which are undertaken solely in order to obtain a profit by forecasting future interest trends, and which are therefore inherently speculative. From this the Charity Commissioners infer that transactions which are 'entirely unrelated' to the charity's debts are speculative; and, furthermore, that once a loan agreement has been entered into, any subsequent agreement to introduce a swap element is necessarily speculative.[91] Lord Templeman contrasted this sort of transaction with one under which the borrower is in a position to borrow only at a variable rate, but needs the security of a loan whose rate is fixed. In such circumstances, the borrower might reasonably consider it to be in his best interests to borrow from the outset by means of a swap arrangement, if this is the only means by which he can obtain a fixed rate. A swap transaction of this nature is not inherently speculative.[92]

---

[87] [1985] Ch Com Rep 23 (para 67)
[88] [1992] 2 AC 1
[89] [1990] Ch Com Rep 37
[90] [1992] 2 AC 1, 31
[91] [1990] Ch Com Rep 37
[92] ibid (where the Charity Commissioners summarize Lord Templeman's comments)

The Charity Commissioners have recently explained, by reference to a number of   **16.45**
illustrations, the exceptional circumstances in which it might be appropriate for a
charity to use a particular form of derivative:[93]

> (1) a charity may need a swap arrangement to stabilise the interest payable by it on a
> loan where the borrowing is substantial and a rise in interest rates would present the
> charity with problems of repayment; or
> (2) a charity may need an option to acquire foreign currency at a particular price in
> order to fund a specific project and does not wish to exceed that price; or
> (3) when a fixed capital sum (to be used in pursuit of the charity's objects) is needed
> at a specific date in the future then part of a charity's invested portfolio could be sold
> forward so as to secure the availability of funds.

In these circumstances, the use of the derivative is not to be considered to be trading or speculative in nature, but is to be treated as an investment.

The general power of investment conferred on trustees of charitable trusts by the   **16.46**
Trustee Act 2000 would now permit them to acquire derivatives where they are acquired as investments. The risk in relying on the general power of investment,
however, is that the Charity Commissioners might argue that any derivatives so
acquired were in fact unauthorized acquisitions, as being for the purposes of trading or speculation, and not investments at all. For this reason, even if a charity
might appropriately invest in derivatives, it may be preferable for the governing
instrument expressly to authorize the purchase of derivatives as investments.

Whilst charities may borrow pursuant to an express or implied power in order to   **16.47**
carry out their purposes, a swap transaction cannot be regarded as ancillary to a
general power to borrow.[94] If a charity is to enter into a swap transaction, it should
have express power in its governing instrument.

F. Widening powers of investment

(1) Power in the charity's constitution
Charitable trust or charitable unincorporated association

The introduction of the general power of investment by the Trustee Act 2000 re-   **16.48**
duces the circumstances in which the trustees of a charitable trust will need to
consider a widening of their investment powers. In practice, a widening is likely
to be needed in future only where a trust created after the Trustee Act 2000 came
into force itself restricts, excludes, or modifies the general power of investment.
It might also be desirable where the trustees wish to make investments which

---

[93] (1995) 3 Decisions 25–6. These criteria relax the Charity Commissioners' earlier view expressed at [1985] Ch Com Rep 22–3 (paras 65–8)
[94] *Hazell v Hammersmith and Fulham LBC* [1992] 2 AC 1, 28–31 (Lord Templeman)

individually involve a degree of speculation (such as the purchase of derivatives), where there is a risk that the Charity Commissioners might argue that their acquisition is for trading or speculation, and so is not authorized by the general power of investment.

16.49 If the constitution of a charitable trust or of an unincorporated charity confers on the trustees or members an express power to amend its provisions, such power can be utilized to extend the powers of investment without the need for the Charity Commissioners' approval. In *Motor and Cycle Trades Benevolent Fund v Attorney-General*,[95] rule 19 of the unincorporated charity provided that no rule should be made, altered, or rescinded except by a four-fifths majority of votes at a general meeting. The trustees sought to alter the rules to confer wider powers of investment than those conferred by the Trustee Investments Act 1961; but, because counsel for the Attorney-General advised that such an amendment was beyond the charity's powers, the Charity Commissioners authorized the trustees to apply to the court for the point to be determined. Whitford J held that, although rule 19 was expressed in the negative, it plainly contemplated that new rules could be made, and that the purported addition to the rules conferring wider powers of investment was valid.

Charitable company incorporated under the Companies Act 1985

16.50 If the company's express powers of investment are set out in a list of ancillary powers contained in the objects clause, such investment powers may be altered or extended only by an amendment to the objects clause, which requires a special resolution.[96] Whether the investment powers are set out in the objects clause or in another clause of the memorandum, their amendment will be ineffective without the prior written consent of the Charity Commissioners.[97] As obtaining such consent can be an expensive procedure, it is important to include a suitably wide investment clause in a charitable company's constitution from the outset.[98]

16.51 If the constitution of a charitable company contains no express power of investment, the company's powers of investment are limited to those which can be implied. A charitable company would no doubt have an implied power to invest in a manner incidental to the carrying out of its charitable objects, especially given that its directors, as fiduciaries, are under a general duty to invest the company's property. The scope of such implied powers is, however, uncertain. It has been

---

[95] Noted at [1982] Ch Com Rep 42. See also ch 8, paras 8.46–8.51
[96] Companies Act 1985, s 4(1)
[97] CA 1993, ss 64(2)(a) (alteration of objects clause), 64(2)(b) (alteration of any other provision in the memorandum or articles which directs or restricts the manner in which the company's property may be used or applied)
[98] The position of a charitable company whose constitution expressly confers the powers of investment contained in the TIA 1961 (now partially repealed) was considered above, para 16.34

suggested[99] that, if a company has no express investment clause, then unless the directors seek to amend the constitution to include an express power of investment, their safest course of action is to apply to the Charity Commissioners in writing, seeking their opinion or advice as to the scope of their investment powers.[100] If the directors act on such opinion or advice, they are treated as having acted in accordance with the charity's constitution.[101]

(2) Application to the court or to the Charity Commissioners

Jurisdiction

Charitable trust or charitable unincorporated association

If the provisions of a charitable trust or the rules of an unincorporated charitable association restrict the trustees' powers of investment, in the absence of a power in the governing instrument to extend the trustees' powers of investment, any extension of such powers will need the approval of the Charity Commissioners or of the High Court.

16.52

The High Court has always had an inherent power, upon application to it by the trustees, to authorize investments not permitted by the general law or by the trust instrument itself.[102] An application to the court can also be made under the statutory power contained in the Trustee Act 1925.[103]

16.53

The Charity Commissioners' jurisdiction to approve an extension of a charity's investment powers falls within section 16 of the Charities Act 1993, as it involves 'a scheme for the administration of a charity'.[104] The Commissioners also have a separate statutory power under section 26 of that Act to sanction an action proposed or contemplated in the administration of a charity when it appears to them to be 'expedient in the interests of the charity'.[105] The difference between the two sections is that the former involves a change to the terms of the trust; whereas the latter does not—it merely authorizes a particular transaction or confers a more general authority to do that which would not otherwise be within the trustees' powers. The Charity Commissioners could, for instance, use section 26 to authorize trustees of a charity to purchase land as an investment where such a power is excluded by the trust instrument;[106] but section 26 is more appropriate to

16.54

---

[99] See M Harbottle, *Investing Charity Funds* (Jordans, 1995) 31
[100] CA 1993, s 29(1)
[101] ibid, s 29(2)
[102] This power was preserved by TIA 1961, s 15; but, being inherent, the power survives that provision's repeal by TA 2000, s 40 & Sch 2, para 1(1)
[103] TA 1925, s 57
[104] CA 1993, s 16(1)(a)
[105] ibid, s 26(1)
[106] See [1988] Ch Com Rep 16–17 (paras 73–5), where (16–17, para 74) the Charity Commissioners expressed their willingness to authorize such investment when the trustees would otherwise lack the power to invest in land

authorize a particular transaction only (for example, to authorize a disposition which might otherwise be set aside as giving rise to a conflict of interests).

Charitable company incorporated by Royal charter

16.55   The court has no inherent jurisdiction to approve an extension of the investment powers of a charity incorporated by Royal charter unless the company holds its property upon trust, and even then only to the extent that such extension would not require an amendment of the charter. Only the sovereign can amend the charter, so the Privy Council Office needs to be involved. Where an amendment is needed, the Charities Act 1993 enables the court[107] or the Charity Commissioners[108] to make a scheme for the charity which is not to take effect until Her Majesty has thought fit to amend the charter.[109]

Charitable company incorporated by special Act of Parliament

16.56   The court has no inherent jurisdiction to amend an Act of Parliament, unless the Act confers jurisdiction on the court, either in such terms or through the creation of an express trust.[110] Subject to this, if a charity is a corporation established by a special Act of Parliament, and any alteration to its investment powers requires an amendment to the statute, such amendment could be effected through a special statutory procedure which can be set in motion by the Charity Commissioners.[111]

16.57   The constitution of a charity established by special Act of Parliament may be impliedly modified by a later general Act, such as the Trustee Act 1925. This was held to have occurred in *Re Shipwrecked Fishermen and Mariners' Royal Benevolent Society*.[112] The Society (a charity) had been incorporated by a special Act of Parliament of 1850, which specified the authorized investments. Over the years these had steadily fallen in value, and the Society applied to the court for a scheme increasing its investment powers. Danckwerts J approved the scheme, and his preferred ground was that section 57 of the Trustee Act 1925 had modified, and was therefore to be read into, the earlier statute of incorporation.[113]

Criteria for extension of investment powers

16.58   Before 1961, when the general law was very restrictive, the courts were usually willing to accede to an application to widen trustees' powers of investment beyond those permitted by the general law. In the years immediately after the passing of the Trustee Investments Act 1961, however, the courts treated the new

---

[107] CA 1993, s 15(1)
[108] ibid, s 16(1)(a)
[109] See further ch 15, paras 15.07–15.11
[110] See also CA 1993, s 15(3); and see ch 15, paras 15.12–15.13
[111] CA 1993, s 17. See further ch 15, paras 15.15–15.17
[112] [1959] Ch 220
[113] Contrast *Re Royal Society's Charitable Trusts* [1956] Ch 87

wider powers of investment as appropriate to most trusts, and were not, therefore, prepared to sanction additional investment powers except in very special circumstances. This restrictive approach applied not merely to private trusts, but also to charitable trusts.[114] By the 1980s, however, when it was becoming recognized that the restrictions imposed by the 1961 Act were out of date, the courts were also beginning to relax their former strict approach, and to agree to extensions of trustees' powers where the trust fund involved was exceptionally large.[115] The general power of investment conferred on trustees by the Trustee Act 2000 effectively relieves many charitable trusts from the need to apply to the Charity Commissioners (or, exceptionally, to the courts) for an extension of the trustees' powers of investment, and much of the learning contained in the existing case law is now redundant.

The only circumstance in which an application for a widening of investment powers is now likely to occur is where a charitable trust's governing instrument contains an express restriction on the trustees' investment powers that the Trustee Act 2000 does not remove (which will therefore include not merely charitable trusts created after the Trustee Act 2000 came into force, but also a number of such trusts set up during the period that the Trustee Investments Act 1961 was in force). In the light of the new statutory investment regime, it would seem that the only criterion for the widening of the investment powers of such charitable trusts is that such widening is expedient in the best interests of the charity. **16.59**

Before the Trustee Act 2000 was enacted, the Charity Commissioners had said that they would consider on its individual merits any application made to them to permit investment in derivatives; and if they considered that sort of transaction appropriate, they would confer the authority by way of an order under section 26 of the Charities Act 1993, rather than by means of a scheme.[116] The general power of investment conferred on trustees by the Trustee Act 2000 now effectively authorizes trustees of charitable trusts to invest in derivatives. Where trustees have such power, their only concerns now will be, first, whether the purchase of particular derivatives ranks as an investment at all, and, secondly, whether such purchase is compatible with their general duties relating to investment, including the duties to choose suitable investments and to diversify as is appropriate to the trust. Until the Charity Commissioners' attitude to the acquisition of derivatives **16.60**

---

[114] *Re London Univ's Charitable Trusts* [1964] Ch 282

[115] See *Trustees of the British Museum v A-G* [1984] 1 WLR 418, where Megarry V-C sanctioned very wide investment powers, but subject to the requirement that one third of the fund be invested in narrower-range securities. Cf *Steel v Wellcome Custodian Trustees Ltd* [1988] 1 WLR 167, where Hoffmann J authorized an extension of the trustees' powers to enable them to invest the whole fund (worth some £3.2 billion) in any property as if they were beneficial owners. For the Charity Commissioners' attitude to extension of investment powers before TA 2000, see (1995) 3 Decisions 21

[116] (1995) 3 Decisions 26

pursuant to the general power of investment is established, it might still be wise for charity trustees who intend to invest in derivatives to seek the Commissioners' prior approval.

G. Ethical investment

16.61   In a private trust, the basic duty of the trustees to secure for the trust the best financial return appears to admit of only one qualification: namely, where another policy receives the unanimous support of beneficiaries who are sui juris.[117] Without such agreement of the beneficiaries, the trustees are not permitted to let the trust lose a financial benefit at the expense of any moral code or ethical scruples of their own.[118] In a charitable trust, however, the basic duty to obtain the maximum return is subject to four qualifications laid down by Nicholls V-C in *Harries v Church Commissioners for England.*[119]

16.62   First, charity trustees should not invest in a company engaged in a particular type of business if they are satisfied that to do so would conflict with the very objects their charity is seeking to achieve.[120] Nicholls V-C mentioned the 'much-cited' examples of cancer research charities and tobacco shares, trustees of temperance charities and brewery and distillery shares, and trustees of the Society of Friends and shares in companies engaged in the production of armaments.[121] It might be inferred from this that if the charity trustees were to invest the charity's funds directly into a clearly 'conflicting' investment, such investment might amount to a breach of trust.[122] In practice, however, matters are rarely as simple as this. It may be difficult in many instances both to identify 'conflicting' investments and also to ascertain whether such investments are actually being made. The latter is a particular problem where the investment is indirect. If charity trustees invest in unit trusts or common investment funds, for example, they may discover only later that they have invested indirectly in companies with conflicting objects.[123]

---

[117]   *Cowan v Scargill* [1985] Ch 270

[118]   Hence, trustees of a private trust who entered into a contract of sale which did not comply with the statutory formalities were held to be under a duty to gazump on receiving a higher offer from another prospective purchaser: *Buttle v Saunders* [1950] 2 All ER 193

[119]   [1992] 1 WLR 1241

[120]   ibid, 1246

[121]   ibid

[122]   The Charity Commissioners had previously expressed this view: [1987] Ch Com Rep 10–11 (paras 41–5); and it seems to derive implicit support from the *Harries* case

[123]   See D Morris, 'Charity investment in the UK: some contemporary issues for the 1990s' [1995] 3 Web JCLI, noting that in 1995, the Imperial Cancer Research Fund discovered that it had unwittingly invested in a common investment fund which had 5% of its investments in tobacco companies

Secondly, trustees are entitled or required (as the case may be) to take non-financial criteria into account if the trust instrument so provides.[124] Nicholls V-C does not indicate what limits, if any, there are upon this qualification. If the direction seeks to exclude certain types of investment from the trustees' portfolio altogether, the exclusion would need to be certain.[125] If the direction relates instead to the manner in which the trustees are to exercise their discretion in selecting investments, as by way of a preference clause, it appears that the same degree of certainty is not required. In either event, however, it is difficult to appreciate why a settlor should be able to specify non-financial criteria which have no relation to the charitable purposes of the trust itself. It might be appropriate to treat such provisions as void to the extent that they are not ancillary to the carrying out of the charity's purposes. This would be an application to the sphere of investment of the general principle that charity trustees are permitted to engage in certain non-charitable activities which can be considered to be means of achieving the charity's charitable purposes.[126] If the trustees consider a direction relating to non-financial criteria too restrictive, they can apply to the Charity Commissioners[127] or to the court under its inherent power to have the direction deleted or amended on the ground that it is expedient to do so.

16.63

Thirdly, there will be rare cases[128]

16.64

> where trustees' holdings of particular investments might hamper a charity's work either by making potential recipients of aid unwilling to be helped because of the source of the charity's money, or by alienating some of those who support the charity financially. In these cases the trustees will need to balance the difficulties they would encounter, or likely financial loss they would sustain, if they were to hold the investments against the risk of financial detriment if those investments were excluded from their portfolio.

This third qualification has been criticized as potentially leaving charity trustees open to political manipulation in the broadest sense.[129] It might, for instance, enable a substantial donor who has a personal dislike of certain types of companies effectively to manipulate the trustees' investment decisions. If such a donor were threatening to cease making donations unless the trustees, for instance, disinvested in companies which employed union labour, or which manufactured contraceptives,[130] the trustees might well consider it in the financial interests of the charity to comply with the donor's whims. In such an extreme instance, this

---

[124] *Harries v Church Commissioners for England* [1992] 1 WLR 1241, 1247
[125] cf *Re Kolb's Will Trust* [1962] Ch 531 ('blue chip' securities held void for uncertainty)
[126] cf *Re Hood* [1931] 1 Ch 240; and the Charity Commissioners' revised guidelines, *Political Activities and Campaigning by Charities*, CC9 (Feb 1997), discussed ch 7, paras 7.40–7.65
[127] CA 1993, s 16(1)(a)
[128] *Harries v Church Commissioners for England* [1992] 1 WLR, 1241, 1247
[129] P Luxton, 'Ethical investment in hard times' (1992) 55 MLR 587, 589–91
[130] cf examples in JH Langbein and RA Posner, 'Social Investing and the Law of Trusts' (1980) 79 Mich L Rev 72, 83–4

would surely be an unacceptable interference with the independence of decision-making by trustees.

16.65 Fourthly, some investments, whilst not in conflict with the purposes of the trust, might be considered by those involved with the charity (that is, not merely the charity trustees) to be ethically unsuitable. Subject to the duty on trustees not to make moral statements at the expense of the charity, and to their being satisfied that there is no risk of significant financial detriment, charity trustees may, in selecting investments, take ethical considerations into account. Nicholls V-C gave as an example the situation where those who supported or benefited from a charity took widely different views on a particular type of investment on moral grounds. He considered that, so long as they were satisfied that the course would not involve a risk of significant financial detriment, trustees might accommodate such views.[131]

16.66 The action in the *Harries* case had been brought by the Bishop of Oxford and some other clergy, with the support of the Christian Ethical Investment Group. The plaintiffs claimed declarations that, in managing their assets, the Church Commissioners, an incorporated body with charitable objects, were obliged to have regard to the object of promoting the Christian faith through the established Church of England. Nicholls V-C refused to make the declarations on the ground that the plaintiffs' policy would result in the exclusion from the Church Commissioners' investments of 37 per cent of listed United Kingdom companies (by value), which would involve a risk of significant financial detriment. In fact, the Church Commissioners were already pursuing an ethical investment policy, albeit one more limited than that sought by the plaintiffs. Since their constitution in 1948, the Church Commissioners had pursued a policy of excluding investment in companies whose main business was in armaments, gambling, or tobacco, or which had more than a small part of their business in South Africa. Nicholls V-C evidently treated this policy as falling within the scope of his fourth qualification. Although there were differing views in the Church as to the morality of investing in such companies, the trustees were able to exclude them from their investment portfolio because they comprised only some 13 per cent of listed United Kingdom companies (by value): an adequate width of alternative investments remained open to them, and so there was no risk of significant financial detriment.[132]

---

[131] *Harries v Church Commissioners for England* [1992] 1 WLR 1241, 1247–8

[132] Somewhat ironically, in view of the decision in *Harries v Church Commissioners*, the Church Commissioners subsequently considered relaxing their ban on investment in breweries and distilleries. The reason for the recommended change was said to be the Church's concern with the burgeoning trade in the sale of alcoholic lemonades and other drinks (known as 'alcopops') to young people. A report to the General Synod (debated in the summer of 1997) recommended a selective easing of the ban so that the Church, as an investor, could make a positive contribution to the issues being debated within the industry. See R Gledhill, 'Church may buy brewery shares to fight alcopops' *The Times*, 20 Nov 1996

H. Delegation

(1) Delegation of investment function

Under the Trustee Act 2000, subject to certain qualifications, trustees may autho-   **16.67**
rize any person to exercise any or all of their delegable functions as their agent.[133]
In the case of a charitable trust, the trustees' delegable functions include any function relating to the investment of assets subject to the trust (including, in the case
of land held as an investment, managing the land and creating or disposing of an
interest in the land).[134] The person or persons to whom the trustees may delegate
such functions include one or more of their own number.[135] The trustees may also
delegate such functions to a person even though he is also appointed to act as their
nominee or custodian.[136] Any delegation of the trustees' investment function[137]
must be authorized by an agreement in, or evidenced in, writing.[138] Before making the delegation, the trustees must have prepared a policy statement that gives
guidance relating to the exercise of the investment function, and the agreement
under which the agent is to act must include a term to the effect that he will secure
compliance with such policy statement, or with any revised or replacement policy
statement.[139] The trustees must formulate any guidance given in the policy statement with a view to ensuring that the functions will be exercised in the best interests of the trust.[140] The policy statement must itself be in, or evidenced in,
writing.[141] Trustees are under a general statutory duty to review the arrangement
under which an agent acts, and must consider, in appropriate circumstances,
whether they should give that agent directions or revoke his authorization or appointment.[142] A trustee is not liable for any act or default of the agent unless he has
failed to comply with the statutory duty of care.[143]

A person authorized under the Trustee Act 2000 to exercise a general power of in-   **16.68**
vestment is subject to the statutory duties in relation to that power.[144] He must, for
example, exercise the general power of investment subject to the duty to have regard to the standard investment criteria laid down in section 4 of the Trustee Act

---

[133] TA 2000, s 11(1)
[134] ibid, s 11(3)(b)
[135] ibid, s 12(1)
[136] ibid, s 12(4)
[137] This is an 'asset management function' within ibid, s 15(5)(a)
[138] ibid, s 15(1)
[139] ibid, s 15(2)
[140] ibid, s 15(3)
[141] ibid, s 15(4)
[142] ibid, s 22
[143] ibid, s 23(1). The duty of care is specified ibid, s 1(1); for its application to the use of agents,
see ibid, s 2 & Sch 1, para 3. See further ch 9, paras 9.78–9.81
[144] TA 2000, s 13(1)

2000.[145] He is not, however, subject to the duty imposed by section 5 to obtain advice if he is the kind of person from whom it would have been proper for the trustees, in compliance with the requirement of that section, to obtain advice.[146]

(2) Appointment of nominees

16.69 Charity trustees may wish to appoint nominees in order to facilitate dealings by a discretionary fund manager. Under the Trustee Act 2000, trustees may, subject to certain qualifications, appoint a person to act as their nominee in relation to all or any of the assets of the trust.[147] The appointment must be in, or be evidenced in, writing.[148] The nominee must be a person who carries on a business which consists of, or includes, acting as a nominee, or it must be a body corporate controlled by the trustees, or a body Corporate recognized under section 9 of the Administration of Justice Act 1985.[149] The persons who may be appointed a nominee include one of the trustees themselves, if it is a trust corporation, or two or more of their number, if they are to act as joint nominees.[150]

16.70 These new statutory criteria are in fact less stringent than the criteria for appointment of nominees which were previously applied by the Charity Commissioners. Before the Trustee Act 2000, where the trust instrument contained no power to authorize the appointment of nominees, the Commissioners' sanction was required by order under section 26 of the Charities Act 1993.[151] It was the Charity Commissioners' practice to require nominees to be either trust corporations with a place of business in England and Wales, or (where the nominee was overseas) to lay down conditions relating to the regulation and review of the nominee and its manner of holding the property.[152] The Law Commission considered that, whilst legislation should not impose rigid requirements on the use of nominees by charitable trustees, such use should be subject to guidance issued by the Charity Commission.[153] In accordance with the Law Commission's recommendation,[154] the Trustee Act 2000 provides that, in selecting a person for appointment as a nominee, the trustees of a charitable trust which is not an exempt charity must act in accordance with any guidance given by the Charity Commissioners.[155]

---

[145] TA 2000, s 13(1); see above, paras 16.17–16.19
[146] TA 2000, s 13(2)
[147] ibid, s 16(1)(a)
[148] ibid, s 16(2)
[149] ibid, s 19(2)
[150] ibid, s 19(5)
[151] (1994) 2 Decisions 30
[152] See Law Commission, *Trustees' Powers and Duties* (Law Com No 260, 1999) 62 (para 5.8 & n 15)
[153] ibid, 62 (para 5.8)
[154] ibid, 62–3 (para 5.9). The Law Commission pointed out that the Charity Commission might, for example, wish to issue guidance against the use of nominees in certain states outside the European Economic Area where the procedures for protecting charitable trusts are considered to be inadequate: ibid, 62 (para 5.8, n 16)
[155] TA 2000, s 19(4)

Trustees are under a general statutory duty to review the arrangement under **16.71** which a nominee acts, and must consider, in appropriate circumstances, whether they should give that nominee directions or revoke his authorization or appointment.[156] A trustee is not liable for any act or default of the nominee unless he (the trustee) has failed to comply with the statutory duty of care.[157]

I. Common investment funds

(1) Introduction

The idea of a common investment fund (CIF) is that several charities pool their **16.72** separate funds to make one single fund for investment, thus enabling them to invest more profitably, and to save the expense of separate management costs. In practice, the setting up of CIFs is effected by investment funds rather than by the charities themselves.

Before the Charities Act 1960, a pooling scheme could be made by the court in **16.73** exercise of its inherent jurisdiction to make schemes;[158] and the Charity Commissioners made such schemes in exercise of their concurrent jurisdiction. A severe restriction, however, was that, in order to avoid contravention of the rule (since modified)[159] that trustees had no power under the general law to delegate investment decisions, a pooling scheme could be made on this basis only if the same persons were the trustees of all the separate trusts in the pool. The Charities Act 1960 relaxed the requirements for a CIF by authorizing delegation of investment decisions to the trustees of the common investment fund,[160] so that such a fund could be set up even if the trustees of the participating charities were different persons. The power to make a scheme (called a 'common investment scheme') setting up a CIF is now contained in the Charities Act 1993.[161] More than £2 billion is currently invested in such funds,[162] which have been of growing importance since the investment function of the Official Custodian for Charities was wound up over the period 1994–5.[163]

---

[156] ibid, s 22
[157] ibid, s 23(1). The duty of care is specified ibid, s 1(1); for its application to the use of nominees, see ibid, s 2 & Sch 1, para 3. See further ch 9, paras 9.78–9.81
[158] *Re Royal Society's Charitable Trusts* [1956] Ch 87
[159] See TA 2000, s 11(3)(b), and above, paras 16.67–16.68
[160] CA 1960, s 22
[161] CA 1993, s 24
[162] See R Marlow, 'Common Investment Funds' (1996–7) 4 CL & PR 21
[163] Under CA 1992, s 29, and see [1995] Ch Com Rep 28 (paras 125–6), and ch 9, paras 9.65 and 9.72. The reduction of the Official Custodian's role began (inter alia) the winding up of the Charities Official Investment Fund (COIF), which had been established by the Charity Commissioners in 1962; it was one of the first CIFs created under CA 1960, and open to all charities: see [1962] Ch Com Rep, 9–16 (paras 21–49), and 34–9 (App B) (where the scheme is set out). Pursuant to her divestment obligation, the Official Custodian for Charities ceased to be registrar of

(2) Common investment schemes made under statute

General

16.74 A common investment scheme may provide for property to be transferred to the fund by a participating charity to be invested under the control of trustees appointed to manage the fund, and for the participating charities to be entitled (subject to the provisions of the scheme) to the capital and income of the fund in shares according to the amount or value of the property transferred to it by each of them and to the value of the fund at the time of the transfers.[164] In practice, this means that when a charity joins a scheme, it is allocated new units in the fund, and when it leaves the scheme, these units are cancelled, the purchase and sale prices of the units being based on the fund's net asset value. A scheme can be made on the application of any two or more charities.[165] The scheme may in terms admit any charity to participate or restrict its right to participate in any manner.[166]

16.75 The scheme may also make provisions for the establishment, investment, management, and winding up of the CIF.[167] In particular it may restrict the size of the fund and provide for the regulation of transfers of property, withdrawals, and advancements out of the fund. It may also provide for income to be withheld from distribution with a view to avoiding fluctuations in the amounts distributed, and generally for regulating distributions of income. The scheme may also provide for money to be borrowed temporarily to meet payments out of the fund. It may also make provision to enable questions arising under the scheme as to the right of a charity to participate, or as to the rights of participating charities, or as to any other matter, to be conclusively determined by the decision of the trustees managing the fund or in any other manner. Finally, it may regulate the accounts and information to be supplied to participating charities.[168]

16.76 A common investment scheme may also make provision for enabling sums to be deposited by or on behalf of a charity at a rate of interest to be determined

---

the COIF on 11 Dec 1992, and the register was transferred to trustees of COIF, pending the return of the investments to their respective trustees: [1992] Ch Com Rep 16 (para 60), 32 (App C, para 7). This encouraged the setting up of other CIFs. By 1996, there were in existence more than 20 other CIFs open to all charities (including one pure overseas-equity fund): see R Marlow, 'Common Investment Funds' (1996–7) 4 CL & PR 21, 23–4. There are also several other restricted CIFs designed for particular types of charities, such as almshouse and Church of England charities. The Commissioners' leaflet on common investment funds (CC15) has been withdrawn

[164] CA 1993, s 24(1)
[165] ibid, s 24(2)
[166] ibid, s 24(3)
[167] ibid, s 24(4). It should be noted that TA 2000, Pts II–IV (ie provisions relating to investment, the acquisition of land, and the appointment of agents, nominees, and custodians) do not (subject to a specified exception) apply to trustees managing a fund under a common investment scheme made, or having effect as if made, under CA 1993, s 24: TA 2000, s 38(a)
[168] CA 1993, s 24(4)

under the scheme and with the right of repayment of the sum deposited with interest.[169]

Except so far as a common investment scheme provides to the contrary, the rights **16.77** of a participating charity under it cannot be assigned or charged, and a trustee or other person concerned in the management of the fund is not required or entitled to take account of any trust or other equity affecting a participating charity or its property or rights.[170]

The powers of investment of every charity include power to participate in com- **16.78** mon investment schemes unless the power is excluded by a provision specifically referring to common investment schemes in the trusts of the charity.[171]

A CIF is deemed for all purposes to be a charity; and if the scheme admits only ex- **16.79** empt charities, the fund is itself an exempt charity.[172] This deeming provision also extends to a similar fund established for the exclusive benefit of charities by or under any similar enactment relating to any particular charities or class of charity.[173] Unless the CIF is an exempt charity, it will therefore require to be registered with the Charity Commissioners. An advantage flowing from the charitable status of these funds is that distributions from them are paid (in contrast to income from other investments) without deduction of tax, thereby relieving the trustees of the need to reclaim tax from the Inland Revenue.[174]

Regulation and structure

Introduction

Until recently, 'a person acting in his capacity as a manager of a fund established **16.80** under' section 24 of the Charities Act 1993, or section 22 of the Charities Act 1960, was an exempt person for the purposes of the Financial Services Act 1986.[175] It was clear that a trustee of a CIF was an exempt person; but in practice all CIF trustees had delegated their management functions to professional fund managers. To the extent that such fund managers gave investment advice to the trustees, they were obliged to act in accordance with the rules of the Investment Management Regulatory Organization Ltd (IMRO) concerning the relationship between adviser and client. The Charity Commissioners and the Treasury took the view that the exemption did not extend to the fund manager of a CIF in respect of the

---

[169] ibid, s 24(5)
[170] ibid, s 24(6)
[171] ibid, s 24(7)
[172] ibid, s 24(8)
[173] ibid, s 24(9)
[174] [1989] Ch Com Rep 30 (para 117)
[175] By virtue of FSA 1986, s 45(1)(j), before the scope of that para was restricted by Financial Services Act 1986 (Restriction of Exemption) Order 1999, SI 1999/2999, reg 2

functions he carried out on behalf of the trustees. The matter was not, however, beyond doubt.[176]

16.81 The exemption for trustees meant that no authorization under the Financial Services Act 1986 was required to operate a CIF (which, for the purposes of that Act, ranks as a 'collective investment scheme'[177]). By default, the Charity Commissioners had taken on the role of regulating the establishment of schemes creating CIFs. In performing this function, the Commissioners applied the same principles as they applied to any charitable trust. For example, although the Charities Act 1993 expressly states that the scheme may make provision for re-munerating the trustees of the fund,[178] the Charity Commissioners would not reg-ister any scheme as a charity if the governing instrument permitted the trustees to be remunerated. Furthermore, the Charity Commissioners would need to be satisfied that there was a need for the scheme, that it had reputable trustees, and that such trustees had no connection with the fund manager. The Charity Commissioners' powers under the Charities Act 1993 did not, however, enable them to regulate CIFs in the same way that collective investment schemes are su-pervised under the Financial Services Act 1986; and the Charity Commissioners also lacked the expertise and experience of financial service regulation possessed by the Securities and Investments Board and IMRO.[179]

16.82 In a joint Consultation Document issued in 1996, the Charity Commissioners and the Treasury expressed the view that the regulatory regime applicable to CIFs was inadequate.[180] Although all fund managers of CIFs were IMRO-regulated firms, and no major problem had arisen, the Charity Commissioners believed that more specific safeguards for investing charities were needed, especially with the growth of the voluntary sector and the increasing number of proposals for CIFs which it was receiving. In particular, the exemption for trustees meant that in-vestors in CIFs were not eligible to seek redress under the investor compensation arrangements. The recommended solution involved both the removal of the ex-emption for a trustee of a statutorily created CIF, and the requirement for new CIFs to adopt one of the model structures to be created by the Charity Commissioners, under which the trustee of a CIF must be a corporate trustee. This last requirement was considered necessary to avoid an individual trustee's in-

---

[176] Charity Commission and HM Treasury Consultation Paper, *The Structure and Regulation of Common Investment Funds* (1996), 3 (para 9)

[177] FSA 1986, s 75

[178] CA 1993, s 24(4)

[179] The Securities and Investment Board was re-named the Financial Services Authority in 1997

[180] Charity Commission and HM Treasury Consultation Paper, *The Structure and Regulation of Common Investment Funds* (1996)

curring extensive personal liability for breach of trust in relation to his investment duties;[181] but it adds to the cost of operating a CIF.[182]

Common investment funds created after 30 November 1999

After 30 November 1999, a person acting in his capacity as manager of a fund es- **16.83** tablished under section 24 of the Charities Act 1993, or under section 22 of the Charities Act 1960 (except in relation to a pooling-scheme fund), has ceased to be an exempt person under the Financial Services Act 1986.[183] Furthermore, CIFs created after that date ('new CIFs') must adopt one of the Charity Commissioners' model structures.[184] The effect of the removal of the exemption is that IMRO[185] now has to satisfy itself that the corporate trustee is not only fit and proper but that it also has the systems and experience necessary to be able to fulfil the duties of an authorized unit trust. Additionally, the trustee of a CIF who is undertaking investment business, and the manager of a CIF, has each to act in accordance with IMRO's Conduct of Business Rules for trustees (in the case of a CIF trustee) or operators (in the case of a CIF manager) of unregulated collective investment schemes.

The Charity Commissioners require each new CIF to be managed by a corporate **16.84** trustee (the Trustee) and a fund manager (the Manager), and, optionally, by a board of individuals (the Board), and to be set up in a form similar to the model scheme set out in Annexe B to the Commission's Policy Statement.[186] Under this scheme, the Trustee and the Manager must each be a body corporate, a member of IMRO, and independent of each other,[187] and neither must be disqualified from acting as the trustee or manager (respectively) of an authorized unit trust.[188]

---

[181] ibid, 4 (para 14)

[182] An advantage of CIFs used to be that their management fees were generally lower than those of unit trusts: see R Marlow, 'Common Investment Funds' (1996–7) 4 CL & PR 21, 23. In response to the Consultation Document, the CLA suggested that, in view of the more expensive structure which a corporate trustee would entail, consideration should be given either to a compulsory corporate custodian trustee (with individual managing trustees), or to indemnity insurance: CLA, *Response to the Charity Commission/HM Treasury Consultation Document on the Structure and Regulation of Common Investment Funds* (Dec 1996), 2–3 (paras 14.1–14.3). In the event, however, the Charity Commissioners adhered to their original proposal for a corporate trustee

[183] FSA 1986, s 45(1)(j), as restricted in scope by Financial Services Act 1986 (Restriction of Exemption) Order 1999, SI 1999/2999, reg 2

[184] Charity Commission, *Common Investment Funds: Policy Statement* (1996)

[185] Since 1999, IMRO has delegated its supervisory functions to the Financial Services Authority (FSA), and its staff have been transferred to the FSA, with a view to the creation of a single regulator under the Financial Services and Markets Act 2000

[186] Charity Commission, *Common Investment Funds: Policy Statement* (1996), 1. A summary of the division of responsibilities amongst the Trustee, Manager and (if there is one) the Board, is set out ibid, Ann A

[187] Within the meaning of the Financial Services Authority Guidance release 1/90, Feb 1990

[188] Charity Commission, *Common Investment Funds: Policy Statement* (1996), Ann B, cl 2, which also provides that 'authorized unit trust' means a unit trust scheme authorized for the purposes of FSA 1986: ibid

Where a Board has been appointed, the new CIF's structure is similar to that of an open-ended investment company,[189] although the new CIF is not itself a corporate body.[190]

16.85 A CIF which adopts the model scheme in Annexe B may provide that any charity is qualified to participate in the fund except one whose trusts expressly exclude the power to participate in common investment schemes.[191] Alternatively, the CIF may restrict entry to charities established for particular purposes.[192]

16.86 Under the model scheme, the Trustee is responsible for the following (inter alia): the supervision and oversight of the manager's compliance with the scheme; the custody and control of the fund's property and the collection of income; the creation and cancellation of units in accordance with the Manager's instructions; the making of distributions to participating charities; the appointment or dismissal of staff; the making of an annual report on the discharge of its management responsibilities; and the fund's winding up.[193] The Trustee's liability for the acts or defaults of the Manager in relation to the exercise of the powers conferred on the Manager by the scheme is excluded if the Trustee has acted with all due skill, care, and diligence in satisfying itself that the Manager is competently exercising those powers and discharging those duties.[194] There is also provision for the Trustee to delegate any of its functions.[195] The Trustee is responsible for all documents of title relating to the property of the fund, but it may permit such documents to be in the possession or under the control as custodian of some other person who has authority under the Financial Services Act 1986 to undertake the safe custody of documents.[196] The Trustee may appoint a body corporate as its nominee to hold the property of the fund.[197]

16.87 The Manager's responsibilities under the model scheme include the following: giving instructions to the Trustee with respect to the creation and cancellation of units; the management of the investments of the fund; the duty to carry out regular valuations of the property of the fund and to ensure that the units are correctly priced; the making and revision of the written statement of the investment policy and of the scheme particulars; keeping a daily record of units purchased or sold; making all records in respect of the fund available for inspection by the Trustee; preparing a report and accounts of the fund in respect of every accounting period; the appointment of the auditor of the fund and settling his terms of

---

[189] ie within the meaning of FSA 1986, s 75(8)
[190] Charity Commission, *Common Investment Funds: Policy Statement* (1996), 1
[191] ibid, Ann B, cl 6; and see CA 1993, s 24(7)
[192] Charity Commission, *Common Investment Funds: Policy Statement* (1996), Ann B, cl 6
[193] ibid, Ann B, cl 9
[194] ibid, cl 11(2)
[195] ibid, cl 12
[196] ibid, cll 13–14
[197] ibid, cl 15

engagement; and taking all other action as necessary for the administration and management of the fund other than those duties and powers conferred by the scheme on the Trustee.[198] There is also provision for the Manager to delegate any of its functions (except where prohibited by the scheme) to any person, including the Trustee.[199]

The first Trustee and Manager are appointed by the scheme.[200] Either may retire **16.88** by giving notice to the other and to the Charity Commissioners; and the Manager must use its best endeavours to find a body corporate qualified to act which is willing to be appointed in place of a retiring Trustee, or (where it is the Manager who is retiring) in place of itself.[201] In regard to removal, the Trustee and the Manager are on an equal footing. Each may apply to the Charity Commissioners for an order to discharge the other from the trusts of the scheme, where it is of the opinion for good and sufficient reason that a change of Trustee or Manager (as the case may be) is desirable in the interests of the participating charities. The Trustee or Manager making such application must serve notice of it on the other. The applicant must use its best endeavours to find a body corporate which is qualified and willing to act as Trustee or Manager (as the case may be). A Trustee or Manager is discharged from the trusts of the scheme only by order of the Charity Commissioners, and its replacement must be appointed by an order of the Commissioners. A Trustee or Manager who retires or who is removed, is discharged from the trusts of the scheme only by an order of the Commissioners, and any replacement Trustee or Manager must also be appointed by an order of the Commissioners.[202]

As charity trustees, CIF Trustees and Managers continue to be subject to the gen- **16.89** eral jurisdiction of the Charity Commissioners. The model scheme recites that, to the extent of their respective duties and powers in respect of the administration and management of the fund and its property, each of the Trustee and the Manager is a 'charity trustee' of the fund within the meaning of the Charities Act 1993.[203]

The Charity Commissioners have also changed their previous policy on the re- **16.90** muneration of CIF trustees, since the model scheme provides for the remuneration of the Trustee and Manager at a rate to be determined in accordance with the scheme particulars.[204]

---

[198] ibid, cl 19(1)
[199] ibid, cl 20
[200] ibid, cll 7 (Trustee), 17 (Manager)
[201] In practice, therefore, most replacement Trustees will be appointed by the Manager, which parallels the position under unit trusts
[202] Charity Commission, *Common Investment Funds: Policy Statement* (1996), Ann B, cls 25 (retirement of Trustee), 26 (retirement of Manager), 27(1) (replacement of Trustee), 27(2) (replacement of Manager)
[203] ibid, cll 8 (Trustee), 18 (Manager)
[204] ibid, cll 23–4

16.91 Although an individual cannot be a Trustees or a Manager of a new CIF, the Charity Commissioners recognize that individuals with skills and experience of the voluntary sector may nevertheless contribute to CIFs. For this reason, a new CIF may make provision for a board of individuals in accordance with the model form in Annexe C to the Charity Commission's Policy Statement. This provides that the scheme may assign to the Board any of the following powers: the appointment and discharge of the Manager; setting the investment policy of the fund; acting as an advisory body to the fund manager on the fund's investment policy; appointing the auditor to the fund, and determining the rate of remuneration of the Trustee and Manager.[205] To the extent of those duties and powers, the model scheme recites that the Board members are 'charity trustees' of the fund within the meaning of the Charities Act 1993.[206] Each member of the Board must be appointed for a specified number of years;[207] and no Board member is entitled to receive any remuneration or benefit at the cost of the fund, except to the extent authorized by the scheme.[208] The Board is not permitted to delegate any of its functions to any person.[209] The model scheme does not require a member of the Board to have any experience of the financial services industry, but it provides that no Board member is entitled to offer investment advice or to conduct investment business in relation to the fund unless he is individually authorized to do so under the Financial Services Act 1986, or is exempt from obtaining such authorization under that Act.[210] Given the limited powers of the Board, the potential liability of its members, and the fact that the members are unlikely to be remunerated, it is questionable whether many persons will wish to sit on such Boards.[211]

Transitional provisions

16.92 A person acting in his capacity as manager of a fund (other than a pooling-scheme fund) established by a common investment scheme that took effect before 1 December 1999 did not cease to be an exempt person as respects his management of that fund until either 1 June 2000 or, if earlier, the date upon which a further common investment scheme took effect in relation to the fund.[212]

---

[205] Charity Commission, *Common Investment Funds: Policy Statement* (1996), Ann C, cl 15
[206] ibid, cl 14
[207] ibid, cl 1–2
[208] ibid, cl 13
[209] ibid, cl 17
[210] ibid, cl 3(2)
[211] See CLA, *Response to the Charity Commission/HM Treasury Consultation Document on the Structure and Regulation of Common Investment Funds* (Dec 1996), 4 (para 27), which expressed doubt whether individuals would wish to sit on the proposed Consultative Committees, where they would be 'neither fish nor fowl', and which recommended instead the establishment of a new Ombudsman to whom charity investors could address individual complaints and through whom fund managers could consult
[212] Financial Services Act 1986 (Restriction of Exemption) Order 1999, SI 1999/2999, reg 3

Existing CIFs which were set up under an interim scheme (in accordance with the **16.93** model structure in Annexe D to the Charity Commission's Policy Statement) during the period of consultation (which began in 1996) are required to restructure by adopting the model scheme in Annexe B.[213] Existing CIFs set up before the consultation period are not required to adopt the model structure in Annexe B; but, as they are affected by the removal of the exemption for CIF fund managers from the Financial Services Act 1986 in the same way as other CIFs, they are likely to wish to apply to the Charity Commissioners in order to have their fund restructured to that model.[214]

(3) Pooling schemes

The court and the Charity Commissioners continue to possess the right to make **16.94** a pooling scheme (that is, one where the participating charities have the same trustees) outside the statutory provision for common investment schemes. It appears, however, that a pooling scheme is also a CIF for the purposes of section 24 of the Charities Act 1993.[215] For the avoidance of doubt as to their jurisdiction, the Charity Commissioners' practice is to prepare all their pooling schemes pursuant to that section.[216] The exemption of a manager of a pooling-scheme fund from the Financial Services Act 1986 survives the removal of the exemption from managers of other CIFs.[217]

J. Cash deposits

(1) Generally

Pursuant to the general power of investment,[218] trustees may place sums of money **16.95** on deposit.[219] Such deposits might be appropriate to provide a charitable trust with accessible sums of money to meet regular expenditure, or as an interim short-term measure in relation to donations or legacies which await medium- or

---

[213] Charity Commission, *Common Investment Funds: Policy Statement* (1996), 2. The interim model scheme reserved to the Charity Commissioners the power to make a further scheme affecting the fund without an application for such a scheme being required under CA 1993 (Ann D, cl 44)

[214] Charity Commission, *Common Investment Funds: Policy Statement* (1996), 2

[215] *Re London Univ's Charitable Trusts* [1964] Ch 282; and see H Picarda, *The Law and Practice Relating to Charities* (3rd edn, Butterworths, 1999) 514

[216] [1963] Ch Com Rep 17–18 (para 47)

[217] The exemption for the manager of a pooling-scheme fund is expressly preserved by Financial Services Act 1986 (Restriction of Exemption) Order 1999, SI 1999/2999, reg 2

[218] TA 2000, s 3

[219] Before TA 2000, the default position was that trustees could place money on deposit in accordance with TIA 1961. Under that Act, deposits in the National Savings Bank and in certified banks were narrower-range investments not requiring advice; deposits with a building society within the meaning of the Building Societies Act 1986 were narrower-range investments requiring advice. These specific restrictions have gone with the coming into force of TA 2000. For the significance of 'narrower-range' investments under the 1961 Act, see ch 1, paras 1.128–1.132

longer-term investment. The Charity Commissioners have issued guidance to trustees in relation to deposits.[220] They recommend that, if a large sum of money is to be deposited, the trustees should obtain and consider the advice of a professional money manager who is a member of IMRO. If the sum to be deposited is smaller, the advice of an independent adviser who is a member of the Financial Intermediaries Managers and Brokers Regulatory Association or the Personal Investment Authority[221] might be appropriate. If the charity frequently receives sums for deposit, the Charity Commissioners recommend that the trustees draw up a written policy statement for distribution to their relevant staff covering such matters as where deposits might be made, how long sums should be on deposit, and the maximum amount that should be invested in any one account. The Commissioners' leaflet also gives guidance on the choice of institution and type of account. Amongst other relevant considerations, the trustees should ascertain whether the interest is paid (or can be paid) gross, or (if it is paid net of basic rate tax) whether it is recoverable. They should also enquire whether a deposit with a bank or building society is protected by a deposit protection scheme.[222] The Charity Commissioners also recommend that deposits should require the authorization of at least two trustees.

(2) Common deposit funds

16.96 The advantage of a common deposit fund is that it enables a number of charities to pool sums of money which they have available for deposit with a view to benefiting from the higher rates of interest that larger deposits can command. Because such funds can make deposits with a number of different institutions, they help to spread the risk.

16.97 Common deposit funds were originally introduced in the Charities Act 1992,[223] following a recommendation of the Charity Commissioners,[224] who had reluctantly concluded that it was not possible to constitute a CIF restricted solely to the deposit of money. Such deposit facilities had to be included in a common investment scheme, with the consequence that investing charities had shares in a fund of fluctuating value. The law was subsequently amended, and funds restricted to the deposit of money can now be constituted under section 25 of the Charities Act 1993. To date, however, it appears that only one common deposit fund has been created.[225]

---

[220] Charity Commission, *Depositing Charity Cash*, CC14(a) (Aug 1995)
[221] Since 1999, the Personal Investment Authority has delegated its supervisory functions to the Financial Services Authority, with a view to the creation of a single regulator to be established under the Financial Services and Markets Act 2000
[222] Under the Credit Institutions (Protection of Depositors) Regulations 1993, a deposit protection scheme provides protection for up to 90% of the investment, up to a maximum investment of £20,000. The maximum recoverable in compensation under such a scheme is therefore £18,000
[223] CA 1992, s 16, adding s 22A to CA 1960
[224] [1989] Ch Com Rep 31 (paras 120–2)
[225] See M Harbottle, *Investing Charity Funds* (Jordans, 1995) 139 (para 9.28)

A common deposit fund must be established by a scheme (called a 'common de- **16.98** posit scheme') made by the court or by order of the Charity Commissioners.[226] The trusts of such a scheme must provide for sums to be deposited by or on behalf of a participating charity and invested under the control of trustees appointed to manage the fund, and for any such charity to be entitled (subject to the provisions of the scheme) to repayment of any sums so deposited and to interest thereon at a rate determined under the scheme.[227] Most of the statutory provisions relating to the creation of a CIF also have effect in relation to common deposit schemes.[228] Any two or more charities may therefore apply for a scheme; the powers of invest-ment of every charity include power to participate in such a scheme (unless specifically excluded); and such a scheme is deemed for all purposes to be a char-ity. It is provided that a common deposit scheme may in particular make provision for regulating as to time, amount, or otherwise, the right to repayment of sums de-posited in the fund. Such scheme may also expressly authorize the creation out of income of a reserve account to counteract losses to the fund and to regulate the manner of determining the rate of interest on deposit from time to time.[229]

It remains unclear whether it is possible to create what might be termed a 'pooling **16.99** deposit scheme', analogous to a pooling scheme under section 24 of the Charities Act 1993, whereby persons who are the same trustees of several charities would be enabled to pool funds for deposit in a common deposit scheme.[230] None has yet been constituted.

K. Charities' reserves

A charity's income must be applied to its charitable purposes. As a general rule this **16.100** duty is fulfilled by such income being expended on such purposes; but it may be fulfilled in two other ways.

First, the trustees of a charitable trust may have a power (or may be subject to a **16.101** duty) to accumulate income for a lawful period of accumulation. Income so ac-cumulated is capitalized and is no longer required to be applied to the charity's purposes.[231] The exercise of the power to accumulate must be the result of an

---

[226] CA 1993, s 25(1)

[227] ibid, s 25(1)

[228] Under ibid, s 25(2), it is provided that sub-ss (2)–(4) & (6)–(9) of s 24 apply to common de-posit schemes and common deposit funds, with some modifications to sub-s (4)(b) & (c): see above, paras 16.74–16.79. It should also be noted that TA 2000, Pts II–IV (ie provisions relating to in-vestment, the acquisition of land, and the appointment of agents, nominees, and custodians) do not apply to trustees managing a fund under a common deposit scheme made, or having effect as if made, under CA 1993, s 25: TA 2000, s 38(b)

[229] CA 1993, s 25(3), which replaces, in this context, CA 1993, s 24(4)(b) & (c) respectively

[230] See M Harbottle, *Investing Charity Funds* (Jordans, 1995) 139 (para 9.29)

[231] On accumulation of income by the trustees of charitable trusts, see ch 2, paras 2.20–2.22

active decision by the trustees: if they simply fail to distribute income without considering whether it should be accumulated, they commit a breach of trust,[232] and there might be adverse tax consequences.[233] The Charity Commissioners have said that, where they have reason to believe a charity may be pursuing that course, they will seek explanations from the trustees and will then take appropriate action if not satisfied by the responses received.[234]

16.102 Secondly, the charity trustees may have an express or implied power simply to retain income for future application to the charity's purposes. Such income retention creates a reserve, which is itself invested. There are no statutory restrictions on the amassing of such reserves; but the building up of excessive reserves may be an indication that the charity is not applying its income or its other property to its purposes and that there is a need for a cy-près scheme.[235] The creation of an income reserve must be the result of a positive decision by the charity trustees taken in the charity's best interests;[236] the charity trustees are not entitled to retain surplus income each year merely as a matter of course.[237]

16.103 The Charity Commissioners expect charities which create income reserves to have a properly agreed reserves policy, which should be formally agreed by the trustees acting as a board and recorded in writing.[238] The Commissioners state that the policy should cover as a minimum the reasons why the charity needs reserves; what level (or range) of reserves the trustees believe the charity needs; what steps the charity is going to take to establish or maintain reserves at the agreed level (or within the agreed range); and arrangements for monitoring and reviewing the policy.[239] Whilst the Charity Commissioners accept that some charities will simply not have the resources to establish reserves, they do expect a charity to have given thought to a reserves policy even if it currently has no reserves.[240] A charity's reserves policy must be informed by a realistic assessment of its reserves needs.[241]

16.104 Quite apart from legal and fiscal issues, charity trustees may need to tread a delicate path. They may consider that a substantial build-up of reserves is appropriate

---

[232] See, generally, *Re Hay's Settlement Trusts* [1982] 1 WLR 202

[233] eg, the undistributed income might not comprise an application for charitable purposes within the meaning of ICTA 1988, s 505(1): see further, ch 3, para 3.07

[234] [1992] Ch Com Rep 25–6 (para 98)

[235] The appropriate grounds under CA 1993, s 13(1), would appear to be para (b) (that the original purposes provide use for part only of the property) or para (c) (that the property could be more effectively used in conjunction with other property given for similar charitable purposes); see Charity Commission, *Charities' Reserves*, CC19 (May 1997), 9 (para 30). For potential problems, see M Chesterman, *Charities, Trusts and Social Welfare* (Weidenfeld & Nicolson, 1979) 379

[236] See Charity Commission, *Charities' Reserves*, CC19 (May 1997), 8 (paras 26–7)

[237] ibid, 11 (para 35)

[238] ibid, 11 (para 36)

[239] ibid, 11 (para 37)

[240] ibid, 12 (para 41)

[241] ibid, 12–13 (paras 42–3)

in order to protect the charity against any future decline or fluctuation in its other sources of income. Yet if the charity has very high reserves and does not explain its reasons for them, it may suffer adverse publicity, leading to a decline in donations and to increased difficulties in fund-raising and in carrying out its purposes.[242] The Charity Commissioners point out that the risk of adverse attention can be greatly reduced by a clear and positive explanation of the reasons why reserves are held.[243]

If trustees of a charitable trust do not wish to expend the whole of the charity's in- **16.105** come in a particular year, they may (if they have a power to accumulate) either capitalize the income through accumulation, or retain it as income for future application to the charity's purposes. Where no power of accumulation is available and the charity trustees would prefer not to create or enlarge an income reserve, they might consider it appropriate to change their investment policy to favour more capital growth. In some circumstances, it might be possible, by such means, and consistently with the charity trustees' general duties, to reduce the charity's income to a level which can be immediately expended on its charitable purposes.

---

[242] ibid, 13–15 (paras 44–52). See also [1992] Ch Com Rep 25–6 (para 98). The criticisms levelled in the 1970s at the policy on retention of reserves practised by St Dunstan's, a charity for those blinded in war, are considered in M Chesterman, *Charities, Trusts and Social Welfare* (Weidenfeld & Nicolson, 1979) 376–81
[243] Charity Commission, *Charities' Reserves*, CC19 (May 1997), 13 (para 44)

17

DEALINGS WITH LAND

Dealings with land by trustees of charities have been governed, since 1 January **17.01** 1993, by provisions now contained in Part V of the Charities Act 1993.[1] Those provisions, however, merely regulate acquisitions and disposals; they do not themselves confer a power on the trustees to acquire or to dispose of land.[2] It is therefore important to consider first if the trustees of a charity have the power to acquire land for the charity or to dispose of charity land which they already hold.

---

[1] CA 1993, ss 36–40, which re-enact provisions introduced in CA 1992, ss 32–7, which came into force on 1 Jan 1993

[2] The point is expressly made by the Charity Commissioners: [1993] Ch Com Rep 14 (para 50)

A. Power to deal with land

(1) Acquisition

Power in governing instrument

17.02 The governing instrument may confer an express power to purchase land, in which case the relevant clause in the instrument must be scrutinized to determine its precise scope. It may be a power to acquire land only for the fulfilment of the charity's purposes, or it may authorize acquisition for ancillary purposes or for investment, or for all or any of these purposes. The constitution of a charitable company will usually contain extensive powers to acquire land, and similar wide express powers to acquire land may also be found in the governing instruments of fairly modern charitable trusts. Each of the model forms of governing instruments for charities drafted on behalf of the Charity Law Association confers a wide power (which must be used only if promoting the charity's objects)[3] 'to acquire or hire property of any kind'.

17.03 Even if the instrument does not currently contain an express power, it may contain a procedure enabling the trustees to amend administrative provisions so as to confer the requisite power. Older trust instruments are less likely to contain either an express power to acquire land or a power to amend the constitution to enable land to be acquired. In these circumstances, the trustees of a charitable trust may now have the statutory power to acquire land conferred by the Trustee Act 2000.[4]

17.04 The statutory duty of care under the Trustee Act 2000[5] applies to a trustee when exercising any power to acquire land, however conferred (including therefore a power conferred by the trust instrument).[6]

Implied power

17.05 If the charity's purposes cannot be fulfilled without the acquisition of land, it may be possible to imply a power to acquire land for those purposes. In the case of charitable trusts, the new statutory power to acquire land reduces the significance of implied powers; but such powers remain important in relation to charitable companies, which are not trustees of the assets held subject to the memorandum, and do not therefore enjoy the statutory power to acquire land which is conferred on trustees.[7] The constitution of a charitable company will usually contain a clause

---

[3] *Trust Deed for a Charitable Trust*, cl 3.8; *Constitution for a Charitable Unincorporated Association*, r 3.8; *Memorandum and Articles of Association for a Charitable Company Limited by Guarantee*, cl 4.8 of memorandum

[4] TA 2000, s 8(1)

[5] ibid, s 1

[6] ibid, s 2 & Sch 1, para 2(b). On the statutory duty of care, see ch 9, paras 9.78–9.81

[7] TA 2000, s 8

conferring wide powers to do all things necessary and expedient in the fulfilment of its objects. Such a clause will empower the company to acquire land for the fulfilment of its charitable objects.[8] Reliance upon an implied power in the absence of such a clause is not entirely satisfactory because its scope may be uncertain. If a charitable company wishes to acquire land, not in fulfilment of its charitable purposes, but merely for purposes ancillary thereto (such as the acquisition of land for use as offices by the charity), it is even less certain that a power will be implied.

Statutory power

Trustees' general statutory power to acquire land

Trustees' statutory powers to acquire land have been greatly extended in recent years.[9] The general power of investment conferred on trustees by the Trustee Act 2000[10] does not permit them to make investments in land other than in loans secured on land.[11] Instead, section 8 of that Act gives trustees a separate power to acquire freehold or leasehold land[12] in the United Kingdom:[13] **17.06**

    (a) as an investment,
    (b) for occupation by a beneficiary, or
    (c) for any other reason.

Although the Trustee Act 2000 does not define the expression 'beneficiary', it would appear that paragraph (b) has no application to charitable trusts, which do

---

[8] *Rosemary Simmons Memorial Housing Assoc Ltd v United Dominions Trust Ltd* [1986] 1 WLR 1440

[9] TIA 1961 (now largely repealed) did not confer on trustees any statutory power to purchase land. A power to acquire a legal estate in land in England and Wales was contained in TLATA 1996, s 6(3) (since modified by TA 2000), but this applied only to trustees of land, and so could not enable trustees to acquire land unless they already held land on trust. The new power to acquire land contained in TA 2000, s 8, is much wider in scope, in that it enables trustees to acquire land regardless of whether they currently hold land on trust. This new statutory power supersedes the previous power of trustees of land to acquire land under TLATA 1996, s 6: see Law Commission, *Trustees' Powers and Duties* (Law Com No 260, 1999) 28, n 90

[10] TA 2000, s 3(1), (2). In its Report, to which was appended the Draft Bill which, with minor modifications, became TA 2000, the Law Commission stated that the reason its Draft Bill excluded the power to purchase land by way of an investment from the general power of investment, but conferred a separate wider power to purchase land, was 'to facilitate consequential amendments to the investment powers of some bodies who, though not trustees, are presently subject to the provisions of the Trustee Investments Act 1961': Law Commission, *Trustees' Powers and Duties* (Law Com No 260, 1999), 27, n 86

[11] TA 2000, s 3(3), (4)

[12] 'Freehold or leasehold land' means (a) in relation to England and Wales, a legal estate in land; (b) in relation to Scotland, (i) the estate or interest of the proprietor of the dominium utile or, in the case of land not held on feudal tenure, the estate or interest of the owner, or (ii) a tenancy; and (c) in relation to Northern Ireland, a legal estate in land, including land held under a fee farm grant: ibid, s 8(2)

[13] ibid, s 8(1). Note the reference to the UK; unlike the more limited power formerly contained in TLATA 1996, s 6(3) (since amended), the power is not restricted to the acquisition of land in England and Wales

not have human beneficiaries.[14] Trustees of a charitable housing trust, for example, therefore cannot rely on paragraph (b) to enable them, in fulfilment of the charity's purposes, to grant short-term leases of flats to individual tenants at low rents. Although each tenant has an interest (a leasehold estate) in the property subject to the trust (the flat), he does not have such interest as a 'beneficiary' under the charitable trust.

17.07   The trustees in the foregoing example could, however, grant such leases in reliance on the general words of paragraph (c). In the Committee Stage of the Trustee Bill, Lord Irvine LC stated that, for the avoidance of any doubt, the words 'for any other reason' in paragraph (c)[15]

> are wide enough to include the purchase of functional land by charitable trusts for carrying out the purposes of the charity, rather than as an investment: for example, a school buying land to serve as a playing field.

Paragraph (c) would also enable trustees of a charitable trust to acquire land for ancillary purposes, for example, to provide office accommodation for the charity's administration.

17.08   For the purposes of exercising his functions as a trustee, a trustee who acquires land under section 8 of the Trustee Act 2000 has all the powers of an absolute owner in relation to the land.[16] One effect of this is that trustees may acquire land with the aid of a mortgage.[17] The statutory duty of care[18] applies to a trustee when exercising the power under section 8 to acquire land.[19]

17.09   The powers conferred on trustees by section 8 are in addition to any other powers conferred on trustees.[20] These could be more limited powers to purchase land which are contained in the trust instrument or which have been previously granted by the court or by the Charity Commissioners.[21] The powers in section 8 are, however, subject to any restriction or exclusion imposed by the trust instrument or by any enactment or any provision of subordinate legislation.[22] A settlor of a charitable trust might, for instance, expressly restrict the trustees' powers of

---

[14]   Paras (a)–(c) of TA 2000, s 8(1), are almost identical in wording to the corresponding paragraphs in TLATA 1996, s 6(4) (repealed). In TLATA 1996, it is provided that 'beneficiary', in relation to a trust, 'means any person who under the trust has an interest in the property subject to the trust (including a person who has such an interest as a trustee or a personal representative)': TLATA 1996, s 22(1). As a charitable trust does not have such a 'beneficiary', such a trust was outside the scope of TLATA 1996, s 6(4)(b). It may therefore be inferred that a charitable trust is similarly outside para (b) of TA 2000, s 8(1)

[15]   Committee Trustee Bill, HL (7 June 2000) col CWH3

[16]   TA 2000, s 8(3)

[17]   Law Commission, *Trustees' Powers and Duties* (Law Com No 260, 1999) 29, para 2.44

[18]   TA 2000, s 1

[19]   ibid, s 2 & Sch 1, para 2(a). On the statutory duty of care, see ch 9, paras 9.78–9.81

[20]   TA 2000, s 9(a)

[21]   Law Commission, *Trustees' Powers and Duties* (Law Com No 260, 1999) 32, para 2.53

[22]   TA 2000, s 9(b)

investment to the investment in shares in specified companies only, thereby excluding the power to acquire land as an investment; or the power to acquire land for investment might be restricted by a direction in the trust instrument relating to ethical investment.[23]

The statutory powers conferred on trustees by section 8 do not apply in relation   **17.10**
to a trust to which the Universities and College Estates Act 1925 applies.[24] Subject to this, section 8 applies in relation to trusts whenever created.[25]

Special provisions affecting trustees of land

Special provisions relating to trustees of land are contained in section 6 of the   **17.11**
Trusts of Land and Appointment of Trustees Act 1996 (the 1996 Act).[26] For the purpose of exercising their functions as trustees, the trustees of land have in relation to the land subject to the trust all the powers of an absolute owner.[27] Trustees of land,[28] meaning trustees of a trust of land,[29] have power to acquire land under the power conferred by section 8 of the Trustee Act 2000.[30] The powers of trustees conferred by the 1996 Act must not be exercised in contravention of, or of any order made in pursuance of, any other enactment[31] or rule of law or equity,[32] and this includes an order of any court or of the Charity Commissioners.[33] The powers may not be exercised so as to contravene any restriction, limitation, or condition on the trustees' authority to act conferred by any other enactment.[34] Section 6 of the 1996 Act cannot be excluded or modified by the terms of the instrument creating a trust of land which comprises charitable, ecclesiastical, or public trusts.[35] The duty of care under section 1 of the Trustee Act 2000 applies

---

[23] cf Law Commission, *Trustees' Powers and Duties* (Law Com No 260, 1999) 31, n 106

[24] TA 2000, s 10(1)(b). The Law Commission's proposal to exclude from s 8 trustees who have special statutory powers to invest or apply trust funds was dropped from TA 2000. See Law Commission, *Trustees' Powers and Duties* (Law Com No 260, 1999) 27–9 (paras 2.42–2.43)

[25] TA 2000, s 10(2)

[26] As amended by ibid, s 40(1) & Sch 2, paras 45–49

[27] TLATA 1996, s 6(1)

[28] ibid, s 1(1)(b). Land held for the purposes of a charitable unincorporated association is held on a trust of land, so the trustees are trustees of land for this purpose

[29] ibid, s 1(1)(a), (b)

[30] ibid, s 6(3), as amended by TA 2000, s 40(1) & Sch 2 , para 45(1)

[31] eg CA 1993, ss 36–9

[32] TLATA 1996, s 6(6). Relevant rules of equity might include, eg, the duties of a trustee to act in good faith and to exercise a power for its proper purpose

[33] ibid, s 6(7)

[34] ibid, s 6(8)

[35] ibid, s 8(1), (3). Following TA 2000, the effect of this limitation is now reduced, since the trustees' power to acquire land is no longer contained in TLATA 1996, s 6(3), but in TA 2000, s 8(1). The latter sub-s, like TLATA 1996, s 8(1), is subject to any restriction or exclusion imposed (inter alia) by the trust instrument; but it differs from TLATA 1996 in that it contains no provision equivalent to TLATA 1996, s 8(3), excluding charitable, ecclesiastical, or public trusts: TA 2000, s 9(b). It is difficult to avoid the conclusion that TLATA 1996, s 8(3) does not sit very easily next to TA 2000, s 9(b)

to trustees of land when exercising their powers conferred by section 6 of the 1996 Act.[36]

17.12 Since a charitable corporation registered under the Companies Act 1985 does not hold its general assets upon trust, but beneficially subject to its objects clause,[37] a charitable corporation is not a trustee of its assets so held, and so does not have the statutory power of a trustee to acquire land conferred by section 8 of the Trustee Act 2000. The position is otherwise where land is held by a charitable corporation that does hold its property upon trust, or where a charitable corporation holds land subject to special trusts (but only as regards the property subject to such special trusts).

Procedure in absence of a power

17.13 Although the new statutory power is likely to meet the needs of most charitable trusts, in some instances trustees may still find their particular powers inadequate. The trust instrument may contain a restriction on, or an exclusion of, the trustees' powers to acquire land.[38] Even if there is no such restriction or exclusion, the trustees may wish to purchase land outside the United Kingdom, and such a purchase is beyond the statutory power.[39] If trustees of a charitable trust wish to acquire land which they have no power to acquire, they will need either to amend their constitution (if they have power to do so) to confer upon themselves the requisite power, or to try to obtain the requisite order from the Charity Commissioners.[40] If the charity is a company incorporated under the Companies Act 1985 and its constitution does not confer power to acquire land, the power to do so may be obtained by an appropriate amendment to the company's constitution, which will need the prior written consent of the Charity Commissioners.[41]

(2) Disposal

Pre-1997: Settled Land Act 1925

17.14 Before 1 January 1997, land vested in trustees for charitable purposes was deemed to be settled land within the Settled Land Act 1925, and the trustees had all the powers conferred by that Act on a tenant for life and on the trustees of a settlement, subject to the obtaining of such consent or order (for example, where appropriate, the Charity Commissioners' consent to a disposal) as would have been

---

[36] TLATA 1996, s 6(9), inserted by TA 2000, Sch 2, para 45(3). On the statutory duty of care, see ch 9, paras 9.78–9.81

[37] *Liverpool and District Hospital for Diseases of the Heart v A-G* [1981] Ch 193

[38] TA 2000, s 9(b)

[39] ibid, s 8(1)

[40] ie either by means of a scheme of administration extending the trustees' powers to include a power to acquire land, under CA 1993, s 16(1), or by way of the authorization of an action which is expedient in the interests of the charity, under s 26(1)

[41] ibid, s 64(2)

required in any event.[42] The statutory powers conferred on such trustees were somewhat restrictive; and, although such powers could be extended by express provision in the governing instrument,[43] additional powers were not always to be found, especially in the constitutions of older charities. In many instances, therefore, the trustees were obliged to obtain the consent of, or an order from, the Charity Commissioners, to authorize a disposal which would otherwise lie beyond their powers.

Post-1996: Trusts of Land and Appointment of Trustees Act 1996

The law has now been changed by the Trusts of Land and Appointment of **17.15** Trustees Act 1996 (the 1996 Act). From 1 January 1997, land held on charitable trusts is not settled land, and land previously held subject to charitable trusts ceased to be settled land from that date.[44] Land held on charitable trusts is now held on a trust of land.[45] There is a limited exception to this in that the 1996 Act does not apply to land subject to the Universities and College Estates Act 1925.[46]

Under section 6 of the 1996 Act, for the purpose of exercising their functions as **17.16** trustees, the trustees of land have in relation to the land subject to the trust all the powers of an absolute owner,[47] which clearly include the power of sale. The statutory duty of care under the Trustee Act 2000[48] applies to a trustee when exercising any power in relation to land acquired under section 8 of that Act or when exercising any other power to acquire land, however conferred.[49]

Land held by a charitable company according to its objects clause is not held by **17.17** the company upon charitable trusts, and so is not subject to the provisions of the 1996 Act. The 1996 Act will, however, apply to land held by a charitable company upon special trusts.

Restrictions in governing instrument

The powers conferred on trustees of land held on charitable trusts by section 6 of **17.18** the 1996 Act cannot be restricted by the trust instrument.[50] Any such purported

---

[43] *Re Booth & Southend-on-Sea Estate Co's Contract* [1927] 1 Ch 579
[44] TLATA 1996, s 2(5)
[45] ibid, s 1(1)
[46] ibid, s 1(3). The Universities and College Estates Act 1925 applies to the Universities of Oxford, Cambridge, and Durham, and to the Colleges of Winchester and Eton
[47] TLATA 1996, s 6(1)
[48] TA 2000, s 1
[49] ibid, s 2 & Sch 1, para 2(c). On the statutory duty of care, see ch 9, paras 9.78–9.81
[50] TLATA 1996, s 8(1),(3). If the disposition creating a trust makes provision requiring any consent to be obtained to the exercise of a power conferred by ibid, s 6, the power may not be exercised without that consent: ibid, s 8(2). This sub-s does not fall within the exclusion in s 8(3), and does therefore apply to charitable, ecclesiastical, or public trusts

restriction is therefore void. It cannot, however, have been intended that the 1996 Act should enable trustees of land held on charitable trusts to dispose of land the identity of which is essential to the charity's purposes. This is considered further below.[51] Subject to this, the effect is that a settlor cannot impose restrictions on the trustees of a charity which would prevent them from later disposing of the land conveyed (for example, by a direction in the conveyance that the trustees are to hold the land for the charitable purposes 'for ever').[52]

Identity of land essential to charity's purposes

17.19 If the continued holding of a particular piece of land is essential to the charity's purposes, its disposal will be permissible only if there is a cy-près circumstance.[53] The identity of the land will be essential to the charity's purpose if, for instance, it comprises a particular house once owned by a particular historical figure, or a particular building of architectural merit, or a particular area of land of outstanding natural beauty, and the purpose of the trust in each case is to preserve the building or the area of land for the public benefit.[54] Land is not essential to a charity's purpose, however, merely because it was given to the charity by a settlor or testator who specified in the governing instrument that the land was to be used for the specified purpose 'for ever'.[55] In *College of St Mary's Magdalen, Oxford (President and Scholars) v Attorney-General*,[56] Lord Cranworth LC stated:

> [I]t is plain that persons who give lands to a charity, devote them for ever to the purposes of that charity, and such is always the expression used in such gifts, the gifts being made to the charitable object 'for ever'. With the belief that the charity will endure for ever, it is extremely improbable that they can have contemplated the sale of the lands.

---

[50] TLATA 1996, s 8(1),(3). If the disposition creating a trust makes provision requiring any consent to be obtained to the exercise of a power conferred by ibid, s 6, the power may not be exercised without that consent: ibid, s 8(2). This sub-s does not fall within the exclusion in s 8(3), and does therefore apply to charitable, ecclesiastical, or public trusts

[51] See below, paras 17.19–17.20

[52] See *Re Colston's Hospital* (1859) 27 Beav 16 (Romilly MR), where the court approved the removal of a school from the centre of Bristol to a site outside the city, notwithstanding that the settlor had directed that the land conveyed should be used 'for ever after' for the purpose of the charity

[53] ie within CA 1993, s 13

[54] See Dillon LJ in *Oldham BC v A-G* [1993] Ch 210, 222

[55] But note that land held in trust for a charity on trusts which stipulate that it to be used for the purposes, or any particular purposes of the charity, cannot be disposed of unless the trustees comply with the public notice provisions contained in CA 1993, s 36(6) (discussed further below, paras 17.67–17.73

[56] (1857) 6 HL Cas 189, 205. This extract was quoted with approval by Dillon LJ in *Oldham BC v A-G* [1993] Ch 210, 220. But contrast, *Brisbane City Council v A-G for Queensland* [1979] AC 411 (PC), where it was found that the council held upon charitable trusts land which had been transferred to it for use 'permanently' for park and recreation purposes and for the holding of annual agricultural shows. The council proposed to sell the land to a company which intended to develop it as a shopping centre; and it seems to have been assumed by the parties that the council would not be entitled to sell the land if it were found to be subject to charitable trusts

In *Oldham Borough Council v Attorney-General*,[57] a settlor had (in 1962) conveyed   **17.20**
a plot of land to trustees, who declared that they would 'hold the said land upon
trust to preserve and manage the same at all times hereafter as playing fields . . . for
the benefit and enjoyment of the inhabitants of Oldham'. The present trustee (the
Council) proposed to sell the land at a high price for development, and to acquire
a new site for the playing fields which would, because of the proceeds of sale, have
better facilities than those currently provided. The Charity Commissioners had
consented to the sale of the land;[58] but the issue came to court on the narrow question of whether the sale of the land required a cy-près circumstance within what is
now section 13 of the Charities Act 1993. The Court of Appeal decided that it did
not. They held that the 'original purposes' of a charitable gift in that section do not
include the intention and purpose of the donor that the land given should be used
for ever for the purposes of the charity. Both before and after the Charitable Trusts
Acts 1853 and 1855, the court had decreed that charity land should be sold,
otherwise than by way of a scheme cy-près, where the court was satisfied that the
sale was for the benefit of the charity.[59] The identity of the land in the *Oldham* case
was therefore merely in the nature of an administrative provision;[60] the purpose of
the charitable trust, the maintenance of playing fields for the inhabitants of a particular area, could be performed on other land, and the disposal of the existing site
was not restricted by what is now section 13 of the Charities Act 1993.

B. Sales, leases, and other dispositions (excluding mortgages) of charity land

(1) Introduction

Before 1993, the consent of the courts or of the Charity Commissioners was re-   **17.21**
quired for certain dealings with charity land.[61] Such consent was required to mortgage, charge, lease, sell, or otherwise dispose of land which formed part of a
charity's permanent endowment, or which had at any time been occupied for the
purposes of the charity. In certain exceptional cases consent was not required, the
most important such case being the granting of a lease for a term not exceeding
twenty-two years, if not granted in consideration of a fine. The Charity
Commissioners' consent was never required to dispose of land held purely as an investment. The consent procedure was considered to have two merits: it might result in the charity trustees' obtaining a better price for the land; and, in some

---

[57] [1993] Ch 210 (CA)
[58] Under CA 1960, s 29 (now replaced by CA 1993, s 36)
[59] *Re Ashton Charity* (1856) 22 Beav 288; *Re Parke's Charity* (1842) 12 Sim 329; *Re North Shields Old Meeting House* (1859) 7 WR 541
[60] cf *Re JW Laing Trust* [1984] Ch 143, 153
[61] CA 1960, s 29 (repealed)

instances, it might alert the Charity Commissioners to the fact that the charity was in need of attention, for example by way of a cy-près scheme. There were, however, some admitted drawbacks: the need for the Commissioners' consent inevitably involved some delay, which led to some sales being lost; and the consent-giving machinery consumed much staff time and effort at the Commission.[62] The aim of the new legislation was to remove the detriments of the existing system, whilst so far as possible retaining its advantages by different means.

17.22 Part V of the Charities Act 1993 retains the basic requirement to obtain the consent of the court or of the Charity Commissioners before disposing of charity land (by sale, lease, or otherwise).[63] Section 36(1) states that, subject to the following provisions of that section and to section 40 of the Act, 'no land held by or in trust for a charity shall be sold, leased or otherwise disposed of without an order of the court or of the Commissioners.'

17.23 The new regime differs from the old in that it applies to dispositions of all charity land, not (as formerly) only to land which is part of the charity's permanent endowment or which is (or has been) occupied for the purposes of the charity (functional land). Land held merely as an investment is therefore within the new provision.

17.24 The new regime also differs significantly from the old because it introduces a procedure which, if followed, enables the consent of the court or the Charity Commissioners to be dispensed with in the majority of cases. This procedure, which is discussed more fully below,[64] essentially involves the trustees obtaining and considering either the written report of a qualified surveyor,[65] or (where the disposition is the grant of a lease for seven years or less) the advice of a person reasonably believed by the trustees to have the ability and practical experience to give it.[66]

17.25 The only instance in which the consent of the court or the Charity Commissioners must be obtained to a disposition made on or after 1 January 1993 is where the disposition is to what is called a 'connected person',[67] which includes a charity trustee or trustee for a charity; an officer, agent, or employee of the charity; certain of their relatives; and institutions and companies controlled by them or in which they have a substantial interest.[68]

---

[62] Woodfield noted that, in 1986, 31 staff at the Commission were involved in dealings with charity land: *Efficiency Scrutiny of the Supervision of Charities*, Report of the Woodfield Committee, Sir Philip Woodfield (chairman) (HMSO, 1987) 36 (para 96)

[63] CA 1993, s 36(1)

[64] See paras 17.50–17.66

[65] CA 1993, s 36(3)

[66] ibid, s 36(5)

[67] ibid, s 36(2)(a)(i); Sch 5

[68] On dispositions to connected persons, see further below, paras 17.47–17.49

If the disposition is to a person who is not a connected person, the trustees could   **17.26**
still seek the consent of the court or the Charity Commissioners to the disposition
as an alternative to using the new procedures; and trustees might be under the impression that by seeking the Charity Commissioners' approval they might save the
expense of surveyor's fees. In practice, however, this will not be so. In deciding
whether to give their consent to a disposition, the Commissioners will as a matter
of practice (as they did for a number of years before 1993) require the charity
trustees in any event to obtain the advice of a surveyor or other suitable person.
Furthermore, since one of the reasons for the introduction of the procedure was
to reduce the Commissioners' involvement in land dispositions to enable them to
devote more resources to some of their other functions, the Charity Commissioners do not welcome unnecessary applications; they expect all dispositions to
non-connected persons to make use of the new procedures.

It is important to note from the outset that the restrictions in section 36 of the   **17.27**
Charities Act 1993 apply notwithstanding anything in the trusts of a charity.[69] It
is not therefore possible for a settlor to avoid the restrictions by stating in the trust
instrument that the land may be sold or otherwise disposed of without either obtaining the consent of the court or the Charity Commissioners or obtaining and
considering the requisite advice.

(2) The meaning of 'land'

'Land' is defined in Part V of the Charities Act 1993 to mean land in England and   **17.28**
Wales.[70] In the absence of further definition in the Act, it is necessary to turn to the
Interpretation Act 1978, which provides that 'land' includes 'buildings and other
structures, land covered with water, and any estate, interest, easement, servitude
or right in or over land.'[71] A disposition of land therefore includes not merely a disposition of an estate in land (such as a conveyance of a freehold or the grant or assignment of a lease), but also the grant or assignment of an interest in land (such
as an easement or a profit à prendre), and the creation or transfer of any other
interest or right (whether legal or equitable) in or over land.

(3) Licence to occupy land

Unless it is coupled with the grant of an interest, such as a profit à prendre, a li-   **17.29**
cence (whether a bare licence or a contractual licence) does not confer an interest
in land. This is so even though revocation of a contractual licence may be

---

[69] CA 1993, s 36(9)
[70] ibid, s 36(11)
[71] Interpretation Act 1978, s 3 & Sch. 1
[72] cf *Verrall v Great Yarmouth BC* [1981] QB 202 (where there was an award of specific performance)

restrained by an injunction.[72] The grant of a licence therefore falls outside section 36(1) of the Charities Act 1993, and so does not need either the Charity Commissioners' consent or the advice of a surveyor. Nevertheless, if the charity trustees allow another body to occupy the charity's premises under a licence, they must ensure (unless the licensee is itself an object of the charity or another charity with similar objects) that the licence is granted for full consideration; otherwise the charity trustees could be in breach of their duty to ensure that a proper return is obtained for the exploitation of the charity's assets. Charity trustees may not, therefore, permit the charity's subsidiary trading company to occupy the charity's premises free of any rent or fee, even if the occupation is under a bare licence.

Lease or licence?

17.30   Whether a transaction creates a lease or a licence is to be determined according to the general principles laid down in *Street v Mountford*.[73] There will be a lease if the occupier has exclusive possession for a fixed term at a rent. An agreement which has these characteristics creates a lease, and the parties cannot turn what is in substance a lease into a licence by using language in the agreement which would be more appropriate to the latter.[74] The meaning of an agreement (for example, as to the extent of the possession which it grants) depends upon the intention of the parties objectively ascertained by reference to the language and relevant background.[75] If substantial services are provided which require entry into the occupier's room, there may be no exclusive possession; as, for instance, is likely to be the case where the charity provides a home for elderly people.[76]

17.31   An occupier who enjoys exclusive possession is not necessarily a tenant: he may, for instance, be an object of charity.[77] If the circumstances and conduct of the parties show that the parties intended that the occupier should be granted a personal privilege with no interest in the land, he will be held to be only a licensee.[78] The House of Lords in *Street v Mountford*[79] approved dicta of Denning LJ in *Faccini v Bryson*,[80] where he had observed:

> In all the cases where an occupier has been held to be a licensee there has been something in the circumstances, such as a family arrangement, an act of friendship or generosity, or such like, to negative any intention to create a tenancy.

---

[73] [1985] AC 809 (HL)
[74] ibid, 819, 821 (Lord Templeman); *Bruton v London & Quadrant Housing Trust* [2000] 1 AC 406, 413 (Lord Hoffmann)
[75] *Bruton v London & Quadrant Housing Trust* [2000] 1 AC 406, 413 (Lord Hoffmann)
[76] *Abbeyfield (Harpenden) Society v Woods* [1968] 1 WLR 374
[77] *Street v Mountford* [1985] AC 809, 818 (Lord Templeman)
[78] *Errington v Errington* [1952] 1 KB 290, 298 (Denning LJ), approved by Lord Templeman in *Street v Mountford* [1985] AC 809, 820–1
[79] [1985] AC 809
[80] [1952] 1 TLR 1386, 1389

These words aptly describe many of the arrangements which charities for the relief of the sick or the distressed enter into in order to provide what is usually short-term accommodation during a period of rehabilitation. In the recent past the court has been more willing to accept a term in the arrangement which would have the effect of denying the occupier the status of a tenant if the licensor has a genuine need to deny such status.[81] If a charity's carrying out of its objects involved the provision of accommodation for its 'beneficiaries', the charity could argue that the performance of its charitable objects required that such occupiers be merely licensees.[82]

In *Gray v Taylor*,[83] the charity provided accommodation in almshouses for poor   **17.32**
persons of good character and not less than 60 years of age who were residents of Peterborough. The trustees permitted the defendant to occupy one of the rooms as an almsperson under what was called a licence, under which she was required to pay a contribution towards the provision of the accommodation. The agreement also provided that her appointment could be set aside, so that the trustees could take possession of her room, if she persistently disturbed the quiet occupation of the almshouses or behaved vexatiously or offensively. Although she had exclusive possession of her room, the Court of Appeal held that such possession was referable to an arrangement other than a tenancy. Sir John Vinelott said:[84]

> A person who is selected as an almsperson becomes a beneficiary under the trusts of the charity and enjoys the privilege of occupation of rooms in the almshouses as a beneficiary.

Another factor which influenced him was that the trustees' powers to let land did   **17.33**
not extend to functional land. The creation of such a tenancy of functional land would therefore be inconsistent with the trustees' performance of their duties as trustees of a charity because, if the occupiers were tenants, the trustees would be unable to restrict the almspersons to persons who continued to meet the qualifying conditions. The occupiers might, for instance, join together in the purchase of a winning ticket in the National Lottery, and would so cease to be proper objects of the charity. Furthermore, the payment which the defendant made in respect of her occupation was not rent payable under a tenancy, but merely liberated the charity's income for purposes relating to the maintenance and improvement of the almshouses.[85] As Sir John Vinelott pointed out:[86]

---

[81] See the speech of Lord Templeman (with which their other Lordships agreed) in *Westminster City Council v Clarke* [1992] 2 AC 288, 300–2 (HL)
[82] ibid
[83] [1998] 1 WLR 1093 (CA)
[84] ibid, 1097
[85] ibid, 1098
[86] ibid

it is historically the case that, until comparatively recently, almspersons were not required to pay any weekly sum. The introduction of a weekly sum came with the introduction of housing benefit, to which almspersons would normally be entitled; payment of a weekly sum not exceeding the housing benefit would not result in any net loss to the almsperson and in effect the housing benefit would be available to the charity.

17.34 In some circumstances, a charity, in order to ensure that its 'beneficiaries' occupied merely as licensees, might have two strings to its bow: it might have been able to rely both on its charitable objects and on the absence of possession. If the licensor is providing temporary housing for vulnerable homeless people,[87] or for persons who are mentally disturbed or who are drug-users or alcoholics, or who might be violent, the licensor may have a genuine need to move the occupiers around. In such circumstances, the courts have accepted that a provision in the agreement entitling the licensor to move occupiers will indicate the existence of a licence only.[88]

Retreat from the *Faccini v Bryson* 'charity' exception

17.35 The recent decision of the House of Lords in *Bruton v London & Quadrant Housing Trust*[89] suggests that the courts will in future be less impressed by arguments based on the altruistic objects of the soi-disant licensor. It now seems that the element of 'charity' will not itself preclude an arrangement from being a lease if that is what it genuinely is in substance.[90]

17.36 The *Quadrant Housing* case concerned a charitable trust that provided short-term accommodation for the homeless and which had obtained a licence from a local authority to use a block of flats for this purpose. The charity allowed the plaintiff into occupation of one of the flats after he had signed an agreement stating that he was allowed to occupy on a temporary basis on a weekly licence for the sum of £18 per week. The agreement recited that the charity had the property on licence from the council in order to provide temporary housing accommodation, and that it was offered to the plaintiff on condition that he would vacate upon receipt of reasonable notice, which would not normally be less than four weeks. It also provided that the staff of the charity and the owners were to be allowed access at all times during normal working hours for all purposes connected with the work of the charity. The plaintiff claimed that the charity was in breach of an implied statu-

---

[87] As in *Westminster City Council v Clarke* [1992] 2 AC 288 (HL) (local authority providing temporary accommodation for homeless persons in accordance with its statutory duty)

[88] *Carr Gomm Society v Hawkins* [1990] CLY 2811 (where the licensor was a registered charity)

[89] [2000] 1 AC 406 (HL)

[90] *Family Housing Association v Jones* [1990] 1 WLR 779 (CA); the status of that decision seemed in doubt in view of the observations of Lord Templeman in *Westminster City Council v Clarke* [1992] 2 AC 288 (HL); but it was recently approved by the House of Lords in *Bruton v London & Quadrant Housing Trust* [2000] 1 AC 406, 414 (Lord Hoffmann)

tory obligation to keep the premises in repair,[91] and this depended upon his establishing that he was a tenant, not a licensee.

At first sight, it would appear that there were two factors which would preclude **17.37** the plaintiff's acquisition of a lease. First, the object of the charity, to provide short-term accommodation for the homeless, involved an element of bounty, and the attainment of this object would be thwarted were the occupiers to acquire the status of tenants. Secondly, the charity's lack of title meant that it was incapable of granting a legal estate; and the plaintiff's knowledge of such lack of title would preclude his claiming even a tenancy by estoppel.

The House of Lords, reversing the lower courts, nevertheless held that in the cir- **17.38** cumstances the plaintiff had acquired a lease. Dealing with the first point, Lord Hoffmann (with whose speech the other Law Lords agreed) held that, applying the test in *Street v Mountford*,[92] the plaintiff had a lease because he had a right to exclusive possession. In his Lordship's opinion, the circumstance that the charity was a responsible landlord performing socially valuable functions could not make an agreement to grant exclusive possession something other than a tenancy: the character of the landlord was irrelevant.[93] On the second point, Lord Hoffmann said that the term 'lease' simply describes a relationship between two parties who are designated landlord and tenant, and that it was wrong to say that whether an agreement is a lease depends upon whether it creates a proprietary interest.[94] Estoppel was irrelevant, since, in his Lordship's view, 'it is not the estoppel which creates the tenancy, but the tenancy which creates the estoppel'.[95] This dealt with the point at issue, and Lord Hoffmann chose not to express any view on whether the plaintiff was a secure tenant, or whether the council might recover possession from him.[96]

With respect to Lord Hoffmann, the notion that a lease can be granted out of thin **17.39** air might be described as a novel one; and it is submitted that the judgment of Millett LJ in the Court of Appeal (which the House of Lords overturned) was both more consistent with principles of property law and more satisfactory in its result.[97] Although the precise consequences of what must now be recognized as a 'non-proprietary' lease have yet to be determined, this decision of their Lordships'

---

[91] Landlord and Tenant Act 1985, s 11
[92] [1985] AC 809 (HL)
[93] [2000] 1 AC 406, 414. Although the House of Lords did not refer to *Gray v Taylor* [1998] 1 WLR 1093 (CA), its reasoning would seem to have been seriously undermined by Lord Hoffmann's speech. *Gray v Turner* might still be sustainable on the basis that the occupiers' payments were not in substance rent; but it might be objected that such characterization of the money payments itself sprang from the licensor's status as a charity and from its charitable objects
[94] [2000] 1 AC 406, 415
[95] ibid, 416
[96] ibid
[97] [1998] QB 834, 842 (CA)

House now makes it extremely difficult for housing charities (or any other charities) to allow persons into occupation of their premises on a short-term basis under a contractual licence. The finding that an agreement which both parties believed and intended to be a licence is in fact a lease, will saddle the charity that granted it with the statutory obligations of a landlord which, to use the words of Millett LJ, 'it never intended to undertake, and which [will] effectively disable it from carrying out the socially valuable function which it performs'.[98]

Licences not conferring rights of occupation

17.40 Where the issue is not whether the right is a licence or a lease, but whether it is a licence or a proprietary interest which does not confer a right of occupation (such as an easement), the courts place greater weight on how the right is described in the document itself, at least where both parties have been professionally advised. The Court of Appeal, for instance, has held that a document which purported to grant a 'licence' to use a fire-escape took effect as a licence only, even though the document was a deed, it used the word 'grant', and it defined the parties as including their successors in title.[99]

Business occupiers

17.41 A charity may have land for investment purposes which it permits to be occupied for business purposes. Under a lease, the occupier may obtain security of tenure under Part II of the Landlord and Tenant Act 1954, unless the lease is for a term certain not exceeding six months,[100] or unless the court approves an exclusion of the tenancy from the statutory protection.[101] The occupier does not have the protection of the Act if the occupation is not referable to a tenancy, but merely under a licence. In determining whether a business occupier is a tenant or a licensee, the principle of *Street v Mountford*[102] is applied. It has, however, been said that, in respect of commercial premises, no inference of exclusive possession can be made.[103]

(4) Contract for the sale or disposition of an interest in land

General requirements

17.42 To be valid, a contract for the sale or other disposition of an interest in land must, if entered into after 26 September 1989, comply with the formalities laid down by the Law of Property (Miscellaneous Provisions) Act 1989. The contract must be

---

[98] ibid, 846 (Millett LJ)
[99] *IDC Group Ltd v Clarke* [1992] 2 EGLR 184
[100] Landlord and Tenant Act 1954, s 43(3)
[101] ibid, s 38(4)
[102] [1985] AC 809 (HL)
[103] *Venus Investments Ltd v Stocktop Ltd* [1996] EGCS 173; *Hunts Refuse Disposals Ltd v Norfolk Environmental Waste Services Ltd* [1997] 1 EGLR 16 (CA)

made in writing and incorporate all the terms which the parties have expressly agreed in one document or, where contracts are exchanged, in each.[104] The document incorporating the terms or, where contracts are exchanged, one of the documents incorporating them (but not necessarily the same one) must be signed by or on behalf of each party to the contract.[105] In this context, 'disposition' has the same meaning as in the Law of Property Act 1925,[106] and therefore includes a conveyance;[107] and 'interest in land' in this context means 'any estate, interest or charge in or over land'.[108]

Requirements specific to sale of charity land

17.43 Since section 36(1) of the Charities Act 1993 states that no charity land shall be 'sold' without the appropriate order, it is clear that it applies (like its statutory predecessor[109]) to a contract for the sale of charity land. Any disposition of an interest in land, however, falls within the sub-section. Since the grant of an option to purchase land confers an equitable interest in the land on the grantee,[110] it too is caught by section 36(1). The grant of a right of pre-emption does not create an interest in land;[111] so that a contract conferring such a right is not within the sub-section. However, an interest in land would be created if and when the vendor decided to dispose of the land. It is therefore necessary that the contract conferring the right of pre-emption complies with section 36, otherwise the right could not become a valid contract for the sale of land.

Conditional contracts

17.44 If the charity trustees propose to lease the charity land on a tenancy for a terms of years certain to a business tenant or to an unincorporated association, the tenancy may be protected by Part II of the Landlord and Tenant Act 1954. If the charity trustees intend that the tenancy should be denied the protection of that Act, it will be necessary for the parties jointly to apply to the court to obtain its approval for a contracting out.[112] If the parties wish to enter into a contract before the agreement of the court has been obtained, the contract should be expressed to be conditional upon the leave of the court being obtained.[113] Even if such condition

---

[104] LP (Misc Provs) A 1989, s 2(1)
[105] ibid, s 2(3)
[106] ibid, s 2(6)
[107] See definition of 'conveyance' and 'disposition' in LPA 1925, s 205(1)(ii)
[108] LP (Misc Provs) A 1989, s 2(6), as amended by TLATA 1996, s 25(2) & Sch 4
[109] ie CA 1960, s 29(1), which used the same wording: 'sold, leased or otherwise disposed of'. See *Milner v Staffordshire Congregational Union (Inc)* [1956] 1 Ch 275
[110] *London and South Western Rly Co v Gomm* (1882) 20 ChD 562, 581 (Jessel MR)
[111] *Pritchard v Briggs* [1980] Ch 338
[112] Landlord and Tenant Act 1954, s 38(4)
[113] *Essexcrest Ltd v Evenlex Ltd* (1987) 55 P & CR 279 (CA)

is not expressed, however, the court may be able to infer that the agreement was conditional upon the obtaining of such approval.[114]

17.45 As before 1993, a contract for the sale of land may be expressed to be conditional upon the obtaining of the Charity Commissioners' consent.[115] Such a conditional contract is not caught by section 36(1) of the Charities Act 1993 because the condition is treated as a condition precedent, so that there is no contract for the sale of land until the condition is satisfied. The contract arises when the condition is met, because the satisfying of the condition lies exclusively with a third party (the Charity Commissioners) and is therefore outside the control of either of the contracting parties. A contract will need to be conditional upon the obtaining of the requisite consent if it involves a disposition to a connected person.[116]

17.46 In most cases, however, charity trustees who intend to dispose of charity land will be going through the procedure of obtaining and considering appropriate advice[117] which will relieve them of the need to obtain the court's or the Charity Commissioners' consent. If the charity trustees wish to enter into a contract before such procedure has been completed, the question arises whether they may do so by means of a conditional contract. It would seem that this is not possible, since the fulfilment of this condition lies within the control of the charity trustees, that is, the condition will not be met unless they decide that they are satisfied that the terms are the best that can reasonably be obtained.[118] In *Ee v Kaker*,[119] a contract for the sale of property 'subject to survey' was held valid on the basis that the purchaser would be bound to act in good faith, and so would effectively be unable to reject a basically satisfactory report.[120] Such reasoning may not, however, be applicable where the vendor comprises charity trustees, who owe to the charity both general fiduciary duties and a specific statutory duty[121] to consider whether the terms are the best that can be reasonably obtained for the charity. If the charity trustees were to have imposed upon them a duty to act bona fide towards the purchaser, it might be argued that they would be placed in a position of conflict, since they owe a similar duty to the charity itself as one aspect of their fiduciary duties.[122] At first instance in *Don King Productions Inc v Warren*,[123] a case not involving char-

---

[114] *Cardiothoracic Institute v Shrewdcrest Ltd* [1986] 1 WLR 368
[115] *Michael Richards Properties Ltd v St Saviour's, Southwark* [1975] 3 All ER 416 (on CA 1960, s 29)
[116] On dispositions to connected persons, see below, paras 17.47–17.49
[117] ie under CA 1993, s 36(3) or s 36(5). See further below, paras 17.51–17.66
[118] CA 1993, s 36(3)(c), s 36(5)(b)
[119] (1980) 40 P & CR 223
[120] See note by JE Adams [1980] Conv 446
[121] ie CA 1993, s 36(3)(c), s 36(5)(b)
[122] Indeed, charity trustees, like other trustees, are under a duty to gazump any purchaser if they can obtain a higher price for the trust: *Buttle v Saunders* [1950] 2 All ER 193
[123] [1998] 2 All ER 608, 633; Lightman J's judgment was affirmed on appeal: [1999] 2 All ER 218 (CA)

ity law, Lightman J pointed out that it is a matter of everyday experience that someone may owe fiduciary duties to different persons at the same time; but his Lordship did not consider this to give rise to a conflict of interests because, in his view, one set of these duties is in each case paramount. In the present context, this would mean that there would be no conflict of interests because charity trustees' paramount duty would not be to the purchaser, but to the trust, to which they owe a duty of undivided loyalty. This explanation, however, merely gives rise to a different objection: namely, it is difficult to see how charity trustees can owe any meaningful duty of good faith towards a purchaser when such duty is in every case overridden by the trustees' duty of undivided loyalty to the trust.

(5) *Dispositions to connected persons*

Although the Charities Act 1993 makes substantial inroads into the need for the **17.47** court's or the Charity Commissioners' consent to dispositions of land, in no case can consent be dispensed with if the disposition is made to a 'connected person', or to his trustee or nominee.[124] For these purposes, 'connected person' in relation to a charity has a complex definition which needs to be set out in full. It means:[125]

(a) a charity trustee or trustee for the charity;
(b) a person who is the donor of any land to the charity (whether the gift was made on or after the establishment of the charity);
(c) a child,[126] parent, grandchild, grandparent, brother or sister of any such trustee or donor;
(d) an officer, agent or employee of the charity;
(e) the spouse[127] of any person falling within any of sub-paragraphs (a) to (d) above;
(f) an institution which is controlled—[128]
    (i) by any person falling within any of sub-paragraphs (a) to (e) above, or
    (ii) by two or more such persons taken together; or
(g) a body corporate in which—
    (i) any connected person falling within any of sub-paragraphs (a) to (f) above has a substantial interest, or
    (ii) two or more such persons, taken together, have a substantial interest.[129]

---

[124] CA 1993, s 36(2)(a)

[125] ibid, s 36(2)(a) & Sch 5, para 1

[126] 'Child' includes a stepchild and an illegitimate child: CA 1993, s 36(2)(a) & Sch 5, para 2(1)

[127] A person living with another as that person's husband or wife is to be treated as that person's spouse: CA 1993, s 36(2)(a) & Sch 5, para 2(2)

[128] A person controls an institution if he is able to secure that the affairs of the institution are conducted in accordance with his wishes: CA 1993, s 36(2)(a) & Sch 5, para 3

[129] For the purposes of para 1(g), a person has a substantial interest if he (a) is interested in shares comprised in the equity share capital of the body corporate of a nominal value of more than one-fifth of that share capital, or (b) is entitled to exercise, or control the exercise of, more than one-fifth of the voting power at any general meeting: CA 1993, s 36(2)(a) & Sch 5, para 4(1). For these purposes, the rules of interpretation set out in Companies Act 1985, Sch 13, Pt 1, apply: CA 1993, s 36(2)(a) & Sch 5, para 4(2). 'Equity share capital' and 'share' have the same meaning as in Companies Act 1985: CA 1993, s 36(2)(a) & Sch 5, para 4(3)

The reason for including a donor of land to charity appears to be to preclude the possibility that the charity might lease the land back to the donor at a low rent, as part of a scheme to avoid inheritance tax.[130]

17.48 Since a charity will control its subsidiary trading companies, any disposition by the charity to such a company (for example, a lease of the charity's premises to the trading subsidiary) will always need consent.

17.49 The categories of persons who rank as 'connected persons' within section 36 will often also be persons in a fiduciary position to the charity, so that a disposition of the land to them would be prima facie voidable in equity. However, in accordance with the principles discussed below,[131] a purported disposition without consent to a 'connected person' within the meaning of section 36 of the Charities Act 1993 is void ab initio. The special treatment accorded to connected persons by this section reflects what was already the Charity Commissioners' practice before 1993: they would always ask trustees seeking the requisite consent to certify that a purchaser was not someone closely connected with the charity.[132]

(6) Avoiding the need to obtain consent

Dispositions other than short leases

17.50 The consent of the court or of the Charity Commissioners to a disposition of land is not required if the charity trustees comply with the alternative procedure set out in the Charities Act 1993. Except where the proposed disposition is the granting of a lease for a term of not more than seven years,[133] the procedure involves three duties that the charity trustees must fulfil before entering into an agreement for the sale, or (as the case may be) for a lease or other disposition, of the land.

Duty to obtain and consider written report from qualified surveyor

17.51 The charity trustees must obtain and consider a written report on the proposed disposition from a qualified surveyor instructed by the trustees and acting exclusively for the charity.[134]

---

[130] FA 1986 contains rules which deem property given with a reservation of benefit to remain that of the donor for the purposes of inheritance tax: FA 1986, s 102 & Sch 20. A benefit which the donor obtains by virtue of associated operations (as defined in IHTA 1984, s 268) is treated as a benefit to him by contract or otherwise for the purposes of FA 1986, s 102: FA 1986, Sch 20, para 6(1)(c). However, the granting of a lease for full consideration in money or money's worth is not to be taken to be associated with any operation effected more than three years after the grant: IHTA 1984, s 268(2)

[131] See paras 17.83–17.85
[132] See [1985] Ch Com Rep 21 (para 63)
[133] ie within CA 1993, s 36(5)
[134] CA 1993, s 36(3)(a)

For this purpose, a person is a qualified surveyor if he is a fellow or professional **17.52**
Associate of the Royal Institution of Chartered Surveyors or of the Incorporated
Society of Valuers and Auctioneers,[135] and he is reasonably believed by the charity
trustees to have ability in, and experience of, the valuation of land of the particular kind, and in the particular area, in question.[136] In practice, the charity trustees
are likely to have to pay for this professional advice. There is nothing in the section to preclude the advice from being given by one of the charity trustees themselves if such person is a qualified surveyor as there defined. This would result in
the surveyor, as one of the trustees, instructing himself; but there seems to be
nothing objectionable in this, at least where there are at least two other charity
trustees who are able to consider the report independently. However, a charity
trustee who acts as a qualified surveyor for the charity will generally not be permitted to charge for such services.[137]

The qualified surveyor's report must contain such information, and deal with **17.53**
such matters, as may be prescribed by regulations so made.[138] Under the present
regulations,[139] the information to be included in the report is very detailed, including the dimensions of rooms, and particulars of easements and other rights.

Duty to advertise the proposed disposition

The charity trustees must advertise the proposed disposition for such period and **17.54**
in such manner as the surveyor has advised in his report (unless he has there advised that it would not be in the best interests of the charity to advertise the proposed disposition).[140] In most circumstances, it is likely that it will be in the best
interests of the charity to advertise; but there may be instances where it may not
be needed, for example, if the charity is exchanging small strips of land with the
owner of adjoining premises in order to improve the boundary between the two
properties, the small area of land exchanged may well not have any value on its
own other than to the adjacent owners themselves.

Duty to decide that the terms are the best reasonably obtainable

The charity trustees must decide that they are satisfied, having considered the sur- **17.55**
veyor's report, that the terms on which the disposition is proposed to be made are
the best that can reasonably be obtained for the charity.[141]

---

[135] Or if he satisfies such other requirements as may be prescribed by regulation: CA 1993,
s 36(4)(a)
[136] CA 1993, s 36(4)(b)
[137] See generally ch 9 above, paras 9.97–9.115 (trustee remuneration)
[138] CA 1993, s 36(4)
[139] Charities (Qualified Surveyors' Reports) Regulations 1992, SI 1992/2980
[140] CA 1993, s 36(3)(b)
[141] ibid, s 36(3)(c)

17.56 If the charity trustees engage in many dispositions of land, it may be impractical for all of them to meet to decide on each individual transaction, especially if there is a large body of charity trustees. It is therefore important, in such instances, that the charity trustees have a power to delegate to a small number of themselves (the committee) the power to make decisions in individual cases. Under the Trustee Act 2000, trustees of charitable trusts have a statutory power to delegate in this manner, in the absence of a contrary indication in the trust instrument.[142] In practice, an express power should require the body of charity trustees as a whole to specify the general policy for disposals, and should require the committee to report back to the general body of trustees at regular intervals.

17.57 The phrase 'the terms on which the disposition is proposed to be made' is intended to ensure that auction sales and sales by tender are included.[143] The wording suggests that the charity trustees must decide whether any offer meets the criteria after the offer has been made. In the case of a sale of charity land by auction, however, it is of course impossible for the charity trustees actively to consider each bid as it is made. It is suggested that, where charity land is sold by auction, the charity trustees meet the requirements of the sub-section if they make their decision on the basis of the reserve price. In other words, land sold by charity by means of an auction sale must always have a suitable reserve price.

17.58 Whether the terms are the best reasonably obtainable will generally be decided by financial criteria, that is, the best offer will usually be the highest offer; although the charity trustees might consider a slightly lower offer to be the best if there are other financial advantages, for example, an earlier completion date. If the trustees receive a higher offer before they have entered into a valid contract with an existing offeror, they are not entitled to go ahead with the original lower offer merely because they regard themselves as morally bound: effectively, they are under a duty to gazump.[144]

17.59 What is less clear is the extent to which charity trustees might take non-financial criteria, such as purely ethical considerations, into account. It could be argued that charity trustees are, by analogy with *Harries v Church Commissioners for England*,[145] prohibited from selling land or other assets to a company with 'conflicting' objects. Since such a sale does not involve an investment in the purchasing company, it does not fall within the letter of that decision; on the other hand, it could be argued that a cancer charity that sells land to a tobacco company for the construction of a cigarette factory is engaging in a transaction contrary to its purposes. If charity trustees who advertise land for sale receive the highest offer

---

[142] TA 2000, ss 11(3), 12(1), (2). See further ch 9, paras 9.149–9.159, esp 9.153 and 9.154
[143] The wording in the Charities Bill 1992 had originally been 'the terms of the proposed agreement', for which were substituted the present words for the reasons stated in the text
[144] *Buttle v Saunders* [1950] 2 All ER 193
[145] [1992] 1 WLR 1241; see ch 16, paras 16.61–16.62

from a company with 'conflicting' objects, their safest course of action would be to seek the consent of the Charity Commissioners to the sale,[146] although the delay thereby occasioned might result in the loss of one or more of the offers. The Charity Commissioners have expressed the view that charity trustees *may* reasonably reject an offer where they have reasonable grounds for believing that the purchaser will use the land in a way which will either affect other land which they are retaining or be directly contrary to the purposes of the charity; but that if the trustees accept a lower offer it must be clear that it is to the overall advantage of the charity.[147]

This suggests that in other circumstances, the charity trustees must generally accept the highest offer, even if it is made by a purchaser who intends to use the premises for what the trustees would regard as merely 'unsuitable' purposes vis-à-vis the charity, for example, for use as a bookmaker's, or for the offices of a political party. If the charity is merely intending to lease the premises, it may wish to insert some restriction on the user of the premises, so that certain trades or uses are prohibited. The wider such restrictions are, of course, the lower the market rent that might be expected to be obtainable for such a lease. The wording of section 36(3)(c) of the Charities Act 1993 might assist here, since a restriction would be one of the 'terms' on which a proposed disposition by way of lease is proposed to be made. The sub-section does, not, however, assist if the charity trustees' objection relates merely to the identity of the purchaser, since the identity of the purchaser is not itself a 'term' of the proposed disposition. The criteria laid down in *Harries*' case[148] would seem to be applicable here by analogy, that is, whilst charity trustees must not impose their own moral or political code in the sale of charity land, they might nevertheless reasonably take into account the possible adverse consequences for the charity (such as bad publicity) which might flow from a sale to certain types of purchasers or for certain types of purposes, and which might result in an overall loss of funds into the charity. **17.60**

Short leases

If the proposed disposition is the granting of a lease for a term ending not more than seven years after it is granted (other than one granted wholly or partly in consideration of a fine), the procedure with which the charity trustees must comply in order to avoid having to obtain consent is slightly less stringent. Before entering into the agreement for a lease, the charity trustees must comply with merely two duties. **17.61**

---

[146] ie by an order under CA 1993, s 36(1)
[147] See Charity Commissioners' leaflet, *Disposing of Charity Land* (CC28) (May 1994)
[148] [1992] 1 WLR 1241; see further ch 16, paras 16.64–16.65

Duty to obtain and consider competent advice

17.62   The charity trustees must obtain and consider the advice on the proposed disposition of a person who is reasonably believed by them to have the requisite ability and practical experience to provide them with competent advice on the proposed disposition.[149]

17.63   As all that is required is 'competent' advice, it may be that, in the circumstances, the charity trustees might reasonably seek the advice of a person such as a bank manager or an estate agent. It should also be noted that there is no requirement that the advice be given in writing; but written advice should nevertheless be obtained, in order to provide evidence that the charity trustees have complied with the statutory requirement. A further difference is that, in this instance, the advice does not have to contain all the details which are required in the report of a qualified surveyor.

Duty to decide that the terms are the best reasonably obtainable

17.64   The charity trustees must decide that they are satisfied, having considered that person's advice, that the terms on which the disposition is proposed to be made are the best that can reasonably be obtained for the charity.[150]

17.65   There is no basic statutory obligation to advertise the proposed disposition in this instance; but the advice might itself contain recommendations regarding advertising, which the charity trustees could not in practice safely ignore.

17.66   It should be noted that the relaxation in this sub-section applies to the granting of a lease 'for a term ending not more than seven years after it is granted', which does not mean that every lease for a term of seven years or less falls within its scope. A lease is granted on the date it is executed, whereas the commencement of the term may be either back-dated or deferred (a reversionary lease). Therefore the proposed grant of a lease of merely six years will not come within this sub-section if the term is expressed to commence more than one year after the proposed grant. Even if a short lease does fall within the sub-section, it may be difficult for the charity to regain possession at the end of the term if the tenant has security of tenure, for example, under the Landlord and Tenant Act 1954, Part II. A business tenancy for a term of seven years commencing on the date of execution of the lease is a lease within the sub-section, even though the tenant may have a basic statutory right to a new lease at the end of the term. This is an evident weakness of the provisions; since the rationale for a less stringent regime under section 36(5) of the Charities Act 1993 is that any loss which the charity might suffer from the disposition will be restricted to the short period of the lease—which is not necessarily so.

---

[149]   CA 1993, s 36(5)(a)
[150]   ibid, s 36(5)(b)

(7) *Stipulations in the trusts that the land is to be used for the purposes of the charity*

Special provisions apply where the trusts stipulate that the land is functional land, **17.67**
that is, land which is used for the purpose of the charity and not merely as an investment. Where any land is held by or in trust for a charity,[151] and the trusts on which it is so held stipulate that it is to be used for the purposes, or any particular purposes, of the charity,[152] then (subject to certain exceptions[153] and without prejudice to the preceding provisions of section 36 of the Charities Act 1993) the land is not to be sold, leased, or otherwise disposed of unless the charity trustees have complied with a public notice procedure.[154]

Public notice procedure

In such circumstances, the charity trustees must have given public notice of the **17.68**
proposed disposition, inviting representations to be made to them within a time specified in the notice which must be not less than one month from the date of the notice),[155] and they must have taken into consideration any representations made to them within that time about the proposed disposition.[156]

The right of objectors is therefore very limited. An objector has no right to prevent **17.69**
a sale or other disposition.[157] If, however, a person has evidence of misconduct or mismanagement in the administration of the charity, or that the charity property needs protecting, he could bring such evidence to the attention of the Charity Commissioners, who would, in an appropriate case,[158] be able by order to restrict the proposed disposition without their consent.[159]

---

[151] ibid, s 36(6)(a)
[152] ibid, s 36(6)(b)
[153] These are specified in CA 1993, s 36(7) & (8)
[154] CA 1993, s 36(6)
[155] ibid, s 36(6)(i)
[156] ibid, s 36(6)(ii)
[157] An amendment tabled at Committee stage during the Parliamentary passage of the Charities Bill 1992 would have enabled an objector to notify the Charity Commissioners, who would then have been empowered to order that the disposition could not proceed without their consent. The amendment was rejected as contrary to the spirit of the legislation
[158] ie if they are satisfied, after an inquiry under CA 1993, s 8, that there has been misconduct or mismanagement, or that it is necessary or desirable to act to protect the charity's property or to secure its proper application: CA 1993, s 18(1). On inquiries under s 8, see further ch 10, paras 10.140–10.145. On the Charity Commissioners' powers under s 18, see ch 10, paras 10.158–10.162
[159] CA 1993, s 18(1)(vi)

Exceptions

Replacement property or very short lease

17.70   The public notice procedure does not apply if the disposition is effected with a view to acquiring by way of replacement other property which is to be held on the same trusts,[160] or is the granting of a lease for a term ending not more than two years after it is granted[161] (other than one granted wholly or partly in consideration of a fine).[162]

17.71   The first of these exceptions would apply, for instance, if a recreational charity were to decide to sell its site in order to move to another nearby:[163] the acquisition would rank as replacement property, and so the sale of the first site would be outside the scope of the public notice procedure. There is no specified time-limit by which the replacement property has to be acquired; it is enough that the disposition is effected 'with a view to acquiring' replacement property. It is therefore possible to envisage circumstances in which, although such acquisition was intended at the time of disposition, no replacement property is ultimately purchased.

Direction of Charity Commissioners

17.72   The Charity Commissioners may direct that the public notice procedure is not to apply to dispositions of land held by or in trust for a charity or class of charities (whether generally or only in the case of a specified class of dispositions or land, or otherwise as may be provided in the direction).[164] The Charity Commissioners may alternatively direct that the public notice procedure is not to apply to a particular disposition of land held by or in trust for a charity.[165] The Commissioners are not to make either type of direction, however, except on an application made to them in writing by or on behalf of the charity or charities in question, and then only if the Commissioners are satisfied that it would be in the interests of the charity or charities for them to give the direction.[166]

17.73   The aim of this saving is to make life less difficult for charities which make many dispositions of functional land each year. The paradigm case is the National Trust, which has some 10,000 properties leased out on relatively short leases (usually eight years).[167] The sub-section enables the Charity Commissioners to make ap-

---

[160]   CA 1993, s 36(7)(a)

[161]   This is not synonymous with a lease of two years: see comments on CA 1993, s 36(5) above, para 17.66

[162]   CA 1993, s 36(7)(b)

[163]   cf (under the pre-1993 law) *Oldham BC v A-G* [1993] Ch 210

[164]   CA 1993, s 36(8)(a)

[165]   ibid, s 36(8)(b)

[166]   ibid, s 36(8). In 1994, the Charity Commissioners made some 50 directions dispensing with the need to publish notices: [1994] Ch Com Rep 10–11

[167]   *Hansard*, HL (series 5) vol 535 Report on the Charities Bill cols 418–420 (6 Feb 1992) (Lord Chorley). The exception in CA 1993, s 36(8), was not in the Charities Bill 1992 as originally laid before Parliament, but was added in debate for the reasons stated in the text

propriate directions to relieve it, or charities in a similar position, of the burden of having to serve thousands of public notices each year.

(8) Exceptions to section 36 of the Charities Act 1993

Disposition authorized by statute or scheme

The restrictions in section 36 do not apply to any disposition for which general or **17.74** special authority is expressly given (without the authority being made subject to the sanction of an order of the court) by any statutory provision contained in or having effect under any Act of Parliament or by any scheme legally established.[168]

The following are examples of dispositions which can therefore be effected with-**17.75** out having to comply with section 36: a sale by a mortgagee (where the mortgage is by deed) when the mortgage money has become due, pursuant to his statutory power of sale;[169] a lease granted by a mortgagee in possession, pursuant to his statutory power of leasing;[170] a sale or other disposal by an administrator or an administrative receiver;[171] and, on a winding up by the court, the sale by a liquidator of a company's property pursuant to his statutory power of sale.[172]

Authorized disposition to another charity

The restrictions imposed by section 36 do not apply to a disposition of land held **17.76** by or in trust for a charity which is made to another charity otherwise than for the best price that can reasonably be obtained, and is authorized to be so made by the trusts of the first charity.[173] To interpret the requirement that the disposition be 'authorized by the trusts' to mean that the particular disposition has to be specifically authorized in the trusts of the first charity would be too restrictive. It appears to require merely that it be clear from the trusts of the first charity that such a disposition of its land comprises an application of its property to its charitable purposes.

The exception is particularly useful where a charitable trust or unincorporated **17.77** charitable association decides to incorporate; the voluntary conveyance or transfer of its land to the new incorporated charity will not need to comply with section 36.

Lease at low rent for occupation by beneficiary for purposes of charity

The restrictions imposed by section 36 do not apply to the granting by or on be-**17.78** half of a charity, and in accordance with its trusts, of a lease to any beneficiary

---

[168] CA 1993, s 36(9)(a)
[169] LPA 1925, s 101(1)(i)
[170] ibid, s 99(2)
[171] Insolvency Act 1986, s 14 (administrators), s 42 (administrative receivers) & Sch 1
[172] ibid, s 167 & Sch 3, Pt III, para 6
[173] CA 1993, s 36(9)(b)

under those trusts where the lease is granted otherwise than for the best rent that can reasonably be obtained, and is intended to enable the demised premises to be occupied for the purposes, or any particular purposes, of the charity.[174]

17.79   The aim of this exemption is to ensure that charities whose purposes comprise the provision of subsidized accommodation for the poor or otherwise disadvantaged are able to continue letting to such persons other than at a commercial rent.[175] The Charity Commissioners have stated that where a charity for the relief of unemployment leases land and buildings at below-market or subsidized rents to businesses starting up, they will regard such dispositions as being to the 'beneficiaries' of the charity, in furtherance of its objects. Such dispositions will therefore fall within this exemption.[176]

Disposition by an exempt charity

17.80   Section 36 does not apply to any disposition of land held by or in trust for an exempt charity.[177] The rationale for the exemption of exempt charities is that these are generally subject to other statutory safeguards. The statutory requirements relating to statements in contracts, conveyances, and leases, however, do apply to dispositions by exempt charities.[178]

Mortgages, charges, and advowsons

17.81   Also exempt from section 36 is any disposition of land by way of mortgage or other security,[179] or to any disposition of an advowson.[180] Dispositions by way of mortgage or other security are exempt because they are subject to the slightly different requirements of sections 38 and 39.

(9) Sales by personal representatives of land given to charity by will

17.82   The Charity Commissioners have stated that, in their view, section 36 of the Charities Act 1993 does not apply to the sale of land given by will to a charity where the sale is effected by personal representatives in the course of administration of the estate.[181] They point out that section 36(1) applies only to land 'held

---

[174] CA 1993, s 36(9)(c)

[175] See HL, Official Report of the Committee on the Charities Bill col 166 (10 Dec 1991) (Lord Allen of Abbeydale); *Hansard*, HL (series 5) (vol 535) Report on the Charities Bill cols 420–1 (6 Feb 1992) (Earl Ferrers)

[176] Charity Commission, *Charities for the Relief of Unemployment*, RR3 (Mar 1999), 6

[177] CA 1993, s 36(10)(a). The list of exempt charities is set out in CA 1993, Sch 2. Exempt charities were also relieved of the need to obtain the court's or the Commissioners' consent under the previous law. On exempt charities generally, see ch 10, paras 10.03–10.26

[178] CA 1993, s 37(1). These requirements are considered further below, paras 17.86–17.95

[179] CA 1993, s 36(10)(b)

[180] ibid, s 36(10)(c)

[181] See (1995) 4 Decisions 26–7

by or in trust for a charity'. If the gift of land is a residuary gift, the charity will have a right in equity to see that the estate is properly administered, but it will acquire no beneficial interest in the land during the period of administration.[182] During this period, therefore, the land cannot be said to be held either 'by or in trust for' a charity. If the gift is contained in a specific devise, there is some authority to suggest that the devisee does acquire a defeasible interest in equity;[183] although the matter is not beyond doubt.[184] However, the Charity Commissioners suggest that a sale by personal representatives in the course of administering the estate would be an exercise by them of a statutory power of disposal, conferred by the joint effect of several statutory provisions,[185] and so would in any event fall outside section 36.[186]

(10) Effect of non-compliance with section 36 of the Charities Act 1993

The Charities Act 1993 does not specify the effect of non-compliance with section 36. However, in accordance with normal principles of statutory interpretation, it would appear that a disposition of land which falls within section 36(1) but which is either made without the requisite consent or not made in accordance with the appropriate procedures specified in sub-sections (3) or (5), is void for the purposes of conveying or transferring a legal estate. The consequence of non-compliance therefore appears to be the same as that pertaining before 1993, when a disposition made without the consent of the court or the Charity Commissioners (where this was required) was void.[187] If the purchaser obtained registration of title at HM Land Registry he would obtain the legal estate by virtue of the magic of registration;[188] but would stand to have the legal estate divested from him by rectification. In practice, the Land Registry will not register a purchaser from a charity or from charity trustees where there is non-compliance with section 36(1), (3) or (5), if the Land Registry is aware of the status of the vendor, which should be apparent from the registered title. **17.83**

More difficulty might arise in practice where the charity purports to grant a lease for a term not exceeding twenty-one years, which is not registrable substantively at HM Land Registry.[189] If a charity purports to grant a term of years to a **17.84**

---

[182] *Comr of Stamp Duties (Queensland) v Livingston* [1965] AC 694

[183] *IRC v Hawley* [1928] 1 KB 578, 583; *Re Neeld* [1962] Ch 643, 687–8; *Williams v Holland* [1965] 1 WLR 739, 743–4

[184] cf *Comr of Stamp Duties (Queensland) v Livingston* [1965] AC 694; Law Commission, *Transfer of Land: Overreaching: Beneficiaries in Occupation* (Law Com No 188, 1989), para 2.16. The Charity Commissioners themselves consider that the position of a devisee under a specific devise is the same as that of one under a gift of residue: (1995) 4 Decisions 26

[185] The relevant statutory provisions are: Administration of Estates Act 1925, s 39(1)(iii); and (in respect of deaths after 31 Dec 1996), TLATA 1996, ss 6(1), 18(1)

[186] CA 1993, s 36(9)(a)

[187] *Bishop of Bangor v Parry* [1891] 2 QB 277

[188] Land Registration Act 1925, s 9 (registration with absolute title)

[189] ibid, ss 19(2), 22(2)

purchaser without complying with the requirements of section 36(1) or (2), the lease will be void for the purpose of creating that term of years; but if the purported lessee goes into possession and pays rent, ostensibly in accordance with the lease, he might obtain a legal estate under a yearly tenancy at common law. This was held to be the position before 1993, in *Bishop of Bangor v Parry*,[190] although it was there pointed out that the lessee would not be able to bring an action for breach of the covenant for quiet enjoyment.

17.85 If the same result were to ensue under the modern provisions, the purpose of the statute would be undermined where the tenant is carrying on a business on the premises, since he would, as a yearly tenant, have security of tenure under Part II of the Landlord and Tenant Act 1954. The position since 1993 may, however, be different. Under the previous law, no consent was required for the grant of a lease for a term not exceeding twenty-two years. Therefore, although the purported creation of a term of years for a longer period was held void in *Bishop of Bangor v Parry*[191] the applicable statute did not preclude the court from holding that the tenant became a yearly tenant. In contrast to this, even a yearly tenancy would now be caught by section 36 of the Charities Act 1993, and would be void unless granted with prior consent or in compliance with the procedures specified in section 36(3) or (5). Since the occupier can acquire no legal estate in the land, it is submitted that he should be treated as a licensee, who will therefore be liable to pay the charity trustees a licence fee for his occupation, such licence fee to be equivalent to mesne profits for occupation under a yearly tenancy.[192]

C. Statements in instruments

17.86 Whereas section 36 of the Charities Act 1993 applies only to contracts and other dispositions of land made by a charity, section 37 applies to contracts and other dispositions of land made either by a charity or to a charity.

(1) Statements in contracts, conveyances, leases, etc

Where charity is disponor

17.87 Section 37(1) applies to any of the following instruments:[193]

(a) any contract for the sale, or for a lease or other disposition, of land which is held by or in trust for a charity, and
(b) any conveyance, transfer, lease or other instrument effecting a disposition of such land.

---

[190] [1891] 2 QB 277
[191] ibid
[192] cf *Javad v Aqil* [1991] 1 WLR 1007
[193] CA 1993, s 37(1)(a) & (b)

Such instrument must state three things:[194]

(i) that the land is held by or in trust for a charity;
(ii) whether the charity is an exempt charity[195] and whether the disposition is one falling within paragraph (a), (b) or (c) of sub-section (9) of section 36 above,[196] and
(iii) if it is not an exempt charity and the disposition is not one falling within any of those paragraphs, that the land is land to which the restrictions on disposition imposed by that section apply.

17.88 In the context of registered land, if the disposition to be effected by any such instrument as is mentioned in section 37(1)(b) will be a registered disposition, or will on taking effect be any instrument to which compulsory registration of title[197] applies, the statement to be contained in the instrument must be in the prescribed form.[198]

17.89 The obligations imposed by section 37(1) also apply to an exempt charity.

Where charity is disponee

17.90 Section 37(5) applies to any of the following instruments:[199]

(a) any contract for the sale, or for a lease or other disposition, of land which will, as a result of the disposition, be held by or in trust for a charity, and
(b) any conveyance, transfer, lease or other instrument effecting a disposition of such land.

Such instrument must state three things:[200]

(i) that the land will, as a result of the disposition, be held by or in trust for a charity,
(ii) whether the charity is an exempt charity,[201] and
(iii) if it is not an exempt charity, that the restrictions on disposition imposed by section 36 above will apply to the land (subject to sub-section (9) of that section).[202]

17.91 In the context of registered land, if the disposition to be effected by any such instrument as is mentioned in section 37(5)(b) will be a registered disposition, or will on taking effect be any instrument to which compulsory registration of title[203]

---

[194] ibid, s 37(1)(i)–(iii)
[195] For the meaning of an exempt charity and its position under CA 1993, see ch 10, paras 10.03–10.26
[196] ie para (a) (disposition authorized by statute or scheme) (see above, paras 17.74–17.75); para (b) (authorized disposition to another charity) (see above, paras 17.76–17.77); and para (c) (lease at low rent for occupation by beneficiary for purposes of charity) (see above, paras 17.78–17.79)
[197] ie under Land Registration Act 1925, s 123A
[198] CA 1993, s 37(7). The prescribed form is specified in the Land Registration (Charities) Rules 1992, SI 1992/3005
[199] CA 1993, s 37(5)(a) & (b)
[200] ibid, s 37(5)(i)–(iii)
[201] For the meaning of an exempt charity and its position under CA 1993, see ch 10, paras 10.03–10.26
[202] For the scope of CA 1993, s 36(9), see above, paras 17.74–17.79
[203] ie under Land Registration Act 1925, s 123A

applies, the statement to be contained in the instrument must be in the prescribed form.[204] On an application for registration, where the instrument by which the disposition is made contains the statement required by sub-section (5), then, unless the charity is an exempt charity, the registrar will enter a restriction in the register.[205] If land with registered title becomes land held in trust for a charity (other than an exempt charity) as a result of a declaration of trust by the registered proprietor, the charity trustees must apply to the registrar for a restriction to be entered in the register.[206]

17.92   The obligations imposed by section 37(5) also apply to an exempt charity.

Does s 37(5) apply to wills?

17.93   Section 37(5) applies to a will only if the will can be considered to be an instrument effecting a disposition of the land. If the gift of land to a charity is contained in a residuary gift, it cannot be a disposition because a residuary legatee or devisee does not acquire any beneficial interest in the subject matter of the gift during the period of administration,[207] but only from the time when the residue is ascertained.[208] In contrast to this, it may be that a specific legatee or devisee acquires an equitable interest in the subject matter of the gift from the moment of the testator's death, albeit that such interest is defeasible in that the personal representatives may need to dispose of the property in the course of administration of the estate in order to pay the testator's debts. Subject to this, the doctrine of relating back means that, when the gift vests, the legatee or devisee is considered retrospectively to have enjoyed a beneficial interest since the testator's death.[209]

17.94   In some other contexts a gift by will can rank as a disposition.[210] It is submitted, however, that a will is not an instrument effecting a disposition of land for the purposes of section 37(5)(b).[211] Even if the will can be considered to pass an equitable interest to a specific devisee, it is suggested that it does not fall within section 37(5). Paragraphs (a) and (b) of that sub-section effectively draw a distinction between contract and conveyance respectively.[212] Whilst a specific devise of land

---

[204] CA 1993, s 37(7). The prescribed form is specified in the Land Registration (Charities) Rules 1992, SI 1992/3005

[205] CA 1993, s 37(8). If a restriction has been entered in the register and the charity becomes an exempt charity, the charity trustees must apply to the registrar for the restriction to be removed: ibid, s 37(9). Conversely, if an exempt charity ceases to be an exempt charity, the charity trustees must apply to the registrar to have a restriction entered in the register: ibid, s 37(10)

[206] CA 1993, s 37(10)

[207] *Comr of Stamp Duties (Queensland) v Livingston* [1965] AC 694

[208] *Barnardo's Homes v Special Income Tax Comrs* [1921] 2 AC 1

[209] *IRC v Hawley* [1928] 1 KB 578. See the discussion of sales of land given by will to charity by personal representatives in the course of administration above, para 17.82

[210] eg LPA 1925, s 53(1)(c)

[211] The sub-section is set out above, para 17.90

[212] See further the discussion of the scope of s 37(2) below, paras 17.103–17.107, esp 17.105

probably passes a defeasible interest to the devisee, it is not a contract and so falls outside paragraph (a). For the purposes of paragraph (b), the instrument giving effect to the devise is not the will, but the executors' vesting assent; and it is submitted that it is that assent alone which must contain the statements set out in section 37(5). If the will itself had to comply with section 37(5), the sub-section would operate as a modern law of mortmain, and invalidate devises of land to charity which omitted the requisite statement to the advantage of the testator's residuary beneficiaries or next of kin. This cannot be correct: the sub-section is clearly intended to protect charity land, not to invalidate testamentary devises of land to a charity.

Effect of omission of statement required by s 37(1) or (5)

Although there is no express sanction for omission to include the statement re- **17.95**
quired by section 37(1) or (5), it can be inferred that the effect of non-compliance is the invalidity of the instrument in question. If, however, the charity trustees also fail to certify in accordance with section 37(2), discussed below,[213] when such certificate is required, the disposition is valid in favour of a purchaser in good faith for money or money's worth.[214]

(2) Charity trustees' certificate

Where any land held by or in trust for a charity is sold, leased, or otherwise dis- **17.96**
posed of by a disposition to which section 36(1) or (2) of the Charities Act 1993 applies, the charity trustees must certify in the instrument by which the disposition is effected either that the disposition has been sanctioned by the appropriate order;[215] or that the charity trustees have power under the trusts of the charity to effect the disposition, and that they have complied with the provisions of that section so far as applicable to it.[216] The duty to certify does not apply if the charity is an exempt charity, because a disposition of land by an exempt charity does not fall within section 36(1) or (2).[217]

Form of certificate

It is recommended that the charity trustees certify in the body of the instrument, **17.97**
in a form of words as close as possible to those of the statute. An appropriate form of words in a conveyance of land by charity trustees who have complied with the requirements of section 36(3) (that is, who have obtained and considered the advice of a qualified surveyor) would be:

---

[213] See below, paras 17.96–17.110, esp paras 17.109–17.110
[214] CA 1993, s 37(4)
[215] ibid, s 37(2)(a)
[216] ibid, s 37(2)(b)
[217] ibid, ss 36(10), 37(2)

The charity trustees hereby certify that they have power under the trusts of the charity to effect the disposition hereunder, and that they have complied with the provisions of section 36 of the Charities Act 1993 so far as applicable to it.

Signatures of charity trustees

17.98 The question then arises whether it is necessary for all the charity trustees to append their signatures to the certificate, which in some circumstances may be impractical. It is suggested that this is not necessary, and that the valid execution of the instrument itself will suffice.

17.99 Under section 82 of the Charities Act 1993, charity trustees may (subject to the trusts of the charity) authorize any two or more of their number to execute deeds or other instruments on behalf of all the trustees.[218] Any deed or instrument executed in pursuance of such authority is of the same effect as if executed by the whole body of trustees.[219]

17.100 In the case of an unincorporated charity, therefore, if the instrument giving effect to the disposition is executed pursuant to such authority, it seems that the instrument can be treated as executed by all the trustees for the purposes of certification also.

17.101 If the charity is a corporation, it may execute a document by attaching the common seal;[220] but this will not comprise a certificate of the directors (the charity trustees). A corporate charity can effect contracts and other dispositions of land by an alternative method: namely, by the signatures of two directors (or by a director and the secretary) expressed to be executed by the company.[221] If signed by two directors, the deed or other instrument would then be signed by two of the charity trustees, but the Companies Act 1985 does not itself expressly provide that a document so executed is deemed to have been executed by all the directors. The signatures of two directors alone may not therefore meet the certification requirements of the Charities Act 1993.

17.102 Section 82 of the Charities Act 1993 is evidently primarily concerned with unincorporated charities, since the doctrine of separate corporate personality means that the directors of a charitable company are not themselves parties to a contract entered into, or to a conveyance executed by, the company. It seems, however, that directors of a charitable company might be able to use the power of delegation which that section confers. Where the disposition by a charitable company requires the certificate of its directors, it could be contended that the directors' need to furnish a certificate means that the directors are a necessary party to the instrument for the purposes of giving effect to the transaction (which includes the provision of the certificate). If

---

[218] CA 1993, s 82(1)
[219] ibid
[220] Companies Act 1985, s 36A(2)
[221] ibid, s 36A(4)

this is so, then directors of charitable companies can themselves take advantage of section 82, and can confer upon any two or more of their number the power to provide the requisite certificate. Execution of the instrument by the signature of two directors would then meet the requirements of both the Companies Act 1985 for the execution of a document by a company, and the Charities Act 1993 for the purposes of certification. Until the issue is resolved judicially, however, the safest course of action is for all the directors to append their signatures to the certificate.

Is charity trustees' certificate needed in a contract to dispose of charity land?

Whereas it is expressly stated that a contract for the sale of charity land must contain the statements set out in section 37(1), it is by no means clear whether a contract for the sale of charity land must contain a charity trustees' certificate.   **17.103**

It could be argued that it must, because section 37(2) applies where charity land is (inter alia) 'sold . . . by a disposition to which sub-section (1) or (2) of section 36 . . . applies'; and the trustees must certify 'in the instrument by which the disposition is effected'. Section 36(1) clearly applies to a contract for the sale of land; and it can therefore be contended that the contract in writing is the instrument by which such disposition (of an equitable interest) is effected. Hence, the contract must contain the charity trustees' certificate.   **17.104**

A counter-argument can, however, be constructed. If a contract for sale of charity land has to contain the charity trustees' certificate, the practical result is that the obligations imposed by sub-sections (1) and (2) of section 37 apply to the same instruments. Why then, it might be asked, has the draftsman used a different form of wording for each sub-section? It would, after all, have been simpler merely to make the certification requirements of paragraphs (a) and (b) of sub-section (2) additional sub-paragraphs (iv) and (v) of section 37(1).[222] The difference in wording suggests that the instruments to which the respective obligations apply are not synonymous. It will be noted that section 37(1) expressly distinguishes between a contract for sale in paragraph (a), and 'any conveyance, transfer, lease or other instrument effecting a disposition of such land' in paragraph (b). This indicates that, for the purposes of section 37(1), it is the subsequent conveyance, not the prior contract of sale, which is the instrument effecting a disposition of the land. Section 37(2) requires the charity trustees to certify 'in the instrument by which the disposition is effected'. It therefore seems to be drawing the same distinction between contract and conveyance as was drawn in section 37(1); in which case only the subsequent conveyance need contain the certificate, not any prior contract.[223]   **17.105**

---

[222] CA 1993, s 37(1) is set out above, para 17.87
[223] See further P Luxton, 'Charity land: dispositions, statements and certificates' (1995) NLJ 67 Appeals Suppl 14, 18. See also the discussion of whether a will is an instrument effecting a disposition for the purposes of s 37(1), above, paras 17.93–17.94; cf (under a different statutory provision) *R v Hackney LBC, ex p Structadene Ltd* The Times 28 Nov 2000

17.106 If the latter argument is wrong, and the certificate has to be contained even in a contract for the sale of land, problems can arise with conditional contracts. If the contract is entered into before either consent has been obtained or the appropriate procedure has been complied with, the contract will need to be conditional upon compliance with such requirements; yet, to satisfy section 37(2), the charity trustees will have to certify in the contract that such requirements have already been fulfilled! There can be no objection to this in principle, since the instrument will not become a contract unless and until the condition to which it is subject is satisfied; the charity trustees' certificate is therefore of no effect until the condition is met, at which instant, the certificate speaks the truth! Nevertheless, the absurdity of such a requirement in these circumstances is a further indication that section 37(2) should not be interpreted to require the charity trustees to certify in a contract for the sale of charity land.

17.107 Until the point is resolved judicially, the safest course of action is for the charity trustees to certify in contracts for the sale of land, and for such certification to be repeated in the subsequent transfer or conveyance.

Protection of purchasers

Conclusive presumption of facts as stated in certificate

17.108 Where the instrument effecting the disposition has been certified in accordance with section 37(2), then in favour of a person who (whether under the disposition or afterwards) acquires an interest in the land for money or money's worth, it is conclusively presumed that the facts were as stated in the certificate.[224]

Where charity trustees fail to certify

17.109 If a disposition is made which requires the trustees' certification and they fail to provide it, the disposition is nevertheless valid in favour of a person who (whether under the disposition or afterwards) in good faith acquires an interest in the land for money or money's worth.[225]

17.110 A purchaser in good faith for money or money's worth can therefore acquire a valid title where the charity trustees have omitted to certify. A purchaser probably cannot be in good faith if he is aware that he is purchasing land from a charity or from charity trustees. He will usually be aware of this: if the title to the land is registered, a restriction will have been entered in the register of title at HM Land Registry; and, even if the title is not registered, a purchaser will usually discover that the vendor is a charity or charity trustees from an investigation of title.

---

[224] CA 1993, s 37(3)
[225] ibid, s 37(4)

(3) Sales by personal representatives of land given to charity by will

For the same reasons as have been stated above[226] in relation to section 36 of the **17.111** Charities Act 1993, the Charity Commissioners take the view that sales by personal representatives of land given to charity by will do not have to comply with the requirements of section 37.[227]

(4) Statement of charitable status by charitable company

Where a company is a charity and its name does not include the words 'charity' or **17.112** 'charitable', the fact that it is a charity must be stated in English in legible characters in (inter alia) all conveyances purporting to be executed by the company.[228] For this purpose, 'conveyance' means any instrument creating, transferring, varying, or extinguishing an interest in land;[229] it therefore includes a lease and a valid contract for the sale of land.

D. Mortgages of charity land

(1) Introduction

Sections 38–9 of the Charities Act 1993 contain provisions relating to mortgages **17.113** of charity land which broadly parallel those relating to other dispositions in sections 36–7.

There is a statement of the basic prohibition: no mortgage of land held by or in **17.114** trust for a charity may be granted without an order of the court or of the Charity Commissioners.[230] For this purpose, 'land' means land in England and Wales,[231] and 'mortgage' includes a charge.[232] The prohibition on mortgaging or charging does not apply to an exempt charity.[233]

In one respect, this basic prohibition is wider than the law before 1993, in that **17.115** (like section 36(1) in the context of sales, leases, and other dispositions of land) it applies to land held merely as an investment. In another respect, the provision is narrower than previous law, since it applies only to land.[234] Charity trustees may therefore mortgage assets of the charity other than land without compliance with

---

[226] See above, para 17.82
[227] (1995) 4 Decisions 26–7
[228] CA 1993, s 68(1)(d)
[229] ibid, s 68(2)
[230] ibid, s 38(1)
[231] ibid, s 38(6)
[232] ibid, s 38(6)
[233] ibid, s 38(7)
[234] The equivalent prohibition in CA 1960, s 29 (repealed) prohibited the mortgaging or charging of any 'property' forming part of the permanent endowment; whereas the restrictions in that section in relation to sales, leases, and other dispositions applied only to land

sections 38–9, although the charity trustees will be subject to the other restrictions imposed by law or by the governing instrument.[235]

(2) Avoiding the need to obtain consent

17.116 The Charity Commissioners' consent to mortgage is not required where the charity trustees have, before executing the mortgage, obtained and considered proper advice in writing on the following matters,[236] which are set out in section 38(3):

> (a) whether the proposed loan is necessary in order for the charity trustees to be able to pursue the particular course of action in connection with which the loan is sought by them;
> (b) whether the terms of the proposed loan are reasonable having regard to the status of the charity as a prospective borrower; and
> (c) the ability of the charity to repay on those terms the sum proposed to be borrowed.

Proper advice

17.117 Proper advice is that of a person who is reasonably believed by the charity trustees to be qualified by his ability in and practical experience of financial matters,[237] and who has no financial interest in the making of the loan in question.[238] Such advice may constitute proper advice notwithstanding that the person giving it does so in the course of his employment as an officer or employee of the charity or of the charity trustees.[239] The section applies notwithstanding anything in a charity's trusts, but not to any mortgage for which general or special authority is given by statute.[240]

(3) Supplementary

17.118 There are supplementary provisions in regard to statements in mortgages, the trustees' certificate, and the protection afforded to purchasers, which parallel those applicable to sales, leases, and other dispositions of charity land.[241]

---

[235] ie they will be in breach of trust unless they exercise the duty of care laid down in TA 2000 s 1(1), which applies to the mortgaging of land: ibid, s 8(3) and s 2 & Sch 1, para 2. See also *Speight v Gaunt* (1883) 9 App Cas 1

[236] CA 1993, s 38(2)

[237] ibid, s 38(4)(a)

[238] ibid, s 38(4)(b)

[239] ibid, s 38(4)

[240] ie under ibid, s 36(9)(a): ibid., s 38(5)

[241] ibid, s 39. These parallel the provisions discussed above, paras 17.87, 17.96 and 17.108–17.110

18

DISCLAIMER OF PROPERTY AND *EX GRATIA* PAYMENTS

18.01 A charity cannot as a general rule apply its property other than for its wholly and exclusively charitable objects. A charity is permitted to apply its funds in ways which are not themselves charitable if this is ancillary to the attainment of its charitable objects; and the court or the Charity Commissioners may authorize the charity to make payments which are expedient in the interests of the charity.[1] A charity might be justified in making a voluntary payment which is reasonably incidental to the carrying on of its charitable purposes: it may, for instance, be good business for a charity to give a member of its staff on retirement a pension in excess of that to which he or she is contractually entitled.[2] Where the charity trustees are unsure as to whether a proposed payment may lawfully be made within the terms of the charity's governing instrument, they may apply in writing to the Charity Commissioners for their opinion or advice.[3]

A. Disclaimer

(1) Disclaimer of legacies and other gifts

18.02 The general principle is that a charity may not generally disclaim a legacy made to it, since the charity will have become entitled in equity on the testator's death, and

---

[1] CA 1993, s 26(1) (power of the Charity Commissioners to authorize dealings with a charity's property)
[2] *Re Snowden, Re Henderson* [1969] 3 All ER 208, 212 (Cross J)
[3] CA 1993, s 29

a disclaimer would comprise an application of the charity's assets for non-charitable purposes.[4] A charity would be permitted to disclaim a gift which comprises onerous property, for example the freehold reversion of flats previously let on very long leases at a premium where the tenants pay only nominal rents. As the principle of disclaimer (or renunciation) was introduced for the benefit of beneficiaries, a charity which has disclaimed a legacy is allowed to retract its disclaimer unless anyone has acted on the faith of it and has altered his position to his detriment in consequence thereof.[5]

18.03 Onerous property apart, it might be possible to envisage instances where a disclaimer of a legacy might be permitted as being expedient in the best interests of the charity; as where the charity has a strong moral objection to the identity of the testator and where the publicity resulting from the acceptance of the legacy might be detrimental to the work of the charity or discourage future gifts from other prospective donors.[6] In view of the lack of specific authority on this point, however, the charity trustees would be unwise to disclaim without seeking the advice of the Charity Commissioners.

18.04 A charity which is a corporate body is not obliged to accept a gift which imposes special charitable trusts, and it may even be obliged to decline to accept the gift unless its constitution permits it to receive and hold property subject to special trusts. If a charity declines such a trusteeship, the property may still be applicable to those purposes under a scheme, or (where the purposes cannot be carried out or the acceptance of the specified charity as trustee was essential to the testator's purpose) it may be possible to apply it cy-près if there is a general charitable intention.[7]

18.05 Charity trustees are not precluded from indicating that they are unwilling to accept a proffered inter vivos gift, since, unless and until the gift is made, it is not part of the charity's property. If, however, the charity trustees were to deter potential donors for reasons unconnected with the needs or interests of the charity, this might constitute misconduct or mismanagement in the administration of a char-

---

[4] A private Act of Parliament, the Alcoholics Anonymous (Dispositions) Act 1986, was passed in order to permit The General Service Board of Alcoholics Anonymous (Great Britain) Ltd, the charitable arm of Alcoholics Anonymous (AA), to disclaim legacies. All the activities of this charity were in practice undertaken in connection with AA, one of whose principles was that those seeking to recover from alcoholism should rely largely on their own resources of character. Large sums of money would therefore undermine the self-reliance of AA members. Under the statute, any gift disclaimed by the charity takes effect as a gift to the Alcohol Education and Research Fund, so that the legacy is preserved for charity. See [1986] Ch Com Rep 32–3 (App D)

[5] *Re Cranstoun, Gibbs v Home of Rest for Horses* [1949] 1 Ch 523, 528 (Romer J), where the Home renounced a gift of residue because it mistakenly thought that it carried with it onerous liabilities

[6] cf (in the sphere of investment) *Harries v Church Comrs for England* [1992] 1 WLR 1241

[7] *Re Woodhams* [1981] 1 WLR 493

ity, which could lead, following an inquiry by the Commissioners, to the charity trustees' suspension or removal.[8]

(2) Disclaimer of onerous property upon liquidation

18.06 If a charity which is a company goes into liquidation, the liquidator is entitled, as he is in the winding up of any company, to disclaim onerous property.[9] The most common example of onerous property is a lease, since it subjects the tenant to various obligations, including the covenant to pay rent. As between a landlord and a corporate tenant that is being wound up, disclaimer determines, from the date it is made, the tenant's rights, interests, and liabilities in respect of the lease.[10]

B. *Ex gratia* payments

(1) Authorization by the court or the Attorney-General

18.07 Charity trustees are not generally entitled to give away the charity's funds or other property merely because they consider the charity to be under a moral obligation to do so, where this is not for the benefit of the charity; and, in most circumstances, neither the courts, the Attorney-General, nor the Charity Commissioners can authorize such a gift. There is, however, an exceptional power that may be used to justify an *ex gratia* payment in special circumstances. The power of the court or the Attorney-General to authorize charity trustees to make *ex gratia* payments out of charitable funds was considered in two applications heard together in *Re Snowden* and *Re Henderson*.[11]

18.08 In *Re Snowden*, the testator, by his will made in 1954, had made a number of small legacies to various individuals, and had (by clause 3) specifically bequeathed shares in three companies upon trust in specified shares among three of his relatives. He also bequeathed (by clause 6) legacies of amounts of between £2,000 and £200 and totalling £5,600 among eleven named charities, and (by clause 8) he also gave his residuary estate on trust to be divided in the same proportions amongst those charities. Mostly within the year before his death in 1964, the testator had sold his shareholdings in the three companies named in clause 3, with the consequence that the gifts made in that clause were adeemed, whereas the value of the residuary estate was considerably increased. The testator's relatives would receive only what minor legacies the testator had specifically provided for them. Their loss, however, was the charities' gain; since, by virtue of their entitle-

---

[8] CA 1993, s 18(1)(i), (2)(i)
[9] Insolvency Act 1986, ss 178–82 (liquidation)
[10] ibid, s 178(4) (liquidation)
[11] [1969] 3 All ER 208 (Cross J)

ment to the residue, the named charities would each receive more than eleven times what the testator had bequeathed to them by clause 6.

18.09   Cross J noted that the value of the company shares bequeathed by clause 3 represented, at the time of the will, a large part of the value of the estate, and he thought that it was unlikely that the testator had contemplated at that time that the value of his residuary estate would be of much value: the form of the residuary gifts, making proportionate additions to a number of comparatively small legacies, supported that view. There was no evidence to suppose that the testator's feelings for his relatives had changed in the year before his death. Cross J found that, in these circumstances, it was highly likely that the testator had overlooked the effect which the sale of the shares would have on his testamentary dispositions; and that, if he had realized what the effect would be, he would have left the three relatives pecuniary legacies of a substantial amount, although not necessarily equivalent to the purchase price, in order to compensate them for the loss of the shares. Taking that view, four of the eleven legatee charities under clause 6 expressed their wish to give up 50 per cent, one expressed its wish to give up 40 per cent, and one expressed its wish to give up 100 per cent, of the share of the residue to which they were respectively entitled in favour of the legatees under clause 3. The surviving executors took out a summons to ascertain whether effect could be given to the wishes of those six charities.

18.10   In *Re Henderson*, the testatrix, by her will made in 1963, bequeathed £3,000 to each of her nephew, Keith Green, and her niece, Anne Green, and after various other smaller pecuniary legacies to other individuals gave the residue of her estate to charity. At some date which could not be identified as being before or after the execution of her will, the testatrix had added in red ink the words 'or ½ each of my shares' to the right of the names of Keith Green and Anne Green. The testatrix died in 1965, and the will as proved did not include such additions. The value of the residuary estate to pass to charity was just over £6,500. The value of the testatrix's shares at her death was just over £11,000. Cross J thought it probable that, by the red ink additions, the testatrix had intended that, in the event of her shares being worth more than £6,000, the two legatees were to share the excess, and that she did not contemplate that so large a sum as £6,500 would pass under the residue to charity. If one were to increase the legacies to Keith and Anne Green to £5,500 so as to make each of them approximately equivalent to half the value of the testatrix's shares at her death, the value of the residue passing to charity would be reduced from £6,500 to £1,500. The administrator of the testatrix's estate issued a summons asking in effect that he be at liberty to increase the two legacies in question by £2,500 each.

18.11   Although there was no direct authority on whether the court or the Attorney-General had power to authorize charity trustees to make a voluntary payment out of charity funds in pursuance of what they considered to be a moral obligation, Cross J drew support by analogy from cases in which there had been, possibly unconscious, maladministration of a charitable trust over a long period, and where it might be hard to expect the trustees or managers to pay very large sums in full. In such cases, the court had asked the Attorney-General to consider whether it would be proper for the charity to accept a lesser sum than was found to be due to it.[12] He also drew support from the court's power to authorize trustees of a private trust to make a payment out of a minor beneficiary's interest as being for the moral benefit of the minor, even though it might be to his financial detriment.[13]

Given the existence of such a power, Cross J was satisfied that the court and the Attorney-General have power to give trustees authority to make *ex gratia* payments out of funds held on charitable trusts. He thought, however, that it was a power which was not to be exercised lightly or on slender grounds, but only in cases where it could be fairly said that, if the charity were an individual, it would be morally wrong of him to refuse to make the payment. His Lordship thought that there might well be a considerable difference between cases, like those before him, where it appears that the testator never intended the charity to receive so large a gift as it did receive, and cases where the testator intended the charity to receive what it had received, but the testator's relatives considered that he was not morally justified in leaving his money to charity rather than to them. The charity might well feel under a moral obligation to hand over the estate or part of it to the relatives in the former circumstances, but there is no reason why it should feel under such an obligation in the latter, unless, perhaps, in making the gift to charity, the testator was breaking a solemn, though legally unenforceable, promise, to leave it to someone else.[14] He thought that cases in which an *ex gratia* payment would be justified would be rarer in the second category than in the first. Applying these principles to the applications before him, he authorized the making of the *ex gratia* payments sought in each case.

(2) Procedure for applying for ex gratia *payments*

Cross J in *Re Snowden* and *Re Henderson*[15] considered that the charity or the trustees wishing to make an *ex gratia* payment should apply to the Charity Commissioners if (as in the *Snowden* case) the payments desired would come out

18.12

18.13

---

[12] *A-G v Exeter Corp* (1827) 2 Russ 362 (Lord Eldon LC); *A-G v Brettingham* (1840) 3 Beav 91; *A-G v Pretyman* (1841) 4 Beav 462
[13] *Re Clore's Settlement Trusts* [1966] 1 WLR 955 (advancement by way of a gift in trust for charitable purposes approved under Trustee Act 1925, s 32; here the beneficiary felt the moral obligation himself); see also *Re CL* [1969] 1 Ch 587 (variation of trust under the Variation of Trusts Act 1958 approved on behalf of a mentally disordered beneficiary as being for the benefit of that person even though it involved his giving his property away)
[14] *Re Snowden, Re Henderson* [1969] 3 All ER 208, 213–14, referring to *National Provincial Bank Ltd v Moore* (1967) 111 Sol Jo 357; The Times, 27 Apr 1967
[15] *Re Snowden, Re Henderson* [1969] 3 All ER 208

of the funds of a particular charity or charities, and to the Treasury Solicitor if, as in the *Henderson* case, the funds in question were held in trust for general charitable purposes. The Charity Commissioners or the Treasury Solicitor, as the case might be, would look into the facts and make a report to the Attorney-General, who would decide whether or not the trustees should be given authority to make a payment. The Attorney-General would not normally bring the question before the court, though if in any particular case he was in doubt what course to take he could apply ex parte[16] to the court for guidance.

18.14 This procedure, which was used to authorize *ex gratia* payments in the years following *Re Snowden*,[17] is still available, but a statutory procedure introduced in the Charities Act 1992 and now contained in the Charities Act 1993 enables the Charity Commissioners to authorize *ex gratia* payments,[18] and it is this new procedure which is now followed in the majority of cases.

(3) Authorization of ex gratia payments by the Charity Commissioners

18.15 Under section 27 of the Charities Act 1993 the Charity Commissioners may by order exercise the same power as is exercisable by the Attorney-General to authorize the charity trustees of a charity to make any application of property of the charity, or to waive, to any extent, on behalf of the charity, its entitlement to receive any property, in a case where the charity trustees otherwise have no power to do so, but in all the circumstances regard themselves as being under a moral obligation to do so.[19] Such power is exercisable by the Commissioners under the supervision of, and in accordance with such directions as may be given by, the Attorney-General.[20] Any such directions may in particular require the Commissioners in such circumstances as are specified to refrain from exercising that power, or to consult the Attorney-General before exercising it.[21] The Commissioners must refer to the Attorney-General any application made to them, if they consider that it would be desirable for the application to be entertained by him instead of by themselves.[22] A refusal by the Commissioners to authorize the charity trustees to make an *ex gratia* payment or to waive the charity's entitlement to property does not preclude the Attorney-General, on an application subsequently made to him by the trustees, from authorizing the trustees to do those things.[23] Any application to the court from the Commissioners' refusal

---

[16] ie without notice, as it is now termed
[17] See, eg [1969] Ch Com Rep 13–14 (para 31); [1970] Ch Com Rep 30 (para 84)
[18] See paras 18.15–18.18 below
[19] CA 1993, s 27(1)
[20] ibid, s 27(2)
[21] ibid, s 27(2)(a) and (b)
[22] ibid, s 27(3)
[23] ibid, s 27(4)

comprises 'charity proceedings' and requires the consent of the Commissioners or (if they refuse to consent) that of a judge of the Chancery Division.[24]

The Charity Commissioners state that they need firm evidence that the making of an *ex gratia* payment is justified.[25] Where the proposed payment is to be made out of property left to charity under a will, the Commissioners require the trustees to state the facts of the case as clearly as possible and to provide a copy of the will and probate. They also require the trustees to provide evidence to show that the will does not dispose of the testator's estate in the manner in which the testator really intended, and evidence to show why the testator was prevented from giving effect to his real intention. The Commissioners point out that it will not be enough to indicate that the testator expressed a wish to benefit someone if he had the opportunity to give effect to his wish but did nothing about it.[26] **18.16**

The Charity Commissioners require clear and impartial evidence. A statement by someone who claims he is morally entitled to a proportion of the estate would therefore not normally suffice on its own. Statements under oath are not normally necessary, but if the strongest evidence available can be given only by someone who has an interest in the outcome of the application, the Commissioners consider that a statutory declaration may be appropriate. The Commissioners suggest that other evidence might include: statements or statutory declarations by independent persons as to the testator's true intentions; statements in writing by the testator himself, expressing his true intentions; and the actions of the person to whom the *ex gratia* payment is proposed to be made, for example, someone who has been promised a legacy by the testator might make commitments or take actions on the strength of that promise.[27] **18.17**

The Charity Commissioners will ask the trustees for further information or evidence if they believe it to be necessary to enable them to come to a decision. Any order authorizing a payment should be preserved as evidence that the *ex gratia* payment was made with the Commissioners' authority, and for production on request to the charity's auditor or independent examiner.[28] **18.18**

---

[24] ibid, s 33(2), (5)
[25] See the Charity Commissioners' explanatory leaflet, *Ex Gratia Payments by Charities* CC7 (1995), 4
[26] ibid
[27] ibid
[28] ibid, 5

PART VI

CHARITABLE GIVING AND
FUND-RAISING

19

CHARITABLE GIVING AND TAXATION

This chapter examines the restrictions on giving to charity by individuals, **19.01** trustees, and companies, and examines the fiscal consequences of charitable giving. Value added tax is afforded separate treatment at the end of the chapter, since its application does not distinguish between individual and corporate donors.

A. Individual giving

(1) Potential pitfalls

Capacity to give

An adult of sound mind has unlimited capacity to enter into all transactions, in- **19.02** cluding the making of gifts to charity or the creation of charitable trusts. A minor (that is, a person under the age of eighteen[1]) cannot hold a legal estate in land,[2] and so cannot dispose of the legal title to land to charity. A minor cannot generally make a valid will of any property, and so cannot make a testamentary gift to charity.[3]

If a person is incapable, by reason of mental disorder, of managing and adminis- **19.03** tering his affairs ('a patient' under the Mental Health Act 1983) and a receiver has

---

[1] Family Law Reform Act 1969, ss 1–2
[2] LPA 1925, s 1(6)
[3] Wills Act 1837, s 7; but a minor on actual military service or a seaman being at sea can make a valid will (and so a testamentary gift to charity): ibid, s 11; Wills (Soldiers and Sailors) Act 1918, ss 1–3

been appointed, it is generally thought that any purported inter vivos disposition by him (including, therefore, a gift to charity) is void.[4] But such a person may make a valid will (which may therefore comprise or include a gift to charity) during a lucid interval.[5]

Preparation of will

19.04   A testator is said to have *animus testandi* if he has the requisite mental capacity,[6] the intention to make a will,[7] and, in making it, exercises a genuine free choice; a will is not valid if the testator lacks *animus testandi*. If the will is prepared by a beneficiary, the court will require evidence that the testator knew and approved of its contents.[8] Suspicion will also be cast on a will if the instructions for it were made through a third party.[9] Another ground of invalidity of a will is the presence of undue influence; although such influence is not presumed, and the burden of proving it is on the person alleging it.[10]

19.05   Some charities become involved in meeting the costs of drawing up a testator's will, either because this is in the course of carrying out their purposes (as where a charity which cares for the sick pays for the cost of drawing up the will of one of its patients) or because they offer this service in a fund-raising campaign. The charity involved may, in some instances, itself be given a legacy under that will. In such circumstances, those who suffer by reason of the legacy to charity (generally the next of kin or those who would have been entitled under an earlier will) may try to allege that the will should be set aside on one or more of the foregoing grounds. Allegations of undue influence or want of knowledge and approval might well be made, and surrounding circumstances may lend weight to them (as where the testator is dependent on the charity for his welfare). If charities pay the costs of preparing testators' wills, it is important that they, as well as the solicitors involved, take particular care to ensure that any such allegations cannot be sustained.

19.06   The Charity Commissioners have produced 'best practice' guidance on this matter.[11] They recommend strongly that charity employees should not become involved in drafting a will, so that there can be no suspicion if the charity is a legatee. More generally, they recommend that charity trustees considering becoming

---

[4]   *Re Walker* [1905] 1 Ch 160 (CA); *Re Marshall* [1920] 1 Ch 284
[5]   *Re Beaney* [1978] 1 WLR 770
[6]   *Banks v Goodfellow* (1870) LR 5 QB 549, 567 (Cockburn CJ)
[7]   *Lister v Smith* (1868) 3 Sw & Tr 282, 288
[8]   *Wintle v Nye* [1959] 1 All ER 552
[9]   *Re Ticehurst* The Times, 6 Mar 1973
[10]   *Low v Guthrie* [1909] AC 278
[11]   Charity Commission, *Paying for wills with charity funds*, guidance notes (Oct 1999). See further Institute of Charity Fundraising Managers, *Legacy Fundraising: Code of Practice* (ICFM, 1999); S Wilberforce (ed), *Legacy Fundraising* (Charities Aid Foundation, 1998)

involved with the payment of the preparation of wills should consider three matters. First, they should consider the difficulty of measuring the benefit obtained by the charity against the costs incurred in having the will prepared. The Commissioners recommend that charities either develop a measuring tool, or else agree only to pay the costs up to an agreed maximum. Secondly, the charity trustees should be aware of the possibility of legal challenge to any legacy they receive. Thirdly, they should be aware of the danger of giving the impression that the charity is over-resourced or lavish with its resources.

In order to avoid the possibility of a successful legal challenge, the Charity Commissioners suggest that charity trustees might reasonably ensure:[12] **19.07**

(a) that written clarification is given to the testator and to the solicitor explaining the basis upon which the charity is offering to meet the cost of preparation of the will and the procedure to be followed;

(b) that the solicitor makes it clear to all that he or she is acting exclusively in the interests of the testator, even though the costs are to be borne by the charity;

(c) that the solicitor takes instructions directly from the testator rather than from the charity (and preferably obtains confirmation of the instructions in writing); and

(d) that before the will is executed, the solicitor is satisfied that the testator fully understands the effect of the will, that it reflects his or her intentions, and that this is recorded.

The Charity Commissioners would not expect a solicitor to suggest to the testator that any particular charity should benefit under the will, and would expect a solicitor to advise adequate provision for the testator's family and dependants.[13] They also suggest that charities might prepare checklists for the solicitor to follow, and for signature by the testator;[14] and that they might seek confirmation from the solicitor that the testator was not subject to undue influence, fully understood and intended the contents of the will, and that the charges made (indirectly) to the charity correspond to the normal charges for preparing a will.[15]

The Charity Commissioners also recommend that the charity should suggest that **19.08**
the individual's own solicitor is instructed to prepare the will,[16] and that the charity should avoid any contractual relationship between itself and the solicitor.[17] The solicitor's relationship with the testator must be a normal professional one;

---

[12] Charity Commission, *Paying for wills with charity funds*, guidance notes (Oct 1999) para 14
[13] ibid, para 15
[14] ibid, para 16
[15] ibid, para 17
[16] ibid, para 18
[17] ibid, para 20

the instructions for the will should be taken from the testator alone, and it is the testator who should be primarily liable for the fees involved. As a result, the charity will have no right to information about the contents of the will (including therefore information about whether it has been given any legacy) unless the testator authorizes the solicitor to inform the charity.[18]

19.09 If a client is referred to a solicitor by a third party, the solicitor can agree to be paid by the third party, provided the referral arrangements comply with the Solicitors' Introduction and Referral Code 1990.[19]

Family provision legislation

19.10 An individual is generally free of any legal constraints on making gifts to charities or for charitable purposes. The only legal restraint is the restriction on testamentary freedom contained in the Inheritance (Provision for Family and Dependants) Act 1975.[20] If a testator who dies domiciled in England and Wales does not, by his will or under the intestacy rules, or a combination of them, make reasonable financial provision for a spouse and certain other persons,[21] they have a right to apply to the court under that Act for reasonable financial provision to be made for them.[22] The persons who may apply are a spouse, a former spouse who has not remarried, a child, and certain other dependants.[23] The court's exercise of this power overrides the dispositions made by the will or under the intestacy rules.

19.11 The details of this legislation are beyond this scope of this book; but it should be borne in mind when preparing a will for a testator who has dependants but chooses to leave all or most of his estate to charity. A gift to charity by will receives no preferential treatment in this regard over other testamentary gifts. For example, in *Millward v Shenton*,[24] a case on the earlier family provision legislation, the testatrix, who died in 1970, by her will left her entire estate, valued at a little over £3,000, to a named cancer charity. She did, however, have an invalid son, who was entirely dependent on state assistance, and he applied to the court for reasonable financial provision to be made for him out of the estate. In the circumstances, the Court of Appeal decided that, after the payment of the costs of administration, he should be awarded a lump sum equal to 11/12 of the remainder of the estate, the other 1/12 going to the charity.[25]

---

[18] Charity Commission, *Paying for wills with charity funds*, guidance notes (Oct 1999), para 21
[19] ibid, paras 22–3
[20] As amended by Law Reform (Succession) Act 1995
[21] Inheritance (Provision for Family and Dependants) Act 1975, s 1(1)
[22] ibid, s 2
[23] ibid, s 1(1)(a)–(e)
[24] [1972] 2 All ER 1025 (CA)
[25] Other illustrative cases are *Re Parkinson* [1969] 1 Ch 283 (where provision for the testator's widow was at the expense of the RSPCA); and *Re Besterman* [1984] Ch 458 (CA) (where the testator had left virtually his entire estate of some £1.4 million to the University of Oxford; this was

(2) Income tax

Gift Aid

Introduction

Tax relief for one-off donations by individuals to charity (commonly called Gift **19.12**
Aid) was introduced in the Finance Act 1990 for gifts made on or after 1 October
1990 which comprise qualifying donations.[26] It is available only for gifts of
money; gifts of chattels are not eligible.[27] Before 6 April 2000, Gift Aid had been
available only on a gift of a sum of not less than £250;[28] but since that date such
restriction has been abolished.[29] A gift of any sum, no matter how small, is now eligible for Gift Aid, provided it meets the other statutory requirements. Gift Aid is
therefore now of the utmost importance.

Until 6 April 2000, a separate form of tax relief was available to individuals on **19.13**
payments made to charity under a deed of covenant, provided the payment
ranked as a 'covenanted payment to charity';[30] but such relief was abolished in respect of covenanted payments by individuals falling to be made by individuals
after 5 April 2000.[31] The abolition of this form of relief does not, of course, preclude individuals from entering into deeds of covenant with charities after that
date. Tax relief on a payment made under a deed of covenant, however, is now provided under Gift Aid instead, so that the payment must be a qualifying donation
for the purposes of Gift Aid. The deed of covenant retains the advantage for the
charity that the covenantor binds himself to make payments over a period of years,
which to some extent enables the charity to make plans on the basis of estimated
future income. In practice, however, charities rarely enforce such covenants, and
a reasonably assured income stream can be almost as well assured through donations made by standing order or direct debit. Nevertheless, this latest extension of
Gift Aid is unlikely to render the use of deeds of covenant obsolete.[32] A charity
might feel more confident about entering into longer-term financial obligations if

---

reduced by the financial provision of a lump sum which the first-instance judge made for his widow,
such provision being increased by the Court of Appeal to £378,000)

[26] FA 1990, s 25. Equivalent tax relief for one-off donations by companies to charity (also called
'qualifying donations') was introduced at the same time (ibid, s 26), and is now contained in ICTA
1988, s 339(1)–(4). See further below, paras 19.81–19.84

[27] For a suggested widening of the scope of Gift Aid, including its extension to gifts of chattels,
see R Venables, 'Gift Aid Relief for Gifts in Kind' (1995–6) 3 CL & PR 139

[28] The minimum sum of £250, which was abolished from 6 Apr 2000, had been substituted for
the original sum of £400 by FA 1993, s 67(2), (4), in respect of gifts made after 15 Mar 1993. There
had also been a maximum sum eligible for Gift Aid, but this ceiling had been removed in respect of
gifts made after 18 Mar 1991 by FA 1991, s 71(5), (6)

[29] FA 2000, s 39(3)(a), repealing FA 1990, s 25(2)(g)

[30] ICTA 1988, s 347A(2)(b), (7), (8) (repealed in relation to covenanted payments falling to be
made by individuals after 5 Apr 2000): FA 2000, s 41(2), (9)(a)

[31] FA 2000, s 41(9)(a)

[32] See J Smith & S Macdonald, 'Wither the Deed of Covenant?!' (2000) 6 CL & PR 211

promises of regular donations are backed up by deeds of covenant. The deed of covenant is also likely to remain the usual means by which a charity's trading subsidiary returns its profits to the parent charity.[33] Finally, members of religious orders who are under a vow of poverty will no doubt continue to use the deed of covenant as the means of passing their income to the order.[34]

Qualifying donation

19.14 For a gift to charity[35] by an individual[36] to be eligible for Gift Aid, it must be a qualifying donation, which means a payment of a sum of money which is not subject to a condition as to repayment, which is not a sum paid under the payroll deduction scheme,[37] and in respect of which the donor gives an appropriate certificate to the charity.[38] In addition, the donation must not be part of an arrangement involving an acquisition of property by the charity from the donor or a person connected with him,[39] and neither the donor nor a person connected with him may receive any benefit in connection with the donation which exceeds the statutory limit.[40] The limit of the benefit is:[41]

(a) 25% of the amount of a gift which does not exceed £100;
(b) £25, if the amount of a gift exceeds £100 but not £1000;
(c) 2.5% of the amount of a gift which exceeds £1,000.

19.15 The value of the benefit or the amount of the gift is adjusted (that is, annualized) for a series of gifts made, or benefits received[42] (or which the donor has a right to receive[43]), at intervals of less than twelve months.[44] If more than one benefit is received by the donor or a person connected with him, the relevant value of the benefit is the aggregate of all the benefits so received.[45] The following illustration of the intended operation of these rules is based upon guidance produced by the Inland Revenue:[46]

> A taxpayer makes a single payment of £120 to a charity, in consequence of which she receives the right to receive six free monthly magazines worth £2.50 each. The benefit of the right to receive the magazines is therefore worth £15 (£2.50 × 6).

---

[33] See further, ch 20, paras 20.31–20.34
[34] J Smith & S Macdonald, 'Wither the Deed of Covenant?!' (2000) 6 CL & PR 211, 217
[35] For this purpose, 'charity' has the same meaning as in ICTA 1988, s 506, and includes each of the bodies mentioned in s 507 of that Act: FA 1990, s 25(12)(a)
[36] For an equivalent form of Gift Aid by companies, see below, paras 19.81–19.84
[37] FA 1990, s 25(2)(a), (b), (d)
[38] ibid, s 25(2)(c), as amended by FA 2000, s 39(2)
[39] The meaning of 'connected person' is that contained in ICTA 1988, s 839: FA 1990, s 25(11)
[40] FA 1990, s 25(2)(e)
[41] FA 1990, s 25(5A), inserted by FA 2000, s 39(5). See also FA 1990, s 25(4), (5)
[42] FA 1990, s 25(5B)(b), inserted by FA 2000, s 39(5)
[43] FA 1990, s 25(5B)(a), inserted by FA 2000, s 39(5)
[44] FA 1990, s 25(5B), (5C), (5D), inserted by FA 2000, s 39(5)
[45] FA 1990, s 25(4)(b)
[46] Inland Revenue, 'Getting Britain Giving: Inland Revenue Guidance Note for Charities' (Mar 2000), para 7.16, Example 3

The right to receive the magazines is a right to receive the benefits at intervals over a period of less than twelve months,[47] so annualizing applies. The statutory limit on the benefit is therefore applied by reference to the annual amount of the donation (£120 × 12 ÷ 6 = £240) and the annual value of the right to receive the magazines (£2.50 × 12 = £30). As the latter figure exceeds the limit of £25 (that is, the limit for donations which exceed £100 but not £1,000), the donation fails the relevant value test and so cannot qualify as a Gift Aid donation.

A benefit of any right of admission[48] to view property, or to observe wildlife, of a charity whose sole or main purpose is the preservation of property, or the conservation of wildlife, for the public benefit, is to be disregarded in determining whether a gift to such a charity is a qualifying donation.[49] **19.16**

A further requirement for a qualifying donation is that either:[50] **19.17**

(i) at the time the gift is made, the donor is resident in the United Kingdom or performs duties[51] which by virtue of section 132(4)(a) of the Taxes Act 1988 (Crown employees serving overseas) are treated as being performed in the United Kingdom; or
(ii) the grossed up amount of the gift would, if in fact made, be payable out of profits or gains brought into charge to income tax or capital gains tax.

Declaration

For a payment to comprise a qualifying donation for Gift Aid, a final requirement is that the donor must give an appropriate declaration to the charity,[52] this being a declaration given in such manner, and containing such information and statements, as may be prescribed by the Board of the Inland Revenue.[53] The effect of this requirement is that Gift Aid is not available where the donor does not provide a declaration, for example where he declines to do so, or places a donation in a collection box anonymously. **19.18**

The Inland Revenue allow a declaration to be made before, after, or at the time that, the donation is made.[54] A post-donation declaration is subject only to the **19.19**

---

[47] FA 1990, s 25(5B)(a)

[48] 'Right of admission' refers to admission of the person making the gift (or any member of his family who may be admitted because of the gift) either free of the charges normally payable for admission by members of the public, or on payment of a reduced charge: FA 1990, s 25(5G), inserted by FA 2000, s 39(5)

[49] FA 1990, s 25(5E), (5F), (5G), inserted by FA 2000, s 39(5). This disregard applies only if the opportunity to make gifts which attract such a right is available to members of the public: FA 1990, s 25(5E)

[50] FA 1990, s 25(2)(i) & (ii), substituted by FA 2000, s 39(3)(c)

[51] The duties to which reference is made are contained in ICTA 1988, s 132(4)(a)

[52] FA 1990, s 25(1)(c). This replaces the previous requirement of a certificate, which was both less flexible and more complicated

[53] FA 1990, s 25(3), as substituted by FA 2000, s 39(4). See Donations to Charity by Individuals (Appropriate Declarations) Regulations 2000, SI 2000/2074

[54] Inland Revenue, 'Getting Britain Giving: Inland Revenue Guidance Note for Charities', (Mar 2000), para 5.2

usual time-limits (normally six years) for the recovery of tax.[55] A single declaration may cover one or more donations.[56] The declaration may be made in writing, orally, or by electronic communication.[57] Posted, faxed, or emailed declarations are therefore acceptable, as is a declaration made by telephone.[58]

19.20 The Regulations require a Gift Aid declaration to contain the donor's name and address, the charity's name, a description of the donations to which the declaration relates, and a declaration that the donations are to be treated as qualifying donations for the purposes of section 25 of the Finance Act 1990 (that is, as Gift Aid donations).[59] There is no requirement for a declaration to contain the donor's signature.[60] Where the declaration is given in writing, it must also contain a note explaining the requirement that the donor must pay an amount of income tax or capital gains tax equal to the tax deducted from the donation.[61] In the case of a written declaration, the information may be pre-printed on the declaration form; in the case of an oral declaration, the information may be recited to the donor, who may be then asked merely to confirm it.[62]

19.21 The Regulations require oral declarations to be supported by written records if they are to be effective.[63] A charity which receives an oral declaration must send the donor a written record showing:[64]

> (i) all the details provided by the donor in his or her oral declaration;
> (ii) a note explaining the requirement that the donor must pay an amount of income tax or capital gains tax equal to the tax deducted from his or her donation;
> (iii) a note explaining the donor's entitlement to cancel the declaration retrospectively;[65]

---

[55] Inland Revenue, 'Getting Britain Giving: Inland Revenue Guidance Note for Charities' (Mar 2000), para 5.2

[56] ibid

[57] Donations to Charity by Individuals (Appropriate Declarations) Regulations 2000, SI 2000/2074, reg 3

[58] Inland Revenue, 'Getting Britain Giving: Inland Revenue Guidance Note for Charities, (Mar 2000), para 5.2

[59] Donations to Charity by Individuals (Appropriate Declarations) Regulations 2000, SI 2000/2074, reg 4(1)(a)–(d). Inland Revenue, 'Getting Britain Giving: Inland Revenue Guidance Note for Charities', (Mar 2000), contains examples of forms of wording which a charity might choose (ibid, ch 5), and a model Gift Aid declaration (ibid, App)

[60] Inland Revenue, 'Getting Britain Giving: Inland Revenue Guidance Note for Charities', (Mar 2000), para 5.7

[61] Donations to Charity by Individuals (Appropriate Declarations) Regulations 2000, SI 2000/2074, reg 4(1)(e)

[62] Inland Revenue, 'Getting Britain Giving: Inland Revenue Guidance Note for Charities', (Mar 2000), para 5.8

[63] Donations to Charity by Individuals (Appropriate Declarations) Regulations 2000, SI 2000/2074, regs 5 & 6

[64] Inland Revenue, 'Getting Britain Giving: Inland Revenue Guidance Note for Charities', (Mar 2000), para 5.9, explaining the requirements now contained in Donations to Charity by Individuals (Appropriate Declarations) Regulations 2000, SI 2000/2074, reg 5

[65] Discussed below, paras 19.21

(iv) the date on which the donor gave the charity the declaration;

(v) the date on which the charity sent the written record to the donor.

A donor who has made a written declaration may cancel it at any time;[66] cancellation is effected by notifying the charity by any form of communication[67]—charities should keep a record of cancellations, including the date of the donor's notification.[68] If a donor who has made an oral declaration cancels it within thirty days of the charity's sending the written record, the cancellation operates retrospectively,[69] so that the charity will lose Gift Aid even on donations already made.[70] Subject to this, a cancellation of a declaration (whether oral or in writing) has effect only in relation to any donation which the charity has not yet received.[71]

As payments to charity made under deed of covenant have been brought within **19.22** Gift Aid, such payments made under covenants entered into after 5 April 2000 must be supported by a declaration. As a transitional measure, the Inland Revenue does not require a Gift Aid declaration in respect of payments which fall due on or after 6 April 2000 under covenants entered into before that date.[72] If a payment under a covenant is made on or after 6 April 2000 but fell due before that date, the previous rules relating to covenanted payments to charity will apply to it.[73]

Tax treatment

Where a donor makes a qualifying donation, the gift is treated (both for income **19.23** tax and capital gains tax purposes) as if it had been made after deduction of income tax at the basic rate. A donor who pays higher-rate tax can claim relief for the donation against either income tax or (since 6 April 2000) against capital gains tax. In order to make Gift Aid attractive to lower-rate taxpayers, a donor is able to meet basic rate tax that the charity reclaims on his donation with an equivalent amount of tax paid on his income or capital gains, whether at the basic or lower rate.[74]

In the hands of the recipient charity, a Gift Aid payment is treated for tax purposes **19.24** as the receipt, under deduction of tax at the basic rate, of an annual payment of an

---

[66] Donations to Charity by Individuals (Appropriate Declarations) Regulations 2000, SI 2000/2074, reg 7(3)

[67] ibid

[68] Inland Revenue, 'Getting Britain Giving: Inland Revenue Guidance Note for Charities, (Mar 2000), para 5.11

[69] Donations to Charity by Individuals (Appropriate Declarations) Regulations 2000, SI 2000/2074, regs 5(3), 6(1) & (4)

[70] Inland Revenue, 'Getting Britain Giving: Inland Revenue Guidance Note for Charities', (Mar 2000), para 5.13

[71] ibid, para 5.12

[72] ibid, para 5.28

[73] ibid, para 4.2

[74] FA 1990, s 25(6)–(9A), substituted by FA 2000, s 39(6)

amount equal to the grossed up amount of the gift.[75] The effect is that the charity is entitled to reclaim the basic rate tax from the Inland Revenue.

Millennium Gift Aid (gifts of money for relief in poor countries)

19.25 In the Finance Act 1998,[76] when the minimum sum entitled to tax relief under Gift Aid was £250, a special form of Gift Aid, popularly called Millennium Gift Aid, was introduced, under which the amount that an individual had to pay to charity for the gift to fall within Gift Aid was reduced to £100, provided the Inland Revenue was notified. For reasons explained below,[77] Millennium Gift Aid survives the widening of Gift Aid generally, but it has, from its inception, been limited by time. To qualify for Millennium Gift Aid, the gift must be made in the period beginning on 31 July 1998 and ending on 31 December 2000, and the circumstances must give rise to a reasonable expectation that the sum given will be applied for, or in connection with, one or more specified purposes.[78]

19.26 The specified purposes are:[79]

(a) the relief of poverty in any one or more countries or territories designated for the purposes of this paragraph; and
(b) the advancement of education in any one or more designated countries or territories, and
(c) the relief of poverty in the case of persons from any country or territory designated for the purposes of this paragraph who are refugees or who have suffered displacement as a result of organised intimidation or oppression or of war or other armed conflict.

A country or territory is a designated country or territory for the purpose of paragraphs (a), (b), or (c) if it is designated as such by an order made for those purposes by the Treasury, or if it is of a description specified in an order so made,[80]

and a description specified in such an order may be expressed by reference to the opinion of any person so specified or by reference to the contents from time to time of a document prepared by a person so specified.

19.27 The abolition of the £250 minimum for Gift Aid payments made by individuals after 5 April 2000 effectively renders the Millennium Gift Aid scheme redundant in respect of payments made after that date. The scheme continues to apply to gifts made before 1 January 2001, however, because of the principle of aggregation with earlier payments. Where a payment of less than £100 was made by an

---

[75] FA 1990, s 25(10)
[76] FA 1998, s 48
[77] See para 19.27
[78] FA 1998, s 48, as amended by FA 1999, s 56, in relation to gifts made on or after 6 Apr 1999, and by FA 2000, s 42
[79] FA 1998, s 48(2), as amended by FA 1999, s 56(3), including the addition of para (c)
[80] FA 1998, s 48(9), as amended by FA 1999, s 56(4)

individual to a charity before 6 April 2000, it can be aggregated with later gifts by that individual to the same charity.[81] Where the aggregated amount is £100 or more, Millennium Gift Aid can be claimed on the entire gift, which is treated as being made at the time of the making of the last.[82] The individual must give an appropriate declaration in relation to that aggregate to the charity.[83]

Payroll deduction

The payroll deduction scheme (which was introduced in 1987[84]) enables employees to make regular payments for the benefit of charity by way of deductions from their salary or wages.[85] There used to be a ceiling on the amounts which could be deducted under the scheme in any one year of assessment, but this was abolished from 6 April 2000.[86] The tax advantage for an employee who is in a payroll deduction scheme is that sums he has effectively paid under the scheme are deductible expenses in calculating his liability to income tax under Schedule E of the Income and Corporation Taxes Act 1988. **19.28**

Payroll deduction applies only if the sums are withheld in accordance with a scheme which is (or is of a kind) approved by the Commissioners of Inland Revenue (the Board). The setting up of a scheme is entirely voluntary in that an employer and each individual employee can choose whether to participate in it or not. Under a scheme, a participating employer deducts an agreed amount from the salary or wage of an employee who has joined. The sums withheld by the employer must constitute gifts by the employee to the charity or charities concerned, and must fulfil any conditions set out in the terms of the scheme.[87] The employer must pay sums so withheld to an agent approved by the Board, and the agent must pay them to a charity or charities.[88] The agent may itself be a charity.[89] **19.29**

For three years from 6 April 2000, the sums paid to charities under payroll deduction schemes are being supplemented by an additional 10 per cent payable out **19.30**

---

[81] FA 1998, s 48(4), as amended by FA 2000, s 42(2)
[82] ibid
[83] ibid
[84] By FA 1986, ss 27–8. Provision for such schemes is now contained in ICTA 1988, s 202, and in the Charitable Deductions (Approved Schemes) Regulations 1986, SI 1986/2211, as amended by the Charitable Deductions (Approved Schemes) (Amendment) Regulations 2000, SI 2000/759
[85] See R Singh, 'An assessment of a decade of payroll giving' (1996) 68 NLJ Charities Appeals Suppl 20
[86] FA 2000, s 38(7), repealing ICTA 1988, s 202(7). For the years of assessment from 1996–7 to 1999–2000 inclusive there had been a ceiling of £1,200: ICTA 1988, s 202(7), as substituted by FA 1998, s 109. The previous limit of £900 had applied from the year of assessment 1993–4: FA 1993, s 68
[87] ICTA 1988, s 202(6). The former additional requirement that the sums were not to be paid by the employee under a covenant has been abolished: FA 2000, s 38(5)
[88] For this purpose, 'charity' has the same meaning as in ICTA 1988, s 506, and includes the bodies mentioned in s 507 of that Act: ICTA 1988, s 202(11), as amended by FA 2000, s 38(5)
[89] Charitable Deductions (Approved Schemes) Regulations 1986, SI 1986/2211, reg 5

of public funds. The supplement must be paid to the charity by the agent, who is entitled to claim reimbursement from the Inland Revenue.[90]

19.31 The circumstances in which the Board may grant or withdraw approval of schemes (or kinds of schemes) or of agents are as prescribed by the Treasury in regulations.[91] The regulations set out what a scheme must provide in order to be approved,[92] and deal with the approval (and the withdrawal of approval) of agencies (including appeals against the Board's decision),[93] the return of information by the approved agency to the Board and the keeping of records,[94] the termination of employers' contracts,[95] and the duty of an employer to provide an employee on his leaving that employment with a statement of the total amount withheld in that tax year.[96]

Deductible expenditure of a trade, profession, or vocation

19.32 Money wholly and exclusively laid out for the purposes of a trade, profession, or vocation are deductible in computing the profits charged under Case I or Case II of Schedule D of the Income and Corporation Taxes Act 1988.[97] Such sums may include some gifts to charity of a revenue nature, including the expenses incurred in continuing to pay an employee whom the employer makes available to the charity on a temporary basis.[98] The principles applied are the same as those applicable in relation to corporation tax, and are discussed more fully in that context below.[99]

Gifts of certain articles by a person carrying on a trade, profession, or vocation

19.33 The Finance Act 1999 has reduced the tax disadvantages of certain gifts in kind to charity made by those carrying on a trade, profession, or vocation. From the point of view of the donor, there were two potential tax problems. First, it is a general rule of tax law that if a trader disposes of his stock-in-trade otherwise than in the course of trade, he is deemed to dispose of it at market value and must enter that figure as a trading receipt in his accounts.[100] The application of this rule naturally

---

[90] FA 2000, s 38(1), (2). Claims by agents for reimbursement must be made before 6 Apr 2004: ibid, s 38(6)

[91] Charitable Deductions (Approved Schemes) Regulations 1986, SI 1986/2211; as amended by the Charitable Deductions (Approved Schemes) (Amendment) Regulations 2000, SI 2000/759

[92] ibid, regs 3–4

[93] ibid, regs 5–8

[94] ibid, regs 9–12

[95] ibid, reg 13

[96] ibid, reg 14

[97] ICTA 1988, s 74(1)(a)

[98] ibid, s 86, as amended by FA 1999, s 57

[99] See paras 19.85–19.86

[100] This is the rule in *Sharkey v Wernher* (1955) 36 TC 275. The rule apparently has no application to those engaged in a profession: *Mason v Innes* (1967) 14 TC 326, so that, eg, an author could

tended to discourage traders from making gifts of trading stock to charity. Secondly, if a person carrying on a trade, profession, or vocation makes a gift of machinery or plant in respect of which he has obtained a capital allowance,[101] he must, under general principles, bring its disposal value into account.[102] The disposal value in respect of a gift is the open-market value at the time of the disposal;[103] and if this exceeds his qualifying expenditure for a chargeable period, he will have to pay a balancing charge.[104] Since this principle applied equally to gifts to charity, there could be a distinct disadvantage to businesses in making charitable donations of valuable machinery and plant.

These disincentives were initially removed in relation to gifts of specified articles to designated educational establishments.[105] More recently, they were removed in relation to specified gifts in kind to a charity for certain types of relief in designated poor countries.[106] They have now been removed entirely by the insertion of a new section 83A into the Income and Corporation Taxes Act 1988[107] in relation to specified gifts in kind to a charity made on or after the passing of the Finance Act 1999.[108] **19.34**

Section 83A applies where a person[109] carrying on a trade, profession, or vocation gives to a charity[110] an article which is either:[111] **19.35**

(a) . . . an article manufactured, or of a class or description sold, by the donor in the course of his trade; or

(b) . . . an article used by the donor in the course of his trade, profession or vocation which for the purposes of Part II of the 1990 Act[112] constitutes machinery or plant[113] used by him wholly or partly in the course of that trade, profession or vocation.

---

assign the copyright in his books to a charity by way of a gift without having to enter the market value as a receipt of his profession whilst still retaining the tax benefit of the deduction of expenses incurred in the creation of the copyright

[101] ie under Capital Allowances Act 1990, Pt II, esp ss 22–3, 27

[102] ibid, s 24(6)(c)(ii)

[103] ibid, s 26(1)(f)

[104] ibid, s 24(5)

[105] The current provision is ICTA 1988, s 84

[106] FA 1998, s 47, repealed by FA 1999, s 55(2)

[107] Inserted by FA 1999, s 55

[108] ie 27 July 1999

[109] The section therefore also applies to companies

[110] This means a charity for the purposes of ICTA 1988, s 506, ie, 'any body of persons or trust established for charitable purposes only': s 83A(1)(a). Gifts to the bodies listed in s 507(1) are also included: ibid, s 83A(1)(b)

[111] ibid, s 83A(2)

[112] ie Capital Allowances Act 1990

[113] There is no statutory definition in the Capital Allowances Act 1990 or elsewhere of 'machinery and plant'. It has been said to include 'whatever apparatus is used by a businessman for carrying on his business—not his stock-in-trade which he buys or makes for sale; but all goods and chattels, fixed or moveable [*sic*], live or dead, which he keeps for permanent employment in his business': *Yarmouth v France* (1887) 19 QBD 647, 658 (Lindley LJ). The purchase of law reports by a barrister is included: *Munby v Furlong* [1977] 2 All ER 953 (overruling *Daphne v Shaw* (1926) 11 TC 256)

Where such a gift is made,[114]

(a) no amount shall be required, in consequence of the donor's disposal of that article from trading stock, to be brought into account for the purposes of the Tax Acts[115] as a trading receipt of the donor; and
(b) section 24(6) of the 1990 Act[116] shall not require the donor to bring into account any disposal value in respect of the article for the purposes of that section.

If such relief has been given, and the donor or any person connected with him[117] has in any chargeable period received any benefit which is any way attributable to the gift, the donor is to be charged to tax in respect of that chargeable period on an amount equal to the value of that benefit.[118]

Gifts of shares and securities to charities

19.36   The Finance Act 2000[119] introduced a new tax relief for disposals to a charity by way of gift or at an undervalue of quoted shares and securities and of certain other types of investment. The new relief, which has been inserted into the Income and Corporation Taxes Act 1988 as section 587B, applies to disposals both by individuals and by companies, the latter being considered below.[120] The relief is additional to the existing relief for gifts to charity of shares, securities, and other assets for the purposes of capital gains tax.[121]

19.37   The relief on a disposal by an individual applies where, otherwise than by way of a bargain made at arm's length, an individual disposes of the whole of the beneficial interest in a qualifying investment to a charity[122] after 5 April 2000.[123] The relief is not, therefore, available on a disposal of only part of the beneficial interest, such as a disposal to the charity for a specified period of time only. A 'qualifying investment' means any of the following:[124]

(a) shares or securities which are listed or dealt in on a recognised stock exchange;
(b) units in an authorised unit trust;

---

[114]   ICTA 1988, s 83A(3)
[115]   ie ICTA 1988 and all other enactments relating to income tax: ibid, s 831(1) & (2)
[116]   ie Capital Allowances Act 1990
[117]   The definition of 'connected person' in ICTA 1988, s 839 applies for this purpose: s 83A(5)
[118]   ibid, s 83A(4). The charge to tax is under Cases I or II or Schedule D, or, if the donor is not chargeable to tax under either of those Cases for that chargeable period, under Case VI of Schedule D: ibid
[119]   FA 2000, s 43, inserting new s 587B into ICTA 1988
[120]   See below, paras 19.88–19.89
[121]   See below, paras 19.40–19.42 and 19.47
[122]   ICTA 1988, s 587B(1). In this section, 'charity' has the same meaning as in s 506, and includes each of the bodies mentioned in s 507(1): ibid, s 587B(9)
[123]   FA 2000, s 43(3)(a)
[124]   ICTA 1988, s 587B(9). If the disponor is unsure whether shares or securities qualify for the scheme, advice is obtainable from the Inland Revenue's Financial Intermediaries and Claims Office (FICO): see Inland Revenue, 'Getting Britain Giving: Inland Revenue Guidance Note for Charities', (Mar 2000), para 10.8

(c) shares in an open-ended investment company; and

(d) an interest in an offshore fund.

On a claim to the Board, the disponor is entitled to a deduction in calculating his total income tax for the year of assessment in which the disposal is made,[125] so the disponor can claim relief at his top rate of tax. The deduction is of 'the relevant amount'.[126]

Where the disposal is a gift, the deduction is of the market value of the qualifying investment[127] at the time when the disposal is made[128] together with the disponor's incidental costs of disposal.[129] The disponor therefore obtains full relief. **19.38**

Where the disposal is at undervalue, the basic principle is that the disponor is entitled to a deduction for the market value of the investments less the value of the consideration for the disposal.[130] The disponor is entitled to an additional deduction for his incidental costs of disposal only if the disposal consideration is less than the notional consideration would be were the investments treated as being disposed of on a 'no gain, no loss' basis.[131] Where the disponor or a person connected with him[132] receives one or more benefits in consequence of making the disposal, the relevant amount is reduced by the value of that benefit, or the aggregate value of those benefits.[133] **19.39**

Where a disponor obtains relief under section 587B, and the disposal comprises a gift to charity for capital gains tax purposes,[134] the charity's base cost for capital gains tax is reduced by a corresponding amount from what it would have been on a disposal on a 'no gain, no loss' basis.[135] If the amount of the reduction exceeds the latter figure, the charity's base cost is treated as nil.[136] **19.40**

The operation of the foregoing principles may be illustrated by the following example: **19.41**

---

[125] ibid, s 587B(2)(a)(i)

[126] ibid, s 587B(2)(a)

[127] The market value is to be determined for the purposes of s 587B as for the purposes of TCGA 1992, except in relation to certain offshore funds: ICTA 1988, s 587B(10), (11)

[128] ICTA 1988, s 587B(4)(a)

[129] ibid, s 587B(6). The incidental costs of making the disposal are to be construed in accordance with TCGA 1992, s 38(2): ICTA 1988, s 587B(9)

[130] ibid, s 587B(4)(b)

[131] ie by virtue of TCGA 1992, s 257(2)(a): ICTA 1988, s 587B(7)(a). For this purpose, TCGA 1992, s 48 (consideration due after time of disposal) applies in relation to the computation of the relevant amount as it applies in relation to the computation of a gain: ICTA 1988, s 587B(7)(b)

[132] The definition of 'connected persons' in ICTA 1988, s 839, applies for this purpose

[133] ibid, s 587B(5)

[134] ie within TCGA 1992, s 257(2)

[135] ICTA 1988, s 587B(3)

[136] ibid, s 587B(3)(b)

A taxpayer acquired for £20,000 in 1999 shares that comprise a qualifying investment. He disposes of them to a charity in the tax year 2000–1 when their market value is £40,000, incurring incidental disposal costs of £400.

(1) If the disposal is by way of gift, the taxpayer is entitled to a deduction from total income tax of £40,400. For capital gains tax purposes, the disposal is a gift to charity within section 257(2) of the Taxation of Chargeable Gains Act 1992, under which the charity would otherwise be treated as acquiring the asset on a 'no gain, no loss' basis, that is at a base cost of £20,000. However, since this is a disposal within that sub-section, under which the market value and disposal costs exceed such base cost, the charity's acquisition cost is treated as nil: section 587B(3) of the Income and Corporation Taxes Act 1988.

(2) If, instead, the disposal is by way of a sale at an undervalue, being for a consideration of £30,000, otherwise than by a bargain made at arm's length, the taxpayer is entitled to a deduction from total income tax of £10,000 (that is, market value of £40,000 less consideration of £30,000). The taxpayer does not, in this instance, receive an additional deduction for his disposal costs since the shares are disposed of for more than £20,000, that is, for more than the notional consideration which would result in a disposal on a 'no gain, no loss' basis.

(3) If, however, the taxpayer had sold his shares to the charity for less than the notional 'no gain, no loss' consideration of £20,000, he would have been entitled to an additional deduction for his disposal costs. If, for instance, he had sold the shares to the charity for £15,000, incurring disposal costs of £150, he would have been entitled to a deduction from total income of £25,150. This would have been calculated as follows: from market value of £40,000 deduct consideration of £15,000, leaving £25,000. To this, add incidental disposal costs of £150.

19.42 A practical application of this new relief for gifts of shares and securities to charity is that it provides a method by which donors can retain the entire benefit of tax deduction for themselves, instead (as under Gift Aid[137]) of effectively passing on the benefit of basic rate tax saving to the charity. If a substantial sum is to be given, shares to this amount could be bought by the donor and given to the charity, which immediately sells them. The effect is that, rather than the charity receiving the benefit of the basic rate tax as an addition to the donor's gift, the donor is able to deduct the full value of his gift from his taxable income for that year.

Gifts to charity from settlor-interested trusts

19.43 Chapter 1A of Part XV of the Income and Corporation Taxes Act 1988 contains provisions which, in certain circumstances, deem the income arising under a settlement to be the income of the settlor and not that of any other person. Chapter 1A applies to settlements under which the settlor or the settlor's spouse retains an interest,[138] and to settlements under which, during the life of the settlor, income

---

137 See above, paras 19.23–19.24
138 ICTA 1988, s 660A

arising under the settlement is paid to or for the benefit of an unmarried minor child of the settlor.[139] A relief introduced by section 44 of the Finance Act 2000 provides, however, that Chapter 1A[140] does not apply to any qualifying income which arises after 5 April 2000[141] under a trust whose trustees are resident[142] in the United Kingdom (a UK trust) if:[143]

(a) it is given by the trustees to a charity [144] in the year of assessment in which it arises; or

(b) it is income to which a charity is entitled under the terms of the trust.

For the purposes of this relief, 'qualifying income' means:[145]

(i) income which is to be accumulated;

(ii) income which is payable at the discretion of the trustees or any other person (whether or not the trustees have power to accumulate it); or

(iii) income which (before being distributed) is income of any person other than the trustees.

If in any year of assessment the income arising to a UK trust includes qualifying and non-qualifying income, both the amount of income entitled to the relief and any management expenses for that year are to be apportioned between such income rateably.[146]

Loans to charities

The Finance Act 2000 provides that, in Chapter 1A of Part XV of the Income and Corporation Taxes Act 1988, 'settlement' does not include any arrangement so far as it consists of a loan of money made by an individual to a charity[147] either for no consideration or for a consideration which consists only of interest.[148] This provision has effect in relation to income arising after 5 April 2000 on loans whenever made.[149]

19.44

---

139 ibid, s 660B

140 For the purposes of FA 2000, s 44, the reference to Ch 1A includes a reference to that chapter as it has effect by virtue of s 660E of that Act (application to settlements by two or more settlors): FA 2000, s 44(5)

141 FA 2000, s 44(6)

142 For this purpose, 'resident', in relation to the trustees of a trust, is to be construed in accordance with FA 1989, s 110: FA 2000, s 44(5)

143 FA 2000, s 44(1)

144 In this section, 'charity' has the same meaning as in ICTA 1988, s 506, and includes each of the bodies mentioned in s 507 of that Act: FA 2000, s 44(5)

145 FA 2000, s 44(5)

146 ibid, ss 44(2), (4)

147 For this purpose, 'charity' has the same meaning as in FA 2000, s 44: ibid, s 45(2). For discussion of FA 2000, s 44, see above, para 19.43

148 FA 2000, s 45(1)

149 ibid, s 45(3)

(3) Capital gains tax

19.45 Under ordinary principles of capital gains tax, tax is charged on the gain accruing to a person on the disposal of an asset.[150] If a taxpayer makes a disposal by way of gift, he is normally treated as disposing of the asset for a sum equal to its market value, but is permitted to make various deductions from that sum in order to compute his gain,[151] the most important of which in practice are likely to be his acquisition cost and any expenditure he has incurred on the asset. The value at which the disposal is treated as being made might for convenience be called the disponor's base cost. There is also a system of taper relief which reduces the percentage of the gain chargeable according to the number of years the asset has been held.[152] The first £7,200 of an individual's capital gains each tax year are exempt;[153] but any gains made in excess of this are taxed at his marginal rate of income tax.[154]

19.46 These ordinary principles are modified where there is a disposal of an asset otherwise than under a bargain at arm's length to a charity or to certain other specified bodies.[155] If the disposal is by way of gift (or for a consideration not exceeding the sums allowable as a deduction[156]), the disposal and acquisition are treated for the purposes of capital gains tax as being on a 'no gain, no loss' basis.[157] In effect, the disponee charity takes over the base cost of the disponor. The same principle of disposal on a 'no gain, no loss' basis applies when assets are disposed of to charity on the termination of an interest (other than on the death of a person with a life interest) in settled property.[158]

19.47 The principle that the disponee takes over the base cost of the disponor is qualified where the gift is one of shares and securities which comprise qualifying investments within section 587B of the Income and Corporation Taxes Act 1988.[159] This has been considered above.[160]

---

[150] TCGA 1992, s 1(1)

[151] ibid, s 38

[152] ibid, s 2A

[153] ibid, s 3(2), the specified amount being substituted for the tax year 2000–1 by the Capital Gains Tax (Annual Exempt Amount) Order 2000, SI 2000/808

[154] TCGA 1992, s 4

[155] ibid, s 257(1). The bodies referred to are set out in IHTA 1984, Sch 3 (Gifts for national purposes, etc)

[156] ie under TCGA 1992, s 38

[157] ibid, s 257(2)(a)

[158] ibid, s 257(3)

[159] As inserted by FA 2000, s 43(1). See further above, paras 19.36–19.42 and below, paras 19.88–19.89

[160] See above, paras 19.40–19.42

(4) Inheritance tax

General principles

Under general principles, inheritance tax is charged on the value transferred by a **19.48** chargeable transfer,[161] which is a transfer of value made by an individual that is not an exempt transfer.[162] A transfer of value is a disposition made by a person (the transferor) as a result of which the value of his estate immediately after the disposition is less than it would be but for the disposition; and the amount by which it is less is the value transferred by the transfer.[163] Most transfers of value by individuals (other than transfers into a discretionary trust) are likely to be potentially exempt transfers; such a transfer becomes an exempt transfer if the transferor survives the transfer by seven years.[164] On an individual's death, inheritance tax is charged as if, immediately before his death; he had made a transfer of value of an amount equal to the value of his estate immediately before his death.[165] In other words, there is a deemed transfer on death.

For inheritance tax purposes, chargeable transfers made by an individual are cu- **19.49** mulated with other chargeable transfers made by him within the previous seven years.[166] If the cumulative total of chargeable transfers exceeds a specified amount,[167] inheritance tax is paid at the rate of 20 per cent on lifetime transfers, and 40 per cent on the deemed transfer on death.[168]

An anti-avoidance provision designed to prevent donors from 'having their cake **19.50** and eating it' is that concerned with gifts subject to a reservation.[169] An example of such a gift would be a voluntary transfer of land made by a donor who remains in occupation after the conveyance. For inheritance tax purposes, property subject to a reservation is, in effect, treated as forming part of the donor's estate until such time (if any) as the reservation ceases.[170]

Gifts to charities

By virtue of section 23 of the Inheritance Tax Act 1984, transfers of value are ex- **19.51** empt to the extent that the values transferred by them are attributable to property

---

[161] IHTA 1984, s 1
[162] ibid, s 2
[163] ibid, s 3
[164] ibid, s 3A
[165] ibid, s 4(1)
[166] ibid, s 7(1)
[167] ie £234,000 in respect of chargeable transfers made after 5 Apr 2000: IHTA 1984, s 8(4); Inheritance Tax (Indexation) Order 2000, SI 2000/803. The annual amount is linked to increases in the retail prices index: IHTA 1984, s 8(1)
[168] IHTA 1984, s 7 & Sch 1
[169] FA 1986, s 102, Sch 20
[170] ibid, s 102(3)

which is given to charities.[171] The exemption under section 23 does not apply if the disposition (whether testamentary or otherwise):

(a) takes effect on the termination of any interest or period;[172]
(b) depends on a condition which is not satisfied within twelve months after the transfer;[173]
(c) is defeasible;[174]
(d) if the interest given is less than the donor's (to be decided twelve months after the transfer);[175] or
(e) if the property is given for a limited period.[176]

19.52 The general provisions concerning gifts subject to a reservation[177] do not apply to exempt gifts to charities.[178] Instead, special provisions apply to such gifts. Thus the exemption under section 23 of the Inheritance Tax Act 1984 does not apply to property if:[179]

(a) the property is land or a building and is given subject to an interest reserved or created by the donor which entitles him, his spouse or a person connected with him to possession of, or to occupy, the whole or any part of the land or building rent-free or at a rent less than might be expected to be obtained in a transaction at arm's length between persons not connected with each other, or

(b) the property is not land or a building and is given subject to an interest[180] reserved or created by the donor other than—

(i) an interest created by him for full consideration in money or money's worth, or

(ii) an interest which does not substantially affect the enjoyment of the property by the person or body to whom it is given.

19.53 The exemption from inheritance tax of gifts to charity does not aply if the property or any part of it may become applicable for purposes other than charitable purposes or those of certain specified other bodies.[181]

---

[171] IHTA 1984, s 23(1). For the purposes of s 23, property is given to charities if it becomes the property of charities or is held on trust for charitable purposes only, and 'donor' is to be construed accordingly: ibid, s 23(6)
[172] ibid, s 23(2)(a)
[173] ibid, s 23(2)(b)
[174] ibid, s 23(2)(c). For this purpose, any disposition which has not been defeated 12 months after the transfer of value and is not defeasible after that time is treated as not being defeasible (whether or not it was capable of being defeated before that time): ibid, s 23(2)
[175] ibid, s 23(3)(a)
[176] ibid, s 23(3)(b)
[177] FA 1986, s 102, Sch 20
[178] ibid, s 102(5)(d)
[179] IHTA 1984, s 23(4)
[180] For this purpose, whether property is given subject to an interest is to be decided 12 months after the transfer of value: ibid, s 23(4)
[181] ibid, s 23(5). The other bodies are those mentioned in ss 24 (gifts to political parties) or 25 (gifts for national purposes, etc), and (where the property is land) of a body mentioned in s 24A (gifts to housing associations)

Gifts to housing associations

Under section 24A of the Inheritance Tax Act 1984, a transfer of value is exempt **19.54** to the extent that the value transferred by it is attributable to land in the United Kingdom given to a registered social landlord or to a registered housing association.[182] The general provisions concerning gifts subject to a reservation[183] do not apply to exempt gifts to such bodies.[184] The exemption under section 24A does not apply if the gift is postponed, conditional, limited, or subject to a reservation, in the same way that, had it been an exempt gift to a charity, the exemption under section 23[185] would not have applied.[186]

Gifts for national purposes

By virtue of section 25 of the Inheritance Tax Act 1984, a transfer of value is an ex- **19.55** empt transfer to the extent that the value transferred by it is attributable to property which becomes the property of a body within Schedule 3 to that Act.[187] The general provisions concerning gifts subject to a reservation[188] do not apply to exempt gifts for national purposes.[189] The exemption under section 25 is lost in the same circumstances as the exemption under section 24A would have been lost if the gift had been to a housing association;[190] except that a transfer by way of a gift for national purposes does not cease to be exempt merely because the property consists of the benefit of an agreement restricting the use of land.[191]

Miscellaneous transfers

There are other exemptions for transfers which, although not gifts to charity, re- **19.56** sult in property becoming available to the public.

---

[182] ibid, s 24A(1) & (2); for this purpose, these terms are defined in s 24A(2)

[183] FA 1986, s 102

[184] ibid, s 102(5)(ee) (inserted by FA 1989, s 171(5) in respect of transfers of value made after 16 Mar 1988)

[185] See above, paras 19.51–19.53

[186] IHTA 1984, s 24A(3); ie s 23(2)–(5) apply in relation to s 24A(1) also. Additionally, in relation to gifts to registered social landlords or registered housing associations, and for the purposes of s 23(2)–(5), property is given to any person or body if it becomes the property of or is held on trust for that person or body, and 'donor' is construed accordingly: ibid, s 24A(3), applying s 24(4) to s 24A(1)

[187] ibid, s 25(1). The bodies named in Sch 3 include the major national art galleries, museums, and libraries in the UK, any local authority, government department, any university or university college in the UK, and other specified bodies including the National Trust, the National Trust for Scotland, and the Historic Churches Preservation Trust. Many of these are charities; but some (eg local authorities and government departments) are not

[188] FA 1986, s 102

[189] ibid, s 102(5)(f)

[190] See above, para 19.54

[191] IHTA 1984, s 25(2)

Conditionally exempt transfers

19.57 On a claim being made, a transfer of value of property which is designated by the Treasury and in respect of which requisite undertakings are given, may be granted conditional exemption.[192] This exemption can apply to the deemed transfer of value on death; but it does not apply to inter vivos transfers unless the transferor or his spouse (or both) have been beneficially entitled to the property for six years, or unless the transferor himself acquired the property when it passed to him on the occasion of a conditionally exempt transfer on the death of the previous owner.[193]

19.58 The Treasury may designate:[194]

(a) any relevant object[195] which appears to the Board[196] to be pre-eminent for its national, scientific, historic or artistic interest;
(aa) any collection or group of relevant objects which, taken as a whole, appears to the Board to be pre-eminent for its national, scientific, historic or artistic interest;[197]
(b) any land which in the opinion of the Treasury is of outstanding scenic or historic or scientific interest;
(c) any building for the preservation of which special steps should in the opinion of the Treasury be taken by reason of its outstanding historic or architectural interest;
(d) any area of land which in the opinion of the Treasury is essential for the protection of the character and amenities of such a building as is mentioned in paragraph (c) above;
(e) any object which in the opinion of the Treasury is historically associated with such a building as is mentioned in paragraph (c) above.

19.59 The requisite undertaking varies according to the paragraph within which the property falls. Common features of the undertakings are that the property will be preserved, that steps will be taken to secure reasonable access to the public, and that any land will be maintained. In the case of land falling within paragraph (b), an undertaking must also be given for the preservation of its character. Other specific undertakings are that objects within paragraphs (a) and (aa) will be kept permanently in the United Kingdom and not leave it temporarily except for a purpose and a period approved by the Treasury; and that objects falling within paragraph (e) should be kept associated with the building concerned.[198]

---

[192] IHTA 1984, s 30(1)
[193] ibid, s 30(2)
[194] ibid, s 31(1)
[195] In s 31, 'relevant object' means a picture, book, manuscript, work of art or scientific object, or anything else that does not yield income; and in determining whether an object or a collection or group of objects is pre-eminent, regard is to be had to any significant association of the object, collection or group with a particular place: ibid, s 31(5)
[196] ie the Commissioners of Inland Revenue: ibid, s 272
[197] In s 31, 'national interest' includes interest within any part of the UK: ibid, s 31(5)
[198] ibid, s 31(2)–(5)

Where there has been a conditionally exempt transfer of property, inheritance tax   **19.60**
is charged on the first occurrence thereafter of what is called 'a chargeable event'.[199]
A failure to observe an undertaking in a material respect is a chargeable event,[200] as
is a disposal of the property (whether on death or inter vivos, and whether on sale
or by way of gift[201]) unless the transfer made on such disposal is itself conditionally exempt.[202] A death or disposal is also not a chargeable event if, within three
years of the death, the personal representatives of the deceased (or, in the case of
settled property, the trustees or the person next entitled) dispose of the property
(either by sale by private treaty or otherwise than by way of sale) to a body mentioned in Schedule 3 to the Inheritance Act 1984,[203] or by a disposal in pursuance
of section 230 (see below).[204]

A disposal in pursuance of section 230 refers to the acceptance of property by the   **19.61**
Commissioners of Inland Revenue (the Board) in satisfaction of tax or interest.[205]
The property which the Board may agree to accept includes land and buildings,
and in some cases objects kept in such buildings.[206] It also includes any picture,
print, book, manuscript, work of art, scientific object, or other thing which the
Secretary of State is satisfied is pre-eminent for its national, scientific, historic, or
artistic interest,[207] and any collection or group of the items mentioned, if the
Secretary of State is satisfied that the collection or group, taken as a whole, is pre-
eminent for any of those qualities.[208]

Potentially exempt transfer of property subsequently held for national purposes

If a potentially exempt transfer proves to be a chargeable transfer (because the   **19.62**
transferor dies within seven years), a liability to inheritance tax may arise. In
specified circumstances, however, the potentially exempt transfer will be treated as
an exempt transfer to the extent that the property transferred has been or could
have been designated under section 31(1) of the Inheritance Tax Act 1984. The
specified circumstances are that, between the date of the transfer and the date of
the transferor's death, the property has been disposed of by sale by private treaty

---

[199] ibid, s 32(1)
[200] ibid, s 32(2)
[201] ibid, s 32(3)
[202] ibid, s 32(5)
[203] ie including various national museums, art galleries, and libraries. For bodies within Sch 3,
see above, para 19.55
[204] IHTA 1984, s 32(4)
[205] ibid, s 230(1)
[206] ibid, s 230(2), (3)
[207] In s 230, 'national interest' includes interest within any part of the UK: ibid, s 230(5)
[208] ibid, s 230(4). In determining whether an object or collection or group of objects is pre-
eminent, regard is to be had to any significant association of the object, collection, or group with a
particular place: ibid, s 230(5)

or otherwise than by sale to a body mentioned in Schedule 3 to that Act, or has been disposed of in pursuance of section 230.[209]

Maintenance funds for historic buildings

19.63 A transfer of value is an exempt transfer to the extent that the value transferred by it is attributable to property which by virtue of the transfer becomes comprised in a maintenance fund, that is, in a settlement in respect of which a Treasury direction[210] either has effect at the time of the transfer or is given afterwards.[211] This exemption for a maintenance fund does not apply in the case of a direction given after the transfer unless the claim for the direction (if not made earlier) is made no more than two years after the date of the transfer, or within such longer period as the Board may allow.[212]

19.64 On a claim being made, the Treasury must give a direction if specified conditions are fulfilled in respect of settled property.[213] The conditions are two-fold. First, the Treasury must be satisfied that the trusts on which the property is held comply with specified requirements, and that the property is of a character and amount appropriate for the purposes of those trusts.[214] Secondly, the trustees must be approved by the Treasury, they must include a trust corporation, a solicitor, an accountant, or a member of such other professional body as the Treasury may allow, and, they must, at the time the direction is given, be resident in the United Kingdom.[215]

19.65 The first specified requirement relating to the trusts on which the property is held is that none of the property held on the trusts can at any time within six years from the date on which it became so held be applied otherwise than:[216]

(i) for the maintenance, repair or preservation of, or making provision for public access to, property which is for the time being qualifying property, for the maintenance, repair or preservation of property held on the trusts or for such improvement of property so held as is reasonable having regard to the purposes of the trusts, or for defraying the expenses of the trustees in relation to the property so held;
(ii) as respects income not so applied and not accumulated, for the benefit of a body within Schedule 3 to this Act or of a qualifying charity.

The other requirements are that none of the property can, on ceasing to be held on the trusts at any time in that period, or, if the settlor dies in that period, at any

---

[209] IHTA 1984, s 26A (inserted by FA 1986, Sch 19, para 6, with respect to transfers of value and other events occurring after 17 Mar 1986). For a disposal in pursuance of s 230, see above, para 19.61
[210] This is a Treasury Direction under IHTA 1984, Sch 4, para 1
[211] IHTA 1984, s 27(1)
[212] ibid, s 27(1A) (inserted by FA 1998, s 144(1), with effect in respect of transfers of value made after 16 Mar 1998)
[213] IHTA 1984, Sch 4, para 1(1)
[214] ibid, para 2(1)(a)
[215] ibid, para 2(1)(b)
[216] ibid, para 3(1)(a)

time before his death, devolve otherwise than on any such body or charity,[217] and that income arising from property held on the trusts cannot at any time after the end of that period be applied except as mentioned in paragraph (a)(i) or (ii).[218]

For this purpose, 'qualifying property' means land or buildings (including objects historically associated with such buildings) which have been designated under section 31(1) of the Inheritance Tax Act 1984, or under similar provisions[219] in earlier capital transfer tax legislation.[220]   **19.66**

A charity is a 'qualifying charity' if it exists wholly or mainly for maintaining, repairing, or preserving for the public benefit buildings of historic or architectural interest, land of scenic, historic, or scientific interest or objects of national, scientific, historic, or artistic interest.[221]   **19.67**

There are detailed provisions relating to the charge to tax when property leaves maintenance funds,[222] and for exempting from a charge to inheritance tax the occasion on which property held on trusts in which no interest in possession subsists[223] becomes held as a maintenance fund.[224]   **19.68**

B. Giving by trustees of private trusts

In exceptional circumstances it may be within the power of trustees of an exclusively private trust to make donations out of the trust funds to charities or for charitable purposes. Everything turns on the powers conferred on them, either under the general law or by the trust instrument itself.   **19.69**

In *Re Clore's Settlement Trusts*,[225] the trustees had a power under clause 8 of the trust instrument to raise any part not exceeding two-thirds of a beneficiary's vested or presumptive share in the trust fund and to 'pay or apply the same for his or her advancement or benefit in such manner as the trustees in their absolute discretion think fit' (a power which, except as to amount, is broadly similar to the power of advancement contained in section 32 of the Trustee Act 1925. The trustees asked the court whether they were permitted, pursuant to this power, to pay a proportion of the trust fund to one of the beneficiaries either directly, with a view to his   **19.70**

---

[217] ibid, para 3(1)(b)
[218] ibid, para 3(1)(c)
[219] ie FA 1975, s 34(1), and FA 1976, s 77(1)
[220] IHTA 1984, Sch 4, para 3(2)
[221] ibid, para 3(4): 'national interest' here includes interest within any part of the UK: ibid, para 3(4)
[222] ibid, paras 8–15A
[223] ie primarily discretionary trusts
[224] IHTA 1984, Sch 4, paras 16–18
[225] [1966] 1 WLR 955

paying the amount over to charity, or whether they could pay that proportion directly to charity. The intention was that one-seventh of that beneficiary's share should be paid to the trustees of an existing charity, the Charles Clore Foundation. The beneficiary in question was very wealthy, and the trust fund was of considerable value. Everyone concerned—the trustees, both beneficiaries under the trust, and the settlor—was in favour of the proposed gift.

19.71   Pennycuick J accepted the argument of counsel for the trustees which had been formulated in five propositions:

(a)   that payment or application for the advancement or benefit of a person means 'any use of the money which will improve the material situation of the beneficiary';[226]

(b)   that the improvement of the material situation of a beneficiary is not confined to his direct financial advantage, but includes the discharge of certain moral or social obligations on the part of the beneficiary, for example towards members of his family;[227]

(c)   that the court has always recognized that a wealthy person has a moral obligation to make appropriate charitable donations;

(d)   that a wealthy person can discharge his moral obligation at less cost to himself if he makes a charitable settlement; and

(e)   that any advance of an appropriate sum under the settlement is capable of improving his material situation by enabling him to discharge his moral obligation without undue burden to himself.

Dealing with proposition (c), Pennycuick J said that the court had generally been concerned with relatively small sums of income,[228] but he did not consider that the proposition was restricted to income payments. He stated:[229]

> It seems to me that a beneficiary under a settlement may indeed in many cases be reasonably entitled to regard himself as under a moral obligation to make donations towards charity. The nature and amount of those donations must depend upon all the circumstances, including the position in life of the beneficiary, the amount of the fund and the amount of his other resources. Once that proposition is accepted, it seems to me that it must lie within the scope of a power such as that contained in clause 8 of this settlement for the trustees to raise capital for the purpose of relieving the beneficiary of his moral obligation towards whatever charity he may have in mind. If the obligation is not to be met out of the capital of the trust fund, he would have to meet it out of his own pocket, if at all. Accordingly, the discharge of the obligation out of the capital of the trust fund does improve his material situation. The precise amount which the trustees can in any given case apply for this purpose

---

226   *Re Pilkington's Will Trusts* [1964] AC 612, 635 (Lord Radcliffe)
227   As in *Re Pilkington's Will Trusts* [1964] AC 612
228   eg *Re Walker* [1901] 1 Ch 879
229   *Re Clore's Settlement Trusts* [1966] 1 WLR 955, 958–9

must depend, I think, on the particular circumstances, and in this respect quantum is a necessary ingredient in the proper exercise of the power.

Later in his judgment, his Lordship emphasized that, where it is proposed to make an advance of capital to discharge the moral obligation of a beneficiary towards charity, it is essential to a valid exercise of the power that the beneficiary himself should recognize the moral obligation.[230] It was not, in other words, for the trustees to impose on the beneficiary their own view of his moral obligations. On the facts of the case, the beneficiary did recognize his moral obligation. His Lordship added that it would be difficult to see how the trustees under such a power as that contained in clause 8 could validly pay over the whole of the autho-rized amount to charitable purposes; but it was not for the court to say where the line should be drawn.[231] In the circumstances of the case before him, he thought that a proposed portion of one-seventh was on the right side of the line.

Turning to propositions (d) and (e), Pennycuick J accepted that the particular beneficiary in the case could confer the same benefit upon the charity at much less expense to himself than if he were to make a corresponding payment to the char-ity personally out of income, which (at the rates of income tax then in force) it would be impossible for him to do. His Lordship thought, however, that, whilst this last consideration emphasized the desirability of making the proposed ad-vance, it was not essential to the power of the trustees to make the advance.[232]   **19.72**

C. Corporate giving

(1) Restrictions on corporate giving

In *Re Lee, Behrens & Co Ltd*,[233] Eve J stated that the validity of corporate gifts:[234]   **19.73**

> is to be tested . . . by the answers to three pertinent questions: (i) Is the transaction reasonably incidental to the carrying on of the company's business? (ii) Is it a bona fide transaction? and (iii) Is it done for the benefit and to promote the prosperity of the company?

More recent authorities, however, indicate that these questions do not distinguish between the power of the company to make gifts and the fiduciary duties of the di-rectors in relation to the exercise of such power;[235] and it has been suggested that, in determining whether a company has a power to make gifts, 'the tests should be

---

[230] ibid, 959
[231] ibid
[232] ibid
[233] [1932] 2 Ch 46
[234] ibid, 51–2
[235] *Charterbridge Corp Ltd v Lloyds Bank Ltd* [1970] Ch 62, 70–1 (Pennycuick J)

finally laid to rest'.[236] The *Lee, Behrens* tests continue to have some bearing on whether directors have abused the powers vested in them;[237] and they still appear to apply to gratuitous dispositions by directors under implied powers.[238] Only some of the questions, however, are now applied to gratuitous dispositions made pursuant to express powers.[239]

19.74 The modern authorities suggest that corporate giving to charity involves three separate issues: first, whether the company itself has power to make the gift; secondly, whether the gift has been authorized by the proper organ of the company; and, thirdly, whether the directors' decision to make a gift to charity can otherwise be impugned.

Company's power to make a charitable gift

19.75 A company has power to make a charitable gift if the making of such gifts is an express object of the company. As Buckley LJ stated in *Re Horsley & Weight Ltd,*[240]

> The objects of a company do not need to be commercial; they can be charitable or philanthropic; indeed, they can be whatever the original incorporators wish, provided that they are legal. Nor is there any reason why a company should not part with its funds gratuitously or for non-commercial reasons if to do so is within its declared objects.

Many objects clauses of commercial companies contain a list of express objects and express powers. If the objects clause contains a power to make gifts to charities, it is a matter of construction whether such power is merely an ancillary power (so that it can be exercised only in pursuit of the authorized objects) or an independent object in its own right. If the description of objects and powers is followed by an 'independent objects clause', declaring that all the objects are to be read and construed as separate and distinct objects, the power will be an express object.[241]

19.76 If the making of charitable gifts is not an express object of the company, it can make such gifts only in pursuance of any ancillary power it has to further the company's express objects. In the absence of such an express power, the company will have to rely on those powers that are implied by law, and these are restricted to those powers which can be fairly regarded as incidental to, or consequential upon, the company's objects.[242] A power to make a gift will not be implied merely be-

---

[236] *Rolled Steel Products (Holdings) v British Steel Corp* [1986] Ch, 246, 288 (Slade LJ)
[237] ibid (where Slade LJ did not distinguish between express and implied powers)
[238] *Re Halt Garage Ltd* [1982] 3 All ER 1016, 1032 (Oliver J)
[239] *Charterbridge Corp Ltd v Lloyds Bank Ltd* [1970] Ch 62
[240] [1982] Ch 442, 450. In that case, one of the objects of the company was the making of grants for charitable, benevolent, or public purposes or objects
[241] ibid
[242] *A-G v Great Eastern Rly* (1880) 5 App Cas 473 (HL); *Tomkinson v South-Eastern Rly Co* (1887) 35 ChD 675; *Re Lee, Behrens & Co* [1932] 2 Ch 46, 51 (Eve J's first question)

cause it can be shown that the gift would be of benefit to the company.[243] Evidence of benefit to the company used to be thought to be an additional requirement for the implying of a power,[244] but this view has not found favour in more recent decisions.[245]

If one of the objects of a company is to make gifts to charity in very general terms, **19.77** a charitable gift made pursuant to that object cannot be challenged on the ground that it is ultra vires.[246] If the company has only an ancillary power to make such gifts, it appears that any gifts made can be challenged on this ground unless they can be considered to be ancillary to the attainment of the company's objects.[247] If the company is relying merely on an implied power, the gift will need to be reasonably incidental to the company's objects. In *Evans v Brunner, Mond & Co*,[248] a chemical manufacturing company (a forerunner of ICI) resolved to give money to various universities and scientific bodies 'for the furtherance of scientific education and research'. Eve J held that the proposed expenditure would be reasonably incidental or conducive to the company's main object, and so dismissed a claim that it would be ultra vires. It can nevertheless be difficult to determine whether a particular charitable gift will be considered to be incidental to a company's objects, and there is clearly a risk that gifts made pursuant to such a power might be open to challenge. To reduce the risks of this, a gift to a charity which has very wide objects might be made subject to an express trust for those objects most closely connected to the objects of the donor company.[249] In practice, however, the safest way to ensure that a gift to charity is not challenged as being ultra vires is to ensure that the power to make such gifts is an independent express object of the company, if necessary by an amendment to the objects clause.

Authorization by appropriate organ of company

If the making of gifts to charity is an object of the company or within the com- **19.78** pany's powers (express or implied), the decision to make such a gift must be made by the appropriate organ of the company (either the board of directors or the company in general meeting) according to the company's articles of association. If one

---

[243] *Evans v Brunner, Mond & Co* [1921] 1 Ch 359
[244] ibid
[245] eg *Re Horsley & Weight Ltd* [1982] Ch 442
[246] ibid
[247] ibid. See also *Simmonds v Heffer* [1983] BCLC 298 (Mervyn Davies J) (gift by the League Against Cruel Sports Ltd, a non-charitable company limited by guarantee, to the Labour Party). Although this view appears inconsistent with *Rolled Steel Products (Holdings) v British Steel Corp* [1986] Ch 246, the principle in the latter case might be considered to be restricted to commercial transactions, and to have no application to gifts: see *Boyle & Birds' Company Law* (3rd edn, Jordans, 1995) 105 (para 4.13.2)
[248] [1921] 1 Ch 359
[249] cf *Simmonds v Heffer* [1983] BCLC 298

or more directors make the gift without approval of the board, the gift may never-theless be ratified subsequently with the approval of all the shareholders.[250]

Impugning decision of directors to make charitable gift

19.79 Directors are under a fiduciary duty to exercise their powers in good faith; a deci-sion of the board to make a gift to charity may therefore be impugned if lack of bona fides can be shown.[251] It has been expressly stated that the question whether the gift is for the benefit of the company as a whole[252] has no application to express powers.[253] Such question continues to be applicable to implied powers, however; so that, where the directors make a gift pursuant to such a power, their decision can be impugned if it can be shown that the making of the gift is not for the benefit of the company as a whole.[254]

Disclosure in directors' report

19.80 If a company (not being the wholly-owned subsidiary of a company incorporated in Great Britain) has in the financial year given more than £200 for charitable pur-poses, the directors' report for the year must state the amount of money given for those purposes.[255] If a company (not being the wholly-owned subsidiary of a com-pany incorporated in Great Britain) has subsidiaries, and the company and such subsidiaries have in that year between them given more than £200 for charitable purposes, the directors' report for the year must state the purposes for which money has been given by the company and the amount of money given for those purposes.[256] In each case, money given for charitable purposes to a person who, when it was given, was ordinarily resident outside the United Kingdom is to be left out of account.[257] In relation to these disclosure requirements, 'charitable pur-poses' means purposes which are exclusively charitable.[258]

(2) Corporation tax

Corporate Gift Aid

Payment by any company

19.81 In 1990, at the same time as Gift Aid was introduced to provide tax relief for one-off donations to charity by individuals,[259] an equivalent tax relief (also sometimes

---

[250] As it was in *Re Horsley & Weight Ltd* [1982] Ch 442

[251] *Re Lee, Behrens & Co* [1932] 2 Ch 46, 51 (Eve J's second question)

[252] ibid (Eve J's third question)

[253] *Charterbridge Corp Ltd v Lloyds Bank Ltd* [1970] Ch 62, 70–1 (Pennycuick J); cf *Re Halt Garage Ltd* [1982] 3 All ER 1016, 1034 (Oliver J)

[254] *Re Horsley & Weight Ltd* [1982] Ch 442

[255] Companies Act 1985, Sch 7, para 3(1), (2)(a)

[256] ibid, para 4(2)

[257] ibid, para 5(3)

[258] ibid, para 5(4)

[259] FA 1990, s 25

known as Gift Aid) was introduced for one-off donations to charity by companies.[260] Important changes to Gift Aid in respect of such donations have been made by the Finance Act 2000. Before 1 April 2000, Gift Aid payments made by a company to a charity were paid net of tax and had to be supported by a Gift Aid declaration. From 1 April 2000, all Gift Aid payments made by a company are paid gross,[261] and the company is entitled to claim tax relief on such payment when calculating its profits for corporation tax. In the hands of the charity, the gift is treated for tax purposes as if it were an annual payment.[262] From 1 April 2000, no Gift Aid declaration need be given.[263]

The Finance Act 2000 has also extended Gift Aid to a payment made by a company to a charity under a deed of covenant. Before 1 April 2000, provided it ranked as 'a covenanted donation to charity',[264] such payment was made net of tax, the tax deducted being reclaimable by the charity. The system of tax relief based on covenanted donations to charity does not apply to a payment under a deed of covenant (whenever entered into) made by a company to a charity after 31 March 2000. Such a payment (provided it is eligible) obtains tax relief under Gift Aid instead. If Gift Aid applies, the payment is (like any other Gift Aid donation by a company) paid gross, the company is entitled to tax relief on the payment when calculating its corporation tax profits, and the receipt is treated as an annual payment in the charity's hands. A payment made by a company after 31 March 2000 is subject to Gift Aid even if the payment fell due on or before that date.[265]   **19.82**

A payment by a company is entitled to Gift Aid if it is a 'qualifying donation' to charity. In relation to payments made after 31 March 2000, a qualifying donation is[266]   **19.83**

> a payment of a sum of money made by a company to a charity,[267] other than—
>> (a) a payment which, by reason of any provision of the Taxes Acts (within the

---

[260] ibid, s 26, amending ICTA 1988, s 339. Because unincorporated associations, such as clubs and societies, are subject to corporation tax, donations which such associations make to charity are similarly governed by the Gift Aid regime applicable to corporations

[261] This is an important difference between Gift Aid payments by companies and by individuals, as gifts by the latter are paid net of basic rate tax: see above, paras 19.23–19.24

[262] ICTA 1988, s 339(4), substituted by FA 2000, s 40(6)

[263] This is another difference between individual and corporate Gift Aid

[264] As defined in ICTA 1988, s 339(8), repealed by FA 2000, s 40(3)

[265] FA 2000, s 40(11)

[266] ICTA 1988, s 339(1), as amended by FA 2000, s 40(2), substituting new para (a)

[267] For the purposes of ICTA 1988, s 339, 'charity' includes each of the bodies mentioned in s 507 (Trustees of the National Heritage Memorial Fund; Historic Buildings and Monuments Commission for England; Trustees of the British Museum; and Trustees of the Natural History Museum), and any association of a description specified in s 508 (scientific research organizations); subject to that, 'charity' has the same meaning as in s 506: ibid, s 339(9), as amended by FA 2000

meaning of the Management Act)[268] except section 209(4),[269] is to be regarded as a distribution; and

(b) a payment which is deductible in computing profits or any description of profits for purposes of corporation tax.

A payment made by a company is not a qualifying donation if the company is itself a charity.[270]

Payment by close company

19.84 Special restrictions apply to payments made by a close company.[271] A payment made by a close company is not a qualifying donation if it is made subject to a condition as to repayment, or the company or a connected person[272] receives a benefit in consequence of making it which in value exceeds either £250 or the statutory limit.[273] The statutory limit is the same as that which applies in relation to Gift Aid donations by individuals.[274] Similarly, where more than one donation or benefit is made or received (or both), they are to be aggregated to determine whether the limit is exceeded.[275] There are also parallel provisions relating to benefits received over a period of less than twelve months, and to a payment which is one of a series.[276] A payment made by a close company is also not a qualifying donation if it is conditional on, or associated with, or part of an arrangement involving, the acquisition of property by the charity, otherwise than by way of gift, from the company or a connected person.[277] Since a charity's subsidiary trading company will usually be a close company, these restrictions must be borne in mind by a charity which makes loans to, or otherwise invests in, its trading subsidiary.[278]

---

[268] 'Taxes Acts' has the same meaning as in the Taxes Management Act 1970, s 118(1), viz, the Income and Corporation Taxes Act 1988 and other Income Tax and Corporation Tax Acts, the Taxation of Chargeable Gains Act 1992, and all other enactments relating to capital gains tax

[269] ie transfer of assets or liabilities between a company and a member where the amount or value of benefits received by the latter exceeds any new consideration given by him

[270] ICTA 1988, s 339(3G)

[271] A close company is essentially a company under the control of 5 or fewer participators, or of participators who are directors: ibid, ss 414(1), 832(1)

[272] For this purpose, a connected person is a person connected with the company, or with a person connected with the company, and ibid, s 839 (which defines 'connected persons' for the purposes of the Tax Acts) applies: ibid, s 339(7A)

[273] ibid, s 339(3B)

[274] ie (a) where the amount of the payment does not exceed £100, 25% of the amount of the payment; (b) where the amount of the payment exceeds £100 but does not exceed £1,000, £25; (c) where the amount of the payment exceeds £1,000, 2.5% of the amount of the payment: ICTA 1988, s 339(3DA), substituted by FA 2000, s 40(5)

[275] ICTA 1988, s 339(3C), (3D)

[276] ibid, s 339(3DB), (3DC), (3DD), inserted by FA 2000, s 40(5). For examples of how these rules operate, see the discussion of Gift Aid by individuals, above, paras 19.14–19.17

[277] ICTA 1988, s 339(3E)

[278] See ch 20, para 20.26

Payment deductible in computing profits

The income of a company is computed in accordance with principles of income **19.85**
tax.[279] In computing a company's profits to be charged to tax, the Income and
Corporation Taxes Act 1988 specifies a number of types of expenditure which are
not deductible; one of these is:[280]

> (a) any disbursements or expenses, not being money wholly and exclusively laid out
> or expended for the purposes of the trade, profession or vocation.

Money which is 'wholly and exclusively' spent 'for the purposes of the trade' is
therefore deductible; and gifts to charity are deductible if they can satisfy this test.
The item of expenditure will, under general principles, be deductible only if it is of
a revenue rather than a capital nature. This issue has been considered on a number
of occasions by the courts in relation to commercial expenditure, and they have
stated that a relevant factor is whether there is an element of recurrence.[281] In commercial cases the element of recurrence is not decisive, since a capital transaction
may be worded to give the appearance of revenue expenditure;[282] but in the cases of
gifts, the element of recurrence is a significant factor. A one-off gift to charity is
therefore less likely to be treated as revenue expenditure than a series of regular gifts.
In *Bourne & Hollingsworth Ltd v Ogden*,[283] regular subscriptions of 100 guineas to a
local hospital were allowed under this paragraph, whereas a couple of special subscriptions of 1,000 guineas were not. A regular subscription by a company to a trade
association that has charitable status is also deductible under this paragraph, unless
the company pays such subscription on behalf of its employees.[284]

If a person ('the employer') carrying on a trade, profession, vocation, or business, **19.86**
makes available to a charity,[285] on a temporary basis, the services of an employee,
the expenditure incurred (or disbursed) by the employer which is attributable to
the employment of that employee is deemed to continue to be deductible as an
expense in computing the profits of the employer[286] during such period of secondment.[287]

---

[279] ICTA 1988, s 9(1)
[280] ibid, s 74(1)
[281] *Vallambrosa Rubber Co v Farmer* (1910) 5 TC 529 (Lord Dunedin); *Pitt v Castle Mill Warehousing Ltd* [1974] 1 WLR 1624 (Megarry V-C)
[282] *IRC v Land Securities Investment Trust Ltd* [1969] 1 WLR 604 (HL). See also *British Insulated & Helsby Cables Ltd v Atherton* [1926] AC 205 (Viscount Cave LC)
[283] (1929) 14 TC 349
[284] *Hutchinson & Co (Publishers) Ltd v Turner* [1950] 2 All ER 633
[285] 'Charity' has the same meaning as in ICTA 1988, s 506, ie 'any body of persons or trust established for charitable purposes': ibid, s 86(2). The expense of secondment of employees to certain
educational establishments is deductible on the same basis: ibid, s 86(3)–(6), as amended and added
by FA 1999, s 57
[286] ICTA 1988, s 86(2)
[287] ibid, s 86, as amended by FA 1999, s 57

Gifts of certain articles by company carrying on a trade

19.87   Until 27 July 1999, a company which disposed of trading stock or machinery and plant by way of gift to a charity could suffer tax disadvantages as a consequence in the same way as an individual trader.[288] These disadvantages have been removed (both in the case of individual traders and companies) by the Finance Act 1999. This has been discussed (in relation to individual traders) earlier in this chapter.[289]

Gifts of shares and securities to charities

19.88   The Finance Act 2000[290] introduced a new tax relief for disposals to a charity by way of gift or at an undervalue of quoted shares and securities and of certain other types of investment. The relief applies to disposals both by individuals and by companies. The former has been considered above.[291]

19.89   The relief on a disposal by a company applies where, otherwise than by way of a bargain made at arm's length, a company which is not itself a charity disposes of the whole of the beneficial interest in a qualifying investment to a charity[292] after 31 March 2000.[293] On a claim to the Commissioners of Inland Revenue, the company is entitled to a charge on income for the purposes of corporation tax for the accounting period in which the disposal is made.[294] The deduction is of 'the relevant amount',[295] which is calculated in the same way as in relation to disposals by individuals[296] except that special rules apply where the disposal is by a company which is carrying on life assurance business.[297]

D. Charitable giving and value added tax

(1) Monetary donations, sponsorship, and fund-raising

19.90   A genuine monetary donation to charity does not involve a taxable supply of goods and services and is outside the scope of value added tax (VAT). If, however, the charity supplies goods or services in return for such 'donation', the amount of the payment to the charity will be consideration for a supply and will not be

---

[288]   ie by reason of the rule in *Sharkey v Wernher* (1955) 36 TC 275 and under Capital Allowances Act 1990
[289]   See above, paras 19.33–19.35
[290]   FA 2000, s 43, inserting new s 587B into ICTA 1988
[291]   See above, paras 19.36–19.42
[292]   ICTA 1988, s 587B(1). In this section, 'charity' has the same meaning as in s 506, and includes each of the bodies mentioned in s 507(1): ibid, s 587B(9)
[293]   FA 2000, s 43(3)(b)
[294]   ICTA 1988, s 587B(2)(a)(ii)
[295]   ibid, s 587B(2)(a)
[296]   ibid, s 587B(4)-(7). See further, above, paras 19.37–19.39
[297]   ICTA 1988, s 587B(8)

accepted by HM Customs and Excise as a genuine donation. Donations given in exchange for an emblem for which there is no fixed minimum charge, for example, a 'flag' or Remembrance Day poppy, are, however, accepted as genuine.[298]

Whether the sponsoring of a charity has VAT consequences depends on the na- **19.91** ture of the sponsorship. A person who makes a monetary donation may be called a 'sponsor' or a 'patron', but if the payment is genuinely a donation and is not made in return for the supply of goods or services by the charity, it is outside the scope of VAT. For this purpose, a mere acknowledgement by the charity of the support of named donors does not attract VAT in respect of their gifts. If a donation is made, for example, to a university to endow a chair, the university may name the chair after the donor with no VAT consequences, since there is no supply.[299] If, however, the payment is conditional on the charity's supplying clearly identifiable benefits in return (such as advertising or publicity, or the making available of the charity's facilities, perhaps at a reduced price[300]) the charity will be making a supply, which will be chargeable to VAT in accordance with the normal rules.[301] If the charity is not itself otherwise carrying on a business, the supply by it of goods or services in return for sponsorship money on only one occasion is unlikely itself to comprise a business for the purposes of VAT. If, however, a charity engages in a number of sponsorship arrangements of this nature, it is probably carrying on a business for the purposes of VAT.[302]

If a sponsorship arrangement involves the supply of goods or services by the char- **19.92** ity, VAT is charged on the supply by reference to the whole of the sponsorship money, even if this far exceeds the value of the benefit conferred.[303] Where there is a single supply, HM Customs and Excise will permit a division into consideration and gift elements only if the sponsor clearly makes such apportionment before or at the time the donation is made.[304] Alternatively, the sponsor could make two separate gifts, where it is clear that one is genuinely voluntary. These devices will be acceptable, however, only if the amount attributed to the supply is realistic in relation to the benefits provided.

---

[298] HM Customs and Excise, 'VAT: Treatment of donations to charities', Press Notice 1026, 24 July 1985. In some circumstances, the supply to their members by certain public interest bodies of services and goods without payment other than a membership subscription is an exempt supply: VATA 1994, Sch 9, Group 9. See ch 3, paras 3.65–3.66

[299] HM Customs and Excise, 'VAT and donations to universities', News Release 84/88, 10 Nov 1988

[300] eg *High Peak Theatre Trust v Comrs of Customs and Excise* [1995] STI 202 (Name-a-Seat scheme organized by the Opera House, Buxton, offered sponsors (inter alia) priority booking and discounts on seat prices. The charity was held to be making a taxable supply

[301] HM Customs and Excise, 'VAT and donations to universities', News Release 84/88, 10 Nov 1988. (in relation to donations to universities)

[302] For further discussion of the meaning of 'business' for VAT purposes, see ch 3, paras 3.34–3.40

[303] *Comrs of Customs and Excise v Tron Theatre Ltd* [1994] STC 177

[304] HM Customs and Excise, 'Charities: Sponsorship', Notice 701/41/95, para 6

19.93   The sponsorship of a fund-raising event may fall within the exemption for charity fund-raising events.[305] The supply of goods or services by a charity in connection with a fund-raising event organized for charitable purposes by a charity or jointly by more than one charity is an exempt supply,[306] provided that no more than fifteen events of the same kind involving the charity are held at the same location in its financial year.[307] If the number of such events is exceeded, every such event is taxable at the standard rate.[308] If the same event (such as a concert) is repeated on successive days, it ranks as a number of separate events;[309] but an event can take place over several days and remain a single event.[310] In calculating the number of events for this purpose, any event held in a week during which the aggregate gross takings do not exceed £1,000 is disregarded.[311] Fund-raising by minor means, such as by coffee mornings and jumble sales, therefore remains exempt, even if such events are held frequently.

19.94   The organization by a charity that is not otherwise conducting a business, of a single fund-raising event, is unlikely to comprise a business for the purposes of VAT; but it will be treated as a business if an admission fee is charged.[312] If a charity makes an admission charge to a charitable function, such as a fund-raising concert or dinner, the whole of any such charge will be treated as consideration for a supply by the charity. A charity might try to reduce the VAT on such sales by selling the tickets at a lower price, but suggesting to purchasers that they make an additional donation; HM Customs and Excise will accept this, provided the admission charge is realistic and any additional sums are genuine gifts, completely at the discretion of the purchaser of the ticket (which must be made clear in all publicity and advertising for the event).[313]

---

[305] See J Warburton, 'Charities, Sponsorship and Value Added Tax' (1996–7) 4 CL & PR 105

[306] VATA 1994, Sch 9, Group 12, Item 1, as substituted by Value Added Tax (Fund-raising Events by Charities and Other Qualifying Bodies) Order 2000, SI 2000/802. See further ch 3, paras 3.74–3.77

[307] VATA 1994, Sch 9, Group 12, Item 1, Note (4)

[308] HM Customs and Excise, 'Exemption for fund-raising events held by charities and other qualifying bodies', Notice 701/59, para 3.9

[309] *Northern Ireland Council for Voluntary Action v Comrs of Customs and Excise* [1991] VATTR 32 (7 performances of the play *Look Back in Anger* over 5 consecutive days held to be outside the exemption)

[310] *Reading Cricket and Hockey Club v Comrs of Customs and Excise* [1995] STI 1979

[311] VATA 1994, Sch 9, Group 12, Item 1, Note (5)

[312] HM Customs and Excise, 'VAT: charities', leaflet 701/1/95

[313] HM Customs and Excise, 'VAT: Treatment of donations to charities', Press Notice 1026, 24 July 1985. The promoters of the Live Aid Concert in 1985 had advertised tickets for the concert without making it clear that the sale price was to be £5 with a voluntary donation of £20. Because a genuine mistake had been made, HM Customs and Excise, with the authority of the Chancellor of the Exchequer, decided as an extra-statutory concession not to insist on the VAT on the gift element of the admission charge. HM Customs and Excise pointed out that such concession was exceptional, and did not set a precedent for treatment of fund-raising events in the future

(2) *Gifts of goods or services*

Gifts of goods and land

A supply for the purposes of VAT does not generally include anything done other- **19.95** wise than for a consideration.[314] This general principle is, however, subject to exceptions.[315] One of these provides that, where goods owned by a business are transferred or disposed of by the person carrying on the business, whether or not for a consideration, there is a supply by him of goods.[316] For this purpose, 'goods' includes land.[317] The effect of this exception is that if, for instance, a business makes a gift of computer equipment to a university, the gift comprises a supply which is liable to VAT based on the cost of the equipment to the business.[318]

Where goods are 'given' to a charity subject to an obligation that the charity will **19.96** do something in return, the transaction is a form of barter. Each party to the agreement, if registered for VAT, will have to account for tax on the open market value of the goods or services supplied.

Gifts of services

A business may donate some of its employees' time to performing services for the **19.97** charity. The general principles of VAT apply. This is a supply of services, but if it is purely voluntary on the part of the business, there are no VAT implications. If there is a benefit which comprises consideration for the supply, and that benefit is itself the supply of goods or services by the charity, there is a barter, and the VAT consequences are as stated in the previous paragraph.

Sale by charity of donated goods

The supply by a charity of goods which have been donated for sale or hire is zero- **19.98** rated for VAT, as is the supply of such goods by a taxable person who has entered into a written agreement or another obligation (such as a trust) to transfer the profits of that supply to a charity.[319] To qualify for zero-rating, the goods must be offered for sale or hire to the general public or to persons who are disabled or in receipt of means-tested benefits.[320] Supplies of land and of other things deemed to

---

[314] VATA 1994, s 5(2)(a)

[315] ibid, s 5(1)(2)

[316] ibid, Sch 4, para 5(1); this sub-paragraph does not apply to a gift of goods made in the furtherance of the business where the cost of the goods to the donor does not exceed £15: ibid, para 5(2)

[317] ibid, Sch 4, para 9(1)

[318] HM Customs and Excise, 'VAT and donations to universities', News Release 84/88, 10 Nov 1988

[319] VATA 1994, Sch 8, Gp 15, Items 1, 1A. These items were substituted by the VAT (Charities and Aids for the Handicapped) Order 2000, SI 2000/805, in respect of supplies made on or after 1 Apr 2000

[320] VATA 1994, Sch 8, Group 15, Notes (1) & (1C), as substituted by VAT (Charities and Aids for the Handicapped) Order 2000, SI 2000/805

be a supply of goods are excluded from these reliefs;[321] the sale by a charity of land which has been donated to it, whether inter vivos or by will, does not therefore qualify for zero-rating.

---

[321] VATA 1994, Sch 8, Gp 15, Note (1F). This exclusion puts into statutory form the view which HM Customs and Excise had previously held: see HM Customs and Excise, 'VAT on expenses of sale of dwellings bequeathed to charities', Business Brief No 12/92, 29 July 1992

20

CHARITIES AND TRADING

A. Introduction

The most obvious form of trading involves the sale of goods; but trading can also **20.01** be in other forms of property (such as land or the supply of services). If a charity which preserves old buildings charges an entrance fee to the public, or a charity school or hospital levies admission fees, each is trading. The first important issue is to determine the extent to which charities are permitted in English law to carry on a trade.

B. Trading and charity law

The first problem that a charity wishing to trade faces is the principle of charity **20.02** law that a charity, being set up for wholly and exclusively charitable purposes, is required to apply its funds solely for those purposes. It has been held that raising funds for charity is not itself a charitable purpose.[1] Therefore the Charity Commissioners will not register a charity whose purpose (or one of whose

---

[1] cf *Oxfam v City of Birmingham DC* [1976] AC 126 (HL); *Blackpool Marton Rotary Club v Martin* [1988] STC 823, affd [1990] STC 1 (CA)

purposes) is the carrying out of a trade. In some instances, however, the trade will involve a carrying out of the purposes of the charity, for example, the charging of tuition fees by a university, or the sale of goods made by disabled people by a charity whose purpose is to assist disabled people to set up in trade. For most charities, however, trading will not be a fulfilment of their main purpose; but this does not mean that they are prohibited from engaging in any form of trade. So far as charity law is concerned, they are permitted to engage in trade (and so to apply the funds of the charity) so far as the trade is merely ancillary to the carrying out of their wholly and exclusively charitable objects. The consequence is that the activity in question must be carried out on a fairly limited scale, otherwise it will be treated as the carrying out of a non-charitable purpose. So the odd jumble sale, or the sale of tickets for the occasional fund-raising dinner, is acceptable; but if these activities are carried out regularly, the Charity Commissioners may contend that a non-charitable purpose is being pursued.

20.03 In practice, if the trading falls within the statutory exemption for small trading[2] or within the Inland Revenue's extra-statutory concession,[3] the Charity Commissioners are likely to treat the trading as merely ancillary to the carrying out of the charitable purposes, so there is no breach of that aspect of charity law. Speculative activity is a different matter. A charity might engage in a business venture which, whilst falling within the statutory exemption or the extra-statutory concession, is highly speculative in nature and exposes the charity's assets to considerable risk. In these instances, it seems that the Charity Commissioners will treat such activities as a breach of charity law, even if such activities fall within the letter of the statutory exemption or the concession.[4]

C. Charity trading and tax law

20.04 The second problem—closely related to the first—is one of tax law. Any person who, or institution which, carries on a trade may be liable to pay income tax (or corporation tax) on the profits of the trade. If the charity is a trust, trading profits would be prima facie liable to income tax; if it is a corporation or an unincorporated association, its trading profits would be prima facie liable to corporation tax (which is essentially calculated on the same principles[5]).

---

[2] FA 2000, s 46; see below, para 20.09
[3] Inland Revenue, ESC C4 (Mar 2000); see below, paras 20.12–20.13
[4] See the response of a team of lawyers from the Charity Commission to questions put at a meeting of the CLA: see report of CLA 'Brains Trust', 16 Mar 2000. The answers do not bind the Commissioners, but they do at least suggest what their approach is likely to be
[5] ICTA 1988, s 9(1)

(1) The meaning of 'trade'

Trade is statutorily (but not very helpfully) defined to include 'every trade, manu- **20.05**
facture, adventure or concern in the nature of trade'.[6] For the purposes of income
or corporation tax, a transaction comprises trading if it satisfies one or more of the
so-called 'badges of trade', which were identified by the Radcliffe Committee,[7]
and which were derived from the relevant tax cases. The badges of trade are:

(1) *The subject-matter involved*: if a charity buys 100,000 T-shirts (bearing the
charity's logo perhaps) for resale, the nature of the subject matter suggests
trade, since it is difficult to see what other reason there can be for their acquisition.[8]

(2) *Length of period of ownership*: if the sale follows soon after acquisition, this
points to trade.[9]

(3) *The frequency of the transaction*: trade generally involves repetition.[10] Thus
in *British Legion Peterhead Branch Remembrance and Welcome Home Fund
v Inland Revenue Commissioners*,[11] the charity organized regular dances on
Saturday nights, and this was held to be trading. A one-off transaction,
such as a sale of a plot of land, is not likely to be trading; but even a single
disposal can be an 'adventure . . . in the nature of trade', if one or more of
the other badges is present.[12]

(4) *Supplementary work*: carrying out work on the asset before resale may suggest trade.[13]

(5) *Circumstances of the realization*: that is, the reasons for the sale. If the charity makes what is in effect a forced sale (because it needs the money) or receives an offer it cannot refuse, there may not be trading.[14] Conversely, if
the charity disposes of the assets through a form of organization, for example through advertising in newspapers, this suggests trade.[15]

(6) *Profit-motive*: this is a relevant factor,[16] at least at the time of purchase,[17] but

---

[6] ibid, s 832(1)
[7] *Final Report of the Royal Commission on the Taxation of Profits and Income*, Cmd 9474 (1954),
para 116
[8] See generally *Martin v Lowry* (1926) 11 TC 297; *Rutledge v IRC* (1929) 14 TC 490; *IRC v
Fraser* (1942) 24 TC 498; *IRC v Reinhold* (1953) 34 TC 389; *Wisdom v Chamberlain* (1969)
45 TC 92; *Johnson v Heath* (1970) 46 TC 463
[9] See generally *Turner v Last* (1965) 42 TC 517; *Marson v Morton* [1986] STC 463
[10] *Pickford v Quirke* (1927) 13 TC 251; *Leach v Pogson* (1962) 40 TC 585
[11] (1953) 3 STC 84
[12] As in *Rutledge v IRC* (1929) 14 TC 490 and *Johnson v Heath* (1970) 46 TC 463
[13] *IRC v Livingston* (1926) 11 TC 538; *Cape Brandy Syndicate v IRC* (1927) 12 TC 358; but contrast *Taylor v Good* [1974] STC 148
[14] See generally *Hudson's Bay Co v Stevens* (1909) 5 TC 424; *West v Phillips* (1958) 38 TC 203
[15] cf *Martin v Lowry* (1926) 11 TC 297, and *Rutledge v IRC* (1929) 14 TC 490
[16] *Simmons v IRC* [1980] STC 350, 352 (Lord Wilberforce); applied in *Kirkham v Williams*
[1989] STC 333 (Vinelott J)
[17] *Taylor v Good* [1974] STC 148

it is not decisive and is by itself insufficient, since to sell some day at a profit is the expectation of most investors.[18] By contrast, there can be trading even in the absence of an intention to make a profit:[19] a charity can be trading even though its motive is to raise funds to enable it better to carry out its charitable purposes.[20] If it is clear, however, that the activity can never make a profit under any circumstances (that is, that it can only ever be run at a loss) then there is no trading. In *Religious Tract and Book Society of Scotland v Forbes*,[21] the charity sold religious tracts through bookshops and through door-to-door salesmen, who also acted as missionaries. The Scottish court held that there was no trading, as the evidence showed that the activities of the salesmen (colporteurs) could never make a profit. The result was that the charity could not deduct the losses from the colportage from the trading profits made by its bookshops.

(2) Exempt charity trading

Primary purpose trading and beneficiary-workers

20.06   Some trading by charities is exempt from income or corporation tax; but the scope of the exemptions is narrow.[22] A charity is exempt from tax on the profits of a trade only if the profits are applied solely to the purposes of the charity and either:[23]

(i) the trade is exercised in the course of the actual carrying out of a primary purpose of the charity; or
(ii) the work in connection with the trade is mainly carried out by beneficiaries of the charity.

20.07   An example of (i) is the sale by Oxford University Press (a charity) of books which it has itself published. Similarly, a charity school which levies fees for admission is engaged in a trade, but the trade is exercised in the course of carrying out a primary purpose of the charity. The sale of mugs and T-shirts by a theatrical charity, however, is not a trade exercised in the course of the actual carrying out of one of its primary purposes, and will not fall within this exemption. In *Dean Leigh Temperance Canteen v Inland Revenue Commissioners*[24] a charity, one of whose objects was the promotion of temperance, ran a coffee shop open to the public. The profits of the shop were held to fall within the exemption because there was evidence that when the charity had been created there had been many public houses in the area; the trading from the shop was therefore exercised in the course of the

---

[18] *IRC v Reinhold* (1953) 34 TC 389
[19] *Grove v YMCA* (1903) 88 LT 696
[20] ibid
[21] (1896) 3 TC 415
[22] See I Dawson, 'Taxation of Trades in the Charities Sector' in *The Voluntary Sector, the State and the Law* (ed A Dunn) (Hart Publishing, 2000), 177–92
[23] ICTA 1988, s 505(1)(e)
[24] (1958) 38 TC 315

actual carrying out of the charity's primary purpose of promoting temperance. By contrast, in *Grove v Young Men's Christian Association*,[25] the charity, one of whose purposes was the provision of hostel accommodation, also ran a restaurant which was open to outsiders; its profits were held to be taxable as the profits of a trade. Had the restaurant been open only to residents of the hostel, the activity would probably not have ranked as trading, since the trading would then have been exercised in the course of carrying out one of the charity's main purposes.

In exemption (ii), the word 'mainly' means that not all the work has to be carried **20.08** out by the beneficiaries themselves; presumably more than half is enough. A classic example of trading within this exemption is the sale by a charity for the blind of goods made by blind persons in workshops run by the charity. Additional instances are furnished by case law. In *Inland Revenue Commissioners v Glasgow Musical Festival Association*,[26] a charitable society, in pursuance of its objects, promoted an amateur music festival; the public were admitted to the concerts on payment of a fee, and the performers received the profits. It was held that the profits were the profits of a trade, but fell within this exemption because the persons who carried on the work in connection with the trade, the performers, were also the beneficiaries. In *Brighton Convent of the Blessed Sacrament v Inland Revenue Commissioners*,[27] a convent school which charged admission fees was held entitled to relief on the profits of such trade because the nuns carried on the trade, and they could be regarded as the charity's beneficiaries.

Small trading income

A new statutory exemption was introduced from April 2000 which exempts a **20.09** charity from tax whose trading income is small,[28] so relieving such a charity from the need to establish a subsidiary trading company. A charity is entitled to claim this exemption if its gross income for a chargeable period does not (or if at the start of that period there was a reasonable expectation that it would not) exceed the requisite limit. This limit is 25 per cent of the charity's incoming resources (including income from all sources, donations, and grants), but subject to the qualification that the limit is never less than £5,000 and cannot exceed £50,000. The exemption is considered in more detail in chapter 3.[29]

---

[25] (1903) 88 LT 696
[26] (1926) 11 TC 154
[27] (1933) 18 TC 76
[28] FA 2000, s 46. The new statutory exemption supersedes the much narrower de minimis exemption for small trading income that the Inland Revenue formerly applied outside its ESCs
[29] See ch 3, paras 3.14–3.18

Profits from certain types of lottery

20.10 There is exemption from tax under Schedule D[30] in respect of the profits accruing to a charity from a lottery which is promoted and conducted either as a small lottery incidental to exempt entertainments[31] or as a society's lottery,[32] provided the profits are applied solely to the charity's purposes.[33]

(3) Inland Revenue practice and concessions

Sale of donated goods

20.11 The Inland Revenue does not treat the sale of donated goods as trading.[34] The donation of funds to a charity is not trading (since there is no consideration by the charity), and the Inland Revenue takes the view that the sale of such goods is merely a way of realizing their value. There are, however, other reasons why a charity may still prefer to sell donated goods through a trading subsidiary rather than directly itself—such as to avoid the charity trustees of a charitable trust being personally liable for any losses which the trade may produce, and for any liability to purchasers under the Sale of Goods Act 1979 or to a third person who is injured by the goods sold.[35]

Fund-raising events within the corresponding exemption from value added tax

20.12 Since April 2000, the concessionary income tax exemption and the previous value added tax (VAT) exemption for fund-raising events have been extended and aligned. The revised extra-statutory concession published by the Inland Revenue provides as follows:[36]

> Certain events arranged by voluntary organisations or charities for the purpose of raising funds for charity may fall within the definition of 'trade' in Section 832 ICTA 1988, with the result that any profits will be liable to income or corporation tax. Tax will not be charged on such profits provided:
> a. the event is of a kind which falls within the exemption from VAT under Group 12 of Schedule 9 to the VAT Act 1994 and
> b. the profits are transferred to charities or otherwise applied for charitable purposes.

20.13 The Group 12 exemption from VAT[37] exempts (inter alia) fund-raising by one or more charities, where the primary purpose of the event is the raising of money,

---

[30] ICTA 1988, s 505(1)(f). See ch 3, para 3.13
[31] Lotteries and Amusements Act 1976, s 3
[32] ibid, s 5
[33] ICTA 1988, s 505(1)(f)
[34] IR 75, para 4
[35] S Lloyd, *Charities, Trading and the Law* (Charities Advisory Trust in association with the Directory of Social Change, 1995), para 3.4
[36] Inland Revenue, ESC C4 (Mar 2000)
[37] VATA 1994, Sch 9, Group 12, as substituted by the Value Added Tax (Fund-raising Events by Charities and Other Qualifying Bodies) Order 2000, SI 2000/802

and where the event is promoted as being primarily for that purpose.[38] The exemption does not apply if more than fifteen events of the same kind involving the same charity are held at the same location in its financial year;[39] but, for this purpose, an event held in a week in which the aggregate takings do not exceed £1,000 is disregarded.[40] The scope of the exemption is more fully considered in chapter 3.[41]

(4) Consequences for a charity of taxable trading

What are the consequences if a charity's trading does not fall within the limits mentioned above? **20.14**

If the trading is carried on in such a way that income or corporation tax is payable, there is a risk that this will be treated as a breach of the requirement that the charity must carry out wholly and exclusively charitable purposes, so there could be questions from the Charity Commissioners. Furthermore, since charity trustees are, as trustees, under a duty to act in the best interests of the charity, they may be in breach of trust if they fail to organize the trading activities in a way that minimizes the tax payable. The Charity Commissioners have, indeed, expressly stated that charity trustees may be personally liable to account for taxation liabilities which are unnecessarily incurred directly or indirectly as a result of the inefficient administration of the charity.[42] This is tantamount to saying that, in many cases, charity trustees will be effectively under a duty to have the trading carried out by a subsidiary trading company rather than by the charity itself. **20.15**

D. Subsidiary trading companies

Although the changes introduced in April 2000 affecting charity trading, both statutory and by way of concession, have widened the scope for a charity to trade directly, they are not sufficient to exempt from tax the trading income of many of the larger charities. Furthermore, a charity might prefer not to trade directly, even if it could do so within the new extended tax limits. If the charity is not itself an incorporated body, the charity trustees run the risk of personal liability if the trade produces a loss, or of actions in contract or tort for selling defective goods; and the charity's assets are similarly at risk. If the charity is incorporated, its directors will generally escape personal liability, but the risk to the charity's assets remains. **20.16**

---

[38] VATA 1994, Sch 9, Group 12, Items 1(b), (c), 2(b), (c), 3(c), (d)
[39] ibid, Note (4)
[40] ibid, Note (5)
[41] See ch 3, paras 3.74–3.75
[42] See [1988] Ch Com Rep 11 (para 44)

20.17 For all these reasons, it is advantageous for many charities not to trade themselves, but to have the trading activities carried on by a subsidiary trading company.[43] Indeed, both the Charity Commissioners and the Inland Revenue recognize and approve of charities establishing subsidiary trading companies. Thus the Charity Commissioners have stated:[44]

> Where a charity wishes to benefit substantially from permanent trading for the purpose of fund-raising we advise that it does so through a separate non-charitable trading company, so that its charitable status is not endangered.

(1) Setting up a subsidiary trading company

20.18 The subsidiary trading company will not be a charity itself. It will be a commercial company limited by shares, and therefore outside the jurisdiction of the Charity Commissioners. There are significant tax advantages in relation to profit-shedding if the trading company is wholly owned by the charity. First, if the company returns its profits to the charity by way of Gift Aid, it may, if it is wholly owned by the charity, make the payment within nine months after the end of its accounting period (when it can actually calculate what its profits are).[45] Secondly, a supply of goods and services by a charity's subsidiary trading company in connection with a fund-raising event will be an exempt supply for the purposes of value added tax[46] only if (inter alia) such company is wholly owned by the charity.[47]

20.19 In order for it to be able to own its trading subsidiary's shares, the charity must have power to invest in such a subsidiary. The constitution of a charitable company is likely to contain a power to set up and invest in a subsidiary company in its 'incidental activities' clause.[48] The constitution of a charitable trust or association, particularly if it was created many years ago, may not contain any express power which would enable it to invest in a subsidiary trading company. Before the Trustee Act 2000, such an investment would not have been authorized under the general law;[49] so that, in the absence of any special power of investment or of a power to amend its constitution, a charitable trust would have needed the Charity

---

[43] Given the advantages of trading through a subsidiary company, it is surprising that more charities do not use such means. In 1994, the accountancy firm KPMG conducted a survey into trading by charities: KPMG Tax Advisers, *Charities and Trading: a recent survey* (Dec 1994). It sent questionnaires (inter alia) to over 1,114 of the largest fund-raising charities in the UK, and received 317 replies. Of these, the survey revealed that 65% did not have any trading subsidiary at all; 26% had one; and only between 1% and 3% had more than one. The statistics also showed that only 60% of charities with a trading income of more than £10m had a trading subsidiary. For charities with a trading income of less than £1m the corresponding figure was merely 16%

[44] [1980] Ch Com Rep 8 (para 10)

[45] See below, paras 20.31–20.34

[46] VATA 1994, Sch 9, Group 12

[47] ibid, Note (2). See further ch 3, paras 3.74–3.77, esp para 3.77

[48] See ch 8, paras 8.97

[49] ie under TIA 1961

Commissioners' consent[50] for the requisite power to be conferred.[51] Since the Trustee Act 2000, however, trustees now have, subject to any restriction or exclusion in the trust instrument, a general power of investment,[52] and investment in the charity's trading subsidiary falls within this general power. The general power of investment does not permit trustees to speculate with trust funds, and it could be argued that the purchase by a charitable trust of shares in its subsidiary trading company might, in some instances, be considered not to be an investment at all.[53] The trustees should take appropriate steps, therefore, to be able to satisfy themselves (and the Charity Commissioners) that the venture is a sound one: they should, for instance, do proper market research, draw up a business plan and a budget, and provide figures for estimated cash flows.[54] In addition, before exercising any power of investment, whether under the Trustee Act 2000 or under an express power, the trustees must comply with the duty to obtain and consider proper advice,[55] unless they reasonably conclude that in the circumstances it is unnecessary or inappropriate to obtain such advice.[56]

There is, however, a tax problem here, caused by the restrictions on the tax exemptions now contained in sections 505 & 506 of the Income and Corporation Taxes Act 1988.[57] These complex provisions essentially provide that charities can lose part of the tax relief on their income if they incur expenditure which does not satisfy the criteria which the sections lay down. The sections distinguish between 'qualifying' and 'non-qualifying expenditure'. Investment in shares in an unquoted company is not 'qualifying expenditure' unless the Commissioners of Inland Revenue are satisfied that such investment 'is made for the benefit of the charity and not for the avoidance of tax (whether by the charity or any other person)'.[58] The trading subsidiary will inevitably be an unquoted company; with the result that, if the charity uses its own funds to set up the trading subsidiary (which could run into a few hundred pounds at least) and to acquire the subsidiary's shares, it will lose part of its exemption from income or corporation tax unless it can satisfy the Inland Revenue as to the purpose of the investment. In practice, it is generally possible to persuade the Revenue that the investment is made otherwise than for the avoidance of tax, notwithstanding that the avoidance of tax is

20.20

---

[50] CA 1993, s 16
[51] The Charity Commissioners would in practice give their consent if it was in the interests of the charity—which in practice it generally was
[52] TA 2000, s 3
[53] cf the position before TA 2000, when the Charity Commissioners would not consent to a widening of a charitable trust's powers to acquire shares in its trading subsidiary if they considered the purchase to be too speculative: [1980] Ch Com Rep 8 (para 10)
[54] See S Lloyd, *Charities, Trading and the Law* (Charities Advisory Trust in association with the Directory of Social Change, 1995), 83–4 (para 7.7)
[55] TA 2000, s 5(1)
[56] ibid, s 5(3)
[57] For a general discussion of these provisions, see ch 3, paras 3.19–3.25
[58] ICTA 1988, Sch 20, para 9(1). See also, ibid, s 506(4)

manifestly at least one purpose of the investment. In this, as in some other aspects of charity trading, the system works because the Revenue are effectively prepared to turn a blind eye to the reality of what is going on. Failing this, it may be necessary to find a benefactor who is willing to put up the money to set up the trading company and to buy the shares in the subsidiary in the name of the charity. The latter expense does not need to be great: it is usually an outlay of just £2 (that is, the acquisition of two shares at £1 each, and which are probably never paid for or the payment for which effectively gets lost in the wash); but nominal amounts of this sort are insufficient to fund the trading subsidiary.

(2) Funding the trading subsidiary

20.21   Even though the trading subsidiary is set up, it cannot trade without capital to enable it to get started before its profits begin to come in. It may need capital to enable it to acquire premises from which to trade, to fit them out, to acquire stock-in-trade, and to pay staff and meet other expenses, such as electricity, gas, and stationery.

20.22   There are problems of both charity law and tax law in the charity's funding the trading subsidiary. As explained by Hill and De Souza,[59] there are three basic ways in which the subsidiary might obtain funding, and these are now considered in turn.

Subscription by the charity for more shares

20.23   The difficulty is that this will be a non-qualifying investment unless the Revenue agree that the investment is made for the benefit of the charity and not to avoid tax.[60] Given the amount that the subsidiary is likely to need, unless the Revenue do so agree, the charity's investment could result in its losing a substantial part of its tax exemptions. Such a loss can be avoided if the charity invests from sources (such as legacies) which are not 'relevant income and gains' under the Income and Corporation Taxes Act 1988.[61] From a tax point of view, the receipt by a charity of a large legacy is likely to provide a good opportunity to set up and fund a trading subsidiary.

Loan by the charity

20.24   The Charity Commissioners consider that any funding which a charity provides to its subsidiary trading company should be viewed as an investment.[62] For this reason, any loan which the charity makes to its subsidiary should normally be

---

[59]   Judith Hill, & J De Souza, 'Charities and trading' (1989) 4 TL & P 98
[60]   ICTA 1988, s 506(4) & Sch 20, para 9(1)
[61]   ibid, s 505(5). See further ch 3, paras 3.19–3.25
[62]   See Charity Commission, *Charities and Trading*, CC 35 (Feb 1997), 18 (para 52). For the investment aspect of loans, see further ch 16, paras 16.39–16.40

secured and on market terms.[63] If charity trustees lend the charity's money to the subsidiary without taking security, they take a great risk that the debt will eventually be irrecoverable, and such lending will usually amount to a breach of trust.[64]

The Charity Commissioners will be concerned to see that the loan is made at a **20.25**
market rate of interest; a loan which is interest-free or at less than a market rate would be equivalent to the charity's making a donation of part of its funds to a non-charitable purpose—which is prohibited under charity law. Even a loan at a market rate of interest will rank as non-qualifying expenditure under section 506 of the Income and Corporation Taxes Act 1988, unless the Inland Revenue is satisfied that the loan is a qualifying loan as being made for the benefit of a charity and not for the avoidance of tax.[65] The charity trustees can never write off the loan: if they do so, they are effectively giving the charity's assets away, and they can be required to pay the amount out of their own pockets. The Charity Commissioners will take appropriate action to see that the sums are recovered for the charity.[66] In practice, the Charity Commissioners will expect loans to contain a suitable timetable for repayment. A mere statement that the loan is repayable on demand is not sufficient, since in practice it means the loan might never be repaid at all. [67]

Merely entering the interest payments due in the loan account in the books of the **20.26**
charity and the subsidiary is not evidence that the amount has been paid: rather it is evidence that it has not been paid, so the subsidiary company will not be able to claim tax relief on the basis that its profits have been reduced by the payment of interest.[68] A charity might be tempted to keep its trading subsidiary in funds by making a loan to the subsidiary each year of an amount equal to the subsidiary's profits for that year, the latter being made over to the charity in the form of payments (usually under a deed of covenant) which qualify for Corporate Gift Aid. The risk in such an arrangement is that it might be found to transgress the special restrictions which payments made by a close company must satisfy to qualify for Corporate Gift Aid.[69] In particular, there is a danger that the receipt of the loan

---

[63] Charity Commission, *Charities and Trading*, CC 35 (Feb 1997), 19 (para 55)

[64] ibid, 20 (para 57)

[65] ICTA 1988, Sch 20, para 10(1)(d)

[66] See eg the action taken by the Charity Commissioners in one instance mentioned at [1990] Ch Com Rep 10 (para 52), where a charity had lent substantial sums of money to a trading company connected with the charity's deceased founder. The company had sustained heavy trading losses, and the investment had been largely lost. The Charity Commissioners considered that the charity trustees had breached their duties in regard to the loan. They referred the matter to the Attorney-General to institute proceedings, but the action was settled by the trustees agreeing to make good part of the losses personally, including the payment of a further sum to cover the additional tax which the charity had had to pay

[67] See further S Lloyd, *Charities, Trading and the Law* (Charities Advisory Trust in association with the Directory of Social Change, 1995), 88 (para 7.8)

[68] *Minsham Properties Ltd v Price* [1990] STC 718

[69] See ch 19, para 19.84

might be treated as a benefit received by the company in consequence of the payment.[70] In *Nightingale v Price*,[71] which did not concern Gift Aid payments, the fact that the charity made loans to the subsidiary of amounts equal to the sums it received from the subsidiary in interest payments and under a deed of covenant was held not to result in a loss of tax relief to either the charity or the subsidiary. The Special Commissioners there accepted that the charity's policy was to increase its own resources. The courts may therefore be well disposed to these sorts of arrangements.[72] It is, however, important that the respective payments made by the subsidiary and the charity to each other are not expressed to be conditional or to be part of any reciprocal arrangement.

Borrowing on the markets by the subsidiary

20.27 This is fine in principle; but the practical problem is who is likely to be willing to lend to a trading company which has no assets on which to give a security? The lender is therefore likely to require personal guarantees from someone else that the loan will be repaid. The issue is: can the charity give such a guarantee? In *Rosemary Simmons Memorial Housing Association Ltd v United Dominion Trust Ltd*,[73] the judge stated obiter that the giving of such a guarantee by a charity for no consideration amounted to the charity's giving away its assets for a non-charitable purpose. The clear answer, therefore, is that the charity cannot give such a guarantee.[74]

(3) Making the charity's assets available to the subsidiary

Generally

20.28 The charity cannot simply give an asset to its non-charitable trading subsidiary. It could sell an asset to the subsidiary at market value, but this will not usually be desirable, since it will reduce the capital of the subsidiary—the opposite of what is generally intended. A sale in consideration for the allotment of shares in the trading subsidiary has its own objections, in that it might comprise a non-qualifying investment resulting in a loss of tax relief.[75] In the case of land (but not in respect of other assets[76]), a rental arrangement may prove satisfactory, provided the subsidiary is making sufficient profits to cover the rent as it falls due, since the rent will usually be deductible in computing the subsidiary's trading profits, and the rental

---

[70] See ICTA 1988, s 339(3B)
[71] [1996] STC (SCD) 116
[72] For the Revenue's attitude to donor benefits, see below, para 20.31
[73] [1986] 1 WLR 1440
[74] The KPMG survey (see note to para 20.17, above), reported, however, that in 1 in 6 of the cases where charities had set up a trading subsidiary, the charity had guaranteed the subsidiary's debts: KPMG Tax Advisers, *Charities and Trading: a recent survey* (Dec 1994), para 11.4
[75] ICTA 1988, s 506; see further above, para 20.20
[76] ICTA 1988, s 505

income may be receivable by the charity in a way which is free of tax.[77] In some cases, it may be possible for the charity simply to make an asset available to the subsidiary without charge, but particular problems can occur with regard to copyrights.[78]

Disposals concerned with the development of land

If the charity has land which it wishes to dispose of for development, it is impor-   **20.29** tant to consider the most tax-efficient manner by which this can be effected. If the charity were simply to sell the land to a developer without itself having carried out any works on the land, the gain on the sale would be exempt from capital gains tax as being a gain accruing to a charity.[79] The charity trustee are, however, under a general duty to dispose of any of the charity's assets for the best price obtainable. This duty is reinforced by the statutory requirement that, before disposing of charity land, the charity trustees must obtain and consider a written report from a qualified surveyor.[80] Such advice may well be that an outright disposal will not obtain for the charity the best terms, and that it would be more profitable for the charity to make the disposal by another method, for example by leasing the land to a development company in consideration of a rent and a premium calculated as a proportion of the estimated price which the company would obtain on disposal.[81] The difficulty with disposal by this means, however, is that it appears to be an arrangement or scheme whereby land is developed with the sole or main object of realizing a gain from disposing of the land when developed;[82] in which case the gain is treated, not as a capital gain (from which the charity would be exempt), but as chargeable to tax under Case VI of Schedule D[83] (in respect of which a charity has no exemption).[84]

To avoid a charge to tax on a disposal by this latter means, the disposal should be   **20.30** effected, not by the charity, but by its trading subsidiary, and in such a way that the latter receives the sale proceeds as trading profits. These can then be returned to the charity in the usual manner, by means of Gift Aid. The initial disposal by the

---

[77] ibid. A grant of a lease by the charity to its trading subsidiary comprises a disposition to a connected person, and so requires the consent of the court or the Charity Commissioners: CA 1993, s 36(2)(a) & Sch 5, para 1. See further ch 17, paras 17.47–17.49

[78] See the discussion in Judith Hill, & J De Souza, 'Charities and trading', (1989) 4 TL & P 98, 101

[79] TCGA 1992, s 256(1)

[80] CA 1993, s 36(3)(a)

[81] See eg *Page v Lowther* (1983) STC 799

[82] ICTA 1988, s 776(2)(c); *Page v Lowther* (1983) STC 799

[83] ICTA 1988, s 776(3)(a)

[84] ibid, s 505(1), which provides no exemption in respect of income arising under Case VI of Sch D. Case VI is a residual Case, under which is taxed income in respect of any annual profits or gains not falling under any other Case of Sch D and not charged by virtue of Schs A or E: ibid, s 18(3)

charity to its subsidiary will have to be at market value, and it will probably be necessary for the subsidiary to fund the purchase price through a commercial loan; but this should cause no problems as the cost of the loan will be a deductible expense in the computation of the subsidiary's profit on the purchase and sale.[85]

(4) Returning the subsidiary's taxable profits to the charity

Gift Aid

20.31 Since 1 April 2000, the former method of returning profits under a deed of covenant is no longer needed for tax purposes, since the system of tax relief on 'covenanted payments to charity' has been abolished. Tax relief on payments made after 31 March 2000 under deed of covenant (whenever entered into) are now dealt with under Gift Aid. Since Gift Aid does not require the payment to be made under a covenant, there is now no tax advantage in a subsidiary trading company entering into a deed of covenant with the charity.[86] In view of this change in the method of tax relief, and the fact that existing covenants might have been worded in ways more suited to the old regime than the new, some charities might prefer to release their trading subsidiaries from their deeds of covenant and to receive future profits by way of Gift Aid payments unsupported by such covenants. Since a release would preclude the charity from the possibility of suing on the covenant, a voluntary release might be considered to be not in the charity's best interests. There could be no objection, however, if the subsidiary company were, in consideration for the release, to enter into a separate obligation (whether by way of contract or trust) to transfer its profits to the charity. It seems that the Inland Revenue are not likely to claim that the release is a donor benefit which might, if it exceeds the statutory limits, prevent the payments qualifying for Gift Aid.[87]

20.32 The Finance Act 2000 has extended and modified Gift Aid in relation to payments by companies after 31 March 2000.[88] First, Gift Aid payments by a company are now paid gross; the company is entitled to claim tax relief on such payment in calculating its profits for corporation tax, and the gift is treated as an annual payment in the charity's hands. Secondly, no Gift Aid declaration need be given. Thirdly, the extended timetable for payment, which used to be available only under the system of 'covenanted payments to charity', is now applied to payments under Gift Aid.

---

[85] See Judith Hill, & J De Souza, 'Charities and trading' (1989) 4 TL & P 98, 101–2, where the authors caution that care should also be taken to avoid falling foul of the judicial anti-avoidance doctrine enshrined in the series of cases beginning with *WT Ramsay Ltd v IRC* [1982] AC 300 (HL)

[86] Although there are other reasons why a charity will generally prefer to have a deed of covenant in place: see below, para 20.34

[87] ICTA 1988, s 339(3B)(b) (close companies); see further ch 19, para 19.84. See also the response of a team of lawyers from the Charity Commission to questions put at a meeting of the CLA: see report of CLA 'Brains Trust', 16 Mar 2000

[88] See further ch 19, paras 19.81–19.84

Before 1 April 2000, if a subsidiary trading company wished to transfer its profits   **20.33**
to the charity by Gift Aid, it had to make such payment before the end of the relevant accounting period. In nearly all instances this meant that the subsidiary had
to estimate what its profits were likely to be before they could actually be calculated. Where a Gift Aid payment is made after 31 March 2000, however, there is
provision for late payment in order to give the company an opportunity to calculate its profits first.[89] Thus, the Income and Corporation Taxes Act 1988 now provides:[90]

> Where—
> (a) a qualifying donation to a charity is made by a company which is wholly owned
>   by a charity, and
> (b) the company makes a claim for the donation, or any part of it, to be deemed for
>   the purposes of section 338 to be a charge on income paid in an accounting
>   period falling wholly or partly within the period of nine months ending with the
>   date of the making of the donation,
> the donation or part shall be deemed for those purposes to be a charge on income
> paid in that accounting period, and not in any later period.

The effect is that a wholly owned subsidiary can make a Gift Aid payment up to
nine months after the end of its accounting trading period and claim a charge on income
as if the payment had been made in that previous accounting period. The company must, however, make the claim within two years following the accounting
period in which the donation is made, or such longer period as the Revenue may
allow.[91]

Although a voluntary payment may qualify for Gift Aid, the trading subsidiary   **20.34**
should still enter into a written agreement or subject itself to an obligation (such
as a deed of covenant or trust) to transfer its profits to the charity. One reason for
this is to enable sales of goods donated to the trading subsidiary for resale to qualify for zero-rating for VAT.[92] Zero-rating of such supplies will apply only if the
trading company ranks as a 'profits-to-charity' person in respect of the goods.[93] A
person is a 'profits-to-charity' person in respect of any goods if[94]

> (a) he has agreed in writing (whether or not contained in a deed) to transfer to a char-
> ity his profits from supplies and lettings of the goods, or

---

[89] Similar provision for late payment had been introduced by FA 1997, s 64(1), in relation to
covenanted donations to charity; but this provision was swept away with the abolition of separate
tax relief for covenanted donations to charity by FA 2000, s 40: see ch 19, para 19.82

[90] ICTA 1988, s 339(7AA), substituted by FA 2000, s 40(7)

[91] ibid, s 399 (7AA)

[92] VATA 1994, Sch 8, Group 15, as amended by the Value Added Tax (Charities and Aids for
the Handicapped) Order 2000, SI 2000/805. Before this amendment, such zero-rating on donated
goods had applied only if a trading company had covenanted by deed to give all the profits of the
supply to a charity

[93] VATA 1994, Sch 8, Group 15, Item 1A

[94] ibid, Note (1E)

(b) his profits from supplies and lettings of the goods are otherwise payable to a charity.

Another reason why the trading company should enter into an agreement or other legal obligation to transfer its profits to the charity is so that the charity can satisfy both itself and the Charity Commissioners that it is inevitable that the company's profits will reach the charity. Since the deed of covenant is the established method of transferring a subsidiary company's profits to the charity, it is in practice likely to remain the usual means by which such obligation is imposed. Therefore, despite the removal of the tax advantages formerly accorded to payments made under deeds of covenant *per se*, most charities will probably still prefer to receive the profits of their trading subsidiaries under deeds of covenant, the payments thereunder qualifying for Corporate Gift Aid.

Other methods

20.35 Another possible method of profit-shedding in favour of the charity is by the subsidiary trading company's payment of a dividend. Since 6 April 1999, however, this method has suffered from the distinct disadvantage that the right of a non-taxpayer (such as a charity) to recover the tax credit attributable to a dividend has been removed.[95] The dividend method also has the drawback that the payment must be made in the company's relevant accounting period, with no return for over-payment.

20.36 Another possible method, where the subsidiary is leased premises owned by the charity, is the return of the profits in the form of rent payments; but this is subject to the same difficulty that the payment has to be made in the company's relevant accounting period. There is the additional problem that a market rent (which the charity must obtain) is unlikely to be satisfied by a rent which is measured precisely by the potentially highly variable trading profits of its subsidiary.

(5) Potential conflict of interests

20.37 Since the trading subsidiary will be a commercial company, the fiduciary duties which each of its directors owes *qua* director are owed to, and enforceable by, the trading subsidiary alone; and, if the director has a service contract, he will additionally owe the trading company various contractual duties. As director of the subsidiary, he must act bona fide for the benefit of the company:[96] in other words, in the interests of the company as a commercial enterprise. He must therefore act, essentially, in the interests of the shareholders—which, in the case of a wholly-

---

[95] F(No 2)A 1997, s 30. The full cost of this measure to charities will not be felt until 2004, as recovery of tax credits by charities is being progressively withdrawn over a 5-year period from 6 Apr 1999: ibid, s 35

[96] *Re Smith & Fawcett Ltd* [1942] Ch 304, 306 (Lord Greene MR)

owned trading subsidiary, means in the interests of the charity, although he must also have regard to the interests of the company's employees in general.[97] If the charity is itself a company, so that the relationship between it and the trading company is one of holding company and subsidiary, the directors of the latter are permitted to take into account the interests of the holding company and the subsidiary together, provided that an 'intelligent and honest man' in their position could reasonably consider this to be in the interests of the subsidiary.[98] If, however, the trading subsidiary is insolvent, or is facing insolvency, the interests of its creditors are paramount.[99]

Because the trading subsidiary's shares will belong to the charity, it would seem **20.38** that the trustees of the charity might be in breach of their duty to protect the charity's assets if they were not to ensure that they receive an adequate flow of information from the trading subsidiary.[100] Complying with such a duty might well encompass putting at least one of their own number, or perhaps a nominee, on the board of directors of the subsidiary.[101] There is, however, a potential for a conflict of interests where the same, or some of the same, persons are both trustees of the charity and directors of the trading subsidiary. In their capacity as trustees, they owe fiduciary duties to the charity, which might conflict with the various duties imposed upon them in their capacity as directors of the subsidiary. The Charity Commissioners have pointed out the risks that a charity runs from one or more of its trustees being put into a position of conflict of interests:[102] namely, that the person occupying the dual role may be unable to separate the interests of the charity from those of the subsidiary. It might, for instance, be difficult to ascertain whether a trustee-director who, in his capacity as trustee, encourages his

---

[97] Companies Act 1985, s 309(1)

[98] *Charterbridge Corp Ltd v Lloyds Bank Ltd* [1970] Ch 72, 74

[99] *Lonrho Ltd v Shell Petroleum Ltd* [1980] 1 WLR 627, 634 (Lord Diplock); *Brady v Brady* [1989] AC 755 (HL)

[100] See the comments of Cross J in *Re Lucking's Will Trusts* [1968] 1 WLR 866, 875

[101] ibid, 875–6; but compare *Bartlett v Barclays Bank Trust Co Ltd* [1980] Ch 515, 533, where Brightman J considered representation on the board to be merely one means by which a trustee might ensure that he has sufficient information to make an informed decision on what action is appropriate to protect the trust assets

[102] (1994) 2 Decisions 20–1, and referring to the Charity Commissioners' inquiries into War on Want and the Royal British Legion. The Commissioners' inquiry into War on Want reported grave deficiencies in the administration of the charity, including failure to recover sums owed to it by WOW Campaigns and War on Want Trading Ltd: see *War on Want: Report of an Inquiry* (HMSO, 1991) and [1992] Ch Com Rep 20–2 (paras 119–27). See also the Charity Commissioners' inquiry into the affairs of the Royal British Legion: *Royal British Legion: Final Report of the Inquirer* (Charity Commission, 1992) discussed [1992] Ch Com Rep 26 (paras 99–104), and (1993) 1 Decisions 24–5. The Royal British Legion (RBL) had made loans to the Legion Leasehold Housing Association (LLHA), which was not a charity. LLHA later went into liquidation owing debts of nearly £900,000 to RBL. The Charity Commissioners expressly criticized the overlap of membership of those controlling RBL and LLHA, and pointed out that this gave rise to a conflict of interests which caused particular problems when LLHA fell into financial difficulties: see (1993) 1 Decisions 25

co-trustees to leave outstanding a loan which the charity has made to the trading company, is acting purely in the interests of the charity. The potential for conflict is most acute when the trading company is in difficulties. The trustee may in fact be acting in the interests of the trading subsidiary, or in his own interests, lest he incur personal liability for wrongful trading in the event that the trading subsidiary should go into insolvent liquidation. The Charity Commissioners recommend that there should be at least one person who is a trustee of the charity and not a director of the trading company, and vice versa.[103]

20.39 The trading subsidiary itself will be a commercial company, and will be entitled to pay remuneration to its directors; but the 'no conflicts' rule means that a trustee who becomes a director of the trading subsidiary cannot generally retain any fees paid to him in the latter capacity, since the directorship will usually flow from the trusteeship.[104] Payment to directors cannot, therefore, be used as a 'back-door' method of remunerating charity trustees.[105] The Charity Commissioners are not generally willing to register bodies as charities which seek to restrict the 'no conflicts' rule by permitting the trustees to retain any directors' fees which they might receive from a trading subsidiary, because they consider that this would be an application of the charity's assets to non-charitable purposes and the body in question would therefore not have purposes that are wholly and exclusively charitable. Similarly, applying the decisions of the courts,[106] the Commissioners are not willing to authorize an amendment to the constitution of a registered charity to allow the trustees to retain fees which might be paid to them *qua* directors of a subsidiary. The Charity Commissioners will be prepared to accept a provision in the charity's governing instrument permitting the retention of directors' fees only if they are satisfied (and the onus of proof is on the trustees) that such remuneration is necessary from the point of view of the charity and that the level of remuneration received by the directors is reasonable having regard to the services which they actually render.[107] Since the Charity Commissioners are strongly in favour of independent directors, these criteria are difficult for the trustees to meet.

---

[103] See Charity Commission, *Charities and Trading*, CC 35 (Feb 1997), 17

[104] *Re Macadam* [1946] Ch 73

[105] Charity Commission, *Charities and Trading*, CC35 (Feb 1997), 18

[106] Note esp in the context of charity, *Re Smallpiece Trust, Smallpiece v A-G*, noted [1990] Ch Com Rep 36 (App D, para (c)) (Paul Baker QC, sitting as a judge of the Chancery Division). On trustee remuneration generally, see *Re Duke of Norfolk's Settlement Trusts* [1982] Ch 61 (CA); and, most recently, *Foster v Spencer* [1996] 2 All ER 672 (Paul Baker QC, sitting as a judge of the Chancery Division)

[107] (1994) 2 Decisions 20–1, referring to *Re Smallpiece Trust, Smallpiece v A-G*, noted [1990] Ch Com Rep 36 (App D, para (c)). See also [1988] Ch Com Rep 9 (paras 38–9)

E. Trading and rate relief

Non-domestic rate relief for charities in respect of premises occupied by them is **20.40** considered generally in chapter 3.[108]

Rate relief is available if the ratepayer is a charity or trustees for a charity and the **20.41** premises are wholly or mainly used for charitable purposes.[109] There is therefore no question of rate relief where the occupier of a charity shop is a charity's trading company, because the occupier is not a charity or a trustee for a charity.[110] In practice, however, many local authorities either do not notice the difference between a charity and its trading subsidiary, or simply fail to take the point; the result is that many shop premises occupied by trading subsidiaries do obtain the benefit of rate relief, even though they are not legally entitled to it. If the charity is itself the occupier of premises, its use of them mainly to raise money for its charitable purposes by the sale of bought-in goods is not an occupation mainly for charitable purposes, so the charity is not entitled to rate relief in respect of those premises.[111] If, however, the charity uses the premises mainly for the sale of goods manufactured by the persons who are its principal beneficiaries, it will be treated as using them mainly for charitable purposes.[112] If a charity's purpose is the relief of poverty overseas, and in pursuance of that the charity runs a programme to develop local industry in developing countries, its sale of articles manufactured within that programme can be regarded as a sale of goods made by its principal beneficiaries.[113] If the charity uses the premises wholly or mainly for the sale of goods donated to a charity and the proceeds of sale of the goods (after deduction of expenses) are applied for the purposes of a charity, the premises are treated as wholly or mainly used for charitable purposes (and so the charity is entitled to rate relief).[114] In these circumstances, therefore, there is no loss of rate relief merely because a minor use of the premises occupied by the charity is the sale of goods by its trading subsidiary.

F. Liability of charity or trading subsidiary

(1) Trading carried on by the charity or charity trustees

If the charity takes the form of a trust, contracts which it enters into are entered **20.42** into by the charity trustees. Both the charity trustees and the charity's assets are

---

[108] See ch 3, paras 3.79–3.93
[109] Local Government FA 1988, s 43(5), (6)
[110] ibid, s 43(5), (6)
[111] *Oxfam v City of Birmingham DC* [1976] AC 126 (HL)
[112] ibid, though the point was there conceded
[113] ibid
[114] Local Government FA 1988, s 64(10). See further ch 3, paras 3.82–3.83

therefore potentially at risk. The risk for the trustees is that they are personally liable on the contracts, so that their own assets are at risk in the event of losses being incurred, with the potential for bankruptcy, particularly where the charitable trust's trading activities are substantial. The risk for the charity is that, where the trustees have acted properly in entering into trading contracts, they are entitled to an indemnity out of the trust's assets. If the charity takes the form of an unincorporated association, the charity's contracts will be entered into by the committee members, who (assuming that they contract as principals) will incur personal liability under the contracts, but with a similar right of indemnity out of the association's assets where they acted properly in entering into them. In each instance, if such indemnity extends to the charity's entire assets, the charity (whether trust or unincorporated association) will effectively cease to exist, and (if it is a registered charity) the Charity Commissioners must remove it from the register of charities.[115]

20.43 If the charity is incorporated, contracts which it enters into, although effected by its directors or governors (or whatever they choose to call themselves) will be made in the charity's own name. In such circumstances, creditors have a direct right of action against the charity, and its assets are at immediate risk. The directors of the company will incur no personal liability under such contracts unless the veil of incorporation is lifted, whether by statute (as where the directors have engaged in fraudulent or wrongful trading) or judicially.[116] Insolvency of a charitable company will usually lead ultimately to dissolution, whether by means of a winding-up order, or simply through the company's being struck off the register of companies. If the charitable company ceases to operate, the Charity Commissioners must remove it from the register of charities.[117] Such a company could therefore be removed from the register of charities before it has been dissolved; but it must in any event be removed from the register when it ceases to exist,[118] which will be the date of dissolution.[119]

(2) Trading carried on by a subsidiary company

20.44 If a charity's subsidiary trading company becomes insolvent, its creditors generally have actions only against the subsidiary. They may be able to recover against the subsidiary company's directors if they can establish fraudulent or wrongful trad-

---

[115] CA 1993, s 3(4). See further ch 26, para 26.04. For a more detailed analysis of the personal liability of trustees of charitable trusts, and of the committee members and ordinary members of a charitable unincorporated association, see further ch 9, paras 9.192–9.209

[116] On the personal liability of directors of charitable companies, see further ch 9, paras 9.210–9.212

[117] CA 1993, s 3(4)

[118] ibid, s 3(4)

[119] On dissolution of incorporated charities generally, see ch 26, paras 26.12–26.25

ing. The subsidiary's creditors will not normally have any right of action against the charity itself, even if (as is usual) the charity holds all its shares.

A creditor will, however, be able to proceed against the charity itself if he can **20.45** establish that the subsidiary entered into the contract as the charity's agent. Although incorporation under the Companies Acts does not itself make the company an agent for its members or for those who control it,[120] evidence may show that an agency was in fact created.[121] A charity must therefore be careful to make sure that, whilst its subsidiary is permitted to indicate to customers and suppliers that its profits will benefit the charity, the subsidiary does not represent to them that they are in fact dealing directly with the charity itself rather than with a non-charitable trading company.[122] The Charity Commissioners strongly advise all charities acting closely with an associated fund-raising company to ensure that in all publicity material directed to raising funds and in the contractual relationship of such companies with suppliers, the status of the two bodies is made clear.[123]

---

[120] *Salomon v Salomon & Co* [1897] AC 22 (HL)
[121] *Smith, Stone & Knight Ltd v Birmingham Corp* [1939] 4 All ER 116
[122] Allegations of this sort were made, eg, by some creditors in the insolvency of Sport for Sport Aid Ltd, which was a trading company established to raise funds for a charity called Sport Aid '88, and which owed debts of between £2m and £3m. See [1988] Ch Com Rep 11 (para 45)
[123] ibid 12 (para 48)

21

REGULATION OF FUND-RAISING

A. Introduction

The use by charities of professional fund-raisers has increased significantly since **21.01** the 1980s, and new methods of fund-raising have also been developing, such as the encouraging of donations by credit card. Charities have also been entering into more agreements with business organizations for their mutual advantage, a simple, and not untypical, arrangement being an agreement between a charity and, for example, a baked-bean manufacturer, under which the latter undertakes to give, say, 5 pence to the charity for every tin of baked beans that is sold, a message to this effect appearing on each tin. Although many of these relationships are beneficial to charity, some reports published in the 1980s identified scope for fraud, both on the charities entering into them, and on the public.[1]

---

[1] See esp *Malpractice in Fundraising for Charity*, report of a working party of the NCVO, Harry Kidd (chairman), 1986; *Efficiency Scrutiny of the Supervision of Charities*, report of the Woodfield Committee, Sir Philip Woodfield (chairman), 1987; *Charities: a Framework for the Future*, White

21.02 Part II of the Charities Act 1992,[2] which was brought into force on 1 March 1995,[3] together with regulations made under it,[4] introduced controls on what are termed 'professional fund-raisers'[5] and 'commercial participators'.[6] Part II seeks to combat abuse where such persons are involved in four ways. First, it requires that there be an agreement between a charitable institution[7] and such a person, which agreement must be in a prescribed form and contain prescribed information.[8] Secondly, it requires what might be called 'up-front' disclosure to the public of key information.[9] Thirdly, it gives donors in some instances a right to a cooling-off period.[10] Fourthly, it provides for the making of regulations to specify the manner in which money or other property is to be transmitted to charitable institutions.[11]

21.03 Part II is not limited in scope to institutions or purposes which are charitable within the Charities Act 1993, but also applies to institutions or purposes that are benevolent or philanthropic. In the interests of brevity, however, Part II provides that the term 'charitable institution' means a charity or an institution (other than a charity) which is established for charitable, benevolent, or philanthropic purposes.[12] It was pointed out in the House of Lords, when the Charities Bill was making its way through Parliament, that such shorthand is potentially confusing,[13] particularly in a statute which bears the words 'Charities Act' in its short title.[14] The confusion is worse compounded because, in Part II, the expression 'charity' retains the narrower meaning which it has in the Charities Act 1993.[15]

21.04 Although Part II mostly concerns professional fund-raisers and commercial participators, it also contains important provisions of wider import, which can affect other persons too.[16] The regulations made under Part II regulate fund-raising for

---

Paper, Cm 694 (1989). See further, P Luxton, *Charity Fund-raising and the Public Interest: an Anglo-American Legal Perspective* (Avebury, 1990) 37–9

[2] CA 1992, ss 58–64
[3] CA 1992 (Commencement No 2) Order 1994, SI 1994/3023
[4] Charitable Institutions (Fund-raising) Regulations 1994, SI 1994/3024
[5] Explained below, paras 21.08–21.28
[6] Explained below, paras 21.29–21.42
[7] Explained below, paras 21.05–21.07
[8] See below, paras 21.43–21.47
[9] See below, paras 21.48–21.56
[10] See below, paras 21.57–21.59
[11] See below, paras 21.60–21.65
[12] CA 1992, s 58(1)
[13] Official Report of the Committee on the Charities Bill, HL, col 214 (11 Dec 1991) (Lord Allen of Abbeydale and Lord Brightman)
[14] ibid cols 254–5 (12 Dec 1991) (Lord Renton). It seems that it was for this reason that Pts II & III were not consolidated into CA 1993; rather, the intention was that they should be consolidated in due course into a separate, more appropriately named, statute. To date, however, this has not occurred
[15] CA 1992, s 58(1), as amended by CA 1993, s 98(1) & Sch 6, para 29(5). CA 1993 does not define 'charity' but it is clear that it refers to an institution with 'charitable purposes', ie purposes that are exclusively charitable according to the law of England and Wales: CA 1993, s 97(1)
[16] See below, paras 21.66–21.71

charitable, benevolent, or philanthropic purposes by persons in business who do not rank as professional fund-raisers or commercial participators.[17] Part II also confers a right on a charitable institution to prevent unauthorized fund-raising,[18] and makes it a criminal offence falsely to represent in a solicitation for a charity that it is a registered charity when that is not so.[19]

B. Definitions

(1) Charitable institution

For the purposes of Part II of the Charities Act 1992, a charitable institution **21.05** means a charity or an institution (other than a charity) which is established for charitable, benevolent, or philanthropic purposes.[20] Benevolent or philanthropic purposes are not defined in the Act, but evidently include purposes that are not in law charitable.

There is scant case law in England on the meaning of benevolent;[21] but in **21.06** Australia, a public benevolent institution has been construed to mean an institution which promotes the relief of poverty, sickness, destitution, or helplessness.[22] Since the promotion of a purpose is not charitable in English law unless it involves a public benefit, an appeal for funds to enable a child to be sent overseas for a medical operation could not be a charitable purpose, but would seem to be a benevolent one, since an act may be benevolent if it indicates goodwill to a particular individual only.[23] Lord Bramwell suggested that a fund for providing oysters for Benchers at one of the Inns of Court, whilst not charitable, might be benevolent; as might a trust to provide a band of music on the village green.[24]

Since philanthropy connotes a love of mankind, it may take many different forms, **21.07** including the giving of money to a beggar. In *Re Macduff*,[25] Stirling J considered 'philanthropic' to be a word of narrower meaning than benevolent, and that an act cannot be said to be philanthropic unless it indicates goodwill to mankind at large. He nevertheless thought that it could include purposes not technically

---

[17] Charitable Institutions (Fund-Raising) Regulations 1994, SI 1994/3024, reg 7
[18] CA 1992, s 62
[19] ibid, s 63(1)
[20] ibid, s 58(1)
[21] *James v Allen* (1817) 3 Mer 17 (bequest in trust for 'benevolent' purposes held not exclusively charitable, and so void)
[22] *Perpetual Trustee Co Ltd v FCT* (1931) 45 CLR 224; *Commission of Pay-roll Tax (Vic) v Cairnmillar Institute* (1990) 90 ATC 4752
[23] *Re Macduff* [1896] 2 Ch 451, 457 (Stirling J)
[24] *Comrs for Special Purposes of the Income Tax v Pemsel* [1891] AC 531, 565 (Lord Bramwell)
[25] [1896] 2 Ch 451, 457. Similarly, observations of Lindley LJ in the same case on appeal: ibid, 464 (CA)

charitable.[26] In *McGovern v Attorney-General*,[27] Slade J referred to Amnesty International (which essentially seeks to secure the observance of human rights throughout the world) as a 'philanthropic' organization.[28]

(2) Professional fund-raiser

21.08 The expression 'professional fund-raiser' means:[29]

    (a) any person (apart from a charitable institution[30] or a company connected with such an institution[31]) who carries on a fund-raising business, or

    (b) any other person (apart from a person excluded by virtue of subsection (2) or (3)[32]) who for reward solicits money or other property for the benefit of a charitable institution, if he does so otherwise than in the course of any fund-raising venture undertaken by a person within paragraph (a) above.

The meaning of certain phrases in this definition will now be considered in turn.

'fund-raising business'

21.09 The expression 'fund-raising business' means any business carried on for gain and wholly or primarily engaged in soliciting or otherwise procuring money or other property for charitable, benevolent, or philanthropic purposes.[33] The meaning of 'wholly or primarily' and 'soliciting or otherwise procuring' will now be considered in turn.

'wholly or primarily'

21.10 A person who carries on a business which is not wholly or primarily engaged in raising money for charitable, benevolent, or philanthropic purposes is not, therefore, a professional fund-raiser within paragraph (a) of the definition contained in section 58(1) of the Charities Act 1992; but he may be a professional fund-raiser within paragraph (b) if he solicits for reward.

'soliciting'

21.11 To 'solicit' means to solicit in any manner whatever, whether expressly or impliedly, and whether done by speaking directly to the person or persons to whom the solicitation is addressed (whether when in his or their presence or not), or by

---

[26] [1896] 2 Ch 451, 457
[27] [1982] Ch 321
[28] ibid, 329, 354
[29] CA 1992, s 58(1)
[30] 'Charitable institution' means a charity or an institution (other than a charity) which is established for charitable, benevolent, or philanthropic purposes: ibid, s 58(1)
[31] The exclusion of a company connected with such an institution was inserted by the Deregulation and Contracting Out Act 1994, s 25. For the meaning of a company connected with a charitable institution, see CA 1992, s 58(5), considered below, para 21.24
[32] For the exclusions in subsection (2) and (3), see below, paras 21.23–21.24
[33] CA 1992, s 58(1)

means of a statement published in any newspaper, film or radio or television pro-gramme, or otherwise.[34] Soliciting may take place whether any consideration is, or is to be, given in return for the money or other property or not.[35]

'or otherwise procuring'

A person may 'otherwise procure' money or other property whether any consid- **21.12**
eration is, or is to be, given in return for the money or other property, or not.[36]

The phrase 'or otherwise procuring' caused some concern during the passage of **21.13**
the Charities Bill through Parliament, lest it bring within the definition of a pro-fessional fund-raiser a whole range of outside agencies which, whilst wholly or primarily engaged in providing support services for fund-raising for charitable in-stitutions, did not themselves directly solicit. Examples might be a marketing consultant who gives advice to a charity on how to prepare its fund-raising pam-phlets, an organization which specializes in writing fund-raising copy, a firm which merely prints the fund-raising leaflets or merely puts the appeal letters into envelopes, or a direct-mailing firm which sends out letters of appeal on behalf of a charity. In Committee, Earl Ferrers assured the House that there was no inten-tion to catch such persons, who were merely providing a service to the charity in the same way that a catering contractor might supply the charity with food.[37] These assurances were repeated at the Report stage, where Viscount Astor ex-plained that the words were intended to deal with the situation where, although an appeal or campaign is undertaken solely by a professional fund-raiser, the ap-peal letter appears to come from the charity itself, with the name and address of the fund-raiser appearing, sometimes inconspicuously, as the recipient of dona-tions.[38] He said that the key factor in such circumstances is that the fund-raiser is the agent who makes the appeal and gathers in the funds, and a reference to solic-iting alone might be inadequate to bring the fund-raiser within the definition of a professional fund-raiser. In his view, the expression 'or otherwise procure' makes it clear that the fund-raiser must actively achieve the obtaining of funds for char-itable purposes, and not simply be a passive recipient by accident.

'Any other person . . . who for reward solicits'

Moral benefit insufficient

Reward in this context presumably requires some monetary, or other financial or **21.14**
proprietary, benefit. It is therefore necessary to exclude any purely moral benefit

---

[34] ibid, s 58(6)(a)
[35] ibid, s 58(6)(b)
[36] ibid
[37] Official Report of the Committee on the Charities Bill, HL, col 220 (11 Dec 1991)
[38] Hansard, HL (series 5) vol 535, Report on the Charities Bill, cols 1202–3 (18 Feb 1992)

which a person might derive from soliciting as a volunteer. It is also necessary to exclude consequential benefits that do not flow directly from the soliciting. Some public figures, for instance, may enjoy favourable publicity by soliciting unpaid for a charity; but any resultant financial benefits which they might thereby obtain, such as additional engagements, are too uncertain and remote to comprise the rewards of solicitation.

No contractual entitlement

21.15 Presumably a person can solicit for reward even if he has no contractual entitlement to any payment, provided that there is an understanding that the charity might be prepared to make him some payment. If, therefore, a number of persons solicit voluntarily but subject to the promise that the one whose solicitations raise the largest total amount for the charity will receive £1,000, each can probably be treated as 'soliciting for reward'.[39] It is, however, possible to envisage that a body set up to encourage good practice in fund-raising might make an exceptional award to a person in recognition of many years devoted to soliciting funds for charity on a voluntary basis.[40] Such a person would not have solicited with a view to obtaining such award, and his acceptance of it would not thereby turn him retrospectively into a professional fund-raiser. Were the position otherwise, no volunteer could safely solicit without complying with Part II of the Charities Act 1992.

Employees or agents of paragraph (a) professional fund-raisers

21.16 An agent or employee of a person who is a professional fund-raiser within paragraph (a) of the definition contained in s 58(1) of the Charities Act 1992 is not also deemed to be a professional fund-raiser merely because it is he who actually makes the solicitation.[41]

Companies or firms which solicit for reward

21.17 A company or firm which is not wholly or mainly engaged in fund-raising for charitable, benevolent, or philanthropic purposes will nevertheless become a professional fund-raiser under paragraph (b) if it solicits (for a charitable institution) for reward. It cannot escape from paragraph (b) by arguing that the soliciting is performed by its employees or agents, since the act of an employee in the proper

---

[39] cf income tax cases which hold that a sum received by an employee from his employer can comprise an emolument of the employment (and so fall to be taxable within Sch E; ICTA 1988, s 19) even if the employee has no contractual entitlement to it: *Laidler v Perry* [1965] AC 16 (HL)

[40] cf income tax cases which hold that an irregular payment, with no foreseeable element of recurrence, paid to a professional sportsman in recognition of his sporting achievements, might not be taxable as an emolument within Sch E, if he has no contractual right to it. Such a sum might be more in the nature of a testimonial or an accolade rather than a reward for services: *Seymour v Reed* (1927) 11 TC 625 (HL); *Moore v Griffiths* (1972) 48 TC 338 (Brightman J)

[41] See proviso to para (b) of definition of professional fund-raiser in CA 1993, s 58(1)

course of his employment, or the act of an agent within the actual scope of his agency, is treated as performed by the employer or principal itself.

Employees or agents of companies or firms which solicit for reward

An agent or employee of a person who is a professional fund-raiser under para- **21.18**
graph (b) cannot shelter behind the exclusion at the end of paragraph (b), because
that paragraph only excludes them from the definition of professional fund-raiser
if their principal or employer is a professional fund-raiser under paragraph (a). It
is therefore arguable that if a professional fund-raiser within paragraph (b) solicits
through its employees or agents, those employees or agents also become professional fund-raisers within paragraph (b) because they are the persons who actually
solicit.

Such agents or employees will become professional fund-raisers, however, only if **21.19**
they solicit 'for reward', and whether a solicitation can be said to be for reward in
a particular case is not necessarily clear.

A company which normally conducts marketing campaigns for the commercial **21.20**
sector may employ staff on employment contracts which require them to perform
whatever work is allotted to them by the employer. If the company is hired by a
charity to conduct a fund-raising campaign, some of its employees might be given
the task of soliciting funds; but it is arguable that (unless they are paid a commission which varies according to the amount which they raise) such employees are
not soliciting 'for reward'; they are merely performing the duties allocated to them
by their employer from time to time. It is only the company which is soliciting for
reward through the acts of its employees.

Secondment to charity of employee or agent

It is important to consider how the provisions operate in the case of a secondment. **21.21**
If, for example, a bank were to volunteer the services of one of its employees to a
charity and continue to pay his salary, it has been suggested that, if that employee
solicits for the charity, he becomes a professional fund-raiser within paragraph (b):
he cannot shelter behind the exclusion in paragraph (b) because his employer is
not a professional fund-raiser within paragraph (a).[42] However, as has been argued
above, it is debatable whether the employee can in these circumstances be considered to be soliciting for reward at all; it could be contended that the employee is
remunerated for working for the bank, and that his soliciting for the charity is to
be treated as gratuitous. However, even if the employee is a professional fund-
raiser within paragraph (b), the mere fact that the bank authorized its employee to
solicit does not make the bank a professional fund-raiser, since the bank is not soliciting for reward.

---

[42] See F Middleton, & S Lloyd, *The Charities Handbook* (Jordans, 1996) 83–4

'for the benefit of a charitable institution'

21.22 A person cannot be a professional fund-raiser within the definition in section 58(1), paragraph (b), of the Charities Act 1992 if he solicits merely for charitable, benevolent, or philanthropic purposes, rather than for a charitable, benevolent or philanthropic institution. However, under the general law, a person who solicits for such purposes and who intends to keep some of the funds so raised for himself must make this clear to the persons solicited at the time of solicitation, otherwise the donors are entitled to expect that the whole of the money so contributed will be applied to the stated purposes.

Exclusions

21.23 The exclusions contained in section 58(2) of the Charities Act 1992 are:

(a) any charitable institution or any company connected with any such institution;

(b) any officer or employee of any such institution or company, or any trustee of any such institution, acting (in each case) in his capacity as such;

(c) any person acting as a collector in respect of a public charitable collection (apart from a person who is to be treated as a promoter of such a collection by virtue of section 65(3));[43]

(d) any person who in the course of a relevant programme, that is to say a radio or television programme[44] in the course of which a fund-raising venture is undertaken by—

    (i) a charitable institution, or

    (ii) a company connected with such an institution,

makes any solicitation at the instance of that institution or company; or

(e) any commercial participator.

21.24 For the purpose of Part II of the Charities Act 1992, a company is connected with a charitable institution if the institution (together if necessary with one or more other such institutions) is entitled (whether directly or through one or more nominees) to exercise, or to control the exercise of, the whole of the voting power at the company's general meeting.[45]

21.25 In-house fund-raisers are excluded by paragraph (b). The risk of the charity being unfairly exploited is clearly reduced where the charity itself controls a fund-raising company or employs its own fund-raisers. There remains the possibility that less reputable firms of fund-raisers might set up their own (captive) charities to employ themselves as fund-raisers at exorbitant salaries. They would then be outside the reach of Part II of the Charities Act 1992, although not necessarily beyond the reach of the Charity Commissioners.[46]

---

[43] For this purpose, 'collector' and 'public charitable collection' have the same meaning as in CA 1992, Pt III: see ch 22, paras 22.56 and 22.60. For the circumstances in which a collector is to be treated as a promoter by virtue of ibid, s 65(3), see ch 22, para 22.66

[44] A 'radio or television programme' includes any item included in a programme service within the meaning of the Broadcasting Act 1990: CA 1992, s 58(1)

[45] CA 1992, s 58(5)

[46] eg by exercising their remedial powers under CA 1993, s 18, following a s 8 inquiry

At the Committee stage of the Charities Bill, fears were expressed that persons **21.26** such as Terry Wogan who appear on the television in fund-raising programmes, and others who receive a small appearance fee, might themselves rank as professional fund-raisers.[47] The exclusion in paragraph (d) was inserted to clarify that such persons are outside the statutory definition. This express exclusion may, however, be unnecessary, since it might be argued that if the person in question has a contract to appear on a number of television programmes over a specified period, his soliciting on the fund-raising programme is not for reward.[48] The exclusion means that even a person paid a very large fee specifically to make a solicitation in a radio or television programme is not a professional fund-raiser.

The owner of a restaurant who places an advertisement in the window stating that **21.27** he will give 10 per cent of the cost of each meal eaten in the restaurant to a named charity prima facie appears to be a professional fund-raiser, since he seems to be soliciting or otherwise procuring money for that charity for reward (that is, through increased profits). He does, however, fall within the definition of a commercial participator, and the exclusion in paragraph (e) makes it clear that he is therefore to be treated as a commercial participator, and not as a professional fund-raiser.

Section 58(3) of the Charities Act 1992 excludes from the definition of profes- **21.28** sional fund-raiser[49] any person who does not receive more than £5 per day or £500 per year in remuneration in soliciting for the benefit of the institution; or not more than £500 in connection with any fund-raising venture. The aim of this is to exclude persons who are essentially volunteers, but who receive a small honorarium.[50]

(3) Commercial participator

Definition

A commercial participator in relation to any charitable institution means any **21.29** person (apart from a company connected with the institution[51]) who carries on for gain a business other than a fund-raising business, but in the course of that business engages in any promotional venture in the course of which it is represented that charitable contributions are to be given to or applied for the benefit of

---

[47] See Official Report of the Committee on the Charities Bill, HL, cols 222–3 (11 Dec 1991)
[48] ibid, cols 222–3 (Lord Astor)
[49] ie from paragraph (b) of the definition of professional fund-raiser contained in CA 1992, s 58(1): see above, para 21.08
[50] See Official Report of the Committee on the Charities Bill, HL, col 219 (11 Dec 1991) (Earl Ferrers)
[51] The words in parentheses were added by the Deregulation and Contracting Out Act 1994, s 25. For the meaning of a company connected with a charitable institution, see above, para 21.24

the institution.[52] The meaning of the phrases 'promotional venture', 'it is represented', and 'charitable contributions' will now be examined in turn.

'promotional venture'

21.30 'Promotional venture' means any advertising or sales campaign or any other venture undertaken for promotional purposes.[53]

'it is represented'

21.31 To 'represent' means to represent in any manner whatever, whether expressly or impliedly and whether done by speaking directly to the person or persons to whom the representation is addressed (whether when in his or their presence or not), or by means of a statement published in any newspaper, film or radio or television programme, or otherwise.[54]

21.32 The use of the passive voice indicates that the representation could be made by somebody other than the commercial participator, so long as it is made in the course of the latter's promotional venture. The wording is probably intended to ensure that the provisions relating to commercial participators apply even if the representation is made by the charity rather than by the commercial participator. If, for instance, a charity, pursuant to an agreement with a retail chain of pizza restaurants, itself advertises that the chain will donate to it 10 pence for each pizza sold by that chain, the representation is made in the course of the pizza chain's promotional venture. The owner of the chain is therefore a commercial participator even though it does not itself make the representation. It suffices that there is a representation that contributions are to be made by the pizza chain.

'charitable contributions'

21.33 In Part II, 'charitable contributions', in relation to any representation made by any commercial participator or other person, means:[55]

    (a) the whole or part of—
        (i) the consideration given for goods or services sold or supplied by him, or
        (ii) any proceeds (other than such consideration) of a promotional venture undertaken by him, or
    (b) sums given by him by way of donation in connection with the sale or supply of any such goods or services (whether the amount of such sums is determined by reference to the value of any such goods or services or otherwise).

'services'

21.34 'Services' in Part II includes facilities, and in particular:[56]

---

[52] CA 1992, s 58(1)
[53] ibid, s 58(1)
[54] ibid, s 58(6)
[55] ibid, s 58(1)
[56] ibid, s 58(9)

(a) access to any premises or event;
(b) membership of any organisation;
(c) the provision of advertising space; and
(d) the provision of any financial facilities.

Examples of who is or is not a commercial participator

Manufacturer

A manufacturer of chocolate bars whose chocolate wrappers state that 10 pence **21.35** out of the purchase price of each bar sold will be given to a specified charitable institution is a commercial participator. The manufacturer is carrying on a business other than a fund-raising business, and the activity is clearly an advertising or sales campaign, and so comprises a promotional venture. The statement on the wrappers is an express representation that charitable contributions are to be given to the specified charitable institution. The manufacturer is a commercial participator whether he sells the bars himself or (as is more likely) supplies them to a retailer. In the latter case, the 'charitable contributions' comprise part of the consideration given for goods 'supplied by him'.

Retail shops and supermarkets

It has been suggested that the shop which sells such chocolate bars is also a com- **21.36** mercial participator. The shop is a business other than a fund-raising business, and the display of the bars would appear to comprise a promotional venture by the shop 'in the course of which it is represented' that charitable contributions (that is, part of the consideration given for goods sold by the store) are to be given to the charitable institution. It could be argued that, in the present context, the representation is made by the shop as well as by the manufacturer; but the use of the passive voice in the phrase 'it is represented' indicates that the shop can be a commercial participator even if the representation is made by the manufacturer alone, since it is made in the course of the shop's promotional venture. Nevertheless, it cannot have been intended that the definition should include a retailer in such circumstances, since it may be impractical for a retailer (especially a large supermarket chain) to enter into a separate contract with each charity concerned.[57]

Manufacturer contracting with charity's trading company

In the foregoing example, the manufacturer of chocolate bars may contract with **21.37** the charity's trading company rather than with the charity itself. The agreement between them may provide that the manufacturer is to pay the appropriate sums to the trading company. However, if the wrappers represent that the sums in question are to be given to the charity, the manufacturer is a commercial participator.

---

[57] See Judith Hill, 'Enter the Commercial Participator' (1995–6) 3 CL & PR 17, 21–2

Particular problems resulting from the application of Part II to agreements with a charity's trading company are considered more fully below.[58]

Credit card companies issuing affinity cards

21.38 A credit card company which issues affinity cards, under which a specified charity is to benefit each time the card is used, is a commercial participator. The credit card company is carrying on a business other than a fund-raising business, and the activity is a promotional venture. The credit card company is supplying services in that it is providing financial facilities.[59] The mere use of the charity's name and logo on the card is an implied representation that charitable contributions (meaning sums given by way of donation in connection with the supply of such services[60]) are to be given to that charity.

Commercial organizers of lotteries

21.39 A commercial organization which runs a lottery for a specific charity is probably a commercial participator. It is carrying on a business which (unless it is wholly or primarily engaged in procuring money for charitable, benevolent, or philanthropic purposes) is not a fund-raising business.[61] It will also be representing that charitable contributions are to be given to the charity. 'Charitable contributions' in this context means part of the consideration given for 'services' supplied by the organization.[62]

Business sponsors

21.40 If a charity organizes a fund-raising event, such as a concert or a play, and obtains a promise of sponsorship from a commercial company to assist with the expenses of holding the event, the sponsor may require the sponsorship to be acknowledged in any advertisements for the event and in the programme. The commercial company will be carrying on a business other than a fund-raising business, and the arrangement for publicity as part of the sponsorship might be considered to be an advertising campaign and so a promotional venture in which the commercial company engages in the course of its business. Can it be argued that, in the course of such promotional venture, it is represented that charitable contributions are to be given to the charity concerned? The answer seems to be no, since neither the sponsorship money which the company will pay to the charity,[63] nor the purchase

---

[58] See below, paras 21.47, 21.56, and 21.64–21.65
[59] CA 1992, s 58(9)(d)
[60] ibid, s 58(1)
[61] ibid, definition of 'fund-raising business' in s 58(1)
[62] ibid, definition of 'charitable contributions' in s 58(1). See S Lloyd, *Charities, Trading and the Law* (Charities Advisory Trust, 1995) 133–4; Lloyd argues that a lottery is an 'event', so that the provision of a lottery comprises 'services' as being the provision of access to an event within CA 1992, s 58(9)(a)
[63] Such sponsorship money falls outside the definition of 'charitable contributions' in CA 1992, s 58(1), because (for the purposes of para (a) of that definition), it is neither consideration for goods

price (or a part of it) paid by members of the public for their tickets that is represented to go to charity,[64] falls within the definition of 'charitable contributions'.

Commercial organizations selling by mail order or catalogue

A commercial organization which sells goods by mail order or through a cata- **21.41**
logue, indicating that part of the purchase price will go to a specific charity, is
clearly a commercial participator.

Business which indicates that part of proceeds will benefit charitable, benevolent, or
philanthropic purposes (as opposed to one or more specific charitable institutions)

If a florist, for instance, puts a notice in his shop window that he will give 5 per **21.42**
cent of his profits for one week for charitable purposes, he is not a commercial participator. He is carrying on a business other than a fund-raising business, and the
activity seems to comprise a promotional venture; but one essential ingredient is
missing, namely, he is not representing that charitable contributions are to be
given to a specific charitable institution. Since, however, he is representing that
contributions are to be applied for charitable purposes, he is obliged, under the
regulations made pursuant to Part II of the Charities Act 1992, to accompany
such a representation with prescribed information.[65] This is dealt with further
below.[66] There is clearly a risk that somebody in such a position may not be aware
of such a statutory obligation, breach of which is a criminal offence.[67] There is a
defence of reasonable excuse,[68] but it is difficult to see that ignorance of the existence of the relevant legislative provision can be a reasonable excuse.

C. Contract with charitable institution

(1) Statutory requirements

It is unlawful for a professional fund-raiser to solicit for the benefit of a charitable **21.43**
institution, or for a commercial participator to represent that charitable contributions are to be given to or applied for the benefit of a charitable institution, unless
(in each case) he does so in accordance with an agreement with that institution

---

or services sold or supplied by the company, nor the proceeds of a promotional venture undertaken
by it; and (for the purposes of para (b)), it is not a sum given by the company by way of donation in
connection with the sale or supply of any such goods or services

[64] This is because the services in question (the putting on of the performance) are supplied by the
charity, not (as required by CA 1992, s 58(1)), by the company itself
[65] Charitable Institutions (Fund-Raising) Regulations 1994, SI 1994/3024, reg 7(2)
[66] See below, paras 21.67–21.69
[67] This offence is punishable on summary conviction by a fine not exceeding the 2nd level on the
standard scale: Charitable Institutions (Fund-Raising) Regulations 1994, SI 1994/3024, reg 8
[68] ibid, reg 7(2)

satisfying the prescribed requirements.[69] The institution may obtain an injunction restraining any contravention of these statutory prohibitions.[70]

21.44 An agreement which does not satisfy the prescribed requirements is not enforceable against the institution except to such extent (if any) as the court may allow.[71] In particular, the professional fund-raiser or commercial participator is not entitled to remuneration or expenses unless these are provided for in an agreement which satisfies the prescribed requirements.[72]

(2) The requirements prescribed by regulation

21.45 Most of the requirements prescribed by regulation are common to agreements with both professional fund-raisers and commercial participators. The agreement must be in writing and signed by or on behalf of the charitable institution and the professional fund-raiser or the commercial participator (as the case may be).[73] The agreement must specify the name and address of each of the parties to it, the date on which it was signed, the period for which it is to subsist, and any terms relating to its termination or variation during that period.[74] It must also contain a statement of its principal objectives and the methods used to pursue them.[75] If more than one charitable institution is party to the agreement, it must also contain provision as to the manner in which the proportion in which such institutions are respectively to benefit is to be determined.[76] The agreement must also provide for any amount by way of remuneration or expenses which the professional fund-raiser or commercial participator is to be entitled to receive, and the manner in which that amount is to be determined.[77]

21.46 An agreement with a commercial participator must additionally contain provision as to the manner in which is to be determined:[78]

> (ii) the proportion of the consideration given for goods or services sold or supplied by the commercial participator, or of any other proceeds of a promotional venture undertaken by him, which is to be given to or applied for the benefit of the charitable institution, or

---

[69] CA 1992, s 59(1)(2)
[70] ibid, s 59(3)
[71] ibid, s 59(4)
[72] ibid, s 59(5)
[73] Charitable Institutions (Fund-raising) Regulations 1994, SI 1994/3024, regs 2(2) (professional fund-raiser), 3(2) (commercial participator)
[74] ibid, regs 2(3) (professional fund-raiser), 3(3) (commercial participator)
[75] ibid, regs 2(4)(a) (professional fund-raiser), 3(4)(a) (commercial participator). The statement of methods must, where the agreement is with a commercial participator, include, in relation to each method, a description of the type of charitable contributions which are to be given to or applied for the benefit of the charitable institution and of the circumstances in which they are to be given or applied: ibid, reg 3(5)
[76] ibid, regs 2(4)(b) (professional fund-raiser), 3(4)(b)(i) (commercial participator)
[77] ibid, regs 2(4)(c) (professional fund-raiser), 3(4)(c) (commercial participator)
[78] ibid, reg 3(4)(b)(ii)(iii)

(iii) the sums by way of donations by the commercial participator in connection
with the sale or supply of any goods or services sold or supplied by him which are
to be so given or applied,
as the case may require.

(3) Need for tripartite arrangement with commercial participator

It has been pointed out that the regulations are fundamentally flawed in that they **21.47**
require the contract to be entered into with the charity itself; whereas, in practice,
in order that the charity can avoid liability to tax on trading income, a commercial participator will be hired, not by the charity, but by its subsidiary trading company. The whole point of such arrangement would be lost if the charity were to be
a principal party to the agreement, since the share of the profits would be taxable
as trading profits in its hands. It has been suggested that the difficulty can be surmounted by the use of a tripartite arrangement, under which the trading company is a principal party, and the charity merely joins in to indicate that it has no
objection to the agreement between the trading company and the commercial
participator.[79]

D. Disclosure statement accompanying solicitation
or representation

(1) Professional fund-raiser

Solicitation for particular charitable institution or institutions

If a professional fund-raiser solicits for a particular charitable institution or insti- **21.48**
tutions, the solicitation must be accompanied by a statement clearly indicating:[80]

(a) the name or names of the institution or institutions concerned;
(b) if there is more than one institution concerned, the proportions in which the institutions are respectively to benefit; and
(c) (in general terms) the method by which the fund-raiser's remuneration in connection with the appeal is to be determined.

Solicitation for charitable, benevolent, or philanthropic purposes

If a professional fund-raiser solicits for charitable, benevolent, or philanthropic **21.49**
purposes of any description (rather than for the benefit of one or more particular
charitable institutions), the solicitation must be accompanied by a statement
clearly indicating:[81]

---

[79] See Judith Hill, 'Enter the Commercial Participator' (1995–6) 3 CL & PR 17, 20–1
[80] CA 1992, s 60(1)
[81] ibid, s 60(2)

(a) the fact that he is soliciting money or other property for those purposes and not for the benefit of any particular charitable institution or institutions;

(b) the method by which it is to be determined how the proceeds of the appeal are to be distributed between different charitable institutions; and

(c) (in general terms) the method by which his remuneration in connection with the appeal is to be determined.

21.50 What the professional fund-raiser must do to comply with paragraph (c) in each of these respective sub-sections is by no means clear, and there can be no certainty until their scope has been considered by the court. The more complex the formula by which the professional fund-raiser's remuneration is to be determined, the more difficult it becomes to ascertain what his disclosure statement must contain. If the amount of detail required in the statement is in inverse proportion to the complexity of that formula, a complex formula might be used in order to reduce the statement to a useless level of abstraction.

21.51 If, for example, a professional fund-raiser's contract with the charity entitles him to take by way of remuneration 10 per cent of the sums which he raises, the paragraph could be interpreted in different ways so as to require him to state that his remuneration is to be determined by any one of the following methods:

(a) according to the total amount that he raises;

(b) according to (an unspecified) percentage of the total amount that he raises; or

(c) by calculating 10 per cent of the total amount that he raises.

21.52 Since (a) does not indicate the 'method' by which payment is to be determined, it must be insufficient. It could be argued that the 'method' is merely the calculation of a percentage, so that, as in (b), it is not necessary to state what the particular percentage is. Such an interpretation, however, would give the contributor no idea at all of the proportion that the professional fund-raiser is to take, and would therefore rob the statutory requirement of its intended purpose. It therefore seems that, in these circumstances, the professional fund-raiser would have to make a statement in accordance with (c).

21.53 According to the same principle, if the professional fund-raiser is paid on the basis of time spent, it would seem that the statement would need to specify that his remuneration is to be determined 'according to the time spent fund-raising at the rate of £x per hour.'

21.54 If, however, the professional fund-raiser is paid by a more complex formula, it may be difficult to summarize it 'in general terms' without some loss of detail. If, for example, his contract provides for him to receive a flat fee of £10,000 supplemented by 10 per cent of the total amount raised up to £50,000, 7½ per cent in respect of any excess up to £100,000, and 5 per cent in respect of any excess above £100,000, it cannot be realistic to suppose that the statement should include all this information. It is submitted that, in such circumstances, a statement 'in general terms' requires merely an indication that the professional fund-raiser is paid: '£10,000 plus a varying percentage depending on the amount raised, but not exceeding 10 per cent.'

(2) Commercial participator

A commercial participator who represents that charitable contributions are to be **21.55** given to or applied for the benefit of one or more particular charitable institutions must accompany the representation by a statement clearly indicating:[82]

> (a) the name or names of the institution or institutions concerned;
> (b) if there is more than one institution concerned, the proportions in which the institutions are respectively to benefit; and
> (c) (in general terms) the method by which it is to be determined—
>> (i) what proportion of the consideration given for goods or services sold or supplied by him, or of any other proceeds of a promotional venture undertaken by him, is to be given to or applied for the benefit of the institution or institutions concerned, or
>> (ii) what sums by way of donations by him in connection with the sale or supply of any such goods or services are to be so given or applied,
>
> as the case may require.

If the commercial participator's contract requires him to make payments to the **21.56** charity's trading company, it is unlikely that the charity will ultimately receive the full amount, since the trading company will have its own trading costs, and will pay over only its net profits after deductions in respect of those trading costs have been made. Indeed, if a sales campaign, for instance, should prove unsuccessful, there is even the risk that there will be no trading profit to transfer to the charity at all. It has been suggested, however, that, where the commercial participator pays a fixed percentage of its sales to a trading company which covenants all its profits to charity, the statutory requirement will be met by a statement to the effect that 'x per cent of each item sold will be paid to XYZ Ltd, a company which covenants all its profits to Y Charity'.[83]

E. Cooling-off period

In certain circumstances, a donor has a right to claim repayment of any donation **21.57** made or to cancel any agreement entered into. This right applies in each case only if the sum paid or agreed to be paid is £50 or more,[84] and in each case permitted administrative expenses may be deducted from any refund.[85]

---

[82] ibid, s 60(3)
[83] See Judith Hill, 'Enter the Commercial Participator' (1995–6) 3 CL & PR 17, 24–5
[84] CA 1992, s 61(1)–(3)
[85] ibid, s 61(4)

(1) Radio or television appeals seeking credit or debit card payments

21.58 If the solicitation or representation is made by a professional fund-raiser or a commercial participator in the course of a radio or television programme, and in association with an announcement to the effect that payment may be made by means of a credit or debit card, the disclosure statement must include details of the right to have any payment of at least £50 refunded under section 61(1) of the Charities Act 1992.[86] The contributor has a right to cancel by notice in writing within a period of seven days beginning with the date of the solicitation or representation.[87]

(2) Indirect oral appeals

21.59 If a solicitation or representation by a professional fund-raiser or commercial participator is made orally but not by speaking directly to the particular person or persons to whom it is addressed and in his or their presence, or in the course of a radio or television programme, the professional fund-raiser or commercial participator must, within seven days of any payment of £50 or more being made to him in response to the solicitation or representation, give the contributor a written statement of the matters which must be contained in the disclosure statement[88] together with details of the right to cancel or to have refunded under section 61(1) of the Charities Act 1992 any payment of £50 or more.[89] The contributor has a right to cancel in writing within seven days of his receiving such written statement.[90]

F. Transmission of money to charitable institutions

21.60 Part II of the Charities Act 1992 expressly empowers the Secretary of State to regulate the manner in which money or other property acquired by professional fund-raisers or commercial participators for the benefit of charitable institutions is to be transmitted to such institutions.[91] This is specified in regulation 6 of the Regulations made in 1994,[92] which lays down the manner in which such money or property is to be transmitted, notwithstanding any inconsistent term in an agreement made for the purposes of section 59 of the Charities Act 1992.

---

[86] CA 1992, s 60(4)
[87] ibid, s 61(1)
[88] For contents of disclosure statement, see above, paras 21.48–21.56
[89] ibid, s 60(5)
[90] ibid, s 61(2)
[91] ibid, s 64(2)(c)
[92] Charitable Institutions (Fund-raising) Regulations 1994, SI 1994/3024, reg 6(1)

If the professional fund-raiser or commercial participator fails to comply with the   **21.61**
obligations which this regulation imposes, without a reasonable excuse,[93] he commits an offence punishable on summary conviction by a fine not exceeding the
second level on the standard scale.[94]

(1) Money, negotiable instruments, and the proceeds of sale or disposal of other property

Each of these must be paid, as soon as is reasonably practicable after its receipt,   **21.62**
and in any event within twenty-eight days after its receipt or such other period as
may be agreed with the institution, either to the person or persons having the general control and management of the administration of the institution, or into a
bank, or building society, account in the name of or on behalf of the institution
which is under the control of any such person or persons.[95]

(2) Property pending sale or other disposal

Until it is sold or otherwise disposed of, any property (other than money or nego-   **21.63**
tiable instruments) acquired by a professional fund-raiser or commercial participator must be dealt with in accordance with any instructions given for that
purpose, either generally or in a particular case, by the institution. This is subject
to the requirement that any property in the possession of the professional fund-raiser or commercial participator, either pending the obtaining of such instructions or in accordance with such instructions, must be securely held by him.[96]

(3) Practical difficulties involving charities' trading companies

It has been pointed out that regulation 6 of the Charitable Institutions (Fund-   **21.64**
raising) Regulations 1994[97] can cause difficulties where, as is often the case, a commercial participator enters into an agreement with a charity's trading company.[98]
If the agreement provided for the commercial participator to pay the sums to the
charity itself, the arrangement would not be tax efficient, since the profit would be
taxable as trading income in the charity's hands. In many instance, therefore, the
commercial participator's contract requires him to pay the sums due to the trading subsidiary, in order that they can ultimately be made over to the charity by a
suitably tax-efficient means, such as by payments under deed of covenant that
qualify for Corporate Gift Aid.[99]

---

[93] ibid, reg 6(2)
[94] ibid, reg 8
[95] ibid, reg 6(2)(a) (money or negotiable instruments); reg 6(2)(b)(ii) (proceeds of sale or disposal of other property)
[96] ibid, reg 6(2)(b)
[97] SI 1994/3024
[98] See Judith Hill, 'Enter the Commercial Participator' (1995–6) 3 CL & PR 17, 22–3
[99] For a discussion of Corporate Gift Aid, see ch 19, paras 19.81–19.84

21.65   Regulation 6, however, is evidently drafted on the footing that the commercial participator will pay the sums due to the charity directly. Where, therefore, the commercial participator pays the sums to the trading subsidiary, the former will be committing an offence if the trading subsidiary fails to transfer such sums to the charity within twenty-eight days after such sums were received by the commercial participator. In this context, the 28-day time-limit is commercially wholly unrealistic, since the trading subsidiary is most likely to pay over its profits to the charity at intervals of considerably more than twenty-eight days—perhaps only annually. Regulation 6 does, however, permit the parties to agree a different time-limit for transmission to the charitable institution.[100] It might therefore be desirable, in the tripartite arrangement to which the commercial participator, the trading company, and the charitable institution, will be parties, to provide for a longer period than twenty-eight days.[101]

G. Provisions of more general application

21.66   Some provisions in Part II of the Charities Act 1992 are of more general application, in that they can also apply to persons who are not professional fund-raisers or commercial participators.

(1) Fund-raising by other persons in business

21.67   The Charities Act 1992 empowers the Secretary of State to make provision which, inter alia, regulates the raising of funds for charitable, benevolent, or philanthropic purposes, whether by professional fund-raisers or commercial participators or otherwise.[102]

21.68   Pursuant to this, regulation 7 of the Charitable Institutions (Fund-raising) Regulations 1994[103] applies to any person who carries on for gain a business other than a fund-raising business but, in the course of that business, engages in any promotional venture in the course of which it is represented that charitable contributions are to be applied for charitable, benevolent, or philanthropic purposes of any description (rather than for the benefit of one or more particular charitable institutions).

---

[100] Charitable Institutions (Fund-raising) Regulations 1994, SI 1994/3024, reg 6(2)(a). See above, para 21.62

[101] But see Judith Hill, 'Enter the Commercial Participator' (1995–6) 3 CL & PR 17, 22–3. On the tripartite arrangement, see above, para 21.47

[102] CA 1992, s 64(2)(e)

[103] SI 1994/3024, see reg 7(1)

Where such a person makes a representation to that effect, he must, unless he has **21.69**
a reasonable excuse, ensure that the representation is accompanied by a statement
clearly indicating:[104]

> (a) the fact that the charitable contributions referred to in the representation are to
> be applied for those purposes and not for the benefit of any particular charitable in-
> stitution or institutions;
> (b) (in general terms) the method by which it is to be determined—
>> (i) what proportion of the consideration given for goods or services sold or sup-
>> plied by him, or of any other proceeds of a promotional venture undertaken by
>> him, is to be applied for those purposes, or
>> (ii) what sums by way of donations by him in connection with the sale or supply
>> of any such goods or services are to be so applied,
> as the case may require; and
> (c) the method by which it is to be determined how the charitable contributions re-
> ferred to in the representation are to be distributed between different charitable in-
> stitutions.

Breach of this provision is an offence punishable on summary conviction by a fine
not exceeding the second level on the standard scale.[105]

(2) *Prevention of unauthorized fund-raising*

Under section 62 of the Charities Act 1992, a charitable institution may be able **21.70**
to obtain an injunction to prevent a person soliciting for its benefit or from making representations that it is to benefit from charitable contributions. The court
must be satisfied that the person is using methods of fund-raising to which the institution objects, or that the person is not a fit and proper person to raise funds for
the institution, or (in the case of representations) that the institution does not
wish to be associated with the particular promotional or other fund-raising venture.[106]

(3) *False representation that solicitation is for registered charity*

It is an offence for a person soliciting money or other property for the benefit of **21.71**
an institution which is not a registered charity to represent that it is so registered.[107] There is a defence that the accused believed on reasonable grounds that
the institution was a registered charity.[108]

---

[104] ibid, reg 7(2)

[105] ibid, reg 8

[106] CA 1992, s 62(2)

[107] ibid, s 63(1). An offender is liable on summary conviction to a fine not exceeding the 5th level
on the standard scale: ibid, s 63(1). In s 63, 'registered charity' means a charity which is for the time
being registered in the register of charities kept under CA 1993, s 3: CA 1992, s 63(2), as amended
by Deregulation and Contracting Out Act 1994, s 26(3), and by CA 1993, s 98(1) & Sch 6,
para 29(6)

[108] ibid, s 63(1A), added by Deregulation and Contracting Out Act, 1994, s 26(2)

22

PUBLIC CHARITABLE COLLECTIONS

Part III of the Charities Act 1992, when brought into force, will repeal the legislation governing public charitable collections (that is, the House to House Collections Act 1939 and section 5 of the Police, Factories, etc (Miscellaneous Provisions) Act 1916) and replace it with a single unified regime applying to collections made both in the street and from house to house. The date for bringing Part III into force has, however, been continually deferred, and, at the time of writing, no regulations to this end have been made. The delay appears to be due to concern about the detailed operation of the new regime, particularly its lack of flexibility. At present, for instance, the chief officer of police for the relevant police area may grant a certificate authorizing certain local short-term house-to-house collections, thereby relieving the promoter of the need to obtain a licence from the local authority.[1] This exemption, which involves less formality than the obtaining of such a licence, has proved useful for door-to-door collections for charity by groups such as carol-singers and Scouts, but will be lost if Part III is brought into force without amendment. **22.01**

It is understood that the Home Office is keeping Part III under review, with the intention of bringing it into force (with such amendments as may prove necessary) at some future date. As things stand at present, therefore, it is necessary to consider both the current legislation governing public charitable collections, and the new regime of Part III that may eventually replace it. **22.02**

---

[1] House to House Collections Act 1939, s 1(4). See below, para 22.50

22.03 It should be noted that some earlier statutes formerly impinging on charitable collections, notably the War Charities Act 1940 and the Trading Representations (Disabled Persons) Act 1958, have been repealed by an order made under the Charities Act 1992.[2]

A. The present legal regime

22.04 There are separate statutory regimes for collections made in the street and from house to house.

(1) Street collections

22.05 Section 5 of the Police, Factories, etc (Miscellaneous Provisions) Act 1916 (the 1916 Act) permits the relevant authority[3] to make regulations with respect to the places where and the conditions under which persons may be permitted, in any street or public place, within its area, to collect money or sell articles for the benefit of charitable or other purposes. Many authorities have made regulations pursuant to this section, but only those regulations applicable in the metropolis have been published.[4] In those areas where no regulations have been made, section 5 does not apply.

22.06 The section applies to street collections for all purposes, not only those which are charitable,[5] and there are in fact no reported cases involving collections for charitable purposes.

Meaning of 'street or public place'

22.07 'Street' is expressly defined to include 'any highway and any public bridge, road, lane, footway, square, court, alley, or passage, whether a thoroughfare or not'.[6]

---

[2] Both Acts (together with the National Assistance Act 1948) were repealed in their entirety as from 1 Sept 1992 by CA 1992, s 78(2) & Sch 7, by virtue of CA 1992 (Commencement and Transitional Provisions) Order 1992, SI 1992/1900, made under CA 1992, s 79(2). The War Charities Act 1940, which applied only to war charities and to charities for the disabled, sought to lay down additional safeguards for public appeals and fund-raising for such charities, but it was in practice a dead letter long before its repeal. The Trading Representations (Disabled Persons) Act 1958 made it unlawful, with specified exceptions, when selling or soliciting orders for goods in the course of a business, to make representations in the course of visits from house to house, or by post or telephone, that blind or otherwise disabled persons were employed in the production, preparation, or packaging of the goods, or benefited (other than as users) from the sale or the carrying on of the business

[3] The relevant authorities are: the Common Council of the City of London, the police authority for the Metropolitan Police District, and the council of each district; but regulations made by a district council do not have effect within the Metropolitan Police District: Police, Factories, etc (Miscellaneous Provisions) Act 1916, s 5(1A), inserted by Local Government Act 1972, s 251 & Sch 29, para 22

[4] Street Collections (Metropolitan Police District) Regulations 1979, SI 1979/1230, as amended by Street Collections (Metropolitan Police District) (Amendment) Regulations 1986, SI 1986/1696

[5] eg it applies to (non-charitable) street collections for striking miners: *Meadon v Wood* The Times, 30 Apr 1985

[6] Police, Factories, etc (Miscellaneous Provisions) Act 1916, s 5(4)

'Public place' is not defined in the 1916 Act, and the use of the expression in other statutes provides but little guidance, as the meaning is affected by the context in which the expression is used. A public place clearly includes a place to which the public have access as of right; it is not clear whether it includes a place to which the public have access by permission only. A public place could arguably include such areas as the inside of a railway station or airport, the common parts of a shopping precinct, or the concourses of supermarkets, even though the latter are likely to be in private ownership. It almost certainly does not include areas to which members of the public have access only for a more restricted purpose, such as the interior of a bank, shop, or public house or supermarket, or private land open to the public for a fête on particular days only. Given that section 5 of the 1916 Act imposes criminal sanctions for breach, it ought on general principles to be construed narrowly. On this footing, it is suggested that the better view is that a 'public place' excludes private land entirely.

Regulations applicable in the metropolis

Within the Metropolitan Police District, the body empowered to make regula- **22.08**
tions is the police authority for that area, that is, the Home Secretary. It has been held that, within the metropolis, the 1916 Act empowers the Home Secretary to delegate the power of issuing permits to the Commissioner of Police for the Metropolis.[7] The only published regulations made under the 1916 Act are those applicable to the metropolis; those currently in force date from 1979,[8] and were amended in 1986.[9]

Need for permit

Under the published regulations, no collection may be made unless a permit has **22.09**
been obtained from the Commissioner of Police of the Metropolis (the Commissioner).[10] An application for a permit must be made in writing, in a pre-scribed form, and generally not later than the first day of the month preceding the month in which it is proposed to hold the collection.[11] Every application must be made by a society, committee, or other body consisting of no fewer than three members.[12] The Commissioner must refer every application to an Advisory Committee appointed by him with the approval of the Secretary of State, and, in

---

[7] *Meadon v Wood* The Times, 30 Apr 1985
[8] Street Collections (Metropolitan Police District) Regulations 1979, SI 1979/1230, which came into force on 1 Jan 1980. The regulations were published in the *London Gazette*: ibid, reg 1(2)
[9] Street Collections (Metropolitan Police District) (Amendment) Regulations 1986, SI 1986/1696
[10] Street Collections (Metropolitan Police District) Regulations 1979, SI 1979/1230, reg 4
[11] ibid, reg 5(1). The prescribed form is set out in Sch 1 to the Regulations
[12] ibid, reg 5(2)

deciding whether to grant a permit, he may have regard to any recommendation of such committee.[13]

Restrictions imposed on collections and collectors

22.10 No collection may be made except upon the day and between the hours stated in the permit.[14] The Commissioner may, in granting a permit, limit the collection to such districts, streets, or public places, or such parts thereof, as he thinks fit.[15]

22.11 No person may assist or take part in any collection unless he is in possession of a written authority signed on behalf of the chief promoter.[16] Any person so authorized must produce that authority forthwith for inspection on being requested to do so by any constable.[17]

22.12 No collection may be made in any part of the carriageway of any street, unless allowed by the Commissioner where the collection has been authorized to be held in connection with a procession.[18] No collection may be made in such a manner as to cause, or be likely to cause, danger, obstruction, inconvenience, or annoyance to any person.[19] No collector may importune any person to the annoyance of such person.[20] While collecting, a collector must remain stationary; and collectors must be at least twenty-five metres apart.[21]

22.13 No promoter,[22] collector, or person who is otherwise connected with a collection may permit a person under the age of 16 years to act as a collector.[23] No collector may be accompanied by any animal.[24]

---

[13] Street Collections (Metropolitan Police District) Regulations 1979, SI 1979/1230, reg 5(3)

[14] ibid, reg 6

[15] ibid, reg 7

[16] ibid, reg 8(1). For the purposes of the regulations, 'chief promoter' means a society, committee, or other body consisting of not less than three persons to which a permit for a street collection has been granted: ibid, reg 2

[17] ibid, reg 8(2)

[18] ibid, reg 9

[19] ibid, reg 10

[20] ibid, reg 11

[21] ibid, reg 12. The Commissioner may, however, waive these requirements in respect of a collection which has been authorized to be held in connection with a procession: ibid, reg 12

[22] In the Regulations, 'promoter' means a person, authorized in that behalf by the chief promoter, who causes others to act as collectors: ibid, reg 2

[23] ibid, reg 13. In the case of a collection which has been authorized to be held in connection with a procession, the Commissioner may authorize the chief promoter to permit persons of not less than 14 years to act as collectors, after receipt of a written assurance by such chief promoter that each of such persons under the age of 16 years will at all times be accompanied by a responsible able-bodied adult: ibid, reg 13

[24] ibid, reg 14

Mandatory use of collecting boxes

Every collector must carry a collecting box;[25] and all collecting boxes must be **22.14** numbered consecutively and must be securely closed and sealed in such a way as to prevent them being opened without the seal being broken.[26] All money received by a collector from contributors must immediately be placed in a collecting box.[27] Every collector must deliver, unopened, all collecting boxes in his possession to a promoter.[28]

A collector may not carry or use any collecting box, receptacle, or tray which does **22.15** not bear displayed prominently thereon the name of the charity or fund which is to benefit, or any collecting box which is not numbered.[29]

A collecting box must be opened in the presence of a promoter and another **22.16** responsible person,[30] unless it is delivered unopened to a bank, when it may be opened by an official of the bank.[31] As soon as a collecting box has been opened, the person opening it must count the contents and enter the amount with the number of the collecting box on a list which must be certified by that person.[32]

Restrictions on payments to collectors and other persons

No payment by way of reward may be made to any collector.[33] No payment may **22.17** be made out of the proceeds of a collection, either directly or indirectly, to any other person connected with the promotion or conduct of such collection for, or in respect of, services connected therewith, except such payments as may have been specified in the form of application for a permit and approved by the Commissioner.[34]

Accounting and certifying requirements

Within three months after the date of a collection, the chief promoter must for- **22.18** ward to the Commissioner a statement in a prescribed form[35] showing the amount received and the expenses and payments incurred in connection with the collection and certified by two of the persons responsible for the collection[36] and by a

---

[25] ibid, reg 15(1)
[26] ibid, reg 15(2)
[27] ibid, reg 15(3)
[28] ibid, reg 15(4)
[29] ibid, reg 16
[30] ibid, reg 17(1)
[31] ibid, reg 17(2)
[32] ibid, reg 17(3)
[33] ibid, reg 18(1)
[34] ibid, reg 18(2)
[35] The prescribed form is set out in Sch 2 to the Regulations
[36] ie by at least two out of the persons who made the application under reg 5(2), which must have been a society, committee, or other body of at least three members

qualified accountant;[37] a list showing the names of the collectors;[38] and a list of the amounts contained in each collecting box.[39] The chief promoter must also, if required by the Commissioner, satisfy him as to the proper application of the proceeds of the collection.[40]

22.19 The chief promoter must also, within the same period, at his own expense, and after any required certification, publish in such newspaper or newspapers as the Commissioner may direct a statement showing the name of the chief promoter, the area to which the permit relates, the name of the charity or fund to benefit, the date of the collection, the amount collected, the amount distributed to each charity or fund to benefit, and the amount of the expenses and payments incurred in connection with such collection.[41] Not later than seven days after the publication of a newspaper containing such statement, the chief promoter must send a copy of that newspaper to the Commissioner.[42]

Christmas carol collections

22.20 A less formal system of certification exists for carol collections, which enables them to be held without the need for a permit from the Commissioner of Police of the Metropolis.[43] Instead, the Chief Superintendent in charge of the police division where a carol collection is to be held may issue a certificate in respect of such a collection to be made in the period from 1st to 24th December in any year.[44] A carol collection means a collection in connection with the singing or playing (including the reproduction of recordings) of Christmas carols by two or more persons assembled together.[45] Where a carol collection is certified by the Chief Superintendent, it is relieved from several of the regulations applicable to street collections in the metropolis, including the obligation to obtain a permit and to submit an account after the collection to the Commissioner of Police for the Metropolis.[46]

---

[37] Street Collections (Metropolitan Police District) Regulations 1979, SI 1979/1230, reg 19(1)(a). The definition of a qualified accountant is set out in reg 19(4). If no more than £400 has been collected, the Commissioner may, instead of the requirement for certification by a qualified accountant, require merely certification by an independent responsible person: ibid, reg 19(1)(a), as amended by Street Collections (Metropolitan Police District) (Amendment) Regulations 1986, SI 1986/1696, reg 2

[38] Street Collections (Metropolitan Police District) Regulations 1979, SI 1979/1230, reg 19(1)(b)

[39] ibid, reg 19(1)(c)

[40] ibid, reg 19(1)

[41] ibid, reg 19(2). The Commissioner may waive these requirements if the collection has raised no more than £400: ibid, reg 19(2), as amended by Street Collections (Metropolitan Police District) (Amendment) Regulations 1986, SI 1986/1696, reg 2

[42] Street Collections (Metropolitan Police District) Regulations 1979, SI 1979/1230, reg 19(3)

[43] ibid, reg 20, as amended by Street Collections (Metropolitan Police District) (Amendment) Regulations 1986, SI 1986/1696, reg 3

[44] Street Collections (Metropolitan Police District) Regulations 1979, SI 1979/1230, reg 20(1)

[45] ibid, reg 20(2)

[46] ibid, reg 20(3). More specifically, a certified carol collection is not subject to regulations 4 and 5 (obligation to obtain permit), 12(b) (minimum distance between collectors), 17 (opening of

(2) House-to-house collections

Scope of House to House Collections Act 1939

The House to House Collections Act 1939 (the 1939 Act) prohibits a 'collection **22.21** for a charitable purpose' except in accordance with the licensing provisions which that Act lays down.[47] The 1939 Act empowers the Secretary of State to make regulations thereunder,[48] specifically including the making of regulations relating to the use by collectors of badges and certificates[49] and for their authentication,[50] to prohibit persons below a prescribed age from collecting,[51] to prevent annoyance to the occupants of houses visited by collectors,[52] and for the submission and authentication of accounts.[53] Regulations including these specific matters have been made in the form of the House to House Collections Regulations 1947,[54] which apply to the whole of England and Wales.

For the purposes of the 1939 Act, a 'collection' means:[55]   **22.22**

an appeal to the public, made by means of visits from house to house, to give, whether for consideration or not, money or other property.

The Act applies only to a collection 'from house to house', which premises a collection from one house to another; a collection at a single house does not therefore fall within its scope.[56] 'House' includes a place of business.[57]

The expression 'whether for consideration or not' makes it clear that a sale of **22.23** goods, as well as a donation, can fall within the ambit of the 1939 Act.[58]

For the purposes of the 1939 Act, a 'charitable purpose':[59]   **22.24**

---

collecting boxes), and 19 (accounting and certifying requirements); it is also exempt from the obligations relating to the numbering of collecting boxes contained in regulations 15(2) and 16: ibid, reg 20(3)(a)

[47] House to House Collections Act 1939, s 1(1). The whole Act was repealed, in relation to Scotland, by the Civic Government (Scotland) Act 1982, ss 119(15), 137(8) & Sch 4. For a survey of the applicable law in Scotland, see CR Barker, 'Fundraising' in *Charity Law in Scotland* (ed CR Barker, PJ Ford, SR Moody, & RC Elliot) (W Green/Sweet & Maxwell, 1996) 190, 190–4

[48] House to House Collections Act 1939, s 4
[49] ibid, s 4(2)(a)
[50] ibid, s 4(2)(b)
[51] ibid, s 4(2)(c)
[52] ibid, s 4(2)(d)
[53] ibid, s 4(2)(e)
[54] SR & O 1947/2662
[55] House to House Collections Act 1939, s 11(1)
[56] *Hankinson v Dowland* [1974] 1 WLR 1327
[57] House to House Collections Act 1939, s 11(1)
[58] *Cooper v Coles* [1986] QB 230 (DC), appl *Carasu Ltd v Smith* [1968] 2 QB 383 (DC), and not following *Murphy v Duke* [1985] QB 905 (DC). See P Luxton, 'Charity Collections: a Need for Consideration?' [1986] Conv 53
[59] House to House Collections Act 1939, s 11(1)

means any charitable, benevolent or philanthropic purpose, whether or not the purpose is charitable within the meaning of any rule of law.

The expressions 'benevolent' and 'philanthropic' are not terms of art, and are indeed not charitable for the purposes of the general law of charities.[60] A purpose may be benevolent, even though it lacks the element of public benefit to qualify as charitable: a collection to raise money to send a particular child abroad for a medical operation would probably rank as collection for a benevolent, but not a charitable, purpose.[61] Some assistance might be obtained from Australia, where a 'public benevolent institution' has been construed to mean an institution which promotes the relief of poverty, sickness, destitution or helplessness'.[62] 'Philanthropic' indicates goodwill to mankind at large.[63] Presumably organizations such as Amnesty International and Greenpeace are to be considered 'philanthropic' bodies for this purpose.

Licensing requirements

22.25 A promoter[64] of a collection within the meaning of the 1939 Act must obtain a licence authorizing him, or another under whose authority he acts, to promote such collection, otherwise he is guilty of an offence.[65] Similarly, a collector commits an offence unless he, or a promoter under whose authority he acts, is authorized by licence to promote the collection in the particular locality.[66]

22.26 A promoter, or a person proposing to promote a collection in any locality for a charitable purpose, must apply to the licensing authority for the area comprising that locality in a prescribed manner, specifying the purpose of the collection and the locality (whether being the whole of the area of the authority or a part thereof) within which the collection is to be made, and must furnish the licensing authority with prescribed information.[67] Subject to the provisions of the 1939 Act, the authority must grant him a licence authorizing him to promote such collection.[68]

---

[60] *Chichester Diocesan Fund and Board of Finance Inc v Simpson* [1944] AC 341 (HL) (benevolent); *Re Macduff* [1896] 2 Ch 451 (philanthropic). See further ch 21, paras 21.06–21.07

[61] See P Luxton, 'Public Charitable Collections: the New Régime' (1992–3) 1 CL & PR 35, 36

[62] *Perpetual Trustee Co Ltd v FCT* (1931) 45 CLR 224; *Comr of Pay-roll Tax (Vic) v Cairnmillar Institute* (1990) 90 ATC 4752

[63] *Re Macduff* [1896] 2 Ch 451, 457

[64] In relation to a collection, 'promoter' means a person who causes others to act, whether for remuneration or otherwise, as collectors for the purposes of the collection: House to House Collections Act 1939, s 11(1)

[65] ibid, s 1(2)

[66] ibid, s 1(3)

[67] ibid, s 2(1), as amended by Local Government Act 1972, ss 251, 272 & Sch 29, para 23(1), Sch 30. An application must be in the form set out in Sch 2 to the House to House Collections Regulations 1947, SR & O 1947/2662, and it must give the particulars there specified: ibid, reg 4(1). An application must be made not later than the first day of the month preceding that in which the collection is proposed to begin, although an application may be granted out of time if there are special reasons for so granting it: ibid, reg 4(2)

[68] House to House Collections Act 1939, s 2(1)

The licensing authority to which the application must be made is, in relation to **22.27** the City of London, the Common Council; in relation to the Metropolitan Police District, the Commissioner of Police for the Metropolis; and in relation to a district council entirely outside the Metropolitan Police District, the district council.[69]

A licence may be granted for such period, not exceeding twelve months, as is **22.28** specified in the application, and, if granted, it remains in force for such specified period unless previously revoked.[70] The licensing authority may, however, substitute a shorter date from that specified in the application, or a longer date not exceeding eighteen months, if this is expedient to provide for the simultaneous expiration of licences.[71]

Grounds for refusal, or revocation, of licence

There are several grounds upon which a licensing authority may refuse to grant a **22.29** licence, or may revoke a licence already granted.[72] The grounds are that it appears to the authority:[73]

(a) that the total amount likely to be applied for charitable purposes as the result of the collection (including any amount already so applied) is inadequate in proportion to the value of the proceeds likely to be received (including any proceeds already received);

(b) that remuneration which is excessive in relation to the total amount aforesaid is likely to be, or has been, retained or received out of the proceeds of the collection by any person;

(c) that the grant of a licence would be likely to facilitate the commission of an offence under section three of the Vagrancy Act 1824,[74] or that an offence under that section has been committed in connection with the collection;

(d) that the applicant or the holder of the licence is not a fit and proper person to hold a licence by reason of the fact that he has been convicted in the United Kingdom of any of the offences specified in the Schedule to this Act,[75] or has been convicted in any part of His Majesty's dominions of any offence conviction for

---

[69] ibid, s 2(1A), added by Local Government Act 1972, s 251 & Sch 29, para 23(2)

[70] House to House Collections Act 1939, s 2(2)

[71] ibid, s 2(2)

[72] ibid, s 2(3)

[73] ibid, s 2(3)(a)–(f)

[74] Vagrancy Act 1824, s 3 (as amended), provides that '[e]very person wandering abroad, or placing himself or herself in any public place, street, highway, court or passage, to beg or gather alms, or causing or procuring or encouraging any child or children so to do; shall be deemed an idle and disorderly person' and may be committed by a magistrate to a term of imprisonment not exceeding one calendar month

[75] Schedule to House to House Collections Act 1939, as modified by Theft Act 1968, s 33(2) & Sch 2, Pt III, specifies the following offences: offences under ss 47–56 of Offences Against the Person Act 1861; robbery, burglary, and blackmail; offences in Scotland involving personal violence or lewd, indecent, or libidinous conduct, or dishonest appropriation of property; offences under Street Collections Regulation (Scotland) Act 1915; and offences under s 5 of Police, Factories, etc (Miscellaneous Provisions) Act 1916

which necessarily involved a finding that he acted fraudulently or dishonestly, or of an offence of a kind the commission of which would be likely to be facilitated by the grant of a licence;

(e) that the applicant or the holder of the licence, in promoting a collection in respect of which a licence has been granted to him, has failed to exercise due diligence to secure that persons authorised by him to act as collectors for the purposes of the collection were fit and proper persons, to secure compliance on the part of persons so authorised with the provisions of regulations made under this Act, or to prevent prescribed badges or prescribed certificates of authority being obtained by persons other than persons so authorised; or

(f) that the applicant or holder of the licence has refused or neglected to furnish to the authority such information as they may have reasonably required for the purpose of informing themselves as to any of the matters specified in the foregoing paragraphs.

22.30   Where a licensing authority refuses to grant a licence, or revokes a licence which has been granted, it must forthwith give written notice to the applicant or holder of the licence, stating upon which one or more of the grounds the decision was made, and informing him of the right of appeal given by section 2 of the 1939 Act.[76] Appeal against the refusal or revocation lies to the Secretary of State,[77] and must be brought within fourteen days from the date of the written notice.[78] If the Secretary of States allows the appeal, the licensing authority must forthwith issue a licence or cancel the revocation as the case may be.[79]

Collectors

22.31   A promoter must exercise all due diligence to secure that persons authorized to act as collectors are fit and proper persons, and to secure their compliance with the regulations.[80] No person under the age of 16 years may act or be authorized to act as a collector of money.[81]

22.32   No collector may importune any person to the annoyance of such person, or remain in, or at the door of, any house if any occupant requests him to leave.[82]

Use of certificates, badges, and collecting boxes or receipt books

22.33   A promoter must issue every collector with a prescribed certificate of authority signed by or on behalf of the chief promoter,[83] with a prescribed badge which gives

---

[76]   House to House Collections Act 1939, s 2(4)
[77]   ibid, s 2(4)
[78]   ibid, s 2(5)
[79]   ibid, s 2(6)
[80]   House to House Collections Regulations 1947, SR & O 1947/2662, reg 5
[81]   ibid, reg 8, substituted by House to House Collections Regulations, 1963, SI 1963/684
[82]   House to House Collections Regulations 1947, SR & O 1947/2662, reg 9
[83]   ibid, reg 6(1)(a). In the regulations, 'chief promoter', in relation to a collection, means a person to whom a licence has been granted authorizing him to promote that collection, or a person who

a general indication of the purpose of the collection,[84] and (if money is to be collected) a collecting box or receipt book marked with a clear indication of the purpose of the collection and a distinguishing number.[85] In the case of a receipt book, such indication and number must also be marked on every receipt in addition to the consecutive number of the receipt.[86]

The promoter must also keep a list of the names and addresses of collectors to whom certificates, badges, and either collecting boxes or receipt books, have been issued, which list must also specify the distinguishing numbers of the boxes or receipt books issued to each collector.[87] The promoter must also exercise all due diligence to secure that every such item which he has issued is returned when the collection is completed or when for any other reason a collector ceases to act.[88]   **22.34**

The prescribed badges and the forms for prescribed certificates of authority must be obtained from Her Majesty's Stationery Office.[89] Such certificates must be authenticated, and such badges must provide a general indication of the purpose of the collection, in a manner approved by the chief officer of police for the area in respect of which the licence is granted.[90]   **22.35**

A collector must sign the certificate issued to him and must produce it when demanded by the police or by any occupant of a house visited by him for the purposes of the collection.[91] A collector must also sign the badge issued to him, and must wear it prominently when collecting.[92] A collector must keep such certificate and badge in his possession and return them to a promoter on replacement, or when the collection is completed, or at any other time on the demand of a promoter.[93]   **22.36**

Where a collector is collecting money by means of a collecting box, he is not permitted to receive any contribution save by permitting the person from whom it is received to place it in a collecting box issued to him by a promoter.[94] If money is collected where no collecting box is used, a collector must (forthwith and in the presence of the contributor) enter the date, the name of the contributor and the   **22.37**

---

is exempt from the obligation to obtain such a licence by virtue of an exemption order (ie in the case of a collection made over a wide area): ibid, reg 2(1). For exemption orders in respect of collections over a wide area, see below, paras 22.43–22.49

[84] ibid, reg 6(1)(b)
[85] ibid, reg 6(1)(c)
[86] ibid, reg 6(1)(c)
[87] ibid, reg 6(2)(a)
[88] ibid, reg 6(2)(b)
[89] ibid, reg 6(3)(a)
[90] ibid, reg 6(3)(b)
[91] ibid, reg 7(a)
[92] ibid, reg 7(b)
[93] ibid, reg 7(c)
[94] ibid, reg 10(1)

amount in a receipt book (including on the counterfoil or duplicate), and must hand the receipt to the contributor.[95]

22.38 When a collecting box is full or a receipt book is exhausted, the collector to whom it was issued must return it to a promoter. A collecting box must be returned with the seal unbroken; a receipt book must be returned with a sum equal to the total amount of the contributions (if any) entered therein. A collecting box or receipt book must also be returned in this way upon the demand of a promoter, or when the collector does not desire to act as a collector, or upon the completion of the collection.[96]

22.39 The chief promoter must exercise all due diligence to secure that all prescribed certificates of authority and badges are destroyed when no longer required in connection with the collection or in connection with a further collection which he has been authorized to promote for the same purpose.[97]

Examining and accounting obligations

Opening and examination of collecting boxes and receipt books

22.40 A collecting box when returned must be examined by, and, if it contains money, be opened in the presence of, a promoter of the collection and another responsible person.[98] If, however, a collecting box is delivered unopened to a bank, it may be examined and opened by an official of the bank in the absence of a promoter.[99] As soon as a collecting box has been opened, the contents must be counted and the amount entered with the distinguishing number of the collecting box on a list, which must be certified by the persons making the examination.[100]

22.41 A receipt book when returned, and all sums received with it, must be examined by a promoter of the collector and another responsible person, and the amount of the contributions entered in the receipt book must be checked with the money and entered with the distinguishing number of the receipt book on a list, which must be certified by the persons making the examination.[101]

Duty to furnish accounts

22.42 The chief promoter must furnish an account of the collection to the licensing authority within one month of the expiry of the licence, although there is provision for the furnishing of combined accounts where the collections took place in more

---

[95] House to House Collections Regulations 1947, SR & O 1947 No 2662, reg 10(2)
[96] ibid, reg 11
[97] ibid, reg 17
[98] ibid, reg 12(1)
[99] ibid, reg 12(2)
[100] ibid, reg 12(3)
[101] ibid, reg 12(4)

than one licensing authority area.[102] The licensing authority may extend the period for furnishing an account, if satisfied that there are special reasons for doing so.[103] Where a house-to-house collection is made in connection with a street collection, there is provision for the submission of a combined account.[104]

Exemption order for collections over wide area

Requirements for exemption order

Where the Secretary of State is satisfied that a person pursues a charitable purpose **22.43** throughout the whole of England (which in this context includes Wales[105]), or a substantial part thereof, and is desirous of promoting collections for that purpose, the Secretary of State may by order direct that he is to be exempt from the requirement to obtain a licence for the promotion[106] as respects all collections for that purpose in such localities as may be prescribed in the order.[107] Whilst such an order is in force, the provisions of the Act have effect in relation to the person exempted, to a promoter of a collection in that locality for that purpose who acts under the authority of the person exempted, and to a person who so acts as a collector for the purposes of any such collection, as if a licence authorizing the person exempted to promote the collection in that locality for that purpose had been in force.[108] Any order so made may be revoked or varied by a subsequent order of the Secretary of State.[109]

It should be noted that the exemption applies only where the person who wishes **22.44** to promote collections 'pursues a charitable purpose throughout the whole of England [including Wales] or a substantial part thereof'. No exemption order can therefore be made in favour of a person who pursues a charitable purpose overseas. Strictly, what must be pursued throughout a substantial part of England and Wales is the charitable purpose, not the collections themselves; a trustee of a national charity might therefore satisfy this criterion even if he intends to promote

---

[102] ibid, reg 14(1). The forms of the account is set out in ibid, 5th, 6th, & 7th Schs: ibid, reg 15. An account in respect of money collected must be accompanied by vouchers for each item of the expense and application of the proceeds, and by any receipt books and the lists of collectors: ibid, reg 16(1). These documents need not be submitted if the account is certified by a professional auditor, but they must be made available for submission to the licensing authority on request within three months after the account is submitted: ibid, reg 16(2)

[103] ibid, reg 14(3)

[104] ibid, reg 14(4)

[105] Although House to House Collections Act 1939, s 3(1), refers only to 'England', in any Act passed before 27 July 1967 (ie before the now-repealed Welsh Language Act 1967), a reference to 'England' includes a reference to Wales; similarly, in any Act passed before 1 Apr 1974, a reference to England includes Berwick-upon-Tweed and Monmouthshire (which now mostly comprises Gwent): Interpretation Act 1978, s 5 & Sch 2, Pt I, para 5(a)

[106] ie under House to House Collections Act 1939, s 1(2); see above, para 22.25

[107] ibid, s 3(1)

[108] ibid, s 3(1)

[109] ibid, s 3(2)

collections for the purposes of that charity in a few licensing authorities' areas only. Nevertheless, the Home Office will grant an order only if satisfied that the charity collects on a substantial basis across the country. It operates on the rule of thumb that the charity should have been collecting in at least 70–100 local licensing authorities' areas a year, for at least two years, and should be able to produce the relevant accounts.[110]

22.45 A charity with an exemption order is in a very favourable position, since it is relieved of the obligation to negotiate individually with each separate licensing authority in England and Wales in whose area it wishes to collect. A potentially unfavourable consequence is that some households might, as a result of uncoordinated collections, be subjected to multiple collections over the same week, or even the same day—one of the problems that the licensing requirements of the Act were designed to prevent. There is a convention that an exemption order holder inform the licensing authority of the dates upon which it plans to make collections from house to house;[111] but it appears that in recent years such voluntary co-operation has been breaking down.[112]

22.46 For these reasons, no doubt, the Home Office keeps a tight rein on the issue of exemption orders. No form of application for such an order is prescribed by the regulations; but the Home Office requires an application to be accompanied by full details, including information on the organization and persons involved in the proposed collections.[113] The Home Office will not grant the order unless its subsequent investigations satisfy it that the scheme will be properly conducted. A delay of a few months can therefore result before the outcome of an application is known. In practice, relatively few exemption orders have been issued.[114]

---

[110] See the standard letter which the Home Office's Voluntary and Community Unit sends in response to inquiries about applications for an exemption order

[111] See Home Office Consultation Paper, *The Regulation of Charitable Appeals in England and Wales* (1988), para 31

[112] See *Charities: a Framework for the Future*, White Paper, Cm 694 (1989), para 10.10

[113] An application for an exemption order must be made not later than the first day of the month preceding that in which the collection is proposed to begin, although the Secretary of State may grant a later application if satisfied that there are special reasons for doing so: House to House Collections Regulations 1947, SR & O 1947/2662, reg 4(2)

[114] As at Sept 1988, only 40 exemption orders had been made: Home Office Consultation Paper, *The Regulation of Charitable Appeals in England and Wales* (1988), para 29. By September 2000, the number of exemption holders had increased to 50: information supplied by Home Office Voluntary and Community Unit. Exemption orders are held in respect of many of the largest national charities, including, eg, Christian Aid, Barnardo's, British Heart Foundation, British Red Cross Society, Children's Society, Imperial Cancer Research Fund, Help the Aged, National Society for the Prevention of Cruelty to Children, Royal National Institute for the Blind, Oxfam, Royal National Lifeboat Institution, St John's Ambulance, Save the Children Fund, Royal Society for the Prevention of Cruelty to Animals, Scope, and World Wide Fund for Nature. It appears that the only order held in respect of a non-charitable body is held for Amnesty International (British Section). See further below, para 22.75

The chief promoter of a collection in respect of which an exemption order has **22.47** been made must furnish an account annually to the Secretary of State so long as the order remains in force.[115] If the order is revoked, a final account must be furnished within three months of the date of revocation.[116] The Secretary of State may extend these time-limits if satisfied that there are special reasons for doing so.[117]

Envelope collections

The regulations make provision for envelope collections,[118] but only in respect of **22.48** a promoter to whom an exemption order has been granted. A promoter holding an exemption order who wishes to promote an envelope collection must inform the Secretary of State, who may permit it if he is of the opinion that the collection is for a charitable purpose of major importance and is suitably administered.[119]

In an envelope collection, every envelope must have a gummed flap by means of **22.49** which it can be closed securely,[120] and no collector may receive a contribution except in an envelope which has been so closed.[121] The other regulations governing house-to-house collections remain applicable to envelope collections, with modifications to take account of the fact that envelopes replace collecting boxes.[122]

Short-term local collections

A more informal procedure exists to authorize certain short-term local collec- **22.50** tions. If the chief officer of police for the police area comprising a locality in which a collection for a charitable purpose is being, or is proposed to be, made is satisfied that that purpose is local in character and that the collection is likely to be completed within a short period of time, he may grant a certificate in the prescribed form to the person who appears to him to be principally concerned in the promotion of the collection.[123] Where a certificate is so granted, most of the provisions of the 1939 Act do not apply in relation to such a collection made within such period as may be specified in the certificate, in relation to the person to whom the

---

[115] House to House Collections Regulations 1947, SR & O 1947/2662, reg 14(2)
[116] ibid, reg 14(2)
[117] ibid, reg 14(3)
[118] An 'envelope collection' means a collection made by persons going from house to house leaving envelopes in which money may be placed and which are subsequently called for: ibid, reg 13(3)
[119] ibid, reg 13(1)
[120] ibid, reg 13(2)(a)
[121] ibid, reg 13(2)(b)
[122] ibid, reg 13(2)(c)
[123] House to House Collections Act 1939, s 1(4). The certificate must be in the form set out in the First Sch to the Regulations: House to House Collections Regulations 1947, SR & O 1947/2662, reg 3(1)

certificate is granted, or to any person authorized by him to promote the collection or to act as a collector.[124]

Miscellaneous offences

22.51 It is an offence for a person to display or use a prescribed badge or prescribed certificate of authority in connection with an appeal to the public in association with a representation that the appeal is for a charitable purpose if the badge or certificate is not held for the purposes of the appeal pursuant to the regulations made under the 1939 Act.[125] It is also an offence to use a badge or device, or any certificate or other document, so nearly resembling a prescribed badge or prescribed certificate of authority as to be calculated to deceive.[126] A police constable may require any person whom he believes to be acting as a collector for the purposes of a collection for a charitable purpose to declare to him immediately his name and address and to sign his name; failure to comply comprises an offence.[127]

(3) Static boxes

22.52 A static collecting box is one which is unaccompanied by a collector, and which is, for example, merely deposited on the counter of a shop or public house. Such boxes fall outside the legislative machinery applicable to boxes used in the street or for collections from house to house.[128] There is, therefore, no statutory obligation to seal or number static boxes; neither is there any statutory obligation regarding the identity of the persons who may open them, or the circumstances in which they may be opened. There is some evidence of lapses of care in the use of such boxes, as where they are left unsealed, or where money is borrowed from them when change is required, and such boxes are often left for excessively long periods without being emptied.[129]

---

[124] House to House Collections Act 1939, s 1(4). The provisions which remain applicable are those of ss 5 (unauthorized use of badges), 6 (collector to give name, etc, to police on demand), & 8 (penalties), so far as such penalties relate to ss 5 and 6. Ss 5, 6 & 8(4), (5) must be set forth on the back of the certificate: House to House Collections Regulations 1947, SR & O 1947/2662, reg 3(1)

[125] House to House Collections Act 1939, s 5(a)

[126] ibid, s 5(b)

[127] ibid, s 6

[128] Static boxes are also expressly excluded from the scope of CA 1993, Pt III: ibid, s 65(2)(c); see below, para 22.60

[129] See *Malpractice in Fundraising for Charity*, report of a working party of the NCVO, Harry Kidd (chairman), 1986, para 5.35. See in particular the defaults relating to static boxes in the *Sanctuary* case: see jdgt of Brightman J in *Jones v A-G*, The Times, 10 Nov 1976, noted [1976] Ch Com Rep 10–11 (paras 26–9). For a complete survey of the *Sanctuary* litigation, see [1971] Ch Com Rep 26–9 (paras 90–6); [1972] Ch Com Rep 27 (para 80); [1976] Ch Com Rep 10–11 (paras 25–9); [1977] Ch Com Rep 13 (paras 31–3). The only stage of the proceedings reported is *Jones v A-G* [1974] Ch 148 (CA). See also B Nightingale, *Charities* (Allen Lane, 1973), 283–7; M Chesterman, *Charities, Trusts and Social Welfare* (Weidenfeld & Nicholson, 1979), ch 16; and P Luxton, *Charity Fund-raising and the Public Interest* (Avebury, 1990), 51–4

In *Jones v Attorney-General*,[130] where static boxes had been simply abandoned as   **22.53**
uneconomical to collect, Brightman J pointed out that a collecting box in the
wrong hands is a potential instrument of fraud, and that a charity which uses them
is under a duty to safeguard them. In particular, a promoter has a duty to ensure
that static boxes are emptied regularly; there could be no justification for aban-
doning boxes simply because it is believed that the contents are not worth collecting. Commenting generally upon security techniques with regard to boxes, his
Lordship stated that it should not be possible for a collector to break the seal on a
box, empty it, and then reseal it without detection. He observed that a way of
preventing this was to provide a sensible system for numbering all seals, and to
maintain a complete and continuous record showing where and to whom seals are
issued. Charities using static boxes should clearly be advised to take heed of
Brightman J's suggestions.[131]

Where static boxes are left unattended for long periods, the Charity Commis-   **22.54**
sioners, having instituted an inquiry, may (where appropriate) be able to act to
protect the money contained in such boxes by (inter alia) making an order vesting
it in the Official Custodian for Charities.[132] No proposals have been laid before
Parliament for the specific statutory regulation of static boxes.[133]

B. The legal regime in Part III of the Charities Act 1992

If and when brought into force, Part III of the Charities Act 1992 will establish a   **22.55**
unified regime for public charitable collections, although it remains to be seen
whether a distinction between collections made in public places and from house
to house will be drawn in the accompanying regulations, when they eventually appear. In the rest of this chapter, except where the context indicates otherwise, it is
assumed that Part III is already in force.

---

[130] The Times, 10 Nov 1976; noted [1976] Ch Com Rep 10–11 (paras 26–9)
[131] See also *Malpractice in Fundraising for Charity*, report of a working party of the NCVO,
Harry Kidd (chairman), 1986, recommendation 21
[132] CA 1993, s 18(1)(iii). This power has been used on a number of occasions: see *Hansard*, HL
(series 5) vol 532, Second Reading of the Charities Bill, col 856 (19 Nov 1991) and Committee
Stage of Bill, cols 252–4 (3 Dec 1991)
[133] The exclusion of static boxes from the Charities Bill laid before Parliament in 1991 was raised
by Lord Brightman in debate in the House of Lords. The explanation for the exclusion was that the
amounts raised by such boxes is usually small, that such boxes tend to be in place for long periods
(whereas the collecting legislation is concerned with relatively short-term collections), that collections by way of static boxes are less intrusive to the public, and that the Charity Commissioners'
powers to deal with such boxes are already adequate: see *Hansard*, HL (series 5) vol 532, Second
Reading of the Charities Bill, col 856 (19 Nov 1991), and Committee Stage of the Bill, cols 252–4
(12 Dec 1991). Whether this response is sufficient to justify the public's confidence in the use of static boxes must surely be in doubt

(1) Scope of Part III

22.56 Part III deals with 'public charitable collections'. A 'public charitable collection' means a charitable appeal which is made in any public place, or by means of visits from house to house.[134] Part III therefore has no application to appeals made in other ways—such as through the medium of radio or television, or by means of advertisements in newspapers and magazines or on hoardings, or via solicitation letters and telephone calls.

Meaning of 'charitable appeal'

22.57 A 'charitable appeal' means an appeal to members of the public to give money or other property (whether for consideration or otherwise) which is made in association with a representation that the whole or any part of its proceeds is to be applied for charitable, benevolent, or philanthropic purposes.[135] 'Proceeds' in this context means all money or other property given (whether for consideration or otherwise) in response to the charitable appeal in question.[136]

22.58 The meaning of 'charitable, benevolent, or philanthropic' has been considered above in relation to the House to House Collections Act 1939, which (in this respect) Part III follows.[137] In view of the extended scope of Part III, however, the short title to the Act which contains it, the Charities Act 1992, is somewhat misleading.[138]

22.59 The words in parentheses—'whether for consideration or otherwise'—ensure that sales (such as sales of goods) are included, the position therefore being the same as under the House to House Collections Act 1939.[139] For the avoidance of doubt, however, Part III in effect provides that an appeal can fall within the definition of a 'public charitable collection' if it consists in or includes the making of an offer to sell goods or to supply services, or the exposing of goods for sale, to members of the public, provided the other requirements for a 'public charitable collection' are met.[140]

22.60 Excluded from Part III is a charitable appeal which is made in the course of a public meeting;[141] or in a churchyard, burial ground, or place of public worship, being (in each case) land which is enclosed or substantially enclosed (whether by any

---

[134] CA 1992, s 65(1)(a)

[135] ibid, s 65(1)(b)

[136] ibid, s 65(4)

[137] See above, para 22.24; see also (in relation to CA 1992, Pt II) ch 21, paras 21.05–21.07

[138] See the suggestion of Lord Renton in this regard: Official Report of the Committee on the Charities Bill, HL, cols 254–5 (3 Dec 1991)

[139] See above, para 22.23

[140] CA 1992, s 65(7)

[141] ibid, s 65(2)(a)

wall or building or otherwise);[142] or which is an appeal to members of the public to give money or other property by placing it in an unattended receptacle.[143] A receptacle is for this purpose unattended if it is not in the possession or custody of a person acting as a collector.[144] A static collecting box is therefore not within the scope of Part III.[145]

Meaning of 'house'

'House' includes any part of a building constituting a separate dwelling.[146]

22.61

Meaning of 'public place'

'Public place', in relation to a charitable appeal, means:[147]

22.62

(a) any highway; and

(b) (subject to subsection (9)) any other place to which, at any time when the appeal is made, members of the public have or are permitted to have access and which either—

(i) is not within a building, or

(ii) if within a building, is a public area within any station, airport or shopping precinct or any other similar public area.

Part III therefore supplies a definition of 'public place' which is lacking in the existing legislation governing street collections.[148] This definition of 'public place' is, however, subject to two important qualifications, which are given in section 65(9), namely that it does not apply to:

22.63

(a) any place to which members of the public are permitted to have access only if any payment or ticket required as a condition of access has been made or purchased; or

(b) any place to which members of the public are permitted to have access only by virtue of permission given for the purposes of the appeal in question.

These qualifications were added during the progress of the Charities Bill through Parliament. Many charities were concerned about the breadth of the definition of 'public place' in the Bill,[149] and feared that it would seriously undermine the enthusiasm of volunteers.[150] A private house at which a ticket-only fund-raising dinner was held, might, for example, comprise a public place. Again, if a person

22.64

---

[142] ibid, s 65(2)(b)

[143] ibid, s 65(2)(c)

[144] ibid, s 65(2)(c). In Part III, ibid, the expression 'collector' means any person by whom the appeal is made (whether made by him alone or with others and whether for remuneration or otherwise): ibid, s 65(3)(b)

[145] On static boxes generally, see above, paras 22.52–22.54

[146] CA 1992, s 65(8)

[147] ibid

[148] ie Police, Factories, etc (Miscellaneous Provisions) Act 1916, s 5: see above, para 22.07

[149] See *Hansard*, HL (series 5) vol 532, Second Reading of Charities Bill, col 836 (19 Nov 1991) (Lord Richards) and ibid, cols 886–7 (Earl Ferrers, replying)

[150] See comments of A Phillips, *The Guardian*, 3 Dec 1991

organized a coffee morning in his own home, any profits to go to charity, and placed a notice about it in the village post office, it appeared that the house would become a public place,[151] with the result that a local authority permit would be needed. The qualifications contained in paragraph (a) and (b) respectively ensure that such venues are removed from the definition of 'public place'.

(2) Local authority permit

22.65 No public charitable collection may be conducted in the area of any local authority except in accordance with a permit issued by the authority under section 68 of the Charities Act 1992, unless an order has been made by the Charity Commissioners under section 72 (that is, in respect of a national appeal).[152] In Part III, 'local authority' means the council of a Welsh county or county borough, the council of a district or of a London borough, the Common Council of the City of London, or the Council of the Isles of Scilly.[153]

Application for permit

22.66 Application must be made by the person or persons proposing to promote a public charitable collection[154] to the local authority in whose area the collection is proposed to be made.[155] The application must specify the period (not exceeding twelve months) for which it is desired that the permit should have effect, and it must contain such information as may be prescribed by regulations.[156] The application must be made at least one month (or such later date as the local authority may allow) before the collection is to begin.[157]

22.67 The local authority must consult the chief officer of police of the relevant police area, and may make such other inquiries as it thinks fit, before determining any

---

[151] See *Hansard*, HL (series 5) vol 532, Second Reading of the Charities Bill, col 851 (19 Nov 1991) (Lord Allen of Abbeydale)

[152] CA 1992, s 66(1). Orders made by the Charity Commissioners in respect of national appeals are considered further below, paras 22.72–22.77

[153] ibid, s 65(4), as amended by Local Government (Wales) Act 1994, s 66(6) & Sch 16, para 99. The functions exercisable under Pt III by a local authority are exercisable, as respects the Inner Temple, by its Sub-Treasurer, and as respects the Middle Temple, by its Under Treasurer, and references in Part III to a local authority or to the area of a local authority are to be construed accordingly: CA 1992, s 65(6)

[154] In relation to a public charitable collection, 'promoter' means a person (whether alone or with others and whether for remuneration or otherwise) who organizes or controls the conduct of the charitable appeal in question: ibid, s 65(3)(a); but if no person acts in such a manner, any person who acts as a collector in respect of it is treated as a promoter as well: ibid, s 65(3)

[155] ibid, s 67(1)

[156] ibid, s 67(2)

[157] ibid, s 67(3), as amended by the Deregulation and Contracting Out Act 1994, ss 27, 81, & Sch 17

application.[158] The local authority must either issue the permit or refuse the application on one or more of the grounds specified in section 69.[159]

Conditions attached to permit

If it issues the permit, the authority may attach such conditions as it thinks fit, having regard to the local circumstances.[160] Such conditions may (for instance) specify the day of the week, time and frequency of the collection, the locality or localities in which it may be conducted, and the manner in which it is to be conducted.[161]   **22.68**

Grounds for refusal of permit

A local authority may refuse to issue a permit on any of the following grounds: **22.69**

(a) that it appears to them that the collection would cause undue inconvenience to members of the public by reason of the day of the week or date on which, the time at which, the frequency with which, or the locality or localities in which, it is proposed to be conducted;[162]

(b) that another public charitable collection is already authorized to be conducted in the local authority's area on the same day, or on the immediately preceding day, or the immediately succeeding day, as that proposed;[163]

(c) that it appears to them that the amount likely to be applied for charitable, benevolent, or philanthropic purposes in consequence of the collection would be inadequate, having regard to the likely amount of the proceeds of the collection;[164]

(d) that it appears to them that the applicant or any other person would be likely to receive an excessive amount by way of remuneration in connection with the collection;[165]

(e) that the applicant has been convicted of certain offences relating to public collections (whether under Part III or regulations made under it, or under similar legislation and regulations made under it applicable to Scotland,[166] or under the street collections legislation[167]) or of any offence involving

---

[158] CA 1992, s 67(4)

[159] ibid, s 68(1)

[160] ibid, s 68(2)

[161] ibid, s 68(3)

[162] ibid, s 69(1)(a)

[163] ibid, s 69(1)(b). A local authority may not, however, refuse to issue a permit on this ground if it appears to them that the collection would be conducted only in one location, which is on land to which members of the public would have access only by virtue of the express or implied permission of the occupier of the land, and that such occupier consents to the collection being conducted there: ibid, s 69(2)

[164] ibid, s 69(1)(c)

[165] ibid, s 69(1)(d)

[166] ie Civic Government (Scotland) Act 1982, s 119

[167] ie under Police Factories, etc (Miscellaneous Provisions) Act 1916, s 5

dishonesty or of a kind the commission of which would in their opinion be likely to be facilitated by the issuing to him of a permit;[168]

(f) where the applicant is a person other than a charitable, benevolent, or philanthropic institution for whose benefit the collection is proposed to be conducted, that they are not satisfied that the applicant is authorized (whether by any such institution or by any person acting on behalf of any such institution) to promote the collection;[169] or

(g) that it appears to them that the applicant in promoting any other public charitable collection authorized under Part III of the Charities Act 1993, or under section 119 of the Civic Government (Scotland) Act 1982, failed to exercise due diligence to secure that persons authorized by him to collect were fit and proper persons and complied with the regulations made under the respective Acts, or to prevent badges or certificates of authority being obtained by unauthorized persons.[170]

22.70 There is also provision for withdrawal of a permit, attaching conditions to one already granted, and for the varying of an existing permit.[171]

Appeals against local authority's decision

22.71 Appeals against a decision of a local authority in regard to permits may be made to the magistrates' court.[172]

(3) National exemption order

22.72 Under section 72 of the Charities Act 1992, where the Charity Commissioners are satisfied, on the application of any charity, that the charity proposes to promote (or to authorize others to promote) public charitable collections throughout England and Wales, or throughout a substantial part of England and Wales, it may make an order authorizing the collections.[173]

---

[168] CA 1992, s 69(1)(e)

[169] ibid, s 69(1)(f). This ground has no equivalent in the House to House Collections Act 1939. It appears to serve a similar function to a provision in the War Charities Act 1940 (now repealed), which, in the context of war charities and charities for the disabled, made it an offence to appeal to the public unless (inter alia) approval in writing had been given by the management committee or persons responsible for the administration of the charity. Collections for other purposes could be made without the charity's knowledge or consent. This state of affairs was hardly desirable; yet many charities opposed the extension of such obligation to collections for all charitable purposes, fearing that it would deter the genuine volunteer. The new provision is therefore a compromise: collecting for a charity without its consent is not itself an offence, but the absence of such consent is a ground for refusing a permit

[170] CA 1992, s 69(1)(g)

[171] ibid, s 70

[172] ibid, s 71

[173] ibid, s 72(1). The provisions as to orders made by the Charity Commissioners contained in CA 1993, s 89(1), (2) & (4), apply to an order made by them under CA 1992, s 72: CA 1992, s 72(5), substituted by CA 1993, s 98(1) & Sch 6, para 29(7)

Such an order may be made subject to conditions, and it may be expressed to be **22.73** without limit of time or for a specified period only; it may also be revoked or varied by a further order of the Charity Commissioners.[174] Section 72 does not lay down an express obligation upon exemption holders to inform the relevant local authorities. There is a convention that holders of equivalent orders under the House to House Collections Act 1939 keep local authorities informed of their intended collecting areas and dates, and it is to be hoped that charities with exemption orders under section 72 will adhere to that convention. Apart from this, an order under section 72 could presumably include an obligation to notify the relevant local authorities, and failure to abide by such a condition might be a ground for revocation of an order previously made. Furthermore, the Secretary of State may make regulations relating to the conduct of public charitable collections authorized under orders made by the Charity Commissioners.[175] Such regulations could therefore include an express obligation to inform (and perhaps to consult).

It is important to note that, for the purposes of section 72, 'charity' and 'charitable **22.74** purposes' have a more restricted meaning than in the rest of Part III of the Charities Act 1992, in that it is expressly provided that, within that section, they have the same meaning as in the Charities Act 1993.[176] A national exemption order will not, therefore, be available in respect of a collection for a purpose which, though benevolent or philanthropic, is not in law charitable. In this regard, the exemption is narrower than that which can currently be granted by the Home Office under the House to House Collections Act 1939.[177] The transfer of the power to grant such an order from the Home Office to the Charity Commissioners, which will come about when Part III is brought into force, created the problem that, unless the width of the national exemption order were restricted, the Charity Commissioners would be making orders in respect of non-charitable bodies. In order to avoid this, the Government preferred to reduce the availability of exemption orders. The transfer of the power to the Charity Commissioners was designed to ensure that such orders would be subject to the closest possible scrutiny, and the Commissioners would be able to exercise this jurisdiction only in respect of those bodies which fell within their general jurisdiction.[178]

The body which most clearly stands to lose if this change is implemented is **22.75** Amnesty International (British Section), which is not a charity, but which has appeals for what would probably be considered to be benevolent or philanthropic purposes. Amnesty International (British Section) appears to be the only

---

[174] CA 1992, s 72(3)
[175] ibid, s 73(1)
[176] ibid, s 72(6), substituted by CA 1993, s 98(1) & Sch 6, para 29(7)
[177] See above, paras 22.43–22.49
[178] See *Hansard*, HL (series 5) vol 535, Report Stage of Charities Bill, col. 1225 (18 Feb 1992) (Earl Ferrers); see generally ibid, cols 1220–8

non-charitable body in respect of which a national exemption order is held under the House to House Collections Act 1939.[179] Greenpeace (which also fails to qualify for charitable status but does not have a national exemption order) might also be concerned. On the same basis, a non-charitable disaster fund appeal, whilst no doubt benevolent or philanthropic, will be ineligible for an exemption order. Collections for such appeals in public places and from house to house will therefore need separate permits from each local authority. This may not be too serious a disadvantage for non-charitable disaster appeals, however, as such appeals tend to be made on television or radio, and appeals made in this manner are outside the scope of Part III.

22.76 It should also be noted that the criterion for an exemption order for collections over a wide area contained in the House to House Collections Act 1939 (that what must be pursued throughout a substantial part of England and Wales is the 'charitable purpose'),[180] will be replaced under Part III by a requirement merely that the collections themselves are made throughout at least a substantial part of England and Wales.

22.77 It is an offence for any person knowingly or recklessly to provide the Charity Commissioners with false or misleading information if the information is provided in circumstances in which he intends, or could reasonably be expected to know, that it would be used by them for the purposes of discharging their functions under section 72.[181]

(4) Regulations

22.78 The Secretary of State may make regulations prescribing the information to be contained in applications for permits and for the purpose of regulating the conduct of public charitable collections.[182] In particular, such regulations may provide for the keeping and publication of accounts, the prevention of annoyance to the public, the use by collectors of badges and certificates of authority, and the prohibiting of persons under a prescribed age from acting as collectors and prohibiting others from causing them so to act.[183] The unauthorized use of badges or certificates of authority is an offence.[184]

22.79 The White Paper indicated that the general regulations will follow the Scottish provisions.[185] These include a requirement that collectors be at least 14 years of age

---

[179] *Hansard*, HL (series 5) vol 535, Report Stage of Charities Bill, col 1226, and see above, para 22.46
[180] See above, para 22.44
[181] CA 1992, s 74(3A), inserted by CA 1993, s 98(1) & Sch 6, para 29(8)
[182] CA 1992, s 73(1)
[183] ibid, s 73(2)
[184] ibid, s 74
[185] ie the Public Charitable Collections (Scotland) Regulations 1984, SI 1984/565, and the Public Charitable Collections (Scotland) Amendment Regulations 1988, SI 1988/1323. See *Charities: a Framework for the Future*, White Paper, Cm 694 (1989), para 10.13. On Scottish

for street collections and 16 years of age for collections from house to house. Holders of exemption orders will be required to appoint qualified accountants as auditors,[186] although in many instances this will already be required under the general auditing requirements contained in the Charities Act 1993.[187]

The White Paper anticipates, however, that the regulations will differ from those **22.80** applicable in Scotland in that (inter alia) the payment of collectors will not be prohibited.[188] The prohibition on the payment of street collectors contained in the regulations applicable in the metropolis[189] (and in those other areas which have adopted regulations containing a similar prohibition) will therefore cease. This change will have the effect of breaking the association between street collecting and begging which goes back to the latter part of the nineteenth century.[190]

(5) Other changes to be made by Part III

Loss of exemption for local short-term collections

The useful exemption currently available under the House to House Collections **22.81** Act 1939 in respect of short-term local collections will be lost if Part III is brought into force in its present form. This exemption, which enables the chief officer of police for a particular police area to grant a certificate relieving the promoter of the need to obtain a licence within the period specified,[191] is not contained in Part III and has not been replaced by any equivalent exemption.

National applicability

At present, the legislation relating to street collections does not apply in a local au- **22.82** thority area unless that authority has made regulations under that legislation.[192] In contrast to this, Part III of the Charities Act 1992 and the regulations made under it will apply to the whole of England and Wales.

---

regulations see CR Barker, 'Fundraising' in *Charity Law in Scotland* (eds CR Barker, PJ Ford, SR Moody, & RC Elliot) (W Green/Sweet & Maxwell, 1996), 190, 190–4

[186] *Charities: a Framework for the Future*, White Paper, Cm 694 (1989), para 10.13
[187] CA 1993, ss 43–4
[188] *Charities: a Framework for the Future*, White Paper, Cm 694 (1989), para 10.14
[189] Street Collections (Metropolitan Police District) Regulations 1979, SI 1979/1230, reg 18(1). See above, para 22.17
[190] See further P Luxton, *Charity Fund-raising and the Public Interest* (Avebury, 1990), 26–31, 100–1
[191] House to House Collections Act 1939, s 1(4); see above, para 22.50
[192] ie under the Police, Factories, etc (Miscellaneous Provisions) Act 1916, s 5

C. General legal controls on collectors

22.83 Apart from the specific legislation relating to public charitable collections, the general law may also impinge on the activities of collectors.

(1) The Theft Act 1968

22.84 If it can be established that a collector intended from the outset to appropriate funds collected for charity, he may be guilty of criminal deception.[193] In appropriate circumstances there might also lie a charge of conspiracy to defraud. The dishonest appropriation of goods donated by members of the public to a charity is an act of theft. Similarly, if a collector or other person were dishonestly to appropriate money contained in a collecting box, being money collected for a charity or for charitable purposes, he would be guilty of theft,[194] since it would be difficult to dispute that money in such a collecting box is property 'belonging to another'[195] for the purposes of the Theft Act 1968.

22.85 In *Jones v Attorney-General*,[196] Brightman J stated that 'a person who solicits money for a charity is a trustee of the money for the purpose of handing it to the charity'. Although his Lordship was speaking in the context of collections involving collecting boxes, it appears that he intended his analysis to apply even when no boxes are used. If this analysis were applied in the law of theft, money solicited for a charity could be treated as property belonging to another (namely, the charity) within section 5(1) of the Theft Act 1968.[197] The criminal courts are, however, reluctant to make a conviction turn on nice points of the civil law, particularly those pertaining (in the absence of an express declaration) to the imposition of a trust.[198] Not surprisingly, therefore, arguments in recent reported theft cases involving charity collections have relied instead on section 5(3). This sub-section provides that:

> Where a person receives property from or on account of another, and is under an obligation to the other to retain and deal with that property or its proceeds in a particular way, the property or proceeds shall be regarded (as against him) as belonging to the other.

---

[193] ie obtaining property by deception under Theft Act 1968, s 15

[194] ibid, s 1

[195] ibid, s 1(1)

[196] The Times, 10 Nov 1976

[197] Theft Act 1968, s 5(1) states: 'Property shall be regarded as belonging to any person having possession or control of it, or having in it any proprietary right or interest'

[198] See *Re A-G's Reference (No 1 of 1985)* [1986] QB 491 (CA), where the court declined to apply the doctrine of constructive trusts in a criminal context. The case concerned a barman who had supplied his own beer to his employer's customers and retained the profit. There could be no conviction of theft under Theft Act 1968, s 1, unless the profit could be treated as belonging to another on the basis that the barman held it on a constructive trust. Lord Lane CJ said that if the facts of that case constituted stealing, a whole host of activities would be brought within the ambit of crime which no layman would think were criminal

In *Lewis v Lethbridge*,[199] the defendant obtained sums of cash from persons whom **22.86**
he had persuaded to sponsor his employer for running in the colours of the Lanz
Charity in the London Marathon. The runner duly took part; but, despite repeated requests, the defendant failed to account for the money. Convicted of
theft, the defendant appealed successfully on the basis that the prosecution had
not established as a matter of law that the appropriation had been of property belonging to another.

The decision turned upon a construction of section 5(3). The appellant had **22.87**
clearly received property, namely the cash, on account of another. It was, however,
found that there was no obligation to deal with the moneys in a particular way.
The Divisional Court was able to reach such a conclusion upon the ground that
there was no rule of the Lanz Charity which required the appellant either, first, to
hand over the actual notes or coins received; or, secondly, to maintain any fund
consisting of that money in cash or in the form of any account which could be said
directly to represent that money. There had been an alternative argument that the
debt which the appellant owed the charity could, for the purposes of section 5(3),
be regarded as the 'proceeds' of the money which he received. Not surprisingly,
this argument found little favour with the court; neither could a debtor be said to
have appropriated a debt simply by not paying it.

Delivering the judgment of the Divisional Court in *Lewis v Lethbridge*, **22.88**
Macpherson J pointed out that the lesson to be learned by charities and others is
that they should impose upon collectors an obligation to maintain a separate
fund. It is, however, difficult to see how a charity can impose such an obligation
upon collectors who raise funds for the charity without notifying it in advance.
Perhaps a statement in the charity's fund-raising rules or constitution might
suffice, on the ground that a collector should be taken to have constructive notice
of such details of a charity's collection rules as he would have discovered had he
made reasonable inquiries.

Since this decision, however, the matter has been further considered in the Court **22.89**
of Appeal in *R v Wain*.[200] In this case the appellant took part in raising money for
a 'Telethon' held for charity by Yorkshire Television (the Telethon Trust). He organized a number of events which raised nearly £3,000; he paid this sum into a
separate bank account which he had opened for the purpose, and which was designated the Scarborough Telethon Appeal. Payment into a separate account was
in accordance with a recommendation made to organizers by the Telethon Trust
(although the appellant denied that he had received such information). Yorkshire
Television later permitted him to pay the sum in that account into his own bank

---

[199] [1987] Crim LR 59 (DC). See M Stallworthy & P Luxton, 'Dishonest Fund-raisers: an
Uneasy Balance Between Theft and the Civil Law' (1988) 51 MLR 114
[200] [1995] 2 Crim App Rep 660; noted (1994) 2 Decisions 34–5

account. He signed several cheques for the sum which he handed to the organizers, but all were dishonoured, and he later withdrew £640 from the account in cash. He was convicted of theft, but appealed, arguing that, for the purpose of section 5(3) of the Theft Act 1968, the debt owed to the charity could not be said to be the proceeds of the money which he had been paid—an argument which relied entirely upon *Lewis v Lethbridge*.

22.90 The Court of Appeal disapproved of *Lewis v Lethbridge*, which it also considered contrary to existing authority on the scope of section 5(3).[201] McCowan LJ, giving the judgment of the court, quoted the words of Professor Smith, who had pointed out[202] that, in *Lewis v Lethbridge*,

> [n]o consideration was given to the question whether any obligation was imposed by the sponsors. Sponsors surely do not give the collector (whether he has a box or not) the money to do as he likes with. Is there not an overwhelming inference (or, at least, evidence on which a jury might find) that the sponsors intend to give the money to the charity, imposing an obligation in the nature of a trust on the collector?

22.91 McCowan LJ considered that, leaving authorities aside, the appellant in the case before him was, by virtue of section 5(3), plainly under an obligation to retain, if not the actual notes and coins, at least their proceeds, that is, the money credited to the bank account which he opened for the trust with the actual property. When he took the money credited to that account and moved it over to his own bank account, it was still the proceeds of the notes and coins donated which he proceeded to use for his own purposes, thereby appropriating them. The appeal therefore failed.

22.92 In the light of *R v Wain*, it may now be inferred that sponsors of charity events who hand over their money or cheques to a collector intend that the collector should maintain a fund equal in amount to their contributions, so that the property or its proceeds can be regarded as belonging to another (that is, the charity) for the purposes of section 5(3). Whether collecting boxes need to be used, or whether such an obligation is imposed by the charity's rules, is no longer important for this purpose, although, in order to safeguard the funds themselves, it is clearly important that charities should continue to require those raising funds by way of sponsorship to keep such funds separate.

22.93 Although the court in both *Lewis v Lethbridge* and *R v Wain* was concerned with sponsorship money, the principle established in the latter case would appear to be equally applicable to donations. It might, however, be more difficult to apply the

---

[201] *Davidge v Bunnett* [1984] Crim LR 297, where the obligation on the defendant had been 'to keep in existence a fund sufficient to pay [a] bill'
[202] JC Smith, *The Law of Theft* (6th edn, Butterworths, 1989), 38–9; McCowan LJ also quoted from JC Smith's commentary on the case at [1987] Crim LR 60

principle to a sale of goods for a charitable purpose that is accompanied by a representation that any profits will be applied to such purpose. It may be impossible to determine at the time of sale what (if any) part of the sale proceeds will comprise the profit, and this is likely to cast doubt on the intention of such purchasers to impose any obligation in respect of any part of the money they hand over.

(2) Rights of donors

On general principles, once a donor to a charity has made the gift, he ceases to **22.94** have any rights in respect of the donation. If, however, a gift to charity is induced by the fraud of the collector (as where the collector intends from the outset to keep all donations for himself), the donor has a right to revoke the gift; furthermore, the fraud might be considered to negative the intention to give, in which case there would be a resulting trust for the donor. In the case of money collected in collecting boxes, where the sums given are usually small and the donors anonymous, the resulting trust device is impracticable, and the better view is that such donors give out and out to charity.[203] An identifiable donor, however, who can establish that his contribution was obtained by fraud, might be able to claim it back on a resulting trust. Apart from this, it is unclear whether a donor to a charity is a person 'interested' for the purpose of bringing charity proceedings.[204] In practice, a donor's best course of action in most cases where he has been induced to contribute to a collection through the fraud of the collector, or where there is an irregularity in collecting, will be (depending upon the circumstances), simply to inform one or more of the police, the local authority, or the Charity Commissioners.

---

[203] cf (in the context of non-charitable funds) *Re Gillingham Bus Disaster Fund* [1958] Ch 300, affd [1959] Ch 62, and *Re West Sussex Constabulary's Widows, Children and Benevolent (1930) Fund Trust* [1971] Ch 1
[204] ie under CA 1993, s 33. See further ch 13, paras 13.25–13.32

23

ADVERTISING AND BROADCAST
APPEALS

This chapter examines the statutory and voluntary controls affecting charity ap- **23.01**
peals and charity advertising. It is necessary to consider separately advertisements
and appeals which are broadcast on television or radio, and advertisements which
appear in other forms, such as in newspapers, magazines and at the cinema. The
former are subject to a number of statutory controls, whereas the latter (apart
from the general law relating to fair trading) are regulated only by voluntary
codes.[1]

A. Broadcast appeals and advertisements

(1) British Broadcasting Corporation (BBC)

The BBC does not accept charity advertisements, but it does broadcast charity ap- **23.02**
peals. The scope of appeals broadcast by the BBC is determined by decisions
taken by its Board of Governors on the recommendations of the Appeals Advisory
Committee, which comprises a panel of experts from the charity sector. The BBC
broadcasts regular charitable appeals in *Lifeline* on BBC1 Television and *The
Week's Good Cause* on Radio 4, and the allocation of these appeals similarly rests
with the BBC Board of Governors on the recommendations of the Appeals

---

[1] For a general survey, see D Morris, 'The Media and the Message: an Evaluation of Advertising
by Charities and an Examination of the Regulatory Frameworks' (1995–6) 3 CL & PR 157. See also
D Morris, 'Broadcast Advertising by Charities' [1990] Conv 106, which contains useful background material

Advisory Committee.[2] In addition, the BBC is involved in its own fund-raising projects such as Children in Need, which are subject to the same scrutiny. When serious emergencies occur, there is a special approval procedure for any emergency broadcast appeal.

23.03 In relation to the regular charitable appeals, the Committee aims to spread appeals as widely and equitably as possible among suitable charities. It meets three times a year to consider applications from charities and to make recommendations to the Governors on the allocation of appeals. Detailed guidelines concerning the suitability of charities and the conduct of broadcast appeals are available from the Appeals Secretary.

23.04 Besides the main BBC Appeals Advisory Committee, there are Appeals Advisory Committees in Scotland, Wales, and Northern Ireland, whose function is to advise on the broadcast of charitable appeals in those regions. All regionally based charities must apply to the Appeals Advisory Committee in their region.

23.05 The first Appeals Advisory Committee was established in 1927, and its essential policy remains the same.[3] In summary, its main provisions require that organizations should be concerned directly, or indirectly through preventative work, with the alleviation of human suffering, or they should aim to promote social, physical, cultural, or moral well-being; but this remit may be widened to include animal charities and charities concerned with preservation of the national heritage, the general aim being to achieve a catholic range of interest over a period of time. The policy continues with a list of working principles and rules, as follows:[4]

(a) A charity should have gained or be likely to gain public support.

(b) It should be registered with the Charity Commission, or give evidence of recognition of charitable status with another appropriate body, e.g. the Registrar of Friendly Societies or the Inland Revenue.

(c) It should have attained or have a good prospect of attaining an established track record of charitable achievement and be able to demonstrate financial viability.

(d) It must demonstrate a need for funds over and above those available from income or reserves.

(e) Charitable work undertaken by certain religious organisations is eligible provided that the funds will be used for the relief of suffering or promotion of physical, mental or moral well-being, that these activities represent a substantial part of the work of the organisation and that the benefits from the appeal are available to all sections of society.

(f) Restoration or repair of cathedrals and churches of genuine historical and architectural interest is eligible, but not new buildings or extension work.

---

[2] See *BBC Appeals Policy* (1999), and *Producers' Guidelines* (1999)
[3] See *BBC Appeals Policy* (1999), 1–2
[4] ibid, 2–3

(g) Memorial funds are not recommended unless set up for charitable purposes and of great general interest.

(h) Hospitals outside the National Health Service may be considered, as also may 'Friends' of Hospitals, provided that they are appealing for projects not covered by the NHS and that their work is national in scope.

(i) Educational charities are considered only if their work has some special and additional social interest, is national in scope, and the purpose of the appeal is to fund capital projects and not running costs.

(j) An appeal is not considered justifiable if the benefits would be of a kind which would normally be provided by a trade or professional organisation's benevolent fund.

(k) Organisations which exist primarily to raise funds for medical or other research should provide evidence that their work is of national significance and that they have appropriate procedures for ensuring that the research they fund is of the highest quality and is of public benefit.

(l) When some serious or major disaster occurs at home and a public fund is set up, a special appeal may be arranged. If it occurs abroad, the request must be referred to, or have been advanced by, the Disasters Emergency Committee.

(m) Assurance must be given that the applicants' [*sic*] work is either national (or international) in scope or has some national (or international) significance.

(n) Regular weekly and monthly appeals are principally fundraising opportunities. Organisations wishing to recruit volunteers or promote campaigns can do so by applying for a news item in the monthly **Lifeline** programme on BBC1 Television.

(o) Charities which are members of the Disasters Emergency Committee are prevented under the terms of their membership from applying for a broadcast appeal.

23.06 Normally, no organization may apply for an appeal more than once in three years, or two years if their previous application was unsuccessful. Exceptions to this rule may be allowed at the Committee's discretion if, for example, one or more of the following conditions apply: (1) if the organization is mainly dependent on the proceeds of broadcast appeals; or (2) if a number of organizations combine to present a joint appeal, with individual participants of the joint appeal excluded thereafter so long as the combination lasts; or (3) if a need arises which could not possibly have been foreseen at the time of the earlier appeal.[5]

23.07 Normally, every application will be accepted or rejected at or before its second consideration in committee.[6]

23.08 The BBC is also a party to the British Appeals Consortium, which has drawn up a charter of good practice for television and radio appeals,[7] and appeals broadcast on the BBC must therefore also conform to the standards of conduct therein prescribed. The charter and the recommendation which it contains are considered more fully below.[8]

---

[5] ibid, 3
[6] ibid
[7] Broadcast Appeals Consortium, *Charter and Recommendations for the Conduct of Broadcast Appeals* (1994)
[8] See below, paras 23.22–23.24

(2) Independent television

23.09 Under the Broadcasting Act 1990, it is a statutory duty of the Independent Television Commission (ITC) to draw up and enforce a code governing standards and practice in television advertising and the sponsoring of programmes.[9] Amongst its specific obligations is a duty to draw up, review, and enforce, a code giving guidance as to the rules to be observed with respect to the inclusion of appeals for donations in programmes showing violence, or the inclusion of sounds suggestive of violence.[10] In pursuance of its statutory obligations, the ITC has published the *ITC Code of Advertising Standards and Practice* (the Code).[11] The Code applies to all television programme services licensed by the ITC under the Broadcasting Acts 1990 and 1996.[12]

23.10 All holders of relevant ITC licences are required to ensure that any advertising they transmit complies with the Code and to satisfy the ITC that they have adequate procedures to fulfil this requirement. The ITC can require advertising which does not comply to be withdrawn.[13] Television companies are not obliged to accept advertising they do not wish to carry or provide access to; but, under the Broadcasting Act 1990, they must not, in accepting advertisements, discriminate unreasonably either against or in favour of any particular advertiser.[14] The ITC is not prepared to make rulings on the acceptability in relation to the Code of particular advertisements in advance of their broadcast; requests for approval or guidance on the likely acceptability of particular advertising proposals should be directed to the relevant television company, or, if appropriate, to the Broadcast Advertising Clearance Centre.[15]

---

[9] The ITC also has a duty to consider complaints about television advertisements which are alleged to be misleading, under the Control of Misleading Advertisements Regulations 1988, SI 1988/915, as amended by Broadcasting Act 1990, s 203 & Sch 20, para 51, and Sch 21; Banking Co-ordination (Second Council Directive) Regulations 1992, SI 1992/3218, reg 82(1) & Sch 10, para 51; Public Offers of Securities Regulations 1995, SI 1995/1537, reg 17 & Sch 2, para 11; Investment Services Regulations 1995, SI 1995/3275, reg 57 & Sch 10, para 18; and Control of Misleading Advertisements (Amendment) Regulations 2000, SI 2000/914

[10] Broadcasting Act 1990, s 7(1)(b)

[11] Published by the ITC in 1998. In drawing up the Code, the ITC also had regard to the Code of Practice issued by the Broadcasting Standards Commission and to the need to give effect to a number of requirements relating to television advertising in the EU Directive on Television Broadcasting (89/552/EEC of 1989 as amended by Directive 97/36/EC of 1997) and the 1989 Council of Europe Convention on Transfrontier Television

[12] ie (at the time of writing) channel 3 (ITV and GMTV), Channel 4, Channel 5, satellite television services provided by broadcasters established in UK, licensable programme services (which include those cable channels established in the UK which are not also in any of the previous licensing categories), digital programme services, and services provided under Restricted Licences. The Code applies to the Welsh Fourth Channel which is regulated by S4C. In some cases, the Code makes different provisions for different types of services

[13] *ITC Code of Advertising Standards and Practice* (1998), iii (para (e))

[14] Broadcasting Act 1990, s 8(2)(b)

[15] *ITC Code of Advertising Standards and Practice* (1998), iv (para (h))

The Code lays down four general principles: first, that television advertising **23.11** should be legal, decent, honest, and truthful; secondly, that advertisements must comply in every respect with the law, both common law and statute, and licensees must make it a condition of acceptance that advertisements do so comply; thirdly, the detailed rules set out in the Code are intended to be applied in the spirit as well as the letter; and, fourthly, the standards in the Code apply to any item of publicity inserted in breaks in or between programmes, whether in return for payment or not, including publicity by licensees themselves, and the term 'advertisement' is to be so construed for the purposes of the Code.[16]

In addition to provisions of general application, the Code deals specifically with **23.12** charities.[17] Under the Code, advertisements soliciting donations for or promoting the needs or objects of United Kingdom bodies whose activities are financed wholly or mainly from donations may be accepted only from registered charities or those able to produce satisfactory evidence that their charitable status has been officially recognized. Such advertisements must comply with the provisions of Appendix 4 to the Code, which also specifies the circumstances in which such advertisements may be accepted where they are submitted on behalf of bodies based outside the United Kingdom. In the case of charities with religious affiliations, other parts of the Code may also apply.[18]

In accordance with Appendix 4,[19] licensees must satisfy themselves either that an **23.13** organization is registered as a charity with the Charity Commissioners or that its charitable status has otherwise been officially recognized. Advertisers must be prepared to submit full details of their constitution, aims, and objectives; membership of governing body; recent and current activities; and such additional information as may be appropriate, including, for example, audited accounts, for the purposes of establishing that a charity is not misrepresenting its activities in any way, or that its status does not conflict with certain other requirements of the Code.[20] Before accepting advertising for charities based outside the United Kingdom, licensees must obtain a written assurance that the organization complies with all relevant legislation in the country in which it is based, and they must both conduct a full investigation of the other matters referred to above, and seek the assurances listed below.[21] In case of doubt following investigations, the Code strongly advises licensees to consult the ITC before accepting advertising from such organizations.[22]

---

[16] ibid, rr 1–4
[17] ibid, r 12
[18] ie r 11 and App 5 (Religious Advertising)
[19] ibid, App 4 (Charity Advertising)
[20] ibid, App 4, para 2. The other requirements of the Code referred to are rr 10 (Politics, Industrial and Public Controversy) and 11 (Religion)
[21] ibid, App 4 (para 3)
[22] ibid

23.14   Advertisers are required to give the following assurances: first, that they do not involve themselves in transactions in which members of their governing bodies or staff have a financial interest; secondly, that the response to their proposed advertising, whether in cash, in kind, or in services, will be applied solely to the purposes specified or implied in the advertising; and, thirdly, that they will not publish or otherwise disclose the names of contributors without their prior permission and that they comply with the requirements of current United Kingdom data protection legislation.[23] The Commission reserves the right to seek assurances on other matters where it considers this appropriate. The Commission also reserves the right to reconsider the acceptability of advertising where it has reason to doubt the validity of any assurances or other information provided.[24]

23.15   Advertisements by commercial advertisers which promote, either as a main or incidental purpose, the needs or objects of organizations which would be acceptable in their own right as not contravening the provisions of the main Code relating to politics,[25] industrial and political controversy,[26] religion,[27] or charities,[28] are also acceptable subject to the following conditions. First, evidence must be provided that the organization concerned has given its consent to the proposed advertising. Secondly, in the case of advertisements including an offer to donate part of the proceeds of sales to charity, each advertisement must specify the charity or charities which will benefit and make clear the basis on which the sums to be donated will be calculated. Offers of this kind should not depend on sales reaching a given level, or be subject to any similar condition. Thirdly, offers of this kind in connection with advertisements for medicinal products are not acceptable.[29]

23.16   Advertisements for charities must handle with care and discretion matters likely to arouse strong emotion in the audience; must not suggest that anyone will lack proper feeling or fail in any responsibility through not supporting a charity; must respect the dignity of those on whose behalf an appeal is being made; must not address any fund-raising message specifically to children; must not contain comparisons with other charities; must avoid presenting an exaggerated impression of the scale or nature of the social problem to which the work of the charity is addressed, for example, by illustrating the message with non-typical extreme cases; and must not mislead in any way as to the field of activity of the charity or the use to which donations will be put.[30]

---

[23] *ITC Code of Advertising Standards and Practice* (1998), para 4(a)
[24] ibid, para 4(b)
[25] ibid, r 10
[26] ibid, r 10
[27] ibid, r 11
[28] ibid, r 12
[29] ibid, App 4, para 5
[30] ibid, App 4, para 6

Charity advertisements may not be scheduled in immediate juxtaposition to **23.17** programme appeals or community service announcements;[31] and regular station presenters may not feature in paid-for advertisements broadcast on their own station.[32]

(3) Independent radio

The Radio Authority licenses and regulates the independent radio industry in ac- **23.18** cordance with the statutory requirements of the Broadcasting Act 1990.[33] The Radio Authority is required to draw up, and periodically to review, a code giving guidance (inter alia) as to the rules to be observed with respect to the inclusion in programmes of appeals for donations.[34]

Furthermore, the Radio Authority is statutorily obliged to do all it can to secure **23.19** that a licensed service does not include (inter alia) any advertisement which is inserted by or on behalf of any body whose objects are wholly or mainly of a political nature,[35] or which is directed towards any political end.[36] A political object in this context includes those objects which were treated as political for the purposes of the law of charity in *McGovern v Attorney-General*,[37] that is including, for instance, the object of procuring a reversal of government policy or of particular decisions of governmental authorities in this, or in a foreign, country.[38] However, whilst an independent political object suffices to deny a body charitable status, such an object will not necessarily deny it the right to advertise on radio: in relation to the Radio Authority's duties to prohibit political advertising, the expression 'wholly or mainly' has been interpreted restrictively to refer only to objects that are substantially or primarily political, this meaning more than 75 per cent.[39]

The Radio Authority must also do all it can to secure that, in the acceptance of ad- **23.20** vertisements for inclusion in a licensed service, there is no unreasonable discrimination either against or in favour of any particular advertiser.[40]

---

[31] ibid, para 7(a)
[32] ibid, para 7(b)
[33] Broadcasting Act 1990, Pt III
[34] ibid, s 91(1)(b)
[35] ibid, s 92(2)(a)(i)
[36] ibid, s 92(2)(a)(ii)
[37] [1982] Ch 321 (Slade J)
[38] *R v Radio Authority, ex p Bull* [1997] 2 All ER 561, 570–2, where Lord Woolf MR quoted and applied a passage from the judgment of Slade J in *McGovern v A-G* [1982] Ch 321, 340. The other members of the Court of Appeal in *R v Radio Authority* adopted a similar approach: Aldous LJ (ibid, 575), and Brooke LJ (ibid, 579–80). For a commentary on the case, see J Stevens & DJ Feldman, 'Broadcasting advertisements by bodies with political objects, judicial review, and the influence of charities law' [1997] PL 615
[39] *R v Radio Authority, ex p Bull* [1997] 2 All ER 561, 570 (Lord Woolf MR), with whom Brooke LJ agreed: ibid, 578. Aldous LJ, however, would not have sought to define the expression 'wholly or mainly', but would have treated it as a jury-type question: ibid, 575
[40] Broadcasting Act 1990, s 92(2)(b)

23.21 The Radio Authority is obliged to draw up, and from time to time to review, a code governing standards and practice in advertising and in the sponsoring of programmes, and prescribing the advertisements and methods of advertising or sponsorship to be prohibited, or to be prohibited in particular circumstances, and to do all that it can to secure that the provisions of the code are observed in the provision of licensed services.[41] In pursuance of its statutory obligation, the Radio Authority has published an *Advertising and Sponsorship Code*.[42] The Code expands upon the statutory prohibition upon advertisements involving political, industrial, and public controversy.[43] The Code's rule on charity advertising on radio,[44] and its amplification in an appendix,[45] are in wording almost identical to the corresponding provisions applicable to television advertising contained in the *ITC Code of Advertising Standards and Practice*,[46] which have been described above.[47] For this reason, they are accorded no separate treatment here.

(4) Charter and Recommendations of the Broadcast Appeals Consortium

23.22 The Broadcast Appeals Consortium was formed by BBC Children in Need, Charity Projects/Comic Relief and ITV Telethon, together with Broadcasting Support Services, Community Service Volunteers, and the Disasters Emergency Committee, in order to establish high standards of conduct for charitable broadcast appeals to supplement the framework of charity law and broadcasting regulations. The Consortium has drawn up and published a *Charter and Recommendations for the Conduct of Broadcast Appeals*,[48] and it is envisaged that the Recommendations will be updated when appropriate.

23.23 The Charter provides that a charitable broadcast appeal may be large or small, on radio or television, for a single cause or many. It states that all broadcast appeals must:

(a) be based on written agreements which reflect the partnership between broadcaster and charity, and cover the financial arrangements, the organization and content of the appeal, the collection and distribution of donations, evaluation, and follow-up;

(b) ensure that broadcasters, trustees, and directors are aware of their responzibilities under the law;

(c) organize in advance the support needed to back the appeal and distribute the proceeds;

---

[41] Broadcasting Act 1990, s 93(1)
[42] March 1997 (latest revision)
[43] *Advertising and Sponsorship Code* (Radio Authority, 1997), r 9
[44] ibid, r 30
[45] ibid, App 5
[46] (1998)
[47] See above, paras 23.12–23.17
[48] (1994)

(d) ensure that any companies connected to or established for the appeal are controlled by an appeal charity, to which all profits must be covenanted;

(e) retain copyright of all appeal logos, images, and slogans;

(f) convey clearly the purpose for which donations are being sought and how they can be made;

(g) respect the dignity of the beneficiaries in the promotion of the appeal and the distribution of the funds;

(h) discourage any activities which do not meet high standards of fund-raising, grant-making, and presentation;

(i) honour all reasonable requests from individuals seeking a refund of their donation; and

(j) make clear how the funds raised will be distributed and publicize the result.

23.24 The Recommendations amplify the Charter by setting out general principles and considerations on which those involved in broadcast appeals can build. The Recommendations cover the five key aspects of charity broadcast appeals:

(a) the organization, structure, and relationships required;

(b) the content and style of the broadcast itself;

(c) the seeking and collection of money or other responses;

(d) the administration and distribution of money or other assistance offered; and

(e) the following up and evaluation of the appeal.

B. Other appeals and advertisements

23.25 A self-regulatory body, the Committee of Advertising Practice (CAP), has drawn up and enforces *The British Codes of Advertising and Sales Promotion*.[49] These comprise an Advertising Code and a Sales Promotion Code. The Codes used to contain an exemption for advertisements which addressed controversial issues of public policy or practice, with the result that many non-commercial advertisements, including those of charities, could not be tested under the Codes for their factual accuracy. This exemption was, however, withdrawn in 1993, so that the Codes now extend to such advertisements.

23.26 The Codes apply to advertisements in newspapers, magazines, brochures, leaflets, circulars, mailings, fax transmissions, catalogues, follow-up literature and other electronic and printed material; to posters and other promotional media in public places; to cinema and video commercials; to advertisements in non-broadcast

---

[49] 10th edn, 1999, which came into force on 1 Oct 1999

electronic media; and to sales and advertisement promotions.[50] The Codes do not apply (inter alia) to broadcast commercials (which are the responsibility of the ITC or the Radio Authority).[51]

23.27   The Codes are interpreted by the Council of the Advertising Standards Authority (ASA), and the Council's interpretation is final.[52] It is stated that their interpretation will reflect their flexibility.[53] The Codes do not have the force of law, but breach of the Codes may have unwelcome consequences for the advertiser. First, there may be adverse publicity, as the ASA produces monthly reports of complaints and adjudications, which contain the name of the advertiser, agency, and media involved, and the reports are circulated to journalists, Government agencies, the advertising industry consumer bodies, and the public. Secondly, the media's standard terms of business require compliance with the Codes, and they may decide to refuse further advertising space to an advertiser until an advertisement has been amended. Thirdly, posters which are the subject of complaints upheld on grounds of taste and decency and social responsibility are subject to a two-year vetting procedure by the CAP. Fourthly, non-compliance with the Codes may lead to advertisers and their agencies losing their membership of trade or professional associations. Fifthly, and ultimately, the ASA can refer a misleading advertisement to the Office of Fair Trading,[54] which can seek an injunction to restrain the use of similar claims in future advertisements.[55]

23.28   The first general principle of the Advertising Code is that all advertisements should be legal, decent, honest, and truthful,[56] that they should be prepared with a sense of responsibility to consumers and to society,[57] that they should respect the principles of fair competition generally accepted in business,[58] and that they should conform with the Codes,[59] which are to be applied in the spirit as well as in the letter.[60] Before submitting an advertisement for publication, advertisers must hold documentary evidence to prove all claims, whether direct or implied, that are capable of objective substantiation, and must send it without delay if requested by the ASA.[61] The general provisions of the Code that might be of particular rele-

---

[50] *The British Codes of Advertising and Sales Promotion* (10th edn, Committee of Advertising Practice, 1999) para 1.1
[51] ibid, para 1.2
[52] ibid, para 1.4.a
[53] ibid, para 1.4.d
[54] Control of Misleading Advertisements Regulations 1988, SI 1988/915, reg 4. These Regulations were made pursuant to European Communities Act 1972, s 2
[55] ibid, reg 5
[56] *The British Codes of Advertising and Sales Promotion,* Advertising Code, para 2.1
[57] ibid, para 2.2
[58] ibid, para 2.3
[59] ibid, para 2.5
[60] ibid, para 2.8
[61] ibid, para 3.1

vance to some charity advertising include a provision that advertisements should contain nothing that is likely to cause serious or widespread offence,[62] although advertisements may be distasteful without necessarily conflicting with this requirement.[63] Another general provision that charity advertisers should bear in mind is that no advertisement should cause fear or distress without good reason, and that advertisers should not use shocking claims or images merely to attract attention.[64]

The Sales Promotion Code contains provisions dealing specifically with charity-linked promotions. These state that promotions claiming that participation will benefit registered charities or causes should:[65]   **23.29**

> a   name each charity or cause that will benefit, and be able to show the ASA the formal agreement with those benefiting from the promotion
> b   when it is not a registered charity, define its nature and objectives
> c   specify exactly what will be gained by the named charity or cause and state the basis on which the contribution will be calculated
> d   state if the promoters have imposed any limitations on their own contribution
> e   not limit consumers' contributions. If an amount is stated for each purchase, there should be no cut-off point for contributions. If a target total is stated, any extra money collected should be given to the named charity or cause on the same basis as contributions below that level
> f   be able to show that any targets set are realistic, and should not exaggerate the benefit to the charity or cause derived from individual purchases of the promoted product
> g   if asked, make available to consumers a current or final total of contributions made
> h   take particular care when appealing to children.

The specific rules dealing with children state that advertisements and promotions addressed to children (inter alia) should not exploit their susceptibility to charitable appeals and should explain the extent to which their participation will help in any charity-linked promotions.[66]   **29.30**

The Code also contains provisions dealing with environmental claims.[67]   **23.31**

---

[62]   ibid, para 5.1
[63]   ibid, para 5.2
[64]   ibid, para 9.1
[65]   Sales Promotion Code, para 42.1
[66]   ibid, para 47.4.e
[67]   ibid, para 49

24

LOTTERIES, COMPETITIONS, AND AMUSEMENTS

A. Lotteries

Although lotteries are regulated by a considerable body of legislation, there is no **24.01** statutory definition of a lottery. Whether an activity constitutes a lottery is therefore to be determined by the common law. Case law has established that a lottery is a scheme for distributing prizes by (and only by) lot or chance.[1] If, therefore, competitors can enhance their chances of success by the use of skill, the scheme cannot be a lottery.[2]

Lotteries are unlawful except as provided for by the Lotteries and Amusements **24.02** Act 1976 and by the National Lottery etc Act 1993.[3] The earlier of these Acts provides for several different types of lawful lotteries: small lotteries which are incidental to exempt entertainments;[4] private lotteries;[5] societies' lotteries;[6] and local lotteries.[7] Sums from the National Lottery are allocated to a number of what are popularly called 'good causes', one of which is charitable expenditure. The importance to charities of each of these lawful lotteries will be considered in turn.

---

[1] *Taylor v Smetton* (1883) 11 QBD 207 (DC); *Barclay v Pearson* [1893] 2 Ch 154

[2] *Hall v Cox* [1899] 1 QB 198; *Hobbs v Ward* (1929) 93 JP 163 (DC). Spot-the-ball type competitions, involving skill, are therefore not lotteries

[3] Lotteries and Amusements Act 1976, s 1, as amended by National Lottery etc Act 1993, s 2(2) & Sch 1, para 2(1)

[4] Lotteries and Amusements Act 1976, s 3

[5] ibid, s 4

[6] ibid, s 5

[7] ibid, s 6

(1) Small lotteries incidental to exempt entertainments

General requirements

24.03 An 'exempt entertainment' means a bazaar, sale of work, fête, dinner, dance, sporting or athletic event, or other entertainment of a similar character, whether limited to one day or extending over two or more days.[8] To fall within the exemption, the whole proceeds of the entertainment (including the proceeds of the lottery), after permitted deductions, must be devoted to purposes other than private gain.[9] The permitted deductions are the expenses of the entertainment (excluding expenses incurred in connection with the lottery), the expenses incurred in printing the lottery tickets, and up to £50 as the promoters of the lottery think fit to appropriate on account of any expenses *incurred by them* in the purchase of prizes.[10] The emphasized words mean that if the prizes are provided by someone else, such as a sponsor, they may exceed £50 in value. Monetary prizes are prohibited.[11]

24.04 Tickets[12] or chances[13] in such a lottery must be sold, and the result of the lottery declared, only on the premises on which the entertainment takes place and while it is in progress.[14] A final requirement is that the facilities for participating in such lotteries, together with any other facilities for participating in lotteries or gaming, must not be the only, or the only substantial, inducement to persons to attend the entertainment.[15]

Tax exemption

24.05 A charity is entitled to claim exemption from tax under Schedule D of the Income and Corporation Taxes Act 1988 in respect of profits accruing to it from a lottery promoted and conducted as a small lottery incidental to exempt entertainments, provided the profits are applied solely to the charity's purposes.[16]

---

[8] Lotteries and Amusements Act 1976, s 3(1)

[9] ibid, s 3(3)(a)

[10] ibid, s 3(3)(a), which also empowers the Secretary of State by order to specify a different sum

[11] ibid, s 3(3)(b)

[12] For the purposes of the Lotteries and Amusements Act 1976, 'ticket', in relation to any lottery, includes any document evidencing the claim of a person to participate in the chances of the lottery: ibid, s 23(1)

[13] In *Rogers v Cowley* [1962] 1 WLR 770, 778, Winn J considered that the word 'chance', in the context of the Betting and Gaming Act 1962, s 16, meant an opportunity to win money or a prize of money's worth

[14] Lotteries and Amusements Act 1976, s 3(3)(c)

[15] ibid, s 3(3)(d)

[16] ICTA 1988, s 505(1)(f)

(2) *Private lotteries*

A private lottery means a lottery in Great Britain which is (inter alia) promoted for **24.06** members of one society[17] established or conducted for purposes not connected with gaming, betting, or lotteries, or for persons who all work, or who all reside, on the same premises.[18] The lottery must be promoted by persons each of whom is a person for whom the lottery is promoted; and, in the case of a lottery promoted for the members of a society, it must be promoted by persons each of whom is authorized in writing by the society's governing body to promote the lottery.[19] The sale of tickets or chances must be confined to the persons for whom the lottery is promoted (although, in the case of a lottery promoted for the members of a society, the sale may extend to any other persons on the society's premises).[20] The whole proceeds of a private lottery, after deducting only expenses incurred for printing and stationery, must be devoted to the provision of prizes for purchasers of tickets or chances, unless it is a lottery promoted for the members of a society, when all or part of such proceeds may also be applied to the purposes of the society.[21] Furthermore, no written notice or advertisement of the lottery may be exhibited, published, or distributed other than by a notice on the society's premises (or on the premises where the persons for whom it is promoted work or reside) and on the tickets (if any) themselves.[22] The price of each ticket or chance must be the same, and the price of the ticket must be stated on the ticket.[23] Every ticket must bear upon its face (inter alia) the name and address of each of the promoters and a statement of the persons to whom the sale of tickets or chances is restricted.[24] No ticket or chance may be issued or allotted except upon receipt of its full price,[25] and no tickets may be sent through the post.[26]

A private lottery could be used as a means of raising funds for a charitable society, **24.07** but as the restrictions upon them are so stringent, and as the profits of such lotteries do not enjoy the exemption from tax available to societies' lotteries, charitable bodies much prefer to use societies' lotteries instead.

---

[17] For this purpose, each local or affiliated branch or section of a society is to be regarded as a separate and distinct society: Lotteries and Amusements Act 1976, s 4(2)

[18] ibid, s 4(1), as substituted by National Lottery etc Act 1993, s 47

[19] Lotteries and Amusements Act 1976, s 4(1A), as substituted by National Lottery etc Act 1993, s 47

[20] Lotteries and Amusements Act 1976, s 4(1B), as substituted by National Lottery etc Act 1993, s 47

[21] Lotteries and Amusements Act 1976, s 4(3)(a)

[22] ibid, s 4(3)(b)

[23] ibid, s 4(3)(c)

[24] ibid, s 4(3)(d)

[25] ibid, s 4(3)(e)

[26] ibid, s 4(3)(f)

(3) Societies' lotteries

Meaning of 'society's lottery'

24.08 A 'society's lottery' means a lottery promoted on behalf of a society which is established and conducted wholly or mainly for one or more of the following purposes: charitable purposes; participation in or support of athletic sports or games or cultural activities; or other purposes which are neither of private gain nor of any commercial undertaking.[27] Any purpose for which a society is established and conducted and which is calculated to benefit the society as a whole is not to be held to be a purpose of private gain by reason only that action in its fulfilment would result in benefit to any person as an individual.[28]

Registration

24.09 A society's lottery is not unlawful if it is promoted in Great Britain by a society which is for the time being registered under the appropriate Schedule to the Lotteries and Amusements Act 1976, and is promoted in accordance with a scheme approved by the society.[29] Registration is either with the Gaming Board (under Schedule 1A) or with the appropriate local authority (under Schedule 1).

Registration with the Gaming Board

24.10 The society must be registered with the Gaming Board under Schedule 1A to the Act[30] if the total value of the tickets or chances sold or to be sold in the lottery is more than £20,000,[31] or if the combined total value of tickets or chances sold or to be sold in that lottery and in all earlier lotteries held by the same society in the same year exceeds £250,000.[32] If either of these circumstances applies, the society must also be registered under Schedule 1A for the following three years.[33] For these purposes, a lottery is earlier than another lottery if any tickets or chances in it are sold, distributed, or offered for sale before any tickets or chances in the other lottery are sold, distributed, or offered for sale.[34] A lottery is held in the year in which the date of the lottery falls,[35] and 'year' in relation to societies' lotteries means a period of twelve months beginning with 1 January.[36]

---

[27] Lotteries and Amusements Act 1976, s 5(1)
[28] ibid, s 5(2)
[29] ibid, s 5(3), as amended by National Lottery etc Act 1993, ss 48(2), 49(1), 64, Sch 10
[30] Lotteries and Amusements Act 1976, s 5(3A)(b)
[31] ibid, s 5(3B). Sub-ss (3A)–(3F) were added by National Lottery etc Act 1993, s 48(3)
[32] Lotteries and Amusements Act 1976, s 5(3C)
[33] ibid, s 5(3D)
[34] ibid, s 5(3E)(a)
[35] ibid, s 5(3E)(b)
[36] ibid, s 5(3F)

An application for registration of a society under Schedule 1A requires an appli- **24.11** cation to be made to the Gaming Board[37] and payment of a prescribed fee.[38] The application must specify the society's office or head office, and the society's purposes, and it must attach a copy of any scheme which the society has approved.[39] The society must also provide the Gaming Board with such information, and permit the Board to inspect and copy such documents, as the Board may require.[40] The Board must refuse to register a society if the scheme approved by the society is contrary to law.[41] The Board may refuse registration upon specified grounds including the following: that a person connected with a lottery promoted, or to be promoted, by the society has been convicted of an offence involving lotteries or of any offence involving fraud or dishonesty;[42] that any lottery promoted by the society within the previous five years has not been conducted properly;[43] non-payment of any fees;[44] and failure to provide the Board with such information, or to permit it to inspect and copy such documents, as it may require.[45] Another discretionary ground for refusal is that a person connected with a lottery[46] caused registration of another society to be refused or revoked for failure to comply with the requirements relating to lotteries, or was a cause of another society's lottery registered with the Board not being properly conducted[47] within the previous five years.[48] The Secretary of State may direct the Board to register a society whose registration has been refused.[49]

A society registered under Schedule 1A must send a return to the Board within **24.12** three months of the date of a lottery promoted on the society's behalf.[50] If the total value of tickets or chances sold in all lotteries held in any one year and promoted on behalf of the same society exceeds £100,000, and any of those lotteries satisfy other requirements,[51] the society must send to the Board accounts in respect of those lotteries, together with a report on them prepared by a qualified auditor.[52]

---

[37] ibid, Sch 1A, Pt I, para 1
[38] ibid, para 2(1). The fee payable on an application for registration is currently £710: Lotteries (Gaming Board Fees) Order 2000, SI 2000/1210, Art 3
[39] Lotteries and Amusements Act 1976, Sch 1A, Pt I, para 1
[40] ibid, Pt II, para 12
[41] ibid, Pt I, para 3(1)
[42] ibid, para 3(2)(a)
[43] ibid, para 3(2)(d)
[44] ibid, para 3(2)(e)
[45] ibid, para 3(1)(f)
[46] For meaning of 'a person connected with a lottery', see ibid, para 3(4)
[47] ibid, para 3(3)
[48] ibid, para 3(2)(g)
[49] ibid, para 4(1)(a)
[50] ibid, Sch 1A, Pt II, para 9(1)
[51] ie namely that any of those lotteries is a lottery to which ibid, s 5(3B), (3C), or (3D) applies: see above, para 24.10
[52] Lotteries and Amusements Act 1976 Sch 1A, Pt II, para 13(1). The expression 'qualified auditor' is explained ibid, para 13(5), (6)

The accounts must be sent to the Board within ten months of the end of the year in which the lotteries were held.[53] No accounts or report on them need be sent to the Board, however, in relation to any year in which the promotion of every lottery promoted on behalf of the society held in that year is managed by a person certified under Schedule 2A as a lottery manager.[54] A society registered with the Gaming Board must also notify the Board in writing of any change in the address of its office or head office within twenty-one days.[55] It must also notify the Board of any modification of a scheme approved by the society,[56] attaching a copy of the scheme as modified;[57] notice must be given at least four weeks before any tickets or chances are sold, distributed, or offered for sale.[58] A society registered with the Gaming Board must pay a prescribed fee at continuing intervals during its registration,[59] and a further prescribed fee for each society's lottery promoted on behalf of the society while it is so registered.[60]

24.13 The grounds on which the Gaming Board may revoke a society's registration comprise those grounds on which it may refuse registration,[61] and some additional grounds.[62] The Board may therefore revoke registration if, for example, false information was submitted to obtain registration,[63] or if the society fails to pay the requisite fees.[64] The Board may also revoke registration if the society fails to submit a return and (if necessary) audited accounts.[65] The Board must revoke registration if a modified scheme is contrary to law.[66] Revocation of registration does not affect any lottery in respect of which any tickets or chances have already been sold.[67] The Secretary of State may direct the Board to restore to the register a society whose registration has been revoked.[68]

---

[53] Lotteries and Amusements Act 1976 Sch 1A, Pt II, para 13(2). For this purpose, 'year' means a period of 12 months beginning with 1 Jan: ibid, para 13(12)

[54] ibid, para 13(10)

[55] ibid, Pt II, para 7

[56] ibid, para 8(1)

[57] ibid, para 8(2)

[58] ibid, para 8(3)

[59] ibid, Pt I, para 6(1)(a). The fee is currently £75, payable at intervals of three years after the society's registration: Lotteries (Gaming Board Fees) Order 2000, SI 2000/1210, Art 5

[60] Lotteries and Amusements Act 1976, Sch 1A, Pt I, para 6(1)(b). The current fee is variable (primarily according to the total value of tickets or chances sold), no fee being payable if the total value of tickets or chances sold does not exceed £2,000: Lotteries (Gaming Board Fees) Order 2000, SI 2000/1210, Art 6

[61] Lotteries and Amusements Act 1976, Sch 1A, Pt I, para 3(2)

[62] ibid, para 3(5)

[63] ibid, para 3(2)(b)

[64] ibid, para 3(2)(e)

[65] ibid, para 3(5), and Pt II, para 13

[66] ibid, Pt I, para 3(1)

[67] ibid, para 3(8)

[68] ibid, para 4(1)(b)

Registration with the appropriate local authority

If the circumstances for registration with the Gaming Board do not apply, so that the **24.14** society is not required to be registered under Schedule 1A, then it must instead be registered under Schedule 1.[69] Registration must be effected with the 'registration authority', which means, in England, a London borough council, a district council, the Common Council of the City of London, or the Council of the Isles of Scilly, and in Wales, a county council or county borough council, being (in either case) the authority in whose area the office or head office of the society is situated.[70]

An application for registration must specify the society's purposes[71], and the soci- **24.15** ety must pay an application fee of £35.[72] The registration authority must refuse or revoke registration under Schedule 1 if the Gaming Board has refused or revoked registration under Schedule 1A within the previous five years.[73] The registration authority may refuse registration if it appears to the authority that any person connected with a lottery[74] promoted on behalf of the society has been convicted of specified offences,[75] that the society does not (or ceases to) comply with the conditions for registration,[76] or that information which the society submitted in order to obtain registration was false in a material particular.[77] The registration authority may also revoke a registration if the society fails to allow it to inspect documents or to access information held on a computer.[78] There is provision for appeal to the Crown Court against a refusal or revocation of registration.[79] Every society registered under Schedule 1 must pay an annual fee of £17.50 to the registration authority on 1 January.[80]

Unless the society is registered with the Gaming Board under Schedule 1A,[81] the **24.16** promoter of a society's lottery must send a return to the registration authority

---

[69] ibid, s 5(3A)(a)
[70] ibid, Sch 1, Pt I, para 1(2), as amended by National Lottery etc Act 1993, ss 48, 64 & Sch 7, para 2, Sch 10, and Local Government (Wales) Act 1994, s 66(6) & Sch 16, para 50(2)
[71] Lotteries and Amusements Act 1976, Sch 1, Pt I, para 2, as amended by National Lottery etc Act 1993, s 48(5) & Sch 7, Pt I, para 3
[72] Lotteries and Amusements Act 1976, Sch 1, Pt I, para 3, with amount substituted by Lotteries (Registration Authority Fees) Order 1991, SI 1991/2178
[73] Lotteries and Amusements Act 1976, Sch 1, Pt I, para 3A(1). Para 3A was added by National Lottery etc Act 1993, s 48 & Sch 7, para 4
[74] For meaning of 'any person connected with a lottery' in this context, see Lotteries and Amusements Act 1976, Sch 1, Pt I, para 4(3)
[75] ibid, para 4(1)(a). These are essentially offences under the Lotteries and Amusements Act 1976 and the Betting, Gaming and Lotteries Act 1963, and offences involving fraud or dishonesty: Lotteries and Amusements Act 1976, Sch 1, Pt I, para 4(2)
[76] Lotteries and Amusements Act 1976, Sch 1, Pt I, para 4(1)(b)
[77] ibid, para 4(1)(c)
[78] ibid, para 4A & Pt II, para 16
[79] ibid, Pt I, paras 5, 7
[80] ibid, para 9; amount substituted by Lotteries (Registration Authority Fees) Order 1991, SI 1991/2178
[81] Lotteries and Amusements Act 1976, Sch 1, Pt II, para 12

within three months of the lottery.[82] The return must be certified by two other members of the society appointed in writing by the society's governing body; and it must show (inter alia) a copy of the scheme, the whole of the proceeds of the lottery, sums appropriated on account of expenses and prizes, the purposes to which the lottery proceeds were applied, the amount so applied, and the date of the lottery.[83]

Application of proceeds

24.17 The whole proceeds of a society's lottery, after deducting sums for expenses and the provision of prizes, must be applied to the society's purposes (these being charitable purposes, the participation in or support of athletic sports or games or cultural activities, or other purposes being neither of private gain nor of any commercial undertaking).[84]

Frequency

24.18 The Secretary of State may by order prescribe the maximum number of lotteries which the same society may promote in any period of twelve months, and the minimum number of days between any two such lotteries.[85]

Rules for societies' lotteries

24.19 The rules for societies' lotteries are contained in section 11 of the Lotteries and Amusements Act 1972.[86]

Promoter

24.20 The promoter must be a member of the society authorized in writing by its governing body.[87]

Tickets and chances

24.21 Every ticket distributed or sold must specify the name of the society, the name and address of the promoter, and the date of the lottery.[88] No ticket or chance may be sold for more than £1,[89] and the price of any ticket distributed or sold must be

---

[82] Lotteries and Amusements Act 1976, Sch 1 para 11

[83] ibid, para 11

[84] ibid, s 5(4)

[85] ibid, s 10(1), as substituted by National Lottery etc Act 1993, s 51. As yet, no such order has been made

[86] As amended by National Lottery etc Act 1993, s 52(1)–(6), (7)(a), (8), and with amounts substituted by Lotteries (Variation of Monetary Limits) Order 1989, SI 1989/1218, art 2 & Sch, and Lotteries (Prizes and Expenses: Variation and Prescription of Percentage Limits) Order 1997, SI 1997/43, Arts 2–4

[87] Lotteries and Amusements Act 1976, s 11(1)(a)

[88] ibid, s 11(1)(b)

[89] ibid, s 11(2)

stated thereon.[90] The whole price for the ticket or chance must be paid before a person is permitted to participate in the lottery, and no money may be returned.[91] No other payment may be required in order to participate.[92]

The total value of tickets or chances sold in any one lottery must not exceed £1 **24.22** million.[93] Furthermore, the total value of tickets and chances sold in all such lotteries held in any one year, and promoted on behalf of the same society, must not exceed £5 million.[94]

Prizes and expenses

No prize may exceed £25,000 or 10 per cent of the total value of tickets or chances **24.23** sold (whichever is the greater);[95] and the total prize-money must not exceed 55% per cent of the whole proceeds of the lottery.[96]

The lottery expenses (exclusive of prizes) must not exceed the specified amounts.[97] **24.24** The amount is 35 per cent of the proceeds if these do not exceed £20,000,[98] and 15 per cent of the proceeds if they do; in the latter case, however, the Gaming Board[99] may authorize a larger percentage (not exceeding 35 per cent in respect of a particular lottery).[100] Expenses met by the society, or by any beneficiary of the lottery, are for this purpose treated as lottery expenses.[101]

In addition to the separate limits upon the amount of the lottery proceeds which **24.25** can be appropriated in prizes and expenses, there is also a limit upon the aggregate of these amounts, which must not exceed a prescribed percentage of the whole proceeds of the lottery,[102] currently 80 per cent.[103]

---

[90] ibid, s 11(3)

[91] ibid, s 11(4)

[92] ibid, s 11(4A)

[93] ibid, s 11(6)

[94] ibid, s 11(7). For this purpose, a lottery is held in the year in which the date of the lottery falls: ibid, s 11(8). In s 11, 'year' means the period of 12 months beginning on 1 Jan: ibid, s 11(9), which also made special provision for the period from 1 May 1977, when s 11(7) came into force, until 31 Dec 1977

[95] ibid, s 11(5)

[96] ibid, s 11(11); Lotteries (Prizes and Expenses: Variation and Prescription of Percentage Limits) Order 1997, SI 1997/43, Art 2

[97] Lotteries and Amusements Act 1976, s 11(12)

[98] ibid, s 11(13)(a); Lotteries (Prizes and Expenses: Variation and Prescription of Percentage Limits) Order 1997, SI 1997/43, Art 3

[99] Lotteries and Amusements Act 1976, s 23(1): 'the Board' means the Gaming Board for Great Britain

[100] ibid, s 11(13)(b); Lotteries (Prizes and Expenses: Variation and Prescription of Percentage Limits) Order 1997, SI 1997/43, Art 4

[101] Lotteries and Amusements Act 1976, s 11(14). A 'beneficiary of the lottery' means a person (other than the society promoting the lottery) to whom, or for whose benefit, any of the lottery proceeds are lawfully paid or applied, other than by way of expenses or prizes: ibid, s 11(15)

[102] ibid, s 11(16), inserted by National Lottery etc Act 1993, s 52(8)

[103] Lotteries (Prizes and Expenses: Variation and Prescription of Percentage Limits) Order 1997, SI 1997/43, Art 5

Schemes

24.26 The Secretary of State may make regulations to be included in any scheme approved by a society for the purposes of a society's lottery,[104] and with respect to the promotion of such lotteries.[105] Under the regulations,[106] no ticket or chance in a society's lottery may be sold to a person under sixteen,[107] or in the street,[108] or by means of a machine.[109] Every ticket distributed or sold in a society's lottery must specify either the name of the registration authority with which the society is registered under Schedule 1 to the Lotteries and Amusements Act 1976, or that the society is registered under Schedule 1A with the Gaming Board.[110] The regulations also set out the requirements for lottery schemes.[111]

Tax exemption

24.27 A charity is entitled to claim exemption from tax under Schedule D of the Income and Corporation Taxes Act 1988 in respect of profits accruing to it from a lottery promoted and conducted as a society's lottery provided the profits are applied solely to the charity's purposes.[112]

(4) Local lotteries

24.28 A 'local lottery' means a lottery promoted by a local authority.[113] Such a lottery is not unlawful if it is promoted in Great Britain in accordance with a scheme which is approved by the local authority and registered with the Gaming Board before any tickets or chances are sold.[114] A local authority may promote a local lottery for any purpose for which it has power to incur expenditure.[115] The local authority must give such publicity to the object of a local lottery as will be likely to bring it to the attention of persons purchasing tickets or chances.[116] It must apply money accruing from a local lottery only to the object of the lottery,[117] unless the Secretary of State consents to its use for another purpose, which he may do only in specified circumstances.[118]

---

[104] Lotteries and Amusements Act 1976, s 12(1)

[105] ibid, s 12(2)

[106] Lotteries Regulations 1993, SI 1993/3223, amended (by the repeal of reg 6 only) by Lotteries (Amendment) Regulations 1996, SI 1996/1306

[107] Lotteries Regulations 1993, SI 1993/3223, reg 3

[108] ibid, reg 4(1); but this is stated not to apply to sales in a kiosk or shop premises having no space for the accommodation of customers: ibid, reg 4(2)

[109] ibid, reg 5

[110] ibid, reg 7

[111] ibid, Sch 2

[112] ICTA 1988, s 505(1)(f)

[113] Lotteries and Amusements Act 1976, s 6(1)

[114] ibid, s 6(2)

[115] ibid, s 7(1)

[116] ibid, s 7(2)(a)

[117] ibid, s 7(2)(b)

[118] ibid, s 7(4). The circumstances are broadly similar to those required for an application of charitable property cy-près under CA 1993, s 13(1)

The rules for local lotteries are essentially the same as those for societies' lotter- **24.29**
ies.[119]

(5) Charitable expenditure under the National Lottery

Introduction

Charities may benefit from the National Lottery, which is authorized and regu- **24.30**
lated by the National Lottery etc Act 1993.[120] 'The National Lottery' means all the
lotteries that form part of the National Lottery, taken as a whole.[121] To form part
of the National Lottery, the lottery must be promoted either by the body licensed
to run the National Lottery,[122] or in pursuance of an agreement between that body
and the lottery's promoter or proposed promoter.[123] The promotion of the lottery
must be authorized by a licence that has been granted to its promoter or proposed
promoter.[124] A lottery that forms part of the National Lottery is not unlawful.[125]

The National Lottery is now regulated by a corporate body called the National **24.31**
Lottery Commission,[126] which (together with the Secretary of State) is charged
with the responsibility of securing that the National Lottery is run, and that every
lottery that forms part of it is promoted, with all due propriety, and that the interests of every participant in such a lottery are protected.[127] Subject to this, the
Secretary of State and the National Lottery Commission must do their best to secure that the net proceeds of the National Lottery[128] are as great as possible.[129]

The National Lottery Commission may by licence authorize a body corporate to **24.32**
run the National Lottery,[130] but it may license only one body at any one time.[131]

---

[119] The relevant parts of Lotteries and Amusements Act 1976, s 11, apply also to local lotteries
[120] For background to the National Lottery etc Act 1993, see *A National Lottery: raising money for good causes*, White Paper, Cm 1861 (1992); P Luxton, 'Charity Lotteries Past and Present' (1993–4) 2 CL & PR 17, 24–8
[121] National Lottery etc Act 1993, s 1(1)
[122] ie under s 5
[123] National Lottery etc Act 1993, s 1(3)
[124] ie under s 6: ibid, s 1(4)
[125] ibid, s 2(1)
[126] ibid, s 3A & Sch 2, inserted by National Lottery Act 1998, s 1(3), which came into force on 1 Apr 1999: National Lottery Act 1998 (Commencement) Order 1999, SI 1999/650, Art 2. The National Lottery Commission in effect replaces the post (now abolished) of Director-General of the National Lottery: National Lottery Act 1998, s 1(2)
[127] National Lottery etc Act 1993, s 4(1), as amended by National Lottery Act 1998, s 1(5) & Sch 1, para 4
[128] 'the net proceeds of the National Lottery' means the sums that are paid to the Secretary of State by virtue of s 5(6): National Lottery etc Act 1993, s 4(3)
[129] National Lottery etc Act 1993, s 4(2), as amended by National Lottery Act 1998, s 1(5) & Sch 1, para 4
[130] National Lottery etc Act 1993, s 5(1)
[131] ibid, s 5(2). The Commission may also by licence authorize a body corporate to promote lot-teries as part of the National Lottery: ibid, s 6(1)

The National Lottery etc Act 1993 specifies the criteria for the granting of such a licence.[132] The licence must include a condition requiring the licensee to pay to the Secretary of State such sums out of the proceeds of lotteries forming part of the National Lottery as may be determined under the licence.[133] The Secretary of State must pay such sums to the National Lottery Distribution Fund[134] (the Distribution Fund[135]), which is also a creature of the Act.[136]

Distribution amongst good causes

24.33 After deduction for various expenses, including those incurred by the Secretary of State,[137] the balance of sums paid into the Distribution Fund are to be apportioned as specified in the Act.[138] Sums paid into the Distribution Fund after 20 August 2001[139] are apportioned amongst five purposes as follows: the arts;[140] sport;[141] the national heritage;[142] charitable expenditure;[143] and health, education, or the environment.[144] A sixth purpose, namely projects to mark the year 2000 and the beginning of the third millennium, ceases to receive sums paid into the Distribution Fund after 20 August 2001.[145] After that date, its share (20 per cent) is effectively reallocated to the purpose of health, education or the environment, whose allocation is thereby increased from 13⅓ per cent to 33⅓ per cent.[146] Each of the other four surviving purposes continues to receive 16⅔ per cent.[147]

---

[132] ibid, s 5(3)–(5)

[133] ibid, s 5(6). The licence may also include a condition requiring the licensee to make arrangements for securing that such sums as may be so determined are paid to the Commission for distribution to participants in lotteries forming part of the National Lottery: ibid, s 5(7)

[134] ibid, s 21(2), as amended by National Lottery Act 1998, s 2(3)

[135] National Lottery etc Act 1993, s 44(1)

[136] ibid, s 21(1)

[137] ibid, s 22(2). The expenses to be deducted are specified in s 31

[138] ibid, s 22(3), as amended by National Lottery Act 1998, s 26 & Sch 5, Pt II, and by the following orders (made pursuant to the power to substitute different percentages contained in National Lottery etc Act 1993, s 28(1)): Apportionment of Money in the National Lottery Distribution Fund Order 1999, SI 1999/344, Arts 2–3; Apportionment of Money in the National Lottery Distribution Fund Order 2000, SI 2000/3356, Art 2.

[139] Date substituted for 31 December 2000 by Millennium Commission (Substitution of a Later Date) Order 2000, SI 2000/3355, Art 2

[140] National Lottery etc Act 1993, s 22(3)(a)

[141] ibid, s 22(3)(b)

[142] ibid, s 22(3)(c)

[143] ibid, s 22(3)(d)

[144] ibid, s 22(3)(f), inserted by National Lottery Act 1998, s 6(2), in relation to sums paid into the Distribution Fund on or after 14 Oct 1997: ibid, ss 6(9), 27(4)

[145] National Lottery etc Act 1993, s 30(1)(a); date substituted by Millennium Commission (Substitution of a Later Date) Order 2000, SI 2000/3355, Art 2

[146] Apportionment of Money in the National Lottery Distribution Fund Order 2000, SI 2000/3356, Art 2

[147] ie the percentages substituted from 17 May 1999 by Apportionment of Money in the National Lottery Distribution Fund Order 1999, SI 1999/344, Arts 2–3

Allocation of charitable expenditure by the Charities Board

Allocation is effected by specified distributing bodies; in the case of sums allocated **24.34** for charitable expenditure, the distributing body is the National Lottery Charities Board[148] (the Charities Board[149]), which is a body corporate established by the National Lottery etc Act 1993.[150] The Charities Board consists of a chairman and twenty-one other members, all of whom are appointed by the Secretary of State.[151] It is required to establish four committees to exercise its functions in relation to applications by charities for grants in respect of appropriate activities in England, Scotland, Wales, and Northern Ireland respectively.[152] For this purpose, 'charities' includes institutions established for charitable, benevolent, or philanthropic purposes.[153] The Charities Board may make grants to such charities and institutions,[154] and may impose such conditions as it thinks fit, including conditions for repayment on breach of any condition.[155] The Charities Board also has power to acquire and dispose of land.[156]

As a distributing body, the Charities Board may delegate its functions relating to **24.35** the distribution of money[157] to various bodies, including any charity[158] or any charitable, benevolent, or philanthropic institution.[159] There is provision for joint schemes among distributing bodies,[160] and the Secretary of State can require

---

[148] National Lottery etc Act 1993, s 23(4). The other distribution bodies are as follows. For the arts: the Arts Council of England, the Arts Council of Wales, the Arts Council of Northern Ireland, and the Film Council: s 23(1). For sport: the Sports Council of England, the Scottish Sports Council, the Sports Council of Wales, the Sports Council of Northern Ireland, and the United Kingdom Sports Council: s 23(2). For the national heritage, the Trustees of the National Heritage Memorial Fund: s 23(3)). For projects to mark the year 2000 and the beginning of the third millennium, the Millennium Commission (established under s 40): s 23(5) but only in respect of sums paid into the Distribution Fund before 1 Jan 2001. For health, education, or the environment, the New Opportunities Fund (established under s 43A): s 23(6)

[149] ibid, s 44(1)

[150] ibid, s 37 & Sch 5, as amended by National Lottery Act 1998

[151] National Lottery etc Act 1993, Sch 5, para 1(1), as amended by National Lottery Charities Board (Increase in Membership) Order 1995, SI 1995/1645, Art 2

[152] National Lottery etc Act 1993, Sch 5, para 2(1)

[153] ibid, Sch 5, para 2(2); ie including the institutions mentioned in s 44(1) in para (b) of the definition of 'charitable expenditure'

[154] ibid, s 38(1)

[155] ibid, s 38(2)

[156] ibid, s 38(3), inserted by National Lottery Act 1998, s 14(1)

[157] National Lottery etc Act 1993, s 25A(1). S 25A was inserted by National Lottery Act 1998, s 11(1): National Lottery Act 1998, s 27(4)

[158] For this purpose, 'charity' means a body, or the trustees of a trust, established for charitable purposes only: National Lottery etc Act 1993, s 25A(9)

[159] National Lottery etc Act 1993, s 25A(4)(b); 'charitable, benevolent or philanthropic institution' means a body, or the trustees of a trust, which is established for charitable purposes (whether or not those purposes are charitable within the meaning of any rule of law), benevolent purposes or philanthropic purposes, and which is not a charity: ibid, s 25A(9)

[160] National Lottery etc Act 1993, s 25B, inserted by National Lottery Act 1998, s 12(1): National Lottery Act 1998, s 27(4)

distributing bodies to prepare, adopt, and review, a strategic plan,[161] which means a statement of their policies for the distribution of money.[162] A distributing body must also comply with any directions which the Secretary of State gives to it relating to the distribution of money.[163] The Charities Board must keep proper accounts[164], and it must report to the Secretary of State on the exercise of its functions at the end of every financial year.[165]

B. Competitions and amusements

24.36 It is unlawful to conduct in or through any newspaper,[166] or in connection with any trade or business or the sale of any article to the public, certain types of competition.[167] The type of competition prohibited is one in which prizes are offered for forecasts of the result either of a future event, or of a past event the result of which is not yet ascertained or not yet generally known,[168] and any other competition in which success does not depend to a substantial degree on the exercise of skill.[169]

24.37 It is lawful to provide at any exempt entertainment amusements with prizes if these constitute a lottery or gaming or both, but do not constitute gaming to which Part II of the Gaming Act 1968 applies, or gaming by means of a machine to which Part III of that Act applies.[170] Whether or not such amusement constitutes a lottery, however, certain conditions must be met:[171] namely, the whole proceeds of the entertainment, after deducting expenses, must be devoted to purposes other than private gain, and the facilities for winning prizes at such amusements must not be the only, or the only substantial, inducement to persons to attend the entertainment.[172]

---

[161] National Lottery etc Act 1993, s 25C, inserted by National Lottery Act 1998, s 13: National Lottery Act 1998, s 27(5)

[162] National Lottery etc Act 1993, s 25C(2)

[163] ibid, s 26(1)

[164] ibid, s 39

[165] ibid, s 34(1)

[166] 'Newspaper' includes any journal, magazine, or other periodical publication: Lotteries and Amusements Act 1976, s 23(1)

[167] ibid, s 14(1). As to the meaning of 'competition', see *Whitbread & Co Ltd v Bell* [1970] 2 QB 547; *Imperial Tobacco Ltd v A-G* [1979] QB 555 (CA). The prohibition does not apply to pool-betting carried on by a bookmaker: Lotteries and Amusements Act 1976, s 14(2)

[168] Lotteries and Amusements Act 1976, s 14(1)(a). As to the meaning of 'forecasts of the result ... of a future event', see *News of the World v Friend* [1973] 1 WLR 248 (HL) ('Spot-the-ball' competition held not unlawful: entrants used their skill to arrive at a result)

[169] Lotteries and Amusements Act 1976, s 14(1)(b)

[170] ibid, s 15(1)

[171] ibid, s 15(3)

[172] ibid, s 15(4)

25

DISASTER FUNDS

A. Introduction

A disaster fund is the term generally used to describe a fund raised by means of an **25.01** appeal to the public following an accident, natural disaster, or war, involving almost always loss of life, or at least serious injury or distress. Sometimes the terms of the appeal provide for the relief of the distress and suffering, or the poverty, of the survivors of the accident and for the relatives of those killed, but the terms of the appeal may be wider or narrower.

Disaster funds give rise to special legal problems, which are highlighted in this **25.02** chapter. The law apart, however, potential promoters would do well to satisfy themselves beforehand of the wisdom of setting up such a fund, especially where the relief is to be provided abroad. The Charity Commissioners have suggested that those without the experience or organizational structures to support disaster relief overseas might be better advised to support the well-established charities engaged in disaster relief overseas, rather than attempting to establish their own charities for such purposes. The Commissioners point out that common problems encountered when inexperienced bodies launch small relief programmes overseas include the loss of funds or goods resulting from inadequate controls; ineffective control over, and unnecessary risk to, volunteers while abroad; and a loss of confidence by local communities in aid organizations generally.[1]

---

[1] [1995] Ch Com Rep 17–18 (paras 69–73)

B. The terms of the appeal

25.03 Appeals to the public for contributions are often made within a matter of hours of a disaster having occurred, and thereby provide an immediate channel for public contributions.[2] An initial difficulty, however, is that such appeals may well precede the preparation of the trust instrument setting out the precise terms of the appeal. There may therefore be a problem in ascertaining whether the terms of the appeal fund are charitable.

(1) Importance of specifying if appeal is charitable

25.04 The difficulty of determining whether an appeal fund is, by its terms, charitable or otherwise, is illustrated by the circumstances surrounding the main appeal fund set up immediately following the Penlee Lifeboat Disaster just before Christmas, in 1981, when a number of Cornish lifeboatmen lost their lives when their boat capsized in heavy seas while they were attempting to rescue the crew of a ship, the *Union Star*. Three days later, Penwith District Council issued a press release which announced the creation of an appeal fund, and which indicated that the total fund would be used directly for the benefit of the dependants. In a further press release of the following day, however, the Council announced that they had obtained legal advice to the effect that the fund was charitable in nature, and that the trustees would be able to distribute to the bereaved amounts which were limited to their reasonable needs only, and that any surplus would have to be applied cy-près. It appears that this second announcement was prompted by the fact that contributions were coming in at a rate which exceeded all expectations, so that very much more would be available for distribution than could have been envisaged initially. In the event, the Attorney-General decided not to contend that the fund was charitable, with the result that the trustees were able to treat the fund as a private trust, and distribute the entire amount among the bereaved families.

(2) The Attorney-General's Guidelines on Disaster Appeals

25.05 As a direct result of the Penlee Lifeboat Disaster Fund, the Attorney-General issued guidelines for organizers of disaster appeals in order to avoid the same uncertainty recurring in future cases.[3]

---

[2] The problems of spontaneous donations, which are made before an appeal has been announced, are considered below, para 25.22

[3] Attorney-General, *Disaster Appeals* (1981): see [1981] Ch Com Rep 7 (para 8) & 40–3 (App A). The Guidelines have since been reprinted by the Charity Commission; *Disaster Appeals: Attorney General's Guidelines*, CC40 (Aug 1994)

Making the appeal

The Guidelines suggest that it may be desirable to take advice before the appeal is **25.06** issued, on whether or not a charitable appeal is called for, and whether the proposed appeal takes account of potential difficulties, whether personal, administrative, or fiscal.[4] Once the terms are agreed, it is generally best to publish the appeal as soon as possible, and as widely as appropriate in the circumstances.[5] If gifts are made before the publication of the appeal fund, and these are too numerous to be acknowledged individually, the published appeal should indicate that gifts already made will be added to the appeal fund unless the donors notify the organizers (say within ten days of the published appeal) that this is not their wish.[6]

Forms of appeal

The most important part of the Guidelines comprises the forms of appeal. Three **25.07** model forms are set out—a charitable appeal, a non-charitable appeal, and a mixed appeal—it being evidently envisaged that the appropriate form can be adapted for use in an emergency. The advantage of the forms of words suggested is that they make it plain on the face of the appeal what its precise legal nature is.

Charitable fund

If a charitable fund is intended, the appeal could take the following form:[7] **25.08**

> This appeal is to set up a charitable fund to relieve distress caused by the accident/disaster at on . The aim is to use the funds to relieve those who may be in need of help (whether now or in the future) as a result of this tragedy in accordance with charity law. Any surplus after their needs have been met will be used for charitable purposes designed:
>   (i)   to help those who suffer in similar tragedies;
>   (ii) to benefit charities with related purposes;
>   (iii) to help the locality.

Non-charitable fund

If a non-charitable fund is intended and those affected are to take the entirety of **25.09** the fund in such shares as the trustees think fit, the appeal could be worded as follows:[8]

> This appeal is to set up a fund, the entire benefit of which will be used for those injured or bereaved in the accident/disaster at on , or their families and dependants as the trustees think fit. This fund will not be a charity.

---

[4] Attorney-General, *Disaster Appeals* (1981), para 1(1)
[5] ibid, para 1(2)
[6] ibid, para 1(3)
[7] ibid, para 3(1)
[8] ibid, para 3(2)

Non-charitable fund with surplus to charity

25.10 A non-charitable fund in which the trustees would have a discretion to give as much as they think fit to those who have suffered, with any surplus going to charity, could be established as follows:[9]

> This appeal is to set up a fund for those injured or bereaved in the accident/disaster at   on   and their families and dependants. The trustees will have a discretion how and to what extent to benefit individual claimants: the fund will not itself be a charity but any surplus will be applied for such charitable purposes as the trustees think most appropriate to commemorate those who died.

Appeals for individuals

25.11 The Guidelines also make suggestions with regard to appeals for individuals, such as an appeal for a child who is suffering from a disease. They recommend that those making such appeals should indicate whether or not the appeal is for a charitable fund. It is also desirable that donors say whether their gift is meant for the benefit of the individual or for charitable purposes, including helping the individual so far as that is charitable. The Guidelines suggest that if no such intention is stated, the donation should be acknowledged with an indication of how it will be used if the donor does not dissent. Those making the appeal should bear in mind the possibility that more may be raised than is appropriate for the needs of the individual, and should therefore consider how any surplus should be dealt with.[10] Thus, those setting up an appeal for a sick child should consider the appropriateness of the form of the appeal to the particular circumstances. If the child is not expected to live for long, there may be a greater need to consider how to deal with any surplus than if the child is expected to survive but to face a lifetime of suffering.[11]

(3) Respective merits of charitable and non-charitable appeals

Charitable fund

25.12 The use of the charitable trust for an appeal may be of advantage to the donors in that their gifts are exempt from inheritance tax and (in the case of gifts of chargeable assets) capital gains tax.[12] The appeal fund itself also enjoys the fiscal benefits of charitable status, so that the investment income from the appeal fund is exempt from income tax (provided it is applied for charitable purposes only) and disposals by the trustees are exempt from capital gains tax. The fund is also exempt from

---

[9] Attorney-General, *Disaster Appeals* (1981), para 3(3)
[10] ibid, para 4(1)
[11] ibid, para 4(2)
[12] The tax treatment of disaster funds (both charitable and non-charitable) is described in a leaflet issued jointly by the Inland Revenue and HM Customs and Excise: *Guidelines on the Tax Treatment of Disaster Funds*. See [1989] Ch Com Rep 12 (para 37)

the rule against perpetuities, so that the capital can be tied up indefinitely. On the other hand, the charitable status of the appeal restricts the trustees in their application of the fund, in that they may not apply to the 'beneficiaries' any more than is sufficient to relieve their reasonable needs.[13] If a surplus remains after all the specified charitable purposes have been fully performed, it will be necessary to apply the surplus cy-près. The fund may also be required to register, and to file appropriate documents, with the Charity Commissioners. Whilst this has the merit of providing public access to important information about the fund, including its constitution and its filed accounts, the duty to comply with these and other obligations of charity law does make the position of a trustee of a charitable trust more onerous than that of a trustee of a private trust.

Non-charitable fund

Donations to non-charitable appeal funds may give rise to inheritance tax and (in **25.13** the case of gifts of chargeable assets) capital gains tax consequences for the donors. This is generally of little practical significance, however, since most donations to appeal funds are of relatively small amounts. If the fund takes the form of a discretionary trust, the trustees will be liable to income tax on accumulated income,[14] whereas income paid to an object is treated as that object's income for the purposes of income tax.[15] If the fund takes the form of a fixed trust, the income is treated as that of the beneficiary entitled to it, whether or not it is paid out to him.

A non-charitable fund is subject to the general law relating to private trusts. It **25.14** must therefore satisfy the requirement of certainty of objects from which charitable trusts are exempt. It is also subject to the rule against perpetuities, but is, on the other hand, outside the regulatory machinery of the Charity Commissioners.

An appeal for funds to even a private disaster fund, however, is likely to be an ap- **25.15** peal for a 'benevolent' or 'philanthropic' purpose, and so will be subject (according to the manner in which fund-raising is conducted) to the regulatory regimes governing public charitable collections[16] and fund-raising.[17]

More than one appeal fund

A disaster which led to the launching of two separate appeal funds was the fire at **25.16** the grounds of Bradford City Football Club in 1985, in which fifty-six people died and more than 300 were injured. The first appeal fund, called the Bradford Disaster Appeal, was set up in the immediate aftermath of the disaster, and took

---

[13] See ch 4, para 4.81

[14] This is at 'the rate applicable to trusts', currently 34%: ICTA 1988, s 686(1), (1A)

[15] See ibid, s 687. The payment is treated as a net amount from which income tax has been deducted at 'the rate applicable to trusts' for the year in which the payment is made: ibid, s 687(2)

[16] CA 1992, Pt III (when brought into force); see further ch 22

[17] CA 1992, Pt II; see further ch 21

the form of a private discretionary trust, with the trustees having the power to apply any surplus to charitable purposes. Some months later, the trustees set up another fund with exclusively charitable purposes, called the Bradford City Disaster Charitable Trust, to receive donations from persons who wished to contribute specifically to a charitable fund. This means of proceeding, with the initial main fund being a private discretionary trust, seems to have been followed in several subsequent disaster appeals.[18]

(4) Creation of a disaster fund with charitable status

Public benefit

25.17 Like any other trust, a disaster appeal fund can be charitable only if the persons to benefit under it comprise a sufficient section of the community. This is clearly satisfied where the number of persons involved is large[19], but there may be doubt where the number is small. In *Cross v Lloyd-Graeme*,[20] an appeal for the widows, orphans, and dependants of six fishermen who drowned when their boat capsized was held charitable. On the other hand, the main appeal fund set up following the Penlee Lifeboat Disaster,[21] which was similarly for the benefit of the dependants of a small number of men, was treated (without litigation) as a valid private trust.[22] In some other instances, the effect of holding of an appeal fund non-charitable will be to render it void (whether for uncertainty of objects, for lack of a beneficiary to enforce it,[23] or for contravening the rule against perpetuities).

Relief of poverty

25.18 If the aim is to create a charitable appeal fund in circumstances where the class of persons to benefit is small, any doubt as to the charitable status of the fund can be avoided by restricting the purposes of the trust to the relief of poverty, as trusts for such purposes are outside the public benefit requirement[24] (unlike trusts which are merely for the relief of distress[25]). It might also be possible to infer poverty from

---

[18] Thus the Channel Disaster Fund, set up following the loss of life on the passenger-ferry *Herald of Free Enterprise*, off Zeebrugge early in 1987, also took the form of a private discretionary trust: see J Laurance, 'Disastrous Disaster Funds' *New Society*, 20 Mar 1987. The Hungerford Tragedy Fund (set up following the murder of 16 people by a psychopathic gunman in that small town in 1987) was also created as a private discretionary trust: B Amiel, 'Behind disaster funds . . .', The Times 4 Sept 1987, 17. Similarly the Hillsborough Disaster Appeal Fund (launched following the loss of life and serious injuries when spectators were crushed at Sheffield Wednesday's Hillsborough Stadium in Apr 1989): see The Times 22 Apr 1989, 4, and The Times 18 Apr 1989, 3

[19] See *Pease v Pattinson* (1886) 32 ChD 154; *Re Hartley Colliery Accident Relief Fund* (1908) 102 LT 165n, where a trust to relieve the relations of 204 miners killed in a pit disaster was held charitable

[20] (1909) 102 LT 163

[21] See H Picarda, 'Spontaneous Disaster Funds' (1982) 132 NLJ 223

[22] See above, para 25.04

[23] *Re Gillingham Bus Disaster Fund* [1959] Ch 62

[24] *Dingle v Turner* [1972] AC 601 (HL); see further ch 5, paras 5.05–5.06

[25] *Re Hobourn Aero Components Ltd's Air Raid Distress Fund* [1946] Ch 194

other forms of wording (such as relieving need). Whilst need might be relieved in ways other than the payment of sums of money (such as the provision of counselling services), where monetary payments are made to the beneficiaries, relieving need means, for the purposes of charity law, relieving financial need. If, therefore, the intention is to create a charitable appeal under which the fund (or any part of it) is to be applied in the form of direct monetary payments to the intended beneficiaries, the purpose of the fund can be charitable (regardless of the numbers of potential beneficiaries) only if it is restricted to the relief of need, meaning, in this context, the relief of poverty.

Restricting the trust's purposes to the relief of poverty can give rise to difficulties for the trustees, however, when they come to the sensitive matter of distributing the funds, since they will need to assess the financial needs of each person considered for benefit. These difficulties were particularly acute in the circumstances of the Aberfan Disaster Fund, which was set up in 1966 after a coal tip in the Welsh village of Aberfan collapsed, causing a mud slide that swiftly engulfed a school and other buildings. In the devastation, 116 children and 28 adults were killed, and many others (including children) were injured. The principal purpose of the Aberfan Disaster Fund was 'the relief of all persons who have suffered as a result of the said disaster and are thereby in need'. The criterion of 'need', which effectively meant that cash allocations had to be based on financial need, had been put into the trust deed in order to avoid problems with charitable status. The trustees found, however, that the task of means-testing beneficiaries caused so much distress that they finally allocated the fund by giving equal amounts to each bereaved family, even though this appears to have comprised a breach of trust.[26]   **25.19**

(5) Drawing up the trust instrument after the appeal

It is permissible to appeal for funds before the trust instrument has been prepared, provided that the basic terms of the appeal are themselves clear, so that a trust instrument embodying these terms can be drawn up at a later date. It is good practice for the appeal to refer to the fact that a trust instrument is being prepared and that it will be made available for public inspection as soon as it has been executed.[27]   **25.20**

It was held in *Attorney-General v Mathieson*[28] that, where donations are made to a charity for its general purposes, the trustee or committee entrusted with the money is taken to have the implied authority of the donors to declare the precise   **25.21**

---

[26] See M Chesterman, *Charities, Trusts and Social Welfare* (Weidenfeld & Nicolson, 1979) 343. On the Aberfan Disaster generally, see I McLean & M Johnes, 'Regulating gifts of generosity: the Aberfan Disaster Fund and the Charity Commission' (1999) 19 LS 380

[27] As occurred in the case of the appeal in connection with the Bradford Disaster Appeal

[28] [1907] 2 Ch 383 (CA); applied *Re Darwin Cyclone Tracy Relief Trust Fund* (1979) 39 FLR 20

terms of the trusts upon which the sums so contributed are to be held.[29] In so declaring the terms of the trusts, the trustee or committee is to be considered to be acting *in loco fundatoris*.[30] This principle extends to the donation of funds to a disaster fund before the trust instrument has been prepared. It can, however, be invoked only where it is reasonable to infer in the first place that the terms of the appeal were themselves wholly and exclusively charitable; it cannot, therefore, be invoked to render charitable an appeal for purposes (such as 'worthy causes'[31]), which are clearly not charitable.

25.22 Some donations may be received before even an appeal has been made. This occurred, for instance, in the Bradford Disaster Appeal, where some persons sent spontaneous donations to Bradford City Council before the release of the press statement launching the appeal. The trustees dealt with such contributions by referring to them in the press release and stating that the trustees intended applying them to the non-charitable discretionary trust to be set up; but that persons who had already contributed to the appeal before reading such announcement, who felt that the present appeal did not meet the purposes for which they had made their contributions, could apply by a specified date to have their contributions refunded.[32]

C. The use of private discretionary trusts

(1) Defining the class

25.23 As a non-charitable appeal is subject to the general law of trusts, it is necessary to ensure that there is certainty of objects. Trusts for abstract non-charitable purposes are likely to be void both for uncertainty of objects[33] and for offending the beneficiary principle, namely that there must be somebody in whose favour the court can decree performance.[34] A private appeal fund should therefore have human objects, who must be specified (either individually or as members of a class) with a sufficient degree of certainty.

25.24 If the appeal takes the form of a private discretionary trust for the benefit of a class of persons, the test for certainty of objects is that of individual ascertainability: the

---

[29] *A-G v Mathieson* [1907] 2 Ch 383, 394, (Cozens-Hardy MR, with whose jdgt the other members of the CA agreed). In regard to whether the trustees have such implied authority to provide for their own remuneration, see ch 9, para 9.105

[30] *A-G v Mathieson* [1907] 2 Ch 383, 389 (counsel for the A-G, *arguendo*)

[31] cf *Re Gillingham Bus Disaster Fund* [1959] Ch 62

[32] See press release in connection with the Bradford Disaster Appeal, reproduced in RW Suddards, *Bradford Disaster Appeal: the administration of an appeal fund* (Sweet & Maxwell, 1986) 78

[33] *Leahy v A-G for New South Wales* [1959] AC 457 (PC)

[34] *Morice v Bishop of Durham* (1804) 9 Ves Jun 399, 404 (Grant MR)

court must be able to say of any given person whether he is or is not a member of the class.[35] The expressions 'relatives' and 'dependants' have been held to satisfy this test,[36] so that a discretionary trust may specify, for example, a discretionary class comprising 'the victims of the disaster, their relatives and dependants'. Nevertheless, the precise scope of the word 'relatives' remains unclear—whether it is to be restricted to the persons who could take the residuary estate upon an intestacy as specified in the Administration of Estates Act 1925,[37] or includes any person to whom one is related in blood, no matter how remote.[38] It is therefore desirable that the trust instrument define this expression more precisely.

The trustees may wish to retain a power to decide whether a person falls within the **25.25** specified class or not. In the Bradford Disaster Appeal, which comprised a private discretionary trust, the expression 'Beneficiaries' was defined as 'such persons being victims of the disaster or relatives or dependants of such victims as the Trustees shall from time to time determine shall be regarded as beneficiaries'.[39] Such a definition enables the trustees to determine evidentially whether a person falls within the class of objects or not. It seems, however, that the better view is that the trust instrument cannot itself either cure conceptual uncertainty or confer on the trustees the power to interpret the meaning of the terms used to define the class, since this would be to oust the jurisdiction of the court.[40] It is therefore submitted that the definition of the class of 'beneficiaries' in the Bradford Disaster Appeal enabled the trustees to determine factually if a person was a victim of the disaster, or the relative or dependant of such a person; but it did not oust the jurisdiction of the court to determine what was meant by the word 'victim', 'relative', or dependant'.

(2) Perpetuity period

A non-charitable fund is subject to the rule against perpetuities, so a lawful period **25.26** of perpetuity should be specified in the trust instrument, which should generally be a period not exceeding eighty years.[41] A non-charitable fund will also be subject

---

[35] *McPhail v Doulton* [1971] AC 424 (HL)
[36] *Re Baden's Deed Trusts (No 2)* [1973] Ch 9 (CA)
[37] AEA 1925, s 46
[38] In *Re Baden's Deed Trusts (No 2)* [1973] Ch 9 (CA), Stamp LJ adopted the former interpretation; whereas Sachs LJ adopted the latter. Megaw LJ's jdgt is more in line with that of Sachs LJ
[39] Bradford Disaster Appeal, Declaration of Trust, cl 2(4)
[40] *Re Raven* [1915] 1 Ch 673; *Re Wynn* [1952] Ch 271; *Dundee General Hospital Board v Walker* [1952] 1 All ER 896. The tenor of the jdgt of Lord Denning MR in *Re Tuck's Settlement Trusts* [1978] Ch 49, 60–2, is to the contrary; but his Lordship's remarks were obiter, as he was speaking in the context of an individual gift subject to a condition precedent. His comments are also out of line with the prior case law and the objection of public policy on which the earlier authorities were founded. Lord Denning MR's comments have, nevertheless, received some extra-judicial support: see JE Martin (ed), *Hanbury and Martin's Modern Equity* (15th edn, Sweet & Maxwell, 1997), 103
[41] Perpetuities and Accumulations Act 1964, s 1. An 80-year period was adopted for the private discretionary trust which comprised the Bradford Disaster Appeal, this being the main appeal fund

to the rules against accumulations of income;[42] so that, after a lawful period of accumulation, all the income must be paid out annually.

(3) Decisions of trustees

25.27 For practical purposes, it may be desirable for the trust instrument to vary the general rule that trustees of a private trust must be unanimous in the exercise of their powers, so as to provide that majority decisions, made at a meeting or after consultation among all the trustees, are to be binding.[43]

(4) Trustee remuneration and other benefits

25.28 There is more scope in a private trust than in a charitable trust for the trust instrument to provide for remuneration for professional trustees and to permit trustees to retain any other incidental benefits of trusteeship. Such relaxations of the no-conflicts rule should not, however, be excessive; even a non-charitable appeal fund is likely to receive considerable public attention, and evidence of the trustees retaining even authorized benefits from the fund may lead to adverse publicity for the fund itself, and may damage future appeals by trustees of other disaster funds.

(5) Public accountability

25.29 Although a private appeal fund is outside the regulatory machinery of the Charity Commissioners, the objects have rights in equity to inspect the trust documents, although not those which relate to the exercise of discretions;[44] but neither the public generally, nor even the contributors in particular, have any right to see the trust's constitution or accounts or other key documents. It is nevertheless good practice for the trustees to make the trust instrument available to the public as soon as it has been executed, and for this to be stated in the terms of the appeal.[45] It is also good practice for the trustees to publish accounts in due course.[46]

---

in respect of that disaster: see cl 2(6) of the Declaration of Trust (reproduced RW Suddards, *Bradford Disaster Appeal: the administration of an appeal fund* (Sweet & Maxwell, 1986), 68

[42] LPA 1925, s 164; Perpetuities and Accumulations Act 1964, s 13
[43] As was done in Bradford Disaster Appeal: see cl 13 of the Declaration of Trust
[44] *Re Londonderry's Settlement* [1965] Ch 918
[45] This was the practice adopted by the trustees of the Bradford Disaster Appeal: see RW Suddards, *Bradford Disaster Appeal: the administration of an appeal fund* (Sweet & Maxwell, 1986), 77–8 (press statement).
[46] As was done in the case of the Bradford Disaster Appeal

Part VII

DISSOLUTION OF CHARITIES

26

DISSOLUTION OF CHARITIES

A. Introduction

This chapter considers the circumstances in which a charity can or must be dis- **26.01**
solved, and the process and consequences of dissolution. The expression 'dissolution of charity' is ambiguous in that it can mean either the dissolution of the
institutional machinery by which property is devoted to charity, or the dissolution
of the charity as an abstract conception independent of such machinery.[1]

Where the charity exists in the form of a corporation, the distinction between the **26.02**
two is clear; but where the charity exists in the form of a trust or an unincorporated association it is more elusive. Although the question of whether a charity
continues or has ceased to exist may seem purely academic, it can in fact be of great
practical importance—in determining, for instance, whether a legatee institution
still exists (perhaps in a different form) for the purpose of taking a gift or legacy.

B. Charitable trust

(1) Power or obligation in trust instrument to dispose of assets

If the charity exists in the form of a trust, it is generally presumed that it holds its **26.03**
property subject to an endowment. The trust instrument may, however, expressly

---

[1] See Buckley J in *Re Vernon's Will Trusts* [1972] Ch 300n. The same principle may explain Lord
Simonds' observation in *National Anti-Vivisection Society v IRC* [1948] AC 31, 74: 'A charity once
established does not die, though its nature may be changed'

or impliedly permit the trustees to spend or apply capital. Where such a power is present, the trustees (depending on the terms of the trust) may be able to exhaust the assets, either by spending all the capital directly on the charitable purposes, or by transferring the assets to another charitable institution with the same purposes. The trust instrument may even provide that the whole of the assets subject to the trust must be applied to the charitable purposes by a specified date.[2] Pursuant to a power in the trust instrument, the trustees may be able to transfer the entire fund to another institution with similar (or indeed other) charitable purposes. In *Re Roberts*,[3] the trust instrument conferred on the trustees of the Sheffield Boys' Working Home a power to sell its property and distribute the proceeds to other charities. Pursuant to this power, the trustees sold the property and paid over most of the proceeds of sale to the Sheffield Town Trust. Wilberforce J held that the exercise of this power involved a termination of the institution. The Sheffield Town Trust was therefore not entitled to take a legacy to the Sheffield Boys' Working Home made by a testatrix who died after the latter's property had been sold.

26.04 When the assets of a charitable trust have been exhausted, the charity ceases to exist. If a charity has ceased to exist, the Charity Commissioners must remove it from the register of charities.[4] The charity trustees (or the last charity trustees) of a registered charity are under an obligation to inform the Charity Commissioners if the charity ceases to exist.[5] If they fail to inform the Commissioners, the institution may remain on the register of charities after it has ceased to exist. Such continued registration does not, however, effect a deemed continuance of the charity. The conclusive presumption that an institution is a charity during the time it is on the register[6] is meaningful only where there is an 'institution' capable of being deemed a charity; and a charity that has ceased to exist is no institution at all.

26.05 If the charitable trustees decide to incorporate (pursuant to a power to do so, which must be contained in the trust instrument), the new incorporated charity will be a separate institution with another charity registration number. If the old charitable trust ceases to exist after the transfer, it will be removed from the register of charities. The change is essentially a matter of machinery, however: the purposes of the charitable trust (now the objects of the charitable company) are not thereby changed. The charity as an abstract conception therefore continues to exist, and it seems appropriate that the incorporated body should prima facie be entitled to take a legacy made to the unincorporated charity by a testator who dies

---

[2] ie a charity of limited duration. See *South Atlantic Fund* [1982] Ch Com Rep 13 (para 33) (5 years from date of deed in absence of special reason to the contrary); *Re JW Laing Trust* [1984] Ch 143 (10 years of settlor's death); *Women's Service Trust* (Whitford J), noted [1977] Ch Com Rep 14–15 (paras 34–6) (perpetuity period)

[3] [1963] 1 WLR 406

[4] CA 1993, s 3(4); and see ch 10, paras 10.80–10.82

[5] CA 1993, s 3(7)(b)

[6] ibid, s 4(1)

after the assets have been transferred. Nevertheless, in order to avoid any doubt about which body is entitled to a legacy made to the unincorporated charity, it might be worth the trustees' considering maintaining the unincorporated charity in existence for at least a few years after the incorporated charity is created, so that the former can receive any legacies and other bequests made specifically to it.[7] This ensures that such legacies vest in the old charity; and such legacies can then be dealt with according to the transfer of undertaking and so transferred to the newly incorporated charity.[8] To avoid the risk of removal from the register,[9] the unincorporated charity will need to continue to satisfy the registration requirements.[10]

Even if the purposes of the charity have become impossible or impracticable to carry out, there should be no need for any application of its assets cy-près where the trust instrument contains a power to terminate the charity (and apply its assets to other charities or charitable purposes). It may, however, become necessary for the Charity Commissioners or the court to prepare such a scheme if the institution becomes moribund in the sense that no trustees can be found who can exercise the power to terminate. **26.06**

(2) Endowed charities

The capital of an endowed charitable trust (or any property a charity holds subject to an endowment) cannot be exhausted by being applied to the charitable purposes. Therefore, unless its assets are destroyed or lost, or become valueless,[11] such a trust is potentially indestructible. It must continue indefinitely unless it can be brought to an end. This might occur in one of three ways. First, the charity trustees of a small charity might use the statutory power (exercisable with the Charity Commissioners' consent) to transfer the assets to another charity.[12] Secondly, the charity trustees of a small charity might have been able to meet the statutory requirements enabling them (with the Charity Commissioners' consent) to spend capital,[13] and might in fact have used this power to exhaust the **26.07**

---

[7] See *The Royal Association for Disability and Rehabilitation* [1977] Ch Com Rep 19–20 (para 57). This incorporated charity was formed by the transfer to it of the assets of two existing charities. In substance this was a merger, but the two original charities were to remain in existence for some years in order to receive any legacies made to them specifically

[8] To ensure that there is no uncertainty about the identity of a legatee charity, it is good practice for the draftsman of the will to specify, not merely the charity's name, but also its registration number

[9] CA 1993, s 3(2)

[10] ie under ibid, s 3(5)(c); so that, if it has neither any permanent endowment, nor the use or occupation of any land, it must ensure that its income from all sources exceeds £1,000 a year. The charity could still be removed from the register if it does not operate: ibid, s 3(4)

[11] The loss of the trust fund through fraud or theft does not necessarily result in the destruction of the charity: the right to recover the trust property or its product or to recover damages (whether for breach of trust, breach of contract, or in tort) itself represents trust property

[12] CA 1993, s 74

[13] ibid, s 75

charity's assets. A third possibility is that the charity ceases to exist because its assets are applied cy-près. Whether, however, an application of an endowed charity's assets under a cy-près scheme causes a termination of the endowed charity is by no means clear. It was apparently held in *Re Faraker*[14] that the endowed charity in the case was to be treated as having survived the making of a cy-près scheme so as to entitle it to receive a legacy under the will of a testatrix who had died several years before the scheme had been settled. The principle in that case has been applied since in *Re Lucas*.[15] In neither of those cases, however, was the alteration substantial, and it is submitted that if a cy-près scheme were to substitute substantially different purposes the charity would be treated as coming to an end. This issue is considered more fully in chapter 15.[16]

C. Charitable unincorporated association

26.08 Since a charitable unincorporated association holds its assets on trust for its objects, the dissolution of such associations is essentially governed by the principles developed in relation to the charitable trust.[17] Even if the members agree to dissolve the association, its assets will continue to be held on trust by the trustees until such assets have been applied, in accordance with the law, either to other similar charitable purposes, or to other charities with similar objects.

26.09 If the rules of association do not give the members an express power to select such similar charitable purposes or charities, the assets will need to be made the subject of a scheme, usually by the Charity Commissioners. The members will generally prefer to reserve such power to themselves, which can be done by express provision in the association's constitutional documents.

26.10 The rules of association should also provide for the Committee members to remain in office as charity trustees after a resolution to dissolve has been passed, in order to clarify that their management powers under the constitution survive such resolution and so that they can ensure that the association is wound up in an orderly way. It is, however, desirable that the Charity Commissioners be informed of (and effectively approve) the proposed application of the assets; and the Committee will, of course, need to file with the Charity Commissioners a final report and account.[18]

---

[14] [1912] 2 Ch 488
[15] [1948] Ch 427
[16] See ch 15, paras 15.98–15.101
[17] See above, paras 26.03–26.07
[18] See r 14 of the Constitution for a Charitable Unincorporated Association, drafted on behalf of the CLA

By these means, the need for the Charity Commissioners to become involved in **26.11** preparing a scheme on dissolution can be reduced; although a scheme may be needed if the association becomes moribund or if its members dissolve it without having exercised their power to select appropriate transferee objects or institutions.

D. Charitable corporation

(1) Methods of dissolution

A charity incorporated under the Companies Acts is dissolved (and therefore **26.12** ceases to exist) when its name is removed from the register of companies.[19] The process of winding up, leading to dissolution, may occur voluntarily, when the members so decide, or compulsorily, as when there is an insolvency. The company is dissolved without any winding up when the company is simply struck off the register of companies as having ceased to operate.[20] The Attorney-General may petition for a charitable corporation to be wound up,[21] and the Charity Commissioners may also petition[22] in certain circumstances,[23] with the Attorney-General's agreement,[24] after they have instituted an inquiry.[25]

(2) Having dissolution declared void

Where a company has been dissolved, the court may, on the application of the liq- **26.13** uidator, the Charity Commissioners,[26] or any other person appearing to the court to have an interest, declare the dissolution to be void.[27] This power will not, however, be exercised in order to enable a charitable corporation to take a legacy under the will of a testator who dies after the date of dissolution.[28] To do so 'would

---

[19] The Charity Commissioners must remove from the register of charities any charity which ceases to exist or does not operate: CA 1993, s 3(4) (see ch 10, paras 10.80–10.82). It is therefore possible that a charitable company may be removed from the register of charities (eg where it has no assets) before it has been removed from the register of companies. Removal of a charitable company from the register of charities before the date of dissolution, however, does not mean that the company ceases to be a charity: see *Re ARMS (Multiple Sclerosis Research) Ltd, Alleyne v A-G* [1997] 1 WLR 877, discussed below, para 26.23

[20] Companies Act 1985, s 652

[21] CA 1993, s 63(1)

[22] ibid, s 63(2)

[23] ie where they are satisfied of the matters specified in CA 1993, s 18(1)(a) & (b), namely that there has been misconduct or mismanagement, or that it is necessary or desirable for the purpose of protecting the charity's property or securing its proper application for the purposes of the charity

[24] CA 1993, s 63(5)

[25] Under CA 1993, s 8

[26] The power of the Charity Commissioners to apply under Companies Act 1985, s 651, is specifically conferred by CA 1993, s 63(3)

[27] Companies Act 1985, s 651

[28] *Re Servers of the Blind League* [1960] 1 WLR 564

dispossess other persons who obtained a vested interest in the asset under a title not derived from the company'.[29]

(3) Application of dissolved charitable company's assets

'Transfer-on-dissolution' clause in memorandum

26.14 The memorandum of a charitable company incorporated under the Companies Acts will usually contain a clause enabling the members, before dissolution, to direct that any surplus assets on a winding up be transferred to some other charity with similar objects. Strictly speaking, these do not have to be charitable objects cy-près those of the dissolved charity.[30] Subject to the power to transfer the assets to another charity, the constitution will also usually provide for a transfer of the assets 'to charitable objects'. In the vast majority of instances, therefore, the use of such a clause obviates the need to apply to the court or to the Charity Commissioners for a scheme.

26.15 The model memorandum of association for a charitable company limited by guarantee prepared on behalf of the Charity Law Association provides that any surplus assets on dissolution must be applied in one or more of the following ways:[31]

> 8.1.1 by transfer to one or more other bodies established for exclusively charitable purposes within, the same as or similar to the Objects
> 8.1.2 directly for the Objects or charitable purposes within or similar to the Objects
> 8.1.3 in such other manner consistent with charitable status as the Commission approve in writing in advance.

26.16 It also states (what is of course a legal requirement) that a final report and statement of account must be sent to the Charity Commissioners.[32]

Need for corresponding clause in articles

26.17 In addition to a clause providing for transfer on winding up being contained in the memorandum, a corresponding clause should also (as is usual practice[33]) be contained in the articles. This can be effected briefly in the manner of the model articles of association for a charitable company limited by guarantee prepared on behalf of the Charity Law Association, which contain an article stating simply:

> 8. The provisions of the Memorandum relating to dissolution of the Charity take effect as though repeated here.

---

[29] *Re Servers of the Blind League* [1960] 1 WLR 564, 565 (Pennycuick J)
[30] J Claricoat & H Phillips, *Charity Law A to Z* (2nd edn, Jordans, 1998), 162
[31] Cl 8
[32] ibid, cl 8.2
[33] *Liverpool and District Hospital for Diseases of the Heart v A-G* [1981] Ch 193, 204

The transfer-on-dissolution provision needs to be repeated in the articles because   **26.18**
of the statutory provisions relating to winding up. On a voluntary winding up,
section 107 of the Insolvency Act 1986[34] provides that the company's assets must
be applied in satisfaction of its liabilities, and that any surplus assets are to be distributed (unless the articles otherwise provide) among the members according to
their rights and interests in the company. Creditors of a charitable company are
entitled to rely on this section in claiming payment; but the provision for distribution of surplus assets to the members is clearly inappropriate for a charitable
company, where the members can have no proprietary interest *qua* members in
the company's property. Nevertheless, a charitable company is not expressly
exempt from this provision,[35] and it is applicable when a charitable company is
wound up voluntarily. On a winding up by the court, section 154 of the
Insolvency Act 1986[36] provides that the court is to 'distribute any surplus among
the persons entitled to it'. It has been pointed out that it would be a paradoxical
result if the ultimate distribution of the net assets were to differ according to
whether the winding up were voluntary or effected by the court.[37] For these
reasons, the articles should indeed 'provide otherwise'.

Even in the absence of a contrary provision in the articles, however, the members   **26.19**
will still be precluded from claiming surplus assets on a winding up. Several
reasons for this were advanced by Slade J in *Liverpool and District Hospital for
Diseases of the Heart v Attorney-General*,[38] in which the charitable company was the
subject of a compulsory winding-up order. First, having regard to what is now section 14(1) of the Companies Act 1985, the members must be deemed to have
contracted with the charitable company on the basis of the memorandum. By
necessary implication of law, the provisions of the clause in the memorandum
requiring the assets to be transferred to another similar charity on dissolution can
properly be deemed to be included in the articles for the purposes of what is now
section 154 of the Insolvency Act 1986. Secondly, his Lordship considered that,
even if that conclusion were incorrect, the members could not be said to be 'entitled' to the surplus assets within the meaning of that section, or to have any 'rights
and interests in the company' within the meaning of what is now section 107 of
that Act, because the provision of the memorandum expressly stating that surplus
assets on dissolution were to be transferred to other charitable institutions was
binding on both the liquidator and the court. Thirdly, under the terms of a charitable company's constitution, its assets are at all times held subject to a legally

---

[34] Re-enacting Companies Act 1985, s 597, which itself replaced Companies Act 1948, s 302
[35] See *Liverpool and District Hospital for Diseases of the Heart v A-G* [1981] Ch 193, 203, where
the court was concerned with a predecessor to Insolvency Act 1986, s 107, namely Companies Act
1948, s 302
[36] Re-enacting Companies Act 1985, s 558, which itself replaced Companies Act 1948, s 265
[37] *Liverpool and District Hospital for Diseases of the Heart v A-G* [1981] Ch 193, 203
[38] [1981] Ch 193

binding obligation which binds the company to apply them for charitable purposes. The position of a charitable corporation in relation to its assets can therefore be said to be 'analogous to that of a trustee for charitable purposes. This ... suffices to give rise to the jurisdiction of the court to order a cy-près scheme'.[39]

Dissolution without application of surplus assets

26.20 If dissolution were to take place without an application of the surplus assets pursuant to such clause or to judicial cy-près (which is possible if the charitable company is struck off the register of companies as being defunct[40]), the undistributed assets will vest in the Crown as bona vacantia.[41] The Crown will, however, permit the assets to be applied to charitable purposes through an exercise of prerogative cy-près.[42]

(4) Legacies to charitable companies in course of winding up

Charitable company solvent

26.21 If the charitable corporation has not been dissolved by the date of the testator's death, any legacy to the corporation vests in it. If the legacy is paid over before dissolution, it will form part of, and go with, the corporation's general assets.

26.22 Difficulties can arise if the dissolution occurs before the legacy has been paid over. As has been stated, if the company was incorporated under the Companies Acts, any property to which it was entitled at the date of dissolution vests in the Crown as bona vacantia.[43] An exception is made for property held by a company immediately before its dissolution on trust for any other person.[44] This would appear to exclude property held by a charitable corporation subject to special trusts, but not a legacy given to it beneficially. Such legacy therefore 'falls to be administered by the Crown, who will apply it according to custom, for some analogous purpose of charity'.[45]

Charitable company insolvent

26.23 A charitable company may be wound up compulsorily and be found to be insolvent. In this event, the members may be called upon to contribute to the assets to the extent of their guarantees.[46] These contributions are unlikely to add substantially to the company's assets, however, as such guarantees are usually of nominal

---

[39] ibid, 214
[40] Companies Act 1985, s 652
[41] ibid, s 654
[42] cf *Re Slevin* [1891] 2 Ch 236
[43] Companies Act 1985, s 654(1); see above, para 26.20
[44] Companies Act 1985, s 654(1)
[45] *Re Slevin* [1891] 2 Ch 236, 243 (Kay LJ, delivering jdgt of CA)
[46] See ch 8, paras 8.79–8.80

amounts. There remains the possibility that the liquidator might be able to claim legacies made to the charity by testators who die even after the date of the winding-up order. In *Re ARMS (Multiple Sclerosis Research) Ltd, Alleyne v Attorney-General*,[47] the charity, which had been incorporated under the Companies Acts, got into difficulties through overspending and was being wound up with debts of some £1.5 million. The liquidator claimed various legacies, made by testators who had died after the winding-up order were beneficial gifts and therefore available to the creditors. Neuberger J, applying *Re Vernon's Will Trusts*,[48] held that a bequest without limitation or trust, to a limited company, takes effect if the company exists at the testator's death, and there was nothing in any of the wills to rebut the presumption of a beneficial gift. One testator had in fact used the word 'charities' in making his bequests; but Neuberger J held that this made no difference because, although the company had gone into insolvent liquidation, it was still registered as a charity with the Charity Commissioners, and the Charities Act 1993 treated a charitable company as a charity at all times until actually dissolved.[49] What authority there was, moreover, suggested that a charitable company retains its charitable purposes even when it goes into liquidation.[50]

In the light of this decision, it would seem to be advisable, when taking instructions from a testator intending to make a gift to a charitable company, to consider the issue of the application of the gift in the event of the company being wound up before the testator's death. Instead of making an absolute gift, the testator could impose an express charitable trust for its (or some of its) purposes, but this may unduly restrict the charitable corporation, whose constitution must expressly permit it to hold property subject to special trusts, and which will in any event need to maintain such legacy separately from its general funds. A more suitable approach might be to subject the legacy to a condition precedent that no winding-up order shall have been made by the date of the testator's death. **26.24**

If a charitable corporation is compulsorily wound up after the death of the testator, but before the legacy is paid over, the liquidator or any other person interested may apply to the court to have the dissolution declared void,[51] so enabling the legacy to benefit the charity's creditors. **26.25**

---

[47] [1997] 1 WLR 877
[48] [1972] Ch 300n
[49] CA 1993, s 63; see also ibid, s 4(1)
[50] *Bowman v Secular Society Ltd* [1917] AC 406
[51] Companies Act 1985, s 651

APPENDICES

APPENDIX A

Trustee Act 2000

2000 CHAPTER 29

ARRANGEMENT OF SECTIONS

An Act to amend the law relating to trustees and persons having the investment powers of trustees; and for connected purposes.

[23rd November 2000]

BE IT ENACTED by the Queen's most Excellent Majesty, by and with the advice and consent of the Lords Spiritual and Temporal, and Commons, in this present Parliament assembled, and by the authority of the same, as follows:

PART I
THE DUTY OF CARE

The duty of care

1. (1) Whenever the duty under this subsection applies to a trustee, he must exercise such care and skill as is reasonable in the circumstances, having regard in particular—

(a) to any special knowledge or experience that he has or holds himself out as having, and

(b) if he acts as trustee in the course of a business or profession, to any special knowledge or experience that it is reasonable to expect of a person acting in the course of that kind of business or profession.

(2) In this Act the duty under subsection (1) is called "the duty of care".

Application of duty of care

2. Schedule 1 makes provision about when the duty of care applies to a trustee.

PART II
INVESTMENT

General power of investment

3. (1) Subject to the provisions of this Part, a trustee may make any kind of investment that he could make if he were absolutely entitled to the assets of the trust.

(2) In this Act the power under subsection (1) is called "the general power of investment".

(3) The general power of investment does not permit a trustee to make investments in land other than in loans secured on land (but see also section 8).

(4) A person invests in a loan secured on land if he has rights under any contract under which—

(a) one person provides another with credit, and

(b) the obligation of the borrower to repay is secured on land.

(5) "Credit" includes any cash loan or other financial accommodation.

(6) "Cash" includes money in any form.

Standard investment criteria

4. (1) In exercising any power of investment, whether arising under this Part or otherwise, a trustee must have regard to the standard investment criteria.

(2) A trustee must from time to time review the investments of the trust and consider whether, having regard to the standard investment criteria, they should be varied.

(3) The standard investment criteria, in relation to a trust, are—

(a) the suitability to the trust of investments of the same kind as any particular investment proposed to be made or retained and of that particular investment as an investment of that kind, and

(b) the need for diversification of investments of the trust, in so far as is appropriate to the circumstances of the trust.

Advice

5. (1) Before exercising any power of investment, whether arising under this Part or otherwise, a trustee must (unless the exception applies) obtain and consider proper advice about the way in which, having regard to the standard investment criteria, the power should be exercised.

(2) When reviewing the investments of the trust, a trustee must (unless the exception applies) obtain and consider proper advice about whether, having regard to the standard investment criteria, the investments should be varied.

(3) The exception is that a trustee need not obtain such advice if he reasonably concludes that in all the circumstances it is unnecessary or inappropriate to do so.

(4) Proper advice is the advice of a person who is reasonably believed by the trustee to be qualified to give it by his ability in and practical experience of financial and other matters relating to the proposed investment.

Restriction or exclusion of this Part etc.

6. (1) The general power of investment is—
- (a) in addition to powers conferred on trustees otherwise than by this Act, but
- (b) subject to any restriction or exclusion imposed by the trust instrument or by any enactment or any provision of subordinate legislation.

(2) For the purposes of this Act, an enactment or a provision of subordinate legislation is not to be regarded as being, or as being part of, a trust instrument.

(3) In this Act "subordinate legislation" has the same meaning as in the Interpretation Act 1978.

Existing trusts

7. (1) This Part applies in relation to trusts whether created before or after its commencement.

(2) No provision relating to the powers of a trustee contained in a trust instrument made before 3rd August 1961 is to be treated (for the purposes of section 6(1)(b)) as restricting or excluding the general power of investment.

(3) A provision contained in a trust instrument made before the commencement of this Part which—
- (a) has effect under section 3(2) of the Trustee Investments Act 1961 as a power to invest under that Act, or
- (b) confers power to invest under that Act,

is to be treated as conferring the general power of investment on a trustee.

PART III

ACQUISITION OF LAND

Power to acquire freehold and leasehold land

8. (1) A trustee may acquire freehold or leasehold land in the United Kingdom—
- (a) as an investment,
- (b) for occupation by a beneficiary, or
- (c) for any other reason.

(2) "Freehold or leasehold land" means—
- (a) in relation to England and Wales, a legal estate in land,
- (b) in relation to Scotland—
  - (i) the estate or interest of the proprietor of the dominium utile or, in the case of land not held on feudal tenure, the estate or interest of the owner, or
  - (ii) a tenancy, and
- (c) in relation to Northern Ireland, a legal estate in land, including land held under a fee farm grant.

(3) For the purpose of exercising his functions as a trustee, a trustee who acquires land under this section has all the powers of an absolute owner in relation to the land.

Restriction or exclusion of this Part etc.

9. The powers conferred by this Part are—
- (a) in addition to powers conferred on trustees otherwise than by this Part, but

(b) subject to any restriction or exclusion imposed by the trust instrument or by any enactment or any provision of subordinate legislation.

Existing trusts

10. (1) This Part does not apply in relation to—

    (a) a trust of property which consists of or includes land which (despite section 2 of the Trusts of Land and Appointment of Trustees Act 1996) is settled land, or

    (b) a trust to which the Universities and College Estates Act 1925 applies.

(2) Subject to subsection (1), this Part applies in relation to trusts whether created before or after its commencement.

Part IV

Agents, Nominees and Custodians

Agents

Power to employ agents

11. (1) Subject to the provisions of this Part, the trustees of a trust may authorise any person to exercise any or all of their delegable functions as their agent.

(2) In the case of a trust other than a charitable trust, the trustees' delegable functions consist of any function other than—

    (a) any function relating to whether or in what way any assets of the trust should be distributed,

    (b) any power to decide whether any fees or other payment due to be made out of the trust funds should be made out of income or capital,

    (c) any power to appoint a person to be a trustee of the trust, or

    (d) any power conferred by any other enactment or the trust instrument which permits the trustees to delegate any of their functions or to appoint a person to act as a nominee or custodian.

(3) In the case of a charitable trust, the trustees' delegable functions are—

    (a) any function consisting of carrying out a decision that the trustees have taken;

    (b) any function relating to the investment of assets subject to the trust (including, in the case of land held as an investment, managing the land and creating or disposing of an interest in the land);

    (c) any function relating to the raising of funds for the trust otherwise than by means of profits of a trade which is an integral part of carrying out the trust's charitable purpose;

    (d) any other function prescribed by an order made by the Secretary of State.

(4) For the purposes of subsection (3)(c) a trade is an integral part of carrying out a trust's charitable purpose if, whether carried on in the United Kingdom or elsewhere, the profits are applied solely to the purposes of the trust and either—

    (a) the trade is exercised in the course of the actual carrying out of a primary purpose of the trust, or

    (b) the work in connection with the trade is mainly carried out by beneficiaries of the trust.

(5) The power to make an order under subsection (3)(d) is exercisable by statutory instrument which shall be subject to annulment in pursuance of a resolution of either House of Parliament.

Persons who may act as agents

12. (1) Subject to subsection (2), the persons whom the trustees may under section 11 authorise to exercise functions as their agent include one or more of their number.

(2) The trustees may not authorise two (or more) persons to exercise the same function unless they are to exercise the function jointly.

(3) The trustees may not under section 11 authorise a beneficiary to exercise any function as their agent (even if the beneficiary is also a trustee).

(4) The trustees may under section 11 authorise a person to exercise functions as their agent even though he is also appointed to act as their nominee or custodian (whether under sections 16, 17 or 18 or any other power).

Linked functions etc.

13. (1) Subject to subsections (2) and (5), a person who is authorised under section 11 to exercise a function is (whatever the terms of the agency) subject to any specific duties or restrictions attached to the function.

Linked functions etc. For example, a person who is authorised under section 11 to exercise the general power of investment is subject to the duties under section 4 in relation to that power.

(2) A person who is authorised under section 11 to exercise a power which is subject to a requirement to obtain advice is not subject to the requirement if he is the kind of person from whom it would have been proper for the trustees, in compliance with the requirement, to obtain advice.

(3) Subsections (4) and (5) apply to a trust to which section 11(1) of the Trusts of Land and Appointment of Trustees Act 1996 (duties to consult beneficiaries and give effect to their wishes) applies.

(4) The trustees may not under section 11 authorise a person to exercise any of their functions on terms that prevent them from complying with section 11(1) of the 1996 Act.

(5) A person who is authorised under section 11 to exercise any function relating to land subject to the trust is not subject to section 11(1) of the 1996 Act.

Terms of agency

14. (1) Subject to subsection (2) and sections 15(2) and 29 to 32, the trustees may authorise a person to exercise functions as their agent on such terms as to remuneration and other matters as they may determine.

(2) The trustees may not authorise a person to exercise functions as their agent on any of the terms mentioned in subsection (3) unless it is reasonably necessary for them to do so.

(3) The terms are—

(a) a term permitting the agent to appoint a substitute;

(b) a term restricting the liability of the agent or his substitute to the trustees or any beneficiary;

(c) a term permitting the agent to act in circumstances capable of giving rise to a conflict of interest.

Asset management: special restrictions

15. (1) The trustees may not authorise a person to exercise any of their asset management functions as their agent except by an agreement which is in or evidenced in writing.

(2) The trustees may not authorise a person to exercise any of their asset management functions as their agent unless—

(a) they have prepared a statement that gives guidance as to how the functions should be exercised ("a policy statement"), and

(b) the agreement under which the agent is to act includes a term to the effect that he will secure compliance with—

(i) the policy statement, or

(ii) if the policy statement is revised or replaced under section 22, the revised or replacement policy statement.

(3) The trustees must formulate any guidance given in the policy statement with a view to ensuring that the functions will be exercised in the best interests of the trust.

(4) The policy statement must be in or evidenced in writing.

(5) The asset management functions of trustees are their functions relating to—

    (a) the investment of assets subject to the trust,

    (b) the acquisition of property which is to be subject to the trust, and

    (c) managing property which is subject to the trust and disposing of, or creating or disposing of an interest in, such property.

Nominees and custodians

Power to appoint nominees

16. (1) Subject to the provisions of this Part, the trustees of a trust may—

    (a) appoint a person to act as their nominee in relation to such of the assets of the trust as they determine (other than settled land), and

    (b) take such steps as are necessary to secure that those assets are vested in a person so appointed.

(2) An appointment under this section must be in or evidenced in writing.

(3) This section does not apply to any trust having a custodian trustee or in relation to any assets vested in the official custodian for charities.

Power to appoint custodians

17. (1) Subject to the provisions of this Part, the trustees of a trust may appoint a person to act as a custodian in relation to such of the assets of the trust as they may determine.

(2) For the purposes of this Act a person is a custodian in relation to assets if he undertakes the safe custody of the assets or of any documents or records concerning the assets.

(3) An appointment under this section must be in or evidenced in writing.

(4) This section does not apply to any trust having a custodian trustee or in relation to any assets vested in the official custodian for charities.

Investment in bearer securities

18. (1) If trustees retain or invest in securities payable to bearer, they must appoint a person to act as a custodian of the securities.

(2) Subsection (1) does not apply if the trust instrument or any enactment or provision of subordinate legislation contains provision which (however expressed) permits the trustees to retain or invest in securities payable to bearer without appointing a person to act as a custodian.

(3) An appointment under this section must be in or evidenced in writing.

(4) This section does not apply to any trust having a custodian trustee or in relation to any securities vested in the official custodian for charities.

Persons who may be appointed as nominees or custodians

19. (1) A person may not be appointed under section 16, 17 or 18 as a nominee or custodian unless one of the relevant conditions is satisfied.

(2) The relevant conditions are that—

    (a) the person carries on a business which consists of or includes acting as a nominee or custodian;

    (b) the person is a body corporate which is controlled by the trustees;

    (c) the person is a body corporate recognised under section 9 of the Administration of Justice Act 1985.

(3) The question whether a body corporate is controlled by trustees is to be determined in accordance with section 840 of the Income and Corporation Taxes Act 1988.

(4) The trustees of a charitable trust which is not an exempt charity must act in accordance with any guidance given by the Charity Commissioners concerning the selection of a person for appointment as a nominee or custodian under section 16, 17 or 18.

(5) Subject to subsections (1) and (4), the persons whom the trustees may under section 16, 17 or 18 appoint as a nominee or custodian include—

(a) one of their number, if that one is a trust corporation, or

(b) two (or more) of their number, if they are to act as joint nominees or joint custodians.

(6) The trustees may under section 16 appoint a person to act as their nominee even though he is also—

(a) appointed to act as their custodian (whether under section 17 or 18 or any other power), or

(b) authorised to exercise functions as their agent (whether under section 11 or any other power).

(7) Likewise, the trustees may under section 17 or 18 appoint a person to act as their custodian even though he is also—

(a) appointed to act as their nominee (whether under section 16 or any other power), or

(b) authorised to exercise functions as their agent (whether under section 11 or any other power).

Terms of appointment of nominees and custodians

20. (1) Subject to subsection (2) and sections 29 to 32, the trustees may under section 16, 17 or 18 appoint a person to act as a nominee or custodian on such terms as to remuneration and other matters as they may determine.

(2) The trustees may not under section 16, 17 or 18 appoint a person to act as a nominee or custodian on any of the terms mentioned in subsection (3) unless it is reasonably necessary for them to do so.

(3) The terms are—

(a) a term permitting the nominee or custodian to appoint a substitute;

(b) a term restricting the liability of the nominee or custodian or his substitute to the trustees or to any beneficiary;

(c) a term permitting the nominee or custodian to act in circumstances capable of giving rise to a conflict of interest.

Review of and liability for agents, nominees and custodians etc.

Application of sections 22 and 23

21. (1) Sections 22 and 23 apply in a case where trustees have, under section 11, 16, 17 or 18—

(a) authorised a person to exercise functions as their agent, or

(b) appointed a person to act as a nominee or custodian.

(2) Subject to subsection (3), sections 22 and 23 also apply in a case where trustees have, under any power conferred on them by the trust instrument or by any enactment or any provision of subordinate legislation—

(a) authorised a person to exercise functions as their agent, or

(b) appointed a person to act as a nominee or custodian.

(3) If the application of section 22 or 23 is inconsistent with the terms of the trust instrument or the enactment or provision of subordinate legislation, the section in question does not apply.

Review of agents, nominees and custodians etc.

22. (1) While the agent, nominee or custodian continues to act for the trust, the trustees—

(a) must keep under review the arrangements under which the agent, nominee or custodian acts and how those arrangements are being put into effect,

(b) if circumstances make it appropriate to do so, must consider whether there is a need to exercise any power of intervention that they have, and

(c) if they consider that there is a need to exercise such a power, must do so.

(2) If the agent has been authorised to exercise asset management functions, the duty under subsection (1) includes, in particular—

(a) a duty to consider whether there is any need to revise or replace the policy statement made for the purposes of section 15,

(b) if they consider that there is a need to revise or replace the policy statement, a duty to do so, and

(c) a duty to assess whether the policy statement (as it has effect for the time being) is being complied with.

(3) Subsections (3) and (4) of section 15 apply to the revision or replacement of a policy statement under this section as they apply to the making of a policy statement under that section.

(4) "Power of intervention" includes—

(a) a power to give directions to the agent, nominee or custodian,

(b) a power to revoke the authorisation or appointment.

Liability for agents, nominees and custodians etc.

23. (1) A trustee is not liable for any act or default of the agent, nominee or custodian unless he has failed to comply with the duty of care applicable to him, under paragraph 3 of Schedule 1—

(a) when entering into the arrangements under which the person acts as agent, nominee or custodian, or

(b) when carrying out his duties under section 22.

(2) If a trustee has agreed a term under which the agent, nominee or custodian is permitted to appoint a substitute, the trustee is not liable for any act or default of the substitute unless he has failed to comply with the duty of care applicable to him, under paragraph 3 of Schedule 1—

(a) when agreeing that term, or

(b) when carrying out his duties under section 22 in so far as they relate to the use of the substitute.

Supplementary

Effect of trustees exceeding their powers

24. A failure by the trustees to act within the limits of the powers conferred by this Part—

(a) in authorising a person to exercise a function of theirs as an agent, or

(b) in appointing a person to act as a nominee or custodian,

does not invalidate the authorisation or appointment.

Sole trustees

25. (1) Subject to subsection (2), this Part applies in relation to a trust having a sole trustee as it applies in relation to other trusts (and references in this Part to trustees—except in sections 12(1) and (3) and 19(5)—are to be read accordingly).

(2) Section 18 does not impose a duty on a sole trustee if that trustee is a trust corporation.

Restriction or exclusion of this Part etc.

26. The powers conferred by this Part are—

(a) in addition to powers conferred on trustees otherwise than by this Act, but

(b) subject to any restriction or exclusion imposed by the trust instrument or by any enactment or any provision of subordinate legislation.

Existing trusts.

27. This Part applies in relation to trusts whether created before or after its commencement.

Part V

Remuneration

Trustee's entitlement to payment under trust instrument

28. (1) Except to the extent (if any) to which the trust instrument makes inconsistent provision, subsections (2) to (4) apply to a trustee if—

    (a) there is a provision in the trust instrument entitling him to receive payment out of trust funds in respect of services provided by him to or on behalf of the trust, and

    (b) the trustee is a trust corporation or is acting in a professional capacity.

(2) The trustee is to be treated as entitled under the trust instrument to receive payment in respect of services even if they are services which are capable of being provided by a lay trustee.

(3) Subsection (2) applies to a trustee of a charitable trust who is not a trust corporation only—

    (a) if he is not a sole trustee, and

    (b) to the extent that a majority of the other trustees have agreed that it should apply to him.

(4) Any payments to which the trustee is entitled in respect of services are to be treated as remuneration for services (and not as a gift) for the purposes of—

    (a) section 15 of the Wills Act 1837 (gifts to an attesting witness to be void), and

    (b) section 34(3) of the Administration of Estates Act 1925 (order in which estate to be paid out).

(5) For the purposes of this Part, a trustee acts in a professional capacity if he acts in the course of a profession or business which consists of or includes the provision of services in connection with—

    (a) the management or administration of trusts generally or a particular kind of trust, or

    (b) any particular aspect of the management or administration of trusts generally or a particular kind of trust,

and the services he provides to or on behalf of the trust fall within that description.

(6) For the purposes of this Part, a person acts as a lay trustee if he—

    (a) is not a trust corporation, and

    (b) does not act in a professional capacity.

Remuneration of certain trustees

29. (1) Subject to subsection (5), a trustee who—

    (a) is a trust corporation, but

    (b) is not a trustee of a charitable trust,

is entitled to receive reasonable remuneration out of the trust funds for any services that the trust corporation provides to or on behalf of the trust.

(2) Subject to subsection (5), a trustee who—

    (a) acts in a professional capacity, but

    (b) is not a trust corporation, a trustee of a charitable trust or a sole trustee,

is entitled to receive reasonable remuneration out of the trust funds for any services that he provides to or on behalf of the trust if each other trustee has agreed in writing that he may be remunerated for the services.

(3) "Reasonable remuneration" means, in relation to the provision of services by a trustee, such remuneration as is reasonable in the circumstances for the provision of those services to or on behalf of that trust by that trustee and for the purposes of subsection (1) includes, in relation to the provision of services by a trustee who is an authorised institution under the Banking Act 1987 and

provides the services in that capacity, the institution's reasonable charges for the provision of such services.

(4) A trustee is entitled to remuneration under this section even if the services in question are capable of being provided by a lay trustee.

(5) A trustee is not entitled to remuneration under this section if any provision about his entitlement to remuneration has been made—

    (a) by the trust instrument, or

    (b) by any enactment or any provision of subordinate legislation.

(6) This section applies to a trustee who has been authorised under a power conferred by Part IV or the trust instrument—

    (a) to exercise functions as an agent of the trustees, or

    (b) to act as a nominee or custodian,

as it applies to any other trustee.

Remuneration of trustees of charitable trusts

30. (1) The Secretary of State may by regulations make provision for the remuneration of trustees of charitable trusts who are trust corporations or act in a professional capacity.

(2) The power under subsection (1) includes power to make provision for the remuneration of a trustee who has been authorised under a power conferred by Part IV or any other enactment or any provision of subordinate legislation, or by the trust instrument—

    (a) to exercise functions as an agent of the trustees, or

    (b) to act as a nominee or custodian.

(3) Regulations under this section may—

    (a) make different provision for different cases;

    (b) contain such supplemental, incidental, consequential and transitional provision as the Secretary of State considers appropriate.

(4) The power to make regulations under this section is exercisable by statutory instrument, but no such instrument shall be made unless a draft of it has been laid before Parliament and approved by a resolution of each House of Parliament.

Trustees' expenses

31. (1) A trustee—

    (a) is entitled to be reimbursed from the trust funds, or

    (b) may pay out of the trust funds,

expenses properly incurred by him when acting on behalf of the trust.

(2) This section applies to a trustee who has been authorised under a power conferred by Part IV or any other enactment or any provision of subordinate legislation, or by the trust instrument—

    (a) to exercise functions as an agent of the trustees, or

    (b) to act as a nominee or custodian,

as it applies to any other trustee.

Remuneration and expenses of agents, nominees and custodians

32. (1) This section applies if, under a power conferred by Part IV or any other enactment or any provision of subordinate legislation, or by the trust instrument, a person other than a trustee has been—

    (a) authorised to exercise functions as an agent of the trustees, or

    (b) appointed to act as a nominee or custodian.

(2) The trustees may remunerate the agent, nominee or custodian out of the trust funds for services if—

(a) he is engaged on terms entitling him to be remunerated for those services, and

(b) the amount does not exceed such remuneration as is reasonable in the circumstances for the provision of those services by him to or on behalf of that trust.

(3) The trustees may reimburse the agent, nominee or custodian out of the trust funds for any expenses properly incurred by him in exercising functions as an agent, nominee or custodian.

Application

33. (1) Subject to subsection (2), sections 28, 29, 31 and 32 apply in relation to services provided to or on behalf of, or (as the case may be) expenses incurred on or after their commencement on behalf of, trusts whenever created.

(2) Nothing in section 28 or 29 is to be treated as affecting the operation of—

(a) section 15 of the Wills Act 1837, or

(b) section 34(3) of the Administration of Estates Act 1925,

in relation to any death occurring before the commencement of section 28 or (as the case may be) section 29.

PART VI
MISCELLANEOUS AND SUPPLEMENTARY

Power to insure

34. (1) For section 19 of the Trustee Act 1925 (power to insure) substitute—

"Power to insure.

19. (1) A trustee may—

(a) insure any property which is subject to the trust against risks of loss or damage due to any event, and

(b) pay the premiums out of the trust funds.

(2) In the case of property held on a bare trust, the power to insure is subject to any direction given by the beneficiary or each of the beneficiaries—

(a) that any property specified in the direction is not to be insured;

(b) that any property specified in the direction is not to be insured except on such conditions as may be so specified.

(3) Property is held on a bare trust if it is held on trust for—

(a) a beneficiary who is of full age and capacity and absolutely entitled to the property subject to the trust, or

(b) beneficiaries each of whom is of full age and capacity and who (taken together) are absolutely entitled to the property subject to the trust.

(4) If a direction under subsection (2) of this section is given, the power to insure, so far as it is subject to the direction, ceases to be a delegable function for the purposes of section 11 of the Trustee Act 2000 (power to employ agents).

(5) In this section 'trust funds' means any income or capital funds of the trust."

(2) In section 20(1) of the Trustee Act 1925 (application of insurance money) omit "whether by fire or otherwise".

(3) The amendments made by this section apply in relation to trusts whether created before or after its commencement.

Personal representatives

35. (1) Subject to the following provisions of this section, this Act applies in relation to a personal representative administering an estate according to the law as it applies to a trustee carrying out a trust for beneficiaries.

(2) For this purpose this Act is to be read with the appropriate modifications and in particular—

(a) references to the trust instrument are to be read as references to the will,

(b) references to a beneficiary or to beneficiaries, apart from the reference to a beneficiary in section 8(1)(b), are to be read as references to a person or the persons interested in the due administration of the estate, and

(c) the reference to a beneficiary in section 8(1)(b) is to be read as a reference to a person who under the will of the deceased or under the law relating to intestacy is beneficially interested in the estate.

(3) Remuneration to which a personal representative is entitled under section 28 or 29 is to be treated as an administration expense for the purposes of—

(a) section 34(3) of the Administration of Estates Act 1925 (order in which estate to be paid out), and

(b) any provision giving reasonable administration expenses priority over the preferential debts listed in Schedule 6 to the Insolvency Act 1986.

(4) Nothing in subsection (3) is to be treated as affecting the operation of the provisions mentioned in paragraphs (a) and (b) of that subsection in relation to any death occurring before the commencement of this section.

Pension schemes

36. (1) In this section "pension scheme" means an occupational pension scheme (within the meaning of the Pension Schemes Act 1993) established under a trust and subject to the law of England and Wales.

(2) Part I does not apply in so far as it imposes a duty of care in relation to—

(a) the functions described in paragraphs 1 and 2 of Schedule 1, or

(b) the functions described in paragraph 3 of that Schedule to the extent that they relate to trustees—

(i) authorising a person to exercise their functions with respect to investment, or

(ii) appointing a person to act as their nominee or custodian.

(3) Nothing in Part II or III applies to the trustees of any pension scheme.

(4) Part IV applies to the trustees of a pension scheme subject to the restrictions in subsections (5) to (8).

(5) The trustees of a pension scheme may not under Part IV authorise any person to exercise any functions relating to investment as their agent.

(6) The trustees of a pension scheme may not under Part IV authorise a person who is—

(a) an employer in relation to the scheme, or

(b) connected with or an associate of such an employer,

to exercise any of their functions as their agent.

(7) For the purposes of subsection (6)—

(a) "employer", in relation to a scheme, has the same meaning as in the Pensions Act 1995;

(b) sections 249 and 435 of the Insolvency Act 1986 apply for the purpose of determining whether a person is connected with or an associate of an employer.

(8) Sections 16 to 20 (powers to appoint nominees and custodians) do not apply to the trustees of a pension scheme.

Authorised unit trusts

37. (1) Parts II to IV do not apply to trustees of authorised unit trusts.

(2) "Authorised unit trust" means a unit trust scheme in the case of which an order under section 78 of the Financial Services Act 1986 is in force.

Common investment schemes for charities etc.

38. Parts II to IV do not apply to—

(a) trustees managing a fund under a common investment scheme made, or having effect as if made, under section 24 of the Charities Act 1993, other than such a fund the trusts of which provide that property is not to be transferred to the fund except by or on behalf of a charity the trustees of which are the trustees appointed to manage the fund, or

(b) trustees managing a fund under a common deposit scheme made, or having effect as if made, under section 25 of that Act.

Interpretation

39. (1) In this Act—

"asset" includes any right or interest;

"charitable trust" means a trust under which property is held for charitable purposes and "charitable purposes" has the same meaning as in the Charities Act 1993;

"custodian trustee" has the same meaning as in the Public Trustee Act 1906;

"enactment" includes any provision of a Measure of the Church Assembly or of the General Synod of the Church of England;

"exempt charity" has the same meaning as in the Charities Act 1993;

"functions" includes powers and duties;

"legal mortgage" has the same meaning as in the Law of Property Act 1925;

"personal representative" has the same meaning as in the Trustee Act 1925;

"settled land" has the same meaning as in the Settled Land Act 1925;

"trust corporation" has the same meaning as in the Trustee Act 1925;

"trust funds" means income or capital funds of the trust.

(2) In this Act the expressions listed below are defined or otherwise explained by the provisions indicated—

asset management functions	section 15(5)
custodian	section 17(2)
the duty of care	section 1(2)
the general power of investment	section 3(2)
lay trustee	section 28(6)
power of intervention	section 22(4)
the standard investment criteria	section 4(3)
subordinate legislation	section 6(3)
trustee acting in a professional capacity	section 28(5)
trust instrument	sections 6(2) and 35(2)(a)

Minor and consequential amendments etc.

40. (1) Schedule 2 (minor and consequential amendments) shall have effect.

(2) Schedule 3 (transitional provisions and savings) shall have effect.

(3) Schedule 4 (repeals) shall have effect.

Power to amend other Acts.

41. (1) A Minister of the Crown may by order make such amendments of any Act, including an Act extending to places outside England and Wales, as appear to him appropriate in consequence of or in connection with Part II or III.

(2) Before exercising the power under subsection (1) in relation to a local, personal or private Act, the Minister must consult any person who appears to him to be affected by any proposed amendment.

(3) An order under this section may—

    (a) contain such transitional provisions and savings as the Minister thinks fit;

    (b) make different provision for different purposes.

(4) The power to make an order under this section is exercisable by statutory instrument which shall be subject to annulment in pursuance of a resolution of either House of Parliament.

(5) "Minister of the Crown" has the same meaning as in the Ministers of the Crown Act 1975.

Commencement and extent

42. (1) Section 41, this section and section 43 shall come into force on the day on which this Act is passed.

(2) The remaining provisions of this Act shall come into force on such day as the Lord Chancellor may appoint by order made by statutory instrument; and different days may be so appointed for different purposes.

(3) An order under subsection (2) may contain such transitional provisions and savings as the Lord Chancellor considers appropriate in connection with the order.

(4) Subject to section 41(1) and subsection (5), this Act extends to England and Wales only.

(5) An amendment or repeal in Part II or III of Schedule 2 or Part II of Schedule 4 has the same extent as the provision amended or repealed.

Short title

43. This Act may be cited as the Trustee Act 2000.

SCHEDULES

SCHEDULE 1

Application of Duty of Care

Investment

1. The duty of care applies to a trustee—

    (a) when exercising the general power of investment or any other power of investment, however conferred;

    (b) when carrying out a duty to which he is subject under section 4 or 5 (duties relating to the exercise of a power of investment or to the review of investments).

Acquisition of land

2. The duty of care applies to a trustee—

    (a) when exercising the power under section 8 to acquire land;

    (b) when exercising any other power to acquire land, however conferred;

    (c) when exercising any power in relation to land acquired under a power mentioned in sub-paragraph (a) or (b).

Agents, nominees and custodians

3. (1) The duty of care applies to a trustee—

    (a) when entering into arrangements under which a person is authorised under section 11 to exercise functions as an agent;

    (b) when entering into arrangements under which a person is appointed under section 16 to act as a nominee;

    (c) when entering into arrangements under which a person is appointed under section 17 or 18 to act as a custodian;

    (d) when entering into arrangements under which, under any other power, however conferred, a person is authorised to exercise functions as an agent or is appointed to act as a nominee or custodian;

    (e) when carrying out his duties under section 22 (review of agent, nominee or custodian, etc.).

(2) For the purposes of sub-paragraph (1), entering into arrangements under which a person is authorised to exercise functions or is appointed to act as a nominee or custodian includes, in particular—

    (a) selecting the person who is to act,

    (b) determining any terms on which he is to act, and

    (c) if the person is being authorised to exercise asset management functions, the preparation of a policy statement under section 15.

Compounding of liabilities

4. The duty of care applies to a trustee—

    (a) when exercising the power under section 15 of the Trustee Act 1925 to do any of the things referred to in that section;

    (b) when exercising any corresponding power, however conferred.

Insurance

5. The duty of care applies to a trustee—

    (a) when exercising the power under section 19 of the Trustee Act 1925 to insure property;

    (b) when exercising any corresponding power, however conferred.

Reversionary interests, valuations and audit

6. The duty of care applies to a trustee—

    (a) when exercising the power under section 22(1) or (3) of the Trustee Act 1925 to do any of the things referred to there;

    (b) when exercising any corresponding power, however conferred.

Exclusion of duty of care

7. The duty of care does not apply if or in so far as it appears from the trust instrument that the duty is not meant to apply.

Schedule 2

Minor and Consequential Amendments
Part I
The Trustee Investments Act 1961 and the Charities Act 1993

The Trustee Investments Act 1961 (c.62)

1. (1) Sections 1, 2, 5, 6, 12, 13 and 15 shall cease to have effect, except in so far as they are applied by or under any other enactment.

(2) Section 3 and Schedules 2 and 3 shall cease to have effect, except in so far as they relate to a trustee having a power of investment conferred on him under an enactment—

    (a) which was passed before the passing of the 1961 Act, and

    (b) which is not amended by this Schedule.

(3) Omit—

    (a) sections 8 and 9,

    (b) paragraph 1(1) of Schedule 4, and

    (c) section 16(1), in so far as it relates to paragraph 1(1) of Schedule 4.

The Charities Act 1993 (c.10)

2. (1) Omit sections 70 and 71.

(2) In section 86(2) in paragraph (a)—
  (a) omit "70", and
  (b) at the end insert "or".

(3) Omit section 86(2)(b).

Part II

Other Public General Acts

The Places of Worship Sites Act 1873 (c.50)

3. In section 2 (payment of purchase money, etc.) for "shall be invested upon such securities or investments as would for the time being be authorised by statute or the Court of Chancery" substitute "shall be invested under the general power of investment in section 3 of the Trustee Act 2000".

The Technical and Industrial Institutions Act 1892 (c.29)

4. In section 9 (investment powers relating to proceeds of sale of land acquired under the Act) for subsection (5) substitute—

"(5) Money arising by sale may, until reinvested in the purchase of land, be invested—
  (a) in the names of the governing body, in any investments in which trustees may invest under the general power of investment in section 3 of the Trustee Act 2000 (as restricted by sections 4 and 5 of that Act), or
  (b) under the general power of investment in section 3 of that Act, by trustees for the governing body or by a person authorised by the trustees under that Act to invest as an agent of the trustees.

(6) Any profits from investments under subsection (5) shall be invested in the same way and added to capital until the capital is reinvested in the purchase of land."

The Duchy of Cornwall Management Act 1893 (c.20)

5. The 1893 Act is hereby repealed.

The Duchy of Lancaster Act 1920 (c.51)

6. In section 1 (extension of powers of investment of funds of Duchy of Lancaster) for "in any of the investments specified in paragraph (a) of section one of the Trustees Act 1893 and any enactment amending or extending that paragraph" substitute "under the general power of investment in section 3 of the Trustee Act 2000 (as restricted by sections 4 and 5 of that Act)".

The Settled Land Act 1925 (c.18)

7. In section 21 (absolute owners subject to certain interests to have the powers of tenant for life), in subsection (1)(d) for "income thereof" substitute "resultant profits".

8. In section 39 (regulations respecting sales), in subsection (2), in the proviso, for the words from "accumulate" to the end of the subsection substitute "accumulate the profits from the capital money by investing them and any resulting profits under the general power of investment in section 3 of the Trustee Act 2000 and shall add the accumulations to capital."

9. In section 73 (modes of investment or application), in subsection (1) for paragraph (i) substitute—

"(i) In investment in securities either under the general power of investment in section 3 of the Trustee Act 2000 or under a power to invest conferred on the trustees of the settlement by the settlement;".

10. (1) In section 75 (regulations respecting investment, devolution, and income of securities etc.), for subsection (2) substitute—

"(2) Subject to Part IV of the Trustee Act 2000, to section 75A of this Act and to the following provisions of this section—

    (a) the investment or other application by the trustees shall be made according to the discretion of the trustees, but subject to any consent required or direction given by the settlement with respect to the investment or other application by the trustees of trust money of the settlement, and

    (b) any investment shall be in the names or under the control of the trustees."

(2) For subsection (4) of that section substitute—

"(4) The trustees, in exercising their power to invest or apply capital money, shall—

    (a) so far as practicable, consult the tenant for life; and

    (b) so far as consistent with the general interest of the settlement, give effect to his wishes.

(4A) Any investment or other application of capital money under the direction of the court shall not during the subsistence of the beneficial interest of the tenant for life be altered without his consent.

(4B) The trustees may not under section 11 of the Trustee Act 2000 authorise a person to exercise their functions with respect to the investment or application of capital money on terms that prevent them from complying with subsection (4) of this section.

(4C) A person who is authorised under section 11 of the Trustee Act 2000 to exercise any of their functions with respect to the investment or application of capital money is not subject to subsection (4) of this section."

(3) Nothing in this paragraph affects the operation of section 75 in relation to directions of the tenant for life given, but not acted upon by the trustees, before the commencement of this paragraph.

11. After section 75 insert—

"Power to accept charge as security for part payment for land sold.

75A. (1) Where—

    (a) land subject to the settlement is sold by the tenant for life or statutory owner, for an estate in fee simple or a term having at least five hundred years to run, and

    (b) the proceeds of sale are liable to be invested,

the tenant for life or statutory owner may, with the consent of the trustees of the settlement, contract that the payment of any part, not exceeding two-thirds, of the purchase money shall be secured by a charge by way of legal mortgage of the land sold, with or without the security of any other property.

(2) If any buildings are comprised in the property secured by the charge, the charge must contain a covenant by the mortgagor to keep them insured for their full value against loss or damage due to any event.

(3) A person exercising the power under subsection (1) of this section, or giving consent for the purposes of that subsection—

    (a) is not required to comply with section 5 of the Trustee Act 2000 before giving his consent, and

    (b) is not liable for any loss incurred merely because the security is insufficient at the date of the charge.

(4) The power under subsection (1) of this section is exercisable subject to the consent of any person whose consent to a change of investment is required by the instrument, if any, creating the trust.

(5) Where the sale referred to in subsection (1) of this section is made under the order of the court, the power under that subsection applies only if and as far as the court may by order direct."

12 Omit section 96 (protection of each trustee individually).

13. In section 98 (protection of trustees in particular cases), omit subsections (1) and (2).

14. Omit section 100 (trustees' reimbursements).

15. In section 102 (management of land during minority or pending contingency), in subsection (2) for paragraph (e) substitute—

"(e) to insure against risks of loss or damage due to any event under section 19 of the Trustee Act 1925;".

16. (1) In section 104 (powers of tenant for life not assignable etc.)—

    (a) in subsection (3)(b) omit "authorised by statute for the investment of trust money", and

    (b) in subsection (4)(b) for the words from "no investment" to "trust money;" substitute "the consent of the assignee shall be required to an investment of capital money for the time being affected by the assignment in investments other than securities, and to any application of such capital money;".

(2) Sub-paragraph (1) applies to the determination on or after the commencement of that sub-paragraph of whether an assignee's consent is required to the investment or application of capital money.

17. In section 107 (tenant for life deemed to be in the position and to have the duties and liabilities of a trustee, etc.) after subsection (1) insert—

"(1A) The following provisions apply to the tenant for life as they apply to the trustees of the settlement—

    (a) sections 11, 13 to 15 and 21 to 23 of the Trustee Act 2000 (power to employ agents subject to certain restrictions),

    (b) section 32 of that Act (remuneration and expenses of agents etc.),

    (c) section 19 of the Trustee Act 1925 (power to insure), and

    (d) in so far as they relate to the provisions mentioned in paragraphs (a) and (c), Part I of, and Schedule 1 to, the Trustee Act 2000 (the duty of care)."

The Trustee Act 1925 (c.19)

18. Omit Part I (investments).

19. In section 14 (power of trustees to give receipts) in subsection (1) after "securities," insert "investments".

20. In section 15 (power to compound liabilities), for "in good faith" substitute "if he has or they have discharged the duty of care set out in section 1(1) of the Trustee Act 2000".

21. Omit section 21 (deposit of documents for safe custody).

22. In section 22 (reversionary interests, valuations, and audit)—

    (a) in subsection (1), for "in good faith" substitute "if they have discharged the duty of care set out in section 1(1) of the Trustee Act 2000", and

    (b) in subsection (3), omit "in good faith" and at the end insert "if the trustees have discharged the duty of care set out in section 1(1) of the Trustee Act 2000".

23. Omit section 23 (power to employ agents).

24. Omit section 30 (implied indemnity of trustees).

25. In section 31(2) (power to invest income during minority) for "in the way of compound interest by investing the same and the resulting income thereof" substitute "by investing it, and any profits from so investing it".

The Land Registration Act 1925 (c.21)

26. In section 94(1) (registered land subject to a trust to be registered in the names of the trustees), at the end insert "or in the name of a nominee appointed under section 16 of the Trustee Act 2000".

The Administration of Estates Act 1925 (c.23)

27. In section 33, in subsection (3) (investment during minority of beneficiary or the subsistence of a life interest) for the words from "in any investments for the time being authorised by statute" to the end of the subsection substitute "under the Trustee Act 2000".

28. In section 39 (powers of management) after subsection (1) insert—

"(1A) Subsection (1) of this section is without prejudice to the powers conferred on personal representatives by the Trustee Act 2000."

The Universities and College Estates Act 1925 (c.24)

29. In section 26 (modes of application of capital money) in subsection (1) for paragraph (i) substitute—

"(i) In investments in which trustees may invest under the general power of investment in section 3 of the Trustee Act 2000 (as restricted by sections 4 and 5 of that Act);".

The Regimental Charitable Funds Act 1935 (c.11)

30. In section 2(1) (application of funds held on account of regimental charitable funds)—

(a) in paragraph (a) for "in some manner" to "trusts" substitute "under the general power of investment in section 3 of the Trustee Act 2000";

(b) in paragraph (b) after "the income" insert "or the other profits".

The Agricultural Marketing Act 1958 (c.47)

31. (1) In section 16 (investment of surplus funds of boards) for paragraph (a) substitute—

"(a) the moneys of the board not for the time being required by them for the purposes of their functions are not, except with the approval of the Minister, invested otherwise than in investments in which trustees may invest under the general power of investment in section 3 of the Trustee Act 2000 (as restricted by sections 4 and 5 of that Act); and".

(2) Any scheme made under the 1958 Act and in effect before the day on which sub-paragraph (1) comes into force shall be treated, in relation to the making of investments on and after that day, as including provision permitting investment by the board in accordance with section 16(a) of the 1958 Act as amended by sub-paragraph (1).

The Horticulture Act 1960 (c.22)

32. In section 13 (miscellaneous financial powers of organisations promoting home-grown produce) for subsection (3) substitute—

"(3) A relevant organisation may invest any of its surplus money which is not for the time being required for any other purpose in any investments in which trustees may invest under the general power of investment in section 3 of the Trustee Act 2000 (as restricted by sections 4 and 5 of that Act)".

The House of Commons Members' Fund Act 1962 (c.53)

33. (1) In section 1 (powers of investment of trustees of House of Commons Members' Fund)—

(a) in subsection (2) omit "Subject to the following provisions of this section";

(b) omit subsections (3) to (5).

(2) In section 2 (interpretation etc.) omit subsection (1).

The Betting, Gaming and Lotteries Act 1963 (c.2)

34. In section 25(1) (general powers and duties of the Horserace Betting Levy Board) for paragraph (e) substitute—

"(e) to make such other investments as—

(i) they judge desirable for the proper conduct of their affairs, and

(ii) a trustee would be able to make under the general power of investment in section 3 of the Trustee Act 2000 (as restricted by sections 4 and 5 of that Act);".

The Cereals Marketing Act 1965 (c.14)

35. (1) In section 18, in subsection (2) (Home-Grown Cereals Authority's power to invest reserve funds) for "in accordance with the next following subsection" substitute "in any investments in which trustees may invest under the general power of investment in section 3 of the Trustee Act 2000 (as restricted by sections 4 and 5 of that Act)."

(2) Omit section 18(3).

The Agriculture Act 1967 (c.22)

36. (1) In section 18, in subsection (2) (Meat and Livestock Commission's power to invest reserve fund) for "in accordance with the next following subsection" substitute "in any investments in which trustees may invest under the general power of investment in section 3 of the Trustee Act 2000 (as restricted by sections 4 and 5 of that Act)."

(2) Omit section 18(3).

The Solicitors Act 1974 (c.47)

37. In Schedule 2, for paragraph 3 (power of Law Society to invest) substitute—
"**3.** The Society may invest any money which forms part of the fund in any investments in which trustees may invest under the general power of investment in section 3 of the Trustee Act 2000 (as restricted by sections 4 and 5 of that Act)."

The Policyholders Protection Act 1975 (c.75)

38. In Schedule 1, in paragraph 7, for sub-paragraph (1) (power of Policyholders Protection Board to invest) substitute—
"(1) The Board may invest any funds held by them which appear to them to be surplus to their requirements for the time being—
  (a) in any investments in which trustees may invest under the general power of investment in section 3 of the Trustee Act 2000 (as restricted by sections 4 and 5 of that Act); or
  (b) in any investment approved for the purpose by the Treasury."

The National Heritage Act 1980 (c.17)

39. In section 6 for subsection (3) (powers of investment of Trustees of National Heritage Memorial Fund) substitute—
"(3) The Trustees may invest any sums to which subsection (2) does not apply in any investments in which trustees may invest under the general power of investment in section 3 of the Trustee Act 2000 (as restricted by sections 4 and 5 of that Act)."

The Licensing (Alcohol Education and Research) Act 1981 (c.28)

40. In section 7 (powers of investment of Alcohol Education and Research Council) for subsection (5) substitute—
"(5) Any sums in the Fund which are not immediately required for any other purpose may be invested by the Council in any investments in which trustees may invest under the general power of investment in section 3 of the Trustee Act 2000 (as restricted by sections 4 and 5 of that Act)."

The Fisheries Act 1981 (c.29)

41. For section 10 (powers of investment of Sea Fish Industry Authority) substitute—
"Investment of reserve funds.
10. Any money of the Authority which is not immediately required for any other purpose may be invested by the Authority in any investments in which trustees may invest under the general power of investment in section 3 of the Trustee Act 2000 (as restricted by sections 4 and 5 of that Act)".

The Duchy of Cornwall Management Act 1982 (c.47)

42. For section 1 (powers of investment of Duchy property) substitute—
"Powers of investment of Duchy property.

1. The power of investment conferred by the Duchy of Cornwall Management Act 1863 includes power to invest in any investments in which trustees may invest under the general power of investment in section 3 of the Trustee Act 2000 (as restricted by sections 4 and 5 of that Act)."
43. In—
   (a) section 6(3) (Duchy of Cornwall Management Acts extended in relation to banking), and
   (b) section 11(2) (collective citation of Duchy of Cornwall Management Acts),

for "Duchy of Cornwall Management Acts 1868 to 1893" substitute "Duchy of Cornwall Management Acts 1863 to 1868".

The Administration of Justice Act 1982 (c.53)

44. In section 42 (common investment schemes) in subsection (6) for paragraph (a) substitute—
   "(a) he may invest trust money in shares in the fund without obtaining and considering advice on whether to make such an investment; and".

The Trusts of Land and Appointment of Trustees Act 1996 (c.47)

45. (1) In section 6 (general powers of trustees), in subsection (3) for "purchase a legal estate in any land in England and Wales" substitute "acquire land under the power conferred by section 8 of the Trustee Act 2000".

   (2) Omit subsection (4) of that section.

   (3) After subsection (8) of that section insert—

   "(9) The duty of care under section 1 of the Trustee Act 2000 applies to trustees of land when exercising the powers conferred by this section."
46. In section 9 (delegation by trustees) omit subsection (8).
47. After section 9 insert—
"Duties of trustees in connection with delegation etc.
9A. (1) The duty of care under section 1 of the Trustee Act 2000 applies to trustees of land in deciding whether to delegate any of their functions under section 9.

   (2) Subsection (3) applies if the trustees of land—
   (a) delegate any of their functions under section 9, and
   (b) the delegation is not irrevocable.

   (3) While the delegation continues, the trustees—
   (a) must keep the delegation under review,
   (b) if circumstances make it appropriate to do so, must consider whether there is a need to exercise any power of intervention that they have, and
   (c) if they consider that there is a need to exercise such a power, must do so.

   (4) "Power of intervention" includes—
   (a) a power to give directions to the beneficiary;
   (b) a power to revoke the delegation.

   (5) The duty of care under section 1 of the 2000 Act applies to trustees in carrying out any duty under subsection (3).

   (6) A trustee of land is not liable for any act or default of the beneficiary, or beneficiaries, unless the trustee fails to comply with the duty of care in deciding to delegate any of the trustees' functions under section 9 or in carrying out any duty under subsection (3).

   (7) Neither this section nor the repeal of section 9(8) by the Trustee Act 2000 affects the operation after the commencement of this section of any delegation effected before that commencement."
48. Omit section 17(1) (application of section 6(3) in relation to trustees of proceeds of sale of land).
49. In Schedule 3 (consequential amendments) omit paragraph 3(4) (amendment of section 19(1) and (2) of Trustee Act 1925).

Part III

Measures

The Ecclesiastical Dilapidations Measure 1923 (No. 3)

50. In section 52, in subsection (5) (investment of sums held in relation to repair of chancels)—
    (a) for "in any investment permitted by law for the investment of trust funds, and the yearly income resulting therefrom shall be applied," substitute "in any investments in which trustees may invest under the general power of investment in section 3 of the Trustee Act 2000, and the annual profits from the investments shall be applied"; and
    (b) in paragraph (iii) for "any residue of the said income not applied as aforesaid in any year" substitute "any residue of the profits from the investments not applied in any year".

The Diocesan Stipends Funds Measure 1953 (No. 2)

51. In section 4 (application of moneys credited to capital accounts) in subsection (1) for paragraph (bc) substitute—
    "(bc) investment in any investments in which trustees may invest under the general power of investment in section 3 of the Trustee Act 2000 (as restricted by sections 4 and 5 of that Act);".

The Church Funds Investment Measure 1958 (No. 1)

52. In the Schedule, in paragraph 21 (range of investments of deposit fund) for paragraphs (a) to (d) of sub-paragraph (1) substitute—
    "(aa) In any investments in which trustees may invest under the general power of investment in section 3 of the Trustee Act 2000 (as restricted by sections 4 and 5 of that Act);".

The Clergy Pensions Measure 1961 (No. 3)

53. (1) In section 32 (investment powers of Board), in subsection (1), for paragraph (a) substitute—
    "(a) in any investments in which trustees may invest under the general power of investment in section 3 of the Trustee Act 2000 (as restricted by sections 4 and 5 of that Act);".

    (2) Omit subsection (3) of that section.

The Repair of Benefice Buildings Measure 1972 (No. 2)

54. In section 17, in subsection (2) (diocesan parsonages fund's power of investment), for "who shall have the same powers of investment as trustees of trust funds:" substitute "who shall have the same power as trustees to invest in any investments in which trustees may invest under the general power of investment in section 3 of the Trustee Act 2000 (as restricted by sections 4 and 5 of that Act)".

The Pastoral Measure 1983 (No. 1)

55. In section 44, for subsection (6) (Redundant Churches Fund's power of investment) substitute—
    "(6) The powers to invest any such sums are—
    (a) power to invest in investments in which trustees may invest under the general power of investment in section 3 of the Trustee Act 2000 (as restricted by sections 4 and 5 of that Act); and
    (b) power to invest in the investments referred to in paragraph 21(1)(e) and (f) of the Schedule to the Church Funds Investment Measure 1958."

The Church of England (Pensions) Measure 1988 (No. 4)

56. Omit section 14(b) (amendment of section 32(3) of the Clergy Pensions Measure 1961).

The Cathedrals Measure 1999 (No. 1)

57. In section 16 (cathedral moneys: investment powers, etc.), in subsection (1)—

    (a) for paragraph (c) substitute—

      "(c) power to invest in any investments in which trustees may invest under the general power of investment in section 3 of the Trustee Act 2000 (as restricted by sections 4 and 5 of that Act),", and

    (b) omit the words from "and the powers" to the end of the subsection.

SCHEDULE 3

Transitional Provisions and Savings

The Trustee Act 1925 (c.19)

1. (1) Sub-paragraph (2) applies if, immediately before the day on which Part IV of this Act comes into force, a banker or banking company holds any bearer securities deposited with him under section 7(1) of the 1925 Act (investment in bearer securities).

    (2) On and after the day on which Part IV comes into force, the banker or banking company shall be treated as if he had been appointed as custodian of the securities under section 18.

2. The repeal of section 8 of the 1925 Act (loans and investments by trustees not chargeable as breaches of trust) does not affect the operation of that section in relation to loans or investments made before the coming into force of that repeal.

3. The repeal of section 9 of the 1925 Act (liability for loss by reason of improper investment) does not affect the operation of that section in relation to any advance of trust money made before the coming into force of that repeal.

4. (1) Sub-paragraph (2) applies if, immediately before the day on which Part IV of this Act comes into force, a banker or banking company holds any documents deposited with him under section 21 of the 1925 Act (deposit of documents for safe custody).

    (2) On and after the day on which Part IV comes into force, the banker or banking company shall be treated as if he had been appointed as custodian of the documents under section 17.

5. (1) Sub-paragraph (2) applies if, immediately before the day on which Part IV of this Act comes into force, a person has been appointed to act as or be an agent or attorney under section 23(1) or (3) of the 1925 Act (general power to employ agents etc.).

    (2) On and after the day on which Part IV comes into force, the agent shall be treated as if he had been authorised to exercise functions as an agent under section 11 (and, if appropriate, as if he had also been appointed under that Part to act as a custodian or nominee).

6. The repeal of section 23(2) of the 1925 Act (power to employ agents in respect of property outside the United Kingdom) does not affect the operation after the commencement of the repeal of an appointment made before that commencement.

The Trustee Investments Act 1961 (c.62)

7. (1) A trustee shall not be liable for breach of trust merely because he continues to hold an investment acquired by virtue of paragraph 14 of Part II of Schedule 1 to the 1961 Act (perpetual rent-charges etc.).

    (2) A person who—

      (a) is not a trustee,

      (b) before the commencement of Part II of this Act had powers to invest in the investments described in paragraph 14 of Part II of Schedule 1 to the 1961 Act, and

      (c) on that commencement acquired the general power of investment,

shall not be treated as exceeding his powers of investment merely because he continues to hold an investment acquired by virtue of that paragraph.

The Cathedrals Measure 1963 (No. 2)

8. While section 21 of the Cathedrals Measure 1963 (investment powers, etc. of capitular bodies) continues to apply in relation to any cathedral, that section shall have effect as if—

 (a) in subsection (1), for paragraph (c) and the words from "and the powers" to the end of the subsection there were substituted—

"(c) power to invest in any investments in which trustees may invest under the general power of investment in section 3 of the Trustee Act 2000 (as restricted by sections 4 and 5 of that Act).", and (b) in subsection (5), for "subsections (2) and (3) of section six of the Trustee Investments Act 1961" there were substituted "section 5 of the Trustee Act 2000".

SCHEDULE 4

Repeals

Part I

The Trustee Investments Act 1961 and the Charities Act 1993

Chapter	Short title	Extent of repeal
1961 c. 62.	The Trustee Investments Act 1961.	Sections 1 to 3, 5, 6, 8, 9, 12, 13, 15 and 16(1). Schedules 2 and 3. In Schedule 4, paragraph 1(1).
1993 c. 10.	The Charities Act 1993.	Sections 70 and 71. In section 86(2) in paragraph (a), "70" and paragraph (b).

Note: the repeals in this Part of this Schedule have effect in accordance with Part I of Schedule 2.

Part II

Other Repeals

Chapter	Short title	Extent of repeal
1893 c. 20.	The Duchy of Cornwall Management Act 1893.	The whole Act.
1925 c. 18.	The Settled Land Act 1925.	Section 96. Section 98(1) and (2). Section 100. In section 104(3)(b) the words "authorised by statute for the investment of trust money".
1925 c. 19.	The Trustee Act 1925.	Part I. In section 20(1) the words "whether by fire or otherwise". Sections 21, 23 and 30.
1961 No. 3.	The Clergy Pensions Measure 1961.	Section 32(3).
1962 c. 53.	The House of Commons Members' Fund Act 1962	In section 1, in subsection (2) the words "Subject to the following provisions of this section" and subsections (3) to (5). Section 2(1).
1965 c. 14.	The Cereals Marketing Act 1965.	Section 18(3).
1967 c. 22.	The Agriculture Act 1967.	Section 18(3).

1988 No. 4.	The Church of England (Pensions) Measure 1988.	Section 14(b).
1996 c. 47.	The Trusts of Land and Appointment of Trustees Act 1996.	Section 6(4). Section 9(8). Section 17(1). In Schedule 3, paragraph 3(4).
1999 No. 1.	The Cathedrals Measure 1999.	In section 16(1), the words from "and the powers" to the end of the subsection.

APPENDIX B(1)

CHARITABLE TRUST

TRUST DEED FOR A CHARITABLE TRUST

Drafted by Francesca Quint of Counsel

on behalf of
Charity Law
Association

Approved by
Charity Commission for
England and Wales

CHARITY LAW ASSOCIATION MODEL DOCUMENTS

A charity needs to have its objects and powers and administrative arrangements set out clearly in its governing document. If it does not, it is likely to be less well governed. I am pleased to recommend the use of this model. It incorporates the essential powers and provisions and expresses them in plain English with explanatory notes. It will prove of great assistance to those intending to set up a charitable trust.

RICHARD FRIES
CHIEF CHARITY COMMISSIONER

The first and certainly one of the most important decisions facing individuals who want to establish a new charity is choosing which legal structure will be right for the charity. Although there are quite a few structures to choose from, most charities are established as trusts, companies or associations. The Charity Commission's registration information pack explains the factors to be considered in choosing between them.

The Charity Commission's registration information pack also contains guidance on the objects or purposes which are recognised by law as charitable. Many worthwhile not-for-profit organisations have objects which are not charitable so it is wise to check before you spend time working on this document.

Copies of the Commission's registration information pack are available from its offices at:

St Alban's House	Woodfield House	2nd Floor
57–60 Haymarket	Tangier	20 Kings Parade
London	Taunton	Queens Dock
SW1Y 4QX	Somerset TA1 4BL	Liverpool L3 4DQ
☎ 0207 210 4556	☎ 01823 345 000	☎ 0151 703 1500

The Charity Law Association has also produced model documents for charitable companies and associations. Copies of these models are available in printed and disk format from:

NGO Finance, 1a Tradescant Road, London SW8 1XD
Tel: 0207 793 0001   Fax: 0207 735 2009

DETAILS NEEDED TO COMPLETE THE MODEL

Before you can complete the model you will need to have made decisions on the following matters. It may help you in this process to refer to the appropriate clause (shown in the right-hand column below) and the accompanying notes.

	Clause
1. The Trustees—you will need full names and residential addresses for each of them.	
2. The name of the charity.	2.1
3. The objects or purposes of the charity.	2.2
4. If the charity is to operate in a limited geographical area, a description of that area.	2.2
5. If the charity is to benefit a special class of beneficiaries, a description of that class.	2.2
6. Whether the charity is to be permanently endowed.	2.3
7. Number of Trustees.	4.2
8. Whether any qualification is going to be required for Trustees.	4.2
9. Whether Trustees are to serve for life (or until they retire) or for a fixed period.	4.3
10. If Trustees are to serve for a fixed period:	
What is that period?	4.4
In which order will the First Trustees retire?	4.3
Is there to be any restriction on the number of times a Trustee may be reappointed before taking a break?	4.5
11. Whether any of the Trustees are to be appointed by other bodies or are to serve as Trustees automatically upon holding some other office.	4.3/4
12. The number of consecutive meetings a Trustee may miss before ceasing to hold office.	4.7.3
13. Are the Trustees to have power to remove a Trustee?	4.7.6
14. Minimum number of Trustees' meetings each year.	5.1
15. Quorum at Trustees' meetings.	5.2
16. Title to be given to the Trustee who will chair meetings.	5.4
17. Minimum number of Trustees to serve on committees.	5.7.2
18. Who is to be able to hold the investments and property of the charity?	6.6
19. Is it intended that it should be possible to amend the Trust Deed and if so, what percentage of the Trustees need to approve?	8
20. Is it intended that it should be possible for the charity to be amalgamated? If so, what percentage of the Trustees need to approve?	9
21. Is it intended that it should be possible to dissolve the charity? If so, what percentage of the Trustees need to approve?	10

Trust Deed for a Charitable Trust

USING THIS MODEL

This model is intended for use by individuals wishing to establish a charitable trust in England and Wales. Legal advice will be needed to adapt it for use in Scotland or Northern Ireland.

Every effort has been made to make the model clear and easy to use. However it is a legal document and so considerable care must be taken to ensure that it is completed in a manner which is appropriate for the intended charity. The Charity Law Association cannot accept any responsibility for its use and neither can the author or the Charity Commission. If in doubt, seek help from a charity lawyer!

Whilst it is possible for the model to be adopted by simply completing the gaps in the text we do not recommend it—it is intended that the text of the model (which appears below the headings on the unshaded pages which follow) should be reproduced as a new and a complete document and a disk is available to make this easier. On the inside back cover of this model we have set out the traditional form of cover or front page for a Trust Deed.

The left-hand pages of this document contain notes to assist you to complete the Trust Deed. The notes may also be useful when the new charity has been established, as a guide to the interpretation of the Trust Deed: for this reason we recommend that you retain them.

On the previous page we have included a checklist of all the details that you will need to complete the model. This list shows the clauses where the details are required in case you need to refer to them or to the corresponding notes.

If you are not a lawyer the task of completing the model may at first sight seem daunting but we have included various aids to help you:
- Where a word or phrase needs to be inserted a brief description appears *[in italics in square brackets]*.
- Where there is a suggestion or choice between alternatives it appears [in normal type in square brackets].
- There is an interpretation clause at the end of the document. Words and phrases which are defined or explained there appear **in bold type** when they first occur.

These aids (with the possible exception of the emboldened terms) should not appear in the final Deed. In preparing the Deed you should also remember that:
- If you do not wish to include an optional clause or if you wish to add in new provisions, you will need to adjust the clause numbering accordingly.
- If you decide to redesignate a term (eg changing "Chairman" to "Chair"), you will need to make the change every time the term appears in the document.

There are differing views on the desirability of punctuation in legal documents. The model has been prepared without punctuation but it can, of course, be added.

You may also wish to include a contents page or index for ease of reference.

When you have completed the document and it has been signed by the Trustees and their witnesses you should send it with a cheque or postal order (made payable to "Inland Revenue, Stamp Duty Only") for 50p to South-West Wing, Bush House, Strand, London WC2B 4QD.

After the Trust Deed has been stamped you will be ready to begin the process of registering the charity. The Charity Commission's registration information pack explains this process and contains copies of the forms which you will need to complete.

NOTES

TRUSTEE DETAILS

This model has been designed for the situation in which a group of individuals (the "First Trustees") have collected money or property for the new charity and now wish to record the terms of the charity. Sometimes all the charity's funds will be donated by one person who wishes to be named as the Founder or Settlor. He or she may also wish to control certain aspects of the charity (for example, by having a right to veto amendments to the Trust Deed). This model can be adapted for use in such a situation but we recommend that you see a lawyer for the task.

There should be at least three trustees (see clause 4.2). A majority of the trustees should be resident in England and Wales.

1. **INTRODUCTION**

    This introduction (sometimes called the "recitals") should contain any information necessary for a full understanding of the Trust Deed. The name by which the charity will be known is specified in clause **2.1**. In the Trust Deed it is referred to simply as "the Trust" (see clause **1.1**): if preferred it can be called "the Charity" or some other designation but it is important to be consistent throughout the document.

2. **NAME & OBJECTS**

    This clause is fundamental to the identity and purposes of the charity.

2.1 The charity's name should be chosen with care. It should be consistent with the purposes of the charity. It must not be misleading, eg by misrepresenting the purposes or status of the charity, or cause confusion with other charities. The Charity Commission can require a charity to change its name: see sections 6 and 7 of the Charities Act 1993 and the Charities (Misleading Names) Regulations 1992. Once a name has been chosen it is worth contacting the Commission's Central Register of Charities to see whether a charity has already been registered with the same, or a similar, name.

2.2 The Objects (ie the main purposes) of the charity must be exclusively charitable under English law, or the organisation will not be a charity and registration will therefore be refused. The Objects should clearly and accurately reflect the true purposes of the charity's intended activities. It may be appropriate to refer to a geographical area as the "area of benefit" of the charity and/or to describe the people the charity will benefit as the "beneficiaries" (see clause **11.1**).

    Legal advice may be required to be certain that the Objects are correctly expressed.

2.3 If you delete the words in square brackets the Charity will continue indefinitely because the Trustees will be restricted to spending only the income of the charity—the charity will be known as "permanently endowed". This could limit the effectiveness of the charity and should therefore be considered carefully.

CHARITABLE TRUST DEED

THIS DECLARATION OF TRUST is made _____ *[date]* by the
First Trustees

_____

_____

_____

_____

_____

[Full names and residential addresses of all of the First Trustees.]

WITNESSES AS FOLLOWS

1. INTRODUCTION

1.1 The First Trustees hold _____ *[details]* on the trusts
declared in this Deed ("the **Trust**")

1.2 Further money or property may be paid or transferred to the **Trustees** for the Trust

1.3 _____

_____ [any other explanatory statement]

2. NAME & OBJECTS

2.1 The Name of the Trust is _____ *[Name]*
(or any other name chosen by resolution of the Trustees)

2.2 The objects of the Trust are ———————————————————

_____

_____

_____

_____

[Objects] (the "**Objects**")

2.3 The Trustees must use the income [and may use the capital] of the Trust in promoting the
Objects

NOTES

3.   POWERS

The powers are not themselves charitable objects, but consist of the legal means by which the Objects in clause **2** may be promoted. It must be stressed that the powers cannot be exercised for any other purpose. Thus, any research carried out under clause **3.1**, or advice or information supplied under clauses **3.2** or **3.3**, must be about a subject which is relevant to the Objects. Co-operation under clause **3.4** can only be in respect of a project relevant to the Objects, so the other organisation involved would need to have some concern with the Objects. Any new charity set up or supported under clause **3.5** needs to have the same or similar Objects.

The powers included in this clause are those most commonly required by charities, but if it is known that the charity will be engaged in specific activities which are not mentioned it is advisable to insert additional provisions to cover them.

3.6   The Trustees should have regard to the law applicable to any fundraising activities the charity is to undertake. The prohibition of "taxable trading" (see clause **11.1**) is essential to avoid an objection from the Inland Revenue. Where a charity will be relying on taxable trading to raise funds, it is recommended that a separate, non-charitable trading company should be used for the purpose, and specialist legal or accountancy advice will be needed.

3.7   The restrictions on mortgaging charity land are contained in sections 38 and 39 of the Charities Act 1993. In some cases the Charity Commission's consent is required. In others, a special procedure must be followed. Legal advice may well be required.

3.9   The restrictions on sales, exchanges and leases of charity land are contained in sections 36 and 37 of the Charities Act 1993. In some cases the Commission's consent is required. In others, a special procedure must be followed. Legal advice will normally be required.

3.10   This clause sets out ways in which financial assistance can be given, whether to individual beneficiaries (where the charity is set up to help individuals) or to other bodies. It will be necessary to consider the need for a licence under Consumer Credit legislation if the charity is to make loans to individuals. In setting the amount of any grant or loan or the extent of any guarantee (which is a *contingent* liability) the Trustees must consider the resources of the charity as well as the needs of the recipient.

3.11   This clause enables the Trustees to designate funds for particular purposes, or as reserves. It is prudent for a charity to maintain reserves to cover planned expenditure (eg repairs to buildings) and to meet the kind of expenditure which may be required at short notice, but reserves are not an end in themselves and should not be built up without a deliberate policy decision, or be excessive in relation to the amount known or reasonably estimated to be required.

3.12   This clause is designed to confer a wide power of investment but to ensure that it is exercised responsibly. An "investment" is an asset which (i) is capable of producing income and (ii) may also increase in capital value. In setting an investment policy and selecting investments the Trustees should have regard to the needs of the charity for both income and capital growth, and act prudently. They should avoid trading and speculation.

3.13   The Charity Commission considers that if discretionary powers are to be given to investment managers an express power to delegate the management of investments is required. It must always be accompanied by safeguards, as here.

3.14   Charity property, whether buildings, equipment or other property, should normally be insured up to its full reinstatement value. Depending on the nature of the charity, other kinds of insurance may be necessary or prudent (eg public liability, employers' liability).

CHARITABLE TRUST DEED

3. POWERS

The Trustees have the following powers, which may be exercised only in promoting the Objects:

3.1 To promote or carry out research

3.2 To provide advice

3.3 To publish or distribute information

3.4 To co-operate with other bodies

3.5 To support, administer or set up other charities

3.6 To raise funds (but not by means of **taxable trading**)

3.7 To borrow money and give security for loans (but only in accordance with the restrictions imposed by the Charities Act 1993)

3.8 To acquire or hire property of any kind

3.9 To let or dispose of property of any kind (but only in accordance with the restrictions imposed by the Charities Act 1993)

3.10 To make grants or loans of money and to give guarantees

3.11 To set aside funds for special purposes or as reserves against future expenditure

3.12 To deposit or invest funds in any manner (but to invest only after obtaining advice from a **financial expert** and having regard to the suitability of investments and the need for diversification)

3.13 To delegate the management of investments to a financial expert, but only on terms that:

   3.13.1 the investment policy is recorded **in writing** for the financial expert by the Trustees

   3.13.2 every transaction is reported promptly to the Trustees

   3.13.3 the performance of the investments is reviewed regularly with the Trustees

   3.13.4 the Trustees are entitled to cancel the delegation arrangement at any time

   3.13.5 the investment policy and the delegation arrangement are reviewed at least once a **year**

   3.13.6 all payments due to the financial expert are on a scale or at a level which is agreed in advance and are notified promptly to the Trustees on receipt

   3.13.7 the financial expert must not do anything outside the powers of the Trustees

3.14 To insure the property of the Trust against any foreseeable risk and take out other insurance policies to protect the Trust when required

---

NOTES

3.15 This type of insurance requires a special clause because it provides a benefit to the Trustees as "charity trustees" (see clause **11.1**). It may be helpful where the charity is involved in particular commercial risks, but it does *not* protect the Trustees from liability towards third parties, and they must therefore be sure never to commit the charity to expenditure it cannot afford.

3.17 This clause covers employees, independent contractors and volunteers, and enables salaries and pensions, or fees, or expenses (or none of these) to be provided. All necessary advice about Employment Law should be obtained. A charity should not pay more than a reasonable rate for the task, but should aim to be a good employer. If there will be a significant number of employees it is wise to consider the incorporation of a charitable company (see clause **3.5**). Special care is required if it is proposed to employ a Trustee (see clause **6.3**).

3.18 This clause will be relevant in the increasing number of cases in which charities enter into contracts to provide services to local or health authorities. A charity can only enter into a contract of this kind if the work it will be doing will promote its Objects. It may be wise to consider the incorporation of a charitable company (see clause **3.5**) if the charity will be involved in significant contractual commitments.

3.19 This "blanket provision" is intended to cover any other power not expressly mentioned. It is still restricted to promoting the Objects.

4.   THE TRUSTEES

This clause sets out the composition of the charity's governing body, ie the charity trustees (see clauses **4.1** and **11.1**). In this Deed they are called the "Trustees" but they could equally well be called the "Governors" or some other term.

4.2 The minimum number of trustees should be at least three. In some cases it is appropriate for the Trustees to have special qualifications, eg residence in the area of benefit or membership of a particular religion. (See also the optional clause **4.7.5**.)

4.3 It may be considered best for the First Trustees to be appointed for life (in which case use the first option in clause **4.3**), or it may be preferred to provide for fixed terms of office. If it is intended that Trustees will serve for a fixed term of office it will be necessary to select the second option in clause **4.3** and to include the chosen period in clause **4.4**. With fixed terms it is wise (for the sake of continuity) to ensure that the First Trustees do not all retire together and so in clause **4.3** you should stagger their retirements. For example if trustees are to serve for 4 years you should ensure that by year 4 they have all retired (they can of course be reappointed at the end of their term of office, but on this subject see clause **4.5**).

It is sometimes desirable for some of the Trustees to be appointed by outside bodies (such as local authorities, other charities in the same field of work or the same area of benefit) or to be *ex officio* trustees, ie to hold office automatically on holding some other office (such as the minister of a particular place of worship). In this situation you will need a bespoke amendment to the model for which you may need legal advice. Every Trustee, however appointed, is a charity trustee, and owes a duty towards the charity rather than to the person or body who makes the appointment. There should therefore be no power for the appointing body to remove the person appointed.

4.4 This clause provides for new Trustees to be appointed by resolution of the other Trustees. A memorandum as required by section 83 of the Charities Act 1993 should be provided as evidence of each such appointment, and, if the property of the charity includes any land vested in the Trustees individually, the memorandum should be executed as a deed in order to pass the legal estate: section 83(2).

CHARITABLE TRUST DEED

3.15 To insure the Trustees against the costs of a successful defence to a criminal prosecution brought against them as **charity trustees** or against personal liability incurred in respect of any act or omission which is or is alleged to be a breach of trust or breach of duty (unless the Trustee concerned knew that, or was reckless whether, the act or omission was a breach of trust or breach of duty)

3.16 To pay reasonable fees to any nominee or **holding trustee**

3.17 Subject to clause 6.3 to employ paid or unpaid agents, staff or advisers

3.18 To enter into contracts to provide services to or on behalf of other bodies

3.19 To pay the costs of forming the Trust

3.20 To do anything else within the law which promotes or helps to promote the Objects

4. THE TRUSTEES

4.1 The Trustees as the charity trustees have control of the Trust and its property and funds

4.2 The full number of Trustees is _____ *[number]* individuals _____
    _____ *[add special qualification if any is to be required]*

4.3 Subject to clause 4.7 the First Trustees are entitled to hold office for life

OR

Subject to clause 4.7 the First Trustees shall each hold office for the following periods:

_____ *[Trustee's name]* _____ *[No. of]* years

_____ *[Trustee's name]* _____ *[No. of]* years

_____ *[Trustee's name]* _____ *[No. of]* years

_____ *[Trustee's name]* _____ *[No. of]* years

4.4 Future Trustees must be appointed [for terms of office of _____ *[number]* years] by resolution of the Trustees

NOTES

4.5 This clause will only be necessary if there are to be fixed periods of office for the Trustees (ie you have chosen the second option in clause **4.3**). The words in the square brackets beginning "but a Trustee . . ." should be retained if it is intended that Trustees should take a break after serving for a number of terms of office. This can be a useful way of ensuring that the charity benefits from the introduction of "fresh blood".

4.6 This provision is important: it is designed to ensure as far as possible that everyone who takes on the task of being a Trustee of the charity is aware of the legal responsibilities it entails.

4.7 Various events can terminate trusteeship.

    4.7.1 Disqualification occurs under section 72 of the Charities Act 1993 if a Trustee is involuntarily removed by the Court or the Charity Commission, in the event of bankruptcy or the like, where the Trustee is disqualified under the Company Directors Disqualification Act or the Insolvency Act, and where the Trustee has been convicted of an offence involving dishonesty.

    4.7.2 Embarrassing problems can arise when a trustee becomes too ill or infirm to be expected to take full responsibility for the task. The Trustees may wish to make a rule under clause **5.7.3** to require a Trustee who appears incapable to undergo a medical examination. Such a request would in most cases lead to a voluntary resignation.

    4.7.3 The period of absence which gives rise to automatic termination of Trusteeship will depend on the normal frequency of meetings.

    4.7.4 The law does not permit Trustees to walk away from their responsibilities leaving no-one in charge of the charity.

    4.7.5 This sub-clause can be deleted if no special qualification for trusteeship is included in clause **4.2**.

    4.7.6 This may be a wise precaution, especially if Trustees will otherwise hold office for life or for lengthy terms, but any resolution to remove a Trustee must be justifiable. Others may feel that such a provision undermines the independence of the Trustees. A memorandum under section 83 of the Charities Act 1993 is again required (see note to clause **4.4**).

4.8 This clause acts as a reminder of the general rule that trustees are entitled to recover from the charity whatever funds they may be obliged to pay out as a consequence of running the charity, eg paying for goods or services ordered by them and supplied to the charity. Of course the indemnity is of no value if the charity does not have the funds to meet it.

4.9 Occasionally a mistake occurs in appointment procedures. If a mistake of this kind is discovered, it does not retrospectively invalidate previous decisions but should be put right before further decisions are taken.

5. PROCEEDINGS OF TRUSTEES

This clause deals with the meetings and proceedings of the Trustees.

5.1 The number of meetings per year will depend on (a) the nature of the charity's activities and (b) the extent to which work is delegated to sub-committees. Two is normally a minimum.

5. The quorum should normally be fixed at (at least) one more than the number nearest one-third of the full number of the Trustees.

5.3 Many charities do not have provision for a telephone conference. It is not necessary to include it unless difficulty in arranging meetings in person is expected (eg where the Trustees are geographically scattered). If the provision is included, it should be borne in mind that (i) a

CHARITABLE TRUST DEED

[4.5   A retiring Trustee who is competent to act may be re-appointed at the end of his/her term of office [but a Trustee shall not be eligible for re-appointment until _____ *[period]* after the end of _____ *[number]* consecutive terms of office]

4.6   Every future Trustee must sign a declaration of willingness to act as a Trustee of the Trust before he or she is eligible to vote at any meeting of the Trustees

4.7   A Trustee automatically ceases to be a Trustee if he or she:

    4.7.1   is disqualified under the Charities Act 1993 from acting as a charity trustee or trustee for a charity

    4.7.2   is incapable, whether mentally or physically, of managing his or her own affairs

    4.7.3   is absent from _____ *[number]* consecutive meetings of the Trustees

    4.7.4   resigns by **written** notice to the Trustees (but only if at least two Trustees will remain in office)

    [4.7.5   ceases to be _____ *[specially qualified]*]

    [4.7.6   is removed by a resolution passed by all the other Trustees after inviting the views of the Trustee concerned and considering the matter in the light of any such views]

4.8   A retiring Trustee is entitled to an indemnity from the continuing Trustees at the expense of the Trust in respect of any liabilities properly incurred during his or her trusteeship

4.9   A technical defect in the appointment of a Trustee of which the Trustees are unaware at the time does not invalidate decisions taken by the Trustees

5.   PROCEEDINGS OF TRUSTEES

5.1   The Trustees must hold at least _____ *[number]* meetings each year

5.2   A quorum at a meeting is _____ *[number]* Trustees

[5.3   A meeting may be held either in person or by suitable electronic means agreed by the Trustees in which all participants may communicate with all the other participants]

NOTES

conference call is not the same as a series of separate telephone calls, which do *not* amount to a meeting; and (ii) the same rules about notice of meetings, the quorum, chairmanship, voting, minutes etc apply to a telephone conference as to a meeting in person.

5.4   There is no need for the chairman of their meetings to be called the "Chairman" if some other term, such as "chair" or "chairperson" is preferred.

5.5   An alternative to a decision taken at a meeting is a written resolution, but this will not be valid unless signed by *all* the Trustees.

5.6   It is normal for a casting vote to be given in favour of the *status quo*, to enable further debate to take place on a future occasion.

5.7   This clause sets out the Trustees' powers in the detailed running of the charity.

    5.7.1   An honorary Treasurer, or Finance Officer, is essential. There may be an honorary Secretary, although it is often more convenient for the Secretary's role to be undertaken by a paid employee. There may be other specific offices, which may alter from year to year according to the charity's activities.

    5.7.2   A specific provision is essential if the Trustees are to be able to delegate to committees. The Trustees will be legally responsible for the committee's acts, and for this reason it is prudent for at least one Trustee to be a member of each committee. The Trustee should, for this reason, define the terms of reference with care. It is essential in all cases to provide for reporting back, and this may have to be in writing (see clause 7.2.2). Although the power to delegate is not limited to particular functions it is usually appropriate for final decisions on major matters of policy to be reserved to the Trustees themselves.

    5.7.3 &   These clauses allow the Trustees to make rules of various kinds to govern different
    5.7.4   different aspects of the running of the charity. There is no need to call them "rules" and "regulations": they can all be called "rules" if preferred.

        You will need to retain the words in one (but not both) of the square brackets in clause 5.7.4. If the charity is to be permanently endowed (see clause 2.3) retain "income", otherwise retain "property and funds".

6.   PROPERTY & FUNDS

This clause reflects the legal position that the property of a charitable trust is held *on trust for the Objects* rather than belonging to Trustees in a private capacity.

6.1   These sub-clauses reflect the legal principle that trustees must not benefit from their trust
&   except so far as expressly permitted by the trust. They prevent a Trustee from being either
6.2   an employee (or other paid worker) or a beneficiary of the charity, although a limited amount of work paid by fees is allowed subject to procedural safeguards in clause 6.3.

In some cases circumstances may require further exceptions to be added to provide for a limited number of employee-Trustees or beneficiary-Trustees to receive benefits, but this will necessitate additional safeguards to protect the charity, and legal advice should be obtained.

CHARITABLE TRUST DEED

5.4 The [**Chairman**] of the Trustees or (if the Chairman is unable or unwilling to do so) some other Trustee chosen by them presides at each meeting

5.5 Except where otherwise provided in this Deed, every issue may be determined by a simple majority of the votes cast at a meeting of the Trustees but a resolution which is in writing and signed by all the Trustees is as valid as a resolution passed at a meeting and for this purpose the resolution may be contained in more than one document and will be treated as passed on the date of the last signature

5.6 Except for the chairman of the meeting, who has a second or casting vote, every Trustee has one vote on each issue

5.7 The Trustees have the following powers in the administration of the Trust:

5.7.1 to appoint a Chairman, Treasurer and other honorary officers

5.7.2 to delegate any of their functions to committees consisting of two or more persons appointed by them [(but at least _____ *[number]* member(s) of every committee must be a Trustee)] and all proceedings of committees must be reported promptly to the Trustees

5.7.3 to make rules consistent with this Deed to govern proceedings at their meetings and at meetings of committees

5.7.4 to make regulations consistent with this Deed to govern the use and application of the [income] [property and funds] of the Trust including regulations about the operation of bank accounts and the commitment of funds

6. PROPERTY & FUNDS

6.1 Any Trustee who possesses specialist skills or knowledge, and any firm or company of which such a Trustee is a member or employee, may charge and be paid reasonable fees for work carried out for the Trust on the instructions of the other Trustees (but only if the procedure prescribed by clause 6.3 is followed in selecting the Trustee, firm or company and setting the amount of the fees and provided that this provision may not apply to more than one half of the Trustees in any one financial year)

6.2 No Trustee may receive from the Trust any payment of money or other **material benefit** (whether direct or indirect) except

6.2.1 under clauses 3.15 (indemnity insurance) and 6.1 (fees)

6.2.2 reimbursement of reasonable out-of-pocket expenses (including hotel and travel costs) actually incurred in the administration of the Trust

6.2.3 interest at a reasonable rate on money lent to the Trust

6.2.4 a reasonable rent or hiring fee for property let or hired to the Trust

6.2.5 an indemnity in respect of any liabilities incurred in or about the administration of the Trust (including the costs of a successful defence to criminal proceedings)

NOTES

6.5 It is important that the Trustees should have sufficient control of the charity's property, and this clause sets out various alternatives for holding title to it. The charity is not a legal person and cannot therefore hold legal title to property or investments in its own name. Incorporation of the trustee body by certificate of the Charity Commission under sections 50 to 62 of the Charities Act 1993 (which will be granted on application by the charity trustees if the Commission consider that it is in the charity's interests) is convenient for many charities but should not be confused with incorporation of a limited company under the Companies Acts. "Trust corporation" in clause **6.5.3** is a technical legal term and "holding trustee" is defined in clause **11.1**.

7. **RECORDS & ACCOUNTS**

7.1 & The keeping of adequate records is essential if a charity is to be properly run. In
7.2 addition, there is detailed legislation in sections 41 to 49 of the Charities Act 1993 and the regulations made under it, as well as guidance in the Charity SORP, about accountability. The rules cover accounting records, the audit or independent examination of accounts (see clause **11.1**) and the provision of an annual report, statement of account and annual return, all of which have to be sent to the Charity Commission.

7.3 This provision is designed to ensure that the Trustees have access to the financial records as well as the published report and statements of account.

CHARITABLE TRUST DEED

6.2.6 in exceptional cases, other payments or benefits (but only with the written approval of the **Commission** in advance)

6.3 Whenever a Trustee has a personal interest in a matter to be discussed at a meeting of the Trustees or any committee, the Trustee concerned must:

6.3.1 declare an interest before discussion on the matter begins

6.3.2 withdraw from the meeting for that item unless expressly invited to remain in order to provide information

6.3.3 not be counted in the quorum during that part of the meeting

6.3.4 withdraw during the vote and have no vote on the matter

6.4 Funds which are not required for immediate use or which will be required for use at a future date must be placed on deposit or invested in accordance with clause 3.12 until needed

6.5 Investments and other property of the Trust may be held:

6.5.1 in the names of the Trustees (or in the name of the trustee body if incorporated under the Charities Act 1993)

6.5.2 in the name of a nominee (being a corporate body registered or having an established place of business in England and Wales) under the control of the Trustees or of a financial expert acting on their instructions

6.5.3 in the name of a **trust corporation** as a holding trustee for the Trust which must be appointed (and may be removed) by deed executed by the Trustees

6.5.4 in the case of land, by the Official Custodian for Charities under an order of the Commission or the Court

7. RECORDS & ACCOUNTS

7.1 The Trustees must comply with the requirements of the Charities Act 1993 relating to the keeping of financial records, the audit or independent examination of the accounts and the preparation and transmission to the Commission of:

7.1.1 annual reports

7.1.2 annual returns

7.1.3 annual statements of account

7.2 The Trustees must maintain proper records of:

7.2.1 all proceedings at meetings of the Trustees

7.2.2 all reports of committees

7.2.3 all professional advice obtained

7.3 Financial records, annual reports and statements of account relating to the Trust must be available for inspection by any Trustee

NOTES

7.4   This sub-clause reflects section 47(2) of the Charities Act 1993, which requires a charity to provide a copy of the latest statement of account to anyone who asks for it in writing and pays a reasonable fee to cover the charity's costs, within two months.

8.   AMENDMENTS

Amendments to the Trust Deed may well be needed as the charity develops. The Deed will be incapable of amendment, except by a scheme of the Charity Commission, if a specific power to amend it is not included. Unless it is intended that the charity should be permanently endowed it is usual to include such a power. It is usual to require more than a simple majority of the Trustees to vote in favour.

It is of the utmost importance that the Deed should not be amended in a way which makes it impossible for the charity to continue to operate. Therefore it is provided that certain amendments are not valid, ie if adopted they will not count as amendments and will not be registered by the Commission. The two cases are (i) where there is a fundamental change in the Objects, ie where the new purposes are of a kind which a previous supporter could not reasonably be expected to have foreseen when contributing to the charity's funds (see clause **11.1**), and (ii) where the change in the Constitution would cause the charity to become a non-charitable body. In addition, where it is proposed to alter the provisions concerning benefits to Trustees (clauses **6.2** and **6.3**) the Commission's consent will be needed in advance.

Any amendment (even one which does not appear to affect the Objects) will have to be considered from the point of view of both charitable status and workability. It will normally be appropriate to seek legal advice or consult the Commission before the proposed amendments are drawn up. The Commission should be notified promptly of all amendments that are made.

9.   AMALGAMATION

This clause is not an essential provision, but it may be useful if, as the charity develops, it is found to be duplicating work done by another charity or to have a considerable overlap with another charity's work. It enables the charity's property to be passed to another charity with similar Objects. Legal advice will probably be needed to deal with the matters referred to in clause **9.2**. An alternative is for the other charity's assets to be passed over to this charity, but that procedure does not require a specific provision in the trusts of the recipient charity.

10.   DISSOLUTION

This is another optional provision, which again is inappropriate in some cases. If it is not included, the charity will remain in existence as long as it has any funds, and if the capital cannot legally be spent it will remain in existence indefinitely.

Where a dissolution provision is included, and the Trustees decide to dissolve the charity, the debts and liabilities (including for example staff pensions) must first be provided for. There may be assets remaining. Those assets must be used for furthering the Objects or for charitable purposes which are within or similar to the Objects, and this clause sets out various alternatives. The Trustees will not be relieved of their responsibilities as charity trustees until they have completed their task, and sent in a final report and statement of account to the Charity Commission. The Commission will then remove the charity from the register of charities.

CHARITABLE TRUST DEED

7.4 A copy of the latest available statement of account must be supplied to any person who makes a written request and pays the Trustees' reasonable costs (as required by the Charities Act 1993)

[8.   AMENDMENTS

This Deed may be amended by supplemental deed on a resolution passed by _____ *[percentage]* of the Trustees but no amendment is valid if it would make a **fundamental change** to the Objects or to this clause or destroy the charitable status of the Trust. No amendment may be made to clauses 6.2, 6.3 or 6.4 without the prior written consent of the Commission]

[9.   AMALGAMATION

9.1 The Trustees may at any time on a resolution passed by at least _____ *[percentage]* of the Trustees transfer the assets and liabilities of the Trust to another charity established for exclusively charitable purposes within, the same as or similar to the Objects _____ _____ *[add any special qualification]*

9.2 On a transfer under clause 9.1 the Trustees must ensure that all necessary steps are taken as to:

9.2.1 the transfer of land and other property

9.2.2 the novation of contracts of employment and the transfer of any pension rights

9.2.3 the trusteeship of any property held for special purposes]

[10. DISSOLUTION

10.1 The Trustees may at any time decide by resolution passed by at least _____ *[percentage]* of the Trustees that the Trust is to be dissolved. The Trustees will then be responsible for the orderly winding up of the Trust's affairs

10.2 After making provision for all outstanding liabilities of the Trust, the Trustees must apply the remaining property and funds in one or more of the following ways:

10.2.1 by transfer to one or more other bodies established for exclusively charitable purposes within, the same as or similar to the Objects

10.2.2 directly for the Objects or charitable purposes within or similar to the Objects

10.2.3 in such other manner consistent with charitable status as the Commission approve in writing in advance

NOTES

11. INTERPRETATION

This clause is an aid to the interpretation of the Deed. Clause **11.1** defines a number of terms used in it.

The statutory definitions referred to are:

"charity trustees" (section 97(1) of the Charities Act 1993) are "the persons having the general control and management of the administration of a charity"

an "independent examiner" (section 43(3)(a) of the Charities Act 1993) is "an independent person who is reasonably believed by the Trustees to have the requisite ability and practical experience to carry out a competent examination of the accounts". An independent examination of the accounts is sufficient where the annual income or expenditure in either of the two previous financial years was no more than £250,000. Above that figure a professional audit is required.

"trust corporation" (see section 205(1)(xxviii) of the Law of Property Act 1925, and section 35 of the Charities Act 1993) means a corporate body either (i) appointed by order of the court or the Charity Commission in a particular case to be a trustee or (ii) authorised under rules made under section 4(3) of the Public Trustee Act 1906 to act as custodian trustee or (iii) having the certificate of the Lord Chancellor. The Public Trustee, though a trust corporation, is not permitted to act in relation to charities.

11.2 This sub-clause should avoid the need to amend the Deed merely to reflect technical changes in the law.

CHARITABLE TRUST DEED

10.3 A final report and statement of account relating to the Trust must be sent to the Commission]

11. **INTERPRETATION**

In this Deed

11.1 The following expressions have the following meanings:

["area of benefit" means _____ *[geographical area]*]

["beneficiaries" means _____ *[qualifications of beneficiaries]*]

"the Chairman" means the person appointed by the Trustees to preside at their meetings

"charity trustees" has the meaning prescribed by section 97(1) of the Charities Act 1993

"the Commission" means the Charity Commissioners for England and Wales

"financial expert" means an individual, company or firm who is an authorised person or an exempted person within the meaning of the Financial Services Act 1986

["fundamental change" means such a change as would not have been within the reasonable contemplation of a person making a donation to the Trust]

"holding trustee" means an individual or corporate body responsible for holding the title to property but not authorised to make any decisions relating to its use, investment or disposal

"independent examiner" has the meaning prescribed by section 43(3)(a) of the Charities Act 1993

"material benefit" means a benefit which may not be financial but has a monetary value

"the Objects" means the charitable objects of the Trust set out in clause 2

"taxable trading" means carrying on a trade or business on a continuing basis for the principal purpose of raising funds and not for the purpose of actually carrying out the Objects and the profits of which are liable to tax

"the Trust" means the charity created by this Deed

"trust corporation" has the meaning prescribed by section 205(1)(xxviii) of the Law of Property Act 1925 but does not include the Public Trustee

"Trustee" means a charity trustee of the Trust

"written" or "in writing" refers to a legible document on paper [not] including a fax message

"year" means calendar year

11.2 References to an Act of Parliament are references to the Acts as amended or re-enacted from time to time and to any subordinate legislation made under it

IN WITNESS of the above the parties have executed this Deed

SIGNED AS A DEED BY

_____   _____

[Name of Trustee]   *[Signature of Trustee]*
in the presence of:

_____   _____

_____   _____

_____   _____

[Name, address and occupation of witness]   *[Signature of Witness]*

SIGNED AS A DEED BY

_____   _____

[Name of Trustee]   *[Signature of Trustee]*
in the presence of:

_____   _____

_____   _____

_____   _____

[Name, address and occupation of witness]   *[Signature of Witness]*

SIGNED AS A DEED BY

_____   _____

[Name of Trustee]   *[Signature of Trustee]*
in the presence of:

_____   _____

_____   _____

_____   _____

[Name, address and occupation of witness]   *[Signature of Witness]*

[Repeat for each of the Trustees]

DATED   **200**

DECLARATION OF TRUST

constituting

[name of charity]

Model front page for a Trust Deed

First published July 1997
© Charity Law Association 1997

A catalogue record for this document is available from the British Library.

ISBN 0 9521604 2 0

Designed by Rachel Fletcher and published by Plaza Publishing

PRODUCED BY PLAZA,
PUBLISHERS OF *NGO FINANCE*
1A TRADESCANT ROAD, LONDON SW8 1XD
TEL: 0207 793 0001   FAX: 0207 735 2009

NGO Finance magazine

APPENDIX B(2)

CHARITABLE ASSOCIATION

CONSTITUTION FOR A CHARITABLE UNINCORPORATED ASSOCIATION

Drafted by Francesca Quint of Counsel

on behalf of
Charity
Law Association

Approved by
Charity Commission
for England and Wales

CHARITY LAW ASSOCIATION MODEL DOCUMENTS

A charity needs to have its objects and powers and administrative arrangements set out clearly in its governing document. If it does not, it is likely to be less well governed. I am pleased to recommend the use of this model. It incorporates the essential powers and provisions and expresses them in plain English with explanatory notes. It will prove of great assistance to those intending to set up a charitable trust.

RICHARD FRIES
CHIEF CHARITY COMMISSIONER

The first and certainly one of the most important decisions facing individuals who want to establish a new charity is choosing which legal structure will be right for the charity. Although there are quite a few structures to choose from, most charities are established as trusts, companies or associations. The Charity Commission's registration information pack explains the factors to be considered in choosing between them.

The Charity Commission's registration information pack also contains guidance on the objects or purposes which are recognised by law as charitable. Many worthwhile not-for-profit organisations have objects which are not charitable so it is wise to check before you spend time working on this document.

Copies of the Commission's registration information pack are available from its offices at:

St Alban's House	Woodfield House	2nd Floor
57–60 Haymarket	Tangier	20 Kings Parade
London	Taunton	Queens Dock
SW1Y 4QX	Somerset TA1 4BL	Liverpool L3 4DQ
☎ 0207 210 4556	☎ 01823 345 000	☎ 0151 703 1500

The Charity Law Association has also produced model documents for charitable trusts and companies. Copies of these models are available in printed and disk format from:

NGO Finance, 1a Tradescant Road, London SW8 1XD
Tel: 0207 793 0001   Fax: 0207 735 2009

DETAILS NEEDED TO COMPLETE THE MODEL

Before you can complete the model you will need to have made decisions on the following matters. It may help you in this process to refer to the appropriate clause (shown in the right-hand column below) and the accompanying notes.

		Clause
1.	The name of the charity.	1
2.	The objects or purposes of the charity.	2
3.	If the charity is to operate in a limited geographical area, a description of that area.	2
4.	If the charity is to benefit a specified class of beneficiaries, a description of that class.	2
5.	Whether the charity is to have members who are organisations (who attend and vote at meetings through an authorised representative).	4.1
6.	Period of notice for general meetings.	5.2
7.	Quorum for general meetings.	5.3
8.	Title to be given to the individual who will chair the meetings.	5.4
9.	Number of members required to demand an EGM.	5.9
10.	Total number of members of the Committee.	6.2
11.	Number of members of the Committee to be elected at the AGM.	6.2.2
12.	Whether any members of the Committee are to be nominated by other bodies and if so the names of those bodies, the number of members of the Committee they may appoint and the term of office of nominated Committee members.	6.2.3
13.	Number of co-opted members of the Committee.	6.2.4
14.	The number of consecutive meetings a Committee member may miss before ceasing to hold office.	6.5.3
15.	Whether the Committee is to have power to remove a member of the Committee.	6.5.6
16.	Minimum number of Committee meetings each year.	7.1
17.	Quorum at Committee meetings.	7.2
18.	Methods of giving notice to members of the charity.	11
19.	Percentage of the members to approve amendments to the Constitution.	12
20.	Whether it is to be possible for the Committee and/or the charity to be incorporated.	13

Constitution for a charitable
unincorporated association

USING THIS MODEL

This model is intended for use by individuals wishing to establish a charitable association in England and Wales. Legal advice will be needed to adapt it for use in Scotland or Northern Ireland.

Every effort has been made to make the model clear and easy to use. However it is a legal document and so considerable care must be taken to ensure that it is completed in a manner which is appropriate for the intended charity. The Charity Law Association cannot accept any responsibility for its use and neither can the author or the Charity Commission. If in doubt, seek help from a charity lawyer!

Whilst it is possible for the Constitution to be adopted by simply completing the gaps in the text we do not recommend it—it is intended that the text of the model (which appears below the headings on the unshaded pages which follow) should be reproduced as a new and a complete document and a disk is available to make this easier.

The left-hand pages of this document contain notes to assist you to complete the Constitution. The notes may also be useful when the new charity has been established, as a guide to the interpretation of the Constitution: for this reason we recommend that you retain them.

On the previous page we have included a checklist of all the details that you will need to complete the model. This list shows the clauses where the details are required in case you need to refer to them or to the corresponding notes.

If you are not a lawyer the task of completing the model may at first sight seem daunting but we have included various aids to help you:
- Where a word or phrase needs to be inserted a brief description appears *[in italics in square brackets]*.
- Where there is a suggestion or choice between alternatives it appears [in normal type in square brackets].
- There is an interpretation clause at the end of the document. Words and phrases which are defined or explained there appear **in bold type** when they first occur.

These aids (with the possible exception of the emboldened terms) should not appear in the final document. In preparing the Constitution you should also remember that:
- If you do not wish to include an optional clause or if you wish to add in new provisions, you will need to adjust the clause numbering accordingly.
- If you decide to redesignate a term (eg changing "Chairman" to "Chair"), you will need to make the change every time the term appears in the document.

There are differing views on the desirability of punctuation in legal documents. The model has been prepared without punctuation but it can, of course, be added.

You may also wish to include a contents page or index for ease of reference.

When you have completed the document and it has been adopted by the association you will be ready to begin the process of registering the charity. The Charity Commission's registration information pack explains this process and contains copies of the forms which you will need to complete.

NOTES

1. **NAME**

    The name and objects of the charity are fundamental to its identity and purposes.

    The charity's name should be chosen with care. It should be consistent with the purposes of the charity. It must not be misleading, eg by misrepresenting the purposes or status of the charity, or cause confusion with other charities. The Charity Commission can require a charity to change its name: see sections 6 and 7 of the Charities Act 1993 and the Charities (Misleading Names) Regulations 1992. Once a name has been chosen it is worth contacting the Commission's Central Register of Charities to see whether a charity has already been registered with the same, or a similar, name. The charity need not be called "the Association": if preferred it can be called "the Charity", "the Society", "the Friends" or whatever other designation is preferred, but it is important to be consistent throughout the document.

2. **OBJECTS**

    The Objects (ie the main purposes) of the charity must be exclusively charitable under English law, or the association will not be a charity and registration will therefore be refused. The Objects should clearly and accurately reflect the true purposes of the charity's intended activities. It may be appropriate to refer to a geographical area as the "area of benefit" of the charity and/or to describe the people the charity will benefit as the "beneficiaries" (see clause **15.1**).

    Legal advice may be required to be certain that the Objects are correctly expressed.

3. **POWERS**

    The powers are not themselves charitable objects, but consist of the legal means by which the Objects in clause **2** may be promoted. It must be stressed that the powers can not be exercised for any other purpose. Thus, any research carried out under **3.1**, or advice or information supplied under **3.2** or **3.3**, must be about a subject which is relevant to the Objects. Under **3.4** the charity can only co-operate in a project relevant to the Objects, so the other organisation involved must also have some concern with the Objects. Any new charity set up or supported under **3.5** needs to have the same or similar objects.

    The powers included in this clause are those most commonly used by charities, but if it is known that the charity will be engaged in specific activities which are not mentioned it is advisable to insert additional provisions to cover them.

CONSTITUTION FOR A CHARITABLE UNINCORPORATED ASSOCIATION

1. **NAME**

   The name of the Association is

   _____ *[Name]* (["the Association"])

2. **OBJECTS**

   The objects of the Association are _____

   _____

   _____

   _____

   _____

   _____ *[Objects]* ("the Objects")

3. **POWERS**

   The Association has the following powers, which may be exercised only in promoting the Objects:

   3.1   To promote or carry out research

   3.2   To provide advice

   3.3   To publish or distribute information

   3.4   To co-operate with other bodies

   3.5   To support, administer or set up other charities

NOTES

3.6   The Committee should have regard to the law applicable to any fundraising activities the charity is to undertake. The prohibition of "taxable trading" (see clause **15.1**) is essential to avoid an objection from the Inland Revenue. Where a charity will be relying on taxable trading to raise funds it is recommended that a separate, non-charitable trading company should be used for the purpose, and specialist legal or accountancy advice will be needed.

3.7   The restrictions on mortgaging charity land are contained in sections 38 and 39 of the Charities Act 1993. In some cases the Charity Commission's consent is required. In others, a special procedure must be followed. Legal advice may well be required.

3.9   The restrictions on sales, exchanges and leases of charity land are contained in sections 36 and 37 of the Charities Act 1993. In some cases the Commission's consent is required. In others, a special procedure must be followed. Legal advice will normally be required.

3.10   This clause sets out ways in which financial assistance can be given, whether to beneficiaries (where the charity is set up to help individuals) or to other bodies. It will be necessary to consider the need for a licence under Consumer Credit legislation if the charity is to make loans to individuals. In setting the amount of any grant or loan or the extent of any guarantee (which is a *contingent* liability) the Committee must consider the resources of the charity as well as the needs of the recipient charity.

3.11   This clause enables the Committee to designate funds for particular purposes, or as reserves. It is prudent for a charity to maintain reserves to cover planned expenditure (eg repairs to buildings) and to meet the kind of expenditure which may be required at short notice, but reserves are not an end in themselves and should not be built up without a deliberate policy decision, or be excessive in relation to the amount known or reasonably estimated to be required.

3.12   This clause is designed to confer a wide power of investment but to ensure that it is exercised responsibly. An "investment" is an asset which (i) is capable of producing income and (ii) may also increase in capital value. In setting an investment policy and selecting investments the Committee should have regard to the needs of the charity for both income and capital growth, and act prudently. They should avoid trading and speculation.

3.13   The Commission consider that if discretionary powers are to be given to investment managers an express power to delegate the management of investments is required. It should always be accompanied by safeguards, as here.

3.14   Charity property, whether buildings, equipment or other property, should normally be insured up to its full reinstatement value. Depending on the nature of the charity, other kinds of insurance may be necessary or prudent (eg public liability, employer's liability).

3.15   This type of insurance requires a special clause because it provides a benefit to the Committee as "charity trustees" (see clause **15.1**). It may be helpful where the charity is involved in particular commercial risks, but it does *not* protect the Committee from liability towards third parties, and the Committee must therefore be sure never to commit the charity to expenditure it cannot afford.

3.16   This clause covers employees, independent contractors and volunteers, and enables salaries and pensions, or fees, or expenses (or none of these) to be provided. All necessary advice about Employment Law should be obtained. A charity should not pay more than a reasonable rate for the task, but should aim to be a good employer. If there will be a significant number of employees it is wise to consider incorporation as a charitable company (see clause **13.2**). Special care is required if it is proposed to employ a Committee member (see clause **9.2**).

910

CONSTITUTION FOR A CHARITABLE UNINCORPORATED ASSOCIATION

3.6 To raise funds (but not by means of **taxable trading**)

3.7 To borrow money and give security for loans (but only in accordance with the restrictions imposed by the Charities Act 1993)

3.8 To acquire or hire property of any kind

3.9 To let or dispose of property of any kind (but only in accordance with the restrictions imposed by the Charities Act 1993)

3.10 To make grants or loans of money and to give guarantees

3.11 To set aside funds for special purposes or as reserves against future expenditure

3.12 To deposit or invest funds in any lawful manner (but to invest only after obtaining advice from a **financial expert** and having regard to the suitability of investments and the need for diversification)

3.13 To delegate the management of investments to a financial expert, but only on terms that:

    3.13.1 the investment policy is recorded **in writing** for the financial expert by the **Committee**

    3.13.2 every transaction is reported promptly to the Committee

    3.13.3 the performance of the investments is reviewed regularly with the Committee

    3.13.4 the Committee are entitled to cancel the delegation arrangement at any time

    3.13.5 the investment policy and the delegation arrangement are reviewed at least once a **year**

    3.13.6 all payments due to the financial expert are on a scale or at a level which is agreed in advance and are reported promptly to the Committee on receipt

    3.13.7 the financial expert must not do anything outside the powers of the Committee

3.14 To insure the Association's property against any foreseeable risk and take out other insurance policies to protect the Association where required

3.15 To insure members of the Committee against the costs of a successful defence to a criminal prosecution brought against them as charity trustees or against personal liability incurred in respect of any act or omission which is or is alleged to be a breach of trust or breach of duty (unless the member concerned knew that, or was reckless whether, the act or omission was a breach of trust or breach of duty)

3.16 Subject to clause 9.2, to employ paid or unpaid agents, staff or advisers

NOTES

3.17   This clause will be relevant in the increasing number of cases in which charities enter into contracts to provide services to local or health authorities. A charity can only enter into a contract of this kind if the work it will be doing will promote its Objects. It may be wise to consider incorporation as a charitable company (see clause **13.2**) if the charity will be involved in significant contractual commitments.

3.19   This "blanket provision" is intended to cover any other power not expressly mentioned. It is still restricted to promoting the Objects.

4.   **MEMBERSHIP**

    Members are essential to an unincorporated association: it cannot function without them.

4.1   This clause provides for an "open" membership. Open membership is essential if the members are to receive benefits, and do not simply join to support the charity. Some charitable unincorporated associations confine membership to individuals, and do not therefore provide for member organisations.

4.2   Apart from "individual" and "corporate" members, it may be considered helpful to provide for eg associate, junior or honorary members with different rates of subscription and voting rights.

4.3   In practice it is often difficult to find out whether a person is or is not a member (and entitled to vote). A register of members' names and addresses enables this to be checked. If the register is kept on computer, Data Protection legislation may apply.

4.6   It is uncommon for a member of a charity to be removed from membership, but if this happens it must only be done for a good reason. Under the rules of Natural Justice, the member concerned must be given an opportunity of stating his or her case before a final decision is taken, and any decision to remove a member must be justifiable.

5.   **GENERAL MEETINGS**

    A general meeting is a formal gathering of the members.

5.1   This clause states who has a right to attend and vote at general meetings, ie individual members and the "authorised representatives" (see clause **15.1**) of member organisations. The charity may invite others (eg other members of member organisations) to observe or participate, but not to vote (see clause **5.6**).

5.2   Notice is dealt with in clause **11**, and "written" is defined in clause **15.1**. 14 days notice should be regarded as a minimum; 21 days is more usual.

5.3   The quorum chosen should be realistic.

5.4   Many charities prefer "Chairman" or "Chairperson" to "Chair" (see clause **15.1**). Others may wish to use "convenor" or some other term. The choice of term used is not vital, but must be consistent throughout the document.

5.5   It should be noted that the required majority is not a majority of the members present at the meeting, but of the votes cast. If the charity has grown so large that it is necessary to consider proxy voting or postal votes it is wise to consider incorporation as a charitable company (see clause **13.2**).

CONSTITUTION FOR A CHARITABLE UNINCORPORATED ASSOCIATION

3.17 To enter into contracts to provide services to or on behalf of other bodies

3.18 To pay the costs of forming the Association

3.19 To do anything else within the law which promotes or helps to promote the Objects

4. MEMBERSHIP

4.1 **Membership** of the Association is open to any individual [or organisation] interested in promoting the Objects

4.2 The Committee may establish different classes of membership and set appropriate rates of subscription

4.3 The Committee must keep a register of **members**

4.4 A member whose subscription is six months in arrears ceases to be a member but may be readmitted on payment of the amount owing

4.5 A member may resign by **written** notice to the Association

4.6 The Committee may terminate the membership of any individual or organisation whose continued membership would in the reasonable view of the Committee be harmful to the Association (but only after notifying the member concerned in writing and considering the matter in the light of any written representations which the member puts forward within 14 **clear days** after receiving notice)

4.7 Membership of the Association is not transferable

5. GENERAL MEETINGS

5.1 All members are entitled to attend general meetings of the Association in person [or (in the case of a member organisation) through an **authorised representative**]

5.2 General meetings are called by [21] clear days' written notice to the members specifying the business to be transacted

5.3 There is a quorum at a general meeting if the number of members [or authorised representatives] personally present is a least _____ *[number]* (or _____ *[percentage]* of the members if greater)

5.4 The **Chair** or (if the Chair is unable or unwilling to do so) some other member elected by those present presides at a general meeting

5.5 Except where otherwise provided in this Constitution, every issue at a general meeting is determined by a simple majority of the votes cast by the members present in person [or (in the case of a member organisation) through an authorised representative]

NOTES

5.6   The casting vote given to the person who presides at a meeting is intended to enable the meeting to proceed with its business. It is normal for the casting vote to be given in favour of the *status quo* to allow further debate on the matter on a future occasion.

5.7 &   The annual general meeting (AGM) is the regular occasion for the members to gather, and
5.8   is essential to the proceedings of a charitable unincorporated association.

  5.8.5 A registered auditor or an independent examiner (see clause **15.1**) will be required to audit or examine the charity's accounts in accordance with section 43 of the Charities Act 1993 (see also clause **10.1**). A professional audit is required if the charity's income or expenditure for either of the two preceding financial years was more than £250,000. In other cases an independent examination will be sufficient. A charity whose income and expenditure respectively amounted to no more than £10,000 in its last financial year does not legally require an independent examination, but it is still advisable to have one.

  5.8.6 A Patron, President or Vice-President has no constitutional responsibilities but may be invited to address the members or to represent the charity on formal occasions or when seeking public support.

5.9   Where an urgent or important matter (such as the amendment of the Constitution) which must be decided at a general meeting cannot conveniently be dealt with at an AGM, the meeting specially called for the purpose is an extraordinary general meeting (EGM).

6.   **THE COMMITTEE**

        This clause sets out the composition of the charity's governing body, ie the charity trustees (see clauses **6.1** and **15.1**). They are all required to be members of the charity. In this Constitution they are called the "Committee" but they could equally well be called the "Trustees", the "Council", the "Management Committee" or some other term. Under section 83 of the Charities Act 1993 a written memorandum should be executed whenever a Committee member is elected or appointed.

6.2   Many charitable associations elect all the members of their governing body each year at the AGM. Others provide for a number of Committee members to be nominated by one or more outside bodies operating in the same area (eg local authorities) or in the same field of work (eg other charities)—see optional clause **6.2.3**. It is usually helpful to allow the Committee to co-opt a number of its members (for example to enlist members with particular skills)—see clause **6.2.4**. The total number of Committee members in clauses **6.2.1, 6.2.2, 6.2.3** (if included) and **6.2.4** should be equal to the number specified in clause **6.2**. Every Committee member, however appointed, is a charity trustee and owes a duty towards the charity rather than to the person or body who makes the appointment. There is therefore no power for the appointing body to remove the person appointed.

CONSTITUTION FOR A CHARITABLE UNINCORPORATED ASSOCIATION

5.6 Except for the chair of the meeting, who has a second or casting vote, every member present in person [or (in the case of a member organisation) through an authorised representative] is entitled to one vote on every issue

5.7 An **AGM** must be held in every year (except that the first AGM may be held at any time within 18 **months** after the formation of the Association)

5.8 At an AGM the members:

    5.8.1 receive the accounts of the Association for the previous financial year

    5.8.2 receive the report of the Committee on the Association's activities since the previous AGM

    5.8.3 elect **elected Committee members** to replace those retiring from office

    5.8.4 elect from among the members of the Association the **Chair** of the Association for the following year

    5.8.5 appoint an auditor or **independent examiner** for the Association where required

    5.8.6 may confer on any individual (with his or her consent) the honorary title of Patron, President or Vice-President of the Association

    5.8.7 discuss and determine any issues of policy or deal with any other business put before them

5.9 An **EGM** may be called at any time by the Committee and must be called within 14 days after a written request to the Committee from at least _____ *[number]* members

6. THE COMMITTEE

6.1 The Committee as **charity trustees** have control of the Association and its property and funds

6.2 The Committee when complete consists of at least three and not more than _____ *[number]* individuals, all of whom must be members (but must not be paid employees) of the Association, i.e.

    6.2.1 the Chair

    6.2.2 _____ *[number]* elected Committee members

NOTES

6.3   Retirement of the elected Committee members by rotation helps to ensure continuity. At the second AGM of the charity the elected Committee members to retire (who will have held office for only a year) will be chosen by lot.

6.4   This provision is important: it is designed to ensure as far as possible that everyone who takes on the task of being a member of the charity's Committee is aware of the legal responsibilities it entails.

6.5   Various events can terminate a Committee member's trusteeship.

      6.5.1 Disqualification occurs under section 72 of the Charities Act 1993 if a trustee is involuntarily removed by the Court or the Charity Commission, in the event of bankruptcy or the like and where the trustee has been convicted of an offence involving dishonesty.

      6.5.2 Embarrassing problems can arise when a Committee member becomes too ill or infirm to be expected to take full responsibility for the task. The Committee may wish to make a rule under clause **8.4** to require a Committee member who appears incapable to undergo a medical examination. Such a request would in most cases lead to a voluntary resignation.

      6.5.3 The length of absence which gives rise to automatic termination of membership will depend on the normal frequency of meetings (see clause **7.1**).

      6.5.5 The law does not allow trustees to walk away from their responsibilities leaving no-one in charge of the charity.

      6.5.6 May be a wise precaution. Others may feel that it undermines the independence of Committee members. A memorandum under section 83 of the Charities Act 1993 is again required (see note to clause **6** generally, above).

6.6   This clause acts as a reminder of the general rule that trustees are entitled to recover from the charity whatever funds they may be obliged to pay out as a consequence of running the charity, eg paying for goods or services ordered by them and supplied to the charity. Of course the indemnity is of no value if the charity does not have the funds to meet it.

6.7   Occasionally a mistake occurs in appointment procedures. If a mistake of this kind is discovered it does not retrospectively invalidate previous decisions but should be put right before further decisions are taken.

CONSTITUTION FOR A CHARITABLE UNINCORPORATED ASSOCIATION

[6.2.3 _____ *[number]* members, to be appointed by _____

_____

_____ *[name of appointing body]* to
hold office for terms of _____ *[number]* years ("**nominated Committee members**")]

6.2.4 up to _____ *[number]* members co-opted by the Committee to hold office until the next AGM ("**co-opted Committee members**")

6.3 One third (or the number nearest one third) of the elected Committee members must retire at each AGM, those longest in office retiring first and the choice between any of equal service being made by drawing lots

6.4 Every Committee member must sign a declaration of willingness to act as a charity trustee of the Association before he or she is eligible to vote at any meeting of the Committee

6.5 A Committee member automatically ceases to be a member of the Committee if he or she:

6.5.1 is disqualified under the Charities Act 1993 from acting as a charity trustee

6.5.2 is incapable, whether mentally or physically, of managing his or her own affairs

6.5.3 is absent from _____ *[number]* consecutive meetings of the Committee

6.5.4 ceases to be a member of the Association [(but such a person may be reinstated by resolution of all the other members of the Committee on resuming membership of the Association)]

6.5.5 resigns by written notice to the Committee (but only if at least two Committee members will remain in office)

[6.5.6 is removed by a resolution passed by all the other members of the Committee after inviting the views of the Committee member concerned and considering the matter in the light of any such views]

6.6 A retiring Committee member is entitled to an indemnity from the continuing Committee members at the expense of the Association in respect of any liabilities properly incurred while he or she held office

6.7 A technical defect in the appointment of a Committee member of which the Committee are unaware at the time does not invalidate decisions taken at a meeting

NOTES

7. COMMITTEE MEETINGS

This clause deals with the meetings and proceedings of the Committee.

7.1 The number of meetings per year will depend on (i) the nature of the charity's activities and (ii) the extent to which work is delegated to sub-committees and/or staff.

7.2 Bearing in mind that decisions may be taken on a majority vote (clause 7.5), the quorum should normally be fixed at (at least) one more than the number nearest one third of the members of the Committee.

7.3 Many charities do not have provision for telephone or video conferences. It is not necessary to include it unless difficulty in arranging meetings in person is expected (eg where the Committee members are geographically scattered). If the provision is included it should be borne in mind that (i) a telephone conference call is not the same as a series of separate telephone calls, which do *not* amount to a meeting; and (ii) the same rules about notice of meetings, the quorum, chairmanship, voting, minutes etc apply to a meeting held by electronic means as to a meeting in person.

7.5 An alternative to a decision taken at a meeting is a written resolution, but this will not be valid unless signed by *all* the Committee members.

7.6 See note to clause **5.6** above.

8. POWERS OF COMMITTEE

8.1 In this Constitution the Chair is appointed by the AGM but other honorary officers are appointed by the Committee (who will be better able to judge their particular talents and abilities) from among their number. A Treasurer is essential. There may be an honorary Secretary, although it is often convenient for the Secretary's role to be undertaken by a paid employee. There may also be a membership secretary or holders of other specified offices, which may alter from year to year according to the charity's activities.

8.2 A specific provision is essential if the Committee is to be able to delegate to sub-committees. The Committee will be legally responsible for the sub-committee's acts, and for this reason it is prudent for at least one Committee member to be a member of each sub-committee. The Committee should also define the terms of reference of each sub-committee with care. It is essential in all cases to provide for reporting back, and this may have to be in writing (see clause **10.2.3**). Whilst the power to delegate is not limited to any particular functions, it is usually appropriate for the final decision on major matters of policy or resources to be reserved to the main Committee.

8.3 & 8.4 & 8.5 The Committee is allowed to make rules of various kinds to govern different aspects of the running of the charity. There is no need to call them "Standing Orders", "Rules" and "Regulations": they can all be called "Rules" if preferred.

8.6 This clause is designed to place the responsibility for finding a solution to internal disputes on the Committee, given the damage which can result to a charity from such arguments, especially when they become public.

CONSTITUTION FOR A CHARITABLE UNINCORPORATED ASSOCIATION

7. COMMITTEE MEETINGS

7.1 The Committee must hold at least _____ *[number]* meetings each year

7.2 A quorum at a Committee meeting is _____ *[number]* members

[7.3 A Committee meeting may be held either in person or through electronic means agreed by the Committee in which each participant may communicate with all other participants]

7.4 The Chair or (if the Chair is unable or unwilling to do so) some other member of the Committee chosen by the members present presides at each Committee meeting

7.5 Every issue may be determined by a simple majority of the votes cast at a Committee meeting but a resolution which is in writing and signed by all members of the Committee is as valid as a resolution passed at a meeting and for this purpose the resolution may be contained in more than one document and will be treated as passed on the date of the last signature

7.6 Except for the chair of the meeting, who has a second or casting vote, every Committee member has one vote on each issue

8. POWERS OF COMMITTEE

The Committee have the following powers in the administration of the Association:

8.1 to appoint a Treasurer and other honorary officers

8.2 to delegate any of their functions to sub-committees consisting of two or more persons appointed by them (but at least [one] member of every sub-committee must be a Committee member and all proceedings of sub-committees must be reported promptly to the Committee)

8.3 to make Standing Orders consistent with this Constitution to govern proceedings at general meetings

8.4 to make Rules consistent with this Constitution about the Committee and sub-committees

8.5 to make Regulations consistent with this Constitution about the running of the Association (including the operation of bank accounts and the commitment of funds)

8.6 to resolve or establish procedures to assist the resolution of disputes within the Association

8.7 to exercise any powers of the Association which are not reserved to a general meeting

NOTES

9.   **PROPERTY & FUNDS**

This clause reflects the legal position that the property of a charitable unincorporated association is held *on trust for the Objects* rather than belonging to the members (as would be the case in a private club).

9.2 &   These clauses reflect the legal principle that the Committee, as charity trustees, must not
9.3   benefit from the charity except so far as expressly permitted by the Constitution. They prevent a Committee member from being an employee although clause **9.2.6** allows a restricted number with special skills to be paid fees for work done, subject to the procedural safeguards in clause **9.3**. Without express provision in the constitution, a Committee member cannot be a beneficiary of the charity (see clause **9.2.7**).

9.4   "Trust corporation" is a technical legal term and "holding trustee" is defined (see clauses **15.1, 9.6.3** and **9.6.4**).

9.5   It is obvious that prudent trustees do not allow significant amounts of money to be kept as cash, or leave funds on current account unless they are likely to be applied in the near future.

CONSTITUTION FOR A CHARITABLE UNINCORPORATED ASSOCIATION

9. PROPERTY & FUNDS

9.1 The property and funds of the Association must be used only for promoting the Objects and do not belong to the members of the Association or the Committee

9.2 No Committee member may receive any payment of money or other material benefit (whether direct or indirect) from the Association except

9.2.1 under clauses 3.15 (indemnity insurance) and 9.2.6 (fees)

9.2.2 reimbursement of reasonable out-of-pocket expenses (including hotel and travel costs) actually incurred in the administration of the Association

9.2.3 interest at a reasonable rate on money lent to the Association

9.2.4 a reasonable rent or hiring fee for property let or hired to the Association

9.2.5 an indemnity in respect of any liabilities properly incurred in running the Association (including the costs of a successful defence to criminal proceedings)

9.2.6 any Committee member who possesses specialist skills or knowledge, and any firm or company of which such a person is a member or employee, may charge and be paid reasonable fees for work carried out for the Association on the instructions of the other Committee members but (i) only if the procedure prescribed by clause 9.3 is followed in selecting the member, firm or company concerned and setting the fees and (ii) provided that this provision may not apply to more than one half of the Committee members in any financial year

9.2.7 in the case of an individual member, charitable benefits in his or her capacity as a beneficiary

9.2.8 in exceptional cases, other payments or material benefits (but only with the prior written approval of the **Commission**)

9.3 Whenever a Committee member has a personal interest in a matter to be discussed at a Committee meeting, the Committee member must

9.3.1 declare an interest before discussion begins on the matter

9.3.2 withdraw from that part of the meeting unless expressly invited to remain in order to provide information

9.3.3 not be counted in the quorum for that part of the meeting

9.3.4 withdraw during the vote and have no vote on the matter

9.4 Any **trust corporation** which is appointed as a **holding trustee** or any nominee for the Association may be paid reasonable fees

9.5 Funds which are not required for immediate use or which will be required for use at a future date must be placed on deposit or invested in accordance with clause **3.12** until needed

NOTES

9.6   The charity is not a legal person and cannot therefore hold the legal title to property or investments in its own name. It is often inconvenient for the members of the Committee, who may change quite frequently, to hold property in their individual names. Yet it is important that the charity should retain control of its property. This clause provides several alternatives. For incorporation of the Committee see the note to clause **13.1**.

10.   **RECORDS & ACCOUNTS**

10.1   The keeping of adequate records is essential if a charity is to be properly run. In addition, there is detailed legislation in Part VI (sections 41 to 49) of the Charities Act 1993 and the regulations made under it, as well as guidance on accountability in the Charity SORP (the Statement of Recommended Practice "Accounting by Charities" approved by the Accounting Standards Board and published by the Charity Commission). The rules cover accounting records, the audit or independent examination of accounts (see note to clause **5.8.5**) and the provision of an annual report, statement of account and annual return, all of which have to be sent to the Commission.

10.3   This provision is designed to ensure that the members of the charity have access to the published report and statements of account.

10.4   This clause reflects section 47(2) of the Charities Act 1993. A copy of the latest statement of account must be sent within two months to anyone who asks for it in writing and pays a reasonable fee to cover the charity's costs.

11.   **NOTICES**

Reference is made to "notice" in various places in the Constitution (see clauses **4.5, 5.2, 6.5.5** and **12.1**). This clause deals with the practical problems which could otherwise arise about when a notice was received by a member (or the charity). Where a number of clear days' notice be specified each "day" starts at midnight, and the day on which notice is given does not count (see clause **15.1**).

Some charities may prefer *not* to have the option of placing a notice to the members in a newspaper or newsletter, or by fax or e-mail, in which case the relevant words should be omitted from clauses **11.1** and **11.3**. It may also be desirable to save postage by restricting postal service to the member's address in the United Kingdom—in which case amendments will be required to clauses **11.2** and **11.3.3**.

CONSTITUTION FOR A CHARITABLE UNINCORPORATED ASSOCIATION

9.6 Investments and other property of the Association may be held:

9.6.1 in the names of the Committee members for the time being (or in the name of the Committee if incorporated under the Charities Act 1993)

9.6.2 in the name of a nominee (being a corporate body registered or having an established place of business in England and Wales) under the control of the Committee or of a financial expert acting on their instructions

9.6.3 in the name of at least two and up to four holding trustees for the Association who must be appointed (and may be removed) by a resolution of the Committee.

9.6.4 in the name of a trust corporation as a holding trustee for the Association, which must be appointed (and may be removed) by deed executed by the Committee

9.6.5 in the case of land, by the Official Custodian for Charities under an order of the Commission or the Court

10. RECORDS & ACCOUNTS

10.1 The Committee must comply with the requirements of the Charities Act 1993 as to the keeping of financial records, the audit or independent examination of accounts and the preparation and transmission to the Commission of:

10.1.1 annual reports

10.1.2 annual returns

10.1.3 annual statements of account

10.2 The Committee must keep proper records of:

10.2.1 all proceedings at general meetings

10.2.2 all proceedings at Committee meetings

10.2.3 all reports of sub-committees

10.2.4 all professional advice obtained

10.3 Annual reports and statements of account relating to the Association must be made available for inspection by any member of the Association

10.4 A copy of the latest available statement of account must be supplied to any person who makes a written request and pays the Association's reasonable costs (as required by the Charities Act 1993)

11. NOTICES

11.1 Notices under this Constitution may be sent by hand, or by post or by suitable electronic means or (where applicable to members generally) may be published in any suitable journal or [national] newspaper [circulating in the area of benefit] or in any newsletter distributed by the Association

NOTES

12.   AMENDMENTS

Amendments to the Constitution may well be needed as the charity develops. The Constitution will be incapable of amendment, except by a scheme of the Charity Commission, if a specific power to amend it is not included. It is usual to include such a power and to require more than a simple majority for a vote on the matter.

12.1   The members must be given advance notice of proposed amendments to the Constitution. The period of notice should be the same as included in clause **5.2**.

12.2 &   It is of the utmost importance that the Constitution should not be amended in a way which
12.3   makes it impossible for the charity to continue to operate. Therefore, under this clause certain amendments are not valid, ie if adopted they will not count as amendments and will not be registered by the Commission. The two cases are (i) where there is a fundamental change in the Objects, ie where the new purposes are of a kind which a previous supporter could not reasonably be expected to have foreseen when contributing to the charity's funds, and (ii) where the change in the Constitution would cause the charity to become a non-charitable body.

Any amendment will have to be considered from the point of view of both charitable status and workability. It will normally be appropriate to seek legal advice or consult the Commission before the proposed amendments are drawn up. The Commission should be notified promptly of all amendments that are made.

13.   INCORPORATION

This clause is not an essential provision, but it may be useful as the charity develops. It deals with two kinds of incorporation.

13.1   The first kind of incorporation may be brought about by the Charity Commission. The Committee as charity trustees may apply to the Commission for a certificate under Part VII (sections 50 to 62) of the Charities Act 1993 incorporating them, ie the Committee, and allowing them to operate as a legal entity. It is not the same as the incorporation of a company (see the note to clause **13.2**). The Commission will normally grant a certificate if they consider that it would be in the charity's interests. This can be administratively helpful in some cases, but since it represents a major change in the structure of the charity this clause requires the Committee to consult the members before making such an application.

13.2 &   The second, and more usual, kind of incorporation does not involve the Commission
13.3   directly. In essence, the unincorporated association is replaced by a limited liability company formed under the Companies Acts. A number of charities which began as unincorporated associations have found it convenient or prudent to transfer their assets and liabilities to a charitable company with a similar name and similar Objects. In this case specialist legal advice is required. Special care is needed to transfer leasehold or freehold land, property held on special trusts, contracts of employment and other contracts. It will also be necessary to make arrangements to collect future payments under existing covenants (or persuade covenantors to execute fresh covenants) and to notify those who may be intending to leave legacies or make other gifts to the charity.

CONSTITUTION FOR A CHARITABLE UNINCORPORATED ASSOCIATION

11.2 The address at which a member is entitled to receive notices is the address noted in the register of members (or, if none, the last known address)

11.3 Any notice given in accordance with this Constitution is to be treated for all purposes as having been received:

11.3.1 24 hours after being sent by electronic means or delivered by hand to the relevant address

11.3.2 two clear days after being sent by first class post to that address

11.3.3 three clear days after being sent by second class post or overseas post to that address

11.3.4 on the date of publication of a journal or newspaper containing the notice

11.3.5 on being handed to the member [or its authorised representative] personally or, if earlier,

11.3.6 as soon as the member acknowledges actual receipt

11.4 A technical defect in the giving of notice of which the members or the Committee members are unaware at the time does not invalidate decisions taken at a meeting

12. AMENDMENTS

This Constitution may be amended at a general meeting by a [two-thirds] majority of the votes cast, but

12.1 The members must be given [21] clear days' notice of the proposed amendments

12.2 No amendment is valid if it would make a **fundamental change** to the Objects or to this clause or destroy the charitable status of the Association

12.3 Clauses 9.2 and 9.3 may not be amended without the prior written consent of the Commission

[13. INCORPORATION

13.1 The Committee may apply to the Commission under the Charities Act 1993 for a certificate of incorporation relating to the Committee but only after consulting the members at a general meeting

13.2 The members at a general meeting may authorise the Committee to transfer the assets and liabilities of the Association to a limited company established for exclusively charitable purposes within, the same as or similar to the Objects and of which the members of the Association will be entitled to be members

NOTES

14.   **DISSOLUTION**

It is not unusual for unincorporated charitable associations to reach the end of their useful life and decide to dissolve. If so, the debts and liabilities must be provided for and there may be assets remaining. Those assets must be used for furthering the Objects or for charitable purposes which are within or similar to the Objects, and this clause sets out various alternatives. The Committee will not be relieved of their responsibilities until they have completed their task, and sent in a final report and statement of account to the Charity Commission. The Commission will then remove the charity from the register of charities.

15.   **INTERPRETATION**

15.1   The statutory definitions referred to are:

"charity trustees" (section 97(1) of the Charities Act 1993) are "the persons having the general control and management of the administration of a charity"

an "independent examiner" (section 43(3)(a) of the Charities Act 1993) is "an independent person who is reasonably believed by the trustees to have the requisite ability and practical experience to carry out a competent examination of the accounts"

"trust corporation" (section 205(1)(xxviii) of the Law of Property Act 1925) means a corporate body either (i) appointed by the court in a particular case to be a trustee or (ii) authorised under rules made under section 4(3) of the Public Trustee Act 1906 to act as custodian trustee or (iii) having the certificate of the Lord Chancellor. The Public Trustee, though a trust corporation, is not permitted to act in relation to charities.

15.2   This clause should avoid the need to amend the Constitution merely to reflect technical changes in the law.

adopting the constitution

The usual procedure is for an association to adopt its Constitution by a formal resolution, often at its first meeting. The Chair of the meeting at which the Constitution is adopted and a witness should complete the text at the end of this model (see page 929).

CONSTITUTION FOR A CHARITABLE UNINCORPORATED ASSOCIATION

13.3 On a transfer under clause 13.2 the Committee must ensure that all necessary steps are taken as to:

13.3.1 the transfer of land and other property

13.3.2 the novation of contracts of employment and transfer of pension rights and

13.3.3 the trusteeship of any property held for special purposes]

14. DISSOLUTION

14.1 If at any time the members at a general meeting decide to dissolve the Association, the members of the Committee will remain in office as charity trustees and will be responsible for the orderly winding up of the Association's affairs

14.2 After making provision for all outstanding liabilities of the Association, the Committee must apply the remaining property and funds in one or more of the following ways:

14.2.1 by transfer to one or more other bodies established for exclusively charitable purposes within, the same as or similar to the Objects

14.2.2 directly for the Objects or charitable purposes within or similar to the Objects

14.2.3 in such other manner consistent with charitable status as the Commission approve in writing in advance

14.3 A final report and statement of account relating to the Association must be sent to the Commission

15. INTERPRETATION

In this Constitution:

15.1 "AGM" means an annual general meeting of the members of the Association ["area of benefit" means _____

_____*[geographical area]*]

"the Association" means the charity comprised in this constitution

["authorised representative" means an individual who is authorised by a member organisation to act on its behalf at meetings of the Association]

["the beneficiaries" means _____

_____ *[definition]*]

"the Chair" means the chair of the Association elected at the AGM

"charity trustees" has the meaning prescribed by section 97(1) of the Charities Act 1993

"clear day" means 24 hours from midnight following the triggering event

CONSTITUTION FOR A CHARITABLE UNINCORPORATED ASSOCIATION

"the Commission" means the Charity Commissioners for England and Wales

"the Committee" is the governing body of the Association

"co-opted Committee member" means a member of the Committee appointed by the members of the Committee in accordance with clause 6.2.4

"EGM" means a general meeting of the members of the Association which is not an AGM

"elected Committee member" means a member of the Committee elected at an AGM

"financial expert" means an individual, company or firm who is an authorised person or an exempted person within the meaning of the Financial Services Act 1986

"fundamental change" means such a change as would not have been within the reasonable contemplation of a person making a donation to the Association

"holding trustee" means an individual or corporate body responsible for holding the title to property but not authorised to make any decisions relating to its use, investment or disposal

"independent examiner" has the meaning prescribed by section 43(3)(a) of the Charities Act 1993

"material benefit" means a benefit which may not be financial but has a monetary value

"member" and "membership" refer to members of the Association

"months" means calendar months

["nominated Committee member" means a member of the Committee appointed by an outside person or body in accordance with clause 6.2.3]

"the Objects" means the charitable objects of the Association set out in clause 2

"taxable trading" means carrying on a trade or business on a continuing basis for the principal purpose of raising funds and not for the purpose of actually carrying out the Objects and the profits of which are liable to tax

"trust corporation" has the meaning prescribed by section 205(1)(xxviii) of the Law of Property Act 1925 but does not include the Public Trustee)

"written" or "in writing" refers to a legible document on paper including a fax message

"year" means calendar year

15.2 References to an Act of Parliament are references to the Act as amended or re-enacted from time to time and to any subordinate legislation made under it

CONSTITUTION FOR A CHARITABLE UNINCORPORATED ASSOCIATION

ADOPTED AT A MEETING HELD

AT _____ *[Place]*

ON _____ *[Date]*

SIGNED

NAME _____

SIGNATURE _____

[Name and signature of chair of meeting]

WITNESSED

NAME _____

ADDRESS _____

_____

OCCUPATION _____

SIGNATURE _____

[Name, address, occupation and signature of witness]

First published July 1997
© Charity Law Association 1997

A catalogue record for this document is available from the British Library.

ISBN 0 9521604 3 9

Designed by Rachel Fletcher and published by Plaza Publishing

PRODUCED BY PLAZA,
PUBLISHERS OF *NGO FINANCE*
1A TRADESCANT ROAD, LONDON SW8 1XD
TEL: 0207 793 0001   FAX: 0207 735 2009

NGO Finance magazine

APPENDIX B(3)

CHARITABLE COMPANY

MEMORANDUM AND ARTICLES OF ASSOCIATION FOR A CHARITABLE COMPANY LIMITED BY GUARANTEE

Drafted by Francesca Quint of Counsel

on behalf of
Charity Law
Association

Approved by
Charity Commission
for England and Wales

CHARITY LAW ASSOCIATION MODEL DOCUMENTS

A charity needs to have its objects and powers and administrative arrangements set out clearly in its governing document. If it does not, it is likely to be less well governed. I am pleased to recommend the use of this model. It incorporates the essential powers and provisions and expresses them in plain English with explanatory notes. It will prove of great assistance to those intending to set up a charitable company.

RICHARD FRIES
CHIEF CHARITY COMMISSIONER

The first and certainly one of the most important decisions facing individuals who want to establish a new charity is choosing which legal structure will be right for the charity. Although there are quite a few structures to choose from, most charities are established as trusts, companies or associations. The Charity Commission's registration information pack explains the factors to be considered in choosing between them.

The Charity Commission's registration information pack also contains guidance on the objects or purposes which are recognised by law as charitable. Many worthwhile not-for-profit organisations have objects which are not charitable so it is wise to check before you spend time working on this document.

Copies of the Commission's registration information pack are available from its offices at:

St Alban's House	Woodfield House	2nd Floor
57–60 Haymarket	Tangier	20 Kings Parade
London	Taunton	Queens Dock
SW1Y 4QX	Somerset TA1 4BL	Liverpool L3 4DQ
☎ 0207 210 4556	☎ 01823 345 000	☎ 0151 703 1500

The Charity Law Association has also produced model documents for charitable trusts and associations. Copies of these models are available in printed and disk format from:

NGO Finance, 1a Tradescant Road, London SW8 1XD
Tel: 0207 793 0001   Fax: 0207 735 2009

DETAILS NEEDED TO COMPLETE THE MODEL

Before you can complete the model you will need to have made decisions on the following matters. It may help you in this process to refer to the appropriate clause (shown in the right-hand column below) and the accompanying notes.

(A) The Memorandum	Clause
1. The name of the charity.	1
2. The objects or purposes of the charity.	3
3. If the charity is to operate in a limited geographical area, a description of that area.	3
4. If the charity is to benefit a specified class of beneficiaries, a description of that class.	3
5. Full names and residential addresses of the Subscribers to the Memorandum and Articles (who will be the charity's first Trustees).	

(B) The Articles	Article
1. Membership structure.	1.3, 1.4
2. Quorum for general meetings of the members.	2.2
3. Number of members to call an EGM.	2.10
4. Minimum and maximum number of Trustees.	3.2, 3.5.7
5. Whether any qualification is going to be required for Trustees.	3.2, 3.6.7
6. Number of consecutive meetings a Trustee may miss before ceasing to hold office.	3.6.3
7. Required majority of members to approve removing a Trustee.	3.6.6
8. Minimum number of Trustee meetings each year.	4.1
9. Quorum for Trustee meetings.	4.2
10. Number of Trustees to sit on each committee.	5.3

For the purpose of completing the Companies House forms to incorporate the charitable company you will also require the following additional information for each of the Trustees:

- Title
- Any previous surname/s
- Date of Birth
- Nationality
- Occupation
- Directorships of other UK companies held now or in the last five years.

Memorandum and Articles of Association
for a Charitable Company

USING THIS MODEL

This model is intended for use by individuals wishing to establish a charitable company in England and Wales. Legal advice will be needed to adapt it for use in Scotland or Northern Ireland.

Every effort has been made to make the model clear and easy to use. However it is a legal document and so considerable care must be taken to ensure that it is completed in a manner which is appropriate for the intended charity. The Charity Law Association cannot accept any responsibility for its use and neither can the author or the Charity Commission. If in doubt, seek help from a charity lawyer!

Whilst it is possible for the model to be adopted by simply completing the gaps in the text we do not recommend it—it is intended that the text of the model (which appears below the headings on the unshaded pages which follow) should be reproduced as a new and a complete document and a disk is available to make this easier. On the inside back cover of this model we have set out the traditional form of cover or front page for Memorandum and Articles of Association.

The left-hand pages of this document contain notes to assist you to complete the model. The notes may also be useful when the new charity has been established, as a guide to the interpretation of the document: for this reason we recommend that you retain them.

On the previous page we have included a checklist of all the details that you will need to complete the model. This list shows the clauses where the details are required in case you need to refer to them or to the corresponding notes.

If you are not a lawyer the task of completing the model may at first sight seem daunting but we have included various aids to help you:
- Where a word or phrase needs to be inserted a brief description appears *[in italics in square brackets]*.
- Where there is a suggestion or choice between alternatives it appears [in normal type in square brackets].
- There is an interpretation clause at the end of the document. Words and phrases which are defined or explained there appear **in bold type** when they first occur.

These aids (with the possible exception of the emboldened terms) should not appear in the final document. In preparing the document you should also remember that:
- If you do not wish to include an optional clause or if you wish to add in new provisions, you will need to adjust the clause numbering accordingly.
- If you decide to redesignate a term (eg changing "Chairman" to "Chair"), you will need to make the change every time the term appears in the document.

There are differing views on the desirability of punctuation in legal documents. The model has been prepared without punctuation but it can, of course, be added.

You may also wish to include a contents page or index for ease of reference.

When you have completed the document and it has been signed by the Trustees (at the end of both the Memorandum *and* Articles of Association) you will be ready to incorporate the company. For this you will need various forms which can be obtained from Companies House, Crown Way, Maindy, Cardiff CF4 3UZ (Tel: 01222 388588). When you have completed these forms you will need a solicitor or notary to "swear" a declaration before returning them (with a cheque for the incorporation fee) to Companies House.

After the company has been incorporated you will be ready to begin the process of registering the charity. The Charity Commission's registration information pack explains this process and contains copies of the forms which you will need to complete.

NOTES

(A) The Memorandum of Association

The memorandum sets out the name and the basic principles by which the charity is governed.

1. **NAME**

    The name and objects are fundamental to the identity and purposes of the charity.

    The charity's name should be chosen with care. It should be consistent with the purposes of the charity. It must also comply with Company Law. It must not be misleading, eg by mis-representing the purposes or status of the charity or cause confusion with other companies or charities. The Charity Commission can require a charity to change its name: see sections 6 and 7 of the Charities Act 1993. Once a name has been chosen it is worth contacting Companies House and the Commission to see whether a charity or a company has been registered with the same, or a similar, name.

    Private companies are required by law to include the word "Limited" in their name. Charities can (and most do) elect not to use the word in their name by completing an additional Companies House form in the pre-incorporation process.

    In the model the charity is called "the Charity": if preferred it can be called "the Company", the "Society" or some other designation, but it is important to be consistent throughout.

2. **REGISTERED OFFICE**

    The registered office (a requirement of Company law) must be in England or Wales if the charity is to be within the jurisdiction of the High Court and the Charity Commission and eligible for charity registration: see section 96(1) of the Charities Act 1993.

3. **OBJECTS**

    The Objects (ie the main purposes) of the charity must be exclusively charitable under English law, or the company will not be a charity and registration as a charity will therefore be refused. The Objects should clearly accurately reflect the true purposes of the charity's intended activities. It may be appropriate to refer to a geographical area as the "area of benefit" of the charity and/or to describe the people the charity will benefit as the "beneficiaries" (see Article **9.1** on page 27).

    Legal advice may be required to be certain that the Objects are correctly expressed.

4. **POWERS**

    The powers are not themselves charitable objects, but consist of the legal means by which the Objects in clause **3** are to be promoted. It must be stressed that the powers cannot be exercised for any other purpose. Thus, any research carried out under **4.1** or advice or information supplied under **4.2** or **4.3**, must be about a subject which is relevant to the Objects. Under **4.4** the charity can only co-operate in a project relevant to the Objects, so the other organisation involved must also have some concern with the Objects. Any new charity set up or supported under **4.5** needs to have the same or similar objects, or come within the Objects.

    The powers included in this clause are those most commonly required by charities, but if it is known that the charity will be engaged in specific activities which are not mentioned it is advisable to insert an additional provision to cover them.

MEMORANDUM & ARTICLES OF ASSOCIATION FOR A CHARITABLE COMPANY

Companies Acts 1985 & 1989

Company limited by guarantee and not having a share capital

Memorandum of Association of

_____ *[Name]*

1. **NAME**

    The name of the Company is _____

    _____ *[Name]* (**"the Charity"**)

2. **REGISTERED OFFICE**

    The registered office of the Charity is to be in England and Wales

3. **OBJECTS**

    The objects of the Charity are _____

    _____

    _____

    _____

    _____ *[Objects]* (**"the Objects"**)

4. **POWERS**

    The Charity has the following powers, which may be exercised only in promoting the Objects:

4.1 To promote or carry out research

4.2 To provide advice

4.3 To publish or distribute information

4.4 To co-operate with other bodies

4.5 To support, administer or set up other charities

NOTES

4.6   The Trustees should have regard to the law applicable to any fundraising activities the charity is to undertake. The prohibition on "taxable trading" (see article **9.1**) is essential to avoid an objection from the Inland Revenue. Where a charity will be relying on taxable trading to raise funds it is recommended that a separate, non-charitable trading company should be used for the purpose, and specialist legal or accountancy advice will be needed.

4.7   The restrictions on mortgaging charity land are contained in sections 38 and 39 of the Charities Act 1993. In some cases the Charity Commission's consent is required. In others, a special procedure must be followed. Legal advice may be required.

4.9   The restrictions on sales, exchanges and leases of charity land are contained in sections 36 and 37 of the Charities Act 1993. In some cases the Commission's consent is required. In others, a special procedure must be followed. Legal advice will normally be required.

4.10   This clause sets out ways in which financial assistance can be given, whether to individual beneficiaries (where the charity is set up to help individuals) or to other bodies. It will be necessary to consider the need for a licence under Consumer Credit legislation if the charity is to make loans to individuals. In setting the amount of any grant or loan or the extent of any guarantee (which is a *contingent* liability) the Trustees should consider the resources of the charity as well as the requirements of the recipient.

4.11   This clause enables the Trustees to designate funds for particular purposes, or as reserves. It is prudent for a charity to maintain reserves to cover planned expenditure (eg repairs to buildings) and to meet the kind of expenditure which may be required at short notice, but reserves are not an end in themselves and should not be built up without a deliberate policy decision, or be excessive in relation to the amount known or reasonably estimated to be required.

4.12   This clause is designed to confer a wide power of investment but to ensure that it is exercised responsibly. An "investment" is an asset which (i) is capable of producing income and (ii) may also increase in capital value. In setting an investment policy and selecting investments the Trustees should have regard to the needs of the charity for both income and capital growth, and act prudently. They should avoid trading and speculation.

4.13   The Charity Commission consider that if discretionary powers are to be given to investment managers an express power to delegate the management of investments is required. It should always be accompanied by safeguards, as here.

4.15   Charity property, whether buildings, equipment or other property, should normally be insured up to its full reinstatement value. Depending on the nature of the charity, other kinds of insurance may be necessary or desirable (eg public liability, employers' liability).

4.16   This type of insurance requires a special clause because it provides a benefit to the Trustees as charity trustees (see Article **9.1**). It may be helpful where the charity is involved in particular commercial risks, but it does *not* protect the Trustees from liability towards third parties in the event that the charity operates while technically insolvent. They should therefore be sure never to commit the charity to expenditure it cannot afford.

MEMORANDUM & ARTICLES OF
ASSOCIATION FOR A CHARITABLE COMPANY

4.6   To raise funds (but not by means of **taxable trading**)

4.7   To borrow money and give security for loans (but only in accordance with the restrictions imposed by the Charities Act 1993)

4.8   To acquire or hire property of any kind

4.9   To let or dispose of property of any kind (but only in accordance with the restrictions imposed by the Charities Act 1993)

4.10 To make grants or loans of money and to give guarantees

4.11 To set aside funds for special purposes or as reserves against future expenditure

4.12 To deposit or invest funds in any manner (but to invest only after obtaining advice from a **financial expert** and having regard to the suitability of investments and the need for diversification)

4.13 To delegate the management of investments to a financial expert, but only on terms that:

    4.13.1 the investment policy is set down **in writing** for the financial expert by the **Trustees**

    4.13.2 every transaction is reported promptly to the Trustees

    4.13.3 the performance of the investments is reviewed regularly with the Trustees

    4.13.4 the Trustees are entitled to cancel the delegation arrangement at any time

    4.13.5 the investment policy and the delegation arrangement are reviewed at least once a **year**

    4.13.6 all payments due to the financial expert are on a scale or at a level which is agreed in advance and are notified promptly to the Trustees on receipt

    4.13.7 the financial expert must not do anything outside the powers of the Trustees

4.14 To arrange for investments or other property of the Charity to be held in the name of a nominee (being a corporate body registered or having an established place of business in England and Wales) under the control of the Trustees or of a financial expert acting under their instructions and to pay any reasonable fee required

4.15 To insure the property of the Charity against any foreseeable risk and take out other insurance policies to protect the Charity when required

4.16 To insure the Trustees against the costs of a successful defence to a criminal prosecution brought against them as charity trustees or against personal liability incurred in respect of any act or omission which is or is alleged to be a breach of trust or breach of duty, unless the **Trustee** concerned knew that, or was reckless whether, the act or omission was a breach of trust or breach of duty

NOTES

4.17   This clause covers employees, independent contractors and volunteers, and enables salaries and pensions, or fees, or expenses (or none of these) to be provided. All necessary advice about Employment Law should be obtained. A charity should not pay more than a reasonable rate for the task, but should aim to be a good employer. Special care is required if it is proposed to employ a Trustee (see clause 5.3).

4.18   This clause will be relevant in the increasing number of cases in which charities enter into contracts to provide services to local or health authorities. A charity can only enter into a contract of this kind if the work it will be doing will promote its Objects.

4.19   This power is not intended for use where a trading company is to be set up, but only where a separate company is regarded as necessary or desirable for purposes which could be carried out by the charity itself.

4.21   This "blanket provision" is intended to cover any other power not expressly mentioned. It is still restricted to promoting the Objects.

5.   **BENEFITS TO MEMBERS AND TRUSTEES**

This clause reflects the legal position that although a charitable company is a legal person and owns its property, the assets are treated in many ways as though they were held *on trust for the Objects* rather than belonging to the members (as would be the case in a non-charitable company). It is therefore necessary to restrict the occasions on which a Trustee may benefit from the charity, and avoid conflicts of interest and duty as far as possible. It cannot be amended without the Charity Commission's consent (see clause 5.5).

5.1 & These clauses reflect the legal principle that the Trustees as charity trustees (and to a lesser
5.2   extent the members, who are also in a fiduciary position) must not benefit from the charity except so far as expressly permitted by the Memorandum of Association. Trustees cannot benefit as beneficiaries.

5.3 & These provisions permit up to one half of the Trustees in any financial year to enter into a
5.4   contract to supply goods or services to the charity, and provide additional safeguards to protect the charity.

MEMORANDUM & ARTICLES OF
ASSOCIATION FOR A CHARITABLE COMPANY

4.17 Subject to clause 5, to employ paid or unpaid agents, staff or advisers

4.18 To enter into contracts to provide services to or on behalf of other bodies

4.19 To establish subsidiary companies to assist or act as agents for the Charity

4.20 To pay the costs of forming the Charity

4.21 To do anything else within the law which promotes or helps to promote the Objects

5. BENEFITS TO MEMBERS AND TRUSTEES

5.1 The property and funds of the Charity must be used only for promoting the Objects and do not belong to the **members** of the Charity but

    5.1.1 members who are not Trustees may be employed by or enter into contracts with the Charity and receive reasonable payment for goods or services supplied

    5.1.2 members (including Trustees) may be paid interest at a reasonable rate on money lent to the Charity

    5.1.3 members (including Trustees) may be paid a reasonable rent or hiring fee for property let or hired to the Charity

    5.1.4 individual members who are not Trustees but who are beneficiaries may receive charitable benefits in that capacity

5.2 A Trustee must not receive any payment of money or other **material benefit** (whether directly or indirectly) from the Charity except

    5.2.1 as mentioned in clauses 4.16, 5.1.2, 5.1.3 or 5.3.

    5.2.2 reimbursement of reasonable out-of-pocket expenses (including hotel and travel costs) actually incurred in running the Charity

    5.2.3 an indemnity in respect of any liabilities properly incurred in running the Charity (including the costs of a successful defence to criminal proceedings)

    5.2.4 payment to any company in which a Trustee has no more than a 1 per cent shareholding

    5.2.5 in exceptional cases, other payments or benefits (but only with the written approval of the **Commission** in advance)

5.3 Any Trustee (or any firm or company of which a Trustee is a member or employee) may enter into a contract with the Charity to supply goods or services in return for a payment or other material benefit but only if

    5.3.1 the goods or services are actually required by the Charity

    5.3.2 the nature and level of the remuneration is no more than is reasonable in relation to the value of the goods or services and is set in accordance with the procedure in clause 5.4

    5.3.3 no more than one half of the Trustees are subject to such a contract in any financial year

NOTES

6. & 7. LIMITATION OF LIABILITY, GUARANTEE

These provisions are required by Company law.

8. DISSOLUTION

It is not unusual for charitable companies to reach the end of their useful life and decide to dissolve. If so, the debts and liabilities must be provided for and there may be assets remaining. Those assets must be used for the Objects or charitable purposes within or similar to the Objects, and this clause sets out various alternatives. The Trustees will not be relieved of their responsibilities as charity trustees until they have completed their task, and sent in a final report and statement of account to the Charity Commission. The Commission will then remove the charity from the register of charities. Removal from the register of companies is a separate matter.

9. INTERPRETATION

Various terms used in the Memorandum are defined in article **9**.

Trustees

This model has been designed so that the individuals whose details and signature will appear and will automatically be the charity's first Trustees. It is therefore important that their number falls within the minimum and maximum number of Trustees set out in article **3.2**.

MEMORANDUM & ARTICLES OF
ASSOCIATION FOR A CHARITABLE COMPANY

5.4 Whenever a Trustee has a personal interest in a matter to be discussed at a meeting of the Trustees or a committee the Trustee concerned must:

    5.4.1 declare an interest at or before discussion begins on the matter

    5.4.2 withdraw from the meeting for that item unless expressly invited to remain in order to provide information

    5.4.3 not be counted in the quorum for that part of the meeting

    5.4.4 withdraw during the vote and have no vote on the matter

5.5 This clause may not be amended without the prior written consent of the **Commission**

6. LIMITED LIABILITY

The liability of members is limited

7. GUARANTEE

Every member promises, if the Charity is dissolved while he, she or it remains a member or within 12 months afterwards, to pay up to [£1] towards the costs of dissolution and the liabilities incurred by the Charity while the contributor was a member

8. DISSOLUTION

8.1 If the Charity is dissolved the assets (if any) remaining after provision has been made for all its liabilities must be applied in one or more of the following ways:

    8.1.1 by transfer to one or more other bodies established for exclusively charitable purposes within, the same as or similar to the Objects

    8.1.2 directly for the Objects or charitable purposes within or similar to the Objects

    8.1.3 in such other manner consistent with charitable status as the Commission approve in writing in advance

8.2 A final report and statement of account must be sent to the Commission

9. INTERPRETATION

9.1 Words and expressions defined in the Articles have the same meanings in this Memorandum

9.2 References to an Act of Parliament are references to the Act as amended or re-enacted from time to time and to any subordinate legislation made under it

NOTES

MEMORANDUM & ARTICLES OF
ASSOCIATION FOR A CHARITABLE COMPANY

We wish to be formed into a company under this Memorandum of Association

NAMES & ADDRESSES OF SUBSCRIBERS	SIGNATURES OF SUBSCRIBERS
[List the full name and residential address of each of the subscribers]	*[signature of each of the subscribers]*

Date _____ *[Date]*

Witness to the above signatures

_____   _____

_____   _____

_____   _____

_____   _____

[Name, address and occupation of witness]   *[Signature of witness]*

945

NOTES

(B)   Articles of Association

The Articles set out the procedures for running the charity.

1.   **MEMBERSHIP**

Members are essential to a company: it cannot function without them.

1.2   The register of members is required by company law. If it is kept on computer Data Protection legislation may be applicable.

1.3   This clause provides for an "open" membership. This is essential if the members are to receive benefits, and do not simply exist to support the charity. Some charitable companies confine membership to individuals, and do not therefore provide for member organisations.

1.4   Apart from "individual" and "corporate members", it may be considered helpful to provide for eg associate, junior or honorary membership. Members of a company have certain rights under company law (eg to vote at general meetings and to receive copies of the company's accounts). It can be expensive and time consuming for a charitable company to comply with the company law requirements for a large membership. In cases where a high proportion of the members do not wish to participate in the management of the charity (for example, where they wish to be members only for the purpose of being informed of the charity's activities) it may be appropriate for the charity to establish one or more categories of "supporter members" who are not members under company law. Legal advice may be required.

1.5.4 It is uncommon for a member of a charity to be removed from membership, but if this happens it must only be done for a good reason. Under the rules of Natural Justice, the member concerned must be given an opportunity of stating his or her case before a final decision is taken and any decision to remove a member must be justifiable.

MEMORANDUM & ARTICLES OF
ASSOCIATION FOR A CHARITABLE COMPANY

Companies Acts 1985 & 1989

Company limited by guarantee and not having a share capital

Articles of Association of

_____ *[Name]*

1. **MEMBERSHIP**

1.1 The number of members with which the company proposes to be registered is unlimited

1.2 The Charity must maintain a register of members

1.3 **Membership** of the Charity is open to any individual [or organisation] interested in promoting the Objects who

   1.3.1 applies to the Charity in the form required by the Trustees

   1.3.2 is approved by the Trustees

   and

   1.3.3 signs the Register of members or consents in writing to become a member [either personally or (in the case of a member organisation) through an **authorised representative**]

1.4 The Trustees may establish different classes of membership and prescribe their respective privileges and duties and set the amounts of any subscriptions

1.5 Membership is terminated if the member concerned

   1.5.1 gives written notice of resignation to the Charity

   1.5.2 dies [or (in the case of an organisation) ceases to exist]

   1.5.3 is six **months** in arrears in paying the relevant subscription (if any) (but in such a case the member may be reinstated on payment of the amount due)

   or

   1.5.4 is removed from membership by resolution of the Trustees on the ground that in their reasonable opinion the member's continued membership is harmful to the Charity (but only after notifying the member in writing and considering the matter in the light of any written representations which the member concerned puts forward within 14 **clear days** after receiving notice)

1.6 Membership of the Charity is not transferable

NOTES

2.   GENERAL MEETINGS

A general meeting is a formal gathering of the members. Company law contains detailed provisions related to the convening of and the nature and conduct of business at general meetings (there are, for example, six different types of resolutions a company may pass with different rules applicable to each). These rules apply to charitable companies and the Trustees must be aware of their provisions. If none of the Trustees have experience in this area legal advice or a good book on the subject will be required.

2.1   This article states who has a right to attend general meetings, ie individual members and the authorised representatives (see article **9.1**) of member organisations. The charity may invite others (eg other members of member organisations) to observe or participate, but not to vote (see article **2.4**). Notice is dealt with in article 7 and "written" is defined in article **9.1**. It may be necessary in some cases, eg where the charity's membership is numerous and widespread, to provide for proxy voting: if so, details should be included expressly in the articles.

2.2   The quorum chosen should be realistic.

2.3   Many charities prefer Chair or Chairperson to Chairman (see article **13.2**). Others may wish to use "convenor" or some other term. The choice of term used is not vital, but it is important to be consistent throughout the document.

2.4   It should be noted that a majority of the members present at the meeting is not required: merely a majority of the votes cast. See also the general note above.

2.5   The casting vote given to the person who presides at a meeting is intended to enable the meeting to proceed with its business. It is normal for the casting vote to be given in favour of the *status quo* to allow further debate on the matter on a future occasion.

2.6   The practical value of this article, which avoids the need for a general meeting if all the members sign a resolution, depends on there being a relatively small number of members.

2.7   The annual general meeting (AGM) is the regular occasion for the members to gather, and
& 2.8   is essential to the proceedings of a charitable company.

2.8.5   A professional audit is required under company law.

2.8.6   A Patron, President or Vice-President has no constitutional responsibilities but may be invited to address the members or represent the charity on formal occasions or when seeking public support.

2.9 &   Where an urgent or important matter (such as the amendment of the Constitution) which
2.10   must be decided a general meeting cannot conveniently be dealt with at an AGM, the meeting specially called for the purpose is an extraordinary general meeting (EGM).

MEMORANDUM & ARTICLES OF
ASSOCIATION FOR A CHARITABLE COMPANY

2. GENERAL MEETINGS

2.1 Members are entitled to attend general meetings [either] personally [or (in the case of a member organisation) by an authorised representative]. General meetings are called on at least clear 21 days written notice specifying the business to be discussed

2.2 There is a quorum at a general meeting if the number of members [or authorised representatives] personally present is at least _____ *[number]* (or _____ *[percentage]* of the members if greater)

2.3 The [**Chairman**] or (if the Chairman is unable or unwilling to do so) some other member elected by those present presides at a general meeting

2.4 Except where otherwise provided by the **Act**, every issue is decided by a majority of the votes cast

2.5 Except for the chairman of the meeting, who has a second or casting vote, every member present in person [or through an authorised representative)] has one vote on each issue

2.6 A written resolution signed by all those entitled to vote at a general meeting is as valid as a resolution actually passed at a general meeting (and for this purpose the written resolution may be set out in more than one document and will be treated as passed on the date of the last signature)

2.7 The Charity must hold an **AGM** in every year which all members are entitled to attend. The first AGM may be held within 18 months after the Charity's incorporation

2.8 At an AGM the members:

    2.8.1 receive the accounts of the Charity for the previous financial year

    2.8.2 receive the Trustees' report on the Charity's activities since the previous AGM

    2.8.3 accept the retirement of those Trustees who wish to retire or who are retiring by rotation

    2.8.4 elect persons to be Trustees to fill the vacancies arising

    2.8.5 appoint auditors for the Charity

    2.8.6 may confer on any individual (with his or her consent) the honorary title of Patron, President or Vice-President of the Charity

    and

    2.8.7 discuss and determine any issues of policy or deal with any other business put before them

2.9 Any general meeting which is not an AGM is an **EGM**

2.10 An EGM may be called at any time by the Trustees and must be called within 28 days on a written request from at least _____ *[number]* members

NOTES

3. **THE TRUSTEES**

This clause sets out the composition of the charity's governing body, ie the people who are the directors of the company and the charity trustees (see articles **3.1** and **9.1**). They are all required to be members of the charity. Here they are called the Trustees but they could equally well be called the "Directors", the "Council" or some other term. Whatever term is chosen should be used throughout the document.

3.2   The minimum number of Trustees should be at least three. It is possible to make provision for some or all of the Trustees to be appointed by outside bodies instead of being elected at the AGM but this will require bespoke amendments to the model. Every Trustee is a charity trustee, however appointed, and owes a duty towards the charity rather than to the person or body who makes the appointment. There should therefore be no power for the appointing body to remove the person appointed. Special qualifications which may be appropriate include eg residence in the area of benefit or membership of a particular religion. Co-option is dealt with in article **3.7**.

3.3   This provision automatically appoints as the charity's first Trustees the individuals who sign the Memorandum and Articles of Association as "subscribers".

3.4   This provision is important: it is designed to ensure as far as possible that everyone who takes on the task of being a Trustee is aware of the legal responsibilities it entails.

3.5   Retirement by rotation helps to ensure continuity.

3.6   Various events can terminate trusteeship.

   3.6.1 Disqualification occurs under section 72 of the Charities Act 1993 if a charity trustee is involuntarily removed by the Court or the Charity Commission, in the event of bankruptcy or the like, where the Trustee is disqualified under the Company Directors Disqualification Act or the Insolvency Act, and where the Trustee has been convicted of an offence involving dishonesty.

   3.6.2 Embarrassing problems can arise when a Trustee becomes too ill or infirm to be expected to take full responsibility for the task. The Trustees may wish to make a rule under article **5.5** to require a Trustee who appears incapable to undergo a medical examination. Such a request would in most cases lead to a voluntary resignation.

   3.6.3 The length of absence which gives rise to automatic termination of a Trustee's term of office will depend on the normal frequency of meetings.

   3.6.5 The law does not allow charity trustees to walk away from their responsibilities leaving no-one in charge of the charity.

   3.6.6 Provision for the removal of a Trustee by the members in general meeting will not be appropriate in all cases.

   3.6.7 This provision will only be necessary if a special qualification has been included in article **3.2**.

3.7   Co-opted Trustees have exactly the same voting powers and responsibilities as those elected at the AGM.

3.8   Occasionally a mistake occurs in appointment procedures. If a mistake of this kind is discovered it does not retrospectively invalidate previous decisions but should be put right before further decisions are taken.

MEMORANDUM & ARTICLES OF
ASSOCIATION FOR A CHARITABLE COMPANY

3.   THE TRUSTEES

3.1   The Trustees as **charity trustees** have control of the Charity and its property and funds

3.2   The Trustees when complete consist of at least [three] and not more than _____ *[number]* individuals, [all of whom must be members _____ *[specify any special qualification]*]

3.3   The subscribers to the Memorandum are the first Trustees of the Charity

3.4   Every Trustee must sign a declaration of willingness to act as a charity trustee of the Charity before he or she is eligible to vote at any meeting of the Trustees

3.5   One third (or the number nearest one third) of the Trustees must retire at each AGM, those longest in office retiring first and the choice between any of equal service being made by drawing lots

3.6   A Trustee's term of office automatically terminates if he or she:

    3.6.1   is disqualified under the Charities Act 1993 from acting as a charity trustee

    3.6.2   is incapable, whether mentally or physically, of managing his or her own affairs

    3.6.3   is absent from _____ *[number]* consecutive meetings of the Trustees

    3.6.4   ceases to be a member [(but such a person may be reinstated by resolution passed by all the other Trustees on resuming membership of the Charity before the next AGM)]

    3.6.5   resigns by written notice to the Trustees (but only if at least two Trustees will remain in office)

    3.6.6   is removed by resolution passed by at least _____ *[number or percentage]* of the members present and voting at a general meeting after the meeting has invited the views of the Trustee concerned and considered the matter in the light of any such views]

    or

    [3.6.7   ceases to _____ *[have the required qualification]*]

3.7   The Trustees may at any time co-opt any person duly qualified to be appointed as a Trustee to fill a vacancy in their number or as an additional Trustee, but a co-opted Trustee holds office only until the next AGM

3.8   A technical defect in the appointment of a Trustee of which the Trustees are unaware at the time does not invalidate decisions taken at a meeting

NOTES

4. **PROCEEDINGS OF TRUSTEES**

    This article deals with the meetings and proceedings of the Trustees.

4.1 The number of meetings per year will depend on (i) the nature of the charity's activities and (ii) the extent to which work is delegated to committees and/or staff. Two is a minimum.

4.2 Bearing in mind that decisions may be taken on a majority vote (article 4.6), the quorum should normally be fixed at (at least) one more than the number nearest to one third of the Trustees.

4.3 Many charities do not have a provision for a telephone or video conference. It is not necessary to include it unless difficulty in arranging meetings in person is expected (eg where the Trustees are geographically scattered). If the provision is included it should be borne in mind that (i) a conference call is not the same as a series of separate telephone calls, which do *not* amount to a meeting; and (ii) the same rules about notice of meetings, the quorum, chairmanship, voting, minutes etc apply to a telephone or video conference as to a meeting in person.

4.5 An alternative to a decision taken at a meeting is a written resolution, but this will not be valid unless signed by *all* the Trustees.

4.6 See notes 2.5 and 4.2 above.

5. **POWERS OF TRUSTEES**

5.1 There must be a company Secretary, and it is often best for the Secretary's role to be undertaken by a paid employee rather than one of the Trustees.

5.2 Here the Chairman and other honorary officers are appointed by the Trustees. In some charities these officers, or some of them, are appointed by the AGM. A Treasurer is essential. There may also be a membership secretary or holders of other specified offices, which may alter from year to year according to the charity's activities.

5.3 A specific provision is essential if the Trustees are to be able to delegate to committees. The Trustees will be legally responsible for the committees' acts, and for this reason it is prudent for at least one Trustee to be a member of each committee. The Trustees may wish, for this reason, to define the terms of reference with care. It is essential in all cases to provide for reporting back. Although the power of delegation is not limited to specific functions it is generally appropriate for decisions on major matters of policy or resources to be reserved to the Trustees themselves.

5.4 & These articles allow the Trustees to make rules of various kinds to govern different aspects of
5.5 & the running of the charity. There is no need to call them "Standing Orders" "Rules" and
5.6 "Regulations": they can all be called "rules" if preferred. See also the note to article 2.

5.7 This provision is designed to place the responsibility for finding a solution to internal disputes on the Trustees, given the damage which can result to a charity from such arguments, especially when they become public.

5.8 See note to article 2.

MEMORANDUM & ARTICLES OF
ASSOCIATION FOR A CHARITABLE COMPANY

4. PROCEEDINGS OF TRUSTEES

4.1 The Trustees must hold at least _____ *[number]* meetings each year

4.2 A quorum at a meeting of the Trustees is _____ *[number]* Trustees

[4.3 A meeting of the Trustees may be held either in person or by suitable electronic means agreed by the Trustees in which all participants may communicate with all the other participants]

4.4 The Chairman or (if the Chairman is unable or unwilling to do so) some other Trustee chosen by the Trustees present presides at each meeting

4.5 Every issue may be determined by a simple majority of the votes cast at a meeting but a written resolution signed by all the Trustees is as valid as a resolution passed at a meeting (and for this purpose the resolution may be contained in more than one document and will be treated as passed on the date of the last signature)

4.6 Except for the chairman of the meeting, who has a second or casting vote, every Trustee has one vote on each issue

4.7 A procedural defect of which the Trustees are unaware at the time does not invalidate decisions taken at a meeting

5. POWERS OF TRUSTEES

The Trustees have the following powers in the administration of the Charity:

5.1 to appoint (and remove) any member (who may be a Trustee) to act as Secretary to the Charity in accordance with the Act

5.2 to appoint a Chairman, Treasurer and other honorary officers from among their number

5.3 to delegate any of their functions to committees consisting of two or more individuals appointed by them (but at least _____ *[number]* member of every committee must be a Trustee and all proceedings of committees must be reported promptly to the Trustees)

5.4 to make Standing Orders consistent with the **Memorandum, these Articles** and the Act) to govern proceedings at general meetings

5.5 to make Rules consistent with the Memorandum, these Articles and the Act to govern proceedings at their meetings and at meetings of committees

5.6 to make Regulations consistent with the Memorandum, these Articles and the Act to govern the administration of the Charity and the use of its seal (if any)

5.7 to establish procedures to assist the resolution of disputes within the Charity

5.8 to exercise any powers of the Charity which are not reserved to a general meeting

NOTES

6. RECORDS & ACCOUNTS

6.1 The keeping of adequate records is essential if a charity is to be properly run. In addition,
& 6.2 there is detailed legislation in the Companies Acts and the regulations made under it, and in sections 45 to 49 of the Charities Act 1993, as well as guidance in the Charity SORP, about accountability. The rules cover accounting records and the provision of an annual report, statement of account and an annual return, all of which have to be sent to the Charity Commission as well as the Registrar of Companies.

6.3 This provision is designed to ensure that the Trustees have access to the published report and statements of account. The Trustees may also feel that members should be able to inspect the accounting records of the charity.

6.4 This article reflects section 47(2) of the Charities Act 1993.

7. NOTICES

Reference is made to the giving of notice in various places in the Articles (see articles **1.5**, **2.2** and **3.5**). This clause deals with the practical problems which could otherwise arise about when a notice was received by a member (or the charity). Where a number of clear days' notice is mentioned each "day" starts at midnight, and the day on which notice is given does not count (see article **9.1**).

Some charities may prefer not to have the option of placing a notice to the members in a journal, newspaper or newsletter (articles **7.1** and **7.3.4**), or by fax or e-mail (article **7.3.1**), in which case the relevant words should be omitted. It may also be desirable to save postage by restricting postal service to the members addresses in the United Kingdom (articles **7.2** and **7.3.3**).

8. DISSOLUTION

See the note to clause 8 of the Memorandum.

9. INTERPRETATION

This article is an aid to the interpretation of the Memorandum and Articles. Article 9.1 defines a number of the terms used.

9.1 In Section 97(1) of the Charities Act 1993 the term "Charity trustees" is defined as "the persons having the general control and management of the administration of a charity".

9.3 This article should avoid the need to amend the Articles merely to reflect technical changes in the law.

MEMORANDUM & ARTICLES OF
ASSOCIATION FOR A CHARITABLE COMPANY

6. RECORDS & ACCOUNTS

6.1 The Trustees must comply with the requirements of the Act and of the Charities Act 1993 as to keeping financial records, the audit of accounts and the preparation and transmission to the Registrar of Companies and the Commission of:

6.1.1 annual reports

6.1.2 annual returns

6.1.3 annual statements of account

6.2 The Trustees must keep proper records of

6.2.1 all proceedings at general meetings

6.2.2 all proceedings at meetings of the Trustees

6.2.3 all reports of committees and

6.2.4 all professional advice obtained

6.3 Accounting records relating to the Charity must be made available for inspection by any Trustee at any reasonable time during normal office hours and may be made available for inspection by members who are not Trustees if the Trustees so decide

6.4 A copy of the Charity's latest available statement of account must be supplied on request to any Trustee or member, or to any other person who makes a written request and pays the Charity's reasonable costs, within two months

7. NOTICES

7.1 Notices under these Articles may be sent by hand, or by post or by suitable electronic means or (where applicable to members generally) may be published in any suitable journal or [national] newspaper [circulating in area of benefit] or any newsletter distributed by the Charity

7.2 The only address at which a member is entitled to receive notices is the address shown in the register of members

7.3 Any notice given in accordance with these Articles is to be treated for all purposes as having been received

7.3.1 24 hours after being sent by electronic means or delivered by hand to the relevant address

7.3.2 two clear days after being sent by first class post to that address

7.3.3 three clear days after being sent by second class or overseas post to that address

7.3.4 on the date of publication of a newspaper containing the notice

NOTES

MEMORANDUM & ARTICLES OF
ASSOCIATION FOR A CHARITABLE COMPANY

    7.3.5 on being handed to the member [(or, in the case of a member organisation, its authorised representative)] personally or, if earlier,

    7.3.6 as soon as the member acknowledges actual receipt

7.4   A technical defect in the giving of notice of which the Trustees are unaware at the time does not invalidate decisions taken at a meeting

8.   DISSOLUTION

The provisions of the Memorandum relating to dissolution of the Charity take effect as though repeated here

9.   INTERPRETATION

In the Memorandum in and in these Articles:

9.1   ["beneficiaries" means ——————————————————————

——

——

————————————————————————————— *[qualifications of beneficiaries]*]

"The Act" means the Companies Act 1985

"AGM" means an annual general meeting of the Charity

["area of benefit" means ——————————————————— *[geographical area]*]

"these Articles" means these articles of association

["authorised representative" means an individual who is authorised by a member organisation to act on its behalf at meetings of the Charity and whose name is given to the Secretary]

"Chairman" means the chairman of the Trustees

"the Charity" means the company governed by these Articles

"charity trustee" has the meaning prescribed by section 97(1) of the Charities Act 1993

"clear day" means 24 hours from midnight following the relevant event

"the Commission" means the Charity Commissioners for England and Wales

"EGM" means an extraordinary general meeting of the Charity

"financial expert" means an individual, company or firm who is an authorised person or an exempted person within the meaning of the Financial Services Act 1986

"material benefit" means a benefit which may not be financial but has a monetary value

"member" and "membership" refer to membership of the Charity

NOTES

MEMORANDUM & ARTICLES OF
ASSOCIATION FOR A CHARITABLE COMPANY

"Memorandum" means the Charity's Memorandum of Association

"month" means calendar month

"the Objects" means the Objects of the Charity as defined in clause 3 of the Memorandum

"Secretary" means the Secretary of the Charity

"taxable trading" means carrying on a trade or business on a continuing basis for the principal purpose of raising funds and not for the purpose of actually carrying out the Objects and the profits of which are liable to tax

"Trustee" means a director of the Charity and "Trustees" means all of the directors.

"written" or "in writing" refers to a legible document on paper [not] including a fax message

"year" means calendar year

9.2   Expressions defined in the Act have the same meaning

9.3   References to an Act of Parliament are to the Act as amended or re-enacted from time to time and to any subordinate legislation made under it

959

MEMORANDUM & ARTICLES OF
ASSOCIATION FOR A CHARITABLE COMPANY

NAMES & ADDRESSES OF SUBSCRIBERS	SIGNATURES OF SUBSCRIBERS
[List the full names and residential addresses of each of the subscribers]	*[signatures of each of the subscribers]*

Date _____ *[Date]*
Witness to the above signatures

_____

_____

_____

_____   _____

[Name, address and occupation of witness]   *[Signature of witness]*

THE COMPANIES ACT 1985 AND 1989

———————————

———————————————————————

MEMORANDUM
AND
ARTICLES OF ASSOCIATION
OF THE

———————————

[name]

———————————————————————

Incorporated on   *[date]*

Model front page for Memorandum and Articles of Association

First published July 1997
© Charity Law Association 1997

A catalogue record for this document is available from the British Library.

ISBN 0 9521604 2 0

Designed by Rachel Fletcher and published by Plaza Publishing

PRODUCED BY PLAZA,
PUBLISHERS OF *NGO FINANCE*
1A TRADESCANT ROAD, LONDON SW8 1XD
TEL: 0171 793 0001   FAX: 0171 735 2009

NGO Finance magazine

INDEX